DISCOVERING
GLOBAL CUISINES

TRADITIONAL FLAVORS
AND TECHNIQUES

NANCY KRCEK ALLEN

PEARSON

Boston   Columbus   Indianapolis   New York   San Francisco   Upper Saddle River
Amsterdam   Cape Town   Dubai   London   Madrid   Milan   Munich   Paris   Montréal   Toronto
Delhi   Mexico City   São Paulo   Sydney   Hong Kong   Seoul   Singapore   Taipei   Tokyo

Editorial Director: Vernon R. Anthony
Senior Acquisitions Editor: William Lawrensen
Assistant Editor: Alexis Duffy
Editorial Assistant: Lara Dimmick
Project Manager: Kris Roach
Director of Marketing: David Gesell
Senior Marketing Manager: Alicia Wozniak
Marketing Manager: Stacey Martinez
Marketing Assistant: Les Roberts
Associate Managing Editor: Alexandrina Benedicto Wolf
Operations Specialist: Deidra Skahill
Art Director: Jayne Conte
Cover Designer: Bruce Kenselaar
Cover Art: Brian Confer
Lead Media Project Manager: Karen Bretz
Full-Service Project Management: S4Carlisle Publishing Services
Composition: S4Carlisle Publishing Services
Printer/Binder: R.R. Donnelley/Willard
Cover Printer: Lehigh-Phoenix Color/Hagerstown
Text Font: 10.5/12, ITC Giovanni Std

Credits and acknowledgments borrowed from other sources and reproduced, with permission, in this textbook appear on the appropriate page within text.

Chapter opening photos and all uncredited on page photos are from Brian Confer. Cooking Tools photo is © Martin Kemp/Shutterstock.com.

Library of Congress Cataloging-in-Publication Data not available upon publication.

10 9 8 7 6 5 4 3 2 1

ISBN 10:   0-13-511348-2
ISBN 13: 978-0-13-511348-6

CONTENTS

RECIPES

CHAPTER THREE

SOUTHEAST ASIA: THAILAND, VIETNAM, AND INDONESIA

CHAPTER SIX

ITALY: GENEROUS AND GENUINE

CHAPTER SEVEN

SPAIN: IBERIAN LAND OF CONTRASTS

CHAPTER EIGHT

GREECE AND TURKEY

CHAPTER NINE

LEBANON: THE HEART OF THE MIDDLE EAST

CHAPTER TEN

THE MIDDLE EAST AND CAUCASUS: PERSIA-IRAN AND REPUBLIC OF GEORGIA

CHAPTER ELEVEN

AFRICA

Of course the patterns vary from place to place, from culture to culture, from age to age; they are all manmade, they all depend on culture. But still, in every age and every place the structure of our world is given to it, essentially, by some collection of patterns which keeps on repeating over and over again.

— Christopher Alexander from *The Timeless Way of Building*

INTRODUCTION

Cuisine is a mark of civilization, one of the most simple and direct ways to enjoy life. It offers a place where diverse peoples can connect, discover their ancient bonds, and celebrate their creative differences. Learning about and respecting other people and their food helps to soften the rigid lines separating country from country and people from people.

For most of the world, skills like cooking or woodworking pass from parent to child, friend to friend, or master to apprentice through demonstration. Aspiring woodworkers discover the feel, scent, and look of pine, birch, and maple, how to hammer a nail, turn a table leg, or join two corners. Aspiring cooks learn the perfume of parsley and cilantro, the feel of properly risen bread dough, the look of perfectly cooked rice, and how to chop and sauté. They begin to intuitively interact with food and experience the taste, texture, color, and scent of properly prepared dishes. Because this approach originates with skills, senses, and intuition, it's fluid and flexible. It makes room for whatever the surroundings offer.

Successful professional cooks, instead of relying solely on recipes, need to master taste and cooking skills. How can an aspiring cook ever learn to really "swim" if he or she always wears the life jacket of recipes? *Discovering Global Cuisines* is designed to build a structure of traditional technique and seasoning skill by providing an understanding of the structure of each culture's dishes, flavor-balance, and cuisine-shaping cultural, historical, and geographic influences. From this, students will hopefully discover the commonalities and connections between cuisines as well as fascinating creative differences.

Ultimately, the goal of a good culinary training is to teach the basics and encourage taste, passion, and imagination. This book can't make anyone an expert global cook. The richness and depth of creativity of each cuisine is mind-boggling and cannot be captured in one volume. Instead, it is meant to introduce some important timeless, fundamental cooking techniques, foods, and dishes. Hopefully students will incorporate the knowledge into their personal repertoire, and become inspired to search deeper. The study of world cuisines offers new, exciting perspectives, which can inspire students to eventually translate what they learn into fresh, original dishes. *Discovering Global Cuisines* can provide a solid reference that will accompany culinary professionals throughout their careers.

The cuisines in this book were chosen for their successful flavor combinations, strong techniques, and creativity. Though desserts are an important part of cuisine, because there is far more material than is possible to cover, *Discovering Global Cuisines* chooses to focus only on savory dishes. Although nutrition isn't directly addressed, it is fundamental to every one of the cuisines represented. Ayurveda and other diet-health modalities in Indian and Asian cuisines have blurred the lines between food and medicine, and the West is awakening to this way of thinking.

Successful cuisines (and many successful culinary professionals!) seem to share several characteristics: early interactions with other cultures, creative transformation of new or foreign foods, and techniques to suit personal tastes and, most importantly, access to and respect for good quality food grown locally. Prepared with whole, fresh, high-quality ingredients, most of the dishes in this book can satisfy not only good nutrition, they can satisfy good taste.

- Slowly read through a recipe (to the end) before starting.

- Take notes the first time a dish is prepared.

- Each recipe ingredient in this book is arranged in this order: weight, piece size, and volume. They are all useful. It's helpful to know the weight of something if multiplying the recipe and ordering the food for a catering or restaurant event. Weight is the most accurate measure, and it saves time when preparing small amounts of food to know that 1/4 ounce of garlic will yield approximately 1-1/2 teaspoons peeled and minced, and that 1 large trimmed (peeled) green onion weighs 1/2 ounce and yields 2 to 3 tablespoons chopped. Piece size is helpful to know when running to the cooler to grab something. Volume is a simple check for consistency since scales are not always available.

- Flour weights and volumes vary in this book. Depending on how flour is placed into a measuring cup, 1 cup of all-purpose flour may weigh between 4-1/2 to 5 ounces. For most recipes this is not a problem, but always add the lesser amount and hold back the extra to add as required.

- Please pay attention. Although every attempt at accuracy has been made through research, recipe testing, and editing *Discovering Global Cuisines*, some errors are inevitable. Please bring them to the attention of the book's publisher and author.

- Water, salt, and pepper are not included in the ingredient list but do appear in the text of the recipe. Always have water, kosher salt, and a pepper grinder on hand.

- The recipes assume that all of cilantro (except the very thickest stems) will be finely sliced from top to stems and rarely chopped. Most cuisines that use cilantro do not pick off the leaves and toss away the flavorful stems.

- Likewise, both Italian parsley leaves and tender stems may be used when a recipe calls for chopped parsley. Large or tough stems may be saved for stock.

- Salt is one of the most important tools of culinary success. Taste a dish and season it with salt several times throughout cooking. If unsure of how to use salt, refer to the Primer Essay on salt.

- Make it a habit to taste a dish before it goes out.

- Some chapters, like Southeast Asia, cover more than one country. This close juxtaposition demonstrates how cuisine melts borders. Notice the overlaps and influences of each cuisine and how each has, similarly or differently, absorbed and transformed the foodstuffs and cooking techniques that came its way.

- If a dish or cuisine sparks an interest, investigate! Cook with home cooks from that culture. Pick up a book listed in the bibliography. Read and cook through it. Practice will get a passionate student-cook further than a recipe alone ever could.

ACKNOWLEDGMENTS

Richard Simpson, director of education at the Institute for Culinary Education in Manhattan, who first hired me to teach professional cooking and gave me the first opportunity to write curriculum and discover how much I loved it.

Bill Lawrensen, my Pearson editor, for giving me the opportunity to write this book.

Alexis Duffy, my Pearson assistant editor, for answering my questions promptly and kindly.

Diane Sukiennik of www.FoodandWineAccess.com for referring me, after a short talk at a conference, to her Pearson editor and making this all possible.

The peer reviewers, chef-instructors, friends, and acquaintances who took time to advise or look over chapters: Lucy House, Kathy Kaufmann, Menkir Tamrat, Roxanne O'Brien, Misaeng Liggett, Judy Chu, Robert George, Marvine and Stathis Stamatakis, Roo Heins, Ammini Ramachadran, Randy Chamberlain, Paddy Rawal, Rakesh and Asha Gupta, Sreedevi and Damodaran Olappamanna, Linda Kurniawan, Parvaneh Holloway, Mariam Habibi, Miriam Nahas Delamielleure, Francisco Rodriguez, Annie Landfield, Richard Messina, Professor James C. McCann, Harry Kloman, Tim Nielsen, Katie Brown, Karen Mauk, and Karen Good.

Summer recipe test diners and organic C.S.A. farm owners Jenny Tutlis and Jon Watts, farm manager Robert Bartle, and the Friday crew at Meadowlark Farm in Leelanau County, Michigan.

My cooking class students at Chateau Chantal, Northwestern Michigan College and Oryana Natural Foods Co-op in Traverse City, Michigan.

My dear friends and relatives, who saw little of me except when I needed them to eat and honestly critique dishes at many potlucks and dinner parties.

A thousand thanks to photographer Brian Confer and the talented crew who prepared the food for the photos and procedures: Cre Woodard, Janice Binkert, Misaeng Liggett, Rose Hollander, Rebecca Tranchell, Mary Buschell, Bryan Rowles, Sue Bourne, Brad Boyer, Alexis Walworth, Nolan Racich, Emily Mitchell, and Mimi Wheeler.

To Fred Laughlin, the director of Northwestern Michigan College's Great Lakes Culinary Institute in Traverse City, Michigan, for his long friendship and kind generosity.

The Traverse Area District Library for their great stacks and kind, helpful librarians.

For their enormously important and savvy comments, a huge thanks to the Pearson peer reviewers and recipe testers working in culinary schools around the country. They are Leonard G. Bailey II, National Institute for Culinary Arts; John Bandman, The Art Institute of New York City; Mark Cosgrove, County College of Morris; Kelli Dever, Boise State University; Stephen C. Fernald, Lake Tahoe Community College; Marian Gruber, West Virginia Northern Community College; Scott Howard, Athens Technical College; David Jurasinki, State University of New York; Roxanne O'Brien, American River College; Stanley Omaye, University of Nevada, Reno; and Janet M. Thomas, Bentley University.

Last, but not least, my beloved husband and artist, William M. Allen, for supporting me and putting up with more than four years of my self-absorption. He did get to eat well.

ABOUT THE AUTHOR
NANCY KRCEK ALLEN

Chef-educator Nancy Krcek Allen has traveled extensively, and has worked in kitchens and classrooms for more than thirty years. Allen graduated from California Culinary Academy in San Francisco. While living in New York City, Allen worked full-time teaching recreational and professional cooking for the Institute of Culinary Education (ICE) and the Natural Gourmet Institute in Manhattan, and in Viareggio, Italy, for Toscana Saporita. During her time at ICE, Allen wrote curriculum for the professional and recreational programs. While living in New York, Allen was a member of the New York Association of Culinary Teachers, Women Chefs and Restaurateurs, and the International Association of Culinary Professionals, where she attained a Certified Culinary Professional rating.

Allen has traveled extensively to learn about food, owned a restaurant and cooking school, catering business, and has worked as a freelance writer for various publications. She currently works as a cooking teacher and writer. Allen lives in Leelanau County in northern Michigan along the glacial moraines of Lake Michigan.

PRIMER ESSAYS

ESSAY ONE SALT

High Salting, Hyper Seasoning

The *New Yorker* writer Adam Gopnik has noted that professional cooks use a technique he calls "high salting." It's what he feels helps to make a professional cook's food taste professional. The liberal use of salt sets the professional cook apart from salt-timid home cooks, but "hyper seasoning" and the proper amount of salt can allow even amateur cooks to produce highly satisfying meals.

Salt is the premier flavor-enhancer. Not only are human tastebuds hard-wired for it, human blood salt level is very close to that of the ocean. Until recently salt was always in short supply. Although it was all around—the seas, oceans, and inside the earth—extracting it was slow and tedious. Modern technology has made salt cheap and abundant, available to all, for use in everything from pies to potato chips. Salt's overabundance has turned it into a dangerous exile. What's a cook to do?

Salt serves many masters, but none better than cooks. Though it's a valuable colleague in the kitchen, salt is no substitute for a lack of flavor from fresh, quality ingredients. But used well, salt will bond with olive oil to bring the best flavor out of salad greens or a pan of sautéed aromatic vegetables headed for a soup or stew. Not only will salt help to soften vegetables, draw out moisture, and concentrate their flavor, it will embed itself into them to subtly heighten their flavor. Two exceptions: salt toughens eggs and corn during poaching or boiling: season them with salt after cooking.

Salt insinuates itself into meat or fish when you sprinkle it on just before cooking to boost flavor. Short brining helps salt move into meat fibers to increase its juiciness and texture. Notice how salt plays off apples and watermelon or atop caramel, the contrast making fruit and caramel taste sharper and sweeter. Salt softens "off tastes" and inhibits bitterness: Japanese and Chinese cooks salt raw fish or seafood briefly and rinse to remove fishy odors and improve texture.

Many cooks wait to the end of a dish to salt, or justify under-salting by saying that diners can salt at the table. To achieve balance and complexity, a properly salted dish doesn't spend all its salt in one place; it's salted in layers. At the beginning of cooking, use salt to brine, with an aromatic vegetable sauté base, or in blanching water (it will set green color). Use salt in the middle of a dish as food simmers, and again at the end as a final correction, or as a garnish to hit the tastebuds with pre-emptive salty pinpricks. Layered salting assures that each element of a dish will take just enough salt into itself to be properly enhanced.

Taste a dish many times as it's seasoned: too little salt and your dish won't achieve its full flavor potential; add too much and salt will be the first, last, and only thing remaining on the tongue. Salt should make food taste more intensely of itself but leave little trace of itself.

A good salt collection can be split into four basics: sea salt for the table; kosher salt for cooking, preserving, blanching, brining, or where large amounts are needed; a specialty salt (like fleur de sel) for garnishing salads, sliced tomatoes, or dishes like polenta with a few crunchy grains just before serving; and rock salt for use as a salt bed and ice cream making.

Salt measures differently depending on shape: granulated, flake, or rock. There is more saltiness per teaspoon of granulated than flaked: 2 teaspoons granulated table salt equals the saltiness of about 3 to 4 teaspoons flaked kosher salt. When salt amounts are important, as in confit or preserving, weigh the salt.

Salt comes from salt mines that are remnants of ancient seas, and from evaporated seawater. Theoretically salt tastes, well, salty, but at a world salt tasting, tasters would discover subtle differences. Unrefined sea salts taste more of the sea and its minerals. Shape, and mineral and moisture content determine how salt will interact and play up food flavor. Larger flakes add drama. Expensive small-grained salts used as a finish endow dishes with a salty snap that hits the tongue and blossoms.

Where does the ubiquitous box of iodized salt fit in? Good chefs avoid it for cooking. The added iodine masks the pure salt flavor and leaves a chemical aftertaste. Flaked kosher salt has cleaner taste than iodized, but good French or Italian sea salt without additives has the most distinct, clean salt taste. It's good sense to have a varied selection of salt on hand:

* Hawaiian ala'e pink salt, colored by iron-rich, red clay salt ponds, tastes of the earth that colors it. Good on grilled fish, rice, and pasta.

* Sel gris or Celtic sea salt is a moist, unrefined, coarse, mineral-rich gray salt, from the French Atlantic coast, that tastes less salty-sharp.

* Korean gray salt is similar to Celtic sea salt, and found in Korean markets. Good on meat, root vegetables, and fish.

* Indian black salt is a sulfurous, pinkish, not-so-salty component of chat masala, the favored spice mixture of pregnant Indian princesses who sprinkled it on summer fruit salads to cool themselves.

* Fleur de sel is the premier salt gathered by hand from crackly thin layers of salt bloom on sea salt ponds off the coasts of northwestern and southern France and Portugal. Good on buttered toast, caramel, fruit, and salad.

* Maldon salt, from Essex on the English coast, is soft and flaky with a salty crunch. Try it on steamed vegetables, baked potatoes, or fries.

* Trapani salt, a dry-grained crystalline salt from Sicily, is considered the best-tasting sea salt. Good on vegetables, seafood, pasta, risotto, and to top polenta.

ESSAY TWO   UMAMI

Big Taste

Writer and chef Paula Wolfert coined the term "Big Taste." Food with Big Taste is sensually fulfilling food that imbeds its flavor, taste, and aroma deeply in memory.

Umami is the Japanese term for deep, rich, savory flavor. Many people hail umami as a "new" discovery, the fifth taste after sweet, sour, salty, and bitter. (Spicy-hot, pungent, and astringent are sensations, not tastes.) But umami isn't really new.

In the early twentieth century, Professor Kikunae Ikeda of Tokyo Imperial University noticed that kelp gave a rich flavor to dashi broth. He observed that there was a taste "common to asparagus, tomatoes, cheese and meat," but wasn't one of the big four tastes. Ikeda linked umami with foods that naturally contain the flavor-enhancing and protein-building-block amino acid salts monosodium glutamate, sodium inosinate, and sodium guanylate.

Professor Ikeda began experimenting, and extracted crystals of glutamic acid from kelp broth. From glutamic acid, he isolated monosodium glutamate salt, a product with similar physical characteristics as sugar and salt, which enhances the flavor of other foods. Ikeda's discovery is also known as MSG, Accent, hydrolyzed vegetable protein, amino acids, or "natural flavorings." They sometimes cause havoc in sensitive diners. But, unlike MSG, the amino acids responsible for umami don't naturally occur alone: they are part of many foods and not usually harmful.

Soy sauce, miso (fermented soybean paste), kimchi, seaweed, beef, bonito (fish in the mackerel family), onions, Parmesan cheese, tart cherries, tomatoes, mushrooms (shiitake and porcini), Thai fish sauce, sardines, and green tea are umami-rich foods. Long cooking (stews, curries, and chilli) and fermentation (kraut, kimchi, and fish sauce), break down amino acid bonds to release umami.

Umami-rich foods synergistically enhance other ingredients in a dish. Notice how tomatoes make anything taste better. Think of the flavors of gazpacho, tart cherry pie, long-cooked beef stew, mushrooms simmered with soy sauce, or soup simmered with a rind of Parmesan cheese. Teamed together with other foods, umami-rich foods can increase a dish's flavor eight- or nine-fold. The result is every cook's dream: really big flavor with lots less work. Think of the mysterious umami as food packed with charisma: a cook's secret voodoo.

ESSAY THREE   PARTNERSHIPS

A truly fulfilling dish often contains a special partnership of foods. The familiar combinations of tomato, mozzarella cheese, and oregano on pizza or apples; maple syrup and cinnamon in applesauce and pie are examples of partnerships that work.

Partnerships infuse dishes with style and vivid, memorable flavor. Investigate the dishes that leave a lasting impression: that's where to strike gold. Long-lasting dishes contain combinations that have been sifted by a jury of ancestors: pork, prunes, and cream; potato and leek; basil, garlic, pine nuts, and olive oil; tomato, onion, chili, and garlic; or white wine, garlic, parsley, and clams.

Partnerships have benefits. They keep a dish from being overly fussy and confusing for the diner by offering a clear personality. Working with a partnership a cook won't be tempted to add "everything but the kitchen sink." Partnerships invite improvisation. They can transform everyday techniques into surprising and original meals. Pizza's team of tomato, mozzarella, and oregano also works well in a rice pilaf. Carry duck sausage, sun-dried tomatoes, and goat cheese into a sandwich or salad, and shrimp, cilantro, and dried cherries might go well tossed into pasta or stuffed into an egg roll.

Partnerships are everywhere. Query friends for their favorite food combinations. Search through cooking magazines or menus from local restaurants or borrow from restaurant meals or dinner with relatives. Keep a journal of favorite partnerships. If a cooking rut hits, pull them out to spark a spontaneous creation.

Tomato, brown butter, and cinnamon

Almonds, garlic, and grapes

Rabbit, red wine, and chocolate

Bananas, chocolate, marshmallow, and graham crackers

Orange, fennel, and olives

Salmon, fennel, and lemon

Shallots, mushrooms, and nutmeg

Watermelon, feta, and mint

Dates, mascarpone cheese, and caramel

Sweet potatoes, lime, and cilantro

Wheat, honey, and cardamom

Pear, honey, lemon, and olive oil

Pear, walnut, blue cheese

Mushrooms, sherry, and shallots

Pecans, dried cherries, and maple syrup

Smoked salmon, dill, and cucumbers

Chicken, tarragon, and cream

Garlic, parsley, and lemon

Feta, olive, and oregano

Potatoes, chilies, and cheese

Grapefruit, avocado, and orange

Pineapple, coconut, and lime

Asparagus, egg, and orange

Fish sauce, lime juice, and palm sugar

Basmati rice, cashew, and golden raisins

Apples, onions, and cabbage

Beans, bacon, and molasses

Eggs, bacon, and toast

Beets, caraway, and dill

Carrots, caraway, and butter

Cheddar cheese, beer, and mustard

Tomato, vodka, and cream

Arugula, papaya, and red onion

Broccoli, peanuts, and garlic

Golden raisins, pine nuts, garlic, and parsley

Peaches, basil, and honey

Butternut squash, onions, and pecans

Apple cider, butternut squash, and apples

Lamb, tomato, and artichoke

Roasted red bell pepper, walnuts, and Parmigiano-Reggiano cheese

ESSAY FOUR   CULTIVATE FLAVOR MEMORY

Storing Flavor Memories

Indian chef, writer, and teacher Madhur Jaffrey relates how before she learned to cook she had stored many strong flavor memories from her early life in India like cumin and tamarind. When Jaffrey began to cook they were ready, waiting, and available to help.

For some, the flavor of grandmother's chicken soup, mom's mac-and-cheese, or dad's barbecue ribs unexpectedly fleet across mind and tastebuds. Repetition of specific flavors can lodge them permanently into memory. Tie those flavors to a positive event and they will embed even deeper. Scent, taste, and memory are then inextricably united into flavor memory.

Smell and taste work as one to make flavor: about 75 percent of flavor is aromatic scent and 25 percent is taste. When a person chews, food molecules vaporize into scent and travel to the nose's 1,000 scent receptors. Scent is a hugely complex mix of elements: it's possible to discern up to 10,000 different elements. Taste is perceived on the tongue. Taste covers just five: sweet, sour, salty, bitter, and umami. The addition of scent multiplies those simple five into an infinite variety of flavors.

Dr. Avery Gilbert, smell scientist, sensory psychologist, and author of *What the Nose Knows: The Science of Smell in Everyday Life*, has found that humans use some of the same "cognitive processes" to interpret smells that they use to determine information coming in from their other senses. Gilbert believes that how someone responds to scent "can change with experience and learning." He says that humans can "educate" their noses and learn to recognize and evaluate smells and this, in turn, can lead to a better understanding of our responses to them.

Flavor recall may be an important key to a food professional's success. It helps cooks to set a benchmark of flavor and teaches them to recognize (and pair) certain flavors like the resiny bite of rosemary or the sweet-sour perfume of strawberry. It also helps a cook to untangle the flavors in a dish, which ultimately may increase her or his culinary skill.

No one starts out with an intuitive, perfect sense of flavor, but everyone has a flavor memory that can be developed. Like all skills, building a sense of flavor and a solid memory of it takes time, attention, and practice. Take the time to form a flavor memory with the ten steps below.

1. Prime the senses: collect food experiences.

Artists study and copy the masters to develop their artistic eye and writers read the classics. Cooks should dine at the tables of masters and great granny cooks, local and international. Travel to foreign lands or an ethnic neighborhood and explore native food. Try everything: eat kimchi with your Korean neighbor or boudin blanc in Louisiana.

2. Start memory-tasting with simple combinations.

Dishes with too many flavors don't allow tasters to easily discern each component. Start simple: sauté a batch of onions with Spanish smoked paprika. Toss the onions with rice to clearly taste, and commit to memory, the flavor of pimentón (Spanish smoked paprika).

3. Pay attention.

The more the focus is on tasting, the deeper a certain flavor will lodge in memory.

4. Play favorite music.

Tie memory-tasting with good music. Positive emotions cement memories into place.

5. Cut down on stimulation. Blind taste foods.

Perform memory-tastings alone whenever possible; it will help to better focus on flavor. Blind taste foods: cut a potato, apple, celery root, and jicama into similar sizes and toss into a bowl. Close the eyes, pinch the nose, and lick each piece of food. Then un-pinch and lick again. Buddhists-in-training sit in deep quiet, with eyes shut, and slowly experience the taste and texture of one raisin or grape. Try it with one pomegranate seed or a dab of tamarind paste.

6. Explore new flavors.

Cook nothing but Indian, Greek, Ethiopian, or Mexican food for a month. It's guaranteed to build strong flavor memories.

7. Taste and smell a dish as it cooks.

Notice how a chicken curry or pot of chili at first tends to smell and taste dissonant, how it comes together after simmering for 20 minutes, and how it forms a cohesive, delicious taste-team after an hour or after an overnight rest in the refrigerator. Some cooks swear that a dish smells different, fuller, after salting.

8. Keep a journal. Take photos.

Recording food experiences reminds cooks of dishes they've had and can be a source of future inspiration. Keeping track of cooking and dining experiences forces cooks to pay close attention to each dish and embed their flavors in memory. Learn from both successful flavors and those that miss the mark.

9. Educate.

Learn herbs and spices. Taste them over and over again until they've deeply embedded themselves in memory. Get to know the citrusy snap of coriander seed, the smoky exotic flavor of nigella seed, and the flowery surprise of Kaffir lime leaf. Discern cilantro from Italian parsley and know the difference between fruity-aromatic Thai basil and the stronger kick of Italian basil.

10. Practice. Be persistent.

The more a cook practices, the faster the flavor memory will fill with tools to boost culinary creativity.

ESSAY FIVE   THE MOST IMPORTANT COOKING SKILL

Chef-Educator Nancy Krcek Allen

During culinary school my chef-instructors dropped gems of advice, which I eagerly collected. My favorite gem came from an esteemed chef early in my culinary training. It instantly embedded itself into my memory: The most important cooking skill a cook can cultivate is to learn to pay attention.

What I have learned after chewing on that piece of advice is that when I cook I must set aside distractions and focus on my cooking. If I entered a kitchen and began to gossip, worried about my boyfriend, or carried anger about a driver cutting me off, my onions burned and my broccoli turned yellow. Paying attention in the classroom and in the kitchen had other benefits: I noticed important details that others missed.

Meditation is about focusing on one thing, usually the breath, to the exclusion of all else. Meditation asks the practitioner not to follow his or her thoughts; instead to allow thoughts to arise and just fall away. No judgments or criticisms, just a noticing and letting go. Zen masters might call paying attention during an activity a sort of moving meditation that enables the practitioner to "be one" with whatever he or she is doing. This practice can become a sort of culinary sixth sense, a kitchen intuition that alerts you to check the boiling potatoes, sautéed onions, or roast beef at just the right moment.

Paying attention has become my most treasured cooking skill. We pay attention to what we love and cherish, and I love and cherish cooking. I often say that paying attention can help cooks to avoid kitchen mishaps that no amount of skill can fix.

UNIT I
ASIA

CHAPTER ONE

CHINA: COMPLEX AND CREATIVE

This chapter will:

- Introduce the history of China, its geography, far-reaching philosophical, religious, and cultural influences and its climate.

- Discuss the importance of the Silk Road, how it connected China across continents to the Middle East, Mediterranean, and Rome, and its effects on Chinese cuisine.

- Introduce China's culinary culture, its four main regional cuisines, and dining etiquette.

- Identify Chinese foods, flavor foundations, seasoning devices, and famous cooking techniques.

- Teach by technique and recipes the major dishes of China.

FIGURE 1.1 Map of China.

The Balance of Opposites

Chef and writer Barbara Tropp has observed how the Chinese dualistic philosophy of yin (dark and yielding) and yang (light and firm) are deeply fundamental to Chinese culture and cuisine. Chinese people know that successfully blending these opposites results in balance and harmony. Chinese cooks, from a humble street cook and the home cook to the restaurant chef, have the knowledge of yin and yang bred into them. Working intuitively with this concept, Chinese cooks incorporate it into every meal, whether they're aware of it or not.

To know Asia one must begin with China. Over millennia, the Chinese birthed many strains of thought and doctrines, more than twenty dynasties, over a dozen kingdoms, several empires, and many wars. Paradoxically, between 403 BCE and 221 BCE, a time of frequent deadly conflicts, philosophies of humanist Confucianism, Taoism (dao-ism), which preached compassion, moderation, and humility, yin-yang, the balance and interdependence of opposites, and the Five Elements, or Wu Xing, arose. The Five Elements described relationships between phenomena, and between foods. Fire, earth, metal, water, and wood connected to five tastes: fire–bitter, earth–sweet, metal–spicy and pungent, water–salty, and wood–sour. Cooks and doctors consider all five when planning a balanced dish or menu. A balancing of yin-yang and the Five Elements affected all aspects of Chinese life, from Chinese medicine, feng shui, the martial arts, military strategy, and the I Ching to Chinese culinary culture.

China has arguably the world's oldest continuous civilization. Primitive humans first lived in what is now China more than a million years ago. They evolved to the upright walking, tool- and fire-using Peking Man and, independently of the Mediterranean, they eventually developed agriculture, animal husbandry, and metal-working.

The Han Dynasty (202 BCE to AD 220) saw the beginning of the 7,000-mile Silk Road, a series of land and sea trade routes begun for the Chinese silk trade. It spanned two continents and crisscrossed Eurasia, from Xian, China, through the Tian Shan Mountains, Iran, Iraq, down to India, and ended in Istanbul. Smaller land and sea branches connected Korea, Japan, the Indonesian Spice Islands, Turkey, Ethiopia, and imperial Rome.

The intersections, introductions, and trade among Chinese and peoples from diverse cultures along the way inextricably linked China to India, Persia, Arabia, Greece, and Rome. Through the fourteenth century, the Silk Road promoted an unprecedented sharing of ideas, arts, sciences, innovations, cooking techniques, and foods like onions, dates, figs, olives, oranges, apples, grapes, spices and herbs, tea, salt, potatoes, melons, sesame seed, walnuts, almonds, carrots, cucumbers, peanuts, wheat, chickens, and pomegranates.

From the seventh to the fourteenth centuries, China was the world's most advanced civilization, the epicenter of Asian influence. Through trade, China's 6,000-year-old culture filtered into and shaped every culture in Asia and Southeast Asia, most especially Korean and Japanese. China, Korea, and Japan are like three sparring sisters cut of the same cloth. They share wok, chopsticks, rice, fresh produce, seafood with accents of meat, and similar beliefs and background, yet each is a highly evolved individual. Korea, Japan, and China have influenced each other's cuisines and cultures; it's difficult to determine who influenced the other's first.

Chinese civilization survived and changed through warring dynasties and foreign incursions from Mongols and the British. The Chinese fought with the British in the Opium Wars (1839–1842 and 1856–1860) over diplomatic, trade disputes, and restriction of the lucrative British opium trade—and lost. This eventually led to uprisings, rebellions, and the end of dynastic China.

The Chinese endured the domestic strife of Mao Tse Tung's Great Leap Forward (1958–1961), which attempted to transform China from an agrarian economy to a modern communist one. Mao failed, causing mass deaths through violence and starvation. Mao initiated the Cultural Revolution in 1966 in an attempt to stop capitalism in China. It became a campaign of extreme violence that pitted many young communists against the Chinese connected with the "bourgeois" West and its education, art, music, calligraphy, and gourmet food.

The Chinese developed many things we take for granted: paper-making, printing, the compass, gunpowder, written characters, currency, written laws, a tax system, and agriculture. Chinese literature, painting, calligraphy, pottery, porcelain, sculpture, and a delightful, complex cuisine continue to influence Asia, Southeast Asia, and the world. China has the fastest growing major economy since the 1978 initiation of market-based reforms; it is the world's largest exporter—and the second largest importer—of goods.

About the size of the fifty United States, China boasts the world's largest population—20 percent—and over a billion more people than the United States's 300 million plus. With nuclear capabilities and the largest army in the world, China is fast becoming a world superpower.

LANGUAGE, PHILOSOPHY, AND RELIGION

Unlike the United States and Canada, China, Korea, and Japan have linguistically and culturally homogenous populations. Though China is home to fifty-six ethnic groups, more than 90 percent of its population is Han Chinese—originating from a dynasty begun in 202 BCE.

The philosophies of Confucius, Taoism, and Buddhism helped form fundamental Chinese, Japanese, and Korean cultural and culinary practices, values, and beliefs. Confucius, a Chinese sage (551 BCE to 479 BCE), shaped Chinese and Korean philosophical and ethical codes. Confucius attached great importance to food, naming it as one of three conditions (along with an army and trust) for founding a state. He wrote that proper relationships are the basis of society and that maintaining group harmony is fundamental.

Buddhism (see *India*) and Taoism came to China from Persia, Central Asia, and India through the Silk Road in the first century, to Korea in the fourth century, and Japan in the sixth century. Taoism, based on the writings of Lao Tzu in the *Tao Te Ching*, considered to be the most influential Taoist text, spoke about concepts that have filtered into Western culture: the unchanging nature of the universe, nonaction, yin-yang, qi (pronounced *chee*)—the life force, and moving in concert with nature. These philosophical and religious beliefs influence every part of Asian life from family conduct and politics to cooking and health.

China's most revealing concept is that of "being One." In *China, Japan, Korea, Culture and Customs*, John and Ju Brown disclose that Chinese people feel that *unity* means "order, strength, and unified power" while *division* means "chaos, disruption, and war." Chinese believe their beliefs and culture are superior and apply the unified concept of "being One" to their land, people, and culture. It is part of the strength that has helped them survive throughout the best and worst times of their long history.

GEOGRAPHY AND CLIMATE

China is a land of three "stair-step" plateaus, plains, basins, foothills, and mountains. These rugged areas occupy nearly two-thirds of China and have fostered her varying customs and cuisines. China's highest point (over 13,000 feet) is the western Qinghai-Tibet Plateau, home to the Himalayas, the Kunlunshan range, Qilianshan range, and Hengduan mountain chain. The Himalayan peak Mt. Everest (29,003 feet), Earth's highest mountain, lies on the borders of China, Nepal, and Tibet. Moving east in China, the mountains ease down to large basins and plateaus 3,000 to 6,000 feet high, then give way to broad, fertile plains sprinkled with lower mountains and foothills around 1,500 feet. This last, easternmost stair-step of China is home to North and Northeast China and the Yangtze Plains, which produce abundant crops.

China's diverse and extensive geography, dominated by monsoons and dry periods, leads to large differences in climate. Generally, winters are warmest south of the Yangtze River, with warm, moist winds from the South China Sea, heat and monsoons, and coldest further north where cold, dry winds blow from higher latitudes.

FARMING AND AGRICULTURE

China's climate and geography varies widely and, consequently, so do its crops. Western China is rugged, dry, and cold with a short growing season. Crops include wheat, barley, potatoes, cotton, sugar beets, fruit, and melons. Livestock are sheep and yak. Northern and northeastern China is dry with long, cold winters. Millet, wheat, corn, cotton, flax, soybeans, and peanuts are the main crops. Central China, known as the rice bowl, is the richest and most productive region with alluvial soil, mild winters, year-round cultivation, and abundant rainfall. Rice, cotton, tea, oil seed, and much produce grows here. South China lies within the tropics so it has a long growing season, lots of rain with primary crops of rice, sugarcane, mulberries, fruit and vegetables, and freshwater fish raised in rice paddies or ponds.

CHINESE CUISINE: ECONOMY, HARMONY, AND BALANCE

Asia's philosophy emphasizing harmony and balance reaches most deeply into food and determines the character of its cuisine. Asians consider food as medicine and a seriously important pleasure. Cooks and doctors alike label foods and cooking techniques either *yin*—dark, cool, watery, and feminine (tofu, watercress, cabbage) or *yang*—light, hot, dense, fatty, and masculine (beef, ginger, mushrooms), though none is purely either. Cooks place complementary pairs in a dish and meal to balance their qualities to create harmony: sweet and sour, soft and crunchy, hot and cold, watery and dense or oily. Doctors prescribe certain dishes to balance or heal certain conditions. All Asian cooks balance the five senses intuitively, weaving together contrasting and complementary colors, textures, flavors, and cooking methods into pleasing meals.

To the Chinese, indeed all of Asia, food is life, health, and a symbol of luck and prosperity. Long, uncut noodles are prized because they mean "long life." Dishes with words that are spelled similarly or sound like *luck* or *prosperity* are often chosen for celebrations: turnip sounds like "good luck," fish sounds like "plenty." Whole chickens and fish symbolize happiness and prosperity. Oranges represent wealth and good fortune because they are China's most plentiful fruit.

Chinese culinary culture is vastly versatile, often quite complex, and adapted to economy. They have always welcomed new ingredients; an old Cantonese aphorism says, "If it has two legs and doesn't talk, and has four legs and isn't a table, you can eat it." Through war, forced migration, and famine, cooks had to be resourceful. These difficulties and opportunities spawned a delightful blend of flavor, texture, and inventiveness. Preparation is everything: cooks cut foods for eye appeal as well as quick, even cooking to save on expensive fuels. Deceptively simple in method, the chef must be part artist, part technician. Top-of-the-stove cooking rules with boiling, steaming and stir-frying, braising, stewing, deep-frying, roasting, and smoking.

Chinese meals revolve around rice or grain. In Northern China (and Korea) wheat, millet, and barley are important. Vegetables, soybeans, and soybean products (soy sauce and fermented pastes) are important secondary foods, while meat, poultry, and fish are supplementary. Foods fall into two categories: *fan* (rice and grain dishes) and *t'sai* (meat and vegetable dishes). Fan and t'sai are not mixed together, allowing each to retain its unique characteristics. With a balance between fan and t'sai, between yin and yang, and the five elemental tastes, Chinese cooks blend inventiveness, flavor, and economy to create an ideal meal.

REGIONAL CHINA: FOUR SCHOOLS OF FOOD, FLAVOR, AND TECHNIQUE

1. **Northern China Region, Beijing: Robust, Pungent, and Delicate**
   Beijing, the political, educational, and cultural center of the People's Republic of China, is China's second largest city and its capital. Imperial food traditions mix with great street food and home cooking. Descendants of imperial chefs have preserved recipes and opened small restaurants featuring dishes that were lost for centuries.

   China's northern region (with the Great Wall) sees weather extremes, from the Gobi Desert to the Siberian mountains. Hearty, earthy dishes with strong, pungent flavors, and refined imperial dishes with lighter, delicate tastes, form this cuisine. Meats like pork, chicken, lamb, goat, and beef are prized. Northern Chinese cooks favor smoking meat, pickling vegetables, braising, roasting, and boiling.

   Unlike in the rest of China, wheat instead of rice predominates as staple food; clever cooks fashion it into flatbreads, steamed yeasted buns, dumplings, and wheat noodles. Garlic chives, leeks, garlic, scallions, onions, vinegars, and bean pastes form the northern seasoning pantry. Famous dishes include Mongolian fire pot, Peking duck, moo shu pork with Peking pancakes, bird's nest soup, beggar's chicken, scallion pancakes, sweet-and-sour dishes, and pork dumplings.

2. **Coastal /Eastern China Region, Shanghai: Refined, Subtle, Cosmopolitan, Creative**
   Shanghai is the largest city in China. Located on China's central eastern coast at the mouth of the Yangtze River, it boasts the world's largest cargo port and the largest center of commerce and finance in Mainland China. Modern, cosmopolitan influences and elegant, discerning touches with seasoning, sauces, and technique (steaming, braising, and clay pot cooking) reveal its refinement. Rice is staple food teamed with salty, saucy fish, shellfish, and vegetable dishes seasoned highly with soy sauce and sugar. The southeastern province of Fujian, south of Shanghai, produces the best soy sauce in China. Famous dishes include soup dumplings, West Lake fish, potstickers, red cooked fish or chicken, drunken shrimp, and scallion pancakes.

3. **Western China or Inland Region, Szechwan, Yunnan, Hunan Spicy, Complex**
   This region lies near the Himalayas and the tropics, giving rise to weather extremes. Myanmar (Burma), Nepal, Thailand, Laos, North Vietnam, India, and Pakistan influence this cuisine. Szechwan cooks love heat. A signature ingredient is red chili, fresh, fermented into paste, dried whole or finely ground. Hunan cooking is smokier and more assertive than Szechwan, to which it is often compared.

   This region's cuisines arise from mountain basins and alongside tributaries of the Yangtze with spicy barbecued fish, braised pork with star anise and five-spice, chicken with red chili, and lamb with cumin and pepper. Rice, citrus, chilies, bamboo, onions, garlic, ginger, peanuts, and sesame are predominate flavors along with soy sauce, tofu, fermented black beans, bean paste, beef, lamb, smoked duck, and fish. Stir-frying, simmering, steaming, stewing, braising, and pan-frying are common. Famous dishes include *mapo doufu* (spicy, braised tofu), carp with hot bean sauce, chicken with walnuts and chilies, Kung Pao chicken, sweet-sour poultry or seafood, hot and sour soup, scallion pancakes, spicy sesame noodles, and Szechwan duck.

4. **Southern China Region, Canton, Guangzhou, Taiwan: Simple, Light, Innovative**
   Canton, or Guangzhou, is the most populated city in the south and the third largest city in China. Located on the Pearl River, which empties into the South China Sea, Canton is only 75 miles northwest of Hong Kong and north of Macao. China's south has a warm, subtropical climate that produces rice and a lush supply of vegetables and fruits like orange, tangerine, lemon, grapefruit, star fruit, litchi, melons, and peaches.

   Rice is at the center of southern meals, and pork the most common meat, used mainly as seasoning. Frog, squab, shrimp, and fish are common. Centering in Guangdong with its history of outside, foreign influences and ingredients, Cantonese cooking may be China's most adventurous. Ginger, rice vinegar, mustard, and soy sauce are big flavorings. Cantonese cooks stir-fry, braise, roast, simmer, and steam. Famous dishes include seafood with black bean sauce, egg rolls, roast pork, egg foo yung, varied dim sum, crabs steamed with ginger, shrimp dumplings, roast meats such as *chaosiu* (pearl-white chicken gently dipped in boiling water), and brilliant green bundles of blanched and dressed, fresh *choisam* (thick-stemmed leafy green).

DINE AT HOME IN CHINA

In a Chinese home, diners sit at a table. The Chinese saying *chīfàn* or "eat rice" means to have a meal; a large bowl of long-grain rice is central to any meal. The hosts will bring out platters of food, in a pre-chosen order depending on flavors or symbolism, and everything will stay on the table. The meal will be well balanced with, for example, no more than one spicy dish or one beef dish in the meal. There will be texture and taste contrasts: a crisp dish followed by a soft one, a bland dish preceding something spicy.

The meal might begin with an appetizer; fresh salads are rare. Chinese consider soup a beverage so a liquid soup will come with the main meal and might appear once or twice to act as palate cleanser. Diners hold a small bowl of rice under the chin, pick morsels of food from platters and shovel the rice with chopsticks into the mouth. Because familial respect is paramount, the best morsels of food will go first to eldest family members. Tea will come after the meal. Dessert will be fresh fruit, which might also come during the meal.

FIGURE 1.2 The Ulong River near Yangshuo in southern China.
Source: Mikhail Nekrasov/Fotolia.

FIGURE 1.3 Chinese clay pot.
Source: bonchan/Shutterstock.

FIGURE 1.4 Chinese strainer.
Source: sunsetman/Shutterstock.

TASTES OF CHINA

Fat: rapeseed (canola) oil, vegetable, peanut oil, lard, sesame oil, and roasted (Asian) sesame oil

Sweet: rock sugar, sugar, maltose, sorghum syrup, honey, sugar cane juice

Sour/Alcohol: lemon, rice vinegar, white vinegar, black vinegar, red vinegar, Shaoxing wine

Salty: light and dark soy sauce, salt, MSG, mushroom soy sauce

Spicy-Hot: ginger, chilies, chili oil, paste, black pepper, hot bean paste, Szechwan peppercorns, fermented red chili paste

Spice: star anise, cinnamon, fennel, allspice, nutmeg, clove, anise, licorice

Aromatic Seasoning Vegetables: scallions, ginger, garlic, garlic chives, onion, young leek

Herbs, Seasonings and Condiments: fermented black beans; hoisin, plum and oyster sauces, bean pastes, black and brown sesame pastes, cilantro, preserved cassia blossoms, dried shrimp, dried tangerine peel, hot mustard

Other Important Foods: short- and long-grain rice, bean curd products (soft, medium, and firm tofu, dried bean curd sheets, fermented bean cakes, and much more), tapioca, millet, wheat, barley, nuts (peanuts, almonds, pine nuts), white radish (*lo bak*), red beans, fruit (citrus, Asian pears, apples, peaches, plums, bitter, winter and sweet melons, rambutan, longan, lychee), many leafy greens, *gai lan* (Chinese broccoli), long beans, mushrooms, cloud ear and wood ear mushrooms, *jujube* (small, dried red dates), dried lily buds, bamboo shoots, lotus root, snow peas, straw mushrooms, water chestnuts, wild and domestic meat (pork, duck, chicken, lamb), river and ocean fish and seafood, insects

Popular Dishes: bird's nest soup, dim sum, pot-sticker dumplings, soup dumplings, kung pao chicken, claypot seafood, peanut noodles, West Lake fish, hot and sour soup, Cantonese roast duck, dan dan noodles, *congee* (rice gruel with toppings), Szechwan long beans, egg drop soup, *mapo doufu* (spicy tofu stew), Peking duck and Peking pancakes, almond chicken, eggplant with garlic sauce, red cooked pork, scallion pancakes, sweet and sour dishes, tea smoked duck or fish, *law bok gau* (turnip cake), shaved ice dessert, steamed egg custard, moon cakes, sweet red bean soup, mango pudding, almond or sesame pudding, hand-pulled noodles, *dim sum*: chicken feet, dumplings, egg rolls, steamed buns and *nor mai gai* (sticky rice and chicken in lotus leaf) and many more

Drinks: various regional black and green teas; chrysanthemum, hibiscus, rose, and jasmine teas; liquor, beer, whiskey, almond milk, soy milk, bubble teas

CHINESE BOTTLED CONDIMENTS

Chinese Bean Sauces

There at least five types of bean sauce made with either soybeans or black beans: **Bean** or **Brown Bean Sauce** is made from the soybean pulp leftover after brewing. **Sweet Bean Sauce** is the Peking sweetened version. **Hot Bean Sauce** typically has Szechwan chilies and Asian sesame oil added. The black bean sauces are made from puréed or crushed black beans. **Black Bean Garlic Sauce** has garlic added and **Black Bean Chili Sauce** is spicier with chilies.

Chili Sauce with Garlic

This thick, red, spicy paste is made from salted red chilies, garlic, sugar, rice vinegar and cornstarch. It is used for stir-fries and marinades.

Hoisin Sauce

This spicy-sweet, thick, reddish-brown sauce is prepared from soybeans, sugar, flour, vinegar, salt, garlic, chili, and sesame. It's used as a barbecue sauce, marinade, and dipping sauce with Peking duck or moo shu pork and Mandarin pancakes.

Oyster Sauce

This rich and concentrated thick, brown sauce is made from soy sauce and oyster extract. Its smoky flavor and big, savory flavor that Japanese call *umami*, make it popular in dipping sauces or on stir-fries. Look for the best.

Plum Sauce (Duck Sauce)

This thick, jammy sauce is made from a type of fruit species related to both plums and apricots, but more closely to the apricot and the Japanese umeboshi plum. The apricot-like plums, sugar, vinegar, salt, ginger, chili, and garlic yield a clear yellow sauce with light, sweet and tart flavor. It is especially good with poultry, spring rolls and egg rolls.

Traditional Chinese Medicine's Five Flavors and Health

Chinese medicine says that foods' five flavors correspond to health. Many Chinese believe that balanced meals including these five flavors improve internal organ function. They are related to the Five Elements (see Glossary). There are pharmacies with restaurants attached, where a doctor of Chinese medicine diagnoses patients and prescribes meals, which the restaurant prepares.

Sour contracts and coalesces, stanches the flow of blood, roughens, and congests.

Bitter dries out, depresses, subdues, or damps down.

Sweet regulates, evens out, harmonizes, softens, buffers, and supports.

Pungent or Sharp opens up, dissolves, and mobilizes active energy (qi).

Salty softens, moistens, and purges or purifies.

CHINESE FLAVOR FOUNDATIONS

Chinese Signature Aromatic Vegetable Combo: Bao Syang

Bao syang, the Chinese signature set of aromatic vegetables consists of green onions, gingerroot and garlic and sometimes chilies. Use bao syang as a base of flavor to give a dish a Chinese flavor.

Signature Seasonings

Liquid/Paste

Chinese Soy Sauce

This dark, salty liquid is fermented from soybeans, wheat, and water. It is less refined and more densely flavored than Japanese soy sauce. Chinese soy sauce ranges from light to medium-thin to heavy, dark, or double dark. Delicate, subtle *light* soy sauce is used as a dipping sauce or with mild fish or chicken. Full-flavored *medium-thin* soy sauce is an all-purpose soy sauce. Full-bodied and slightly sweet *dark* soy sauce ("superior") often has molasses added, and is used in stews and marinades and to coat meats for roasting and barbecuing.

Dajiang (Chinese Soybean Paste)

Northeast China's fermented soybean paste is similar in taste and texture to Korean doenjang. Manchurians are said to have introduced it more than four centuries ago to this region. Chinese eat dajiang with raw summer vegetables or as a salad dressing.

Mushroom Soy Sauce

This smooth, meaty-flavored soy sauce is the dark Chinese soy sauce infused with dried shiitake mushrooms. It's used as a seasoning in stir-fries and marinades and with meat and poultry.

Chinese Rice Vinegar

This pale, mild-flavored vinegar is fermented from glutinous (sweet or sticky) rice. It's used for cooking, salads, pickling, and in sauces.

Red Rice Vinegar

This pale, slightly sweet red vinegar is fermented and distilled from red rice, barley, and sorghum. It's especially prized for crabs, fried noodles, and soup. It is said to aid digestion.

Chinkiang Black Vinegar

This dark, fermented and aged vinegar is made from glutinous rice. It is milder than other vinegars with a smoky, slightly sweet taste. Black vinegar is used with noodles, as a dip, or as seasoning in soups or cold dishes. Balsamic vinegar can be used as a substitute.

Chinese (Roasted) Sesame Oil (Asian Sesame Oil)

A seasoning (not cooking) oil made from roasted brown or black sesame seeds.

FIGURE 1.5 Chinese Jinhua ham.
Source: Gary Sergraves/DK Images.

Shaoxing Wine (Chinese Rice Wine)

This nutty, amber, rice wine is brewed from glutinous rice, millet, and yeast and aged 10 to 100 years. Similar in alcohol content and full-bodied flavor to sherry, Shaoxing wine is used for drinking, marinating, and cooking. Avoid salted varieties. Dry sherry may substitute.

See *Chinese Bottled Condiments* for more bottled Chinese products.

Animal

Chinese Jinhua Ham

The 8- to 10-month process of salting, soaking, drying, and dry-curing results in hams similar in taste and texture to the Iberian and Parma hams. Chinese cooks sometimes soak Chinese ham to remove its saltiness before using in stewed and braised dishes, stock, and soup. Currently the Jinhua ham is not imported into the United States, but Chinese here substitute a Jinhua-style ham made in Brooklyn, New York, or Westphalian or Smithfield ham or prosciutto.

Dried Shrimp

Fresh shrimp are salted and dried to intensify their flavor. Chinese use dried shrimp to enhance vegetable dishes. The best are bright pink and about 1 inch from head to tail. Avoid older, gray-colored shrimp. To soften their flavor, soak in sherry or shaoxing wine. They keep indefinitely.

Vegetable/Fruit

Chinese Dried Black Mushrooms

These flavorful mushrooms range in color from black and brown to gray and in size from 1 to 3 inches; the larger ones are more costly. Look for medium-sized, but thick caps. Rinse then

FIGURE 1.6 Bags of dried shrimp.
Source: Philip Blenkinsop/DK Images.

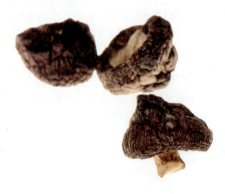

FIGURE 1.7 Dried black mushrooms.
Source: defun/Fotolia.

soak mushrooms in warm water until soft, 20 to 30 minutes, before using. Reserve soaking water and use in dish. Discard tough stems or use for stock-making. It takes 1 pound of fresh shiitakes to yield 3 ounces dried.

Fermented Black Beans

These deeply savory beans are made by salting and fermenting black soybeans. They have an almost chocolate flavor. They pair well with garlic and should be rinsed or soaked briefly before chopping to remove the saltiness. Fermented black beans keep indefinitely unrefrigerated.

(Continued)

FIGURE 1.8   Chinese chives.

Source: JIANG HONGYAN/Shutterstock.

Herbal/Spice

Gow Choy (Garlic Chive)
This long, narrow and wide-leafed pungent garlic-flavored herb is used to season dumpling fillings, stir-fries, and soups.

Star Anise
The seeds of this 8-pointed star-shaped, brown spice have a mildly licorice-fennel flavor and are used in red-cooked dishes.

Szechwan Pepper, Sansho, Prickly Ash or Fagara
The Szechwan peppercorn is a small reddish spice with an outer husk and an inner dark

FIGURE 1.9   Star anise.

Source: Dave King/DK Images.

seed. Japanese use a close relative called *sansho*. The husk is used for seasoning and the bitter seeds discarded. Whole Szechwan pepper and sansho are often lightly dry-toasted before use. Szechwan pepper isn't hot, it is citrusy and mouth-numbing. Duck, chicken,

FIGURE 1.10   Szechwan peppercorns.

Source: Paul Williams/DK Images.

and pork dishes go well with Szechwan peppercorns, which are made into a roasted Szechwan salt good for dipping. Different varieties of this spice are used in China, Japan, Korea, Tibet, Indonesia, Bhutan, Goa, and Nepal. Sansho's lemony-fragrant leaves, *kinome*, are used in Japanese cooking, dried or fresh, with bamboo shoots or as soup garnish.

SEASONING AND PASTE MIXTURES

CHINESE FIVE-SPICE POWDER AND FIVE-SPICE SALT

Classically the five spices are Szechwan peppercorns, cinnamon, star anise, fennel, and clove. Depending on its use, this mixture could also contain allspice, white pepper, chili, fennel, ginger, or licorice root.

Yields 3 to 4 tablespoons

1 tablespoon Szechwan peppercorns
2 whole star anise
1 teaspoon ground cinnamon
1/2 teaspoon fennel seed
6 whole cloves

1   Toast Szechwan peppercorns in a dry frying pan until fragrant. Don't walk away; they'll burn.

2   Cool and grind spices to a fine powder. Inhale the scent.

Vary! Improvise!

☞ **Five-spice salt:** *Grind together equal parts kosher or sea salt and five-spice powder. Use as a dipping medium for fried foods. Dip food in soy sauce then into five-spice salt mixture.*

☞ **Five-spice sugar:** *Make five-spice powder with sugar instead of salt; use with desserts or sweets.*

SZECHWAN CHILI OIL (HONG YU)

Use this oil stirred into sauces or drizzled over noodles and dumplings.

Yields about 1 cup

2/3 to 3/4 ounce crushed red chili flakes, 1/4 cup
1 cup canola or vegetable oil
Optional Seasonings: 1 slice gingerroot, crushed, and/or 1 star anise

1 Pour chili flakes and optional seasonings into 1-pint heat-proof glass canning jar. Heat oil to 225 degrees F.

2 Pour oil over chilies and **optional seasonings**. Cool. Chili oil may be used immediately, but flavor and fragrance will improve after several hours and deepen over several days. Refrigerate.

SAUCE

Simple-to-make Asian sauces don't require the complex flavor techniques of French or European cuisine, but they're no less flavorful. Asian sauces make expert use of umami-rich ingredients and highly flavored seasonings that grab you and make you lust for more. Some chefs cook garlic, scallions, ginger, or spices before simmering; others add everything raw and marinate to allow flavors to mingle. Asian sauces thicken naturally by simmering or with the help of rice flour or cornstarch. Resting sauces is the key to flavor success.

SIMPLE CHINESE DUMPLING DIPPING SAUCE

Yields 7 tablespoons

Scant 1/2 ounce gingerroot, 2 teaspoons peeled and finely minced
4 tablespoons red or black vinegar or balsamic vinegar
2 tablespoons Japanese shoyu *or* thin Chinese soy sauce
1 teaspoon Chinese chili oil *or* Asian sesame oil *or* Chinese chili paste with garlic

1 Mix all ingredients together. Taste and adjust flavors.

SZECHWAN MYSTERIOUS FLAVORS SAUCE

Great paired with fish or meat.

Yields about 5 fluid ounces, scant 2/3 cup

2 tablespoons plain sesame *or* vegetable oil (*not* Asian toasted sesame oil)
1/2 ounce gingerroot, 1 tablespoon peeled and minced
1/2 ounce garlic, 2 large cloves, 1 tablespoon peeled and minced
1 ounce trimmed green onions, 2 large, 4 tablespoons minced, white and green separated
1/2 cup Chinese rice wine or sherry
1 teaspoon Chinese chili paste
2 tablespoons soy sauce
1 tablespoon Chinese black vinegar *and* 1 teaspoon balsamic vinegar *or* balsamic vinegar to taste
1 to 2 teaspoons maple syrup *or* brown sugar, to taste

1   Heat oil in a small 6- to 7-inch saucepan over medium heat. Stir in ginger, garlic, and white part of green onion; cook until soft and infused into the oil, 2 minutes. Add rice wine, raise heat, and boil until reduced by half.

2   Remove pan from heat and stir in chili paste, soy sauce, vinegar, and sweetener. Taste and adjust seasonings with more sugar, soy sauce, vinegar, or chili.

3   Pour sauce over fish or serve on side. Garnish with green part of green onions or stir them into sauce.

Source: *The Modern Art of Chinese Cooking* by Barbara Tropp.

CHINESE SWEET AND SOUR DIPPING SAUCE

Yes, the Chinese really do use ketchup for this sauce. Use it as a dip for fried fish or shrimp, meatballs, or as a quick stir-fry sauce.

Yields about 1 cup

3 tablespoons rice vinegar
4 tablespoons sugar
2 tablespoons ketchup
2 teaspoons soy sauce
2 tablespoons plain sesame *or* vegetable oil (not Asian roasted sesame oil)
1/2 ounce garlic, 2 large cloves, 1 tablespoon peeled and minced
1/2 ounce gingerroot, 2 to 3 teaspoons peeled and finely minced
2 teaspoons cornstarch dissolved in 2 tablespoons cold water

1   Combine vinegar, sugar, ketchup, and soy sauce with 1/2 cup water and set aside.

2   Heat a 2-quart saucepan over medium heat and add the oil. When it is hot, stir in garlic and gingerroot. Simmer until fragrant without browning, about 1 minute.

3   Stir in ketchup mixture and bring to a boil. Reduce heat to medium-low. Give cornstarch mixture a stir and scrape into simmering sauce while stirring it. Cook until clear and glossy, about 20 seconds. Cool and serve at room temperature. Sauce will last about 5 days, refrigerated.

Source: *The Modern Art of Chinese Cooking* by Barbara Tropp.

SPECIAL METHODS

Signature Technique: Hot Wok-Smoking

Chinese cooks use smoking as a flavoring, not cooking, technique. There are two types of smoking: hot and cold. Wok-smoking is a hot smoke technique used for flavor and texture, not preservation. It requires short brining or marinating and temperatures from 90 to 150 degrees F, resulting in fully or partially cooked moist food. Cold smoking keeps foods longer; it requires longer brining, lower temperatures, and longer smoking. Wok-smoking opens a new world of flavor: smoke ears of corn, okra, tomatoes, eggplant, peppers, poultry, pork, or tofu. Fatty fish like salmon absorb smoke faster and stay moist.

1   **Brine or Marinate:** (Skip this step for vegetables.) Brine or marinate moist protein ingredients like fish, seafood, or meat 15 minutes (for seafood) to 8 hours (for meat and poultry). Set on oiled wok-steaming rack or stainless steel wok-steaming basket.

2   **Precook Moist Protein:** Steam seafood, meat, or tofu in wok covered with lid until slightly under-cooked. Drain water from wok and wipe dry.

3 **Protect the Wok:** Line wok (with a lid) with aluminum foil for quick clean-up. Fold edges of foil over top edges of wok.

4 **Choose Aromatics:** Pour smoking ingredients into bottom of lined wok. Loose tea leaves, herbs, and herb stems like rosemary, basil, or thyme; rice, grain, citrus peel, dried flowers, or leaves like bay or Kaffir lime, and spices are options. Chinese add sugar or brown sugar.

5 **Set It Up:** *For non-marinated or brined foods:* Place food on an oiled circular wok rack. Set rack into wok over smoking ingredients. A 6-inch-deep hotel pan with rack and lid or hotel pan topped with a 2-inch deep perforated pan and lid also works. Line the bottom pan with foil.

6 **Seal It Well:** Seal lid onto wok by ringing it with aluminum foil or a wet towel.

7 **Smoke It:** Set wok on medium heat. When it begins to smoke, start timing.

8 **Time It and Check It:** The timing depends on how much smoked taste is desired. Three to 5 minutes produces delicate smoke flavor in fish. For deeper smoke flavor, smoke food longer, but check on it every 2 minutes.

CHINESE TEA AND SPICE SMOKED FISH

4 servings

1-1/2 pounds salmon fillet, boned, but skin on

Marinade

Yields about 1/2 cup

1 ounce trimmed green onions, 2 large
1-1/2 tablespoons Chinese rice wine or sake
4 tablespoons soy sauce
1 tablespoon sugar
1 tablespoon kosher salt
1 ounce peeled gingerroot, 2 to 3 tablespoons finely matchstick cut

Smoking Mixture

1 to 1-1/4 ounce dry black tea leaves, 1/3 cup
2-1/3 ounces raw rice, about 1/3 cup
1-1/2 to 2 ounces brown sugar, 1/3 cup packed
1 teaspoon Szechwan peppercorns
One 3- to 4-inch cinnamon stick, broken up
2 large slices orange zest *or* 2 tablespoons crumbled dried orange peel

Garnish: Asian sesame oil

1 If using a whole fish, score it in a deep cross-hatch on both sides; for a fillet, score just the flesh side.

2 **For marinade:** Halve green onions lengthwise, cut into 2-inch lengths, and smash lightly. Mix together green onions and remaining marinade ingredients. Pour over fish. Work marinade, green onions, and ginger into score marks.

3 Marinate fish 10 to 15 minutes room temperature—or 30 minutes refrigerated. Turn whole fish once and spoon marinade over fish. Lay fillet into marinade, flesh side down.

4 Set fish on an oiled metal wok steaming rack or perforated 2-inch-deep hotel pan. Discard marinade. Bring water to a boil in the bottom of a wok, steamer, or a 6-inch-deep hotel pan. Place fish on rack or perforated pan, cover with a lid or foil and steam until fish is faintly pink at its thickest point, about 6 minutes per inch of thickness. Remove fish to cool. Leave on rack.

5 Meanwhile set up a second 6-inch-deep hotel pan or wok. Line it with heavy aluminum foil. Pour in smoking mixture and spread evenly over bottom of pan—over areas of burners. Set rack with fish in wok at least 2 inches above smoking mixture. Set hotel pan over two burners on medium high heat. Cover tightly with lid and/or foil to seal. When smoke seeps out, lower heat to medium. Smoke fish 5 to 10 minutes depending on desired taste. Rest fish in smoker with heat off 2 to 3 minutes. Check fish: if it seems pale, sprinkle more brown sugar in bottom of wok or hotel pan and smoke longer.

6 **To Serve:** Remove fish from pan or rack onto platter. Brush with sesame oil. Serve warm or room temperature.

Vary! Improvise!

☛ *Devise smoking combos to give flavor to duck, chicken, or pork.*

Chinese Stir-Fry Preparation Methods

SIGNATURE RECIPE

SALT-WHISKED SHRIMP

For stir-fries, crystallizing or salt whisking removes stickiness and gives seafood a crystalline look and firmer texture.

1 pound 26/30 shrimp, peeled and deveined
3 teaspoons kosher salt, *divided*

1 Place shrimp into a large mixing bowl and sprinkle with 1 teaspoon salt. Stir rapidly 1 minute.

2 Pour shrimp into a colander and rinse with cold water. Drain and blot with paper towels.

3 Place shrimp back into mixing bowl; add 1 teaspoon salt. Stir rapidly 1 minute. Drain, place shrimp back into mixing bowl, and repeat process a third time with 1 teaspoon salt.

4 Rinse and drain shrimp a third time, blot-dry in paper towel. Shrimp are ready for stir-frying.

VELVETING IN OIL OR WATER

A two-step process from southern China, velveting speeds cooking, tenderizes proteins, keeps food from sticking, and food absorbs less oil. Velveted proteins go into a stir-fry after the sauce is simmering, contrary to the usual method of stir-frying primary proteins with aromatics in the beginning of a dish. Chinese expert chef Barbara Tropp says that oil-velveted foods are firm and plush while water-velveted foods are bouncy and soft.

1 pound 26/30 shrimp, peeled and deveined
  or 1 pound boneless, skinless chicken
    or 1 pound skinned fish fillets

Velveting Ingredients

1 teaspoon kosher salt
1 teaspoon Chinese rice wine *or* dry sherry
1-1/2 tablespoons cornstarch
Optional: 1 large egg white

1 Dice chicken or fish fillets into 3/4-inch cubes. Chicken should not be frozen before velveting; the plush texture will be lost.

2 Mix together **velveting ingredients**.

3 Mix protein in velveting mixture and refrigerate 30 minutes to 1 hour.

4 Cook velveted ingredients in oil or water:

Velveting in Oil

- *If using wok:* Heat over high heat; when hot, lower heat to medium and add 2 cups oil. Bring oil to 212 degrees F (on deep-fry thermometer). When velveting in oil, a hot wok keeps velveted food from sticking.

- *If using 4-quart saucepan:* Pour in oil and heat to 212 degrees F over medium-high heat. Set a strainer over a metal bowl. When oil reaches 212 degrees F on a deep-fry thermometer, give velveted chicken, fish, or shrimp a stir, and pour into oil. (Overly hot oil toughens proteins.) Remove pan from heat. With chopsticks or slotted spoon, quickly but gently separate pieces of meat, fish, or shrimp. Cook protein until set and lightly opaque on surface, 15 to 20 seconds.

- Quickly scoop protein into strainer and drain. Protein is ready to be stir-fried—do this immediately. Strain and reuse oil in stir-fry dish or for more velveting.

Velveting in Water

Bring 1 quart water to a boil and add 1 tablespoon oil. Turn off heat. Stir velveted chicken or fish, and scatter into water. Stir gently with chopsticks to separate. Occasionally stir until food is set and opaque on surface, 15 seconds. Lift meat or seafood into a strainer to drain. Shake gently to remove excess water. Use food immediately.

HANDMADE TOFU (DOUFU)

The Chinese first developed tofu around 164 BCE, but it didn't reach Japan until the eighth century. Twelve hundred years later, with the influence of the Japanese macrobiotic movement, tofu arrived in the United States. Associated with the Buddhist meatless diet, most of the earliest tofu shops were in large temple or monastery complexes. Nigari is the traditional curding agent in Japan. In China, calcium sulfate or gypsum is traditional; it produces a softer, custard-like tofu with more tofu yield than nigari.

Yields 33 to 39 ounces fresh tofu

About 10 ounces organic soybeans, 1-1/2 cups
About 5-1/2 quarts nonchlorinated water, *divided*

Curding Agent

Subtle and Sweet: 2 teaspoons calcium chloride (refined nigari) or magnesium chloride
   or 2 teaspoons granular nigari
      or 2 to 4 teaspoons commercial liquid nigari
   or
Mild and Soft: 2 teaspoons gypsum (calcium sulfate) or Epsom salts (magnesium sulfate)

For Serving

High-quality soy sauce
Minced green onions

1   **Soak beans:** Wash and drain soybeans. Place in bowl and cover beans with 6 cups cold, nonchlorinated water. Soak 10 hours. Drain and rinse beans and pour back into bowl.

2   **Prepare draining vessels:** Place a non-reactive colander into a large, clean pot. Line colander with a 24-inch square of dampened, triple-layered cheesecloth; set aside. Line a strainer or tofu box "settling" container with dampened triple-layered cheesecloth so that it overhangs the container.

3   Over high heat in a heavy, 8-quart pot, bring 7-1/2 cups nonchlorinated water to a boil.

4   **Purée beans:** Pour half the drained, soaked beans and 2 cups nonchlorinated water into a blender and purée on high until beans are very smooth, about 3 minutes. Add purée (go) to water heating in pot. Repeat with remaining beans and another 2 cups water. Pour beans into pot and rinse blender with 1/2 cup water and pour into pot.

5   **Cook purée:** Stir bean mixture frequently so it doesn't boil over or scorch to the bottom of the pot. When the foam rises, turn off the heat. Pour bean mixture through cheesecloth-lined strainer. Scrape out beans from pot into the colander. Rinse out pot and place back on stove.

6   **Drain soymilk:** Twist cheesecloth closed and press out soymilk from the soybean solids (okara). Open cheesecloth sack, shake the solids, twist closed and press again to express the milk. Pour soybean solids into a bowl and stir well with 3 cups nonchlorinated water. Pour back into cheesecloth and express milk as before. Set solids aside. Measure curding agent into 1 cup nonchlorinated cold water to form curding solution; set aside until needed.

7   **Cook the soymilk:** Pour soymilk into the rinsed-out 8-quart pot and place back onto stove. Bring soymilk to a boil over high heat; stir frequently in a Z pattern to prevent scorching. Lower heat to medium, and cook soymilk 7 minutes. Remove pot from heat.

8   **Curd the soymilk:** Stir soymilk vigorously 5 to 6 times. Give curding solution a stir and while stirring soymilk, pour in 1/3 cup curding solution. Stir 5 to 6 times in a Z motion, reaching bottom and sides of pot. Bring spoon to a halt upright in soymilk. When all movement has ceased, lift spoon out. Sprinkle 1/3 cup curding solution over surface of soymilk, cover pot and allow curds to form for 3 minutes. Uncover pot and drizzle in remaining curding solution.

9   Slowly stir upper 1/2-inch layer of curdling soymilk for 20 seconds. Cover pot and wait 3 to 4 minutes for nigari or magnesium chloride, and 6 minutes for calcium sulfate or Epsom salts. Uncover pot and stir surface layer until the milky liquid curdles, 20 to 30 seconds. White curds should float in clear, pale yellow whey. If whey is milky, wait 1 minute and stir gently until it curdles. If it still persists, make a mixture of 1/3 cup water mixed with 1/2 teaspoon curding agent, and stir gently into milky whey.

10 **Transfer curds, and press:** Ladle curds into strainer or settling container. Fold edges of cheesecloth over curds. Place a flat board or plate on top and weight with 1/2- to 1-pound weight until whey stops dripping, 10 to 15 minutes. *For firm tofu:* Press curds with 2 pounds of weight for 30 to 40 minutes.

11 **To firm-up tofu:** Immerse tofu in water 3 to 5 minutes, unwrap and transfer to plate to drain. *To store tofu:* Place in storage container, cover with cold, nonchlorinated water, and refrigerate. Tofu will firm and lose its sweet flavor the longer it sits in water. Change water daily. (Tofu is a moist protein and should be handled carefully like fish, eggs, or chicken.)

12 **To Serve:** For a delightful treat, dice tofu into cubes *before* immersing into water. Drizzle with a little soy sauce and garnish with green onions.

Source: *The Book of Tofu: Food for Mankind* by William Shurtleff and Akiko.

SIMMER, STEW, POACH, AND STEAM

> ### COOK'S VOICE: MARTIN YAN
>
> ### Chinese Chef, Author, Teacher, and Television Personality
> ### San Francisco, California
>
> "You can do almost anything with soup stock, it's like a strong foundation. When you have the right foundation, everything tastes good."

Chinese Soup

Good soup is the same around the world. It starts with great-tasting stock and fresh ingredients. Chinese cooks prepare two kinds of broth or stock: a clear, light broth made from chicken and a rich broth made with pork and pork bones. Both are flavored with ginger and scallions.

Asians have a soup style for every dining occasion. Chinese soups eaten with meals at home are lighter, modest, and sipped throughout a meal as a beverage and tasty food. Chinese banquet, formal, or occasion soups are made from expensive ingredients like bird's nests and shark fin. By technique, soups fall into three categories: simmered, poached, and mixed.

- **Simmered soups** are rich, hearty, chunky, and substantial. They consist of broth or water simmered with meat and vegetables. Simmered soup ingredients and broth should be equally flavorful. Cooks put meat and ingredients into boiling liquid and cook only until meat or vegetables are tender, and still retain flavor.
- **Poached soups** are fast cooked to retain individual flavors. Main ingredients are cut smaller, marinated, or velveted and cooked briefly in broth until vegetables are crisp-tender and meat is just cooked through.
- **Mixed soups** are a mixture of many tastes, textures, and ingredients, usually finely diced and quickly cooked; mixed soups are often thickened with cornstarch or eggs, which offsets their strong seasonings of soy sauce, sesame oil, vinegar, chili, and pepper.

SZECHWAN SOUR AND HOT SOUP

Dried shiitakes or Chinese black mushrooms, with their intense, concentrated flavors, are excellent in this soup. This is a typical Chinese mixed soup.

Yields about 12 cups, 8 to 12 servings

4 ounces fresh shiitake mushrooms
  or 1 ounce dried shiitakes, about 3/4 cup
12 ounces firm tofu, 2 cups finely and evenly diced into 1/4-inch cubes
4 ounces water-packed, not canned, bamboo shoots, 1 cup julienned
1 ounce prosciutto (3 thin slices), Smithfield *or* Westphalian ham, about 1/3 cup finely diced
Optional: 1 teaspoon Szechwan peppercorns
2 quarts chicken stock
4 tablespoons soy sauce
4 tablespoons rice vinegar, more to taste
Optional: 2 tablespoons cornstarch mixed with 2 tablespoons cold water
2 large eggs, about 1/4 cup lightly beaten

Garnish

Ground white pepper *or* Asian hot chili sesame oil
1 ounce trimmed green onion, 2 large, about 1/4 cup minced, more to taste

> ### COOK'S VOICE: JUDY CHU
>
> ### Traverse City, Michigan
>
> "I was brought up the daughter of a Northern Chinese father. His region claims this soup (hot and sour soup) as its own. And I grew up with some contempt at all the restaurants that would flavor this soup with hot chili sauce . . . the one I consider the purest uses white pepper, not Szechwan pepper and certainly not chili pepper oil."
>
> Source: Courtesy of Judy Chu.

1 Finely slice mushroom caps into thin julienne strips. Slice off stems and use for stock or finely mince. There will be 1 to 1-1/4 cups mushrooms. *If using dry mushrooms*, soak in boiling water until soft, 20 minutes. Julienne-cut the caps, but discard tough stems. (Reserve 1/2 cup soaking liquid and substitute for part of the chicken stock.)

2 *If using Szechwan peppercorns:* Heat a small sauté pan (not nonstick) over medium heat. Toast Szechwan peppercorns until fragrant, 30 seconds to 1 minute. Cool and crush finely.

3 Heat stock in a saucepan and add mushrooms, tofu, bamboo shoots, and ham. Bring to a boil and immediately lower heat to a simmer. Simmer 2 minutes and stir in soy sauce, toasted Szechwan pepper, and vinegar, adding more to taste.

4 Stir optional cornstarch and water together, if using. While stirring soup, pour cornstarch slurry into simmering soup. (Using cornstarch to thicken sour and hot soup is not classical in China, but done in Chinese restaurants in the West.) Bring soup to a boil and cook until slightly thickened, 1 minute. While stirring the boiling soup in circles, slowly pour in egg, and cook until it coagulates into shreds. Taste and adjust seasonings.

5 **To Serve:** Ladle soup into bowls and garnish with white pepper or a few drops of hot chili oil, and minced green onion.

Egg Drop Soup

Make egg drop soup by stirring 1/2 cup beaten eggs (about 2 large) into 2 quarts boiling, plain chicken stock, as in method for *Szechwan Hot and Sour Soup*. Garnish with minced green onions.

CHICKEN SOUP WITH WATERCRESS

This is a typical Chinese poached soup.

Yields 5-1/2 to 6 cups

8 ounces boneless, skinless chicken breast

Velveting Ingredients

1 large egg white
2 teaspoons cornstarch
2 teaspoons vegetable oil

6 to 7 ounces fresh watercress, 1 bunch
1 ounce Smithfield ham, Westphalian ham, or prosciutto, 1/4 to 1/3 cup thinly sliced
4 cups chicken stock
Optional: 1 tablespoon Chinese rice wine or dry sherry

1 *Marinate chicken in* **velveting ingredients:** Slice chicken breast in half lengthwise. Slice each half cross-grain into 1/8-inch thick slices to yield 1 cup. Sprinkle chicken with 1/2-teaspoon kosher salt. Beat egg white, cornstarch and vegetable oil together until smooth, fold mixture into chicken and refrigerate 30 minutes or up to 3 hours in advance.

2 Fill a 3-quart saucepan with cold water. Set a colander or strainer out. Bring water to boil and lower to a slow simmer. Stir chicken, and immediately slide it into the simmering water. Stir gently, and cook chicken until firm and white, 40 to 60 seconds. Pour water and chicken through strainer and drain chicken. Set chicken aside or refrigerate until ready to construct soup.

3 **Blanch watercress:** Refill saucepan with water and bring to a boil. Lightly trim bottom stems off watercress. Blanch watercress in boiling water until bright green and wilted, 30 to 60 seconds, and immediately drain. Rinse with cold water and squeeze-drain. Slice watercress crosswise into 2-inch lengths to yield about 1 cup. Set watercress aside until serving.

4 Slice ham into 1/4-inch by 1- to 1-1/2-inch strips. Bring the stock to a boil. Lower heat to a simmer and stir in ham and chicken. Cover pan partially and simmer soup 2 minutes. Taste soup, and season with salt and sherry.

5 **To Serve:** Place 1/4 cup watercress into each of 4 serving bowls. Ladle hot soup over and serve immediately.

Source: The Key to Chinese Cooking by Irene Kuo.

GREAT FISH DISHES BEGIN WITH THE FISHMONGER

The secret of any good fish dish is to form a relationship with your fishmonger and to balance strong fish flavors. Asian rice wine, acids like vinegar or citrus and ginger do this well—the added bonus, they firm up fish flesh.

Purchase fish with scales and gills intact—scales keep fish fresher and bright red, oxygen-filled gills tell of its freshness. If fresh whole fish is unavailable, use fillets with bone-in. If a fish is too large for the cooking vessel, cut it, but leave bones in. Chinese cooks say that meat is sweetest nearest the bone. Fish cheeks are also tasty, don't discard the head: Asian cooks prepare stock and whole soups from tasty fish heads.

Fresh Fish has:
- Moist red gills
- Round bright, clear eyes, not cloudy or sunken
- Firm, bouncy flesh that springs back when poked
- Shiny skin with scales firmly attached
- No strong fishy odor—only a slight sea odor

Chinese Liquid-Cooking Techniques

Chinese and Korean cooks stew in clay or stone pots over charcoal or gas heat. Tougher, flavorful portions like ribs, shoulder, and shank are ideal. Long, slow cooking transforms them into tender, succulent food. Cooks thicken stew liquid with cornstarch or simmer to reduce and intensify. Poaching, clear-simmering, and stewing all use low, moist direct heat. Water boils vigorously at 212 degrees F. Poaching, simmering, and stewing cook at lower temperatures; they raise large, lazy bubbles and ripple the water's surface gently at around 170 to 185 degrees F.

CLEAR-SIMMERED

This important technique combines water or stock and a main course meat or fish into one dish. Very fresh meat, poultry, large fish, or sturdy vegetables may be fried in oil with ginger and green onion (or not), covered with water or stock and slow-cooked, traditionally in a clay pot; the broth remains clear or reduces and thickens.

A minimum of seasonings keeps the spotlight of flavor on the main ingredient. Wine, salt, rich stock, dried mushrooms, cured ham, dried shrimp or scallops, and green onions add flavor and color to poultry; soy sauce, pepper, garlic, ginger, and green onions are used with fish. A garnish of oil and seasonings is sometimes used.

WHITE-CUT OR ICE-CHILLED

White-cut is a method that cooks pork or whole chicken by simmering partway and steeping partway in plain (or seasoned without soy sauce) water or stock until just done. Some cooks submerge small whole chickens into boiling water (covered by 2 inches), turn off the heat, cover the pot and let the chicken cook in the hot water until cooked through. The meat must be very fresh, and chicken never frozen. The meat is plunged into ice water 15 to 20 minutes; it contracts, the juices gel and flavor is locked in. The meat may be used as a base for salads, combined with vegetables, or served alone with a sauce poured on top or on the side for dipping.

SALT-CURED OR SALT-WATER-MARINATED

Salt-curing involves rubbing meat or poultry with roasted Szechwan peppercorns and salt for a few hours or days. The meat is simmered or steamed, and chilled. This method intensifies flavor, and results in a firm, silky texture. The salt-water-marinated technique simmers small cuts of shellfish, duck (with bone), or offal in salt water and Szechwan peppercorns. The protein is chilled in the brine before serving. These techniques result in firm, fresh-tasting foods that may be used as a main dish or appetizer.

RED-COOKED

Chinese (and Koreans) stew meat, fish, and tofu in a soy-sauce-based broth infused with star anise or five-spice powder, Chinese rice wine, and sometimes rock sugar. Red-cooked foods take on the "red" hue of soy sauce. Often the foods are seared before simmering in the rich broth. Red-cooked foods are served warm or cold and the liquid may be reduced to act as a glaze or sauce. Leftovers keep well. Red-cooking is popular in Eastern China, where the finest soy sauce is made.

FLAVOR-POTTED

Chinese flavor potting is similar to red-cooking. Ingredients are precooked, simmered, and steeped in a sauce, but at slightly higher heat for a shorter time, drained and cooled. While red-cooked foods can be served hot or cold, flavor potted foods are sliced and served room temperature or cold as nibbles or lunch dishes; they are not as intensely flavored as red-cooked foods. Reused red cooking or flavor potting liquid gets richer flavored the longer it's used.

CLEAR-SIMMERED WHOLE FISH

2 to 4 servings

2 pounds whole fish

Seasonings

2 tablespoons rice wine
1/4 ounce gingerroot, 2 slices smashed
1/2 ounce trimmed green onion, 1 large, 2 tablespoons sliced

Garnish

1/4 cup vegetable or plain sesame oil
1/2 ounce gingerroot, 1 tablespoon peeled and finely matchstick cut
1 ounce trimmed green onions, 2 large, 4 tablespoons finely julienned
Soy sauce
Cilantro leaves

1 **Prepare the fish:** scale, gut, and rinse. Slice fish on both sides in 2 to 3 diagonal cuts to the bone. Cut fish crosswise if necessary to fit cooking vessel. Alternately use 3/4-inch thick halibut or flounder steaks.

2 **Prepare the clear simmering liquid:** Fill a skillet or pan large enough to hold fish in single layer with cold water to cover fish by 1 inch and add **seasonings**. Bring to a boil over medium heat.

3 **Poach fish:** Slide cleaned fish into liquid and lower heat to gently simmer. Simmer fish until flesh is opaque and flaky when pierced with a knife tip, 6 to 8 minutes. Fish should be very slightly undercooked at bone. Drain fish, remove to platter, cover and keep warm.

4 **Garnish:** Heat oil in wok or small sauté pan. When hot, add ginger and scallions. Immediately pour oil and seasonings over fish. Drizzle with soy sauce and cilantro leaves.

5 **To Serve:** Fish have a two-part skeleton: flat spine from tail to neck and two-dimensional ribs. Flesh from cooked fish like bass, rockfish, snapper, and trout come away from the bone easily. Use a fork and spatula to loosen flesh at the top and back of fish and lift fillet from the flat bones. No need to flip the fish; instead lift tail and attached spine and ribs away from the second, bottom fillet. Leave the head; it has succulent fish cheeks. Tiny bones may still lurk in fillets, so warn guests.

Vary! Improvise!

☛ *Prepare serving-sized fillets with this method.*

FIGURE 1.11 Red cooked pork belly.

Source: uckyo/Fotolia.

RED-COOKED CHICKEN OR TOFU

For a saltier taste, increase the soy sauce.

2 to 4 servings

Broth Ingredients

Yields 2-1/3 cups

4 tablespoons soy sauce
1/2 cup dry sherry or Chinese cooking wine
1 scant ounce rock sugar, 2 tablespoons
   or 2 tablespoons brown sugar
1/2 ounce gingerroot, 4 twenty-five-cent-sized slices, bruised
1 ounce green onions, 2 large, sliced into 1-inch pieces and bruised
2 whole star anise
1/2 teaspoon fennel seed
1 four-inch stick cinnamon, lightly crushed
Zest of one orange

Vegetable oil for browning

Red Cooked Chicken *or* Tofu

1 pound bone-in chicken legs and thighs or breast, skinned
   or 1-1/2 pounds boneless, skinless chicken breast
     or 1-1/2 pounds tofu, diced into 1-inch cubes

For Serving

1 tablespoon Asian sesame oil for brushing
Finely sliced cabbage or romaine lettuce
Sliced tomato

1   Pour red-cooking **broth ingredients** plus 2 cups water into saucepan. Bring to a boil, cover pot partially, lower heat, and simmer broth 15 minutes. Cool 5 minutes and strain into a 4-quart sauce-pan. Discard spices.

2   It's not necessary to brown the protein food, but it gives better color. If browned food is desired, heat a wok or 9-inch skillet over high heat and drizzle in vegetable oil. Blot food dry. When oil is hot, brown chicken.

3   Bring red-cooking broth to a near boil. Transfer meat or tofu to the sauce and lower heat to a gentle simmer. Simmer food until just done—don't overcook: bone-in chicken 30 to 45 minutes, boneless, skinless chicken 15 to 20 minutes, and tofu about 20 minutes.

4   Turn off heat and allow chicken or tofu to cool in red-cooking broth. The longer the food sits, the more flavor (and saltiness) it acquires. Some cooks cool chicken or tofu overnight in red-cooking sauce.

5   **To Serve:** Drain red-cooked food and brush with Asian sesame oil. Slice boneless chicken or tofu into 3/8-inch slices and serve on top of shredded cabbage or lettuce and sliced tomatoes.

Vary! Improvise!

☛ *Red-cook fish or pork.*
☛ *Choose light, crisp, and finely chopped dishes to pair with red-cooked food.*
☛ *Red-cook a whole duck or cubed beef and turnips.*

BONG BONG CHICKEN (BANG BANG JI)

This dish, prepared using the "white-cut" method for cooking the chicken, is popular Szechwan street food. In Chengdu, carts and stalls serve this "small eats" topped with hot chilies, and a dipping sauce of Asian sesame oil, oyster sauce, and salt or MSG.

Yields 6-1/2 to 7 cups, serves 4 to 6

1-1/2 pounds boneless, skinless chicken breasts
1/4 cup Shaoxing wine *or* sherry
1 ounce trimmed green onions, 2 large, cut in 2-inch lengths and lightly smashed
1/2 ounce gingerroot, peeled, finely sliced into 4 to 5 "coins" and smashed
1 teaspoon Szechwan peppercorns
1 pound English cucumbers, lightly peeled

Dressing

Yields *about 2/3 cup*

2 teaspoons finely crushed Szechwan peppercorns
6 tablespoons soy sauce
2 tablespoons Chiankiang black vinegar
   or 4 teaspoons balsamic vinegar and 2 teaspoons rice vinegar
2 tablespoons Asian sesame oil
1 tablespoon Asian chili oil
1/4 ounce gingerroot, 1-1/2 teaspoons peeled and minced
1/4 ounce garlic, 1 large clove, 1-1/2 teaspoons peeled and minced
2 teaspoons sugar
1/4 ounce trimmed cilantro, 3 to 4 tablespoons finely sliced

Garnish

1/2 ounce cilantro, 1/2 cup finely sliced
1 ounce trimmed green onions, 2 large, 1/4 cup minced
1/4 ounce toasted sesame seed, 1 tablespoon
   or about 1 ounce crushed, roasted peanuts, 1/4 cup

1. **Poach the chicken:** Pour 4 cups cold water, wine or sherry, green onions, ginger, and peppercorns into 4-quart saucepan. Bring to a boil. Reduce the heat to low, add the chicken breasts, and simmer uncovered 5 minutes. Remove pan from heat and cover. Rest chicken in hot broth 30 minutes. Remove chicken from broth, cool, and pull into fine shreds to yield about 4 cups. Set aside.

2. **Prepare cucumbers:** Cut cucumber lengthwise in half. Remove seeds with spoon. Slice cucumber crosswise into 2-inch lengths. Slice lengths into 1/4-inch-thick matchsticks to yield about 2-1/2 cups. Set aside.

3. **Prepare dressing:** Heat a small skillet over medium heat, and toast Szechwan peppercorns until fragrant but not burned. Crush in mortar or with the side of a chef's knife. Combine soy sauce, vinegar, sesame oil, chili oil, Szechwan pepper, ginger, garlic, sugar, and cilantro. Whisk together by hand or in a food processor. (Dressing without cilantro can be stored up to 5 days ahead in the refrigerator. Stir in cilantro before using.)

4. **To Serve:** Arrange cucumbers on a platter. Toss chicken with half the dressing. Pile chicken on top of cucumbers. Drizzle remaining dressing over chicken and cucumbers. Garnish chicken with cilantro, green onions, and sesame seeds or peanuts (or both).

Source: The Seventh Daughter: My Culinary Journey from Beijing to San Francisco by Cecilia Chiang with Lisa Weiss.

FIGURE 1.12 Mapo doufu.

Source: uckyo/Fotolia.

FIGURE 1.13 The center of a Chinese meal.

Source: Elenathewise/Fotolia.

SPICY WESTERN CHINESE STEW (MAPO DOUFU)

This classic Chinese dish comes from Western China, where hot chilies are beloved. It braises quickly. Scarce and expensive fuel keeps Chinese cooking times short.

Yields 4 cups, 4 servings

2 to 3 tablespoons vegetable oil
2 tablespoons fermented black beans, rinsed and drained
1/2 ounce gingerroot, 1 tablespoon peeled and minced
1/4 to 1/3 ounce garlic, 2 medium cloves, 2 teaspoons peeled and minced
8 ounces ground pork
2 to 4 teaspoons Chinese chili paste
2 ounces trimmed green onions, 4 large, 1/2 cup finely sliced total, white and green separated
1 cup chicken stock
1 pound medium to soft tofu, about 3 cups diced into 1/2-inch cubes
3 to 4 teaspoons soy sauce
Cornstarch Slurry: 1 teaspoon cornstarch mixed with 1 tablespoon cold chicken stock
1 teaspoon dry-toasted, ground Szechwan peppercorns
2 teaspoons Asian sesame oil

For Serving

Cooked rice

1 Have all ingredients prepped and ready. Set out on half sheet pan by the stove.

2 Heat a 12-inch skillet or wok over medium-high heat. When wok is hot, drizzle oil in around sides. Add black beans, ginger, and garlic and cook until they sizzle well, 30 seconds. Lower heat and add ground pork. Break up meat, and stir-fry until done.

3 Stir in chili paste and white of green onions; cook 1 minute. Pour in chicken stock and tofu, lower heat to a simmer, and cook until tofu is done, 5 to 7 minutes. Season dish with soy sauce to taste.

4 Give cornstarch slurry a stir and slowly pour it in while stirring gently. When it has thickened and cleared, 1 minute, stir in Szechwan pepper and sesame oil. Remove pan from heat and scrape *ma po dou fu* into serving vessel.

5 **To Serve:** Top *ma po dou fu* with green part of green onions and serve with rice.

Chinese Rice

Rice is a staple for all of China except the North, where they grow and eat more wheat. Most Chinese prefer long-grain white rice. In some areas Chinese eat short-grain or glutinous rice and black rice. Most Chinese eat rice boiled, steamed, or as *congee* (rice porridge). With condiments and additions, congee serves as breakfast and as a meal for babies and delicate stomachs, and as a way to stretch rice. Fried rice, glutinous rice "pearl balls," sizzling rice cake soup, and sticky rice dumplings are also popular rice dishes.

FIGURE 1.14 Rice paddy.

Source: spaceport9/Fotolia.

SIGNATURE RECIPE

CHINESE WAY TO COOK RICE

It's best to cook at least 14 ounces rice (2 cups): the rice will cook more evenly and efficiently.

One pound of raw rice yields about 7 cups cooked

- 7 ounces long-grain white rice, 1 cup *needs* 16 fluid ounces water

- 14 ounces rice, 2 cups *or* more *needs* 12 to 14 fluid ounces water *per cup* rice

1 Rinse white rice in strainer or swish rice in pot with cold water until water runs clear. Drain rice. The right size and weight of pot is crucial so choose appropriately. Ideally rice should fill no more than about 1/3 of the pot.

2 Bring rice, salt, and measured cold water to a boil. Many Chinese cover rice with enough water to come up to the first finger joint. This works for long-grain rice, but it will be too much water for short-grain rice.

3 Cover pot, lower heat to a simmer, and cook rice 12 to 15 minutes. Alternatively, use a rice cooker.

4 Turn off heat, do not disturb rice. You may pour a little water in around the edges of the rice: listen for the crackling sound. Older or aged rice needs more water. Don't overdo or you'll end up with soggy rice. Allow rice to steam and settle 10 minutes. It will firm up and break less easily. Rice should be tender at center, but chewy. Don't let rice cool completely or it will turn into a brick.

5 **To Serve:** Uncover pot and fluff hot rice with a fork. Don't stir! (Fluff even if it will be awhile until rice is used.) Turn rice out into serving dish, pile high, and serve hot.

Noodles

Historians find evidence that Chinese dined on noodles as early as 200 BCE and they still hold an important place in the Chinese diet. In northern China, where wheat is available, noodles are the staple food over rice. In southern China, a rice growing region, rice noodles are more prevalent. Long noodles symbolize longevity to Chinese so they appear at birthday celebrations. Xi'an, or Shaanxi, a western Chinese province, is famous for noodles formed by slapping, pulling, and stretching the dough into long, narrow strands. Students in cooking schools learn how to swing and stretch dough by hand. In Beijing markets noodle-swingers make them in minutes.

There are many Chinese noodle dishes, but the most popular are cooked and chilled noodles tossed with a savory dressing, pan-fried noodle "cake," savory stir-fry over noodles, and cooked noodles stir-fried with meat and vegetables. A popular Chinese noodle dressing is rice vinegar, soy sauce, chili sesame oil, minced scallion, and salt and pepper. *Mien* is Mandarin for noodle; in China, *chow mein* is made with soft noodle that is boiled then stir-fried.

Chinese cooks prepare noodles six ways:

- in soup
- cooked and seasoned
- in hot gravy
- in cold gravy
- steamed
- stir-fried

PEANUT NOODLES (CHENGDU DAN DAN)

Chengdu is in the western Szechwan province where some of the spiciest and most flavorful Chinese food reigns. Chili oil is a beloved condiment. For a heartier dish, add fried (or baked) tofu, diced cooked chicken, or shrimp. Be sure to mince garlic and ginger finely.

4 to 6 servings

Sauce Ingredients

Yields *scant 1 cup sauce*

1 ounce gingerroot, 2 tablespoons peeled and finely minced or grated
1 ounce garlic, about 4 large cloves, 2 tablespoons peeled and finely minced
2 tablespoons peanut butter
2 tablespoons sesame butter (tahini)
5 teaspoons Asian sesame oil
2 teaspoons Chinese chili oil, more to taste
6 tablespoons soy sauce
4 teaspoons balsamic vinegar or Chinese black vinegar
Optional: 1 tablespoon rice vinegar
Optional: 2 teaspoons sugar

8 ounces mung bean sprouts, about 3 cups packed
1 pound dried thin egg noodles
2 teaspoons Asian sesame oil

Garnish: 2 ounces trimmed green onions, 4, about 1/4 cup trimmed and finely chopped

1 Combine **sauce ingredients** in large mixing bowl, taste, and set aside.

2 Bring 4 quarts water to a boil. Place sprouts into a handled sieve and lower into water. Cook several seconds. Rinse under cold water and drain. Place in mixing bowl.

3 Add noodles to boiling water and cook until tender, but still resistant to the tooth. Drain and rinse under cold water. Drain noodles well, toss with 2 teaspoons Asian sesame oil and chill.

4 **To Serve:** Toss noodles with sauce. With chopsticks, gently fold in sprouts and most of the green onions. Mound noodles on a platter and garnish with remaining green onions.

Vary! Improvise!

☛ *Restaurant Service: Prepare sauce, steamed vegetables, and cooked noodles separately. Reheat one order of noodles and vegetables briefly and toss with some of the prepared peanut sauce. Garnish with green onions (and ground roasted peanuts if desired).*

Asian Dumplings

Though pretty much every culture makes some sort of stuffed dumpling, follow the wheat and it seems that they probably originated in the early wheat growing regions of Mesopotamia (Iraq and parts of Syria and Turkey) and northern-central China. A Japanese traveling monk named Ennin, who visited China around AD 840, noted that dumplings were special food presented during feasts and celebrations. In present-day China dumplings are still important for Chinese New Year and for going-away parties.

Chinese cooks steam, boil, or pan-fry-steam dumplings with filling choices ranging from rich and savory, fresh and light, to sweet. Meat, seafood, vegetable, tofu, and sweet bean filled dumplings are enhanced with vinegar, soy sauce, rice wine, chili, and sesame oil based sauces. Korean dumplings, called *mandu*, are most commonly beef, pork, vegetable, kim chi, or tofu stuffed, and served as pot-stickers, in soup or with a dipping sauce. The Japanese pork *gyoza* has more garlic, and its wrappers are thinner than Chinese *jiaozi*.

FIGURE 1.15   Steamed dim sum.
Source: JPL Designs/Shutterstock.

ANIMAL HOUSE

Students in Chinese culinary schools learn to make dumplings in the shape of animals: goldfish, turtles, rabbits, penguins, hedgehogs, frogs, and chicks. Their dexterous hands, some crimpers, tiny scissors, and a small rolling pin are all that's necessary to produce an incredible dumpling zoo.

FIGURE 1.16   Hedgehog dumplings.
Source: Invisible/Shutterstock.

HANDMADE DUMPLING WRAPPERS

Chef Andrea Nguyen relates that medium-thick homemade wrappers—a scant 1/8-inch thick in the center and 1/16-inch thick at the rim—work well for boiled, steamed, or pan-fried dumplings. Hot-water dough makes medium-thick wrappers that are more yielding than cold-water dough, and the wrappers need little or no water to seal.

Yields about 17-1/2 ounces dough, thirty-five 1/2-ounce dumplings, 3-1/4- to 3-1/2-inch diameter

11-1/4 to 12 ounces unbleached all-purpose flour, 2-1/2 cups
1 cup boiling water, rested 2 minutes to cool slightly

1 Pour flour into food processor or mixing bowl. Pour boiling water into heat-proof liquid measure to 3/4 cup plus 3 tablespoons. Slowly add water to processor as it runs. Check dough: it should be rough, feel *earlobe soft*, and hold its shape when pinched. Add water by the teaspoon until it does. Knead by processing dough 10 to 20 seconds more. Dough will form a ball.

   *Alternatively, pour flour into mixing bowl. Make a well in center of flour and pour in 3/4 cup hot water. Mix and knead dough to earlobe soft, adding more water by the teaspoon until dough comes together.

2 Knead dough on work surface 30 seconds to 2 minutes. (If too much water is added and dough is sticky, lightly flour board, otherwise, refrain from extra flour.) The dough should be smooth, elastic, and when pressed, slowly bounce back with only a light impression of a finger.

3 Wrap dough in plastic or in plastic baggie tightly. Rest dough 15 minutes to 2 hours. Dough should be earlobe soft after resting.

Signature Technique: Rolling Dumpling Dough

1 *Assemble:*
   A metal tortilla press
   Tiny rolling pin or clean pencil
   Two 7-inch squares cut from heavy freezer baggies
   Flour
   Parchment-covered sheet pan

2 Divide dough into two halves: one 8-1/2 ounces and the second one 9 ounces. Rewrap one half, set aside, and place remaining half on work surface.

3 Roll first half into 17-inch log, square thinner ends so they are the same diameter as the middle of the dough log. Cut log into 17 equal-sized pieces, 1/2 ounce each. Weigh for consistency. Repeat with second half of dough, but roll it to 18 inches and repeat process.

4 Cover cut dough well with plastic wrap. Dip **cut** sides of one piece lightly into flour, and shake off excess. Lay one plastic square on tortilla press. Lay the dough disk, cut side down, in the center and cover with remaining plastic square. Close tortilla press, fold handle over top plate and press down *only once* with moderate pressure. Remove dough and set dough wrapper on parchment-covered sheet pan. Repeat flattening with remaining dough disks. **Keep dough covered with plastic wrap.**

5 Lightly flour work surface. Place a flattened disk on work surface and, with *small* rolling pin or pencil, apply pressure on outer 1/2- to 3/4-inch border of wrapper. This will result in a small "belly" in the center of the wrapper. Frilly edges are fine.

6 Set wrapper aside on sheet pan and repeat with remaining dough. If dough seizes and is hard to roll, let it rest a few minutes and reroll. If they look really misshapen, roll into a ball and rest, and press out in tortilla press again. Repeat entire process with remaining half of dough.

7 Form dumplings according to recipe directions. The wrappers will take about 1 tablespoon filling each.

Vary! Improvise!

☛ *Golden Dough: Add 1 teaspoon turmeric to flour.*

Freeze

Freeze dumplings for later use: place on sheet pan and freeze. Remove to freezer baggies and freeze dumplings up to 2 months. Don't defrost before cooking. Boil in broth or water. When dumplings rise, cook 2 minutes more.

CHINESE SOUP DUMPLINGS

Bite into a soup dumpling and experience the gush of hot, savory liquid. How did the cook do that?

- Start by reducing 1 cup homemade chicken stock to 1/4 cup. Preferably stock made with young, flexible chicken bones, which make a more gelatinous broth.
- Chill chicken gelatin until it firms up into jello-like consistency. (You can cheat and use powdered gelatin, but the flavor won't be as intense.) Dice gelatin finely and keep chilled.
- Fold gelatin cubes into chilled pork or meat and cabbage mixture and stuff dumplings.
- It's best to make your own, sturdier wrappers for soup dumplings.
- Steam or pan-fry soup dumplings.

FIGURE 1.17   Soup dumplings.
Source: leungchopan/Shutterstock.

CHINESE DUMPLING SKINS AND WRAPPERS

Keep all wrappers and skins covered when not using; they dry out quickly. Always buy extra wrappers. They freeze well up to 1 month. Thaw overnight in the refrigerator.

Steamed Shao-mai Dumplings

Three- to 3-1/2-inch diameter paper-thin round wrappers work best for delicate shao-mai. You'll be able to see your fingers through them when held up to the light. Cut square wrappers with a round cutter if round wrappers are not available. Thinner wrappers tend to get soggy if left to stand too long. Steam dumplings as soon as possible after shaping.

Pot-Stickers, Soup Dumplings, and Boiled Dumplings

Commercially made, thick, 3- to 3-1/2 inch diameter, round wrappers, or handmade wrappers stand up best to pan-frying, steaming, and boiling.

Wontons

Thin, square wonton skins are best for wontons. For soup wontons, bring the points together to form a flat triangle. For deep-fried wontons, bring the points together to form a flat triangle, then bring the sides together.

Spring Rolls

Chinese cooks use two types of fresh wheat flour wrappers about 7- to 8-inches square. *Shanghai wrappers* are made with flour without egg and are thin but sturdy with a papery, dry texture. *Spring roll skins* are more like a fresh noodle. They often contain egg and wheat. Both need refrigeration.

NORTHERN CHINESE PORK AND CABBAGE POTSTICKERS (JIAOZI)

Yields 2 cups filling, enough for about 32 dumplings

Filling

7 ounces Napa cabbage
11 ounces ground pork
1 ounce trimmed green onions, 2 large, 1/4 cup minced
1/2 ounce gingerroot, 1 tablespoon peeled and finely minced
2 teaspoons Asian sesame oil
2 teaspoons Chinese rice wine
 or sherry wine

32 thick round dumpling wrappers
 or 1 recipe *Homemade Dumpling Wrappers*

Dipping Sauce

1/2 cup Chinese red vinegar
1/2 ounce ginger, 1 tablespoon peeled and finely slivered

1 **Prepare filling:** Stack cabbage leaves, halve lengthwise, and finely slice to yield about 3 cups. Place cabbage in large colander and toss with 1 tablespoon kosher salt. Lay a small plate with a heavy can on top to weight it.

2 Rest cabbage 20 minutes and squeeze out moisture with your hands. The cabbage should look cooked. Squeeze the liquid life out of the cabbage until it is wilted to yield about 1 cup firmly packed wilted cabbage.

3 Combine 1/2 teaspoon kosher salt, pork, green onions, ginger, sesame oil, and rice wine with cabbage and mix well. Lightly oil a sheet pan and set aside.

4 **Stuff dumplings:** Place a 3-1/4- to 3-1/2-inch round wrapper on work surface. If using commercial wrapper, lightly wet inside edges and top back edge with water or egg yolk. Place 1 tablespoon **filling** across the center. Pleat top (back) edge with 3 or 4 pleats in center. Bring top and bottom edges together. Press to seal shut.

5 **Finish remaining dumplings:** Place on oiled tray and keep covered with damp towel or plastic wrap. At this point you may refrigerate, freeze, or pan-fry the potstickers (see *Signature Technique: Pan-Fry/Pan-Steam Potstickers*). Alternatively, steam dumplings until done, 5 to 7 minutes (see *Steaming Technique*).

6 **Prepare dipping sauce:** Stir together red vinegar and ginger and rest 15 to 20 minutes. Serve with dumplings.

Source: *The Wisdom of the Chinese Kitchen* by Grace Young.

FIGURE 1.18 Northern Chinese pork and cabbage potstickers.

Signature Technique: Pan-Fry/Pan-Steam Potstickers

1 Heat a heavy 12- or 14-inch cast-iron or nonstick skillet (have a cover nearby) over medium-high heat until a drop of water evaporates on contact. Add enough oil to coat the bottom well and heat it to almost smoking.

2 Remove pan from heat and quickly place dumplings, bottom smooth side down, in concentric rings, fitting tightly next to each other. They should sizzle. Place pan back on medium-high heat and cook until bottoms brown. Check by lifting a dumpling with a spatula.

3 Add enough stock or water to come less than 1/4 way up the sides of dumplings. Lower heat to a moderate bubble and cover pan.

4 After 5 minutes, lift lid and check dumpling bottoms. They should be crispy and liquid should be absorbed. Taste one. If not done, add *a little* more stock or water and cook until done and liquid is fully absorbed.

5 Move pan off burner and loosen dumpling bottoms with spatula. Invert serving platter over skillet, flip and remove skillet. Serve dumplings with browned bottoms up. Eat immediately with dipping sauce, a porcelain spoon, and chopsticks.

CHINESE WHEAT STARCH

Wheat starch is a by-product from making wheat gluten flour. To make gluten, mix bread flour and water into a bread-like dough. Knead it well. Immerse the dough ball in a large bowl of cold water and knead. The wheat starch will flow out as the dough is "washed." Allow the white starch to settle, pour off excess water, and dry the wheat starch. Wheat starch and tapioca flour are available in Chinese or Asian groceries.

FIGURE 1.19 Chinese shrimp bonnets (har gow).

CHINESE SHRIMP BONNETS (HAR GOW)

These shrimp dumplings are also called Crystal Dumplings because the wrapper becomes clear as it steams. They are a favorite dim sum. The dough is pliable and fun to work.

Yields about 32 (3-1/2-inch) dumplings

1 recipe *Shrimp Filling, see Southern Chinese Seafood Dumplings (Shao-mai)*

Crystal Wrapper Dough

Yields *18 ounces dough*

About 7-1/2 ounces wheat starch, 1-1/2 cups
About 3 ounces tapioca flour, 1/2 cup plus 1 tablespoon
    or about 3 ounces cornstarch, 1/2 cup plus 1 tablespoon
1/4 teaspoon kosher salt
2 tablespoons canola oil, *divided*, more as needed for rolling

1 Prepare *filling* according to recipe, and refrigerate.

2 **Prepare wrapper dough:** Bring a small pot of water to boil. Place wheat starch, tapioca flour, and salt into a strainer or sifter and sift into mixing bowl. Make a well in the center. Pour 1-1/2 table-spoons oil and 9 fluid ounces boiling water into well. Quickly stir with rubber spatula until well mixed. Add up to another 2 tablespoons boiling water if dough is dry.

3 Knead dough until smooth, 2 minutes. It should be medium-firm and bouncy, like Play-Doh, not soft and mushy. If dough is too mushy, knead in more wheat starch. When pressed, dough should not crack. If it does, knead in remaining 1-1/2 teaspoons oil. Place dough in zipper baggie and rest 5 minutes. Dough will keep up to 6 hours at room temperature in plastic baggie.

4 **For 3-1/2-inch dumplings:**
   • Weigh dough and divide into two 9-ounce balls. Keep dough covered at all times.
   • Roll one ball into an 18-inch log of even thickness and square off the edges.
   • Cut log into 18 equal pieces; each piece should weigh 1/2 ounce. Keep dough pieces on parchment-covered sheet pan covered well with plastic wrap.
   • Repeat with remaining log. There will be a total of 36 pieces of dough, each weighing 1/2 ounce, 4 more pieces than needed.

5 **Form the dumplings:** Cut four 7-inch squares of plastic wrap and place two on tortilla press. To keep from sticking, lightly oil the cut sides of each piece of dough. Place dough cut side down on plastic wrap-covered tortilla press and flatten each piece into 3-1/2 inch circles.

6 Transfer plastic wrap with dough on it to work surface and cover press with another piece of plastic wrap. Place 1 level tablespoon filling along center. Fold skin over to make a half-moon. Pleat outer edge. Repeat process with remaining dough. Set dumplings on their bottom with the pleated edge standing upright on parchment-covered sheet pan. Cover tightly with plastic wrap.

7 Place dumplings into steamer basket atop squares of parchment paper, lettuce, or cabbage. Bring water in steamer to a hard boil, and set steamer basket over the water. Steam until done, 3 to 4 minutes. If dough cracks, it was steamed too long. Serve with sweet soy dipping sauce.

8 **To make dumplings ahead:** Freeze cooked dumplings up to 1 month. Thaw dumplings in refrigerator and steam 2 minutes to reheat.

Source: *Asian Dumplings* by Andrea Nguyen.

FIGURE 1.20 Steamed shrimp shao mai made with handmade wrappers.

Source: dreambigphotos/Fotolia.

FIGURE 1.21 Southern Chinese dumpling (Shao-mai).

Vary! Improvise!

☛ *Wasabi Shao-mai: Include 1 teaspoon wasabi paste in filling.*

☛ *Purée chopped cilantro into filling.*

SOUTHERN CHINESE SEAFOOD DUMPLINGS (SHAO-MAI)

Shao-mai are steamed open-faced dumplings made with very thin shao-mai wrappers or circles cut from won ton skins. Quick to prepare, shao-mai can be made with just about any type ground meat or seafood. The fresher the seafood, the better the texture. A "mousse" made with old fish (which dehydrates and loses viscous collagen tissue that binds fish fibers together) will be soggy. Shrimp or scallops are more "gluey" or gelatinous than others, so mixing a little of them with fish helps the filling's texture.

Yields 15 fluid ounces filling, 30 dumplings

32 thin 3-inch round dumpling skins
   or 1 pound *Homemade Dumpling Wrappers*

Shrimp Filling

16 ounces 26/30 shrimp, 12 to 13 ounces shelled and deveined

Weigh shrimp after shelling and add enough extra seafood to equal 16 ounces:

3 to 4 ounces white fish *or* scallops, as needed

Fish Filling

16 ounces very fresh catfish, sole *or* whitefish

Scallop Filling

16 ounces scallops, muscles removed

Seasonings

1-1/2 ounces gingerroot, 1-1/2 tablespoons peeled and minced
1/2 ounce garlic, about 2 large cloves, 1 tablespoon peeled and minced
1-1/2 ounces trimmed green onions, about 3 large, 1/2 to 2/3 cup coarsely chopped
1 tablespoon rice wine or sherry

Garnish: 2 ounces water chestnuts *or* carrot, scant 1/2 cup peeled and diced into 1/8-inch cubes

To Serve: *Dipping Sauce* of choice

1 Prepare dumpling skins if using *Homemade Dumpling Wrappers*. If only square wrappers are available, use a 3-inch round cutter to cut them into rounds.

2 **Prepare filling:** Pat seafood dry. Cube fish or scallops *or* chop shrimp. Place seafood into a food processor with **seasonings:** ginger, garlic, green onions, rice wine, and 1 teaspoon kosher salt. Pulse to mix, then purée ingredients until evenly mixed into a thick paste.

3 Fold in water chestnut or carrot garnish by hand. Chill mixture until ready for use.

4 Prepare a **dipping sauce**. For steaming dumplings: cut parchment into 30 two-inch squares.

5 **Fill dumplings:** Place 1 level tablespoon filling in center of 1 wrapper. Bring all sides up to form a beggar's purse. Push and pleat sides together so dumpling has an "empire" waist and some filling pushes out the top. Place shao-mai on prepared parchment squares on a sheet pan, and cover with a damp cotton towel until ready to cook.

6 **Steam dumplings:** (See *Chinese Wok-Steaming.*) Bring water to boil in wok or pot. Set dumplings on their parchment in a steamer basket. Place steaming basket on pot or in wok. Place a lid lined with a cotton towel on the steamer or pot, and cook dumplings until the seafood is opaque and wrapper is cooked, 4 to 6 minutes. Test by tasting.

7 **To Serve:** Serve dumplings hot with dipping sauce.

PORK AND SHRIMP WONTONS

Chinese cooks believe that pork and shrimp complement each other perfectly. For extra flavor, use fresh water chestnuts.

Yields 2-1/2 cups filling, about 40 wontons

12 ounces boneless country style ribs, diced
10-1/2 to 11 ounces 26/30 shrimp, 8 ounces shelled and deveined, chopped
About 1-1/4 ounces peeled water chestnuts or jicama, 1/4 cup diced into 1/16-inch cubes
1-1/2 ounces trimmed green onions, 3 large, 1/3 cup finely sliced
1/2 ounce gingerroot, 1 tablespoon peeled and finely minced
2 tablespoons oyster sauce
2 teaspoons soy sauce
2 tablespoons Chinese rice wine or dry sherry
2 teaspoons Asian sesame oil
40 wonton wrappers
For Sealing: water, beaten egg or cornstarch slurry

For Serving

Dipping Sauce of choice

1 Place pork and shrimp into food processor. Pulse chop until slightly pasty, but with texture. Scrape pork and shrimp mixture into a bowl and combine with water chestnuts or jicama, green onions, ginger, oyster sauce, soy sauce, rice wine or sherry, and sesame oil. Season with salt and pepper.

2 To fill the wontons, lay one won ton skin on work surface. (Cover the remaining won ton skins with plastic wrap to keep from drying). Lightly moisten bottom edges wrapper with water, beaten egg, or cornstarch slurry. Place 2 to 3 teaspoons filling in center. Don't overfill. Fold wrapper in half so two pointed ends meet. Press down firmly on the edges to seal. Repeat with remaining wontons.

3 Fill a large 6- to 8-quart pot with salted water and bring to a boil. Working in 2 or 3 batches to avoid overcrowding, quickly add the dumplings one at a time, making sure they don't stick to each other. Lower the heat to medium and continue to gentle-boil, gently stirring occasionally, until the dumplings float and are cooked through, 3 to 5 minutes. Check for doneness with instant read thermometer (about 150 degrees F) or cut one open. Remove won ton with a slotted spoon and transfer to platter.

4 **To Serve:** Arrange dumplings on platter and serve while hot with a dipping sauce. Filled, uncooked won tons freeze well.

Vary! Improvise!

☞ **Deep-Fry:** *Heat oil for deep-frying to 365 degrees F. Add wontons in small batches and fry, turning occasionally, until golden, about 2 minutes. Remove with a slotted spoon and drain on paper towels.*

☞ **Won Ton Soup:** *Place steamed or raw wontons into hot chicken stock and simmer to heat or cook through. Ladle stock and 3 to 5 wontons per serving into bowl. Garnish with cilantro or finely sliced green onions and serve.*

☞ **Nurse's Cap Won Ton:** *Bring bottoms of won tons together with one overlapping the other, and seal.*

FIGURE 1.22 Basic Chinese steamer.

Source: lullabi/Fotolia.

BASIC CHINESE BUN DOUGH

Don't forget to add the baking powder before rolling, cutting, and stuffing the dough!

Yields 1-1/2 pounds dough, 20 buns

2-1/2 teaspoons sugar
1 teaspoon active dry yeast
1 pound unbleached all-purpose flour, 3-1/3 to 3-1/2 cups, plus more for rolling
1 teaspoon Asian sesame oil
1 teaspoon double acting baking powder

1 Dissolve sugar in 1 cup plus 2 tablespoons warm water and stir in yeast. Rest mixture 10 minutes, until foamy.

2 Pour flour in mixing bowl. Stir in yeast mixture slowly and mix ingredients to a rough dough. Slowly add more warm water if dough doesn't come together. Turn dough out onto a lightly floured surface. Dough shouldn't be sticky so it shouldn't need much flour. Knead until the dough is smooth and elastic, 8 to 10 minutes. The dough should bounce slowly back when pressed.

3 Oil a large bowl, place dough in and turn so dough is evenly coated. Seal bowl tightly with plastic wrap, and set in a warm spot without drafts. Let dough rise until doubled, 1 to 1-1/2 hours. Fully risen dough should not spring back when pressed. (For a lighter dough, press down and allow dough to rise a second time.)

4 Uncover dough, press down into a pancake, and turn out onto a lightly floured surface. Sprinkle baking powder over dough and gather up the edges to enclose it. Knead dough to mix baking powder evenly, to fingertip firm: a fingertip impression will bounce back slowly.

5 Cover dough with a dry towel and rest 5 to 10 minutes before using. If not using dough immediately, place dough in zipper baggie. Refrigerate dough until ready to use, but no longer than overnight.

Source: *The Modern Art of Chinese Cooking* by Barbara Tropp.

Signature Technique: Chinese Steamed Buns

To practice rolling and pleating "buns," use Play-Doh; making 100 puts a cook past the novice stage.

Yields twenty 2-1/2-inch buns

1 **Prepare dough and filling:** About 2-1/2 cups filling from *Three Chinese Steamed Bun Fillings* or *Chinese Barbequed Pork (Char Siu)*. Cool filling to room temperature. For the best flavor, prepare filling and dough the day before using. Let dough rise in refrigerator overnight.

2 **Prepare work area for stuffing:** Set up 2 half-sheet pans. Cut twenty 2-inch squares of parchment. Oil them on one side and set on sheet pans. Place a bowl of filling, two clean dry (lint-free) towels, a child-size rolling pin or dowel, and a ruler alongside dough.

3 *Cut dough* into equal halves. Return half to bowl and cover. Roll remaining half into a smooth and even cylinder 10-inches long. With ruler as guide, slice dough log into ten equal 1-inch-thick slices. Set slices cut side down and cover. Or scale out **1-1/4 ounce balls of dough**.

4 **Roll dough:** Dust both sides of one dough slice and flatten. With a small rolling pin, roll dough round from outer edge into almost the center of dough. Keep turning dough round and rolling almost to the center of dough. The wrapper should be round with a 4-1/2-inch diameter with a nickel-sized belly button in the center. (Alternatively, press dough into shape with fingers.)

5 **Fill dough:** Set dough circle onto a prepared parchment square. Mound 2 tablespoons filling in center of wrapper. Don't overfill.

6 **To pleat bun wrapper:** Place filled wrapper on work surface.
   • Grasp right side of dough at "3 o'clock" with right thumb inside wrapper and right index finger outside.

FIGURE 1.23 Shaping steamed Chinese buns.

Source: lianxun zhang/Fotolia.

- Fold a 1/2 inch of dough over (outside of bun) to the thumb and index finger, and catch the pleat with the index finger.
- Press pleat down with thumb and index finger to secure.
- Fold another 1/2-inch pleat over to the right index finger thumb and tack down as before.
- Continue to fold, pleat, and rotate bun until fully pleated.

Remember: Right thumb stays still while left hand grabs and brings dough pleat over. Right index finger collects the new dough and pinches down. Lefties should reverse the process.

- Remove thumb and pinch together the open top of bun.
- Twist it firmly closed, counterclockwise, into a topknot.
- Round and shape the finished bun gently with your hands.

7 Set finished buns 2 inches apart on oiled side of paper set on sheet pans. Finish cutting, rolling, and stuffing remaining dough.

8 Bring water to boil in wok or bottom of steamer (see *Chinese Wok-Steaming*). Line lid of steamer with clean towel to keep steam from dripping onto buns.

9 Set buns on paper in steamer basket (no more than two baskets high) *or* perforated pans for commercial steamer; place in wok or steamer. Steam buns 12 minutes at high heat. Steam 2 baskets in wok 12 to 15 minutes and 10 to 12 minutes for 1 basket.

Signature Technique: Chinese Wok-Steaming

Asians use two steaming methods: food sits directly on a steaming basket or rack, or on a plate or in a bowl set into a steaming basket or wok to retain flavorful juices. Asian steamers include round bamboo stacking baskets that fit into a wok or round stainless steel "baskets" with perforated holes. Steamed foods retain a pure and subtle taste and more nutrients. Cantonese chefs favor steamed dishes.

1 Soak bamboo steamers in hot water 15 to 20 minutes. Drain. Fill wok with enough water to come up 1 inch from bottom of steaming rack to prevent water touching food while boiling. Bring water to a boil. (Place a penny in the wok: when the rattling slows or ceases, it's time to add more water.

2 Meanwhile, fill steaming baskets with food. Steam no more than 3 baskets at a time. Place foods that need long cooking nearest the bottom. Set items that stick, like dumplings, on squares of parchment paper or cabbage leaves, or set food and seasonings in shallow bowls or on plates that will fit into the steaming basket leaving room for steam to circulate.

3 Steam will drip from the lid, so line it with a clean cotton towel. Keep a pot of hot water with a ladle nearby to continually refill water around the sides of the steamer—the bottommost (bamboo) steamer can burn—a good reason to visit a Chinese restaurant supply to buy stainless steel steaming trays. (They're good for smoking food too.)

SOUTHERN CHINESE STEAMED SCALLOPS WITH FERMENTED BLACK BEANS

2 servings

1 tablespoon fermented black beans, soaked 10 minutes, drained and minced
1/8 ounce garlic, 1 small clove, about 3/4 teaspoon peeled and finely minced
1/4 ounce peeled ginger, about 1 teaspoon minced
1/2 ounce trimmed green onion, 1 large, 2 tablespoons minced
8 ounces large sea scallops, "feet" removed
2 to 3 teaspoons vegetable oil
1 tablespoon soy sauce
2 tablespoons Chinese rice wine *or* dry sherry

Garnish: 1/2 ounce trimmed green onion, 1 large, about 2 tablespoons bias-cut

1 Mix black beans, garlic, ginger, and minced green onion together. Set up steamer basket in wok and bring water to a boil.

2 Place scallops on a heat-proof plate that will fit in steamer and spoon black bean mixture over. Drizzle with oil, soy sauce, and rice wine. Place plate in steamer. Steam until scallops are tender and almost cooked through, 3 to 5 minutes.

3 **To Serve:** Transfer scallops to a serving plate and pour the sauce over them. Garnish with bias-cut green onions. Serve hot.

Vary! Improvise!

☞ *Substitute Asian sesame oil for vegetable oil.*
☞ *Try other proteins in place of scallops, like fish or chicken breast.*

STEAMED WHOLE FISH WITH HAM AND BLACK MUSHROOMS

The combination of ham and black mushrooms is a classic Chinese pairing.

4 to 6 servings

Marinade

4 tablespoons Chinese rice wine or sherry
1/2 ounce gingerroot, 5 thin slices, peeled and smashed
1 ounce trimmed green onions, 2 large, sliced into 1-inch lengths and smashed

1/2 ounce small dried Chinese black mushrooms, about 5
3-1/2- to 4-pound whole, firm-flesh fish like red snapper or flounder, gutted and scaled
2 ounces Chinese ham, Smithfield ham, or prosciutto, 3 to 5 thin slices

Fish Seasonings

1/2 ounce trimmed green onion, 1 large, 2 tablespoons finely sliced on diagonal
1 ounce gingerroot, about 2 tablespoons peeled and finely matchstick cut
1 tablespoon soy sauce
2 tablespoons Asian sesame oil

1 *Prepare* **marinade:** Mix together 2 teaspoons kosher salt, rice wine, ginger, and green onions. Set aside to marinate.

2 Place dried mushrooms in small mixing bowl and cover with hot water. Weight mushrooms with a plate, and soak until tender, 30 minutes. Remove and discard stems. Slice mushroom caps in half, and set aside.

3 Rinse fish, pat dry, and place into 2-inch-deep hotel pan. Make 5 deep slices along fish flanks on each side from base of head to tail at a 45-degree angle about 1 inch apart. Remove ginger and green onions from marinade and discard. Rub remaining liquid into cuts on fish and all over skin

on both sides. Marinate fish 30 minutes. Divide ham or prosciutto equally into 10 parts (about 2 inches by 3-1/2 inches, and stuff one part plus a mushroom half into each cut in fish.

4 Prepare a 6-inch-deep hotel pan with 1 inch of water. Set pan on two burners. (Alternatively, use a commercial steamer.) Place a folded sheet of parchment into a 2-inch-deep perforated hotel pan with pointed edges hanging slightly out the long sides. Transfer fish to parchment. The paper will help to move the fish when it is finished cooking.

5 Mix together **fish seasonings** in small bowl, and set aside.

6 Bring water to a boil over high heat. Cover steamer and steam fish until it flakes when probed deeply at the thickest part to the bone with the tip of a knife, 15 to 25 minutes. To steam fish more evenly, carefully flip it after 10 to 12 minutes.

7 **To Serve:** Transfer fish to platter. Sprinkle fish seasonings over fish and serve immediately.

Source: *Classic Chinese Cuisine* by Nina Simonds.

STIR-FRY, PAN-FRY, AND DEEP-FRY

Chinese cooks and chefs use three methods when cooking with oil: stir-fry, shallow-fry, and deep-fry. They choose a refined vegetable oil that can withstand high heat without breaking down and smoking.

Stir-Fry

What is the ideal utensil to take on a desert island? Consider the wok. It can perform a multitude of tasty tasks (stir-fry, deep-fry, steam, braise, simmer, smoke, and boil) while saving fuel, time, and money. The wok hasn't survived and thrived by looks alone. Stir-frying in a well-seasoned steel wok is the most characteristic cooking method in the Asian/Chinese repertoire. Students in Chinese culinary schools line up outdoors to flip handfuls of dirt in light, one-handled woks. As they practice, they strengthen wrists and memorize the motion so it becomes embedded and automatic.

The stir-fry method unites not only China's regional cuisines, but also all of Asia. Its quick cooking retains food's color, flavor, texture, and nutrients. In a skilled cook's hands, stir-fried meats are juicy and flavorful, vegetables are lightly seared and crisp-tender, and the finished dish is fresh and brightly colored. Stir-frying takes only minutes; however, ingredient preparation takes longer. Because stir-frying goes so quickly, everything must be prepared before heating the wok. There are three types of stir-fry:

- **Raw:** raw ingredients are stir-fried with seasonings and little sauce.
- **Precooked:** foods are precooked before they are stir-fried.
- **Soft:** foods are batter-coated and velveted before stir-frying.

Shallow or Pan-Fry

Shallow or pan-frying involves frying floured or battered proteins at a moderate temperature in a shallow amount of oil so that the food is immersed only halfway. The food is fried without much movement until browned on both sides. Cooks feel that this method draws out more flavor and scent from the food than deep-frying. Noodles are cooked this way until browned and crunchy-crusty, and dumplings are often reheated by shallow or pan-frying.

FIGURE 1.24 Restaurant chef in China.
Source: erwinova/Fotolia.

Deep-Fry, Oil-Velveting, and Passing-Through-Oil

Deep-frying may be used as a preparation stage or a cooking method on its own. The Chinese method of deep-frying has many nuances:

- **Clear or dry deep-frying:** Seasoned but not battered deep-fried food
- **Soft deep-frying:** Batter-coated and fried at a lower temperature to maintain tenderness
- **Crisp deep-frying:** Marinated food, steamed and deep-fried until crisp
- **Quick-frying:** Foods deep-fried in hot oil, the oil drained, and seasonings added to the food in the wok
- **Velveting:** Food is starch-coated, fried at a lower temperature, and finished in a stir-fry
  See *Signature Technique: Velveting in Oil or Water* for more information.
- **Passing-through-oil:** Deep-fried, battered food cooked through, removed, then fried a second time in hot oil

DEVISE A STIR-FRY DISH

Asian cuisine is all about balance: texture, color, flavor, cooking method, season, and temperature. Start with color and texture; contrast them. Think like an artist first and like a cook second.

- **Cook by color and texture:** Choose three to five colorful, differently textured, contrasting and flavorful combinations of *protein* and *assisting vegetables*.
- **Choose seasonings** like chili or curry pastes, soy, fermented black beans, Szechwan peppercorns or sherry.
- **Choose aromatic vegetables** like garlic, onions, green onions, and ginger and/or a prepared sauce like hoisin, plum, or devise one (with or without cornstarch).
- **Organize; advance preparation is everything:** slice, dice, precook or pretreat/marinate food and seasonings. Make food pretty, uniform, and bite-sized. Expose as much surface area as possible so food cooks quickly. Food should be dry.
- **Line up everything needed** next to the cooking area, including utensils before beginning to cook.
- **Prepare a condensed cheat sheet** of procedure. Hang sheet where it can be seen easily during cooking.

CHINESE CULINARY CRAFT

When in culinary school in China, chef and author Jen Lin-Liu relates how she and the other students watched a highly respected, skilled Chinese chef, working only with a wok, cutting board, and 8-inch cleaver, demonstrate the fundamental simplicity and freshness of Chinese cooking. He marinated thin slices of pork tenderloin and placed them in one layer in a wok over high heat. When the pork was done on the first side the chef, in one fluid motion, masterfully flipped the meat "like a pancake" then seasoned the "*guota liji*" or "sunken wok tenderloin" with leeks and ginger. This simple and satisfying dish revealed to her and her fellow students the chef's culinary expertise and mastery.

FIGURE 1.25 Chinese cleaver on traditional wood chopping block.
Source: Maitree Laipitaksin/Shutterstock.

Signature Technique: Stir-fry

1 Heat a 14-inch dry wok or a heavy skillet over the highest heat the burner can muster. The wok should be as close to heat source as possible. If the wok is round-bottomed, flip gas burner over to form a cup. Avoid wok rings; they keep wok too far from heat source. For a round-bottomed wok and immoveable burner, use the ring to avoid catastrophe.

2 **Hot wok, cold oil:** When the wok is very hot, dribble cold oil in around the edges, **two or three teaspoons per batch**. Swirl oil to coat sides of wok. It should not smoke. Choose a mild-flavored oil that can maintain a high temperature without smoking.

3 **Exploding quick infusion:** Toss seasonings into hot oil, lower heat and toss briefly. Start by infusing hot oil with smashed whole pieces of garlic and ginger, but pull them out when they begin to color. (Add minced garlic later, so that it doesn't burn.)

4 **Rapid searing:** Slowly scatter meat or protein into hot, seasoned oil (in batches if necessary). Flip and toss protein with hot oil until they cook to desired doneness. The aim of this constant movement is to give the metal little opportunity to draw out moisture or scorch the protein, although sometimes browning is desired. Remove seared food to a bowl to keep warm; continue to stir-fry remaining protein or vegetables.

5 **Don't overfill wok.** Fill wok about *one-third* full. Listen for the crackling-searing noise that means a dry wok or skillet. If a wok gets too full, food will stew, not stir-fry.

6 **Regulate heat** as you cook so food cooks evenly, sears evenly, and at a reasonable pace without burning. Use stove knobs to turn heat higher and lower. Stand facing the stove. Stir-fried dishes need constant attention. Don't be guilty of neglect.

7 **Steaming and blossoming** give vegetables a crisp tenderness and bright color. Add small amount of liquid and/or seasonings, cover wok to trap steam and allow the seasonings' flavor to "blossom," about 1 minute—listen for the crackling noise.

8 **Final blending with sauce or seasonings.** Return all ingredients back to wok. If desired, prepare a slurry to thicken the stir-fry (see below). Season finished stir-fry with Asian sesame oil, green onions, or other seasonings.

   *To thicken sauce with slurry: Mix **1 teaspoon cornstarch or arrowroot with every 2-1/2 to 3 fluid ounces (1/3 cup) cold liquid and seasonings.** Pour in slurry mixture and bring to a boil. Cook until the sauce clears and thickens, stirring and tossing stir-fry constantly. Overcooking can cause sauce to break and become watery.

9 **Pile the stir-fry high** onto a platter and bring it to the table immediately.

10 **Don't leave the wok.** Please take it while hot to the sink and rinse it with water.

FIGURE 1.26 Food cooked in wok.

Source: Marcus/Fotolia.

RICE BRAN OIL WINS OVER CANOLA

According to *Cook's Illustrated*, rice bran oil has a smoke point of 497 degrees F versus canola oil at 456 degrees F. Taste testers loved its light, nutty flavor over foods cooked in the oilier-tasting canola oil.

Season a Stir-Fry in Stages

For richer, more complex flavor, divide and add seasonings at the beginning, middle, and end.

EXERCISE: IMPROV STIR-FRIED GREEN BEANS

When adding more ingredients to this stir-fry, work in batches. Cooking each food separately ensures that it will be perfectly cooked. Begin with proteins; start with hard vegetables and work to tender ingredients. Keep in mind flavor and color contrast. Try to work with no more than three to five main ingredients. Too many flavors and foods and the dish is muddy with no strong personality. Less is more.

2 servings

1 tablespoon canola or vegetable oil, more as needed

1/4 ounce garlic, 1 large clove, lightly smashed and peeled

1/2 ounce green onion, 1 large, white part smashed gently and green saved for garnish

(Continued)

FIGURE 1.27 Long beans.

Source: Silkstock/Fotolia.

1 thin crosswise slice peeled ginger-root, bruised

5 to 8 ounces whole green beans or trimmed Chinese long beans, 2 cups stemmed

2 tablespoons chicken stock or vegetable broth, as needed

Soy sauce

Asian sesame oil

1. Prep ingredients and have them ready on a sheet pan in order of use. Write a "cheat sheet" with each step outlined; referring to a recipe scatters attention.
2. Hot wok, cold oil. Don't wimp out: use *high* heat to heat the wok before adding oil. Adjust the heat lower later if necessary, but most home burners don't put out enough heat. When wok radiates heat, dribble oil in around sides. Swirl oil. Use only as much oil as absolutely necessary.
3. Add aromatic seasonings: garlic, white part of green onion, and ginger. Mash into oil to infuse flavor into oil. Remove them when garlic turns golden.
4. Add green beans and sear over high heat until they are seared brown approaching black and wrinkled. Don't be in a hurry. The searing is what gives a stir-fry its unique flavor.
5. Steam: Add 1 to 2 tablespoons chicken broth or water to beans and cover wok. Steam 1 minute. Beans will turn bright green. Add more stock if necessary, but liquid should evaporate.
6. Taste-test: Uncover beans and taste for crisp-tender texture. Cook until texture is right.
7. To Serve: When beans are done, drizzle with soy sauce and sesame oil to taste. (Garnish with reserved minced green onion.) Pile beans onto plate and eat immediately.

EXERCISE: IMPROV REGIONAL CHINESE STIR-FRIED GREEN BEANS

Decide how to prepare green beans with the flavors below. Use *Improv Stir-Fried Green Beans Technique* for guidance and inspiration. The order of the ingredients can give a clue of how to proceed.

2 servings

1 tablespoon oil

5 ounces green beans, about 2 cups top stems removed and sliced into 2-inch lengths

Robust: Northern-Style (Beijing) Green Beans

Sear beans first then add:

1/4 ounce garlic, 1 clove peeled and lightly smashed

1 ounce white and tender green of leeks, 1/4 cup finely diced

1 ounce ground lamb, about 2 tablespoons

1 tablespoon Chinese bean paste

Refined: Eastern-Style (Shanghai) Green Beans

1 quarter-sized slice peeled ginger, lightly smashed

1/4 ounce garlic, 1 large clove, halved and smashed lightly

1 ounce finely cubed pork loin, about 2 tablespoons

Add green beans and 1 tablespoon water/cover and steam. Season with and cook until slightly thickened/caramelized:

1 teaspoon each: soy sauce, rice wine, and sugar

Light and Creative: Southern-Style (Cantonese) Green Beans

1 ounce green onions, 2 large, 3 tablespoon bias cut, white and green separated (green for garnish)

(Continued)

1/4 ounce gingerroot, about 1 teaspoon peeled and minced

1/2 ounce prosciutto or Westphalian ham, 1 tablespoon finely diced

Add green beans and 1 to 2 tablespoons water/cover and steam. Uncover, garnish with green onion greens. Season with salt or soy sauce.

Sweet-Sour: Southern-Style (Cantonese) Green Beans

Sear green beans and add:

1/8 ounce garlic, 1/2 to 3/4 teaspoon peeled and minced

1/2 teaspoon minced gingerroot

Mix together and add at end, cook until thickened:

2 teaspoons rice vinegar

1 tablespoon sugar

2 teaspoons ketchup

1 teaspoon soy sauce

2 tablespoons water

1/2 teaspoon cornstarch

Spicy: Western-Style (Szechwan) Dry-Fried Seared Green Beans

Sear green beans and add:

Two 3-inch dried red chilies, stemmed and seeded

  or 1 teaspoon chili paste

1/2 ounce green onion, about 1 large, about 2 tablespoons thinly bias cut

1/8 ounce garlic, 1 small clove, 1/2 teaspoon peeled and minced

1/4 ounce gingerroot, about 1 teaspoon peeled and minced

Season with soy sauce or salt, to taste.

BROCCOLI IN FERMENTED BLACK BEAN SAUCE

Try this dish with cauliflower, celery, or asparagus in place of broccoli.

Yields, 3 cups, 2 to 4 servings

1 pound broccoli, 1 large bunch
4 teaspoons fermented black beans
2 tablespoons vegetable oil
1/2 ounce garlic, 2 large cloves, 1 tablespoon peeled and minced
1/2 ounce ginger, 1 tablespoon peeled and minced
1/2 cup cold chicken stock
1 teaspoon cornstarch dissolved in 3 tablespoons cold water
2 teaspoons Asian sesame oil

1 **Prepare broccoli:** Cut off large stems, trim away bottoms, and peel away tough skin. Slice stems into thin coins. Break apart florets into small, bite-sized pieces in roughly equal size. Do not cut through florets; instead, slice through stem and pull floret apart to yield 4 cups broccoli.

2 Place black beans into small strainer and rinse. Drain and chop beans coarsely; set aside.

3 **Cook:** Heat wok or heavy skillet until hot over medium-high heat. Swirl in oil, wait 20 to 30 seconds, and stir in black beans, garlic, and ginger. Cook 15 seconds, stirring constantly. Fold in broccoli and lower heat to medium. Stir-fry broccoli until the color deepens, about 30 seconds.

4 **Steam:** Stir in chicken stock. Bring to a boil and cover pan. Steam broccoli until crisp tender, 3 to 5 minutes. Remove lid and pour cornstarch over broccoli. Stir and toss until sauce thickens. Stir in sesame oil. Taste stir-fry, and adjust seasonings.

5 **To Serve:** Immediately pile broccoli onto platter and serve hot.

Source: from *The Key to Chinese Cooking* by Irene Kuo.

Vary! Improvise!

☞ *Chicken: Dice or finely slice 1/2 pound boneless, skinless chicken breast. Stir-fry chicken with 1 tablespoon oil (before cooking black beans, garlic, and ginger). Remove chicken from pan after cooking and set aside. When broccoli is done, fold in chicken and heat through.*

CLEAN WOK, GOOD HEART

Maintain a wok: Clean it while it is still hot and put it away dry.

- Sprinkle wok with kosher or coarse salt and gently scrub with a rag, sponge, or bristled vegetable scrubber to loosen cooked-on food.
- Rinse wok with water only.
- Place wok on burner and heat over low heat until dry.
- Remove wok from heat and rub lightly with oil while still warm to re-season.
- Cool wok completely and towel off excess oil.
- Stack wok with paper towel in between to prevent rust. Rust never sleeps.

MASTER THE WOK TOSS

Want to be a wok master? Purchase a one-handled, 12- to 14-inch thin steel wok. Heavier woks will strain the wrist. Grab the wok handle with the dominant hand. Rapidly propel wok forward, and ever so slightly up, and as the food moves forward, jerk wok backward. This forces food to propel itself up and against the wok's curve then flip forward and down. *Remember:* A rapid back and forth, slightly rounded motion, to flip and toss.

Practice 1   Flip 1 whole domestic mushroom. Then add four more and flip.
Practice 2   Fill wok 1/4 full of dry rice. Flip.
Practice 3   Fill wok 1/3 full of dry beans. Flip.

FRIED RICE

Adaptable and delicious, fried rice is another great way to use up stray leftovers. This comfort food originated in the eastern Chinese city of Yangzhou, but is has become popular in southern China. Day-old cooked rice is a must. The outer starch layer firms up and allows rice to fry without turning to sticky mush as freshly cooked rice would.

Yields about 4 cups, 4 servings

2 tablespoons oil, *divided*
2 large eggs, about 1/2 cup lightly beaten
1 ounce trimmed green onions, 2 large, 4 tablespoons minced
4 cups cooked day-old cooked rice
1 tablespoon soy sauce *or* 1 teaspoon kosher salt

1   Refer to *Signature Technique: Stir-fry.* Heat wok over medium heat, add 1/2 tablespoon oil, pour in eggs and cook until set, but not hard, scrambling eggs into smaller pieces. Transfer to bowl and reheat wok over medium heat with 1/2 tablespoon oil. Stir-fry green onions until bright green, 30 seconds. Transfer to bowl with eggs.

2   Heat wok over medium-high with 1 tablespoon oil. Add rice and heat through. Stir in eggs and green onions. Season with soy sauce and/or salt, to taste.

3   **To Serve:** Scrape hot rice out of wok, and pile high onto a platter. Serve hot. Clean the wok.

NORTHERN CHINESE MOO SHU CHICKEN

A sort of Chinese enchilada, moo shu needs everything to be cut long and thin to fit into the round pancakes. This is equally good with pork, shrimp or tofu, or just vegetables. Chinese chefs make "paint brush" scallions for painting hoisin onto the pancakes before filling them.

Yields 3-1/2 to 4 cups, 2 to 4 servings

Sauce Ingredients

1-1/2 tablespoons chicken stock
2 tablespoons soy sauce
2 tablespoons Chinese rice wine
1/2 teaspoon sugar
2 teaspoons cornstarch
Optional: 1/2 teaspoon *Five Spice Powder*

1 large egg, about 1/4 cup lightly beaten
1 teaspoon Asian sesame oil

Aromatic Vegetable Seasonings

1/2 ounce garlic, 2 large cloves, 1 tablespoon peeled and minced
1/2 ounce gingerroot, 1 tablespoon peeled and minced
About 4 ounces shiitake mushrooms, 5 to 6 large, 1 cup stemmed and finely sliced

3 tablespoons vegetable oil for stir-frying, more as needed, *divided*
6 to 7 ounces boneless, skinless chicken breast, about 1 cup cut into 1-inch by 1/8-inch shreds
6 to 8 ounces Savoy cabbage leaves, 2-1/2 to 3 cups halved lengthwise and finely sliced cross-wise
About 3 ounces carrot, 1 cup shredded or grated
2 ounces trimmed green onions, 4 large, about 1/2 cup julienned
About 3 ounces mung bean sprouts, 1 cup

For Serving

1/2 cup prepared hoisin sauce
4 to 8 Mandarin pancakes, steamed soft
  or flour tortillas, steamed soft

1 Combine **sauce ingredients** in small bowl, blend well and set aside. In another bowl, whisk egg with sesame oil; set aside. Prep **aromatic vegetable seasonings**, but don't mix them together.

2 Heat a wok and swirl in 2 to 3 teaspoons oil. When hot, add chicken. Don't move it for a minute; it will form a crust. Stir-fry until chicken is just cooked. Remove chicken to a bowl. Wipe wok clean if it is crusted.

3 Reheat wok and add 2 teaspoons oil. When oil is hot, pour in eggs. They will puff up and begin to firm. Move them gently aside so wet egg can cook. When eggs are cooked, place on a cutting board and slice into a julienne. Place them with the chicken. Wipe wok clean if necessary.

4 Reheat wok, add 2 to 3 teaspoons oil, and when hot, add ginger and garlic and cook 10 seconds. Add mushrooms, cover and cook until soft. Uncover wok, add cabbage and carrots, and stir-fry until crisp-tender.

5 Add green onions, bean sprouts, meat, and **sauce ingredients** and toss and cook until mixture thickens and clears. Taste and adjust seasonings with salt and pepper if desired. Heap moo shu mixture onto a serving platter.

6 **To Serve:** Paint a little hoisin sauce on a hot flour tortilla or Mandarin pancake and spoon moo shu mixture in a log down the middle. Roll up and eat like an enchilada.

Vary! Improvise!

☞ *Personal Stir-Fry: Consider stir-frying minced garlic and/or ginger, peeled shrimp, finely sliced or minced boneless, skinless chicken, sausage, or finely sliced boneless pork, finely diced carrots, mushrooms, broccoli, matchstick cut snow peas, or green peas, and stirring into the rice at the end.*

FIGURE 1.28 Cantonese velvet shrimp with walnuts and shiitakes.

CANTONESE VELVET SHRIMP WITH WALNUTS AND SHIITAKES

Notice how the sauce is prepared before shrimp are added to finish cooking in the sauce.

Yields about 3-1/2 cups, 4 servings

1 pound 21/25 or 26/30 shrimp, peeled and deveined
About 4 ounces fresh shiitake mushrooms, 5 to 6 large
About 1-1/2 ounces broken walnuts, 1/3 cup

Seasonings

1/4 ounce garlic, 1 large clove, 1-1/2 teaspoons peeled and minced
1/2 ounce ginger, about 2 teaspoons peeled and minced
2 ounces green onions, 4 large, 1/2 to 2/3 cup finely sliced on the diagonal

Sauce Ingredients

2 teaspoons soy sauce
2 tablespoons Chinese wine or sherry
4 teaspoons cornstarch
8 ounces cold fish stock *or* clam juice

Garnish: 2 teaspoons Asian sesame oil

For Serving

Hot, cooked rice or egg noodles

1 *Salt Whisk* shrimp then *Velvet* shrimp in oil. Reserve oil from velveting shrimp. Slice shiitake caps into thick slices and mince stems to yield about 1-1/3 cups; set aside.

2 Preheat oven to 350 degrees F. Spread walnuts on a sheet pan and roast in oven until fragrant.

3 Prepare **seasonings** and set aside separately. Mix together **sauce ingredients** in small bowl and set aside.

4 Heat wok or deep 10-inch skillet over high heat. Swirl in 2 tablespoons reserved oil. Stir in mushrooms and ginger and cook until tender. Stir in garlic and green onions and cook until soft.

5 Stir **sauce ingredients** to recombine, and pour them into vegetables. Stir constantly and cook until sauce boils, thickens, and clears. Fold shrimp and walnuts into sauce. Lower heat and simmer until shrimp are opaque. Remove pan from heat, stir in sesame oil.

6 **To Serve:** Heap mixture onto a serving platter with rice or noodles. (Wash the wok.)

Vary! Improvise!

☞ *What other combinations besides walnuts and shiitakes would work together in this shrimp dish?*

THREE CHINESE STEAMED BUN FILLINGS

Roasted Pork

Yields *3 cups*

1-1/2 pounds pork shoulder butt
    or 1-1/4 to 1-1/2 pounds pork loin with fat cap
        or *Chinese Barbequed Pork (Char Siu)*
            or leftover grilled pork chops
2 tablespoons cornstarch
1 tablespoon vegetable oil

4 to 5 ounces onion, 1 cup peeled and minced
Scant 1/2 ounce ginger, about 2 teaspoons peeled and minced
2 tablespoons soy sauce
1 to 2 tablespoons hoisin sauce
2 ounces trimmed green onions, 4 large, 1/2 cup minced

1 Preheat oven to 400 degrees F. Rub pork with oil and season with salt and pepper. Place in roasting pan and roast in oven until shoulder butt registers 150 to 155 degrees F and loin registers 145 to 150 degrees F internally. Tent pork with foil and rest 10 minutes.

2 Dice pork into 1/4-inch cubes, discarding fat and gristle to yield 3 cups diced pork. (Alternatively, use leftover grilled pork.)

3 In a small bowl, stir together cornstarch and 1/4-cup cold water. Set aside.

4 Heat oil in wok or 9-inch skillet over medium heat. Cook onion until soft and add ginger; cook 30 seconds. Stir in 2 tablespoons water (or pork juices) to deglaze, then add diced pork, soy sauce, and 1 tablespoon hoisin. Season with salt and pepper and more hoisin to taste. If using *Chinese Barbequed Pork*, use less soy sauce and hoisin. Taste. Pour in cornstarch mixture. Stir and boil until it thickens and clears, 1 minute. Mix in green onions, and cool. Taste and re-season. Scrape into bowl.

Chicken Curry

Yields *2-1/2 cups*

3 tablespoons cornstarch, *divided*
18 ounces trimmed raw chicken breast, finely diced
4-1/2 tablespoons chicken broth
4 tablespoons oil, *divided*
3 tablespoons rice wine *or* sherry
6 to 7 ounces onion, 1-1/2 cups peeled and finely diced or minced
1-1/2 tablespoons curry powder
2 teaspoons sugar
2 ounces trimmed green onions, 4 large, 1/2 cup minced
Freshly squeezed lemon juice to taste

1 In a small mixing bowl, stir together 1 tablespoon cornstarch and 1/2 teaspoon kosher salt. Stir in chicken breast. In another bowl, stir together remaining cornstarch with chicken broth and set both bowls aside.

2 Over medium heat, heat wok or 10-inch skillet with half the oil. Cook chicken until pieces have separated, stirring constantly, 1 minute. Deglaze pan with rice wine and scrape into bowl.

3 Reheat wok or skillet with remaining oil and cook onion until soft. Add curry powder, cook 30 seconds to 1 minute and add sugar, salt, and chicken. Stir cornstarch slurry, and pour into chicken. Cook until sauce thickens and clears. Fold in green onions. Cool. Season with lemon juice, to taste, and salt, as necessary.

Vegetarian Mushroom

Yields *2-1/2 cups*

1 pound domestic mushrooms, 3-3/4 to 4 cups cleaned and quartered
8 ounces fresh shiitake mushrooms, 3 to 4 cups quartered and stems finely chopped
2 to 3 tablespoons vegetable or canola oil
1/2 ounce gingerroot, 1 tablespoon peeled and finely minced
1/2 ounce garlic, 2 large cloves, 1 tablespoon peeled and finely minced
6 tablespoons Chinese rice wine *or* sherry
1-1/2 tablespoons cornstarch mixed with 2 tablespoons cold broth *or* water
2 to 3 ounces trimmed green onions, 4 to 6 large, 1/2 to 2/3 cup finely chopped
Freshly squeezed lemon juice, to taste
Soy sauce, to taste

1 In a food processor with a couple quick pulses, or by hand, lightly chop mushrooms. Don't over chop or the texture will be lost and they will turn into oatmeal. Leave chickpea-sized pieces.

2 Heat wok or 12-inch skillet over medium heat and swirl in oil. Add ginger and garlic. Cook briefly until just tender and add mushrooms. Cook until they exude moisture and begin to dry. Add sherry or rice wine and cook until almost dry.

3 Stir in cornstarch slurry, and cook stirring constantly, until mixture thickens and clears. (If there is too much moisture in the mushrooms they will be soupy. *To correct*, make another cornstarch slurry and slowly add just enough, while cooking mushrooms over low heat, until they thicken.)

4 Stir in green onions. Remove mixture from heat, and season with lemon juice and salt or soy sauce to taste. Cool before using.

Source: *Chinese Noodles, Dumplings and Breads* by Florence Lin.

SHALLOW-FRIED CANTONESE EGG NOODLE CAKE WITH BEEF AND BROCCOLI

Yields 4 cups meat and broccoli with sauce, 2 to 4 servings

8 ounces dried, thin Chinese egg noodles
2 teaspoons Asian sesame oil

Meat Marinade

1 tablespoon soy sauce
1 tablespoon Chinese rice wine *or* sherry
1/2 teaspoon sugar
1/2 teaspoon Asian sesame oil
1/4 ounce garlic, 1 large clove, 1-1/2 teaspoons peeled and minced
1 teaspoon cornstarch

12 ounces top sirloin roast *or* other meat

Sauce Ingredients

Yields about 1-3/4 cups
1-1/2 cups chicken broth
3 tablespoons oyster sauce
2 tablespoons soy sauce
1 tablespoon Chinese rice wine or sherry
1 teaspoon sugar
1 teaspoon Asian sesame oil

Cornstarch Slurry

2 tablespoons cornstarch mixed with 2 tablespoons cold chicken broth or water

Seasonings

1/2 ounce gingerroot, 1 tablespoon peeled and minced
1 ounce trimmed green onions, 2 large, 4 tablespoons minced

About 12 ounces bite-sized broccoli florets, 4 cups
Vegetable oil for stir-frying

1   **Cook noodles:** Heat 3 quarts water to boiling and add noodles. Cook until al dente. Drain—do not rinse. Oil 8-inch cake pan with sesame oil. Press hot noodles into it, and set aside to cool.

2   Stir together **meat marinade** in mixing bowl. Trim fat away from meat and slice meat cross-grain into 1/8-inch thick slices, 1-1/2 inches wide. Place meat into a bowl with **meat marinade** ingredients and marinate 30 minutes at room temperature.

3   Mix together **sauce ingredients** in one bowl and cornstarch slurry in another. Prepare **seasonings** and set aside by the stove.

4   Bring a pot of water to boil and blanch broccoli until tender, 4 minutes, *or* steam broccoli. Run blanched broccoli under cold water to refresh. Drain florets and pour into a bowl; set aside.

5   Preheat oven to 350 degrees F.

6   Heat a wok or 10-inch skillet on medium-high heat, and when hot, drizzle in 2 tablespoons oil. Swirl it around and up the sides. Invert noodle cake into skillet or wok and brown one side, 4 to 5 minutes. Invert or slide noodle cake onto large plate. Reheat skillet over medium-high heat and add 1 to 2 tablespoons oil. Slide or invert noodle cake onto uncooked side and sauté until browned, 4 to 5 minutes. Slide noodle cake onto a parchment-covered sheet pan and place in oven to stay warm.

7   Reheat wok over medium-high heat. Add 2 to 3 teaspoons oil and when hot, stir-fry meat in batches—until it browns and cooks to medium. Remove beef to a bowl as you cook it. If wok or skillet begins to crust and brown, stir in 2 tablespoons water and scrape up bits. Cook until almost dry and remove.

8   Add 1 teaspoon oil to wok or skillet and when hot, stir in seasonings. Stir-fry 10 seconds and stir in *sauce ingredients*. When sauce boils, give **cornstarch slurry** a stir and scrape it in. Stir and boil until it thickens and clears. Taste and adjust seasonings.

9   **To Serve:** Add cooked meat and broccoli to *sauce* and heat through. Transfer noodle cake to deep, large platter, and pour sauce over. Serve hot.

Source: *Classic Chinese Cuisine* by Nina Simonds.

Vary! Improvise!

☛ *Substitute boneless, skinless chicken thighs for the beef.*
☛ *Increase the broccoli or matchstick-cut and steam or blanch 1 large carrot*

Signature Technique: Egg and Spring Roll Commonsense

1   To create a filling, balance the textures:
   - Use dense, chewy, tender meats or tofu and marinate for more flavor.
   - Use light, crisp foods like mung bean sprouts, bamboo shoots, carrots, and water chestnuts.
   - Use rich foods as accent like peanuts, pine nuts, or ham.
   - Use soft-cooked background vegetables like cabbage and bok choy.

2   **Cut everything into a small dice or fine shred** so that it rolls easily without poking through and tearing wrappers.

3   **Drain cooked fillings** or use cornstarch to thicken. Wet fillings soggy-up wrappers and split them. If you use an uncooked filling, this isn't a problem.

4   **Don't overload wrappers.** They will split when deep-fried.

5   **Be careful to fold the edges of the wrapper in** and to neatly tuck in the floppy edges. This is important to avoid potential explosions and greasy messes.

6   **Use a flour and water slurry or beaten egg wash to seal wrapper.**

7   **Set egg or spring rolls onto a sheet pan dusted with cornstarch.** Don't let rolls sit long, or they will get very soggy and tear. Heat oil while rolling. As the rolls fry, finish rolling.

8   **Heat oil** to 375 degrees F. Deep-fry until golden. Taste-test one.

9   **Drain rolls and consume while hot.** Or cool them and freeze. To reheat rolls, place on a sheet pan in preheated 350 degree F oven until warm and crisp.

FIGURE 1.29   Spring rolls.
Source: JJAVA/Fotolia.

CHINESE EGG ROLLS/SPRING ROLLS

Yields 3 cups filling, 12 medium rolls or 9 large rolls

Marinade

1/2 ounce gingerroot, 1 tablespoon peeled and minced
1/2 ounce trimmed green onion, 1 large, 2 tablespoons minced
1 tablespoon cornstarch *or* arrowroot
1 tablespoon soy sauce
1 tablespoon Chinese rice wine *or* sherry
1-1/2 teaspoons hoisin sauce

Meat

8 ounces raw boneless, skinless pork, about 1 cup finely slivered
  or raw boneless, skinless chicken breast, finely slivered

Filling

3 tablespoons vegetable oil for stir-frying
4 ounces fresh shiitake mushrooms, 1-1/2 to 2 cups stemmed and finely sliced
3 ounces carrots, about 3/4 cup peeled and finely shredded
1 pound Savoy cabbage leaves, about 6 cups de-ribbed and finely sliced
6 ounces mung bean sprouts, 2 to 2-1/2 cups

1/4 cup chicken stock or water
1/2 ounce green onion, about 1 large, 2 tablespoons minced
1 package 5-1/2- by 6-inch square egg roll skins

Egg wash: 1 egg yolk whisked with 1 teaspoon water
To Serve: Dipping sauce of choice

1 Mix together **marinade ingredients** and toss with **meat**. Place in refrigerator to marinate while you assemble remaining ingredients.

2 *Prepare* filling. Heat a wok over high heat. When oil is hot, but not smoking, swirl in 1 tablespoon oil and stir-fry mushrooms until tender. Add carrots and cook until tender. Scrape vegetables into bowl.

3 Reheat wok over high heat and add 1 tablespoon oil. Stir-fry cabbage until seared and wilted, 5 to 10 minutes. Add sprouts and cook until wilted. Scrape vegetables into bowl with carrots and mushrooms.

4 Heat wok again and swirl in 1 tablespoon oil over medium heat. When hot, scrape meat mixture into wok. Stir-fry until meat is fully cooked, adding 1/4 cup chicken stock or water to deglaze (it will stick). Don't use too much liquid or filling will be too wet. Cook until sauce thickens. Remove wok from heat and stir in cooked vegetables and green onion. Toss together well, taste and adjust flavors, seasoning with salt to taste. Cool.

5 Line up a cornstarch-dusted sheet pan, cooled filling in a bowl, wrappers, and egg wash.

6 **Fill rolls:** Lay an egg roll wrapper with point at top and bottom, like a diamond, on work surface. Place 1/3-cup filling 2-inches up from the bottom point, centered in the middle of wrapper. Paint top half of inside of wrapper with egg. Roll the bottom point of wrapper up and then tuck in the sides neatly and firmly. If there are openings, the egg roll will leak. Finish rolling up egg roll. Place egg rolls on prepared sheet pan covered with plastic wrap. (Fill egg rolls only just before cooking them or the wrapper will disintegrate.)

7 **Cook rolls:** Set up deep-frying utensils and sheet pan lined with paper toweling. Heat oil to 375 degrees F in wok or deep-fryer. Deep-fry or shallow-fry rolls until crispy and brown. Remove with strainer or slotted spoon. Set egg rolls on a paper-towel-covered sheet pan to drain. Egg rolls may be frozen at this point. Reheat in 375 degree F oven straight from freezer.

8 **To Serve:** Cut egg rolls in half, arrange on serving plate or plate, and serve hot with dipping sauce.

Vary! Improvise!

☛ **Bake the rolls:** *Preheat oven to 450 degrees F. Paint rolls with oil and set on parchment-covered sheet pan. Place pan on bottom of oven and bake rolls until bottoms are browned, 8 to 10 minutes. Turn rolls and finish baking second side, 7 to 10 minutes.*

☛ **Vegetarian:** *substitute finely diced baked firm tofu for chicken.*

SHALLOW-FRIED CHINESE SCALLION BREAD

Chef Eileen Yin-Fei Lo, who teaches hands-on classes at Manhattan's China Institute, fills her pancakes with a paste made from scallions, salt, sugar, and Crisco. A contemporary Chinese restaurant in Shanghai called 1221 makes these in miniature.

Yields 13 ounces dough, two 6-1/2 ounce 9-inch breads

Dough

4 ounces cake flour, 1 cup
4-1/2 to 5 ounces all-purpose flour, 1 cup
1 teaspoon baking powder
1 teaspoon kosher salt
1-1/2 teaspoons Asian sesame oil, *divided*
2/3 cup boiling water

2 ounces trimmed green onions, 4 large, 1/2 cup finely chopped
1-1/2 tablespoons all-purpose flour
2 teaspoons Asian sesame oil, *divided*
Additional flour for rolling dough

For Pan-Frying: 4 tablespoons canola or vegetable oil

For Serving

Soy sauce-based dipping sauce

1 **Prepare the dough:** Pour flours, baking powder, salt, and 1 teaspoon sesame oil into food processor and process a few seconds to mix. With machine running, slowly add boiling water until the dough forms a broken mass or a ball forms. If dough doesn't form a mass or ball, scrape down sides and add boiling water by teaspoons until it does.

2 Remove dough from processor, scrape out all stray bits, and knead dough into a ball with heel of your hand a few times until it is smooth. Dough should be earlobe soft. Cut dough into two equal pieces and form into balls. Pour 1/2 teaspoon sesame oil into small mixing bowl and roll dough balls in it to coat. Cover bowl with plastic wrap and rest dough 30 minutes to 1 hour.

3 Mix green onions with 1-1/2 tablespoons flour and set aside.

4 Place 1 dough ball onto lightly floured work surface—use as little flour as possible—the more flour added, the tougher the pancake will be. Roll dough into 8- to 9-inch circular thin pancake. If dough becomes hard to roll out, cover and wait 10 to 15 minutes. The gluten will relax.

5 Brush the round lightly with 1 teaspoon sesame oil and sprinkle evenly with 1 teaspoon kosher salt. Spread half the green onions over the dough and lightly press them into it.

6 Roll dough into a cylinder. Then gently roll and stretch cylinder so it measures at least 14-inches long. Taking one end of cylinder, wind it around itself, taking care to keep the seam side facing in. Tuck the remaining end under and press cake together. Place spiraled cake on work surface, cover and let it rest 10 minutes while repeating the process with the second ball of dough, remaining sesame oil, salt, and green onions.

7 Flatten spiral cake gently with the heel of a hand. Roll it out as thinly as possible, 8- to 9-inches. Dust with flour as necessary. Cover pancake while skillet heats.

8 **Cook bread:** Heat a 10-inch heavy nonstick skillet over medium heat. Add 2 tablespoons oil. When oil is hot, lower heat to medium-low, and add bread. It should sizzle. With fingers, press and swirl dough out into 9- to 10-inch pancake. Cover pan and cook until bottom of bread is evenly golden, occasionally uncovering, swirling and lightly pressing bread, about 4 minutes. Lower heat to low or uncover if bread cooks too fast—high heat results in tough bread.

9 **Flip bread:** Lower heat to low, cover pan, and cook until remaining side is golden, again swirling and pressing bread occasionally. Turn bread in the pan often to ensure even cooking. It should be browned, slightly flaky, and crisp.

10 **To Serve:** Blot bread with paper towel. Slide onto cutting board, cool 2 minutes, and cut bread into pie-shaped wedges. Place wedges on platter and serve warm with dipping sauce.

FIGURE 1.30 Small Chinese scallion breads.
Source: dreambigphotos/Fotolia.

Vary! Improvise!

☛ *Substitute finely sliced white and tender green of leeks or spring ramps for green onions.*

☛ *Toast and crush 1 teaspoon Szechwan peppercorns. Mix with green onions and roll into dough.*

FRESH OR RECYCLED OIL

Recycled deep-fry oil heats more slowly and burns more quickly so it colors food darker than fresh oil. Properly recycled oil can be reused once or twice if it hasn't been heated to smoking for too long. Fresh oil has the best flavor and isn't as toxic: heated oil breaks down and disintegrates into toxins known as *free radicals*. It's not good to feed guests free radicals.

- Cool oil.
- Strain oil through cheesecloth-lined mesh strainer.
- Store oil airtight in a cool, dark spot or a refrigerator. Use fish frying oil only for fish.
- Discard oil when it foams, burns easily, thickens at room temperature, smells, or colors food too darkly.

Deep Fry

Most Asian kitchens don't have ovens so they make full use of top-of-the-stove techniques to produce brown and crisp foods. Deep-frying methods vary; each produces a different end result. Raw ingredients can be deep-fried **naked**, with a **light coating** of cornstarch or flour, or with a **batter**.

- Cut foods into uniform pieces so that they cook evenly. Slash fish to the bone so oil will penetrate.
- Choose quality oil with a high smoke point.
- No thermometer? Test oil temperature with a day old bread cube. For 360 degrees F to 375 degrees F, a cube of bread will turn light brown in 60 seconds.
- Reduce splattering: food should be dry and at room temperature.
- Slide food into oil gradually, in small batches, to avoid sudden temperature drop.
- Return oil to its proper temperature between batches.
- Remove cooked food from oil with wire strainer or slotted spoon and place on sheet pan lined with paper towel to drain. Keep warm in 200 degree F oven.

Signature Technique: Scary but Fun, Chinese Deep-Fried Whole Fish

Asian kitchen wisdom says that you'll know when a whole fish is very fresh: the cooked flesh will come away from the bones easily. To emerge from this lesson unscarred:

1 **Prepare fish.** Fish should be gutted through a small undercut toward the tail so it doesn't flop open. Cut out gills (they taste bitter). Wash and dry fish; sprinkle inside with kosher salt. Score outside flanks almost to the bone. (Avoid the tail so not to weaken it.) The meat will be easy to eat, cook more evenly and quickly.

2 **Heat wok before adding oil.** This opens metal pores, which allows oil to enter and seal so fish won't stick.

3 **Account for displacement.** Add only enough oil so when the fish takes its nosedive into oil it won't displace that oil all over the cook.

4 **Heat oil higher than necessary:** to about 375 degrees F. When the cold fish goes in, it will lower oil temperature to the ideal 365 degrees F. Monitor oil temperature.

5 **Prepare for splattering.** Barbara Tropp says to brandish the wok lid like a shield—but the cook isn't Lancelot, the fish is certainly not a sword, and the oil is not an enemy. Just wear an apron, long sleeves, asbestos gloves and a welding mask, and be careful.

6 **Slide, don't slam.** Holding it by the tail, slide fish face-first into hot oil. Don't toss it. Slide fish in slowly.

7 **Baste the fish.** If fish isn't immersed and turning is difficult, spoon hot oil over fish constantly as it lies in hot oil. Move fish around to prevent sticking. Chinese chefs use long-handled wide, flat metal strainers on which they lay fish, lower into oil, and ladle hot oil over.

8 **Remove the fish.** Two Chinese mesh strainer-spoons or metal offset spatulas with holes work. Have a lettuce-covered platter ready nearby. Insert one utensil under each end of fish and lift. Allow oil to drain. Tip fish so oil in the cavity drains off. Blot with paper toweling (have it ready and waiting), and place onto platter. Garnish and serve immediately.

CHINESE NUDE FISH WITH MYSTERIOUS FLAVORS SAUCE

Fish cheeks and tail bits are most succulent.

3 to 4 servings

Mysterious Flavors Sauce
2 pounds whole fish, red snapper, sea bass, rock cod or pompano, gutted, scaled, head and tail on
Water chestnut flour, white rice flour or cornstarch, as needed

1 Prepare *Mysterious Flavors Sauce*.

2 First wash, dry, and salt the inside cavity of the fish. Score outside of fish with a crosshatch or crosswise at 1-1/2 inch intervals, almost to the bone. This will make it considerably easier to eat.

3 Follow *Signature Technique: Scary but Fun, Chinese Deep-Fried Whole Fish* for deep-frying fish. Preheat oven to 325 degrees F. Heat oil to 375 degrees F. Dust fish with water chestnut flour, white rice flour, or cornstarch. Fry the fish: 2-pound fish will take about 8 minutes total.

4 **To Serve:** Transfer to preheated heatproof platter and keep fish warm in oven if necessary. Serve fish with *Mysterious Flavors Sauce* for dipping.

Source: *The Modern Art of Chinese Cooking* by Barbara Tropp.

GRILL, GRIDDLE, ROAST, BROIL, BAKE, AND BARBECUE

Most Chinese homes do not have ovens. Roasted meats are sold in shops that specialize in the process. Duck and pork are the favored meat; beef is expensive, and lamb is too strong-smelling for many Chinese. Crisp-skinned roast duck is a prized and highly evolved procedure: the duck is scalded in boiling liquid to remove fat, air-dried until the skin becomes taut and hard; coated with sugar and seasonings for crunch, flavor, and color; then roasted vertically to drain excess fat. Marinated chickens wrapped in cheesecloth are buried in very hot salt and roasted to yield silky, moist, tender meat.

FIGURE 1.31 Chinese roasted ducks.

Source: philipus/Fotolia.

CHINESE BARBECUED PORK (CHAR SIU)

This flavorful, juicy meat shows the Chinese mastery of cooking pork. Serve with rice and vegetables or in noodles, soups, and stir-fries. It makes a particularly tasty steamed dumpling filling.

Yields about 4 cups, 4 to 8 servings

Marinade

1/2 ounce garlic, about 2 large cloves, 1 tablespoon peeled and minced
1 ounce gingerroot, 2 tablespoons peeled and minced
1/2 cup soy sauce
1/4 cup Chinese rice wine or sherry
1/4 cup hoisin sauce
1 ounce brown sugar, 2 tablespoons
2 teaspoons dry mustard powder
1 teaspoon *Chinese Five-Spice Powder*

2-1/2 to 3 pound pork shoulder butt, butterflied

Basting Mixture

1/2 cup honey
About 1-1/2 ounces brown sugar, 1/4 cup packed

1 Whisk together **marinade** ingredients.

2 Pour marinade over pork and turn it to marinate evenly. Refrigerate pork 8 to 24 hours, turning in marinade periodically. Remove pork from marinade, place on a rack set inside a roasting pan, and rest pork 30 minutes at room temperature.

3 Preheat oven to 400 degrees F. Mix together **basting mixture** ingredients in a small bowl. Place pork in oven and roast to internal temperature 150 to 155 degrees F. Brush 3 times with basting mixture during roasting. Baste one last time just before removing pork from the oven.

4 **To Serve:** Tent pork with foil and rest in warm place 10 minutes before slicing.

Source: *The Complete Meat Cookbook* by Bruce Aidells and Denis Kelly.

Vary! Improvise!

☞ *Substitute pork loin and marinate 2 days. Roast to internal temperature 145 to 150 degrees F.*
☞ *Substitute 3 pounds country style ribs or 1-1/2 inch thick pork chops.*

PICKLE AND PRESERVE

Chinese Preserving

For millennia, vegetables cured by salting, fermenting, pickling in vinegar, citrus or brine, oil or spices, and dehydration have been the mainstay of Asian winter meals. Curing transforms tofu, vegetables, fruit, nuts, eggs, beans, and meat. Fermented and salted soybeans turn into Chinese fermented black beans or soy sauce and bean pastes.

Two famous Chinese pickles are Szechwan cabbage (dehydrated, brined, and pickled in a hot spicy mixture) and Swatow mustard cabbage, a tangy preserve from southern China, which should be rinsed before using in stir-fried dishes.

CHINESE PICKLED MUSTARD GREENS

Use as a stir-fry condiment with poultry or pork. Dishes with them need less salt.

Yields 2 quarts

Brine Ingredients

3 tablespoons kosher salt
2 tablespoons white vinegar

1 pound Chinese mustard greens
   or 1 pound mustard greens
      or 1 pound Chinese cabbage

1 **Prepare brine:** Mix salt and vinegar with 2 cups boiling water. Stir to dissolve salt. Set aside to cool to lukewarm.

2 **Prepare greens:** Wash and drain greens. Remove stems and reserve. Chop or tear leaves into bite-sized squares. Slice stems into 1-inch lengths. Yields about 10 to 12 cups packed.

3 Tightly pack greens into two 1-quart wide-mouth glass canning jars or 2-quart lidded Cambro container. Cover greens with brine. Weight vegetables so they stay under the liquid. Cap tightly.

4 **Develop flavor:** Leave vegetables at room temperature. Taste after 3 days: greens should be pleasantly salty-sour. If not, leave at room temperature up to 3 days longer. Store in refrigerator up to 2 months.

PICKLED CHINESE CABBAGE

Serve this refreshing pickle as an appetizer before a Chinese meal or as a condiment on the table with meal dishes.

Yields about 2 quarts

1 tablespoon Szechwan peppercorns
1-1/2 pounds Chinese or Napa cabbage
3/4 to 1 ounce thinly sliced ginger, 5 to 6 large slices
1-3/4 ounce sugar, 1/4 cup
4 teaspoons kosher salt
1-1/4 cups rice vinegar
4 ounces carrot, 1 large, 1 cup peeled and matchstick cut
About 3 ounces red bell pepper, 1/2 medium, 1/2 to 3/4 cup slivered
6 to 12 one-inch long dried red chilies, as desired

1 Heat a small skillet and add the peppercorns. Dry-toast just until fragrant, but not browned. Set aside in small bowl.

2 Slice off a thin slice from base of the cabbage; separate the leaves. Wash leaves and drain well. Stack leaves and slice in half lengthwise. Slice crosswise into 1-inch widths to yield about 7 cups.

3 Place ginger, sugar, salt, vinegar, and 2 cups water into a small saucepan. Bring to a boil over medium heat. Stir until sugar and salt are dissolved. Remove from heat and set aside.

4 In a very clean 2-quart (half gallon) glass canning jar or two 1-quart jars, layer part of the cabbage, carrots, bell pepper, chilies, ginger slices (from liquid) and peppercorns in several layers. Press vegetables down with clean fist to compress. Pour vinegar solution over. Seal jar with cap.

5 Set vegetable pickle aside for 8 hours. Refrigerate 2 days. Pickle may be eaten after 1 day, but it improves in flavor after 2 to 3 days and lasts well up to a month.

REVIEW QUESTIONS

1. What was the Silk Road? How and why was it developed? What did it eventually promote?

2. Name foods that moved along the Silk Road.

3. Name the three main aromatic vegetables used in Chinese cooking.

4. What is the main difference between Cantonese food and Szechwan food?

5. What are three important steps to a good stir-fry?

6. Discuss the important Chinese philosophies regarding food.

CHAPTER TWO

JAPAN AND KOREA

This chapter will:

- Introduce the histories of Japan and Korea, each country's geography, cultural influences, and climate.
- Introduce Japanese and Korean culinary culture, their regional variations, and dining etiquette.
- Discuss the influences of Japanese and Korean cuisines on each other and their differences and similarities.
- Identify major aesthetic, philosophical, and religious influences.
- Identify Japanese and Korean foods, flavor foundations, seasoning devices, and favored cooking techniques.
- Offer the major dishes of Japan and Korea through techniques and recipes.

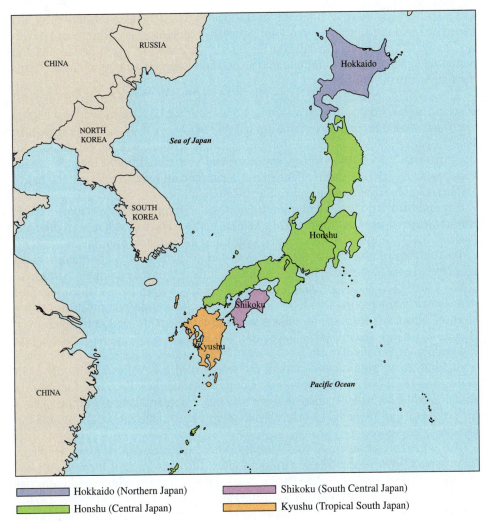

Hokkaido (Northern Japan) Shikoku (South Central Japan)

Honshu (Central Japan) Kyushu (Tropical South Japan)

FIGURE 2.1 Map of Japan.

Japanese Seasonal Artistry

Japanese author and highly respected cooking teacher Shizuo Tsuji explains that a desire to combine artistry with seasonal food likely gave birth to modern Japanese cuisine. Japanese people feel that greater variety of dishes in a meal exhibits greater hospitality, so formal cuisine consists of many small courses and dishes—a large departure from Western cuisine. Each bowl, cup, or plate used to hold the food is also considered an integral part of the dish and meal. Much of Japanese tableware and garnish is seasonal—some pieces are cherished art. The choice of tableware is as important as the choice of food, cooking technique, and presentation in the dining experience.

Both of the Asian countries, *Hanguk* (Korea) and *Nippon* (Japan), live in volcanic and seismic uncertainty. Japan, an archipelago, is home to more than 6,800 islands, 60 active volcanoes, and a history of violent earthquakes. Korea is a peninsula with a rocky, mountainous landscape perched at the edge of a catastrophic earthquake zone with one active volcano.

JAPAN: SMALL, BUT STRONG

Japanese diet, culture, recreation, work, and lifestyle contribute to the highest life expectancy of any country in the world, a very high standard of living, and the third lowest infant mortality rate. Origami, lacquerware, kabuki, noh theater, the martial arts of akido and judo, famed pottery, architecture, sword-making, poetry, gardens, shamisen music, famed writers and painters, reverence for nature and cooking, tea ceremony, and its formal *kaiseki* cuisine reflect the Japanese dedication of decades of life to developing and perfecting a skill and transforming it into an art form. Japanese culture, at its best, turns the simple into the sublime.

Archaeologists postulate that 30,000 years ago Japan's earliest inhabitants migrated over land bridges from Northeast Asia; possibly some arrived later from Southeast Asia by sea. The first culinary influences came around 300 BCE when Chinese and Koreans also brought pottery, metal-working, and wet-rice farming. Chinese writing, Zen Buddhism, Confucianism, Taoism, the soybean, soy sauce, and tofu arrived from China along with Buddhist art and architecture via trade routes. Japanese continued to practice their native animist religion, Shinto, and blended it with Zen Buddhism.

The samurai warrior-caste evolved in Japan when powerful feudal clans took over law enforcement and taxation. From 1192 to 1867 rulers rose and fell with deadly, dramatic power struggles between Japan's Imperial House and the military governments.

Political and cultural influences came from Europe in 1543 when Portuguese ships sailed in Japanese harbors to trade; the Spanish, Dutch, and English followed. Portuguese brought foods and cooking techniques like battering and deep-frying, which Japanese transformed into tempura. Dutch traders brought potatoes and sweet potatoes. Fearing takeover, Japan shut its doors to missionaries and foreigners in 1633 until 1853. Only Dutch and Chinese traders were allowed into two Japanese ports and no Japanese were allowed out under pain of death.

Another strong political and cultural influence sailed into Tokyo Bay in July 1853 in the form of United States naval officer Commodore Matthew Perry and four heavily armed "black ships" (the Japanese thought they might be giant dragons puffing smoke) to "negotiate" a treaty with Japanese officials and to open trade. On March 31, 1854, a nervous Japan signed.

Two wars, *Sino-Japanese* and *Russo-Japanese*, and the annexation of Korea followed. Japan joined WWI on the side of victorious allied forces. It brought them wealth, influence, territorial holdings in the Pacific, recognition as a great military and industrial world power, occupation of Russian Manchuria and oil-rich Sakhalin, and entrance to the League of Nations. Japan embarked on an aggressive course of conquest to obtain scarce raw materials. Worried Western powers stonewalled Japan. Rather than lose face and declare economic collapse, Japan declared war. Their plan was to negotiate with the foreign powers by first attacking the U.S. Pacific fleet at Pearl Harbor and seizing the Philippines, Malaya, Hong Kong, Java, and Sumatra to isolate Australia and New Zealand.

On December 7, 1941, in a preventative strike designed to keep the United States out of World War II, Japan bombed U.S. troops at Pearl Harbor, Hawaii. The next day the United States declared war on Japan. The United States firebombed sixty-seven Japanese cities for six months, but the Hirohito regime would not surrender. To end World War II, in 1945, President Harry S. Truman ordered U.S. troops to drop the nuclear weapon "Little Boy" on Hiroshima on Monday, August 6, 1945, and "Fat Man" on Nagasaki on August 9. Together the bombs killed more than 250,000 Japanese, devastated large cities, industries, transportation, and food supplies. Japan surrendered, and the United States occupied Japan from 1945 to 1952. Today, Japan is one of the world's leading industrial countries, but much of her natural beauty has been destroyed by overpopulation, pollution, and industry.

JAPANESE LANGUAGE, PHILOSOPHY, AND RELIGION

Japan is 99 percent Japanese with the remainder of the population made up of native Yamato, indigenous Ainu from the northern island of Hokkaido, and foreign workers like Koreans, Chinese, Brazilians, Filipinos or Peruvians, and Western expats. Japanese (*Nihongo*) is Japan's official language. Three scripts form the written language: Chinese *kanji,* and two scripts modified from Chinese characters: *hiragana* and *katakana.*

More than half of Japanese still practice *Shintoism*, an ancient polytheistic belief system that originated in prehistoric times and part of many family holiday rituals. Buddhism came to Japan in the sixth century from Korea: Buddha encouraged meditation as a path to enlightenment and talked about the interdependence of all things. (See *Chinese Religion*.) Zen Buddhism in Japan led to the meditative practices of tea ceremony and ikebana flower arranging. Now there are many schools of Buddhism. Most modern Japanese incorporate the beliefs of Shintoism and Buddhism into their lives. Japan grants religious freedom to Christianity, Islam, and Sikhism. Seventy percent of Japanese are not religious; less than half claim a belief in God or Buddha.

GEOGRAPHY AND CLIMATE: THE RING OF FIRE

Japan is an archipelago consisting of the four main islands of northernmost, winter-snowy *Hokkaido*, temperate central *Honshu*, south-central *Shikoku*, southernmost, tropical *Kyushu*, plus 6,848 smaller islands. Japan's highest peak is the volcano Mt. Fuji-san. Most of Japan is mountainous, with fertile valleys, volcanoes, and hot springs. The Japanese archipelago is located on the Pacific *Ring of Fire*, where continental and oceanic plates meet. It is the cause of its frequent earthquakes, which can trigger tidal waves (*tsunami*) and cause untold damage. With over 30 million inhabitants, the Greater Tokyo Area on Honshu, which includes the capital city of Tokyo and several surrounding prefectures, is the largest metropolitan area in the world.

FARMING AND AGRICULTURE

Japan comprises four islands (1,000 miles from north to south) on which Japanese farmers grow rice, vegetables, citrus fruits, and cattle. Japan has a striking shortage of farmland, but it makes the most of what it has by cultivating available land intensively. Most Japanese farms are small and family-oriented with an aging generation tending crops, but a renaissance agricultural movement is growing among the young.

JAPANESE CUISINE: MASTERS OF ARTISTIC RESTRAINT AND SEASONALITY

Rice is at the center of Japanese cuisine. Japanese farmers have cultivated the favored short-grain and sticky varieties for centuries. Japanese cooks prepare rice in some fashion for every meal. The most basic is steamed rice, which serves as an integral part of a meal or as part of many dishes like *sushi* (seafood, often raw, with rice). Cooked and pounded sticky rice turns into *mochi*, a sweet rice cake, rice flour turns into *wagashi* (tea ceremony sweets) or sweet dumplings and fermented rice transforms into rice vinegar or *sake* (brewed rice beverage).

The soybean, which came from China, is not far behind rice in importance. Cooked, salted, and fermented, it becomes *shoyu* (soy sauce) and *miso* (fermented bean paste). Cooked soybean "milk" mixed with *nigari* (magnesium chloride) forms curds, which become *tofu*.

Since the ocean and rich fishing surround Japan, the Japanese diet has always relied on fish and seafood. Fish salted and preserved in rice was the basis of sushi, which evolved to modern-day fresh sushi during the seventeenth and eighteenth centuries. Japanese cooks excel at *sashimi* (raw seafood), grilled fish, *okonomiyaki* ("as-you-like-it" pancakes) and *dashi* (seafood broth), *oden* (stew), and soups.

Buddhism banned meat eating for more than a thousand years until mid-1800. Creative thirteenth-century Japanese monks developed *shojin ryori*: artful, small, all vegetable dishes using seasonal produce and foraged ingredients like wild mushrooms and sea vegetables and gingko nuts. *Shojin ryori* is based on five cooking techniques (simmer, steam, grill, deep-fry, and vinegar-marinate), five colors (green, red, yellow, white, and black/purple), and the five tastes (sweet, sour, salty, bitter, and umami).

Japanese cuisine was born of austerity so its cooks have learned to make the most of what comes their way. *Washoku* is the modern term for traditional-style Japanese food guided by a set of principles. These principles honor and elevate color, taste, methods of preparing food, the diner's sensitivity and the cook's sensibilities on both the cooking and the dining experience. With an abundance of seafood and the use of many *umami*-ingredients like *shoyu* (soy sauce), *kombu* (kelp), and *katsuobushi* (dried fish flakes), the flavors of Japanese cuisine are rich and complex. Seemingly less complicated than its Asian sister cuisines, Japanese cooks tend to focus intensely on quality, technique, and on attracting and satisfying the eye.

Throughout history, Japanese cooks have absorbed and creatively redeveloped foreign ingredients and techniques into a cuisine wholly their own. Sixteenth-century Portuguese traders introduced sugar, corn, chilies, and deep-frying, which led to the popular deep-fried vegetable and seafood delicacy called *tempura*. Japanese cooks and chefs excel at choosing and aesthetically arranging the freshest food in season. With the restraint of natural artists, they carefully and skillfully prepare food to bring out its best qualities.

From mid-1800 onward, the West introduced more meat and dairy, and Japan's vegetarian history began to decline. Japanese raised Wagyu cattle beginning around the second century for plowing but not eating. This unique grass-fed breed, developed in isolated farms, has delicious, juicy, intensely fat-marbled, tender meat. The famed *Kobe beef* is from Wagyu cattle from Hyogo province.

Japanese cuisine and cooking methods may seem deceptively simple, but they are exacting and meaningful. Many chefs and cooks take decades to master one skill. For example, soba making, though it takes just flour and water, is fraught with details about the type of buckwheat, where it's grown, how to grind the flour and how to roll, cut, and cook the noodles.

Meaning and ritual are deeply layered into Japanese cuisine. A home cook dedicated to *chanoyu* or tea ceremony, might study for a lifetime. In the ritual of preparing and serving *matcha* (powdered green tea) with *wagashi* (traditional Japanese sweets), the student pours attention into artful and ritualistic movements. Chanoyu is not just drinking tea: it's about aesthetics, deep symbolic and artistic meaning, and an offering of hospitality from one's heart to honored guests.

Traditional Japanese breakfast is rice, *miso* soup, fried fish, and pickled vegetables. Lunch might be *soba* (buckwheat noodles) in broth or with *tempura* and dipping sauces, *donburi* (rice topped with chicken and egg), or an artful *bento box* (an elegant box-shaped container filled with rice and several small preparations of vegetables and seafood or meat). A typical dinner might comprise clear soup and three main dishes: rice with *sashimi* (raw fish), *yakimono* (grilled dish), *nimono* (simmered dish), and pickled vegetables. Even the simplest cooks present dishes and garnishes in the way of *washoku*: with artistry in thoughtfully chosen plates and dishes that reflect the season.

REGIONAL JAPAN: SURROUNDED BY OCEAN

1. **Northern Japan, Hokkaido: Seafood Heaven**
   Located in the colder north, this island is home to a large variety of fresh fish and processed seafood. Hokkaido's bounty includes several types of excellent crab, scallops,

sea urchins, salmon roe, salmon, herring, flounder, cod, squid, octopus, shrimp, abalone, surf clams, and kelp. Well-known dishes are *ramen*, *ishikari-nabe* (salmon, miso, and vegetable stew cooked by the Ainu people) and *Jingisukan* (basted and roasted dish of thinly sliced lamb, bean sprouts, cabbage, and pumpkin). The cities of Sapporo and Hakodate are here.

2. **Central Japan, Honshu: Cosmopolitan, Abundant Choice**
Honshu is the largest island with the most arable land (and rice farming) and three-fourths of the population. Located in the temperate center, Honshu is made up of six regions: northernmost *Tohoku* (Sendai); eastern *Hokuriku* (Niigata and Kanazawa); western *Kanto* (Tokyo, Saitama, Chiba, and Yokohama); mid-western *Chubu Tokai* (Nagoya and Shizuoka); southern *Kansai* (Kyoto, Osaka, and Kobe) and *Chugoku* (Hiroshima). *Tonkatsu* and *misokatsu* (fried pork cutlets), *fugu* (puffer fish), oysters, and buckwheat *soba* noodles are popular.

Tohoku is known for *kamaboko* (steamed fish paste). Kanto and Kyoto are known for dishes made from *yuba* or boiled soymilk skin and boiled tofu. Osaka loves savory octopus dumplings. Shizuoka and Tokyo excel at charcoal-broiled eel, and Hokuriku for sake and sake-cooked dishes. Hiroshima is known for *okonomiyaki* (savory pancakes) and Kyoto for *shojin-ryori* (vegetarian temple cuisine) and *kaiseki* restaurants featuring beautifully presented, understated dishes set by the chef and using ingredients at their seasonal peak.

3. **South Central Japan, Shikoku: Fish and Fruit**
An island lying just south of Honshu, Shikoku (Kochi) sits surrounded by the Inland Sea and the North Pacific. High quality *katsuo* (fish high in umami) and an exceptional *tai* (snapper) are prized here, along with *sanuki-udon*, supple wheat flour noodles with kelp broth and a variety of toppings.

4. **Tropical South Japan, Kyushu: Chicken, Spirits, and Produce**
Located in the subtropical south, Kyushu is the southern-most island in Japan's chain. Its cities are Fukuoka, Nagasaki, Kumamoto, and Kagoshima. This island loves chicken and eats more of it than anywhere else in Japan. From around 1868, Kyushu's cooks, inspired by Western consommé have simmered chicken and vegetables in chicken broth. They dip the boiled meat and vegetables into *ponzu* (soy and citrus sauce) and serve with chopped leek relish. They cook rice in the leftover broth to make *okayu*. *Saraudon* (crunchy lard-fried thick, or oil-fried thin wheat noodle teamed with seafood and bamboo shoots) or *kikurage* (mushrooms and pork) are popular.

DINE AT HOME IN JAPAN

In a Japanese home diners enter, slip off shoes, and slide into slippers. Bring a small gift to show appreciation: a special seasonal food, chocolate, or something from the West. Diners sit at a low table, on cushions, or at a Western-style table. Japanese hosts will have considered the season when choosing not only the menu, but also the serving vessels, creatively matching food with serving dishes.

Before eating diners say *itadakimasu*, which means, "I humbly receive." If offered a hot towel, use it to clean the hands only. Manners dictate picking up a rice or soup bowl with the left hand and use chopsticks with the right, or vice versa for lefties. Lift bowls to the mouth, but do not allow them to touch, except when drinking soup. Never bite chopsticks, pass them around, stick them into rice upright or use them to spear food or to point. The hosts, never the guest, will pour tea, beer or *sake*, although diners may pour for others. Hold a glass with both hands and say *domo arigato*, which means "thank you." Drinking alcohol usually begins with the toast, *kanpai* (cheers).

The rice bowl will be on the left, the soup bowl on the right, and each *okazu* on small plates (for each diner) just behind them. When serving from communal dishes, turn chopsticks around or use the serving utensils. The hosts will consider it rude to pour soy sauce on a perfectly seasoned meal (fresh tofu is an exception) and ruder yet to waste soy sauce, so go easy while pouring it for sushi or dipping.

Good manners require eating what the hosts offer, even just a little. It shows respect. A Japanese meal will typically consist of *gohan* (short-grain rice), several different *okazu* or side dishes, a bowl of soup, and *tsukemono* or pickles. The cook will vary the *okazu* by cooking technique: raw, as in *sashimi*; grilled, simmered in broth, steamed, deep-fried, vinegar marinated, or dressed with a sauce. Some form of seafood will likely be a feature of the meal. Since rice is revered it is rarely wasted, even one grain. Conclude the meal by telling the hosts, *gochisosama deshita*, or "It was a feast."

FIGURE 2.2 Yokohama City and Mt. Fuji.
Source: shirophoto/Fotolia.

TASTES OF JAPAN

Fat: Sesame oil (plain and Asian roasted), vegetable oil

Sweet: Sugar, millet jelly, rice syrup, *anko* (sugar-sweetenened bean jam)

Sour/Alcohol: *Su* (rice vinegar), lemon, *yuzu* (citrus), sake, *mirin* (fortified rice wine seasoning)

Salty: *Tamari* and *shoyu* (soy sauces), salt, miso, *kombu* (kelp), MSG, *umeboshi* (salted plums)

Spicy-Hot: Chili oil, chili paste, red chilies, black pepper, *shoga* (ginger), *wasabi* (spicy tuber), Japanese mustard, *ichimi* chili, *shichimi-togarashi* (seven-spice mixture)

Aromatic Seasoning Vegetables: Onion, garlic, *negi* (large green onion), ginger, *nira* (garlic chives), carrots, *shishito* (small, mild green chili)

Spice: *Sansho* (pricky ash buds)

COMMON JAPANESE COOKING TOOLS

Hocho (Japanese style knives), *do-nabe* (earthen pots), *otoshi-buta* (wooden drop lid), *hangiri* (wooden tub for sushi rice), *ryoribashi* (long, cooking chopsticks), *makisu* or *sudare* (bamboo-rolling mat), rice cooker, *suribachi* and *surikogi* (ridged mortar and pestle), *oroshi-gane* (toothed grater for grinding daikon or ginger), *hashi* (chopsticks), *tamago yaki nabé* (square omelet pan)

Herbs, Seasonings, and Condiments: *Shiso* or *ohba* (green and red perilla leaf), *mitsuba/trefoil* (Japanese parsley), kinome leaf, *dashi* (broth), *katsuobushi* (savory fish flakes), *niboshi* (dried fish), dried shiitake mushrooms

Other Important Foods: Short-grain rice, tofu, *age-dofu* (fried tofu), *koya-dofu* (freeze-dried tofu), *yuba* (soymilk skin), *okara* (pulp leftover from soymilk), *natto* (fermented soy beans), sesame seeds, gingko nuts, azuki beans, *daizu* (dried soybean), *edamame* (fresh soybean), *kuromame* (black soybean), barley, corn (in northern Hokkaido), *kyuri* (Japanese cucumber), *komatsuna* (mustard spinach), *myoga* (flower buds), buckwheat and millet, bamboo shoots, lotus root, *yurine* (lily root), ume plum, eggplant, daikon radish and sprouts, *kabu* (turnip), soy and mung bean sprouts, *gobo* (burdock root), *kabocha* (Japanese pumpkin), mushrooms, *mizuna* (water greens), spinach, Chinese cabbage, *nasu* (Japanese eggplant), poultry, beef, pork and seafood, *nagaimo* (true yam), *satsuma-imo* (yellow-fleshed sweet potato), *yamaimo* (mountain potato), sea vegetables, *sato-imo* (taro), *kabocha* (winter squash), *kaki* (persimmon), *mikan* (tangerine), *sudachi* (bitter orange), *nashi* (Japanese pear), *kampyo* (dried gourd ribbons)

Popular Dishes: *Donburi*, sushi, sashimi, *oden* (simmered ingredients), *tonkatsu* (fried pork cutlet), *okonomi-yaki* (pancake), tempura, *oshinko* ("pickled" foods), *yakitori* (grilled, skewered chicken), *dengaku* (miso-grilled foods), *mochi* (pounded rice cake), *shabu-shabu* or *sukiyaki* (beef and vegetables cooked in flavored broth), *nabe* (stew) soba, and udon, *kareraisu* (curry and rice), *onigiri* (rice balls), *tamagoyaki* (slightly sweet, delicate rolled "omelet"), *wagashi* (various beautiful Japanese tea snacks), *dorayaki* (small pancakes filled with bean paste), *ohagi* (glutinous rice cakes), *tokoroten* (chilled agar noodles), *anmitsu* (kanten and sugar syrup), sponge cake

Drinks: Twig, black tea and green teas, barley tea, beer, sake, hard liquor, *shochu* (liquor)

FIGURE 2.3 How to hold chopsticks.
Source: Robbert Ross/Fotolia.

JAPANESE MUSHROOMS (KINOKO)

Japanese (and Koreans) use many mushrooms for flavor, texture, and presentation. They give flavor, elegance, and heft to vegetarian dishes.

Enokitake (Winter Mushroom)

Pale mushrooms with long, thin stems and small caps that are often used in soups for their texture and elegant look. Mild flavored, enokitake are crisp when raw and chewier when cooked.

Eryngii (King Oyster or Trumpet Mushroom)

Similar in taste to porcini mushrooms, the meaty, thick-stemmed king oyster's flavor and aroma develop when cooked. Native to the Mediterranean, eryngii mushrooms have become popular in Japan.

FIGURE 2.4 Enoki mushrooms.
Source: Will Heap/DK Images.

FIGURE 2.5 King oyster mushroom.
Source: sassyphotos/Fotolia.

(Continued)

(Continued)

Hiratake (Oyster Mushrooms)

An elegant, petaled pale smoky gray mushroom with little stalk and a chewy texture, this mushroom lives up to its name with a delicate scent and flavor of oysters.

FIGURE 2.6 Oyster mushroom.
Source: Neil Fletcher/DK Images.

Maitake (Hen of the Woods)

A fleshy, pale to dark brown mushroom that forms large, bushy clusters. Known for its immune supportive properties, maitake's flavor and aroma are rich but mild; its texture firm.

FIGURE 2.7 Maitake mushrooms.
Source: soulgems/Fotolia.

Matsutake (Pine Mushroom)

This high-priced fall mushroom grows in red pine forests. Its firm but juicy texture, spicy scent, and deep flavor make it prized among Japanese gourmets for grilling or with rice.

FIGURE 2.8 Matsutake mushroom.
Source: Picture Partners/Fotolia.

Nameko

Small headed, tawny orange-brown, covered with a clear gelatin-like substance, these mushrooms are sold canned or bottled and used in miso soup or with grated daikon radish.

FIGURE 2.9 Nameko mushroom.
Source: quayside/Fotolia.

Shiitake (Black Mushroom)

This meaty, umami-rich mushroom has a chewy texture and strong but pleasant flavor, which pairs well with meat and soy sauce. Dried shiitake are often used to make the vegetarian broth called *dashi*.

FIGURE 2.10 Fresh shiitake mushroom.
Source: Chris leachman/Fotolia.

Shimeji (Beech Mushroom)

Firm textured and crunchy cultivated mushroom that looks like an enlarged version of Western button mushrooms, with a long stem and small, pale brown or cream cap. Raw, it is slightly bitter, but bitterness disappears with cooking and turns nutty. They are good with meat or seafood, or grilled, sautéed, or roasted alone.

FIGURE 2.11 Shimeji mushroom.
Source: joloei/Fotolia.

JAPANESE FLAVOR FOUNDATIONS

Japanese Signature Aromatic Vegetable Combo

Onion or green onions, gingerroot, and sometimes garlic

Signature Seasonings

Liquid/Paste

Goma Abura (Sesame Oil)

Sesame oil is pressed from *raw* seeds to produce a pale-colored, nutty cooking oil. Pressed from *roasted* seeds, the fragrant, nutty oil is used as a beloved seasoning, never for cooking.

Japanese Soy Sauce (Shoyu, Tamari, and Usukuchi Shoyu)

This intense, umami-rich liquid condiment is made when cooked soybeans, roasted wheat, and salt are allowed to ferment. Japanese shoyu is a higher quality soy sauce than Chinese and has a more refined flavor. There are three types: the all-purpose *shoyu* is brewed from roasted wheat, soybeans, and salt; *tamari* is brewed from only soybeans, giving it a deeper flavor preferred as a condiment; and the pale "white" *usukuchi shoyu* made with more salt and barely roasted wheat and preferred in dishes where dark, rich-flavored soy sauce would clash.

Mirin (Fermented Rice Wine Seasoning)

This fortified sweet alcoholic seasoning, when made traditionally, is brewed from rice, koji bacteria and water and fortified with 80 proof alcohol. Eden brand is traditionally brewed. Low-cost mirins (aji-mirin or mirin-fu) are mixtures of chemicals, molasses, and glucose. Traditional mirin is called *hon-mirin* or "real mirin." This mirin should be refrigerated and used within several months after opening. Mirin should be brought to a boil before using to remove raw alcohol flavor.

Miso (Fermented Bean and Grain Paste)

Live, lactobacillus-rich paste traditionally made from cooked soybeans and rice (or other grains and legumes) fermented with koji. Japanese cooks use miso to flavor soup broths, as part of sauces, and to marinate foods.

Sake (Brewed Rice "Wine")

An alcoholic liquid (12 to 16 percent) brewed from steamed rice, filtered, and aged in casks. It is used for drinking and cooking. The best sakes are served cold. Along with dashi, shoyu or soy sauce, and miso, sake is one of the four big flavors of Japanese cuisine.

Animal

Katsuobushi (Dried Bonito or Skipjack)

Katsuobushi is dried, fermented, and smoked skipjack tuna fillets high in umami. Most

FIGURE 2.12 Katsuobushi flakes.
Source: MaMi/Fotolia.

FIGURE 2.13 Konbu/kelp.
Source: Ian O'Leary/DK Images.

commonly used as the base for dashi broth along with kelp, kasuobushi is also used to boost the flavor of sauces and to garnish salads. Traditionally, cooks kept large chunks of katsuobushi and shaved them as needed on a tool similar to a wood plane. Now, most katsuobushi is sold as pink shavings in bags.

Vegetable/Fruit

Konbu/Kombu (Kelp)

This sea vegetable is among many that Japanese and Korean cooks employ. Known for its high glutamate content, kelp is a flavor-booster, much like its derivative, MSG. The white bloom on its surface is salt and minerals; do not rinse them away.

Togarashi (Hot, Red Chilies)

These small red chilies may be used fresh in season or dried. Japanese remove the seeds. The coarsely ground red chili is called ichimi. Ao-togarashi also refers to sweet green chilies (lion head) that look like a large jalapeño or Anaheim chili.

Wasabi Root

The green rhizome of the wasabi plant, this fresh product is grated as a high-end condiment with sushi or added to sauces. Dried, powdered "wasabi" is not true wasabi, but rather a mixture of horseradish, mustard, and

FIGURE 2.14 Wasabi root.
Source: matin/Fotolia.

food coloring. See *Glossary: India and Asia* for more information.

Yuzu

A fragrant, but sour gnarly-skinned Japanese citrus the size of a tangerine. Its aromatic rind is slivered and used as garnish; the juice is used to season dishes. Yuzu is also available as a bottled juice or dry powder.

(Continued)

(Continued)

FIGURE 2.15 Yuzu citrus.
Source: Gary Segraves/DK Images.

Herbal/Spice

Mitsuba or Trefoil (Japanese Parsley)
The flavor of this long-stemmed, three-leaved herb is refreshing and slightly bitter, like a cross between sorrel, celery, and Italian parsley. It is grown in two ways: plain and with dirt piled around the stems so they grow tall and leggy and blanched white. Japanese cooks use blanched stems in chawan mushi, in cooking and for tying sushi. The leaves are added as garnish after cooking to soups like miso and donburi. It becomes bitter if overcooked.

FIGURE 2.16 Mitsuba.
Source: Dave King/DK Images.

SEASONING AND PASTE MIXTURES

JAPANESE SEVEN-SPICE PEPPER (SHICHIMI-TOGARASHI)

This seven-spice combo contains two hot spices and five aromatics. Use it on yakitori or noodles.

Yields 2-1/2 tablespoons

1/2 teaspoon dried, crushed tangerine peel
1 teaspoon sesame seed
1 teaspoon white poppy seed
1 teaspoon Japanese sansho *or* Szechwan peppercorns
2 teaspoons red chili flakes
1 teaspoon nori flakes
1 teaspoon dried shiso leaves or seeds

1 Lightly grind ingredients together. Place in a small jar and keep tightly covered.

WALNUT DRESSING (KURUMI AÉ)

Dry-toasted or parched sesame seeds ground into goma-shio are a major staple in Japanese and Korean kitchens, used in everything from salad dressings seafood. (See recipe in chapter Korea.) This variation is made in northern Japan and tossed on cooked vegetables and konnyaku.

Yields about 1/2 cup

3 ounces coarsely chopped, unsalted walnuts, about 2/3 cup
2 teaspoons sugar
1 tablespoon soy sauce

For Using

2 tablespoons *Dashi* or water
Steamed vegetables like matchstick carrots, cauliflower florets, or broccoli florets

1 **Toast:** Preheat oven to 350 degree F. Spread nuts on a sheet pan. Roast in oven until lightly roasted or parched and fragrant.

2 **Grind:** Place nuts in suribachi, mortar or blender and grind until pasty with small bits of nut. Add sugar and grind to a fine paste.

3 **Mix:** Stir in soy sauce and grind mixture to a sticky paste. Transfer to an airtight container and refrigerate up to 4 days.

4 **To Use:** Toss paste with dashi or water to thin. Toss paste, to taste, on carrots, cauliflower, or broccoli florets.

Source: *At Home with Japanese Cooking* by Elizabeth Andoh.

SAUCE

JAPANESE PONZU SAUCE

Yields about 5 fluid ounces

1 tablespoon mirin
2 tablespoons dried *katsuobushi* flakes (bonito flakes)
1/2-inch square kelp or kombu
2 tablespoons rice vinegar
1/4 cup Japanese soy sauce
1/4 cup fresh lemon juice, 1 to 2 lemons

1 **Express Method:** Pour mirin, bonito flakes, kelp, and vinegar into a small saucepan. Bring mixture to a boil and turn off the heat. Let mixture sit until cool. Stir in soy sauce and lemon juice. Strain mixture after 2 to 3 hours. Refrigerate.

2 **Traditional Method:** Pour ingredients into a jar and refrigerate overnight. Strain and keep in refrigerator.

3 **To Use Ponzu:** Drizzle it onto a dish as a garnish. Marinate shrimp, chicken, pork, fish, or tofu. Use in place of vinaigrette for salads of any sort. Use as a dipping sauce for grilled shrimp or dumplings. Use to boost the flavor of ground meat preparations like chicken meatballs.

Sesame Seed: Goma

Japanese and Korean cooks use black, brown-unhulled and white-hulled sesame seeds, whole and ground. Refrigerate or freeze seeds; they go rancid quickly. Black and brown unhulled seeds are stronger flavored than the delicate white sesame. Sesame seeds are high in calcium, not to mention good flavor.

FIGURE 2.17 Daikon radish.
Source: Will Heap/DK Images.

TWO JAPANESE TEMPURA DIPPING SAUCES

Grated raw daikon radish is traditionally served with tempura as a digestive. Serve your tempura with dipping sauce and shredded daikon radish on side as garnish.

Each yields about 9 fluid ounces, 4 servings

Tempura Dipping Sauce 1

1/2 cup *Dashi*
1-1/2 tablespoons soy sauce
1-1/2 tablespoons mirin

3 ounces daikon radish, 1 cup peeled and finely grated

Tempura Dipping Sauce 2

1/2 ounce gingerroot, 1 tablespoon peeled and finely minced
1/2 cup *Dashi*
1-1/2 tablespoons Japanese soy sauce
1-1/2 tablespoons mirin
1 to 2 teaspoons fresh lemon juice *or* brown rice vinegar
1/2 ounce trimmed green onion, 1 large, 1-1/2 to 2 tablespoons finely slivered

1 Mix ingredients:

Tempura Sauce 1: Mix dashi, soy sauce, and mirin together.

Tempura Sauce 2: Place gingerroot into cheesecloth and squeeze out 1/2 to 1 teaspoon juice. Mix to taste with remaining ingredients.

2 Taste and adjust sauces. Serve **Tempura Sauce 1** with grated daikon on side.

FIGURE 2.18 Suribachi with gomasio.
Source: Egidia Degrassi/Fotolia.

Vary! Improvise!

☞ *On Noodles:* Add 1 to 1-1/2 tablespoons rice vinegar to sesame-sugar-soy dressing, increase soy sauce by 1 to 2 tablespoons, add 1 tablespoon Asian sesame oil, 1 tablespoon minced ginger, and 4 tablespoons minced green onion. Toss on 1 pound warm cooked noodles.

ROASTED SESAME DRESSING (GOMA AÉ)

This is one of Japan's most popular dressings. The delicate, hulled, white sesame seeds are a better (and less bitter) choice for this dressing than the unhulled brown ones. This dressing is traditionally served tossed on steamed spinach, but it may be used on any cooked vegetables like green beans, carrots, or Brussels sprouts. See Japanese Sesame and Sesame Miso Dressed Salads.

Yields 1/2 to 2/3 cup, enough for 2 pounds vegetables

5 tablespoons white sesame seeds
2 tablespoons sugar
3 tablespoons soy sauce

Optional for Thinning Dressing

1 to 2 tablespoons *Dashi* or water
2 teaspoons rice vinegar or freshly squeezed lemon juice

Sesame-Miso Dressing

2-1/4 ounces white shiro miso, 3 tablespoons

1 Place sesame seeds with a pinch of kosher salt in a small skillet. Over medium to medium-low heat, dry roast seeds until golden and fragrant. Place warm seeds into a suribachi and grind until they become fine and powdery. Add sugar and grind seeds until very well crushed. Blend in soy sauce.

2 **Optional:** If a thinner sauce is desired, stir in dashi, water, and/or rice vinegar or lemon juice, as desired. For **sesame miso dressing**, stir white miso into **roasted sesame dressing**.

JAPANESE MISO DRESSING

Use this dressing as marinade, salad dressing, dipping sauce, drizzle on cooked vegetables, fish, meat, or pasta, or drizzle into stew or soup.

Yields 4 to 5 fluid ounces

2 tablespoons mirin
2 tablespoons saké
2 ounces sweet white (shiro) miso, 3-1/2 tablespoons
2/3 to 3/4 ounce sugar, 1-1/2 tablespoons
1-1/2 teaspoons lemon juice or rice vinegar
Optional: 1/2 tablespoon wasabi powder mixed with 1 teaspoon water

1 Pour mirin and saké into small saucepan and bring to a boil. Remove from heat and cool.

2 Mix white miso, mirin, saké, sugar, and lemon or vinegar together to taste. Thin with warm water to desired consistency. Stir in wasabi paste to taste.

JAPANESE MISO: WONDER FOOD

Japanese traditionally made miso at home. They inoculated steamed soybeans and grain with *koji bacteria*, blended them with water and salt, then aged the mixture in cedar vats. The difference in grain, proportion of soybeans, salt, time, temperature, and pressure created miso ranging from white, mellow-light, and red to dark and black. Light-colored miso contains less salt and ferments for a short time; dark miso contains more salt and ferments longer.

White and light misos are made from a larger proportion of rice and less soybeans. Rice miso accounts for 80 percent of miso sold in Japan. Barley miso, from southern Japan, and soybean miso from central Honshu are darker, stronger-flavored, and more regional. Miso can be made with rye, buckwheat, hemp seed, adzuki beans, or chickpeas; its texture can be smooth or chunky. It pays to buy good, live-cultured miso from companies like *Mitoku*, *South River*, and *Miso Master*, which contain tasty, beneficial bacteria and enzymes that support digestive and immune health.

Modern Miso

Modern chefs have found creative ways, other than in soup or as a marinade, to use this complex, savory, high-umami food. Mix 2 tablespoons into 1 cup mayonnaise for a dip. Prepare miso butter with 1/2 cup unsalted butter and 4 tablespoons miso; use it to braise seafood or vegetables like sweet potatoes or broccoli. Dehydrate miso, and crumble on or into dishes. Mix miso with maple syrup and smear on bacon. Bake until crisp. Mix miso with equal parts sesame butter. Thin with lemon juice and water for a sauce.

By Color, Salt, and Fermentation Time

- **Shiromiso** or white miso (7 days to 2 months)
- **Mellow, light miso** (2 months)
- **Akamiso** or red miso (1 to 1-1/2 years)
- **Hatcho** or brown soybean miso (up to 3 years)

Light misos are best for light foods, seafood, and summery dishes. Dark misos are good with beef, meat, and wintery meals. Mix together different misos for more complex flavor.

WHITE MISO TOPPING (DENGAKU)

Yields 5 to 5-1/2 fluid ounces, enough for 15 to 20 pieces of vegetable, about 2 teaspoons per piece, depending on size.

3 tablespoons saké
3 tablespoons mirin
4 ounces sweet white (shiro) miso, 7 tablespoons
2 tablespoons sugar, more to taste
Optional: 1 large egg yolk
2 to 3 tablespoons *Dashi*, as needed
    or 2 to 3 tablespoons chicken or vegetable stock
Optional: 1/8 to 1/4 ounce ginger, 1 to 2 teaspoons peeled and minced

1 Set a stainless steel bowl into a pot so it forms a double boiler. Remove bowl and heat enough water in pot so that it is 2 to 3 inches from bottom of bowl.

   *If not using egg skip the double boiler. Prepare topping in saucepan:

2 Pour sake and mirin into small saucepan and bring to a boil to burn off raw alcohol taste. Remove from heat and scrape into double boiler bowl.

3 In double boiler bowl (or saucepan), whisk together miso, sugar, egg yolk, 2 tablespoons broth, and optional ginger with sake and mirin. If using egg, set bowl over simmering water. Fold and simmer topping until smooth and thickened, 2 to 3 minutes. Cool. Taste and adjust seasonings. The consistency should be like cake frosting. If too thick, thin with extra broth, stock or water.

4 **To Use:** Spread miso topping onto boneless, skinless chicken breast or thigh, slices of pork loin or whole pork tenderloin, vegetables (like zucchini or salt-wilted slices of eggplant), fish fillets, seafood, or tofu slabs, and broil or grill. **White Miso Topping** is especially good as a marinade: Spread or toss with chosen food and marinate several hours to overnight before broiling or grilling.

Vary! Improvise!

☛ *Green Miso Topping: Add 1 tablespoon squeezed dry and puréed, cooked spinach.*
☛ *Hearty Red Miso Topping: Substitute half the white miso for red Hatcho miso.*
☛ *Sesame Topping: Add 1 tablespoon toasted, ground sesame seed or 2 teaspoons Asian sesame oil.*

SPECIAL METHODS

SIGNATURE RECIPE

SUSHI ROLLS (HOSO-MAKI)

Hoso-maki are the small rolls made with a half sheet of nori. When eating sushi out, pay attention. Take mental pictures of how great sushi looks and tastes. Aim to achieve it.

Yields enough for 5 to 6 whole sheet or 10 to 12 half sheet hoso-maki

14 to 15 ounces short-grain sushi rice, 2 cups *or* 6 cups cooked, seasoned sushi rice
Sushi Seasonings

Maki-zushi Filling Combos

Each filling enough for about 6 half-sheet hoso-maki *or* 3 "trainer-maki" made with whole nori sheet
3 nori sheets, cut in half for each type of hoso-maki

Cucumber Roll (Kappa-Maki)

About 8 ounces English cucumber
3 tablespoons umeboshi plum paste or 3 tablespoons chopped, pitted umeboshi plums

FIGURE 2.19 Sushi-maki (Futo-maki, temaki, cucumber hoso-maki (kappa-maki) and spicy tuna inside out roll (ura-maki)).

Tuna or Toro and Onion Roll (Tekka-Maki)

About 9 ounces sashimi grade tuna or fatty tuna
1 ounce trimmed green onions, 2 large, 4 tablespoons minced

Spicy Tuna Roll

12 ounces flesh scrapings from skin and leftover pieces of sashimi grade tuna, 1-1/2 cups
1 tablespoon Asian sesame-chili oil
1 tablespoon mayonnaise
2 teaspoons rice vinegar or fresh lemon juice
1 ounce trimmed green onion, 2 large, 4 tablespoons finely sliced or minced
1-1/2 teaspoons toasted sesame seeds
Optional: 1 tablespoon crunchy bits leftover from frying tempura (*tenkasu*) *or*
1 tablespoon rice crispy cereal

California Roll

12 ounces ripe avocadoes, 1-1/2 large, thinly sliced, about 1/4 avocado per roll
6 to 8 ounces English *or* Kirby cucumbers, peeled, seeded, and finely slivered
12 ounces steamed crabmeat, picked over for shells
Optional: 6 tablespoons flying fish roe *or* 2 ounces dry-toasted black or brown sesame seeds, 6 tablespoons

Shrimp California Roll

12 ounces ripe avocadoes, 1-1/2 large, about 1/4 avocado per roll
6 to 8 ounces English *or* Kirby cucumbers, peeled, seeded, and finely slivered
About 12 ounces 26/30 shrimp, 18 peeled, deveined and steamed
Optional: 6 tablespoons flying fish roe (*tobiko*) *or* 2 ounces dry-toasted black or brown sesame seeds, 6 tablespoons

Boston Roll

6 to 9 ounces cured salmon or lox
8 to 10 ounce avocado, 1 large *or* 6 to 8 tablespoons mayonnaise
6 to 8 ounces Boston or Bibb lettuce, 1 small head, 6 whole leaves, washed and dried

Pickled Herring and Ginger Roll

8 ounce jar wine-pickled herring, drained
4 tablespoons drained, Japanese pickled ginger slices

1 *Cook* sushi rice according to *Signature Technique: Japanese (and Korean) Short-Grain Rice* and fold in **sushi seasonings**.

2 *Choose* a filling combo and prepare:

Cucumber Roll

Peel, seed, and slice cucumber into thick julienne or long strips. Pit and chop whole umeboshi plums. Use 2 to 3 tablespoons cucumber and 1-1/2 teaspoons umeboshi paste per roll.

Tuna Roll

Slice tuna into six 1-1/2 ounce, long oblongs about 1/4- to 3/8-inch by 1/4- to 3/8-inch by 3- to 6-inches. Use 1-1/2 ounces log cut tuna and 2 teaspoons green onions per roll.

Spicy Tuna Roll

On very clean cutting boards, wearing gloves, finely chop or mince tuna. Mix with remaining ingredients except crunchy flakes. Refrigerate tuna until ready for use. Taste and re-season. Stir in optional crunchy flakes or cereal. Use about 1/4 cup per maki.

California Roll

Halve avocadoes, pit, but do not peel. Finely slice each 1/2 avocado, still in shell, lengthwise into 4 to 6 thin slices. Peel and seed cucumber then sliver. Roe or sesame seeds are for pressing on the outside rice if roll is an inside-out roll.

Shrimp California Roll

Halve avocadoes, pit, but do not peel. Finely slice each 1/2 avocado, still in shell, lengthwise into 4 to 6 thin slices. Peel and seed cucumber then sliver. Steam shrimp and cool. Roe or sesame seeds are for pressing on the outside rice if roll is an inside-out roll.

Boston Roll

Thinly slice lox or cured salmon into long slices; use between 1 and 1-1/2 ounces cured salmon per roll. Slice avocado as described for **California Roll** or use mayonnaise. Halve lettuce leaf lengthwise and remove spine. Allow tops of each lettuce half to hang out both ends of the rolls.

Pickled Herring and Ginger Roll

Slice pickled herring into long, thin pieces and use a scant ounce per maki. Use 2 teaspoons ginger per maki.

3 *Set up* work table with ingredients for use: rice and each distinct roll's ingredients. Group them together in small bowls or on plates. Set up a bowl of warm, lightly vinegared water for hands (even if wearing gloves), and clean, dry cotton towels. Everything should be meticulously clean.

   Equipment to have on hand: cotton towel dampened with water-diluted vinegar, bamboo-rolling mat completely covered with saran wrap, cutting board, and very sharp knife.

4 **With clean, dry hands or gloved hands:** Place rolling mat on workspace so that the bamboo runs parallel to the edge of the table. Look at a sheet of nori. Notice the lines on it. Notice a shiny and a rough, dull side. Always lay the shiny side facing rolling mat. The shiny side of nori goes on the outside.

5 Lay one sheet of nori for a "trainer-maki" *or* one-half sheet of nori for a hoso-maki onto mat, longest side parallel to table edge. To cut nori in half, fold it in half parallel with the lines on it and cut with either scissors, or bend it back and tear gently. Place open bag of nori sheets into a ziploc bag and seal tightly. Air and water are enemies of nori. Wet nori becomes slimy.

6 *Lightly moisten hands* in vinegared water and blot excess on towel. Pick up a handful of rice. With a *light* touch, begin to cover nori with rice. For "trainer-maki," leave 1/3 to 1/4 of the nori sheet empty at top (it'll be too much rice otherwise). For hoso-maki, leave 1/4 inch clear at the top. Press a few rice grains along the top to act as glue to hold the edge in.

7 **Don't press and mash the rice.** Rice kernels should remain whole, not flattened. Layer rice no more than about 2 to 3 grains of rice thick—better too little rice than too much. Leave a small "trench" near the bottom third of hoso-maki, parallel to the edge of the table or counter.

8 Moisten hands and dry them. Place thin strips of ingredients along trench. If using a half sheet of nori, don't overfill. The perfect maki is a balance between rice and filling.

   Use neither too much nor too little of each. If necessary, place a few grains of rice on the top edge of rolls made with large sheets of nori to seal.

9 Roll mat and bottom third of nori up and over filling, like a wave, keeping the feeling and intention of a rounded shape. Don't flatten maki. This requires a firm but light touch. Place a few grains of rice along the bare top edge of nori if you haven't already. Continue to roll maki, gently but firmly, in baby steps, pulling the mat out as it catches.

10 When rolling is finished, press mat lightly around the rounded form of the maki, and down lightly on seam, to seal and shape roll.

11 Remove mat and slice roll into 6 or 8 pieces. Let a sharp knife, slicing back and forth gently, do the work. Refrain from pressing knife. Wipe knife on damp cotton towel after each cut.

12 Set slices with cut side up decoratively onto a plate with a small bit of shoyu, a small pyramid of wasabi and a small mound of *Gari* (pickled ginger).

Vary! Improvise!

☞ *Sushi-maki fillings are tricky: when they have no distinct personality, they are less than memorable. A winning combo can't have too many elements and must taste balanced. Less is more: choose three items that work well together like yellowtail, avocado, and pickled jalapenos with cilantro on the outside or asparagus, tuna, and spicy mayonnaise.*

SEASONED SUSHI RICE

14 to 15 ounces sushi rice, 2 cups
   or 6 cups cooked sushi rice

Sushi Seasonings

3 tablespoons unseasoned rice vinegar
2 tablespoons sugar
2 teaspoons kosher salt

1 Cook rice according to *Signature Technique: Japanese (and Korean) Short-Grain Rice*. Rinse wooden *hangiri* or hotel pan with cold water and drain. Leave the drops; do not dry pan. Turn cooked, hot rice out into wooden *hangiri* or hotel pan.

2 Stir together **sushi seasonings** in small saucepan. Heat until dissolved. Cool in bowl set in ice bath.

3 Drizzle and fold sushi seasonings into rice with wooden or rubber spatula. Take care not to break, mash, stir, or squash rice.

4 Fan and fluff rice occasionally until it is room temperature, 10 minutes. (This drives away excess moisture and stops the cooking.) Cover rice lightly with damp cotton towel. Use rice the same day, within 2 hours. Refrigerated rice becomes hard. Microwave or steam before reusing.

THE MANY TYPES OF SUSHI

Sushi is, at its simplest, cooked, seasoned rice. Here is a lineup of how the Japanese transform humble cooked rice into gloriously addictive sushi:

- **Maki-zushi:**
  Futomaki: Very thick roll, 2 inch diameter using 1 sheet nori
  Hoso-maki: Thin sushi rolls made with 1/2 sheet of nori
  Temaki: Hand rolls, cone shaped, 1/2 sheet nori
  Gunkan-maki: Small pingpong rice ball surrounded with nori strip, designed to hold loose ingredients like fish roe or quail's egg
  Ura-maki: Inside-out roll
  Oba-zushi: Nori rolls prepared with cooked soba noodles instead of rice
- **Bou-zushi:** Rice bar covered with ingredients on the outside with the help of plastic wrap
- **Nigiri-zushi:** Small rice pingpong ball squeezed, shaped and topped with wasabi and sliced topping of raw or cooked seafood (*neta*), omelet (*tamagoyaki*), or cooked vegetable
- **Chirashi-zushi:** Scattered sushi, cooked or raw vegetables, and seafood loosely tossed with rice in a bowl; topped with slices of sweet omelet
- **Oshi-zushi or Battera-zushi:** Rice pressed and layered with fish, seafood, omelet, or vegetables in wooden box, and cut into squares
- **Fukusa-zushi:** Thin square or round egg omelet, like beggar's purse, filled with rice and vegetables or seafood
- **Inari-zushi:** Deep-fried bean curd pocket filled with seasoned rice and vegetables

SUSHI CONDIMENTS AND INGREDIENTS

- **Gari:** Pink pickled ginger. The lighter the color, the better the quality.
- **Wasabi:** Dried and powdered horseradish colored green, made into paste with warmish water and rested 5 to 10 minutes to develop flavor. Real wasabi is not horseradish but a root in the watercress family. Look for powdered real wasabi or fresh or frozen, grated real wasabi.
- **Nori:** Seaweed formed and dried into 8-inch by 6-7/8-inch sheets. Nori varies in price, quality, and flavor. Look for dark, thick, shiny, crisp sheets. Keep cool in airtight container. If it gets damp, pass over a flame or burner.
- **Kanpyo:** Dried ribbon strips of gourd. Soak and simmer in flavored dashi before use.
- **Katsuobushi:** Dried shaved skipjack tuna. Big umami. Use as condiment, topping, or in dashi.
- **Oshinko:** Japanese pickles like pickled daikon radish.
- **Shiso leaf:** Cinnamon-minty leaf used as sashimi garnish (green variety)
- **Takuan:** Rice bran pickled daikon radish
- **Tamagoyaki:** Slightly sweet egg "omelet" made in a square sauté pan in thin layers and rolled
- **Umeboshi:** Salt-pickled Japanese plums, whole or in paste; actually a kind of apricot
- **Shishimi or Seven-Spice Powder:** Powdered condiment consisting of red pepper flakes (*togarashi*), Japanese sansho pepper, dried orange peel, white poppy and/or black hemp seed, nori flakes, and white sesame seed
- **Natto:** Strong-tasting, gooey fermented whole soybeans
- **Yukari:** Minced salted shiso leaf

MOST POPULAR VARIETIES OF SUSHI AND SASHIMI GRADE SEAFOOD

Purchase seafood to be served raw only from reputable suppliers of sashimi-grade seafood to Japanese restaurants. Almost all fish to be served raw is carefully frozen and thawed to control parasites. Because of their popularity and overfishing (with nets), tuna and other popular seafood have been declining rapidly.

Tuna (Maguro)

    Blue-fin (Hon-Maguro)

    Big-Eye (Mebachi-Maguro)

    Albacore (Shiro-Maguro)

    Yellowfin (Ahi)

Parts of Tuna

    Akami (Lean Tuna)

    O-toro/Toro (Fatty Belly Tuna)

    Chu-toro (Medium Fatty Belly Tuna)

Yellowtail (Buri)

Young Yellowtail (Hamachi and Kanpachi)

Prepared Freshwater Eel (Unagi)

Prepared Saltwater Eel (Anago)

Japanese Sea Bream (Tai)

Cured Mackerel (Saba)

    Spanish or Horse (Aji)

    Japanese (Sanma)

    Spanish (Sawara)

Sardine (Iwashi)

Halibut (Hirame)

Salmon (Shake)

Cooked Octopus (Takko)

Blanched Squid (Ika)

Clam (Hokkugai and Mirugai)

Scallop (Hotate)

Cooked Crab (Kani)

Sea Urchin (Uni)

Sweet Shrimp (Ama-ebi)

Cured Fish Roe/Eggs

    Salmon (Ikura)

    Herring (Kazunoko)

    Cod (Mentaiko)

    Flying Fish (Tobiko)

    Pollock (Tarako)

FIGURE 2.20 Frozen tuna in Tokyo fish market.
Source: paylessimages/Fotolia.

MAGICAL SHISO-PERILLA LEAF

Is it cinnamon-like, minty, taste of apple, or is it reminiscent of basil? High in vitamins A and C, the fragrant green shiso or perilla leaf has antiseptic properties. Japanese use green shiso with raw fish (sashimi), in dressings, sliced in salads, with red miso and saké, mayonnaise, or rice or noodles. The red or purple variety is used for pickling. Koreans call perilla "wild sesame" and use it to wrap bulgogi or season and wrap rice. Shiso can be grown in a small pot on a windowsill.

FIGURE 2.21 Green shiso.
Source: Craig Knowles/DK Images.

Temaki Method (Cone-Shaped Handrolls)

1 Choose and prep three to four ingredients that harmonize and contrast: shrimp tempura, lettuce and avocado, or yellowtail, avocado, pickled jalapeños, and cilantro sprigs. Prepare *Seasoned Sushi Rice.*

2 With 1/2 sheet nori, shortest side parallel to the counter edge, cover the bottom half of nori with rice 3 grains thick.

3 Lay filling diagonally across the rice. Roll up nori and rice into a cone and seal edge with a few grains of rice.

Ura-Maki Method (Rice Outside/Nori Inside Roll)

1 Prepare *Seasoned Sushi Rice.* Choose filling combinations from *Signature Technique: Sushi Rolls (Maki)* and prep.

2 Cover rolling mat completely with saran wrap, and seal. Lay 1/2-sheet nori onto it. Cover nori completely, edge to edge with rice 2 to 3 grains thick. Sprinkle on toasted black sesame seeds or flying fish roe.

3 Pick up a corner of the rice-covered nori and flip it so that the nori is now on top and its longest side is parallel to the counter edge and rice-covered side is on the bottom. Lay filling ingredients along the bottom third of nori and roll up, taking care not to get mat stuck while rolling.

FIGURE 2.22 Rolling ura-maki.
Source: Lerche & Johnson/Fotolia.

FIGURE 2.23 Futo-maki.

Futo-Maki Method (Big Fat Roll)

Japanese Omelet (Tamagoyaki)
Red bell pepper
Fresh shiitake mushrooms
Avocado, peeled and sliced lengthwise
Cucumber, lightly peeled, seeded, and julienned
Carrots, peeled and julienned
Thin asparagus
Green beans, halved lengthwise
Takuan (pickled daikon radish), julienned
Konnyaku (yam cake), julienned
Kanpyo (dried gourd strips)

1 Prepare *Seasoned Sushi Rice.*

2 Choose and prepare color-contrasting ingredients. Prepare Japanese omelet according to directions, and slice into logs about 1/4-inch thick. Roast bell pepper, remove skin, and slice into long thin strips. Remove stems from shiitakes and slice caps into thick slices. Refer to *Flavored Rice (Takikomi Gohan)* for **Simmering Broth**, and simmer shiitakes, carrots, asparagus, green beans, and konnyaku in it until tender. To prepare kanpyo, soak into warm water 10 minutes. Blanch in boiling water 3 minutes, and drain. Rinse under cold water while rubbing and scrubbing kanpyo. Place in enough **Simmering Broth** to just cover strips, and simmer until evaporated, about 12 to 15 minutes.

3 Cut one sheet of nori in half with the lines. Lay the half piece down on rolling mat with narrowest end parallel to counter edge. Cut remaining half piece in half again, but across the lines, not with them. Place a few rice grains at the top of the sheet on the mat, and stick the second cut sheet at the top, lining it up narrow end to narrow end. It should measure 4 inches wide by 10 inches long.

4 Spread 1/4-inch thick rice evenly from bottom edge to 1-1/2 inches shy of the top of nori. Build a "dam" at the top end of rice: lightly pile rice up 1/2-inch high.

5 Lay filling ingredients in 1 layer all along the length of rice from the bottom to the top "dam" of rice. Beginning at the bottom, bring nori up and around ingredients, rolling up slightly so that a spiral forms. Nearing the top, the dam will break and spill into the naked nori space and help to seal it. Press lightly on seam side.

6 Without pressing knife, cut futomaki into 4 equal slices with a very sharp knife.

STUFFED JAPANESE RICE BALLS (ONIGIRI)

Onigiri is common in bento box lunches in Japan and is known as omusubi or nigirimeshi. Onigiri means "to take hold of with hands." Japanese often take large oval or triangle-shaped onigiri for lunch, to flower-viewing in the spring or to sporting events in the autumn. Onigiri are served warm or room temperature. The filling inside is salty, which balances well with the rice. Onigiri molds are available as an alternative to molding the rice with hands.

FIGURE 2.24 Onigiri.
Source: BRAD/Fotolia.

Yields 6 to 12 onigiri

6 cups *Seasoned Sushi Rice*
1-1/4 ounces, 1/4 cup toasted sesame seeds

Umeboshi Filling

Yields *4 tablespoons, about 6 two-teaspoon portions*

4 ounces umeboshi plums, about 16 to 18, 4 tablespoons pitted and chopped
   or 4 tablespoons umeboshi paste

Katsuobushi Filling

Yields *1/2 cup, about 12 two-teaspoon portions*

1/2 to 3/4 ounce katsuobushi fish flakes, 1 cup packed
2 to 3 teaspoons sugar *or* 2 to 3 teaspoons maple syrup
2 tablespoons soy sauce

Salmon Filling

Yields *1/2 cup flaked, cooked fish, about 12 two-teaspoon portions*

4 ounces skinned and boned salmon fillet
2 to 3 tablespoons soy sauce, more as needed
Optional: 3 sheets nori seaweed

1   Prepare *Seasoned Sushi Rice* and keep warm. Toss rice with sesame seeds before constructing onigir.

   *To make onigiri, rice must be warm. It's best to use cooked rice within an hour, but if it cools, heat the rice in a microwave. Cooked rice may be refrigerated in an air-tight container overnight, and microwaved until very warm, but not burning hot, before making onigiri.

2   With scissors, cut each nori sheet lengthwise into 2-inch wide by 7-inches long strips to yield 4 strips per sheet.

3   Prepare filling or fillings:

   Katsuobushi: Place fish flakes into small bowl. If using sugar, heat soy sauce and sugar in small saucepan until sugar dissolves and mix with fish flakes. If using nontraditional maple syrup, mix it with soy sauce and fish flakes.

   Salmon: Preheat oven to 400 degrees F. Place fish in baking dish. Pour soy sauce over fish, making sure both sides are covered with soy sauce. Bake fish until cooked through but moist, 15 to 20 minutes. Alternatively, brush fish with oil and season with salt and pepper; grill until done. Cool fish and flake with fingers. Season fish with soy sauce, salt and pepper to taste.

4   **Set up:** Place a bowl of warm, salted water and a small bowl of kosher salt on work surface. Set filling(s), nori strips and rice on work surface.

5   **Construct onigiri:** With very clean hands: Dampen hands, shake off excess and, if desired, sprinkle hands lightly with kosher or sea salt. Pick up 1/2 cup warm cooked rice and firmly form into a compact ball. Similar to making a clay "pinch pot," stick a thumb into the center of the ball and begin widening and pressing the rice to make a pocket. Place 2 teaspoons filling into the pocket, press rice over filling and form rice into a compact ball again. As desired, press into a traditional triangular shape, a ball, or a log. If not serving immediately, wrap onigiri in plastic wrap up to 2 hours (depending on filling) before serving, and keep in a cool but not refrigerated spot.

6   **To Serve:** Japanese serve onigiri oiled and grilled (*yaki-onigiri*) or wrapped with nori. If crisp nori is desired, wrap rice triangle, log, or ball with one strip (or more) nori just before serving. If nori is wrapped ahead it will become soggy, which is another alternative. Onigiri may be briefly refrigerated, but the rice hardens unpleasantly after several hours; it's best to serve them within an hour of preparation.

Vary! Improvise!

☞ Use chopped, cooked shrimp as filling.

☞ Substitute drained, flaked high-quality canned tuna mixed with mayonnaise and wasabi for salmon.

☞ Use Teriyaki Salmon for a filling.

☞ Roll finished onigiri in toasted black or brown sesame seeds.

TOFU: FOOD FOR MANKIND

Curded soymilk (bean curd or tofu) was developed in China and 800 years later came to Japan by way of traveling Buddhist monks. Tofu can be found made in more ways than just fresh tofu "pudding," silken-soft, medium, firm, extra-firm, and super-firm: creative cooks have made tofu into noodles, dried sticks, fermented curd, and fried pockets. In China there is a mind-boggling offering of textures, shapes, and flavors of bean curd not available in the West. Refer to chapter *China* for a recipe for handmade tofu. Two books are good resources for aspiring tofu makers: *The Book of Tofu: Food for Mankind* by William Shurtleff and Akiko Aoyagi, and *Asian Tofu* by Andrea Nguyen.

SIMMER, STEW, POACH, BOIL, AND STEAM

THE JAPANESE WAY OF DINNER

Japanese chef and author Hiroko Shimbo reveals that the Japanese don't construct a meal, as we do in the West, with soup, salad, and main dish. Instead the most common meal is a complementary selection of rice, soup, grilled fish or another protein, several vegetable side dishes, and pickled vegetables that is designed to balance flavor, texture, color, cooking method, and nutrition. Apart from formal restaurants (or the special kaiseki meal), food is served all at one time rather than as in a Western meal with one dish or course after another. Soup and rice are served as the last course in a Japanese meal before dessert.

Japanese Soup

Japanese use three types of "dashi" or broth as a base for soup: one made with *katsuobushi* (shaved, dried fish flakes) and *kombu* (kelp), one with *kombu* alone, and a third with *niboshi* (tiny dried sardines) and *kombu*. In Japan, light chicken stock is used only with chicken soups. Banquet, formal, or occasion soups are made from expensive seasonal ingredients like matsutake mushrooms.

Japanese categorize soup into two types: *thick* and *clear*. They love hearty miso soup for breakfast, lunch, and dinner. Clear garnished soups (*suimono* or something to drink) made with dashi broth act as first course appetizers or palate refreshers between courses. Japanese soups come in small lacquered bowls with lids. When the diner removes the lid a delicate soup fragrance wafts up to entice the appetite.

SIGNATURE RECIPE

JAPANESE DASHI BROTH

Use bonito-katsuobushi dashi for clear soups and light miso soup and the stronger flavored anchovy dashi for noodles, soups, stews, and with dark miso or toenjang-seasoned soups. Look for the curly anchovies; they dried faster and will be fresher tasting. Soak kombu (and shiitake) overnight in cold water for a richer flavored dashi.

Vegetarian Kombu and Shiitake Dashi

Yields 3-1/2 cups

1/2 ounce kelp (*kombu*), two to three 2-inch by 5-inch pieces
1 to 1-1/2 ounces dried shiitake mushrooms, 6 to 8

Classical Bonito-Katsuobushi and Kombu Dashi

Yields 3 to 3-1/2 cups

1/2 ounce dried kelp (*kombu*), two to three 2-inch by 5-inch pieces
1/2 to 3/4 ounce dried *katsuobushi* flakes, 1 cup packed

1   Fill stockpot with 1 quart cold water and kombu (and shiitake if using). Heat pot uncovered on medium heat. Bring water to near boiling, about 10 minutes.

2   Remove kombu when small bubbles start to surface; stock may turn bitter if kombu boils. Kelp should be soft enough for a thumbnail to pierce. If not, lower heat and add 1/4 cup cold water and bring to just near boiling once again. Remove kombu just prior to water boiling.

3   To finish:
    Vegetarian Dashi: Remove from heat and rest shiitake in broth 15 minutes. Strain out shiitake.
    Bonito Dashi: Bring kombu stock to a boil and add 1/4 cup cold water and bonito flakes. Bring stock to a boil again and remove from heat at once. Allow flakes to settle 5 to 7 minutes, and strain.

4   Broth will have its best flavor with immediate use, but will keep 3 days refrigerated. Reserve used kelp and bonito for a second dashi. Repeat procedure for second dashi with 1/2 ounce more fresh bonito and 1 quart cold water. Use secondary dashi for noodles.

JAPANESE MISO SOUP

In Japan, miso soup arrives in special lidded lacquered bowls. Diners lift the lid to get a blast of the soup's enticing aroma. Typically two ingredients garnish a bowl of miso.

Yields 8 to 9 ounces, 1 serving

Per Serving: 6 to 8 ounces *Vegetarian* or *Classical Bonito Dashi*
Garnishing Ingredients (about 1 tablespoon *total* per serving)

- Slivered daikon radish and finely sliced green onion
- Soft or firm tofu, diced into 1/4-inch cubes and small squares of *wakame* (seaweed)
- Steamed potato, diced into 1/4-inch cubes and minced green onion

Optional:

- 1 tablespoon lightly cooked, artfully cut vegetables

Per Serving: Miso 2 teaspoons to 1 tablespoon shiro *or* other miso, to taste

1   Prepare **dashi**.

2   Prepare **garnishing ingredients**.

3   Place miso in a small mixing bowl and whisk in 1 to 2 tablespoons hot dashi until smooth. Sweet white miso is less salty so more may be used. Darker misos are saltier; start with less.

4   Pour miso mixture back into hot but not boiling dashi and whisk to mix well. Don't boil soup after adding miso. It will kill the beneficial bacteria.

5   To Serve: Place **garnishing ingredients** into each serving bowl. Pour 6 to 8 ounces hot miso broth over the garnish, and serve immediately.

Vary! Improvise!

☞ *Create a miso soup combination in the restrained but artistic Japanese style.*

☞ *Research and try the colorful and flavorful array of misos at the local health food store like chickpea and adzuki bean.*

TWO JAPANESE CLEAR SOUPS

Fatty tuna, or toro, *is the most expensive and luscious part of the tuna from the belly of the fish.* Chu-toro *is slightly less fatty.*

4 servings

3 cups *dashi*

Tuna and Scallion Soup Ingredients

4 ounces sashimi grade fatty tuna (*chu-toro*), cut cross-grain 1/4-inch thick, 1 inch wide
1 ounce trimmed green onions, 2 large, about 1/4 cup thinly bias sliced
Shichimi seven-spice mixture

Shrimp, Lotus Root, and Watercress Soup Ingredients

1 ounce fresh lotus root, peeled and sliced cross-wise into four 1/8-inch thick slices
About 4 ounces 36/40 shrimp, 12 peeled and deveined
1 ounce trimmed watercress, about 4 sprigs

2 tablespoons saké
1-1/2 teaspoons soy sauce

1 Prepare **dashi**. Prepare **soup ingredients** for *Tuna and Scallion* or *Shrimp, Lotus, and Watercress*.

2 Bring 4 cups water in small saucepan to boil with 2 tablespoons saké. Cook soup ingredients:

Tuna and Scallion

Place tuna into a small sieve (in batches) and plunge into boiling water and out again immediately. Rinse under cold water. Drain. Refrigerate tuna if soup won't be served immediately.

Shrimp, Lotus Root, and Watercress

Boil lotus root until crisp-tender, 2 minutes. Remove and rinse with cold water. Bring water to boil again and add watercress. Cook until bright green and tender, 20 to 30 seconds. Remove watercress with small sieve and rinse under cold water. Drain. Bring liquid to boil again and turn off heat, add shrimp and cover. Allow shrimp to cook until they are just opaque, 1 minute. Drain.

3 Heat dashi in saucepan and season with soy sauce and salt to taste. Finish soup:

Tuna and Scallion

Lower heat to a simmer and add tuna and green onions to dashi. Turn off heat and cover. Rest soup 1 minute. Ladle 2/3 cup dashi and 1/4 of the tuna and green onions into each soup bowl. Sprinkle with shichimi seven-spice mixture.

Shrimp, Lotus Root, and Watercress

Arrange 1/4 of the shrimp, 1 slice lotus root, and 1 sprig watercress in each bowl. Ladle 2/3 cup hot dashi over vegetables and shrimp.

4 **To Serve:** Serve soup immediately, while hot.

Source: *Japanese Cooking, A Simple Art* by Shizuo Tsuji.

Vary! Improvise!

☞ *Devise a stylish, elegant, and simple clear soup.*

Japanese Savory Simmered Foods (Ni Mono)

Simmered and braised foods are the backbone of Japanese meals. They may consist of sautéed meat, vegetables, or seafood, or ingredients simmered in seasoned liquids. The cooking broth reduces and semi-glazes the food, similar to *teriyaki*.

Nabé mono are tabletop-cooked dishes like *sukiyaki*, thin slices of beef sirloin, grilled bean curd, *shirataki* (yam noodles), Chinese cabbage, and mushrooms, briefly seared then simmered in soy sauce, saké, and dashi. Fish, pork, and meat stews are part of this method as well as simmered fresh vegetable dishes that serve as sides to rice, meat, and fish dishes.

SIMMERED DAIKON (DAIKON NO NIMONO)

Yields 2 cups, 4 servings

1 pound daikon radish with 3-inch diameter
1 cup *Dashi*
1 teaspoon soy sauce
1 teaspoon mirin

Garnish: Shaved katsuobushi flakes

1 Peel daikon and trim ends. Slice in half lengthwise. Slice each half crosswise into 1-1/2 inch widths to yield 2-1/2 to 3 cups.

2 Place daikon into 2- to 3-quart saucepan. Pour dashi, 1/2 teaspoon kosher salt, soy sauce, and mirin over. Bring mixture to a boil over medium heat. Reduce heat, cover pan, and simmer daikon until very tender, about 15 minutes. Uncover pan and allow liquid to reduce until about 1 to 2 tablespoons remain, about 10 minutes.

3 **To Serve:** Pile 1/4 of daikon and liquid into a small bowl. Top with shaved katsuobushi flakes. Repeat with 3 more small bowls. Daikon may be served warm or at room temperature. This side is excellent with fish or meat dishes.

SIMMERED JAPANESE PUMPKIN (KABOCHA NO NIMONO)

Yields 6 to 7 cups

2-1/2 to 3 pounds kabocha squash
2 cups *Dashi*
4 tablespoons mirin
2 tablespoons soy sauce
Optional: 2 teaspoons sugar, more to taste

Garnish: 1/2 ounce thinly sliced ginger, 2 to 3 teaspoons peeled and very thinly julienned

1 Slice kabocha in half and scrape out seeds with a metal spoon. Slice each half into 1-inch wide slices then crosswise into 1-inch cubes to yield 7 to 8 cups.

2 Pour kabocha cubes into 4-quart saucepan. Mix dashi, mirin, soy sauce, and optional sugar together in medium mixing bowl. Pour over squash; it should reach 2/3 of the way up the squash. Bring mixture to a boil. Reduce heat and cover pan partially. Simmer squash until just tender, 10 to 12 minutes. If squash overcooks it will be mush. Fold in ginger.

3 **To Serve:** Spoon squash and liquid into small serving bowls. This is excellent with rice and fish, chicken, or meat.

FIGURE 2.25 Kabocha.
Source: Peter Anderson/DK Images.

Vary! Improvise!

☞ **Buttery Braise:** *Braise squash or 2-1/2 pounds Yukon Gold potatoes (peeled and diced into 1-inch cubes) with 1 cup dashi, 1-1/4 cups saké, and 3 tablespoons unsalted butter. Cook uncovered in a 12-inch skillet until liquid evaporates. Stir in soy sauce to taste.*

☞ *Fold in 1 tablespoon rice vinegar or fresh lemon juice at the end.*

Japanese Rice (Gohan or Meshi)

Japanese prefer short-grain white rice cooked in a rice cooker. At most meals, they eat plain rice with toppings, or in *donburi*, in *okayu* (thick congee), or as sushi. Leftover rice is never wasted: it might be mixed with green tea, or used in fried rice. Rural markets called *seimaijo* have automated rice-polishing machines where shoppers can polish brown rice to their liking.

JAPANESE RICE

Uruchi mai: Unpolished white Japonica short-grain rice. This is the rice that is always used for sushi.

Genmai: Unpolished Japonica brown rice; it goes well with rustic dishes and has a strong, nutty flavor.

Haigamai: Half-polished Japonica brown rice; lighter than genmai, this rice is similar to white rice, but has more nutrients.

Mochi gome: Sweet or glutinous short grain (rounder than uruchi mai) rice. This rice is usually soaked and steamed and pounded into *mochi* (rice cakes).

SIGNATURE RECIPE

JAPANESE (AND KOREAN) SHORT-GRAIN RICE

14 to 15 ounces/2 cups dry short-grain sushi-type rice yields 5 to 6 cups cooked rice

For: 7 ounces short-grain (Japonica) sushi rice, 1 cup, rinsed, soaked, and drained
Use: 10 fluid ounces water
For: 14 ounces, 2 cups short-grain sushi rice (or more), rinsed, soaked, and drained
Use: 8 to 9 fluid ounces water per cup of rice

1 Rinse rice in strainer or swish rice in pot with cold water until water runs clear. Drain rice. The right size and weight of pot is crucial, so choose appropriately. Ideally rice should fill no more than about 1/3 of the pot. Soak rice 15 to 30 minutes in cold water and drain.

2 Pour rice and measured cold water into small saucepan. Bring rice to a boil. Cover pot, lower heat to a simmer, and cook rice exactly 15 minutes. (You may also use a rice cooker.)

3 Turn off heat, do not disturb rice. Pour 1 to 2 tablespoons water in around the edges of the rice. Listen for the crackling sound that means the rice needs more water. Don't overdo adding water, or the rice will be soggy.

4 Allow rice to steam, sit, and "settle" 10 to 15 minutes before disturbing. It will firm up and break less easily. Rice should be tender at center and chewy. Fluff rice into hotel pan to cool. If desired, toss with Japanese sushi or Korean kimbap seasonings.

KONNYAKU (DEVIL'S TONGUE)

Konnyaku is a firm, jello-like cake made from the root of the konnyaku plant, a variety of yam. It is boiled, mashed, and poured into a wooden box, to form a dense, slippery rectangle that can be translucent white or gray flecked with brown (seaweed). With no distinct flavor, konnyaku soaks up the taste of what it is cooked in. With zero calories and a chewy, satisfying texture, konnyaku is a popular diet food. It can be found as white, partially translucent noodles called *shirataki*, which are used for *suki-yaki* and simmered dishes called *nabe*.

FIGURE 2.26 Konnyaku.
Source: Reika/Shutterstock.

JAPANESE FLAVORED RICE (TAKIKOMI GOHAN)

Yields about 7 cups, 6 to 8 servings

3/4 ounce dried shiitake, about 4 medium

Simmering Broth
3 cups *Dashi*
2 tablespoons soy sauce
2 tablespoons saké or mirin
2 teaspoons sugar

6-1/2 ounces konnyaku, about 1 cup diced into 1/2-inch cubes
3 ounces carrot, 1 medium, about 1/2 cup peeled and diced into 1/2-inch cubes
3 ounces snow peas, 1 cup stringed and sliced on the diagonal
14 ounces sushi rice, 2 cups, rinsed and drained

Garnish: Asian sesame oil

1 Place dried shiitake in small bowl and cover with 1 cup boiling water. Soak until soft, about 30 minutes. Drain and reserve soaking water. Slice shiitake into thin strips and set aside.

2 *Prepare* **simmering broth:** Pour dashi, soy, saké or mirin, and sugar into saucepan. Bring to a boil. Add konnyaku and simmer 5 to 10 minutes. The longer it simmers, the more flavor it takes on. Remove konnyaku with slotted spoon and transfer to mixing bowl. Repeat this simmering process with the sliced shiitakes (5 to 6 minutes), carrot and snowpeas (2 minutes), and transfer to bowl with konnyaku as each is cooked crisp-tender.

3 Pour rice into 4-quart saucepan. Measure simmering liquid and reserved shiitake soaking liquid to make 2-1/2 cups liquid. If more is needed, use water. Pour liquid into rice and bring to a boil. Reduce heat and cover pan. Simmer rice 15 minutes. Remove pot from heat, but do not disturb. Rest rice 10 minutes. Uncover pot and toss with simmered konnyaku and vegetables. Season rice with salt and Asian sesame oil to taste.

4 **To Serve:** Pile rice into small bowls and serve hot.

Vary! Improvise!

☞ *Substitute other seasonal vegetables for carrot and snowpeas like asparagus or squash.*

☞ *Grill, or simmer chicken breast in simmering liquid. Dice into 1/2-inch cubes and toss with hot rice and vegetables.*

Japanese Noodles

The Japanese adore noodles. Noodle shops, stands, and stalls are easy to locate for a quick, cold snack or quickly slurped hot lunch. Made from wheat or buckwheat flour, Japanese noodles are cut into several distinctive shapes: Tokyo and northern Japanese favor buckwheat soba or green tea soba while Osaka and southern Japanese favor wheat-based thick *udon, kishimen* (large, flat wheat noodle), *hiyamugi* (spaghetti-type wheat noodle), *Chuka-soba* (ramen), and summery, thin *somen*.

FIGURE 2.27 Hand-rolling soba dough.
Source: Dementeva Marina&NatashaNaSt/ Shutterstock.

FIGURE 2.28 Cutting dough into noodles.
Source: Dementeva Marina&NatashaNaSt/ Shutterstock.

HANDMADE SOBA

If given the chance, visit a Japanese soba restaurant and watch as soba-makers expertly prepare and cut 100 percent buckwheat noodles. It's a real skill since buckwheat has no gluten. Hand-made soba takes on an earthy, rich flavor when flour is fresh-ground from roasted buckwheat groats. Grind groats (in small batches) to a fine powder in a coffee grinder, or purchase stone-milled Cold Mountain buckwheat flour from health food or Japanese markets. The freshest flour makes the best noodles. These noodles are a challenge: if they are too frustratingly delicate to work, use more white flour and less buckwheat. Or take a class at the Tsukiji Soba Academy in Tokyo.

1-1/2 pounds dough or 4 to 6 servings

10 to 12 ounces finely ground roasted buckwheat groats *or* light buckwheat flour, 2 cups
4-1/2 to 5 ounces all-purpose white flour, 1 cup
10 fluid ounces hot water, as needed

1 Sift flours together into a large bowl. Stir in half the water and mix with hands until dough looks like small pebbles. Continue to drizzle water until flour comes together into an earlobe soft, moist but not wet, smooth ball.

2 Knead dough by folding inward and pressing down hard with the heel the hands, and rotating a quarter turn each time. Work dough until smooth and shiny with no air pockets, 10 to 15 minutes. As the flour is kneaded, water-soluble proteins break down and the dough begins to bind, a stage often referred to by soba experts as "blossoming of the dough."

3 Form dough into a flat square and place in plastic baggie. Rest at room temperature 30 minutes. Divide dough into 6 pieces. Keep 5 pieces in baggie. Lightly dust work surface with white flour. Shape dough into a square and roll it out slightly so it can fit the pasta machine.

4 Place a 6-quart pot of water on to boil.

5 **Roll and cut dough by hand:** Spread counter with flour and roll dough into 8-inch wide sheets about 1/16-inch thick. Fold up long ends of dough into thirds, over each other. Slice dough into long 1/16-inch wide noodles.

Roll and cut dough by machine: Roll dough through widest setting of pasta machine. Fold it over and roll again through same setting. Lightly flour dough if it sticks. Fold and roll dough through a third time. It should be about 1/8-inch thick. Roll dough through the finest pasta cutter, used for angel hair, directly into metal strainer.

6 Shake off excess flour, and submerge noodles into boiling water. Cook al dente, 1 to 2 minutes. Drain noodles and rinse well with cold water. Don't shake noodles, they are very delicate and will break up. Alternatively, steam the noodles in a commercial steamer or in a bamboo steamer lined with parchment paper.

7 **To Serve:** Serve noodles hot in dashi broth or cold with a dipping sauce. Garnish each. Dough keeps (wrapped tightly) 1 month frozen and 2 days refrigerated.

JAPANESE COLD SOBA AND DIPPING SAUCE (TSUKEJIRU)

In hot weather, Japanese serve soba noodles cold with garnishes and dipping sauces on bamboo-lined plate. In cold weather they come in a bowl with hot broth and garnishes. Soba shops serve soba garnished hundreds of ways from grated daikon radish to tiny specks of nori (seaweed) confetti. The nutty, hearty flavor of buckwheat makes a surprisingly satisfying meal.

Yields 1-1/2 cups, 4 servings of 4 ounces noodles per person

Tsukejiru Sauce

3-1/2 tablespoons soy sauce
1-1/2 teaspoons sugar
1-1/2 cups *Dashi*
Scant 1/4 ounce, dried katsuobushi flakes, 1/4 cup packed

Garnish

Nori strips
Finely sliced green onions
Toasted sesame seeds
Wasabi paste

1 pound dry soba noodles

1 **Make tsukejiru sauce:** Heat soy sauce and sugar together until sugar dissolves. Add dashi and bring sauce to a boil over medium heat. Set up a fine strainer over a heatproof bowl.

2 Add katsuobushi flakes to boiling dashi. Remove pot from heat. Rest 2 minutes. Pour sauce through strainer; discard fish flakes. Cool sauce. Refrigerate if not using immediately; use within 3 days.

3 Prepare desired **garnish**.

4 Bring 2 quarts cold water to a rolling boil. Add salt and soba noodles. Stir soba with chopsticks so they don't stick together. Lower heat and boil until soba are tender but with a very slight resistance, but not as much resistance as al dente pasta, 5 to 8 minutes.

5 Meanwhile, fill a bowl with ice water. When soba are done, drain and plunge into ice water. By hand, gently wash excess starch from noodles. Add fresh water and ice cubes if water warms. Drain noodles. Rinse with cold water and drain well.

6 **To Serve:** Divide chilled noodles onto four plates or special Japanese bamboo-lined platters. Garnish noodles with prepared garnishes. Serve noodles with tsukejiru sauce on side in bowls for dipping.

FIGURE 2.29 Cold soba.
Source: 54613/Shutterstock.

JAPANESE SOBA OR UDON NOODLES IN HOT BROTH (KAKEJIRU)

Shrimp tempura is another classical hot soba garnish. Place on top of the noodles and broth just before serving.

2 servings

8 ounces soba or udon noodles

Garnishes

Grated daikon radish
Sliced Japanese fish cake
Sliced green onions
Fresh enoki mushrooms
    or 2 to 6 shrimp tempura made with 16/20 to 26/30 size shrimp

Kakejiru Broth

Yields *2 cups*

2 cups *Dashi*
2 teaspoons sugar
2 teaspoons shoyu or soy sauce

1 Preboil soba or udon as for *Japanese Cold Soba*. Prepare a choice of **garnishes**.

2 Bring pot of water to a boil. Dip cooked soba (or udon) into water 1 minute to heat through. Drain well, and place in serving bowl with chosen **garnishes**.

3 **To Serve:** Bring **kakejiru broth** ingredients to a boil over medium heat. Season with salt, to taste. Ladle broth over hot soba.

JAPANESE SAVORY STEAMED CUSTARD (CHAWAN MUSHI)

Mushi means to steam, and steamed foods are known as mushi mono. Chawan mushi is savory custard steamed in small, lidded china cups. Japanese traditionally mix the savory custard base with gingko nuts and mitsuba (Japanese parsley). Koreans serve al jjim, their version of steamed savory custard, filled with shrimp or pollack roe, and marinated beef garnished with sesame oil, red chili powder, and green onion. Serve this tender, tasty custard chilled in summer or hot in winter. The amount of garnish is traditionally spare. For more customer value, double the shrimp or chicken.

Yields 32 fluid ounces, four 8-fluid ounce servings

Shrimp Garnish

About 3 ounces raw 26/30 shrimp, 4 peeled and deveined
1/2 ounce trimmed green onions, 1 large, about 2 tablespoons finely minced

Chicken and Vegetable Garnish

2 ounces raw chicken breast, about 4 tablespoons thinly sliced
1/2 ounce snow peas, about 4
1/2 ounce trimmed green onions, 1 large, about 2 tablespoons finely minced

Custard for 4 servings

1 cup eggs, 4 to 5 large
3 cups dashi *or* 3 cups chicken stock
1 tablespoon mirin
1 tablespoon Japanese soy sauce

1 *Prepare* **garnish** *ingredients:* for either shrimp or chicken and vegetable. Blanch, steam, or microwave snow peas 20 seconds and finely slice on diagonal.

2 *Prepare* **custard (1 part egg to 3 parts stock):** Place eggs in mixing bowl and whisk dashi *or* stock into eggs slowly and gently—no bubbles, please. Stir in mirin, soy sauce, and 1/2 to 3/4 teaspoon kosher salt. Strain custard into a bowl.

3 *Arrange* **garnish** *ingredients:* Divide equally into bottom of 4 heatproof 8- to 10-ounce cups, glasses, or ramekins.

4 **Set up steamer:** See *Signature Technique: Chinese Wok-Steaming* in chapter China. Bring water to a boil. Or use commercial steamer. Ladle egg custard into containers. Cover with plastic wrap (or lid) and place in steamer.

5 **Cook:** Steam chawan mushi over medium heat until it is firm, but still slightly jiggly like jello, about 15 minutes. Check water levels in steamer every 5 minutes.

6 **To Serve:** Remove cups from steamer, unwrap or uncover and cool chawan mushi. Serve as hot as a first course in winter, or chill completely and serve cold in summer.

Vary! Improvise!

☞ *Compose two garnish combos for chawan mushi.*

SAUTÉ, PAN-FRY, AND DEEP-FRY

Since Japanese cooks consider pan-frying part of *yaki mono*, which means "foods seared with heat," pan-fried and teriyaki dishes are listed under **Grill, Griddle, Roast, Broil and Barbecue**.

JAPANESE DONBURI

This rice dish is similar to Korean bibimbap: both are bowls of rice topped with meat or seafood, vegetables, egg, and seasonings. Donburi, a century old, is a popular lunch and an original Japanese fast food. Since this dish can creatively accommodate leftovers, precooked meat is fine, but donburi made from raw meat tastes best. Noodle toppings make great donburi. Small "mom-and-pop" Japanese restaurants serve this satisfying, filling comfort food.

Each dish (beef or chicken) yields 1-1/2 cups, 2 to 4 servings

10-1/2 ounces white sushi rice, 1-1/2 cups
    or about 4 cups cooked, hot short-grain rice

Sauce

1 cup *Dashi or* chicken stock
2 tablespoons soy sauce, to taste
1 tablespoon sugar

Gyudon (Beef Bowl)

1-1/2 tablespoons vegetable oil
4 ounces onion, about 1 cup peeled and finely slivered
8 ounces thin-sliced beef

Garnish: 1/4 ounce pickled ginger, 1 to 2 teaspoons finely chopped

Oyakodon (Chicken and Egg)

4 ounces raw boneless, skinless chicken thigh, diced into 1/2-inch cubes
1 ounce trimmed green onions, 2 large, 1/4 cup cut into 1-inch lengths
2 eggs, 1/2 cup lightly stirred

Garnish: 1/2 ounce trimmed green onion, 1 large, about 2 tablespoons finely sliced

1 Cook short-grain rice according to *Signature Recipe: Japanese and Korean Short-Grain (Sushi) Rice.*

2 Combine **sauce** ingredients in small saucepan.

3 Prep ingredients for beef **gyudon** or chicken and egg **oyakodon**.

4 Bring **sauce** ingredients to a simmer over medium heat.

5 Finish cooking donburi:

Gyudon-Beef

Heat oil over medium-high heat in 9-inch skillet; stir-fry onion until soft and slightly browned. Stir in meat and cook until slightly pink. Stir in sauce ingredients and simmer mixture 1 minute.

Oyakodon-Chicken

In a small saucepan, simmer chicken and green onion lengths in **sauce** ingredients until almost fully cooked, 2 minutes. Pour eggs into **sauce** in slow, steady stream; don't stir. When egg bubbles at edges, stir once. Egg should be set, but moist.

6 Divide rice into 2 or more serving bowls. Scoop meat, vegetables, and **sauce** over rice.

7 **To Serve:** Garnish with either pickled ginger *or* green onions, and serve immediately.

Source: *Japanese Cooking: A Simple Art* by Shizuo Tsuji.

Vary! Improvise!

☞ *Create a quick donburi lunch special with leftover cooked rice.*
☞ *Tempura on Rice (Tendon): For 2 servings, prepare 4 large shrimp tempura. Place 2 on top of each bowl of hot rice, ladle the sauce over top, and garnish with thinly cut nori strips.*

JAPANESE FRIED CHICKEN (CHIKIN KARA-AGE)

Cut into nuggets, fried chicken is popular in lunchtime bento boxes.

4 servings

2 pounds chicken thighs, about 6

Marinade

2 tablespoons soy sauce
2 tablespoons saké or mirin
1/4 ounce garlic, 1 large clove, 1-1/2 teaspoons peeled and minced
1/8 to 1/4 ounce gingerroot, 1 teaspoon peeled and minced

Vegetable oil for deep-frying
2-1/3 ounces corn starch or *katakuriko* (potato starch), 1/2 cup

For Serving

Shichimi togarashi or sansho pepper or sweet chili sauce

1 Trim chicken thighs of excess skin, but leave a square of skin attached to the meat. Remove bone from thighs. (Yields 24 to 26 ounces boneless chicken thighs.) Cut each thigh into quarters for chicken "nuggets." Place in mixing bowl.

2 In a small bowl, mix together soy sauce, sake or mirin, garlic, and ginger. Fold evenly into chicken, turning to coat evenly. Marinate chicken 30 minutes at room temperature.

3 Heat an 11- to 12-inch skillet over medium heat. Pour in enough oil to reach a depth of 1/2 inch. Pour cornstarch or potato starch into bowl. When the oil shimmers and is hot: drain each piece of chicken and lay into the corn or potato starch. Turn to coat evenly. Place chicken into oil, skin side down.

4 Fry the chicken until crisp and browned, about 4 to 6 minutes for nuggets. Turn chicken and fry the second sides until crisp and browned, 4 to 6 minutes. Chicken should be cooked through completely. Drain chicken on platter covered with paper towels. Keep warm in 200 degree F oven if necessary.

5 **To Serve:** Place chicken on platter and serve with shichimi togarashi, sansho pepper, or sweet chili sauce to shake on top. May be served warm, room temperature, or cold.

Deep-Fried Foods (Agé Mono)

Modern Japanese cooks use deep-frying frequently to cook fish, shellfish, meats, poultry, and vegetables. Stuffed eggplant, chicken balls, bean curd patties, and pork cutlets (*tonkatsu*) are popular. The foods are coated with cornstarch, flour, batter, or Japanese breadcrumbs (*panko*) and lightly seasoned before cooking. They are served with spicy, highly flavored sauces, vinegared salads, and pungent pickles at the table. The original influences came from Chinese and European visitors. Tempura was a direct result of the Portuguese introduction of fritters to Japanese cooks in the sixteenth century.

FIGURE 2.30 Tempura.
Source: Monkey Business/Fotolia.

JAPANESE TEMPURA

Low-gluten flours like cake flour, rice flour, arrowroot, or cornstarch make a crisper batter than higher gluten all-purpose flour.

Fish Tempura

8 ounces skinned fish fillets, cut into 1/2- to 1-inch wide "fingers"

Shrimp Tempura

8 ounces 21/25 to 16/20 shrimp, shelled and deveined—tail shell left on

Vegetable Tempura

4 ounces carrots, about 1 cup matchstick cut or slivered
4 ounces green beans, about 1 cup matchstick cut or slivered
About 5 ounces sweet potato, 1 medium, 1 cup peeled and sliced into 1/8-inch thick
    half moons

Japanese Dipping Sauce of choice
3 ounces daikon radish, peeled

Batter One: Plain with Seltzer

Yields a scant 1 cup

3 ounces cake flour, 3/4 cup
1/8 teaspoon kosher salt
4 to 5 fluid ounces plain seltzer *or* soda water, as needed

Batter Two: With Leavening and Egg Yolk

Yields a generous 1 cup

4 ounces cake flour, 1 cup
1/2 teaspoon baking soda
1 large egg yolk, about 1 tablespoon
5 fluid ounces ice water, as needed

Oil for deep-frying

1 **Prepare fish, shrimp, or vegetables:** Cut uniformly and small or thin enough to cook through in a couple minutes. Make 2 or 3 shallow crosswise cuts on underside (not the back) of each shrimp. Gently pull shrimp out flat. Arrange tempura ingredients on half sheet pan.

2 Prepare *Japanese Dipping Sauce* of choice, and set aside.

3 Grate daikon radish finely to yield 1 cup, and set aside in small bowl in refrigerator.

4 *Assemble* **batter ingredients** *for either* **One** *or* **Two:** Mix dry ingredients together. Assemble wet ingredients, but do not mix with dry ingredients yet.

5 Heat deep-fat fryer, or heat an empty wok over low heat before adding oil. Oil should be at least 3 inches deep. The oil will rush up as food is added, so vessel should accommodate this. Use fresh oil every time for best-flavored, lightest tempura.

6 **As the oil heats and not before, mix dry and wet batter ingredients:** Using chopsticks or fork, make a well and stir in 3/4 of the liquid. For a light, crisp batter, water should be ice-cold. Some cooks add crushed ice to batter to keep it cold. An addition of 50 percent to 100 percent carbonated water

will make a lighter batter. Don't overmix batter. Check consistency and add more water if necessary. Batter should be the consistency of heavy cream. It should coat a spoon or food and run off lightly.

7 Heat oil a little higher than needed. When adding food the temperature will go lower. When deep-frying, avoid distractions and pay attention.

- Deep-fry dense vegetables at about 350 degrees F.
- Deep-fry light vegetables or shrimp at 350 degrees F to 360 degrees F.
- If oil is too hot, food browns but doesn't cook. Too cool, oil seeps in and makes tempura soggy and greasy. Stable oil temperature is critical to successful tempura. Use a candy/deep fat thermometer to regulate if not using a commercial or electric deep-fryer. Don't overfill and crowd oil. This lowers oil temperature.

8 Dry food with paper towel, and dredge damp foods like shrimp or fish in flour before dipping in batter to help batter stick. Shake off excess.

Fish or Shrimp Tempura

Dip prepared fish or shrimp in flour, shake off excess, and dip batter. Let excess run off 2 to 3 seconds. Place in hot oil and fry until golden and seafood is cooked through, 2 to 4 minutes.

Vegetable Tempura

Place carrots and green beans together into batter. With chopsticks, pull out a small batch, drain 1 to 2 seconds, and set into hot oil. Hold onto them 30 seconds so they stay together. Flip and cook remaining side. Drain. Dip sweet potato into batter. Let it run off and fry until tender and cooked through, 5 to 7 minutes.

9 As food cooks, remove all of one batch before adding fresh uncooked pieces to oil. Allow oil to come back up to temperature in between batches. Skim away burnt bits frequently. They contribute to off flavors. Salt breaks down oil, so use none or very little in batter recipes.

10 Drain hot tempura on rack set over pan or on paper towels and don't let pieces touch. Season tempura with salt while hot or not at all, as desired. Remember that the dipping sauce is salty. Keep warm up to 5 minutes in preheated 300 degree F oven.

11 **To Serve:** Serve tempura immediately. Arrange it attractively on a plate with dipping sauce and freshly grated or shredded daikon radish on the side.

Vary! Improvise!

☞ *Texture Tip: Save cooked bits of tempura batter for a spicy tuna sushi filling. Add crunchy bits for a textural and taste temptation.*

☞ *Try making tempura with herbs like shiso or other Japanese ingredients like shiitake mushrooms. Choose interesting combos.*

☞ *Panko Crunch: Dip battered foods into panko before deep-frying.*

GRILL, GRIDDLE, ROAST, BROIL, AND BARBECUE

Yaki Mono

The Japanese call foods that are seared with heat *yaki mono*. Pan-fried, grilled, or pan-grilled and broiled foods fall into this category. The foods are often seasoned lightly and served with a dipping sauce. Teriyaki or glaze-grilling, miso-marinated, and broiled or grilled foods, and the thick, log-like rectangular and the thin, crepe-like Japanese omelet used for handkerchief sushi called *fukusa* also fall into this category.

Signature Technique: Salt-Grilling (Shio Yaki)

Salt-grilling is one of the oldest methods of cooking in the Japanese repertoire. It may be practiced on small whole fish, fish steaks or fillets, unshelled shrimp, boned (but not skinned) chicken breast, or boneless chicken thighs. Fatty fish like salmon and mackerel and small whole trout or snapper are excellent when salt-grilled.

1 Allow a 4- to 5-ounce cleaned and boned fish fillet or steak per person, or an 8-ounce whole small fish, scaled and gutted. The skin may be left on the fillet or removed. Wash fish and pat dry. Slice several deep cuts into side flanks of whole fish so salt may penetrate.

2 Heat a grill or grill pan. The fish may be grilled directly on an oiled grilled or grill pan, skewered with two oiled skewers and grilled (usually done with small whole fish) or set on an oiled wire mesh and set on grill to cook. Skewering keeps seafood from shrinking and curling. Japanese cooks use an indoor "grill" to grill food, which is a square pan that sits on the burner with a wire mesh insert.

3 Salt the seafood on all sides with about 2 teaspoons coarse sea salt or kosher salt per 1 pound of fish. Whole fish require two saltings: the fins and tail, and then the fish.

4 Grill the skin side (if using skin) first. Depending on thickness of fish, grill on first side until opaque half-way up, about 5 minutes. Carefully flip fish and grill on remaining side until done, 3 to 5 minutes. If using skewers, twist them periodically so they can be removed easily after grilling.

5 Transfer cooked fish to plate and remove skewers. Serve fish hot or at room temperature with lemon, grated daikon radish, and soy sauce. Each diner mixes the trio into a dipping sauce at the table. Serve whole fish with cucumber, lemon, and soy sauce.

SALT-GRILLED SALMON (SHIOYAKI SHAKE)

This simple dish is a favorite throughout Japan. The classic plates for grilled or broiled fish are long, rectangular, and flat. Serve with small bowls for mixing dipping sauce if desired.

4 servings

1 pound skinned and boned thick salmon fillet
3 ounces daikon, 1 cup peeled and grated
1 lemon, sliced into 4 to 6 wedges

For Serving

Soy sauce
Rapini with Spicy Miso Sauce (Nanohana no Karashi Miso-ae)
Simmered Daikon (Daikon no Nimono)
Simmered Pumpkin (Kabocha no Nimono)

1 Wash fish and pat dry. Cut fillet evenly and attractively into four 4-ounce pieces.

2 Heat a grill, grill pan, or broiler over medium heat. Sprinkle 2 teaspoons kosher or sea salt on all sides of the fillet.

3 Place fillet on oiled grill or grill pan and cook on first side, without moving, until fillet turns opaque about halfway up, about 5 minutes. Flip fish and cook remaining side, 3 to 5 minutes. (If broiling, set fillet on a foil-wrapped broiler tray and broil each side until browned, about 5 minutes per side depending on how close the fillet is to the heating element.)

4 While fish cooks, arrange 1/4 cup grated daikon in a pile on each of four plates. Place a wedge of lemon next to it.

5 **To Serve:** When fish is done cooking, place a small dipping sauce bowl at each setting and a small container of soy sauce on the table. Place one fillet on each plate. Instruct diners to mix a dipping sauce with daikon, lemon, and soy, or just squeeze lemon on both daikon and fish before eating. Serve with one or more of the vegetable side dishes. For a full meal, serve grilled salmon and vegetables with miso soup and cooked rice.

Signature Technique: Japanese Omelet-Log (Tamagoyaki)

Tamagoyaki is traditionally made in a heavy, rectangular or square pan called a tamago yaki nabé. A round sauté pan may be used, but the omelet won't have quite the same solid log-like look as an omelet made in an oblong or square pan. The egg batter is seasoned with dashi, soy sauce, salt, mirin, and/or sugar and sometimes saké. Tamagoyaki is often included in scattered sushi bowls or bento lunch boxes.

A similar rolled omelet is also made in Korea where it is called gaeran mari. Korean cooks sometimes mix chopped kimchi, leek, grated onion, or carrot into the batter. They may lay pieces of nori on the barely set egg before rolling it up, or garnish with finely sliced green onions before serving.

- Prepare egg batter with dashi, sugar, soy sauce, and salt. Japanese cooks make tamagoyaki very sweet with up to 1/3 cup sugar per 1-1/4 cups egg. Whisk the eggs lightly with fork so they don't form air bubbles. For a Korean style omelet, stir in a choice of minced green onion, finely diced ham, kimchi, leek or onion, or grated carrot or vegetable. Season highly.

- The size of the finished omelet depends on the volume of egg to the size of the pan. More batter will produce a larger log.

  *1-1/2 cups batter made in a 6-inch wide by 7-1/2-inch long oblong pan yields a 3-inch wide by 6-inch long by 1-1/2-inches high log.

  *1-1/2 cups batter made in a round 10-inch skillet with a 7-inch bottom diameter yields a 2-1/2 to 3-inch wide by 8-inch long by 1-1/2 to 2-inch high log.

- Pan should be heavily oiled over medium-low to medium heat. Too high heat will burn and toughen the egg; too low heat won't produce a fluffy omelet.

- Pour in about 1/4 to 1/3 of volume of batter and cook until egg is set but top is still barely set; the wet batter will allow the layers to adhere. The wet egg will cook more as each layer is produced. Lubricate pan well with oil before pouring in next layer of egg. Make 3 to 4 more thin layers with 1/3 to 1/4 the volume of the remaining batter for each. Log should be shaped with squared off sides, like a rectangle.

- Finish cooking egg log on four sides until browned. While omelet is hot, place on a sushi-rolling mat completely covered with plastic wrap. Gently press omelet into a rectangular shape, and cool. Slice omelet crosswise into thick slices before serving. Serve hot or at room temperature.

JAPANESE OMELET (TAMAGOYAKI)

One 3-inch wide by 6-inch long by 1-1/2-inches high log, 4 servings

1/4 cup *Dashi*
2 to 4 tablespoons sugar
1-1/2 teaspoons soy sauce
5 to 6 large eggs, 1-1/4 cups
Vegetable oil or plain sesame oil

For Serving

1/2 ounce trimmed green onion, 1 large, 2 tablespoons finely sliced on the diagonal
3 ounces daikon radish, 1 cup peeled and grated
1 teaspoon soy sauce, more to taste

1　Combine dashi, sugar, soy sauce, and 1/2 teaspoon kosher salt in small bowl. Stir until dissolved.

2　Pour eggs into a medium bowl and lightly beat with a fork until blended; avoid whisking air into them. Stir in dashi mixture and blend to yields about 1-1/2 cups egg batter.

3　Heat a **6-inch by 7-1/2-inch oblong Japanese omelet pan** (with 2-1/2 cup capacity) over medium-high heat. Pour in 2 teaspoons oil. When oil is hot but not sizzling, pour in 1/3 of the egg mixture (about 1/2 cup). Immediately tilt and rotate pan. Cook egg, gently pushing cooked egg toward center and allowing wet egg to fill in the space, until barely set, but not overly runny. Prick air bubbles with chopsticks and allow egg to flow into the space.

4　Fold omelet into thirds toward handle of pan and push omelet back. An edge should be peeking out from under the omelet. Oil the exposed part of the pan. When the oil is hot, pour in 1/3 of the remaining egg (about 1/3 cup). Lift the edge of the omelet to allow egg to run under and to connect with it. Cook until barely set, but not overly runny.

5　Repeat the process with 2 more layers, rolling the omelet forward and pushing it back. When the layers are done, cook the omelet on all sides until browned. Lay it on a plastic wrap covered sushi mat and press omelet lightly to form a rectangle. Cool.

6　Place green onions in strainer and pour 1/2 cup hot water over. Lightly squeeze to drain and set in bowl; set aside. Mix grated daikon with soy sauce to taste, and set aside in a separate bowl.

7　**To Serve:** Slice omelet crosswise into 8 equal slices, each about 3/4-inch thick. Lay two slices per serving overlapping on each of four plates. Garnish with green onions. Pile 1/4 of the radish alongside omelet slices.

*For a round, nonstick, 9- to 10-inch diameter sauté pan with 7-inch inner bottom diameter:

Heat pan over medium heat and lightly lubricate with oil. Pour in 1/2 cup batter, and cook as in Step 3. Follow Step 4 four more times with 1/4 cup batter each time, and fold omelet in thirds or fourths as it rolls forward. Tilt pan and allow wet egg to run in under and set, especially around the two ends of log; this will fill and strengthen the edges. Finish and serve as with omelet from oblong pan.

FIGURE 2.31 Japanese omelet (Tamogoyaki).

BENTO BOX, BENTO BALANCE

Bento is the ultimate takeout food. Modern bento is attractively packed, colorful food in charming takeout containers. Bentos reflect the Japanese belief that each meal should be beautifully presented and reflect a balance of five colors, five cooking methods, five flavors, and five textures. Bento boxes can be found in convenience stores, train stations, and airports. Originally bento boxes were made at home for family members to take for lunchtime. The food was beautifully presented in black, red, and gold lacquerware boxes partitioned off to hold the various ingredients.

The boxes traditionally included rice or onigiri (stuffed rice balls), a fish or meat dish like teriyaki salmon, tempura, fried chicken or tamagoyaki, and one or more cooked or pickled vegetable dishes like salt-pickled vegetables, seasoned mushrooms, rapini in miso sauce, or rice salad. Bento balance can apply to lunch combinations from any cuisine if the food is made and arranged carefully, and served in a beautiful segmented box.

FIGURE 2.32 Traditional bento box.
Source: Yury Zap/Shutterstock.

FIGURE 2.33 Take out bento box.
Source: kentoh/Fotolia.

JAPANESE TERIYAKI

Teri means gloss or luster. Strong-flavored, fatty fish, chicken, beef, or pork work best with this method. This classic dish may be more popular in the United States than in Japan. Serve it with cooked rice or a salad dressed with rice vinegar and sesame oil. Korean cooks add garlic, ginger, and chilies to chicken teriyaki, and garnish with roasted sesame seeds.

Yield 2 to 4 servings

Teriyaki Sauce

2 tablespoons shoyu or quality soy sauce
2 tablespoons mirin
2 tablespoons saké or dry sherry
Optional: 1 tablespoon sugar

1 pound skinned and boned salmon fillet
   or 1 pound 1-inch thick sirloin steak, about 2
1 tablespoon saké or dry sherry for steak
Sansho pepper or black pepper

1 Pour **teriyaki sauce** ingredients into a saucepan and bring to a boil over medium heat. Lower heat and simmer sauce until reduced and slightly thickened, 4 to 5 minutes.

2 Prepare fish or steak:

Salmon

Cut fish crosswise into four equal pieces. Sprinkle 1-1/2 teaspoons kosher salt on plate or pan and place fish skin side down onto it. Sprinkle 1-1/2 teaspoons kosher salt over top of fish. Rest fish 15 to 20 minutes. Salting extracts moisture and odor and firms fish. Rinse fish and blot dry.

Steak

Salt steaks lightly on both sides.

3 Heat a 10- to 12-inch skillet over medium-high to high heat.

Salmon

When skillet is hot, add 1 tablespoon oil, swirl around, and place fish in skinned side down. Sauté fish 2 minutes, flip, and cook until fish is almost done. To remove excess oil, remove skillet from heat and blot away oil with paper towel. Pour teriyaki sauce over fish. When sauce bubbles, tilt pan and turn fish to coat it in sauce. Simmer over low heat until fish is done to taste.

Steak

Swirl 1 tablespoon oil into heated skillet. When oil is hot, sear steak on one side until browned, 3 minutes. Turn once and sear second side. Splash 1 tablespoon saké or sherry to deglaze, cover steaks, and cook until done to taste, 1 to 3 minutes. Remove steaks and keep warm.

   Pour teriyaki sauce into pan and bring it to a boil, stirring and scraping. It will begin to thicken after a minute. Return steaks to the pan and coat in sauce.

Vary! Improvise!

☛ *Broiled Teriyaki Fish: Combine 2 tablespoons soy sauce, and 1 tablespoon each mirin and saké. Marinate four 4-ounce yellowtail (hamachi), mackerel, or other oily fish fillets in mixture 30 minutes. Broil fish skin-side down until it begins to brown, 4 to 5 minutes. Flip fillets and broil skin-side up until skin bubbles and browns, 4 to 5 minutes. Serve fish hot.*

☛ *Chicken Thighs: Skewer boneless, skinless chicken thighs. Grill until halfway done. Place a little thickened teriyaki sauce into a separate bowl. Brush it onto skewers several times as the meat finishes grilling. Serve skewers drizzled with remaining (untouched) teriyaki sauce.*

4 Season fish or meat with sansho pepper.

Salmon

Plate fish and drizzle sauce remaining in skillet over.

Steak

Slice steaks 1/4-inch thick cross grain. Arrange meat on plates and spoon pan sauce over.

Japanese Dengaku

Less common than other grilled foods in Japan, dengaku is a simple, versatile food-on-a-stick. According to Shizuo Tsuji, author of *Japanese Cooking: A Simple Art, dengaku* takes its name from a medieval Japanese festival entertainment. It began as popsicle-handled grilled tofu smeared with miso that reminded people of the "dengaku hoshi" or single-stilted dancers. Dengaku now includes grilled, miso-dressed, and broiled konnyaku cake, a starchy, bland-tasting tuber (a.k.a. devil's tongue), eggplant, large shiitake mushrooms, and seafood.

For a topping see *Dengaku Miso Topping* or mix white shiro miso with dashi or stock to thin until spreadable. Slice tofu into 3/8-inch thick by 1-inch by 2-inch slab and press between paper towels 20 minutes. Slice eggplant into 1/2-inch thick rounds, salt, rest 20 minutes, rinse, and blot dry. Cook food until tender, spread with miso topping about 1/16-inch thick and broil or grill until speckled. Food may also be slathered with miso and marinated overnight before cooking.

MISO-GLAZED BLACK COD

This classic dish can be prepared with other fish, but the luscious black cod and the sablefish (also called black cod) suit it perfectly.

6 servings

Miso Topping (Dengaku) without egg
Six 6- to 7-ounce skinless black cod or sablefish fillets, about 1-1/2 inches thick

Garnish

Toasted white sesame seeds
Finely sliced or minced whole green onion
Japanese Pickled Ginger (Gari)

For Serving

Cooked short-grain rice

1 Prepare *Miso Topping (Dengaku)* without egg. Cool to room temperature.

2 Wash fish and pat dry. Slather fish with miso mixture, set in pan or bowl, cover with plastic wrap and refrigerate. Marinate fish in miso at least 8 hours and up to 48 hours.

3 Heat broiler to high. Scrape marinade from fish. Place fish in baking pan (nonaluminum). Broil until brown speckled on top, 2 to 4 minutes. Remove pan from broiler and preheat oven to 400 degrees F. Place fish into oven and finish roasting until flaky, 8 to 10 minutes.

4 **To Serve:** Transfer fish to serving plates and garnish with sesame seeds, green onions, and pickled ginger. Serve with rice.

Source: *Nobu: The Cookbook* by Nobuyuki Matsuhisa.

Vary! Improvise!

☞ **Vegetarian Version:** Substitute 1/2-pound-long Japanese eggplant per serving. Slice eggplant in half lengthwise and score cut side in a shallow crosshatch. Remove stem. Salt cut sides of eggplant and rest 15 to 20 minutes. Rinse and pat dry. Brush eggplant with oil. Broil eggplant halves cut-side down, until tender and golden but not burned. Turn and repeat on cut side, about 6 to 8 minutes total. Eggplant should be tender all the way through; if not, bake or microwave to finish. Carefully spread cut sides with miso, about 1/16- to 1/8-inch thick. Broil until miso is brown speckled. Garnish eggplant with sesame, green onions, and pickled ginger.

Japanese Style: Negimaki

Japanese cooks make something similar to Korean bulgogi called *negimaki*. Thinly sliced beef is basted in teriyaki sauce, wrapped around blanched long green onions (*negi*), secured with a toothpick, brushed with oil, and grilled medium-rare.

FIGURE 2.34 Traditional yakitori restaurant.
Source: buckeyeinjapan/Fotolia.

Vary! Improvise!

☞ *What other meats or vegetables could stand in as yakimomo?*

JAPANESE CHICKEN AND SCALLION KABOBS (YAKITORI)

Yakitori is made from skewered bite-sized chicken: cubes, meatballs, heart, liver, skin, wing, tail, intestines, or gizzard. Workers on their way home stop to eat and drink at small yakitori shop with seats set at a long, narrow, shallow charcoal brazier. The chef presides over his skewers, working with sure hands. At other similar shops, chefs grill kushiyaki (skewered foods) like tofu, pork belly, mushrooms, and gingko nuts seasoned with salt, lemon juice, or tare (yakimono sauce).

Yields 8 kabobs, 4 servings

8 metal or bamboo skewers

Yakimono Sauce

Yields *about 5 to 6 fluid ounces*

3 tablespoons saké
6 tablespoons soy sauce
2 tablespoons mirin
1 tablespoon sugar

1 pound boneless, skinless chicken thighs
6 ounces trimmed green onions, 12 large green onions, about 2 bunches
2 tablespoons vegetable oil for brushing

Garnish: Togarashi or Black Gomasio

1 Soak bamboo skewers if using. Mix **yakimono sauce** ingredients together in a small saucepan. Bring to a boil; lower heat to medium. Cook until slightly reduced, 2 to 5 minutes. Divide sauce into 2 bowls.

2 **Prepare skewered food:** Dice chicken into 1/2-inch cubes. Cut green onions into 1-inch lengths with white and some green. Marinate chicken and green onions with a little yakitori sauce 15 to 20 minutes.

3 Preheat grill or broiler. Arrange 8 metal or soaked bamboo skewers, chicken, green onions, a brush, and a bowl with 2 tablespoons oil on work table.

4 On one skewer, slide a piece of chicken, a piece of green onion (through its side), chicken, green onion, and ending with chicken. Finish remaining 7 skewers with meat and green onions. Gently brush oil over meat and green onions. Place on grill or under broiler. Cook meat until halfway done, turning once, 2 to 3 minutes.

5 Use 1 bowl **yakimono sauce** for brushing: Brush meat and vegetables with sauce and return them to grill or broiler to cook until 3/4 done. Remove and baste again. Place skewers back on or under heat source to finish cooking.

6 **To Serve:** Platter cooked yakitori. Pour reserved bowl of sauce over and serve. (Boil leftover basting sauce to kill bacteria before serving.) Sprinkle yakitori with *togarashi* or *black gomasio*.

THE POWER OF FIVE

Japanese people believe in the "power of five":

- **Five Senses:** The Japanese cook considers taste, scent, feeling or texture, sight, and sound when preparing a meal. The way the dish looks, what food is put on what tableware is very important. It should be seasonal and of the proper color and shape for the food. The sounds of nature when dining are highly prized: trickling water, wind in the trees, or birdsong.
- **Five Colors:** Japanese cooks try to incorporate the colors black, white, red, green, and yellow. Contrasts add interest and nutritional balance. Even a garnish of black sesame on white rice helps relieve monotony, and spark flavor.
- **Five Tastes:** They are salty, sweet, sour, bitter, and umami and all should be reflected in a meal.
- **Five Methods:** The five cooking preparation methods of raw, simmered, fried, steamed, and roasted/grilled should be used in a balanced meal. Kaiseki cuisine serves a series of small dishes that begin with raw and move on through the remaining methods.
- **Five Attitudes:** The five attitudes come from Zen Buddhism and vegetarian temple cuisine: The diner acknowledges the work that went into the food, considers his or her worthiness of the food, refrains from greed and favoritism, consumes the food to support health, and affirms that it support the work of enlightenment. The attitudes help diners reflect and give gratitude before dining.

SALAD AND VEGETABLE METHODS

Japanese "Salad": Aemono and Sunomono

Aemono means *dressed things*. Most aemono dressings are thicker and based on puréed tofu, sesame paste, egg, or miso. *Sunomono* (vinegared things) are aemono dressed with vinegar-based dressings. Japanese serve small portions of fresh-tasting and colorful aemono before a meal, to complement a main dish or at the end of a meal before rice. Ingredients can be raw or cooked vegetables, nuts, mushrooms, cooked or raw seafood, tofu, edamame, noodles, rice, and seaweed.

Aemono technique allows cooks unfamiliar with the cuisine to enter the Japanese sensibility and begin to create simple and beautiful dishes. Food freshness, cutting technique, and a good dressing are crucial. Taste everything, and season it so it becomes almost addictive. Japanese never use warm ingredients for their "salads." Cool hot ingredients to room temperature in winter and chill them in summer. Blot ingredients dry before dressing them or the salad will be watery and tasteless.

EXERCISE: SUMOMONO AND AEMONO

Choose main ingredient or ingredients and dressing by color, seasonality, and flavor. Here are combinations from *New Salads, Quick, Healthy Recipes From Japan* by Shinko Shimizu:

- Steamed Cauliflower with Sea Urchin Mayonnaise
- Deep-fried Potato Cubes with Hot Cucumber-Daikon Dressing
- Blanched Cabbage with Soy Dressing
- Steamed Broccoli with Vinegar and Miso Dressing
- Steamed Eggplant with White Miso and Ginger Dressing
- Boiled Peanuts with White Miso-Onion Dressing
- Thinly Sliced Red Radishes Tossed with Black Sesame Goma-sio
- Grilled Shiitake Topped with Ponzu Sauce

1. Prepare a Japanese salad from the descriptions above. Chop, shred, dice, slice, salt-wilt, and press or cook ingredients as necessary. Blot food or squeeze dry.
2. To salt-wilt: Toss finely sliced raw vegetables with salt. Rest 20 to 30 minutes. Squeeze or press to drain.
3. Mix together or prepare dressing.
4. Toss together ingredient/s and dressing *or* plate ingredient and top with sauce. Garnish.

JAPANESE VINEGAR DRESSINGS FOR SEAFOOD

Yields about 2-1/4 cups with cucumbers and seafood, 2 to 4 servings

Nihaizu (Two-Flavor Dressing)

Yields 1/2 cup

3 tablespoons rice vinegar
1 tablespoon soy sauce
1/3 cup *Dashi*

Sanbaizu (Three Flavor Dressing)

2 teaspoons sugar added to *Nihaizu*

Main Ingredients

6 ounces small Kirby *or* Persian cucumbers, 1 to 1-1/3 cup ends trimmed and thinly sliced
16 ounces cleaned octopus, squid, or whitefish, about 1-1/2 cups sliced into bite-sized pieces
    or 10 ounces cooked fresh crabmeat, 1-1/2 cups picked through for shells

1 Mix chosen **dressing** ingredients together.

2 Toss thinly sliced cucumbers with 1 tablespoon kosher salt; mix and rest 10 minutes. Lightly knead until wilted, 2 to 3 minutes. Rinse cucumbers and drain well. Blot dry, and toss into mixing bowl.

3 Steam octopus, squid, or whitefish until just done. Pick through cooked crabmeat for shells and discard. Toss *Nihaizu* or *Sanbaizu*, cucumbers, and octopus, squid, whitefish, or crab together. Taste and readjust flavors.

4 **To Serve:** Pile high onto serving plates or a platter.

SEASONAL ATTENTION

Japanese cooks consider the seasons when choosing what to eat. This attention, called *kisetsukan*, is deeply embedded in the Japanese psyche. Its origin goes to the roots of the indigenous nature-loving Shinto religion, and to Japan's agrarian past. Seasonal celebrations such as rice planting and harvest festivals continue to modern-day and underlie Japanese culture.

Celebration of food at its peak is called *shun*. Japanese people are sensitive to the moment when strawberries reach their sweetest or fish is most flavorful, and seek out the best they can afford. Tableware, art, clothing, and activities like cherry-blossom viewing are part of the Japanese celebration of the seasons.

JAPANESE SESAME AND SESAME-MISO DRESSED SALADS

Roasted Sesame and Sesame Miso Dressing may be used on steamed asparagus, carrots, daikon radish, cauliflower, or broccoli. Cut the vegetables into bite-sized pieces before steaming.

4 to 6 servings

Roasted Sesame Dressing (Goma Aé)

Vegetables for Salad

1 pound Japanese or Kirby cucumbers, thinly sliced
   or 1 pound Chinese cabbage, finely sliced
   or 1 pound baby spinach, steam-wilted
   or 1 pound mung bean sprouts, blanched 5 seconds
   or 1 pound snowpeas, halved on the bias
   or 1 pound green beans, sliced into 1-1/2 inch lengths
   or 1 pound trimmed asparagus, sliced into 1-1/2 inch lengths
   or 1 pound daikon radish, 3-1/2 cups peeled and sliced into 1/4-inch thick half moons
   or 1 pound new potatoes, cut into bite-sized pieces

1 Prepare **Roasted Sesame Dressing** or **Sesame-Miso Dressing** variation. Set aside.

2 *Prepare chosen* **vegetables for salad:** Salt and press cucumbers or Chinese cabbage to wilt (see *Signature Technique: Salt-Pressed Pickles (Shio-Zuké)*). Drain. Steam fresh spinach. Squeeze lightly to remove moisture to yield 1 cup. Blanch mung sprouts 30 to 45 seconds. Drain. Steam snowpeas until crisp-tender, about 2 minutes. Steam green beans or asparagus until tender, about 5 minutes. Steam daikon or potatoes until tender, 7 to 10 minutes.

3 **To Serve:** Toss each pound of vegetables with 4 to 6 tablespoons dressing, about half, to taste. Serve at room temperature or chilled.

RAPINI WITH SPICY MISO SAUCE (NANOHANA NO KARASHI MISO-AE)

This popular spring dish is served at elegant kaiseki restaurants where it is served in small portions in beautiful, seasonal tableware.

Yields about 3 cups, 4 to 6 servings

1-1/4 pound bunch rapini (broccoli rabe)
2 tablespoons mirin
1 tablespoon saké
About 2-1/2 ounces white (shiro) miso, 1/4 cup
1 teaspoon dry mustard or Japanese dry hot mustard (neri-karashi)

Optional Garnish: 1 to 2 teaspoons toasted sesame seeds

1 Fill a 4-quart saucepan with cold water and bring to a rolling boil over high heat. Season water with salt.

2 **Prepare rapini:** Trim off 1 to 2 inches from bottom of stalks. Cut remaining rapini into 1-inch lengths to yield 7 to 8 cups (12 ounces). Place rapini into boiling water, lower heat to medium, and boil until crisp-tender, about 3 minutes. Immediately drain through colander and rinse with cold water. Do not immerse in ice water. Drain rapini well by lightly pressing.

3 **Prepare dressing:** Pour mirin and saké into small saucepan and bring to a boil. Pour into medium mixing bowl and stir in miso and mustard powder. Toss dressing with well-drained rapini.

4 **To Serve:** Pile rapini into small bowls and optionally garnish with sesame seeds. Serve at room temperature with a Japanese meal.

WAKAME SALAD (KYURI TO WAKAMÉ NO SUNOMONO)

The sesame oil is not traditional, but with it the salad tastes similar to sushi bar seaweed salad.

Yields about 2 cups, 4 servings

1 ounce dried wakame, 1 heaping cup
5 tablespoons rice vinegar
2 tablespoons soy sauce
1 tablespoon sugar
Optional: 2 to 3 teaspoons Asian sesame oil
5 to 6 ounces English or Kirby cucumber
　　or 3 ounces daikon radish, peeled

Garnish: 1 tablespoon toasted white or brown sesame seeds

1 Place wakame into small bowl and cover with warm water. Let sit until seaweed is tender, but with a slight crunch, 20 minutes. Meanwhile, mix together rice vinegar, soy sauce, sugar, and optional sesame oil in a medium mixing bowl and set aside.

2 Peel cucumber lightly, leaving thin green stripes; slice in half lengthwise and remove seeds with a spoon. Finely slice cucumber into thin half rounds to yield 1 cup. If using daikon radish, peel, slice in half lengthwise, and finely slice into thin half rounds to yield 1 cup.

3 Drain wakame and gently squeeze out excess water. Toss seaweed with rice vinegar mixture. Toss cucumber or radish with wakame and dressing. Rest salad at room temperature or in refrigerator until chilled, 20 minutes.

4 **To Serve:** Pile salad into small serving bowls and sprinkle with sesame seeds.

PICKLE AND PRESERVE

Tsukemono: Japanese Pickles

Japanese cooks know that fermentation and pickling elicit deeper flavor from food. They employ salt, vinegar, miso, or rice bran flakes (*nuka*) to prepare *takuan* (nuka-pickled daikon radish), *gari* (vinegar-pickled ginger), and the gooey, blue-cheese-like *natto* (*Bacillus subtilis natto* inoculated cooked soybeans). Tokyo department stores offer a huge array of these tasty tidbits. Look for *nara-zuké* (eggplant and zucchini-like vegetables pickled in malt paste), *sakura-zuké* (daikon pickled with aka-jiso and sweet wine, which turn them pink), *shiba-zuké* (assorted vegetables), *hiroshimana-zuké* (greens in brine), and *béni shoga* (red pickled ginger).

FIGURE 2.35 Pickled vegetables in a Japanese market.
Source: Theodore Scott/Shutterstock.

Signature Technique: Salt-Pressed Pickles (Shio-Zuké)

Pressed "pickles" are essentially salted raw vegetables wilted with pressure and transformed to tender, crunchy, and sweet-salty. Japanese cooks use a special press that screws down and presses the ingredients, but a plate with a weight works. These pickles go well with plain Japanese rice and sweet-simmered dishes.

1 **Choose ingredients:** One to five ingredients make a tasty, colorful pressed pickle (or salad). Contrast flavors and colors. Cabbage, carrots, cucumbers, red radishes, apples, firm pears, and daikon radish may be used.

2 **Peel and cut:** Peel and finely slice, matchstick-cut, or dice produce. Place prepared produce in a Japanese pickle press (*shokutaku tsuké mono ki*) or into a bowl. For pickles consumed the same day, toss produce with 2 rounded teaspoons kosher salt per 16 ounces of produce (2 percent of produce weight). For longer maturing pickles (ready in 2 to 3 days) use kosher salt to 4 percent of weight of produce, about 4 rounded teaspoons kosher salt per 16 ounces produce.

3 **Arrange:** Lay produce into press or bowl.

4 **Press:** If using a press, tighten it down until it is snug against the vegetables then twist twice more. If not, place vegetables into a bowl and place a plate over them. Weight the plate with plastic bag wrapped cans or stones press the produce.

5 **Timing:** Harder vegetables will take longer than soft vegetables. Test the vegetables and drain off excess moisture as it collects. Pressing is finished when the produce tastes crunchy, but tender. Thinner or smaller vegetables will take less time to wilt.

6 **Rinse:** Rinse vegetables with cold water to get rid of salt. Drain well and squeeze out excess moisture with hands.

7 **Dress:** Pressed pickles may be simply dressed with soy sauce or made into salads and dressed with a vinegar, sugar, soy, and mirin dressing.

ALL-SEASON SALT PICKLES
(ICHINEN JU NO SHIO ZUKÉ)

Japanese cooks traditionally serve pickles alongside main dishes and rice. They would make an interesting filling for sushi-maki.

Yields about 2 cups

7 ounces trimmed daikon radish, peeled
8 ounces zucchini, ends trimmed
1 ounce trimmed carrot, peeled
2 rounded teaspoons kosher salt

For Serving

1 teaspoon soy sauce

1 Thinly slice the radish on a diagonal and slice into 1/8-inch thick matchsticks to yield about 1-1/2 cups. Repeat cutting method with zucchini to yield 2 cups, and carrot to yield 1/4 cup.

2 Place vegetables into a bowl and toss with salt and lightly squeeze. Transfer vegetables and liquid to a Japanese press or bowl. Screw press down tightly. If using bowl, place a clean plate to cover and weight with 2 pounds of weight (two 16-ounce cans) set into a clean baggie.

3 A brine will form after an hour. Allow the pickles to mature 4 to 6 hours at room temperature or in refrigerator overnight. Rinse pickles and squeeze dry; they are ready to eat. Refrigerate pickles up to 3 to 5 days.

4 **To Serve:** Toss with soy sauce to taste.

JAPANESE PICKLED GINGER
(AMAZU SHOGA OR GARI)

Overnight salting draws out moisture and is the secret to crisp pickles. Mild, nutty rice vinegar is essential; don't substitute. Avoid old, stringy, tough ginger. It won't work. Young ginger comes into the market in early spring and fall. Look for it in Southeast Asian markets. Its skin is transparent and its tips are pink.

Yields about 1 quart pickled ginger

18 to 20 ounces very young tender gingerroot
1-1/2 tablespoons kosher salt
10 fluid ounces rice vinegar
3 fluid ounces water
2-2/3 to 3 ounces sugar, 1/3 to 1/2 cup

1 Bring a small saucepan filled with water to a boil; set a strainer nearby. Peel ginger (the skin will scrape away easily with a spoon) and rinse. Pat dry. Slice ginger cross-grain into paper-thin disks with a very sharp Benriner or mandoline. Remove saucepan of boiling water from heat and place ginger into water. Pour immediately through a strainer and drain well. Toss ginger in a nonmetallic bowl with kosher salt, cover and refrigerate 8 hours, turning once.

2 **The next day:** Squeeze ginger gently, drain, and pack into clean 1-quart glass jar. Discard liquid.

3 Mix vinegar, water, and sugar in small saucepan. Bring to a boil and stir until dissolved. Pour over ginger and press it down so it is fully immersed. Young ginger will turn pink. Cool ginger and seal tightly.

4 Refrigerate ginger at least 1 week before using; it will taste best up to 6 months refrigerated.

Source: *At Home with Japanese Cooking* by Elizabeth Andoh.

Vary! Improvise!

☞ *Use this recipe to pickle wild leeks (ramps). About 2-1/2 pounds yield 1 pound trimmed ramps.*

☞ *What other vegetables could be pickled this way?*

KOREA: LIKE A SHIP IN A STORM

Korea's Secret Fifth Element: Kimchi

Kim Man-Jo and Lee Kyou-Tae, and Lee O-Young relate in The Kimchee Cookbook: Fiery Flavors and Cultural History of Korea's National Dish *that with the creation of kimchi, Koreans have added a fifth taste, "pungency," to the four important tastes of Western cuisine (sweet, sour, salty, and bitter). Pungent flavor activates saliva and awakens the appetite. "Controlled spoilage" breaks down amino acids to give kimchi and fermented foods like bean and chili pastes their unique, pungent, and umami-rich flavor.*

Korea, also known as *The Land of the Morning Calm*, holds a 5,000-year-old rich cultural heritage that is less known to the West than Japan's or China's. Korea is ethnically "one" except for a small number of Chinese. Despite its unforgiving landscape, harshly divided people, tumultuous politics, and the hardships of a Japanese occupation, famine, and the Korean War, Koreans have survived. The strength and resiliency of the people are reflected in their culture and cuisine: simple but strong, pungent flavored food, vibrant colored clothing, martial arts, lively folk and drum dances, and literature dealing with the pain and chaos of war.

The Korean peninsula, like China, is one of the world's oldest continuous civilizations. Its earliest inhabitants migrated from northwestern Asia. Early Koreans produced celadon pottery, the world's first metal-based movable type printing press, and carved Buddhist scriptures onto woodblocks They created the Korean Hangul alphabet, invented the first Asian sundial, and the world's first water-powered clock.

Around 108 BCE, the Chinese Han dynasty established a military presence in Korea. Between the first and seventh centuries, three Korean kingdoms competed for supremacy. The *Silla* kingdom eventually united the peninsula in AD 668, but by AD 935 was supplanted by the *Koryo* dynasty. From the fourteenth through the early twentieth centuries, Japan and China repeatedly invaded Korea. General Yi Seongye overthrew the Koryo king and set up the last feudal dynasty, the *Choson*. Korea, because of hostile Western policies toward China, rejected contact with Europeans through the eighteenth and nineteenth centuries. Competition for influence in Korea between China, Japan and Russia resulted in the Sino-Japanese War (1894 to 1895) and the Russo-Japanese War (1904 to 1905).

In 1910 victorious Japan annexed Korea and ruthlessly tried to obliterate Korean culture. After Japan's defeat in World War II, Korea was split up: Russia took over North Korea, and the United States occupied South Korea. Russia refused to allow United Nations elections, and North Korea subsequently invaded South Korea. The Korean War (1950 to 1953) ended without a peace treaty, and U.S. troops remained in South Korea. South Korea's agrarian economy suffered postwar because it was left without North Korea's industrial base, and North Korea suffered severe economic and food shortages without South Korean agriculture. Foreign aid has helped to develop industries in South Korea.

North Korean politics have made life there as unstable as living on a ship in a violent storm. For the most part it is closed to South Korea and the United States. The 4-kilometer-wide region that divides the country is known as the DMZ (demilitarized zone); it sees constant conflict.

From 1950 to 1960 South Korea suffered under repressive rule, which the people eventually overthrew. Military officials took over in 1961 and ruled into the *Sixth Republic*, which began in 1987 and continues. In 1992 the first nonmilitary president in three decades was elected. The country is now a democracy but still fraught with corruption. North Korea has not fared well. Beginning in 1995, because of greed, economic mismanagement, weather-related disasters, and imported grain shortages, North Korea endured serious famine for several years, resulting in the death of as many as 2 million people. Despite outside help, chronic food shortages and malnutrition continue because of the oppressive, tyrannical dictators, and now-deceased presidents Kim Il-sung and son Kim Jong-il. Kim Jong-un succeeded his grandfather and father as ruler in 2011.

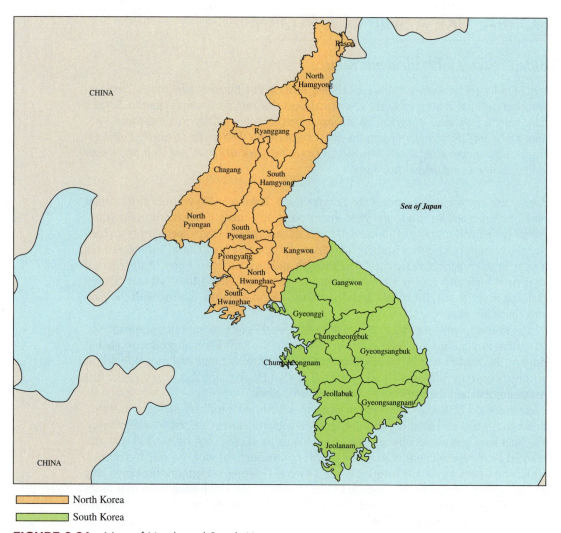

North Korea
South Korea

FIGURE 2.36 Map of North and South Korea.

KOREAN LANGUAGE, PHILOSOPHY, AND RELIGION

Korean is the official language of Korea. Its simplified phonetic alphabet system, commissioned by Sejong the Great in the fifteenth century, is called *Hangul*.

In the fourth century, Buddhism became Korea's official religion. From the fourteenth through the early twentieth centuries Confucianism replaced Buddhism and extreme conservation ruled. More than 40 percent of South Koreans have a religious affiliation, which is divided between Buddhism (34 percent), Christianity (30 percent), Confucianism, and shamanism. Most Koreans hold Buddhism and Confucianism as a set of values, rather than a religion. *Cheondogyo* (Heavenly Way), Muslim, and Bahai faiths have developed in recent years. Although religion is almost nonexistent in North Korea, Buddhism, Protestantism, and Catholicism have followers there.

GEOGRAPHY AND CLIMATE: SEA IN A HEAVY GALE

Korea is a strikingly beautiful country. Some describe its topography as "a sea in a heavy gale" because of the many mountains with uplands and deep valleys crisscrossing the country. Most of the Korean peninsula's population resides in fertile coastal plains or lowlands with a temperate four-season climate: warm, humid summers, short rainy season, and cold, dry winters. Spring and summer are normally longer in South Korea, and autumn and winter are longer in North Korea.

South Korea's eastern coast is smooth while the southern and western coasts are jagged. Its largest city is the capital, Seoul, located on relatively flat Han River in the center of the Korean Peninsula with more than 10 million inhabitants. North Korea is home to the Korean peninsula's highest mountains, with Paektu-san Mountain at 9,003 feet, and the 491-mile-long Amnok River. Its largest city is Pyongyang, the capital, with a population of over 3 million.

FARMING AND AGRICULTURE

The Korean peninsula extends south into warm seas, which create micro-environments where farmers grow rice, beans, and vegetables in the valleys. People forage in the mountains for mushrooms and wild plants such as bracken fern and bellflower. North Korea, with its colder weather and mountainous terrain, has less agriculture than South Korea. South Korea, the peninsula's major agricultural area, suffers serious droughts every few years.

KOREAN CUISINE: MASTERS OF THE ROBUST, PRACTICAL, AND PUNGENT

China strongly influenced early Korean cuisine: rice, fermented soy foods and pastes, and the use of chopsticks. Chinese influences show up in the emphasis on five flavors, five elements, and five colors in food preparation and presentation, and the habit of serving grain as the central part of a meal surrounded by side dishes. During repeated invasion and occupation, the Japanese introduced cooking techniques, foods, and dishes like *kimbap*, which are similar to sushi-maki. Koreans have transformed their Chinese heritage and Japanese influences into a very different, distinctive cuisine.

New York Times food writer Mark Bittman calls Korean food "Japanese food with guts . . . an endorsement of Korean cuisine's vigorous, muscular, completely unsubtle flavor profile and aggressive seasoning." Invigorating and idiosyncratic, Korean food is heartier and more robustly seasoned than Chinese or Japanese cuisine, with lots of garlic, chili, black pepper, green onions, sesame oil and seeds, soy sauce and fermented soy and chili pastes, seafood, and a fondness for beef, pork, and chicken. *Bulgogi*, thinly sliced marinated and grilled beef and *galbi*, marinated and grilled beef or pork short ribs, are national dishes. Though modern Koreans eat meat, for centuries ordinary folk depended on vegetables, grains, and legumes supplemented with seafood. Meat eating became widespread in South Korea with the arrival of American troops and economic growth.

Alive with beneficial bacteria, lacto-fermented vegetables like Chinese cabbage and daikon radish, known as *kimchi*, aid digestion. Served daily and with every meal, the highly popular red chili powder, green onion, ginger, and garlic-spiked kimchi enhances the flavor of rice and meat or vegetables. Modern Korean cooks also enjoy a wide choice of vegetables, and many forage wild ferns, bracken, mushrooms, nuts, herbs, and greens.

As in the rest of Asia, *bap* (rice) is an important staple along with barley, millet, wheat, sorghum, and buckwheat. Korean cooks use rice as a base for every meal, boil it into *juk* (rice gruel), grind it for rice cakes, and ferment it into rice wine. Two of Korea's most beloved dishes are *bibimbap* (hot rice garnished with meat and vegetables and seasoned with red chili paste), and *kimbap* (large sushi-type rolls filled with beef and spinach). Soybeans are used to make soymilk, tofu, and fermented seasoning pastes. Mung beans are sprouted and cooked for side dishes or ground and made into pancakes and noodles. Adzuki beans are cooked and ground into a thick gruel, tossed whole with rice, or ground and stuffed into rice cakes.

As in Japan, fish, seafood, and sea vegetables are widely available. Many types of fresh, dried, and salted seafood are consumed throughout Korea and people seek out the best from various regions. *Myulchi* or plain dried anchovies, which are made into side dishes and soup broth, are popular on every table. Mollusks like octopus, cuttlefish, and squid; shellfish like shrimp (dried and fresh); clams, oysters, and abalone; and fish like mackerel, eel-like hairtail, croaker, and Pacific herring make their way into raw dishes, broths, grilled dishes, or stews. Umami-rich sea vegetables like kelp serve to season sauces, soups, and stews.

Like their Chinese forebears, Korean cooks prepare foods with their medicinal and seasonal qualities in mind. Meals and food choices are governed by level of affluence and how a food maintains specific health concerns as well as the *five tastes* and *five colors*. Soup, rice, meat, or seafood and several side dishes or *banchan* (like *kimchi* or tofu) are served daily even in the poorest homes.

REGIONAL KOREAN PENINSULA: TWO COUNTRIES, ONE CUISINE

As in other parts of Asia, climate, geography, and available ingredients influence Korean dishes. Until the late nineteenth century, transportation was poor, and isolated provincial regions maintained characteristic tastes, ingredients, and cooking methods. Modern transportation and foreign foods have tended to blur regional lines. Though social and political change has marked Korean cuisine or *hansik*, many traditional dishes, handed down through generations, have survived, with variations, throughout the peninsula. *Bulgogi*, stuffed dumplings in soup, barbequed meat, red chili, and seafood stew, *bibimbap*, *kimchi*, and *kimbap* are a favored few. Rich or poor, everyone eats rice, noodles, tofu, vegetables, meat, and fish in some form.

South Korea, Seoul: Spicy and Abundant

Korea's south is warmer and the food is more varied, abundant, and spicy than the north. South Korea is known for seafood, pungent fermented anchovy and shrimp pastes that season this region's spicy kimchi. The northeastern city of Ch'unch'on is known for *dak galbi* (chicken barbecue). Cholla province in the southwest has the reputation of the best food in South Korea with a local kimchi with more seafood than usual, and a pungent stew called *kimchi jiigae*.

North Korea, Pyongyang: Cold and Scarce

Rice, meat, potatoes, barley, millet, sorghum, and beans are staples in northern dishes. Milder, saltier kimchi is favored. The northeastern city of Hamhung is known for *naengmyŏn* or cold noodles made with chilled broth, cucumbers, Korean pear, and boiled egg, or sliced, cold boiled beef.

DINE AT HOME IN KOREA

In a Korean home, guests remove shoes. The hosts will seat diners at a low table with cushions arranged on the floor. In traditional homes men and women dined separately, but that has changed. Wait until the eldest family member picks up chopsticks before beginning. Pace the meal to finish after the elder. Refrain from clashing crockery or talking about unappetizing topics like dirt, bodily functions, or disease.

Diners eat with a set of wooden, silver, or stainless steel chopsticks and a long-handled shallow spoon. The place setting, from the left, is rice bowl, spoon, and chopsticks, soup,

FIGURE 2.37 Seoul, South Korea.
Source: Krzysztof Czuba/Fotolia.

and stew on the right. Hot foods sit on the right side of the table, and cold foods, rice, and vegetable on the left, kimchi at the back, and sauces in the front.

Korean hosts present each diner with a bowl of plain or seasoned short-grain rice. They don't pick up the bowl, instead eating the rice, soup, and stew with a spoon. Using both chopsticks and spoon together is frowned upon. Diners are surrounded by platters and bowls of hearty seafood, meat, or poultry, a rich soup (*guk*), and stunning choices of five or more *banchan*: smaller vegetable (*namul*), tofu or pickled dishes like *kimchi*, and a small bowl of dried and salted fish or anchovies. Tea, beer, or wine will be served. Koreans pour others' drinks for them. When the host offers alcohol, refuse it twice and on the third, receive the drink. Diners should face away from the eldest male and cover the mouth when drinking alcohol.

TASTES OF KOREA

Fat: Sesame oil, dark roasted Korean sesame seasoning oil, vegetable oil, lard

Sweet: Sugar, barley malt powder and syrup, sorghum syrup, honey

Sour/Alcohol: Lemon, *yuzu* citrus, rice vinegar, brown rice vinegar, white vinegar, Korean rice wine

Salty: Sea salt, MSG, soy sauce, fish sauce, *toenjang* (fermented soybean paste), *doenjang* (fermented anchovy and soybean paste)

Spicy-Hot: *Kochukaru* (Korean dried red chili powder), spicy red chili paste, chilies, black pepper, ginger, wasabi

Aromatic Seasoning Vegetables: Onion, green onion, garlic, ginger, garlic chives, carrots, *susam* (fresh ginseng)

Spice: Szechwan peppercorns, shichimi-togarashi, cinnamon

Herbs, Seasonings, and Condiments: Mint, watercress, shiso/perilla leaf, dried anchovies, sea vegetables, salted and dried shrimp, anchovy and katsuobushi broth, dried mushrooms, kim chi, sesame paste, white and black sesame seeds, dried squid, dried pollock

Other Important Foods: *Dubu* (tofu), beans (mung, adzuki, kidney), grains (short grain and glutinous rices, wheat, buckwheat, millet, barley), nuts (pine nuts, chestnuts, walnuts), sesame seeds, mushrooms, wild greens, roots and shoots, lotus root, *boo* and *mu* (white radishes), cucumber, potato, Chinese and Napa cabbage, bok choy, persimmons, *naju bae* (Asian pear), sea vegetables, mung beans and sprouts, mung starch, sweet potato starch, wheat and buckwheat noodles, zucchini, meat (beef, pork and chicken), seafood

Popular Dishes: *Kimchi* (fermented cabbage), *bulgogi* (marinated beef barbecue), *bibimbap* (rice and vegetables), *chapchae* (stir-fried noodles), *chijimi* (spring onion pancakes),

COMMON KOREAN COOKING TOOLS

Wok, cutting board, rice cooker, and cleaver

KOREAN FLAVOR FOUNDATIONS

Korean Signature Aromatic Vegetable Combo

Garlic, green onions, red chilies, onions, and gingerroot

Signature Seasonings

Koreans and Japanese use many of the same seasonings.

Liquid/Paste

Chamgirum (Dark Korean Sesame Oil)

Korean sesame oil tends to be nuttier and more aromatic than roasted Asian sesame oils. It is used as a flavoring, not for cooking.

Doenjang (Fermented Soybean Paste)

Cooked ground soybean paste formed into blocks, sun-dried, and fermented then brined. The liquid rendered is Korean soy sauce (kanjang) and the strong solids become doenjang, a salty seasoning used in jjigae stew or mixed with garlic, sesame oil, and chili paste to produce ssamjang dip or sauce.

Hyeonmi Sikcho (Brown Rice Vinegar)

Brown rice vinegar is fermented from whole-grain brown rice instead of white rice. It has a richer, mellow flavor. Use in both Japanese and Korean cuisines for salads and vegetable dishes.

Kanjang (Korean Soy Sauce)

A deep flavored, earthy soy sauce made from soybeans.

Kochujang (Fermented Chili Paste)

This is an important seasoning paste is made of kochugaru (red chili powder), glutinous rice powder mixed with powdered doenjang and salt, and fermented.

Animal

FIGURE 2.38 Dried anchovy.
Source: bonchan/Shutterstock.

Myulchi (Dried Anchovy)

Koreans use different kinds of dried anchovies for cooking: large anchovies (2 inches long) for broth, medium-sized (about 1 inch), and smaller for side dishes. Anchovy sauce is also used for an important ingredient for kimchi. Dried anchovies are used to flavor broth and sauces; look for the fast-dried curled ones. Scrape out dried guts before using.

Vegetable/Fruit

FIGURE 2.39 Kochu (red chili).
Source: olemla/Fotolia.

Kochu (Korean Red Chili)

The Japanese introduced this long red capsicum to Korea in the seventeenth century. Korea's unique geography, sea air, mountainous regions, soil, and water contributed to the distinctive kochu chili. It has become an essential flavor in the Korean pantry. When dried and ground, kochu is called kochugaru or gochukaru.
See Japanese Mushrooms and Japanese Signature Seasonings.

Cheonggochu or Pootgochu (Green Chilies)

Koreans also use small and large green chilies that can be mildly hot like a jalapeño or sweet.

Jangsung (Garlic Stems or Scapes)

These are long, curly sprouts/stems with flower heads that arise in the spring from fall-planted hard-stem garlic. The stems should be firm, delicate smelling, and pale green. Koreans slice them into 2-inch lengths and stir-fry or pickle garlic stems.

Manul (Garlic)

Korea consumes more garlic per capita than any other country. Koreans grow two types: hard stem with 4 to 6 large cloves and soft stem with many small cloves.

Herbal/Spice

Gochugaro (Red Chili Powder)

This is the essential dried Korean red chili powder, which comes coarse, medium, and finely ground.

FIGURE 2.40 Kkae-ip (perilla or wild sesame leaf).
Source: Dave King/DK Images.

Kkae-ip (Perilla or Wild Sesame Leaf)

This refreshing fragrant green (or purple) leafy herb, unrelated to sesame, tastes of mint, cinnamon, and basil. Both Japanese and Korean cuisines use perilla for its refreshing, lively taste. Korean perilla's flavor and leaf is distinct from Japanese: Korean perilla is larger, rounder, and flatter, with a less serrated edge and a violet coloring on the underside. Koreans often pair it with pork belly and slice into salads. A common practice is to use the whole leaf as a wrap for grilled meat or sliced in strips and mixed into bibimbap. Japanese cooks serve a different variety of green perilla called shiso with sashimi and use a purple variety for pickling.

FIGURE 2.41 Chinese chives.
Source: JIANG HONGYAN/Shutterstock.

Buchu (Korean or Chinese Garlic Chive)

This pungent-flavored, wide, flat and long-leafed chive is used to make kimchi, chive pancakes, and with cucumber pickles. It can be found in Chinese markets called gow choy.

jigae (stew), *pat juk* (sweet azuki bean porridge), *jjigae chongol* (hot pot), *seolleongtang* (oxtail soup), *ddukbokkie* (soft rice cakes in spicy sauce), *dakjuk* (chicken and rice porridge), *danpatjuk* (sweet red bean soup), *hoeddeok* (sweet walnut stuffed pancakes), *yangnyeom tongdak* (sweet fried chicken), *kang jung* (sesame candy), green tea ice cream, *bungeoppang* (fish pastry stuffed with sweet adzuki bean paste), *gotgamssam* (walnuts wrapped in persimmons), *patbingsu* (shaved ice with sweet red beans and fruit)

Drinks: Beer, wine, *makgeolli* (rice wine), *soju* (liquor), *yakju* (fermented rice liquor), roasted corn tea, ginger tea, barley tea, five-grain tea, wild sesame seed tea, candied *yuja* (yuzu) citrus tea, persimmon leaf tea, Korean ginseng tea, milk, soymilk

SEASONING AND PASTE MIXTURES

KOREAN RED CHILI PASTE

Use this to make vegetable kimchi, marinate tofu or meat, or to flavor soup, hot pot, or vegetables.

Yields 3 cups, enough for 5 to 10 pounds diced vegetables

About 1 ounce Korean ground red chili pepper, 1/4 cup packed
1/2 ounce garlic, 2 large cloves, 1 tablespoon peeled and minced
1/8 to 1/4 ounce ginger, 1 teaspoon peeled and minced
1 tablespoon sugar
2 tablespoons fish sauce

1 Mix ingredients together with 2 tablespoons cold water and 1 teaspoon sea or kosher salt.

2 Seal in glass jar up to 2 months.

TOASTED SESAME SEED OR SESAME SALT (KOREAN KKAESOGEUM OR JAPANESE GOMA-SHIO)

Dry-toasted or parched sesame seeds are a major staple in Korean and Japanese kitchens, used in everything from salad dressings seafood. Crushed with salt, toasted sesame becomes a simple, satisfying condiment on vegetables, rice, salt-wilted radishes, daikon, or cucumbers. Use the black or brown, unhulled seeds for hearty flavor and the hulled white seeds for delicate flavor.

Yields 1/2 cup

2-1/2 ounces unhulled brown or black sesame seeds, about 1/2 cup

1 Heat a small sauté pan over medium-low heat. Add sesame seeds. Flip or stir until they begin to smell fragrant and jump. Beware of burning them: white seeds toast quickly and brown or black seeds won't show a color change. Taste one. Toasted properly, brown and black seeds will crush easily with a fingernail.

2 Remove pan from heat and immediately pour seeds onto a plate. Japanese roast sesame seeds moderately. Koreans like sesame seeds deeply roasted.

3 Cool seeds before grinding or chopping. Lightly grind together 3 to 4 teaspoons kosher or sea salt and brown sesame seeds in a *suribachi* or clean coffee grinder until seeds are broken and fragrant but not pasty. Chop cooled black sesame seeds with 2 teaspoons kosher or sea salt.

Source: The Korean Table by Taekyung Chung and Debra Samuels.

Sesame Seed: Goma

Japanese and Korean cooks use black, brown-unhulled, and white-hulled sesame seeds, whole and ground. Refrigerate or freeze seeds; they go rancid quickly. Black and brown unhulled seeds are stronger flavored than the delicate white sesame. Sesame seeds are high in calcium, not to mention good flavor.

SAUCE

THREE FROM ONE KOREAN DIPPING SAUCES

Beware, as the chili powder blooms in the sauce its flavor will become stronger.

Sauce Base

Yields about 1/3 cup

1/4 cup soy sauce
1 tablespoon Asian sesame oil
About 1/3 ounce toasted crushed sesame seed, 1 tablespoon

Korean Seasoned Soy Sauce (Yangnyum Ganjang)

Yields about scant 1/2 cup

Add to *Sauce Base*:

> 1/2 ounce trimmed green onions, 1 large, 2 tablespoons minced
> 1/2 teaspoon Korean red chili powder

Korean Vinegar-Soy Sauce (Cho Ganjang)

Total yield about 5 fluid ounces

Add to *Sauce Base*:

> 1/4 cup rice vinegar

Korean All-Spice Sauce

Total yield about 3/4 cup

Add to *Sauce Base*:

> 4 teaspoons rice vinegar
> 4 teaspoons honey
> 1/2 ounce green onions, 1 large, 1-1/2 to 2 tablespoons minced
> 1/4 ounce garlic, 1 large clove, 1-1/2 teaspoons peeled and finely minced
> Scant 1/4 ounce walnuts, about 2 halves, 2 to 3 teaspoons finely crushed
> 1 teaspoon Korean hot red chili powder

1 In small mixing bowl, mix together **sauce base**.

2 Combine sauce base with one choice of: *Seasoned Soy Sauce, Vinegar-Soy Sauce,* or *All-Spice Sauce.* Season with salt and pepper to taste.

3 Rest sauce 20 minutes for best flavor. Refrigerate unused sauce up to 1 week.

KOREAN CHILI SAUCE (YANGNYEOM GOCHUJANG)

Serve this tasty sauce with bibimbap, *cooked rice, or steamed or raw sliced vegetables.*

Yields 4 to 5 fluid ounces

2-3/4 ounces Korean chili paste (*gochujang*), 4 tablespoons
2 tablespoons Asian sesame oil
1 tablespoon soy sauce
1/4 ounce garlic, 1 large clove, 1-1/2 teaspoons peeled and minced
About 1/3 ounce toasted crushed sesame seeds, 1 tablespoon
1 tablespoon sugar *or* Korean malt syrup (*mool yut*)
1 ounce trimmed green onions, 2 large, 4 tablespoons finely minced

1 Combine ingredients in a bowl. Keep refrigerated in a tightly sealed container up to 1 week.

SPECIAL METHODS

KOREAN RICE ROLLS (KIMBAP)

Japanese maki (rolls) and Korean kimbap share the same technique, rice-covered seaweed (nori or kim) rolled with a filling inside. The flavors differ: Japanese prefer varied combos of seafood, vegetables, and egg while the traditional Korean filling is seasoned spinach, egg, and beef.

8 large rolls

17-1/2 ounces short-grain sushi rice, 2-1/2 cups

Kimbap Rice Seasonings

4 tablespoons rice vinegar
2 teaspoons sugar
1 tablespoon Asian sesame oil
16 to 18 ounces beef tenderloin

Beef Seasonings

1 tablespoon soy sauce
2 tablespoons rice wine *or* sherry
1 tablespoon sugar
3/4 ounces garlic, 3 large cloves, 4-1/2 teaspoons peeled and minced

1-1/2 ounces trimmed green onions, 3 large, 6 tablespoons finely minced, *divided*
3 tablespoons Asian sesame oil, *divided*
20 ounces fresh baby spinach, about 20 cups
   or 1-1/4 cups cooked, drained spinach
1/3 to 1/2 ounce toasted sesame seeds, 4 teaspoons
3 large eggs, 3/4 cup
1 tablespoon vegetable oil, more as needed
8 whole sheets nori

For Serving

Pickled Ginger
Soy sauce *or Korean Vinegar-Soy Sauce*
Hot yellow mustard

1 **Prepare rice:** Soak and cook rice according to *Signature Recipe: Japanese and Korean Short-Grain (Sushi) Rice.* Toss **kimbap rice seasonings** together. Toss with hot rice; season with salt. Set rice aside covered with damp towel. There should be about 7 cups cooked rice.

2 **Prepare beef:** Slice beef into long 1/4-inch thick strips about 1 inch wide. Stir together soy sauce, rice wine, sugar, garlic, 3 tablespoons minced green onion, and 2 tablespoons Asian sesame oil. Pour over beef and marinate 10 to 15 minutes.

3 Heat grill or grill pan over medium heat. Season beef with salt and pepper and place on grill. Grill beef long enough for grill marks on both sides, but leave its center rare. Set beef aside.

4 **Prepare spinach:** Pile washed (but not drained) spinach into pot set over high heat. Cover and cook spinach, tossing and turning with tongs, until wilted, 1 to 2 minutes. Pour into strainer and press out as much liquid as possible to yield about 1-1/4 cups. Toss drained spinach with sesame seeds and remaining 3 tablespoons minced green onion and 1 tablespoon sesame oil. Season spinach with salt and pepper and set aside.

5 **Prepare eggs:** Whisk eggs and season with salt and pepper. Heat 8-inch nonstick skillet over medium-heat vegetable oil. When hot, pour in half the egg and cook until set. Flip and briefly cook opposite side; don't overcook egg. Repeat with remaining oil and egg. Slice egg into 1/2-inch wide strips.

6 **Assemble kimbap:** Set out a small bowl of warm water and one sheet of nori/kim on bamboo rolling mat on counter with the longest side of the nori parallel to the counter edge. Dampen your hands. Spread about 3/4 cup rice on the bottom of the nori all the way to the edges and 3/4 of the way up. Leave about a 1-1/2-inch gap at the top. Dot a few grains of rice at the top edge of nori for sealing. Do not use water to seal.

7 Place 1/8 of the beef, spinach, and egg horizontally across the middle of the rice and press lightly into rice. Roll as directed for Japanese nori-maki. Finish making remaining rolls.

8 **To Serve:** Slice kimbap logs into 8 rounds. Arrange slices on plate with pickled ginger, soy sauce, or *Korean Vinegar-Soy Sauce* and hot yellow mustard on the side.

Source: *Growing Up in a Korean Kitchen* by Hi Soo Shin Hepinstall.

Vary! Improvise!

☞ *Crave Crunchy: Peel, seed, and sliver cucumber, and roll inside kimbap with other fillings.*
☞ *Hot Mustard: Mix water with yellow mustard powder until spreadable. Rest 10 minutes before using as a condiment.*

Korean Ssäm: A Leaf in Hand

Ssäm is one of those dishes that doesn't require a recipe. It's great for a quick, fresh meal and will help you creatively use leftovers. Ssäm consists of leaf vegetables such as red leaf lettuce, sesame leaves, or par-boiled Napa cabbage leaves that Koreans use to wrap thin slices of roasted meat, cooked rice, and condiments like koch'ujang, doenjang, or ssam-jang paste into a packet—which they devour in one or two bites.

Koreans might include kimchi, mint leaves, sliced fresh chilies, bell pepper or onion, Chinese chives, or minced garlic for more flavor. There are many variations of ssäm: with seaweed, crepe, pumpkin leaf, shiso leaf, marinated raw beef, and seafood. Korean-born New York chef and restaurateur David Chang made ssäm famous by putting it on his menu at Momofuku Ssäm Bar. His bo ssäm consists of a brined and slow-roasted pork butt or shoulder thinly sliced and served with kimchi on lettuce leaves.

SIMMER, STEW, POACH, BOIL, AND STEAM

Korean Soup

Korean cooks make dried sardine broth with or without kelp, and beef stock or chicken stock flavored with garlic, scallions, and rice wine. There are four types of Korean soups: *malgeunguk* (clear soup with cooked meat, seafood, or vegetables and soy sauce), *tojang-guk* (with seafood like clams, dried anchovies, and shrimp with doenjang and sometimes kochujang), *gomguk* (rich beef bone and cartilage soup seasoned with salt) and *naengguk* (cold summer soup seasoned lightly with soy sauce and sesame oil). Koreans serve soup as part of the main meal or, like the Japanese, accompanying rice at the end of a meal. Banquet, formal, or occasion soups are made from expensive seasonal ingredients like ginseng.

KOREAN TEMPLE CUISINE

Many Korean families visit Buddhist temples on special holy days (this is also done in China and Japan). The temples, often stunningly beautiful, serve elaborate and beautifully presented vegetarian meals to the public. Korean temple cuisine is traditionally without the "five stimulants," which variously include onions, green onions, garlic, green peppers and *honggo* or dropwort, leeks, chives, and garlic scapes. These are some of the dishes the monks might serve:

Vegetarian juk (seasoned rice porridge)

Watery plain kimchi and regular kimchi

Mixture of rice and vegetables wrapped in spinach-like leaves or in a vermicelli pancake

Wild vegetables, each with its own seasonings like cooked roots of balloon flowers and fern bracken

Fried kelp

Steamed bean curd with burdock, mushrooms, and carrots

Acorn jelly

Small potatoes glazed with soy sauce and millet syrup

Vegetarian chapchae

Seasonal vegetable fritters

Vegetarian jeon

Short grain brown or white rice or glutinous rice with beans, millet, and vegetables

Vegetarian doenjang jjigae

Tea with dessert like fried puffed rice snack called *yugwa*

FIGURE 2.42   Buddhist temple in South Korea.
Source: Maxim Tupikov/Shutterstock.

SIGNATURE RECIPE

KOREAN ANCHOVY BROTH

Use this strong flavored anchovy dashi for noodles, soup, and stew, and with dark miso or toenjang-seasoned soups. Look for the curly anchovies; they dried faster and are fresher tasting. Soak kombu (and shiitake) overnight in cold water for a richer flavored dashi.

Yields 3 cups

About 3/4 ounces kelp (*kombu*), three to four 2-inch by 5-inch pieces
1-1/2 to 2 ounces dried small anchovy sardines, 1 cup packed, heads and black entrails removed

1 Fill stockpot with 1 quart cold water and kombu (and shiitake if using). Heat pot uncovered on medium heat. Bring water to near boiling, about 10 minutes.

2 Remove kombu when small bubbles start to surface; stock may turn bitter if kombu boils. Kelp should be soft enough for a thumbnail to pierce. If not, lower heat and add 1/4-cup cold water and bring to just near boiling once again. Remove kombu just prior to water boiling.

3 **To finish:** Cool kombu stock to warm. Place anchovies into it and bring to boil over high heat. Lower heat and simmer 5 to 7 minutes. Strain through cheesecloth-lined strainer; discard anchovies. Broth will have its best flavor with immediate use, but will keep 3 days refrigerated.

COOK'S VOICE: HANNAH LILY WON

Korean-Born Music Teacher
Los Angeles, California

"When I go home to visit my mother she always makes me stuffed chicken soup. It's my ultimate comfort food. The small whole chicken goes in a bowl, we ladle in the broth, and we add salt, freshly ground black pepper and finely chopped green onion to the broth. We also have a small bowl of equal parts salt and ground pepper on the side, along with another small bowl for all the little bones. Chopsticks to pull pieces of the chicken apart, although theoretically it should fall right off the bone, and we dip one mouthful of chicken into the salt and pepper and then follow up with a sip of the broth with spoon. Mmm . . ."

Source: Courtesy of Hannah Lily Won.

FIGURE 2.43 Dried jujube (Chinese date).
Source: WONG SZE FEI/Fotolia.

FIGURE 2.44 Korean tonic stuffed chicken soup top left: Korean watercress salad.

Vary! Improvise!

☛ *Devise an alternative filling combo instead of chestnuts and dates.*

KOREAN TONIC STUFFED CHICKEN SOUP (SAM GAE TANG)

Stuffed with medicinal foods like jujube dates and ginseng, Koreans consider this soup healing. A whole chicken in the bowl might be disconcerting, but simmered until meltingly tender makes it easy to eat. The stuffing tastes best mixed and eaten with some broth.

2 to 4 servings

Two 1-1/4 to 1-1/2 pound Cornish game hens

Tonic Stuffing

Yields *1-1/2 cups*

7 ounces short-grain rice, 1 cup
    or 1-1/4 to 1-1/2 cups cooked short-grain rice
3/4 ounce peeled, cooked chestnuts, about 2, 2 to 3 tablespoons diced
1 to 1-1/2 ounce dates, 2 large, about 2 tablespoons pitted and diced
    or 1 ounce dried jujubes (Chinese date)
1/4 ounce garlic, 1 large clove, 1-1/2 teaspoons peeled and finely slivered *or* minced
1/3-ounce gingerroot, 2 teaspoons peeled and finely slivered *or* minced
    or 1/3 ounce fresh ginseng root, peeled and finely slivered

1-1/2 to 2 quarts chicken stock
2 ounces trimmed green onions, 4 large, 1/2 cup sliced into 1-inch slivers or finely minced
Korean red chili powder

1   Wash and drain rice. Place in 2-quart saucepan with 1-1/2 cups cold water and 1/2 teaspoon kosher salt. Bring to a boil, lower heat, cover pan, and simmer rice 10 minutes. Remove pan from heat and rest rice (do not disturb) 10 minutes.

2   Meanwhile, wash poultry and pat dry.

3   Mix together 1-1/4 cups cooked rice, chestnuts, dates, garlic, ginger or ginseng, and season with salt and pepper. Stuff cavity of each bird with half the stuffing. Sew chicken cavity closed with needle and thread. Place chicken in 4-quart pot and cover with chicken stock. Bring to a boil, lower heat, and simmer until chicken is tender and internal temperature is at least 170 degrees F, about 1 to 1-1/2 hours.

4   Lift poultry from broth and drain. Place in mixing bowl. Remove skin and thread and discard. Transfer whole chickens to two deep serving bowls, *or* place chickens on cutting board and cut in half through breast bone and place each half with its stuffing in one of four bowls.

5   **To Serve:** Heat broth to boiling, remove from heat and stir in green onions. Ladle broth and onions over chicken. Serve soup with Korean red chili powder, salt and freshly ground black pepper on the side. (Serve extra broth and leftover rice on side or save for another meal.) Dip meat in salt, chili powder, or black pepper. Sip the broth and eat rice stuffing with it.

WHITE RADISH SOUP (MOO GOOK)

The hallmark of moo gook is very tender radish. For a spicier version, stir in 1/8 to 1/4 teaspoon Korean red pepper powder while stir-frying the radish.

Yields 4 to 5 cups, 4 servings

7 ounces daikon radish (about 2 inches by 4 inches), 1 cup diced into 1-inch cubes
2 teaspoons plain sesame oil or vegetable oil

3 cups *Anchovy Broth*
  or 3 cups chicken stock
1 ounce trimmed green onions, 2 large, 1/4 cup finely sliced
1/4 ounce garlic, 1 large clove, 1-1/2 teaspoons peeled and minced
2-1/2 to 3 ounces fresh mung bean sprouts, 1 cup packed, washed, and drained
1 tablespoon soy sauce

Garnish: 1 to 2 teaspoons Asian sesame oil

1 In a 3- to 4-quart saucepan, heat oil over medium heat. Stirring frequently, sauté radish pieces for one minute. Add minced garlic and cook 30 seconds.

2 Add anchovy broth to the radish, bring to a boil. Reduce heat, cover partially with a lid, and simmer soup until radish is tender, 7 to 10 minutes. Stir in green onions and sprouts and remove saucepan from heat.

3 **To Serve:** Season soup with soy sauce to taste. Ladle soup into 4 bowls and drizzle 1/2 teaspoon sesame oil over each. Serve moo gook with cooked rice and several *namul* or side vegetable dishes. Some Koreans add freshly cooked rice to moo gook to form a stew.

PINE NUT PORRIDGE (JAT JUK)

Jat juk is a homey but elegant, sweet and soupy white porridge that Koreans love for breakfast, as a treat or as a restorative. Jat juk would be excellent before or after a spicy-hot meal. For more nutrients short-grain brown rice may be substituted, but the porridge will lose its pristine whiteness. Koreans prepare many types of juk—with pumpkin, chestnuts, or jujubes or from other grains or azuki beans. Juk may be served with flavorful accompaniments like kimchi, sesame, walnuts, pickled cuttlefish, vegetables, or spicy octopus.

Yields 6-1/2 to 7 cups, 4 to 6 servings

7 ounces short-grain white sushi-type rice, 1 cup
3-1/2 to 4-1/2 ounces pine nuts, 3/4 cup, *divided*
Optional: 1 tablespoon sugar

1 Wash rice and soak in 1-1/2 cups water 30 minutes to 2 hours. Drain rice, reserve water, and place rice in blender with 1/2 cup soaking water. Grind rice until smooth, about 2 minutes. Pour rice into 4-quart saucepan. Rinse out blender with remaining soaking water and pour into saucepan. Stir 3 cups cold water into saucepan.

2 If pine nuts have black nibs, remove them. Rinse and drain nuts. Set aside 4 teaspoons nuts for garnish. Place remaining nuts in blender with 1/2 cup water and grind until smooth. Scrape out nut purée into small bowl and set aside. Rinse blender with 1/2 cup cold water and set water aside separately from purée.

3 Bring rice mixture to a boil on medium heat. Stir or whisk rice gruel constantly until thickened and creamy, 5 minutes. Rice will settle to the bottom and clump if not stirred constantly. Reduce the heat to low, cover pan, and simmer rice gruel 15 minutes, stirring occasionally.

4 Stir in ground pine nuts and simmer gruel 1 minute. Thin with reserved blender rinsing water, if desired. Taste gruel, and season with sugar and kosher salt, about 1 teaspoon.

5 **To Serve:** Ladle hot gruel into four bowls and top each with 1/2 to 1 teaspoon reserved pine nuts. Serve.

ONE POT SIMMERING AT THE TABLE

China, Japan, and Korea have developed popular, communal one-pot meals cooked at the home or restaurant table. Chinese from the northern steppes likely first developed *Mongolian hot pot*. The hot pot operates like a samovar; it has a doughnut-shaped trough filled with broth. Live coals fill its chimney-like center to keep broth hot. All one-pot meals around Asia use thinly sliced meat and vegetables and swish in hot broth to cook.

Japanese one-pot meals, called *nabemono*, are usually made in an earthenware *donabe*, cast-iron pot, or skillet. Nabemono are nutritious, often inexpensive, use seasonal fare, easy to prepare, and reinforce the communal table. Sumo wrestlers eat a nabemono called chanko-nabe daily to build up weight. Ishikari-nabe, a regional classic from Hokkaido, consists of salmon and vegetables in a miso-kelp broth. Shabu-shabu and sukiyaki are party food: thinly sliced ingredients can be prepped ahead of time. Each person cooks the food to their liking, dipping it into their choice of small sauces and seasonings.

Chongol is Korea's version of Japanese sukiyaki. A wide, deep pan of simmering broth on top of a gas burner presides at the center of the table. Six to eight diners pick from a large, festive array of ingredients thinly sliced meat and vegetables fanned out on platters. Swished first in a simmering broth, the meat, bean curd, or vegetables might be dipped into a sauce before eating.

KOREAN MISO STEW (DOENJANG JJIGAE [JIG-GAY])

Jjigae, the Korean satisfying stew and national comfort food, is simmered only long enough to cook the ingredients; they are salty from doenjang and spicy with chili powder. Some ingredients are precooked or marinated to shorten cooking time or develop flavor. Cooks typically make jjigae at the table in an electric skillet or in a glazed earthenware pot on a portable butane burner. The secret to a great doenjang-jjigae is the quality of the doenjang (bean paste).

Yields 6-1/2 to 7 cups, 3 to 4 servings

Meat

6 ounces lean pork or beef, thinly sliced
    and/or 4 ounces skinless pork belly, diced into 1/-2 inch cubes

Meat Seasonings

1 tablespoon rice wine or dry sherry
1 tablespoon Asian sesame oil
1 tablespoon soy sauce
1 to 2 teaspoons sugar

Soup Base

1/2 teaspoon *gochujang* paste, more to taste
3 to 4 tablespoons doenjang (or Japanese miso), to taste
4 cups *Korean Anchovy Broth*
    or 4 cups beef or chicken stock

Essential Ingredients

1 ounce garlic, 4 large cloves, 2 tablespoons peeled and minced
4 to 5 ounces onion, 1 cup peeled and sliced

1 ounce trimmed green onions, 2 large, 1/4 cup finely sliced
About 8 ounces firm tofu, 1-1/2 cups cubed 3/4-inch

Vegetables

4 ounces potato, about 3/4 cup peeled and diced into 1/2-inch cubes
About 4 ounces fresh shiitake mushrooms, 4 to 5 large, 1 cup caps sliced, stems minced
4 ounces zucchini, about 1 cup quartered lengthwise and sliced 1/2-inch thick

Vegetable oil, as needed
Optional: 1 red bird's eye chili, stemmed, seeded, and sliced

Garnish: Finely sliced green onions

For Serving

Cooked short-grain rice

1 Mix **meat** and meat seasonings together in small bowl; marinate 1 hour. Drain, and discard seasonings.

2 *Prepare* **soup base:** Stir gochujang and doenjang into anchovy broth or stock, to taste.

3 Prep **essential ingredients** and **vegetables**.

4 Heat 4-quart casserole over high heat, add 1 tablespoon vegetable oil. Sauté meat until browned, 4 minutes. Pour **soup base** into casserole and bring to a boil. Add garlic and potato. (Usually longest cooking ingredients go first and quick-cooking ingredients last.) Cook 5 minutes.

5 Add onion, green onions, tofu, shiitake, and zucchini. Simmer over low heat, partially covered, until vegetables are tender, 7 to 10 minutes. Add optional chili, and cook 1 minute. Total cooking time should be no more than 15 minutes. Taste and season with more doenjang and salt or pepper.

6 **To Serve:** Garnish jjigae with green onions. Set casserole in the middle of the table and serve jjigae with small serving bowls of rice.

Vary! Improvise!

☞ *Refine jjigae into a restaurant style dish.*
☞ *Serve jiigae with Korean Chili Sauce.*

KOREAN FERMENTED SOYBEAN PASTE: DOENJANG/TOENJANG

To make doenjang (or toenjang), soybeans are cooked and ground. The paste, formed into blocks, is known as "meju" or dry soybean paste. When exposed to sunlight and warmth, the blocks ferment and bacteria break down protein in the soybeans.

After several months, meju blocks are brined in large pottery jars and fermented; during this time beneficial bacteria form. The liquid that is produced becomes Korean soy sauce (*kanjang*) and the solid is doenjang. Doenjang, unlike Japanese miso, is very strong-flavored, salty, thick, and chunky. Some commercial doenjang and soy sauce makers add wheat flour and dried ground anchovies. Unlike miso, doenjang retains beneficial qualities after cooking. It is high in lysine, which rice lacks, and linoleic acid.

Koreans mix doenjang with garlic, sesame oil, and chili paste to produce *ssamjang*, which they eat with ssambap: rice wrapped in Chinese cabbage. Doenjang is also popular in meat dishes like *samgyeopsal* and stews like *doenjang jjigae*.

It's Ramen by Any Name

Chinese call them ramen, Koreans call them *ramyun*, and Japanese call them *chukamen* (Chinese noodles), but they are the same wavy, dried noodles compressed into square cakes made popular in college dorms. The instant variety arrives in cellophane with a seasoning packet. Good news: plain ramen are available so it's possible to create fresh-tasting ramen dishes with homemade broth and a choice of seasonings.

FIGURE 2.45 Ramen.
Source: sassyphotos/Fotolia.

SAUTÉ, PAN-FRY, AND DEEP-FRY

FIGURE 2.46 Bibimbap in a stone bowl.

Source: Peter Kim/Fotolia.

Korean Bibimbap

If most Koreans had to choose a dish to eat daily it would be *bibimbap*. Bibimbap is a simple, one-dish combination of rice mixed with an ever-changing choice of vegetables, meat, sometimes a fried egg, and kochujang. Meat is marinated in soy sauce, sesame oil, garlic, ginger, and scallions, and cooked. Ingredients are vigorously mixed together in individual serving bowls before eating. Stone bowl bibimbap, from the southern province of Cholla, is served in a large stone bowl heated over a flame, which turns it into a sizzling dish with a delicious bottom crust.

VEGETARIAN BIBIMBAP

Cooking ingredients separately ensures that they keep their integrity.

Yields 2 large or 4 moderate servings

Seasoned Chili Paste

Yields 1/2 cup

2-3/4 ounces Korean chili paste (gochujang), 1/4 cup
2 tablespoons Asian sesame oil
1 tablespoon soy sauce
1/2 ounce garlic, 2 large cloves, 1 tablespoon peeled and minced
About 1/3 ounce toasted sesame seeds, 1 tablespoon
1 tablespoon sugar *or* Korean malt syrup (*mool yut*)

Rice

Yields about 6 cups

14 ounces sushi rice, 2 cups

Spinach

Yields 1 cup

1 pound baby spinach, washed and drained
1 to 2 teaspoons Asian sesame oil

Mushrooms

Yields 1/2 cup

1 tablespoon vegetable or plain sesame oil
About 6 ounces shiitake mushrooms, about 2 cups caps, and stems trimmed and sliced
About 1/4 ounce garlic, 1 medium clove, 1 teaspoon peeled and minced

Carrots

Yields about 1 cup

2 teaspoons vegetable or *plain* sesame oil
7 ounces carrots, 2 medium, about 2 cups peeled and grated
About 1/4 ounce garlic, 1 large clove, 1 teaspoon peeled and minced

For Rice Crust: 1 tablespoon vegetable or plain sesame oil

For Serving

8 ounces Persian or Kirby pickling cucumbers, 3 small, 2 to 2-1/2 cups trimmed and slivered
2 teaspoons Asian sesame oil

1 *Prepare* **seasoned chili paste:** Combine all the ingredients plus 1 tablespoon hot water in a small bowl and set aside. (Keep refrigerated in a tightly sealed container up to 1 week.)

2 *Cook* **rice:** Place rice in heavy 4-quart saucepan. Rinse with cold water and drain. Pour in 2 cups cold water. Bring rice to a boil, lower heat, and cover pot. Cook rice exactly 12 minutes, lift lid, and pour in 1/2 cup cold water. Simmer rice 2 minutes and remove pan from heat. Rest rice 15 minutes undisturbed. Fluff rice and keep warm until ready to use.

3 *Steam* **spinach:** Bring 1/4-inch water to a boil in a large pot. Stir in spinach, cover, and steam, turning once or twice with tongs, until leaves are wilted, about 2 minutes. Immediately transfer spinach to a colander, and gently squeeze away water to yield about 1 cup. Chop spinach lightly if not using baby spinach. In a small bowl, combine spinach with sesame oil, and season with salt. Set aside.

4 *Prepare* **mushrooms:** Heat oil in a 10-inch skillet over medium heat. Add mushrooms and garlic and sauté until mushrooms soften, release moisture, and begin to dry, about 3 minutes. Remove skillet from the heat. Scrape mushrooms into another small bowl and season with salt. Set aside.

5 *Prepare* **carrots:** In the same skillet, heat oil over medium-high heat. Add carrots and garlic. Sauté until carrots soften, about 3 minutes. Remove skillet from heat. Season carrots with salt, scrape into a third small bowl, and set aside.

6 **When ready to serve:** Place serving bowls into 200 degree F oven to warm.

   On top of stove: Heat 5- to 6-quart pot or deep 11- to 12-inch skillet over medium heat. Add 1 tablespoon oil. When hot, flatten 1 heaping cup cooked rice into it. Cook rice until crisp and slightly golden on underside, about 5 minutes. Flip rice and cook second side until golden and crisp, 5 minutes. Break up crusty rice. Fold in remaining rice and heat through—alternatively, microwave cooked rice until hot and stir into skillet.

7 **To Serve:** Spoon about 1-1/2 cups hot rice into each of 4 warm serving bowls. Divide cooked vegetables and **cucumbers** and arrange on top of 4 bowls of rice. Drizzle 1/2 teaspoon sesame oil over each serving. Pass **seasoned chili paste** for diners to add, to taste.

Source: *Quick and Easy Korean Cooking* by Cecilia Hae-Jin Lee.

Vary! Improvise!

☞ *While rice is still in skillet, arrange vegetables on top of it in wedge-shaped piles. Heat through, bring skillet to the table, add chili sauce, and toss mixture gently to combine ingredients.*

☞ *Substitute or add favorite vegetables including bean sprouts, zucchini, slivered daikon radish, fern bracken, shredded lettuce, or daikon sprouts.*

☞ *Top each bowl with a fried or poached egg.*

☞ *Add grilled or sautéed beef, chicken or pork loin.*

Korean Rice (Bap)

Rice is a sacred Korean staple. Meals revolve around it with many side dishes of vegetables (*namul*) or meat and the ever-present kimchi. Koreans, like the Japanese, prefer plain short-grain and glutinous rice. Sometimes rice is paired with millet, sorghum or barley, vegetables, chestnuts, black beans, or red beans; sometimes rice is cooked halfway, topped with a stir-fry of meat and kimchi or vegetables, cooked until done, then folded together. Fried rice, rice rolled in seaweed, stir-fried rice cake, *ssäm* (rice in lettuce leaf) are only a few of Korea's many *bap* dishes. See *Signature Recipe: Japanese and Korean Short-Grain (Sushi) Rice* for the rice cooking method.

KIMCHI FRIED RICE (KIMCHI BOKUMBAP)

Cooked rice firms after a day and holds together best for fried rice. Serve this comfort food for lunch with soup and a vegetable namul.

Yields about 8 cups, 4 to 6 servings

9 to 10 ounces pork loin or boneless, skinless chicken, about 1-1/4 cups medium dice
2 tablespoons soy sauce, more as needed
1 tablespoon cornstarch
6 tablespoons vegetable oil, *divided*, more as needed
3 eggs, 3/4 cup beaten
2 ounces trimmed green onions, 4 large, 1/2 cup diced, more to taste, *divided*
6 cups day-old cooked short-grained sushi-type brown or white rice
7-1/2 to 8 ounces kimchi, 1-1/2 cups diced, more to taste
1 tablespoon Asian sesame oil

1 **Marinate:** Mix pork or chicken, soy sauce, and cornstarch together in a small bowl, and set aside.

2 **Cook eggs:** Heat wok or deep 14-inch skillet with 2 tablespoons oil over medium heat. When oil is hot, pour in eggs and when they begin to set, scramble eggs lightly. When eggs are fully set but not hard, transfer to a cutting board. Dice eggs into 1/2- to 3/4-inch cubes and set aside in bowl.

3 **Cook pork:** Reheat wok or skillet with 2 tablespoons oil and when hot, stir in meat mixture. Stir-fry until meat is done, 4 to 5 minutes. Stir in 1/3 cup green onion. Transfer meat to bowl with eggs.

4 **Fry rice:** Reheat wok or skillet with 2 tablespoons oil, and when hot, spread cooked rice in the pan. Allow rice to heat through without moving it. If desired, allow rice to sit until crust forms. (More oil or a nonstick skillet will keep rice from sticking and crusting onto pan.)

5 **Heat through:** Toss the hot rice with kimchi, eggs, and meat, and heat through. (Add a small amount of water to deglaze if rice sticks to pan.) Fold in remaining green onions and sesame oil.

6 **To Serve:** Pile hot fried rice into small bowls and serve.

Vary! Improvise!

☞ **Vegetarian:** *Substitute cubed, firm tofu or 1-1/2 cups shelled frozen edamame (green soybeans) for meat. Or omit meat and increase eggs and kimchi.*

☞ **Reduce the fat:** *Use a nonstick skillet.*

☞ **Restaurant service:** *Prepare the elements of this dish. Finish steps 4 and 5 just before serving.*

KOREAN NOODLES (CHAPCHAE)

As in Japan, noodles shops populate Korean streets. The three most popular Korean noodles dishes are chapchae, naengmyon (cold buckwheat noodles) and kuksu (Korean spaghetti).

Absorbent sweet potato starch (or mung/cellophane) noodles seasoned with soy sauce, garlic, and sesame oil form the foundation of chapchae. Add or subtract vegetables, meat, or tofu to tailor to what's available. Spinach, carrots, zucchini, and Napa cabbage are traditional, but shiitake mushrooms, sliced bulgogi, and onion kick up the flavor.

Yields about 6 cups, 4 servings

4 ounces Korean sweet potato starch noodles
  or cellophane (mung bean starch) noodles

Vegetables

4 ounces fresh shiitake mushrooms, about 6 medium caps, 1 cup finely sliced
10 ounces baby spinach, about 10 cups
5 to 6 ounces carrot, 2 to 3 medium, 1-1/2 cups peeled and finely slivered
8 ounces zucchini, 2 medium, 2 cup finely slivered
6 to 7 ounces Napa cabbage, about 2 cups de-ribbed and finely sliced
1-1/2 to 2 ounces green onions, 3 to 4 large, 1/2 cup halved lengthwise and cut into 2-inch sections

3 tablespoons plain sesame or vegetable oil, divided, more as needed
1 ounce garlic, 4 large cloves, 2 tablespoons peeled and minced
1 tablespoon Asian sesame oil
2 to 3 tablespoons soy sauce, to taste

1 Soak noodles in hot water, until transparent and softened, 15 to 20 minutes. Cut with scissors.

2 Prepare **vegetables**. Combine **vegetables** in a bowl. Mix well.

3 Heat wok or heavy 11- to 12-inch 6-quart pot until hot, and swirl in 2 tablespoons oil. When oil is hot add garlic and stir-fry until golden. Stir in half the vegetables and cook until crisp-tender and spinach is wilted, 4 to 5 minutes. Transfer vegetables to a mixing bowl. Reheat wok or pan over high heat and add 1 tablespoon oil. When pan is hot, add remaining vegetables and cook until spinach wilts and vegetables are tender. Combine all vegetables in wok or pot.

4 Lower heat and add drained noodles. Stir well and cook until noodles are tender, 2 to 3 minutes. Season chapchae with Asian/Korean sesame oil, soy sauce, and freshly ground pepper. Taste chapchae and adjust seasonings. Soy sauce should noticeably color noodles. Taste noodles again.

5 **To Serve:** Mound chapchae high onto a platter and serve.

Vary! Improvise!

☞ *Increase noodles by 2 ounces.*

FIGURE 2.47 Kimchi and pork pancake (jeon) with stuffed whole kimchi.

CRISP KOREAN KIMCHI AND PORK PANCAKES (JEON)

Pancakes are a favorite snack or meal all over Korea. The Japanese make a version called okonomiyaki with pork and cabbage, and sometimes with noodles and mayo. Brown rice flour gives a satisfying chewiness and crispy edge to jeon, but it's not strictly necessary. Use imagination to create new combinations. Serve large pancakes cut into pie-shaped triangles or cook the batter into small individual pancakes. Jeon make great hors d'oeuvres and are satisfying as part of a Korean meal.

Yields 3 cups batter, 2 eight 8-inch, 3/8-inch thick pancakes, 2 to 4 servings

Filling

1 large egg, 1/4 cup whisked
5 to 6 ounces lightly drained kimchi, 1 cup
1-1/2 ounces trimmed green onions, 3 large, 1/3 to 1/2 cup finely bias cut
4 ounces raw pork loin, 1/2 cup diced into 3/8-inch cubes
    or 4 ounces ground lean pork

Korean Seasoned Soy Sauce

Basic Batter

4-1/2 ounces unbleached white flour, 1 cup
1-1/2 ounces brown rice flour, 1/4 cup
1 teaspoon kosher salt
1 cup ice water, more as necessary

4 tablespoons vegetable oil, *divided*

1 Mix together **filling** ingredients in a bowl.

2 Prepare *Korean Seasoned Soy Sauce*, and set aside.

3 *Prepare* **basic batter:** Whisk together flours and salt. Pour in ice water and mix with chopsticks; don't overmix, mix just until smooth. If filling ingredients are wet, less water will be needed, so at this point the batter should be slightly thick. Rest batter 10 minutes.

4 Fold **filling** into **batter**. Batter should be thick with ingredients, but should drop off a spoon in a thick stream: halfway between pancake and crepe batter. If batter is too thick, adjust consistency with ice water or kimchi juice to yield approximately 3 cups batter. Cook batter immediately; do not store.

5 **Cook:** Place an 8-inch nonstick skillet over medium-high heat. Swirl in 2 tablespoons oil. Pour half the batter (1-1/2 cups) into pan and spread it out evenly with back of spoon.

6 Turn heat down to medium and cook pancake until bottom is brown and edges crisp, 2 to 3 minutes. Flip and cook remaining side until brown and crisp, 2 minutes. Repeat with remaining oil and batter. If the pancake is difficult to flip, slide it onto a plate. Invert the hot skillet over top of the plate and flip them together. Remove plate and finish cooking remaining side of jeon.

7 **To Serve:** Slice hot jeon into 8 triangles. Serve first-cooked side up with *Korean Seasoned Soy Sauce.*

Vary! Improvise!

☞ Substitute 1/2 cup sliced garlic chives (buchu) for green onions.
☞ Substitute diced chicken, tofu, or shrimp for pork.
☞ Omit meat or seafood and double the green onions.

KOREAN SAUTÉED SUMMER SQUASH
(HOBAK NAMUL)

Yields 3-1/2 to 4 cups, 4 servings

2 pounds zucchini and summer squash, about 8 with 1-inch or less diameter
3 tablespoons oil, more as needed

Sauce

1 tablespoon soy sauce
1-1/2 teaspoons minced salted anchovy
1 tablespoon rice wine *or* sherry
1 ounce trimmed green onions, 2 large, 4 tablespoons thinly sliced
1/2 ounce garlic, 2 large cloves, 1 tablespoon peeled and minced
1/2 teaspoon Korean red chili powder, more to taste

Garnish: 1 tablespoon toasted sesame seeds

1 Slice squash 1/4- to 1/2-inch thick to yield about 8 cups. Blot dry with paper toweling. When cut and exposed to air for very long, summer squash can become bitter, so use immediately or toss in 1 tablespoon oil and cover with plastic wrap.

2 Heat 3 tablespoons oil over medium-high heat in a deep 12-inch skillet. When hot, add half the squash in one layer. Cook until squash is slightly browned and starts to soften and curl at the edges, 3 minutes. Flip only once and cook second side. Remove zucchini to a mixing bowl with a slotted spoon.

3 Reheat skillet with a little more oil, if necessary, over medium-high heat and when hot, spread squash in 1 layer. Repeat browning. Lower heat and fold in first batch of cooked squash. Combine **sauce** ingredients and fold into cooked squash. Toss and heat through, 1 to 2 minutes. Taste squash and adjust seasonings.

4 **To Serve:** Arrange squash on platter and scrape sauce from skillet over the top. Garnish squash with sesame seeds and serve at room temperature.

Source: *Growing Up in a Korean Kitchen* by Hi Soo Shin Hepinstall.

Vary! Improvise!

☞ **Deepen the flavor:** *Drizzle dish with 2 teaspoons Asian sesame oil along with sesame seeds.*

GRILL, GRIDDLE, ROAST, BROIL AND BARBECUE

Korean Barbecue

Bulgogi means "fired meat." Koreans are mad for it and love to pair bulgogi with kimchi. Slices of beef, pork, or even chicken can be marinated in Korean soy sauce, garlic, and sugar and grilled. Many other seasonings like Korean sesame oil, rice wine, ginger, sesame seeds, hot Korean chili paste, grated Asian pear, or other fruit give it even more flavor.

Galbi is popular Korean outdoor grilled picnic food. *Galbi* or *kalbi*, which means *rib*, names a variety of grilled or broiled beef or pork short ribs, or chicken legs, marinated in the same sauce as bulgogi. Pastures for cattle grazing are scarce in mountainous South Korea, so beef is a luxury. Popular galbi houses have grills set in tables. Wrap galbi with lettuce, *perilla*, or other leafy vegetables, dip in *ssamjang*, or sprinkle grilled beef slices with *Toasted Sesame Seed Salt*.

FIGURE 2.48 Bulgogi setup.
Source: Mikko Pitkänen/Fotolia.

FIGURE 2.49 Grilled pork rib galbi.
Source: paul_brighton/Fotolia.

Vary! Improvise!

☞ *Toss green onions cut into 2-inch pieces with oil and salt. Pan-fry or grill and serve with Korean barbecue.*

KOREAN BULGOGI OR GALBI/KALBI

The Korean pear (different from Asian pear) breaks down meat proteins (much like pineapple or papaya); some Koreans substitute kiwi. The key to a good Korean marinade is a lot of sweetener. Beef short ribs are meaty and very flavorful, but are too tough for barbecuing. Slicing them in an accordion cut and marinating 8 to 12 hours helps to tenderize and richly flavor them. Some Koreans like to add a tablespoon or two of (glass bottle) Coke to this marinade.

2 to 4 servings

For Bulgogi

1-1/2 pound boneless beef sirloin tip, rib-eye, or strip steak, thinly sliced (see step 1)

For Galbi

1-1/2 pounds beef short ribs, "English-style" cut 2- to 3-inch thick
  or 1-1/2 pounds "country" style pork ribs, very meaty with small bone attached

Korean Barbecue Marinade

Yields 1/2 cup; with kiwi or pear yields generous 3/4 cup

5 tablespoons Korean soy sauce
2 teaspoons Korean or Asian sesame oil
1/2 ounce garlic, 2 large cloves, 1 tablespoon peeled and minced
1/3 ounce ginger, 2 teaspoons peeled and minced
1 tablespoon sugar or honey
2 teaspoons rice vinegar
2 teaspoons toasted sesame seed
Optional: 3 ounces kiwi or Korean or Asian pear, 1/3 cup peeled, cored and puréed

Garnish: 1 ounce trimmed green onions, 2 large, 4 tablespoons thinly sliced

For Serving

Cooked short-grain rice
Kimchi
Panchan or Korean side dishes

1 Prepare meat:

Bulgogi

Purchase meat pre-sliced or wash, pat dry, and freeze in plastic baggie until meat is firm. Slice 1/16- to 1/8-inch thick with chef's knife or slice meat 1/16-inch thick on meat slicer.

Galbi

Accordion-cut beef short-ribs: Make a 1/4-inch thick slice nearest the bone of a short rib and parallel to it, down to about 1/4-inch from bottom of meat. Don't cut through—the bone/meat should be attached like a hinge. Flip rib over and again make a 1/4-inch thick slice down to 1/4-inch from bottom of meat to form a hinge. Flip and repeat this process, slicing 1/4-inch thick cuts parallel to bone and stopping 1/4-inch short of bottom, once more on each side until you have a strip of meat 8 to 10 inches long. Repeat with remaining ribs.

2 Mix together **Korean barbecue marinade** ingredients (or purée in blender). Season with freshly ground pepper.

3 Place meat in half hotel pan, mix marinade with meat, and cover with plastic wrap *or* place both in plastic zipper baggie. Marinate **bulgogi** sirloin tip 1 hour room temperature. Marinate **galbi** beef ribs 2 hours room temperature, or 8 to 12 hours refrigerated.

4 Heat barbecue to high for bulgogi and medium for galbi. Don't overcook meat.

Bulgogi

Remove beef from marinade, allowing excess to drip back into bowl. Place meat on hot grill. Cook to desired doneness, 1 to 2 minutes per side for medium-rare.

Galbi

Remove ribs, drain excess marinade, and place on barbecue. Cook on both sides until caramelized and crusty, 3 to 4 minutes per side.

5 **To Serve:** Garnish bulgogi or galbi with green onions and serve with cooked rice, kimchi, and other *panchan* (Korean side dishes).

SALAD AND VEGETABLE METHODS

KOREAN GREEN "SALAD" (MINARINAMUL)

This is one of the many namul or vegetable side dishes that Koreans prepare well. Korean water dropwort or minari is traditionally used, but watercress is more readily available in the West.

Yield 2 to 4 servings

6 to 8 ounces watercress, bottom ends trimmed, about 7 cups
1/4 ounce garlic, 1 large clove, 1-1/2 teaspoons peeled and minced
1 tablespoon Asian sesame oil
1 teaspoon honey
2 teaspoons crushed, toasted sesame seed
1 tablespoon rice vinegar

1 Steam watercress until tender, 1 to 2 minutes. Drain and lightly squeeze dry. Chop into bite-sized pieces.

2 Toss watercress with remaining ingredients. Season with salt, to taste. Chill before serving or serve at room temperature. Taste and re-season before serving.

Source: *Flavours of Korea* by Marc and Kim Millon.

Fruit as Meat Tenderizer

Certain fruits like pineapple, papaya, kiwi, and Korean pear contain protease enzymes (bromelain and papain) that break down protein. When you use them in a marinade be careful with them: too long in the marinade will turn meat into mush. Asian pears have about half the proteolytic action of the Korean pear. The fruit adds flavor as well as tenderizes. The heat of cooking stops proteolytic enzymatic activity. Marinate tougher meat like beef 2 hours at room temperature, or 8 hours refrigerated, and delicate meat like chicken for half that time. Seafood is the most delicate of all: 5 minutes with acid or enzymes marinades is enough. Cold slows marination.

FIGURE 2.50 Korean pear.
Source: Dave King/DK Images.

FIGURE 2.51 Traditional vegetable namul.
Source: ivylingpy/Fotolia.

BEAN SPROUT SALAD (SOOKJU NAMUL)

This salad is very strong with garlic. Use half or less if a milder dish is desired.

Yields 3 cups, 4 servings

1 pound mung bean sprouts
1 ounce trimmed green onion, 2 large, 1/4 cup sliced lengthwise and finely sliced crosswise
1/2 ounce garlic, 2 large cloves, 1 tablespoon peeled and minced, to taste
4 teaspoons Asian sesame oil
1 tablespoon toasted sesame seeds
1 tablespoon soy sauce
Optional: 2 to 3 teaspoons rice vinegar

1 Fill a 4-quart saucepan almost full of water. Bring to a rolling boil. Stir in bean sprouts and cook sprouts 1 minute. Drain through fine strainer, rinse sprouts with cold water, and drain well.

2 While sprouts boil, toss green onion, garlic (to taste), sesame oil, sesame seeds, and soy sauce in medium mixing bowl. Immediately fold in drained, blanched sprouts and toss to evenly coat with dressing. Taste salad and season with salt and pepper. Rest salad 5 minutes before serving, or chill 1 hour.

3 **To Serve:** Pile salad onto plates or platters and serve room temperature or chilled.

FIGURE 2.52 Lotus root.
Source: WONG SZE FEI/Fotolia.

LOTUS ROOT WITH SWEET-SOY GLAZE (YEONGEUN JORIM)

Choose a smooth, thick-bodied lotus root.

Yields 4 cups, 4 to 6 servings

1 pound fresh lotus root
   or 1 pound peeled and sliced water-packed lotus root
2 cups *Anchovy Stock*

Jorimjang Sauce

4 tablespoons soy sauce
2 tablespoons sugar
1 tablespoon honey
   or 2 tablespoons Korean malt syrup or maple syrup
1 tablespoon rice wine or saké
1 tablespoon Asian sesame oil

Garnish: 1 tablespoon toasted sesame seeds

1 **If using fresh lotus root:** Peel lotus root and rinse well. Slice lotus crosswise into 1/4-inch slices to yield 4 cups. Rinse. Place lotus root into a 4-quart saucepan with anchovy stock. Bring to a boil over high heat. Reduce heat and boil lotus root 10 minutes.

   If using water packed peeled and sliced lotus root: Simmer 3 minutes. Transfer root slices to a bowl and set aside. Pour all but 1/4 cup stock into storage container, cool, and store in refrigerator for another use. Reserve 1/4 cup stock.

2 Whisk jorimjang sauce ingredients together in 10-inch nonreactive sauté pan. Bring to a boil over medium-high heat, stir in lotus roots, and reduce heat to medium-low. Turn lotus roots in sauce and spoon sauce over lotus roots until they take on the color of the sauce, 5 to 7 minutes.

3 Pour in reserved 1/4 cup stock, raise heat to high, bring sauce to a boil, and cook until lotus root is glazed with a thickened syrup, 3 to 5 minutes. Stir in Asian sesame oil. Remove pan from heat. (If sauce is heated too far and becomes sticky, stir in little stock or water.)

4 **To Serve:** Divide lotus root and pile onto plates. Garnish with sesame seed.

Source: *A Korean Mother's Cooking Notes* by Chang, Sun-Young.

PICKLE AND PRESERVE

Korean Kraut: Kimchi

Koreans are obsessed with fermented foods and they judge restaurants and chefs by their kimchi. Visit Seoul in November during kimchi-curing or *kimjang*. That's when Chinese cabbage metamorphoses into Korean *kimchi*, and its sour-spicy scent wafts through the air. Kimchi is a live-cultured or fermented food similar to sauerkraut. Its live lactobacillus bacteria are good for digestion and gut health.

There are over a hundred types of kimchi; most share the basic techniques of salt-wilting, seasoning, and fermenting, except summer kimchi, which is more like a wilted salad. The region, seasonal vegetables, seasonings, amount of salt, and fermentation time determine kimchi's flavor.

Koreans ferment Chinese or Napa cabbage, radishes, radish greens, pears, cucumbers, and scallions. Their seasonings include red chili powder, ginger, garlic, onion, scallions, shiso leaf, salt, fresh fish or fresh oysters, Chinese chives, and fish sauce or dried anchovies or dried shrimp. Typically South Koreans use more salt, sugar, chili, and seafood to produce a strong, sweet-flavored kimchi in their warm and quick-fermenting climate. In cooler North Korea, kimchi is watery, less salty, and not very spicy-hot.

FIGURE 2.53 Various types of kimchi at a Korean market.
Source: ehpoint/Fotolia.

FIGURE 2.54 Chinese cabbage.
Source: Roger Phillips/DK Images.

SUMMER KIMCHI (NABAK-KIMCHI)

Korean meals are not complete without several varieties of kimchi. It adds crunch to noodle and dumpling dishes and deepens the flavor of soups, stews, and rice. Summer kimchi is closer in technique to Japanese quick-pressed salads: It doesn't have the long fermentation time of winter kimchi. Summer kimchi is salted and left out to ferment no more than 1 to 2 days, resulting in a fresher, clean taste. Add a lesser amount of kimchi paste for a less spicy kimchi.

Yields 1 quart

4 to 5 tablespoons *Korean Kimchi Paste*
About 1-1/2 pounds Chinese cabbage leaves, about 10 cups diced into 1-inch squares
About 8 ounces daikon radish, about 1-1/2 cups peeled and diced into 1/2-inch cubes
4 teaspoons kosher salt, *divided*
1 tablespoon sugar
2 ounces trimmed green onions, 4 large, 1/2 cup sliced into 1-inch lengths and slivered

1 Prepare **Korean Kimchi Paste**. (Use half the chili powder for less heat.)

2 Toss Chinese cabbage with 1 tablespoon kosher salt and 2 cups water in large stainless bowl. In another small bowl, toss daikon with 1 teaspoon kosher salt and 1 teaspoon sugar. Set both bowls aside at room temperature 2 hours. Drain vegetables in colander; blot bowl dry. With gloves, toss wilted vegetables with remaining 2 teaspoons sugar, **kimchi paste**, and green onions.

3 Pack kimchi and liquid into 1 quart plastic zipper baggie or a clean 1-quart glass canning jar. Screw lid on jar lightly. Or roll up kimchi in baggie, but don't close zipper completely, and place in a bowl. Leave jar or baggie at room temperature (70 degrees F) overnight or up to 2 days. The longer it goes, the more sour it will become. Taste and decide.

4 To stop fermentation (transfer baggie kimchi to quart jar), refrigerate kimchi. Summer kimchi will last 2 weeks refrigerated.

Source: *The Korean Table* by Taekyung Chung and Debra Samuels.

Signature Technique: Stuffed Whole Cabbage Kimchi

- **Slice** Napa cabbage lengthwise into quarters with root attached.

- **Wash** cabbage, and drain lightly. Place in bowl.

- **Rub** leaves with kosher salt. Leave 1 to 3 hours to wilt until crunchy like a dill pickle.

- **Mix** together stuffing (*sok*): red chili powder, cooked rice paste, anchovy fish sauce, sugar, scallions, ginger, and garlic.

- **Rinse and drain** Napa cabbage.

- **Smear stuffing** on *each* leaf.

- **Pack** stuffed cabbage quarters into container (or zipper baggie)

- **Cover** kimchi with whole cabbage leaves and a little brine.

- **Weight** kimchi with plate.

- **Ferment** kimchi 3 days to a week depending on ambient temperature and desired sourness of the kimchi. Taste test. The pH should register around 4 to 4.1.

- **Taste test** kimchi. Refrigerate it when it tastes delightfully sour and appealing. Get a consensus.

FIGURE 2.55 Stuffed kimchi.
Source: Ben Fink/DK Images.

AUTUMN-STYLE STUFFED WHOLE CABBAGE KIMCHI (T'ONG PAECH'U KIMCHI)

This kimchi can be eaten in 2 to 5 days, and its flavor will develop more after refrigeration. It will last at least 3 months refrigerated, and become more sour. For a casual kimchi (mak kimchi), toss stuffing with Napa cabbage, which has been diced into 1-1/2 inch squares. Koreans prepare kimchi with many other vegetables like baby bok choy, slivered daikon radish, bell peppers, cucumbers, or eggplant.

Yields about 5 quarts

5-1/2 pounds Napa or Chinese cabbage, preferably 3 medium heads
6-1/2 to 6-3/4 ounces kosher salt, 1-1/4 cups
2 to 3 cups non-chlorinated water, *divided*

Stuffing

Yields about 2 cups

About 2/3 ounce glutinous rice flour, 2 tablespoons
3 to 4 tablespoons chopped salted anchovies
    or 3 to 4 tablespoons Thai (anchovy only) fish sauce
2 to 4 ounces Korean hot red chili powder, 1/2 to 1 cup packed (lesser amount for mild kimchi)
3 ounces trimmed green onions, 6 large, 2/3 to 1 cup sliced into 1/2-inch lengths
1/2 ounce garlic, 2 large cloves, 1 tablespoon peeled and finely minced
Scant 1/2 ounce shelled chestnuts or walnuts, 3 tablespoons finely minced
4 to 5 ounces fresh ginger, about 1/2 cup peeled and finely minced
1-3/4 ounces sugar, 4 tablespoons
1 tablespoon freshly squeezed lemon juice

1 **Trim and cut cabbage:** Remove several outer leaves from cabbage and reserve. Lightly trim cabbage ends, but leave root on so cabbage holds together. If there are 3 cabbages, slice each in half lengthwise from root to top tip. Lay each cabbage on its cut side and slice in half again, taking care to split root end in half so each quarter is held together by a quarter of the root. If there are 2 large cabbages, slice them as directed above into 6 wedges each. Yield for either should be a total of 12 wedges.

2 **Salt-brine cabbage:** Stir 1/4-cup salt into 1-cup lukewarm nonchlorinated water, and set aside to dissolve. Rinse cabbage wedges, and drain lightly. Place cut sides up in a 6-quart nonreactive bowl in one layer. Rub remaining 1-cup salt between leaves of each quarter and over all the cabbage. Drizzle salt and water mixture over cabbage. Weight cabbages with clean plate.

3 **Rest cabbage in brine:** Let cabbage sit 1 to 3 hours, turning it so it wilts evenly. After 1 hour, test cabbage every 20 minutes until it has a crunchy snap. Drain and rinse, drain again in a colander. Discard all but 1/4 cup used brine water, and retain bowl.

4 **Prepare stuffing while cabbage brines:** In a small saucepan, stir rice flour and 1 cup nonchlorinated water together. Bring to a boil, lower heat to medium-low, and cook, stirring constantly with heatproof spatula, until pasty, 2 minutes. Cool. Combine rice paste with anchovy or fish sauce and chili powder. Fold in green onions, garlic, nuts, ginger, sugar, and lemon juice. The consistency should be like ketchup; add nonchlorinated water to thin.

5 **Stuff and pack cabbage:** Wearing plastic or rubber gloves, lay a cabbage quarter in reserved bowl. Smear 1 heaping tablespoon stuffing between the leaves (and cut edges) of each cabbage wedge, beginning with outer leaves and working inward. Repeat with remaining wedges. As each cabbage quarter is finished, press leaves together and pack into 6- to 8-quart food-safe plastic container with a tight-sealing lid. Press down firmly to remove air bubbles.

6 Dredge reserved and loose leaves in remaining stuffing and use to cover kimchi. Pour 1/4 to reserved brine water and 1/4 cup nonchlorinated water into bowl, swirl, and pour over cabbages. Weight with clean plate.

7 **Ferment cabbage:** Tightly seal container. Taste after one day. If more saltiness or sweetness is desired, ladle out some of the brine and adjust by mixing with more salt or sugar then pour over the cabbages. Reseal container. Leave container at room temperature without opening, ideally 70 to 72 degrees F, for another 2 to 4 days. Refrigerate kimchi when it reaches the desired flavor and acidity.

8 **To Serve:** Wearing gloves, slice cabbage quarters crosswise into 1-1/2-inch pieces, and plate.

Source: *Growing Up in a Korean Kitchen* by Hi Soo Shin Hepinstall.

LACTIC ACID FERMENTATION

Lactic acid fermentation of cabbage for sauerkraut or of other vegetables is a live process that cannot be fully controlled. Therein lies its beauty. Fermentation makes some cooks uncomfortable. Here are some fermentation facts:

- Fermentation occurs in two phases. In the first phase salt, water, or cabbage juice and the build-up of carbon dioxide protects against decay until enough lactic acid forms and raises the pH to around 4.1. This must take place quickly, within 3 to 5 days. Temperature plays a huge role. Ideal temperature is 68 to 72 degrees F.
- After 3 to 5 days, the second or flavor maturation phase begins when lactic acid has taken over and booted out bad bacteria. At this point the ambient temperature can be slightly lower, about 64 to 68 degrees F for several weeks for sauerkraut.
- Temperature and salt control the rate of fermentation. Fermentation speeds up at higher temperatures and slows in cooler ones. Salt slows fermentation so cold weather winter kimchi has less salt than warmer weather spring kimchi. Cooler, longer ferments create more flavor. That's why Koreans buried their winter kimchi in the constant temperature of the earth. Modern Korean cooks use a special kimchi refrigerator.

REVIEW QUESTIONS

Japan

1. Discuss key influences on Japanese cuisine.

2. What two foods are at the center of Japanese cuisine?

3. Name two fermented Japanese soy products. Describe one and how it's made.

4. What is katsuobushi and how is it used?

5. What is sashimi? What is sushi? Name two types of sushi.

6. Describe the process and proportions of rice and water for preparing sushi rice.

Korea

1. What culture had the strongest early influence on Korean cuisine? What culture was a second influence?

2. Name three seasonings of Korean cuisine.

3. What is kimchi? How and when is it eaten in Korea?

4. Describe the main difference between bulgogi and galbi.

5. Name two grains that Koreans eat besides rice.

6. How does the food of South Korea differ from the north?

CHAPTER THREE

SOUTHEAST ASIA: THAILAND, VIETNAM, AND INDONESIA

This chapter will:

- Introduce three of the most influential countries of South East Asia, their histories, geography, cultural influences, and climates.
- Introduce the culinary cultures, regional variations, and dining etiquette of Thailand, Vietnam, and Indonesia.
- Identify the foods, flavor foundations, seasoning devices, and favored cooking techniques of Thailand, Vietnam, and Indonesia, and how they differ and where they are similar.
- Teach by technique and recipes the major dishes of Thailand, Vietnam, and Indonesia.

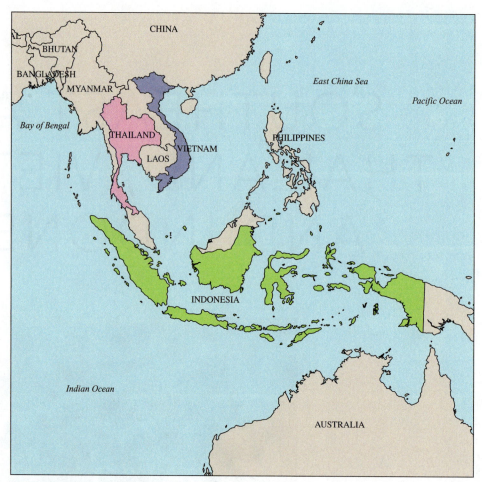

FIGURE 3.1A Map of Southeast Asia.

Southeast Asia is a loosely scattered collection of twelve countries inhabiting a peninsula and thousands of far-flung tropical islands stretching from China to Australia. It's a land of emerald green rice paddies climbing up terraced hills, wide rivers and sinuous tributaries, dark mountains, dry jungle scrub, waterfalls, and glistening fertile deltas. Vegetation runs riot through elaborately carved ancient Buddhist and Hindu temples and Muslim mosques while exotic beaches and ash-crusted live volcanoes illuminate the diverse landscape.

Southeast Asia includes Brunei, Cambodia, Indonesia, Laos, Malaysia, Myanmar, Papua New Guinea, Philippines, Singapore, Thailand, Timor-Leste, and Vietnam. Vietnamese, Cambodian, Lao, Thai, Burmese, Malaysian, and Indonesian cultures are closely linked by proximity and kinship. Though hundreds of miles of sapphire-blue ocean and a dozen salty seas divide the other countries of Southeast Asia, ocean and sea trade and food inextricably bind them.

The cuisines of Thailand, Vietnam, and Indonesia best represent much of the cuisine of Southeast Asia's twelve countries: they are the most developed, dynamic, and influential cuisines. All share a love of rice, seafood, fish sauce, shrimp paste, lemongrass, garlic, galangal, coconut, mung beans and sprouts, peanuts, soy, and chilies.

Just as it takes a village to raise a child, it takes a world of influence to develop a cuisine. War, trade, invasion, colonization, migration, and occupation have played a part in developing each of Southeast Asia's cuisines. The Arab-Iranians, Chinese, Dutch, English, Portuguese, and French influenced Indonesian cuisine because the country sits naturally at an important shipping crossroads. Vietnam, sharing borders with China, founded her cuisine on solid Chinese technique. When the French occupied Vietnam she had a second great cuisine's influence. Thailand, never European-colonized, was influenced early in its history by the indigenous Mon originally from northeastern India, by traders, Indian missionaries, and by migrations from southern China.

THAILAND: LAND OF THE FREE

Thai Culture: A Careful Choice

Rafael Steinberg writing for Time-Life Pacific and Southeast Asian Cooking *notes that Thai cooks seem to have chosen carefully what foreign elements were allowed to dominate their cuisine and culture. In contrast, other Southeast Asian cuisines came together seemingly haphazardly from the myriad influences that buffeted them throughout history. Thai cooks designed a cuisine that is an "integrated, harmonious whole." This reflects the country itself, which, unlike its neighbors, has never been colonized.*

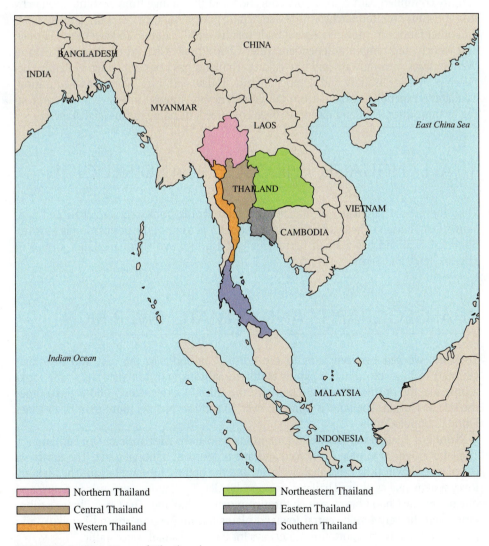

Northern Thailand		Northeastern Thailand	
Central Thailand		Eastern Thailand	
Western Thailand		Southern Thailand	

FIGURE 3.1B Map of Thailand.

The Mon, or Dvaravati, a civilization that originated in India, first inhabited parts of northern and central Thailand. From them came Buddhism, modern Thailand's main religion, and the first wet-rice cultivation plus the use of spices and herbs. Wet rice cultivation influenced the culinary, financial, and cultural course of Asia and Southeast Asia: Arab and Indian merchants came to trade rice and sugar in exchange for foods, spices, silk, cotton, gems, and cooking techniques.

Thailand's 800-year history has five major periods: *Nanchao* (650 to 1250), *Sukhothai/ Lanna* (1238 to 1378), *Ayutthaya* (1350 to 1767), *Thon Buri* (1767 to 1772), and *Rattanakosin* (1782 to present day). Nanchao and Sukhothai/Lanna were the golden eras when benevolent kings governed and asserted their independence from Khmer and Mon kingdoms. Around the tenth century, Tai peoples from northern Vietnam and south China settled in Thailand; later influences came from Cambodian-Khmer and Burmese migrations.

The Ayutthaya Period began with the founding of Ayutthaya as the capital. In 1765 the Burmese invaded Ayutthaya and destroyed most of the city and religious sites. The Thon Buri period was a time of upheaval (the capitol moved to Thon Buri), military defense against the Burmese, and disintegration from a lack of central authority. The Portuguese established an embassy in Thailand in 1511.

During the Rattanakosin period the capital moved to Bangkok and restoration of the country continued with compulsory education and the change from absolute monarchy to a constitutional monarchy with a democratic government. In 1833 the United States and other European countries signed trade treaties with Thailand. To keep out the British and French, and remain independent, ruler Chao Phraya Chakkri modernized Siam in Western ways with railways and universities. Thailand has bounced (often violently) between periods of military and democratic rule. Today, with high literacy and education, Thailand is experiencing rapid economic growth despite intense anti-government protesting by minorities. Thailand has never been colonized; its name means *land of the free*.

THAI LANGUAGE, PHILOSOPHY, AND RELIGION

Thai, the official language of Thailand, contains words borrowed from Pali and Sanskrit. Most Thais are Theravadic Buddhists. About 5 percent of the population is Muslim. Southern Thailand has a small percentage of Catholics and there are small groups of Hindus, Jews, and Sikhs.

THAI GEOGRAPHY AND CLIMATE: RIVER RICH

Thailand, wedged between Laos to the north, Cambodia to the east and Myanmar (Burma) to the west, shares a skinny southern isthmus with Malaysia. Its shape looks a little like the profile of an elephant with the isthmus as its trunk. About three times the size of Florida, Thailand is home to over 65 million people, more than three times Florida's population.

Northern Thailand is mostly mountainous with deep river valleys. Doi Inthanon is Thailand's highest point at 8,451 feet, and one of fourteen national parks. The northeast is a place of low rolling hills, shallow lakes, and the upland Khorat Plateau. The Mekong River system snakes along Thailand's eastern border. Thailand's seven minor rivers, and one major, the Chao Phraya, stretch through much of Thailand. The Chao Phraya's tributaries feed the very fertile central lowland plains farming region around Bangkok, and provide abundant transportation waterways for large and small water traffic.

Southern Thailand's narrow isthmus offers vacationers long coastline beaches, islands offshore, and mangrove forests. Three main seasons rule Thailand's mostly sunny and humid, subtropical climate: the cool, dry season from November to February, the hot season in April and May, and the wet, monsoon season June through October.

FARMING AND AGRICULTURE

Farmers in Thailand's rich central plain and fertile valley raise most of the country's cash crops like rice, corn, sugarcane, vegetables, produce, and fruit. Two-thirds of Thailand is mountainous and hilly, with stony, shallow soil, but farmers manage to cultivate it. In less arable, rugged, and dry regions like the Northeast and South, farmers raise rice and secondary crops for subsistence. Many of the northern Hill tribes practice shifting cultivation to allow the soil to restore fertility. With over 50 million acres of farmland (half of that in rice cultivation), Thailand also produces and exports soybeans, peanuts, cocoa, shrimp, fish, and most of the world's tapioca (cassava). To discourage opium and marijuana growing and deforestation, the government encourages mountain villagers to grow coffee, apples, strawberries, kidney beans, and other temperate crops instead.

THAI CUISINE: MASTERS OF GREAT FLAVOR CONTRASTS

Rice, the foundation of self-sustaining and prosperous Thai communities for centuries, is of sacred importance. At the geographic halfway point between China and India, and with Persian and Portuguese visitors, it's no surprise that Thai cooking is strong on flavor and method. The real surprise: the sophistication, coherence, elegance, and refinement of purist Thai cuisine.

Thailand contains two flourishing cuisines: the *palace cuisine* and the simple, practical *peasant cuisine*. (Street food is a much-relished third.) Peasant cuisine is spicy and robust, fast-cooked with stir-fried noodles or meat. Palace cuisine is sweeter, less intense, with richer ingredients like coconut milk and lots of fruit and vegetable carving and elaborate presentation. Rice, fish, and seafood are important to both.

Thais wove together a variety of influences to create the classic palace cuisine. Originally it was a cuisine instigated by harem wives. Kings were "patrons of the kitchen." Culinary contests between the many wives helped create a complex, formal cuisine with coherent style, refined techniques, elegant traditions, and tongue-contrasting flavor. Descendants of royal wives opened restaurants so this cuisine continues today.

Thai entrées are either something served with rice or noodle dishes. Thai *kaeng* dishes include foods served in liquid like soup or the famous coconut curry that go with rice, and *krueng kieng*, side dishes of dry cooked food or noodles. The harmonious Thai blending of contrasts: spicy, sweet, sour, hot and salty with wet, dry, crisp, soft, smooth and chunky, give this cuisine its world-renowned character and wake-up-and-take-notice flavor.

REGIONAL THAILAND

Thailand has four distinct regions (that include 73 provinces), which differ greatly in geography and cultural influence.

1. **Northern Thailand: Poor and Spicy**

   The poorest northern region contains forests and cool mountains with wild mushrooms, roots and greens, droughts, and poor soil. The Burmese (Myanmar) influence comes out in dishes mildly hot with ginger, chilies, onion, and turmeric and thin curries without coconut milk. The Shan of China also contributed *nam prik*, a spicy dipping sauce with raw or cooked vegetables. Laotians contributed steamed sticky rice with meals and the use of dill. Barbecue chicken, green papaya salad, egg noodles, grubs, worms, ant eggs, and grasshoppers are popular.

2. **Northeastern Thailand: Rustic and Creative**

Thailand's northeastern region with a semi-arid plateau between Laos, Cambodia, and the Mekong River is the largest. Home to a popular, rustic cuisine partial to grilled, marinated meats and robust sauces with steamed sticky rice with a strong Laotian influence, cooks of this region deal daily with a lack of money, poor ingredients, poor soil, and poor climate. Bamboo shoots, wild watercress, toasted ground rice (condiment), river fish, hot and sour soup, green papaya salad, grilled beef salad, and meat are popular.

3. **Central Thailand: Mild and Sweet**

Thailand's central region is its heartland. A vast, flat plain with Bangkok and the Chao Phraya River and its network of canals and rivers, this is the richest growing region with an abundance of jasmine rice and exotic fruit like mango, durian, mangosteen, rambutan, guava, pomelo, and many vegetables. Central Thais eat jasmine rice boiled and soft, mild and sweet curries, Thai salads (*yum*) with roast beef, Thai omelet, vegetables, and local herring (*platoo*).

4. **Southern Isthmus and The Gulf: Two Regions, Tropical, Simple, and Flavorful**

The southern isthmus and the Gulf of Thailand are mountainous, tropical and, with eight months of rains, lush green. It has coconut, pineapple, and rubber plantations. With Malaysia nearby, there is a distinct Muslim and Chinese influence in the cuisine. Fishing, seafood, and tourism are abundant. Coconut curries with chili, grilled, steamed and baked seafood; claypot dishes and *satay* with *Massaman* (Muslim) curry paste are prepared simply but with big flavor.

DINE AT HOME IN THAILAND

An invitation to a Thai home for a meal would be rare in the poorer areas. If invited, it's likely there will be stairs to climb to the main living area. Greet the hosts with the *wai* as a sign of respect by raising both hands, palms joined, fingers pointing upwards, lightly touching the body somewhere between the chest and the forehead. The higher the hands and the lower the bow of the head, the more respect shown. A small gift of flowers or chocolates would be welcome. Step over, not on the threshold, remove shoes at the door, and squat on a bamboo mat-covered wooden floor, or sit at a table.

The host or hostess might offer a predinner snack of green papaya salad, cashews, or spicy sausage. In a non-Muslim home they might offer beer or spirits, or water, tea, or Thai iced tea. A large bowl of rice will sit in the center of the table or bamboo floor mat, and surrounding it, a clear soup, a steamed dish, a fried dish, dishes of curry, meat or fish tossed "salad," and spicy condiments. Very little meat will be part of the meal: Thais, like Chinese, use meat and seafood as condiment and stretch it as far as they can. Wait for the host to summon guests to the meal and say *kin khao* or "eat rice," before digging in. The food will be room temperature. Thais eat with the right hand or with a spoon, fork, bowl, and plate. They use chopsticks only for noodles.

Since there is an emphasis on sharing and community, take a small portion of each dish on the first pass. The host and hostess will urge guests to eat more, but be polite. Wait to be asked before taking food, never take the last serving and when finished leave a little food, but *never* rice, on the plate to signal satisfaction. Diners do not lick their fingers!

FIGURE 3.2 Phi Phi Island, Thailand.
Source: Iakov Kalinin/Fotolia.

TASTES OF THAILAND

Fat: Coconut oil, lard, peanut oil, plain sesame oil, vegetable oils

Sweet: Palm sugar, sugar

Sour/Alcohol: Tamarind, lemon, lime, distilled vinegar

Salty: Fish sauce (*nam pla*), shrimp paste, soy sauce

Spicy-Hot: Red and green chilies (bird's eye), black and white peppercorns, ginger, galangal

Spice: Cinnamon, clove, cumin, coriander, cardamom, turmeric

Aromatic Seasoning Vegetables: Shallot, onion, ginger, galangal, garlic, green onion, cilantro root, lemongrass

Herbs, Seasonings, and Condiments: Cilantro, mint, Thai basil, garlic chives, Kaffir lime leaf, dried shrimp, banana leaves, pandan leaves

Other Important Foods: Coconut, wing beans, tomatoes, small round eggplant, bitter gourds, long beans, soybeans, snow peas, green beans, mung beans, tapioca (cassava), tofu, peanuts, sesame, rice (jasmine, purple glutinous, white glutinous), tropical fruits (green papaya, mango, pineapple, durian, mangosteen, bananas, melons, see *Tastes of Vietnam*), Thai pumpkins, okra, bean sprouts, bamboo shoots, water chestnuts, water lily stem, daikon radish, sweet corn and baby corn, cucumbers, asparagus, sweet potato, yam bean, greens (Thai broccoli, pak choy, Chinese cabbage, Thai mustard greens, amaranth), mushrooms (oyster, shiitake, straw mushrooms, mouse ear fungus), meat (beef, chicken, pork, lamb, sausage), grubs and insects, fish, seafood (crab, shrimp, cuttlefish, mussels, squid), rice noodles, mung starch noodles

Popular Dishes: *Satay* (grilled skewered meat or seafood), *nam chim sate* (peanut sauce), coconut curry (yellow, green, massaman, jungle, red), *khai yat sai* (crab, pork, or prawn stuffed omelet), *som tum* (green papaya salad), *yum* salads of grilled beef, sausage, pork, or fried fish), *laab* or *larb* (minced meat "salad"), *pad Thai* (stir-fried rice noodles), *tom kha kai* (chicken coconut soup), *tom yum* (hot and sour lemongrass soup), *khao niao mamuang* (sticky rice with mango), *pla nueng manao* (steamed fish with garlic, chilies, and lime), steamed dumplings, fish cakes, *khao tom mat sai kluai* (banana and sticky rice steamed in banana leaf)

Drinks: Hot tea, beer, liquor, rice wine, Thai whiskey, spiced Thai iced tea and Thai iced coffee, soymilk, fruit juices

COMMON THAI COOKING TOOLS

Cleaver, wok, steamer, mortar and pestle

THAI FLAVOR FOUNDATIONS

Thai Signature Aromatic Vegetable Combo

Shallots, ginger, galangal, garlic, lemongrass, chilies, and cilantro root

Signature Seasonings

Many of these seasonings are used throughout Southeast Asia.

Liquid/Paste

Nam Pla (Fish Sauce)
See *Vietnam, Signature Seasonings.*

Palm Sugar
Palm sugar is the sap of the coconut palm tree, which is cooked down to crystalline form and used as a sweetener in soups, sauces, and desserts.

FIGURE 3.3 Palm sugar.
Source: phloen/Shutterstock.

Animal

FIGURE 3.4 Shrimp paste.
Source: leungchopan/Fotolia.

Shrimp Paste
Pungent seasoning paste made from ground, salted, and fermented shrimp. Though it smells like long neglected gym socks, when

(Continued)

(Continued)

cooked this flavoring device delivers an exotic salty, smoky flavor. The best fermented salted shrimp pastes come from Thailand. They are known as kapi in Thailand, in Vietnam as mam tom or mam ruoc, and trasi, terasi or belacan in Malaysia and Indonesia. Dry-roast the firm, powerful cake version in a wok or 400 degree F oven wrapped in foil, or fry in oil at the beginning of a stir-fry. The softer shrimp paste is available in a small tub. When in doubt, use less rather than more.

Vegetable/Fruit

FIGURE 3.5   Thai Bird's Eye chilies.
Source: EW CHEE GUAN/Fotolia.

Bird's Eye Chilies
Tiny, hot, red or green chilies used in Southeast Asia.

Coconut
See *Glossary: Asia and India.*

FIGURE 3.6   Galangal.
Source: Dave King/DK Images.

Galangal
Resiny, hot, peppery rhizome used as seasoning. Looks like gingerroot.

Herbal/Spice

FIGURE 3.7   Cilantro.
Source: Reika/Fotolia.

Cilantro
This pungent, soapy, meaty flavored delicate green herb is sometimes mistaken for the tougher and greener Italian parsley.

FIGURE 3.8   Trimmed lemongrass.
Source: Ian O'Leary/DK Images.

Lemongrass
Lemongrass has long, narrow, pale green woody stalks with a tender, bulb-like base. It has a refreshing and delicate, grassy, citrus flavor and scent.

FIGURE 3.9   Fragrant (kaffir) lime.
Source: Ian O'Leary/DK Images.

Lime Leaves (Also known as Kaffir)
See *Vietnam: Signature Seasonings.*

FIGURE 3.10   Thai basil.
Source: Clive Streeter and Patrick McLeavy/DK Images.

Thai Basil (húng qué or rau qué also known as cinnamon basil or horapha)
A variety of basil native to Southeast Asia, Thai basil has narrow leaves (with purple stems) that taste of licorice and cinnamon. It is more heat stable than Italian basil. Thai holy basil (*kaprow*) and Thai lemon basil (*maenglak*) are two other popular varieties used in Southeast Asia.

SLICING CILANTRO

In countries where dishes use a lot of cilantro cooks don't laboriously pick off the leaves and toss away the stems. Instead, the cook takes a bunch of clean, dry cilantro and begins finely slicing from the root end.

Cooks discard the first quarter or half-inch of stems, but from there all the cilantro will be used. Too much chopping renders delicate cilantro into a pasty mush.

SEASONING AND PASTE MIXTURES

GARLICKY THAI CILANTRO PASTE

Peppercorns, galangal, and ginger provided heat before chilies arrived in Thailand. Use this paste to season a stir-fry, curry, rice, or vegetables.

Yields 1/4 cup

1 teaspoon white peppercorns
1/4 ounce cilantro stems, 2 tablespoons finely minced
1 ounce garlic, 4 large cloves, 2 tablespoons peeled and chopped
1 teaspoon to 1 tablespoon canola or rice bran oil

1   Grind peppercorns to powder. Place them with cilantro and garlic into a wet-dry spice grinder, mortar with pestle, or into a blender, and grind or purée until smooth.

2   To facilitate grinding, pour in oil slowly while machine is running.

Source: *Real Thai* by Nancie McDermott.

THAI CURRY PASTE

Thai and Indian curries differ in flavor and ingredients. South India's influence shows in the use of coconut milk and the similarity between Thai curry pastes and South Indian wet masalas. Thai cooks prepare many different types of curry paste, but red and green are the most popular.

- *Yellow* curry paste is the mildest with turmeric and dried chilies. It goes well with vegetables, chicken, and beef.

- *Red* curry paste is hot with fresh red chilies, cilantro roots, galangal, and lemongrass. It pairs well with poultry, eggs, and fish.

- *Green* curry paste is the hottest made with green chilies, cilantro, and spices. It is good with vegetables, poultry, and fish.

- *Jungle* curry paste, from central-northern Thailand, is made with white peppercorns, green chilies, galangal, lemongrass, *krachai* (wild ginger), shallots, shrimp paste, and lots of garlic. It is not tempered with coconut so it is very hot. Traditionally jungle curry is used to prepare wild boar.

FIGURE 3.11 Cayenne chilies.
Source: Dave King/DK Images.

TRADITIONAL THAI CURRY PASTES

Although canned Thai curry pastes are fine, making them fresh gives the cook control over flavor and heat, not to mention the brighter and fresher taste.

*To trim lemongrass: cut away all but the bottom 3 to 4 inches of bulb, peel away dry outside layers, and trim off hard root base.

Red Curry Paste

Yields about 6-1/2 fluid ounces

2 ounces fresh long red chilies, about 4 to 8, stemmed
1-1/2 ounces trimmed lemongrass, about two 4-inch bulbs
1/2 to 1 ounce garlic, 2 large cloves, 1 tablespoon minced
1/4 ounce cilantro roots or stems, 2 tablespoons minced
2 large Kaffir lime leaves, minced
1-1/2 ounces galangal or gingerroot, about 1 inch, 3 tablespoons peeled and chopped
1 teaspoon coriander seed
1 teaspoon cumin seed
1/2 teaspoon white peppercorns
1 teaspoon shrimp paste
1 teaspoon kosher salt

Green Curry Paste

Yields about 4-1/2 fluid ounces

1 ounce jalapeño chili, 1 large stemmed
3/4 to 1 ounce trimmed lemongrass, one 4-inch trimmed bulb
1/4 ounce cilantro stems, 2 tablespoons finely minced
1/2 ounce gingerroot or galangal, 1/2 tablespoon peeled and chopped
3/4 ounce garlic, about 3 medium cloves, 1-1/2 tablespoons peeled and chopped
1/3 ounce shallots, 1 small, peeled
1 teaspoon lime zest, from 1 large lime
1-1/2 teaspoons coriander seed
1/2 teaspoon cumin seed
1/2 teaspoon black peppercorns
2 teaspoons fresh lime juice
1/2 teaspoon shrimp paste
1 teaspoon fish sauce
1/2 teaspoon palm sugar

1 **Collect:** ingredients for either **red** or **green** curry paste. (Seed chilies for less heat.) Chop all fresh ingredients including trimmed lemongrass.

2 **Toast:** coriander, cumin, and peppercorns in a dry sauté pan just until fragrant. Cool and grind to a powder in spice grinder.

3 **Grind:** all ingredients for either **red** or **green** curry paste together in blender or a small wet-dry grinder, or with mortar and pestle, until smooth. Add up to 2 tablespoons water to aid in blending.

4 **Store:** Curry paste will keep for 1 week sealed and refrigerated. To freeze, top paste with oil and seal tightly. Chilies lose their bite the longer they are frozen. Enliven thawed paste with ground fresh chilies.

THAI ROASTED CHILI PASTE (NAM PRIK PAO)

Nam prik is the name Thais give to spicy chili pastes. Similar to Indonesian sambal, nam prik can be prepared in many ways: with minced pork, fish or dried seafood, garlic, fresh or dried chilies, fish sauce, lime juice, tamarind pulp, unripe mango, or nuts. Use nam prik like a salsa: with cooked rice, raw vegetables, omelet, grilled meat, poultry, and seafood or as a dip.

Yields 1-1/3 cups

3 ounces tamarind paste, 1/4 cup plus 2 tablespoons
2 ounces dried red chilies, about 1-1/3 cups stemmed, broken and lightly seeded
1/2 to 3/4 cup canola or vegetable oil
2 ounces shallots, about 4, about 1/2 cup finely sliced
2 ounces garlic, about 8 cloves, 5 to 6 tablespoons peeled and sliced
2 ounces dried shrimp, about 1 cup
1 ounce palm sugar, 2 tablespoons

1 Break tamarind paste up and immerse in 1 cup hot water. Mash tamarind with fingers and soak until it softens into a purée, 15 to 20 minutes. Strain and discard fiber and pits. Reserve tamarind purée-pulp to yield 6 tablespoons thick purée. Set it aside.

2 Heat a wok over moderate heat and dry-toast chilies until they darken and burn in places, 1 to 2 minutes. Move them around to cook evenly, but take care not to inhale. Pour chilies into a bowl to cool.

3 Heat oil in wok over medium to low heat. When hot, toss in shallots and fry until golden. Lower heat if oil begins to smoke. Scoop shallots out with slotted spoon into bowl with chilies.

4 Fry garlic until golden. Scoop garlic into bowl with chilies with slotted spoon.

5 Slide shrimp into hot oil and cook until colored. Transfer to bowl with chilies. Remove wok with oil from heat and reserve.

6 Pour chilies with shallots, garlic, shrimp, palm sugar, and thick tamarind purée into blender or food processor. Grind until smooth. Add up to 1/2 cup water, as necessary, to facilitate grinding and to clean out blender.

7 **Final cooking:** Heat wok with oil over low heat. Pour paste into hot oil and cook until paste darkens to a deep brown and thickens, 4 to 7 minutes. Cool paste. Seal tightly in a jar and refrigerate.

Vary! Improvise!

☞ Use this *nam prik pao* as *tom yum* sauce and stir into *tom yum* noodle soup.

☞ For a less fishy taste, remove or lessen the dried shrimp and increase the shallots.

☞ ***Stir-fried Squid in Thai Roasted Chili Paste (Pla Muek Phat Nam Phrik Phao)***

Slice 1 pound cleaned squid into rings. Stir-fry 2 tablespoons sliced shallot in 2 tablespoons oil until browned. Add squid and stir-fry briefly, 1 to 2 minutes. Pour into serving dish. Reheat wok and add 1 tablespoon oil. Stir-fry 2 teaspoons roasted chili paste and 2 green onions into 1/2-inch lengths until onions are tender, 1 to 2 minutes. Remove wok from heat and stir in shallots and squid. Season with soy sauce to taste. Heat through and scrape into serving bowl. Serve with hot jasmine rice.

THAI (AND VIETNAMESE) ROASTED RICE POWDER

Use this powder as a seasoning or condiment on top of cooked food.

Yields 3-1/2 tablespoons

1-3/4 ounces glutinous white rice, 1/4 cup

1 Select an 8-inch sauté pan (*not* nonstick). It should accommodate rice in one layer. Heat over medium-low and pour in rice. Shaking pan periodically, cook rice until it transforms from white to golden-brown, 8 to 10 minutes.

2 Pour rice onto plate to cool. Grind rice in two batches in clean coffee/spice grinder until its texture resembles sugar.

THAI SKILL AND BALANCE

Chef and author Su Mei-Yu feels that though cooking skill is important to a Thai cook, he or she must also be judged on whether the meal is balanced by flavor, texture, aroma, and an appetizing appearance. Each dish in an ideal Thai meal of five dishes, with "varied amounts of liquid or sauce," must stand on its own *and* in harmony with other dishes.

FIGURE 3.12 Thai dinner.
Source: 29september/Shutterstock.

SAUCE

THAI PEANUT SAUCE

Even Thai cooks use canned red curry paste, but freshly made curry paste makes this sauce bright and full of flavor. Use with satay, as salad dressing or with grilled vegetables or roasted meat.

Yields about 3-3/4 cups

2 ounces tamarind paste, 1/4 cup packed
8 to 9 ounces roasted peanuts, 2 cups
14-ounce can coconut milk
2 tablespoons Thai red curry paste, more to taste
2 to 3 tablespoons fish sauce, more to taste
2 to 2-1/2 ounces palm sugar, 1/4 cup
    or 1/4 cup maple syrup
3 to 4 tablespoons fresh lime juice, about 1 large lime, more to taste

Vary! Improvise!

☞ ***More Flavor:*** *Add 1 tablespoon minced gingerroot, 2 teaspoons minced garlic, and 2 tablespoons minced cilantro stems to curry paste in step 3.*

☞ ***Quick Tamarind:*** *Substitute 1 to 2 teaspoons tamarind concentrate (Tamicon brand from Indian grocers) for tamarind purée. It won't be as fruity-flavored as the block-shaped tamarind paste.*

1 Immerse tamarind paste in 1/2 cup boiling water and set aside 5 to 10 minutes. Knead tamarind until it softens and becomes a purée. Strain to yield at least 3 tablespoons purée; set aside. Discard pits and fiber. Reserve any extra tamarind.

2 Pour roasted peanuts into food processor and pulse-grind until they are finely chopped and begin to clump.

3 Heat coconut milk and curry paste in medium saucepan over medium-low heat and simmer 3 to 4 minutes. Stir in ground peanuts, fish sauce, and sweetener. Bring sauce to a boil and lower heat. Simmer until thickened, 3 to 5 minutes. Stir in lime juice and 3 tablespoons tamarind purée. Simmer 1 minute. Sauce will thicken as it cools. Thin with up to 1/2-cup water and re-season, if necessary, with lime, fish sauce, or more of the extra tamarind.

THAI TAMARIND SAUCE

Serve this big-flavored, multilayered sauce with steamed or deep-fried whole fish or fillets or crusted, pan-fried fillets. See Glossary for more information on tamarind.

Yields about 10 fluid ounces

4 ounces tamarind paste, 1/2 cup, packed
2 tablespoons vegetable oil
1/4 ounce garlic, 1 large clove, 1-1/2 teaspoons peeled and minced
About 1/2 ounce shallot, 2 tablespoons peeled and finely chopped
1-1/2 to 2 ounces ginger, 2 tablespoons peeled and minced
1 tablespoon red or green Thai curry paste, more to taste
1-1/2 ounces palm sugar, 3 tablespoons, more to taste
   or 3 tablespoons maple syrup
2 tablespoons fish sauce
1 ounce trimmed green onions, 2 large, 4 tablespoons finely minced
1/2 ounce cilantro, 1/4 cup finely sliced

1 Break up tamarind paste and place in bowl. Cover with 1-1/2 cups boiling or hot water. Knead tamarind to release the fruity purée. Scrape through mesh strainer to yield 1 cup thick purée; discard pits and fiber.

2 Heat oil in a 2-1/2-quart nonreactive saucepan over medium-low heat. Add garlic, shallot, and ginger. Simmer, taking care not to burn the garlic, until vegetables are soft. Add curry paste and cook 1 minute, mashing into oil so it cooks evenly. Stir in tamarind and bring mixture to a boil. Add palm sugar and fish sauce. Lower heat and simmer sauce 1 to 2 minutes, stirring to mix sugar evenly. Remove sauce from heat and stir in green onions and cilantro. Rest sauce 15 minutes.

3 Taste sauce and adjust flavors if necessary, to balance between salty, sweet, and sour. Call another cook over and gain a tasting consensus. Sauce should coat a spoon. If it thickens too much, thin with water.

4 **To Serve:** Serve sauce at room temperature. (If using on fried fish, garnish platter with sliced cucumbers, tomatoes, and cilantro.)

FIGURE 3.13   Tamarind pod.
Source: Will Heap/DK Images.

SPECIAL METHODS

THAI VEGETARIAN ROLLS

These rolls are made with wheat flour wrappers. Here the wrappers are blanched, filled and eaten. They may also be filled and deep-fried without being blanched.

Yields about 3-1/2 cups filling, enough for 10 spring rolls

Thai Chili Sauce
3/4 to 1 ounce mung bean cellophane vermicelli
10 ounces Savoy cabbage leaves, about 10 medium leaves

> **Seasonings**
> 1 tablespoon soy sauce
> 1 tablespoon oyster sauce or hoisin sauce
> 2 teaspoons palm sugar or maple syrup

2 tablespoons vegetable oil
8 ounces stemmed, fresh shiitake mushrooms, about 3 cups caps sliced
4 ounces carrot, about 2 medium, 1 cup peeled and shredded
About 6 ounces mung bean sprouts, 2 cups, rinsed and drained
8 ounce package 5-1/2-inch by 6-inch square fresh wheat flour egg roll wrappers, 10

1 Prepare *Thai Chili Sauce*.

2 Soak cellophane noodles in hot water till soft, 15 to 20 minutes. Drain and squeeze dry; chop noodles into 1/2-inch lengths; there should be about 1/2 cup. Remove hard stem from cabbage and slice cabbage leaves very finely to yield 5 cups.

3 Mix together **seasonings** in small bowl, and set aside. Heat oil in wok over high heat and stir-fry cabbage and mushrooms until crisp-tender, 5 minutes, adding up to 4 tablespoons water to deglaze, but cook until water evaporates. Lower heat to medium and fold in carrots, cellophane noodles, and **seasonings**. Stir-fry until vegetables are tender, 5 minutes. Fold in mung sprouts and remove pan from heat; toss until sprouts wilt. Scrape filling onto plate to cool. Taste and re-season with salt if necessary.

4 **Set up:** Bring 4-quart saucepan of cold water to boil. Set a bowl of cold water next to the stove with a small strainer nearby. Dampen 2 smooth cotton towels and wring dry. Spread one out on the work surface. Blanch 1 or 2 wrappers at a time in boiling water 1 minute. (Be careful, they tear easily.) Pull out with strainer and drop wrapper into bowl of cold water. Immediately remove with strainer and drain.

5 With fingers, stretch wrapper out flat on damp cotton towel, points facing up and down toward you. Blot top of wrapper dry with second towel if necessary. Place 1/3 cup filling in the center. Spread to form a 4-inch wide log, roll up once, fold and tuck in sides neatly, and finish rolling. Set roll in container seam-side-down. Cover container with plastic wrap. Repeat with remaining wrappers.

6 **To Serve:** Place rolls on platter, and serve with *Thai chili sauce*. To rewarm the rolls, steam 1 minute.

Vary! Improvise!

☞ *Devise an alternative filling with vegetables, seasonings, or vegetarian protein.*

SIMMER, STEW, POACH, BOIL, AND STEAM

Southeast Asian Soup

Southeast Asian soup starts with good broth, infused generously with sinus clearing seasonings. The flavors should ring every taste and sensation bell: savory, salty, sour, sweet, spicy, and pungent. Tender, bite-sized pieces of seafood or meat cook in broth, and a profusion of herbs garnish Southeast Asian soups.

Thai Soup (Tom Yum and Tom Kha)

Two of the best-loved soups of Thailand, *tom yum* and *tom kha*, mirror economical Chinese cooking: they are quick to prepare and deeply satisfying. "Tom" means "to boil"; it signals broth-based soup seasoned with herb and spice paste and a choice of meat, seafood, or vegetables. A great tom yum asserts strong spicy-hot-sour flavor and herbal fragrance. Infuse broth with lemongrass, kaffir lime leaves, galangal, lime juice, fish sauce, and crushed chilies. Prawns, chicken, fish, or mixed seafood are typical, with straw or oyster mushrooms and cilantro leaves as garnish. Tom kha or tom kha gai, with the addition of coconut milk and galangal, is made with chicken. Thai tom yum sauce gives tom yum soup its orange glow.

Signature Technique: Thai Soup

1 Gather ingredients. Prepare or have on hand homemade broth (or water). Cut vegetables into bite-sized pieces. Slice meat thinly and fish or seafood into small chunks so they cook quickly, 2 to 4 minutes.

2 To infuse flavor into broth, simmer seasonings in it 5 to 10 minutes. Water-based soups benefit from a short sauté of flavorings. It softens seasoning vegetables like onion and garlic and releases their flavor. Add whole, bruised, or coarsely pounded lemongrass, ginger, lime leaves, spices, pounded cilantro roots or stems, chili paste, tomato, onion and/or garlic.

3 Add vegetables and meat or seafood and cook until just done. Don't overcook meat or fish; it will become tough.

4 Season soup to taste salty, sour, sweet, and hot with fish sauce, lime juice, palm sugar, and bird's eye chilies or chili paste or sauce.

5 Garnish soup with coconut milk or cream, if using and/or cilantro leaves or other herbs.

THAI HOT AND SOUR SHRIMP SOUP (TOM YUM GOONG)

This classic favorite is from the central and southern regions of Thailand. Broth should be highly seasoned and seafood very fresh.

Yields 7-1/2 cups, 4 to 6 servings

4 cups (to 6 cups, see step 1) fish stock *or* chicken stock
1 pound 26/30 or 41/50 shrimp, peeled and deveined, shells *reserved*
2 teaspoons *Thai Roasted Chili Paste* (nam prik pao)
    or commercial tom yum sauce
6 Kaffir lime leaves, finely sliced
Two 1-ounce (trimmed to bottom 3-inches) stalks lemongrass, smashed
1/2 ounce cilantro stems, 1 heaping tablespoon finely minced
2 tablespoons fish sauce, more to taste
1 teaspoon palm sugar
2 ounces canned straw mushrooms, about 1/3 cup
    or 2 ounces fresh shiitake mushrooms, 1/2 cup finely sliced caps
2 large limes: 3 tablespoons fresh juice and wedges from the rest
1/2 ounce cilantro, 1/4 cup finely sliced
Optional: 1 Thai bird's eye chili, 1/4 teaspoon stemmed and sliced into rounds

1 This step boosts flavor: Bring stock, 2 cups cold water, and shrimp shells to a boil, lower heat, and simmer 10 minutes. Let stock steep and cool 10 to 15 minutes and strain. Discard shrimp shells.

   *If there are no shrimp shells, use 6 cups fish or chicken stock.

2 Mix chili paste, lime leaves, lemongrass, cilantro stems, fish sauce, and sugar with stock. Bring soup to a boil (add fresh mushrooms if using). Simmer 5 minutes. Stir in canned mushrooms, if using, and shrimp. Cover pan and turn off heat. Allow shrimp to cook until opaque, 2 to 3 minutes.

3 **To Serve:** Uncover pan and stir in 3 tablespoons lime juice. Cut remaining limes into wedges. Soup should be decidedly hot and sour, jumping with big flavor. Stir in cilantro leaves and *optional* chili. Serve hot with lime wedges.

Vary! Improvise!

☞ *Devise a vegetarian version of this soup.*

☞ *Substitute poultry or fish for shrimp.*

THAI CHICKEN AND COCONUT SOUP
(TOM KHA GAI)

This soup may be quick to make, but it's full of flavor.

Yields 4 cups, 2 to 4 servings

3 cups chicken stock
2 Kaffir lime leaves, finely sliced
1/2 ounce (trimmed to bottom 3-inches) stalk lemongrass, smashed
1/2 ounce galangal *or* gingerroot, peeled and sliced into thin rounds
4 ounces boneless skinless chicken breast, thinly sliced into 1-inch by 1/2-inch matchsticks
3/4 cup coconut milk, more to taste
1 tablespoon fish sauce, more to taste
2 tablespoons freshly squeezed lime juice, 1/2 large lime, more to taste
1 red Thai bird's eye chili, 1/4 to 1/2 teaspoon sliced into small rounds

Garnish: 1/4 ounce cilantro, 2 tablespoons finely sliced

Vary! Improvise!

Fish or Shrimp-Coconut Soup:
☛ *Use 3 cups fish stock instead of chicken broth and 1/2 pound shrimp, peeled and deveined, or 1/4 pound cubed fish in place of chicken.*

1 In a 4-quart saucepan heat stock, lime leaves, lemongrass, and galangal or ginger over medium heat. Bring to a boil. Lower heat and simmer stock, partially covered 5 to 10 minutes.

2 Lower heat to a bare simmer and add chicken. Cook until meat turns opaque, 1 minute. Remove soup from heat and stir in coconut milk. Season with fish sauce, lime juice, chili and salt until the flavor becomes addictive.

3 **To Serve:** Ladle hot soup into bowls, garnish with cilantro and serve.

FIGURE 3.14   Thai green chicken coconut curry.
Source: Oran Tantapakul/Fotolia.

FIGURE 3.15   Non-coconut pork curry.
Source: wolfmaster13/Fotolia.

Signature Technique: Thai Curry

Thai curry has its roots in Indian curries and Chinese stir-fries. Indian seasonings like coriander and cumin seed are used to prepare the moist Thai curry pastes. They are reminiscent of the southern Indian method of grinding cooked aromatics and spices to form wet masalas. China's influence is in the quick cooking.

- Prepare (or purchase) Thai curry paste.
- Prep a pleasing combination of ingredients with color and texture in mind like shrimp and bok choy or roast duck, pineapple, and tomatoes.
- Meat like chicken thighs with bone-in (but skinless) give a deeper flavor to the dish. Chop meat with bone into bite-sized pieces with a cleaver. Dice flavorful beef like chuck or pork into 1-1/2 to 2-inch cubes.

Coconut-Based Curry Stews

1 Heat coconut oil, vegetable oil, or 1/2 cup coconut cream (scooped from the top of a can of coconut milk) in a nonreactive pan. If using coconut cream, cook over medium heat to reduce it and eliminate liquid. As the coconut cream bubbles and sputters, the water will evaporate and the cream will turn into clear oil.

2 Mash curry paste (and desired additional minced seasonings like ginger, galangal, cilantro roots or stems, or garlic) into fat and cook 1 to 2 minutes. The fat carries the flavor into the dish.

3 Cook meat, tofu, or hard vegetables in paste 2 to 3 minutes to infuse flavor into them.

4 Pour in coconut milk and whole seasonings like smashed lemongrass and lime leaves; simmer until hard vegetables are almost cooked through.

5 Add tender diced vegetables. Simmer curry until vegetables are crisp-tender. Season dish highly with fish sauce, palm sugar, and salt to taste. This is a dish of big contrasts.

6 Garnish Thai curries with finely sliced Thai bird's eye chilies and Thai basil, cilantro leaves, and/or mint. Serve the curry with fluffy jasmine rice.

Non-Coconut Curry Stews

1 Prepare curry paste.

2 *Choose a way to prepare curry:*

Simmer Method

Mix curry paste, soy sauce, or fish sauce and meat, and simmer until meat loses rawness, about 5 minutes. Pour in broth and simmer meat until tender but not falling apart. Stir in seasoning items like shallots, carrots, and lime leaves. Simmer until vegetables are tender. Season curry with fish sauce, tamarind, or lime or palm sugar to taste. Garnish with cilantro and/or Thai basil.

Fry and Simmer Method

Heat oil in skillet or saucepan. Stir-fry curry paste several minutes over medium heat. Stir in bite-size diced or sliced meat and cook until meat is coated in paste and cooked through. Pour in stock and fish sauce, and bring to a boil. Add seasonings like lime leaves and lemongrass, and vegetables of choice. Simmer until meat and vegetables are tender. Season with fish sauce, palm sugar, or lime juice to taste. Garnish with fresh herbs or chilies.

Restaurant Service or Large Crowd Curries

Prepare a curry base ahead: Fry curry paste. Add coconut milk and/or stock and seasonings. Simmer then cool. Steam or blanch each vegetable separately and cool. This will ensure bright green broccoli and green beans and perfectly cooked cauliflower. Marinate meat if desired.

To Serve

Simmer protein in curry base. Add partially cooked vegetables and finish cooking in seasoned hot curry base, garnish and serve.

TWO COCONUT CURRIES

These dishes are from central Thailand, the heartland. Search Chinatown for small, round Thai eggplant and add to the beef curry.

Each yields about 8 cups, 4 to 6 servings

Green Chicken Curry

3 to 4 tablespoons *Green Curry Paste*
16 ounces boneless, skinless chicken breast and thigh meat
8 to 9 ounces trimmed broccoli, 3 cups florets
About 4 ounces cherry tomatoes, half pint, 1 cup halved lengthwise

Red Beef Curry

3 to 4 tablespoons *Red Curry Paste*
16 ounces lean beef
About 1-1/2 pounds butternut squash, 3 cups peeled and diced into 1/2-inch cubes
Optional: 2 ounces cherry tomatoes, 1/2 cup halved lengthwise

1/2 cup coconut cream
   or 2 tablespoons coconut oil
3 cups coconut milk
5 large to 10 small fresh or frozen Kaffir lime leaves

Seasonings

3 tablespoons fish sauce, to taste
1 tablespoon palm sugar *or* maple syrup

Garnish

1/2 ounce cilantro, 1/4 cup finely sliced
   or 1/2 ounce mint or Thai basil leaves, 1/4 cup torn or sliced
Optional: 2 bird's eye chilies, 3/4 teaspoon thinly sliced

For Serving

Cooked jasmine rice

1 Prepare *green or red curry paste.*

2 *Prep meat and vegetables.*

   Green Chicken: *Dice chicken into 1/2-inch cubes. Prepare vegetables.*

   Red Beef: *Slice beef into bite-sized, even, thin strips. Prepare vegetables.*

3 **Reduce coconut cream:** Heat coconut cream or oil in a 6-quart nonreactive pan. If using coconut cream, cook over medium heat to reduce liquid. As the coconut cream bubbles and sputters, globules of clear oil will separate out. Add curry paste and cook 1 to 2 minutes, mashing and melting paste into coconut fat.

4 Add meat (or for vegetarian curries, harder vegetables or tofu) and stir-fry, turning it to coat in the coconut-spice paste mixture. Cook 2 to 3 minutes to infuse flavor.

5 **Simmer curry:** Pour in coconut milk and bring mixture to a simmer; lower the heat if necessary. Add vegetables and lime leaves. Simmer curry until vegetables are almost tender, 4 to 5 minutes. Do not boil coconut milk on high heat; it can separate and become oily. Stir in fish sauce, palm sugar, and salt to taste. Taste. The flavors should pop. This is a dish of big contrasts.

6 **To Serve:** Garnish dish with fresh herb(s) and chilies. Infuse into hot curry 1 minute. Serve immediately with fluffy Jasmine rice.

RUSTIC CURRY STEW (GAENG BAH)

This curry is spicy, but softens when served with rice and other dishes. For more flavor, simmer with a smashed lemongrass stalk and a few lime leaves.

Yields about 4 cups, 4 servings

8 ounces boneless pork or beef
3 tablespoons vegetable oil
3 tablespoons *Red Curry Paste*
2 cups chicken stock
3 tablespoons fish sauce
1 tablespoon palm sugar
3 ounces drained, sliced bamboo shoots, 1/2 cup
7-1/2 to 8 ounces small, round Thai eggplant or regular eggplant, stemmed or 1-1/2 cups stemmed and diced into 1-inch cubes
3-1/2 to 4 ounces green beans, 1 cup stemmed and cut into 2-inch lengths
1/4 ounce Thai basil or basil leaves, torn
1/4 ounce mint leaves, 1/4 cup finely sliced
Optional Garnish: 2 fresh red Thai chilies, 1/2 teaspoon sliced into thin rounds

For Serving

Freshly cooked, hot jasmine rice

1 Slice meat into thin strips measuring about 3/4-inch by 1-1/2-inches to yield 1 cup. Set aside.

2 Heat oil in a 6-quart saucepan over low heat. When oil is hot, stir in curry paste. (If it sizzles and pops, remove briefly from heat.) Mash paste into oil and cook until fragrant, 3 to 4 minutes.

3 Stir in meat and stir-fry until cooked through and coated with curry paste, about 3 minutes. Pour in chicken stock and bring curry to a boil. Stir in fish sauce, sugar, bamboo shoots, and eggplant. When curry boils, reduce heat to a simmer. Simmer eggplant until almost tender, 5 minutes. Stir in green beans and simmer curry until beans are tender, about 7 minutes.

4 Remove pan from heat and stir in herbs; rest curry 5 to 7 minutes. Taste curry, season with fish sauce if desired. Stir in optional chilies or serve on the side for addition at the table.

5 **To Serve:** Serve curry hot or warm with jasmine rice.

Source: *Real Thai* by Nancie McDermott.

Vary! Improvise!

☛ *Make a curry base and vary it with three different combinations of food and seasoning to make three different curries.*

☛ **Quick Curry:** *Fry a spoonful of Thai curry paste in oil, add chicken or shrimp and vegetables and stir-fry until almost done. Pour in coconut milk and simmer; season with fish sauce and cilantro.*

FIGURE 3.16 Tiny Thai Green eggplant.
Source: Will Heap/DK Images.

Vary! Improvise!

☛ **Other Vegetables:** *Substitute summer or winter squash, baby corn, sugar snap peas, snow peas, or carrots and potatoes for the vegetables. Adjust cooking times so the vegetables cook properly.*

THAI STYLE PUMPKIN BRAISED IN COCONUT MILK

This snack food dish straddles the divide between dessert and dinner.

Yields about 3-1/2 to 4 cups, 4 to 6 servings

2 cups coconut milk
1 ounce palm sugar, 2 tablespoons
   or 2 tablespoons maple syrup
1 pound pumpkin, kabocha *or* butternut squash, 3-1/2 to 4 cups peeled and diced
1/2-inch by 1-inch

Garnish

4 tablespoons coconut cream
Optional: Cilantro leaves

1 Heat coconut milk, sweetener, and 1/2 teaspoon salt in 4-quart saucepan over low heat until sweetener melts. Add pumpkin or squash and bring to a boil. Simmer partly covered until tender, about 10 minutes. Don't stir, it'll break up the pumpkin. It should remain whole and tender. Remove pan from heat and taste. Season with more salt or palm sugar, to taste.

2 **To Serve:** Spoon squash and coconut milk into bowls. Drizzle each serving with coconut cream and optional cilantro.

Vary! Improvise!

☞ *Try this dish with other root vegetables.*

TASTE TIP

Don't discard cilantro stems. Turn them into a taste-boosting Thai base: finely mince cilantro stems, shallots, and ginger. Stir-fry this fresh flavor foundation with a spoonful of canned Thai curry paste in place of home-made Thai curry paste for faster, fresh flavor.

Southeast Asian Rice

Like most of Asia, a day in Vietnam, Thailand, and much of Indonesia isn't complete unless diners have eaten rice. Long-grain white rice, long-grain sticky or glutinous rice, short-grain sticky rice, and black glutinous rice are most frequently eaten. Northern Thais eat sticky rice with meals, while the rest of Thailand saves it for dessert and prefers long-grain fragrant rice like nutty jasmine. Vietnamese eat both long and glutinous rice. Grilled, banana leaf-wrapped coconut sticky rice stuffed with finger bananas is a favorite treat in Vietnam and Cambodia. Indonesians favor soft but not mushy rice, and eat both long-grain and sticky rice. For information on cooking long-grain jasmine rice see chapter *India* and the technique for cooking basmati rice, which is similar.

Glutinous Rice

All rice contains two types of starch: *amylose* and *amylopectin*. Differing amounts of these starches determine rice texture and cooking methods. As rice cooks, heat and water penetrate the kernel's outer surface. The rice starch breaks down and absorbs water to form a gel. The type of starch determines whether rice will be fluffy or sticky.

In general, the *shorter* the rice grain, the *higher the amylopectin* (and the glycemic-blood sugar index) and the lower the amylose. Amylose, a long starch molecule, doesn't gelatinize during cooking like amylopectin. Therefore, high-amylose rice like long-grain, Thai jasmine, or Indian basmati, tend to fluff and separate when cooked, harden when cool, but melt when reheated. Medium-grain (risotto-type) rice has both starches, but more amylopectin. Short-grain (sushi) rices have even more amylopectin and less amylose than medium-grain, while glutinous or "sticky" rice has *no amylose*, only amylopectin. It becomes very sticky when cooked, which makes it easier to eat by hand or chopsticks.

Glutinous or waxy rice contains no gluten; the name refers to its glue-like quality. Though glutinous rice is considered low-class (because many eat it with their hands), it is quite popular in parts of Asia and Southeast Asia. Chinese cooks prepare sticky rice dumplings or dim sum style stuffed lotus leaves. Japanese grind glutinous rice into flour or cook and pound it for mochi. Laotians favor glutinous rice as everyday rice while Thai and Vietnamese cooks use it in many sweet and savory dishes. There are two ways to cook glutinous rice: **soak and steam** or **soak and boil**. Soaking and steaming assures the best, chewy texture.

See chapter *China* for instructions on cooking long-grain Thai jasmine or long-grain white rice.

SIGNATURE RECIPE

STEAMED GLUTINOUS (STICKY) RICE

1 pound (2-1/3 cups) short-grain sticky rice **yields about 6 cups cooked rice** *or*
14-ounces (2 cups) short-grain sticky rice **yields about 5-1/4 cups cooked rice**

1 Soak sticky rice in cold water a minimum of 2 hours or up to 8 hours.

2 Drain rice into strainer, and rinse under cold water. Shake off excess water.

3 Set up wok to steam (see chapter *China*). Water should be 1 inch beneath the bottom of the steamer basket. Remove basket from wok. Line steamer basket with a large square, double layer of damp cheesecloth. Allow cheesecloth to hang over steamer edges.

4 Start water in wok boiling. Spread rice (get every grain) into the cheesecloth. Fold excess cheesecloth neatly over the top of rice.

5 Cover steamer, place back on wok, and steam rice 30 to 40 minutes. During this time add boiling water to wok to keep water level up. After 10 to 15 minutes, unfold cheesecloth and give rice a stir with chopsticks to ensure even cooking. Taste to determine doneness; it should be tender and chewy. Fold cheesecloth and cover rice, continue to steam if necessary.

6 When rice is done, it should be shiny, tender, and pleasantly chewy, but cooked through with no hardness. Serve as is or use in another dish. For a treat, mix warm rice with coconut milk. Leave plain at room temperature up to 2 hours and re-steam to serve hot. Fluff with chopsticks.

FIGURE 3.17 Glutinous (sticky) rice.
Source: jreika/Shutterstock.

MANGO ANATOMY 101

All mangoes have a large, flat seed pit that runs parallel to the mango's broadest, rounded, cheeky sides. Cut away a small slice at top and bottom of the mango. Set mango on one flat side onto a cutting board. With a very sharp knife, slice away the peel. Alternately, peel with vegetable peeler. Mangoes are slippery, so be careful. Starting at the top of the peeled mango, cut off one mango "cheek" by feeling the way with the knife flat to the pit and along and down the pit. Turn the other cheek: repeat on remaining side. Place a cheek on its flat side and finely slice into long strips. Keep strips together so they fan attractively.

FIGURE 3.18 Mango.
Source: Andre/Fotolia.

THAI COCONUT STICKY RICE WITH MANGO

4 to 6 servings, debatable

14 ounces glutinous/sticky rice, 2 cups
1-1/2 to 2 cups coconut milk
Finely crushed palm sugar
    or maple syrup
2 pounds ripe mango, 2 large, about 4 cups peeled and sliced (See *Mango Anatomy 101*)

1   Soak and steam sticky rice as in *Signature Technique: Glutinous (Sticky) Rice.*

2   Mix coconut milk, 1/2 teaspoon kosher salt, and palm sugar or maple syrup together to taste. To melt palm sugar, simmer coconut milk and sweetener until sugar melts, but don't boil.

3   Pour hot cooked rice into a bowl and fold half the coconut milk into rice. Cover and let rice sit until coconut milk absorbs fully. Reserve remaining coconut milk.

4   **To Serve:** With a fork, fluff rice and mound individual servings on each plate. Arrange mango slices prettily over rice. Pour reserved sweetened coconut milk over and serve.

HEAVENLY BLACK STICKY RICE

Farmers in southern Thailand grow black sticky rice in patchwork fields. Southern Thais use it mostly for sweet snacks. In Indonesia restaurant menus offer sweetened black sticky rice as a "pudding" drizzled with hot coconut milk. Black glutinous rice, a natural-colored whole-grain rice, is distinctly different than sweet and subtle white sticky rice. It looks like an unevenly colored, purple version of wild rice. Though Southeast Asians use black sticky rice primarily in sweet snacks and desserts, this nutty whole grain makes exotic and chewy rice salads or stir-fries.

FIGURE 3.19   Thai black sticky rice.
Source: Rozmarina/Fotolia.

Signature Technique: Thai Steamed Fish

Thai cooks are the masters of minimalist, big-flavored cooking. Small, whole fish steamed Chinese style, but infused with Thai flavors results in a simple but complex-flavored fish with sauce.

1   **Prepare the fish:** Scale and gut 1-1/2- to 2-pound very fresh fish (per 2 servings) like trout or black bass. Rinse and pat dry.

2   **Pound the seasonings:** In a mortar with a pestle, pound garlic, chilies, cilantro stems or roots, ginger, and green onions or shallots into a coarse paste.

3 **Season the paste:** Stir in fresh lime juice, palm sugar, and fish sauce, and stir into a loose paste.

4 **Score fish deeply:** With a very sharp knife, make diagonal slices on the flanks of the fish. This will allow seasonings to penetrate.

5 **Season fish:** Place fish on heatproof plate. Pour seasoning paste into slits on both sides of fish. When fish goes into steamer, sprinkle on a few tablespoons water, stock, or coconut milk.

6 **Steam fish:** Pour 1 inch of water into a 6-inch-deep hotel pan and bring to a boil. Set a 2-inch-deep perforated pan on top. Set fish on plate inside; there should be adequate space so steamer can move around. Cover plate with a half sheet of parchment to protect against dripping condensation from lid, and cover hotel pan with lid. Steam until fish is cooked through when probed with the tip of a paring knife, 12 to 15 minutes.

7 **Serve:** Transfer fish to serving plate or platter and spoon juice over top. Garnish with lime wedges and cilantro or Thai basil. Serve with jasmine rice.

FIGURE 3.20 Thai steamed fish.
Source: rakratchada/Fotolia.

THAI STEAMED FISH WITH LIME (PLA NEUNG MA NAO)

2 servings

Seasoning Paste

Yields about 1/4 cup

1 ounce garlic, 4 large cloves, peeled and crushed
3/4 to 1 ounce cilantro stems, 2 tablespoons finely sliced
6 to 7 Thai bird's eye, about 1 tablespoon stemmed and sliced
or 1/2 ounce serrano chili, 1 medium
2 tablespoons fresh lime juice, more as needed
2 tablespoons Thai fish sauce
1 tablespoon palm sugar
1/8 teaspoon freshly ground black pepper

1-1/2 to 2 pound trout or other small fish, gutted, scaled, rinsed and patted dry
2 tablespoons fish stock or clam juice

Garnish

1 lime, sliced into thin half moons
Cilantro leaves

For Serving

Hot jasmine rice or sticky rice

1 **Prepare seasoning paste:** Place garlic, cilantro stems, and chilies into mortar and pound into a coarse paste. Stir in lime juice, fish sauce, sugar, and pepper. Ingredients may be pulsed in a small wet-dry processor.

2 **Score and season fish:** Score the flanks of the fish in deep diagonal cuts. Lay fish on heatproof plate. Work soupy paste into fish cuts and cavity.

3 **Steam fish:** Drizzle fish with fish stock or clam juice. Set up steamer and steam fish as directed in *Signature Technique: Thai Steamed Fish.*

4 **To Serve:** Transfer fish and juices to serving platter. Spoon juices over fish. Taste juices and, if necessary, drizzle with more lime juice. Garnish fish with lime slices and cilantro. Serve with hot rice.

Source: Chef Andy Ricker, *Bon Appetit*, January 2012.

POPULAR SOUTHEAST ASIAN GREENS

FIGURE 3.21 Chinese broccoli.
Source: Dorling Kindersley/DK Images.

Chinese broccoli, a hearty, succulent, leafy green, is related to cabbage. It has green clusters of flowering buds (florets) growing on long, thick, leafy stalks. Sweeter than regular broccoli, Chinese broccoli leaves a tangy aftertaste. Leaves, stalks, and florets can be used raw or boiled, steamed, or stir-fried in a wide variety of dishes.

Water spinach or *water convolvulus*, an aquatic green with hollow stems and long and narrow,

FIGURE 3.22 Water spinach.
Source: Clive Streeter and Patrick McLeavy/DK Images.

pale green pointed leaves, grows in the warm, wet climate of Southeast Asia. Related to the morning glory, nutrient-rich water spinach is available in Asian markets May through October. Cooks stir-fry or steam leaves and tender stems, often slipping it into steamed buns, spring rolls, or dumpling fillings.

Bok choy or *pak choi*, a tender, sweet leafy green (from 3 to 12 inches long)

with wide white stalks and deep green leaves, is related to cabbage and mustard greens. *Shanghai bok choy* is pale green all over. The baby size is a delicacy. Bok choy's stems take longer to cook than leaves so they are separated and cooked before the leaves. Baby bok choy stems are tender; many cooks leave the small heads whole. Young leaves and stalks make juicy, sweet raw salads, braise small heads whole and slice mature heads for mixed stir-fries.

FIGURE 3.23 Bok choy.
Source: David Murray/DK Images.

THAI STIR-FRIED CHINESE BROCCOLI

Stir-frying is an ideal way to lock in color, flavor, and nutrients of Asian leafy greens. Blanch vegetables to preserve color, subdue strong flavors, shorten stir-fry time, or to prep ahead.

4 to 6 servings

1 pound Chinese broccoli, about 8 cups florets
2 tablespoons vegetable oil
1 ounce garlic, 2 large cloves, 1 tablespoon peeled and minced
1 tablespoon fermented soybean paste (*dao jiao*)
1 teaspoon palm sugar
1 tablespoon Thai fish sauce

1 **Wash vegetables:** Rinse broccoli in cold water. Make sure to scrub at base where dirt lodges. Discard discolored leaves.

2 **Prep greens and remaining ingredients:** Set up on tray ready to cook. Chop florets and leaves into 2-inch lengths. If stems are tough, peel them; if stems are thick, slice them lengthwise.

Slice stems into 1-1/2-inch lengths.

3 **Stir-fry:** Heat wok or skillet over high heat and swirl in oil. (See chapter *China* for stir-fry technique.) When oil shimmers, stir-fry garlic 30 seconds. Toss in broccoli stems and stir-fry 1 to 2 minutes. Stir in soybean paste, palm sugar, and fish sauce. Stir-fry 30 seconds more. Add florets and 1/2 cup water. Bring to a boil and cover. Steam broccoli until stems are crisp-tender, 3 to 4 minutes and remove lid. Test. Add more water if necessary and continue to steam until broccoli is moist, crisp-tender, and bright green. Taste dish, and adjust seasoning with salt or fish sauce.

4 **To Serve:** Turn greens out onto a platter, piled high, and serve hot or at room temperature.

Vary! Improvise!

☛ *Thai Brussels Sprouts: Create a stir-fry with shaved or halved Brussels sprouts. Brown sliced garlic in oil and set aside. Stir-fry Brussels sprouts in oil, season with oyster sauce, fish sauce, soy sauce, palm sugar, chicken stock, and Thai chilies and boil until sauce reduces and vegetables are crisp-tender. Stir in garlic.*

STIR-FRY, PAN-FRY, AND DEEP-FRY

Signature Technique: Southeast Asian Stir-Fried Noodle Dishes

(Review stir-fry in chapter *China*.)

1 Assemble all ingredients and prepare them:

- Soak rice noodles (for pad Thai) in warm water or rinse fresh noodles.
- If using dried noodles like Chinese egg noodles, boil and rinse with cold water before stir-frying. Leave noodles al dente so they stand up to 1 to 2 minutes stir-frying without falling apart.
- Mince ginger and garlic or other aromatic seasonings.
- Cut, slice, and dice meat and vegetables bite-sized or thinly for quick cooking.
- Arrange prepared ingredients on platter, ready for cooking.

2 Stir-fry ingredients:

- Work in small batches. Fill wok or skillet no more than 1/3 full.
- Add more oil each time, just enough to keep food from sticking, 2 to 4 teaspoons per batch.
- Remove cooked food to large mixing bowl after each batch.

3 Cook food in this order:

- Seasoning paste or aromatic seasoning vegetables like garlic, ginger, onion, and chilies.
- Meat, tofu, or shrimp, to infuse with seasonings.
- Hard vegetables like cabbage, carrots, and celery; cook until crisp-tender. Add a little liquid and cover wok or pan to steam vegetables for a few seconds, if necessary.
- Soft, quick-cooking vegetables like mung bean sprouts, green tops of green onions, and tomatoes.

4 **Add the noodles:** Add enough of a seasoning sauce, stock, or water to keep noodles from sticking. Cook rice or fresh noodles until sauce is absorbed and they taste firm, but tender, 1 to 3 minutes. Heat through cooked noodles or simmer until al dente.

5 **The finish:** Toss stir-fried ingredients into pan or wok with noodles. Heat through and taste. Season dish with salt, pepper, soy sauce, chilies, lime or lemon juice, and herbs or with more of whatever gives the noodle dish its flavor. Make it taste so big and rich that diners must have another bite. Pile noodles onto a platter and garnish with herbs, nuts, fish sauce, chilies, and/or lime wedges.

FIGURE 3.24 Set-up for Thai style stir-fried rice noodles (pad Thai).

FIGURE 3.25 Thai style stir-fried rice noodles (pad Thai).

THAI STIR-FRIED RICE NOODLES (PAD THAI)

Traditional pad Thai ingredients include dried shrimp, seasoned tofu, egg, pickled radish, and garlic chives. This version is unapologetically lush.

Yields about 7 cups, 4 to 6 servings

1 ounce tamarind paste, 2 tablespoons

Seasoning Ingredients

2-1/2 tablespoons fish sauce, more to taste
2-1/2 tablespoons palm sugar *or* maple syrup

8 ounces dried Thai rice stick noodles
5 to 6 ounces Savoy cabbage leaves
2-1/2 to 3 ounces carrots, 1 medium
4 ounces 26/30 shrimp, peeled and deveined
4 tablespoons vegetable oil, as needed
2 large eggs, about 1 cup whisked
1 tablespoon *Thai Red Curry Paste*, more to taste
8 ounces boneless, skinless chicken breast, thinly sliced into ribbons
1 cup chicken stock
1-1/2 ounces trimmed green onions, about 3, 1/2 cup finely sliced
4 ounces mung bean sprouts, about 1-1/2 cups

Garnish

2 ounces roasted peanuts, about 1/4 cup coarsely chopped
or 1/2 cup roasted chopped cashews
1 ounce cilantro, 1/2 cup finely sliced
Lime wedges
Fish sauce

1 **Tamarind:** Soak tamarind paste in 1/2 cup boiling water until very soft, 15 to 20 minutes. Mash tamarind and liquid together to a purée. Push through a fine strainer. Scrape the bottom of strainer to retrieve all the tamarind purée. Discard fiber and seeds remaining in strainer. There should be at least 1/2 cup purée. Mix **seasoning ingredients**, fish sauce, and sweetener with the tamarind purée, and set aside.

2 **Soak noodles:** Cover rice noodles in warm (not hot) water until flexible, 20 minutes; drain. Cut them into smaller lengths if desired, although Thais don't.

3 Remove cabbage leaves from head. Slice each whole leaf in half with the ribs and remove ribs. Stack leaves and finely slice them crosswise into 1/8- to 1/4-inch-wide shreds to yield 2 to 3 cups. Shred or julienne carrots into long, thin lengths to yield about 2/3 cup. Arrange vegetables on a tray, ready for cooking action.

4 **Salt-whisk shrimp:** Pour 1 teaspoon kosher salt over shrimp and stir 1 minute. Rinse, drain, and pat dry. Set shrimp on tray.

5 **Cook egg:** Heat a 10-inch nonstick skillet over medium heat, and swirl in 1 teaspoon oil. Pour in egg and cook until set. Push cooked egg aside so wet egg can run onto the pan and cook, but don't make scrambled egg. When egg is fully cooked, remove it from pan onto a clean cutting board and slice into strips. (Alternatively, cook egg in wok with 1 tablespoon oil.) Set egg on tray with oil, curry paste, chicken, chicken stock, green onions, and sprouts.

6 **Stir-fry curry paste and chicken:** Heat a wok or heavy 11-inch, 6-quart Dutch oven over high heat until hot, and swirl in 2 tablespoons oil. Stir in curry paste and stir-fry, mashing into oil, 30 seconds. Stir in chicken and stir-fry until just cooked through. Transfer chicken to large mixing bowl with slotted spoon and set aside. Deglaze wok or Dutch oven with a little stock or water and scrape into bowl with chicken.

7 **Stir-fry shrimp. Stir-fry cabbage and carrots:** Reheat wok or Dutch oven over high heat, and swirl in 1 tablespoon oil. Stir-fry shrimp until just opaque; transfer to bowl with chicken. Swirl in 1 tablespoon oil and stir-fry cabbage and carrots until fully wilted, about 4 minutes. Transfer to bowl with shrimp and chicken.

8 **Noodles and green onions:** Lower heat to medium under wok or Dutch oven. Stir drained noodles, *seasoning ingredients*, and 1/2 cup chicken broth into cooking vessel, and bring to a boil. Stir and cook noodles gently, but constantly, until just tender, but with some resistance, 2 to 3 minutes. The noodles should absorb the liquid as they cook, leaving moist and slippery but not soupy noodles. Fold in green onions and bean sprouts. If noodles stick to wok, drizzle in more stock or water.

9 **Combine it all:** Fold chicken, shrimp, and vegetables into noodles. If they clump or seem sticky, moisten noodles with remaining stock or just enough water to loosen them.

10 **Last addition:** Fold egg and part of the cilantro gently into noodles. Taste and adjust seasonings.

11 **To Serve:** Mound pad Thai high onto a large platter. Garnish with nuts and remaining cilantro (reserve some for passing at the table). Arrange lime wedges around the edge. Serve with fish sauce and extra cilantro and nuts on the side.

Signature Technique: Southeast Asian Laab or Larb

Part stir-fry and part salad, this highly delicious way of serving meat is much like Indonesian Rendang. Meat is expensive so mincing and seasoning it highly makes it more like a condiment—and it goes further.

- Pre-ground meat isn't suitable for this laab; it produces a mushy texture. Grind or chop the meat from boneless, skinless chicken breasts, trimmed pork loin, or tender steak. Trim away gristle, fat, and tendons from dark meat poultry.
- Stir in roasted rice powder just before meat is fully cooked to thicken, or stir in and use as seasoning.
- Called *laab* in Northeastern Thailand and *larb* in Laos, the Vietnamese make a longer cooked minced version with dark caramel sauce. Scoop larb with vegetables or lettuce leaves or serve with rice.
- Use offal like liver or other meats.
- Stir in sriracha or other chili sauce at the end for a wetter laab/larb.

Vary! Improvise!

☞ *Cilantro Aversion: Substitute mint or Thai basil for cilantro.*

☞ *Peanut Allergy: Substitute toasted cashews, sesame seeds, or pumpkin seeds.*

☞ *No Curry Paste: Substitute an equal amount of Chinese chili paste with garlic.*

FIGURE 3.26 Thai larb.
Source: surut/Fotolia.

THAI STIR-FRIED MINCED MEAT "SALAD"
(LAAB OR LARB)

In Northeastern Thailand, classic laab is made with finely chopped grilled (medium-rare) sirloin, and shredded duck breast, roast chicken, turkey, or grilled fish also show up. To make an authentic-tasting laab, season it to eye-popping strength with lime juice, fish sauce, roasted rice powder, chilies, and lots of herbs.

Yields about 3-1/4 to 3-1/2 cups, 4 to 6 servings

1-1/2 pounds trimmed pork
    or 1-1/2 pounds boneless, skinless chicken breast
2 tablespoons freshly squeezed lime juice
2 tablespoons fish sauce
4 to 5 teaspoons fragrant coconut *or* vegetable oil

Aromatic Vegetables

1-1/2 to 2 ounces shallots, 3 to 4 small, 1/3 cup finely minced
1/2 to 3/4 ounces garlic, 2 to 3 large cloves, 3 to 4-1/2 teaspoons minced
1/4 to 1/2 ounce bird's eye chilies, 3 to 6 chilies, 2 to 4 teaspoons stemmed and sliced
1 ounce gingerroot, 2 tablespoons peeled and minced
Optional: Zest of 1 lime *or* lemon

1 tablespoon *Roasted Rice Powder*
3 tablespoons freshly squeezed lime juice
1 tablespoon palm sugar *or* maple syrup

Garnishes

1 ounce trimmed cilantro, 1/2 cup coarsely chopped leaves and finely chopped stems
1/8 ounce torn mint leaves, about 1/4 cup
    or instead of cilantro and mint, 1/2 ounce Thai basil leaves, 1 cup torn

For Serving

Steamed sticky or jasmine rice
Lettuce leaves
Roasted Rice Powder

1 **The meat:** Dice pork or chicken into even 1-inch cubes and pour into food processor with lime juice and fish sauce. About 30 to 35 one-second pulses should take meat down to 1/8-inch pieces.

2 *Cook aromatic vegetables:* Heat oil in 11-inch skillet and cook **aromatic vegetables** over medium heat until tender, golden, and sizzling, 1 to 2 minutes. Add meat and cook, breaking it up with a spoon, until slightly pink, 3 to 4 minutes. Season meat with roasted rice powder, lime juice, and palm sugar and cook until slightly thickened, about 1 minute.

3 **Put It Together:** Toss meat into serving bowl with **garnishes**. Taste and re-season meat with salt, fish sauce, chili, palm sugar, or fresh lime juice.

4 **To Serve:** Serve larb with cooked long-grain or sticky rice or scoop into lettuce leaves. Garnish with more roasted rice powder if desired.

Vary! Improvise!

☞ *Higher Calling:* Season larb additionally with oyster sauce or chili sauce like sriracha.

☞ *Veggie It Up:* Devise a vegetarian laab or larb.

☞ *Fish or Meat Larb:* Prepare a laab/larb with boneless, skinned fish. Or sirloin or duck breast.

☞ *Translate laab into party finger food.*

☞ *Another Larb:* Finely dice grilled or roasted meat or fish and toss with cooked or uncooked aromatic vegetables, seasonings, and garnishes.

GRILL, GRIDDLE, ROAST, BROIL, AND BARBECUE

THAI GRILLED SKEWERS (SATAY)

Though many cooks think satay originated in Thailand, evidence shows that it was more likely from Java, Indonesia. See Signature Technique: Indonesian Saté for more information.

Yields 8 to 10 fluid ounces, enough for 1-1/2 pounds protein, about 30 to 40 skewers

1 teaspoon whole white peppercorns
1 teaspoon cumin seed
1 teaspoon coriander seed
1 teaspoon ground turmeric
1 cup thick canned coconut milk
1/2 ounce gingerroot, 1 tablespoon peeled and minced
1 ounce (bottom bulb trimmed to 3-inches) lemongrass, almost 3 tablespoons finely minced
   or 2 tablespoons minced lemon zest
2 tablespoons fish sauce
1-1/2 pounds boneless, skinless chicken breast
   or 1-1/2 pounds boneless country ribs or pork loin
     or 1-1/2 pounds trimmed sirloin steak
      or 2 pounds 16/20 or 21/25 shrimp
Lime wedges
Thai Peanut Sauce

FIGURE 3.27 Grilling meat satay.
Source: jiggo/Fotolia.

1 Pan roast whole spices separately until fragrant and 1 shade darker. Cool and grind to powder in clean coffee or spice grinder. Mix together with remaining ingredients.

2 **Prepare chicken, pork, or beef:** Meat must be cut so that it will cook quickly over hot coals. For Thai satay, slice meat into long, thin strips about 1-inch by 4-inches. For shrimp: With scissors, cut open the backs of each shrimp along the vein. Leave shell on, but devein shrimp.

3 **Marinate:** Toss meat or shrimp into bowl with coconut-spice mixture. Marinate meat 1 hour at room temperature. Marinate shrimp or chunks of fish or seafood 15 minutes in refrigerator.

   Chicken, pork, and beef can marinate overnight in refrigerator. Zipper baggies allow easy turning in the marinade.

4 Metal skewers are better, but bamboo is common. If using, soak bamboo skewers in warm water, 20 to 30 minutes. Preheat grill. Remove refrigerated meat or seafood, and bring to room temperature.

5 Thread meat onto bamboo or metal skewers. Thread shrimp tightly so they look as if they're "spooning" with backs nestled to feet. Shake off excess marinade. Grill meat skewers until meat is crispy on the edges and tender on the inside—pork should not be overcooked, and beef may be left pink inside. Grill shrimp until just opaque.

6 **To Serve:** Plate or platter meat or shrimp satay and serve with lime wedges and *Thai Peanut Sauce*.

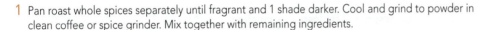

SALAD AND VEGETABLE METHODS

Thai Salads (Yum or Yam)

These hot and sour salads are close to Thai hearts. *Yums* (or *yam*) are a hand-tossed mixture of cooked or raw fruits and/or vegetables and herbs, often with meat or seafood. The dressing is sweet-sour-salty-hot and spicy—the balance makes each dish different. The classic yum salad is sliced grilled beef, but catfish, cucumber, mango, and *laab* salads are popular. Thais serve yums with drinks or as a predinner appetizer.

FIGURE 3.28 Vegetarian yum mushroom salad.
Source: meaothai/Fotolia.

THAI YUM SALAD DRESSINGS

Each dressing yields 1 cup, about 4 servings

Yum Dressing One: Earthy, Creamy, and Spicy

Good with mushrooms, jicama, zucchini blossoms, pea shoots, green mango, star fruit, pineapple, squid, chicken, or pork.

2 tablespoons thick tamarind purée made from 1-ounce tamarind paste
(2 tablespoons)
2 tablespoons fish sauce
1-1/4 ounce palm sugar, 2-1/2 tablespoons crushed
1 ounce sugar, 2 tablespoons
1/4 to 1/2 teaspoon sea salt

4 tablespoons freshly squeezed lime juice
1/4 cup unsweetened coconut cream
1 teaspoon *Thai Roasted Chili Paste-Sauce*, more to taste

Yum Dressing Two: Light, Sweet, Sour, Salty, and Spicy

Good with pork, shrimp, chicken, hard-boiled eggs, spinach, mung sprouts, mushrooms, green beans, lettuce, tomato, cucumber, bamboo shoots, or mung noodles.

1/4 cup fish sauce
2 ounces sugar, 1/4 cup
1 ounce palm sugar, 2 tablespoons crushed
1 teaspoon kosher salt
2 tablespoons rice vinegar
1/2 cup freshly squeezed lime juice, about 2 large limes
1/2 ounce cilantro stems, 1 tablespoon finely minced
2 to 3 bird's eye chilies, 3/4 to 1 teaspoon stemmed and finely sliced

Garnishing Ingredients

Crispy Shallots
Roasted Rice Powder
Dried shrimp
Roasted peanuts or cashews
Toasted unsweetened coconut flakes
Herbs like cilantro, Thai basil or mint

1 For **Dressing One**, soak tamarind paste and 1/4 cup hot water. Knead 3 to 5 minutes. When liquid thickens to a purée, push through strainer to yield at least 2 tablespoons. Set aside extra.

2 **Prepare Dressings:** Taste, and adjust to hot, sour, sweet, and salty. Dressings should be intense-tasting:

Dressing One

Combine 2 tablespoons strained tamarind purée, fish sauce, sugars, and salt in saucepan over low heat. Simmer until dissolved. Remove from heat and cool. Stir in lime juice, coconut, and chili paste-sauce.

Dressing Two

Combine fish sauce, sugars, and salt in saucepan over low heat. Simmer until dissolved. Remove from heat and cool. Stir in rice vinegar, lime juice, cilantro, and chilies.

3 **For a Salad:** Choose fresh herbs, blanched or raw vegetables, fruit, and greens and/or cooked protein. Contrast flavors, colors, and textures. Thinly slice produce to maximize and harmonize flavor. Be creative, but keep the ingredients simple. Try these traditional yum salad combos:

- Shrimp, toasted unsweetened coconut, unripe mango, blanched but crisp green beans
- Squid rings, green onion, chilies, lime, tomato, Thai basil, cilantro
- Chicken, raw, shredded cabbage and carrots, shallot, mint, roasted peanuts
- Grilled chicken, crispy shallots, unripe mango, roasted peanuts or cashews, mint
- Grilled or roast pork, shallots, cilantro, mint, *Roasted Rice Powder*, raw cabbage
- Grilled beef, grilled eggplant, cherry tomatoes, shallots, mint
- Grilled fish, minced ginger, shallots, Napa cabbage, toasted coconut, peanuts, cilantro

4 **To Serve:** Toss salad ingredients with a **dressing** or pile high on platter and drizzle with a **dressing**. Garnish with a choice of **garnishing ingredients**.

Source: *Cracking the Coconut* by Su-Mei Yu.

THAI HOT AND SOUR SHRIMP SALAD (YUM GKOONG)

Make this salad with sea bass, squid, scallops, shelled mussels, clams, firm fish, or a combination of seafood. Just-cooked warm seafood absorbs flavors better than chilled.

Yields about 2 cups, 2 servings

---

16 ounces 26/30 shrimp, peeled and deveined
    or 2 cups peeled and deveined, cooked shrimp
1/2 cup *Yum Dressing Two*
1 ounce 4-inch trimmed bottom bulb lemongrass
1/2 ounce shallot, 1 small peeled halved lengthwise and sliced thinly crosswise
1/4 ounce cilantro leaves, 1 to 2 tablespoons finely sliced
    or 1/4 ounce *culantro* (sawleaf herb)
1/2 ounce mint leaves, 4 tablespoons coarsely chopped

Garnish: mint leaves

1 Shell, butterfly, and devein shrimp. Dissolve 1 tablespoon sea salt in 1/2 cup cold water and soak shrimp 2 minutes for a quick brining. Rinse thoroughly and drain. Steam shrimp 1 minute, turn off heat, and check after 1 and 2 minutes. Shrimp should be fully opaque, but still juicy and tender.

2 Prepare *Yum Dressing Two*.

3 Trim off and discard woody bottom tip of lemongrass and 2 to 3 fibrous outer layers. Slice stalk from bottom end into 3 tablespoons razor thin rounds. Mince, grind in wet-dry grinder or processor, or pound in mortar with shallots, cilantro or culantro and mint leaves until very smooth. Mix with *Yum Dressing Two*. Taste and adjust flavors.

4 **To Serve:** Toss warm shrimp with *Yum Dressing Two*. Taste and adjust seasonings. Pile on serving plates and garnish with mint leaves.

PAPAYA'S LIGHT AND DARK SIDE

Cut into a ripe papaya: its sunny, soft, garish orange-pink flesh beckons. Bite into the flesh. Christopher Columbus reputedly called papaya "the fruit of the angels" because of its sweet, mild, musky flavor and buttery-luscious texture. Ripe papaya offers a rich array of antioxidant nutrients and for skin, joint, spleen, lung, cardiovascular, colon, and eyes. Unripe papaya is high in *papain*, a potent protein-digesting enzyme—it can digest up to 200 times its weight in protein. Green papaya is used not only as a digestive aid and meat tenderizer, but also as a remedy for jellyfish bite, acne, and ruptured discs. Pregnant women should avoid it; too much can cause miscarriage.

FIGURE 3.29 Green papaya.
Source: sommai/Fotolia.

Signature Technique: Sour-Pounded Thai Salad (Som Tum)

The classic som tum (sour-pounded) made with green papaya is the most beloved dish among Thai women. The two most popular versions use either dried shrimp or salted crab. Green papaya salad with dried shrimp and peanuts is called som tum Thai. Green papaya salad with salted crab is called som tum pbooh. This salad highlights the four main tastes of Thai cuisine: lime-sour, chili-spicy, fish sauce-salty, and palm sugar-sweet.

Garlic, shrimp paste, wing beans, long beans, tomatoes, brined crabs, fried shallots, cucumber, shredded carrot, and tamarind also find their way into som tum. Unripe mango makes a particularly delicious, resiny-fruity substitute for the bland papaya. Substitute green beans, snow peas, or shredded cabbage for long beans. The taste-astonishing som tum may be served with steamed sticky rice and barbecued chicken, with rice noodles and other salads or raw vegetables or alone with pork rinds.

1 **Crush seasonings into paste:** Place garlic, chilies, dried seafood, and palm sugar into a large mortar or stainless steel bowl and pound with a pestle.

2 **Cut and shred vegetables and fruits:** Choose a simple, but creative combination of fruit and vegetables for the salad. Cut them into manageable sizes: Slice long beans or green beans into 1–2-inch lengths. Shred peeled papaya or green mango or cabbage leaves into long lengths. Peel, seed, and cut cucumber into long, narrow julienne. Halve cherry tomatoes. *Optional blanch:* Although not traditional, the green beans may be blanched in boiling water 20 seconds to heighten color.

3 **Pound the produce into the paste:** Beginning with the hardest and moving to the softest, add produce to the mortar to infuse flavor. Lightly crush and bruise long or green beans, unripe shredded papaya or mango, cabbage, cucumber, and cherry (or quartered) tomato.

4 **Season and stir:** Stir in lime juice, fish sauce, and herbs. Fold all ingredients together so salad is evenly flavored. Marinate 10 minutes before serving. Taste and adjust flavors. Fold in nuts before serving.

HOW TO SHRED A LARGE GREEN PAPAYA

The large, unripe papaya with pale white or green flesh is about texture. It forms a bland, crisp backdrop for a robust, stinging play of flavors and textures. Peel papaya with vegetable peeler. Slice away stem-top for a flat spot. Lay papaya onto one side. Chop lightly lengthwise on entire side of papaya forming lots of strips or lines. Then, stand papaya on the flat-cut stem and thinly slice down on the long lines of chopped papaya. This will form long, thin spaghetti-like shreds of green papaya. Repeat. Turn papaya and keep chopping and slicing. Or use a wavy-edged vegetable peeler-shredder.

FIGURE 3.30   Cutting green papaya for Thai green (Som Tum Thai).

FIGURE 3.31 Thai green papaya salad.

THAI GREEN PAPAYA SALAD (SOM TUM THAI)

The dressing is the star of som tum—it infuses crunchy papaya with bold flavor. The proportions of the dressing may be varied to taste.

Yields about 7 cups, 4 to 6 servings

Spice Paste

1/4 ounce, 1 large clove (mild) to 1 ounce, 4 large cloves (traditional) garlic, 1-1/2 teaspoons to 2 tablespoons peeled and coarsely chopped garlic
3 (mild) to 8 (traditional) bird's eye chilies, stemmed and sliced into rounds
2 teaspoons small dried shrimp
1 ounce palm sugar, 2 tablespoons, more to taste

Vegetables

8 ounces green beans *or* long beans cut into 1-1/2-inch lengths
2 to 2-1/2 pounds firm, unripe green papaya, 1 medium–large, 4 cups peeled and slivered
4 ounces cherry tomatoes, 1/2 pint, 3/4 to 1 cup halved

Seasonings

1/4 to 3/4 cup freshly squeezed lime juice, 3 to 4 limes
3 tablespoons fish sauce
1/4 to 1/2 ounce cilantro, 4 tablespoons finely sliced
Optional: 1/8 ounce mint or basil leaves, 2 tablespoons torn

Garnish

3 ounces chopped unsalted dry-roasted peanuts, about 1/2 cup
    or 3 ounces unsalted lightly chopped dry roasted cashews, about 1/2 cup

For Serving

Steamed sticky or long-grain white rice

1. *Prepare* spice paste: Grind and pound garlic and chilies together in large mortar or stainless steel mixing bowl with pestle until they form a paste. Add dried shrimp and palm sugar and grind to incorporate into a paste.

2. In a large mortar (in batches) or large mixing bowl, lightly bruise and pound **vegetables** to infuse spice paste into them: Add beans and pound lightly—enough to bruise, but not enough to turn them to mush. Add shredded green papaya to mortar or bowl. Toss well with seasonings and lightly pound to bruise papaya until is tender, but not mushy. Add tomato and optional herbs; stir and bruise lightly to blend.

3. *Toss salad with seasonings:* Stir lime juice, fish sauce, and cilantro into **vegetables**, to taste. Mint and basil are optional. Rest salad at room temperature 10 to 15 minutes to develop flavor. Taste salad and adjust as needed with more fish sauce, lime juice, or palm sugar. Som tum should be hot and sour with a delicate sweetness.

4. **To Serve:** Pile salad high on a serving plate and **garnish** with nuts. Serve immediately with warm rice, which forms the cooling element.

PICKLE AND PRESERVE

Asian Pickles

Asians don't process pickles as in the West. Instead, cooks make small batches of quick vinegar-based pickles and consume them within a few weeks—after that they take on a really sour kick. These crunchy, bright-flavored bites add digestive tang and texture to salads, summer rolls, and sandwiches. Top a creamy soup with diced pickles or pair with grilled meat, poultry, or fish to cut through fat. Brines with citrus or vinegar, salt, and sugar and spices are common. Southeast Asians like their pickled foods crunchy, spicy, and sweet.

SIGNATURE RECIPE

QUICK ASIAN PICKLES

Always use kosher salt. Iodine darkens pickles over time and anti-caking chemicals cloud them. Vinegar and citrus juice add flavor but also inhibit bacteria. Many Asians use white distilled vinegar (5% acidity) for pickling. It is sour and slightly metallic tasting so more sugar will be needed to balance it. Rice vinegar (4.3% acidity), which is milder and less acidic, requires less—or no—sugar. Let taste be the judge. Use these proportions as a jumping-off point and change them to suit personal tastes and needs. Organization and sanitation are keys to good pickles.
Each yields 16 ounces brine, enough for 1-1/2 to 2 quarts of pickles.

Typical Brine Proportions

White Vinegar Brine

8 fluid ounces white vinegar
8 fluid ounces water
4 tablespoons sugar
1 to 2 teaspoons kosher salt

Rice Vinegar Brine

10 fluid ounces rice vinegar
6 fluid ounces water
3 tablespoons sugar
1 teaspoon kosher salt

1 Heat water and vinegar in stainless-steel saucepan and mix in sugar and salt until dissolved. Set aside. Avoid the use of acid- or salt-reactive containers or utensils made of copper, iron, zinc, or brass.

2 Choose vegetables that are super-fresh and blemish-free for best results. Old, tired vegetables will make worn-out pickles.

- Wash, peel, seed, or stem vegetables.

- Cut off cucumber ends: the blossom end releases cuke-softening enzymes.

- Slice, dice, julienne, or cut vegetables into matchstick or bite-sized pieces. The smaller you cut or shred vegetables, the quicker they'll pickle.

- For extra crunch, toss vegetables with kosher salt for 30 minutes to 1 hour. Rinse, drain, press out liquid, and proceed.

3 Bring vinegar brine to a boil. Tightly pack vegetables into sterilized glass canning jars and pour boiling hot brine over them. Cool and screw on lid tightly.

4 **To Serve:** Rest pickle 1 hour before serving, or refrigerate and consume in up to 4 weeks.

THAI PICKLED GARLIC OR SHALLOTS (KRATIEM DONG OR HOM DONG)

Serve these as garnish or condiment, or chop for use in sauce, soup, or stew.

Yields 1 pint

12 ounces garlic cloves *or* shallots, about 3 cups
1/2 cup rice vinegar
1 tablespoon kosher salt
1-1/2 ounces cane sugar or palm sugar, 3 tablespoons
2 small red chilies *or* bird's eye chilies, stemmed and halved lengthwise
Optional: 1 stalk lemongrass, bottom bulb trimmed to 4 inches and bruised

1 Blanch garlic cloves or shallots briefly to loosen skins. Drain and peel. Trim root end, but leave most of the root intact on shallots to hold them together. Slice large shallots in half through root ends. Toss vegetables with 1 tablespoon kosher salt and refrigerate overnight. Rinse, drain, and pat dry before proceeding.

2 Heat vinegar, salt, sugar, and 1/2 cup water together. Simmer until salt and sugar dissolve, 1 minute. Add peeled garlic cloves or shallots, chili, and optional lemongrass, bring liquid to a boil and remove from heat.

3 Transfer vegetables to sterilized pint canning jar. Pour hot liquid over to cover. Cool then cover jar tightly. Store in refrigerator 5 days to develop flavor before using. Will keep refrigerated up to 6 months.

VIETNAM: ACCOMMODATION, ACCULTURATION, AND ADAPTATION

Vietnam: More Than Rice Paddies and Peasants

Rafael Steinberg, writing for Time-Life Pacific and Southeast Asian Cooking, *points out that though many Americans think of Vietnam as "jungle villages, rice paddies and pajamaed peasants caught up in the vortex of catastrophe," it is much more. Indeed, Vietnam is a country with a more than two millennia-old culture, language, and identity, a university established before any in Europe and inhabitants to whom religion, food, and art are deeply important.*

Historians maintain that nomadic tribes of Chinese Mongols and Indonesian immigrants were Vietnam's first ancestors. China ruled an ancient Vietnam, half its modern size, from 111 BCE for more than a thousand years. China's huge influence brought political, bureaucratic, and culinary skills (mainly Cantonese), written and spoken language, and social and spiritual beliefs.

The first Europeans to visit Vietnam were the Portuguese in the early nineteenth century, but by mid-century France began to take control with a brutal, repressive colonial regime. The Japanese set up military bases in Vietnam during World War II, but by 1945 the northern Communist Vietnamese overthrew both Japanese and French rule.

Vietnam was cut in half: the north was strongly communist with Chinese and Soviet backing while the south had anti-communist American and French support. In 1946 France invaded Vietnam again, but in 1954 Communists finally ejected France and a century of their colonial rule. The Communist north tried to forcibly reunify Vietnam, leading to full-scale American intervention in the early 1960s, and the Vietnam War.

South Vietnam surrendered in 1975. Almost two decades of Communist political repression and near famine followed, causing a massive exodus from Vietnam. In 1986 Communist reforms revived agriculture and the vibrant Vietnamese cuisine. Vietnam began to emerge from centuries of wars, devastation, and deprivation. Today economists are optimistic that Vietnam may be among the fastest growing of emerging economies.

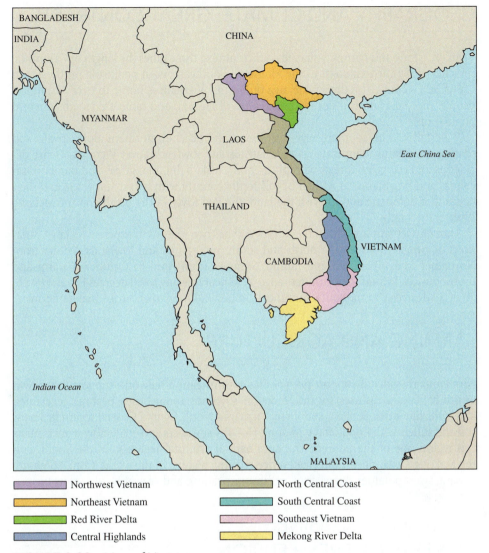

FIGURE 3.32 Map of Vietnam.

Legend:
- Northwest Vietnam
- Northeast Vietnam
- Red River Delta
- Central Highlands
- North Central Coast
- South Central Coast
- Southeast Vietnam
- Mekong River Delta

VIETNAMESE LANGUAGE, PHILOSOPHY, AND RELIGION

Vietnamese is Vietnam's official language. Many words are borrowed from Cantonese and it is interspersed with French words. After the French occupation, the written form of Vietnamese changed from a Chinese system to an adapted version of the Latin alphabet.

Though most Vietnamese consider themselves nonreligious, they do visit temples yearly, and honor ancestors and heroes. Their philosophy and conduct stem from the early religions of Mahayana Buddhism, Confucianism, and Taoism. Roman Catholicism, Cao Dai, and Hoa Hao claim large minorities. Hinduism, Islam, Protestantism, and Theravada Buddhism claim small minorities. Like the Chinese, clan and family guide Vietnamese society, and scholars are highly regarded.

GEOGRAPHY AND CLIMATE: GREAT CONTRASTS

Vietnam, a long and narrow S-shaped country almost three times the length of California, stretches along the east coast of the Mainland Southeast Asian peninsula on the South China Sea. About twice the square area of Florida, Vietnam is home to over 85 million people, more than four times the population of Florida, and ranks thirteenth in world population.

Waterfalls, caves, southern lagoons, dunes, and beaches, northern alpine peaks and soaring mountains, temperate central plateaus and lowlands cover Vietnam. Dense deciduous and evergreen forests with pine, ebony, teak, palm, mangrove, and bamboo, savannas and brushland carpet half of this fertile country with two major rivers and their deltas that dominate and nourish the land: the Red River in the north and the Mekong River in the south.

Though Vietnam lies within the tropics and has two seasons, it experiences large variations in climate between the north and south, mountains and lowlands. Winter from November to April is cold and humid. Summer from April to October is warm and monsoon-wet. Winter temperatures range from near freezing to 60 degrees F in the north, 70 to 80 degrees F in the south. Summer is hotter and rainy with occasional typhoons.

FARMING AND AGRICULTURE

Numerous river deltas support rice paddies. Vast irrigation networks support the growth of rice, coffee, tea, cashews, sugarcane, cotton, soybeans, mung beans, peanuts, vegetables, and fruits like citrus, longan, and litchi. Vietnam's North Central Coastal region has poor soil and suffers with floods and typhoons. Hot, dry summers and cold, rainy winters make this region one of the poorest. The dominant agricultural region is in the South with the Mekong Delta, one of the greatest rice-growing regions in the world. Corn, sorghum, cassava, sweet potatoes, beans, fruit, sugarcane, peanuts, and vegetables also grow there.

VIETNAMESE CUISINE: MASTERS OF FRESH FUSION

Vietnamese cuisine is a meeting of two of the world's greatest cuisines: Chinese and French. It has resulted in a skilled, refined, subtle, highly flavorful and intelligently prepared cuisine that is uniquely its own. Though Vietnamese cuisine's ancient roots are fully Chinese, the lavish use of fine fish sauce and raw aromatic herbs, the spare use of fat and the astonishing range of vegetarian and nonvegetarian food made with fresh produce, beef, pork, chicken, and seafood sets this light and refreshing cuisine apart from any other in Asia.

From the Chinese, Vietnamese cooks learned skilled cooking methods like stir-frying, deep-frying, boiling, and steaming, the use of chopsticks, and how to prepare noodles, soups, and spring rolls. Twelfth-century Mongol raids brought beef. Khmers influenced the central imperial and southern cuisine, and introduced spices from India. French colonialism brought the use of shallots, baked goods, and baguettes (for *banh mi* sandwiches), crème caramel made with coconut, a version of café au lait made with sweet condensed milk, paté, artichokes, and asparagus and refined cooking techniques.

Like the Chinese, Vietnamese cooks don't employ complicated techniques or long cooking. Instead they rely on the freshest ingredients available daily in the market or garden, and flavor layering to achieve satisfaction. Cilantro, *culantro*, mints, basils, *perilla* leaf, *laksa* leaf, and many other herbs provide signature fragrance and freshness to the popular *goi cuon* (pork and shrimp wrapped in lettuce and soft rice paper), *pho* (thick soup of meat, rice noodles, and vegetables), *banh xeo* (sizzling rice flour crepes with seafood and vegetables) and *bun rieu*, (rich crab noodle soup). Vietnam has surpassed her former masters: Each bite is a feast of contrasting sweet, sour, salty, spicy, crunchy, smooth, fresh, pungent, aromatic, and more.

REGIONAL VIETNAM

1. **North Vietnam: Spare and Simple**

   The cuisine of the harsh, mountainous, cooler north shares similarities with its near neighbor, China. The north, unlike the rest of Vietnam, has four seasons, which often determine what food is available. Wartime suffering and lack of means have made this the poorest region of Vietnam, though its Red River delta is a fertile rice-growing region. Hanoi is the principal city. The north's traditional cuisine is milder, simpler, and more spare than the rest of Vietnam, with black pepper, soy sauce, plain sticky rice, beef, snails, corn, grilled fish and pork, *pho* noodle soups, rice pancakes, and rice noodle dishes.

2. **Central Vietnam: Creative, Refined, and Confident**

   The central region of Vietnam was the seat of its ruling dynasty and may have the most culturally authentic food. This region housed the Imperial kitchens of Hué. The lack of agricultural diversity inspired royal cooks to develop their creativity. They refined peasant food with presentation and sophisticated culinary skills turning simple food into a complex, confident, striking cuisine. Central food is spicier than in the south with rice noodles, steamed rice pancakes with shrimp, grilled rice cake with prawns, the famous *bun bo Hue* (thick, round rice noodles in a spicy lemongrass and red chili-flavored broth), and *chao tôm* (shrimp mousse mounded around sugarcane).

3. **South Vietnam: Vibrant and Robust**

   Vietnam's southern Mekong Delta region is a fertile rice and produce-growing area. Ho Chi Minh City (Saigon) is the principal city. This cuisine, open to foreign flavors, is varied, vibrant, robust, and generously seasoned with garlic, shallots, spices, and fresh herbs. It shows influences from nearby Thai and Cambodian cuisines. Southern food tends towards spicy-sweet. Seafood, fresh fruit and vegetables, mussels and rice, fried sticky rice balls with chicken, claypot fish, and fried salted and spiced crabs are popular.

DINE AT HOME IN VIETNAM

At a Vietnamese home, whether to a city apartment or country village compound, remove shoes at the door and hand the hosts a gift of food: cookies, pickles, mangoes, flowers, incense, or something from the garden. Important guests and the elders will face the door, the seat of honor, and eat first. In the north it's common for families to bow to "mother" and allow her the first bite. The entire meal will be in the center of the table. A typical meal will include individual bowls of rice; a communal offering of meat, fish, or seafood; stir-fried, raw, pickled, or steamed vegetables; *canh* (clear broth with vegetables and meat or seafood); and garlic, chili, ginger, or lime juice-spiked fish sauce and/or soy sauce for dipping. Loads of leafy vegetables and herbs will accompany the main dishes.

Younger family members wait for elders to pick up chopsticks, gracefully holding them as far away from the eating ends as possible. There will be a rice bowl, chopsticks, and a spoon. Vietnamese hold the rice-filled bowl in the palm of the hand when taking food from the platter and keep the bowl close to the mouth (Chinese-style) when eating. Avoid clacking chopsticks against the table. The host sometimes will place choice morsels of food in a guest's bowl. (To be extra polite, some Vietnamese refuse food the first time.) Diners take only what they can eat; it's rude to leave rice, but okay to secrete bits of peelings or pits on the table next to the plate. Pass dishes with both hands. Water, or tea served in small cups poured from a small teapot, are common beverages. Rest chopsticks on the empty bowl to signal satisfaction.

FIGURE 3.33 Tam Coc Valley.
Source: Houng Giang Hai/Fotolia.

FIGURE 3.34 Vietnamese market.
Source: drmurphy/Fotolia.

COMMON VIETNAMESE COOKING TOOLS

Wok, Chinese steamer, mortar and pestle

TASTES OF VIETNAM

Fat: Vegetable oil, Asian roasted sesame oil, butter, coconut

Sweet: Sugar, palm sugar

Sour/Alcohol: Tamarind, lime, vinegar, Chinese rice wine, star fruit

Salty: Fish sauce, fish paste, dried shrimp, shrimp paste, soy sauce

Spicy-Hot: Chilies, black pepper

Aromatic Seasoning Vegetables: Lemongrass, ginger, scallions, galangal, garlic, shallot, onion

Spice: Star anise, annatto seed, cinnamon, curry powder, Chinese five-spice, dried red chili flakes, turmeric, cloves, black cardamom

Herbs, Seasonings, and Condiments: Cilantro, dill, mint, red perilla, Thai basil, Vietnamese coriander, culantro or saw-leaf herb, fish mint, rice paddy herb, sorrel, Vietnamese balm, Vietnamese mint, wild betel leaf, Chinese chives, Kaffir lime leaves, pandan leaf, oyster sauce, shrimp sauce, hoisin sauce

Other Important Foods: Long-grain and sticky rice, tofu, wheat gluten, bean curd puffs, pork skins, legumes (mung, black-eyed peas, azuki, hyacinth), tapioca (cassava), coconut, cashews, peanuts, sesame seeds, tropical fruit (see *Tastes of Thailand*, Buddha's hand citrus, apricot, cherimoya, Chinese date, sugar apple, guava, longan, lychee, papaya, rambutan, pomelo, mango, watermelon, Mandarin orange), banana blossoms, plantain, wing beans, green beans, snow peas, leafy greens (see *Tastes of Thailand*), tomato, chrysanthemum leaves, eggplant, water chestnut, water spinach, dropwort, watercress, daikon radish, meat (beef, chicken, goat, pork), fish, seafood (shrimp, anchovy, turtle, frog, snail), insects, agar-agar

Popular Dishes: *Goi cuon* (fresh salad rolls), *banh cuon* (steamed rice roll), *cha gio* (fried pork spring roll), *banh xeo* (sizzling rice crepes), *bahn pho* (noodle soup), *bun* (vermicelli noodle salad with various vegetables and meats) *nuoc cham* (dipping sauce), *che* (sweet soup), hot and sour soup, cured fermented pork, meat "floss," baguette, *bahn mie* sandwich, bahn canh (thick rice noodle dish), dumplings, steamed rice cake, congee, caramel sauce, banh da lon (steamed layer cake from tapioca and rice flours, coconut milk and sugar), banana cake, cassava cake, flan, mooncake, *che banh lot* or *chendol* (coconut milk, rice jellies, shaved ice, and palm sugar dessert), tofu pudding, tapioca pudding, glutinous rice balls stuffed with sweet azuki bean paste

Drinks: Black and chrysanthemum teas, beer, wine, liquor, iced tea and iced coffee, ginseng tea, lotus tea, rice liquor, tropical fruit juices, snake wine, salty-sweet limeade, soy milk

VIETNAMESE FLAVOR FOUNDATIONS

Vietnamese Signature Aromatic Vegetable Combo

Shallots, garlic, chilies, ginger, galangal, lemongrass, green onions

Signature Seasonings

Many of these seasonings are used throughout Southeast Asia.

Liquid/Paste

Nuoc Mam (Vietnamese Fish Sauce)

Vietnam's prized staple, fish sauce, like olive oil and wine, has levels of excellence. Made by fermenting 3 parts anchovies to 1 part salt for one week then recycling the liquid back through the wooden vats daily for a year, high-quality fish sauce is intensely meaty and full of umami complexity. The first extraction is used for sauce and dips, the remainder for cooking. Quality nuoc mam is transparent, salty at first taste with a sweet aftertaste. Use it to up the flavor of meat, soup, or sauce. Author Andrea Nguyen recommends *Three Crabs* and *Flying Lion* brands.

Animal

Dried Shrimp (Tôm Khô)

Also used in other Asian cuisines, Vietnamese cooks use them in soup, vegetable dishes, and fried rice.

FIGURE 3.35 Small dried shrimp.
Source: HONG SIEW MEE/Fotolia.

Herbal/Spice

Vietnamese are wild about fresh herbs, which tend to grace many dishes. These are a few of the most popular.

FIGURE 3.36 Vietnamese coriander/rauram.
Source: Dave King/DK Images.

Vietnamese Coriander (rau ram)

This culinary and medicinal herb tastes of lemon, coriander, and cilantro. It is popular in Southeast Asia and Latin America.

Red Perilla (shiso or rau tio to, also known as wild sesame)

Perilla can be red or green. Red perilla has a slightly spicy anise-basil flavor. Green perilla is spicier and tastes of cinnamon, lemon, and mint. It is popular in Southeast Asia, Korea, Japan, and China.

Thai Basil (húng qué or rau qué also known as cinnamon basil or horapha)

A variety of basil native to Southeast Asia, Thai basil has narrow leaves (with purple stems) that taste of licorice and cinnamon. It is more heat stable than Italian basil. Thai holy basil (*kaprow*) and Thai lemon basil (*maenglak*) are two other popular varieties used in Southeast Asia.

Vegetable/Fruit

Lime and Lime Leaf

The Southeast Asian lime tree (also known as Kaffir) has small, bumpy, green citrus and distinctive, shiny, firm double leaves. The pungent skin of the limes is used to flavor Thai curry pastes. The leaves are heavenly-fragrant and used to perfume soups, curries, and sauces. The juice of this lime can be bitter and so it is not often used. The tree is native to Malaysia, India, Laos, Indonesia, Thailand, and adjacent countries. Lime leaves freeze well.

FIGURE 3.37 Red perilla.
Source: © Le Do/Fotolia.

Saw-Leaf Herb (ngò gai or culantro)

Latin and Southeast Asian cuisines rely on this spiky, slow-growing but strong-flavored herb that Latins call *culantro* and Vietnamese call *ngo gai*. Though it goes by many names (Mexican coriander, saw-tooth herb, and stinkweed), a blindfolded cook could be fooled into mistaking it for an especially earthy cilantro with its soapy, pungent scent. Use it fresh as the Vietnamese do, or cook it in soup or stew, as does much of Latin America. Native to Mexico, this herb has long, slender green leaves with serrated edged leaves. Used in Vietnamese summer rolls, *pho bo*, soups, and salads.

Fish Mint (rau diép cá)

This herb has small heart-shaped leaves with a strong fishy flavor. Popular in home kitchens, it's often eaten raw in noodle dishes and in fresh summer rolls or with grilled meats and fish soups.

Rice Paddy Herb (ngó om)

This tropical herb is native to Southeast Asia, where it flourishes on drained or flooded rice paddies. Its flavor and scent are reminiscent of

(Continued)

(Continued)

FIGURE 3.38 Culantro/saw leaf herb.
Source: Dave King/Dorling Kindersley.

FIGURE 3.39 Fish mint.
Source: © Le Do/Fotolia.

FIGURE 3.40 Rice paddy herb.
Source: Dave King/Dorling Kindersley.

citrus and cumin. Add it to soups, curries, or stir-fries at the end of cooking.

Vietnamese Balm or Vietnamese Mint (rau kinh giới)

Often used in noodles and soups, this gently lemony herb, similiar to lemon balm, is usually eaten raw.

Wild Betel Leaf (la lot)

This peppery herb has shiny heart-shaped leaves that season stir-fries and soups. It pairs well with red meat and is classically wrapped around ground meat and grilled or pan-fried.

FIGURE 3.41 Betel leaves.
Source: Karen Trist/Dorling Kindersley.

FIGURE 3.42 Floating Vietnamese green grocer.
Source: © mkmakingphotos/Fotolia.

SEASONING AND PASTE MIXTURES

VIETNAMESE CRISPY SHALLOTS

Use for garnishing cooked fish, poultry, salads, vegetables, stir-fries, noodle dishes, and soups.

Yields 1/2 cup

1/2 cup canola oil
4 ounces shallots, about 6 medium, 1 cup slivered (sliver shallots evenly so they brown evenly)

1 Pour oil into small saucepan. Heat over medium heat. When oil ripples (but not so hot that it smokes) and a bit of shallot sizzles upon contact, pour in shallots. Cook shallots until browned and crispy, around 10 minutes. Lower heat if the shallots cook too quickly and unevenly.

2 Remove browned shallots from oil with slotted spoon as they brown. Spread on paper towel to drain. Reserve the frying oil for seasoning. Use the crispy shallots as garnish. Keep crispy shallots one to two days in tightly covered container. To re-crisp, microwave for several seconds.

SAUCE

VIETNAMESE CARAMEL SAUCE (NUÓ'C MÀU)

This sauce is a fundamental staple of Vietnamese cooking and reveals the French influence. Vietnamese cooks simmer meat, seafood, eggs, and tofu in it for a deep brown color and rich flavor. Add a tablespoon to a barbecue marinade, stew, sauce, or stir-fry for a mysterious flavor undercurrent.

Yields 3/4 cup

7 ounces sugar, 1 cup
1/8 teaspoon cream of tartar

1 Fill a deep half hotel pan or baking dish with ice cubes. Pour sugar, 1/4 cup water, and cream of tartar into a 2- to 3-quart saucepan with a lid and stir a minute or two until sugar dissolves. Bring saucepan to a boil over medium heat, cover, and lower heat. Cook sugar 5 to 7 minutes and check. Vigorous bubbles should cover the entire surface. Cover pot again.

2 Cook sugar another 8 to 10 minutes. Uncover pot. Sugar will go from pale yellow to light, then dark tea-color.

3 After 15 to 20 minutes total cooking time, smoke will rise. Remove pan from heat and swirl. It will continue to cook and darken to red wine with burnt orange-colored bubbles. When caramel underneath bubbles and turns molasses or coffee dark, immediately set saucepan into pan with ice to stop cooking. The caramel will harden.

4 Pour 1/2-cup cold water into caramel. Return pan to medium heat and stir caramel and water until caramel dissolves. Remove from heat and cool. Pour into glass canning jar, seal, and store indefinitely.

Source: Into the Vietnamese Kitchen by Andrea Nguyen.

Vary! Improvise!

☞ *More Flavor: Simmer 1/3 cup caramel sauce with 1/4 cup fish sauce and 4 tablespoons thinly sliced shallots 3 to 4 minutes. Season with freshly ground black pepper. Use as satay marinade.*

VIETNAMESE-STYLE PEANUT SAUCE (NUÓ'C LEO)

This chunky sauce with peanuts, ground pork, and salty fermented soybean sauce makes a rich, tasty dip for raw vegetables, Southeast Asian-style meatballs, or grilled Asian-flavored meat.

Yields 1-1/2 cups

1 ounce tamarind paste, 2 tablespoons
2 to 3 ounces dry-roasted peanuts, 1/2 cup
1 tablespoon vegetable oil
1 ounce garlic, 4 cloves, about 2 tablespoons peeled and minced
1-1/2 ounces ground pork, 3 tablespoons
3 tablespoons Vietnamese soybean sauce (*tuong* in Vietnamese and *dao jiao* in Thai)
1-1/2 teaspoons palm or cane sugar
2 bird's eye chilies, 3/4 teaspoon stemmed and minced
2 to 3 teaspoons fresh lime juice, more to taste

1 Knead tamarind paste with 5 tablespoons hot water to soften, and soak 15 to 20 minutes. Press softened tamarind through a strainer; reserve purée, and discard pits and fiber to yield about 1/4 cup tamarind purée.

2 Grind nuts in a food processor to a coarse powder and set aside.

3 Heat oil in a 3-quart saucepan over medium-high heat. Stir-fry garlic until it becomes golden, 15 to 20 seconds. Stir in pork to break it up. When the pork is cooked through, stir in soybean sauce, tamarind purée, 3/4 cup water, and all but 1 tablespoon ground peanuts. Bring to a boil. Simmer until sauce thickens to a thick, pourable sauce, 2 to 5 minutes; add water as necessary for desired consistency. Stir in sugar and chilies.

4 **To Serve:** Taste, season with salt, and adjust flavors. Just before serving, stir in lime juice to brighten the flavor. Pour sauce into serving bowl and top with reserved peanuts. Sauce will thicken and flavor will mature overnight. Reheat with a little extra water to thin, and simmer 2 minutes before serving. Add fresh lime juice to brighten flavor. Keep refrigerated 4 days or frozen up to 1 month.

Source: *Hot, Sour, Salty, Sweet* by Naomi Duguid and Jeffrey Alford.

SIGNATURE RECIPE

VIETNAMESE NUOC CHAM

This sauce is the heart and soul of Vietnamese cuisine. Its variations are numerous, but all have the basics of fish sauce, lime juice, palm sugar, and chilies with some water. Start with the basic proportions and personal taste to get the flavor right. If tasting becomes difficult, go away for a moment and return to taste another time, or ask for assistance.

Yields about 2/3 cup, 5 to 6 fluid ounces

Base proportions: 4–3–2–2

4 tablespoons freshly squeezed lime juice, 1 large lime
1-1/2 ounces palm sugar, 3 tablespoons
    or 3 tablespoons maple syrup
2 tablespoons Vietnamese fish sauce
2 tablespoons water, more depending on quality and age of fish sauce

Optional Seasonings

1 small red bird's eye chili, stemmed and finely sliced
About 1/2 ounce shallot, 1 small, 1 tablespoon peeled and finely sliced

Garnish: Finely shredded carrot

1 **Prepare base:** Whisk together lime juice, sweetener, fish sauce, and water. Taste by dipping a leaf into sauce. Mixture should be pleasantly salty and sour balanced with sweet to offset sour. If fish sauce is old or not high quality, use less or adjust sauce with more water and if necessary, lime juice and sweetener. If limes are unavailable it's acceptable to substitute rice vinegar or traditional white distilled vinegar; it will keep fresh longer.

2 **Thirty minutes before serving:** Choose one seasoning. Stir chili or shallot into the base and rest at room temperature. Garnish with a little finely shredded carrot, if desired.

3 **To Serve:** Pour nuoc cham into serving bowl and set a spoon into it. Serve alongside *Vietnamese Fresh Rice Paper Wrapped Rolls (Goi Cuon)* or as a sauce or dipping sauce for meat, rice, or vegetables.

VIETNAMESE SWEET AND SOUR DIPPING SAUCE

Serve with grilled food like Shrimp Mousse on Sugarcane.

Yields 3/4 cup

1/2 ounce shallots, about 2 tablespoons peeled and minced
1/3 to 1/4 ounce garlic, 1 medium clove, 1 teaspoon peeled and finely minced
1-1/2 ounces palm sugar, 3 tablespoons
   or 3 tablespoons cane sugar
2 tablespoons rice or white vinegar
1 to 1-1/2 tablespoons fish sauce

Slurry

1-1/2 tablespoons cornstarch

Garnish

1 tablespoon each finely minced: scallion greens, carrot, and red bell pepper

1 Mix 1 cup water, shallots, garlic, sugar, vinegar, and fish sauce in a small saucepan. Bring to a boil, lower heat, and simmer sauce 5 minutes.

2 Stir cornstarch well into 3 tablespoons cold water. Whisk this slurry into hot liquid. Simmer and stir until it thickens and clears.

3 Remove sauce from heat and stir in garnish of minced vegetables. Cool. Season with salt and pepper to taste.

SPECIAL METHODS

Signature Technique: Rolling Goi Cuon Two Ways

A quick soak in warm water softens and transforms brittle dried rice or tapioca starch paper into a tender wrapper for fresh, uncooked rolls. Filled as they are with fresh ingredients, these rolls double as a salad-in-hand. Vietnamese summer rolls lend themselves to invention, but don't overfill or overwhelm with too many ingredients. They can be constructed two ways:

Two-Tucked Ends Method 1

- Lay folded lettuce leaf on bottom third of rice wrapper, in the center, with 1- to 2-inch margins at the edges.

- Fill lettuce evenly with ingredients: noodles, pork, sprouts, mint, and cilantro leaves in an oblong.

- Roll up once, fold in ends neatly, and roll up a half roll.

- Lay 4 shrimp halves, cut side up, on unrolled part, and chives with frond hanging out, then finish rolling firmly. Shrimp should be visible through wrapper.

One Open-End Method 2

- Fold over right side of round paper to make a straight edge on right side.

- At the bottom third of wrapper, place 2 lettuce leaves horizontally, with the tops of leaves facing out and hanging slightly over the folded edge. Keep a 1- to 2-inch border on the left side.

- Layer cilantro and mint leaves on each lettuce leaf with tops of cilantro hanging out and over like the lettuce leaf.

- Place filling ingredients—cucumber, avocado, and nuts—on top of herbs.

- Roll up, beginning at the bottom and fold over the unfolded left side.

- When the lettuce is visible through the skin, place 4 shrimp halves, cut side up, on the unrolled part. Finish rolling up roll firmly. Shrimp should be visible through wrapper.

Trouble-Shooting

- Rolls need a firm, but gentle hand. Too much pressure will blow them open, too little and they'll be too loose and fall apart when cut.

- If roll tears, fill it with less or prepare with doubled rice papers.

- *Double-Paper Method:* Hold 2 rice paper wrappers together and immerse in warm water until soft, drain, and set on damp towel. Lightly press out excess water and blot. The extra wrapper may add an extra starchy chewiness, but it's great security for nervous novices.

CLASSIC VIETNAMESE FRESH RICE PAPER WRAPPED ROLLS (GOI CUON)

If 16/20 shrimp are unavailable, substitute 21/25 and use 3 per roll. It's smart to have on hand double the amount of wrappers necessary. They often crack and tear. Erawan brand is generally considered the best.

4 large rolls, 2 to 4 servings

Nuoc Cham
or Vietnamese Sweet Sour Dipping Sauce
8 ounces 16/20 shrimp, 8, shelled and deveined
2 ounces rice vermicelli

1-1/2 ounces mung bean sprouts, 1/2 cup

About 4 ounces red leaf or Boston lettuce, 1 small head, whole leaves washed and dried

4 ounces grilled pork *or* grilled boneless skinless chicken breast, thinly sliced

1/3 to 1/2 ounce mint sprigs, leaves removed and stems discarded

1/2 ounce trimmed cilantro sprigs, 8 to 12 three-inch long sprigs

Optional: 1 ounce Chinese chives, about 12

8 to 10 eight-inch round rice or tapioca spring roll wrappers

1 Prepare *Nuoc Cham* or *Vietnamese Sweet Sour Dipping Sauce* and set aside for use later. Set up steamer. Steam shrimp just until opaque, 1 to 3 minutes. Immediately remove from steamer and cool. Slice shrimp into mirror halves.

2 Fill 3-quart saucepan with cold water and bring to a boil. Place vermicelli into small heatproof bowl. Pour enough water over noodles to cover; rest 2 minutes. Drain vermicelli and blot dry. Place mung sprouts in strainer. Pour enough boiling water over them to wilt crisp-tender, about 1 cup. Rinse sprouts under cold water, drain, and blot dry.

3 Tear lettuce into 3- to 4-inch-long pieces. Assemble and divide shrimp, vermicelli, sprouts, lettuce, meat, and herbs into four piles on a parchment-covered sheet pan or clean tray. Keep rice wrappers in their packaging: they will curl up and crack if left uncovered.

4 Fill a large, deep pan or dish with warm water on workspace. Set up filling ingredient tray nearby. Wet and wring out 2 smooth cotton towels, and lay one out near the pan and fillings.

5 Dip 1 spring roll skin in water until pliable, 1 minute. The warmer the water, the faster this will go. Water should not be so hot that it hurts fingers. Replenish water to keep warm.

6 Place spring roll skin onto a damp cotton towel and blot off excess moisture with the other damp towel. If they're too wet, the skins will be slippery, but blotted, the skin should be skin-soft and tacky. With speed it's possible to place another skin into the water to soften while rolling the first one.

7 For a traditional roll tucked on both ends, follow *Method 1* in *Two Ways to Roll Goi Cuon*. (For more secure wrappers, see **Double-Paper Method** under *Signature Technique: Rolling Goi Cuon Two Ways*.) Imagine the rice paper divided into 3 sections horizontally:

   • In the **middle of the bottom third** of the wrapper nearest the edge of the work surface: Lay lettuce down as a base. Then lay vermicelli, sprouts, meat, and herbs on top of the lettuce. (The chives are left long and rolled so a couple inches stick out one end.)

   • The shrimp line up in the **middle of the middle third**, uncut side facing outward, so their ghostly pink shape can be seen through the rice wrapper after wrapping. Bring the lower edge of the paper up and over the filling, fold right and left edges into the center, and finish rolling up like a jelly roll.

   • **The top third** of the paper is the seal.

8 Place roll seam-side-down onto a platter and finish constructing remaining rolls. Cover rolls tightly with damp cotton towel or plastic wrap. Keep in a cool spot, but not refrigerated, up to 2 hours. If rolls must keep longer, spray with warm water before wrapping in plastic wrap or cover with damp towel and plastic wrap. Refrigerate. The texture of the wrapper will be tougher. Remove rolls from refrigerator 30 minutes to 1 hour before serving.

9 **To Serve:** Cut rolls in half diagonally and arrange them decoratively onto a serving plate or platter. Serve with a Vietnamese dipping sauce.

FIGURE 3.43 Vietnamese summer rolls (goi cuon).
Source: © uckyo/Fotolia.

Vary! Improvise!

☞ *Devise three filling combos.*

☞ *Create a goi cuon for a vegetarian-vegan-dairy-and-gluten-free lunch or dinner option.*

IMPROVISED VIETNAMESE FRESH RICE PAPER WRAPPED ROLLS (GOI CUON)

It's wise to have on hand double the number of wrappers necessary. They often crack and tear. Erawan brand is generally considered the best. The shrimp, avocado, and cucumber filling is a riff on the classic California sushi roll. If 16/20 shrimp are unavailable, substitute 21/25 and use 3 per roll.

4 large rolls, 2 to 4 servings

Nuoc Cham
or Vietnamese Sweet Sour Dipping Sauce

8 ounces 16/20 shrimp, 8, peeled, deveined and steamed until opaque
8 ounces English cucumber, 1-1/4 cups lightly peeled, seeded, cut into long matchsticks
12- to 16-ounce head red leaf or Boston lettuce, whole leaves washed and dried
1/3 ounce cilantro sprigs, 8 large sprigs, washed and dried
1/2 ounce mint sprigs, leaves removed and stems discarded, washed, and dried
1/2 ounce Thai or Italian basil sprigs, about 12 leaves, stems discarded, washed, and dried
8 to 10 ounce ripe Haas avocado, 1 large
1-1/2 ounces peanuts, about 1/3 cup coarsely chopped
      or 1 to 2 ounces toasted pumpkin seeds, 1/4 to 1/2 cup

8 to 10 eight-inch round rice or tapioca spring roll wrappers

1 Prepare *Nuoc Cham* or *Vietnamese Sweet Sour Dipping Sauce* and set aside for use later. Set up steamer. Steam shrimp just until opaque, 1 to 3 minutes. Immediately remove from steamer and cool. Slice shrimp into mirror halves.

2 Lightly peel cucumber. Seed cucumber and cut into 3- to 4-inch long matchsticks. Assemble and divide shrimp, cucumbers, lettuce, and herbs into four piles on a parchment-covered sheet pan or clean tray. Just before assembling rolls cut each avocado half into 8 long, thin slices. Keep rice wrappers in their packaging: they will curl up and crack if left uncovered.

3 Fill a large, deep pan or dish with warm water on workspace. Set up filling ingredient tray nearby. Wet and wring out 2 smooth cotton towels, and lay one out near the pan and fillings.

4 Dip 1 spring roll skin in water until pliable, 1 minute. The warmer the water, the faster this will go. Water should not be so hot that it hurts fingers. Replenish water to keep warm.

5 Place spring roll skin onto a damp cotton towel and blot off excess moisture with the other damp towel. If they're too wet, the skins will be slippery, but blotted, the skin should be skin-soft and tacky. With speed it's possible to place another skin into the water to soften while rolling the first one. (For more secure wrappers, see **Double-Paper Method** under *Signature Technique: Rolling Goi Cuon Two Ways*.) Fold in about 1 inch of the wrapper on the right side for one end open OR on the right and left sides of the paper for two open ends.

6 Follow *Method II* in *Two Ways to Roll Goi Cuon*. This gives a sushi look, which leaves one or both ends open to show off graceful fronds of lettuce and herbs. Imagine the rice paper divided into 3 sections horizontally:

• In the **middle of the bottom third** of the wrapper nearest the edge of the work surface:

Lay a whole lettuce down as a base. Leafy ends should hang off one or both folded over ends. Lay cucumber, herbs, avocado, and peanuts on the lettuce.

• The shrimp line up in the **middle of the middle third**, uncut side facing outward, so their ghostly pink shape can be seen through the rice wrapper after wrapping.

• Bring the lower edge of the paper up and over the filling, fold left edge or neither edge into the center. Finish rolling up roll tightly, like a jelly roll.

• **The top third** of the paper is the seal.

7 Place roll seam-side-down onto a platter and finish constructing remaining rolls. Cover rolls tightly with damp cotton towel or plastic wrap. Keep in a cool spot, but not refrigerated, up to 2 hours. If rolls must keep longer, spray with warm water before wrapping in plastic wrap or cover with damp towel and plastic wrap. Refrigerate. The texture of the wrapper will be tougher. Remove rolls from refrigerator 30 minutes to 1 hour before serving.

8 **To Serve:** Cut rolls into 2 to 4 sushi-size pieces, and arrange them decoratively on a plate like sushi, with dipping sauce or vinaigrette pooled around them.

TAPIOCA PEARLS

These clear, chewy balls are used in sweet "pudding" desserts or soups in Vietnam. They are also part of bubble tea or *boba*, thick, sweet drinks made with tea, coffee, and fruits blended with syrup and often milk (coconut, regular milk, or evaporated milk), shaken or blended with crushed ice, and mixed with a few precooked pearls. Bubble-tea pearls are sometimes tinted with caramel or dye to give color. *Che bap* is a classic Vietnamese sweet soup made with corn, coconut milk, and the smaller tapioca seeds. See *Glossary* for more information.

FIGURE 3.44   Cooked tapioca pearls.
Source: joanna wnuk/Shutterstock.com.

SIMMER, STEW, POACH, BOIL, AND STEAM

Vietnamese Soup (Cahn, Chao, Sup, and Pho)

Vietnamese enjoy soup every day and consume it throughout a meal and often flavor rice with soup. Vietnamese recognize *cahn* as light, first-course, everyday family-style soups made with water; *chao* as rice congee-based soups and small bowls of *sup* (derived from the French *soupe*) as special soups made with meaty broths and expensive ingredients. The famed Viet *pho* falls into a category all its own called *mon nuoc* or watery dish. Vietnamese don't consider pho a true soup; it's a noodle-laden breakfast, singular "snack," or quick lunch.

FIGURE 3.45   Beef pho (pho tai).
Source: © Brian Weed/Fotolia.

Signature Technique: Pho (fuh)

Technically Pho is a noodle dish; it's not considered soup. Originally a breakfast from North Vietnam's capitol, Hanoi, pho has become the signature noodle dish or soup of all Vietnam. Vietnamese eat it for breakfast, lunch, or a late-night snack. Prepare it with beef, chicken, shrimp, or pork. Hanoi-style pho bo with beef and pho ga with chicken are the favorites.

Northern pho uses wide noodles and more green onion than southern style pho. Southern Vietnamese pho broth is sweeter and includes bean sprouts and many fresh herbs with variations in meat, broth, and additional garnishes such as lime, hoisin, bean sauce, and chili sauce.

1 **The pho stock is all-important:** Slow-simmer a rich meaty stock until deeply flavorful; it should be slightly clear with a clean, spicy-sweet flavor and little fat.

2 **Spice the stock:** Simmer seasonings and spices in the stock. Pho beef stock uses beef bones, onions, fresh ginger, cinnamon, star anise, coriander seed, whole clove, and cardamom pods. Chicken stock uses meat and bones with similar spices.

3 **Bite-sized cuts:** Ingredients for pho should be cut or sliced bite-sized for easy eating with chopsticks and fast cooking: slice meat thinly and fish or seafood into small chunks.

4 **Quick blanch:** Rice noodles should be soaked until pliable in warm (not hot) water, 15 to 20 minutes, then dipped into boiling water until tender, 30 seconds to 1 minute. Place in bottom of bowl.

5 **Dip in simmering stock:** Blanch mung sprouts in simmering broth until slightly cooked but still crunchy. Cook meat, chicken, or seafood in simmering broth until barely or just done (beef should remain slightly pink) and tender.

6 **Layer:** Layer noodles, sprouts or other vegetables, meat, or seafood and herbs and green onions into a serving bowl. Ladle hot broth over top.

7 **Set up a condiment dipping dish:** The simplest pho with rich broth, beef, shredded green onions, and herbs relies on condiments to achieve the signature flavors of salty, sour, sweet, and hot. Favored condiments are chili sauce, sliced bird's eye chilies, vinegar, black pepper, fish sauce, lime wedges, fried shallots, and/or hoisin sauce. Place condiments into a small dipping dish and dip meat or noodles into it.

VIETNAMESE NOODLE AND BEEF SOUP (PHO TAI)

Yields 14 cups with noodles and meat, 4 to 6 servings

Spiced Stock

2 quarts very rich beef stock
1 to 1-1/2 ounces gingerroot, 3 to 4 tablespoons peeled and thinly sliced cross-grain
3 ounces trimmed green onions, 6 large, 1 cup sliced into 1-inch lengths
3 whole cloves
2 whole star anise
2-inch cinnamon stick

Noodles

8 ounces 1/2-inch wide rice stick noodles (yields about 4 cups soaked and drained)

Garnishing Ingredients

2 ounces cilantro, 1 to 1-1/2 cups lightly packed sprigs
    or saw-leaf herb (culantro)
1/4 ounce Thai basil leaves, about 1/2 cup, torn
1/2 ounce Thai bird's eye chilies, 3 to 4, 1-1/2 to 2 teaspoons stemmed and finely sliced
    or 1 Thai bird's eye chili per person
Fried Shallots
2 limes, cut into 12 wedges
Fish sauce

8 ounces mung bean sprouts, 3 cups rinsed and drained
12 to 16 ounces beef flank, sirloin or round steak, thinly sliced cross-grain into bite-sized pieces
3 ounces trimmed green onions, 6 large, 1/2 to 2/3 cup thinly sliced on the diagonal
    or finely julienned

1 **Prepare spiced stock:** Bring stock, gingerroot, green onions, and spices to a boil in 4-quart saucepan. Lower heat, cover, and simmer stock 20 minutes. Allow stock to steep off heat 15 minutes. Strain into bowl then pour back into saucepan. Discard onions and spices, but save ginger slices if tender. Finely sliver ginger and add back to the stock. Set aside saucepan.

2 **Soak noodles:** Meanwhile, place rice noodles in large bowl and cover with very warm water until pliable, 15 to 20 minutes. Drain noodles, and keep covered.

3 **Prepare garnishing ingredients:** Set each individually into small serving bowls on a platter. Pour fish sauce into small container with spout.

4 **Just before serving:** Bring stock to a simmer over medium heat. Cover partially. Bring a 4-quart pot of water to boil. Set 4 or 6 large serving bowls on platter.

5 **Cook noodles:** Divide soaked noodles into 4 or 6 portions. Place each portion, one by one, into strainer and lower into boiling water. Cook until al dente, about 30 seconds to 1 minute. Drain noodles and divide evenly between serving bowls.

6 **Sprouts:** Bring stock back to boil. Place bean sprouts in strainer and blanch 30 seconds to 1 minute in stock. Divide evenly between bowls.

7 **Beef:** Place a portion of beef into strainer and lower into simmering stock. Blanch until slightly pink, 30 seconds to 1 minute. Repeat with remaining beef and divide meat evenly among the bowls.

8 **Green onions:** Place green onions into strainer and blanch in boiling stock 30 seconds to 1 minute. Divide evenly between bowls.

9 **To Serve:** Ladle 1-1/2 to 2 cups hot spiced stock over each bowl of noodles, sprouts, meat, and green onions. Allow diners to decide what garnishes to put on their pho: cilantro or culantro, basil, fried shallots, lime juice, and fish sauce. Garnishes bring pho alive.

Vary! Improvise!

☛ *Prepare pho with a rich, spiced chicken stock, and chicken breast.*

☛ *Prepare pho with a rich fish stock and 1-1/2 to 2 pounds shrimp.*

VIETNAMESE SWEET SOUP WITH CORN AND TAPIOCA SEEDS (CHE BAP)

Che bap is eaten as a snack at any time of the day, not necessarily as a dessert, and served warm or cold. It can be made with anything from corn to bananas, sweet potatoes, plantains, winter squash, seaweed, or cooked azuki beans in place of corn.

Yields about 4 cups, 4 servings

1-1/2 ounces small tapioca "seeds," 1/4 cup
2 tablespoons palm sugar, more to taste
13-1/2 ounce can unsweetened coconut milk, about 1-3/4 cups
   or 2 cups fresh coconut milk
1-1/2 cups fresh corn kernels, about 2 medium ears
   or about 7-1/2 ounces frozen corn kernels, 1-1/2 cups

Garnish: 2 tablespoons chopped, roasted peanuts
   or 2 tablespoons chopped, roasted cashews

1 Pour 2 cups water into 4-quart saucepan and bring to a boil over medium heat. Reduce heat to medium-low and stir in tapioca and sugar. Cover pan partially and simmer pearls until nearly translucent, 15 minutes.

2 If using canned coconut milk, stir coconut milk, 1/4 cup water and corn kernels into pan, but if using fresh coconut milk, omit the water. Simmer soup uncovered until it has thickened and pearls are completely translucent, 15 minutes longer. Season soup with 1/8 to 1/4 teaspoon kosher salt and if desired, more palm sugar, to taste.

3 **To Serve:** Ladle into bowls and top with peanuts or cashews.

SIGNATURE RECIPE

FOOD SIMMERED IN CARAMEL SAUCE (KHO)

Similar to Chinese red-cooking (see China), simmering foods in Vietnamese Caramel Sauce results in a lacquered-rich color and savory-sweet flavor. Traditionally prepared in earthenware vessels similar to Chinese clay or sand pot stews, these salty-sweet dishes need rice for balance.

Each yields about 4 cups, 2 to 4 servings

Chicken, Ginger, and Garlic Kho

1-1/2 pounds boneless, skinless chicken thighs
1/2 ounce gingerroot, 1 tablespoon peeled and minced
2 tablespoons fish sauce
Optional: 1 tablespoon palm sugar

Shrimp Kho

1-1/2 pounds 21/25 shrimp, peeled and deveined
1-1/2 tablespoons fish sauce
2 tablespoons *Caramel Sauce*

Chicken-Ginger Aromatics

1 tablespoon vegetable oil
1/4 ounce garlic, 1 large clove, 2 teaspoons minced

Shrimp Aromatics

1 tablespoon vegetable oil
4 to 5 ounces onion, 1 cup peeled and thinly slivered

Chicken-Ginger Kho

3 tablespoons *Caramel Sauce*
2 to 3 tablespoons chicken stock
To Serve: Hot, cooked jasmine rice

Garnish: 1 ounce green onions, 2 large, 4 tablespoons finely sliced or minced

1 *Prepare and marinate chicken or shrimp:*

Chicken

Dice chicken into 1-inch cubes and toss with ginger, fish sauce, and optional palm sugar in a mixing bowl. Marinate 30 minutes.

Shrimp

Stir shrimp in bowl with 2 tablespoons kosher salt, rinse under cold water immediately then drain. Blot bowl dry. Combine shrimp with fish sauce and caramel sauce in mixing bowl.

2 *Heat a 10-inch skillet over medium heat and add 1 tablespoon oil then:*

Chicken Aromatics

Sauté garlic until just tender, 30 seconds.

Shrimp Aromatics

Sauté sliced onion until just tender, 1 to 2 minutes.

3 Finish the kho:

Chicken

Add chicken and marinade, caramel sauce, and chicken stock to sautéed garlic. Bring to a boil, lower heat, and simmer kho uncovered, stirring occasionally, until chicken is cooked through, about 15 minutes. Sauce should be reduced to a deep brown. Stir chicken to coat evenly in sauce, cover, and rest off the heat 5 to 7 minutes.

Shrimp

Add shrimp to onion and cook over medium heat until they turn orange-brown and are sweet and appealingly chewy; depending on their size, anywhere from 5 to 10 minutes. Only a few tablespoons of sauce will remain when shrimp are done. If pan begins to dry and sauce sticks, add a little water. Shrimp are purposely slightly overcooked to saturate them with flavor. Remove pan from heat.

4 **Finish kho:** Stir in 1/4 to 1/2 teaspoon freshly ground black pepper, to taste, and cool. Reheat kho before serving. Taste and adjust seasonings with fish sauce or salt and pepper.

5 **To Serve:** Spoon hot kho over bowls of rice. Garnish with green onions, and serve.

Source: *Into the Vietnamese Kitchen* by Andrea Nguyen.

FIGURE 3.46 Vietnamese fishing boats.
Source: © RCH/Fotolia.

Vary! Improvise!

☛ Prepare kho with grilled or roasted pork spareribs.

☛ Serve the chicken or shrimp on skewers as party food.

☛ Prepare Vietnamese caramelized pork (Thit Heo Bam) same as kho, but with lean ground pork or beef. Sauté shallots, add ground pork, and cook until done. Stir in caramel sauce, fish sauce, and palm sugar. Cook until meat is evenly browned. Garnish with green onions, and serve with rice.

VIETNAMESE STYLE PUMPKIN BRAISED IN COCONUT MILK

This dish straddles the divide between dessert and dinner.

Yields about 4 cups, 4 to 6 servings

2 cups coconut milk
1 ounce palm sugar, 2 tablespoons
    or 2 tablespoons maple syrup
1 pound pumpkin, kabocha *or* butternut squash, 3-1/2 to 4 cups peeled
and diced 1/2-by-1-inch
2-1/2 to 3 ounces zucchini, 1/2 cup 1/2-inch cubes
About 2 ounces raw peanuts, 1/2 cup

Garnish: Cilantro leaves

1 Heat coconut milk, sweetener, and 1/2 teaspoon salt in 4-quart saucepan over low heat until sweetener melts. Add pumpkin or squash and bring to a boil. Simmer partly covered until tender, about 10 minutes. Don't stir, it will break up the pumpkin, which should remain whole and tender.

2 **Finish:** Fold in diced zucchini and peanuts. Cook until zucchini is tender, 4 to 5 minutes. Remove pan from heat and taste. Season with more salt or palm sugar, to taste.

3 **To Serve:** Spoon squash and coconut milk into bowls. Sprinkle with cilantro. Serve hot.

Vary! Improvise!

☞ *Substitute roasted peanuts for raw.*

☞ *Substitute unsalted, roasted cashews for peanuts.*

STIR-FRY, SAUTÉ, PAN-FRY, AND DEEP-FRY

VIETNAMESE STIR-FRIED BABY BOK CHOY AND SHIITAKES

Stir-frying is an ideal way to lock in color, flavor, and nutrients of Asian leafy greens. Blanch greens to subdue strong flavors, shorten stir-fry time, or to prep ahead.

4 to 6 servings

1 pound baby bok choy
2 tablespoons vegetable oil
1-1/2 ounces garlic, 3 large cloves, 4-1/2 teaspoons peeled and finely minced
8 to 9 ounces shiitake mushrooms, about 3 cups stems minced, and caps finely sliced *or* cubed 1-inch
1 tablespoon fish sauce
2 tablespoons water
1/2 lime, about 2 tablespoons juice

1 **Wash vegetables:** Rinse bok choy in cold water. Make sure to check the base where dirt lodges. Discard discolored leaves.

2 **Prep remaining ingredients:** Set up on tray ready to cook. Slice 4- to 5-inch-long bok choy in halves or quarters lengthwise, yields about 12 cups quartered. Slice smaller (2- to 3-inch) bok choy in halves or quarters lengthwise.

3 Heat wok or skillet over high heat and swirl in oil. (See chapter *China* for stir-fry technique.) When oil shimmers: Stir-fry garlic until colored, 10 seconds, and add shiitake. Cover and cook until shiitake are wilted, 1 minute, and add bok choy. Stir-fry 1 to 2 minutes and stir in fish sauce and 2 tablespoons water. Bring to a boil, cover, lower heat, and steam bok choy until crisp-tender, 1 to 2 minutes. Uncover, test for doneness, and cook bok choy further if necessary until moist and tender, but still bright green. Toss lime juice over greens, to taste.

4 Taste greens, and adjust seasoning with salt or fish sauce.

5 **To Serve:** Turn greens out onto a platter, piled high, and serve hot or at room temperature.

Vary! Improvise!

☞ **Create Indonesia:** *Prepare Indonesian stir-fried greens with a sambal.*

SIGNATURE RECIPE

RICE CREPE (BANH)

Banh may be refrigerated and reheated, but won't have the crisp-soft texture of those fresh off the heat. There are two ways to prepare bahn: With Sizzling Banh Xeo, *one portion of the filling ingredients cook in the pan then the batter is added.* Happy Banh Khoai *uses precooked ingredients piled onto top of the cooked rice crepe.*

Banh Batter for either *Sizzling Banh Xeo* or *Happy Banh Khoai*

Filling Ingredients

1-1/2 ounces shallots, about 2 medium, 1/3 cup slivered
8 ounces 25/30 or 41/50 shrimp, shelled and deveined
    or 8 ounces lean pork, finely sliced
    or half each of shrimp and pork
1 teaspoon fish sauce
1 teaspoon palm sugar or maple syrup
7- to 8-ounce can straw mushrooms, drained and halved
    or 8 ounces fresh mushrooms, sliced and cooked
1 ounce trimmed green onions, 2 large, 4 tablespoons finely sliced
About 6 ounces fresh mung sprouts, 2 cups

Fresh Vegetable Garnishes

1 pound head Bibb, Boston or leaf lettuce, leaves washed, dried and left whole
8 ounces English cucumber, 1-1/4 cups halved lengthwise, seeded and thinly sliced
1/2 ounce cilantro sprigs, 1 cup, or 1/2 small bunch, large stems trimmed away
About 1/2 ounce mint leaves, 1 cup, or 1/2 small bunch, stems discarded
About 1/2 ounce Vietnamese basil leaves, 1 cup, or 1/2 small bunch, stems discarded

Dipping Sauce

6 to 8 fluid ounces *Nuóc Cham* with finely minced garlic

1 Choose a batter below, and prepare.

2 Prepare **filling** for chosen bahn. Divide the chosen **filling** equally into 5 to 6 portions and set it, with oil, on a sheet pan next to the stove. Arrange bean sprouts and green onions in 5 to 6 portions and set next to stove.

3 Assemble **fresh vegetable garnishes** on a platter.

4 Prepare **dipping sauce**: *Nuóc Cham* with garlic.

5 Cook **Sizzling Banh Xeo** or **Happy Banh Khoai** according to the following directions.

6 **To Serve:** Place platter with **fresh vegetable garnishes** and **dipping sauce** on table. Vietnamese diners tear or cut a bahn with scissors, fold a piece into a lettuce leaf with cucumber and herbs, and dip into *Nuóc Cham* sauce before eating.

FIGURE 3.47   Vietnamese sizzling crepe (banh xeo).

VIETNAMESE RICE CREPES (BANH KHOAI AND BÁNH XÈO)

Banh means "cake." *Bahn khoai* refers to the "delight" or happiness that these savory filled crepes bring. These eggless rice flour crepes originate in central Vietnam, and are another instance of the strong French influence in Vietnamese food. Banhs are made in small, highly seasoned cast-iron skillets with lots of fat. *Bahn xeo* is the modern version, made with coconut milk batter. The name alludes to the sizzling sound the rice-coconut batter makes when it hits the hot pan. Cooks from central Vietnam dip banh in *tuong* sauce, consisting of liver, hoisin sauce, and garlic. Southern cooks make the crepes larger and lacier than in central Vietnam.

SIZZLING CAKE (BANH XEO)

Chef Andrea Nuygen says that older banh recipes traditionally called for a tablespoon or two of cooked, mashed lentils. Nontraditional chickpea flour stands in for lentils. It adds stability, color, and flavor. Do not use glutinous rice flour for the batter.

Yields 2-1/2 to 3 cups batter, enough for five 9-inch or six 8-inch crepes

Batter

5 to 6 ounces Asian white rice flour, 1 cup
About 2/3 ounce tapioca flour, 2 tablespoons
About 1/2 ounce garbanzo bean flour (chickpea) flour, 2 tablespoons
1/2 teaspoon kosher salt
1/2 teaspoon ground turmeric
1/2 cup unsweetened coconut milk
1/2 cup water
1/2 ounce trimmed green onions, 1 large, 2 tablespoons minced

Vegetable or fragrant coconut oil for cooking

1 Whisk together batter ingredients and set aside to rest 30 minutes to 1 hour.

2 Prepare **filling ingredients** under *Signature Technique: Rice Crepe (Banh)*. Toss seafood and/or pork with fish sauce, palm sugar, and black pepper. Divide **filling ingredients** into 5 to 6 portions. Prepare **fresh vegetable garnishes** and nuoc cham **dipping sauce**, and set aside.

3 **Cook filling:** Heat 8- to 9-inch nonstick skillet over medium-high heat, add 1 tablespoon oil and cook **1 portion of filling** until meat or seafood is fully cooked.

4 **Cook bahn xeo:** Check batter: It should be the consistency of thick cream. If not, thin with up to 1/4 cup water. Whisk batter well. Pour 1/4 cup batter (for 8-inch) or 1/3 cup batter (for 9-inch) into hot skillet with filling, swirling around and up the sides so it covers evenly—batter should sizzle, bubble, and become "lacy" as it hits the hot skillet. Pile 1/4 cup sprouts, lower heat to medium, cover pan, and cook *banh xeo* until sprouts wilt, 1 to 2 minutes.

5 Remove lid and continue to cook bahn until edges brown, crisp, and curl away from the pan, bottom is bubbled and browned, but center is tender, 1 to 2 minutes. Check by lifting bottom of pancake with heatproof rubber spatula. Fold over banh, like an omelet, and slide onto plate. Repeat with remaining batter and fillings.

6 **To Serve:** Refer to *Signature Technique: Rice Crepe (Banh)*.

HAPPY CAKE (BANH KHOAI)

Chef Andrea Nuygen says that older banh recipes traditionally called for a tablespoon or two of cooked, mashed lentils. Nontraditional chickpea flour stands in for lentils. It adds stability, color, and flavor. Do not use glutinous rice flour for the batter.

Yields 2-1/2 to 3 cups batter, enough for five 9-inch or six 8-inch crepes

Batter

5 to 6 ounces Asian white rice flour, 1 cup
About 1/2 ounce garbanzo bean flour (chickpea flour), 2 tablespoons
1/2 teaspoon kosher salt
1/2 teaspoon turmeric
1 cup water
1 tablespoon top fat from canned coconut milk
    or 2 to 3 teaspoons fragrant coconut oil

Vegetable or fragrant coconut oil for cooking

1 Whisk together batter ingredients and set aside to rest 30 minutes to 1 hour.

2 Prepare **filling ingredients** in *Signature Technique: Rice Crepe (Banh)*, and set aside. Prepare **fresh vegetable garnishes** and nuoc cham **dipping sauce** and set aside.

3 *Cook filling ingredients:* Heat 9- to 10-inch nonstick skillet with 2 to 3 teaspoons oil. When hot, add slivered shallots, and fry until golden. Remove to bowl. Toss shrimp and/or pork with fish sauce, palm sugar or maple syrup, and black pepper. Heat 2 to 3 teaspoons oil in skillet, and cook shrimp and/or pork until just done; remove to bowl with shallots. If using fresh mushrooms, heat 2 to 3 teaspoons oil in skillet, and cook mushrooms until tender. Toss mushrooms with shallots, seafood, and/or pork. Toss green onions and mung sprouts together in a separate bowl. Divide cooked filling and sprout-green onion mixture into 5 or 6 portions and set aside.

4 **Cook bahn khoai:** Check batter. It should be the consistency of thick cream. If not, thin with water. Heat 8- or 9-inch nonstick skillet with 1 tablespoon oil. Whisk batter well and pour 1/3 cup into pan—it should sizzle, bubble, and crackle. Arrange **1 portion cooked filling** and **sprout-green onion mixture** on top, cover pan, and cook until sprouts wilt, 2 to 3 minutes.

5 Remove lid and continue to cook bahn until edges brown, crisp, and curl away from the pan, bottom is bubbled and browned, but center is tender, 1 to 2 minutes. Check by lifting bottom of pancake with heatproof rubber spatula. Fold over banh, like an omelet, and slide onto plate. Repeat with remaining batter and fillings.

6 **To Serve:** Refer to *Signature Technique: Rice Crepe (Banh)*.

RICE FLOUR

Many cooks from India, Asia, and Southeast Asia use rice flour milled from long-grain rice or glutinous rice (a stickier, starchier flour). White rice flour available from health food stores is coarser than Asian white rice flour. Brown rice flour, available in health food stores, is even coarser. Rice flour lacks gluten so it's good for gluten-free diets, but doesn't bind well in breads or baked goods; add tapioca starch, guar gum, xanthan, or chickpea flour to stabilize. Make rice flour with a clean coffee/spice grinder. Grind small amounts of rice until very fine, and strain through fine mesh strainer. Grind again until rice is desired consistency.

- **Asian white rice flour:** Highly refined rice flour that looks like cornstarch. It is best used as a thickener or in combination with other flours.

- **White rice flour:** White rice flour available in health food stores tends to be coarser than Asian rice flour. It is not a good substitute for the Asian variety.

- **Brown rice flour:** Milled from the whole grain, brown rice flour contains more flavor and nutrients than white rice flour, but most are coarsely milled.

- **Glutinous rice or sweet rice flour:** Made from white glutinous rice, this flour looks like cornstarch and is used for baking and desserts.

- **Roasted red rice flour:** This Indian flour is best for making Indian roti, dosa, or hoppers in Sri Lankan cuisine.

Southeast Asian Fried Rolls

Southeast Asian cooks may have learned to make spring rolls from the Chinese, but their rolls are uniquely their own. The classic tiny Vietnamese spring roll starts with ground pork, minced shrimp or crab, cellophane noodles, vegetables, and seasoning wrapped in rice paper wrappers and deep-fried while the Thai version wraps pork, shrimp, stir-fried vegetables, and mung noodles in steamed or freshly made wheat wrappers to serve fresh or deep-fried.

Signature Technique: Vietnamese Crispy Fried Rice Paper Rolls

Vietnamese serve these crisp-tender treats with lettuce leaves; the trinity of herbs: cilantro, Thai basil, and mint; pickled carrot and radish; a dipping sauce; and lime wedges. Cut them with scissors and roll up into lettuce leaves with herbs. It's fresh, pungent, oily-luscious, and sweet-sour-salty all in one bite. Diners won't want to stop. Dipping sauce is a must. Triangular rice papers are best for mini rolls. If triangular papers are not available, use 13-inch round papers and quarter after soaking.

1 **Prepare filling:** Make it highly seasoned; taste-test it by frying a little patty and sharing a bite with companions. Go with the team taste.

2 **Set up work space:** Dampen and wring out a large smooth cotton towel and place with a half hotel pan of very hot water and tablespoon measure.

3 Dip a rice wrapper into water until soft, 1 minute. Drain wrapper. Place triangular wrapper, with the widest end nearest, pointed edge sticking up, on cotton towel and blot well. (If using 13-inch round wrapper, cut into 4 equal triangles.) Too much moisture and the paper won't stick. Let it rest to absorb moisture and it will become tacky-sticky—a good thing.

4 Place a rounded tablespoon filling in the middle of the wide bottom end and form it into a log about 3-inches by 1-inch. Fold up bottom and then fold in the sides neatly over filling. If this isn't done neatly, the rolls will blow up when fried. Roll up spring roll the rest of the way so wrapper fits filling tightly.

5 Set finished spring rolls seam-side-down on a parchment-covered sheet pan, and cover with a damp, not wet, towel.

6 Heat 1/2-inch canola oil in 10- to 11-inch heavy skillet, enough to immerse spring rolls half way. Heat oil until an instant read thermometer registers 365 degrees F. Slide, don't drop, rolls into hot fat and leave a little space so they don't touch. Fill the pan and leave the rolls alone to fry and harden. They will stick to a nervously probing utensil and tear. Fry until crisp and golden, turning the whole batch to brown on the other side, about 4 to 5 minutes total. Drain on paper towels.

*If rolls don't brown, the oil may not have been hot enough. To reheat and crisp the rolls, place into 425 degree F oven 5 to 7 minutes.

7 **To Serve:** Arrange a platter with garnishing ingredients and a bowl filled with dipping sauce. Place rolls, with scissors nearby to cut rolls in half, and serve.

FIGURE 3.48 Vietnamese fried rolls.
Source: © Kheng Guan Toh/Fotolia.

VIETNAMESE FRIED PORK, SHRIMP, AND CRAB ROLLS (CHÀ GIÒ OR NEM RÁN)

Yields about 2-1/3 to 2-1/2 cups packed filling, about twenty-four 1-inch by 2-1/2-inch rolls each with about a rounded tablespoon filling

Filling

1/2 ounce cellophane noodles
Optional: 1/2 ounce dried cloud/tree ear mushrooms
About 1 ounce shallots, 2 small, 4 tablespoons peeled and minced
1/4 ounce garlic, 1 large clove, 1-1/2 teaspoons peeled and finely minced
2 tablespoons egg white, from 1 large egg
2 teaspoons palm sugar or maple syrup
4 ounces peeled and deveined 26/30 shrimp
2 ounces crabmeat, picked through for shells and shredded
   or 2 ounces extra peeled and deveined shrimp
8 ounces lean ground pork, 1 cup packed
2 tablespoons fish sauce
1 ounce shredded or finely diced carrot, 2 tablespoons
Scant 1/4 ounce mint leaves, 2 tablespoons finely sliced
1/4 ounce cilantro, 2 tablespoons finely sliced
Scant 1/4 ounce Thai or Italian basil leaves, 2 tablespoons finely sliced

Twelve to fifteen 6-1/2- by 6-1/2- by 9-inch triangular tapioca *or* rice paper wrappers,
5 ounces
   or four 13-inch round tapioca *or* rice paper wrappers
Oil for frying

Plate Garnish

1 pound head Boston or bibb lettuce, whole leaves washed and dried
Sliced bird's eye chilies
Mixture of Thai basil, mint, and cilantro leaves

Dipping Sauce

Nuoc Cham

1 Soak cellophane noodles in hot water and mushrooms in another bowl of hot water until soft, 20 minutes. Drain and squeeze each well. Chop or cut noodles with scissors into 1/2-inch pieces to yield about 1/3 cup noodles. Place in bowl and set aside covered.

2 If using, finely chop mushrooms and place with noodles; set aside.

3 Pulse-grind shallots, garlic, palm sugar, and egg white, add shrimp (use extra if not using crab), and pulse-grind until just slightly chunky. Scrape mixture into bowl with mushrooms.

4 In a medium-sized mixing bowl, mix together crab, if using, pork, fish sauce, carrot, and herbs and season with 1/2 teaspoon salt and freshly ground pepper. Fold in noodle-shrimp mixture.

5 To fill, roll and fry rolls, see *Technique: Vietnamese Crispy Fried Rice Paper Rolls.*

6 **To Serve:** Arrange hot rolls on platter with the **plate garnish** and **dipping sauce**: *Nuoc Cham. To eat:* Fill a lettuce leaf with chilies and herbs, add spring roll, fold together, and dip into *Nuoc Cham.*

FIGURE 3.49   Shrimp mousse on sugarcane.
Source: © phloen/Fotolia.

GRILL, GRIDDLE, ROAST, BROIL, AND BARBECUE

Signature Technique: Vietnamese Mousse on a Stick

Traditional cooks prepare chao tom by pounding ingredients with a mortar and pestle, but a food processor makes it fast. The ethereal mousse is a tasty canvas for improvised flavors.

For 12 to 13 ounces shelled shrimp, fish fillets, scallops, or boneless, skinless chicken breast

- *Prepare "mousse"* in food processor with seasonings. Adding oil or minced pork fat enriches low-fat fish, shrimp, or chicken breast mousses. Try coconut oil or bacon for more flavor. Set mousse aside to firm and rest, 20 minutes.

- Prepare Dipping Sauce: Clean greens and herbs for garnish. Slice sugarcane into 12 thin sticks about 1/4- to 1/2-inch diameter and 4 to 5 inches long. If using lemongrass, trim away top and slice it into 4- to 5-inch sections; slice thicker sections lengthwise into thin sticks with root attached. Blot sticks dry with paper towel and set aside.

- Set up a Steamer: Line steamer tray with parchment.

- Rub hands with oil. Divide mousse into 12 equal-sized balls.

- Set up a small bowl of oil, steamer tray, a plate, shrimp mousse balls, and sugarcane or lemongrass sticks on work surface. Rub hands with oil again. Flatten one mousse ball in the palm of a hand into a 2-1/2-inch square. Place a sugarcane or lemongrass stick on top, leaving its ends hanging out, and form mousse around the middle of the stick. Pat and smooth mousse while turning the stick. Set finished stick into steamer. Make remaining 11 sticks. Fill steamer; when it's full, set remaining sticks on plate.

- Bring water in steamer to a boil, set filled steamer tray into it, and cover. Steam mousse sticks until slightly puffed and opaque, 2 to 3 minutes. Remove steamed skewers and set on tray. Fill steamer again and, when boiling, finish steaming remaining skewers. Cool. Refrigerate up to 2 days and bring to room temperature before grilling.

- Steaming isn't strictly necessary; it may be skipped and the skewers can be grilled only. For do-ahead parties, steaming first, grilling later, saves time.

- Set up platter with lettuce leaves, herbs, and dipping sauce.

- Heat grill, cast-iron grill pan, or broiler to medium-high heat. Oil shrimp mousse lightly. Grill chao tom, turning frequently, until sizzling and browned, 5 to 7 minutes. Slice mousse vertically (parallel with stick) into 3 or 4 slices.

- **To Serve:** Transfer sliced mousse and grilled sugarcane sticks to a serving plate. Instruct diners to wrap mousse slice in lettuce leaf with herbs and dip in sauce before taking a bite. Grilled sweet sugarcane is an added bonus on which to chew.

VIETNAMESE SHRIMP MOUSSE ON SUGARCANE (CHAO TÔM)

To moonlight these as 1- to 2-bite party food, make them into smaller 1/2-ounce logs (1-1/2 inch by 1 inch), steam, and grill. Slide them onto bamboo skewers before serving. To tone down the fish sauce, use less, and season with salt, but fish sauce does give an umami-hypnotic quality.

Yields 12 ounces, twelve 1-ounce servings

Mousse Base

Yields about 1-1/2 cups

1 pound 26/30 shrimp, about 12 ounces peeled and deveined
1 tablespoon mild vegetable oil *or* fragrant coconut oil
2 teaspoons tapioca starch *or* cornstarch

Mousse Seasonings

2 to 3 teaspoons fish sauce
2 teaspoons crushed palm sugar *or* maple syrup
1/2 ounce shallot, 1 medium, 2 tablespoons peeled and minced
1 red bird's eye chili, stemmed and minced
    or 1/4 teaspoon freshly ground black pepper
    or 1 teaspoon chili paste

For Serving

3/4 cup *Nuoc Cham* dipping sauce
12 ounce head tender leaf lettuce, bibb, Boston, red leaf, green leaf, or butter leaf
1 ounce trimmed cilantro sprigs, about 12
1/2 ounce mint sprigs, 6 large sprigs, leaves removed and stems discarded
1/2 ounce Thai basil sprigs, 6 sprigs, leaves removed and stems discarded

Three 4- to 5-inch long pieces sugarcane
    or 4 to 6 fat, long stalks lemongrass
    or 20-ounce can sugarcane sticks
Oil as needed for forming mousse

1 Drop shrimp into mixing bowl with 1 tablespoon kosher salt. Stir well for 20 seconds, and pour them into a colander. Rinse shrimp well with cold water, drain, and blot with paper towel. This firms the shrimp. Coarsely chop shrimp and pour into food processor with 1/4 teaspoon kosher salt, oil, tapioca or cornstarch, fish sauce, sugar or syrup, shallot, and chili or pepper or chili paste.

2 Process mousse, in pulses, until a coarse, fluffy paste forms. Scrape into a bowl and cover with plastic wrap; rest shrimp mousse 20 minutes in refrigerator. Fry a small bit of mousse to check for seasonings, if desired.

3 Prepare **nuoc cham** dipping sauce.

4 **Prep elements for serving and forming:** Clean greens and herbs. Slice sugarcane into 12 thin sticks about 1/4- to 1/2-inch diameter and 4 to 5 inches long. If using lemongrass, trim away top and slice it into 4- to 5-inch sections; halve thick sections lengthwise into thin sticks. Blot sticks dry with paper towel and set aside.

5 **Set-up:** If not using commercial steamer, set up two steamer baskets over wok. Add water to wok: it should be 1 inch from bottom of steamer baskets. Steaming isn't necessary—chao tom may just be grilled. Cut out 12 small squares of parchment. Place a small bowl of oil, steamer tray, a parchment-covered half-sheet pan, shrimp mousse, and sugarcane or lemongrass sticks on work surface.

6 **To form:** With oiled hands, divide mousse into 12 equal-sized balls and place on sheet pan. Flatten one ball in the palm of a hand into a 2-1/2-inch square. Place a sugarcane or lemongrass stick on top, leaving the ends hanging out, and form mousse around the middle of the stick. Pat and smooth mousse as around the stick. Set finished stick onto one parchment square, and set on sheet pan. Parchment will keep the mousse from sticking to the steamer basket. Finish forming remaining balls.

7 **To steam:** Bring water in wok to a boil. Fill steamer trays, place on wok, and cover top tray. Steam chao tom until slightly puffed and opaque, 2 to 3 minutes. Remove steamed chao tom and arrange on clean parchment covered sheet pan. Cool. Refrigerate chao tom 1 day; bring to room temperature before grilling.

8 Set up platter with lettuce leaves, herbs, and dipping sauce.

9 Heat grill, cast-iron grill pan, or broiler to medium-high heat. Oil chao tom lightly. Grill chao tom, turning frequently, until sizzling and browned, 5 to 7 minutes if raw and less if cooked. Slice mousse vertically (parallel with stick) into 2 to 3 slices.

10 **To Serve:** Transfer sliced mousse and grilled sugarcane sticks, if using, to a serving plate. Instruct diners to wrap mousse slice in lettuce leaf with herbs and dip in sauce before taking a bite.

FIGURE 3.50 Vietnamese shrimp mousse on lemongrass (chao tôm).

Vary! Improvise!

☞ *Devise and season a chicken chao or scallop chao.*

☞ *Optional Non-Traditional Seasonings: Add 1/4 ounce cilantro leaves (2 tablespoons sliced) and/or 1/2 to 1 ounce gingerroot (1 tablespoon peeled and minced) to* **Mousse Seasonings.**

SALAD AND VEGETABLE METHODS

SIGNATURE RECIPE

VIETNAMESE NOODLE SALAD BOWL (BUN)

Originally from South Vietnam, this dish is a layered salad. Served room temperature, it has six basic elements: rice vermicelli; salad mix with sliced lettuce, herbs, sprouts, and fresh vegetables; stir-fried or grilled meat or seafood; chopped roasted peanuts; nuoc cham; and crispy shallots. Bun gives leftovers a starring role: slice or dice leftover grilled steak or pork or stir-fry or grill extra shrimp, scallops or fish for the next day's Bun Bowl.

4 servings

11 to 12 ounces rice vermicelli

Stir-Fried Beef *or* **Chicken**

2 to 3 tablespoons oil
5 ounces onions, about 1 cup peeled and finely slivered
1 pound flank steak, finely sliced cross-grain, then each slice into 1-inch pieces
    or 1 pound boneless, skinless, trimmed chicken breasts, finely sliced cross-grain
1 to 2 tablespoons fish sauce

Salad and Vegetable Mix

4 ounces Romaine lettuce leaves, about 4 large leaves, 4 cups loosely packed
    or red leaf lettuce, *or* bibb or Boston lettuce
8 ounces cucumber, peeled lightly, 1-1/2 cups halved lengthwise and finely sliced
8 to 9 ounces mung sprouts, about 3 cups rinsed 30 seconds in hot water and drained
1 ounce *or* more mixed herb leaves: cilantro, culantro, mint, red perilla and Thai basil, 2 cups, loosely packed

1 to 1-1/2 cups *Nuoc Cham*
2 to 3 ounces roasted unsalted peanuts, 1/2 cup lightly chopped

Garnishes

Crispy Shallots
Lime wedges

1 Soak rice vermicelli in hot water until pliable, 5 to 10 minutes, and drain to yield 4 cups soaked, drained noodles.

2 Heat wok over high heat and when hot, drizzle in 2 teaspoons to 1 tablespoon oil. Stir-fry onion until it is brown-seared and tender. Scrape into bowl.

3 Reheat wok over high heat, swirl in more oil, and add half the meat and spread out on wok bottom for maximum exposure. Brown and cook meat until partially done and flip to brown remaining side. Leave beef slightly pink for best texture. (Cook chicken in same way, but all the way through.) Repeat with remaining meat. Meat may be grilled for more flavor. Toss cooked meat in bowl with fish sauce and freshly ground pepper.

4 Prepare **salad and vegetable mix**. Remove large ribs from lettuce leaves and slice leaves into fine ribbons. Toss together lettuce leaves, cucumber, mung sprouts, and herbs in a large bowl.

Vary! Improvise!

☞ *Vegetarian Bun:* Devise a vegetarian bun bowl with grilled vegetables. Season it highly.

☞ *Grilled Pork Bun:* Finely slice 1 pound pork tenderloin into coins or half-moons, toss with oil, and grill until almost done. Don't overcook pork or it'll be like shoe leather. Season with 2 cloves minced garlic and 1 to 2 tablespoons fish sauce.

☞ *Grilled Shrimp Bun:* Peel and devein 1 pound 21/25 shrimp. Toss with oil and grill until just opaque. Season with salt and freshly ground black pepper.

5 Prepare **nuoc cham** and set aside in serving container with spout. Chop roasted, unsalted peanuts, place in serving bowl, and set aside. Place **garnishes**, crispy shallots and lime wedges, in small serving bowls.

6 Bring a large pot of water to boil. Set up four large serving bowls. When ready to serve, place 1/4 portion (about 1 cup) noodles into strainer and dip into boiling water 20 to 30 seconds. Drain well, and pour noodles into 1 serving bowl. Repeat with remaining 3 noodle portions. Scatter 1/4 portion of salad and vegetable mix over noodles, then top with cooked meat and onions.

7 **To Serve:** Pass nuoc cham, peanuts, and crispy shallots so diners can garnish the bun bowl to personal taste. A squeeze of lime wouldn't be out of place.

VIETNAMESE CABBAGE, CARROT, AND CHICKEN SALAD (GÒI GÀ OR GA XE PHAY)

This may be served at room temperature or chilled.

Yields about 5 cups, 4 servings

8 ounces green cabbage leaves, 4 to 6 large
6 ounces carrot
1 pound boneless, skinless chicken breast, about 12 ounces baked

Dressing

Yields about 5 fluid ounces

2 tablespoons fish sauce
4 tablespoons freshly squeezed lime juice
2 tablespoon rice vinegar
2 tablespoons vegetable oil
Optional: 2 tablespoons sugar or maple syrup

3/4 ounce shallot, 1 large, 2 tablespoons peeled and thinly sliced
1/4 ounce garlic, 1 large clove, 1-1/2 teaspoons peeled and minced
1 red or green bird's eye chili, finely sliced
1/2 ounce mint leaves, 1/2 cup finely sliced, *divided*
1-1/4 ounces roasted peanuts or cashews, 1/4 cup chopped

1 Remove ribs of each cabbage leaf. Stack leaves and slice cabbage into 1/8-inch by 1/8-inch by 2-inch julienne to yield 3 cups. Slice carrots into 1/8-inch by 1/8-inch by 2-inch julienne to yield 1-1/2 cups. Toss cabbage in a small bowl with 2 teaspoons kosher salt. In another bowl toss carrot with 1 teaspoon kosher salt. Set aside vegetables until soft and wilted, about 30 minutes. Rinse vegetables, and drain well. Place them into a clean cotton or paper towel, and blot dry. Transfer vegetables to large mixing bowl.

2 Steam, poach, roast or grill chicken. Cool meat; shred or slice thinly to yield about 3 cups. Place into small mixing bowl.

3 Stir together **dressing** ingredients (fish sauce, lime juice, vinegar, oil, and optional sweetener) until sugar dissolves. Fold **dressing**, shallot, garlic, and chili into cabbage and carrot in bowl. Marinate 20 minutes. Ingredients may be refrigerated and held several hours at this point.

4 **To Serve:** Reserve 1 tablespoon mint for garnish. Toss chicken and remaining mint with cabbage and carrot mixture. Taste salad, season with salt and pepper, and adjust flavors with lime juice or vinegar. Pile salad on serving plate and garnish with reserved mint and nuts.

Source: *Authentic Vietnamese Cooking* by Corinne Trang.

Vary! Improvise!

☞ *Tuna Salad:* Substitute 1 pound tuna, grilled medium, for chicken. Dice into small cubes.

☞ Add other herbs like Thai basil or cilantro.

☞ Substitute other roasted nuts or seeds for peanuts or cashews.

☞ Add 1/2 cup finely sliced celery for more crunch.

☞ Finely slice 2 ounces green onions, about 4, and toss with dressing ingredients.

☞ *Vietnamese Cole Slaw:* Prepare a salad without chicken and with more cabbage and carrots, but don't wilt them. Add finely shredded cucumber and/or blanched mung sprouts if desired. Garnish with Vietnamese Crispy Shallots. Serve on top of large, round Vietnamese rice and sesame seed wafers (Banh Trang Me) that may be fried or microwaved until cracker-like. They are available at Vietnamese markets.

PICKLE AND PRESERVE

BANH MI: BAGUETTE SANDWICH

Banh mi is the sophisticated sub sandwich of Vietnam. A crusty baguette stuffed with seasoned roasted meat, liver paté, or cold cuts, kissed with mayonnaise and soy sauce, garnished with cucumber, chili, and cilantro, and graced with the sweet-sour bite of pickled daikon radish and carrot make this a sandwich memory not easy to forget.

FIGURE 3.51 Banh mi sandwich.
Source: © uckyo/Fotolia.

VIETNAMESE PICKLED RADISH AND CARROT (DO CHUA)

When purchasing the large, white daikon radish, look for ones that are around 1-1/2 inches wide: larger and they can be spongy, unpleasantly hot and bitter; smaller and they'll lack the bite and sweetness of mature daikon. Serve on sandwiches, with grilled meat or add to soups and stews.

Yields 1 quart

1 cup plus 2 tablespoons white vinegar
2 ounces sugar, 1/4 cup minus 2 teaspoons, reserved separately
1/2 pound carrots
1 pound daikon radish

1 Whisk together 1/2 cup boiling water, 1/2 teaspoon kosher salt, vinegar, and all but the 2 teaspoons sugar. Set aside.

2 Peel, wash, and cut carrots and daikon into 2-inch-long and 1/4-inch-thick matchsticks. Place in bowl. Knead and toss with 2 teaspoons sugar and 1 teaspoon kosher salt until a piece of daikon bends almost enough to touch its ends together without breaking, 15 minutes. Rinse and drain vegetables, pressing to rid them of water.

3 Tightly pack vegetables into a clean 1-quart glass canning jar. Pour hot vinegar mixture into jar until full. If there isn't enough to cover, spoon in 3 teaspoons vinegar and 1 teaspoon water.

4 Screw lid on tightly. Let pickles develop flavor 1 hour or up to 24 hours at room temperature. Refrigerate up to 4 weeks.

Source: *Into the Vietnamese Kitchen* by Andrea Nguyen.

Vary! Improvise!

☞ *Tweak the recipe with more carrots and less daikon or with less or more sugar.*

INDONESIA: UNITY IN DIVERSITY

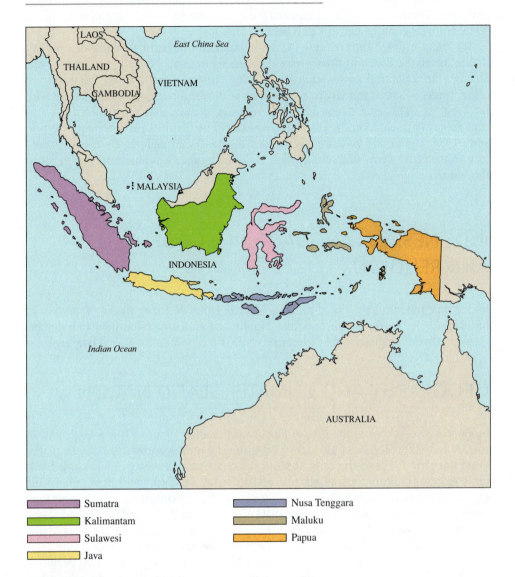

Sumatra
Kalimantam
Sulawesi
Java

Nusa Tenggara
Maluku
Papua

FIGURE 3.52 Map of Indonesia.

Indonesia: An Ancient Center of Trade and Influence

Rafael Steinberg writing for Time-Life Pacific and Southeast Asian Cooking *called Indonesia a "polyglot, cosmopolitan area of many domains (that) lacked in cohesiveness." Despite this difficulty, its location made Indonesia the center of routes of the shipping trade, which helped her to forge cultural and religious links throughout Asia and Southeast Asia. In the thirteenth century Marco Polo called Java "a very rich island" because of its spice production and the "great numbers of ships and merchants" who purchased them. Today Indonesia's national motto is "Unity in Diversity."*

Fossil remains of the "Java Man" gave historians reason to believe that people crossing a land bridge from India first inhabited the Indonesian archipelago. For two millennia, trading ships sailed between India and China via the Indonesian islands purchasing lumber and spice and leaving behind food, cooking techniques, language, political ideas, art, and Hindu, Buddhist, and Muslim religions. Hindu traders and priests had influence in the first and second centuries. Muslims invaded in the thirteenth century, and by the fifteenth century Islam was the favored religion.

During the sixteenth century, Portuguese, British, and Dutch traders greedy for nutmeg, ginger, cinnamon, clove, and mace fought over and plundered the Moluccas, also known as the Spice Islands, a collection of small islands south of the Philippines. The Dutch and their East India Trading Company took control of Indonesia. World War II and a brutal Japanese occupation expelled the Dutch overlords. With Japan's surrender in 1945, an Indonesian named Sukarno became president.

The Dutch invaded and attempted to regain Indonesia, but strong worldwide condemnation forced the Dutch to finally release Indonesia in 1949. Named president for life, Sukarno faced political power struggles; in 1967 General Suharto eased Sukarno from office. Under Suharto's military rule, Indonesia improved its economy and relations with the West. In 1997, after major economic setbacks, demonstrators demanded the corrupt Suharto's resignation. In 1999, Indonesia held its first free parliamentary election since 1955. Unrest and violence has plagued the nation throughout the twentieth century. In the early twenty-first century, four major earthquakes in nineteen months killed thousands.

INDONESIAN LANGUAGE, PHILOSOPHY, AND RELIGION

Multiethnic Indonesia's national motto is *Unity in Diversity*. Today almost 90 percent of Indonesians are Muslim, with Buddhist, Hindu, and Christian minorities. Indonesians speak numerous languages and dialects, but *Bahasa Indonesia* is the official language.

GEOGRAPHY AND CLIMATE: ISLAND NATION

Indonesia, also known as the *Ring of Fire*, means "Indian Islands." It is a large land of islands and 400 volcanoes (100 active) lying directly on three unstable tectonic plates. From the early 1970s to the early 1990s Indonesia endured twenty-nine recorded volcanic eruptions. Sitting on the equator and sprawled between the Indian and Pacific Oceans, this collection of more than 17,500 islands (922 inhabited) in a 2,300-mile long chain has the world's fourth largest population after China, India, and the United States. Squashed together, its landmass would take up the entire Eastern Seaboard from Maine down to Florida and east to Ohio, Kentucky, Tennessee, Mississippi, and Louisiana.

Warm coastal waters ensure fairly constant land temperatures of 70 to 90 degrees F with humidity 60 to 90 percent. June through September is typically the dry season and December through March typically the monsoon season. Typhoon damage is minimal; they weaken before penetrating this archipelago. Some of the world's largest islands make up Indonesia: Sumatra, Java, most of Kalimantan (Borneo), Sulawesi (Celebes), Halmahera, and the west half of New Guinea (Papua) and numerous smaller islands like Bali. Some boast mountain peaks of 9,000 feet (2,700 meters) or more.

FARMING AND AGRICULTURE

In Indonesia, cultivated or forest grown crops like rice, corn, vegetables, sago, coconut, spices, mung beans, cabbage, carrots, peanuts, potatoes, and asparagus prevail. Tropical fruits like bananas, mangos, papaya, oranges, and pineapples, along with plantation-grown coffee, tea, coconuts, sugar, and palm oil, grow in various regions. Farmers in the dry and mountainous areas practice mainly subsistence farming, but do grow root crops like *cassava* (tapioca). Over millennia, Indonesia's 400 volcanoes have rained lava and ash to enrich the soils of Java, Bali, and upland Sumatra, and support rice cultivation. Indonesia practices fixed irrigated rice farming and rotating slash-and-burn crop farming. The Spice Islands still grow and export cloves, nutmeg, and pepper.

INDONESIAN CUISINE: MASTERS OF SEAFOOD AND COCONUT

To develop fully, a cuisine must move from solitary home cooks to professionals for refinement, development, codification, and dissemination. Indonesian cooks are late bloomers. The first Indonesian cookbook was published in 1967. As a consequence, for years Indonesian food lay undeveloped.

Indonesian cuisine features a mixture of Chinese, Indian, Arab, and Western influences. With hundreds of different ethnic groups and rich variety, this cuisine is defined mainly by the use of seafood and coconut. Across the country cooks incorporate these ingredients into simple meals and condiments. The Spanish brought chilies and the Chinese introduced noodles, soy sauce (Indonesians added sugar to soy sauce to create *ketcap manis*), mung beans, tofu, and soybeans. (Indonesians fermented soybeans into *tempeh* cakes.)

Rice is important, but not all people can afford to eat it so the staple starches sago, sweet potatoes, tapioca, or maize substitute. Vegetables do not star in the Indonesian diet as they do in the rest of Asia, but Indonesians do love to forage wild plants and leaves. Star fruit, papaya, water spinach, long beans, eggplant, pumpkin, and cucumber are the most popular produce.

Food stalls or *warung* are the social center of small towns, selling household needs and snacks, fruit, and cooked meals like grilled chicken or fish, soup, mixed rice, or a meat or seafood dish. Pushcart hawkers make lunch or snacks an easy reach with shaved ice drizzled with syrup, jellies, and fruit, or satay or soup.

Sambal is the uniquely Indonesian invention of pounded or ground spices and chilies that, mixed with rice, act as condiment, seasoning, or sauce. *Gado gado*, a salad of raw vegetables, *rendang*, a spicy meat and coconut "stew," fried or grilled fermented soybean cake *tempeh*, meat or shrimp *saté*, peanut sauce, and *nasi goreng* (fried rice) are a small part of this large cuisine. *Rijsttafel* or "rice table," what many foreigners think of as an Indonesian meal, is a smorgasbord-like Dutch interpretation of Indonesian savory dishes and sambals invented during colonial times.

REGIONAL INDONESIA

Java, Sumatra, and Bali

The three islands of Java, Sumatra, and Bali have the greatest variety of food, with fertile gardens, coconut groves, and rice paddies. In the mountainous interiors, fresh fish is rare and salted fish the norm. Though fruit is abundant, those who live in rural areas away from orchards eat it rarely. The affluent and city dwellers have access to more variety and better food. People in poor, rural regions still experience hunger.

In general, Java, with its refined culture has subtle, spicy food. Sumatra, with lots of chilies, garlic, shallots, galangal, turmeric, lemongrass, basil, lime and salam leaves, dried shrimp paste, and coconut, is hot-spicy and complex. Sulawesi is known for its fish dishes: in particular, fish roasted over coals with a spicy dipping sauce. In non-Islamic Bali, spit-roasted suckling pig, slow-cooked spiced duck, chili-hot dishes, and purple sticky rice with coconut are popular. Wild game and boar, plus wild leafy greens, star fruit, ferns, jackfruit, green papaya, and coconut star in Borneo's diet. The rocky, semi-arid eastern islands have poor soil, little rainfall, and therefore, a sparse diet.

FIGURE 3.53 Indonesian rural village.
Source: © rigamondis/Fotolia.

DINE AT HOME IN INDONESIA

Dining in an Indonesian home is relaxed and informal. Guests have a special place, so wait for the hosts to seat the guests. In most homes the hostess or host will prepare the meal early in the day and everyone will eat it at room temperature later. Indonesians value variety in a meal over quantity.

Mealtime in Indonesia is communal: the hostess will place a large bowl of rice with many small dishes like *rendang* and *sambals* around it in the middle of a table or on a mat on the floor. *Silakan makan* is the invitation to "please eat." In Muslim homes, Indonesians eat and pass food with the right hand *only*. Serving spoons will come with each dish; use the left hand to serve. Some homes will provide a spoon and fork.

The host will encourage guests to help themselves first, but it's good manners to insist that others do, then capitulate. Men generally go before women. It's impolite to pile a plate with food, so take small amounts. Indonesians eat *all* of what they take. To counteract spicy sambals, mix them with rice. Coffee, or in non-Muslim homes, beer, arrack, or *brem* (sweet palm wine) might be offered.

TASTES OF INDONESIA

Fat: Coconut oil and milk, vegetable oil, peanut oil

Sweet: Palm sugar, sugar

Sour/Alcohol: Tamarind, lime, lemon, vinegar

Salty: *Ketcap manis* (salty-sweet soy sauce), dried anchovies, *trasi* (shrimp paste), dried shrimp

Spicy-Hot: Ginger, black pepper, red chilies, bird's eye chilies, Java pepper

Aromatic Seasoning Vegetables: Shallots, onions, ginger, garlic, galangal, lemongrass, green onion, fresh turmeric

Spice: Five-spice powder, star anise, anise, fennel, coriander, cinnamon, cardamom, cloves, pepper, cumin, nutmeg, bay leaves, turmeric, nutmeg

Herbs, Seasonings, and Condiments: *Salam* leaf, Kaffir lime leaf, curry leaves, knotgrass leaf (Vietnamese coriander), pandan leaf, cilantro, celery leaves, Thai basil, lemongrass, mint, dill, curry leaf, *tulsi* (holy basil), preserved soybeans, ketchup, dried grated coconut, *serundeng* (spiced and fried grated coconut), *krupuk* (shrimp crackers), *bawang goreng* (crisp fried shallots), *sambal* (chili sauce), *pecel* (vegetables, peanut paste, and shrimp cracker)

Other Important Foods: Rice (black sticky, long-grain rice), tofu, tempeh, mung beans and sprouts, tomatoes, wheat, tapioca (cassava), *kemiri* (candlenuts), peanuts, coconut, fruit (watermelon, jackfruit, bananas, tropical fruit [see *Tastes of Thailand* and *Tastes of Vietnam*], winter melon), chayote squash, avocado, pumpkin, seafood (crabs, prawns, shellfish), dried fish, meat (beef, lamb, goat, chicken, duck), snow peas, asparagus, long beans, green beans, sweet potato, okra, eggplant, daikon radish, taro, lettuce, pumpkin, mustard greens, bell peppers, jicama, potatoes, cabbage, corn, cucumber, mushrooms

Popular Dishes: *Rendang* (spiced, cooked, shredded meat), *sayur asam* (tamarind and vegetable soup), *lemper roll* (meat

COMMON INDONESIAN COOKING TOOLS

Grinding stone, mortar and pestle, coconut grater, wok-like *kuali* or *wajan*

FIGURE 3.54 Komodo Island, Indonesia.
Source: © RCH/Fotolia.

and rice roll in banana leaf), *gado-gado* (vegetable salad with peanut sauce), *soto ayam* (chicken and vegetable soup), *opor ayam* (chicken coconut soup), *nasi goreng* (fried rice with egg, sausage, and vegetables), *saté* (skewered, grilled meat), *sambal* (spicy stew), *rijsttafel* (Dutch-Indonesian buffet), *acar* (vegetable pickle), *krupuk* (prawn cracker), *ayam goreng* (spicy fried chicken), *tempeh* (fermented soy cake), *bakso,* (meatball soup), *semur* (beef stew with kecap manis and seasonings), *bubur* (rice porridge with condiments), *aceh* (spicy noodle and seafood or goat dish either dry or soupy), *nasi padang* (rice, chili, and coconut dish), *perkedel* (fritters), *sambal goreng teri* (anchovy with peanuts), *martabak* (stuffed egg pancake), spring roll, deep-fried dumplings, *rujak* (fruit or vegetable salad), *bubur kacang hijau* (sweet mung bean coconut porridge), sweet coconut cake, *klepon* (glutinous rice balls filled with coconut sugar), battered and fried bananas, *cendil* (coconut and rice jellies cakes)

Drinks: Chinese tea, palm toddy, beer, sweet coffee, sweet iced tea, *bandrek* (ginger and coconut sugar drink), *cendol* (coconut with rice jellies), *dadiah* (water buffalo milk yogurt), *brem* (sweet alcoholic beverage), *kopi luwak* (coffee made from beans digested by palm civet animal)

INDONESIAN FLAVOR FOUNDATIONS

Indonesian Signature Aromatic Vegetable Combo

Onion, garlic, ginger, or galangal and chilies

Signature Seasonings

See *Thailand* and *Vietnam Signature Seasonings* for more Indonesian seasonings.

Liquid/Paste

Ketcap Manis
This thick, sweet, and syrupy soy sauce is best when made sweetened with palm sugar.

Animal

Shrimp Paste
See *Thailand Signature Seasonings*.

Vegetable/Fruit

Candlenuts
Round, fatty nut used to thicken Indonesian curries and add texture and flavor to many dishes. Substitute macadamia nuts or raw cashews. **Candlenuts are toxic when raw and must be cooked before eating.**

Herbal/Spice

Java Pepper or Cubeb Pepper
Java pepper is a pungently aromatic spice similar in appearance to peppercorns, but with the stem attached. Its flavor can be acrid, slightly bitter, and persistent. Some describe its flavor as a cross between warm, woody allspice and black pepper. Arab trade via India brought the spice to Europe and Africa.

Indonesian cooks use it to flavor many dishes, especially curries.

Salam Leaf
Many Indonesian and Malaysian cookbooks call for the subtly flavored salam leaf, from the cassia (cinnamon) family, and suggest that deprived cool-climate cooks substitute bay leaves. Bay leaves are nothing like this aromatic and slightly sour/astringent salam leaf. Available fresh only in Indonesia and Malaysia (the tree grows wild there), salam leaves are available dry in some Southeast Asian groceries catering to Indonesians. Cooks fry the leaves in oil to bring out their delicate flavor. Some cooks substitute the more flavorful Indian curry leaves.

FIGURE 3.55 Candlenuts.
Source: Matthew Ward, Dorling Kindersley.

FIGURE 3.56 Cubeb peppercorns.
Source: Dave King, Dorling Kindersley.

FIGURE 3.57 Salam leaf.
Source: Dave King, Dorling Kindersley.

SEASONING AND PASTE MIXTURES

COOK'S VOICE: LINDA KURNIAWAN

Indonesian-Born Caterer and Homemaker
Sydney, Australia

"Bumbu is a general description for something that you use to spice up your cooking. It could be as simple as garlic and salt, or it could also be a complex combination of different spices and herbs. It could be in powder or paste or freshly ground spices, and it could also be a mix of spice and soy sauce. So basically we call everything that we use in cooking to season as bumbu! The combination of palm sugar, tamarind and chili peppers is especially perfect for a hot day."

Signature Technique: Indonesian Spice Paste (Sambal)

Many Indonesian dishes like sambal goreng and rendang start with this ground aromatic seasoning vegetable paste. It may be used singly or in combination with other seasonings. Sambals are fried in fat before adding other ingredients, much like Thai curry pastes.

1 Indonesian cooks prepare spice pastes with a grinding stone and peeled, sliced, or chopped ingredients. Modern kitchens use a small wet-and-dry grinder.

2 If using a blender, water or coconut milk must be used if the paste will be simmered. Oil is used to grind the paste if the paste will be fried.

3 Pastes melt easily into stir-fries, marinades, soups, and sauces. Indonesian cooks prepare sambals in batches and keep them refrigerated, ready for quick meals.

FIGURE 3.58 Indonesian sambal.
Source: © airdone/Fotolia.

MILD SPICE PASTE (SAMBAL)

Use this sambal to spark a stir-fry, soup, or stew. Add fresh chilies to make it a spicy sambal.

Yields 1-3/4 cups paste

12 ounces shallots, about 12 medium, 2-1/3 cups peeled and chopped
3 to 4 ounces gingerroot, 1/2 cup peeled and coarsely chopped
1-1/2 ounces garlic cloves, 6 large, 1/3 cup peeled and halved lengthwise
About 2 ounces candlenuts or macadamia nuts, 1/2 cup
3 tablespoons canola oil

1 Place shallots, gingerroot, garlic, and nuts into a food processor. Pulse-grind until pasty and evenly puréed.

2 Heat a wok over medium heat and drizzle in oil. When hot, scrape in paste and fry, mashing and turning paste to cook evenly, until vegetables are soft, 5 to 10 minutes.

3 Cool paste and refrigerate in glass jar up to 1 week.

4 **To Use**: Fry spice paste in oil until fragrant and add cubes of meat or vegetables, or simmer it in liquids like chicken stock or coconut milk. Good tossed on vegetables or on a pound of cooked rice noodles or pasta.

CHILI PASTE (SAMBAL ULEK OR SAMBAL OELEK)

Sambal ulek is the most basic sambal. Although any fresh red chili may be used, the longer and milder Indonesian chili known as *lombok* is traditional. Prepare sambal ulek by chopping 3- to 3-1/2-inch-long red chilies, then pounding or grinding them with kosher salt, in a mortar or blender until they become a coarse paste. Will keep refrigerated 1 month. Sambal ulek can be used as a base for other sambals or as an addition to dishes; it may be purchased ready-made in Southeast Asian groceries.

Sambal Trasi

Add a small amount of shrimp paste to sambal ulek, and grind with the salt.

Sambal Manis

Season sambal ulek with tamarind paste (soaked and strained) and palm sugar.

Sambal Bakso

Season sambal ulek with sugar and white vinegar. Use in *bakso* (meatball beef soup).

SAUCE

INDONESIAN PEANUT SAUCE (SAMBAL KACANG)

Fried shallots are available at many Thai markets. Serve this sauce with Saté or Gado-Gado.

Yields about 2 cups, 4 to 6 servings

4-1/2 to 5 ounces dry-roasted roasted peanuts, 1 cup
1/2 ounce garlic, 2 large cloves, peeled and bruised
1/2 ounce bird's eye chilies, 3 to 4, stemmed and finely sliced
   or 1/2 ounce serrano chilies, about 1, 1 tablespoon stemmed and sliced
1-1/2 to 2 ounces galangal *or* gingerroot, 3 tablespoons peeled and chopped
1 Kaffir lime leaf
3 tablespoons ketcap manis
2 to 3 tablespoons freshly squeezed lime juice, 1 large lime

Garnish: 2 to 3 tablespoons *Fried Shallots*

1 Grind peanuts, garlic, chilies, and galangal or ginger in blender until fine. Add 1/2 cup water and grind until smooth.

2 Pour paste into medium saucepan, rinse out blender with 1-1/2 cups water, and pour into saucepan. Stir in lime leaf and ketcap manis.

3 Simmer sauce over low heat, stirring occasionally to prevent sticking, until thick, about 20 minutes. Taste and season with salt and lime juice.

4 **To Serve:** Remove lime leaf. Stir in fried shallots. Serve warm.

INDONESIAN COCONUT DRESSING

The shrimp paste gives this dressing a uniquely Indonesian flavor. This is a basic version of a dressing used on blanched vegetables. Other versions are made into a spiced grated coconut "paste" with galangal, garlic, salam leaves, and tamarind instead of lime juice and tossed on blanched vegetables.

Yields about 1-1/2 cups

1/2 fresh coconut, about 1-1/2 cups shredded fresh *or* frozen fresh coconut
   or 3 ounces unsweetened, dry, shredded coconut, 1 cup
1/2 teaspoon *Sambal Ulek*, mashed bird's eye chilies or chili paste
   or 1/2 teaspoon crushed red chili flakes

1/2 ounce shallot, 1 small, 2-1/2 to 3 teaspoons peeled and minced
6 tablespoons fresh lime juice, about 2 limes
2 teaspoons palm sugar, more to taste
Optional: 1/2 teaspoon shrimp paste

1 If using dried, unsweetened coconut, soak in 1/2 cup warm water 15 to 20 minutes. Grind coconut in blender until milky. Pour into bowl.

2 Whisk coconut with chili, shallot, lime juice, and palm sugar. Whisk in shrimp paste if using. Season sauce with salt to taste and set aside to develop flavors 20 minutes. Taste again and adjust flavors with more lime juice, salt, or sugar.

3 **To Use:** Drizzle coconut dressing on *urap*—a salad made with mixed blanched vegetables (green beans, carrots, chayote squash, shredded cabbage, and spinach), fried tempeh, and mung sprouts or on *jukut murab*—a salad of black-eyed peas, cucumber, green onions, and mint or basil.

SIMMER, STEW, POACH, BOIL, AND STEAM

Indonesian Soup (Sop and Soto)

Indonesians eat soup at any meal; rice is a must-have accompaniment. Soup is like tasty sauce: Indonesians serve it along with everything else and often pour soup over rice or noodles to moisten and flavor. Indonesian soups are simple: clear stock with meat, fish, or vegetables (*sop*) or thicker (*soto*), filled with coconut milk, fried potatoes, noodles, vegetables, or hard-boiled eggs and spice paste.

Signature Technique: Indonesian Soup

1 Cook chicken to make a broth or have stock on hand.

2 Prepare a sambal.

3 Cut vegetables into bite-sized pieces. Slice meat thinly and fish or seafood into small chunks so they cook quickly, 2 to 4 minutes. Or shred cooked chicken from broth.

4 Simmer sambal in broth or fry sambal paste and add broth or stock. Simmer with salam leaves, smashed stalk of lemongrass, and/or lime leaf.

5 Add vegetables and meat (beef, goat, lamb, or chicken and offal) or seafood and cook until just done. Or precook meat and vegetables and layer into serving bowl. Ladle stock or broth over and serve with condiments.

6 Season soup to taste salty, sour, sweet, and hot with lime juice, and bird's eye chilies or chili paste.

7 Garnish soup with saw-leaf, cilantro leaves, lemon basil, or other herbs of choice.

INDONESIAN CHICKEN SOUP (SOTO AYAM)

Soto is Indonesian comfort food. Extra substance comes from the addition of noodles, lontong (compressed rice), or potato croquettes (perkedel). Many soto dishes originate in Java; each small town has its specialty. Some Javanese substitute fried potatoes for perkedel and serve soto ayam with plain rice.

Poyah, a mixture of ground fried shrimp cracker (krupuk udang), ground fried garlic, and salt is a condiment traditionally served on soto ayam.

Yields about 8 cups, 4 servings

2-1/2 pounds chicken thighs, legs, and breast, about 2 pounds skinned and fat removed
2 large eggs
Vegetable oil as needed
14 ounces potatoes, 2 medium potatoes peeled

Sambal

Yields 1/2 cup

2-1/2 ounces shallot, 3 medium, 1/2 cup peeled and coarsely chopped
3/4 ounce garlic, 3 large cloves, crushed and peeled
1/2 ounce gingerroot, 1 tablespoon peeled and coarsely chopped
1/2 ounce candlenuts (*kemiri*), 6 to 8
    or 1/2 ounce macadamia nuts, 6 to 8
2 teaspoons turmeric

1 tablespoon vegetable or fragrant coconut oil
1/2 ounce garlic, 2 large cloves, 4 teaspoons peeled and finely sliced
Scant 1/2 ounce galangal, smashed
    or 1 teaspoon dried, ground galangal
1 stalk lemongrass, bottom bulb trimmed to 4 to 5 inches and smashed
    or 2 teaspoons dried ground lemongrass
3 ounces celery cabbage, 2 leaves, 1 cup leaves halved lengthwise and finely sliced
    or 3 ounces green cabbage, 1 cup finely sliced

Garnish

Fried Crispy Shallots
Poyah (see headnote)

For Serving

1 to 2 limes, sliced into wedges
Hot, cooked long-grain rice
Sambal ulek or sambal soto

1 **Cook chicken:** Place chicken into 4- to 5-quart saucepan and cover with 7 cups cold water. Bring to a boil, partially cover pan, reduce the heat, and simmer chicken until tender, 1 hour. Skim away and discard scum and fat.

2 **Hard-cook eggs:** Place eggs in small saucepan and cover by 1 inch with cold water. Bring to a boil. Remove pan from heat, cover and rest eggs in hot water 12 minutes. Drain eggs, place in bowl of cold water 10 minutes. Crack and peel eggs. Quarter eggs lengthwise and set aside in refrigerator until needed.

3 **Cut and fry potatoes:** Heat several inches of vegetable oil in wok over medium heat, or heat a deep fryer. With a mandoline, slice potatoes 1/16-inch thick to yield about 2 cups. Blot potatoes dry. When hot, add the potatoes to the oil, and fry until golden and crisp. Drain potatoes on paper towel and set aside until needed.

4 Remove chicken from broth and transfer to bowl; cool until easy to handle. Remove meat and discard bones and gristle. Shred meat to yield 3-1/2 cups cooked meat; set aside or refrigerate until ready for use. Strain broth and pour back into saucepan to yield 5 to 6 cups broth.

5 **Prepare sambal:** Meanwhile, grind shallot, garlic, ginger, and nuts in mini-processor or wet-dry grinder into a coarse paste. Scrape paste into bowl and stir in turmeric.

6 **Fry soup seasonings:** Heat oil in a wok or 8-inch skillet over medium heat. When hot, scatter sliced garlic into pan and fry until golden, 1 to 2 minutes. Transfer garlic to small bowl with slotted spoon; set aside. Reheat pan with oil remaining in it over medium-low heat, and add the sambal paste. Stir-fry until cooked through, 3 to 5 minutes.

7 **Season broth:** Bring soup broth to a boil. Place sambal, galangal, and lemongrass into broth. Reduce heat and cover pan; simmer broth 25 to 30 minutes.

8 **Just before serving:** Bring broth to a boil. Crush or chop the fried garlic and add to the reheated broth with cabbage and chicken. Remove pan from heat and rest soup 15 minutes. Season soup to taste with salt and freshly ground pepper.

9 **To Serve:** Ladle soto into 4 large soup bowls. Garnish each with 2 egg wedges, fried potatoes, and fried shallots. Garnish soto with *poyah* if desired. Serve with lime wedges, hot rice, and sambal ulek or sambal soto. Alternatively, spoon hot rice into soup plate and ladle soto over. Garnish with potatoes and eggs. Serve with lime wedges and fried shallots on the side.

Vary! Improvise!

☞ *Fast: Substitute good quality thick potato chips for house-fried potato chips.*

☞ *Faster: Substitute 3-1/2 cups shredded, cooked chicken (from 1 pound boneless skinless chicken breast) and 5 to 6 cups chicken stock for chicken and broth in recipe.*

FIGURE 3.59 Indonesian chicken soup (soto ayam) with Indonesian pickle (acar).

INDONESIAN FISH SOUP (IKAN KUAH KUNING)

This is a humble but spicy yellow-tinged soup. Salt and lemon basil or cilantro are essential.

Yields about 5 cups, 2 to 3 servings

Spice Paste

Yields 2/3 to 3/4 cup paste

3 ounces shallots, about 6 small, about 3/4 cup peeled and chopped
3/4 ounce garlic, 3 large cloves, 4 to 4-1/2 teaspoons peeled and chopped
1 ounce green chilies, 2 serranos or 1 jalapeño, 2 tablespoons stemmed and diced
1-1/2 ounces gingerroot, about 1 inch, 3 tablespoons peeled and chopped
1 teaspoon ground turmeric

1 to 2 tablespoons vegetable oil
1 stalk lemongrass, trimmed to bottom 3 to 4 inches, smashed
1 ounce gingerroot, about 1-inch piece peeled, sliced into 3 slices and smashed
1 Kaffir lime leaf
2 to 3 tablespoons fresh lime juice
1-1/4 pounds boned thick sea bass fillet, skinned

Garnish: About 1 ounce lemon basil leaves (*kemangi*) or trimmed cilantro, 1/2 cup finely sliced

1 Grind **spice paste** ingredients in a blender until smooth. Add 1 tablespoon water to facilitate grinding.

2 Heat oil in 3-quart saucepan over medium heat, and add spice paste, lemongrass, ginger, and lime leaf. Fry paste 2 to 3 minutes to infuse into oil. Pour in 2 cups water and bring to a boil. Lower the heat and simmer covered 15 to 20 minutes.

3 Dice fish into 3/4-inch cubes and toss in a small bowl with lime juice. Rest fish in refrigerator 5 to 10 minutes, but no longer. Fish will turn to mush.

4 **When ready to serve:** Bring soup broth to a boil. Turn off heat, stir fish into hot broth, cover, and rest soup 5 minutes. Give fish a stir to see if it's done. If not, simmer until fish is opaque.

5 **To Serve:** Discard lemongrass, ginger slices, and lime leaf. Season soup to taste with salt and pepper. Stir in lemon basil or cilantro and serve.

SIGNATURE RECIPE

INDONESIAN DRY STEW (RENDANG)

Meat long-cooked in seasonings and coconut milk is known as rendang. The meat simmers, and when the coconut milk evaporates, it fries. When a large buffalo was slaughtered, inhabitants needed to preserve excess meat, so rendang was born. Though buffalo and beef are traditional, parts of Indonesia prepare rendang from duck or chicken. Tamarind or vegetarian versions are made with jackfruit or cassava. This dish may not look like much, but its taste is rich and appealing.

Yields 3 cups, 4 to 6 servings

2 pounds buffalo *or* beef roast

Spice Paste

Yields 1/2 cup paste

2 ounces shallots, about 3 shallots, 1/2 cup peeled and coarsely chopped
1/2 ounce garlic, 2 large cloves, about 1 tablespoon peeled and minced
3 three-inch long dried red chilies, about 1 tablespoon stemmed, seeded, and broken up
2 ounces gingerroot, 1/4 cup peeled and coarsely chopped
    or 2 ounces galangal, 1/4 cup peeled and coarsely chopped
1/2 teaspoon turmeric

5 cups coconut milk
1 large Kaffir lime leaf
1 ounce lemongrass, bottom bulb trimmed to 3 to 4 inches, smashed
2 to 3 tablespoons freshly squeezed lime juice, 1 medium lime

To Serve

Hot sticky rice
Green vegetables

1   Dice meat into 3/4- to 1-inch cubes. There should be about 4 cups meat.

2   **Prepare spice paste:** Place shallots, garlic, chilies, and ginger or galangal into blender with turmeric and 3 to 4 tablespoons coconut milk. Grind seasonings to a smooth paste.

3   Stir meat, spice paste, lime leaf, lemongrass, and 1 teaspoon kosher salt together into a heavy, 4- to 6-quart nonreactive pot with remaining coconut milk. Bring to a boil over medium heat, lower heat to a gentle bubble, and cook until coconut milk has reduced, about 2 hours. Stir occasionally.

    *For quicker cooking poultry or vegetables, first cook spice paste and whole seasonings in coconut milk at a low boil until coconut milk has reduced, about 1 hour. Add poultry pieces (and 1 teaspoon tamarind paste) and continue to cook until liquid is very thick and reduced, 45 minutes to 1 hour.

4   Transfer rendang to a heavy 12- to 14-inch nonreactive skillet and, stirring frequently over medium-high heat, stir-fry and break up meat into shreds until it dries and darkens, and all the liquid and seasonings are absorbed into meat, 30 to 40 minutes. Stir in lime juice.

5   Rendang's finished texture should be brown, thick, dry, but oily and succulent. Remove whole seasonings. Rest rendang 15 to 20 minutes and taste. Adjust flavors with salt or more lime juice, if necessary.

6   **To Serve:** Serve rendang with hot sticky rice and green vegetables for a complete meal.

Vary! Improvise!

☞ **More Authentic Flavor:** Add 1/4 teaspoon shrimp paste to Spice Paste mixture.

☞ Use as a filling for flatbreads, roti, or tacos.

FIGURE 3.60   Beef rendang and sticky rice on a banana leaf.
Source: © paul_brighton/Fotolia.

FIGURE 3.61   Balinese rice terraces.
Source: © TravelPhotography/Fotolia.

INDONESIAN-BALINESE BLACK STICKY RICE WITH HOT COCONUT MILK

When cooked Balinese black rice turns deep purple. It makes an exotic breakfast. For haunting flavor, simmer the syrup with fresh pandan leaf.

Yields 2 cups cooked rice, 4 to 6 servings

8 ounces black "glutinous" sticky rice, 1-1/3 cups
3 ounces palm sugar, 1/4 cup
   or 1/3 cup maple syrup
1/4 teaspoon pandanus extract, available in Southeast Asian markets
12 to 14 fluid ounces fresh coconut milk
   or 13-1/2 to 14 ounce can unsweetened coconut milk
1 pound finger bananas, about 2 cups peeled and sliced
   or 13 to 16 ounce ripe mango, about 2 cups peeled and finely cubed or thinly sliced

1   Follow *Signature Technique: Glutinous (Sticky) Rice* for soaking and cooking glutinous rice. Steam soaked black rice at least 40 minutes; it's a whole grain so it may take longer. Keep rice hot.

2   Pour palm sugar into a saucepan with 2 tablespoons water and simmer, stirring occasionally, until palm sugar dissolves and is slightly syrupy. (Skip this if using maple syrup.) Stir pandanus extract and 1/4 teaspoon salt into palm sugar syrup *or* maple syrup. Toss hot rice with syrup. It's crucial to get sweetener on while rice is still hot because it will absorb better. Let rice sit covered until liquid is absorbed, 10 minutes.

3   Bring coconut milk to a simmer, but do not boil.

4   **To Serve:** Pile 1/2 cup rice in each of 4 serving bowls, pour 1/2 cup hot coconut milk over top. Serve garnished with sliced banana or mango.

MAGICAL PANDANUS LEAF

Though not easily available in the West, the fragrant pandan leaf is worth searching out in Asian markets (or growing indoors). Its flavor, subtle and nutty, adds an exotic hint to the dishes of Malaysia, Indonesia, Thailand, Singapore, and Sri Lanka. Known as "screwpine," this plant forms rosettes of long, arching spiny leaves, 18 to 30 inches long, maturing from all green, to green with pale yellow stripes. Simmer 1 leaf per cup coconut milk.

FIGURE 3.62   Pandan leaf.
Source: Dave King, Dorling Kindersley.

INDONESIAN YELLOW RICE (NASI KUNING)

This is a typical rice pilaf method and it reveals the influence of India and Thailand. See chapter India for more on pilaf technique. Balinese like to shape this rice into a cone in honor of the sacred Hindu mythical Mt. Meru. Yellow is one of four sacred Balinese colors, and the color of royalty.

Yields about 7 to 8 cups depending on the rice, 4 to 6 servings

14 ounces long-grain, jasmine, or basmati rice, 2 cups
2 tablespoons fragrant coconut oil or vegetable oil
2 ounces shallots, about 3 small, 1/2 cup finely sliced or diced
1 teaspoon ground turmeric
13.5 fluid ounce can coconut milk, about 1-3/4 cups
    or 2 cups fresh coconut milk
1 stalk lemongrass, trimmed to bottom 3- or 4-inches and smashed
1 large Kaffir lime leaf
1 cup chicken stock

1   Soak rice in cold water 20 to 30 minutes. Drain well.

2   Heat oil in 4-quart saucepan. Fry shallots until they begin to color, about 3 minutes. Add turmeric and fry 30 seconds. Add drained rice and fry 2 minutes.

3   Pour canned coconut milk into measuring cup and add enough water to make 2 cups total, about 1/4 cup; if using fresh coconut milk, disregard this step. Stir coconut milk and water, lemongrass, lime leaf, stock, and 1-1/2 teaspoons kosher salt into rice, and bring to a boil. Lower heat, cover pot, and simmer rice 15 minutes. Turn off heat and rest rice covered 10 minutes. Uncover rice and fluff. If not serving rice immediately, cover saucepan, and rest in warm spot up to 20 minutes.

4   **To Serve:** Fluff rice and pile into serving dish. Discard lemongrass and lime leaf or use as garnish. Serve rice with fish, meat, and vegetables.

FIGURE 3.63 Active Mt. Merapi volcano, Java, Indonesia.
Source: © Cecilia Lim/Fotolia.

INDONESIAN RICE ROLLS: LEMPER

Banana leaves form an enticing emerald green packet around *lemper* rolls. Steamed glutinous rice mixed with coconut milk, palm sugar, and pandan leaf is flattened onto banana leaves, filled with garlicky-spiced shredded chicken or beef, and rolled into a packet. Kencur or galangal, a gingery-resiny rhizome, and garlic, are central to lemper meat seasoning.

FIGURE 3.64 Savory grilled lemper rolls.
Source: © Blinztree/Fotolia.

Indonesian-Born Caterer and Homecook
Sydney, Australia

I was never taught how to cook step by step, so I just rely on my grandma, and my memory of how a dish tastes. My grandma never measures the ingredients she uses in cooking, so she pretty much describes the taste over the phone. I wish I had paid more attention while she was doing the cooking back then. Now I will make myself take notes while she cooks when I go back to Indonesia. My suggestions on my favorite Indonesian dishes . . . probably very traditional and authentic ones such as:

1. **Empek-empek Palembang:** A mixture of mackerel fish paste combined with tapioca starch, formed into fish shapes, and eaten with spicy palm sugar vinaigrette and diced cucumber.
2. **Sate Padang:** Saté made from beef, especially the tongue, cooked with herbs, then skewered, and eaten with a spicy rice flour-turmeric sauce.
3. **Siomay Bandung:** A mixture of mackerel fish paste combined with shredded *chokoes* (chayote, also called mirlitons), formed into a dough or combined with tofu or bitter gourd and eaten with peanut sauce.
4. **Martabak Telor:** Plain flour dough looks like a spring roll paper filled with beef mince, onions, scallions, and eggs, and pan-fried, eaten with a spicy palm sugar vinaigrette and pickled cucumber, carrots, and shallots.
5. **Gado-gado:** Salad of raw and cooked vegetables, tempeh, and shrimp chips served with peanut sauce.

STIR-FRY, PAN-FRY, AND DEEP-FRY

PALATE AROUSAL: INDONESIAN BASE, SAUCE, AND RELISH (SAMBAL)

Sambals, fiery condiments, can be a soft paste or thick sauce-like relish. Indonesians fry and add them to meat or seafood, eat them like a chutney, atop rice, meat, fish, or vegetables, or mix them with other ingredients. Sambals add a salty spice that arouses the palate. They start with chilies. Sumatra is known for the hottest.

- *Sambal goreng* (fried sambal) is not super hot. Typically it is stir-fried with hard-boiled egg, meat, seafood, tofu, or tempeh. Sambal goreng is ideal for restaurants: prepare spice paste ahead and scoop into pan with chosen protein and vegetables to order.
- *Sambal terasi* (raw sambal) is good tossed with raw vegetables, fried rice, fish, chicken, or tofu. Blanched and peeled tomatoes, chilies, shrimp paste, palm sugar, and lime juice are its main components.

Shallots, garlic, lime leaf, candlenuts (or macadamia nuts), and lemongrass are also ingredients in sambals. Refrigerate fried or raw sambals in glass jars up to 1 week.

SIGNATURE RECIPE

FRIED SPICE PASTE STEW (SAMBAL GORENG)

Sambal goreng, the beloved Indonesian national dish, can be made with meat, fish, or seafood. Prepare it with chicken and it becomes sambal goreng ayam, with shrimp, sambal goreng udang. With fish it's called sambal goreng ikan. This dish is rather spicy the first day, but softens overnight. For less heat, halve the amount of dried chilies in the spice paste.

Yields 8 to 9 cups sauce, enough for 2 to 3 pounds meat or seafood and vegetables, 8 servings

Fried Spice Paste (Sambal Goreng)

Yields 1-1/2 to 1-3/4 cups

6 ounces shallots, 1-1/3 to 1-1/2 cups peeled and coarsely chopped
1-1/2 to 2 ounces garlic, 6 to 8 large cloves, 3 to 4 tablespoons peeled and chopped
1/2 ounce dried stemmed red chilies, 1/2 cup broken up
1 ounce macadamia *or* candlenuts, 1/4 cup
1 ounce gingerroot *or* galangal, 2 tablespoons peeled and coarsely chopped
1 teaspoon ground coriander
1 teaspoon tamarind concentrate
    or 1 tablespoon strained tamarind purée
Optional: 1 teaspoon shrimp paste

Chicken "Stew" (Sambal Goreng Ayam)

2 cups coconut milk, *divided* (up to 1 cup extra to soften the chili-heat)
2 to 2-1/2 pounds boneless, skinless chicken thighs *or* breast
3 tablespoons oil
1 pound green beans, 3-1/2 to 4 cups stemmed and sliced 1-1/2 inch long
(or 4 cups other vegetables, sliced into bite-sized pieces)
1 stalk lemongrass, bottom bulb trimmed to 3-inches
    or zest of 1 large lemon
4 Kaffir lime leaves
1 pound tomatoes, 2 medium, about 2 cups peeled, seeded, and diced

For Serving

1 large lemon
Cooked long-grain rice

1 **Prepare fried spice paste:** In a blender, purée chopped **sambal goreng** ingredients with 1/2 to 3/4 cup coconut milk and 1/2 teaspoon kosher salt until smooth. Sambal sauce without meat or seafood will keep refrigerated 4 to 5 days.

2 **Chicken sambal:** Finely slice chicken into "worm" size pieces and set aside.

3 Heat oil in 5- to 6-quart pan, scrape in spice paste, and fry over high heat 1 minute. Lower heat to a simmer and cook 4 minutes. Stir in chicken and cook over medium heat until almost cooked through.

4 Pour in remaining coconut milk, green beans, lemongrass or lemon zest, and lime leaves. Bring to a simmer, partially cover pan, and lower heat. Simmer sambal until green beans are crisp-tender and chicken is cooked through, about 10 minutes. Stir occasionally. Sauce should be thick. Fold in tomatoes and simmer 2 to 5 minutes more.

5 **To Serve:** Taste sambal and season with salt and lemon juice. Serve with hot rice.

Vary! Improvise!

☞ *Seafood: Substitute 2 pounds firm fish fillets for chicken. Dice fish into 1-inch cubes. Leave shellfish whole. Don't overcook.*

☞ *Vegetarian: Substitute 2 pounds cubed, fried tofu or tempeh for chicken.*

Indonesian Stir-Fried Noodles

Stir-fried noodles are a favorite Southeast Asian quick, one-dish treat morning, noon, or at night. Indonesians stir-fry fresh, round, thick egg noodles, with spice paste, chilies, ketcap manis, and vegetables. For quick meals, substitute instant ramen noodles.

FIGURE 3.65 A Balinese mie goreng.
Source: © JJAVA/Fotolia.

INDONESIAN FRIED NOODLES (MIE GORENG)

Mie goreng means fried noodle; it is the premier midnight snack in Indonesia, Malaysia, and Singapore. Diners prefer fresh egg noodles, but instant ramen noodles often stand in. Mie goreng stands apart from other fried noodle dishes with its lavish use of chilies, garlic, shallots, and ketcap manis. This version isn't searingly hot.

Yields about 8 cups, 4 servings

8 ounces long, thick Chinese or German egg noodles, dried or fresh

Spice Paste

Yields about 1 cup

1/2 ounce garlic, 2 large cloves, peeled
4 to 5 ounces shallots, 1 cup peeled and diced
1/4 ounce macadamia *or* candlenuts, 4 to 6
1/2 teaspoon ground white pepper
1 teaspoon palm sugar

1/4 ounce bird's eye chilies, 3 to 4 whole, about 1/2 tablespoon stemmed and finely sliced
8 ounces 26/30 or 41/50 shrimp, peeled and deveined
   or 4 to 6 ounces, thinly sliced lean pork
8 ounces Napa cabbage, 3 to 4 cups diced into 1-1/2-inch squares
6 to 8 ounces tomato, 1 cup cut into 8 wedges and wedges halved
2-1/2 ounces trimmed green onions, 5 large, cut into 1-inch lengths
6 ounces mung bean sprouts, about 2 cups
3 to 4 tablespoons ketcap manis (sweet soy sauce)
Vegetable or fragrant coconut oil for frying

Garnish

Crispy Shallots
Ketcap manis
Optional: 2 eggs, scrambled
Optional: Fried shrimp crackers

1 **Cook noodles:** Bring large pot of water to boil. Salt the water and stir in noodles. Cook noodles al dente, fresh will take 1 to 2 minutes. Cook dry noodles according to package. Rinse in cold water and drain.

2 *Prepare spice paste:* Grind garlic, shallots, nuts, pepper, and palm sugar to a smooth paste in a mortar with pestle or blender. If using blender, add 2 to 4 tablespoons water to facilitate grinding.

3 **Assemble and prepare remaining ingredients:** Arrange chilies, shrimp or pork, cabbage, tomato, green onions, sprouts, and ketcap manis in bowls on tray ready to cook.

4 **Cook it:** Swirl oil into in a wok or heavy 10- to 12-inch skillet over high heat until hot but not smoking. Toss in spice paste and chilies; stir-fry until chilies are soft and paste is dry and begins to stick. Toss in shrimp or meat and fry in spice paste 2 minutes to infuse flavor. Scrape into bowl.

5 Swirl in more oil and toss in cabbage and tomato; stir-fry until tomato begins to soften, 1 minute. Cover and steam 1 minute. Toss in noodles, green onions, bean sprouts, and sweet soy sauce and cover. Steam 2 to 3 minutes until vegetables are crisp-tender and noodles are hot. Toss noodles once more, and remove from the heat. Don't overcook noodles and don't leave them to sit in the pan: plate them as fast as possible. Taste noodles and season with salt and pepper.

6 **To Serve:** Serve mie goreng warm garnished with fried shallots. Serve with a bottle of ketcap manis on the side. Fancy up and garnish with finely sliced scrambled eggs and fried shrimp crackers.

GRILL, GRIDDLE, ROAST, BROIL, AND BARBECUE

Signature Technique: Indonesian Saté

Though Westerners think of it as Thai, satay or saté with peanut sauce came originally from Indonesia, probably by way of Arab immigrants in the early nineteenth century. Although saté is a national dish and variations around the archipelago are numerous, many Indonesians consider Javanese saté the best. East Javanese eat lamb saté dipped in ketcap manis, and West Javanese favor peanut sauce. Celebratory feasts, traveling vendors, and tented and regular restaurants all offer saté. Indonesians serve it with slivered onions, sliced cucumbers and rice cakes, pineapple sauce, cucumber relish, or ketcap manis.

FIGURE 3.66 Indonesian chicken sate.
Source: © Suprijono Suharjoto/Fotolia.

- Turmeric is important to give meat a golden color.

- Meat must be thinly sliced so that it will cook quickly over hot coals. For Indonesian saté, dice meat into 3/4-inch cubes. For Thai satay, slice meat into long, thin strips 1-inch by 4-inches.

- Zipper baggies allow the cook to turn meat in the marinade easily.

- Cover and refrigerate beef, lamb, or chicken overnight and bring to room temperature before cooking, or leave at room temperature up to 1 hour. Marinate shrimp or chunks of fish or seafood 15 minutes in refrigerator.

- Metal is better, but bamboo is prettier. Soak bamboo skewers in warm water, 20 to 30 minutes before using.

- Thread meat onto bamboo or metal skewers and shake off excess marinade.

- Grill skewers until meat is crispy on the edges and tender on the inside. For cubed meat, cook 2 to 3 minutes per side, turning only once.

- Serve satay/saté with traditional peanut sauce or a sauce of choice.

TRADITIONAL JAVANESE SATÉ

Yields about 2/3 cup spice purée, enough for 2 pounds protein, 4 to 6 servings

1/2 ounce tamarind paste, 1 tablespoon packed
2 tablespoons coriander seed
2 tablespoons cumin seed
4 three-inch dried chilies, about 1 tablespoon stemmed, seeded, and broken
1 teaspoon turmeric powder
1 ounce stalk lemongrass, bottom bulb trimmed to 3 or 4 inches, scant 3 tablespoons finely chopped
1/4 to 1/2 ounce gingerroot, about 2 teaspoons peeled and minced
1 ounce palm sugar, 2 tablespoons
2 pounds boneless, skinless chicken breast or meat, finely sliced cross-grain
4 teaspoons vegetable oil
Lime wedges
    or Indonesian Peanut Sauce

1 Mix tamarind paste with 3 tablespoons hot water. Knead tamarind, and soak until soft, 15 to 20 minutes. Push pulp through strainer and discard fibers and seeds to yield 2 tablespoons thick tamarind purée.

2 **Toast spices:** In a small, dry sauté pan, toast coriander and cumin seeds until they crackle, turn 1 shade darker, and are fragrant. Cool. Grind to a powder with dried chilies.

3 **Grind spice purée:** In a wet-dry grinder or blender, grind lemongrass, ginger, sugar, and toasted spices until fine. Add turmeric and 2 tablespoons thick tamarind purée; purée until mixture is smooth and pasty. Add and purée up to 2 tablespoons water to achieve a thick but pourable consistency.

4 Prepare chicken (or other protein) and marinate in spice purée 1 hour at room temperature or overnight in refrigerator. Preheat grill. Remove refrigerated meat and bring to room temperature. Season meat with salt and toss with oil. Skewer and grill meat until done to taste.

5 **To Serve:** Plate or platter saté and serve with lime wedges or *Indonesian peanut sauce* or both.

INDONESIAN SPICED GRILLED FISH (IKAN BAKAR)

4 servings

Spice Paste (Sambal)

Yields about 1/2 cup

1/2 ounce macadamia nuts or candlenuts, about 6, 1 tablespoon
1 ounce shallots, 3 small, peeled
1/2 ounce garlic, 2 cloves, peeled
3-inch dried red chili, scant teaspoon stemmed, seeded, and chopped
1/2 ounce gingerroot, 2 teaspoons peeled and coarsely diced
1/2 teaspoon ground turmeric
1 teaspoon tamarind concentrate
   or 2 to 3 teaspoons tamarind purée (1/2 tablespoon paste soaked in
   1-1/2 tablespoons warm water and strained)
4 tablespoons coconut milk, more as needed
1 teaspoon palm sugar

2 to 2-1/2 pounds thick fish fillets, skin on

For Serving

Cooked rice
Indonesian Pickle (Acar)

1 **Prepare spice paste:** Coarsely chop ingredients before placing into wet-dry spice grinder, blender, or mortar and pestle. Blend nuts, shallots, garlic, chili, ginger, turmeric, tamarind, coconut milk, sugar, and 1/2 teaspoon kosher salt until smooth. Add more coconut milk as necessary to facilitate grinding.

2 **Divide paste:** Place 2/3 of paste in a small saucepan. Cook paste in saucepan over medium heat until thickened to peanut butter consistency. Set aside. Rub fish fillets with remaining 1/3 of paste. Marinate fish 1-1/2 hours in refrigerator or 1/2 hour at room temperature before cooking.

3 **Preheat grill or broiler:** Spread thick, cooked paste over fish with a small spatula. Grill or broil until spice paste browns. Grill or broil fish on a heatproof platter until it just begins to flake with a fork, 6 to 10 minutes.

4 **To Serve:** Serve fish hot with rice and pickles.

Vary! Improvise!

☞ *Substitute 5 pounds whole snapper, tilapia, or other whole fish. Slash meat to bone and rub with spice paste.*

SALAD AND VEGETABLE METHODS

FIGURE 3.67 Balinese vegetarian meal.
Source: © TravelPhotography/Fotolia.

FIGURE 3.68 Indonesian vegetables with peanut sauce (gado gado) and shrimp chips.

SIGNATURE RECIPE

INDONESIAN VEGETABLES WITH PEANUT SAUCE (GADO GADO)

This classic Indonesian dish demands fresh vegetables perfectly steamed. Ideal food for a festive brunch or lunch, some gado-gado restaurants allow diners to choose vegetables: cabbage, greens, green beans or long beans, carrots, cauliflower, potato, cucumber, or mung bean sprouts.

6 to 8 servings

Indonesian Peanut Sauce
4 tablespoons *Fried Shallots*
  or commercial fried shallots

Steamed Vegetables

5 to 6 ounces cabbage, 2-1/2 cups shredded (steam 3 to 4 minutes)
8 ounces green beans, 1-1/2 cups sliced into 1-inch lengths (4 minutes)
6 ounces carrots, 2 medium, 1-1/2 cups peeled and thinly bias sliced (2 to 3 minutes)
8 ounces cauliflower florets, 2 cups (3 to 4 minutes)
3 ounces mung bean sprouts, about 1 cup (30 seconds)
8 ounces redskin potatoes, 1-1/2 cups diced into 1/2- to 3/4-inch cubes (4 to 5 minutes)

Raw Vegetables

8 ounces Boston or bibb lettuce, 1 small head, 6 cups whole leaves washed and dried
Optional: 8 sprigs watercress, large stems discarded, washed and dried
8 ounces English cucumber, 1-1/2 cups lightly peeled and diagonally sliced
  or 3 to 5 ounces Persian or Kirby pickling cucumbers, 2 small, thinly sliced

Garnish

2 to 3 hard-cooked eggs
Optional: 4 ounces tempeh diced into 1/2- to 3/4-inch cubes and fried until browned
Optional: 4 to 6 shrimp crackers, deep-fried

1 Prepare *Indonesian Peanut Sauce* and *Fried Shallots* for garnish.

2 Steam or blanch **vegetables** separately (according to times after them) until crisp-tender—don't overcook.

3 Prepare **raw vegetables**. Prepare *garnish*.

4 Arrange lettuce and watercress around edge of platter and line vegetables in separate rows over it, contrasting the colors. Arrange cucumbers around edge of platter and top salad with eggs in the center. Or arrange it any way that looks beautiful, artistic, and inviting. Garnish gado-gado with fried shallots, hard-boiled eggs, shrimp crackers, or fried tempeh just before serving.

5 **To Serve:** Reheat peanut sauce. Adjust consistency and taste. Serve on side *or* drizzle over salad.

Vary! Improvise!

☞ *Local and Seasonal:* Prepare gado gado with local, fresh produce and peanut or coconut sauce.

INDONESIAN SALADS

Urap

Since coconuts grow everywhere in Indonesia and are always in season, cooks prepare a more elaborate mixed vegetable salad similar to gado gado called *urap*. Instead of peanut sauce, it's served with a spicy coconut sambal or Spicy Coconut Dressing. Indonesian cook and author Sri Owen says that central Javanese cooks add tempeh and mung sprouts to urap with coconut dressing.

Jukut Murab

This Balinese salad is made with black-eyed peas, cucumbers, scallions, mint or basil, and coconut sambal or Spicy Coconut Dressing.

Rujak

This salad is made with various bite-sized-cut tropical fruits and vegetables: water apple, pineapple, pomelo, green apple, mango, jicama, cucumber, raw sweet potato. Rujak is dressed with a bumbu of palm sugar, tamarind, ground toasted peanuts, shrimp paste, bird's eye chili, and red chili thinned with water.

Asinan

A refreshing sweet and sour vegetable salad (mung bean sprouts, cucumbers, cabbage, carrots) dressed with white vinegar, sugar, garlic, and chilies and garnished with fried peanuts and sweet tamarind sauce. It is often served with deep-fried rice cakes and grilled meat or seafood.

PICKLE AND PRESERVE

Signature Technique: Indonesian Pickles (Acar)

This Indonesian pickle came from Indian traders who brought achar (chutney) to Indonesia. It is a vinegar pickle made in Indonesia, Malaysia, and Singapore with yard-long beans, carrots, and cabbage. There are many varieties of acar: acar ramping, acar kuning, acar ketimun, and acar segar. Acar is commonly served as a condiment and eaten with the main course.

- Cut ingredients into 1/4-inch- by 2-inch-long julienne or finely slice.

- Pickle different types of vegetables or fruits: cabbage, pineapple, daikon radish, jicama, or green beans. Add peeled whole cloves of garlic if desired.

- Soften hard vegetables, if desired, by pouring boiling water over them, and squeeze-draining after 10 to 15 minutes.

- Another version of acar is made with a sambal of ground candlenuts, garlic, ginger, chilies, and spices, which is fried. The vegetables are partially cooked in the paste, scraped into a bowl, and mixed with vinegar, salt, and sugar. Cucumbers are not cooked, and added last.

- Pack vegetables in clean glass jar for best flavor.

- Acar should be slightly sweet, sour, and hot. Adjust flavor of pickling liquid by adding or reducing sugar, salt, or chili or by adding water to dilute the vinegar. For more heat, finely slice the chilies.

- For best flavor, allow acar to rest in refrigerator 2 to 3 days before consumption.

INDONESIAN PICKLE (ACAR)

Yields 1 quart

1 pound English cucumbers
8 ounces carrots, 2 medium, scrubbed or peeled
3 ounces shallots, about 6, 1/2 cup peeled and finely sliced
1/4 ounce bird's eye chilies, about 8, stemmed and slit on one side
6 tablespoons sugar
3/4 cup white vinegar

1   Slice cucumber into 2-inch lengths then slice into 1/4- to 1/2-inch matchsticks to yield 3 cups. Slice carrots into 2-inch lengths and slice into 1/4-inch matchsticks to yield 1-1/2 cups. Toss cucumbers, carrots, shallots, and chilies in large bowl with 1 tablespoon kosher salt; rest 20 minutes, and drain off liquid. Pack vegetable mixture firmly into glass canning jar.

2   In a small saucepan, mix together sugar and vinegar, and simmer until sugar is dissolved. Pour vinegar mixture over vegetables in jar. Cover with lid and refrigerate. For best flavor, rest pickle 2 hours or up to 2 days before using.

3   **To Serve:** Serve with saté, grilled fish, or rice dishes.

REVIEW QUESTIONS

Thailand

1. Name two large countries that influenced Southeast Asian cuisine.

2. What is fish sauce (nam pla) and how is it made?

3. Name three ingredients that could go into a Thai curry paste.

4. Discuss the method for preparing pad Thai or a Thai coconut curry.

5. What two types of cuisine flourish in Thailand? Describe the differences.

6. Name two aromatic vegetables commonly used in Thai cuisine.

Vietnam

1. What two countries influenced Vietnamese cuisine? Discuss their influences.

2. Name one Vietnamese herb and describe its flavor.

3. What are the three main components of nuoc cham?

4. Describe how to prepare dried rice paper wrappers for fresh rice rolls.

5. Name one Vietnamese dish and discuss its preparation.

6. What is tapioca pearl made from? How may it be used?

Indonesia

1. Name the three main islands of Indonesia.

2. What were the key cultural influences on Indonesian cuisine and why?

3. What two foods define the Indonesian diet?

4. What is rendang? Describe its preparation.

5. What is a sambal? What are its components? What is sambal goreng?

6. Describe ketcap manis and its use.

CHAPTER FOUR

INDIA: LAND OF SPICE, RICE, FLATBREADS, AND LEGUMES

This chapter will:

- Introduce the history of India, its geography, cultural influences, and climate.

- Introduce Indian culinary culture, its four main regional variations, and dining etiquette.

- Identify the spices, foods, flavor foundations, seasoning devices, and favored cooking techniques of north and south India, their differences and similarities.

- Reveal how this cuisine feeds more than one billion 300 thousand people from land one-third the size of the United States.

- Teach the loved techniques unique to north and south India through recipes.

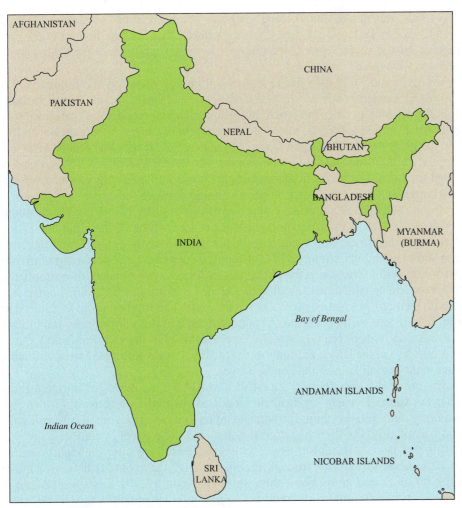

FIGURE 4.1 Map of India.

Mother India

American philosopher Will Durant considered India as the "motherland of our race": of European language through Sanskrit, of philosophy, of mathematics through the Arabs, of Christian ideals through the Buddha, and of democracy through the Indian village and self-government. He felt that possibly she was "the mother of us all."

"There are some parts of the world that, once visited, get into your heart and won't go. For me, India is such a place. When I first visited, I was stunned by the richness of the land, by its lush beauty and exotic architecture, by its ability to overload the senses with the pure, concentrated intensity of its colors, smells, tastes, and sounds. It was as if all my life I had been seeing the world in black and white and, when brought face-to-face with India, experienced everything re-rendered in brilliant technicolor."

Keith Bellows, Vice-President, National Geographic Society

Indian culture is rich with color, contrasts, and contradictions. Imagine if the over 300 million inhabitants of the United States moved to fifteen southern states and almost another billion people followed. Imagine that multitude as six ethnic groups speaking more than fourteen official languages, following more than seven major religions and many smaller ones, all with important dietary restrictions.

India is a land of majestic peaks of the world's highest mountain range, centuries of Turkic, Arabic, Moghul (Persian for Mongol) invasions, and plunderers who introduced new foods, seasonings, and cooking methods. The country has seen great wars and bloodshed over land and religion. It has the princely rich, and the poorest of the poor begging on the streets, with Mother Teresa, an Irish Catholic nun from Macedonia, called to serve them.

The civilization that gave rise to Indian culture was known as the Indus (3300 to 1300 BCE). Contemporaries with the ancient Sumer and Egyptian civilizations, the Indus built highly complex cities and sent trading ships as far as Mesopotamia. Many historians believe that around 1500 BCE, the Aryans (meaning *noble*) migrated from the north. They laid the groundwork for modern Indian cultural traditions: the caste system, Vedic culture, the Sanskrit language, and the development of ancient texts filled with deep wisdom called the Vedas. The Aryans lived alongside the Indus, and eventually moved south into the Ganges Valley, and built large kingdoms around northern India.

Around 500 BCE, Persian kings conquered the Indus Valley, occupying it until around 350 BCE. The Greeks with Alexander the Great conquered the Persians, but Aryan kingdoms continued to develop in the East. By the fifth century BCE, Siddhartha Gautama, also known as Buddha, witnessed life's vicious cycle of suffering. Feeling a deep and compassionate wish to free others from suffering, he found a way through his own suffering to subsequent enlightenment. Siddhartha founded Buddhism, which taught others how to train their minds to attain peace. During the fourth and third centuries BCE, the Mauryan Empire, one of India's greatest, conquered most of the subcontinent and brought Buddhism to most of central Asia. The Empire ushered in the Classical Period, during which India had the largest economy of the medieval world with maritime spice trading links to the Roman Empire and Southeast Asia.

The Imperial Gupta Dynasty, established in AD 319, consolidated northern India. After the Gupta Dynasty, six separate kingdoms ushered in a thriving Golden Age. For many centuries, they built incredible temples and developed artistically, culturally, and scientifically. The decimal numeral system and the concept of zero were invented during this period. Hinduism began to weaken Buddhism after the eighth century. In 1001, Arab armies came through the Khyber Pass; they continually raided Indian cities for more than thirty years, then vanished. Again in 1192 they invaded, and by 1202 Arabs had conquered the most powerful Hindu kingdoms in the North. Southern India, geographically difficult for invasions, continued to be dominated by Hindu dynasties.

Turks and Afghans invaded northern India and established the Delhi Sultanate. They ruled until 1398 when Mongols brutally invaded under Tamerlane. In 1526, the more educated and enlightened Mughal leader Babar came to power. He conquered Punjab and Delhi and founded the Mughal Dynasty with six eventual emperors, who became the most influential Islamic Moghul dynasties in Indian history. The greatest emperor was Akbar, who married a Hindu princess and established cultural tolerance. Akbar's grandson, who eventually succeeded him, built the Taj Mahal to the memory of his beloved dead wife. By the eighteenth century the Mughal Empire declined due to increased brutality on, and distance from, the native population.

Portuguese ships had traded with India beginning around 1510. However, by 1769 the British, through the East India Trading Company and trading posts established in Madras, Bombay, and Calcutta, gained control of European trade in India. Their control came through an organized system called the Raj, which was based on agreements with native princes and an increasing role in local politics. In 1857, Hindu soldiers rebelled against British rule, and the British Crown seized control of India.

Hindu and Muslim tensions were increasing. Mohandas K. Gandhi, a humble man of great peace, called for unity and independence. Fed up with the British Raj and their treatment of the native Indian population, Gandhi and the Indian National Congress led a mass independence movement of nonviolent resistance and noncooperation; the Muslim League later joined them. However, the division between Hindus and Muslims remained. In 1947 the British partitioned India along religious lines: they created Muslim Pakistan and Hindu India. Great violence ensued when minorities in each area were forced to flee. The British returned to restore stability. With partition, Gandhi and his followers finally achieved their goal of full independence.

Disunity and periods of chaos between India and Pakistan continued. A Hindu fanatic assassinated Gandhi in January 1948. Nehru became India's first Prime Minister and guided the country to peace. Then Indira Gandhi, Nehru's daughter, came to power in 1966. She was powerful and brought economic and political changes, but abused her power with moves like suppressing the press and forced sterilization. In 1984 a Sikh fanatic assassinated her.

Modern India's political climate remains divisive: strife, assassination, and corruption have marked much of it. Despite this India is becoming a strong economic power. In the early 1990s, Congress-led government policies instituted economic liberalization and reform, which has opened India to global trade and begun to shake up (but not abolish) the long-held traditions of castes and creeds. Twenty-first century India is a nation remaking itself with a large, educated, and motivated middle class. Despite large economic gains, India faces many problems: overpopulation, environmental degradation, and widespread poverty.

LANGUAGE, PHILOSOPHY, AND RELIGION

Though there are fourteen official languages in India with English as the language of trade and politics, over 40 percent of India's population speaks Hindi with the remainder speaking 1,651 other languages and dialects.

Religion is an integral part of India's fabric of life from food, daily chores, education, and philosophy to politics. India is home to 80 percent or more Hindu, 10 percent Islamic, 5 percent Sikh and Christian, and the remainder Buddhist, Jain, Bahai, and Zoroastrian. Hinduism carries diverse theory and practice—including the caste system. It has no founder, but Hindus consider the ancient texts *Rig Veda*, *Upanishads*, and the *Bhagavad Gita* as sacred. Hindus, mainly vegetarian, don't necessarily worship one main deity. They might explore ultimate reality, pay homage to superhuman gods like Brahma, Shiva, Vishnu, Rama, or Krishna, or worship spirits, trees, or animals. Hinduism's primary beliefs focus on *dharma* (ethics/duties), *samsāra* (cycle of birth, life, death, and rebirth), *karma* (action and subsequent reaction), *moksha* (liberation from samsara), and the *yogas* (paths or practices).

The Islamic faith originated in the early seventh century in Arabia, and was founded by the prophet Muhammad, a religious, military, and political leader. In the early eighth century, Arab traders brought Islamic food and beliefs to India and by the twelfth century, gathered a large following. In its early phase, Islam was aggressive, but Sufi mystics softened the message to one of brotherhood, peace, and love.

Buddha, or Gautama Siddhartha, founded Buddhism in the sixth century BCE. It is based on the principle of impermanence, which says that everything is changeable, and the principle of causation, which says that nothing happens by chance and that natural forces and karma lead to all events. Buddha offered his followers, through meditation and the Middle Path between indulgence and abstinence, a balanced and harmonious way of life. His *Four Noble Truths* are the basis of Buddhist teachings: suffering is universal, it is caused by desire, suffering can be prevented, and letting go of desire eliminates suffering and leads to nirvana or enlightenment.

Each of India's religions directs their followers to eat in a certain way. Since cows are sacred to Hindus, they eat no beef and many are vegetarian. Jains, because of their belief in reincarnation, eat no eggs, seafood, or meat, and don't eat root vegetables, garlic, or onions because harvesting kills the entire plant. Muslims eat no pork, but do consume beef, goat, and lamb. South Indians and members of the highest Hindu Brahmin caste are often vegetarian. Many South Indian vegetarians don't eat onions or garlic (substituting asafoetida) because they are considered too strongly flavored—and they are often paired with meat. Religion makes cooking in India a socially complex but highly creative pursuit.

GEOGRAPHY AND CLIMATE

India is a country of continual wonder. From vast mountains to tropical coasts, desert, and jungle, it spreads over twenty-eight states and seven union territories in an area one-third the size of the United States. The Himalayan mountain range, the north's most influential feature—their peaks are sacred to Hindus and Buddhists alike—echo the scale of this country's enormous diversity of food, culture, religion, race, and language. India shares its northeastern Himalayan borders with China, Nepal, and Bhutan. Pakistan, Iran, and Afghanistan lie to the northwest. India's border with western Pakistan lies in the northwestern Punjab Plain and the great Thar Desert, the seventh largest desert in the world and highly inhospitable for farming.

India is dry and sunny for most of the year. Summers are hot. Her climate ranges from the snow-covered Himalayas to equatorial-tropical humid heat, unpredictable droughts, and monsoons. The capital, Delhi, and north, can be cold December through February, but very hot by April. Southern winters are generally warm, dry, and sunny. In May (September in eastern India) the monsoons arrive to bring a month or more of intense, bucketing rain.

Northern India's Himalayas include two of the world's highest peaks, K2 (28,251 feet) (though K2 is in the Pakistan-administered disputed Kashmir region) and Kanchenjunga (28,209 feet), the highest point within India proper. The highest Himalayan peak, Everest (29,002 feet), lies on the border of Nepal, Tibet, and China. The Vindhya Range (average elevation 9,843 feet) crosses most of central India, extends over 650 miles, and separates northern and southern India.

Three rivers are prominent in India: the ancient Indus, which flows through Pakistan and far northern India, and the holy Ganges and the Brahmaputra, which flow eastward into the Bay of Bengal through Bangladesh. The vast Ganges-Brahmaputra Delta occupies most of northern, central, and eastern India. The Ganges, India's longest river, forms the Indo-Gangetic Plain and provides rich farming. This fertile region's seasonal flooding supports rice paddies.

South India is home to the fertile Deccan Plateau, which makes up much of it. South India is bounded by the Arabian Sea to the west, the Indian Ocean to the south, and the Bay of Bengal to the west. South and east lie two mountain ranges—the Western and Eastern Ghats—a plateau heartland with four rivers.

FARMING AND AGRICULTURE

Food and agriculture are central to Indian life. Roughly three-quarters of India's population live in small rural farming villages. India and the fifteen U.S. southern states mentioned in the first paragraph have similar areas of farmable land—India has more farmable land than any country except the United States—and more water than any country except the United States and Canada. Farmers depend on monsoons. Years with no monsoons mean hunger for those not living near rivers and mountains with snow.

The people of India get by on less food than people in the West. The population of the United States consumes approximately *four shares* of produced food per person; India's average consumption is *1/5 share per person*—and India exports food!

INDIAN CUISINE: MASTERS OF SEASONING

Though there seems to be no one, clear India, cultural similarities and food tie the Indian people together. Classic Indian cuisine evolved from ancient Ayurvedic health principles: a richly flavored cuisine, modest and extravagant, simple yet complex, based on an ancient philosophy of balance and health that still underlies modern Indian cooking. Food, flavors, and seasonings balance the three *doshas* or body types. Spices generating body heat, like cardamom and clove, are warming—and cooling spices, like chilies, cause sweating—and serve to balance "cold" or "warm" conditions.

India's food illustrates its cultural and geographical richness. Religious dietary laws, climate, geography, neighbors, and a history of constant foreign invaders—Aryans, Iranians, Greeks, Parthians, Scythians, Kushans, Arabs, Turks, Persians, Portuguese, Dutch, French, and British—have left marks on India's creatively complex cuisine. Despite this, India's cuisine is all its own, shaped by cooks pushed by necessity to make what was available appealing.

If Italians are masters of big, fresh flavor and the French are masters of technique, surely Indian cooks are masters of seasoning. Indian cooks are evidence for the saying "Limits intensify creativity." They built a world-class cuisine from a simple base of grains, legumes, fresh produce, herbs, and spices. Cooks all over India waltz creatively with these humble staples. Top-of-the-burner cooking still prevails, though more affluent cooks own modern stoves with ovens.

Think of Indian food, and a richly intense, spicy curry will probably come to mind. "Curry" is not an Indian term (though it is used): it's the name the British, who occupied India, gave to dishes with spiced gravy that came with rice or flatbread. "Curry" is a corruption of the South Indian word *kari*, or foods cooked with liquid. In India, curries range from soupy stews to drier stir-fries.

Outside influences shaped Indian curries. The Moghuls from Persia brought saffron, butter, cream, nuts, and clay pot cooking to the North. The international trading ports of the western coastal areas of Goa, Kerala, and Karnataka have Portuguese red chili and

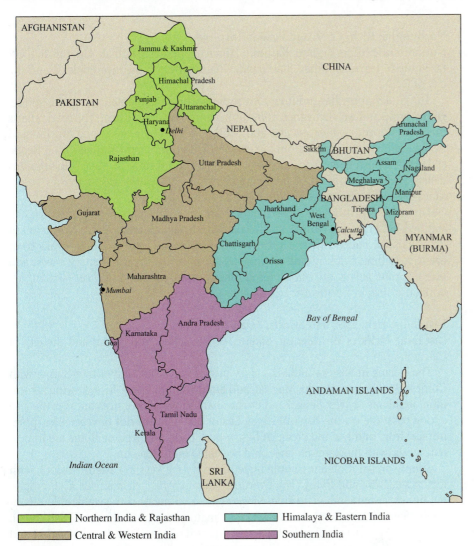

FIGURE 4.2 Map of regions of India.

vinegar-based vindaloos, pork, and deep-frying. The New World contributed tomatoes, chilies, and potatoes. Southern India traded with Southeast Asia and shares similar flavors and techniques. Insulated from Persian conquests and trade of the north, Southern dishes have remained similar throughout the South. Eastern India borrowed Far Eastern cooking techniques and flavors.

The modern Indian kitchen always has a pressure cooker, the stainless steel "masala box" of spices and a rolling pin. Even the most modest meals start with a mound of rice or a flatbread with a minimum of one vegetable and one legume dish and pickle or chutney. A meal might enlarge to include *rasam* broth, spicy curries or *sambals*, vegetable and legume dishes, cooling *raita* or *pachadi* salads and relishes, big-flavored and appetite-stimulating savory, sweet, or sour chutneys and "pickles" with small amounts of meat or seafood. Indian meals don't require courses—diners eat dishes together: a bite of curry, some rice, a bit of chutney, a bite of bread, and perhaps a pickle or raita.

Dinnerware might be banana leaves or the more modern *thali*—a stainless steel tray topped with small stainless steel bowls filled with food. Indian breads serve as scoops, fingers of the right hand act as utensils, and spoons are sometimes used with thali. Most Southern Indians of any religion eat with their right hands. Fingerbowls or hand sinks are common for washing.

REGIONAL INDIA

1. **North India: Rich, Cool, and Persian-Inspired**
   North India includes Jammu, Kashmir, Himachal Pradesh, Punjab, Uttaranchal, Uttar Pradesh, Haryana, Bihar, Jharkhand, Chattisgarh and Madhya Pradesh, and the city of Delhi.

   The cooler north has mountainous regions where tea plantations, grain, and legumes grow, and weather varies from subfreezing to oven-like heat. The food reflects this with warming *garam masalas* and cooling *raitas*. There are strong Muslim and Persian influences here left from the invaders who came over Pakistan's more accessible Hindu Kush range. You can discover Persian "footprints" in the North's famous dishes: *pilau, biryani, kebab, tandoori* cooking, *kofta,* and *helvah*—dishes that are sometimes elaborate, always tasty and pungent, but not spicy-hot.

   Dry *masala* mixtures and roasted spices are the rule. Lamb, yogurt, *ghee* (roasted clarified butter), dairy, wheat, and whole-wheat *chapatis* are favored. Northeastern Bengalis favor *mustard oil* and seafood, but not much lamb. Northern cooks favor roasting, grilling, braising, and stewing. *Mutter paneer* (curry with cottage cheese and peas), *biryani, pullao, dal, chicken tikka, fish Amritsari, samosa,* and *chaat* (snacks) are popular dishes. Tea is the drink of choice.

2. **East India: Fish, Rice, and Sweets, Asian-Influenced**
   East India includes West Bengal, Sikkim, Bihar, Orissa, and Assam and the city of Calcutta.

   The cuisine in Eastern India is a spicy mix of vegetarian and nonvegetarian with Chinese, Mongolian, Hindu, Mughal, and Buddhist influences. Rice growing is common. Residents of West Bengal and Orissa share a love of fish, rice, and sweets—and a long coastline on the Bay of Bengal. Seafood, a colorful riot of vegetables, pork, tropical fruit, and red and green chilies, yogurt, corn, and legume flours are important foods, with mustard oil, ghee, and vegetable oil for cooking.

   Simple preparation and simple ingredients are the keys to eastern cuisines, with lots of steaming and frying. The five-spice mixture *panch phoran* used as a tempering unites eastern Indian cuisine. *Momos* (steamed meat- or vegetable-filled wontons), *thukpa* (clear soup), *tomato achaar* (tomato pickle), *machcher jhol* (fish curry), *jhaal-muri* (spicy snack of puffed rice and mustard oil), and the desserts *sandesh* and *rasgulla* form part of the eastern Indian repertoire.

3. **West India: Fiery, Diverse, and Coastal**
   West India includes Gujarat, Goa, Rajasthan, Maharashtra, and the city of Mumbai.

   This region has the most diverse cuisine in India because of its international ports and Portuguese influences. Largely Hindu and vegetarian, West India tends toward drier, hotter weather inland, so pickled and preserved vegetables are popular. The coastal areas are lush and green with an abundance of seafood. West India's pantry includes rice, peanuts, coconut, red chilies, vinegar, sugar, corn, lentils, legume flour, buttermilk, yogurt, nuts, sesame seeds, pork, and the cooking oils ghee, sunflower, canola, and peanut oils. The fiery *pork vindaloo* is a Portuguese-influenced Goanese curry. Fresh coconut-based hot and sour curries with fish and seafood, *chicken xacuti*, seaside snack *bhelpuri*, *dal*, *bakri* (millet flour chapattis), and many more dishes form the western Indian repertoire.

4. **South India: Tropical Vegetarian Heaven**
   South India includes Karnataka, Andhra Pradesh, Tamil Nadu, and Kerala.

   Indian vegetarians or *Vedics* have the most creative vegetarian diet in the world with a great variety of dishes made with whole legumes and split, skinned lentils (*grams* and *dals*), *paneer* cheese, chickpea flour, and grains such as rice, corn, and millet. Rice and dal act as the solid anchor to every meal along with seasoned vegetables and, occasionally, seafood. The daily meal is generally *sambar* with rice, *rasam* (spicy vegetarian broth), and a cooling yogurt dish (*pachadi*) served with sides like *cachumber* (chopped raw vegetable salads), pickles, or *pappadums* (thin, crisp flatbreads).

   More tropical in climate, the south of India is home to many vegetarians and people who don't consume onions, garlic, or strong spices. The hallmark of southern cuisine is the bright, strong contrasts of flavor, much like Thailand: bland meets hot-spicy, salty meets sweet, and sweet meets sour. South India's creativity shows in their use of dal and rice in a profusion of dishes like *dosa* (rice-dal "crepe"), *iddlis* (rice-dal steamed cakes), and *badas* (lentil dumplings), and their use of spices, particularly their tempered *chaunks*. *Uttapams* (puffy fried pancakes), *payasam* (sweet "pudding"), *thoran* (vegetable curry), *biryani*, *patria* (vegetable leaf rolls), *pongal* (seasoned rice dish), *koottu* (stir-fried vegetable), *aviyal* (multi-vegetable curry), and fish *moli* (curry) are a few of the overwhelming and amazing array of dishes.

   Favored cooking methods are steaming and stewing. Both *wet masalas*—spices ground with onions, garlic, and gingerroot—and *dry masalas* are popular with more fresh seasonings than in the north. Coconut, coconut oil, sesame and sesame oil, mustard seeds, chilies, and abundant tropical fruits and vegetables make this vegetarian heaven. Coffee is the drink of choice.

DINE AT HOME IN INDIA

Indians remove shoes before entering a home. A show of manners requires politely turning down offers of tea, coffee, or snacks several times before agreeing to partake. Since fingers are basic eating utensils in the south and parts of the north, wash them before sitting down for a meal. (Sometimes a large spoon and fork will be offered.)

Guests are seated at a table or on a cushion set on the floor—no elbows on the table and sit up straight. The guest of honor will be served first, followed by men then children. Women typically serve first and eat later. The hostess-cook will set a *banana leaf* or a *thali* (stainless steel platter) before each diner and top it with food, or fill small stainless cups with various dishes. She'll bring communal dishes to the table for second servings. To serve with a serving spoon or reach for something that is not food during dinner, use the left hand.

A meal might include a gram or dal, rice, a vegetable dish or two, and, of course, a chutney or raita. It may be topped by a *roti* (flat bread) sitting close by with vegetables on the right, and salads and chutneys on the left. From the most complex to the simplest dishes, Indians everywhere consider balance and harmony important in a dish and a

FIGURE 4.3 The holy city of Varanasi on the Ganges.
Source: dzain/Fotolia.

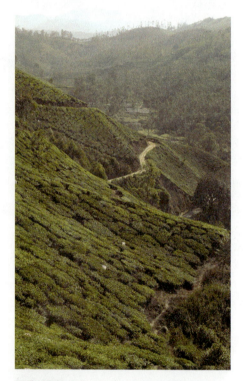

FIGURE 4.4 Indian tea plantation.
Source: Gennady Shingarev/Fotolia.

COMMON INDIAN COOKING TOOLS

Kadhai (shallow metal wok), *tava or tawa*, grinding stones, rolling pin, pressure cooker, masala box (stainless steel box of spices)

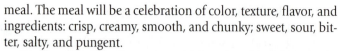

meal. The meal will be a celebration of color, texture, flavor, and ingredients: crisp, creamy, smooth, and chunky; sweet, sour, bitter, salty, and pungent.

Southerners still enjoy eating with hands. With only the right hand, tear off some roti and scoop or dip it into the food while flexing the right thumb to help shove food onto it. If there is no flatbread, roll rice into a ball and dip it into food to scoop—again using that flexed thumb. Licking fingers is a proper sign of great enjoyment. Leave a little food on the plate to signal satisfaction to your host or hostess. Profusely thank host and hostess. Wait for others to leave the table before departing.

TASTES OF INDIA

Fat: Ghee, vegetable oil, peanut oil, fragrant coconut oil, sesame oil, mustard oil, plus lesser use of corn, sunflower, cottonseed, soybean, canola, safflower, palm and almond oils

Sweet: *Jaggery* (unrefined cane sugar), sugar, *gur* (coconut palm sugar), honey, sugarcane

Sour/Alcohol: Tamarind, tamarind powder, *amchur* (green mango powder), lime, lemon, tomatoes, green mango, yogurt, dried pomegranate seeds, coconut vinegar, dried kokum/cocum

Salty: Salt, salt pickles, black salt

Spicy-Hot: Red and green chilies, black pepper, ginger

Spices: See *Signature Seasonings*

Aromatic Seasoning Vegetables: Onion, shallot, ginger, garlic, chilies, horseradish, green onion

Herbs, Seasonings, and Condiments: *Varak* (edible silver foil), cilantro, mint, dill, curry leaf, *tulsi* (holy basil), *methi* (fenugreek greens), rosewater, orange flower water, *kewra* or screwpine essence

Other Important Foods: Dairy (yogurt, buttermilk, cream, paneer cheese, yogurt cheese, condensed milk), coconut milk or cream, many varieties of beans, peas, and lentils; *besan* (chickpea flour) and mung flour, basmati and long-grain rice, millet and flour, barley, *atta* (whole wheat flour), buckwheat, rice flakes, coconut, nuts, and seeds, fresh and dried fruit, many vegetables—gourds, sweet and bitter melon, plantain, squash, taro, yam, taro leaves, spinach, meat (lamb, goat, chicken), edible silver foil (*varak*), fish and seafood

Popular Dishes: *Bonda* or *vada* (lentil-based deep-fried snack), *pakora* (deep-fried chickpea battered vegetables), curry dishes, *roti* flatbreads: *chapatti, paratha, kulcha* (tandoori flatbread stuffed with onions), *naan* (tandoori-bread), *puri* (deep-fried, puffed flatbread), tandoori-made foods, chutney, *dosa* (rice and dal pancake), *dal* (split lentil dish), *iddli* (puffed cakes made of rice and dal), *pullao* (rice pilaf), *raita* (yogurt and vegetable salad/condiment), *samosa* (triangular stuffed and fried savory pastry), *achaar* (pickle), *pappadum* (thin and crisp dried lentil disks, toasted or deep-fried to puff), *biryani* (layered rice pilaf), *vindaloo* (Goanese dish of Portuguese origins made with chilies, vinegar, and garlic) Indian sweets: halva, rice pudding, gulab jamun

Drinks: Tea, coffee, beer

INDIAN TAVA/TAWA

This very shallow, wok-like steel or iron griddle should be 1/4-inch thick and range in diameter from 9 to 12 inches. The *tava* is perfect for cooking breads like chapatti and paratha. Like a wok, a tava must be seasoned—by heating and rubbing with oil. Wash the tava with water immediately after cooking, dry over a burner, and rub with oil. A flat steel or cast-iron griddle or commercial flat-top may be substituted.

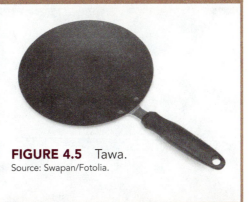

FIGURE 4.5 Tawa.
Source: Swapan/Fotolia.

INDIAN FLAVOR FOUNDATIONS

Indian Signature Aromatic Vegetable Combo

Onion, ginger, garlic, and chili might be called the Indian "mirepoix."

Chefs and cooks all over India use these four as the start or finish to soup, lentil dishes, breads, salads, and meat curry-stews.

Signature Seasonings

Liquid/Paste

Coconut Oil

Firm at room temperature, high-quality coconut oil has the fragrance and flavor of coconuts; the cheaper types have none. Heat stable, coconut oil is used mainly in south India for cooking. The best coconut oil comes from chopped, washed, and dried coconut meat, which is cold-pressed to obtain virgin coconut oil. Cheaper commercial oils use chemicals, refining, bleaching, and deodorizing.

Gingelly Oil (Plain Sesame Oil)

Gingelly oil is pressed from unroasted sesame seeds. South Indians favor it for cooking and skin care.

FIGURE 4.6 Jaggery.
Source: Swapan/Fotolia.

Jaggery (Gur)

Rich and flavorful with a creamy texture and the buttery flavor of caramel and molasses, this unrefined sugarcane juice comes in brown blocks that must be grated or chopped. Palm sugar, made much like maple syrup, from the sap of various palm trees, is sometimes confused with jaggery. Palm sugar is less intense flavored than jaggery. Both are used in India; sometimes palm syrup and cane syrup are mixed together.

Mustard Oil

This spicy, strong smelling oil, similar to horseradish, is pressed from black mustard (Brassica nigra), brown mustard (Brassica juncea), and white mustard seed (Brassica hirta). East Indian cooks use mustard oil as a main cooking oil, while north Indian, Nepalese, and Bangladeshi cooks use it for specific dishes. Indian cooks heat mustard oil to the smoking point and cooled before using to mellow and release the pungent smell. Mixing mustard oil with canola eliminates the need for this process. Mustard oil adulteration (the addition of argemone oil, a poison) has occasionally been reported in India.

Vegetable/Fruit

Anardana (Dried Pomegranate Seeds)

Used to season dishes with a fruity-tart flavor.

Red and Green Chili

Indian cooks use 2- to 3-inch long, fresh green chilies that are similar to Thai bird's eye chilies, also called finger chilies, hari mirch, or mirchi. Serrano chilies may be substituted, but jalapeños tend not to be flavorful enough. Indian cooks are also fond of dried red chilies and red chili powder. They prepare green chili paste, stuffed chilies, curries, chutney, stuffed and dried then fried chilies as well as many other dishes from fresh, dried, or powdered chilies.

Tamarind

See Glossary.

FIGURE 4.7 Dried pomegranate seeds.
Source: Monkey Business/Fotolia.

FIGURE 4.8 Tamarind pod.
Source: Will Heap/DK Images.

Herbal/Spice

Curry Leaf (Sweet Neem or Kadi Patta)

Heavenly aromatic leaves from a small tree native to India, curry leaves are popular in South

(Continued)

(Continued)

FIGURE 4.9 Curry leaves.
Source: Dave King/DK Images.

FIGURE 4.11 Black cardamom.
Source: s4sanchita/Fotolia.

Indian cuisine. They are often infused by the handful into temperings and add a great deal of flavor to various legume, soup, and curried dishes.

FIGURE 4.10 Fresh fenugreek leaves.
Source: Neil Fletcher/DK Images.

Fenugreek Leaves (Methi)

These leaves are popular throughout India. They are used dried or fresh as an herb, a vegetable, or as a remedy. When fresh, the leaves of this small bushy plant, have a clean, slightly bitter taste that increases when they are dried. Fresh fenugreek leaves are used in meat or vegetable dishes, stir-fries, curries, breads, and salads. The dried leaves are used in teas, breads, or sprinkled as a garnish on savory dishes. The fenugreek flowers produce the fragrant spice known as fenugreek.

Lesser-Known Indian Spices

Ajwain (Carom or Bishop's Weed)

These small pungent seeds, related to caraway and cumin, look like small cumin seeds, but are more dominant with an astringent thyme flavor. They help digest legumes and are used in small amounts in cooked dishes.

Amchur (Sour Mango Powder)

Produced from unripe mangos, this dried powder gives a fruity sourness to foods.

Asafoetida (Hing)

A dried latex gum native to India that comes from a rhizome that grows underground, asafoetida is often sold ground. Its pungent scent when uncooked can be off-putting—keep it tightly sealed in a glass jar. Once cooked, asafoetida transforms into a mild, meaty flavor similar to leek, onion, and garlic, and is particularly good with legumes.

Black Cardamom

This large brown seed pod has a strong smoky, camphor flavor derived from drying over smoky fires. It's used in savory legume, soup, and stew dishes. Green cardamom is not a substitute.

Black Cumin (Kala Jeera)

This small, slender crescent-shaped seed smells heavy and earthy at first sniff, but upon cooking it becomes nutty and appealing. It is popular in northern India. In Southern India, nigella (kalonji) seed is often called black cumin.

Black Salt (Kala Namak)

A rock salt with naturally occurring high sulfur content, which gives black salt an intense eggy odor. When ground, the salt turns pink. Black salt is used to season snacks (chaats), chutneys, and raitas (salads with yogurt).

FIGURE 4.12 Nigella seed.
Source: FOOD-pictures/Fotolia.

Kokum (Aamsul or Kokam)

A fruit related to mangosteen indigenous to South India, the dried outer skin is sun-dried and used as a souring agent. It has a mildly fishy taste and is dark, almost black, and shiny. Goanese and South Indians sometimes substitute it for tamarind in curried dishes.

Nigella or Kalonji

Also erroneously called black onion, black cumin, or black sesame, these pungent black seeds taste like a combination of onion, black pepper, and oregano with an edge of bitter like mustard seeds.

SEASONING AND PASTE MIXTURES

SPICES ALL OVER INDIA

Spices, herbs, and their flavors vary tremendously depending on variety and where and how they are grown. Age determines flavor and pungency, so get rid of spices that don't have fragrance. Purchase whole spices; they retain flavor longer. Grind them with a spice grinder as needed.

Getting It Right with Indian Spices

Novice cooks often feel overwhelmed by Indian spices and seasonings. Indian cooks have evolved their methods over centuries of experimentation. The combinations and differing interpretations make it hard to create a "blueprint" for blending spices—most are passed on from elders to children.

Think of Indian seasonings as a medicine cabinet; most have health supportive properties: blood sugar and cholesterol reducer, circulation increaser, warming, anti-arthritic, digestive, laxative, preservative, antioxidant, anti-inflammatory, stimulant, blood purifier, bronchial aid, anti-spasmodic, anti-nausea, calmative, tonic, anti-flatulent, aphrodisiac, and antiseptic/antibacterial/antifungal properties.

Some seasonings build flavor, some add color, and some contribute aroma.

Essential

Brown mustard seed (spicy-warm)

Cilantro or coriander leaf (soapy, meaty, refreshing)

Coriander seed (citrusy)

Cumin seed (earthy, pungent-woody, slightly menthol)

Curry leaf (mildly spicy, curry scented)

Cayenne (hot-spicy)

Fenugreek seed (maple-scented)

Garlic

Gingerroot

Red and green fresh chilies

Turmeric (bitter, acrid)

Paprika (sweet, slightly pungent)

Red chili powder

Important

Asafoetida (pungently garlic and onion-scented)

Black, white, green peppercorns (acrid, pungent)

Green/white cardamom (floral-fragrant, citrus, sweet, complex-spicy)

Black cardamom (smoky, woody)

Cinnamon (sweet, fragrant, spicy)

Nutmeg (sweet, fragrant, spicy)

Mace (pungent nutmeg)

Clove (pungent-warm, smoky, sweet)

Fennel seed (slightly anise)

Caraway seed (woody-spicy, pungent)

Nigella or kalonji seed (onion-black-pepper-oregano)

Fenugreek leaf (mildly pungent, spicy, bitter)

Occasional

Aniseed (licorice)

Ajwain or carom seed (intensely oregano)

Cassia/cinnamon leaf (dried leaf mildly fragrant)

Celery seed (fresh, astringent, bright, slightly bitter celery)

Dill seed/leaf (mild caraway or dill)

Kokum (sweet, acidic, salty)

Saffron (pungent, earthy, slightly bitter)

Star anise (licorice, bitter)

Black cumin (smoky, woody)

Poppyseed; white and black (nutty)

Black salt (sulfur)

Allspice (pungent, clove-cinnamon-nutmeg)

Amchur (fruity-tart)

Santa Fe, New Mexico
Chef-Owner of the Restaurant Raaga

FIGURE 4.13 Ajwain seed.
Source: Swapan/Fotolia.

"Most people don't understand how flavorful *ajwain* is. I use it for multiple dishes—I use it in my grilled seafood dishes. It gives a wonderful flavor. It has a flavor similar to thyme, but a more pungent version."

Masalas

Indian cooks usually prepare masalas (or spice mixtures) as they cook, but for convenience Westerners and busy Indian cooks prepare an all-around masala or "curry powder." Dry roast the spices for an even quicker flavor infusion. Each ingredient in a masala needs to have a purpose:

- Coriander, cumin, caraway, cardamom, cinnamon, fennel, nutmeg, clove, curry leaves, nigella/kalonji seed, and fenugreek give flavor and aroma. Many are digestives.
- Peppercorns and mustard seeds give heat, flavor, and aroma. Cayenne pepper gives heat and color.
- Lentils and split peas are for thickening—when toasted they provide nutty flavor.
- Poppyseeds and coconut give flavor and thicken.
- Turmeric and saffron are for color and flavor.

EXERCISE: MAKE A PERSONAL MASALA

Masalas are like perfume. It's essential to trust personal nose and taste when preparing them. Use fresh spices—crush and smell to determine potency—if weak, dump it. For a longer shelf life, store masala in an airtight jar in refrigerator or dark, cool place.

1. Prepare a base for a curry masala blend.

Grind Together

2 tablespoons coriander seed

1 tablespoon cumin seed

1 tablespoon black peppercorns

   or half of 3-inch dry red chili

1 to 2 teaspoons ground turmeric

2. Grind spices *raw* or *dry toast* whole spices for a head start on flavor. Spices achieve best flavor when toasted before or during cooking, but don't stay fresh as long as whole, raw spices.

   - To dry-toast whole spices: use a heavy (not nonstick) sauté pan.

- Toast coriander seed until it turns 1 to 2 shades darker and pour onto plate.
- Toast cumin seed until 1 to 2 shades darker and fragrant; pour onto plate with coriander.
- Toast peppercorns (or chili) very lightly.
- After seasonings cool, grind in spice/coffee grinder, and pour into bowl. Stir in ground turmeric and sniff.

3. Divide masala base into two or three portions. Decide what seasonings to add to each base.

4. Grind (or toast and grind) other spices separately. Add and sniff like a perfumer. Grind or toast and grind additional spices according to chart on tempering. Stir in small, measured amounts into each portion of masala base until it smells right. Keep it simple.

5. Prepare a simple curry (like *Curry in a Hurry*) with the personal masala.

EASTERN INDIA: FIVE-SPICE MIXTURE (PANCH PHORAN)

A Bengali, Assamese, and Oriyan spice blend of equal parts of five whole spices, panch phoran is a popular East Indian tempering that cooks toss with vegetables (especially potatoes), lentils, beef, or fish.

Yields about 2 tablespoons

1 teaspoon fenugreek seed (methi)
1 teaspoon nigella seed (kalonji)
1 teaspoon brown mustard seed (radhuni)
1 teaspoon coriander seed (dhania) *or* fennel seed (saunf)
1 teaspoon cumin seed (jeera)

1 Mix seeds together. If desired, before using, lightly crush seeds in mortar with pestle.

NORTHERN INDIA: CURRY MASALA

Yields about 1/2 cup

2 tablespoons coriander seed
1 tablespoon poppy seed
1 tablespoon whole black peppercorns
1 tablespoon cumin seed
2 teaspoons ground turmeric
1 teaspoon *each*: fennel seed *and* fenugreek seed
1/2 teaspoon *each*: caraway seed *and* black or brown mustard seed
1/4 teaspoon *each*: ground cinnamon, clove, *and* ground cayenne

1 Grind spices and mix together. Alternatively, roast spice separately, cool, and grind then mix. Store in airtight jar in cool, dark spot.

FIGURE 4.14 Green cardamom.
Source: Dave King/DK Images.

GARAM MASALA

Garam masala is traditionally a blend of four spices: cardamom, cinnamon, cloves, and black pepper, sometimes nutmeg. Originating in North India, it warms the body in cooler weather. The original Mughal garam masala is not toasted and cooks use it primarily in cream, yogurt, and fruit-based sauces. Cumin, coriander, and fennel seed are added to toasted Punjabi garam masala, which is used in tomato and onion-based dishes. Both garam masalas are added as a "top" flavor/fragrance toward the end of cooking.

Mughal Garam Masala

Yields about 5 tablespoons

2 three-inch cinnamon sticks, crushed
1 teaspoon whole cloves
1 tablespoon black peppercorns
1 whole nutmeg, chopped into smaller bits
2 to 3 teaspoons ground cardamom

Punjabi Garam Masala

Yields a generous 3/4 cup

3 tablespoons cumin seeds
3 tablespoons coriander seed
2 tablespoons black peppercorns
1 tablespoon ground cardamom
1 cinnamon stick, 4 inches long, crushed
1 tablespoon fennel seed
2 teaspoons chopped nutmeg
1/4 teaspoon whole cloves

1 Grind **Mughal** masala spices together in spice grinder.

2 Toast **Punjabi** spices separately in a dry skillet until fragrant and one shade darker. Cool and grind together in spice grinder.

3 Store garam masalas in 2 separate airtight jars in cool, dark spot.

WET-DRY GRINDER

Modern Indian cooks use machines to grind dry or wet ingredients. South Indian cooks use a machine fitted with grinding stones to pulverize soaked legumes and rice. Indian cooks living abroad in the West use the *Preethi* grinder. A mini wet-dry spice grinder or food processor works well for grinding small amounts.

Southern Podi

South Indian cuisine wouldn't be complete without these essential spiced powders. South Indian homes keep several on hand to use as Westerners use salt and pepper. Cooks grind combinations of roasted spices, lentils, herbs, ginger, or garlic into delightful crumbly condiments. Sometimes they are mixed on the plate with coconut oil or ghee and used as a sort of dipping sauce. Podis are a quick flavor booster for rice, lentils, or vegetables.

SOUTHERN INDIA: SAMBAR PODI

Yields 1/4 to 1/3 cup

1 teaspoon tiny red split lentils
2 tablespoons coriander seed
2 teaspoons black peppercorns
2 teaspoon cumin seed
1 teaspoon fenugreek seed
1 tablespoon ground turmeric
1 teaspoon ground cayenne pepper

1 Grind spices and mix together. Store in airtight jar in cool, dark spot.

SOUTHERN INDIA: SPICED COCONUT POWDER (THENGA PODI)

This nutty-spicy condiment comes from the Brahmin of southern Tamil Nadu. Roasted sesame seeds, garlic, ginger, and spices might also appear in a thenga podi.

Yields about 1-1/4 cups

1-3/4 ounces (split and skinned) urad dal *or* channa dal, about 4 tablespoons
1 teaspoon dark mustard seeds
2 three-inch dried red chilies, less for milder and more for hotter
3 teaspoons fragrant coconut oil
4 ounces grated fresh or frozen coconut, 1 cup
    or 5 ounces dried, unsweetened coconut, 3/4 to 1 cup
1/2 to 1 teaspoon thick Indian tamarind concentrate (Tamicon brand)

1 In a dry 9-inch skillet or heavy saucepan, over medium-low heat, slowly roast each ingredient separately until lightly golden. Too much roasting makes a podi bitter.
   - Cook ural dal until golden and pour into a small bowl to cool.
   - Cook mustard seeds until they pop and turn grey; pour into bowl with dal.
   - Dry-toast dry chilies evenly, 30 seconds. Break off and discard stems (and inner seeds for less heat), then tear chilies into small pieces and place in a second bowl.
   - Heat 2 teaspoons oil and stir coconut frequently so it browns evenly; slow the cooking by adding 2 teaspoons water. Place in bowl to cool.
   - Heat 1 teaspoon oil and cook tamarind just until it sizzles; scrape into bowl with coconut.

2 Cool roasted ingredients before grinding. Traditionally podis are ground in mortar with pestle, but the modern spice/coffee grinder or blender work well. Don't overgrind. Texture is key.
   - Grind dal (lentils) and mustard seeds into fine powder in spice or coffee grinder.
   - Grind spices and chilies separately and somewhat coarsely.
   - Grind coconut with tamarind in food processor to resemble breadcrumbs.

3 Mix ground ingredients together, and season podi with about 1/2 teaspoon kosher salt. Cool podi thoroughly and taste. Store in airtight container in refrigerator up to 1 month or more.

Vary! Improvise!

☞ *Use this enticing condiment in soup, salad dressing, or noodles, or rub on grilled meat or seafood.*

SAUCE

In the cuisines of India, sauce is not a thing apart from a dish. An Indian "curry" is a good example. As with a Western stew or braised dish, the sauce is an integral part of the dish. It doesn't stand alone to be mixed and matched with other proteins as a French beurre blanc or an Italian pesto might. Curried dishes are therefore listed under *Simmer, Stew, Poach, Boil, and Steam.* Chutneys, which are technically condiments but can serve in a sauce-like capacity, come under the sauce heading.

Some modern Indian home cooks separate the sauce from the curry: it's called a *daag.*

North Indian cook and author Camellia Panjabi says that many Indian working women prepare a daag or curry base weekly and refrigerate. They sauté onion, ginger, garlic, spices, and masala (with or without tomato), but stop short of adding meat, seafood, or vegetables. For a quick dinner, home cooks combine the daag with vegetables, legumes, paneer cheese, meat, or seafood. This method is ideal for restaurant service, too: prepare just the base of a favorite curry, and heat a serving size portion with protein and/or vegetables per order.

Chutney

The East Indian Trading Company coined the word *chutney.* It is of colonial, not Indian, origin. Much like a Western sauce, chutney is a sweet, sour, spicy, or savory condiment, highly flavorful, served with an Indian meal to add sparkle and enhance the dining experience. Cooked or fresh, smooth or chunky, sweet or savory, cooks all over India make chutneys from spices, chilies, fresh herbs, nuts, legumes, fruit or vegetables, and season them highly.

Along with the salty, spicy "pickle," chutneys are an important staple because they uplift a meal and, much as a sauce or salsa in other cuisines, serve to enhance bland foods like breads or rice. Easy to make and store, chutneys give diners an opportunity to alter the meal according to their tastes. Bottled chutneys and fruit chutneys from apples or peaches familiar to Westerners are not common in India; they are more Caribbean-style. Instead tamarind, coconut, peanut, cilantro, or mint and onion chutneys are favored. They can be very spicy with chilies, black pepper, and dried chili. Tamarind and lime add sourness, and jaggery adds sweetness.

FRESH MANGO CHUTNEY

This is a typical South Indian chutney, where mangoes are available year-round. South Indian cooks often make it with sour, unripe mango, but it's also tasty with a ripe one.

Yields 1-1/2 cups

13 to 14 ounce firm-ripe mangoes, about 2 cups peeled and diced
1/2 to 1 teaspoon red chili powder
1/4 ounce trimmed cilantro, about 1/4 cup finely sliced

Tempering

1 tablespoon fragrant coconut oil
1 teaspoon dark mustard seed
1/2 teaspoon cumin seed
1 ounce shallot, 1 medium, 3 to 4 tablespoons peeled and finely diced
1/3 ounce gingerroot, about 1 teaspoon peeled and minced, more to taste
6 to 8 curry leaves
Pinch asafoetida powder

1 lime, about 2 to 3 tablespoons freshly squeezed lime juice

1 Place mango, chili powder, 1/2 teaspoon kosher salt, and cilantro into food processor. Pulse/purée until mango is a chunky purée. Scrape into mixing bowl.

2 Heat oil over medium heat in 2-quart saucepan. Add mustard and cumin seeds and cook 30 seconds. Add shallot, ginger, and curry leaves and cook until shallots soften, 2 to 3 minutes. Add asafoetida and remove pan from heat.

3 Fold tempering into mango mixture. Season with salt and lime juice to taste. Rest chutney to develop flavor 20 minutes before serving.

Vary! Improvise!

☛ *Devise a tomato chutney from this recipe.*

☛ ***Cooked Mango Chutney:*** *Add the chunky mango purée to the tempering and bring to a boil. Simmer a few minutes and remove from heat. Season with fresh lime juice. This will keep slightly longer than the fresh chutney. Sweeten with jaggery if desired.*

SOUTH INDIAN ONION-URAD DAL CHUTNEY (VENGAYAM THOVIAYAL)

This savory, addictive chutney could make a full meal with rice or roti.

Yields 2 to 2-1/2 cups

1 ounce block tamarind paste, 2 tablespoons packed
5 tablespoons oil *or* fragrant coconut oil
4 ounces urad dal, 1/2 cup, rinsed, drained, and patted dry
3/4 teaspoon caraway
1/8 teaspoon ground asafoetida
8 ounces onions, 1-3/4 to 2 cups peeled and finely diced
2 three-inch dried red chilies, stemmed

Tempering

2 teaspoons fragrant coconut oil
3/4 teaspoons dark mustard seeds

1 Break up tamarind and place in small heatproof mixing bowl. Pour 1/3 cup boiling water over and soak until soft, 15 to 20 minutes. Mash pulp. Push through strainer. Discard pits and fiber. Reserve tamarind purée, about 2 tablespoons.

2 Heat oil in 4-quart saucepan over medium heat and stir in urad dal. Stir constantly and cook until evenly golden. Stir in caraway and asafoetida and cook 30 seconds. Stir in onions and cook until soft, 5 to 7 minutes.

3 Lower heat and add 2 tablespoons tamarind purée, red chilies, and season with salt. Simmer and stir 5 minutes.

4 Transfer chutney to blender and add 2/3 cup cold water. Purée chutney to a slightly crunchy, rough paste. Scrape into mixing bowl and rinse out blender with a little more water and use to thin chutney. Taste chutney and season with more tamarind or salt. Place into serving dish.

5 **Temper, temper:** Heat oil in 6-inch sauté pan over medium heat. When hot, add mustard seeds and fry until they sputter and crackle. Immediately pour over chutney. Serve chutney at room temperature.

TASTY TAMARIND

School children in India often wait for the school bus under big tamarind trees. The long pods hang down and the children grab them. They peel away the outside husk and suck away at the tart-sweet sticky stuff inside, spitting out the fiber and large seeds.

TAMARIND CHUTNEY

This delightful fruity, sour chutney is prepared all over India and served with most meals.

Yields 1 to 1-1/4 cups

2 ounces tamarind paste, 1/4 cup packed
1/4 teaspoon ground cumin
1/2 teaspoon ground cinnamon
1 teaspoon garam masala
About 1/2 ounce gingerroot, 1 tablespoon peeled and finely grated
2-1/2 to 3 ounces jaggery, 5 to 6 tablespoons

1 Mix tamarind and 3/4 cup boiling water. Soak 15 to 20 minutes. Knead tamarind to release purée. Strain and scrape through mesh strainer set over bowl to yield about 3/4 cup thick purée; reserve. Discard seeds and fiber.

2 Heat a small saucepan over medium-low heat. Add spices and cook until fragrant, 30 seconds. Stir in tamarind purée. Place ginger in cheesecloth and squeeze ginger juice into tamarind. Stir in jaggery and bring to a boil. Lower the heat and simmer until jaggery is melted, 1 to 2 minutes. Remove pan from heat and cool.

3 Taste and adjust seasonings to sweet-sour, adding sweetener as necessary. Stir in water to achieve desired consistency, thick enough to coat a spoon, but pourable.

Vary! Improvise!

☛ *Toast 1/4 cup yellow raisins in 1 teaspoon ghee until golden and puffed. Mix with spiced tamarind purée and whiz in blender until smooth.*

☛ *Substitute maple syrup for jaggery.*

FRESH CILANTRO (OR MINT) CHUTNEY

Serve this with rice, dal, or deep-fried pakora as a dipping sauce.

Yields 1-3/4 cups, 6 to 8 servings

4 ounces cilantro, 4 cups packed
  or 4 ounces mint leaves, 2 cups packed
1 ounce jalapeño chili, 1 large, 2 tablespoons stemmed and chopped
About 1 ounce gingerroot, 2 tablespoons peeled and chopped
1-1/2 to 2 ounces jaggery, 3 to 4 tablespoons
  or maple syrup, to taste
4 to 6 tablespoons freshly squeezed lime juice, 1-1/2 to 2 large limes

1 In blender, purée cilantro or mint, chili, ginger, 1 teaspoon salt, sweetener, and 4 tablespoons lime juice, scraping down as necessary. Pour in 3/4 cup water and continue to purée until very smooth.

2 Taste chutney and adjust flavors. Scrape mixture into a container or bowl and chill 20 minutes—to give chutney time to develop flavor. If necessary, stir in more water to adjust consistency to a thick soupy consistency. Taste chutney and adjust flavor with more salt, lime juice, or sweetener.

Vary! Improvise!

☛ ***Cilantro-Cashew:*** *Purée 3-3/4 ounces dry-roasted cashews (3/4 cup) in with cilantro. Adjust with more water to achieve thick soupy consistency.*

☛ ***Cilantro-Coconut:*** *Purée 1/2 cup toasted or fresh grated coconut in with cilantro.*

☛ ***Coconut Milk:*** *Substitute coconut milk for half the water.*

FRESH SOUTH INDIAN COCONUT CHUTNEY

Coconut chutney, a staple in many South Indian homes is served with iddlis (steamed fluffy rice cakes) or crisp dosa for breakfast. It often includes a tempering made with brown mustard or cumin seed, fresh curry leaves, and urad dal. Fresh coconut has the best flavor but unsweetened dried will make respectable chutney. One coconut yields 1-1/2 to 2 cups shredded coconut meat.

Yields about 1-1/4 cups

1/2 large fresh coconut, 4 to 5 ounces freshly grated coconut, 1 cup packed
   or 3/4 cup dried, unsweetened, finely shredded coconut
1 teaspoon cumin seed
1/2 ounce trimmed cilantro *or* mint leaves, 1/4 cup packed
1 ounce fresh green chilies, 2 medium serranos, about 2 tablespoons stemmed and chopped
2 tablespoons fresh lime juice, more to taste
1 ounce jaggery, 2 tablespoons, to taste
   or maple syrup, to taste

1 See *Glossary* for preparing fresh coconut. If using dry coconut, soak 10 to 15 minutes just covered in warm water. Press-drain; reserve soaking water.

2 Heat small skillet over medium heat. Add cumin seeds and dry-toast until they crackle. Remove from heat immediately to plate; cool seeds. Lightly crush seeds in mortar with pestle.

3 Combine coconut, cumin, cilantro or mint, and chilies in food processor. Purée until smooth and creamy. Season chutney with lime juice, salt, and sweetener to taste. Add 1/4 cup reserved soaking water or water to adjust chutney to the consistency of a thick salsa.

4 Rest chutney 15 to 20 minutes at room temperature. Adjust consistency if necessary. Taste and re-season—the flavor should speak sweetly and assertively. Coconut chutney keeps 5 to 6 days refrigerated. Serve it as a spread or with chapati, pappadams, or pakora or aside any rice and lentil dish.

BOMBAY SANDWICH

When visiting Bombay/Mumbai, stop at the food stalls for a snack. Slices of toasted or plain bread are layered with fresh coconut chutney and vegetables and called a *Bombay Sandwich*. Prepare one: layer roast chicken, turkey, or egg sandwiches with *Fresh South Indian Coconut Chutney*.

SPECIAL METHODS

KEY FATS: GHEE, PEANUT OIL, MUSTARD OIL, COCONUT OIL, AND SESAME OIL

Fats are a sure indicator of where a person is in India, and the world. They impart a distinct flavor and style. Indian chefs use different oils depending on the region, the dish, and their finances. (Many modern Indians use olive, canola, sunflower, or safflower oil for health benefits.)

- In the more affluent North, ghee and butter are favored, but since they are pricey, vegetable oils and a manufactured "ghee" are also popular.
- Bengal, a northeastern state, and the northernmost state of Punjab, prefers the pungent mustard oil pressed from the seed of Indian mustard plants. It must be heated to smoking to soften its harsh flavor.
- In the central Indian state of Madhya Pradesh, where peanuts grow, peanut oil is favored.
- South Indian cooks have traditionally cooked with coconut and sesame oils, but poor cooks use cheaper vegetable oils like soybean, safflower, sunflower, cottonseed, palm, and corn oil.

ROASTED CLARIFIED BUTTER (USLI GHEE)

Some Indian cooks use a vegetable shortening called vanaspati ghee *for cooking. It is specially processed to look and taste like ghee, but it is a hydrogenated fat made from coconut, cottonseed, rapeseed, and palm oils. There's nothing like the real thing.*

Yields about 12 fluid ounces

1 pound unsalted butter

1 Dice butter into small cubes and place in a heavy 2- to 3-quart saucepan over lowest heat possible. Place a flame tamer under the pan to slow the cooking.

2 Set up strainer over stainless bowl and line it with dampened cheesecloth.

3 The simmering butter will separate into oil and milk solids and form a crust on top and bottom. Cook butter gently until the bottom is golden brown, 35 to 45 minutes or longer depending on the heat. Watch the butter closely as it can easily go from golden to tar black in seconds.

4 Remove saucepan from heat and strain ghee through dampened cheesecloth. Store ghee in a heatproof container, not plastic, and cool. Skim top for the brown, crusty residue and discard it or spread on a chapati. Cover ghee and refrigerate; it will last for several months. The better the ghee is strained the longer it will keep.

FIGURE 4.15 Kadhai with tempering and curry leaves.

Flavor Tempering (Baghar, Tadka, or Chaunk)

Tempering is an important Indian flavor technique and not one meal is without it. *Chaunk, tadka,* or *baghar* are other Indian names for this process of cooking a series of aromatic seasonings, spices, or herbs quickly in hot ghee or oil. The aim is to infuse fat with flavor and to provide quick distribution in a dish. This layering of seasonings is a small part of what makes Indian cooks remarkable magicians of seasoning. The tempering is an essential part of a cook's arsenal of flavoring; it can begin or finish a dish and lend complexity. One or two good temperings bring a pot of cooked plain lentils or cauliflower alive with flavor. Use it in four ways as a flavor device:

As a flavor base or flavor foundation:

- Sauté aromatic vegetables like onions, ginger, garlic, chilies, and spices in ghee or oil to form a *flavor foundation* much like French cuisine's *mirepoix*. This foundation will start a dish. Freeze it in small batches for quick meals. It will become a wonderful base with which to creatively season any Indian dish. Use it alone or add other ingredients like tomato or coconut milk to form your own personal curried dish.

As a flavor-infused addition:

- Cook a series of whole or ground spices and seasonings in hot ghee or oil and pour them into cooked food like lentils, potatoes, beans, or vegetables.

As a corrective or flavor intensifier:

• If a dish doesn't have the desired punch, make another tempering. Indian cooks season a dish with a tempering then sometimes prepare a second tempering to swirl into (for instance) spinach dal just before it goes to the table. At the Indian table, those who want less spice—like children—can dip the serving spoon in around the edges and get a little less spicy portion.

As a garnish:

• Pour a crunchy or colorful tempering on top and leave it for guests to mix into the dish.

Signature Technique: The ABCs of Flavor Tempering

A **Consider the Dish.** Choose from whole and ground seasonings, gingerroot, onions and chillies, channa or ural dal, and curry leaves. Start simple—with three or four—until the flavors are familiar. Think of classic combinations: cooked carrots with ginger, cumin or caraway; cauliflower might beg for the citrus flavor of coriander and the pungent spiciness of chilies and curry leaf; bland cooked legumes would benefit from lots of spices and chilies. Large volume dishes might require several temperings with spices and dal and fresh ingredients divided.

B **Over Moderate Heat** —for more control—in a heavy-bottomed sauté or saucepan, heat ghee or oil until hot, but not smoking. Intensity of flavor depends on heat, how long spices are cooked, and what order they go into the pan—singly or all together.

The general cooking order:

• **Whole spices:** Brown mustard seed should turn ash-grey. Fenugreek gets bitter when over-cooked. Add whole spices in order of toasting:

Dark roast/first additions: Cinnamon stick, clove, black cardamom, star anise, nutmeg, brown mustard

Medium roast/second additions: Coriander, cumin, dry split lentils

Light roast/third additions: Fennel, caraway, fenugreek, kalonji

• **Dal:** Dry split, skinned lentils like urad dal should be browned to impart nutty taste.

• **Fresh chilies:** Slivered fresh chilies should blister.

• **Curry leaves:** Fresh curry leaves should shrivel.

• **Dry chilies, spices, and masalas:** Dry and ground spices should sizzle, foam, and darken a shade. Asafoetida powder should be added last and cooked only a few seconds.

• **Onions, gingerroot, and garlic:** Sliced, minced, or grated. If a large amount of onions are used, cook them separately for best results.

• **Tomatoes:** Moist foods like onions and tomatoes bring heat down and stop the toasting process.

C **Add Other Ingredients** like vegetables, meat, or seafood and cook with the tempering or pour the tempering into a cooked dish. Season with salt and pepper and perhaps lime juice and serve.

BROWN-TEMPERED URAD DAL

Sometimes lentil soup will stick and brown to the bottom of the pot. Stirred into the soup the browned bit enriches flavor. Brown-tempered raw urad dal graces dishes similarly, adding a rich, meaty, and complex nuttiness.

EXERCISE: TEMPERING INTO LENTILS

1. Cook 1 cup red split lentils in 3 to 4 cups water.
2. Divide cooked lentils into 3 portions.
3. Prepare measured ingredients for 3 separate temperings. Keep track.
4. Prepare each tempering and stir into each separate pot of lentils.
5. Season with salt and lime juice.
6. Taste and judge.

THE INDIAN WOK (KADHAI/KARAI)

Similar to a Chinese wok, the kadhai is made of steel or iron. It should be seasoned, washed without soap, dried, and oiled before storing. Substitute a 12- to 14-inch wok for a kadhai.

SIGNATURE RECIPE

INDIAN CHEESE (PANEER OR PANIR)

Chewy, non-melting paneer cheese is a good meat substitute in Indian dishes. Making it is a simple process—its delicate fresh flavor makes it worth the time.

Yields 11 to 12 ounces cheese, 2 cups cubed

2 quarts whole milk (preferably organic)
1/4 cup white vinegar

- The higher the milk fat content, the softer the cheese.

- Substitute fresh lemon juice for vinegar. Rinse wrapped curds before pressing.

- Leftover whey can be used for making Indian breads like chapatti.

1 Heat milk in heavy 4-quart saucepan over medium heat. Stir occasionally. Line a fine strainer with a double layer of cheesecloth or a clean, thin cotton towel, and set over a bowl or pan.

2 When milk comes to a boil, turn off the heat. Gradually and gently stir in vinegar. Curds will form and separate from the whey—remove pan from burner and continue to gently stir until curds form and vinegar smell dissipates.

3 Gently ladle curds and whey through strainer. (At this point, while paneer is warm, you may add spices or herbs to season the cheese.) Form paneer into an even square—still wrapped in cheesecloth—and lay on a cutting board. Lay another cutting board on top and weight paneer 2 hours.

4 Remove paneer from cheesecloth, seal in storage container, and refrigerate if not using immediately. To use, dice into cubes.

Source: *Culture Cheese Magazine*, Spring 2011.

SIMMER, STEW, POACH, BOIL, AND STEAM

Indian Curries

Across India, cooks prepare a mind-boggling choice of spiced dishes. Food available locally and seasonally, location, religion, and economics determine what kind of curry an Indian cook prepares. The richer North and Central regions emphasize available fresh vegetables, fruit, meat, wheat, and dairy. Along coastal areas fish and seafood figure prominently while in the South coconuts and legumes show up.

How the cook builds flavor depends upon a set of traditions that dictate what seasonings and methods go with what foods. Apprentice to an Indian cook or follow the classics to learn when and what seasonings to use. Curries or spiced dishes spring from elemental techniques and flavors.

North India: Vegetable oil and ghee, onion, garlic, ginger, cumin, coriander, dry red chilies, turmeric, chili powder, cardamom, cinnamon, cloves, aniseed, fennel, and garam masala play important roles.

South India: Vegetable and coconut oils, black mustard seed, asafoetida, black peppercorns, tamarind, chilies, fenugreek seeds, and fresh curry leaves form the distinct flavor.

East India: Mustard oil, vegetable and occasionally ghee, mustard seeds, white cumin, nigella, fennel seed, fenugreek, and the five-spice panch phora are trademark flavors.

West India: Vegetable oils, peanut oil and ghee, dry red chilies, kokum, sesame seeds, coconut, and vinegar are typical.

Signature Technique: North Indian Curry

1 **Cook whole spices** in fat over medium-high heat until they smell fragrant and they begin to jump, about 30 seconds. Cooking spices in hot fat brings out the best flavor elements. Add liquid (or watery vegetables) and the temperature drops to 212 degrees F.

2 **Add aromatic vegetables (onion, ginger, and/or garlic).** Cook sliced or diced onions (don't overload the pot) and over medium to high heat until translucent or seared or browned, and tender or caramelized. Brown onion for heavier, richer color and flavor, or cook until soft for lighter dishes. Reduce the heat and add puréed or finely minced ginger and/or garlic and cook for a few seconds.

3 **Add ground spices.** Mix ground spices with water or liquid (water, vinegar, broth, tomato, or coconut milk) to form a loose paste to keep spices from sticking. Cook onion-spice mixture over low to medium-low heat, until liquid evaporates, craters appear—and spices stick to pan and roast, 1 to 2 minutes. (If using meat to infuse flavor into it, cook meat in mixture until moisture evaporates.)

4 **Add liquid ingredients.** Typically, tomato, tamarind liquid, coconut milk, water, or broth provides liquid. Simmer until tomatoes break down, 15 to 20 minutes. At this point the curry sauce or *daag* may be divided and frozen for quick use later.

5 **Add proteins and vegetables.** Meat, seafood, cooked legumes like chickpeas simmer until almost done or infused with flavor. Vegetables go in and simmer until very tender.

- Add cooked beans and peas with harder vegetables and simmer until tender. Add softer vegetables and simmer until tender.

- For seafood, cook vegetables in the curry mixture and add seafood at the very last; it can overcook easily.

FIGURE 4.16 Sacred Indian cows wandering in India.
Source: Daniele Lenzi/Fotolia.

EXERCISE: CURRY IN A HURRY

This American translation of a curry is a simple recipe that makes an excellent *daag* curry base without the chicken.

Yields about 4 cups, 2 to 4 servings

2 tablespoons canola oil, ghee, or coconut oil

1/2 teaspoon cumin seed

1/2 teaspoon brown mustard seed

1/2 teaspoon nigella seed

4 to 5 ounces small yellow onions, 1 cup finely sliced

About 1/4 ounce ginger, 1/2 tablespoon peeled and minced

1/4 ounce garlic, 1 large clove, 1-1/2 teaspoons finely minced

1 tablespoon *Northern Masala*

6 ounces ripe *or* drained, canned tomatoes, 1 cup finely diced

1 pound boneless, skinless chicken breasts, diced into 3/4-inch cubes

Fresh lime juice

1. Follow the technique outlined in *Signature Technique: North Indian Curry.*

INDIAN COOKING TIPS

- Use all the cilantro, not only the leaves. Finely slice it from top to stems. Don't chop.
- Purée garlic and ginger in a blender or small food processor with a little water for a finer and easier purée.
- Use from 1 teaspoon to 1 tablespoon of each ginger, garlic, and ground cumin and coriander per pound of meat.

- Whole spices will liven up a curry with **individual** flavor notes.
- Ground spices mixtures or masalas form a **soft, more muted backdrop**.
- Shallots and small yellow (bag) onions contain less liquid, brown faster, and impart a more intense onion flavor.

FIGURE 4.17 North Indian thali.
Source: Ashwin/Fotolia.

NORTHERN CHICKPEA CURRY (CHANNA MASALA)

This curry is even better tasting the next day. It is mildly hot, but for less heat, omit one chili.

Yields about 6-1/2 to 7 cups, 6 servings

1 ounce tamarind paste, 2 tablespoons packed
   or 1 teaspoon tamarind concentrate
1/4 to 1/2 cup ghee *or* vegetable oil
2 teaspoons cumin seed
6 to 7 ounces small yellow onions, 1-1/2 cups peeled and thinly slivered
1/3 ounce garlic, about 2 medium cloves, 2 teaspoons minced
1/2 ounce gingerroot, 1 tablespoon peeled and finely minced or grated
2 ounces jalapeño chilies, about 2 large, 1/4 cup stemmed and finely diced
2 to 3 tablespoons *Northern Masala*
4 fluid ounces tomato liquid or water, 1/2 cup
8 to 9 ounces ripe tomatoes, 1-1/2 cups finely diced
   or 1-1/2 cups drained canned diced tomatoes, liquid reserved
14 ounces dry chickpeas, 2 cups, soaked, drained, and cooked
   or 5 cups cooked, drained chickpeas
2 teaspoons *Punjabi Garam Masala*

To Serve

Northern Fragrant-Spice Pullao
Tamarind Chutney

1 Bring 1/2 cup water to boil in small saucepan. Break up tamarind paste and place in small, heat-proof bowl. Pour 3 fluid ounces boiling water over and soak until soft, 10 minutes. Knead pulp until it releases from mass and thickens into a purée. Scrape tamarind purée through strainer. Discard pits and fiber and set strained purée aside. Should yield 2 to 3 tablespoons thick purée.

2 **Cook spices:** Heat fat in a 6-quart heavy pot over medium high heat. Add cumin seeds and cook until they darken and jump, 20 to 30 seconds.

3 **Cook aromatics:** Add onions and cook until browned, about 15 minutes. Stir constantly. Add garlic, ginger, and chilies and cook 1 minute. Don't burn the garlic.

4 **Add masala powder:** Stir and cook for 10 seconds then add 1/2 cup tomato liquid or water. Cook until water evaporates and spices begin to stick and toast.

5 **Add tomatoes:** Simmer until fat begins to separate from the gravy, about 5 minutes. Add 2 tablespoons tamarind purée or 1 teaspoon tamarind concentrate and simmer curry 20 minutes. Add extra boiling water (or chickpea cooking liquid) as necessary to keep a thickish sauce. Stir frequently.

6 **Stir in chickpeas and garam masala:** Simmer curry 20 minutes uncovered for a thickish sauce. Taste curry. Season with more tamarind, salt, and cayenne pepper, to taste.

7 **To Serve:** Serve curry with pullao and chutney.

NORTHERN FISHERMAN'S CURRY

This is simple fisherman's food from the village. It contains no onions to sweeten it and no cream or coconut to tame it, which makes it the ultimate, authentic peasant food. Try preparing it with shrimp or boneless, skinless chicken breast.

Yields about 5 cups, 4 servings

1 ounce garlic, 4 large cloves, 2 tablespoons peeled and minced
1/2 ounce ginger, 2 teaspoons peeled and minced

Masala Spices

1 tablespoon ground coriander
3/4 teaspoon ground cumin
3/4 teaspoon ground turmeric
1/2 teaspoon ground black pepper

3 tablespoons ghee, coconut or vegetable oil
1/2 teaspoon mustard seeds
1/4 teaspoon fenugreek seeds
1 pound tomatoes, 2 medium–large, 2 cups finely chopped or puréed
    or 2 cups drained, canned diced tomato
1/4 teaspoon ground cayenne
    or 1/2 to 1 teaspoon ground dry red chili, to taste
1/2 teaspoon garam masala
2 ounces cilantro, 1/2 cup finely sliced
1-1/2 pounds skinned, boned firm white fish like tilapia, diced into 1- to 1-1/2-inch cubes

To Serve: Hot, cooked rice or roti

1 Mix garlic and ginger together and set aside. In another bowl mix *masala spices* with 1/4 cup water and set aside. Bring a small pot of water to boil for later use.

2 Heat oil in a 6-quart saucepan over medium heat. Sauté mustard seed until it pops and turns gray, 30 to 60 seconds. Add fenugreek and cook 10 seconds. Add ginger and garlic and cook 20 to 30 seconds.

3 Scrape in masala spice mixture, and cook over medium to medium-low heat until water evaporates and masala forms craters, spices stick and toast, and oil separates, 8 to 10 minutes.

4 Pour in tomatoes, cayenne or chili, garam masala, and half the cilantro. Simmer curry partially covered until it bubbles and oil separates from mass, 8 to 10 minutes. Taste curry and season with salt. If flavors are not harmonious, simmer longer.

5 Add fish to curry mixture and simmer 1 minute. Slowly pour 1/2 cup boiling water around the sides of fish. Lower heat to a simmer, cover and cook until fish is opaque and cooked through when separated with fork, 5 to 7 minutes. Add more water as necessary to maintain a sauce.

6 **To Serve:** Garnish curry with remaining cilantro. Serve with rice or roti.

NORTHERN CHICKEN KORMA

The royal Moghul korma is a rich curry made with cream or yogurt. Kormas are delicately seasoned—cream softens the seasonings—but richly flavorful. Finely ground nuts and coconut help to thicken while adding flavor. This big-flavored dish will hypnotize guests.

Yields about 6 cups, 4 servings

Marinade

3/4 cup plain whole-milk yogurt
3/4 ounce garlic, about 3 large cloves, 4 to 4-1/2 teaspoons finely minced
About 1 ounce gingerroot, 4 teaspoons peeled and finely minced
2 teaspoons ground coriander

1-1/2 pounds skinned and fat trimmed, bone-in chicken thighs *or* breasts
    or 1-1/4 pounds boneless, skinless chicken breasts and thighs, diced into 1-inch cubes
2 tablespoons ghee
1-inch cinnamon stick
1 piece mace
6 whole cloves
6 whole allspice
10 green cardamom pods
1 teaspoon brown mustard seed
10 black peppercorns
8 to 9 ounces small yellow onions, 2 cups peeled and slivered
1 to 2 ounces green chilies, 1 to 2 large, 2 to 4 tablespoons stemmed and finely diced
1 cup chicken stock or water (use only half if preparing dish for biryani)
2-1/2 ounces unsweetened dried coconut, about 1-1/2 to 1-2/3 cups
1 ounce almonds *or* cashews, about 3 tablespoons
3/4 teaspoon garam masala
1 teaspoon jaggery *or* maple syrup
1/2 ounce cilantro, 1/4 cup finely sliced

To Serve: Hot, cooked rice or roti

1 Mix **marinade** ingredients together in mixing bowl.

2 Slash bone-in chicken so marinade can penetrate. Place meat in marinade and mix well. Marinate chicken at room temperature 1 hour or for best flavor, overnight, covered, in refrigerator. Bring to room temperature before cooking.

3 Heat ghee in large saucepan over medium heat. When hot, add cinnamon, mace, cloves, allspice and cardamom and mustard seed, and cook until they sizzle and darken one shade, 1 to 2 minutes. Add peppercorns and cook 20 seconds. Immediately add onion and green chilies and season with kosher salt. Cook onions and chilies until soft, 6 to 8 minutes.

4 Add chicken and its marinade and chicken stock to spice and aromatic mixture. Simmer korma partially covered, over low heat until bone-in chicken is cooked through and tender, 30 to 40 minutes—or boneless meat is tender, 20 to 25 minutes. Stir occasionally. If korma begins to dry, add small amounts of water or chicken stock.

5 Meanwhile, grind coconut and almonds separately in blender or spice grinder until coconut is fine and almonds are powder. Stir coconut and almonds into korma and simmer, uncovered, until the gravy is creamy and thickened, 3 to 5 minutes. Stir in garam masala, jaggery, and cilantro. Season with salt; taste and adjust seasoning.

6 **To Serve:** Serve korma with rice or roti.

Vary! Improvise!

☛ *Dairy-Free: Substitute 3/4 cup canned coconut milk plus 1 tablespoon fresh lime juice for the yogurt and fragrant coconut oil for ghee.*

PANEER CHEESE AND SPINACH (SAAG PANEER OR PALAK PANEER SAK)

There are many ways to make this classic North Indian dish: with ginger or garlic or without, with tomato or cream or without, browning paneer or not. The simplest version just uses spinach, paneer, chilies, cumin seeds, lemon juice, and cream. Prepare the paneer early in the day.

Yields 6 cups, 4 to 6 servings

2 pounds trimmed, washed and drained baby spinach
   or two 10-ounce boxes frozen chopped spinach, thawed
1 ounce jalapeño chili, 1 large, 2 tablespoons stemmed

Wet Spice Masala

1/2 ounce gingerroot, 2 to 3 teaspoons peeled and minced
1-1/2 teaspoons ground coriander
1/2 teaspoon ground turmeric
1/2 teaspoon ground cumin
1/2 teaspoon red chili powder, more to taste

4 to 6 tablespoons ghee *or* oil
11 to 12 ounces *Indian Cheese (Paneer or Panir)*, 2 cups diced into 1/2-inch cubes
2 ounces garlic, 4 large cloves, 2 tablespoons minced
8 ounces tomatoes, 1 medium, about 1-1/2 cups finely diced
1/2 to 1 teaspoon garam masala
3 tablespoons cream *or* whole milk yogurt

For Serving

Roti or hot, cooked basmati rice

1   Place spinach leaves in 8-quart pot and over medium-high heat, steam over medium-high heat until wilted. Transfer spinach and liquid into a food processor with jalapeño chili. Coarsely purée vegetables and set them aside.

2   *Prepare* wet spice masala: In a small bowl, mix ginger, coriander, turmeric, cumin, and chili powder with 1/4 cup water, and set aside.

3   **Option: brown paneer.** Heat 6 tablespoons ghee or oil in 6-quart Dutch oven or wok (with a lid) over medium-high heat until hot, but not smoking. Blot paneer cheese very dry. Place cheese cubes into hot fat and cook until browned, turn and brown second side. Remove paneer to bowl with slotted spoon. It may stick to the pan; that is fine.

4   Lower heat to medium, and stir in wet spice masala, garlic, and tomatoes. Scrape up browned bits and simmer masala until tomatoes soften, 15 to 20 minutes. Add spinach. Cover pan and cook mixture until heated through, 3 to 4 minutes. Uncover, turn spinach, cover and cook until hot and very soft, another 3 to 4 minutes. Season with salt. Stir in paneer, garam masala, and cream or yogurt, cover and simmer 5 to 10 minutes more.

5   **To Serve:** The dish should be thick but juicy. Taste and adjust seasonings (and consistency if necessary). Serve with *roti* or hot basmati rice.

Vary! Improvise!

☞ *Substitute 2 pounds trimmed mustard greens mixed with spinach, Swiss chard, or stemmed kale for the spinach. Simmer greens until meltingly tender.*

☞ *Add grated carrot or squash for color.*

CROSSROADS CUISINE IN GUJARAT

Gujarat, on India's west coast, roughly halfway between north and south India, is a "crossroads" cuisine. Pushing out into the Arabian Sea, this state has been a center of trade for all of India—a place where North and South meet and where traders return to bring a tradition of new foods and flavors. Quicker cooking stir-fries and steamed dishes are favored, a departure from slow-cooked dishes typical of northern cuisine. Northern and Gujarati cuisines rely on ghee, less on rice, and more on flour made from grains like millet and legumes like chickpeas for flatbreads.

FIGURE 4.18   Market in the southern state of Kerala.
Source: lamio/Fotolia.

INVESTIGATE NORTHERN AND SOUTHERN CURRY TECHNIQUE

Notice that curries made in North and Central India employ dry spices and spice mixtures that cooks fry with onions, ginger, garlic, and chilies. In South and West India, cooks often grind raw or fried onions, ginger, spices, and/or chilies—with shredded fresh or dry coconut or tamarind into a wet masala. Ground wet masalas help thicken and smooth Southern curries.

Ammini Ramachandran Categorizes South Indian Spiced Dishes

It's like herding cats, but Ammini Ramachandran, author of *Grains, Greens, and Grated Coconuts*, born in the South Indian state of Kerala, categorizes the encyclopedic choices of South Indian curries and spiced dishes by texture. "In south India the consistencies of curries vary from thick, to somewhat thick to watery," says Ramachandran. "We use different words than curry to denote most of these dishes. The dry dishes are never called 'curries' in South India."

The first four categories have some form of gravy or sauce and are what Westerners would identify as a "curry." *Somewhat thick* and *yogurt, buttermilk, or coconut-based curries* have similar consistencies but the tartness comes from tamarind in the first and yogurt in the second. Thickening agents are different—dal in the first and coconut in the second.

Coconut milk-based curries are not tart. South Indians mix these dishes with hot rice and serve on a banana leaf.

1. **Watery or Thin Curries**

   These include the tomato and lentil-based watery *rasam* and *kulambu* (rasam without lentils but with yogurt) and are served over rice or drunk, but Indians do not consider them soup. Rasams use either tamarind or lemon to add a refreshing sour flavor.

2. **Somewhat-Thick Curries**

   These are gravy-textured curries, and include tart and spicy *sambar*—based on cooked legumes or ground roasted coconut and spices—similar to Northern dal dishes.

3. **Thick Curries**

   These include *erisseri* (spiced split peas and vegetables or fruit or cooked with coconut and spices), *koottu* and *aviyal* (semi-solid mixed vegetable stew). They are sometimes mixed with yogurt. Often these curries are garnished with toasted coconut, a spoon of coconut oil, or a spice tempering.

4. **Yogurt, Buttermilk, or Coconut Milk-Based Dishes**

   These milder, creamy dishes incorporate cooked and raw ingredients in dishes such as *kichadi*, *oolan*, raita-like *pachadi* ("pounded food")—yogurt and coconut-based dishes with finely chopped or puréed raw or cooked cucumbers, squash, mango, bitter gourd, or pineapple—and *kaalan*—a thick and sour dish with both yogurt and coconut plus a vegetable like cooked plantain or yam. Simmered yogurt curry *pulissery*, long considered "comfort food," is part of this category.

5. **Dry-Spiced Dishes**

   Not true curries, these are vegetable preparations that are either dressed raw, steamed or boiled, and pan-fried with other ingredients or seasonings—or stir-fried. They include *thoran*, *mezukkupuratti*, *poriyal*, and the fresh, chopped, salady *kachumber*.

SOUTH INDIAN FIVE LEVELS OF FLAVOR

Cookbook author Ammini Ramachandran says that South Indian curries, indeed all curries, contain five levels of flavor.

1. Vegetables and Fruit (Vegetarian) and/or Meat and Seafood

2. Whole and Dry Spice Combinations, Masalas and Salt

3. Coconut, Dal, and/or Sesame Seed

4. Sweet and Sour Seasonings

5. **Final Garnish:** Tempering, Herbs, Coconut Oil, and/or Roasted Coconut

FIGURE 4.19 South Indian lunch on a banana leaf.
Source: wong yu liang/Fotolia.

Signature Technique: South Indian Curry

South Indian cuisine relies on specific basic techniques, seasonings, and food combinations. Always test unfamiliar ingredients or techniques before improvising with them. Keep an improvisation simple. Everything-but-the-kitchen sink cooking clouds the personality and flavor of a dish.

1 Sauté aromatic **vegetable seasonings** like onion, shallot, chilies, ginger, or garlic in oil or ghee in a 6- to 8-quart pot until soft or browned depending on the dish.

2 Purée or grind all or part of sautéed aromatic **vegetable seasonings**. Add **ground spices,** a little water, coconut milk, tamarind, or other liquid and flavors to aid puréeing.

3 If using animal protein, marinate meat or seafood with part of the purée.

4 Drain and blot dry meat if using. Heat fat and brown meat if desired.

5 Heat fat in 6- to 8-quart pot, add and quickly sauté whole spices. Add purée (and the purée from marinade if used) and simmer until thick and dry.

6 If using, stir in **cooked legumes** or **vegetables** or **meat** (browned or not) and nonpuréed aromatic **vegetable seasonings** (if any) and coat in spice-purée mixture. Simmer 1 to 2 minutes.

7 Season curry with salt. Enhance the flavor but stop short of saltiness.

8 Add **liquid ingredients** like boiling water, tomato, or coconut milk, bring to a near boil, lower heat, partially cover, and simmer curry until done—vegetables like cauliflower or squash and meat should be tender. Beans or chickpeas should be infused with flavor.

9 If using, now fold **seafood** or **fish** into curry sauce, cover, and remove pot from heat. The residual heat will cook tender morsels of fish, seafood, or chicken breast in a short time.

10 If flavor needs a boost, prepare a tempering or two to enhance and intensify flavor.

NOT ALL COCONUT OIL IS CREATED EQUAL

Regularly used in South Indian cooking, coconut oil can be a good substitute for ghee or oil. Vegetable-based, it contains no cholesterol, but like butter, it hardens at room temperature because of its high saturated fat content. Cheaper, refined coconut oils have no scent or flavor. Search for extra virgin, unrefined brands that carry the delicate fragrance and flavor of coconut. Use the sniff test to determine which is most fragrant.

INDIAN TIPS

- Citrus juice loses flavor as it sits or with long cooking. Squeeze it and stir it in at the end.
- Herbs like cilantro and mint should be added at the end of cooking or as garnish. (Minced cilantro stems can be added during cooking to boost flavor.)
- Roast spices before cooking or during frying for deeper flavor.
- Thicken too-thin curries with rice or chickpea flour—they add flavor and nutrients.
- Pay attention: boiling yogurt or coconut milk causes it to curdle and lentils need stirring while cooking because they tend to clump on the bottom and burn.

INDIAN CURRY LEAVES

Many dishes in South Indian cuisine require fresh curry leaves. These aromatic and enticing narrow green leaves look like a long, narrow bay leaf. They are indispensable for true South Indian flavor, but can be difficult to find unless an Indian market is nearby. Refrigerated, curry leaves last only a week or two before blackening. Freezing turns them to black mush. But there is another way: Place fresh leaves in a storage container in the refrigerator. Leave the lid ajar so there is airflow. The leaves will dry, but retain much of their scent and flavor. After the leaves dry, seal the storage container and keep leaves refrigerated. They will keep flavor several months.

Vary! Improvise!

☞ **Lemon or Lime Rasam:** Substitute 6 to 8 tablespoons fresh lemon or lime juice for tamarind. Garnish with finely julienned gingerroot along with cilantro.

☞ Simmer 1-1/2 cups finely diced tomatoes in rasam after it is strained, instead of adding purée.

Watery or Thin Curries

SOUTHERN RASAM

Rasams are traditionally served early in the meal. Watery and soup-like, they pack more flavor than might be imagined. Tomatoes, tamarind, and citrus add tang and digestibility. South Indians drink rasams or pour them over cooked rice.

Yields 6 cups, 6 to 8 servings

2 ounces tamarind paste, 1/4 cup packed
About 4 ounces *toor dal* (split pigeon peas) *or* yellow split peas, 1/2 cup washed and drained
1/2 ounce serrano chili, about 1, stemmed, halved lengthwise and seeded
1/8 teaspoon turmeric
8 ounces plum tomatoes, 2 medium, 1 cup coarsely chopped
    or 3/4 cup canned tomato purée

Tempering

1 tablespoon coconut or vegetable oil
1 teaspoon mustard seeds
2 teaspoons cumin seeds
3-inches stemmed and seeded dried red chilies, about 1 tablespoon broken
12 curry leaves
1/2 ounce garlic, about 2 medium cloves peeled and smashed
1/8 teaspoon asafoetida

3/4 to 1 teaspoon coarsely ground black peppercorns

Garnish: 1/2 ounce cilantro, 1/4 to 1/3 cup finely sliced

1 Break up tamarind and place into small mixing bowl. Pour 3/4 cup boiling water over and soak and knead until soft, 10 minutes. Scrape through strainer to yield 1/2 cup purée. Reserve pulp and set aside. Discard seeds and fiber.

2 Pour dal or split peas, 3 cups water, green chili, and turmeric into a 4-quart saucepan, and bring to a boil. Reduce heat, cover pot, and simmer dal until soft, 30 minutes. Remove chili and discard. Purée dal with immersion blender or in blender or food processor. (Don't clean blender or processor; it'll be used again.) Scrape dal mixture through a medium strainer back into clean saucepan.

3 Purée fresh tomatoes in blender or food processor (skip this step with canned purée). Pour tomatoes into saucepan with strained dal. Rinse out blender with 2 cups water and pour into dal. Stir in reserved tamarind purée.

4 **Temper, temper:** Heat oil in an 8- to 9-inch skillet or saucepan over medium heat. Add mustard and cumin seeds, red chilies, curry leaves, and garlic. Cook until seeds crackle and leaves shrivel, 1 to 2 minutes. Add asafoetida and cook 20 to 30 seconds more. Pour 1 cup water into tempering, and scrape into saucepan with dal and tomato.

5 Stir pepper into rasam, and bring to a boil. Lower heat and simmer 5 minutes. Rest rasam 15 to 20 minutes. Scrape through strainer and discard solids in strainer. Stir 3/4 cup water into rasam. Taste and adjust seasonings with salt and freshly ground pepper.

6 **To Serve:** Ladle hot rasam into bowls, garnish with cilantro and serve.

SOUTHERN FISH CURRY

Marinating fish in vinegar and lime juice eliminates any strong smells, and grinding coconut without water intensifies flavor. Spicy and pungent, this curry has the true flavor of South Indian home cooking.

Yields 8 to 9 cups, 4 to 6 servings

1-3/4 pounds fish steak *or* skinned and boned fillets (tilapia, halibut, or whitefish)
1 large lime
2 teaspoons cider vinegar
1-1/2 ounces tamarind paste, 3 tablespoons packed
3/4 teaspoon fenugreek seed
3/4 teaspoon cumin seed
8 to 10 ounces grated fresh coconut, about 2 cups
   or 4-1/2 ounces dry, unsweetened finely shredded coconut, 1-1/2 cups
1 ounce gingerroot, 1/2-inch chunk, peeled
1-1/2 ounces garlic, about 6 large cloves, peeled
1 pound tomatoes, 2 to 2-1/2 cups diced
   or 28-ounce can diced tomatoes, 2 to 2-1/2 cups
2 tablespoons poppy seeds, crushed in mortar

Tempering

1/3 cup vegetable *or* coconut oil
1/2 teaspoon dark mustard seeds
8 to 12 ounces small yellow onions, 2 to 3 cups peeled and diced
20 to 30 fresh curry leaves
1 teaspoon ground coriander
1/2 teaspoon turmeric
1 to 2 teaspoons red chili or cayenne powder

For Serving

Hot, cooked long-grain rice

1 Marinate fish with juice from 1/2 lime (about 2 tablespoons) and vinegar 30 minutes. (Save remaining lime half for garnish.)

2 Soak and knead tamarind in 1 cup hot water 15 to 20 minutes. Press pulp through strainer and discard seeds and fiber. Set aside tamarind liquid/purée. Crush fenugreek and cumin seed together and set aside separately.

3 (If using, soak dry coconut in hot water 10 minutes and press-drain.) Pour coconut, ginger, garlic, tomatoes, and poppy seeds into blender or food processor. Purée 30 seconds. Use a little tamarind liquid to facilitate puréeing, if necessary.

4 **Temper, temper:** Heat oil in a deep 14- to 16-inch skillet (it should accommodate fish in a single layer). When oil is hot, pour in mustard seeds. When they begin to sputter, add the onions and fry until light golden. Add curry leaves and cook until wilted. Add coriander, turmeric, and cayenne and fry 30 seconds to 1 minute.

5 Add coconut-spice purée to pan and stir constantly while cooking, about 3 to 4 minutes. Pour 1 cup water into blender or food processor to rinse; pour in half the blender water, all the tamarind liquid, and 3/4 teaspoon kosher salt. Bring sauce to a boil, lower heat, and simmer 3 minutes. Add more of the water remaining in blender, as needed, to maintain medium-thick consistency of sauce.

6 Lay fish into sauce in one layer. Sprinkle fish with salt, fenugreek, and cumin seeds. Cover pan. Let fish cook until opaque when separated with the tip of a knife on one side then flip, a total of 7 to 10 minutes, depending on thickness of fish.

7 **To Serve:** Slice lime half into small wedges. Serve curry and hot rice with lime wedges. Prepare curry a day ahead or early in the day for richer flavor.

Source: *Great Curries of India* by Camellia Panjabi.

FIGURE 4.20 Southern fish curry.

Thick Curries

SOUTHERN CHICKPEA-COCONUT CURRY (KADALAKARI)

Though this curry has no onion or garlic it is surprisingly full of flavor. Very light; perfect for a summer meal. Seed the chilies for less heat.

Yields 6 cups, 4 to 6 servings

14 ounces dried chickpeas, 2 cups
   or 4 cups cooked chickpeas
1/2 teaspoon turmeric
2 tablespoons vegetable *or* fragrant coconut oil
3 ounces dry, unsweetened finely shredded coconut, 1 cup packed
1 tablespoon coriander seed
1 ounce serrano or jalapeño chili, 2 to 4 tablespoons stemmed and sliced
1/2 ounce gingerroot, 1 tablespoon peeled and finely chopped

Tempering

1 tablespoon vegetable or coconut oil
1 teaspoon dark mustard seed
4-inch dried red chili, stemmed and sliced
1/4 teaspoon asafoetida
12 to 15 fresh curry leaves, about 1/4 cup loosely packed

4 tablespoons fresh lime juice, about 1 large lime
1/2 ounce cilantro, 1/4 cup finely sliced

Garnish: finely sliced cilantro leaves

For Serving

Hot basmati rice

1 Quick soak chickpeas with 2 teaspoons kosher salt (this will help tenderize them). Drain chickpeas, place in 4-quart saucepan, and cover with fresh cold water. Bring to a boil, lower heat, cover, and simmer chickpeas until tender, 45 minutes to 1 hour. Cool chickpeas and drain cooking water; reserve both.

2 Heat oil in 6-quart saucepan over medium-high heat. Add coconut and stir constantly until golden, 1 to 2 minutes. Add coriander and green chilies, and sauté 1 to 2 minutes. Cool mixture. Scrape coconut mixture into a blender. Purée coconut and spices with 1 cup chickpea cooking liquid or water to make a thick purée.

3 Scrape coconut-spice purée into 6-quart pan and add chickpeas. Swish blender with 1 cup more chickpea cooking liquid or water. Pour this liquid into chickpeas and season them with salt. Bring curry to a boil, lower heat, and simmer uncovered until sauce reduces and thickens, 10 to 15 minutes. Remove curry from heat.

4 **Temper, temper:** Heat oil for tempering in 9-inch skillet over medium heat. Pour in mustard seeds and when they crackle add the chili, asafoetida, and curry leaves. Cook until curry leaves wilt, 30 seconds to 1 minute. Scrape tempering into hot curry and rinse out pan with 2 tablespoons water or cooking liquid; stir the liquid into the curry.

5 Rest curry 10 minutes, covered, to infuse flavors. It will absorb remaining liquid and the sauce will cling to the chickpeas. Taste curry and season with lime juice, and salt to taste.

6 **To Serve:** Stir in sliced cilantro. Pour curry into serving dish. Garnish with cilantro leaves. Serve with hot basmati rice.

Source: *Grains, Greens and Grated Coconuts* by Ammini Ramachandran.

Vary! Improvise!

☛ *Make this dish with other types of beans: pink beans, red beans, white beans, or split peas.*

☛ *Spread dry, unsweetened shredded coconut on sheet pan and toast in oven instead of on stove; reduce fat for browning it in the pan by half.*

CAULIFLOWER AND COCONUT CURRY

This vegetable curry is from Mangalore on the Hindu southwest coast of India near Goa. Notice the way the spice base is fried then ground. This is typical of South India.

Yields about 6 cups, 4 to 6 servings

4 tablespoons coconut *or* vegetable oil, *divided*
1 ounce jalapeño chili, 1 large, 2 tablespoons stemmed, seeded, and diced, more to taste
8 to 9 ounces small yellow onions, 2 cups finely diced, *divided*
1/2 teaspoon turmeric
1/2 teaspoon ground paprika
1/2 teaspoon thick tamarind concentrate, leveled off (Tamicon brand)
1 tablespoon *Sambar Podi*
About 2 ounces gingerroot, 2 tablespoons peeled and minced
1/2 ounce garlic, 2 large cloves, 1 tablespoon peeled and minced
8 ounces white potato, about 2 cups peeled and diced into 1/2- to 3/4-inch cubes
1 pound trimmed cauliflower, about 6 cups florets cut into 1- to 1-1/2 inch large florets
1-1/2 to 2 cups thick canned coconut milk
Optional: 1 to 2 teaspoons jaggery or maple syrup
3 to 4 tablespoons fresh lime juice

For Serving

Rice pilaf or cooked, hot rice

1 Heat small pot of water to boiling for later use.

2 **Blender paste:** Heat a nonreactive 6-quart pot over medium heat. When hot, add 2 tablespoons oil, chilies, and half the onions. Cook vegetables until soft, 3 to 5 minutes. Scrape vegetables into blender. Add turmeric, paprika, tamarind, and 1/4-cup warm water to blender, and grind to a smooth paste; reserve.

3 **Base:** Reheat pot over medium heat, and add 2 tablespoons oil. Sauté remaining onions until soft. Add ginger and garlic and cook 1 minute. Mix **sambar podi** with 2 tablespoons boiling water to form a loose paste, and fold into onions.

4 **Sauce:** Cook **sambar podi** until the water evaporates and spice sticks to pan. Pour in reserved blender paste. Rinse blender with 1/2 cup boiling water and stir into pot. Simmer until sauce develops craters and thickens, 3 to 5 minutes. Stir in potatoes and cook in paste 1 minute. Add 1/2-cup boiling water, and simmer potatoes 5 minutes uncovered, stirring occasionally.

5 **Finish:** Stir in cauliflower, coconut milk, and jaggery, if using, and season curry with salt. Cover pot, lower the heat, set lid ajar, and simmer mixture until vegetables are tender and sauce is thickened, 15 to 20 minutes.

6 **To Serve:** Season curry with lime juice, salt, and freshly ground black pepper, to taste. Adjust texture of curry with boiling water, if necessary. It should be moist but not watery. Serve with rice pilaf or rice.

Source: *The Great Curries of India* by Camellia Panjabi.

Vary! Improvise!

☛ *Omit potato and use 1-1/2 pounds trimmed cauliflower, about 8 cups florets.*
☛ *Substitute sweet potato for white potato.*
☛ *Toss in sliced green beans at the end and cook uncovered until tender, about 6 minutes.*
☛ *Garnish with finely sliced cilantro.*

SOUTH INDIAN VEGETABLE KOOTTU

Lightly spicy koottus are quick Tamil Nadu vegetable-lentil dishes that fall into a middle category between a saucy curry or sambar and a dry bhuna. Moist, not floating in sauce, and thick, koottus often usurp sambar. Many South Indians eat them with chapatti breads.

Yields About 4 cups, 4 to 6 servings

3-1/2 ounces *chana dal* (split chickpeas), almost 1/2 cup, washed and drained
3/4 teaspoon ground turmeric
1-1/4 pounds sweet potato, about 3 cups peeled and diced into 1/2-inch cubes
  or 1-1/4 pounds butternut squash, peeled and diced into 1/2-inch cubes
    or 1-1/4 pounds plantains, peeled and sliced 1/2-inch thick

Fried Seasonings

1 tablespoon vegetable oil *or* fragrant coconut oil
About 3/4 ounce urad dal, 2 tablespoons
1 to 2 ounces jalapeños, 1 to 2, stemmed, seeded, and quartered lengthwise
1-1/2 to 2 ounces dry, unsweetened shredded coconut, 1/2 cup packed
1 tablespoon cumin seed

Tempering

1 tablespoon fragrant coconut *or* vegetable oil
1 teaspoon brown mustard seed
3- to 4-inch dried red chili, about 1 tablespoon stemmed, seeded, and sliced
12 curry leaves, about 1/4 cup loosely packed

1 lime
To Serve: Hot, cooked rice

1 Pour chana dal, 2 cups water and turmeric into 4-quart saucepan and bring to a boil. Reduce heat and cover pan. Simmer dal until very soft, 20 to 30 minutes. Add sweet potato (or squash or plantains) to dal. Cover and simmer until tender, 10 to 15 minutes.

2 Heat oil for **fried seasonings** over medium heat in 9-inch skillet. Add urad dal and chilies and cook until dal is pale gold. Add coconut and spices and cook until evenly browned/gold. Grind **fried seasonings** in blender with 1/2 cup water to aid grinding. Scrape mixture into cooked squash and dal. Rinse out blender with 1/2 cup more water, and stir into dal mixture (koottu). Simmer koottu until flavors come together, 5 to 10 minutes.

3 **Temper, temper:** In 9-inch skillet heat oil over medium heat. Add mustard seed, chili, and curry leaves. Cook until the seeds crackle and turn gray and curry leaves wilt, 30 to 60 seconds. Scrape into koottu.

4 **To Serve:** Taste and season koottu with salt, pepper, and lime juice. Rest koottu covered 10 minutes to blend flavors. Serve hot with rice.

Source: *Grains, Greens and Grated Coconuts* by Ammini Ramachandran.

Vary! Improvise!

☛ *Control the seasoning and heat with the final tempering: add more or less chili, mustard seed, or other spices and seasonings.*

DON'T SEED THE CHILIES

When Indian cooks are queried about whether one should seed fresh chilies before using in a curry they often reply, "What? And lose all the flavor?"

Yogurt, Buttermilk, or Coconut Milk-Based Dishes

SIMPLE SOUTHERN POTATO OOLAN

Oolan can be made with many different vegetables and legumes. Its special flavor comes from coconut milk, fragrant coconut oil, and earthy curry leaves. In South India this dish would use three unseeded serrano chilies—which are somewhat hotter than jalapeños.

Yields 6 cups, 4 to 6 servings

6-1/2 to 7 ounces dried black-eyed peas, 1 cup
   or 2 cups drained, canned black-eyed peas
1 pound redskin or yellow Finn potatoes, 3 cups peeled and diced into 1/2-inch cubes
1/2 ounce serrano chili, 1 chili stemmed, seeded, and quartered lengthwise
1 teaspoon ground cumin
2 cups coconut milk

Tempering

1 tablespoon coconut oil
1 teaspoon dark mustard seed
12 to 15 fresh curry leaves

To Serve: Hot, cooked rice or chapattis

1 **If using dry peas:** Rinse black-eyed peas and cover with fresh water. Bring to a boil, lower heat, cover pot, and simmer peas until tender but not soft, 30 to 45 minutes. Remove 2 cups drained, cooked black-eyed peas; use remainder for another dish.

2 Place potatoes, chili, and cumin in a small saucepan with 1 cup water and 1/2 teaspoon salt. Cover pot and bring to a boil. Lower heat to medium-low and cook vegetables until crisp-tender, 5 to 7 minutes.

3 Uncover pot and pour in coconut milk and 2 cups black-eyed peas. Simmer until potatoes and peas are very tender and coconut milk is reduced and slightly thickened, 10 minutes. There should be just enough liquid to almost cover the beans and vegetables.

4 **Temper, temper:** Heat coconut oil in a small skillet over medium heat. Toss in mustard seed and curry leaves and sauté until seeds sputter and curry leaves wilt, about 2 minutes. Scrape tempering into cooked vegetable and chilies. Taste and adjust flavors with salt.

5 **To Serve:** Serve hot with steamed rice or chapattis.

Vary! Improvise!

☛ *Prepare oolan with other vegetables like winter or summer squash, okra, or green beans.*
☛ *Substitute chana dal (split and peeled chickpeas) or split mung beans for black-eyed peas.*
☛ *Season oolan with fresh lime juice.*

Indian Rice

Boiled or steamed long-grain and basmati rice are favored, particularly for wet dishes that soak into rice. India produces the nutty, aromatic Indica rice, *basmati*, of which there are many varieties. Basmati rice has a firm, dry texture when properly cooked. The kernel is long and slender like the South Indian long-grain variety, but slightly smaller. When cooked, the kernels increase three times in length, not width. The best Indian basmatis (Dehra Dun is considered one) are aged (dried) six months to one year to intensify texture and nutty flavor. Because of this, basmati costs more.

South Indians grow most of India's rice and eat more rice (*chaval*), but less basmati. North Indian pilafs and biryanis require basmati rice; it has been cultivated for centuries at the foot of the Himalayas. Translated from Hindi, basmati means "pearl of scents."

Indian groceries sell aged basmati, Patna long-grain, and Patna basmati, a less nutty basmati type, South Indian red rice, and parboiled rice. Parboiled rice (long or medium

FIGURE 4.21 Basmati rice.
Source: tycoon101/Fotolia.

grained) begins with unhulled rice that is boiled and steamed. This process forces nutrients back into the grain. After cooling, the rice is milled as usual. Parboiled rice has a firmer texture and glassy look; it takes a bit longer to cook. South Indian cooks prefer it because it doesn't clump together when cooked.

Signature Technique: North Indian Pullao (Pilaf/Pulau/Pilau)

1 Choose rice (or grain) and aromatic vegetables. For a fluffier pilaf, choose long-grain rice like basmati or jasmine. Long-grain rice is best for pilafs and short-grain for sticky dishes. Pullaos are fluffy by nature.

2 Pour rice into fine sieve and rinse rice well in cold water. Drain well.

3 Pour basmati rice into measured cooking water and soak 15 to 20 minutes. The soaking process is essential; it helps basmati to cook evenly and achieve its greatest length. Use meat stock in place of water for a richer flavored pilaf.

- 1 cup rice (7 ounces) needs 2 cups water
- 2 cups rice (14 ounces) **or more** needs 1-1/2 to 1-3/4 cup water **per cup rice**.

4 Sauté slivered or diced onions in fat in suitable saucepan and set aside. Toast flavor-giving foods like nuts, seeds, coconut, or dried fruits and set them aside to be folded in later.

5 Choose a suitable sized and weight pot with good conductive qualities on sides and at base.

- Bring rice to boil in soaking liquid *or*
- Add drained, soaked grain (save soaking liquid) to hot fat or to above-mentioned cooked onions and cook briefly, turning to coat with fat. Sautéing rice hardens the outer starch layer, making for less sticky rice and a toasted, nutty flavor.
- Add cold or boiling liquid. Boiling liquid speeds cooking and makes a fluffier pilaf.

6 Season rice with salt. Lower heat to a simmer and cover pot.

7 Cook until rice is tender (15 minutes for white rice and 45 minutes for brown) *or* bring pullao to a boil, cover, and place oven-safe pot in a preheated 350 degree F oven 20 minutes for white rice and 50 minutes to 1 hour for brown. Don't stir rice; it breaks the grain.

8 Pour in coconut milk (if using) *or* more liquid if pullao seems dry, but **don't stir rice**. When adding liquid, listen for the searing sound, which means it was dry. Add extra liquid sparingly. Allow rice to rest 10 to 15 minutes, covered.

9 Fluff rice and fold in garnish like ghee, butter, peas, raisins or nuts, herbs, or a tempering. Taste. Taste. Taste. Season if necessary.

10 Fluff rice with a fork and serve immediately.

- To keep bright color of green vegetables, blanch them, and add at end of pullao's cooking time. Also add frozen thawed vegetables such as peas and corn during the last 3 to 5 minutes of cooking.
- Season pullao with spices and fresh herbs. Add strong or whole spices in the beginning. Add garnish or delicate herbs (cilantro or mint) at the end.

NORTHERN FRAGRANT-SPICE PULLAO

Yields 6 to 7 cups, 6 to 8 servings

4 tablespoons ghee *or* vegetable oil, *divided*
2 ounces golden raisins, about 3 tablespoons
1-3/4 ounces toasted chopped cashews *or* almond slivers, about 2 tablespoons
14 ounces basmati rice, 2 cups, washed, soaked, and drained
3 cups boiling vegetable broth *or* water
5 cardamom pods

3-inch cinnamon stick
1/4 ounce nutmeg, 1 whole, chopped into large pieces
Optional: 2 tablespoons melted ghee or butter

1 Heat a 4-quart saucepan and add 1 tablespoon ghee or oil. When hot, add raisins. Sauté until they begin to darken and caramelize. With a slotted spoon, transfer raisins into a small bowl to cool.

2 Add 1 tablespoon fat to saucepan. When hot, add nuts, and sauté until golden. Pour into bowl with raisins and set aside to fold in at the end.

3 Add remaining fat to saucepan. Stir in rice and sauté over medium heat until coated with fat and outside of rice begins to harden, 2 minutes.

4 Pour in hot broth or water all at once. When rice boils, reduce heat to low, add 1 teaspoon kosher salt, cardamom, cinnamon, and nutmeg, and cover pan.

5 Simmer rice exactly 15 minutes, and remove from heat. Rest rice undisturbed 10 minutes. Fold in raisins and nuts, and drizzle rice with optional ghee or butter. Fluff rice gently. Serve warm. Warn guests not to eat whole cardamom pods, cinnamon stick, or nutmeg pieces.

Vary! Improvise!

☞ *Devise a pullao that an Indian would love from local ingredients.*

NORTHERN BASMATI PULLAO WITH BROWN-FRIED ONIONS

Brown-fried onions are a form of tempering. Use them to flavor rice, vegetable, meat, or seafood dishes. Small yellow onions have more flavor, less water, and brown more quickly. Substitute 5 to 7 ounces shallots for even quicker browning and more intense flavor.

Yields about 6-1/2 cups, 4 to 6 servings

Brown-Fried Onions

Yields about 3/4 cup

5 tablespoons ghee *or* vegetable oil, *divided*
2 teaspoons black mustard seeds
2 teaspoons cumin seeds
10 ounces small yellow onions, 2 cups thinly slivered and packed
About 1/2 ounce gingerroot, about 2 teaspoons peeled and minced
1/2 ounce garlic, 2 large cloves, about 2 teaspoons peeled and minced

14 ounces basmati rice, 2 cups, washed, soaked, and drained

1 Pour 4 cups cold water into a saucepan and bring to a boil for later use.

2 **Prepare the brown-fried onions:** Heat 4 tablespoons fat over medium heat in a 12-inch skillet. Add spice seeds and fry until mustard seeds grey and sputter, 30 seconds. Raise heat to medium-high, stir in onions, season with salt, and fry, stirring frequently. Fry onions until very brown and shriveled, about 15 to 20 minutes. Add ginger and garlic and cook 30 seconds. Remove brown-fried onions from saucepan and set aside in mixing bowl.

3 Heat 4-quart saucepan with remaining 1 tablespoon fat. Add rice and cook 2 minutes, stirring to cook evenly. Add 3 cups boiling water and 1 teaspoon kosher salt. Bring to a boil, lower heat, and cover pan. Simmer rice 15 minutes exactly. Uncover pan and pour in 2 to 3 tablespoons more water around sides and cover. Rest rice 10 minutes. Do not stir and do not let rice sit longer.

4 **To Serve:** Gently fluff hot rice and fold in brown-fried onions. Serve hot.

SOUTH INDIAN COCONUT RICE

Dried coconut is known as copra *in India. It is pressed to make coconut oil. Though coconut oil is a saturated fat (solid at room temperature), like olive oil, a good quality coconut oil is less refined. Unrefined virgin coconut oil has the divine, delicate scent of coconut and purported health benefits. Prosperous Brahmin estates in southern India pressed their own coconut oil.*

Yields about 7 cups, 4 to 6 servings

14 ounces long-grain rice, 2 cups rinsed and drained
2-1/2 ounces dry, unsweetened coconut flakes, 1 cup packed
1 ounce raw cashew pieces, 1/4 cup

Tempering

2 tablespoons fragrant coconut oil
1 tablespoon brown mustard seed
About 3/4 ounce urad dal, 2 tablespoons
1 ounce serrano chilies, about 2, stemmed, seeded, and finely slivered lengthwise
12 to 15 curry leaves
About 1/2 ounce gingerroot, 2 teaspoons peeled and finely minced
1/4 teaspoon asafoetida

1 Preheat oven to 375 degrees F.

2 In a 3- to 4-quart saucepan mix rice, 3 cups cold water and 1 teaspoon kosher salt. Rest 15 to 20 minutes. Place pan on burner over high heat and bring to a boil. Lower heat, cover pan, and simmer rice 12 minutes. Remove pan from heat and rest undisturbed 15 minutes.

3 Spread coconut on sheet pan and toast in oven until golden, 5 to 7 minutes. Spread nuts on another sheet pan and roast until golden, 10 minutes. Coconut and nuts may also be browned with oil on top of the stove in a large skillet.

4 Temper, temper: Heat oil in small, heavy skillet. When hot, add mustard seed and urad dal. Cook until mustard seed sputters and turns gray and dal turns lightly golden. Add chilies, curry leaves and cook until chilies soften and curry leaves shrivel. Add ginger and asafoetida and cook 10 to 20 seconds.

5 To Serve: Fluff rice into bowl. Gently fold tempering, coconut, nuts, and salt and pepper, to taste, into rice. Serve hot.

Vary! Improvise!

☞ Spice tempering *plus onion, green chili, and tomato folded into cooked rice.*
☞ Spice tempering *plus tamarind liquid folded into cooked rice.*
☞ Spice tempering *plus grated unripe mango and roasted nuts folded into cooked rice.*

SOUTH INDIAN GREEN MANGO RICE (MANGAI SADAM)

South Indian cooks traditionally use ghee for this rich dish, but fragrant coconut oil is also a good combination with mango. This dish has mild flavor, good for pairing with spicy curries.

Yields about 10 cups, 6 to 8 servings

4 to 5 ounces freshly grated coconut, 1 cup
    or 2-1/4 ounces dried, unsweetened finely shredded coconut, 3/4 cup
14 ounces long-grain or Basmati rice, 2 cups, rinsed and drained
1-1/2 pounds firm, unripe mango 1-1/2 large, 3 cups peeled and diced into 3/8-inch cubes
1 teaspoon mustard seeds
1/2 teaspoon asafoetida powder

1/2 teaspoon ground turmeric
Four 3-inch dried red chilies, about 3 tablespoons stemmed, seeded, and slivered, *divided*, more to taste

Tempering

2 tablespoons ghee *or* coconut oil, *divided*
1 tablespoon urad dal
About 3 ounces raw cashews, 1/2 cup lightly chopped
    or about 3 ounces raw peanuts, 1/2 cup
1 sprig curry leaves, stripped off stem, about 12

1   Soak dry coconut, if using, in hot water 5 to 10 minutes. Press-drain, but reserve soaking water and set aside.

2   Bring rice, 2 teaspoons kosher salt, and 3 cups water (use reserved soaking water as part of this) to boil in 3- to 4-quart saucepan over high heat. Lower heat, cover pan, and simmer rice 15 minutes exactly. Remove pan from heat and rest rice 5 to 10 minutes, but no more than 15 minutes. Fluff rice into large bowl.

3   In a food processor, grind together, coconut, 1 cup diced mango, mustard seeds, asafoetida and turmeric powders, and 2 dried red chilies to a fine paste. If necessary, add a little water to facilitate grinding. Ground mango paste mixture should be the consistency of a fine paste, not watery.

4   **Temper, temper:** Heat 2 teaspoons ghee or oil on medium heat in 10-inch sauté pan. Add and fry urad dal until golden and aromatic. Add remaining mango cubes to urad dal, and sauté until mango softens; pour mixture into small bowl. Heat 2 teaspoons ghee or oil and fry cashews or peanuts until fragrant and golden; pour into separate bowl. Heat remaining 2 teaspoons ghee or oil and fry curry leaves and remaining red chilies; cook until curry leaves shrivel and chilies darken. Scrape dal and mango cubes back into pan and stir in ground mango paste. Remove pan from heat.

5   Fold mango and dal **tempering** mixture and nuts into the cooked rice. Taste rice, and season with more salt if necessary.

6   **To Serve:** Pile pilaf high onto serving platter.

Source: *Dakshin, Vegetarian Cuisine from South India* by Chandra Padmanabhan.

Legume Dishes

POPULAR INDIAN LEGUMES (GRAMS AND DALS)

Indian legumes come three ways: whole with skin, split with skin, *or* split without skin. Grams are whole beans, lentils, and dry peas. Indian cooks regularly use pressure cookers to speed legume cooking. *Dal* is the Indian term for split and skinned dried lentils, bean, or peas. Quick cooking split, skinned lentils or mung beans are simmered into spicy stews also called dal, and are eaten daily with chapatis or rice and vegetables.

Grams and dals are the foundation of Indian cuisine, especially in the more vegetarian South.

- **Black-eyed peas/cowpeas** Whole black-eyed peas are *lobia*. Split and husked they are *chowla dal*. Soak overnight.
- **Channa dal/gram lentil/Bengal gram** A smaller, split and husked variety of chickpea, very sweet and nutty and very popular. Soak overnight.

(Continued)

(Continued)

- **Kala chana/brown chickpeas** A small, dark brown chickpea-like pea popular in whole bean dishes, high in iron and protein, known as black chickpeas, very nutty. Soak overnight.
- **Kubli/kabli channa/white chickpea, garbanzo bean** Sweet, meaty and tender. Soak overnight.
- **Kidney beans/rajma dal** Red and kidney shaped. Soak overnight.
- **Mung beans/moong dal/green gram** A small, round, greenish bean comes in three forms—whole with skin, *sabat moong*—split without skin, *moong dal*—and split with skin, *chilke moong dal.*
- **Dew bean/muth** A very small, nutty, greenish-brown bean.
- **Pink lentils/masoor dal** Tiny split and skinned lentils popular in Bengali cuisine that turn yellow when cooked. There is a similar variety of Egyptian red lentil.
- **Yellow lentils/pigeon peas/toovar dal** Split and skinless pale yellow to gold lentils also known as *arhar dal* and *tuar dal*. Larger than pink lentils and paler, these split and skinned lentils take longer to cook. They benefit from soaking 3 to 6 hours and are popular in South India in dal soups and sambhar.
- **Split peas/matar dal** Split and skinned green and white pea. Use as substitute for *toovar dal*. Soak 3 to 6 hours.
- **Patva/lima beans/butter beans** A large white, flat bean that benefits from soaking overnight.
- **Urad dal/black gram** These small, ivory fleshed, black-skinned beans come in three forms: whole with skin—*sabat urad* (earthy tasting), split without skin, *urad dal* (bland and starchy), and split with skin, *chilke urad dal.*
- **Val/hyacinth bean** Nutty and creamy when cooked, this round, buff-colored, plump, ridged bean benefits from soaking overnight.
- **Red Chori/adzuki bean** Very sweet when cooked, this small, oval red bean benefits from soaking for 3 hours, but it is not necessary. Japanese use adzuki beans for desserts.
- **Kulith/horse gram** This farmer's staple resembles *masoor dal* and has a very earthy flavor when cooked. Soak overnight.

Signature Technique: Lentil Dishes (Dal)

1 **Choose a type of dal:** Split and peeled lentils cook quickly, about 20 minutes, and except for split peas, do not need soaking. Soak split peas, split chickpea (channa dal) or whole dal in warm water for 2 hours, drain, and add fresh water before cooking for better texture. Whole dal like mung beans take longer to cook.

2 **Cook dal:** The cooked dal should be soupy and sauce-like. The proportion of lentils to water is usually 1 part lentils to 3 or 4 parts water. If desired, dry spices may be added during cooking. Dried turmeric, garlic cloves, asafoetida, and red chili powder are common additions. Bring dal to a boil, lower the heat, and cover the pot partially. Simmer until dal is very soft. Scrape bottom of pot periodically to ensure that dal is not sticking and burning.

3 **Prepare a tempering:** Depending on tastes and place, Indian cooks might prepare a tempering with whole spices, onions, gingerroot, garlic, dried chilies, fresh chilies, or curry leaves. Infuse these flavors into a fat of choice: plain sesame oil, peanut oil, ghee, or fragrant coconut oil.

4 **Steep the dal:** Scrape the tempering into the cooked dal and cover. Allow dal to steep up to 30 minutes. Reheat before serving if necessary.

5 **Season and garnish:** Season dal with salt, pepper, and lime juice as desired. If the flavor is not intense enough, prepare a second tempering, scrape into dal, and infuse for 15 minutes. Garnish dal with sliced cilantro or green peas, if desired, just before serving.

EASTERN TADKA DAL

Dals are the simplest and most nutritious dishes. Notice how dal cooks with turmeric and asafoetida. Both aid in digestion.

Yields 3-1/2 to 4 cups, 4 to 6 servings

6-1/2 to 7 ounces *masoor dal* (pink split lentils), 1 cup rinsed and drained
1/2 teaspoon turmeric
1/4 teaspoon ground asafoetida

Tempering (Tadka)

3 to 4 tablespoons ghee, vegetable oil, *or* plain sesame oil
1 tablespoon crushed *Ponch Phoran*
1/2 ounce green chili, 1 serrano, stemmed, seeded, and finely slivered
1/2 ounce gingerroot, 1 tablespoon peeled and minced
1/4 ounce garlic, 1 large clove, 1-1/2 teaspoons peeled and finely minced
4 ounces small yellow onions, 1 cup packed, thinly slivered

Juice of 1 large lime, about 4 tablespoons
Optional garnish: 1/2 ounce cilantro, 1/4 cup finely sliced

For Serving

Hot, cooked rice or chapattis

1 Pour lentils, 4 cups water, turmeric, and asafoetida into a 4-quart saucepan. Bring to a boil, reduce heat, partially cover pan, and simmer lentils until mushy, about 25 minutes. Have extra boiling water on the side to add as necessary. Whisk lentils until smooth. The consistency should be soupy thick.

2 **Temper, temper:** Heat half the fat in 9-inch skillet over medium heat until hot. Add seeds and chilies. When seeds sputter, add ginger and garlic and cook until they release fragrance, 10 to 30 seconds. Scrape tempering into lentils.

3 Heat skillet over medium heat with remaining fat. Stir in onions and fry until they wilt and brown, 7 to 10 minutes. Pour onion tempering into cooked lentils. Deglaze skillet with 2 tablespoons water, stir water into pot, and cover. Steep tempering in hot dal 10 to 15 minutes before serving. Reheat over low heat if necessary before serving.

4 **To Serve:** Season dal to taste with lime juice, salt, and freshly ground pepper. Garnish with cilantro if desired. Serve with rice or chapatti.

Vary! Improvise!

☞ **Mukti's (Western) Goanese Dal:** Substitute *moong dal* (split mung beans) for lentils. Brown 6 cloves crushed garlic and 1 teaspoon peppercorns and add to cooked dal along with 2 cups chopped baby spinach, 1 teaspoon turmeric, 1/4 teaspoon chili powder, and 1 table-spoon vinegar. Simmer until spinach is soft. Season to taste.

☞ **Vegetable Dal:** Boil cubed vegetables like carrots, potatoes, tomatoes, or squash with dal.

☞ **Nontraditional:** Stir coconut milk in at the end for richer flavor.

☞ **Southern Tradition:** Add several Indian "curry" leaves with chili to the tempering.

SOUTHERN URAD DAL

This is a typical, simple South Indian vegetarian dal; to increase flavor, use vegetable stock in place of water.

Yields 7 cups, 4 to 6 servings

10-1/2 to 11 ounces split urad dal (black-skinned Indian lentils), 1-1/2 cups
   or 10-1/2 to 11 ounces split lentils like masoor dal, 1-1/2 cups
1/2 teaspoon red chili powder
1/4 teaspoon turmeric
1 teaspoon garam masala
1/2 ounce gingerroot, 1 tablespoon peeled and finely minced
1 tablespoon fragrant coconut oil or vegetable oil

Tempering

1/2 to 1 ounce green chilies, 2 serranos, stemmed, seeded, and finely slivered
   or three 2-1/2 inch dried whole red chilies, stemmed
15 curry leaves
1/2 teaspoon asafoetida

1/2 ounce cilantro, 1/4 cup finely sliced
1 to 2 tablespoons freshly squeezed lime juice, about 1 lime

For Serving

Hot, cooked long-grain or basmati rice or chapattis

1 **Soak and cook dal:** Place dal into mesh strainer and rinse well in cold water. Drain. Pour dal into 4-quart saucepan and add 6 cups cold water. Soak dal 2 hours. Bring dal and water to a boil—be mindful, it can foam over quickly. Skim off foam and discard. Stir in chili powder and turmeric, and lower the heat. Cover pan and simmer dal until soft, 20 to 30 minutes.

2 Stir 2 teaspoons kosher salt, garam masala, and ginger into hot dal. Cover and steep while making the tempering.

3 **Temper, temper:** Heat a small skillet over medium heat. Add chilies and curry leaves and cook until chilies turn color and shrivel. Add asafoetida and cook 20 to 30 seconds. Remove skillet from the heat and scrape spices into hot dal. Deglaze skillet with 1/2 cup water and stir into dal. Place dal back on low heat and simmer 15 minutes. Dal should be loose like a creamy soup. The flavor of this simple dal will improve with a 15-minute resting period before serving.

4 **To Serve:** Taste dal and season with salt to taste. Stir in cilantro and lime juice. Pour dal into serving bowl and serve hot or lukewarm with rice or chapatti.

Source: *Cooking Along the Ganges* by Malvi Doshi.

SOUTHERN GREEN SAMBHAR

Tamarind, dal, yogurt, buttermilk, or a combination forms the base for thick, stew-like, pungent and spicy simmered vegetable sambars—the Southern version of dal. *Topped with a dollop of ghee and served with plain cooked rice, sambars come first in a simple South Indian meal. Notice the absence of garlic or onion; asafoetida takes their place.*

Yields about 6 cups, 4 to 6 servings

2 ounces tamarind paste, 1/4 cup packed
7 ounces dry whole mung beans, 1 cup picked over and washed
1/2 teaspoon ground turmeric

Tempering

1-1/2 tablespoons ghee or coconut oil
1 teaspoon brown mustard seed
3-inch dried red chili, about 1 tablespoon stemmed, seeded, and chopped
8 curry leaves
1 ounce jalapeño, 1 large, stemmed, seeded, and quartered lengthwise
1/2 teaspoon asafoetida powder

1 ounce cilantro, 1 cup finely sliced

For Serving

Chapattis or rice

1   Soak tamarind in 1 cup hot water and knead until soft, 15 minutes. Scrape pulp in a fine mesh strainer, extracting as much tamarind purée as possible, about 7 fluid ounces. Discard pits and fiber. Set tamarind purée aside.

2   Place mung beans, turmeric, and 4 cups water in a saucepan and bring to a boil. Lower heat to a simmer and place a lid on the pot slightly ajar. Simmer beans until tender, 30 minutes. Stir occasionally during cooking so dal doesn't stick to the bottom of the pot and burn. When dal is soft, whisk in tamarind purée.

3   **Temper, temper:** Heat fat in a 9-inch sauté pan over medium heat. Add mustard seed, red chili, curry leaves, and jalapeño. When mustard seeds turn gray and crackle and green chili softens, add asafoetida and cook 30 seconds more. Scrape tempering into cooked dal and reheat. Add a little boiling liquid to tempering pan to deglaze, and stir into sambhar, if necessary, to maintain a thick soup consistency. Simmer dal 2 minutes. Remove pan from heat.

4   **To Serve:** Stir in cilantro, and allow sambhar to steep 2 minutes. Taste and adjust seasonings with salt. Serve with chapattis or rice.

Source: *Dakshin, Vegetarian Cuisine from South India* by Chandra Padmanabhan.

SAUTÉ, PAN OR GRIDDLE-FRY, AND DEEP-FRY

Northern Dry-Spiced Dishes

BHUNA

As in tempering, spices in a bhuna dish sauté and simmer in fat 20 to 30 minutes with only small amounts of liquid added to keep them from sticking. Frying spices in fat releases flavor, an important first step. The liquid in a bhuna cooks down to form a thick sauce to coat meat or vegetables.

BHUNA GHOSHT

Ghosht means meat; any sort may be used; it is typical of northern India.

Yields about 5 cups, 4 servings

3 tablespoons canola or vegetable oil
1 bay leaf
1-inch cinnamon stick
2 whole cloves
5 peppercorns
3 to 4 ounces small yellow onions, 3/4 cup peeled and finely chopped
1 to 1-1/2 ounces gingerroot, 2 tablespoons peeled and minced
1/2 ounce garlic, 2 large cloves, 1 tablespoon peeled and minced
1/2 ounce serrano chili, about 1, 1 tablespoon stemmed and minced
1-1/4 pounds trimmed pork *or* lamb, diced into 1-inch cubes
1/2 teaspoon turmeric
1 teaspoon ground coriander
1/2 teaspoon cayenne pepper
1/2 teaspoon garam masala
10 ounces tomato, about 1 large, 1-1/2 cups finely diced, puréed or grated
Fresh lemon or lime juice
Finely sliced cilantro

For Serving

Rice, Dal, or Chapati and Raita

1 In a 6-quart saucepan, heat oil over medium heat. Add bay leaf and cinnamon stick and when they sizzle and brown, add cloves and peppercorns. Sauté spices 30 seconds, add onions, and sauté until golden, about 10 minutes. Add ginger, garlic, and chilies, and cook 1 minute.

2 Add meat and 1/2 teaspoon kosher salt. Lower heat cook mixture, stirring frequently and as spices stick, add 1 to 2 tablespoons water. Simmer 20 minutes. Mix turmeric, coriander, cayenne, and garam masala with 2 tablespoons water. Scrape into onion-spice bhuna and cook until spices begin to stick and toast, 1 minute.

3 Add tomato. Cook, stirring frequently, 5 to 7 minutes. Add 1 cup more water and simmer bhuna covered to develop flavor 30 to 45 minutes. Uncover bhuna and simmer until it reduces to a thick sauce that coats meat.

4 **To Serve:** Taste bhuna and season with salt and lime juice. Garnish with cilantro. Serve with rice or chapattis, dal and raita.

Source: *Great Curries of India* by Camellia Panjabi.

Vary! Improvise!

☛ **Switch to Seafood:** *Omit meat, but prepare sauce through step 3 until reduced. Slide in 1-1/4 pounds fish cubes or raw, peeled, and deveined shrimp. Simmer seafood just until opaque.*

SHRIMP MASALA

Prepare chaunk mixture separately and refrigerate or freeze for later use. It forms a delicious base that can begin any Indian dish. Use alone or add other seasonings.

Yields about 4-1/2 to 5 cups, 4 to 6 servings

Chaunk (Tempering)

Yields about 1-1/2 cups, enough for 2 pounds seafood, meat, or vegetables

6 tablespoons ghee
1 pound small yellow onions, finely slivered, about 4 cups packed
1 to 1-1/2 ounces gingerroot, 2 tablespoons peeled and minced
1/2 ounce garlic, 2 large cloves, 1 tablespoon peeled and minced
1/2 ounce serrano or 1 ounce jalapeño chili, 1 large chili, 1 to 2 tablespoons stemmed and slivered

2 tablespoons ghee
1 teaspoon dark mustard seed
1 teaspoon cumin seed
2 pounds 36/40 or 26/30 shrimp, peeled and deveined
Freshly squeezed lime juice
Optional garnish: Finely sliced cilantro

To Serve

Hot basmati rice or chapattis

1 **Chaunk:** Heat 6 tablespoons ghee over medium-high heat in a heavy 14-inch skillet or large wok. When ghee is hot, add onions, and sauté, stirring frequently, until browned, 15 to 20 minutes. If they begin to burn, lower heat to medium. The onions should be caramelized. Deglaze pan with a little water as necessary, scrape up brown bits, and cook to evaporate water. Stir in ginger, garlic, and chili and cook until tender, about 3 minutes. Season with salt. Scrape onions into a bowl, and set aside. Drain off 2 tablespoons excess ghee.

2 Set skillet back on burner on medium-high heat. Drizzle in 2 tablespoons reserved ghee. When ghee ripples and is hot, add seeds and cook several seconds, add shrimp, and stir-fry until seared and mostly opaque.

3 Stir in onion **chaunk** and heat through until shrimp are fully cooked, but don't overcook; they will become rubbery. Season shrimp with salt, freshly ground pepper, and lime juice to taste.

4 **To Serve:** Pile shrimp onto platter and serve with hot rice or chapattis. Garnish with cilantro if desired.

Vary! Improvise!

☛ *Prepare this dish with cubed fish, chicken, or lamb.*

NORTHERN DRY-COOKED LAMB (SOOKHA KEEMA)

Keema means ground meat. This keema uses the dry-bhuna technique. Serve it with roti or allow keema to cool and use as filling for samosa, stuffed paratha, or vegetables. If lamb is very lean, no need to precook and drain. Instead, add it raw in step 3 and cook until it just loses its pink blush.

Yields 2 cups

1 tablespoon vegetable oil
16 to 18 ounces ground lamb
4 to 5 ounces yellow onion, 1 cup finely diced
1/2 ounce garlic, 2 large cloves, 1 tablespoon peeled and minced
1/2 ounce gingerroot, 1 tablespoon peeled and minced
1 ounce green chilies, 2 serranos or 1 jalapeño, 4 tablespoons stemmed, seeded, and minced
1/2 teaspoon turmeric
1 tablespoon garam masala
Fresh lemon juice, to taste
1/2 ounce cilantro, 1/4 cup finely sliced
    or about 1/2 ounce mint leaves, 1/4 cup finely sliced

1 Heat 10- to 12-inch skillet over medium heat. Add oil and when hot, add meat. Cook, breaking up meat, until pink is just gone. Set strainer over a mixing bowl and pour meat into strainer. Drain off fat, and reserve meat and fat.

2 Reheat skillet with 1-1/2 tablespoons drained fat over medium heat. Stir in onions and cook until browned, 10 to 15 minutes. Add garlic, ginger, and chilies and reduce heat. Cook 1 minute. Stir in turmeric and cook 30 seconds. Add drained, cooked lamb, 1 teaspoon kosher salt and simmer lamb 15 to 20 minutes. If lamb sticks, add 1 to 2 tablespoons water and continue to simmer mixture until all the moisture has evaporated and meat is dry.

3 **To Finish:** Stir in garam masala, lemon juice, and cilantro or mint leaves. Taste and adjust flavors. (Discard any leftover excess drained fat from lamb.)

Source: *Classic Indian Cooking* by Julie Sahni.

Vary! Improvise!

☛ *Substitute ground goat meat for lamb.*

SPICED POTATOES (MASALA ALOO)

Use this bhurta dish to stuff pani poori, paratha, dosa, or samosa or as a side dish with other curries. Substitute cauliflower for the potatoes for a lighter dish; seed chili for less heat. Two to 3 teaspoons finely chopped ginger is a good addition; cook with the onions.

Yields about 7 cups

3 pounds medium-sized baking potatoes, scrubbed
4 tablespoons oil or ghee
3 teaspoons brown mustard seeds
2 teaspoons cumin seeds
1 ounce jalapeños, 1 large, 2 to 3 tablespoons stemmed and finely diced
1/2 teaspoon turmeric
8 to 9 ounces small yellow onions, 1 cup peeled and finely diced
2 teaspoons *Garam Masala I*
About 1-1/2 ounces fresh or frozen green peas, 1/4 cup
    and/or 1/2 ounce cilantro, 1/2 cup finely sliced

1 **Cook potatoes:** Place potatoes in small saucepan and cover with cold water. Bring potatoes to a boil, reduce heat, and cook until a knife inserts easily but potatoes still hold together, 15 to

20 minutes. Peel potatoes and dice into 1/4- to 1/2-inch cubes, about 7-1/2 to 8 cups. Alternatively, dice potatoes, steam until tender, about 5 minutes, and peel.

2 **Cook seasonings:** Heat ghee or oil in 6-quart pot or 10-inch deep skillet over medium heat. Add seeds and chili. Cook until seeds sputter and chili softens, 30 to 45 seconds. Stir in onions, turmeric, and 1/2 teaspoon kosher salt, and cook until onions are soft.

3 Fold diced potatoes into pot or pan and turn to mix well, mashing lightly to break up potatoes. Cook until potatoes begin to brown. If using for stuffing, break up a bit more. For a side dish, leave larger pieces of potato. Fold in garam masala and season with kosher salt to taste, about 1 teaspoon. Fold in peas and/or cilantro.

Source: *Classic Indian Cooking* by Julie Sahni.

Southern Dry-Spiced Dishes

SOUTHERN PORIYAL AND THORAN: SOUTH INDIAN STIR-FRY

Both poriyal and thoran are served as a dry side dish with rice and curry. *Poriyal* is the Tamil Nadu name for this South Indian spiced stir-fried vegetable dish. *Thoran* is the Kerala name. Vegetables for poriyal and thoran can be diced or shredded and they are sautéed, steamed, or braised in natural juices. Typical seasonings for a poriyal are brown mustard seed, cumin seed, coriander seed, urad dal, lentils or split peas, onion, turmeric, masala, and dry red chili. Both dishes are cooked with shredded coconut, but thorans have no lentils or split peas.

CABBAGE THORAN

Southern Keralites add onion or shallots and garlic, a strict no-no for Northern Keralites. With steamed rice and sambhar, thoran makes a full meal. Beets make an especially colorful thoran. Serve this with grilled or fried fish or seafood, sambhar, and rice.

Yields 4 cups, 4 to 6 servings

3 tablespoons fragrant coconut oil
1 tablespoon dark mustard seeds
3-inch dried red chili, stemmed, seeded, and broken
2 ounces shallots, 3 medium, 1/2 cup peeled and slivered
1 ounce jalapeño chili, 1 medium, 1/4 cup stemmed, seeded, and slivered
3/4 teaspoon turmeric
16 ounces green cabbage, about 6 cups trimmed and finely sliced
20 curry leaves
2-1/4 ounces dried, unsweetened shredded coconut, 3/4 cup
　　or 4 ounces grated fresh coconut, 1 cup
Optional: 1 lime, juiced

1 Heat coconut oil in 6-quart pot over medium heat. When oil is hot, add mustard seeds. Cook until they sputter, 30 seconds, and add red chili, shallots, and green chili. Cook until shallots brown, 2 to 3 minutes.

2 Sprinkle in turmeric and stir in cabbage and curry leaves. Season with a little salt. Stir-fry cabbage until it begins to wilt, 1 to 2 minutes. Cover pot, reduce heat, and simmer thoran until cabbage is tender and completely wilted, 3 minutes.

3 Push cabbage to the edges of the pot and pour in coconut. Smooth cabbage back over top of the coconut. Cover pot and simmer 5 minutes. Remove pan from heat, stir, replace lid, and rest thoran to develop flavors 5 minutes. Taste thoran and season with salt and optional lime juice. Serve warm.

Source: Cooking teacher Nimmy Paul, Cochin, Kerala, India.

Vary! Improvise!

☛ *Prepare thoran with shredded or finely diced beets, cauliflower, zucchini, eggplant, green beans, or green plantains.*

☛ *Substitute 2 ounces cabbage for 2 ounces shredded carrots, about 3/4 cup.*

Indian Breads (Roti)

India's choice of breads or *roti* is wide and tasty. People all over the country eat them. Roti are cooked either on a shallow *tawa (tava)*, or cast-iron griddle, or in a *tandoor* oven, where the cook slaps breads onto the side of the deep clay oven (with coals at its bottom) to grill and bake. *Naan* and *kulcha* are dairy-rich tandoori-oven baked breads. In the north and south, *chapatti*, a thin unleavened whole wheat flatbread is served daily. In the north, rich, rolled or stuffed *parathas* are favored. In the west, millet (*bajra*) or sorghum (*jowar*) flour is made into chapatti-like roti.

South India excels at rice and legume pancake breads. Often served for breakfast, *masala dosa* is the most famous: rice and urad dal are soaked, drained, and ground and allowed to ferment together overnight. The batter is thinly smeared on a cast-iron griddle to a large, round, crisp crepe. It is filled with spiced potatoes and served with coconut chutney. Variations are many—like egg dosa (fried egg on top), onion dosa (fried onions inside), mooli dosa (with radish inside), and Kerala dosa, which is smaller, slightly thicker and spongier.

INDIAN ATTA OR CHAPATTI FLOUR

Atta or *chapatti* flour is whole wheat flour—a fiber-rich food. Lighter in color than whole-wheat, atta is milled until very fine and smooth. Western whole wheat flour is not a substitute. Traditional atta is stone ground. The *chakki* or stone grinder produces friction and temperatures from 212 to 250 degrees F. High temperatures roast carotenes in the bran and contribute to the characteristic atta sweetness and aroma. Atta flour is a soft to medium-hard wheat flour with low to medium gluten content. Some gluten helps in rolling out chappatis very thin, which is desirable in India, while less gluten keeps them tender and less rubbery.

WESTERN INGENUITY

To save time rolling **chapattis** and **phulkas:**
- Dip a ball of dough into flour, shake off excess, and flatten. Place dough in a tortilla press lined with two pieces of a heavy plastic freezer bag. Press, peel off dough, and roll to desired size.

To make samosas:
- Flatten a piece of dough with a rolling pin into a square shape that will fit into pasta machine easily.
- Begin on machine's widest setting and roll dough through.
- Place machine setting down (thinner) one notch. Roll dough through without folding. Continue to roll dough through narrower notches until desired thickness is achieved.
- Cut out rounds with a 6-inch cutter, stuff, and cook according to recipe.

WHEAT FLATBREADS (CHAPATTI, PHULKA, POORI, OR PARATHA)

These breads are best eaten hot and freshly made. But, like tortillas, they can be stored in a plastic baggie after cooling and reheated over a flame or on a griddle. Brush with water to keep from drying.

Yields 25 to 26 ounces dough

Yields 13 (scant 2 ounces each) 6- to 6-1/2-inch phulka or paratha *or* 7-inch chapatti *or* 25 to 26 (1 ounce) 4-1/2- to 5-inch poori

FIGURE 4.22 Chapatti.
Source: Jehangir Hanafi/Fotolia.

About 15 ounces chapatti flour, 3 cups
1 ounce chapatti flour for rolling, about 1/4 cup
Optional: Ghee or fragrant coconut oil for brushing

1 Mix flour and 1-1/2 teaspoons salt. Slowly stir or mix in 1-1/2 cups warm to hot water. Gather dough into a moist ball. For large batches, mix and knead dough in mixer with paddle.

2 Knead dough on lightly floured surface. Be consistent. Knead with heel of hand, pulling up edge toward you and center of dough ball, making quarter turns. Knead until smooth and supple and the consistency of moist playdough, 1 to 2 minutes. Rest dough covered with plastic wrap in bowl *or* in a plastic bag 20 to 30 minutes to allow starch granules to absorb water, gluten to rest, and dough to rise slightly.

3 **Scale dough** into 13 scant 2-ounce pieces for phulka, paratha, and chapatti. **Scale dough** into 25 to 26 1-ounce pieces for poori. Cover dough when not in use to keep it from drying and forming a crusty skin.

   OR roll dough into a log:

   Phulka, Paratha, and Chapatti: 13-inches long and cut into 13 (scant 2 ounce) pieces.

   Poori: 25 to 26 inches long and cut into 25 to 26 (1-ounce) pieces.

4 **Rolling roti: Don't Go Off the Edges—Turn Dough, Not Rolling Pin**
   - Dip cut side of dough piece into flour. Dust work surface with a little flour and place dough onto it.
   - Roll dough into a circle with a consistent up/down motion only—not sideways or crossways.
   - Don't roll pin off top or bottom edges—this thins them.
   - Make quarter turns of dough circle and continue the up/down motion of rolling pin—stopping short of top and bottom edges—the dough has turned all the way around and it is the diameter needed. As the dough turns, the edges should even out. Experienced roti rollers can automatically rotate roti without stopping by gently rocking the pin while rolling.

Forming and Cooking Roti

Griddle-Cooked: Chapatti (cha-pa-tea)

1 Heat griddle over medium to medium-high heat. It should sizzle when water hits it.

2 Roll scant 2-ounce balls of dough out to a thin circle, 7-1/2 inches diameter.

3 Place chapatti on ungreased griddle and cook until dough whitens, bubbles form, and brown speckles appear all over. Flip and repeat on remaining side. Brush with ghee if desired.

Griddle-Cooked and Puffed: Phulka (full-ka)

1 Heat griddle over medium to medium-high heat. Dip dough in flour (enough to keep it from sticking) and roll scant 2-ounce balls of dough to 6- to 6-1/2-inch diameter. Brush off excess flour.

2 Place phulka on griddle and cook until bubbles form, dough whitens, and brown speckles just begin to appear, 20 to 30 seconds. Flip phulka and repeat on remaining side.

Vary! Improvise!

☛ *Chickpea or Missi Roti:* Use 2 cups unbleached white flour and 1 cup chickpea flour for roti dough.

3 Heat gas burner over medium flame. Place phulka on direct flame until it puffs then turn it over and repeat on remaining side until brown speckled and dough is puffed and completely cooked (whitened). Phulka will puff better if they are rolled evenly and without dry stray bits of dough pressed into them—and if care is taken not to puncture them when turning with tongs or fingers.

4 Brush phulka with ghee (or coconut oil if desired). Set aside, wrapped in a clean towel, to keep warm and moist until you've finished cooking all the phulka.

Deep-Fried: Poori or Puri (poor-e)

1 Heat oil in wok or deep-fryer to 365 degrees F.

2 Roll 1-ounce balls of dough to 4-1/2- to 5-inch diameter.

3 Slip poori in one at a time to a wok or 2 to 3 in a deep-fryer. Press the poori down with spoon into fat gently so it fries evenly and puffs, and turn to cook both sides until golden.

Stuffed and Griddle-Cooked: Paratha (pa-rah-ta)

Old Delhi's favorite hole-in-the-wall restaurant Parathey Walli Galli stuffs one popular paratha with roasted chopped cashews, spiced mashed chickpeas, or chopped, cooked, and spiced vegetables.

1 **Prepare filling:** *Spiced Potatoes (Masala Aloo)* (or with cauliflower) or *Lamb Keema* or filling of choice.

2 Heat a griddle to medium heat.

3 Roll scant 2-ounces dough ball into 6-1/2-inch diameter. Mound 1/4 cup filling in center.

4 Bring up sides to center and pleat together, while rotating paratha, to cover filling. Pinch center closed and gently flatten dough. Roll out paratha to 6- to 7-inch diameter on a lightly floured surface.

5 Cook on cast-iron griddle until dough is whitened and speckled golden all over. Brush with oil or ghee. Keep warm, covered, in a 250 degree F oven.

FIGURE 4.23 Spiced potato (Masala Aloo) stuffed wheat flatbread (Paratha) with lime pickle.

Folded and Griddle Cooked: Flaky Paratha

1　Heat griddle over medium heat. Roll 2 ounces dough to 6-1/2-inch circle. Follow one of the methods below for folding and layering.

　　Triangular fold method: Paint dough circle with ghee, fold in half, paint again with ghee, and fold in half again. This will form a triangle. Roll it out until quite thin. Cook according to instructions below.

　　Coil and wind method: Paint dough circle lightly with ghee and roll loosely into a snake. Wind snake tightly around itself to form a circle. Press down and roll out again. Cook according to instructions below.

　　Cone and press method: Paint dough circle with ghee. Make *one* cut from center of dough to outside edge, as if starting to cut a pie. From cut edge, roll dough into a loose cone. Place wide end of cone on surface and lightly press the pointed end down. Roll bread out again. Cook according to instructions below.

2　**To cook flaky paratha:** Place on hot griddle and cook until dough whitens and bubbles appear. Flip dough and cook paratha, pressing it down gently with the back of a large steel spoon until speckled brown and cooked through. Flip and cook first side again, smoothing with spoon, until brown speckled. Some cooks baste or brush parathas with fat as they cook.

3　Brush paratha with ghee and serve hot.

STREET AND HOME FUN FOOD: PANIPURI

Mention *panipuri* to an Indian and his or her eyes will light up. Panipuri are a favorite Indian street snack. Hawkers construct them with tiny, bite-sized poori that are cracked open at the top and filled with spiced cooked lentils or potatoes and topped with tamarind chutney and herb water (*pani* means water and refers to the watery tamarind chutney). Variations abound.

FIGURE 4.24 Panipuri.
Source: Pangfolio.com/Shutterstock.

FLAKY SPINACH PARATHA WITH GREEN CHILIES

Yields about 20 ounces dough, eight 2-1/2 ounce/7-inch parathas

1 pound baby spinach, washed and drained
   or 10 ounces frozen spinach
7-1/2 ounces chapati flour, 1-1/2 cups
3-1/2 ounce all-purpose flour, 3/4 cup
1 teaspoon cumin seed
1/2 ounce serrano chili, about 1, 2 tablespoons stemmed and thinly sliced
1 tablespoon ghee *or* vegetable oil (Julie uses olive oil)
Flour for dusting
1/2 cup ghee *or* vegetable oil for cooking paratha

1 Cook or thaw spinach, squeeze dry, and chop to yield 1 cup packed spinach.

2 Pour spinach, flours, cumin seed, chili, ghee or oil, and 1-1/2 teaspoons kosher salt into food processor. Pulse-process until spinach is evenly ground, about 40 to 60 seconds, and scrape into mixing bowl. Mix 1/4 cup warm water into dough slowly until it comes together into playdough soft, but not wet, dough. Gather dough into a ball.

3 Knead dough on a lightly floured surface with the heel of one hand, pulling dough into the center and turning it a quarter turn each time until smooth, 3 to 5 minutes. Cover dough with plastic wrap or seal into plastic baggie and set aside 30 minutes to one hour.

4 Roll dough into a thick and even 8-inch log. Cut it into 8 equal pieces or scale out 8 pieces weighing 2-1/2 ounces each. Cover dough so it doesn't form a dry crust.

5 Roll one piece of dough into a 6- to 7-inch circle. Brush with ghee or oil, fold it in half, brush again, and fold to make a triangle. Roll into a thin 7-inch triangle. Repeat with remaining dough balls. Keep breads covered on a parchment-covered sheet pan until ready to cook them.

6 Heat a cast-iron griddle or flat top gas griddle on medium to medium-high heat. Brush each side of bread with a little ghee or oil, and place on griddle. With the back of a metal spoon, lightly rub the bread until it whitens and bubbles and golden speckles appear, about 30 seconds to 1 minute per side. Flip paratha and cook the other side. Repeat rubbing with spoon—bread should puff slightly.

7 **To Serve:** Brush bread with ghee or oil and serve warm.

Source: New York cooking teacher Julie Sahni.

Vary! Improvise!

☞ *Choose Another Paratha Rolling Technique: Refer to Flaky, Layered Paratha.*

FIGURE 4.25 Cooking dosa.
Source: © Ruby/Alamy.

SOUTH INDIAN DOSA

This batter is high in protein and acquires a pleasant sourdough flavor from overnight fermenting. Indian cooks use thinned batter for large, thin, crispy, crepe-like dosa and steam thick dosa batter in special steamers (that look like egg poachers) to light, bready oval cakes called iddli. South Indians serve both dosa and iddli for breakfast. Iddli are dipped into soupy, spiced curry and dosa are filled with spiced potatoes or other combinations and served with chutneys.

Yields about 6 cups batter; 10 to 12 large dosa *or* 20 to 24 thicker 2-1/2 to 3-inch cakes, 5 to 8 servings

About 5 ounces urad dal, 2/3 cup
10-1/2 ounces long-grain white rice, 1-1/2 cups
1-1/2 teaspoons kosher salt
6 fluid ounces ghee, coconut oil or vegetable oil, 3/4 cup

For Serving

Coconut Chutney
Spiced Potatoes (Masala Aloo)

1 **Soak overnight:** Wash and drain dal. Pour dal into a mixing bowl and cover with 3 cups water. Wash and drain rice. Pour rice into a second bowl and cover with 3 cups water. Set the dal and rice aside to soak 6 to 8 hours.

2 **Grind rice:** Strain water off rice. Pour drained rice into food processor bowl. Purée 2 minutes, scraping down rice every 20 to 30 seconds, until batter resembles a paste. Pour in 1/4 cup warm water and purée 2 minutes, scraping down every 30 seconds. Slowly pour in 1/2 cup warm water. Purée mixture 4 minutes; it will become a fine batter. Scrape rice into large mixing bowl.

3 **Grind dal:** Drain water off dal and pour drained dal into food processor. Purée dal 3 minutes, scraping down every 30 seconds. The dal will come together into a mass. Slowly pour in 1/4 cup warm water. Process another 2 minutes, scraping down every 20 to 30 seconds. Slowly pour in another 1/2 cup warm water. Process 1 minute longer; dal will be frothy, fluffy, and light.

4 **Mix rice and dal batters:** Scrape dal into large mixing bowl with rice. Stir in 1/2 cup warm water to yield 5 cups batter.

5 **Ferment batter:** Cover bowl with towel and plate, and set batter aside in a warm spot. Batter should smell slightly sour and expand and become bubbly like a sourdough after 24 to 48 hours, depending on the ambient temperature. If batter over-ferments, the dosa will not hold together quite as well, but the batter is still edible; use it for small pancakes instead. Placing batter in a proofer to control temperature will speed up the fermentation. This will yield **about 6 cups batter**. Stir in 1-1/2 teaspoons kosher salt. Leftover batter can be refrigerated for 2 days and frozen up to a month.

6 **Spread and cook dosa batter:** Bring batter to room temperature if refrigerated. Cold batter will stick to the cooking surface:

   Nonstick pan: Place a 12-inch nonstick pan over medium heat. When pan is warm but not hot, ladle 1/2 cup batter into the center of pan. Working quickly, press lightly with bottom of the ladle or a metal spoon, and spread batter in one circular clockwise motion to a 10- to 12-inch diameter to form a paper-thin, unbroken circle.

   Seasoned cast iron griddle: Preheat large cast-iron griddle so that the heat can be felt when a hand is held 2 inches from its surface. Toss a few ice chips onto pan to cool, and lubricate pan with oil-soaked paper towel. If the griddle is too hot, the dosa batter will clump and not spread evenly. Ladle 1/2 cup batter and with the back of the ladle or a large metal spoon, spread batter quickly and evenly with a clockwise motion, to form a paper-thin, unbroken circle roughly 10 inches in diameter.

   Commercial flat top gas griddle: Heat flat top gas griddle to 350 degrees F. Cool it slightly with ice chips, and lubricate with an oil-soaked towel. Ladle 1/2 cup batter and with the back of the ladle or a large metal spoon, quickly and evenly with a clockwise motion, spread the batter to form a paper-thin, unbroken circle roughly 10 inches in diameter. Dosa made on commercial gas griddles may be made much larger with more batter.

7 When dosa begins to sizzle, drizzle 1 teaspoon oil or ghee around the edges of the dosa. Cook dosa until the top is opaque, no longer moist, the bottom side is golden brown, and the dosa starts to curl around the edges, 4 to 6 minutes. Flip the dosa and brown the other side, about 1 minute. (Professional Indian cooks do not flip dosa.) Transfer dosa to a serving plate and proceed with step 8.

   To hold dosa briefly, fold in half or roll and place in one layer on a sheet pan. Place in 200 degree F oven. If the pan gets too hot between dosa, the batter will clump up and will not spread evenly. Rub the skillet or griddle with ice chips, let the water evaporate, and wipe with an oil-soaked towel before making additional dosa.

8 **To Serve:** Place one dosa onto plate with dark side down. In the center, spoon 2 to 3 tablespoons **coconut chutney** and 1/2 cup or more **masala aloo**. Fold dosa in half or into a roll. Serve immediately while still crisp.

Source: *The Art of Indian Vegetarian Cooking* by Yamuna Devi.

FIGURE 4.26 Dosa with chutney.
Source: Mukesh Kumar/Shutterstock.

FIGURE 4.27 Indian iddli with sambar.
Source: graphia/Fotolia.

Vary! Improvise!

☛ *Cooking Teacher Nimmy Paul's Kerala-Style Dosa:* In a nonstick skillet, cook thicker, smaller dosa made with 1/4 cup batter. Don't spread the batter: the cakes should look like silver-dollar pancakes. Perch two or three curried shrimp atop the mini cakes for an elegant presentation.

☛ *Brown Rice Dosa:* Substitute long-grain brown rice for white and soak 8 to 12 hours. Soak dal 6 to 8 hours.

☛ *Use batter for gluten-free, egg-free pancakes:* Add a little sweetener, spices, or vanilla and turn Indian dosa batter into sourdough gluten- and egg-free pancakes.

☛ *Spice It Up:* Stir in seasonings of choice to batter: nigella seed, sesame seeds, ground turmeric, sliced cilantro, or finely sliced chilies.

FIGURE 4.28 Mung beans.
Source: Geoff Brightling/DK Images.

Vary! Improvise!

- ☞ Grind cilantro or mint into batter.
- ☞ Fold shredded carrots into batter.
- ☞ Grind gingerroot into batter.

SOUTHERN MUNG BEAN AND RICE PANCAKE (PESARATTU)

Pesarattu is a breakfast dish. These are slightly thick dosa or savory pancakes made from soaked and ground mung beans and rice ground into a fluffy batter. A blender grinds the batter finer than a food processor.

Yields about 6 cups batter, about twelve 7-inch pancakes

14 ounces mung beans, 2 cups whole or split
About 5 ounces long-grain white rice, 3/4 cup
8 to 9 ounces onion, 2 cups peeled and diced
1 ounce dried, unsweetened, finely shredded coconut, 1/3 cup
   or 2 ounces fresh/frozen grated coconut, 1/2 cup
2 ounces jalapeño chilies, 2 large, about 4 tablespoons stemmed, seeded, and diced
1 teaspoon ground coriander
Oil or fragrant coconut oil for frying
To Serve: Grated jaggery or maple syrup *and* chutney of choice

1 Soak beans and rice together 8 hours. Drain and rinse.

2 **Purée:** Grind half the beans and rice in a blender until beans and rice break up. Add 1/2 cup warm water and grind to a slightly thick, slightly coarse paste: some of the broken bean bits should be visible. Pour into mixing bowl. Repeat with remaining beans and rice and another 1/2 cup warm water. Scrape batter into mixing bowl with first batch.

3 Drop onion, coconut, chilies, coriander, and 1-1/2 teaspoons kosher salt into the blender. Grind vegetables together until smooth, and stir into batter. Rinse out blender with 1/2 cup warm water and reserve. If not using batter immediately, refrigerate until needed. Adjust consistency of batter with water reserved in blender—it should be a thick but pourable purée.

4 **Cook:** Heat a 9-inch nonstick skillet *or* griddle over medium to medium-low heat. Coat with oil or coconut oil and pour in 1/2 cup batter. With the back of the measuring cup or a large spoon, immediately spread batter into 7-inch round pancake. On the nonstick skillet, the batter will adhere better when it cooks a bit.

5 Cook both sides of pancake until browned and firm, 2 to 4 minutes per side. Cover skillet (or pancake) with lid to cook through well. The pancake may stick on a griddle, but don't hurry it. When it forms a firm brown crust it will let go.

6 **To Serve:** While hot, place pesarattu on plate, and spread with jaggery (or maple syrup) and chutney.

PLANT DEFENSE

Plants have defenses. Like many raw legumes, chickpea flour can be toxic when not fully cooked. Cooking inactivates the naturally occurring defensive enzymes.

Pakora

Well-loved and versatile, pakora appear on the street or in Indian homes. Pakora are a quick snack, a light meal with soup, or an offering for company. There are two types: foods dipped into thin batter *or* foods stirred into thick batter and spooned. Both are fried in hot oil and served with tamarind or cilantro chutney.

Basic pakora consists of chickpea flour, water, salt, and sometimes baking powder. Seasonings like cumin, coriander, chilies, or cilantro add zing. Thin batters are best for delicate leaves like spinach or chard and thicker batters for moist foods like vegetables and meat or seafood. For a cakey but light batter, add baking powder. Omit it for a crisper coating. Some Indian chefs just dredge food in sifted chickpea flour and deep-fry.

SIGNATURE RECIPE

CHICKPEA FRITTERS (PAKORA)

Cauliflower, onions, potatoes or plantain, spinach and zucchini, and proteins like seafood, paneer cheese, or chicken are common pakora. Create: Think contrast, color, texture, and flavor or use tried and true combinations.

Dry Ingredients

4-1/2 ounces besan (plain chickpea flour), (1 cup unsifted), 1-1/2 cups sifted
2 teaspoons kosher salt
1 teaspoon vegetable oil

*Water (see amounts below)

Optional: 1/4 teaspoon baking powder

Thick Batter for Vegetable Dumplings

Yields about 3/4 cup

*3 to 4 fluid ounces water

Medium Batter for Coating Most Foods

Yields about 1 cup

*6 fluid ounces water

Thin Batter for Coating Leafy or Delicate Vegetables

Yields about 1-1/4 cups

*8 fluid ounces water

1 **Prepare batter:** Stir together sifted chickpea flour and salt in mixing bowl. Stir in oil and **water**. Whisk batter 1 minute until very smooth.

2 Rest batter 30 minutes. Whisk in optional baking powder just prior to cooking.

Vary! Improvise!

☛ *Add 2 tablespoons rice flour to basic batter for a crisper batter.*

☛ *For a lighter batter good for seafood, substitute 1/2 cup cornstarch for 1/2 cup chickpea flour.*

SPOONED: POLKA DOT PAKORA

1 recipe *Thick Batter* with baking powder
2 teaspoons nigella seed
6 ounces red bell pepper, about 1 cup seeded, stemmed, and finely diced
1/2 ounce cilantro, 1/4 cup finely sliced

1 Prepare *Thick Pakora Batter* and rest 30 minutes.

2 Heat oil to 365 degrees F.

3 Whisk baking powder, nigella, pepper, and cilantro into batter.

4 Spoon batter by tablespoons into hot oil and fry until golden. Break one apart to make sure it is done.

Vary! Improvise!

☞ *Mix 7 ounces diced Vidalia onion and 1-1/2 teaspoons curry masala into thick batter, spoon into hot oil, and fry.*

DIPPED: SWEET POTATO POPPYSEED PAKORA

1 recipe *Medium Batter*
2 tablespoons poppy seed
1/4 teaspoon ground nutmeg
16 ounces sweet potato, 4 cups peeled, sliced into 1/4-inch-thick half-moons

1 Prepare *Medium Pakora Batter* and rest 30 minutes.

2 Heat oil to 365 degrees F.

3 Whisk poppy seed and nutmeg into batter.

4 Dry sweet potato slices or dredge in chickpea flour and shake off excess. Dip into batter, drain 1 second, and slide into hot oil. Fry until golden.

Vary! Improvise!

☞ *Mix 1/4 teaspoon each ajwain and turmeric into thin batter. Dip spinach leaves into it and fry until golden.*

Signature Technique: Deep-Frying Pakora

1 **Organize.** Assemble all utensils, prepared food, and batter to within arm's reach. Do all preparation before even thinking of heating the oil.

2 **Heat kadhai or wok.** This opens the metal's pores and allows oil to seep in, which keeps food from sticking. Or heat deep-fryer to 360 degrees F.

3 **Add oil** and heat to 365 degrees F. When you add food, the temperature will lower. Coated vegetable pakoras are best deep-fried around 350 to 360 degrees F so that vegetables cook through before batter browns too much. In the highest castes, ghee is the frying medium of choice because it imparts rich flavor. Ghee is expensive; its smoking point is 365 degrees F so watch the thermometer carefully if you use it, and keep lower than 360 degrees F.

4 **Dip food** into flour first for thicker crust. (Or stir grated vegetables into batter.) Pick up pieces of vegetables and drain 2 seconds before frying.

5 **Slide pakora** into oil. Be prepared for oil splatters. Don't toss, *gently slide*, to lessen splash and burn.

6 **Do a test pakora.** Note cooking time and color. Break it open and taste it.

7 **Don't overfill frying vessel.** It lowers oil temperature, which makes food soggy and greasy. Oil temperature is crucial; keep it steady (with a thermometer).

8 **Drain foods** either on a rack not touching or on paper toweling.

9 **Serve pakora immediately** while still warm *or* reheat in a hot oven.

NORTH INDIAN SAVORY PASTRIES (SAMOSA)

Yields 11 ounces dough, 30 samosa

About 7 ounces unbleached all-purpose flour, 1-1/2 cups
1/4 teaspoon baking powder
1 teaspoon kosher salt
Optional: 1 teaspoon ajwain seeds, crushed
2 ounces cold ghee *or* unsalted butter, 1/4 cup

Filling

2 cups *Masala Aloo*
  or 2 cups *Lamb Keema*

Canola oil for deep-frying

For Serving

Cilantro Chutney or *Tamarind Chutney*

1 **Prepare dough:** Pulse-mix flour, salt, baking powder, optional ajwain, and fat in a food processor *or* cut them together by hand as for pie dough. Turn out mixture into a bowl. Mix in 1/3 cup cold water until dough comes together into playdough consistency. Add 1 tablespoon more if necessary. Dough texture should be similar to pie dough, tender and soft but not wet. If dough is rough, knead lightly until smooth. Form dough together into a ball and wrap in plastic. Set aside to rest 30 minutes to 1 hour. Prepare chosen **filling**.

2 Roll dough into 15-inch log and cut into 15 even pieces. Or scale off 15 scant 3/4-ounce pieces. Cover dough. Dip one piece of dough into flour on both cut sides and lightly shake off excess. Roll out into a thin circle 5 inches diameter. Cut each round in half to make two semi-circles.

3 Dip a fingertip in water and moisten half of straight edge of one semi-circle. Bring other half over to form a cone. Make a 1/4-inch seam—wet edge over dry edge. Press securely to seal. Holding wrapper like an ice cream cone, dampen top half of inner edge. Fill cone with 1-1/2 tablespoons filling. Press filling deeper into cone with a finger. Pinch dough firmly to seal top edge. If not sealed well, samosa will burst open into cooking oil. Set sealed samosa seam-side-down on parchment-covered sheet pan and allow to air-dry 10 to 30 minutes.

4 **Fry samosa:** Heat oil in a wok or fryer to 365 degrees F. Fry samosas until golden brown, 3 to 4 minutes. Drain on paper towels and keep warm in 250 degree F oven.

5 **To Serve:** Arrange samosas on platter with bowls of cilantro or tamarind chutney.

Source: *Classic Indian Cooking* by Julie Sahni.

Vary! Improvise!

☛ *Lower the Fat:* Brush samosas with oil and bake on parchment-covered sheet pan in preheated 450 degree F oven until golden, 20 minutes.

☛ *Tangy Variation:* Substitute cold buttermilk or yogurt for water.

GRILL, GRIDDLE, ROAST, BROIL, AND BARBECUE

GRILLED CHICKEN OR LAMB SKEWERS (TIKKA)

Cover the exposed part of bamboo skewers with foil or hang them off the edge of the grill to keep them from burning. Or use metal skewers.

About 12 servings

3 pounds boneless, skinless chicken thigh meat
   or 3 pounds boneless trimmed lamb shoulder or leg
2 tablespoons ground coriander
2 tablespoons ground cumin
2 tablespoons *Curry Masala*
1 ounce gingerroot, about 2 tablespoons peeled and grated
1 ounce garlic, 4 large cloves, 2 tablespoons peeled and minced
4 tablespoons fresh lemon juice, about 1 large lemon
8 fluid ounces plain whole milk yogurt, 1 cup

For Serving

Tomato-Chili Cachumber
Chutney of choice
Chapatti or *Phulka*

1 Remove excess fat from meat. Dice meat into 1- to 1-1/4 inch cubes.

2 **Combine dry spices:** Place coriander, cumin, and masala into a small skillet. Over medium-low heat, dry toast spice. Push spices around so they toast evenly. They will darken a shade and smell fragrant. Pour into bowl and cool spices. (Alternatively, dry-toast whole spices separately, cool and grind.)

3 Mix toasted spices, ginger, garlic, lemon juice, yogurt, and 1 teaspoon kosher salt together. Add chicken and mix well. Cover and refrigerate chicken overnight *or* let it sit at least one hour at room temperature.

4 If using bamboo skewers, soak 24 bamboo skewers in warm water 30 minutes. Heat a grill or broiler. Thread about three pieces of meat on a short metal or bamboo skewer. Grill or broil tikka until cooked through and crusty.

5 **To Serve:** Arrange tikka on platter and serve with cachumber, chutney, and chapatti or phulka.

TANDOOR COOKING

Tandoori foods are a specialty of North India. A *tandoor* or Indian clay oven bakes, roasts, and grills at the same time, giving any food cooked in it both the moistness of roasted food and the flavor of grilled food. Tandoori is restaurant food. Few people have these expensive, furnace-like ovens in their homes, though they can be purchased: an electric tandoor oven goes for around $600. Indian chefs slap flatbreads like buttery, yeasty naan on the sides of the oven. They place long metal skewers filled with yogurt and spice-marinated meat, whole chickens, seafood, whole fish, meatballs, and vegetables to roast-grill in a tandoor.

FIGURE 4.29 Naan bread cooked in tandoori oven.
Source: WITTY234/Shutterstock.

NORTH INDIAN TANDOOR FLATBREAD (NAAN)

Naan are not usually made at home; they show up in Indian restaurants boasting a tandoori oven.

Yields about 32 ounces dough, eight 4 ounce, 7-inch by 5-inch naan

2-1/4 teaspoons active dry yeast
1 teaspoon sugar
20 to 21 ounces all purpose flour, 4-1/2 cups, more for dusting and rolling
2 teaspoons kosher salt
1 teaspoon baking powder
3 tablespoons whole milk
2 tablespoons plain, whole milk yogurt
1 large egg, 1/4 cup lightly beaten
2 tablespoons vegetable oil, plus 1 tablespoon more for bowl
3 tablespoons ghee
   or 3 tablespoons melted unsalted butter

1 Mix together yeast, sugar, and 1/4-cup warm water in a small mixing bowl. Rest until foamy, 5 minutes. Pour flour, salt, and baking powder into the bowl of a food processor with a blade or into mixer bowl with a dough hook. Blend the dry ingredients. With machine running, pour in yeast mixture, milk, yogurt, egg, 2 tablespoons oil, and 3/4 cup warm water.

2 Knead and/or pulse dough until smooth and elastic, 2 minutes in a processor, 5 to 8 minutes in a mixer, 8 to 10 minutes by hand on flour dusted surface. Dough should be earlobe soft but not sticky. Add as little flour as possible.

3 Oil large bowl with remaining 1 tablespoon oil, and turn dough in it to coat all sides. Cover bowl with plastic wrap and a kitchen towel. Let the dough rise in a warm place until doubled, 1 to 1-1/2 hours.

4 Press down dough and roll into a log. Divide log into 8 equal pieces, about 4 ounces each. Pat each slice into a 4-inch pattie, place on a lightly floured baking sheet, and cover with a damp kitchen towel. Rise dough a second time until doubled in size, 45 to 60 minutes.

5 To use a tandoor or deck oven, heat to 450 degrees. To use an oven, 30 minutes before baking, place a pizza stone or two overturned aluminum half-sheet pans on the bottom rack and heat oven to 450 degrees. To use a kettle grill, heat to medium-high.

6 Roll out 1 dough ball on a lightly floured work surface into a circle with a 6-inch diameter. Roll and stretch dough from both ends to make a teardrop shape roughly 5 by 7 inches. Brush away excess flour. Repeat with remaining dough balls.

7 *Bake Dough:*

   Tandoor Oven: Drape one piece of dough over a folded towel or round cloth pillow called a *gadhi*. Press bread onto hot wall of tandoor oven. Cook breads until puffed and tops are bubbled and browned, 1 to 2 minutes. Gently pry the bread off clay wall with a metal spatula or tongs without scratching.

   Deck Oven: Slide dough teardrops into oven with wooden paddle. Bake until bottom is browned and top is browned and puffed, 4 to 5 minutes.

   Oven: Lay dough teardrops on preheated pizza stone or overturned sheet pans. Place naan on stone or pans, and bake until the bottoms are browned and the tops blister, puff, and are lightly toasted, 5 minutes. Breads may be turned and the remaining side baked about 2 minutes. The broiler may also be used as finish to obtain the bubbled and golden tops.

   Grill: Oil the clean grill grate. Lightly brush bottom of dough with ghee or butter. Place naan bottom-side-down on grate; leave space in between. Grill until the bottoms are golden and the tops start to puff and bubble, 1 to 2 minutes. Lightly brush the tops with melted ghee or butter. Invert bread, and grill the remaining side until golden and crisp, 1 to 2 minutes.

8 **To Serve:** Remove bread from oven, grill, or tandoori oven. Brush tops of naan with ghee or melted butter, and place in a cloth-lined basket; serve hot. Repeat with remaining dough.

Source: *The New York Times* and Bukhara Grill, Manhattan.

BIRYANI VERSUS PULLAO

Paddy Rawal, chef-owner of the restaurant Raaga in Santa Fe, New Mexico, says, "In culinary school in India one of the questions we had to answer was, 'how do you differentiate biryani from pullao?' The answer is that biryani has a sauce and pullao is moist, but has no sauce. There are many different ways to make biryani—the Moghlai style is layered, the southern Hyderabadi is a dryer, lighter biryani, while with my style—the Avadhi (Awadhi)—nothing is roasted. I mix raw whole spices like star anise, cardamom, red mace and nutmeg, raw rice and raw meat together in a heavy cast iron container, seal it and bake in slow, even heat."

Biryani

Though they are prepared all over India, biryanis originated in the North, brought by Moghal invaders. The many styles of biryani are prepared using the *dum* or pot-roasting method. Derived from the Parsee word "birian," *biryani* means "fried before cooking." It is filled with nuts, fruits, and fragrant seasonings. The name doesn't give a sense of the celebratory and exotic nature of this dish, which was served to royalty.

For biryanis, rice is fried in ghee for a toasted, nutty flavor. Frying hardens the outer rice starch and helps to keep rice fluffier. Rice cooks with spices in water or broth until partially done. Other ingredients like marinated/sauced meat, seafood, chickpeas, or vegetables are cooked separately. The two are layered (sometimes strewn with cardamom pods, whole mace, or rosewater) together into a pot, sealed, and baked in a 325 to 350 degree F oven. Everything is gently folded together before serving.

Signature Technique: Moghal Biryani

- Choose heavy, oven-safe pot with tight-fitting lid.

- Prepare sauced, seasoned meat, bean, or vegetable dish—like a korma or curry or stir-fried seasoned vegetables. It should be on the thicker side.

- Fry rice seasonings and/or garnishes like nuts and raisins in generous amount of fat.

- Preheat oven to 350 degrees F. Parboil rice and drain. Fold in seasonings.

- Layer half the seasoned cooked meat, bean, or vegetable "curry," half the rice, the remaining seasoned meat, bean, or vegetable "curry," and remaining rice. Drizzle with ghee, saffron-soaked water, or milk.

- Seal lid with foil or wet towel. Traditionally dum-cooked pots are sealed with dough.

- Place in oven and cook until rice is done, about 30 minutes. Remove pot from oven and rest biryani 10 minutes or more. Uncover and fold ingredients together.

- Plate biryani and garnish with sautéed raisins and nuts.

CHICKEN BIRYANI

This Moghul dish reveals its Persian roots—it is quite similar to the Persian polo/polows.

Yields about 5 quarts, 10 to 12 servings

Double recipe *Northern Chicken Korma* made with boneless, skinless chicken
    or 3 quarts of another curry
2 tablespoons ghee

21 ounces basmati rice, 3 cups soaked and drained
4-1/2 cups boiling chicken broth *or* water
8 tablespoons ghee *or* vegetable oil, *divided*
1 to 1-1/4 ounces each: slivered almonds, cashews, and pistachios, 1/4 cup each
1-1/4 ounces golden raisins, 1/4 cup
1 pound small yellow onions, 4 cups thinly slivered
1/2 ounce cilantro, about 1/4 cup finely sliced
2 ounces jalapeño chilies, about 2 large, 4 tablespoons stemmed and finely diced
1/2 cup chicken stock, *divided*
2 teaspoon saffron threads

1   Prepare *Chicken Korma* with boneless, skinless chicken or prepare another curry.

2   **Prepare rice:** Heat 2 tablespoons ghee in 4-quart saucepan over medium heat and add drained rice. Cook rice until it begins to stick, 1 to 2 minutes. Pour in boiling chicken broth or water and 2 teaspoons salt. Bring rice to a boil, lower heat, cover, and cook 10 minutes. Remove pot from heat. Rest rice 10 minutes undisturbed to firm up. Fluff rice. Do not let rice sit more than 5 minutes longer before assembling biryani. It will harden into a block.

3   In 12-inch skillet, heat 2 tablespoons ghee and fry almonds, cashews, pistachios, and raisins separately, until nuts are golden and raisins puff. Place each batch in mixing bowl.

4   Heat 4 tablespoons ghee over medium-high heat and fry onions until very browned and crisp, 15 to 20 minutes. Set aside on paper towels for garnish later.

5   Mix cilantro, chilies, and 1/4 cup chicken stock. In a separate bowl, mix saffron with remaining 1/4 cup chicken stock. Set aside.

6   Preheat oven to 325 degrees F.
   • Coat bottom of 6-quart heavy-lidded casserole with remaining 2 tablespoons ghee.
   • Spread 1/4 of cooked rice, about 3 cups on ghee and smooth with spatula.
   • Drizzle half of the cilantro-chili mixture over rice.
   • Spread with half of chicken korma, about 6 cups.
   • Spread 1/4 of rice, about 3 cups, over korma.
   • Drizzle remaining cilantro-chili mixture over rice.
   • Spread remaining half of korma over rice and cover with remaining rice. Press gently to compact it. With a rubber spatula, smooth top of rice to resemble a dome.
   • Dribble saffron and broth over top.

7   Cover casserole and seal edges with aluminum foil. Place casserole in oven 35 minutes, turn off oven, and let it sit another 10 minutes without opening door of oven. Remove casserole from oven and unseal.

8   **To Serve:** Scoop top rice into a bowl and set aside. Fold together meat and rice remaining in casserole and mound mixture on large platter. Cover meat with rice set aside in bowl. Garnish with toasted nuts, raisins, and fried onions. Serve immediately.

Source: *Classic Indian Cooking* by Julie Sahni.

Vary! Improvise!

☛ *Vegetarian Biryani:* Substitute *Cauliflower Coconut Curry* for *Chicken Korma.*

SALAD AND VEGETABLE METHODS

Salads made with delicate lettuces are not common in India due to the heat. Raw chopped vegetables and seasoned cooked vegetables take their place. Raita and pachadi, similar to a yogurt "salad," are served as the cooling element to spicy curries.

Signature Technique: Bhurta/Bharta

Bhurtas are the ultimate North Indian comfort food. Highly seasoned crushed vegetables, bhurta is a sort of cooked "salad." A smoky-flavored bhurta consists of roasted, grilled, or sautéed vegetables like eggplant, boiled, sautéed potatoes, or baked or sautéed tomatoes—mashed together with cooked aromatics and seasonings. Bhurtas consist of:

- **Vegetable:** Aloo-potato, brinjal-eggplant, or tomato
- **Sautéed aromatic vegetables:** Tomato, onion, garlic, ginger, or chili
- **Tempering:** Spices or seasonings cooked in fat
- **Garnish:** Cilantro or herbs
- **Seasoning:** Salt and pepper

COOK'S VOICE: ASHA GUPTA

Homecook and Native of New Delhi Troy, Michigan

"My kids love to make sandwiches from my eggplant bhurta, which they call bhurta sandwich."

Source: Courtesy of Asha Gupta.

Vary! Improvise!

☞ *Add 1 teaspoon minced ginger to onions in tempering.*

☞ *Double the amount of tomato.*

NORTHERN "BROKEN" EGGPLANT (BHARTA)

Yields about 5 cups

3 pounds eggplant

Tempering

3 to 4 tablespoons vegetable oil
1 teaspoon cumin seed
6 to 7 ounces small yellow onions, 1-1/2 cups finely diced
1 tablespoon ground coriander
1/2 teaspoon turmeric
1/4 to 1/2 teaspoon ground Kashmiri *or* red chili
    or 1/2 ounce green chili, 1 to 2 tablespoons stemmed, seeded, and diced
1/4 ounce garlic, 1 large clove, 1-1/2 teaspoons minced
8 ounces tomato, 1 large, about 1-1/2 cups finely diced

1 lime, juiced

For Serving

Finely sliced cilantro

1 **Cook eggplant:** Roast whole eggplant under broiler, on gas grill, or on low gas flame, turning constantly, until skin is blackened and eggplant is soft all the way through. (If eggplant blackens before cooking through, peel away blackened skin and place in microwave to finish cooking.) Peel away skin and wipe away stray black bits with paper towels. Slice off stem and discard. Dice eggplant and slide into mixing bowl, mash lightly to yield about 3 cups. Set aside.

2 **Temper, temper:** Heat oil over medium heat in a 10-inch skillet and add cumin seed. Cook until the seeds sputter and turn one shade darker, 20 to 30 seconds. Add onion and raise heat to medium-high. Cook onion until browned and soft.

3 Stir in ground spices and cook 30 seconds to 1 minute to toast them. Stir in fresh chili, garlic, and tomatoes, lower heat, season with salt, partially cover, and simmer aromatic tempering until vegetables are soft, 5 to 10 minutes. Remove pan from heat and fold mashed eggplant into spiced vegetables. Season bhurta with salt, freshly ground black pepper, and lime juice to taste.

4 **To Serve:** Pile bhurta in serving bowl and garnish with cilantro.

Source: Cooking teacher Jyoti Agarwal, Gourmet Desire, New Delhi, India.

North Indian Raita and South Indian Pachadi

Raitas and pachadis are cooling side dishes, much like Middle Eastern yogurt and vegetable "salads." Indian chef Julie Sahni says no Indian meal is complete without yogurt. *Raita* and its southern cousin *pachadi* are especially popular in summer.

Signature Technique: North Indian Raita Method and Southern Pachadi

The key to these yogurt salads is seasonal produce and homemade whole milk yogurt or the best live-cultured whole milk yogurt available. Thicken runny yogurt by pouring it into a cheesecloth-lined strainer set over a bowl, and draining overnight in the refrigerator. Thick, yogurt-rich pachadis can be made with a variety of raw or lightly cooked vegetables like okra, carrots, or tomatoes.

1 Peel and grate or finely chop fresh fruit or vegetables. Alternatively, prepare a tempering and add diced vegetables like okra, eggplant, zucchini, or anything that is abundantly fresh and cook until tender—like a poriyal. Cool or chill.

2 Fold prepared vegetables or fruit into whole milk yogurt or low-fat yogurt mixed with sour cream.

  *Proportions: 1 to 3 cups grated or cooked vegetable or fruit to 2 cups whole milk yogurt or 1-1/2 cups yogurt and 1/2 cup sour cream.

3 Season raita or *pachadi* with dry toasted ground spices, sweetener, cilantro, mint, green or red chilies, or a tempering made with spices, chilies, and/or curry leaves.

NORTH INDIAN CUCUMBER-YOGURT RAITA

Yields about 4 cups

2 teaspoons cumin seed
24 ounces English cucumbers, 2 medium, about 3-1/2 cups peeled, seeded, and shredded
1/2 ounce jaggery, 1 tablespoon
   or maple syrup, to taste
1/2 ounce cilantro, 1/4 cup finely sliced
1/2 ounce mint leaves, 1/4 cup finely sliced
1/2 to 1 ounce jalapeño or serrano chilies, 1 to 2 tablespoons stemmed and finely diced, to taste
16 fluid ounces whole milk yogurt, 2 cups
3 to 4 tablespoons fresh lime juice, 1 large lime

1 Dry toast cumin seed in small skillet over medium heat until aromatic. Immediately transfer to plate to cool. Grind in spice grinder to a powder, and set aside.

2 Toss cucumber with 1 teaspoon kosher salt and set aside 15 minutes. Gently squeeze excess liquid from grated cucumber and drain well.

3 Fold sweetener, cilantro, mint, chili, and cumin with yogurt. Fold into cucumbers. Refrigerate raita 20 to 30 minutes to mingle flavors. Season with lime juice and salt to taste.

Vary! Improvise!

☛ *Substitute 4 tomatoes, diced or add one tomato, diced, to cucumber yogurt raita.*

☛ *Substitute shredded spinach for cucumbers.*

☛ *Substitute grated baby yellow squash or zucchini.*

☛ *Substitute cooked, cubed winter squash for cukes and cinnamon, ginger, cardamom for spices.*

☛ *Mix grated apples or pears with crystallized ginger, yogurt, and citrus juice and salt.*

☛ **Dairy-Free:** *Mix diced bananas, toasted, finely ground cashews, lime juice, mint leaves, and ginger.*

SOUTH INDIAN MANGO-YOGURT SALAD (MANGAI PACHADI)

Though some south Indian cooks consider pachadi a sort of fresh curry, it's similar to a raita.

Yields 3-1/2 to 4 cups, 4 servings

1-1/2 pounds unripe or slightly ripe mango, 1-1/2 large, 3 cups peeled and diced into 3/8-inch cubes, *divided*
1/2 ounce dried, unsweetened, finely shredded coconut, 3 tablespoons
3 ounces jalapeño chilies, about 3, 6 tablespoons stemmed and diced, to taste
2 ounces cilantro, 1 cup finely sliced
12 fluid ounces whole milk yogurt, 1-1/2 cups
Jaggery or maple syrup

Tempering

1 teaspoon plain sesame oil *or* fragrant coconut oil
1 teaspoon brown mustard seeds
2 teaspoons cumin seed
6 curry leaves
1/4 teaspoon asafoetida

1 Purée half the diced mangoes and all the coconut, chilies, and cilantro in a blender until they become a smooth paste. Add as little water as necessary to blend. Mix mango paste with yogurt in a mixing bowl. Fold in remaining diced mango. Season mixture with salt and jaggery or maple syrup, to taste.

2 **Temper, temper:** Heat oil in a small, heavy sauté pan over medium heat and add mustard seeds. When they turn grey and sputter, about 20 seconds, add cumin seed and curry leaves and cook until leaves wilt. Add and cook asafoetida 10 seconds. Fold into mango-yogurt mixture.

3 **To Serve:** Pour yogurt-mango-tempering mixture into a serving bowl. Taste and adjust seasonings. Serve pachadi at room temperature or chilled.

Source: *Dakshin, Vegetarian Cuisine from South India* by Chandra Padmanabhan.

Vary! Improvise!

☞ *Ripe Mango Pachadi: Instead of unripe mango, peel and finely dice a large ripe mango. Do not purée it with the coconut, chilies, and cilantro. Instead, fold it into the coconut paste, yogurt, and spices.*
☞ *Mixed Vegetable Pachadi: Steam 1/2-inch cubes of vegetables or medley of vegetables and cool. Fold in yogurt, spices, tempering, and fresh cilantro or mint.*

Signature Technique: Southern Cachumbar/Kachumbar

A cachumbar is a side "salad." Indian diners view it as a sort of refreshing relish: think Mexican salsa. It consists of diced or shredded fruit or vegetables seasoned with green chilies, chili powder or dry red chilies, fresh lime or lemon juice, salt, herbs, and sweet or green onion. Some contain nuts. To prepare a cachumber:

- Choose combinations of vegetables for flavor and color: carrots, green onions, and cashews or green mango, tomato, and green onion.

- Shred or finely diced cabbage, carrots, radish, cucumber, tomatoes, melon, or unripe green mango or unripe green papaya so diners may scoop it comfortably with a piece of chapatti bread.

- Finely diced onion and chili. Fold into fruit or vegetable. Chill until ready to serve.

- Season cachumbar with citrus juice and salt just before serving. Some cooks dress and rest cachumbars before serving, others don't. Taste and re-season to achieve bold, bright flavor.

TOMATO-CHILI CACHUMBAR

In the northern Moghul cuisine, cachumbar accompanied grilled kebabs. Garnish with anardana (dried pomegranate seeds) for a burst of flavor.

Yields 5-1/2 to 6 cups, 6 to 8 servings

16 ounces tomatoes, 2 to 2-1/2 cups, diced into 1/2-inch cubes
16 ounces English cucumber, about 2 cups lightly peeled, seeded, and diced into
1/2-inch cubes
2 ounces trimmed green onions, 4 large, 1/2 to 2/3 cup finely sliced
4 ounces trimmed red radishes, 2 cups finely sliced
1/2 ounce cilantro, 1/4 cup finely sliced, more to taste
1 ounce jalapeño chili, 1 medium, 2 to 3 tablespoons stemmed and finely diced
    or 1/2 ounce serrano chili, 1 medium, 1 to 2 tablespoons stemmed and finely diced
1/2 cup fresh lime juice, about 2 large limes

For Serving

Grilled chicken or *Grilled Chicken or Lamb Skewers (Tikka)*

1 Mix tomatoes, cucumber, green onion, radish, cilantro, and chili in a bowl. Refrigerate salad
   20 minutes to chill. Toss with fresh lime juice and salt, to taste.

2 **To Serve:** Pile *cachumbar* into a bowl and serve as part of a larger Indian meal or serve with grilled
   chicken or tikka.

PICKLE AND PRESERVE

Indians love salty, spicy vegetable and fruit pickles. Cooks prepare them from green mango, turnip, lime, lemon, cauliflower, chilies, white radish, or carrot. Pickle makers take advantage of the Indian heat for fermentation, and place them in the sunlight. Pickles mature from 2 weeks to 6 months; the longer maturing pickles last many years. Indian pickles are preserved in salt, lemon or lime juice, and oil. Indian chefs say mustard oil preserves pickles better than other oils.

LIME PICKLE (MASALA BHARA NIMBU ACHAR)

Yields 1 pint

12 ounces small Key limes, 12 to 14

Spice Mixture

1/2 teaspoon fenugreek seeds
1 teaspoons dark mustard seeds
1/2 teaspoon cayenne or chili powder
1/4 teaspoon asafoetida powder
1-1/2 tablespoons kosher salt

1/2 to 3/4 cup fresh lime juice, 2 to 3 large limes
1/3 to 1/2 cup Indian mustard oil *or* plain sesame oil

1   Preheat oven to 200 degrees F. Wash limes very well. Place limes in small baking dish and into oven until fully dry, 10 minutes.

2   In a small skillet over medium heat, dry-toast fenugreek seed and dark mustard seeds until a shade darker and fragrant. Cool. Grind seeds in spice grinder and mix with cayenne, asafoetida, and salt to yield 3 tablespoons spice mixture.

3   Place a lime with the stem-end-down on a cutting board. Slice into quarters so that it remains connected at the stem end and opens like a flower. Spread open lime, stuff 1/2 teaspoon spice mixture into the opening, and rub spices on cut inside of lime.

4   Press lime together and stuff it cut-side-up into a 1-pint wide-mouth glass canning jar. Repeat stuffing with remaining limes. Press them tightly together into jar. Pour lime juice over the stuffed limes, but leave about 1 inch headspace, and seal jar. Place jar in warm spot, preferably in the sun, until limes begin to soften, 5 to 7 days.

5   Heat mustard oil, if using, to smoking for 5 minutes, cool slightly, and pour over limes. If using sesame oil, warm it, and pour over limes. Cool. Cap jar with plastic lid. Keep in warm spot 4 to 6 weeks, shaking daily. Limes should be very tender and yellowed. Test by biting one. If limes are not tender (like preserved lemons), leave in a warm spot 5 weeks or more. The flavor improves with age. Refrigerate to keep indefinitely.

Source: *The Art of Indian Vegetarian Cooking* by Yamuna Devi.

STREET FOOD (CHAAT)

A not-to-be-missed part of Indian food, these savory streetside snacks encompass starchy or beany chopped salads dressed with yogurt, *samosa*, *pakora*, *panipuri* and, possibly the most famous, *bhelpuri*. Here are ten popular Northern chaats—there are many more in other regions of India. Look for stands with lots of people. . .

1. *Aloo Chaat:* Boiled cubed potatoes, sprinkled with chaat masala, cilantro, yogurt, and tamarind chutney.

2. *Golgappe/Panipuri:* Deep fried, wafer thin crisp-walled and hollow *poori*, cracked open to make a hole and filled with spiced potatoes or dal and topped with tamarind chutney and chaat masala plus cilantro water. Eat in one bite or it'll gush all over.

3. *Bhelpuri and Papri Chaat:* Papri chaat is a northern mix of puri, sev (deep-fried thin chickpea noodles), boiled grated potatoes, chickpeas, chutney, yogurt, chaat masala, and chilies.

4. *Sevpuri:* Potato, chutney, and sev (thin shreds of deep-fried chickpea noodles) stuffed into pooris—like panipuri, but no cilantro water.

5. *Aloo Tikka:* Deep-fried mashed potato patties and masala garnished with chopped onion, chutney, cilantro, and chilies.

6. *Pakora or Bhaji:* Chickpea batter-dipped vegetables deep-fried and served with chutney.

7. *Puri Subzie or Curry:* Cooked potatoes dressed with gravy.

8. *Dahi Bhalla:* Deep-fried dal patties marinated overnight in yogurt and garnished with chaat masala and chutney.

9. *Fruit:* Guava, banana, apple, or melon chunks sprinkled with chaat masala.

10. *Kebabs:* Chunks of beef, chicken, or lamb marinated in yogurt and spices, slid onto skewers, and grill-roasted in a tandoori oven.

CHUNKY CHAAT MASALA

Look for boxes of this unique seasoning mix made with *amchoor* (dried mango powder), dried pomegranate seeds, ground cumin and coriander, sulfury black salt, powdered ginger, ground red chili, salt, and black pepper. Pregnant Indian princesses, lacking appetites for food during hot weather, were enticed to the table with dainty chunks of watermelon sprinkled with chaat masala.

BELOVED BHELPURI CHAAT

Originally Gujarati fast, street food, this iconic street snack consists of puffed rice; very thin, fried chickpea noodles (*sev*), potatoes, and tamarind chutney. Travel to West Indian beaches of Mumbai and you'll find numerous roadside hawkers (*chaatwallas*) selling versions with cilantro chutney, dal, tomatoes, cilantro, grated coconut, diced mango, onions, green chilies, and mustard oil. To make *bhelpuri chaat*, toss puffed rice, boiled grated potato, and sev from your nearest Indian market as a base. Dress with chopped tomato, cilantro, onion, cucumber, cooked beans, and cilantro

FIGURE 4.30 Bhelpuri.
Source: highviews/Shutterstock.

or tamarind chutney. Pile it on a plate and eat fast—bhelpuri loses its crunch quickly.

REVIEW QUESTIONS

1. From what ancient philosophy did Indian cuisine evolve?

2. Name two differences between south and north Indian food.

3. What are the four ingredients that make up an Indian "mirepoix"?

4. What is tempering? How may it be used?

5. What is a masala?

6. Name four key fats used in Indian cuisine.

7. Discuss the techniques for preparing a northern versus southern style curry dish.

UNIT II

EUROPE AND THE WESTERN MEDITERRANEAN

CHAPTER FIVE

FRANCE: CONFLICT, CULTURE, AND CREATIVITY ON A CROSSROADS

This chapter will:

- Introduce the fascinating history of France, its geography, cultural influences, and climate.
- Reveal how and why France became the world's most revered and respected culinary capital.
- Introduce French culinary culture and dining etiquette, important techniques that French chefs have codified, and the dishes of the twelve culinary regions of France.
- Identify important French foods, flavor foundations, seasoning devices, and favored cooking techniques.
- Offer recipes for some of the important dishes of regional France.

Northwest France

North, Northeast, & North Central

East & Center

Southeast France

West & South

Central France

North France

Northeast France

Eastern France

Southern France

Central & Southwest

North Central France

FIGURE 5.1 Map of France.

The Beauty of France

French cooking teacher and author Anne Willan writes eloquently about French cuisine. She maintains that France "leads the fight against conformity" in regard to food. She describes her local village and farmer's market, which likely arose during Roman times, with admiration and affection. Willan's market offers a large choice of fresh produce, cheeses, sausages, and pâtés prepared "by a retired policeman," fresh-picked wild mushrooms and maybe a boar leg. She calls it "inspiration and indulgence for a whole week of feasting." In her many cookbooks Willan celebrates her good fortune for having migrated to France from England.

France contains the largest land area in Western Europe and is surrounded by the Mediterranean Sea, Spain, the Atlantic, Andorra, Monaco, Belgium, Luxemborg, Germany, Switzerland, and Italy. This beautiful country, slightly smaller than Texas, offers a range of geography, climate, history, food, and culture that no other country in Europe possesses.

Some might reduce France down to the Eiffel Tower, the Louvre, Notre Dame Cathedral, the extravagant châteaux of Loire, southern Provençal olive trees and lavender fields, the rocky but seafood-rich shores of Normandy and Brittany, the prolific chalky-soil vineyards of Bordeaux and Burgundy, and the cool, sparsely-inhabited eastern alpine meadows of the Alps. But France is too rich, too complex, and too varied to be summarized in these few images.

Paleolithic remains and cave paintings in Dordogne indicate the first communities in the area of modern-day France dated from 25,000 years ago. The first features of a social and political landscape appeared 6,000 years ago with the Neolithic culture. Early cultures clashed, fought, and traded. They eventually connected the Atlantic and the Mediterranean through trade well before the Celts arrived around 1500 BCE. The Celtic Gauls inhabited the land until 500 BCE, and it was known as *Gaul.*

France's location made it a crossroads of trade, travel, settlement, and invasion. The rich land, abundant with lakes and navigable rivers, surrounded by ocean, channel, and sea, made it desirable for Greeks, Phoenicians, English, and Romans. From 57 BCE to 52 BCE, Roman emperor Julius Caesar conquered part of Gaul until the fifth century when, during the fall of the Western Roman Empire, the Franks, a Germanic people, conquered the land. The name *France* is from the Latin *Francia* or "country of the Franks."

During the *Middle Ages* (fifth to fifteenth century), France endured numerous, bloody wars. The 843 Treaty of Verdun divided the territory into France, Germany, and Italy. The Frankish *Capetian Dynasty* (987 to 1328) made France the most powerful land in Europe: they established Paris as capital of the kingdom, increased the royal domain forty times, and made Paris Europe's cultural and intellectual center. During Capetian reign, the French Crusades set off in 1095 to take up arms against "infidels," desecrating their Holy Land shrines. The Crusades, though violent, set up an interchange between East (Islam) and West (Christian) of Arabic cooking methods, political and social ideas, and goods like silk, spices, produce, dyes, figs, oils, and gems.

At the end of the *Hundred Years' War* (1453) with England, France finally gained Burgundy and Brittany to create an approximation of modern-day France. The Valois monarchy (1328 to 1559) made economic progress, and awakened France to the lure of Italy with the arts, and foods like asparagus, melons, and artichokes. Florentine princess Catherine de' Médici, married Valois heir Henry II. Her chefs continued the French culinary style established in the late Middle Ages, which merged Roman, Germanic, and Arab influences.

Centuries of costly and violent domestic and foreign wars over religion and civil and social order followed. Unrelenting displays of sumptuous dining in the French court of Sun King Louis XIV brought changes to haute cuisine: dining in courses and the fork. Enormous expenditures, disparities in wealth, high taxes, and famine due to shortages of grain and bread caused the privileged classes and common people to revolt.

The French Revolution (1789 to 1799) became a period of radical social and political upheaval. During this time many former royal chefs began to open restaurants. In 1792 the French people claimed themselves a republic. The French Revolutionary Wars between France and European monarchies finally led to the French monarchy's downfall. Louis XVI was executed in 1793. General Napoléan Bonaparte led the French Revolution to victory and in 1799 named himself first consul and, eventually, emperor. His abdication and exile in 1814 came as a result of his defeat in the Franco-Prussian War.

World War II saw France divided by German Nazi occupation; Allied forces liberated her and Charles de Gaulle headed a new French Union. War with the rebelling French colonies of Vietnam (French Indochina) and Algeria finally ended, and the French protectorates of Morocco and Tunisia received independence in 1956. Today France is a principal member in the United Nations, the European Union, and NATO, and has become a powerful economic, cultural, military, and political influence.

LANGUAGE, PHILOSOPHY, AND RELIGION

Though French is the official (and highly protected) language of France, certain regions speak dialects like Basque, Catalan, Picard, Norman, Franco-Provençal, Dutch, and Occitan.

About 80 percent of the French population is Roman Catholic, 10 percent Muslim, largely of North African descent, less than 2 percent Protestant and around 1 percent Jewish; the remainder are nonreligious. France is home to the largest Muslim and Jewish populations in Europe.

GEOGRAPHY AND CLIMATE—L'HÉXAGONE

The French call their country *l'héxagone* (hexagon) because of its six-sided shape; it is also a symbol for the country. Three-fourths of France is a triangular great plain from the Rhine River to Brittany and south to the Pyrénées. Deep river valleys, high plateaus, and low hills cut through it. Four rivers flow through France—the Seine, the Loire, the Garonne, and the Rhône. The Rhine runs for about 100 miles along France's eastern border.

The French island of Corsica lies in the Mediterranean, about 115 miles east-southeast of Nice. Mont Blanc (15,781 feet), in the Alps near the Italian and Swiss borders, is Western Europe's highest point; the forest-covered Vosges Mountains are in the northeast, and the Pyrénées tower along the Spanish border.

France has four climate zones. In the west and Atlantic coast, a temperate, *maritime climate* prevails with mild winters, cool summers, and frequent rainfall half the year. The *interior climate* has hot summers and cold winters with moderate rainfall. The eastern and *mountain climate* has long, bitter winters with snow. The southern *Mediterranean climate* has hot, dry summers with mild and humid winters and few rainy days.

FARMING AND AGRICULTURE

France holds about one-third of the agricultural land in the European Union and is its leading food producer and the *world's second largest agricultural producer* after the United States. Northern France has large wheat farms, the west is known for fine dairy products, pork, poultry, apples, and apple products like hard cider and Calvados. Central France produces the most beef; central and southern France produces an abundance of fruits, vegetables, and wine. Coastal regions have fishing industries. The French have worked the land, taming, culturing, polishing, and shaping their natural environment for more than 2,000 years. Genuine wilderness, though scarce, still exists in the Alps.

REGIONAL EUROPE

Northern and Southern Europe

France and Italy have two distinct cuisines, lifestyles, and cultures: southern and northern. The climate and the peoples who passed through formed them. Spain, Portugal, southern Italy, southern France, and Greece make up sunny, Mediterranean-hugged Southern Europe with its reliance on olive oil, wine, wheat, citrus fruits, almonds, pine nuts, almonds, and abundant seafood. Phoenician, Arabic, Greek, and Roman influences predominate. Seasonings like anchovies, capers, anise, fennel, and saffron unite this area.

Colder Northern Europe, with its German, Austro-Hungarian, and Celtic influences, relies more heavily on lard, butter, cheese, meats like pork, beef and game, beans, and produce that does well in four-season climates, like apples, pears, cabbage, root vegetables, and greens. Wine, mustard, caraway, thyme, tarragon, bay leaf, parsley, and sage are common seasonings.

French, Italian, and Spanish dishes have many similarities, but with noticeable differences in seasoning, preparation, and presentation. The differences are the results of the best kind of improvisation—one that bends methods, foods, and dishes introduced by immigrants or invaders to local, seasonal ingredients and culinary know-how.

For instance, fish soups and stews are popular throughout France, Italy, and Spain from the French *bouilliabaise* seasoned with tomato and fennel, to Italian *zuppa di pesce* with tomato, garlic, and parsley, and Spanish *gazpachuelo*, seafood chowder with egg, lemon, Serrano ham, and sherry. All three countries love crusty-brown potatoes—Italians pan-roast cubed potatoes and toss with anchovies and garlic, French cooks deep-fry potatoes in duck fat, and Spanish cooks prepare *patatas bravas*—golden, olive-oil fried potato cubes with spicy tomato sauce. Whether it's French *crudités* salads, Spanish *tapas*, or Italian *antipasti*, each cuisine has developed a way to enrich and enhance the fresh taste of the food that's around them.

FRENCH CUISINE: A NATIONAL CULINARY HABIT

France is the third largest country in Western Europe after Russia and Ukraine, but it is arguably first in agriculture and cuisine. Why did France become the queen of western cuisine, the pinnacle of gastronomy? The "prince of modern gastronomy," Maurice Edmond Sailland (pen name Curnonsky), once noted that to create a national culinary habit a country must have a *haute cuisine*—a grand gastronomy of chefs cooking for king, court, or restaurant, a *cuisine bourgeois*—the cooking of city folk with access to high-quality ingredients, and a *cuisine paysan*—a rustic country cooking of artisans who grow and harvest their own food. France excels in all three.

First and foremost, French people are tied to the land and devoted to fine eating from land, river, ocean, and sea. Their diet takes its meaning and direction from locally abundant food and centuries-old time-tested ancestral cooking that remains simple and seasonal, with quality, flavor, and freshness all-important.

The country, or *pays*, and its soil, or *terroir*, gave France natural advantages: France has more fertile soil in a temperate climate than anywhere in Europe. The Mediterranean Sea, English Channel, and Atlantic Ocean provide superior seafood. Quick, efficient distribution and food cultivated for flavor—not shelf life—harvested at peak, provide a remarkable, superior variety of food and beverages like cider, wine, butter, cream, cheese, poultry, meats, fruit, and vegetables. In short, the French have great reverence and respect for food and the good sense to eat it in season at its freshest.

Two strands of French cuisine continue to emerge and converge—*haute cuisine*, or restaurant cuisine, and the home-cooked *bourgeoise cuisine* or *cuisine de femme*—cuisine of women. Committed to top-quality ingredients and exploration, they provide creative inspiration for each other, a factor that has likely kept French cuisine fresh and vital. The philosophies and revolutions of French cuisine have profoundly influenced cooks around the world. Creative, skilled, strong-spirited home cooks and chefs, from La Varenne, Carême, Escoffier, Point, Bocuse, and beyond, continue to revolutionize French cuisine, while a country of appreciative diners supports their endeavors. Why France? Her people take food seriously and pay close passionate attention to every aspect of it.

CULINARY REGIONS OF FRANCE

Through migrations and conflicts, Celtic, Latin, Arabic, and Teutonic (Germanic-Frankish) peoples contributed to France's complex, diverse cuisine and the unique character of twenty-one mainland administrative areas plus Corsica that contain over *200 microclimates*. Each has a rich history, culture, agriculture, speech, and distinct gastronomy. Neighbors Italy, Spain, Belgium, Switzerland, and Germany share borders with France, and Britain is a short hop across the English Channel; their influences are woven into the fabric of French food. Denizens of Alsace-Lorraine eat German *choucroute garni*, in British/Celtic influenced Brittany you find *far*, a sweet Yorkshire pudding, and the mead-like *chouchenn*. Spain echoes in *cassoulet* from southwestern Toulouse, and in Provence there is a Mediterranean reliance on garlic and olive oil. Starting in the northwest and going clockwise through France, teacher and author Ann Willan accords France twelve important culinary regions. They are described in more detail later in this chapter.

1. **Northwest,** *Dangerous Coastline:* Brittany
2. **North,** *Dairy Pastureland, Norman Influences:* Normandy
3. **North, Northeast and North Center,** *Ancient Crossroads:* Nord Pas de Calais/Flanders, Paris and Île-de France, and Champagne

4. *Northeast, German Influences:* Alsace-Lorraine
5. *East and Center, Gastronomic Heart:* Burgundy, Dijon, and the Lyonnais
6. *East, Alpine Valleys, Dairy and Wine:* Franche-Comté, the Jura, Savoie, and the Rhone Alps
7. *Southeast, Mediterranean, Aromatic and Sun-Drenched:* Provence and the Cote-d'Azur
8. *South, Mediterranean Grape, Rice, and Seafood:* Languedoc-Roussillon
9. *West and South, Peppery and Proud:* Midi Pyrénées, Gascony, and Pays Basque
10. *Central and Southwest, Rich Cooking, Great Wine:* Aquitaine/Bordeaux, Perigord, and Poitou-Charents
11. *Central, Mountains and Volcanic Plateau, Peasant Fare:* Auvergne and Massif Central
12. *North Central, Cradle of Culture, Garden of France:* Centre and Val de Loire

DINE AT A HOME IN FRANCE

Meals are an integral part of French family life so the dining table is central to a French home. When dining at someone's home, dress with care, no sneakers, plunging necklines, or revealing clothes, but good-quality fabric and stylish clothing. It is most courteous to show up late—at least 10 minutes. Bring a small gift like chocolate, but not soap, wine, or flowers. Send flowers before or after the meal.

Follow the hosts in all things. When seated, wait for the hostess to place the napkin on her lap. When the aperitif is served, wait for the host to toast before drinking. Make eye contact and say, *santé* (san-TAY). Allow the hosts to serve wine; it's impolite to study wine labels. Keep hands and wrists, but not arms or elbows, on the table.

The breadbasket, wine bottle, and mineral water are essential elements on the French table. Place bread on the tablecloth for informal meals or on bread plate for a formal meal. The French break bread into small pieces before placing in the mouth. Cut meat, fish, vegetables, and fruit with knife in the right hand and a fork in the left. Cut only one bite at a time. Fold lettuce onto a fork; don't cut it.

A traditional three to five course dinner or Sunday lunch lasts two to four hours, or longer in the country. It's likely that no processed or ready-made food will appear; instead the hosts will prepare fresh, local meat and produce and purchase fresh baguettes daily. A French dinner often consists of *appetizer* like a terrine, sautéed mushrooms, or *paté*, possibly a fish course, the *entrée* or main course, *salade verte* or lettuce with vinaigrette, a *cheese course* with at least three cheeses, *dessert* like fresh or candied fruit, *crème brulée*, chocolate *mousse*, cherry *clafoutis*, or apple *tart Tatin* and lastly, *coffee*. Each course will be passed. Take small a small portion. Leaving food on the plate is an insult. Try *everything* whether it's frog legs, escargot, blood sausage, *fois gras*, raw sea urchin, or tripe. Those with a serious food allergy should speak up ahead of time. Otherwise, eat up. Leave the wineglass nearly full when finished drinking.

During dinner don't discuss money, politics, religion, or recipes. When yawning or coughing, cover the mouth. When leaving a dinner seat temporarily, place the napkin on the chair, not the table. When done eating, fold the napkin and set it on table. It's good manners to thank the host and hostess.

TASTES OF FRANCE

Fat: Butter, sunflower seed oil, peanut oil, olive oil, corn oil, canola or rapeseed oil, grapeseed oil; walnut, hazelnut, pistachio, pine nut, almond oil, cream, milk, crème fraiche, yogurt

Sweet: Sugar, many types of honey like chestnut, blossom, heather, and rosemary

Sour/Alcohol: White wine vinegar, red wine vinegar, cider vinegar, lemon, orange, liqueurs, white and red wine

Salty: Sea salt, Dijon mustard, coarse-grained, violet mustard, olive paste

Spicy-Hot: Black, green, and white pepper, cayenne pepper, paprika, chilies

Spice: White licorice, coriander, cinnamon, clove, aniseed, cumin, star anise

Aromatic Seasoning Vegetables: Onion, carrots, celery, leeks, shallots, garlic, ginger

Herbs, Seasonings, and Condiments: Italian parsley, tarragon, chives, rosemary, bay leaves, thyme, sage, summer savory, marjoram, oregano, fennel, basil, lavender, verbena, chervil, mint

Other Important Foods: *Lentilles du Puy* (French green lentils), white beans, wheat, couscous, Carmargue red rice, walnuts, hazelnuts, almonds, pine nuts, chestnuts, fruit (apples, pears, cherries, peaches, blueberries, raspberries, strawberries, grapes, and plums), mushrooms, truffles, endive, leeks, Espelette pepper, fennel, beets, artichokes, white and green asparagus, celery root, tomatoes, leafy greens, mache, watercress, Belgian endive, Swiss chard, arugula, Burgundian meat (Charolais beef, Bresse chicken, goose, duck, foie gras, pork, wild game, rabbit, *saucisson* [sausages], hams, turkey, quail, guinea fowl, pigeon, capon, cured meat, and sausage), seafood (mussels, *escargots* [snails], oysters, lobster, shrimp, and many varieties of fish), chocolate

Famous Dishes: Crêpes Suzettes, *brandade* (salt-cod mousse), quiche Lorraine, *cassoulet* (rich bean stew), *bouilliabaisse* (fish soup), fois gras terrine, *paté* (savory meat loaf, sometimes in pastry), *babas au rhum* (rich rum-soaked yeast cakes), *bisque* (rice-thickened, creamy soup), *beignets* (sweet fritters), *daube* (Provençal beef stew), *ratatouille* (braised summer vegetables), baguette, *brioche* (egg-rich yeast bread), *croissant* (crescent-shaped buttery, crisp pastry), *gougere* (baked cheese-flavored choux pastries), *mousse* (sweet or savory airy mixture), *madeleine* (small shell-shaped sponge cake), *petit fours* (small two bite cakes), *quenelles* (poached fish or poultry mousseline ovals), *pot-au-feu* (soupy vegetable meat stew), *millas* (thick cornmeal porridge)

Drinks: Wine, hard cider, beer, liquor, various liqueurs, mineral water, tea, coffee, tisanes, cassis

COMMON FRENCH COOKING TOOLS

Chef's knife, pots, sauté pans, and saucepans, fish poachers, strainers, and many other useful items

FRENCH CHEESE (FROMAGE)

French cheese is protected by law and is classified under four categories:

- **Fermier:** Farmhouse cheese produced with milk from farm where cheese is made
- **Artisanal:** Small producer using their own milk or milk from nearby farms
- **Coopérative:** Local milk producers' dairy joined together to produce cheese
- **Industriel:** Factory-made cheese from local or regional French milk sourced locally, depending the regulations for a specific cheese

FIGURE 5.2 French cheese at Provençal market.
Source: ecobo/Fotolia.

Cheeses vary, among other details, depending on the milk—the animal and what it eats (winter hay or summer grass); how the rind is developed (washed, salted, herbed, or ash-covered), how long it ages and where (different fermentation bacteria exist in differing climates and regions). France has more than fifty protected cheeses. These a few top favorites:

Camembert (Normandy): A soft, creamy, buttery cow milk cheese with a thin white rind. Heating destroys Camembert's texture and flavor.

Brie de Meaux (Île de France): Soft, white-crusted, raw cow milk cheese with a soft, creamy, nutty-tasting interior. The slightly chalky-tasting brie becomes runny with age.

Roquefort (Midi-Pyrénées): A rindless, salty, white sheep milk bleu cheese with a tangy flavor that goes from mild to sweet, smoky then salty. It is crumbly and slightly moist, with veins of green mold.

French Feta: See *Greek Cheese*. French feta came about because of an excess of sheep milk for Roquefort production. French feta is milder, creamier, and less salty than the Bulgarian or Greek fetas. For true feta lovers, tangy Greek feta is still the best.

Fromage Blanc (Fromage Frais): This is a fresh, soft, creamy white cheese made from whole or skim cow milk that is heated and curded with a direct-setting cheese culture for 12 hours. The curds are drained in a warm spot 6 to 12 hours, depending on desired consistency. This cheese is eaten fresh and used in cooking; dieters substitute it for cream because it has less calories and cholesterol. It has the texture of crème fraîche—thick and spreadable. In France, fromage blanc comes in two styles: fromage blanc *campagnard* (similar to cottage cheese) and fromage blanc *lissé* (whisked smooth). The French like to pair it with pears and honey.

Reblochon (Savoie): A nutty-tasting, washed-rind cow milk cheese with a soft, uniform center and fine white mold covering its crust. Reblochon is used in *tartiflette*, a Savoyard gratin made with potatoes, cream, onions, and ham.

Munster (Lorraine Region): An unpasteurized, semi-soft, white cow milk cheese washed in brine with an orange rind with an assertive, deep, rich, tangy flavor complemented by a strong, barnyardy aroma.

Pont l'Evèque (Normandy): A cow milk cheese with a soft, washed rind that is white and delicately brown with a fine-textured, tender, creamy interior. It is unpasteurized and not pressed, with a pungent aroma and savory, buttery, and mild grassy flavor.

Chèvre: A goat milk cheese made in various ways—cured for several days for the popular rindless soft logs—to longer for firmer chévres with rinds of ash, salt-washed, leaf-covered, and more. France produces many: *Bucheron* (log-shaped), *Chabis, Clochette, Couronne Lochoise, Crottin de Chavignol, Pélardon, Picodon, Pouligny Saint-Pierre, Rocamadour, Sainte-Maure de Touraine, Chabichou du Poitou, Valençay,* and *Pyramide*. Young chévres are sweet, earthy and slightly tart, and soft and flaky. *Bucherondin de Chévre* (*buche* means log) from Poitou-Charentes is semi-soft, dense and flaky, with a mild flavor that sharpens with age.

Cantal (Auvergne): One of the oldest cheeses in France, it is a semi-hard cheese with a soft interior made two ways: from either raw or pasteurized milk of winter-hay fed cows. Reminiscent of Cheddar, it has a sweet, earthy tang and buttery taste that strengthens with age.

Comté (Franche-Comté): A semi-hard cow milk cheese, aged 4 to 24 months (typically 12 months) with a dusty-brown salted rind and pale, creamy interior. Its taste is strong and delicately sweet with hints of apricot, chocolate, butter, cream, and grilled bread.

FIGURE 5.3 Variety of dry sausages.
Source: Pierdelune/Shutterstock.

FRENCH WINE AND OTHER ALCOHOLIC DRINKS

Most French people consider wine as the lifeblood of a meal. French vineyards produce all the known styles of wine: red, rosé, white, sparkling, and fortified. The French labeling system is based on geography rather than, as in the New World, by major type of grape. Two concepts are important to good French wine: *terroir* and the *AOC system*. Terroir takes into account the earth and climate of a region. In France this produces wines with animal and earth overtones and less obvious fruitiness. Therefore, French wines are designed to pair particularly well with food, but are not as drinkable alone.

The Appellation d'Origine Contrôlée (AOC) system oversees and approves specific grape varieties and wine-making practices for specific regions, villages, or vineyards. France's AOC system protects and classifies wine into four main grades:

AOC (Appellation d'Origine Contrôlée) or regulated wine of origin: This is the highest rank. The vineyard areas, grape yields, varietals, blends of varietals, alcohol content, and bottling within the region are highly controlled. Bottles display geographic designations.

VDQS (Vins Délimités de Qualité Supérieure) or delimited wine of superior quality: This is a rank with a minor level of production. Its wines are waiting to be elevated to AOC. Production is not as strict as AOC, but these wines hold promise and are working to be noticed.

Vin de Pays (Country Wine): Less controlled than the previous two categories, these regional wines are produced widely throughout the country. The larger geographic region and varietals are often designated. They can offer good value.

(Continued)

(Continued)

Vin de Table (Table Wine): This wine sees the least amount of control and is the lowest quality wine. Grapes are grown anywhere in France and require no geographic designation. This category is slowly disappearing; its wines are traditionally consumed locally or distilled.

Top French Wine-Growing Regions

As the second largest wine producer in the world (Spain and Italy vie for first), there are numerous wine-growing regions in France. In *The Essentials of Wine*, John P. Laloganes divides the wine-growing regions of France into three broad areas and seven significant wine regions for world-class wine; each region specializes in certain varieties according to climate, soil, law, and tradition.

The top producers are in this order: Languedoc-Roussillon, Bordeaux, Rhône, Loire, Burgundy, Champagne, and Alsace. Other important regions are Beaujolais, Corsica, Jura, Provence, Savoy, and the Southwest.

One: Northeastern France

Alsace

A region that is squeezed between France and Germany, Alsace shows many German influences in its mainly white wines. The wine has been described as austerely Germanic with a French joie de vivre—German grapes with French winemaking style. White varietals are Riesling, Gewürztraminer, Pinot Gris, and Pinot Blanc. The red varietal is Pinot Noir. Alsace also produces sparkling and dessert wine.

Burgundy

Located in the north-central region of France, this region is plagued with capricious weather. When the weather cooperates, Burgundy can produce memorable wines. White varietals are Chardonnay. Red varietals are Pinot Noir and Gamay.

Champagne

This northern region also has unpredictable weather, but it manages to produce the best sparkling wines in France.

Winemakers combine grape varieties to maintain consistency. White varietals include Chardonnay and red varietals include Pinot Noir and Pinot Meunier.

Two: Western France

Bordeaux

This vast, cool region has the ideal gravel and clay soil to produce its elegant, powerful wines. It is famous for "classifed growth" wines. White varietals include Sauvignon Blanc, Sémillon, and Muscadelle. Red varietals include Cabernet Sauvignon, Merlot, Cabernet Franc, Petit Verdot, and Malbec. Bordeaux also produces dessert wines.

Loire Valley

This region near the chilly Atlantic coast produces mainly white wines like Muscadet, Sauvignon Blanc, and Chenin Blanc. Its red varietals include Cabernet Franc and Cot or Malbec. The Loire also produces dessert and sparkling wines.

Three: Mid-Central and Mediterranean France

Rhône Valley

This region is divided into north and south. The cooler north typically produces strong, spicy reds with Syrah grapes and whites made with Viognier, Marsanne, and Roussanne grapes. The warm south produces ripe, soft, luscious wines with less acid, higher sugar, and higher alcohol that are blends of Genache and Mourvèdre.

Languedoc-Roussillon and Provence

This region, which stretches along the Mediterranean coast, was long known for producing the most wine, but commercial, mediocre wine, in France. Because of the heat the grapes are less acidic with higher sugar and alcohol content. In the last few decades the quality has improved. White varietals include Chardonnay and Grenache Blanc. Red varietals include Grenache, Mourvedre, and Syrah. This region also produces famed versions of fortified wines.

Other Alcoholic Drinks

These drinks are popular for reduction sauces or glazes, apéritifs and digestifs.

Cognac (ko-nyack)

Cognac is made in the region of Charentes in the city of Cognac. Twice-distilled fermented grape juice or *eau de vie* is aged from two to six years in oak casks. As the eau de vie ages, it loses alcohol and water through evaporation. After aging cognac must be 40 percent alcohol by volume. The eau de vie is usually higher so it is blended again to lower its alcohol content.

Armagnac (ar-man-yack)

This distinctive brandy is produced in the Armagnac region of Gascony in southwest France. It is distilled from wine usually made from a blend of white wine grapes using column stills rather than the pot stills used for Cognac. The spirit is aged in black oak barrels before release. Armagnac is distilled once and cognac is distilled twice. Armagnac spends more time in oak barrels, which gives it more finesse and roundness with a bouquet of vanilla, toffee, nougat, pepper, rose, and chocolate.

Calvados (kal-vah-dohz)

Calvados is an apple brandy made in Normandy. It is distilled into an eau de vie from fermented, dry apple cider made from more than 100 apple varieties. It is aged in French oak barrels at least two years, and blended before bottling. Longer aging produces a smoother drink. Reminiscent of apples and pears, Calvados is often served as an apéritif, in cocktails, in sorbet or cooking, as a digestif after a meal, or with coffee.

Cider (Cidre)

The deep amber and aggressively carbonated French cider of Normandy is pressed from ripe, pectin-rich bitter, sweet-bitter, sweet, and acidic varieties of apples. French cider, made from unsweetened, fermented apple juice, often offers more sweetness due to *keeving*, the process of slowing fermentation through enzymatic activity. Full-bodied, sweeter French ciders pair well with cream-based sauces, white meats, or rich cassoulet. The drier, more champagne-like ciders pair well with flaky fish and creamy cheeses.

FRENCH FLAVOR FOUNDATIONS

In European cooking, flavor often builds from the bottom of a pan up—first from the base of an aromatic sauté, on up to simmering and seasoning, and ending with top garnish. French chefs have discovered and developed many ways to enrich flavor. *Mirepoix, caramelized onions*, and mushroom *duxelles* are three beloved aromatic vegetable combos. Infused broths, oils, vinegars, compound butters, and herbal mixtures are also part of the French flavor repertoire.

French Signature Aromatic Vegetable Combo: Mirepoix (meer-pwah)

Mirepoix: Diced onion, carrot, and celery
A mirepoix is the most basic of flavoring bases for soups, stocks, sauces, stews, and braises. Sometimes the white of leek, or in a *classic mirepoix*—ham, will be added. Onions and leeks give off the most flavor, carrots add sweetness, and celery, a slight, refreshing bitterness.

The size and cut of the mirepoix depends on the dish and how it will be cooked. The size also determines how the flavor will be perceived: small-diced vegetables tend to marry flavors and large diced vegetables tend to stay more individual.

- **Roasting and long stewing:** large dice (3/4- to 1-inch or larger)
- **Shorter cooking dishes and sautés:** medium dice (1/2-inch) small dice (1/4-inch)
- **Garnish and raw dishes:** brunoise dice (1/8-inch)

*Basic Mirepoix Proportions

2 parts diced onion

1 part diced carrot

1 part diced celery

Optional: 1 to 2 parts diced white and pale green leek parts

- **Matignon or Classic Mirepoix:** Add 1/2 part diced ham

Signature Seasonings

Liquid/Paste

See *French Wine and Other Alcoholic Drinks*. Many of these alcoholic products are used to prepare sauces and deglaze sautés.

Dijon Mustard (Moutarde de Dijon) and Moutarde à L'ancienne

Moutarde de Dijon, a creamy mustard, was originally made with finely ground brown or black mustard seed. To be labeled Dijon, it adheres to a formula developed over 150 years ago in Dijon, France. Finely ground seeds are mixed with an acidic liquid (vinegar, wine, and/or grape must) and seasoned with salt and sometimes a spice. Dijon is smooth and bright-tasting with a clean, nose-tingling heat. Moutarde a l'ancienne is the grainy Dijon. Both intensify flavors and are particularly good in salad dressings and in sauces for meat and fish.

Animal

Anchovies

These small fish are preserved by being gutted and salted in brine, matured for 6 to 10 months in barrels, then packed in cans or jars in oil or in salt or puréed into paste. The maturation process results in the characteristic strong flavor of anchovies. Anchovies play an important role in the French *anchoiade* (warm purée of anchovy, olive oil, and vinegar), *remoulade* (mayonnaise sauce), and *tapenade* (olives, anchovies, capers, and lemon juice). (See chapter *Spain*, section *Signature Seasonings* for more on Spanish anchovies and

FIGURE 5.4 Fresh anchovy.
Source: antonio scarpi/Fotolia.

FIGURE 5.5 Preserved a anchovy fillets.
Source: Jiri Hera/Fotolia.

chapter *Italy*, section *Signature Seasonings* for Sicilian anchovies.)

Vegetable/Fruit

Capers

A favorite of Mediterranean cooking, capers are small unopened buds of the Mediterranean bush, *Capparis spinosa L.*, closely related to the cabbage family, but they look more like a rose bush. Caper bushes grow wild and are also cultivated throughout the Mediterranean. Pickled in vinegar or preserved in salt (which brings out their flavor), European cooks consider the smallest capers (*nonpareilles*) the best. Capers have a sharp, mustard-like, peppery flavor, which add tang to vinaigrette, sauces, salads, and meat and fish dishes. Cooks in the Mediterranean pair them with anchovies. Use capers whole, crushed, or chopped. Rinse salted capers to remove excess salt, or drain pickled capers—save the salty caper pickling liquid for use in sauces and dressings.

Leeks (Poireaux)

The leek is a long cylindrical vegetable in the lily/onion family that looks like a giant green onion, but its flavor is sweeter and mellower than most onions. Its width can range from 1/2 inch to almost 2 inches. The white of the leek is most flavorful, but both the mild green and white can be eaten. Leeks give great flavor in whatever dish they are cooked. They pair particularly well with potatoes and vegetables and are particularly good in short braises and soup.

FIGURE 5.6 Leeks.
Source: PRILL/Shutterstock.

Shallots (Eschalot)

Bordeaux is known for shallots. The region grows three types: gray, purple-red, and white. Gray are the most prized. Unlike onions, the three are similar in flavor. Much smaller than an onion and larger than a clove of garlic, the intensity of a shallot's flavor falls in between. Shallots tend to be stronger but sweeter than

(Continued)

(Continued)

onions and are often used raw in vinaigrettes. When browned too far, shallots become bitter.

Herbal/Spice

Basil

Basil, a delicate herb in the mint family, originated in India. Though its flavor varies depending on the variety, basil has a distinct anise taste and strong, alluring fragrance. Because of its delicate nature most French cooks add basil as a garnish and refrain from cooking it.

Bay Leaf

A spicy, fragrant leaf of the bay laurel tree, French cooks use fresh or dried leaves in stock, soup, braised dishes, and patés. It is an important part of the bouquet garni.

Chervil

This delicate herb has a mild flavor of licorice/anise. It is in the parsley family and resembles Italian parsley, but is a paler green with finer, fronded leaves. Chervil is part of the mixture *fines herbes* and flavors béarnaise sauce. It pairs well with mild foods like sole and other white fish, chicken, eggs, and zucchini, as well as salads, sauces, and soups. Its flavor is best fresh; add it near the end of cooking.

FIGURE 5.7 Red/purple shallot.
Source: Ian O'Leary/DK Images.

Espelette Chili-Pepper (Piment d'Espelette)

This Appellation Controlled special, small, pointy and red French pepper is grown in Espelette near the Spanish-Basque territory where it is central to the cuisine. It has less heat than cayenne, but has a robust, lightly smoky flavor. The pepper may be purchased dried and ground.

FIGURE 5.8 Chervil.
Source: Roger Phillips/DK Images.

FIGURE 5.9 Basque espelette pepper.
Source: peapop/Fotolia.

FIGURE 5.10 Sorrel.
Source: Roger Phillips/DK Images.

Sorrel

A large green-leafed vegetable-herb with a pleasant, tart, lemony taste, sorrel is one of the first spring arrivals. Sorrel was developed in Italy and France in the Middle Ages. In French cuisine, it is frequently puréed in soups and sauces or mixed with potatoes, eggs, or other vegetables.

French Tarragon

Tall and bushy with slender stems filled with long narrow leaves, this spicy, aromatic herb with hints of anise pairs well with eggs, tomatoes, and poultry. It is found in fines herbes mixture and sauce Bearnaise and is often infused into vinegar or oil. Overuse can overpower a dish.

Thyme

French cooks pair this woody, meaty-flavored herb with lamb, tomatoes, eggs, and meat, and it's part of the bouquet garni. Whole stems with their small round leaves flavor stock, beans, stews, and soup. Varieties of thyme vary, but common or French thyme is the best for cooking.

FRENCH MUSHROOMS AND FUNGUS (CHAMPIGNONS)

Although more than 3,000 mushroom varieties grow wild in France, only a small fraction are edible. More mushrooms grow in the south of France from Aquitaine in the west to the Alpes-Maritimes in the east because of climate. These are the royalty of French mushrooms. All grow wild except champignons de Paris, which are cultivated.

Black Trumpet or Black Chanterelle: This tall vase-shaped mushroom, closely related to the chanterelle, looks like a gray or black version of that mushroom. French cooks consider black chanterelles choice with their intense, nutty flavor.

Cépes (Boletus or Porcini): Fresh, this pale brown mushroom looks a little like a toadstool with caps ranging from 1- to 10-inch diameter. Cépes are prized for their strong, meaty flavor and juicy, velvety-smooth texture. They may be served raw or cooked and are available dried.

Champignons de Paris (White, Crimini, or Portobello): This common supermarket mushroom is meaty when cooked and delicately nutty raw. It varies in color from white (champignons de Paris) and light brown (crimini) to the older, dark brown (portobello). The older portobello is much stronger flavored with very dark, inky gill. Sizes vary from button to jumbo, but white and crimini are dome-shaped; portobellos tend to flatten. Look for white and crimini with tightly closed gills.

Girolles or Golden Chanterelle: These vase-shaped mushrooms are nutty and fruity-aromatic and range in flavor from delicate to mildly peppery. They range from yellow to orange-colored. A very choice fresh mushroom.

Pieds de Mouton (Sheep's Feet or Hedgehog): This mushroom has an irregular shape and an indented, funnel-like cap that can range from 1- to 5-inch diameter. Its color ranges from white to orange. The inner flesh is bright white, sweetly aromatic, somewhat dry, and tastes similar to a chanterelle. These mushrooms are best slow-cooked. It

FIGURE 5.14 Pieds de mouton mushroom.
Source: coco/Fotolia.

is peppery and bitter when raw and should be used fresh.

Pleurote (Oyster): This soft beige, brown or gray mushrooms has a fluted, fan-like cap. The larger caps deliver more flavor. Oyster mushrooms may be eaten raw but when cooked they become velvety, and a delicate flavor, that some say resembles oysters, emerges. The flavor varies from mild to strong with an anise scent depending on when it is harvested.

Morelles (Black Morels) This mushroom is related to the truffle and shares its pronounced earthy, yeasty, nutty flavor. The color ranges from tan to dark brown; the darker the mushroom, the

FIGURE 5.11 Black trumpet or black chanterelle mushroom.
Source: Sébastien Garcia/Fotolia.

FIGURE 5.12 Cépes mushroom.
Source: morchella/Fotolia.

FIGURE 5.13 Golden chanterelle mushroom.
Source: Diana Miller/DK Images.

FIGURE 5.15 Oyster mushroom.
Source: Neil Fletcher/DK Images.

(Continued)

(Continued)

FIGURE 5.16 Morel mushrooms.
Source: Neil Fletcher/DK Images.

stronger the flavor. Morels are cone-shaped and spongy with a dimpled head that can hide dirt and insects. It is available dried.

Mousseron (Fairy Ring) These small, thin-stemmed mushrooms have caps with very deep, lacy gills. They are golden colored with a soft, chewy texture and the scent and rich, nutty flavor close to porcini.

FIGURE 5.17 Mousseron mushroom.
Source: ChantalS/Fotolia.

Truffles, Black This earthy, umami-flavored underground fungus, usually the size of a walnut, carries mystery and prestige: Brillat-Savarin called it "the diamond of the kitchen." Because of their scarcity and high cost, truffles are used carefully and frugally: shaved paper-thin slices might be sprinkled over pasta, eggs, salad, or inserted into meat, stuffing, paté, or cheese. Truffles lose their flavor within a week so are preserved in cognac or oil. Commercially canned truffles are much less flavorful.

FIGURE 5.18 Black truffles.
Source: Ian O'Leary/DK Images.

Duxelles (*dook-cell*)

Mushrooms, high in umami-big-savory-flavor, give an intense jolt of flavor to stuffings, dips, grains, soup, or stew. *To yield 2 cups:* Finely dice 1 to 1-1/2 ounces shallots and 1 pound domestic mushrooms. Cook in butter or oil to oatmeal consistency, deglazing with 1/4 to 1/2 cup Port, sherry, or wine. Season with thyme or nutmeg, salt, and pepper. Improvise with wild mushrooms or shiitake.

SEASONING AND PASTE MIXTURES

Bouquet Garni (*bow-kay gar-nee*)

A typical bouquet garni bundle (or bouquet) is made of fresh or dried savory herbs and seasonings. Usually added at the beginning simmering to marinade, stock, soup, or stew, the bouquet garni imparts its flavor through long contact. The classic bouquet garni consists of 2 sprigs thyme, 1 bay leaf, and 4 parsley sprigs or stems wrapped in leek greens.

Persillade (*per-see-yad*)

Consisting of equal parts finely minced flat leaf parsley and garlic (seasoned with salt and pepper), persillade goes onto hot food toward the end of cooking to maintain a fresh, vibrant flavor. Italian cooks use a similar combo called gremolada with lemon zest. Spanish cooks call it a picada and sometimes add bread or nuts.

FINES HERBES (*FEEN ERBS*)

Sprinkle on hot dishes at the end of cooking, or cook mixture slightly. Good in vinaigrette, on omelets, eggs, in soup or delicate tasting dishes. No chervil? Double the tarragon.

Yields about 1/4 cup

1/4 ounce trimmed Italian parsley, 2 tablespoons minced
1/4 ounce chives, 2 teaspoons trimmed and finely sliced
1/4 ounce chervil, 2 teaspoons trimmed and minced
1/2 ounce tarragon, 2 teaspoons minced leaves

1 Mix together and use immediately.

HERBES DE PROVENCE

A Provençal dried herbal mixture used to marinate grilled fish or meat, simmered in vegetable or legume soups and stews, or to flavor savory dishes. Mix four or more: thyme, wild thyme, marjoram, oregano, rosemary, basil, chervil, savory, lavender, fennel, and bay leaf.

- *Simple Herbes de Provence* consists of 1 part dried marjoram, 1 part dried oregano, 2 parts dried thyme, and 1 part dried summer savory.

QUATRE ÉPICES (*KA-TER E-PEACE*)

Used for meat dishes: patés, terrines, sausage-making, slow-cooked beef stews, chicken, or pork. Some recipes call for equal parts of the four spices.

Yields about 3 tablespoons

2 tablespoons white or black peppercorns
1 teaspoon freshly grated nutmeg (or allspice)
1 teaspoon whole cloves
1/2 teaspoon ground cinnamon or ground ginger

1 Grind together and keep in airtight container.

CARAMELIZED ONIONS

Prepare caramelized onions ahead and freeze for a fast flavor enriching addition. Simmer in broth for onion soup or simmer with vinegar and sweetener for sweet-sour onion jam. Red onions yield deeper color.

Yields 1-1/2 cups

3 tablespoons unsalted butter
3 tablespoons extra virgin olive oil
3 pounds red or Spanish onions, about 12 cups peeled and thinly sliced
1/2 cup port or good red wine, more as needed

1 Heat butter and oil in heavy 6-quart (11-inch) pot over medium-low heat. Add onions and sprinkle with 1/2 teaspoon salt; cover. Sweat onions, stirring occasionally, until soft and juicy, 25 to 30 minutes.

2 Uncover onions and raise heat to medium-high. Stirring frequently, sauté until moisture evaporates. Pay attention. When the bottom of the pot collects caramelization, scrape off into onions. If sides of pot collect caramelization, scrape into onions, but lower heat slightly.

3 When caramelization speeds up, deglaze bottom of pot with small amounts of alcohol and scrape it into the onion mass. Let liquid evaporate fully before adding more.

4 Cook onions until evenly nut brown, 25 to 30 minutes, deglazing several times. Save 2 tablespoons liquor for the end.

5 Stir in last 2 tablespoons liquor and remove pan from heat, cover, and allow pan to rest 5 minutes. At this point use the onions, or cool and freeze, or refrigerate up to 4 days.

Vary! Improvise!

☞ *Sweet and Sour Onion Jam:* Add maple syrup, honey or brown sugar and red wine vinegar to cooked onions, to a larger-than-life sweet-sour taste, and simmer again until onions are thick.

☞ *Filling and Topping:* Mix onions with feta, bleu, or goat cheese and use as a savory stuffing for a tart, chicken breasts phyllo filling, or as a topping on toasts or *pissaladière*—a savory, Provençal caramelized onion tart layered with olives, anchovies, and thyme.

☞ *Apple Animation:* Deglaze onions with 1-1/2 cups sweet cider or 1/2 cup Calvados. Use as part of a filling for crêpes.

SAUCE

SIX FATHERS OF THE FRENCH REVOLUTION OF CUISINE

Before the nineteenth century, the best cuisine in France was found only in the homes of the aristocracy (privileged class). After the French Revolution with the diminishing nobility many chefs were out of jobs. The Revolution ultimately served to expand French cuisine: It abolished the restrictive guild system, which then allowed any chef to produce and sell any culinary item. Chefs opened restaurants that catered to the burgeoning middle class. Ordinary people began to look to the chefs to tell them what and how to eat.

François Pierre de la Varenne was the seventeenth-century author of *Le Cuisinier François*, the founding text of modern French cuisine, and several other culinary texts. La Varenne moved away from Italian traditions—lard to butter, bread to roux and heavy spices—that had revolutionized sixteenth-century medieval French cookery. La Varenne was head of a group of French chefs who wrote cookbooks for professionals. He revolutionized French cooking by codifying seventeenth-century French culinary innovations and food preparation systematically by rules and principals.

Marie Antoine Carême, the first celebrity chef, called the king of chefs or chef of kings, Carême first practiced high (haute) French cuisine, wrote several cookbooks, systematized sauces into four main *mother sauces*, espagnole, velouté, béchamel, and allemande (velouté with mushroom cooking liquid and egg yolk finish), and encouraged chefs to create new derivatives of them. He revolutionized dining through the change of service from all dishes on the table at once to each dish served separately in courses.

Auguste Escoffier simplified nineteenth-century French high cuisine in his essential book *Le Guide Culinaire*. The famed Escoffier standardized and transformed the mother sauces into espagnole, velouté, béchamel, tomato, and the lesser sauces, hollandaise and mayonnaise, and emphasized quality local ingredients prepared simply and directly.

Fernand Point started the nouvelle cuisine revolution in the mid-twentieth century.

Paul Bocuse worked under Point and carried on nouvelle cuisine. Point inspired and encouraged chefs:

- to invent
- to cook regional, local cuisines instead of an inflexible classical menu
- to free themselves from rigid French culinary rules
- to lighten the texture of sauces and dishes
- to simplify cooking techniques

Michel Guérard, in the 1970s, without sacrificing flavor, introduced lower-fat versions of classics in his revolutionary book, *Cuisine Minceur*:

- by preparing sauces without cream, butter, or egg yolks
- by using sabayons, aromatic broths, yogurt, and fromage blanc as sauce liaisons
- by borrowing from foreign cuisines

French Sauce/Mother Sauce

Chefs Antonin Carême and Auguste Escoffier codified sauce-making into five leading or *mother sauces*: **béchamel**, **velouté**, **espagnole**, **tomato**, and **hollandaise**. Their derivatives and other sauces are called **compound** or **small sauces**: mayonnaise, vinaigrette, coulis, beurre blanc, infused butter or oil, salsa, and chutney come under this category. From these classic five mother sauces cooks continue to extrapolate and improvise new variations. The variations represent a French cook's secret shorthand: Provençal means it will likely come with tomatoes, olives, garlic, and basil and Lyonnaise brings to mind onions.

Five Sauce-Making Methods

The mother sauces also represent three sauce-making methods. Adding two compound sauce methods comes to a total of five distinct sauce-making methods:

ONE: STARCH-THICKENED

Sauces like **béchamel** and **velouté** are thickened with roux while some quickly thickened sauces employ cornstarch or arrowroot slurry (jus or fond lié) or potato starch. Sauce Espagnole or brown sauce consists of brown stock flavored with mirepoix, tomato paste, and a bouquet garni, strained and thickened with brown roux. **Sauce Espagnole** is rarely used in this form. Instead it is reduced to *demi-glace* or further to a *glace*. Sauces derived from this mother sauce include Sauce Bordelaise, Sauce Perigeux, and Sauce Bigarade. A *fond lié* is typically a brown sauce thickened quickly with cornstarch or arrowroot slurry.

TWO: REDUCTION

Liquids rich with sugars, or gelatin from bones, will thicken as they boil and reduce. **Demi-glace** is a classic example. The starch has been skimmed away from Sauce Espagnole, and the thickening comes from the gelatin present in veal bones. Balsamic vinegar, cider, wine, and most gelatin-rich stocks like young chicken and veal can be reduced to sauce consistency or further to syrup.

THREE: EMULSIFICATION

An emulsified sauce is one where an emulsifier helps to hold water or liquid in suspension in oil or fat. Dijon mustard, egg yolk, and nut butters or fruit and vegetable purées may act as emulsifiers. Mayonnaise, hollandaise and Bearnaíse, sabayon, and crème Anglaise use egg. Vinaigrettes use Dijon mustard or egg. Rouille uses egg, potato, or puréed roasted bell pepper to help thicken and emulsify. The newer foams are emulsified with lecithin, unflavored gelatin, or agar-agar.

There are two types of emulsified sauces: hot and cold. Hollandaise and its derivative, tarragon-flavored Bearnaíse, are hot emulsions made with eggs and warm whole or clarified butter. Mayonnaise and the garlic mayonnaise *aioli* are made with eggs and room temperature oil.

FOUR: PURÉE

Tomato sauce was the first French classical purée sauce. In modern times cooked or raw vegetable and fruit purées or "coulis" have become popular for their light, fresh, pure flavor.

FIVE: CHUNKY OR FOREIGN CONDIMENTS

The foreign or new wave chunky condiments and sauces like salsa, chutney, and raita form a fifth, lively sauce-making category.

BÉCHAMEL (*BEY-SHA-MEL*) AND VELOUTÉ (*VELL-LOO-TAY*)

Béchamel is still the star of starch-thickened sauces in Europe: Italians call it besciamella and Spanish cooks use it to bind croquetas. Although many chefs have predicted its demise, béchamel is just too useful and reliable to toss out. Béchamel and its sister velouté don't just coat food, they are often ingredients in a dish. They impart body to soups and stews, and add a binding creaminess to gratins or mac and cheese. Cooks in Provence prepare béchamel with olive oil instead of butter. Memorize its proportions.

Yields 1 cup thick or 2 cups medium thick

Roux

1 ounce all-purpose white flour, 3-1/2 to 4 tablespoons
1 ounce whole unsalted butter, 2 tablespoons diced

- **Thick Béchamel**
  1 cups whole milk for béchamel
     or 1 cup chicken or fish stock for *Velouté*

- **Medium Thick Béchamel**
  2 cups whole milk for béchamel
     or 1 cup chicken or fish stock for *Velouté*

1 large shallot sliced in half and stuck with 2 whole cloves
Dusting of nutmeg

1 **Prepare the roux:** Over medium to low heat, heat flour and butter in a small saucepan and cook over low heat until it bubbles and smells like Christmas cookies, 1 to 2 minutes. A white roux should not take on color. Place milk or stock in a small saucepan and heat to a simmer over low heat.

2 **Whisk in hot liquid:** Remove pan from heat. Slowly whisk in simmering milk or prepare with chicken stock or fish stock in place of milk for velouté. Whisk until roux is well incorporated into milk. Raise heat to medium, switch to a wooden spoon, and stir béchamel constantly (remember the corners) until the mixture comes to a boil and thickens.

3 **Simmer:** Reduce heat to low, add shallots with cloves and nutmeg. Simmer béchamel covered, 30 to 45 minutes, stirring occasionally so sauce doesn't stick and burn.

4 **Strain:** Remove shallots and cloves; strain sauce, if necessary. Season béchamel with salt and pepper, and adjust the consistency with more milk, as necessary.

Vary! Improvise!

☞ *Sauce Créme: Finish béchamel or velouté with cream.*

☞ *Sauce Mornay: Finish béchamel with grated cheese.*

☞ *Sauce Choron: Stir in 1 to 2 tablespoons tomato sauce.*

☞ *Dairy-Free: Béchamel prepared with grapeseed or almond oil in place of butter and freshly made almond milk in place of cow milk makes a superlative dairy-free sauce.*

CLASSIC DIJON MUSTARD VINAIGRETTE

Vinaigrettes may consist of oil and vinegar or contain seasonings and an emulsifier like mustard or egg yolk. Always use freshly ground pepper; there is no seasoning worse than stale ground pepper. If using lemon juice, always squeeze it fresh; the juice turns bitter on standing. Fresh greens deserve the best.

Classic Proportions

1 part acid to 3 or 4 parts oil
For each tablespoon acid, emulsify with 1 heaping teaspoon Dijon mustard

For 5 fluid ounces, 3 servings:

2 rounded teaspoons Dijon mustard (no substitutes)
2 tablespoons vinegar
3 to 4 fluid ounces oil: grapeseed or canola oil *or* a mix of canola and olive oil

For 15 to 16 fluid ounces, 7 to 9 servings:

2 heaping tablespoons Dijon mustard
3 fluid ounces vinegar
9 to 12 fluid ounces oil or mixed oils

1 Set bowl up so that it won't move. A damp paper or cloth towel wrapped around the bottom of a bowl forms a solid base. *Alternatively*, prepare this in a blender or food processor.

2 Place Dijon mustard into a mixing bowl and whisk in vinegar or acidic ingredients (like citrus juice).

3 Measure oil or a combination of oils into a container with a spout or lip. *Slowly*, drop by drop, whisk the oil into the acid-mustard mixture. If oil goes in too quickly the vinaigrette will break. The whisk or processor won't be able to break up the oil droplets and emulsify them quickly enough.

4 When vinaigrette begins to visibly thicken and emulsify, increase oil to a thin stream. Taste vinaigrette with a lettuce leaf before you add all the oil. Adjust flavor of vinaigrette with more oil or acid, or a pinch of sugar. Season with salt and pepper and/or herbs.

5 If vinaigrette breaks (it will look separated and oily) place a small amount of mustard into a clean mixing bowl. Slowly, drop by drop, whisk broken vinaigrette into it. Taste and adjust the flavors.

EXERCISE: IMPROVISE MUSTARD VINAIGRETTE

Choose oil or oils, an acid or acids, and an optional aromatic.

- Sauté or lightly cook aromatic vegetable seasonings like onions, shallots, gingerroot, or garlic briefly to help keep vinaigrette fresh longer.
- Choose demonstrative (strong) oil like walnut, hazelnut, or sesame or non-demonstrative (mild) like grapeseed or canola. Mix and taste them in proportions that balance, usually 1/3 nut oil with 2/3 mild oil.
- The acid component could be citrus, fruit, or vegetable juices like cider or carrot, various vinegars like sherry, balsamic, red wine, white wine, coconut, cider, or champagne or wine.

MAYONNAISE AND VARIATIONS

Mayonnaise is an emulsified sauce made with room temperature egg yolks, oil, mustard, and lemon juice or vinegar.

Large Yolks	Acid	Kosher Salt	Dijon Mustard	Oil in Cups
One	2 to 3 tsp	1/2 tsp	1 tsp	1/2 to 3/4 cup
Two	1 to 2 Tbsp	1 tsp	2 tsp	1 to 1-1/2 cups
Three	2 to 3 Tbsp	1 tsp	1 Tbsp	1-1/2 to 2 cups
Four	3 to 4 Tbsp	1 tsp	4 tsp	2-1/2 to 3-1/2 cups
Six	5 to 8 Tbsp	2 tsp	2 Tbsp	3 to 4 cups

Handmade Mayonnaise

In a clean bowl whisk together yolks, acid, lemon juice or vinegar, and mustard. Slowly and in a very thin stream, whisk in oil until incorporated. The sauce will thicken as the emulsion forms. Taste mayonnaise, and season with salt and freshly ground pepper. Refrigerate sauce 30 minutes.

Blender Mayonnaise

Substitute 1 whole egg per 2 yolks in the chart. (Use 1 whole egg for just one yolk and adjust acid to taste.) Pour eggs, acid, salt and mustard into blender and purée to thoroughly combine, 15 seconds. With the machine running, pour in a very thin stream of oil until fully thickened. Taste mayonnaise, and season with salt, pepper, and more acid as necessary.

Tips

- **For a Thicker, Safer Mayonnaise:** Whisk egg yolks, mustard, and acid over a double boiler until *slightly* thickened, not scrambled. Immediately remove from heat and slowly whisk in oil.

- If mayonnaise breaks (separates), whisk it slowly into a fresh egg yolk.

- Olive oil may turn bitter if overworked by overbeating.

- Rest mayonnaise in refrigerator to chill and thicken before using. The flavors will soften and marry.

- Stir water into too-thick mayonnaise to thin. Taste and re-season.

- Store mayonnaise in sterilized plastic, not aluminum, containers with a tight seal.

- Use clean utensils when scooping mayonnaise from container.

- Prepare small batches or just what is needed.

- Keep mayonnaise and mayonnaise-dressed dishes chilled or refrigerated. Discard mayonnaise after 4 days.

Classic Mayonnaise Variations

Aioli

Prepare with 1 cup mayonnaise with extra virgin olive oil and lemon juice. Stir in 2 to 3 teaspoons minced or pounded garlic. Season with more lemon, and salt to taste. This Provençal sauce is good with fish or vegetables.

Sauce Andalouse

Prepare 1 cup mayonnaise and add 1/4 cup thick tomato sauce, 1 tablespoons minced or pureed roasted and skinned red bell pepper, and 1/2 teaspoon minced chives. Andalouse is good with eggs, poultry, vegetables, and fish.

Sauce Chantilly

Prepare 1 cup mayonnaise and just before serving, fold in 1/2 cup whipped cream. Chantilly is good with vegetables and fish.

Sauce Dijonnaise

Prepare 1 cup mayonnaise and add 4 to 5 teaspoons Dijon mustard.

Sauce Gribiche

Prepare 1 cup mayonnaise and add 1/2 chopped hard-cooked egg, 2 teaspoons each minced capers, cornichons, fines herbes, and 1 tablespoon minced shallot. Gribiche is good with fish and deep-fried foods.

Sauce Verte (vairt)

Prepare 1 cup mayonnaise. Blanch 1/3 cup packed fresh parsley, chives, basil, cress or other greens 30 seconds to one minute. Refresh, dry, and purée herbs well. Strain juice, if desired, and stir into mayonnaise, or stir purée into mayonnaise. Good with seafood.

Sauce Rémoulade (ruh-moo-lahd)

Prepare 1 cup mayonnaise and fold in 2 teaspoons each minced cornichons, capers, fines herbes, and 1/4 teapoon chopped anchovies or anchovy paste. Remoulade is good with cold meat, fish and vegetables, classically with grated celery root.

Sauce Suédoise (sway-DWAHZ)

Prepare 1 cup mayonnaise and add 1/2 cup thick applesauce and 1 to 2 tablespoons prepared (drained) horseradish. Suedoise is good with pork, game, and cold meat.

Sauce Tartare

Prepare 1 cup mayonnaise and add 2 teaspoons each minced parsley, chives, cornichons, capers, and 1/2 hard-cooked egg, sieved. Good with fish and cold meats and vegetables.

Source: The Institute of Culinary Education.

FLAVOR INFUSIONS

French cooks use every opportunity to infuse flavor into cooking. One way is to steep seasonings or flavorful food in liquid or fat. Fat carries flavor throughout a dish—liquids do too, but fats are more stable. Preparing an infusion ensures that there are a wide variety of quick flavor components at hand to help layer flavor into dishes. They encourage creativity.

1. **Water Infusions:** Stock and court bouillon are examples of water infusions; coffee, tea, and herbal tisanes are also handy.
2. **Sweet Syrup Infusions:** Sugar syrups infused with herbs, flowers, or fruit, and mixed with bubbly water can stand in for sodas or moisten sponge cake. They give fruit an herbal glow and a boost to sauces. Maple syrup and honey make good flavor-infusion mediums.
3. **Wine Vinegar Infusions:** Infusing herbs or fruit into vinegar preserves their flavor longer than water. Use blackberry or apricot-infused vinegar to prepare a sauce from the drippings of a pork or venison roast. Drizzle leek or cherry-infused vinegar on salad.
   - **Fruit Vinegar:** Mash 4 pounds washed and hulled berries or pitted fruit with 1 quart white wine vinegar, cover and store in a cool place for 3 to 4 weeks, stirring every other day. Strain vinegar through china cap lined with a triple layer of cheesecloth, or through a clean pillowcase—let it hang overnight—don't squeeze. For every cup of vinegar, stir in 1 tablespoon sugar and bring to a boil in a wide, non-reactive pan 3 minutes. Decant into sterilized bottles. Keep in a cool, dark place.
4. **Oil Infusions:** Infused oil might be the most useful way to conserve fleeting flavor. Spice and herb oils perform culinary feats for sautés, as bastes, sauces, and vinaigrettes. Cold infusions (or purées) work well for mild-flavored, tender herbs like basil, tarragon, parsley, and chives or with fresh chilies and citrus zest. Warm infusions work well with strong herbs and seasonings like rosemary, sage, thyme, gingerroot, or garlic and dried spices. To prolong shelf life, containers and utensils should be sterilized in boiling water. Oils should always be

kept sealed and refrigerated to minimize oxidation and extend the life of the oil. Use oils within a month for best flavor. Experiment with olive, grape seed, sunflower, and canola oils.

- **Cold Herb Infusion:** Blanch 1/2 cup packed herb leaves 10 seconds. Chop herbs, and grind in blender with 1 cup oil. Steep 1 to 2 days refrigerated, and strain. Store in sterilized bottles. Refrigerate.
- **Warm Herb Infusion:** Warm 1 cup oil over low heat to 165 to 180 degrees F. Blanch 1/3 ounce or more herb branches 15 seconds in boiling water, blot dry, drop into oil, and simmer 20 minutes. Cool herbs in oil, strain, store in sterilized bottles, and refrigerate.

5. **Butter Infusions**

- **Compound Butters:** A cold butter-infused fat, softened butters mashed or puréed with herbs, spices, aromatics, or fruit and a small amount of citrus (for malleability) have been a popular French seasoning technique. Mashed, and flavored with herbs, spices, citrus, fruit, or vegetables, compound butters top grilled, sautéed, or roasted food in place of a sauce. *Fruit butters* pair with scones, pancakes, and biscuits or meat and fish (mango with snapper). *Herb butters* go well on meat (rosemary or mint with lamb). *Spiced butters* (cardamom or curry) pair well with noodles, rice, and vegetables. Freeze compound butters up to 1 month and refrigerate up to 1 week.
- **Savory Butter:** Mash together 1 pound room temperature unsalted butter, 4 to 8 tablespoons chopped fresh herbs, 4 teaspoons fresh lemon juice, 2 teaspoons salt, and a few grinds of pepper.

6. **Cream and Milk Infusions:** In *The Herbfarm Cookbook*, chef Jerry Traunfeld encourages cooks to infuse fresh herbs into milk or cream. Traunfeld strains, chills, and whips the infused cream for desserts or uses it as a base for others.

- **Herb Infused Cream:** Bring 2 cups cream to a boil. Wash and dry 6 four-inch sprigs lemon verbena *or* 7 four-inch sprigs mint or tarragon *or* 3 teaspoons fresh herb flower buds *or* 6 four-inch sprigs lemon balm. Remove cream from the heat and stir in herbs; steep mixture 30 minutes and strain.
  - Use infused cream as a base for crème brûlée or in a sauce to underscore flavor.
  - Serve infused whipped cream with fresh fruit, with pie or cake: tarragon with apple pie or lemon verbena with berry shortcake or basil cream with peaches.
  - Infuse spices like star anise or cardamom or citrus zest into cream and use the cream in a liaison for *Flemish Chicken and Cream Soup* or *Blanquette de veau*.

CLARIFIED, DRAWN, AND EMULSIFIED BUTTER

Clarified Butter

Melt whole butter and it will stratify into three layers: watery whey on bottom, yellow butter oil in the center, and crusty milk solids on top. Use flavor-rich clarified butter to sauté over high heat without burning. The milk solids, high in sugar, burn when butter is heated to high temperatures. Cut butter into a small, even dice so that it melts evenly and quickly.

Drawn Butter

Melt diced whole butter, or use clarified butter, and season with salt and pepper (maybe fresh lemon juice) for a classic shellfish/lobster dipping sauce.

Emulsified Beurre Monté

Whole butter whisked into a small amount of boiling water over low heat will emulsify into a creamy sauce: Bring 1 tablespoon water to boil over moderate heat. Reduce heat and, bit by bit, whisk in 2 ounces or more small cubes of unsalted butter. The French Laundry in Napa Valley, California, uses beurre monté to poach shelled lobster (at 160 to 180 degrees F, 5 to 6 minutes) or fish, to baste meat, or as a quick sauce. Replace the water with wine, and add shallots and lemon juice for a light, buttery sauce beurre blanc.

SPECIAL METHODS

REVIEW: EGGS

French cooks love eggs and they have elevated them to great heights in soufflés, omelets, and baking. Eggs fill an amazing variety of needs in the French kitchen: they leaven, emulsify, filter, prevent crystallization, and add richness and color.

An egg has a natural coating that blocks pores in its shell and protects it from taking on oxygen, which spoils it. (For sea voyages with no refrigeration some sailors rubbed eggs with oil or fat.) When cracked, the top inside membrane of the egg will reveal how much oxygen it has taken on. Check a whole raw egg's freshness by placing it into a bowl of cold water. If it sinks completely it is very fresh. An egg that floats should be discarded. Older but edible eggs are in between.

Food chemist Shirley Corrither says in *Cookwise* that destroying bacteria is a matter of time and temperature. Salmonella is completely dead at 160 degrees F and eggs scramble at 180 degrees F. Corrither says that you may pasteurize whole eggs or yolks by holding them for 3-1/2 minutes at 140 degrees F. In other words, immerse whole raw eggs in a bowl of hot tap water or place yolks in a double boiler set over simmering water.

To stabilize and render mayonnaise and rouille, prepare a sabayon: Place a bowl of ice or cold water nearby. Heat 2 egg yolks and 1/4 cup liquid (vinegar, water, wine, or juice from recipe) in a small double boiler over, not in, simmering water, over low heat. Stir and scrape constantly with heatproof spatula. At the first sign of thickening, remove pan from the heat, keep stirring, and set pan into cold water.

SIZE	OUNCES PER DOZEN	NUMBER IN 1 CUP		
	Whole Eggs	Yolks	Whites	Whole
Jumbo	30	11	5	4
Extra large	27	12	6	4
Large	24	14	7	4 to 5
Medium	21	16	8	5

Signature Technique: Perfect Hard-Cooked Eggs

Eggs, like any tender protein, become rubbery-tough and dry if cooked too quickly over high heat. Eggs cook best when brought to a boil then removed from the heat and allowed to cook in the hot, not boiling, water. Yolks stay yellow and creamy.

- Have eggs at room temperature.

- Older eggs peel best.

- Place eggs in saucepan just big enough to hold them in one layer.

- Cover with cold water by one inch. Bring water to a boil then immediately cover pan and remove it from the heat.

- For hard-cooked large eggs, leave in hot water 10 to 12 minutes.

- Drain eggs. Lightly crack ends of eggs to make peeling easier. (The broader end of the egg contains the larger air pocket.)

- Rest eggs in cold running water until completely cooled, 5 to 10 minutes. Peel eggs. Chill eggs if not using immediately.

PATE BRISÉE (SAVORY BUTTER PASTRY CRUST)

This universally beloved pastry makes sweet or savory tarts, free-form galettes, quiche, or pie.

Yields about 22-1/2 ounces dough, enough for two 9-inch crusts

8 ounces unsalted cold butter, 1 cup
12 ounces unbleached all-purpose flour, about 2-1/2 cups
1 teaspoon kosher salt
Optional: 2 tablespoons vodka
6 tablespoons ice water (2 tablespoons more if vodka is not used)

1 Cut butter into 1/2-inch cubes, and place into a food processor or a bowl.

2 Measure flour by scooping and leveling. Pour flour into processor bowl with salt. Pulse fat into flour in processor. Pour flour and fat into a bowl. *By hand*, pour flour into mixing bowl. Cut and smear fat into the flour until it resembles cornmeal.

3 Make a well in the center of the flour and pour in optional vodka and 2 tablespoons ice water. Toss it to mix evenly. Add ice water slowly, it takes time to absorb. Add only enough water so that the dough comes together into a ball when pressed. Too much water will yield heavy dough.

4 Place dough on counter and press with the heel of the hand to smear lightly. This is known as *fraisage* and helps to form layers in the dough. Press the dough into a flat disk, wrap in plastic, and refrigerate a minimum of 30 minutes before using.

CRÈME FRAÎCHE

Yields 2 cups

2 cups heavy cream (not ultra-pasteurized)
2 tablespoons live, cultured buttermilk

1 In a small saucepan over medium heat, gently warm whipping cream to 85 degrees F. Remove pan from heat, pour cream into a bowl, and stir in buttermilk.

2 Cover bowl. Set it aside to ferment in a warm (75 degrees F) spot until thick, 12 to 24 hours. Taste should be the guide: shorter ferment time produces a nutty crème fraîche; longer time results in a tart product, more like sour cream. Cooler fermenting temperature will lengthen fermenting time and warmer temperature will shorten it. The mixture should taste pleasantly nutty and mildly tart, and look like slightly whipped cream: thick but somewhat loose.

3 Refrigerate crème fraîche. It will thicken to a creamy, sour cream consistency. Refrigerate up to 10 days.

SIMMER, STEW, POACH, BOIL, AND STEAM

NEW WAVE: SOUS VIDE

Chefs who want a higher level of food safety, precise control, and consistency over their cooking have brought technology into the kitchen. From the early 1970s, French biochemist Bruno Goussalt explored, then taught and systematized sous vide, a low-temperature cooking method.

(Continued)

(Continued)

Fast becoming a vital part of modern gastronomy, sous vide gives chefs the ability to regulate and maintain precise cooking temperatures. It involves sealing chilled foods (with a commercial vacuum sealer) into plastic and immersing the package into simmering water.

Remarkably, the water, programmed and maintained by an immersion circulator, simmers at the temperature the chef wants the food to reach: lamb loin at 140 degrees F or tenderloin at 125 degrees F. Food doesn't overcook, is the same temperature throughout, and has a longer window of holding. The flavor and texture of sous vide food is extraordinary, vibrant-tasting, supple, and succulent. Sous vide isn't a replacement for a solid grasp of cooking fundamentals—how to season, cook vegetables well, or properly sear meat—it's another exciting and helpful tool.

Stocks and Soups

France, Italy, and Spain draw on similar methods for stocks, broths, and soups. They all serve soup before a meal, as a meal, hot, cold, or lukewarm, thick, and thin. When choosing a soup, most chefs take into consideration the rest of the meal and prepare soups to introduce, rather than overwhelm or overshadow, the rest of the meal.

The perfect soup vessel fits ingredients and liquid with room to spare (5-quart for 8 to 12 servings), is nonaluminum/nonreactive, and heavy. To build a soup, start with an aromatic vegetable foundation like *mirepoix*. Water-based soups obtain flavor from fresh, tasty ingredient and seasoning combos. For deeper, easy flavor, use meat, seafood, or vegetable stock, quick shrimp shell broth or dried mushroom infusion, fresh juice, and leftover bean cooking liquid. Mature stewing hens, or tougher short ribs, shank, neck, legs, and hocks deliver the most flavor.

Signature Technique: Meat Stocks Light and Dark

Great stock or broth underlies most memorable soups. Whether it's vegetable, fish, meat, or poultry, don't rely on canned, salty, and chemical enriched pastes and powders. House-made stock gives soups a clarity and integrity that no factory-made facsimile can match. Limited time? Prepare 30-minute mini-infusions with roasted vegetables, dried mushrooms, or the leftover bones from a chicken breast, roasted turkey, or shrimp shells, mirepoix, and parsley stems.

White or Light Colored Stock

Prepare with chicken, veal, or beef bones in water with vegetables and seasonings.

Brown or Dark-Colored Stock

Prepare with roasted chicken, veal, beef, or game bones, and vegetables. Seasonings and dark flavorings like red wine and tomatoes or paste may also be used to add more color and flavor. Leftover roasted turkey bones make strong-flavored dark poultry stock.

- **Choose the Bones:** Young, flexible bones from young chickens and veal give off the most collagen (a protein found in connective tissue) and result in more gelatinous stock. Older bones from older hens or roosters and beef give off strong flavor, but are less gelatinous. Crack the bones for more flavor dispersion.
- **Choose the Cut Depending on Simmering Time:** To extract maximum flavor from mirepoix and vegetables, cut them into small dice for short-cooking stocks (fish). For long-cooking stocks (poultry or meat), cut vegetables into medium to large dice.

Simmering

For tender, succulent food, the low, constant heat of simmering wins. Simmering temperature falls between 180 and 200 degrees F. Look for small bubbles that periodically rise to the surface. Keep lids slightly ajar. Pressure and heat build up in covered pots (similar to a pressure cooker), which makes liquid go to higher temperatures.

Simmering is friend to tough or tender meat, dried beans and lentils, and hard vegetables like turnips, carrots, beets, and potatoes. The quality and flavor intensity of stock and soup is directly related to the heat at which they cook. Simmered soups have richer, deeper flavor. Simmering (versus boiling) draws out and develops flavor by tenderizing ingredients slowly. Simmering produces the clearest stock. Boiling tends to harden and emulsify fat- and protein-laden scum into stock.

- **Begin with Cold Water:** Cold water doesn't allow impurities to coagulate and emulsify into and cloud stock.

- **Simmer Stock Slowly:** Hard-boiling a stock may save time but produces cloudy stock. The fat emulsifies into the water instead of rising to the top where it may be skimmed away.

- **Skim Often:** Remove impurities before they cloud the stock.

- **Strain the Stock Carefully:** Ladle stock into another container to avoid impurities at the bottom. Strain remaining stock through china cap lined with cheesecloth.

- **Chill Stock Quickly:** Stock can sour or grow bacteria if not taken out of the danger zone quickly.

- **Remedy Weak and Watery Stock:** Reduce it over medium heat until rich and flavorful, usually 1/2 or 2/3 of original volume.

- **Stock Cubes:** Reduce stock or broth in wide, shallow pan over medium-low heat until thick and syrupy. Cool and refrigerate or freeze in cubes. Add to sauces, or reconstitute in 1 cup water for every tablespoon syrup.

- **Degreasing Options**

  - Use a degreasing cup or fat separator.

  - Use a ladle or spoon to skim off fat from the surface of the stock.

  - Set a small pot of stock onto the side of a burner and boil. This will push the fat to one side where it can be easily skimmed.

  - Quick-chill broth by setting a shallow pan of it in ice or ice water. When stock is fully chilled, scrape off congealed fat.

CHICKEN STOCK (FOND DE VOLAILLE)

Stock is made with raw bones and it has many uses in the kitchen. The technique for preparing broth is the same except that broth is made with meat and bones, and broths are usually intended for a specific finished dish. Enriched broths may be made with stock instead of just water.

Yields about 2-1/2 quarts

5 pounds raw chicken bones, rinsed

Mirepoix

8 to 10 ounces onions, 1 large, 2 cups large diced
4 ounces carrots, 1 cup peeled and medium diced
4 ounces celery, 4 to 6 stalks, 1 cup medium to large diced
Optional: 8 ounces leeks, 1 large, 1 cup white and tender green large diced

1/4 ounce Italian parsley stems
4 sprigs fresh thyme
2 bay leaves, preferably fresh

1 Place chicken bones in 10-quart stockpot. Cover with 1 gallon (4 quarts) cold water. Bring water to a boil over medium heat. Lower heat and simmer bones 30 minutes. Skim away as much foam as possible.

2 Immerse mirepoix, parsley stems, thyme, and bay leaves into pot. Simmer stock until fragrant, 3 hours. Midway through cooking time, as stock reduces, stir in 2 to 3 cups cold water. If stock boils, the impurities will emulsify into the stock and cloud it.

3 Remove pot from heat and cool stock slightly. Ladle stock through china cap lined with cheesecloth; quickly chill it down. Discard bones and vegetables.

4 Refrigerate stock until fat congeals on top, 4 to 8 hours. Skim and discard fat. Ladle stock into storage containers. Refrigerate stock no more than 4 days. Freeze stock for longer storage.

Signature Technique: Fish Stock

Real fish stock or "fumet" (foo-may) has become all but extinct in restaurant kitchens. Its flavor far surpasses what passes for fish stock. It's easy to cobble together a passable facsimile with clam juice, white wine, shrimp shells, white mirepoix, and a hint of Asian fish sauce. But it won't have the subtle, dynamic flavor of real fish fumet. Build a relationship with the local fish market or sniff out and befriend a top-notch fish purveyor to get first choice of fresh fish as it comes in, and a pile of bones with which to build fish fumet. Prepare fumet whenever ingredients become available. Fumet may be frozen up to 2 months.

Fish Stock with Wine: Fumet (*foo-may*) de Poisson (*pwah-san*)

- **Use Light-Colored, Lean, Mild-Flavored Fish Bones and Head:** Fatty and strong fish like salmon or tuna produce strong-tasting, fatty stock not suitable for all dishes. Use sole, flounder, turbot, or whitefish racks and heads.

- **Chop the Rack:** Chop or break fish racks into smaller pieces for more flavor dispersion. Crack bones from crustaceans.

- **Remove Scales and Gills:** They can result in bitter stock.

- **Rinse Bones and Heads Well in Cold Water:** Rinse away blood and other impurities so they don't cloud stock.

- **Prepare Stock with White Mirepoix:** To keep fish stock light-colored and mild tasting, omit carrots. Some chefs add leeks and mushrooms. Dice the mirepoix small.

- **Sweat:** Over low to medium-low heat, in a small amount of fat, slowly cook fish bones and heads, crustacean shells and white mirepoix and light-colored vegetables until soft but not browned.

- **Begin with Cold Water:** Cold water keeps impurities from coagulating and emulsifying into stock and clouding it.

- **Add an Acid:** White wine or lemon juice will pull out more flavor from bones.

- **Simmer Stock Slowly, and Not Long:** Because of the delicacy of seafood bones, 30 minutes, and no more than 45 minutes, is enough time to extract the maximum flavor. Simmering too long can result in bitter stock.

Nontraditional Flavor Tips

- Mix leftover fish poaching liquid with bottled clam juice for a quick fumet.

- Spike shrimp broth or weak-flavored fish stock with bottled Vietnamese fish sauce.

- Prepare broth from Japanese dried *katsuobushi* (bonito flakes) or dried sardines, dried kelp, vegetables, and water. (See chapter *Japan* for *Dashi*.)

FISH STOCK WITH WINE (FUMET DE POISSON)

Yields about 2 quarts

5 pounds fish bones and heads and/or crustacean bones
2 tablespoons oil or clarified butter
4 to 5 ounces onions, 1 cup peeled and finely diced
2 ounces celery, 1/2 cup finely diced
3 to 4 ounces leek, 1/2 medium, 1/2 cup finely diced
2 ounces mushrooms, 1/2 cup finely sliced
1 cup white wine
1 tablespoon fresh lemon juice
1 bay leaf, preferably fresh
2 small sprigs fresh thyme
1/8 teaspoon white peppercorns
1/4 ounce Italian parsley stems, about 4

1 Crack bones, and rinse away scales and blood. Remove gills from head. Rinse and drain.

2 Heat oil or butter in 6- to 8-quart stockpot over medium-low heat. Add onions, celery, leek, and mushroom and sweat vegetables until soft but not colored, 3 to 5 minutes. Add bones and heads, and sweat until opaque, 2 to 3 minutes.

3 Pour white wine, lemon juice, and 2-1/2 quarts cold water over bones and vegetables. Bring to a simmer and skim away impurities and scum.

4 Add bay leaves, thyme, peppercorns, and parsley stems. Simmer fumet uncovered until stock is flavorful, 30 minutes. Remove pot from heat and cool 15 minutes. Strain stock through a fine-meshed china cap lined with cheesecloth. Chill stock.

COURT-BOUILLON (*BULL-YAWN*)

French cooks often prepare this "short-broth" or flavored liquid with white mirepoix when using to it poach seafood. The method is similar to Fish Stock with Wine.

Yields about 4 to 5 cups, enough for 1-1/2 pounds protein

1 cup white wine
6 to 8 ounces leek, about 1 cup white and pale green finely sliced or diced
4 ounces trimmed celery, 2 medium stalks, 3/4 to 1 cup sliced
6 to 7 ounces onion, 1 medium, 1-1/2 cups sliced or diced
Bouquet garni: 1 bay leaf, 3 large Italian parsley stems and 1 large sprig thyme
For fish: Zest of 1/2 lemon and juice of 1/2 lemon, about 2 tablespoons freshly squeezed

1 Place all ingredients into a 4-quart saucepan and cover with 5 cups cold water. Bring liquid to a boil, cover, lower heat, and simmer on low 20 minutes. Remove pan from heat, and cool 10 minutes.

2 Strain court-bouillon, discard vegetables, and reserve liquid for poaching. Chill if not using immediately.

Vary! Improvise!

Add or Substitute:
☞ *4 ounces/1/2 cup trimmed and sliced fennel stalks and 1/2 teaspoon fennel seed*
☞ *2 stems tarragon for parsley*
☞ *Sliced shallots, red wine vinegar, and fresh dill*
☞ *1 head garlic, excess paper removed and cloves separated*

Types of French Soup

The father of codified French cooking, Georges Auguste Escoffier, in his *Le Guide Culinaire* classifies soups into two main categories: **clear** and **thick**.

- **Clear soups** are made with a base of consommé (or clear stock or broth) and garnished with precooked or raw vegetable, starch, or protein added just before serving. Creative garnish combinations give an endless parade of great soups from one richly flavorful consommé or rich stock.

- **Thick soups** are further divided into **purées**, **cullises**, **bisques**, **veloutés**, **creams**, **special**, **vegetable**, and **foreign** soups. Purées are thickened with starchy vegetables and cooked rice or breadcrumbs. Cullises are soups with meat or fish base thickened with rice, lentils, espagnole sauce, or bread. Bisques are shellfish soups thickened with rice. Veloutés are soups with a velouté base and finished with a liaison of egg yolk and cream. Cream soups have a béchamel base and a cream finish. Special soups veer from the typical velouté or cream techniques. Vegetable soups are rustic soups. Foreign soups are those of foreign origin like mulligatawny.

FRENCH SOUP CATEGORIZED BY TECHNIQUE

Categorized by technique, French soup would fall into four main types.

1. **Garnished** Garnished soups are clear, brothy soups of two types:
   - **Uncooked Garnish:** Garnish chilled or hot, clear consommé, stock, or broth with uncooked ingredients like cheese or herbs.
   - **Cooked Garnish:** Garnish chilled or hot clear consommé, stock, or broth with precooked ingredients like grilled chicken slices, steamed shrimp, cooked or raw bite-sized vegetables, tiny meat balls, cooked noodles or dumplings, crepe strips, or peas.
2. **Sautéed (or Sweated) and Simmered.** Sautéed (or sweated) and simmered soups are thicker and heartier than garnished or simmered soups. Sauté or sweat the aromatic vegetables and seasonings to concentrate flavor. Pour in stock, broth, or water, and additional ingredients like vegetables. Simmer soup until ingredients are tender. Garnish and serve.
3. **Thickened.** Thickened soups are stocks or broths thickened with starches or a liaison of cream and egg during or after soup making.

   - **Flour and Roux:** Sauté aromatic vegetables and sprinkle with flour (to make a roux) or add a premade roux (see *Béchamel*) with the proportions **1 tablespoon roux to 1 cup liquid.**
   - Rice or Breadcrumbs: Simmer soup with rice or breadcrumbs until they soften and disappear into the soup.
   - Slurry, Beurre Manie, or Liaison: Prepare soup and thicken at end with cornstarch or arrowroot slurry, bits of beurre manie, or egg and cream liaison.
4. **Puréed.** A blender, food processor, or an immersion blender purées cooked or raw vegetables, cooked fish, or meat to thicken purée soups. Sometimes small amounts of raw or toasted bread or nuts are puréed in to add stability.
   - **Three Approaches to a Purée**
   - Purée raw vegetables (and nuts or bread) with stock.
   - Sauté aromatic vegetables and simmer vegetables or legumes until tender, and purée.
   - Simmer together ingredients (like potatoes and leeks) in water, milk, broth, or stock until tender, and purée.

CONSOMMÉ

French chefs prepare elegant, crystal clear consommé by "clarifying" and intensifying stock with a mixture of ground raw meat, egg whites and shells, and mirepoix. Make lobster, fish, game, beef, chicken, or vegetable consommé; serve them as cold amber jelly in warm weather and hot with garnishes in cold weather. They may also be used to make aspic.

For 4 servings:

6 cups well-flavored degreased stock

Clearmeat
8 ounces lean ground meat
3 ounces finely diced *mirepoix* (1-1/2 ounces onion, 1 ounce carrot, 1/2 ounce celery)
3 large egg whites, about 1/3 cup lightly whisked
3 washed egg shells, crumbled

For 16 servings:

6 quarts well-flavored degreased stock

Clearmeat
2 pounds lean ground meat
12 ounces finely diced *mirepoix* (6 ounces onion, 4 ounces carrot, 2 ounces celery)
12 egg whites, about 1-1/3 cups lightly whisked
12 washed egg shells, crumbled

1 Pour cool or cold stock into saucepan or stockpot.

2 Combine cold **clearmeat** ingredients (and seasonings) in bowl well. Scrape into cold stock. (Albumin from egg whites and shells grabs "impurities" that cloud stock. Meat and mirepoix impart rich flavor.)

3 Bring stock to a boil slowly over medium to medium-low heat while frequently whisking. Lower heat immediately. Simmer mixture over low to medium-low heat 1 hour without whisking. As the meat raft solidifies, poke a hole in it to relieve pressure.

4 Set up strainer lined with double thickness of dampened cheesecloth set over pot. Ladle consommé through it. Taste consommé and season with salt to taste. It should be richly flavorful and crystal clear.

5 **To Serve:** Garnish hot consommé with one of **garnishes** below.

Clear Consommé Garnishes

- **Printanier:** 4 teaspoons each julienne carrot, turnip, green peas, and green beans cooked in stock and divided among bowls with 2 tablespoons finely sliced (chiffonade) sorrel and lettuce divided. Ladle hot consommé over top, and garnish with chervil leaves.
- **Au Vermicelle:** Divide 2 ounces cooked pasta or noodles per serving. Garnish with herbs.
- **Julienne or Brunoise:** 2 tablespoons slivers or very small dice of vegetables, meat, or seafood first cooked, either by roasting or poaching in hot stock. Distribute among bowls and ladle consommé over top.
- **Crêpes:** Prepare crêpes in small skillet. Cool and slice into thin strips. Layer with meat and herbs in bowl and ladle hot consommé over top.
- **Meatballs or Quenelles:** Poach tiny, seasoned ground chicken, pheasant, or other meat or seafood balls in stock, place into bowls, and ladle hot consommé over top.
- **Tomato:** Peel, seed, and beautifully brunoise tomato, simmer in butter until tender, but not falling apart, add consommé, and simmer 2 to 3 minutes. Ladle into bowls.
- **Make a verrine parfait:** Layer 1/2-inch warmed gelatinous consommé in glass and chill. Layer **garnish** on and cover with another 1/2-inch consommé. Chill. Repeat until glass is filled. Chill before serving.

CREAM OF WATERCRESS SOUP
(POTAGE CRÉME CRESSONIÈRE)

Yields 8 cups, 4 to 6 servings

15 ounces watercress, about 3 bunches, 15 to 18 cups trimmed and lightly packed
1 pound leeks, 2 large
3 tablespoons unsalted butter
8 to 9 ounces onion, 2 cups peeled and finely diced
4 cups chicken stock
2 cups heavy whipping cream
White pepper
2 to 3 tablespoons fresh lemon juice, 1 large lemon

For Garnish: 4 to 6 sprigs watercress

Optional Garnish: **2 tablespoons caviar**

1 Fill a 4-quart saucepan 3/4 full of cold water. Bring to a rolling boil. Remove 4 to 6 sprigs watercress and set aside for garnish. Immerse remaining watercress into boiling water and boil gently until tender, 2 to 3 minutes. Drain watercress and rinse under cold water. Drain again and gently squeeze out as much water as possible. Chop or purée (in blender) watercress very finely to yield about 1-1/2 cups; set aside.

2 Slice leeks in half lengthwise and rinse. Discard or set aside tough green part for another use. Finely slice remaining white and tender green parts to yield 2 cups.

3 Heat butter in 4-quart saucepan over medium heat. Stir in leeks and onions and season with 1 teaspoon kosher salt. Cook until vegetables are tender, 5 to 7 minutes. Stir in stock and 2 cups cream. Bring soup to a simmer over medium heat, lower heat, and simmer soup 30 minutes.

4 **Just before serving:** Remove saucepan from heat. Stir watercress into soup. If desired, purée soup with immersion blender until smooth. Taste soup, and season with lemon juice, salt, and freshly ground white pepper.

5 **To Serve:** Heat soup, but don't boil. Ladle soup into serving bowls. Garnish with reserved watercress leaves and optional caviar. Serve immediately.

Source: The Paris Cookbook by Patricia Wells.

Vary! Improvise!

☞ *Sorrel Soup: Substitute sorrel for watercress. Sorrel is a pleasantly citrusy-sour herb that shows up in French gardens early in the spring. It's used to prepare a sorrel sauce, which goes well with fish. For another treat, purée sorrel leaves with a potato and leek soup.*

☞ *Greener: Blanch 1 to 2 ounces (1 to 2 cups) baby spinach and purée with watercress.*

Hot Soups Hot and Cold Soups Cold

Soup temperature matters as much as flavor. Serve hot soup lukewarm or a chilled soup too icy, and its best flavor won't show. Help soup be all it can be. Heat or chill properly. Warm or chill soup plates or bowls, and get soup to the table quickly.

VERRINES

Verrines (*vair-eens*), elegant miniatures of the food world, will get any creative cook's heart racing. They've swept in from France to charm diners with entertaining style, exciting textures, flavors, and beauty. Transparency and surprise are vital to verrines, small glasses—shot size to wine glass—filled with 3 or more layers of sweet or savory foods.

Usually served at a meal's start or finish, they can be appetizer or dessert. Some diners order several and call them lunch. Devise and improvise verrines by deconstructing classic dishes: layer a cold gelée of rich beef broth seasoned with port into a glass, top with warm caramelized onions and a Parmesan *frico*.

Signature Technique: Poaching

Poaching is a moist method that cooks food by immersing it completely or partially in simmering—not boiling—liquid, about 160 to 175 degrees F. At this temperature the water will form small bubbles that will sit on the bottom of the pan and lazily make their way to the surface. The surface will show a small shimmery (smile) movement. For the best flavor and texture, begin with cold poaching liquid, bring to a simmer, then place food to be poached into it.

- Poaching softens strong-flavored foods (salmon) and strengthens the flavor of mild tasting foods (pears).
- Poaching will cook anything from leeks, apples, fish, beef, and chicken to leg of lamb.

- Poaching removes excess saltiness from dried cod, ham, and corned beef.
- Poaching helps to eliminate excess fat.

1 *Per serving* figure 5 to 6 ounces boned and skinned meat or fish or 1-pound whole fish or chicken with bones.

2 **Prep food to be poached:** scale and gut whole fish, cut fish fillets into thick, even sized pieces, remove skin and excess fat from meat, trim leeks—cut away tough green leaves, but leave root intact. Season meat or fish with salt.

3 **Prepare poaching liquid or court-bouillon:** Strain and pour into poaching vessel that will accommodate food in one layer. For whole fish, improvise a sling with parchment paper or cheesecloth so that the fish will be easy to remove after poaching.

4 Bring liquid to a high simmer. Don't cover the vessel with a lid. It will hold in heat and raise the temperature of the liquid. Instead, cover food with a piece of parchment cut to fit the cooking vessel with a small hole in its center.

5 Immerse food so it is covered in gently simmering liquid. Food may touch but should not overlap. If a low temperature cannot be maintained on the top of the stove, place poaching vessel in preheated 250 degree F oven. The hotter the fluid, the more destructive it is to food, from both the higher temperature, which toughens delicate protein, but also from the increased agitation. A fragile fish fillet will fall apart in boiling water.

6 Start timing and check food doneness every few minutes. Leave fillets to cook until they are opaque and flake easily. Start checking fish after 5 minutes for each inch of thickness. **The lower the heat, the more tender and juicy textured flesh will result.** Leave salmon slightly pink in the center.

7 Remove cooked pieces as they are done with slotted metal spatula or slotted spoon. Pull whole fish up gently and drain. Keep food warm on serving plate or in bowl while you prepare a sauce.

8 **Reduce poaching liquid to make a sauce.** Or prepare separate sauces for poached food. Reduce fish poaching liquid to a couple of tablespoons, and whisk in cold butter off-heat to create a beurre blanc pan sauce. Serve whole fish warm or chill it overnight, and serve cold with sauce on side.

Poaching Terms

Nage or à la Nage: If court bouillon is reduced after poaching, and made into a sauce (usually for fish or shellfish), it is called a *nage*.

Fumet de Poisson: Fish stock made with fish bones and head, white mirepoix (no carrots), a bouquet garni, and white wine simmered 20 to 30 minutes. Fish fumet makes an excellent poaching medium. After cooking fish in court-bouillon it may also be called *fumet*.

REVIEW: PERFECT POACHED EGGS

- Fill a saucepan or nonstick skillet with 2 inches of water and add a little vinegar (this helps firm the white and keep it from forming "clouds").
- Bring water to a simmer. Break eggs into small cups. Slip them one by one into water, starting at 12 o'clock and going around the pan clockwise.
- Cook eggs until white is completely set and yolk is still soft to the touch.

- Remove eggs with a slotted spoon, starting at the first one put in.
- Drain eggs on paper towels before setting on toast or in a cup.
- Serve poached eggs immediately or hold 5 hours in the refrigerator in a bowl of chilled water.
- To reheat, immerse cold poached eggs in simmering water 1 minute. Remove with slotted spoon, drain with paper towel, and serve.

Signature Technique: Braising and Stewing

Though deep-frying and grilling may have bigger star power, homely braising and stewing offer cooks a wondrously succulent return. When whole or cut foods simmer in a covered vessel with a small amount of added liquid, and slow, steady heat, they're braising. Add more liquid and it's a stew. If granny's pot roast or Irish stew comes to mind, braising and stewing may seem fuddy-duddy, but they lay claim to elegant, timeless dishes like Italian osso buco, coq au vin, beef Bourguignon, and rabbit or chicken fricassee.

Most vegetables and delicate fish or shellfish, because they don't require tenderizing, need only short cooking (1 hour or less) to achieve a flavor-enhancing exchange. Long, slow, moist heat (1-1/2 to 4 hours) is best for tough, less expensive cuts of meat because it breaks down collagen and muscle fibers, and renders meat or tough root vegetables into tender spoon-food. The stovetop is the better choice for short braises and stews, and a 300 to 325 degree F oven is best for long braising or stewing.

- Choose the correct size and weight cooking vessel depending on short or long braise.

- Aromatic vegetables, seasonings, and liquid should pair well with main ingredient.

- Marinate meat like beef or venison overnight. Bring wine, aromatics, and seasonings to a boil in a shallow pan and ignite until it will light no more. Cool. Immerse meat in marinade and refrigerate overnight. Strain off aromatics and set aside. Bring marinade to a boil and strain off cloudy meat albumin.

Brown Braise or Stew

Season main animal protein with salt.
Blot meat dry or dust with flour and brown (don't cook through), and remove from pan.
Sauté aromatic vegetables.
Deglaze with marinade, alcohol, or stock, and reduce.

White Braise or Stew

Place main meat/animal protein ingredient back on top of vegetable foundation.
Braise: Liquid (stock or marinade) should barely come halfway up the sides of the food.
Stew: Pour in enough liquid to almost cover.
Bring liquid to a simmer and cover vessel.

For **long cooking** *braise or stew:*

Place oven-proof vessel into oven preheated to 325 degrees F.

For **short cooking** *braise or stew:*

Keep vessel on stovetop on low heat.

- Check braise or stew partway through cooking time. Adjust heat so it simmers not boils.

- Strain liquid and degrease, if necessary. To finish sauce:
  Reduce over moderate heat.
  Thicken with beurre manie, cornstarch, arrowroot, or potato starch.
  Purée cooked vegetables and stir back in to thicken sauce.

STEW, RAGOÛT, BLANQUETTE, NAVARIN, DAUBE, OR FRICASSÉE?

So many names for similar dishes can be confusing:

Stew

An overall term for meat, poultry, seafood, or vegetable dishes cooked at low heat with lots of liquid. French cooks thicken stews with flour, roux, cornstarch, potato starch, or an egg yolk-cream liaison. Italian cooks may use roux or flour, but more often they thicken with tomato, tomato paste, or breadcrumbs. (Spanish cooks might use *picada*, a combination of pounded nuts, bread, garlic, and olive oil.)

Ragoût

French term for deep flavored, thickened or unthickened white or brown stew.

(Continued)

(Continued)

Ragoût à blanc

Light-colored ingredients layered, simmered, and served unthickened.

Ragù

Italian term for thick meat sauce with a little tomato—it's not a stew. Both ragoût and ragù are derived from *ragoûter*, meaning "to stimulate appetite."

Blanquette

A white stew made with veal, chicken, or lamb simmered in light stock and wine without browning and thickened with egg and cream at the end.

Navarin

A brown ragoût made with mutton or lamb and garnished with small cooked potatoes, turnips, peas, and small onions.

Daube

A brown ragoût generally with a whole joint of meat simmered in red wine, dark stock, aromatics, herbs, and sometimes spices. Daubes are popular in Provence.

Fricassée

A dish that is neither braise or stew, but somewhere in between. Typically poultry or rabbit is sweated without browning and it simmers with stock and wine, but not enough to cover, in a lidded pot, and is thickened with *beurre manie*. *Beef Bourguignon* and *coq au vin* are brown fricassées.

SAUTÉ, PAN-FRY, AND DEEP-FRY

Signature Technique: Ten Steps to Pan Sauté/Pan Sauce

1 *Prep* sauce ingredients:
   - **Fat:** Clarified butter, oil, mixture of whole butter and oil, or lard
   - **Main Ingredient:** Tender, quick-cooking cuts of seafood, poultry, and meat like chicken breast, fish fillet, shrimp, scallops, veal scallopini, beef tenderloin, pork tenderloin, or duck breast
   - **Aromatic Vegetables:** Shallots, onion, ginger, green onions, garlic, carrots, celery, or mushrooms
   - **Deglazing Liquid:** Wine, cream, meat, or vegetable broths or liqueurs
   - **Seasonings:** Fresh or dried herbs like Italian parsley, tarragon, rosemary and thyme, spices and spice mixtures like herbs de Provence, and salt and pepper
   - **Thickeners:** Flour, roux, cornstarch slurry or beurre manie, and vegetable and fruit purées
   - **Garnish:** Delicate herbs for top flavor like basil, cheese, and whole butter

2 **Heat pan and add fat:** Pat protein dry and season with salt. (Dust with flour for extra browned crispiness and slight thickening. Flour will burn if cooked too long or at too high heat.) Sauté protein until golden and cooked through but not overcooked.

3 **Remove protein from pan:** It will continue to cook slightly. Keep in a warm spot. Discard excess fat; wipe pan if burned. Or sear/sauté protein and place in a preheated 400 degree F oven to finish cooking while preparing the pan sauce on the top of the stove. **Pan-roasting**, the friend of hurried restaurant cooks, is the offspring of the union of the sauté and the oven roast. Sautéing browns meat or fish for color and flavor. The ovenproof sauté pan goes into a hot oven to roast and finish meat or fish.

4 If glaze looks as if it might burn, deglaze and scrape deglazing liquid and bits into a small bowl and add later. Add fresh fat to pan as necessary, and sauté aromatic vegetables until tender (and golden). Infuse strong seasonings like curry, rosemary, or thyme into fat.

5 *Reduce the* sauce:
   - **First Reduction:** Deglaze pan with wine or acid, and reduce by boiling moderately. Reducing evaporates water, intensifies flavor, and burns off the raw alcohol flavor.

Reduce by 1/2 or 2/3, or to thin syrup. If it goes too far, add water.

- **Second Reduction:** Pour in stock, if using, and reduce by 1/2 to 2/3. Demi-glace or stock reduced to a glaze are excellent flavor enhancers, and require no reduction.

- **Third Reduction:** Pour in optional cream. Reduce until it coats a spoon lightly: *nappé* or sauce consistency.

6 *Thicken the* **sauce:** If not using cream, after reducing with wine or stock, it's possible to thicken a sauce with a vegetable or fruit purée, cornstarch slurry, or beurre manie. Whisk in slowly and boil until sauce thickens. Better to add too little than too much: starch flattens the flavor of a sauce.

7 **Taste and adjust the flavors and seasonings:** Salt, pepper, acids like wine vinegar or citrus juice, and sweeteners like sugar or honey. To add more wine, reduce it in another pan on the side (to remove alcohol rawness) before stirring into sauce.

8 *Garnish the* **sauce:** From sprinkling with chopped, fresh herbs to mounting with whole butter, garnishing finishes and enriches flavor. Remove pan from heat and whisk in cold bits of butter. Do not re-boil sauce or butter will break. Keep sauce hot in a preheated thermos set in a warm spot.

9 *Taste the* **Sauce** *Again.*

10 **To Serve:** Slice protein or leave whole.

Three Serving Options:

- Reheat protein in sauce and plate.
- Plate protein and drizzle or pour sauce over.
- Sauce the plate, and set protein over top. Garnish.

GRILL, GRIDDLE, ROAST, BAKE, AND BROIL

Savory Soufflé (*soo-flay*)

If any dish could be said to inspire discomfort in cooks it would probably be the soufflé. An ethereal puff of delicate and creamy, but fleeting, enjoyment, soufflés probably had their roots in early puddings and meringues. Soufflés gained their reputation as temperamental and demanding when in 1813 and 1814, two French chefs, Beaufilliers and Louis Ude, published soufflé recipes. Billed as low-cost, fashionable suppers, French chefs began to make soufflés in earnest. After almost thirty years of frustration with collapsing soufflés, restaurant chefs finally got some help from famous French chef Carême, who detailed his soufflé techniques in an 1841 cookbook. Now that culinary chemistry has kicked in, chefs understand more of the soufflé's perverse nature. It begins and ends with the egg.

Signature Technique: Savory Soufflé

For a successful soufflé there are three crucial points: soufflé base must be the correct consistency—*too thick, it cannot rise, and too thin will knock the air out of the whites;* egg whites must be stiff, *but not overbeaten into lumps. Beaten whites must be* carefully folded, not stirred, *into the base or they will lose loft. Prepare a soufflé vessel, make the base and separate the eggs early in the day. Thirty minutes before desired serving time: whip the whites and bake the soufflé.*

The Elements

Soufflé dish or ramekins
Butter and breadcrumbs
Thick béchamel or bouille base

Egg yolks
Chopped or puréed vegetable *or* grated cheese
Seasonings like Dijon mustard, herbs or spices like nutmeg or curry
Egg whites

1 **Butter and crumb soufflé dish** or dishes, tap out excess, and set aside. Crumbs, grated cheese (or ground nuts) give the soufflé something to grip onto as it rises. The standard soufflé dish is a tall, straight-sided 1- to 2-quart ovenproof dish, but it will vary according to the recipe.

2 **Separate whites from yolks** with the *three-bowl method* to ensure fat-free whites. Fat impedes egg white whipping. Wipe hands and bowl with vinegared towel to remove fat.
   - Set up 3 clean bowls.
   - Crack an egg. Separate white from yolk; drop white in one bowl and yolk in a second.
   - Crack second egg. Separate white from yolk, drop white into empty bowl and yolk into bowl with first yolk.
   - If second egg white is free of yolk, slide it into bowl with first white.
   - Crack third egg and separate white into empty bowl; yolk goes into third bowl. If white is yolk-free, slide it into bowl with other whites.

3 **Prepare the base.** There are several ways to prepare a savory soufflé base: with mashed potato, cream cheese, *bouille* (*boo-yee*) (milk and flour cooked together), béchamel, or cornstarch. Most savory French soufflés start with a medium-thick to thick béchamel or bouille.

4 **Stir egg yolks** into cooled base.

5 **Prepare grated cheese or cooked vegetable** (chopped or puréed) component. Fold into base.

6 **Choose seasonings** like Dijon mustard or herbs and spice and fold into base. At this point base can sit at room temperature up to 1 hour.

7 **Preheat oven 25 degrees F higher than necessary. Lower oven temperature when soufflé goes in.** Oven temperature and the size of the soufflé are all-important to achieve the desired consistency. High temperatures create a more dramatic rise but will run the risk of overbrowning the outside before the inside is set. Large soufflés (1-1/2 to 2-quart) need 375 degrees F. Small 8-ounce soufflés can bake at 400 degrees F.

8 **Whip whites to stiff peaks with cream of tartar or in copper bowl.** *Cream of tartar* stabilizes beaten whites. A copper bowl will stabilize and give them more loft. Gently pull whisk or beater out of beaten whites. Whites beaten perfectly stiff will stand up in a tender peak. Not stiff enough and the peak will immediately fall over; too stiff and the whites will not peak or incorporate well, begin to separate and to look like "dry" puffs of cloud.

9 **First lighten the base** by stirring in 1/8 of whites. **Fold remaining whites** into base with rubber spatula. Fold batter in bowl from bottom outer edge of whites, and up and over toward center. Turn bowl a quarter turn each time. Once every 3 turns, drag spatula through center of bowl. **Stirring deflates egg whites.**

10 **Completely fill prepared soufflé dishes,** level off the top and run a thumb around the inside edge to form a gutter or trench. This will shape the "top hat." For insurance, tie a buttered parchment collar around the top edge of the soufflé dish to keep the soufflé from falling over.

11 **Place soufflé in the middle of the oven to bake.** Leave room for rising by removing the top rack. Don't open oven door for first 20 minutes. Bake soufflés until they double in size, puff, and are almost firm to touch. The top should be deeply golden. If a soufflé cracks hugely, the oven is too hot; small cracks in cheese soufflés are expected. Some cooks like soufflés firm inside, some like them tender. If unsure whether a soufflé is done, take it out, poke with a thin knife to check if it comes out wet with batter or clean. If it's too soft, pop soufflé back into the oven quickly.

12 **Prepare serving plate:** Place linen napkin on plate. Place soufflé straight from oven on napkin and serve immediately—the soufflé will begin its collapse quickly.

FIGURE 5.19 Egg whites whipped to stiff peaks.
Source: Dave King/DK Images.

CHEESE SOUFFLÉ (SOUFFLÉ AU FROMAGE)

The French like soufflé golden and crisp on the outside and set, but still tender on the inside. If desired, one extra egg white may be used for increased lightness.

Yields 4 cups batter; fits a 1-quart soufflé dish or four 8-ounce soufflé dishes; double the recipe for a standard 2-quart soufflé dish

3 tablespoons unsalted butter, plus 2 teaspoons for buttering dish
2/3 ounce fine, fresh, white breadcrumbs, 3 tablespoons, for crumbing dish
Scant 1 ounce all-purpose flour, 3 tablespoons
1 cup hot whole milk
Optional: 2 teaspoons Dijon mustard
About 3 ounces Gruyère or Swiss cheese, 1 cup grated
5 large eggs, *separated*
Pinch of cream of tartar

1   Preheat oven to 400 degrees F and place rack in center of oven. Butter the inside of a 1-quart soufflé dish or four 8-ounce soufflé dishes. Coat the insides of dishes with breadcrumbs.

2   Melt 3 tablespoons butter in a medium saucepan over medium heat. Whisk in flour and cook flour until slightly colored, 2 minutes. Whisking constantly, pour in the milk slowly. Reduce heat to very low and whisk in mustard, and 1/2 teaspoon kosher salt. Simmer white sauce 5 minutes; it will be very thick. Stir frequently to prevent scorching. Remove pan from heat and stir in Gruyère until mostly melted; set aside to cool. Whisk 4 egg yolks (1/4 cup) into sauce to yield about 1-2/3 cup soufflé base.

3   Place 5 egg whites (3/4 cup), a pinch of salt and a pinch of cream of tartar into a very clean bowl, and beat until stiff. Immediately, gently stir 1/8 of whites into sauce. With a rubber spatula, fold remaining whites into sauce until the whites are almost completely incorporated (a few small areas of white are acceptable).

4   Scrape soufflé batter into prepared baking dish or dishes. Smooth top with spatula. Run a thumb around the edge to form a small gutter. Place soufflé into oven. Reduce temperature to 375 degrees F for one large soufflé, but if baking small soufflés, don't reduce temperature. Bake until soufflé is puffed and deeply browned, 30 to 40 minutes for large; less time for small soufflés.

Vary! Improvise!

☞ *Replace Gruyère with 3/4 cup cooked and puréed or chopped vegetable:* carrot, spinach, broccoli, red bell pepper, peas, corn, zucchini or roasted butternut squash, or cauliflower.

☞ *Prepare tri-colored soufflé: Divide batter into 3 parts and mix in 1/4 cup cooked and puréed vegetables of contrasting colors before adding the whites. Layer finished batters.*

PASSION FOR GRILLING

French cooks haven't latched onto grilling as Americans and other Europeans have. In *The Barbecue! Bible*, (American) author Steve Raichlen recounts how, when on the trail of "the elusive art of French grilling," author Patricia Wells told him about a restaurant that specialized in grilling—400 miles away near the Spanish border. Raichlen and his wife averaged driving speeds of 100 miles per hour to get there, and dined on escargot grilled over vine trimmings and roots that very evening.

SALAD AND VEGETABLE METHODS

French Salads

French salads, though wonderfully varied, fall into two main groups: composed (*composée*) like the classic *Niçoise Salad*, or tossed. A subcategory of composed and tossed salads are "American" salads, which feature meat, starch, and vegetables, all in one salad, and *crudités*, small tossed salads made of raw or lightly cooked vegetables dressed with vinaigrette or mayonnaise. See *Glossary* for more information on lettuce.

Signature Technique: Salad Verte/French Simple Salad

For most French meals, a simple salad of only lettuces or greens, dressed with mustard vinaigrette or oil and vinegar, are served after a meal as a digestive and palate cleanser. Bitter greens get the liver moving and bile flowing. Sweet greens clear the taste of the previous course and set the diner up for the next one.

1 Start with sweet and bitter greens: oak leaf lettuce, red oak leaf lettuce, red and green round lettuce, baby leaves like mizuna, baby chard or beetroot leaves, corn salad, arugula, watercress, baby spinach, or Belgian endive.

2 Greens and vegetables should be the freshest possible. During cleaning, go over greens diligently and remove suspicious stuff and large, tough stems.

3 Start with very clean greens. Crunching on grit is embarrassing and ruinous. Pull leaves from lettuces and rinse well under cold water. Place in salad spinner and spin to rid leaves of excess moisture. For large amounts of greens, fill sink with cold water. Toss leaves in water and drain; repeat if greens are gritty. Place in salad spinner and spin till dry. Wet greens dilute the dressing. Refrigerate clean greens in zip bag, layered with paper toweling up to 2 days.

4 Tear greens into bite-sized pieces. Don't cut greens for *Salade Verte* with a knife. Place clean dry greens in a bowl. Use 1 to 3 ounces cleaned greens per person: one part young romaine or leaf, one part bibb or Boston lettuce, and one part escarole, chicory, or baby frisée.

5 Toss greens with enough oil to lightly coat lettuce leaves and make them glisten. Season with salt and freshly ground pepper. Slowly drizzle on vinegar or squeeze on fresh lemon. The oil will coat the greens and help acids to adhere and distribute evenly. Or toss greens with vinaigrette. It should not pool on the bottom of the bowl, just gently coat leaves.

6 Serve dressed salad immediately—or greens will become wilted and limp.

Signature Technique: French Raw and Cooked Vegetable Salads (Crudités à la Française)

For Americans, crudités (kroo-deh-TAY) conjures images of naked, raw radishes, florets of broccoli and cauliflower, and sticks of carrot and celery cringing on a platter with dip. It's the least visited part of a party. Something has been lost in translation.

True crudités à la Française are colorful, raw or lightly cooked single-vegetable salads dressed with homemade mustard vinaigrette, oil, and vinegar or homemade mayonnaise, seasoned simply with fresh herbs. French home cooks typically serve three salads of contrasting colors and texture—each following the garden as it changes from carrots to cucumbers, tomatoes, celery root, then beets. Crudités à la Française makes an eye-catching buffet or first course. Serve singly or several on a plate, alone, or atop salad greens.

Most French cooks make only a narrow range of traditional salads based on sliced tomato or cucumber, grated celery root, shredded carrot, or roasted beets. Cooks are not bound by convention, so get creative. Season crudités well with salt and freshly ground pepper, mayonnaise or a choice of oils and various vinegars or freshly squeezed citrus juice.

CRUDITÉS SUGGESTIONS

- Thinly sliced fennel bulb dressed with toasted fennel seed, fresh lemon juice, and olive oil
- Roasted, skinned bell pepper with torn basil, olive oil, and red wine or balsamic vinegar

- Shredded, salt-wilted cabbage dressed with chopped Italian parsley or caraway seed, olive oil, and red wine vinegar
- Shredded carrots dressed in a crunchy heap with walnut oil, toasted

(Continued)

(Continued)

walnuts, fresh lemon juice and fresh mint, dill leaves, or fines herbes
- **Wedges of sun-warmed tomatoes** tossed with olive oil, red wine vinegar, and torn basil leaves
- **Finely sliced, salt-wilted cucumbers** dressed with *Mustard Vinaigrette* or oil and vinegar
- **Beets** baked in foil, peeled and finely shredded or cubed, and dressed with dill and vinaigrette or *Crème Fraîche* and dill *or* dress long raw spiral shreds with mustard vinaigrette
- **Celery root or turnips**, peeled and grated or shredded raw with *Sauce Remoulade* or lemon mayonnaise *or* mixed with equal parts grated apple and dressed with remoulade or mayonnaise

CREATE A RATATOUILLE

French *ratatouille* was first made around Provence and Nice in the south of France, but Spanish cooks claim to have created this braised summer vegetable dish made with onion, garlic, tomato, bell pepper, eggplant, and zucchini. The mother of ratatouille, Spanish *alboronia*, is made in Don Quixote's *La Mancha* region, south of Madrid. Catalan cooks prepare a similar dish called *samfaina* (sometimes with grilled vegetables) and Majorcan cooks prepare a layered version with potatoes called *tumbet*. (See *Salad and Vegetable Methods* in chapter *Spain*.)

French chef Joël Robuchon says that the secret of a good ratatouille is to cook the vegetables separately "so each will taste truly of itself." In the classic dish, fresh tomatoes simmer with Provençal olive oil, garlic, and thyme into a sauce. The separately sweated, tender vegetables, parsley, and basil are added to the tomato sauce and just heated through; if the tomatoes aren't ripe and rich, cooks stir in a little tomato paste. In *Mastering the Art of French Cooking (Volume 1)*, Knopf, 1971, Julia Childs roasts the vegetables in a 400 degree F oven then layers them with the sauce and simmers the dish 10 minutes. It may be served hot, warm, or room temperature or used as a base for soup and stew.

These proportions will yield about 2 quarts ratatouille, but it may be tweaked to suit personal tastes.

Extra virgin olive oil, as needed
3/4 ounce garlic, 3 large cloves, peeled and sliced or 4-1/2 teaspoons minced
Fresh or dried thyme
1-1/2 pounds ripe tomatoes, 3 large, about 4 cups skinned and diced
1 pound onions, 2 large, about 4 cups sliced or diced
3/4 to 1 pound eggplant, 1 large, about 5 cups sliced or diced
3/4 to 1 pound green bell peppers, 2 large, 3 to 4 cups stemmed, seeded, and sliced or diced
8 ounces zucchini, 2 medium, about 2 cups sliced or diced
1/4 ounce trimmed Italian parsley, 2 tablespoons chopped
Torn basil leaves

THE REGIONAL FOOD OF FRANCE

Notice that the organization of this chapter differs from the rest of the book. Instead of organization by technique, it is organized by region. Most culinary school training is firmly rooted in dishes and techniques that have been codified by French chefs. Rather than repeat topics and techniques, it seems more beneficial to highlight the regions of France and some of their special dishes.

FIGURE 5.20 Fleur de ael salt flats in Brittany, France.
Source: Philcopain/Fotolia.

REGION ONE: NORTHWEST FRANCE

Brittany—Contrasts of Land and Dangerous Coastline

This wind-swept area of sandy beaches and rocky cliffs is known for superb seafood and salt-marsh fed lamb, crêpes, hard cider, and buckwheat *galettes*. More Celtic than Gallic, this peninsula has poor soil that grows buckwheat but no wheat. The freshest seafood abound: Belon oysters, sea urchins, *mussels à la marinére*, *homard à l'Américaine*, *beurre blanc*, salt cod, and the seafood stew *cotriade*. Potatoes, cabbage, artichokes, cauliflower, strawberries, dried beans, and chestnuts grow inland.

BUCKWHEAT CRÊPES (CRÊPES OR GALETTES AU SARRASIN)

Crêpes originated in Brittany—a century ago Bretons made all crêpes with buckwheat flour. Buckwheat was imported from Asia to Brittany during the Crusades and grew well there. Most crêperies offer the beloved savory or sweet light-as-air crêpes from wheat flour (crêpes au froment) and two styles of buckwheat crêpes or galettes (crêpes au sarrasin)—made thicker in southern Brittany and thinner in the north. When roasted, buckwheat groats are assertive and earthy. Milk in the batter softens their flavor, but buckwheat gives crêpes the strength to stand up to strong Breton fillings like caramelized onions, honey, ham and fried eggs, cheese, and mushrooms.

Yields 20 to 24 fluid ounces, 16 to 18 small and 10 to 12 large crêpes

1/4 cup beaten egg, about 1 large egg
1-1/3 cups water *or* milk
3-1/2 to 4-1/2 ounces buckwheat flour, 3/4 cup
   or 3-1/2 to 4-1/2 ounces roasted buckwheat groats
About 3-1/2 ounces white flour, 3/4 cup
1/4 teaspoon kosher salt
Butter, oil, or lard for cooking

If using groats for fresh flour: Grind buckwheat groats in small batches in a coffee grinder until powdered.

1 Mix the Batter:

   Hand Method: Whisk together eggs with milk or water. Pour flours and salt into mixing bowl. Pour egg mixture into flour and hand-whisk batter. Hand-whisking strengthens the batter.

   Blender Method: Pour eggs and half the liquid into blender or food processor and process 5 seconds then add dry ingredients and process another 5 to 10 seconds. Scrape batter into bowl, rinse out blender with remaining liquid, and mix into batter.

2 Cover bowl with plastic wrap and rest batter 1 to 24 hours; refrigerate if more than 1 hour. Resting batter produces tender crêpes.

3 Bring batter to room temperature. Strain batter if it looks lumpy. Check batter consistency: it should be slightly thinner than heavy cream.

4 Heat a *flat cast-iron, steel crêpe, or nonstick* pan over medium-high heat.

> Use a 6-inch or 7-inch interior diameter pan for small crêpes.
> Use a 9-inch or 10-inch interior diameter pan for large crêpes.

5 When pan is hot, drizzle on melted butter, lard. or oil. Rub it over pan with paper towel. Fat should not pool on pan, just glaze it. *Alternatively*, use similar sized nonstick pans and drizzle on butter, lard, or oil.

6 Lift pan off burner, pour on batter, and spread by tilting pan to form a thin, round film of a crêpe on the pan. (Breton cooks use a wooden T-shaped spreading tool called a *rozell*.)

> 3 tablespoons batter for 6-inch to 7-inch pan (16 to 18 crêpes)
> 1/4 cup batter for 9-inch to 10-inch pan (10 to 12 crêpes)

7 Cook crêpe without touching until top looks dry and set and edges brown and curl, 1 minute. (Crêpe is very tender and will tear easily until it sets.) Flip crêpe with fingers or heatproof rubber spatula, and cook remaining side 30 seconds.

8 Rub crêpe lightly with butter, if desired. Stack crêpes and cover with foil; keep warm in 200 degree F oven covered with foil until ready for filling and eating.

9 Repeat crêpe-making until all batter is used. Fill crêpes, or cool, and place in zipper baggies. Refrigerate 3 days and freeze up to 2 months.

10 **To Use:** Serve crêpes plain, drizzled with honey, or stuffed with fillings like caramelized onions, ham and fried eggs, or cheese and mushrooms. See **Vary! Improvise!** for more suggestions.

Trouble, Trouble

- Batter frothy? Let it rest.
- Crêpes too lacy or edges crack? Batter is too thin or pan is too hot. Add flour or lower heat.
- A few spots were missed when tilting pan? Drop bits of batter into the space.
- Batter won't spread and cover pan? Batter is too thick. Thin with water or milk.
- Batter curdles in pan? Too much fat in pan—wipe out with paper towel.

Vary! Improvise!

☞ *Traditional Filling:* Layer thinly sliced prosciutto or ham, sautéed mushrooms, and grated cheese on top of a buckwheat crêpe, roll into a log or fold into a triangle, and place in baking dish. Bake at 350 degrees F to melt cheese, 10 to 12 minutes.

☞ *Goat Filling:* Prepare 8 ounces goat cheese with 5 tablespoons chopped fresh herbs or *Fines Herbes*. Season with salt and pepper and thin with milk or cream until spreadable. Spread 1 tablespoon filling over each crêpe and roll up or fold.

☞ *Crêpe Cake:* Smear crêpes with a thin layer of apple butter or applesauce and crème fraîche, and stack on top of each other. Cut like a cake.

☞ *Many Ways to Fold 'Em:* Fill and shape crêpes into cigars, triangles, envelopes or quesadillas, or slice into noodles.

☞ *Green Pancakes:* Purée herb leaves into batter.

MIGHTY MUSSELS

FIGURE 5.21 Mussels on the Brittany coast.
Source: Friedberg/Fotolia.

- About 20 to 25 medium-sized mussels make 1 pound and yield about 6 to 8 ounces meat.
- One pound of mussels will serve one person for dinner and 2 to 3 as an appetizer.

Mussels are so savory and succulent that many French chefs consider them one of the most important flavor enhancing foods in a French kitchen. Commercial mussels grow on the sea floor in cultivated beds, attached to poles or on ropes suspended in water. Sedentary mussels attach themselves to a surface and to each other by very strong *byssal threads* or *beards*. In the wild, mussels attach to each other in colonies off sea-washed rocks.

Before spawning, mussels are at their meatiest (October to May). After spawning, meat content drops about 10 per cent. On the West coast, avoid mussels during the toxic *red tide*, which occurs during warm months. Microorganisms called *dinoflagellates*, and their concentrated toxins, cause serious illness and paralytic shellfish poisoning. Low in saturated fat, mussels provide easily absorbed vitamins B and C, amino acids, Omega 3 fatty acids, and minerals iron, manganese, phosphorus, potassium, selenium, and zinc.

FIGURE 5.22 Cleaning a mussel.
Source: David Murray/DK Images.

Vary! Improvise!

☞ *What other combinations of flavorings or seasonings from other regions of France might work here in place of shallots and thyme?*

☞ *Check out Spanish and Italian versions of this mussel dish.*

☞ *Substitute beer or a favorite liqueur for the wine.*

☞ *Enrich mussel broth with a little cream or unsalted butter.*

☞ *Add 2 ounces fresh fennel, 1/2 cup finely diced, to the broth-base before it's cooked.*

MUSSELS STEAMED IN WHITE WINE (MOULES MARINERE)

Diners pull apart the shells and use a half shell as a utensil to scoop out the mussel. Don't ignore the steaming broth; it's richly savory and as important as the mussels. Mussels served with French fries and mayonnaise or aioli *are called* moules et frites *(mool et freet). Remove shells (and discard) and toss cooked pasta with mussels and broth for a great first course or lunch.*

4 servings

2 pounds mussels, about 40 to 50
2/3 to 1 cup good dry white wine
About 1 ounce shallots, 1/4 cup minced
1 bay leaf
2 large sprigs fresh thyme
2 to 3 tablespoons unsalted butter, diced
Garnish: 1/2 ounce trimmed Italian parsley, 1/4 cup chopped

For Serving

Fresh baguette, sliced

1 Place mussels into a colander. Pick through each and scrub carefully. Rinse, drain, and chill.

2 **Prepare flavorful cooking broth-base:** Pour wine, shallots, bay leaf, thyme, and butter into a 6-quart pot. Bring to a boil over high heat until butter melts. Remove from heat until ready to use.

3 **Immediately before cooking:** De-beard mussels—pull away their black threads. De-bearding kills mussels. Dead mussels decay quickly. Do not allow mussels to soak in water. Toss out cracked mussels or any that won't close tightly when tapped or are extra heavy (probably mud-filled). Keep mussels cold and covered with damp towel.

4 **Reheat broth-base:** Add mussels to the bubbling hot base, stir mussels to coat, cover pot, and steam until mussels open, 4 to 5 minutes, shaking pot several times throughout cooking. Remove opened mussels immediately with a slotted spoon and transfer into bowl or on wide soup plates. Discard any that did not open. Reserve mussel broth. Garnish mussel broth with parsley.

5 **To Serve:** Let sand settle to bottom of pot and ladle hot mussel cooking broth with parsley over mussels. Serve with slices of baguette to soak up broth.

MOULES ET FRITES

New York pastry chef and cookbook author Nick Malgieri says that the classic French combination of steamed mussels and French fries served with mayonnaise probably originated in Belgium where mussels are a staple and potatoes were accepted soon after their arrival in Europe. The combo migrated across the border to French cooks who embraced it as their own. Many bistros in Brussels offer a wide range of choices, from mussels steamed with a mirepoix, white wine, and a little butter, to Pernod and cream, or beer-infused mussels.

REGION TWO: NORTHWESTERN FRANCE

Normandy—Dairy Pastureland, Norman Influences

This rich land of apple tree, cow, and sea produces the best pork, cream, and seafood in France. It has twice the cow pasturage of any French province. Norman soil is too rich for grapes, but great for apples. Its apple pies are France's best. Normandy's specialties are *porc normande* (pork with apples and cream), sole Dieppoise, Madame Poulard's omelette, *canard à la Rouennaise. joue de bœuf* (braised beef cheek), shellfish platter, dover sole in brown butter, *moules marinière*, *boudin noir* (blood sausage), *carbonnade* (beef and beer stew), tripe, head cheese, salt-marsh fed lamb, butter, *crème fraîche*, *teurgoule* (rice pudding), hard cider, and the fiery apple brandy and Calvados.

FISH WITH APPLES AND CIDER (POISSON VALLÉE D'AUGE)

The Auge Valley of Normandy is home to the best cider apples in France. Substitute chicken or veal for fish if desired.

4 to 6 servings

1-1/2 pounds skinned and boned turbot or other white fish fillets like loup de mer or sole
Unsalted butter
8 ounces leek, 1 leek, white part only, 1 cup halved lengthwise, cleaned, and sliced crosswise
4 to 5 ounce tart green apple, 1 medium, 1 cup peeled, cored, and thinly sliced
1-1/2 cups dry hard cider
1-1/2 cups fish stock *or* clam juice
8 ounces white mushrooms, about 2 cups halved and finely sliced
2 teaspoons freshly squeezed lemon juice, more to taste
8 ounces *Crème Fraîche*, 1 cup

1 Heat oven to 375 degrees F.

2 Rinse fillets with cold water and pat dry. Season fillets with salt and pepper and fold fillets in half (or roll loosely) with skinned side inside.

3 Butter a 10-inch ovenproof skillet and arrange leeks and apple in it. Arrange fish on top and pour cider and stock or clam juice over fish and vegetables. Cover skillet with buttered parchment cut to fit inside of skillet (buttered side facing fish). Bring to a simmer. Place pan or dish in oven and bake until fish flakes easily, 10 to 15 minutes. Transfer fish to warm platter with slotted spoon and keep warm. Tent fish with aluminum foil. Reserve fish cooking liquid.

4 Meanwhile, heat a 6-quart pot or 12-inch skillet over high heat, add mushrooms and sprinkle with lemon juice, 2 tablespoons water, and season with salt and pepper. Cover vessel and cook mushrooms until they are tender, 5 to 8 minutes. Remove mushrooms with slotted spoon and set aside. Reserve juices in pan.

5 Pour fish cooking liquid along with apples and leeks into pan with mushroom juices. Bring to a boil and reduce liquid to 1/2 cup, 15 to 20 minutes, depending on pan. Apples may either soften or hold their shape. Stir in crème fraîche or cream and reduce the heat. Simmer sauce until reduced by 1/4 and just thick enough to coat a spoon lightly, but leave a mark when a finger is drawn through it, 3 to 5 minutes.

6 **Just before serving:** Stir mushrooms and liquid from fish on platter into sauce. Taste sauce and season with salt, pepper, or lemon juice. Reheat fish in sauce gently over low heat 2 minutes. Don't boil sauce or it will break.

7 **To Serve:** Transfer fish to warm serving plates or platter. Off the heat, whisk in 1 to 2 tablespoons chopped butter. Spoon sauce over fish and serve immediately.

Source: *Country Cooking of France* by Anne Willan.

Vary! Improvise!

☞ *Porc Normande:* Substitute sliced raw pork loin for fish.

☞ *Poulet Normande:* Substitute boneless, skinless chicken breasts for fish.

AGNEAU DE PRÉ-SALÉ

The flavor of lamb from the Norman coastal meadows of Cotentin and Saint-Michel Bay is distinctively salty. The animals dine on grass seasoned by the seawater and salty winds that periodically wash over the meadows. The animals' high consumption of salt, iodine, and more than 60 herbs results in an extraordinarily tender, juicy meat. It's so prized for its special tang and mild herbaceous flavor that in 2009 *agneau de pré-salé* was awarded an Appellation d'Origine Contrôlée (AOC) designation, which protects the name.

LAMB STEW WITH SPRING VEGETABLES (NAVARÍN PRINTANIER DE PRÉ-SALÉ)

Navarin is one of the top ten favorite dishes in France. It is especially good made with the salt-marsh lamb (pré-salé) of Normandy. Young, tender fresh vegetables are the gold standard for this dish.

Yields 9 to 10 cups, 4 to 6 servings

3 to 4 tablespoons vegetable oil, *divided*
Flour, as needed
2 pounds trimmed, boneless lamb shoulder or leg, diced into 1- to 1-1/2-inch cubes
1 cup dry (hard) cider *or* white wine
1-1/2 cups chicken stock
8 ounces tomatoes, 1 large, about 1 cup finely diced
    or 14-1/2 ounce can plum tomatoes, 1 cup drained and diced
1/4 ounce garlic, 1 large clove, 1-1/2 teaspoons peeled and minced
1 tablespoon minced fresh thyme
1 tablespoon minced fresh marjoram
    or 1 teaspoon dried marjoram
1 large bay leaf
1 tablespoon vegetable oil
1 ounce unsalted butter, 2 tablespoons diced
3 ounces small shallots, 12 medium, 1 cup peeled and roots trimmed but not cut off
12 ounces small new potatoes, about 8, 1-1/2 cups scrubbed or peeled and halved
6 to 8 ounces young carrots, about 1-1/2 cups sliced diagonally
6 ounces baby turnips, about 6 small, 1-1/4 cups scrubbed and halved
9 ounces shelled or frozen peas, 2 cups
1/4 ounce trimmed Italian parsley, 2 tablespoons chopped

For Serving

Crusty bagette *or* hot, cooked egg noodles

1 Heat a heavy 6-quart pot (about 11-inch diameter) over medium-high heat with 2 tablespoons oil. Pour flour into a mixing bowl. Season lamb cubes with a little salt and dredge half in flour. Shake off excess flour, and place lamb cubes in hot oil. Lamb should fit in one layer with space in between for good browning. Sauté meat until evenly browned. Turn with tongs. Remove to a bowl, and repeat browning with remaining oil, flour, and lamb.

2 Return all meat to pan. Stir in cider to deglaze and scrape bottom of pan. Boil 1 minute. Stir in stock, tomato, garlic, and herbs. Bring stew to a boil, lower the heat and simmer, partially covered, until meat is tender, 1 hour. Skim away excess fat.

   *Optional: For a finer result, transfer lamb to clean bowl, and push sauce through strainer into clean 6-quart pot. Skim away fat. Stir lamb cubes back into sauce and reheat.

3 Heat oil and butter in 12-inch skillet over medium-high heat. Stir in shallots, potatoes, carrots, and turnips, and season with a little salt. Sauté vegetables until browned, 5 to 7 minutes. Transfer vegetables with slotted spoon (drain excess fat) to the lamb stew. Bring stew to a low boil, reduce heat, and simmer partially covered until vegetables are tender, 15 minutes. If using, stir in fresh shell peas and simmer 4 minutes. Taste stew and season with salt and pepper.

4 **To Serve:** If using frozen peas, stir in and bring stew to a simmer. Stir in parsley and serve stew immediately with crusty baguette or over noodles.

Vary! Improvise!

☞ *Less Fat:* Steam potatoes, carrots, and turnips until just tender instead of sautéing.

☞ *Seasonal and Colorful:* Substitute other garden fresh vegetables by color like green beans.

SOUFFLÉ OMELET MADAME POULARD
(OMELETTE MÈRE POULARD)

This signature omelet is served at the foot of Mont-Saint-Michel, where the Hôtel la Mère Poulard is known for its breakfasts. The chefs whisk the eggs for these light-as-air omelets in copper bowls and cook them over an oak wood-fire. Madame Poulard advises cooks not to let the butter brown or to overcook the eggs.

2 servings

4 large eggs, about 1 cup
2 tablespoons whipping cream
1 to 1-1/2 ounces unsalted butter, 2 to 3 tablespoons diced

1   Preheat oven to 350 degrees F. Clean a mixing bowl with a little vinegar and rinse with water. Blot dry. Set another mixing bowl nearby. Separate eggs, taking care not to mix any yolk with whites. Place whites into the vinegar-cleaned bowl. Place yolks into the other bowl.

2   Whisk egg yolks with cream, salt, and freshly ground pepper until very light-colored and thickened. With a clean whisk, beat egg whites until almost stiff peaked. Lighten yolks by stirring in a little of the beaten whites. Fold in remaining whites.

3   Heat a 9-inch omelet pan or nonstick skillet over medium-high heat and add butter. When it foams, pour the egg batter into the pan and smooth the top. Reduce heat to medium. Cook egg until puffed and lightly browned on bottom, 3 to 5 minutes. (Lift omelet at edge to judge color.) Place skillet in oven, and bake omelet until a knife inserted in center comes out clean, 10 to 12 minutes. Loosen omelet edges with spatula.

4   To Serve:

Serve Folded
With sharp knife, cut along the center of the omelet, but not through to bottom. Fill the center, if desired. Tip skillet. With pancake turner, fold omelet in half on the cut, and invert onto warmed plate or platter with a flip of the wrist.

Serve Open-Faced
Slide omelet from pan onto plate. Spoon or sprinkle filling, if desired, over top. Cut in half or into wedges. Serve immediately.

Vary! Improvise!

☞ *Cheesy: Fold shredded or crumbled cheese into eggs.*
☞ *Sweet: Fold sliced strawberries or fruit marmalade into eggs.*
☞ *Savory Herbs: Fold a combination of Italian parsley, chives, and chervil or basil into batter.*

REGION THREE: NORTHERN FRANCE

Champagne, Paris, and Île-de France—
An Ancient Crossroads

This wide region of mostly flat land is known for cabbage, Belgian endive, potatoes, sugar beets, and root vegetables. *Île de France*, literally an island with Paris in its center, is the historical point zero of France. The surrounding region is its pantry, and known for wheat and Brie. In Champagne, Belgian (Flemish) influences come through in hearty, filling dishes like the yeast-dough quiche, *flamiche*, and in stews: juniper-kissed *hochepot* and mustard-garnished *carbonnade*. Stuffed cabbage, pea soup, crusted pâtés, mussels in cream, and herring in white wine are popular.

FLEMISH CHICKEN SOUP (WATERZOOI DE POULET)

A "waterzooi" is actually a classic Flemish chicken stew, similar to blanquette de veau—meat simmered in chicken stock, aromatic herbs, and vegetables, and finished with a liaison of eggs and cream. Originally made with fish, waterzooi often includes carrots and potatoes, and is served with a baguette to sop up liquid. With the extra stock in this recipe the stew becomes soup.

Yields about 3 quarts, 6 to 8 servings

1 tablespoon unsalted butter, finely diced
About 12 to 16 ounces leeks, 2 cups trimmed and white and tender green thinly sliced
4 ounces trimmed celery, 2 to 3 medium stalks, 1 to 1-1/4 cups thinly sliced
8 to 9 ounces onion, 1 medium, peeled, trimmed, and quartered through root end
2 whole cloves
1/2 to 2/3 ounce Italian parsley, 6 large sprigs, leaves and stems separated
1 cup dry white wine
3-1/2 pound chicken, rinsed
1/4 teaspoon grated nutmeg
2 quarts chicken stock

Liaison

3/4 cup heavy cream
4 large egg yolks

1 Spread butter, leeks, celery, onion quarters stuck with cloves, and parsley stems into a heavy 6-quart soup pot. Heat pot over medium heat. Drizzle vegetables with wine. Cut out a circle of parchment to fit inside of pot and cut and small hole in its center. Place parchment on top of vegetables, lower heat, and simmer/sweat until soft, 20 minutes.

2 Meanwhile, cut chicken into 6 pieces (legs, thighs, breasts), remove skin and excess fat, and discard. When vegetables are tender, remove parchment, discard it, and arrange chicken on top of vegetables. Sprinkle with nutmeg and 1 teaspoon kosher salt. Pour chicken stock over mixture. Bring to a boil, lower heat, cover partially, and simmer soup until chicken is very tender, 1 to 1-1/4 hours. Transfer chicken from pot to mixing bowl with tongs. When cooled enough to handle, remove meat from bones and cut into bite-sized pieces; place back into clean mixing bowl, and keep warm. Discard bones, parsley stems, and onion halves.

3 **Temper and finish with liaison:** Whisk remaining butter, cream, egg yolks, and chopped parsley together in small heatproof bowl. Slowly whisk 1/2-cup hot soup into eggs and cream. Remove soup from heat. Slowly pour, and stir tempered liaison into hot soup. Taste soup and season again if necessary with salt and pepper. Stir in reserved chicken meat.

4 **To Serve:** Ladle hot soup into (preheated) bowls, and garnish with croutons, if desired.

Source: *The Soups of France* by Lois Anne Rothert.

Vary! Improvise!

☛ *More Flavor: Stir in 1 tablespoon chopped tarragon leaves with parsley.*
☛ *Save: Purée or finely chop onion quarters and stir back into soup-stew.*

FIGURE 5.23 Belgian endive.
Source: Eric Gevaert/Fotolia.

ENDIVE SALAD WITH SHALLOT VINAIGRETTE (SALADE ENDIVE AU VINAIGRETTE DU ECHALOTE)

Vary the shallot preparation for different flavor: add them raw, cooked soft, or sautéed brown. To cut endive ahead and keep from browning, cover julienned leaves with cold water and 1 tablespoon fresh lemon juice. Refrigerate. Blot dry before dressing.

4 to 6 servings

Shallot Vinaigrette

Yields about 5 fluid ounces

1 large egg yolk
2 tablespoons white wine vinegar
1 tablespoon Dijon mustard
1/3 cup extra virgin olive oil
1 ounce shallot, 1 large, 2 tablespoons peeled and finely minced

12 ounces Belgian endive, about 3 heads

1 **Prepare vinaigrette:** whisk together egg yolk, vinegar and mustard. Slowly whisk oil into mixture a thin stream until thickened. Stir in shallots (raw or softened). Season dressing with salt and pepper. Refrigerate until serving.

2 **Immediately before serving:** Halve endive heads lengthwise; remove core with a small V-cut at the base of the endive. Julienne endive leaves lengthwise. Transfer to mixing bowl.

3 **To Serve:** Immediately toss endive with dressing. Pile onto a platter or serving plates. Serve immediately.

REGION FOUR: NORTHEASTERN FRANCE

Alsace-Lorraine—German Influences

Set on the alluvial plain of the Rhine, with the wild, forested Vosges Mountains as backdrop, this hilly, rural region is known for wild mushrooms, cabbage, game, trout, fine white wines, *foie gras*, and pork. Specialties are *soupe aux cerise* (cherry soup), braised boar with mushrooms and bilberries, *quiche lorraine, choucroute alsacienne, babas au rhum, spaetzli, kugelhopf*, and boar or deer prepared with red wine, juniper, and currant jelly. Potatoes, Brussels sprouts, bacon, sausage, horseradish, rutabaga, goose, and fruit *eau de vies* are featured.

French Noodles

French cooks rarely make noodles, except in Alsace and Lorraine, near the German border. They are not served alone or as a first course: Instead, noodles are tossed in butter or browned in butter with breadcrumbs, or tossed with cream and vinegar, and served as a side dish. Spaetzli go well with meat dishes like *choucroute garni*, roast goose, foie gras, and quail with juniper berries. A hot noodle salad called *totelots* has a cold dressing of oil, vinegar, cream, shallots, and garlic and is popular in Lorraine.

FIGURE 5.24 Alsace, France.
Source: Zharastudio/Fotolia.

SPAETZLI

Season these tender noodles with a choice of herbs or spices, boil, and serve with butter or fry until golden and heap with fresh herbs like parsley or basil. Boil them in chicken broth or beer for richer flavor.

Yields about 18 fluid ounces dough, 4 to 6 servings

9 to 10 ounces all-purpose flour, 2 cups
2 large eggs, 1/2 cup beaten
1 ounce unsalted butter, 2 tablespoons diced into small cubes

1 Sift flour and salt (and spices if using) into bowl. Make a well in the center of the flour and pour in eggs, 1/2 teaspoon kosher salt, and 2/3 cup lukewarm water. With a spoon, begin stirring in flour from around the edges. Mix until dough is smooth and soft. The softer the dough, the lighter will be the spaetzli, but if dough is too soft, and gooey the noodles will disintegrate when boiled. Cover dough and rest 30 minutes.

2 Melt butter in large sauté pan and set aside.

3 Bring a 4-quart saucepan of cold water to a boil and season with salt liberally. When water boils, lower heat so water simmers.

4 Pour half the dough into a spaetzli press, perforated pan, or colander. Push dough through holes into simmering water. Cook noodles until they rise to the surface and are still al dente when tested, 2 to 3 minutes. Alternatively, drop small spoonfuls of dough into simmering water or place dough on small cutting board, cut small "worms" off dough and scrape into simmering water. Remove cooked noodles with slotted spoon, drain, and drop into melted butter. Repeat process with remaining dough.

5 **To Serve:** Season spaetzli with salt and pepper. Serve just heated through, or fry in butter until golden.

Vary! Improvise!

☞ *Season noodle dough with 1/2 teaspoon ground star anise or 1/2 teaspoon ground nutmeg. Serve with beef* daube, coq au vin, *or any stew or braise.*

☞ *Boil noodles in chicken stock, and use them to garnish hot consommé.*

☞ *Toss noodles with fresh dill or chives and sour cream.*

☞ *Toss noodles with a mass of butter-cooked mushrooms and leeks.*

☞ *Substitute 1/4 of the flour with chestnut flour.*

SAUERKRAUT WITH SMOKED, CURED, AND FRESH PORK (CHOUCROUTE GARNIE À L'ALSACIENNE)

Choucroute shows off the richly varied charcuterie of northeastern Alsace.

Yields 8 to 12 servings

1-1/2 pounds fresh ham hocks, about 3 small or 2 large
   or 1-1/2 pounds smoked ham hocks
1/4 cup duck, goose or pork (lard) fat or oil
1 pound yellow onions, 4 cups peeled and finely diced
4-1/2 pounds sauerkraut, about 9 cups drained, lightly rinsed, and squeezed to drain
1-1/2 pounds boneless pork loin or tenderloin
1 pound smoked ham
8 ounces lean slab bacon
1 pound smoked pork sausages, pricked with fork
2-1/2 to 3 ounce head garlic, about 6 to 8 large cloves, peeled

Spices

3 whole cloves
6 juniper berries
5 coriander seeds

4 to 5 cups Alsatian Riesling or other dry, fruity white wine
1 pound fresh pork sausages

1 tablespoon oil
2-1/2 pounds red potatoes, about 12 medium, peeled and halved *or* quartered
Dijon mustard

1 Place ham hocks in a 4-quart saucepan. Cover with cold water, bring to a boil, lower heat, and simmer fresh hocks 1 to 1-1/2 hours and smoked hocks 30 minutes. Drain and set aside.

2 Preheat oven to 350 degrees F. Melt fat in a 10-quart pot (with a lid) over medium heat. Add onions, cook until soft but not browned, 10 to 12 minutes. Mix in kraut. Remove half the mixture and arrange ham hocks, pork loin, ham, bacon, smoked sausage, garlic, and spices on top. Cover meat with remaining kraut and onions and pour wine over it all. Place in oven and bake until meats are tender, about 2 hours. Or bring to a boil, lower heat, cover, and simmer.

3 Prick fresh sausages with a fork, place in a skillet, cover with water, and simmer over medium heat 10 minutes. Drain. Dry the skillet, add oil, and heat over medium heat. Brown the sausages, turning occasionally. After choucroute bakes 1 hour, place sausages on top and continue baking.

4 **Thirty-five minutes before serving:** Place potatoes in a pot of cold salted water over high heat. Bring to a boil, lower heat to medium, and cook until tender, 10 to 20 minutes. Drain and keep warm.

5 **To Serve:** Spoon sauerkraut onto a large platter. Slice pork loin, ham, and bacon, and arrange on platter with ham hocks, potatoes, and sausages. Serve with mustard.

REGION FIVE: CENTRAL AND EASTERN FRANCE

Burgundy, Dijon, and the Lyonnais—The Gastronomic Heart

Crisscrossed with rivers, ponds, lakes, ponds, and mountains, the central part of this region is a calcareous, stony plain called the *bourguignons*. It is covered with vineyards. In part due to the hospitable dukes of Burgundy, this region is a cultural and culinary force with great wine, the renowned Bresse chicken, Charolais beef, Dijon mustard, wild game, river fish, and a largesse of produce. The red wine *sauce meurette* is paired with fish, poached eggs, meat, and snails. Robust dishes like *beef bourguignon, coq au vin, gougère, saucisson en brioche* (sausage rolled in bread and baked), *gratinée lyonnais* (onion soup), and Burgundy and Chablis wines are favored.

Vary! Improvise!

☛ Layer 1 large, tart apple, peeled, cored, and sliced, into casserole.

☛ Vary the meats with any smoked or raw pork products you like: pork chops, Canadian bacon, or frankfurters.

FIGURE 5.25 Vineyards, Burgundy, France.
Source: PHB.cz/Fotolia.

FOWL FRICASSÉE (COQ AU VIN)

Coq means "rooster" and this dish originally was made with a tough, but flavorful rooster. It was marinated overnight (or longer) to tenderize and flavor it. This is a most succulent dish. The wine reduces in two pans for convenience and speed. Slice off stem end of boiling onions and drop into boiling water. Blanch 2 minutes for easier skin removal. Trim root end very lightly so the onion holds together.

6 to 8 servings

Bottle of Wine

One 750 milliliter bottle of wine yields between 3-1/4 and 3-1/2 cups.

1 bottle fruity, medium to full-bodied red wine like Burgundy, Pinot Noir, or Zinfandel, 3-1/2 cups
5 pounds chicken legs and thighs, about 8 large, 4 pounds skinned

Garnish

8 ounces thick cut bacon, sliced into 1/8 to 1/4-wide inch *lardons*
1/4 cup clarified butter
1 pound small boiling onions, peeled, root end lightly trimmed
1 pound domestic mushrooms, 4 cups halved or quartered

3 tablespoons clarified butter, *divided*, more as needed
4 ounces carrots, 3/4 cup finely diced
3 to 4 ounces celery, 3/4 cup finely diced
1 pound onions, 4 cups peeled and finely diced
About 1 ounce shallots, 1/4 cup finely diced
1/2 ounce garlic, 2 large cloves, smashed and peeled
1 bottle fruity, medium to full-bodied red wine like Burgundy, Pinot Noir, or Zinfandel, 3-1/2 cups
2-1/2 cups chicken stock, more as needed for de-glazing

Bouquet Garni

4 large sprigs thyme
1 ounce Italian parsley, about 4 large sprigs
1 large bay leaf

3 tablespoons oil, as needed
About 1-1/4 ounces all-purpose flour, 1/4 cup
2 teaspoons tomato paste
Beurre Manie: 1 tablespoon flour kneaded with 2 teaspoons butter
Scant 1 ounce trimmed Italian parsley, 1/3 cup finely chopped

For Serving

Noodles or French bread

1 Clean excess fat and skin from chicken, blot dry, and place in large mixing bowl. Twenty-four to 48 hours before beginning coq au vin, stir wine into chicken, turning several time to coat and marinate evenly. Cover bowl with plastic wrap and refrigerate 24 to 48 hours. Remove chicken from bowl, drain, and reserve wine. Pat chicken dry. (For *Beef:* The beef may be marinated in red wine overnight if desired. Drain beef, reserve wine, and pat meat dry before cooking.)

2 Heat a heavy 10-inch skillet over medium heat and add bacon. Cook until bacon is crisp and golden-brown. With a slotted spoon, remove bacon to a paper-lined plate to drain. Pour grease out of pan. Deglaze skillet with 1/2 cup of reserved red wine and set aside in small bowl. Wipe out pan.

*If at any point a skillet burns black, transfer food to another skillet. Do not allow it to become incorporated into the dish. Burned food makes for a bitter dish.

3 Heat skillet over medium heat, and add 2 tablespoons clarified butter. Add small onions, cover pan, and cook until soft. Uncover skillet, raise heat to medium-high, and cook, stirring or shaking pan, until they are evenly browned but not burned. Remove onions to a bowl and set aside. If skillet is browned, deglaze with a little stock or water and reserve liquid. If skillet is burned, discard deglazing liquid.

4 Reheat skillet over medium-high heat, add 1 tablespoon clarified butter, and stir in mushrooms. Cook 2 minutes, lower heat to medium, and cook until mushrooms brown. Transfer mushrooms from skillet into bowl with onions. *For chicken only:* Pour remaining wine reserved from marinade and 1 cup chicken stock into skillet, and bring to boil over medium-high heat. Boil until 2 cups remain.

5 Heat 11- to 12-inch Dutch oven with 2 tablespoons clarified butter over medium-high heat. Stir in carrots, celery, onion, shallots, and garlic, and sauté until vegetables are golden. Pour the remaining bottle of wine, the reserved deglazed wine from step 2, and 1 cup broth into vegetables. (For *Beef:* Pour in 3 cups wine plus 1 cup beef stock.) Add bouquet garni; bring to a boil over medium-high heat. Reduce until 2 cups remain.

6 Heat 3 tablespoons oil in 12-inch skillet over high. Lightly salt meat pieces and toss with flour, shake off excess flour, and add meat to hot fat. Without crowding, sauté meat in 2 to 3 batches until evenly browned. Transfer into a bowl. Deglaze pan with broth in between batches and scrape deglazing liquid into bowl with meat.

7 Combine meat, deglazed and reduced broth, and wine mixtures into Dutch oven. Stir in tomato paste. Bring wine, vegetables, and meat to a boil, and reduce heat to a simmer. Cook meat covered, with lid slightly askew, until tender, turning once or twice, 35 to 45 minutes. Meat should pierce easily with a skewer.

8 With a slotted spoon, transfer meat into ovenproof and stovetop-proof casserole or deep serving dish. Tuck bacon, mushrooms, and onions in and around it. Cover and keep warm.

9 Skim away excess fat from cooking liquid. Pour liquid and vegetables remaining in Dutch oven into a fine strainer into a saucepan. Push and scrape vegetables firmly through strainer into saucepan. Discard vegetable residue. Bring sauce to a boil. Whisk in small amounts of the butter-flour beurre manie slowly until sauce thickens to sauce consistency. **Use only what is needed to thicken sauce.** The sauce should just coat the back of a spoon lightly. Season sauce to taste with salt and pepper.

10 **To Serve:** Ladle hot sauce over hot chicken (or *Beef*) and vegetables in casserole. Garnish with parsley. Serve hot with noodles or French bread.

BEEF STEW FROM BURGUNDY (BEEF BOURGUIGNON)

6 servings

3 pounds trimmed stewing beef (chuck) diced into 2-inch cubes

Garnish

6 ounces lean bacon or pork belly, sliced into 1/8- to 1/4-wide inch *lardons*
1/4 cup clarified butter
1 pound small white boiling onions, peeled, root lightly trimmed so root holds onion together
1 pound fresh domestic mushrooms, 4 cups halved or quartered

3 tablespoons clarified butter, *divided*, more as needed
4 ounces carrots, 3/4 cup finely diced
3 to 4 ounces celery, 3/4 cup finely diced
1 pound onions, 3-1/2 to 4 cups finely diced
3/4 ounce garlic, 3 large cloves, smashed and peeled
3 cups Burgundy wine
2 cups beef stock

Bouquet Garni

2 large sprigs fresh thyme
1 ounce Italian parsley, about 4 large sprigs
1 large bay leaf

3 tablespoons oil, as needed
About 1-1/4 ounces flour, 1/4 cup
1 tablespoon tomato paste
Beurre Manie: 1 tablespoon flour kneaded with 2 teaspoons butter
Scant 1 ounce trimmed Italian parsley, 1/3 cup finely chopped

For Serving

Noodles or French bread

1 Follow the method for *Signature Recipe: Fowl Fricassée (Coq au Vin)* and look for (*Beef*). This recipe uses less wine so it reduces in one pan.

Vary! Improvise!

☞ *Substitute turkey legs for chicken or even rabbit.*

☞ *Prepare with full-bodied white wine instead of red.*

☞ **Butter-Free Manie:** *Mix olive oil with flour to make a paste as cooks do in the South of France.*

FRENCH ONION SOUP (GRATINÉE LYONNAISE)

Although eighteenth-century French chefs polished it with caramelized onions, ancient Greek and Roman home cooks first prepared onion soup with onions cooked until just soft.

Yields about 9 cups, 6 to 8 servings

1 recipe *Caramelized Onions*, 1-1/2 cups
6 cups chicken broth
2 cups beef broth
1 tablespoon balsamic vinegar

Garnish

1 baguette sliced diagonally into six to eight 1/2- to 3/4-inch thick
3 to 4 ounces Gruyère cheese, about 1 cup grated

1 Whisk caramelized onions into stock in a 4-quart saucepan, and bring to a boil. Lower heat to a simmer, and cover pan. For melting onions and deep flavor, simmer soup 1 hour.

2 Stir in balsamic vinegar. Season soup with salt and pepper.

3 Heat broiler. Toast baguette slices on cookie sheet. Top with each with 2 tablespoons Gruyère. Place under broiler briefly to melt.

4 **To Serve:** Ladle hot soup into bowls and top with baguette slices.

SALAD FROM LYON (SALADE LYONNAISE)

For centuries Lyon has been the French capital of gastronomy, probably because two of France's beloved wine-growing regions are near Lyon: Beaujolais lies to the North, and the Côtes du Rhône to the South. Many of France's finest chefs have worked there, notably Paul Bocuse. Beaujolais is the most popular wine served with local dishes. It goes well with this salad. Although lyonnaise usually signals a dish with many onions, some savvy ancestral cook took the combo of toast, eggs, and bacon and transformed it into this celebrated classic Lyonnaise dish.

4 servings

3 ounces country style bread, 3 to 4 cups diced into 1/2-inch cubes
1 tablespoon olive oil
8 ounces thick-cut bacon, cut into *lardons* (1/4-inch wide strips)
12-ounce head frisée or curly endive, about 8 cups washed, dried, and torn or sliced
4 large eggs
1 teaspoon white wine vinegar
3 tablespoons olive oil
5 tablespoons red wine vinegar, *divided*, to taste

1 Preheat oven to 350 degrees F. Toss bread cubes with olive oil. Spread bread in a single layer on a baking sheet and bake until golden brown, 10 to 15 minutes.

2 Lay bacon into a 12-inch skillet. Heat skillet over medium heat and fry bacon until crisp, turning to cook both sides evenly. Discard all but 3 tablespoons bacon fat.

3 Toss frisée into a large mixing bowl.

4 **Poach the eggs:** Fill a 2-quart saucepan with cold water and white wine vinegar, and bring to a boil. Reduce the heat to a bare bubble. Break eggs into pan. Simmer eggs until whites are set and yolks still runny, 3 to 4 minutes. Pour water off eggs and set them aside to keep warm while finishing salad. (To hold eggs overnight or up to two days: chill poached eggs, and reheat in simmering water just before serving.)

5 Add oil to skillet with bacon fat, and heat over high heat. When fat is hot, pour over frisée, and toss well. The heat should wilt the greens slightly (to wilt greens further, place in hot skillet and toss with tongs then remove to bowl). Pour 4 tablespoons vinegar into the hot pan, deglaze, and cook until it has reduced by half, 30 seconds to 1 minute. Pour hot vinegar over salad and toss. Toss again with croutons and bacon. Taste salad, and season with salt and freshly ground pepper and more vinegar, to taste.

6 **To Serve:** Divide salad among 4 plates. Scoop a warm egg with a slotted spoon, blot dry, and place on top of one salad. Finish with remaining eggs and salad, and serve immediately. To eat, break egg yolk and toss it with salad to coat the leaves—smoky, bitter-sharp, sour, and unctuous-rich all in one dish.

EGGS AND RED WINE SAUCE (OEUFS MEURETTE)

This sauce and dish are a specialty of Burgundy. Meurettes are wine-based and flavored with a classic mirepoix, bouquet garni, and bound with beurre manie (kneaded butter). This sauce goes well with fish, beef, and poached eggs. Use the best moderately-priced wine available.

6 servings

6 tablespoons melted clarified butter

Mirepoix

1 ounce onion, 1/4 cup finely diced 1/4-inch cubes
About 1-1/3 ounces carrots, 1/4 cup peeled and finely diced 1/4-inch cubes
About 1 ounce trimmed celery, 1/4 cup finely diced 1/4-inch cubes

1 ounce ham, prosciutto, or Westphalian ham, 2 tablespoons diced into 1/4-inch cubes
3 cups red wine

Bouquet Garni

1 bay leaf
2 large sprigs thyme
5 large stems from Italian parsley

Beurre Manie: 4 teaspoons flour kneaded with 2 teaspoons unsalted butter
4 to 6 ounces thin-sliced white bread, 6 slices, cut into 3- to 4-inch round *croutes*
6 large eggs, raw or poached ahead and chilled (see *Review: Perfect Poached Eggs*)
Minced Italian parsley or *Fines Herbes*

1 Heat 2 tablespoons clarified butter in 2-quart saucepan over medium heat. Add **mirepoix** and ham and sauté until golden, about 8 to 10 minutes. Add red wine and bouquet garni. Reduce heat, and simmer sauce until wine reduces to 1 cup or by 2/3, about 20 minutes. Skim away scum. Strain wine from vegetables into mixing bowl. Press vegetables down in strainer to remove as much liquid as possible. Discard vegetables and return wine to saucepan. Bring to a simmer.

2 **Thicken sauce:** Slowly whisk very small bits of **beurre manie** into simmering sauce. As sauce simmers it will thicken and cook off starchy flour flavor. Don't add too much beurre manie all at once or sauce will become very thick. Add enough so sauce just coats the back of a spoon lightly like heavy cream. Taste sauce, and season with salt and pepper.

3 **Toast croutes:** Preheat oven to 400 degrees F. Place bread rounds into oven and bake until golden, 7 to 10 minutes. Brush toasts lightly on both sides with remaining clarified butter.

4 **Just before serving:** Prepare or reheat poached eggs in simmering water.

5 **To Serve:** Reheat sauce over low heat. Place a hot poached egg on each croute, spoon sauce over the eggs, and garnish with parsley or fines herbes. Serve immediately.

Source: Institute for Culinary Education.

TARRAGON CHICKEN ROASTED IN A CASSEROLE (POULET POELÉ À L'ESTRAGON)

4 servings

3 pound roasting chicken
2 tablespoons unsalted butter
1/2 teaspoon fresh lemon juice
1/3 to 1/2 ounce tarragon leaves, 2 tablespoons chopped

1 to 2 tablespoons unsalted butter, diced, *divided*
2 to 3 tablespoons canola oil, *divided*
2 to 3 ounces onions, 1/2 cup peeled and finely sliced
About 1-1/2 ounces carrots, 1/4 cup peeled and sliced
2 cups chicken broth
Slurry: 1 tablespoon cornstarch or arrowroot mixed with 2 tablespoons Port
4 large sprigs tarragon
1 tablespoon diced unsalted butter
1/4 ounce tarragon leaves, 1 tablespoon chopped lightly

1 Preheat oven to 350 degrees F. Wash, drain, and pat chicken dry. Mash 1/2 teaspoon kosher salt butter, lemon juice, and chopped tarragon together. Insert butter under skin of breast, thighs, and legs. Rub skin with any remaining butter or with buttery hands. Truss chicken.

2 **Brown the chicken:** Heat a heavy 4- to 5-quart casserole or Dutch oven over medium-high heat. Stir in 1 tablespoon butter and 1 tablespoon oil. When butter melts and oil shimmers, lay chicken in breast side down and brown, 2 to 3 minutes. If pan gets too hot and begins to brown too quickly, turn heat down to medium. With 2 large metal spoons, turn chicken until evenly golden all around, adding more oil as necessary, 10 to 15 minutes. Remove chicken.

3 **Cook the vegetables:** If fat has burned, wipe it out and add 1 tablespoon each oil and butter. If not, add onions and carrots and cook over medium heat until soft but not browned. Season vegetables with salt and add 3 tarragon sprigs. Set chicken on top of vegetables breast side up; baste with fat in casserole. Cover casserole tightly and reheat on stove. When chicken sizzles, place casserole in middle of preheated oven.

4 Roast chicken 1 hour. Baste at 20-minute intervals. After 1 hour, drumsticks should move easily in sockets and reach internal temperature of 175 degrees F. If not, place covered casserole back in oven to roast until it does. Remove chicken from casserole to platter. Discard trussing string, and rest chicken in warm spot, tented with foil while making the sauce.

5 **Prepare sauce:** Pour stock into casserole and simmer over medium heat 2 minutes; skim away fat. Whisk slurry, and whisk slowly into boiling stock. Simmer sauce until lightly thickened. Remove sauce from heat, taste, and season with salt and freshly ground pepper. Strain sauce into clean saucepan.

6 **To Serve:** Carve chicken into serving pieces and arrange on platter. Reheat sauce, remove from heat, and whisk in butter. Drizzle chicken with sauce. Garnish with tarragon. Serve immediately.

Source: *Mastering the Art of French Cooking* by Julia Child.

REGION SIX: EASTERN FRANCE

Franche-Comté, Savoie, and the Rhône Alps—Alpine Valleys, Dairy, and Wine

Home to the Jura Mountains and the Alps, this is a scenic region of alpine foothills and meadows, pine forests, and valleys with strong Italian and Swiss influences. *Gruyère, emmental, reblochon,* and *tome de savoie* cheeses, pork, walnut oil, wild mushrooms, river trout, and red Rhône wines are featured. Heartwarming dishes like chicken with morels and cream, *blanquette de veau,* tart cherry soup, *quenelles nantua* (dumplings in crayfish sauce), *gratin dauphinoise* (potato gratin), *fondue,* and *Mont Blanc* (meringue with chestnut cream) are popular here.

FIGURE 5.26 Beaujolais vineyards straddle both Loire Valley and Rhône-Alpes.
Source: david hughes/Fotolia.

WHITE VEAL STEW (BLANQUETTE DE VEAU)

This dish is in the top ten of French diners' favorite meals. Serve with hot rice, buttered noodles, or spaetzli.

Yields about 3 quarts, 6 to 8 servings

1 pound leeks, 2 medium, tough green tops removed
8 to 10 cups chicken stock
3 pounds veal shoulder, diced into 2-inch cubes
8 ounce onion, peeled and wedge-cut into eighths
2 ounces celery, 1 medium stalk trimmed and sliced into 1-inch lengths
1 ounce garlic, about 4 large cloves, 2 tablespoons peeled
and finely sliced
1 pound white button mushrooms, 4 cups cleaned and halved
or quartered, *divided*
5 large sprigs fresh thyme
5 large sprigs Italian parsley
8 ounces pearl onions, 2 cups blanched and peeled
3 tablespoons oil

Roux and Velouté

1-1/2 ounces unsalted butter, 3 tablespoons
About 1-1/4 ounce all-purpose flour, 1/4 cup

3/4 cup heavy cream
3 tablespoons crème fraiche
1/4 teaspoon freshly ground white pepper

For Serving

Hot rice, buttered noodles, or *Spaetzli*

Garnish: 1/2 ounce trimmed Italian parsley, 3 to 4 tablespoons finely chopped

1   Halve leeks lengthwise with root end intact, and rinse between leaves to remove sand. Slice white and tender green into 1-inch wide half moons. Combine leeks with 8 cups stock, veal, onion, celery, garlic, 3 ounces (1/3 cup) mushrooms, thyme, parsley, and 1-1/2 teaspoons kosher salt. Bring to a boil, lower heat, and simmer uncovered 2 hours. Add more stock if necessary.

2   Bring a small pot of water to a boil. Slice off stem end of pearl onions and drop into boiling water. Blanch 2 minutes, drain, and remove skins. Trim root end very lightly so the onion holds together.

3   Heat oil in small saucepan over medium-low heat. Add remaining mushrooms and season with salt. Cook until tender, and do not brown. If mushrooms begin to color, add a little stock, and cover, and continue to cook until tender. Remove mushrooms with slotted spoon into small bowl. Toss pearl onions into saucepan, season with salt, and cook until tender without browning. Add a little more stock as necessary. Scrape into bowl with mushrooms.

4   **Strain Veal and Broth:** At least 3 cups stock should remain. Remove meat from colander and set aside. Reduce stock over medium heat if there is too much, or pour extra chicken stock through the vegetables in the strainer and press through to make up the difference. Discard strained vegetables. Keep stock warm.

5   *Prepare* **Roux** *and* **Velouté:** In a 4-quart saucepan, over medium-low heat, melt butter and stir in flour with spoon. Cook until sizzling and fragrant, but not colored 1 minute. Whisk in 3 cups warm veal stock, 1 cup at a time. Bring to a boil, reduce heat, and simmer sauce until thickened, 5 minutes.

6 **To Serve:** Whisk in cream, crème fraîche, white pepper, veal, pearl onions, and mushrooms. Simmer and stir gently, don't boil, until warmed through, 5 minutes. Serve blanquette over rice, noodles, or spaetzli. Garnish with chopped parsley.

Source: *The Balthazar Cookbook* by Keith McNally.

VEGETABLE GRATIN (*GRAH-TÁN*)

A gratin is a crusty, golden dish of lightly cooked meat, seafood, or vegetables baked in broth, béchamel, or cream, topped with diced butter and cheese or butter-toasted breadcrumbs, or just cheese. The gratin originated with busy French countrywomen who simply poured cream and cheese over cooked vegetables in a gratin dish and baked them.

Signature Technique: Gratin

- Use a gratin type dish, whether round, rectangular, or oval; metal, glass, or porcelain must be ovenproof, wide, and shallow—no deeper than 2 inches— for maximum surface area and lots of crusty topping.

- A 2-inch-deep, 9-inch by 12-inch (4-quart) half hotel pan *or* 9-inch by 14-inch (3-quart) oval gratin dish yields 6 to 8 servings.

- Prepare 2 to 3 pounds vegetables to yield 8 to 10 cups sliced or diced vegetables. Slice hard vegetables 1/8-inch thick. Slice softer vegetables 1/8- to 1/4-inch thick. Or dice vegetables bite-size, 1/2- to 3/4-inch cubes.

- Most vegetables benefit from precooking. It speeds up the cooking time and gives more control. Depending on starchiness and their ability to break down easily and absorb or give off liquid, it's not necessary to precook every vegetable, but do finely slice, dice, or grate them.

- Cream makes the most luscious gratin, but half and half, a whole milk *Béchamel, or* chicken *Velouté* work well, too.

- Precooked caramelized onions, garlic, or sautéed aromatic vegetables imbue vegetable gratins with rich, complex flavor.

- Top gratins with cheese, Béchamel, or Mornay sauce, breadcrumbs, and oil or melted butter. Try traditional Gruyère, good Cheddar, Fontina, blue cheese, or Parmigiano-Reggiano.

- If a gratin doesn't brown and crust, stick it under a broiler, or use a blowtorch.

Vary! Improvise!

☞ *Most vegetables work well gratinéed—potatoes, leeks, turnips, cauliflower, cabbage, Belgian endive, carrots, parsnips, fennel bulb, mushrooms, or squash. Blanch or lightly steam vegetables before preparing gratin.*

☞ ***Onion Gratin:*** *Blanch and trim 2 pounds small onions. Butter gratin dish and arrange onions in one layer. Pour 2 cups cream mixed with a pinch of nutmeg and salt and pepper over onions. Bake uncovered until tender and golden.*

☞ ***Cauliflower Gratin:*** *Substitute cauliflower for potatoes and chicken stock for milk/cream. Top with buttered breadcrumbs or shredded cheese and follow recipe for potato gratin.*

☞ ***Butternut Squash, Caramelized Onion, and Sage Gratin:*** *Alternately layer caramelized onions, finely sliced fresh sage leaves, steamed butternut squash cubes or slices, and minced garlic. Cover with cream and top with butter tossed breadcrumbs. Bake until tender.*

☞ ***Potato, Rutabaga, and Blue Cheese Gratin:*** *Alternately layer 1/8-inch thick sliced rutabaga, 1/8-inch thick sliced potato, crumbled blue cheese, fresh thyme leaves. Cover with cream and top with butter-tossed breadcrumbs.*

FIGURE 5.27 Wild mushroom soup (Soupe aux oronges).

POTATO GRATIN (GRATIN DAUPHINOIS)

This is a classic French gratin. To keep cream from curdling (potatoes are high in acid), simmer thinly sliced potatoes first in milk and drain. Use the milk for another dish.

Yields one 2-inch deep, 9-inch by 12-inch (4-quart) half hotel pan or 9-inch by 14-inch (3-quart) oval gratin dish. 6 to 8 servings

1/4 ounce garlic, 1 large clove, peeled and halved lengthwise
1 ounce unsalted butter, 2 tablespoons diced, *divided*
2-1/2 pounds potatoes, 5 to 6 cups peeled and sliced 1/8-inch thick
3 cups milk for blanching
2 cups heavy cream
1/8 teaspoon grated nutmeg
Optional: 2 ounces Gruyére, about 1/2 cup grated
1 ounce unsalted butter, 2 tablespoons diced

1 Preheat oven to 425 degrees F. Rub baking vessel with garlic then a little of the butter.

2 Peel potatoes and thinly slice on a mandoline. Bring milk, potatoes, and 2 teaspoons kosher salt to a boil in a 4-quart saucepan. Drain. Reserve 1 cup milk.

3 In saucepan, bring heavy cream, reserved milk, nutmeg, and salt and pepper to a low boil. Arrange potatoes overlapping in half hotel pan in rows or in 6-cup gratin dish in concentric circles. Pour hot cream and milk over. Sprinkle potatoes with cheese and dot with remaining butter. Bake until golden brown, 20 minutes or more.

4 **To Serve:** Cool potatoes slightly. Evenly slice or scoop servings onto serving plate or serve in gratin dish.

WILD MUSHROOM SOUP (SOUPE AUX ORONGES)

The Jura Mountains in Franche-Comté contain forests with earthy wild mushrooms called oronges that are unavailable in the United States. Paired with local hazelnuts, this soup is divine. Any fresh wild mushroom will give the soup its characteristic flavor: morels, shiitakes, and chanterelles. Notice the classic use of rice as a thickener. Use nutty basmati or Louisiana "pecan" rice for a deeper layer of flavor.

Yields about 8 cups, 4 to 6 servings

1-1/2 ounces unsalted butter, 3 tablespoons finely diced
6 to 7 ounces onions, 1-1/2 cups peeled and finely diced
8 ounces fresh wild mushrooms, about 3-1/2 cups quartered lengthwise
8 ounces fresh white mushrooms, about 3-1/2 cups quartered lengthwise
6 cups chicken stock, 1 cup more as needed
About 2-1/2 ounces long-grain white rice, 6 tablespoons
1 to 1-1/2 ounces hazelnuts, 4 to 6 tablespoons
1/2 ounce trimmed fresh chopped chervil *or* Italian parsley leaves, 1/4 cup

1 Preheat oven to 400 degrees F. Over medium to medium-low heat in a 5-quart saucepan, melt butter. Stir in onions and 1 teaspoon kosher salt. Cook onions until soft, 5 to 7 minutes. Stir in mushrooms and cook until wilted, 7 to 10 minutes. Remove 8 to 12 pieces of wild mushrooms for garnish, and set aside. Pour 6 cups stock and rice into onion-mushroom mixture. Bring soup to a boil over high heat. Lower heat, cover pot, and simmer soup until rice is tender, 20 minutes.

2 Meanwhile, spread hazelnuts on sheet pan and place in oven. Toast nuts until fragrant and darkened, about 10 minutes. Wrap hot nuts in towel and rub to remove skins. Discard skins, coarsely chop nuts, and set aside.

3   Cool soup slightly and purée in batches in blender. Return purée to clean pot and add more stock as necessary for proper soup consistency. Taste soup and season with salt and freshly ground pepper.

4   **To Serve:** Warm soup over medium-low heat. Ladle hot soup into bowls. Garnish with reserved mushrooms, chopped nuts, and chervil or parsley.

Source: *The Soups of France by Lois Anne Rothert.*

Vary! Improvise!

☞ *Another Nut:* Substitute toasted macadamia nuts (or toasted pecans) for hazelnuts.

☞ *Intensify:* Slice extra wild mushrooms. Sweat in 1 tablespoon butter or olive oil. Stir into soup just before serving.

☞ *Spring:* Substitute wild ramps for onions and use morels for wild mushrooms.

☞ *Dairy-Free:* Replace butter with olive oil.

REGION SEVEN: SOUTHEASTERN FRANCE

Provence and the Côte-d'Azur—Aromatic and Sun-Drenched

Known for olives, olive oil, and garlic, this Mediterranean-south-facing region has distinct Roman, Italian, and Arabic influences. It is a land blessed with fragrant wild herbs (*herbes de Provence*), abundant and varied seafood, tomatoes, honey, grapes, and wheat. Prized fruit and vegetables are grown intensively: citrus, watermelon, fennel, eggplant, artichokes, zucchini, radish, cauliflower, and artichokes. Sea bass with fennel, *bouilliabaisse*, sauce *rouille, tapenade, pissaladiére, tian, ratatouille,* slow-cooked *beef en daube, pistou, pebronata* (pepper and tomato stew), *socca* (chickpea flatbread), anchioade, grilled sardines, ravioli, and potato gnocchi are featured.

TAPENADE

Tapenade is a mixture of finely chopped olives, capers, anchovies, and garlic made in southern France, Italy, and Spain. In the Occitan region in the south of France, the word for capers, an important ingredient, is tapéno, *hence* tapenade. *Roasted almonds or pine nuts, herbs, and wine vinegar appear in tapenade. Smear it on toast, stir into soups, sauces, or pair with cheese.*

FIGURE 5.28   Provence, France.
Source: david hughes/Fotolia.

Yields 9 fluid ounces, about 1 cup plus 2 tablespoons

5 ounces pitted Kalamata olives, 1 cup lightly chopped
1-1/2 ounces drained capers, 1/4 cup
2 oil- or salt-packed anchovy fillets, rinsed and chopped
1/8 ounce garlic, 1 small clove, 3/4 teaspoon peeled and chopped
2 tablespoons olive oil
2 tablespoons freshly squeezed lemon juice

Optional Ingredients

1/4 ounce trimmed Italian parsley, 2 tablespoons chopped
1 teaspoon lemon zest
     or 3 large basil leaves
        or 1 teaspoon fresh thyme leaves
1-1/4 ounces toasted pine nuts, 1/4 cup

1   Pit olives by smashing lightly with the side of a chef's knife if they are not pitted. If capers are salt-packed, soak briefly and drain. Rinse and chop anchovies.

2   Place olives, capers, anchovies, and garlic in a food processor and pulse-chop until ingredients hang together but still have texture. Scrape down sides of processor frequently. With the machine running, pour olive oil into olive mass in a steady stream.

3   Stir in lemon juice, and season with freshly ground pepper, to taste. If desired, stir in **optional ingredients** of choice. Cover and refrigerate tapenade 4 to 6 hours before using. Taste again and adjust seasonings. Will keep up to 5 days refrigerated.

Vary! Improvise!

☞ *Vary the Olives:* Green olive versions include *herbes de Provence,* fresh basil, roasted red peppers, and tomatoes.

☞ Add finely diced soaked sun-dried tomatoes.

☞ Use in vinaigrettes or as a pasta sauce.

☞ Stir a little into tomato sauce at the end of cooking.

☞ Stir into goat cheese or ricotta cheese for a crepe filling.

THREE POPULAR FRENCH OLIVES

Niçoise

These small olives, with their delicate flavor, are essential to *Salad Niçoise* and *Pissaladiere*, a Provençal "pizza."

FIGURE 5.29 Niçoise olives.
Source: Roger Dixon/DK Images.

Nyons

Dry-cured and brine-aged, Nyons are slightly wrinkled, but plump with large pits. Authentic Nyons are a dull black, rich, and very flavorful, not shiny, slick, and flat-tasting as their imposters. French cooks snack on them and dress them with olive oil, thyme, and rosemary.

Picholine

A medium-sized uncracked green olive with a nutty, anise-y flavor. French cooks pair them with fennel and olive oil and add them to chicken or fish stews and braises.

FIGURE 5.30 Nyons olives.
Source: Roger Dixon/DK Images.

FIGURE 5.31 Picholine olives.
Source: © SoFood/Alamy.

WHO HAD THE FIRST FISH STEW?

Food historian Clifford Wright thinks that the likely forerunner of Provençal bouillabaisse was probably an Italian fish stew. He discloses that "the closest thing to a bouillabaisse" appeared in a fifteenth-century Italian cookbook from southern Italy. The medieval stew, called *brodecto de li dicti pisci*, was made with "sardines and anchovies boiled in *vino greco* (strong Neapolitan wine)" and seasoned with black pepper, saffron, and olive oil.

FRENCH FISH STEW

The south coast of France is best known for fish stew and soup, but everywhere there is fishing there are fish stews. *Bouillabaisse, bourride,* and *cotriade* are most famous. The flavor of a good bouillabaisse relies on as many different fish with bones as possible, olive oil, saffron, tomatoes, and fennel with *rouille* stirred into the finished stew. *Bourride* from Provence and Languedoc, relies on garlic, onion, fennel, orange, and thyme and comes with aioli and toast.

Nearer to Italy, saffron-scented fish soup is puréed, and served with *rouille* and croutons. In Brittany, *cortriade*, from "côte" or coast, where the stew originated, features rich fish like eel, monkfish, mackerel, cod, and haddock with sorrel, potatoes, leeks, and cream. *Matelote* ("boatman") is a special fish stew all over France. Most cooks use freshwater fish, some use one type and others, a mixture. In Loire, matelote is made with eels, baby onions, and mushrooms, in Alsace, with Riesling and cream, and in Normandy with cider and crème fraîche. The Burgundian stew, *pochouse*, is made with river fish, bacon, garlic, white wine, and cream.

COMPLEX FISH STEW (BOUILLABAISSE MARSEILLAISE)

Some French chefs believe true bouillabaisse must contain fish of the Mediterranean, but others advise non-Mediterranean dwellers to use a combination of both rich and white-fleshed fish like monkfish, red mullet, bass, snapper, perch, whitefish, haddock, flounder, and mackerel. Whole fish are a must for the important and flavorful fish stock that underlies every good bouillabaisse, but shellfish are unnecessary—rather like gilding the lily.

Yields about 4 quarts, 8 to 10 servings

3 pounds white fleshed fish *with heads* and 2 pounds rich fleshed fish *with heads*
 or 2-1/2 to 3 pounds fish fillets *and* 2 quarts fish stock

Marinade

3 tablespoons olive oil
1/2 ounce garlic, about 2 large cloves, 1 tablespoon peeled and finely minced
1/8 teaspoon crumbled saffron

3/4 cup olive oil
1 pound onions, 4 cups peeled and finely sliced
1 pound leeks, about 2 medium, 2 cups trimmed, halved lengthwise, and sliced
3 to 3-1/2 ounces celery, about 2 medium stalks, 3/4 to 1 cup sliced
1 pound fresh tomatoes, about 2 cups peeled, seeded, and diced
 or 28-ounce can whole plum tomatoes, 2 cups drained and diced
1 ounce garlic, 4 large cloves. 2 tablespoons peeled and minced

Bouquet Garni

5 large stems Italian parsley
1 large bay leaf
2 large sprigs thyme

2 large strips orange zest *or* zest of 1/2 orange
1 teaspoon fennel seed
1/4 teaspoon saffron dissolved in 1 tablespoon water
1 tablespoon tomato paste
1 tablespoon Pernod *or* Pastis
1/2 ounce trimmed Italian parsley, 1/4 cup chopped
16 ounce loaf country bread, 8 to 10 slices toasted
1/4 ounce garlic, 1 large clove, halved lengthwise and peeled

Sauce Rouille

1 **If fish is whole with head and bones:** Early in the day or the day before: scale, gut, and clean fish. Discard fins and gills. Rinse fish and pat dry. Fillet fish, remove, and discard skin, and cut meat into 1-inch cubes. If using filleted fish, remove skin and bones, and cut into 1-inch cubes.

2 Prepare fish stock with fish heads and bony racks (see *Fish Stock*) to yield 1-1/2 to 2 quarts stock.

3 Toss skinned fish chunks in bowl with **marinade** ingredients, cover, and refrigerate 1 hour or up to overnight.

4 In a large casserole or wide soup pot, over medium heat, heat oil, and stir in onions, leeks, and celery. Cook vegetables until soft but not colored, 5 to 10 minutes. Stir in tomatoes, garlic, **bouquet garni**, orange zest, and fennel seed. Cook 2 minutes, and pour in 1-1/2 quarts fish stock and saffron. Bring stew to a boil, lower heat, and simmer 40 minutes.

5 **Fifteen to twenty minutes before serving:** Set white-fleshed fish into stew and simmer gently until fish is half cooked, 3 minutes. Pour in remaining hot fish stock (or water), if necessary, to keep fish covered.

- If using shellfish or bivalves, add next and simmer until shellfish are just opaque or bivalves open, 3 to 5 minutes. Shake, but don't stir pan.

- Some cooks presteam shellfish or bivalves with fish stock or bouillabaisse broth, return broth to bouillabaisse and combine seafood in serving bowl.

6 Taste stew, and season with salt and pepper. Discard **bouquet garni** and orange strips and adjust the consistency with more of remaining stock (or water) if soup is too thick.

- *Optional Classical Technique:* Bring stew to a boil and drop in fatty fish first. Boil hard 3 minutes—don't stir. This may feel counterintuitive, but the boiling emulsifies the fat into the broth so it doesn't float on the surface. (That's why stock shouldn't be boiled: it emulsifies the scum and fat into the stock and renders it as cloudy as a San Francisco summer morning.)

7 **To Serve:** Stir tomato paste and Pernod or Pastis together with a little broth, and fold into soup. Sprinkle bouillabaisse with parsley, and serve with topped with toasts drizzled with **rouille**.

Vary! Improvise!

☞ *Serve Bouillabaisse in Two Courses: Strain out fish. Serve the broth as first course and the fish as the second.*

THE BOUNTY FOR BOUILLABAISSE

Food historian Clifford A. Wright acknowledges that understanding the kind of Mediterranean fish to use for bouillabaisse can present a puzzle for cooks. This is partly because of the difference in fish names around the Mediterranean and partly because of the preference of each coastal village and each cook. Traditionally scorpionfish, sea robin, and conger eel were favored, but bream, turbot, monkfish, mullet, and hake are also popular. *Bouillabaisse du pecheur* was first prepared on the beach by fishermen while untangling nets. They used sea water as a base; the fresh-caught fish, fennel, tomatoes, and seasonings went in when it boiled. Fresh fish is essential and the variety and amount of fish determine flavor. Saffron is the favored seasoning.

Look for these Mediterranean fish in French, Spanish, and Italian grocers around the United States:

Scorpionfish (rascasse)

Sea robin (grondin)

Red gurnard (rouget grondin)

Dorade (gilt-head bream)

Turbot

Wrasse (rouquier, roucaou or roucan)

John Dory (Saint-Pierre)

Weever (vive)

Red mullet (rouget de roche)

Monkfish (baudroie or lotte)

Pandora (pageot rouge)

Spanish bream (pageot blanc or bezique)

Rainbow wrasse (girelle)

Silver hake (whiting or merlan)

Conger eel (European conger or fielas)

Moray eel (murene)

Bass (loup de mer)

Mackerel (maquereau or auriou)

Absinthe to Pernod

In 1916 France banned the anise-flavored *absinthe* because some opponents erroneously accused one ingredient, wormwood, as being poisonous, hallucinogenic, and an aphrodisiac. Absinthe's largest maker, Pernod-Fils, created a new drink that eliminated wormwood and increased the star anise. Traditionally Pernod and absinthe are served in a specially shaped glass with a sugar cube suspended on a small slotted spoon over the glass. Cold water is poured over the sugar and into the Pernod. Star anise, not water-soluble, turns the water cloudy.

RUST-COLORED GARLIC MAYONNAISE
(SAUCE ROUILLE)

Some cooks thicken rouille with potato or bread and egg. Sauce rouille is traditionally served with bouilliabaisse, but is good with grilled fish, hard-boiled eggs, or grilled vegetables.

Yields about 1-1/2 cups

3-inch dried red chili, halved lengthwise, stemmed, seeded, and chopped
    or 1-1/2 ounces red bell pepper, 1/4 medium pepper, roasted, peeled and
      finely diced
1 ounce garlic, 4 large cloves, 2 tablespoons peeled and finely minced
2 large egg yolks
2 tablespoons fresh lemon juice, 1/2 to 1 lemon
1 cup mild-flavored extra virgin olive oil, *divided*
1 tablespoon tomato paste
1 tablespoon red wine vinegar

1 Place chili or bell pepper and garlic into blender or into mortar, and purée or pound until smooth. Add yolks and 1 teaspoon lemon juice. Purée or pound together 1 minute.

2 In blender: with machine running, *gradually*, drop by drop, pour all but 1 tablespoon olive oil into blender to emulsify sauce. In mortar with pestle: scrape pounded rouille base into mixing bowl and whisk in all but 1 tablespoon oil slowly to emulsify sauce.

3 Heat 1 tablespoon oil over medium heat in small skillet and add tomato paste. Stir and cook paste until it darkens slightly. Whisk in vinegar, and cool slightly. Purée or whisk paste into rouille. Taste and adjust seasoning with salt, freshly ground pepper, and lemon or vinegar.

4 Refrigerate rouille until ready for use. Store refrigerated no more than 1 day.

Source: *The Country Cooking of France* by Anne Willan.

Signature Technique: Composed Salad (Salade Composée)

1 Wash and dry lettuce well. Leave leaves whole or tear into large pieces.

2 *Choose composing ingredients.* A good template is *Salade Niçoise*.
- Ingredients should contrast color, taste, and texture, but work together.
- Steal ideas from successful pairings: salmon-dill-asparagus or crab-avocado-cucumber.
- Capture the eye: mix different lettuces and small colorful *crudités* salads.
- Employ the rule of threes: no more than three strong colors or flavors in a dish.
- Choose a protein and two vegetables or several *crudités* salads to delight diners' eyes.

3 Grill, cook, marinate, and/or dress composing elements.

4 Prepare vinaigrette or dressing. Dress small salad elements with vinaigrette for more flavor.

5 Arrange greens on a platter or individual serving plates. Decoratively arrange salad elements on or around greens in attractive rows, circles, or piles.

6 Garnish salad with croutons, crispy bacon, white anchovies, or herbs. Spoon dressing over the salad, pour into squeeze bottle for easy dressing, or pass dressing so that each diner may dress his or her own salad portion.

SALAD FROM NICE (SALADE NIÇOISE) (KNEE-SWAHS)

Composed salads are showy appetizer salads, often with poultry, meat, or fish and a variety of vegetables and garnishes, attractively arranged on a bed of greens. Salade Niçoise makes a satisfying and elegant summer lunch. Basil, anchovies, tomato, and olives are a classically Niçoise garnish, from Nice (niece) in the south of France. Items are purposely and artfully arranged rather than tossed or mixed. Composed salads are usually served as a main course, not as an accompaniment to an entrée.

6 to 8 servings

1 pound fresh sashimi-grade tuna steak cut 1- to 1-1/2-inches thick
   or two 12-ounce cans yellowfin tuna in olive oil, drained
2 to 3 tablespoons extra virgin olive oil
2 pounds small to medium red-skin potatoes, scrubbed
3/4 to 1 cup *Mustard Vinaigrette* with red wine vinegar
   plus scant 1/2 ounce basil leaves, 3 tablespoons finely sliced
3/4 to 1 cup *Mustard Vinaigrette* with white wine vinegar
   plus scant 1/2 ounce tarragon leaves, 3 tablespoons chopped
16 ounces baby green beans (*haricots vert*), stem ends only trimmed
1-1/2 pounds tomatoes, about 3 medium-large, cored, but left whole
16 ounces Boston or bibb lettuce, 2 heads, leaves washed and dried
3 large eggs, hard-cooked (See *The Perfect Hard-Cooked Egg*)
6 anchovy fillets, soaked in water 20 minutes, drained
About 2-1/2 ounces Niçoise olives, 1/2 cup

1 Remove tuna from refrigerator and rub with olive oil. Rest at room temperature 30 minutes. If using canned tuna, break up into big chunks and set aside in small mixing bowl.

2 Place potatoes in a 4-quart saucepan, cover with cold water, bring to a boil, and cook until tender and a knife tip pierces, 15 to 20 minutes. Don't overcook potatoes or them they will fall apart when sliced.

3 **Prepare mustard vinaigrettes:** Mix red wine vinaigrette with basil. Mix white wine vinaigrette with tarragon. Set them aside.

4 When potatoes are done, cool them. Slice potatoes 1/4-inch thick. Pour 2 to 3 tablespoons white-wine tarragon vinaigrette over them while still warm and toss gently so they don't break up.

5 Fill a 4-quart saucepan with cold water and 1 tablespoon kosher salt, and bring to a boil. Blanch green beans in boiling water until tender, 4 to 5 minutes. Refresh beans under cold water. Drain them, and set aside. Heat a grill pan to cook the fresh tuna, if using.

6 Blanch tomatoes in boiling water until skins loosen, 30 to 60 seconds, cool and peel. Slice each into 8 wedges. Toss tomato wedges with 2 tablespoons red wine-basil vinaigrette.

7 If using, lightly salt and pepper the edges of the tuna steak, and grill until medium, about 2 to 3 minutes per side for a 1-inch-thick steak. Cool and slice cross-grain into 1/4-inch-thick slices. Tuna should be red or pink in the center.

8 **To Serve:** Place lettuce leaves on a platter as a bed. Arrange piles of dressed potatoes, green beans, dressed tomatoes and eggs around the sliced tuna in the center. Garnish with anchovies and olives. Serve with vinaigrettes on the side.

Source: The Institute for Culinary Education's Techniques of Fine Cooking.

Vary! Improvise!

☛ *Other Composed Salads (Salades Composées):* Endive layered with cooked beets, toasted walnuts, and goat cheese.

☛ *French Lentils and Pork:* Prepare French Green Lentil Salad. Arrange on Romaine leaves with slices of grilled pork tenderloin or other grilled meat.

☛ *Glorified Sub Sandwich; Pan Bagnat or Composed Salad in a Baguette:* Stuff dressed ingredients for Salade Niçoise into a horizontally sliced and hollowed out roll or half baguette. Wrap sandwich, and refrigerate several hours or overnight. Resting gives the vinaigrette time to saturate ingredients and bread. Great picnic or travel food.

FIGURE 5.32 Pissaladiére and assorted crudités: celery root remoulade, carrots with walnut oil, walnuts, lemon and dill and tomatoes and basil with olive oil and vinegar.

SAVORY PROVENÇAL TART (PISSALADIÉRE)

Romans probably introduced cooks in the south of France to this type of "white" pizza with its distinctive onion-olive-anchovy topping. The dough is wet and sticky, but don't knead in too much flour or dough will become tough. This technique yields a light, crisp crust. For an even lighter crust, refrigerate dough and let it rise overnight. Bring to room temperature before baking.

Yields 15-inch by 17-inch commercial half-sheet pan

Dough

Yields 19 to 20 ounces

1 cup lukewarm water
1 tablespoon active dry yeast
4 tablespoons olive oil, *divided*
About 10-1/2 ounces all-purpose unbleached flour, 2-1/3 cups, more for pan
1-1/4 teaspoons salt

Topping

Yields 2 cups

4 tablespoons olive oil
About 30 ounces onions, 5 medium, 7 cups halved and sliced 1/8-inch thick

3 to 4 ounces anchovies in oil, drained and cut in half
About 4-3/4 ounces black Kalamata or Niçoise olives, 3/4 cup pitted
   or 3 ounces pitted black olives, 3/4 cup

1 **Prepare the dough:** Mix together water and yeast; rest 1 minute. Stir in 3 tablespoons olive oil. Pour flour and salt into a 2-quart mixing bowl and mix together. Make a well in the center and scrape in water-yeast-oil mixture. Stir with a rubber spatula to form a soft, sticky dough. Beat dough lightly until smooth, 1 minute. Clean off dough from spatula back into bowl. Cover bowl tightly with plastic wrap and allow dough to rise in warm spot until doubled in bulk, 1 hour.

2 **Prepare the topping:** Heat a 5- to 6-quart pot over medium heat with olive oil. Add onions and cook until they noticeably sizzle. Lower the heat, cover the pot, and simmer onions until very soft, 30 minutes. Check onions, and stir, every 5 to 10 minutes. Onions should be very moist, not browned. Uncover pot, raise heat slightly, and cook onions until excess moisture evaporates, 5 minutes. Onions should be moist but not wet. Scrape onions into a large mixing bowl to cool.

3 Preheat oven (not a convection) to 450 degrees F and set a rack on the lowest level. Spread 1 tablespoon olive oil remaining from dough on 15-inch by 17-inch half-sheet pan. Sprinkle evenly with 1 tablespoon flour. Set aside.

4 With an oiled rubber spatula, scrape dough away from edges of bowl to form an even ball. Scrape ball in one piece, without folding, onto oiled pan. Lightly flour hands and top of dough, and pat it into the pan. If dough resists, let it rest, covered with plastic wrap, 5 minutes.

5 Press dough firmly and evenly into bottom and sides of pan. Pierce dough at 2-inch intervals with fork. Spread onions evenly over top of dough. Scatter anchovies and olives evenly over onions.

Vary! Improvise!

☛ *Arrange thinly sliced disks of ripe plum tomatoes on top of the onions before baking.*
☛ *Chop the anchovies and add them to the onions after cooking.*
☛ *Arrange anchovies and olives artfully into 1-inch "squares" before baking. Cut and serve the small pissaladière squares as cocktail hors d'oeuvres.*

Bake pissaladière on bottom rack of oven until crust is golden and crisp and onions still moist, 25 to 35 minutes. Cool on baking rack.

6 **To Serve:** Cut pissaladière into squares and serve.

Source: How to Bake by Nick Malgieri.

CHICKPEA FLOUR FLATBREAD (SOCCA)

In France and Italy along the Mediterranean Coast this flatbread is served as snack food near the beach. In Italy it is known as torta de cecina or farinata.

Yields 3 cups batter, one 13- to 14-inch round socca, 8 to 12 servings

About 8 ounces chickpea flour, 2 cups packed
1 tablespoon kosher salt
2 cups warm water
6 tablespoons extra virgin olive oil, *divided*
Freshly ground black pepper

1 Combine chickpea flour, salt, and water in mixing bowl and whisk until smooth. Set batter aside 2 hours or longer to allow the starch to fully expand and ensure good texture. Whisk 2 tablespoons oil into batter just before using.

2 Preheat oven or deck oven to 450 degrees F. Arrange a rack on the lowest setting. Place a 13- to 14-inch round paella or cake pan in oven to heat, 5 to 7 minutes. Remove pan from oven and swirl in remaining 4 tablespoons oil. Immediately pour batter into the center of the pan and gently swirl batter to reach the edges.

3 Return pan to the lowest rack and bake until batter is set and a browned crust forms, 12 to 15 minutes. Remove pan from oven and loosen socca with the aid of a heatproof rubber spatula. Flip socca. Place pan back in oven to brown the second side, 10 to 15 minutes. Remove socca from oven and cool in pan 5 minutes.

4 **To Serve:** Transfer socca to cutting board while warm and cut into pie-shaped slices. Serve sprinkled with salt and freshly ground black pepper.

Vary! Improvise!

☞ *Add 1/4 teaspoon ground cumin to the batter.*

☞ *Add herbs or other whole or ground spices to the batter.*

☞ *Increase recipe by 1/3 to 1/2 and prepare socca in a commercial half-sheet pan (15-inch by 17-inch). Instead of flipping it to brown the second side, place it under a broiler to cook until speckled brown.*

FIGURE 5.33 Tian.

PROVENÇAL SUMMER VEGETABLE CASSEROLE (TIAN)

A tian is the southern French version of gratin. A tian may be topped with olive oil-tossed bread-crumbs, cheese, or both—or just layered in a gratin-type dish and drizzled with olive oil. Baking unifies the ingredients into a delicious whole—a moist, tender interior and crispy brown top crust.

Yields 2-inch deep, 9-inch by 11-1/2-inch rectangular *half* hotel pan *or* a 3-quart oval gratin dish, 6 servings

16 ounces eggplant, 2 medium, about 5 cups trimmed and cut in 1/4-inch thick rounds
12 ounces zucchini, 2 small, about 3 cups trimmed and cut in 1/4-inch thick coins
Olive oil as needed
About 2 pounds leeks, 4 medium, trimmed, 4 cups halved lengthwise and sliced 1/4-inch thick cross-wise
1/2 ounce garlic, 2 large cloves, 1 tablespoon peeled and minced
1/2 to 3/4 cup dry white wine
1 tablespoon chopped fresh thyme leaves
1-1/2 pounds small ripe plum or regular tomatoes, about 3-1/2 cups sliced into 1/4-inch thick rounds

Topping

2-1/2 to 3 ounces fresh (not dried) white breadcrumbs, 1-1/4 cups
2 tablespoons olive oil

1   Toss eggplant rounds with 1 tablespoon kosher salt, and set aside 20 minutes. Rinse, drain, and pat eggplant slices dry. In separate bowls, toss zucchini and eggplant with oil to lightly coat, about 1 tablespoon olive oil each. Season zucchini with salt.

2   Cut parchment paper to fit inside of half hotel pan (to top vegetables), and set aside. Preheat oven to 375 degrees F.

3   Heat a 10-inch skillet with 3 tablespoons olive oil over medium heat until shimmering. Add leeks. Cook until tender, 5 to 7 minutes. Add garlic and cook 1 minute. Scrape leeks and garlic into of 9-inch by 11-1/2-inch rectangular half hotel pan or 3-quart oval gratin dish.

4   Pour white wine into empty skillet (to deglaze) and reserve in small bowl. Spread leek-garlic mixture across bottom of pan or dish. Sprinkle with salt, black pepper, and half the thyme.

5   In a half hotel pan, layer and overlap eggplant in equal rows on top of leeks. *If eggplant and tomatoes have a large diameter, slice each round in half. Tuck zucchini and tomatoes in between eggplant slices, alternating colors. (If working with a circular or oval baking dish, work in the same way, but in fans from the center.) Use all the vegetables. Drizzle vegetables with reserved wine and remaining thyme. Oil one side of prepared parchment. Place oiled side down on top of vegetables and cover vessel tightly with foil. Bake tian until vegetables are very tender, but not falling apart, 45 minutes to 1 hour.

6   Remove tian from oven and uncover. Raise heat to 400 degrees F. Mix breadcrumbs with olive oil and sprinkle **topping** evenly over top of tian. Place back into oven to bake until topping is browned, 15 to 20 minutes. Or broil topping until golden.

7   **To Serve:** Cool tian to room temperature and cut into serving sized portions.

Vary! Improvise!

☞ *Make a tian with just cherry tomatoes, zucchini, or summer squash. They need little or no extra liquid. Don't overcook them, especially tomatoes, or they will turn to sauce.*

☞ *Season tian with precooked caramelized onions, garlic, or sautéed aromatic vegetables for deeper flavor.*

REGION EIGHT: SOUTHERN FRANCE

Languedoc-Roussillon—Mediterranean Grape, Rice, and Seafood

This Mediterranean region comprises two areas: a flat coastline and plain with freshwater, and the rugged Cévennes mountains. It provides France with abundant seafood, fruit and vegetables, chestnuts, chickpeas, lentils, white kidney beans, and couscous. One-fifth of France's wine is grown here and it is the home of Roquefort cheese. *Camargue*, on the marshy Rhône delta, is France's only rice-growing area. Grilled fish, rice-stuffed peppers, stuffed squid, *aioli*, *brandade* (salt-cod purée), *cassoulet*, *bourride* (garlicky fish soup), and chickpea soup are favorites. Catalan influences show in up in the local *paella* and in the use of spicy red peppers.

RED RICE SALAD (SALADE RIZ ROUGE)

The wild marshlands of France's Le Camargue near Marseille are home to the hearty somewhat starchy, medium-grain rice called riz rouge *(ree rooz). It is the only rice grown in France. Cooks there boil it like pasta, toss with olive oil, vinegar, and diced raw vegetables, and serve as a rice salad. Introduced into culinary circles in 1988, this red rice has a nutty flavor, firm texture, and sweet finish.*

Yields about 4-1/2 cups rice salad, 4 to 6 servings

About 6-1/2 ounces French red rice, 1 cup
   or 7 ounces long-grain brown rice, 1 cup
12 to 14 ounces red bell peppers, 2 medium
   or 12 ounces bottled roasted peppers, 1-1/2 cups diced into 1/4-inch cubes
1 ounce capers, 2 tablespoons lightly chopped
1/2 cup *Mustard Vinaigrette*
4 to 6 basil leaves
4 to 6 ounces baby greens, 4 to 6 cups

1 Bring 4 quarts water to boil. Stir in 2 teaspoons kosher salt and rice. Boil until tender, but still slightly al dente, 30 to 35 minutes for red rice and 35 to 45 minutes for brown rice. Drain rice and rinse with cold water. Drain rice well to yield about 3 cups cooked rice.

2 Meanwhile, roast bell peppers until blackened and tender. Cool in covered bowl. Peel away skin and remove all seeds and white membranes. Dice peppers into 1/4-inch cubes to yield about 1-1/2 cups. Toss peppers and capers with rice. Toss rice mixture with vinaigrette to taste, about 3 to 4 tablespoons. Season rice with salt and pepper. Tear basil leaves and toss with rice.

3 **To Serve:** Toss greens with some of the remaining vinaigrette and divide onto 4 to 6 serving plates. Divide rice salad into 4 to 6 portions and place on top of greens. Serve.

French Rice Pilaf

French cooks prepare long-grain rice pilaf with their characteristic flavor layering: first cooking aromatics in fat, cooking the rice briefly to harden its outer starch layer, then adding boiling stock, salt, and seasonings. The rice goes covered into a 350 degree F oven to bake until tender and fluffy. This pilaf method works for other grains as well.

Vary! Improvise!

☞ *Substitute fresh tarragon or Italian parsley in place of basil.*
☞ *Fold in 1/4 to 1/2 cup toasted walnuts or slivered almonds.*

SQUID AND CALAMARI

Squid and calamari are beloved for their tender texture and sweet taste. More than 500 species range in size from about 1 inch to 60 feet long. Available from the last two weeks of March throughout the summer, these meaty mollusks have no shell, only an ink sac for protection. Calamari, which tend to be more tender than squid, have side fins running the full length of the body while squid have shorter, pointed flapfins. Squid are usually larger than calamari. Tender-fleshed calamari is best for frying, grilling, and stir-frying. Squid is best for stuffing and stewing.

To Clean Squid and Calamari

- Pull the tentacles away from the body.

- Pull out the *quill* (like a shard of plastic) from body and discard.
- Pull out any guts and rinse inside the body with cold water.
- Cut the tentacles away from the guts by slicing just below the eyes. Check the center of the tentacles for the hard beak, and discard. Discard guts. Retain the ink sac to use in seafood pasta or risotto.
- Pull away purplish skin and ears (wing-like flaps) from the body to leave only white meat.
- Blot squid dry before cooking.
- Leave bodies whole for stuffing, slice the body into rings, or cut down one side, open, scrape off guts, then score inside lightly in a cross-hatch pattern before frying or stewing.

FIGURE 5.34 Cleaning squid.
Source: Left: Clive Streeter and Patrick McLeavy/DK Images; Right: Ian O'Leary/DK Images.

STUFFED SQUID IN TOMATO SAUCE (LES ENCORNETS FARCIS À LA SAUCE TOMATE)

This stuffing can make use of leftover fish or ground meat. The French use local Mediterranean fish: rougets (red mullet), rascasses (scorpion fish), and others. Sole, cod, and haddock also work well. Chef Vedel prefers to use tiny hot chilies in his tomato sauce, which enliven flavor without adding much heat, rather than black pepper, which can become bitter when long simmered. Encornets, usually served with rice, are sometimes browned and flambéed in cognac before simmering in tomato sauce. Some cooks thicken the tomato sauce with aioli or leftover stuffing.

4 servings

Tomato Sauce

Yields about 2-3/4 cups

3 tablespoons olive oil
8 ounces onion, 2 cups sliced

FIGURE 5.35 Stuffed squid.
Source: Hugh Johnson/DK Images.

2 pounds ripe tomatoes, 3 cups peeled and diced into 1/2-inch cubes
3/4 ounce garlic, 3 large cloves, 4-1/2 teaspoons crushed, peeled, and chopped
3 bay leaves
1-inch dried hot red chili, seeds and stem removed

1-1/2 pounds cleaned squid, *separated*: about eight 3- to 5-inch squid bodies *plus* tentacles, reserved for stuffing

Stuffing

Yields about 2 cups

2 ounces crustless day-old bread, 1 cup finely chopped
6 ounces raw sausage meat, 3/4 cup
    or 6 ounces ground raw peeled and deveined shrimp, 3/4 cup
      or 6 ounces raw or cooked skinned, boned fish, 3/4 cup
1/2 cup finely chopped squid tentacles (from the 1-1/2 pounds squid)
2 tablespoons fresh lemon juice, about 1/2 large lemon
1 ounce trimmed Italian parsley, 1/2 cup chopped
1/2 ounce garlic, 2 large cloves, 1 tablespoon crushed, peeled, and minced

For Serving

Hot, cooked rice

1 **Prepare sauce a few hours or a day ahead:** In a 6-quart lidded pan over medium heat, pour in olive oil and onions. Simmer until onions are translucent, 5 to 7 minutes. Stir in tomatoes and cook until they release juice, about 5 minutes. Stir in garlic, bay leaves, and chili; simmer sauce partially covered 45 minutes to 1 hour. Add squid liquid or water as needed to keep a thick sauce consistency. Chef Vedel's general rule with tomatoes is the more they simmer, the less acidic they'll be. Toward the end of the cooking time, crush tomato chunks in sauce with a potato masher to thicken and smooth sauce.

2 **Prepare the stuffing:** In a medium mixing bowl pour in breadcrumbs, or if using, rice. Stir in sausage *or* shrimp, chopped tentacles, lemon juice, and parsley. Fit a piping bag with a 1/2-inch plain tip and scrape the stuffing into the bag. Insert the tube tip into each squid body and stuff almost full; they will expand as they cook so don't over fill. Close and secure each squid with a toothpick.

3 **Cook:** Place stuffed squids into the simmering tomato sauce, partially cover, and simmer over low heat 1 hour, or place into 350 degree F oven. Test squid by poking with tip of a knife: they should offer no resistance. If they do, simmer longer.

4 **To Serve:** Scoop rice onto platter or serving plate and arrange squid and sauce over top.

Source: Cooking teacher Erick Vedel, Arles, France.

Signature Technique: Cassoulet

Cassoulet, a specialty of Languedoc on the Mediterranean in southwest France, is a long, slow-cooking casserole-stew rich with beans and meat—white beans layered with pork, sausage, and Goose or Duck Confit and topped with a breadcrumb crust. This thick stew has as many variations as cooks, but a good cassoulet should include about 70% beans and their liquid, mirepoix, bouquet garni, and 30% meat. Three famous recipes:

- **Cassoulet de Castelnaudary:** made with pork
- **Cassoulet de Toulouse:** richer than Castelnaudary, with lamb and sausages
- **Cassoulet de Carcassonne:** made with partridge

Vary! Improvise!

☛ *Add 2 ounces (1/3 cup) diced, peeled, and seeded tomato to stuffing.*

☛ *Gluten-Free: Substitute 1 cup packed, leftover cooked rice for the breadcrumbs.*

CASSOULET

Julia Child advises cooks to "use sausages only, or roast or braised pork, lamb, or duck or turkey instead of or along with goose." The must-have is a rich-flavored stock to give the beans deep flavor.

Yields 5-1/2 to 6 quarts, 8 to 12 servings

1 pound dry Great Northern or white kidney beans, 2-1/3 cups, yields 7 cups cooked, and 3 cups cooking liquid
Optional: 1/2 pound salt pork

Bouquet Garni

1/2 ounce Italian parsley sprigs, 4 large sprigs
2 large sprigs thyme
1 large bay leaf

3/4 ounce garlic, 3 large cloves, crushed and peeled

Cassoulet

2-1/2 pounds lamb shoulder or leg with bone, about 2 pounds meat and 1/2 pound bone, meat diced into 1-1/2-inch cubes
Rendered goose fat, lard, or vegetable oil
8 to 9 ounces large onions, 2 cups peeled and sliced or slivered
1/2 ounce garlic, 2 large cloves, 1 tablespoon peeled and minced
2 tablespoons tomato paste
1/2 teaspoon chopped fresh thyme leaves
1 bay leaf
1 cup dry white wine
2-1/2 cups beef stock, more as needed
1 pound garlic sausage
2-1/2 pounds *Goose or Duck Confit*, about 1-1/4 pounds meat only, 2-1/2 to 3 cups diced
2 tablespoons rendered goose fat or lard, more as needed
4 ounces crustless French bread, 2 cups fresh crumbs
1/2 ounce trimmed Italian parsley, 1/2 cup lightly packed

1 **Quick-soak beans:** Pick over beans to remove stones. Wash, drain, and place beans in a large pot. Cover with 3 quarts water and 1 tablespoon kosher salt. Cover and bring to a boil. Cover and let sit 1 hour.

2 **Blanch optional salt pork:** If using salt pork, remove rind and cut pork into slices 1/2-inch thick. Place in 4-quart saucepan and cover with cold water. Bring to a boil. Lower heat and simmer rind and pork 15 minutes to remove excess salt. Drain, rinse pork in cold water, drain again, and set aside.

3 **Cook beans:** Tie **bouquet garni** ingredients into cheesecloth. Drain soaked beans and pour into 4-quart pot. Add optional pork and rind, bouquet garni, garlic, and 2 quarts cold water. Bring to a boil, partially cover pot, reduce heat, and simmer beans until tender, 45 to 60 minutes. (May be done up to 3 days in advance and refrigerated. Bring just to a simmer before assembling.) Drain beans, discard bouquet garni, and reserve liquid.

4 **Brown lamb:** Blot lamb dry if necessary and season with salt. Heat a deep 12-inch skillet with 2 tablespoons fat or oil over medium-high heat until very hot but not smoking. Add lamb (in batches if necessary so they aren't crowded) and brown two sides. Transfer to a bowl. Don't wash skillet.

5 **Prepare lamb "stew":** Heat a 6-quart Dutch oven or casserole over medium heat, and add 1 tablespoon fat. Stir onions into hot fat and sauté until golden. Stir garlic and tomato paste into onions and cook 1 minute. Place lamb in casserole. Add herbs, wine, and stock to just cover lamb. Bring lamb mixture to a boil, cover Dutch oven, lower the heat, and simmer until lamb is tender, about 2 hours.

6 **Brown sausage:** Cut sausage in half lengthwise, then into 3/8-inch-thick half moons to yield about 2-2/3 cups. Heat 1 tablespoon fat in 12-inch skillet over medium heat. Brown sausage

and set aside. (If pan browns too quickly, deglaze with a little water and allow it to evaporate completely.)

7 Pour lamb "stew" into bowl to cool. (Reserve Dutch oven or casserole for later use.) Remove and discard bones. Taste and season lamb with salt and pepper. (This may be cooked up to 3 days in advance. Cover and refrigerate cooled, boned lamb in cooking liquid. Remove congealed surface fat before using.)

8 Remove bone and skin from preserved goose or duck. Dice meat into 1/2-inch cubes. If using salt pork, thinly slice.

9 **Assemble cassoulet:** Preheat oven to 325 degrees F. Arrange 2 cups beans in the bottom of the reserved 6-quart casserole or Dutch oven. Cover with a layer of half the meats: about 2 cups lamb, about 1-1/2 cups confit meat, about 1-1/3 cups browned sausage and, if using, half the salt pork. Repeat with a layer of 2 cups beans, then the remaining meats. End with a layer of remaining beans, about 3 cups, coming to within about 1/4 inch of the rim of the casserole.

10 Ladle lamb-cooking liquid, about 3 cups, plus as much bean cooking liquid as needed (about 1 cup), to just barely reach beans on top. Reserve remaining bean cooking liquid. Partially cover casserole and place in oven to bake 2 hours. An instant-read thermometer placed in the center should reach 212 degrees F.

11 **Remove casserole from oven and uncover:** The liquid should have been absorbed and evaporated so the top inch of the cassoulet is slightly dry looking. If there is too much liquid, the breadcrumb topping won't turn crusty. To reduce excess liquid, uncover casserole and boil, or place in oven. Alternatively, ladle some of the excess liquid into a skillet and boil to reduce by 2/3; scrape back into casserole.

*Recipe may be prepared up to 2 days in advance (without breadcrumbs and parsley). Cover and refrigerate after assembling. Bring to a simmer on top of the stove, then bake in oven as directed above.

12 **Finish cassoulet:** Mix together parsley and breadcrumbs and spread evenly over the top of the cassoulet. Raise oven heat to 450 degrees F. Place casserole back into oven and bake until breadcrumb topping is lightly brown and crusty, 20 to 30 minutes.

13 Break crust into beans with the back of a spoon. Return casserole to oven. Lower temperature to 375 degrees F, and bake until a second crust has formed. Break it into the beans, and if the beans seem too dry, add a little of reserved bean-cooking liquid. When the crust forms a third time, the cassoulet is ready to serve.

Source: *Julia's Menus for Special Occasions* by Julia Child.

> ### COOK'S VOICE: JEAN-JACQUES RACHOU
>
> #### Chef/Owner Manhattan's La Cote Basque
>
> Chef Jean-Jacques Rachou serves cassoulet daily. Rachou, from Toulouse, where cassoulet is believed to have originated, has been making the same cassoulet for over fifty years. "I never change it," he says. "The best cassoulet is from Toulouse and consists of duck confit, saucisson, pork skin, pork, beans, garlic, onion and bouquet garni, slow-cooked at least four hours."

REGION NINE: SOUTHWESTERN FRANCE

Midi-Pyrénées, Gascony, and Pays Basque—Peppery and Proud

Formerly a huge agricultural region, this area is now the main center of France's aerospace and high-tech industries. With Basque country on the Atlantic west coast and Spain and the stony Pyrénées along its southern border, this region is strong with Spanish influence. Sweet bell peppers, the *piment d'Espelette*—a spicy red pepper that is dried, and many types of—seafood—tuna, anchovies, sardines and swordfish, maize, salt cod, Spanish style cured ham, and sausages are favored foods. *Salsa verde* (with peas and asparagus), *garbure* (stew), *pipérade* (onion, peppers, tomatoes and eggs), Basque *axoa* (stew), and *millas*, stiff cornmeal porridge, are featured dishes.

FOIE GRAS

Foie gras is the enlarged liver of ducks or geese—almost pure fat. Grade A is the best available and best for poaching and searing. It should be firm, fine-textured, almost free of green or blood spots with a minimal number of veins. Grade A foie gras weighs between 1 and 3 pounds with color ranging from light beige to pale pink. In France, *foie gras*

FIGURE 5.36 Pays Basque.
Source: Tilio & Paolo/ Fotolia.

FIGURE 5.37 Geese raised for Foie Gras near Le Bougayrou, France.
Source: steve estvanik/Shutterstock.

entier denotes a whole liver. A label with *foie gras* denotes several pieces of the liver and *bloc de foie gras avec morceaux* means pressed liver with large and small pieces.

Grade B foie gras comes with some blemishes and larger veins and weighs between 3/4 and 1-1/2 pounds. It is good for searing and higher heat cooking, pâtés, terrines, and mousses. Vacuum packed foie gras kept very cold will keep 1 week, but use within 2 days of opening. Fresh foie gras can be frozen for up to a year, but some of the creamy texture will be lost. Expect a 15 to 20 percent weight loss when cooking foie gras, depending on the cooking method. Plan 3 to 4 ounces raw foie gras per appetizer serving and 5 to 6 ounces per entrée serving.

Foie gras may be infused with flavor by poaching in simmering liquid. It may be rolled into cheesecloth and simmered in stock then chilled to become *foie gras au torchon*. Foie gras baked in a mold, chilled, and sliced becomes *terrine de foie gras*. The French method of preparing foie gras *mi cuit* or half-cooked brings out its best flavor.

SEARED FOIE GRAS WITH SHALLOTS AND APPLES

Much of French foie gras comes from Gascony, where Armagnac brandy is produced. You may serve this dish as a decadent open-faced sandwich atop toasted brioche.

6 servings

1-1/2 pounds lobe Grade A duck *or* goose foie gras
2 to 3 ounces shallots, about 4 to 5 medium, 1 cup peeled and slivered
8 to 10 ounces ounce tart green apples, 2 medium, 2 cups peeled, cored, and thinly sliced
1/2 to 3/4 cup Armagnac or brandy
Grated nutmeg
6 slices brioche, toasted and halved into triangles

1 Remove foie gras from refrigerator to soften, about 1 hour. Remove bile and blood spots. Gently open lobes with fingers, locate the obvious larger veins. Carefully remove them and any small veins. Do not dig. Press lobes back into original shape and refrigerate until firm, 1 hour. Dip knife in warm water. Slice foie gras crosswise into six 3/4- to 1-inch-thick slices. Lightly season both sides of slices with salt and pepper. Place back in refrigerator.

2 Heat a 10-inch heavy *or* cast-iron skillet over high heat until very hot, just shy of smoking. Sauté foie gras in three batches of 2 slices, until browned, 30 to 60 seconds per side. Periodically pour out fat from skillet, and reserve. Remove foie gras from skillet and transfer to parchment-covered sheet pan and keep warm. Regulate the heat: don't allow skillet to get so hot that it smokes.

3 Pour out all but 1 tablespoon fat in skillet and heat over high heat. Reserve remaining fat. Stir in 1/3 of the shallots, season with salt, and sauté until caramelized, 5 to 7 minutes. Repeat in two more batches with remaining shallots and more fat as necessary. Scrape shallots into bowl and keep warm. Season with salt and pepper.

4 Add 1 tablespoon fat to skillet. Over high heat, sauté 1/3 of the apples until browned and crisp-tender, 5 to 7 minutes. Transfer apples to small bowl and keep warm. Repeat in two batches with remaining apples and more fat as necessary. Transfer to bowl and keep warm.

5 Remove skillet from the heat and add Armagnac. Return pan to medium heat, tip skillet, and flame the Armagnac. Cook until brandy is almost evaporated, 1 to 2 minutes. Pour apples back into skillet. Season with nutmeg, salt, and pepper to taste.

6 **To Serve:** Arrange 1/6 of the shallots and apples on each plate. Top with seared foie gras. Set toasted brioche alongside foie gras. Serve immediately.

FIGURE 5.38 Foie gras (duck or goose liver).
Source: Foodpictures/Shutterstock.

Vary! Improvise!

☞ *Substitute firm pears or mango for apple.*

☞ *For restaurant service, prepare 1 serving of foie gras, shallots, apples, and Armagnac at a time.*

BASQUE MAINSTAY: PIPÉRADE

If *basquaise* is on a menu in France, it means a dish with ham, which a traditional pipérade basquaise often contains. This thick stew of onions, tomatoes, red and green bell peppers, garlic, and the rusty-red Basque Piment d'Espelette hot chili is a favorite on its own (*piper* means a hot red pepper). French cooks traditionally prepare *pipérade* as a medium for scrambled eggs or as an omelet filling. Stir it into cooked rice or employ it as the base of a fish stew with fresh tuna or as a Basque-style chicken stew.

BASQUE CHICKEN (POULET BASQUAISE)

The traditional proportions of pipérade, *the mainstay French cooks use with egg dishes, varies widely, but usually has less peppers than this recipe. For* pipérade basquaise (*with eggs) use 8 ounces onion, 16 ounces mixed green and red bell peppers, 16 ounces tomatoes, and omit thyme and bay leaf. Simmer sauce very thick before adding 5 beaten eggs and gently cooking into small curds.*

6 to 8 servings

4-1/2 to 5 pounds chicken thighs, 3-3/4 to 4 pounds skinned

Pipérade Sauce

Yields about 8 cups

3 tablespoons olive oil
1 pound Spanish onions
2 pounds green bell peppers, 4 large
1-1/2 pounds red bell peppers, 3 large
2 pounds plum tomatoes, peeled and seeded
    or two 28-ounce cans peeled whole plum tomatoes, 4 cups drained
3/4 to 1 ounce garlic, 3 to 4 cloves, 1-1/2 to 2 tablespoons peeled and minced
2 large sprigs fresh thyme
1 bay leaf
1 to 1-1/2 teaspoons *Piment d'Espelette* chili powder
    or 1-1/2 teaspoons paprika and a pinch of cayenne

6 tablespoons canola or olive oil, *divided*
Flour for dredging chicken

For Serving

Hot, cooked rice

1 Remove chicken skin and fat. Wash and pat chicken dry and set aside at room temperature.

2 **Cut the Vegetables:** Halve then quarter each onion through the root. Slice crossways into 1/4-inch-thick slices to yield about 4 cups. Remove stems, cores, and seeds from bell peppers. Slice into 1/2-inch wide strips to yield 6 cups green bell peppers and 4 to 5 cups red bell peppers. Dice tomatoes into 1/2-inch cubes to yield about 4 cups.

3 **Prepare the Sauce:** Heat oil in a heavy 8-quart pot over medium heat. Add onion and cook until soft but not colored, about 7 minutes. Stir in bell peppers, cover pot, and reduce heat to medium-low. Simmer vegetables until tender, 15 to 20 minutes. Stir in tomatoes, garlic, thyme, bay leaf, and chili powder. Season with 1 teaspoon kosher salt. Cover pot, and simmer until vegetables soften and become juicy, 15 to 20 minutes. (If there is a lot of liquid, uncover pot and cook sauce over medium heat until thick and liquid is somewhat reduced, 5 minutes.) Season to taste with salt, pepper, or more chili.

   *At this point, the pipérade sauce may be set aside for up to 2 days or used for other dishes.

4 **Brown the Chicken and Simmer in Pipérade Sauce:** Heat 3 tablespoons oil in 12-inch skillet over medium-high heat. Season half the chicken with salt and dredge in flour. Shake off excess flour. Place chicken in skillet and fry it until browned on both side. Transfer to the pipérade sauce. Wipe out skillet and add 3 tablespoons oil. Reheat over medium-high heat. Season remaining chicken with salt, dredge in flour, shake off excess, and fry until browned. Transfer to pot with pipérade. Immerse cooked chicken into sauce and bring to a boil. Reduce heat, partially cover pot, and simmer until chicken is tender and cooked through, about 45 minutes.

5 **To Serve:** Taste and season dish with salt and pepper as necessary. Serve with rice.

Source: *Around My French Table* by Dorie Greenspan.

Vary! Improvise!

☞ *Add 2 ounces (1/2 cup) pitted black olives to the sauce at the end of cooking.*

☞ *Garnish pipérade with basil chiffonade or chopped Italian parsley before serving.*

☞ *Add 3 to 4 ounces diced prosciutto or ham to onions when making pipérade sauce.*

ROQUEFORT AND CARAMELIZED ONION TART

This classic tart was a specialty of Midi-Pyrénées. Originally from the caves of Mont Combalou, tangy Roquefort cheese is protected by an AOC, or appellation of origin control. If French Roquefort isn't available, use a good-quality blue cheese.

Yields 10-inch tart, 6 to 8 servings

Pate Brisée dough for 10-inch tart pan

Filling

2 tablespoons butter
1 tablespoon vegetable oil
1 pound onions, 4 cups thinly sliced
4 ounces Roquefort cheese, about 1 cup crumbled
2 large eggs
1 cup cream
2 teaspoons chopped thyme leaves

1 Prepare *Pate Brisée*, and chill.

2 Preheat oven to 375 degrees F. Fit pastry into a 10-inch tart pan with removable bottom. Line pastry with parchment paper and fill with dry beans or another tart pan. Place in oven and blind-bake until dough is set but not colored, 15 minutes. Remove pan from the oven and cool 10 minutes. Remove blind-baking beans or top pan.

3 Heat butter and oil in 6-quart pot on medium-high heat. Add onions. When the pan is hot, reduce heat to low and cover. Simmer onions until tender, 30 to 40 minutes, stirring and checking periodically. Uncover pot and raise heat to medium-high. Stirring frequently, sauté onions until golden brown, about 15 to 20 minutes. If the onions begin to stick, deglaze with 1 to 2 tablespoons water or white wine and evaporate liquid each time. Season onions with 1/2 teaspoon kosher salt and scrape into a bowl to cool.

4 Layer caramelized onions then Roquefort cheese onto the pastry. Beat together eggs, cream, thyme, salt, and freshly ground pepper. Pour egg mixture over onions and cheese. Place tart into oven and bake until the eggs are set in the middle, 20 to 30 minutes.

5 **To Serve:** Cool tart slightly, cut into wedges, and serve warm.

REGION TEN: COASTAL SOUTHWESTERN FRANCE

Aquitaine, Bordeaux, and Poitou-Charents— Rich Cooking, Great Wine

Bordered on the west by the Atlantic Ocean and by Midi-Pyrénées to the south, this region, a continuation of the famous Southwest, is home to many kilometers of coastline, rural farmland, an oyster lagoon, and forest. Its variety of food makes for luxurious dining: Atlantic seafood, fresh produce, excellent wine, Cognac, truffles, onion, shallots, foie gras, many types of fruit trees, melons, prunes, walnuts, mussels, lamb, and pork. Hearty dishes like *entrecôte bordelaise* (steak with red wine sauce), sauce *périgueux* (truffle), chicken *fricassée* with cognac, rabbit with prunes, goat cheese salad, and green beans with ham are featured.

Signature Technique: Oil-Braised Poultry (Confit)

Confit (con-fee) is an ancient method that comes from the French word "confire" meaning "to preserve," but modern kitchens make confit because of the meltingly tender and tasty results.

French cooks prepare confit in late fall and winter when the ducks have fattened substantially. It's an economical way to preserve meat since nothing is wasted. All parts of the duck, the breasts, wings, necks, and offal (hearts and gizzards), may be made into confit, not just the leg quarters. Though this ancient preservation method might seem challenging, confit is easily made in three steps:

Step One: Salt and Season

Poultry parts cure in kosher salt. This draws out water in which microorganisms and bacteria thrive, and makes an inhospitable environment. Many recipes call for curing 48 hours, but unless it will be stored it in a crock in a cellar, a shorter time is sufficient. Traditional confit recipes tend to use a lot of salt and cure longer, resulting in saltier meat. Many cooks in France salt their meat without seasonings. If seasoning the meat is desired, rub on dry seasonings after the salt. Scatter sliced shallots, garlic, juniper, or fresh herbs like thyme under and over salted meat. Moist seasonings can shorten the shelf life of confit.

The Salting and Curing Time

Weigh meat. Determine proper amount of salt for the length of cure desired. Modern salting will leave the meat pleasantly salty with a salty broth at the bottom. Traditional salting will extract most of the moisture during curing so there will be little or no broth present after poaching. Traditionally salted meat will taste saltier.

Modern Salt: Cure 24 to 36 hours

- 1/6 ounce salt or 0.18 ounce (about 1.5 teaspoons Diamond Crystal salt) per pound of meat.

Traditional Salt: 36 to 48 hours

- 1/3 ounce salt or 0.36 ounce (about 1 tablespoon Diamond Crystal salt) per pound of meat.

*Diamond Crystal Kosher Salt weighs the least per volume because of its shape. Other salts must be weighed as they vary drastically.

Step Two: Poach Gently Immersed in Fat

Drain away liquid that has collected during curing. Pat duck parts very dry. Place meat in deep baking dish and fully cover with warm, rendered duck or pork fat. Bring meat and fat to a bare simmer on top of the stove. Simmer meat until very tender over very low heat, 4 to 10 hours. Or place into 200 to 250 degree F oven. It will keep the temperature even more easily than a stovetop. Occasionally stir to loosen skin or turn meat that wants to stick.

- Ducks weighing 10 to 12 pounds each will supply enough fat to confit themselves. If you have smaller or leaner ducks or poultry, freshly rendered pork fat (lard) is a good substitute. Older laying hens and turkey with tougher but more flavorful meat, pork, and pork belly make meltingly flavorful, tender confits.

- Leftover fat may be frozen up to 6 months. It may be strained through cheesecloth and re-used for confit twice more before it become too salty. The fat will take on the flavor of the seasonings.

Step Three: Store and Age

Remove poultry from hot fat and pack into sterilized crock or heavy plastic container like Cambro. (It's okay to cut off knobby end of leg if it won't fit.) With a ladle, scoop hot fat off the top of the pan through cheesecloth-lined strainer. Leave moist broth on the bottom—this can sour a confit, but it can be used to season other dishes. Beware, it will be salty. Ladle fat over duck parts so they are fully immersed and airtight with 1 inch of fat on top. Store confit in refrigerator up to 6 months. Confit and duck fat freeze well. Ripen or age confit at least 1 month. Peak flavor is from 2 to 5 months.

SALT-CURED AND FAT-SIMMERED DUCK LEGS (CONFIT DE CANARD)

Two different chefs give two different flavors to confit: Madeleine Kamman and Tom Colicchio.

Yields 5 to 5-1/2 pounds unskinned duck quarters (leg/thigh), about 6 servings

Each leg quarter yields about 4 ounces meat or 1/2 cup shredded

Madeleine's Spice Mixture

Yields about 6 teaspoons, enough for 15 pounds poultry

1 teaspoon ground cumin
1 teaspoon ground coriander
1 teaspoon ground cinnamon
3/4 teaspoon ground allspice
1/2 teaspoon dried, ground ginger
1/2 teaspoon freshly ground nutmeg
3/4 to 1 teaspoon crumbled dried thyme leaves
1/4 teaspoon ground cloves
1 large bay leaf, finely crumbled

1-1/2 ounces garlic, 6 large cloves, crushed and peeled

Tom's Seasonings

Enough for 5 to 5-1/2 pounds poultry

About 2 ounces shallots, about 3 medium, 1/2 cup peeled and sliced
2 ounces garlic, about 8 large cloves, about 1/4 cup peeled and sliced
1/2 ounce fresh thyme, about 12 sprigs, washed and blotted dry
3 bay leaves

The Meat

5- to 5-1/2 pounds unskinned duck leg/thigh quarters, about 6 large

The Salt

- **Modern Salt:** 0.9 to 1 ounce salt, 2-1/2 to 2-3/4 tablespoons *Diamond Crystal* kosher salt

- **Traditional Salt:** 1.8 to 2 ounces salt, 5 to 5-1/2 tablespoons *Diamond Crystal* kosher salt

The Fat

3 to 4 quarts rendered duck fat (1 quart duck fat weighs a little more than 1-3/4 pounds)

1 Prepare either **Madeleine's Spice Mixture** or **Tom's Seasonings**.

- If using **Madeleine's Mixture**, mix dry spices and bay leaf in small bowl. Measure out **2 teaspoons** of the spice mixture for this recipe, and set aside remainder for another confit. Prepare garlic and set aside.

- If using **Tom's Seasonings**, prepare shallots, garlic, thyme, and bay leaves, and mix together in medium mixing bowl.

2 **Salt and Season Meat:** Pat meat dry. Rub with measured salt.

- If using **Madeleine's Mixture**, rub the reserved 2 teaspoons spice mixture over cut sides and skin. Place meat in stainless steel hotel pan in one layer; tuck garlic under meat.

- If using **Tom's Seasonings**, scatter half the seasonings under the meat and the remainder over the meat.

FIGURE 5.39 Raw duck quarters.
Source: Richard Griffin/Shutterstock.

3 **Cure Meat:** Cover pan with plastic wrap. Refrigerate meat and leave to cure 24 to 36 hours.

4 Preheat oven to 200 degrees F. Meanwhile, melt the fat over low heat in a 6-quart saucepan.

5 Drain liquid from meat. Pat dry the duck meat, garlic, and if using, shallots and thyme sprigs. Return legs and garlic, and if using, shallots, thyme, and bay leaf to ovenproof pan in a single snug layer. Cover completely with the hot fat. Place pan in oven.

6 **Cook Meat:** Cook confit slowly at a very slow simmer, just an occasional bubble, until meat is tender (about 190 degrees F internal temperature), can be easily pulled from the bone, the fat is clear, and garlic cloves have turned deep gold, 5 to 6 hours. Remove confit from oven. Cool meat in its fat. (For the "express" method, cook confit at 250 degrees F for 3 to 4 hours. Be aware that lower heat produces a very tender confit.)

7 Transfer duck to sterilized container. Ladle warm fat (but avoid juices on the bottom) through cheesecloth-lined strainer. Discard strainer contents. Pour enough warm fat over meat to cover by at least 1 inch. Cool confit completely, seal the container, and refrigerate up to 6 months. If using duck fat, strain, save and freeze. Reuse fat up to three more times for confit.

8 **To Serve:** To extract leg quarters without tearing, remove confit from refrigerator 2 to 3 hours before serving to allow fat to soften. Set container in large bowl of lukewarm water to hasten the warming process.

- **To Just Reheat Duck:** Preheat oven to 425 degrees F. Place duck quarters on rack set into hotel or baking pan and place into oven until warm, 10 to 15 minutes. At this point duck may be skinned and the meat removed from bone then shredded for use in salads, vegetables, or risotto, as hors d'oeuvres, as a filling for *Buckwheat Crepes*, crepes, or pasta or in soup, *Cassoulet*, or stew.

- **To Serve Duck Quarters Whole and Crisp the Skin:** Preheat oven to 400 degrees F. Arrange duck quarters skin side down into 12-inch ovenproof skillet. Heat skillet over medium heat. Fat will render and skin will become crisp, 5 to 7 minutes. Pour off fat and turn quarters skin side up. Blot off excess fat. Place pan in oven to heat duck through, 10 to 15 minutes.

Source: *The New Making of a Cook* by Madeleine Kamman.

THE OTHER CONFIT: PRESERVING IS NOT THE POINT

The term *confit* can also refer to foods slow-cooked completely immersed in oil or fat: tomatoes, onions, eggplant, tuna, salmon, or shrimp. Unlike steaming, boiling, or sautéing, a slow-cooked bath in fat turns fish and seafood silky and succulent, and locks in a rich flavor and texture for vegetables.

- Choose fish steaks or fillets 3/4 to 1-inch thick: salmon, halibut, tuna, scallops, shrimp, Chilean sea bass, lobster, swordfish, boneless, skinless chicken, and turkey breast are good choices.
- Bring food to room temperature 1 hour before cooking the confit; the food will cook more quickly and evenly. For deeper flavor, toss food with herbs, spices, citrus zest, gingerroot, or garlic to marinate during that hour.

- Olive oil is hands-down the best for flavor and texture, but if using quarts of olive oil seems decadent, cut the oil with high-quality sunflower or safflower oil.
- Cool oil after use, strain it through a coffee filter, and discard the juicy sediment remaining on the bottom of the pan, or incorporate its rich flavor into a sauce. Refrigerate oil and reuse once or twice again. Since, unlike deep-frying, the oil isn't heated very high, it won't break down as quickly. (Salt breaks down oil; salt food when it comes out of oil if planning to reuse the oil.)
- Preheat oven to 225 degrees F. Pour enough oil to cover food (4 to 6 cups oil for 2 pounds seafood) into a high-sided 10- or 11-inch ovenproof high-sided skillet or heavy pan.

(Continued)

(Continued)

- Bring oil to 120 degrees F on an instant-read thermometer, and slide food into hot oil.
- Food should be completely immersed. Place pan into oven.
- Check temperature and fish doneness after 10 minutes. White blobs of albumin will begin to appear when fish is done: 10 minutes for thin cuts, up to 25 minutes for thicker fish, seafood, and tender vegetables, and 45 minutes to 1 hour for hard vegetables.

- The lower the heat of the oil, the more tender and succulent the outcome. Maintain 120 degrees F for animal proteins like fish, seafood, and chicken and 120 to 140 degrees F for vegetables.
- Prepare a vinaigrette or sauce for seafood or vegetables with confit oil or the juicy sediment leftover after cooking. Squeeze lemon juice and sprinkle herbs on confit-cooked food. Use confit-cooked food for composed or tossed salads or as garnish on pasta or in soup.

Pan Sauté/Pan Sauce: Layers of Flavor

One of the most versatile, speedy techniques a cook can master is to make a sauce in a pan that a sautéed piece of chicken, fish, or steak just vacated. It might be as simple as reduced Port or as complex as sautéed aromatic vegetables sautéed, deglazed with three more layers of flavor—wine, stock, and cream—reduced each time. The glaze that forms in the pan jumps off the bottom adding an extra bit of flavor to the pan sauce. Pan sautés are popular in restaurants for their versatility and flexibility. Many cooks reduce wine and stock ahead to save time, or prepare sauces fully and just heat them through in the pan before plating. See *Signature Technique: Ten Steps to Pan Sauté/Pan Sauce* for more information.

STEAK WITH RED WINE SAUCE (ENTRECÔTE BORDELAISE)

Reduce 1 cup unsalted beef stock to 2 tablespoons if demi-glace is unavailable. Entrecôte Bordelaise served with potatoes—mashed, French-fried, or baked—is an ideal pairing.

Serves 2

Red Wine-Shallot Sauce

About 1 ounce shallot, 2 small, 2 tablespoons peeled and thinly sliced crosswise
1 cup good red wine, such as Bordeaux, Cotes du Rhone, or Merlot
2 tablespoons demi-glace *or* reduced beef stock (see headnote)

1/2 ounce unsalted butter, 1 tablespoon, diced
Two 8- to 10-ounce rib, top loin, or sirloin boneless strip steaks, cut 1 inch thick
1 teaspoon unsalted butter, more as needed
1 teaspoon oil, more as needed
Garnish: Finely chopped Italian parsley

1 Prep and measure all ingredients for **red wine-shallot sauce:** shallot, red wine, demi-glace, and butter. Set near stove.

2 Season steaks with salt and pepper on both sides. Heat 9- or 10-inch sauté pan over medium-high heat. Add 1 teaspoon butter and 1 teaspoon oil to pan and swirl. When butter foams, immediately place steaks in pan. Sauté steaks until a brown crust forms and they naturally let go from the pan, 3 minutes or more per side. Do not turn before crust forms. If meat sticks, it's usually not ready to be turned. Cook on second side until an instant-read thermometer reads 125 degrees F for medium-rare or 130 degrees F for medium. Remove meat from pan and keep warm.

3 Over low heat, reheat pan from searing steak without washing. Add more butter and oil if desired, and stir in shallots. Cook until soft, 2 to 5 minutes. Carefully pour in wine and demi-glace or reduced stock. Scrape up browned bits. Add juices that collected under steak to pan. Gently boil sauce until reduced to 1/4 cup or 2 fluid ounces.

4 **To Serve:** Remove pan from heat. Whisk in 1 tablespoon diced whole butter. Season sauce with salt and pepper to taste. Garnish with parsley. Pour over steak and serve.

REGION ELEVEN: SOUTH-CENTRAL FRANCE

Auvergne and Massif Central— Mountains and Volcanic Plateau

The Massif Central range divides east and west, north and south; its high peaks dominate France. The volcanic plateau produces wheat, barley, corn, and grapes along with cattle, game, pork, and Vichy water. This scenic and historic region is known for hearty, homey food like *tartouffe* (potato pie), *potee* (boiled stuffed cabbage), *tourte* (chicken pie), sausages, pâtés, blue cheese, de Puy green lentils, Cantal cheese, and fruit *clafoutis* (puffy custardy-cake).

FIGURE 5.40   Auvergne, France.
Source: david hughes/Fotolia.

FRENCH GREEN LENTIL SALAD (SALAD LENTILLES DU PUY)

Green lentils from Puy, France stay firm when cooked. Dice vegetables the size of lentils. Serve as hors d'oeuvre or summer pique-nique food.

Yields 5 to 6 cups, 4 to 6 servings

About 7 ounces French green lentils, 1 cup
3/4 ounce shallot, 1 small studded with 3 whole cloves
1 bay leaf
3 to 4 tablespoons extra virgin olive oil
   or 3 tablespoons French roasted walnut oil
2 to 3 tablespoons red wine vinegar
1 to 2 ounces red onion, green onion *or* shallot, 4 tablespoons peeled and finely diced
2 tablespoons finely sliced chives
   or 1 tablespoon fresh tarragon leaves
1/4 ounce trimmed Italian parsley, 2 tablespoons finely chopped
About 4 ounces red bell pepper, 1 cup stemmed, seeded, and finely diced

For Serving

4 to 6 ounces lettuce leaves

1 Combine lentils, shallot, bay leaf, 3/4 teaspoon kosher salt, and 3 cups water in a saucepan. Bring to a boil. Lower heat, cover pot, and simmer lentils until tender, 25 minutes.

2 **Optional:** Bring 1 cup water to a boil in a small saucepan. To soften the bite of raw red onion, green onion, or shallot, place into strainer and pour boiling water over. Drain well and set aside.

3 Drain liquid from lentils, and pour lentils into a mixing bowl. While warm, stir in oil, vinegar, onion or shallot, herbs, and bell pepper. Taste and season with salt and pepper. Rest 15 minutes before serving.

4 **To Serve:** Arrange lettuce leaves on serving plates and pile lentils on top. Serve at room temperature. Or serve lentils as a warm side dish with roasted or grilled meat.

FIGURE 5.41   French green lentils.
Source: Elenathewise/Fotolia.

Vary! Improvise!

☞ *Fines Herbes:* Substitute 3 tablespoons fines herbes for chives or tarragon and parsley.

SILKY POTATOES (ALIGOT)

Traditionally made with a soft raw cheese called tomme fraîche from the south-central Auvergne, aligot is addictive. Cooks in the Auvergne use scissors to cut aligot into ribbons and onto plates. Beating transforms these humble potatoes into a stretchy and silky smooth emulsion. It's comfort food at its most elegant, simple best, and great teamed with a steak or roasted herbed chicken.

Yields 4 to 5 cups, 4 to 6 servings

2 pounds Yukon Gold *or* russet baking potatoes
4 tablespoons unsalted butter, finely diced
1/3 ounce garlic, 2 medium cloves, 2 teaspoons peeled and finely minced
1/2 cup whole milk, more if needed
4 ounces mozzarella cheese, 1 cup grated
4 ounces Gruyère cheese, 1 cup grated

1 Peel potatoes and dice into 1/2-inch cubes to yield 5 cups. Place in 4-quart saucepan, cover with 4 cups cold water, and add 1 tablespoon kosher salt. Bring to a boil, lower heat, cover, and simmer potatoes until tender, 10 to 15 minutes. Pour potatoes through strainer to drain; set saucepan back on stove and reserve for later use.

2 Transfer hot potatoes to food processor and add butter, garlic, and 1 teaspoon kosher salt. Pulse until butter is fully incorporated. Pour in 1/4-cup milk and process, scrape down, and process again until potatoes are smooth and creamy.

3 **Ten to 15 minutes before serving:** Scrape potatoes back into reserved saucepan, and place on medium heat. Beat in cheeses, 1 cup at a time, until fully incorporated. Stir potatoes constantly and vigorously (as for risotto or polenta) over the heat until the cheese melts fully and potatoes are smooth and elastic. They will begin to pull away from the bottom or side of the pan and form long ribbons when dropped from a wooden spoon. If potatoes are too thick, stir in up to 1/4 cup more milk.

*To hold potatoes: Spread potatoes out in hotel pan, cover, and set over simmering water to keep warm up to 1 hour.

4 **To Serve:** Taste aligot and season with salt and freshly ground pepper. Stir in more whole milk if potatoes become too thick. Serve aligot very hot.

Source: *Cook's Illustrated.*

Vary! Improvise!

☞ **More Stretch:** *Double the mozzarella for more stretch and richness.*
☞ **Different Flavor:** *Substitute aged white cheddar for Gruyère.*

REGION TWELVE: NORTH-CENTRAL FRANCE

Loire, Orleans, and the Loire Valley—Cradle of Culture, Garden of France

A land of vineyards, rolling green hills filled with more than 1,000 chateaux, and the Loire River, this fertile region is often called the *Garden of France*. Charles VIII brought Italian gardeners here at the height of the Renaissance and they introduced lettuce, artichokes, and green peas. Melons, plums, pears, apricots, wheat, maize, haricots vert, potatoes asparagus, walnuts, and many types of fruit trees flourish.

This region produces most of France's cultivated white mushrooms. Game like quail, venison, and boar is roasted. Pork is made into *rillettes* and pâtés. *Beurre blanc* (white butter sauce) is one of this region's most important culinary contributions. Classic Loire dishes are river pike-perch in beurre blanc, eel in *matelote* (stew), or salmon with sorrel sauce. Loire prunes are paired with pork, cream, and local Vouvray white wine for *porc aux pruneaux*. Fish, rabbit, and chicken are poached in wine. *Tarte tatin*, salads with walnut oil, *pain d'épices* (spiced sweet bread), carp in red wine, and goat milk-*chevre* (cheese) are some of this region's delights.

FIGURE 5.42 Home garden in Loire Valley.
Source: Paul Merrett/Shutterstock.

BROWN MEAT JAM: RILLETTES

FIGURE 5.43 Rillettes.
Source: Ian O'Leary/DK Images.

Rillettes, a specialty of Tours and Le Mans, southeast of Paris (respectively in and near the Loire Valley), is a cross between meat *paté* and duck *confit* (see *Region Ten: Coastal Southwestern France*). Typically rillettes are made with diced pork belly, shoulder, or ribs long and slow-simmered in pork fat. The meltingly tender meat is drained and shredded (bones discarded) and mixed or beaten with some of the fat. It's packed into ramekins and covered with a little more cooking fat and allowed to cure in the refrigerator several days. The soft, smooth meat paste is spread onto bread or toast and eaten as an appetizer or snack.

POACHED SALMON WITH LEMON WHITE-BUTTER SAUCE (SAUMON POCHÉ)

Preparing a beurre blanc for fish from its reduced poaching liquid is a traditional method from the Loire Valley, with its profusion of river fish like pike. It works especially well with cod, halibut, small whole fish, fish steaks, scallops, skate, salmon, or swordfish.

4 servings

4 to 5 cups hot *Court-Bouillon*
Four 5 to 6 ounce skinned salmon fillets

Lemon Beurre Blanc

About 1-1/2 ounces shallots, 2 medium, 2 to 3 tablespoons peeled and finely diced
1-1/2 ounce unsalted cold butter, 3 tablespoons diced
1 teaspoon freshly squeezed lemon juice, to taste
2 teaspoons chopped *Fines Herbes*
    or 2 teaspoons chopped Italian parsley

1 Prepare **court-bouillon**.

2 Preheat oven to 375 degrees F. Season fish with salt and pepper and place into a 9- or 10-inch ovenproof sauté pan. Pour in hot court-bouillon to just cover, or at least 7/8 the way up the sides of the fish.

3 Place pan in oven and poach until fish is almost cooked through, depending on thickness, 6 to 10 minutes. Salmon should be opaque and firm, but tender, to the touch and pink in the center when flaked with tip of knife. Remove fish with slotted spatula carefully, place on warm platter and cover with foil to keep warm. Reserve poaching liquid.

4 *Fifteen to 20 minutes before serving prepare the* **lemon beurre blanc:** Add shallots to poaching liquid and, over medium-high heat, bring to a boil. Reduce court-bouillon until slightly syrupy to about 2 to 3 tablespoons.

5 Remove pan from heat. Whisk in butter, bit by bit. Taste sauce and season with salt, freshly ground pepper, lemon juice, and herbs. Lemon beurre blanc will vary in thickness, depending on the ratio of poaching liquid to butter. For thicker sauce, use more butter. Don't boil the sauce or it'll break.

6 **To Serve:** Place a warm fillet on each serving plate and spoon lemon butter sauce over. Garnish with *fines herbes* or parsley.

Vary! Improvise!

☛ *Add one of the ingredients below to Lemon Beurre Blanc:*

☛ *1 tablespoon roughly chopped capers, more to taste*

☛ *1/2 ounce green onions, 1 to 2 tablespoons trimmed and finely sliced*

☛ *Chopped roasted garlic*

☛ *1 teaspoon French Dijon or whole-grain mustard*

WILD RABBIT SOUP WITH MUSHROOMS (SOUPE AU LAPIN DE GARENNE)

"De Garenne" can be translated to mean a wild or very gamey, flavorful rabbit, for which this soup is ideal (but any will do). Depending on how much liquid is added, the soup can become a stew. The technique is the same.

Yields about 9 cups, 6 servings

3 to 3-1/2 pounds skinned rabbit
1 ounce unsalted butter, 2 tablespoons diced
2 tablespoons oil
Flour as needed
1 teaspoon curry powder
1-1/2 pounds onions, 6 cups peeled and finely diced
1/4 ounce garlic, 1 large clove, 1-1/2 teaspoons finely minced
1 pound fresh white mushrooms, about 4 cups quartered, *divided*

Bouquet Garni

6 large stems Italian parsley
2 bay leaves
2 large sprigs thyme

1 sprig rosemary
1 tablespoon oil or unsalted butter, diced

Optional Liaison

3 large egg yolks
1 cup crème fraîche

1 Rinse rabbit and blot dry. Cut it into 4 to 8 pieces.

2 In 6-quart soup pot over medium heat, add butter and oil. Season rabbit with salt and dredge in flour, shake off excess, and place in hot fat. Brown rabbit on both sides and transfer to a bowl.

3 Sprinkle bottom of soup pot with 1/4 cup water, curry powder, onions, garlic, and 1/2 cup mushrooms. Cook until water evaporates and onions soften, 5 to 7 minutes. Stir in 9 cups cold water, rabbit, **bouquet garni**, and rosemary, and bring to a boil. Reduce heat and simmer soup until meat falls from bone, about 2 hours.

4 Heat 1 tablespoon butter in sauté pan and cook remaining mushrooms until golden and tender, about 5 minutes. Set aside for garnish.

5 Remove rabbit pieces from soup, remove meat from bones. Reserve meat. Discard bones and bouquet garni. Strain soup through fine mesh strainer and push solids through strongly. Return soup broth to soup pot, add mushroom garnish and reserved rabbit meat. (Alternatively, save some mushrooms for garnishing the soup in bowls.) Simmer soup to heat through. Taste soup and season with salt and freshly ground pepper.

6 **To Serve:** Whisk together yolks and crème fraiche for the **liaison**, and temper: whisk in a little hot soup. Slowly whisk egg-soup mixture back into soup. Do not boil soup or it will curdle. Ladle soup-stew into bowls and serve. (Top with reserved cooked mushrooms, if using.)

FIGURE 5.44 Rabbit cut into pieces.
Source: Gary Ombler/DK Images.

Source: *The Soups of France* by Lois Anne Rothert.

BRAISED PORK WITH PRUNES AND CREAM
(PORC AUX PRUNEAUX ET CRÉME)

Most connective tissue in meat consists of either collagen or elastin. Cooked using moist, slow heat, collagen breaks down into gelatin and water. Elastin, under normal cooking conditions, will not break down so it remains stringy and tough. Lean pork contains less collagen and more elastin in the silverskin, tendons, and ligaments, so they should be trimmed away before pork is cooked. The fattier pork shoulder used here is excellent for longer, moist cooking.

8 servings

5 ounces pitted prunes, 24 small, 1 cup loosely packed
2 cups white wine, preferably French Vouvray
4 to 5 pound boneless pork shoulder roast (butt), trimmed of most external fat,
rolled and tied
2 to 3 tablespoons vegetable oil

Mirepoix

4 to 5 ounces onion, 1 cup peeled and medium diced
4 to 5 ounces carrot, 2/3 cup peeled and medium diced
2 to 3 ounces trimmed celery, 1/2 cup medium diced

3 tablespoons unsalted butter, diced
1 cup heavy cream *plus* 2 teaspoons fresh lemon juice
 or 1 cup crème fraiche
2 to 3 teaspoons red currant jelly, to taste
About 1/2 ounce trimmed Italian parsley, 4 tablespoons minced

1 Place prunes in a small saucepan, cover with white wine, and simmer until plump and soft, 8 minutes. Drain. Reserve wine and prunes in separate bowls.

2 **Brown meat:** Preheat oven to 350 degrees F. Blot meat dry and season with salt. Heat oil in a 6-quart Dutch oven over medium-high heat. Brown meat on all sides, 7 to 8 minutes. Transfer meat to a bowl and set aside.

3 **Brown mirepoix:** Lower heat under Dutch oven to medium, and stir in **mirepoix** ingredients. Sauté vegetables until lightly browned, 8 minutes. If bottom of Dutch oven browns too quickly, deglaze with 2 tablespoons reserved wine and continue to cook mirepoix until soft and browned. Deglaze Dutch oven with reserved wine and scrape up bits from bottom.

4 **Roast pork:** Place pork on top of the mirepoix. Cover Dutch oven and place in oven. Roast pork until very tender with an internal temperature of 160 to 165 degrees F, about 1 hour. Remove pork from pot, cover with foil, and keep warm. Rest pork 10 minutes minimum. (After resting, the meat should reach between 170 to 175 degrees F.)

5 **Prepare the sauce:** Strain contents of Dutch oven through a fine strainer into a bowl. Press down to extract all the liquid. Return juices from bowl to Dutch oven, about 2 cups. Over high heat, bring liquids to a boil, skim away excess fat, and reduce liquids by half to about 1 cup.

6 Stir in cream and lemon juice or crème fraîche, and boil until sauce turns light beige and just coats the back of a spoon. Whisk in red currant jelly, and season sauce with salt and pepper to taste to yield about 1-1/2 cups sauce. Stir in prunes and heat through.

7 **To Serve:** Carve meat into 1/2-inch-thick slices and plate. Top each serving with 3 prunes and spoon about 3 tablespoons sauce over prunes and pork. Garnish with parsley and serve hot.

Source: *The Institute for Culinary Education's* Techniques of Fine Cooking.

Vary! Improvise!

☞ *Lean Pork: Substitute 4 pork tenderloins (3 to 4 pounds) for the pork butt. Cut vegetables into small dice. Season meat with salt and tie two tenderloins together; repeat with remaining two tenderloins. Brown meat and vegetables following steps 2 and 3. Place tenderloins on vegetables and roast to internal temperature of 145 to 150 degrees F, 12 to 15 minutes. Remove meat and rest on platter covered loosely with foil 5 minutes. Slice meat into 1/2-inch-thick medallions and top with prunes and sauce.*

VINEGAR AND OIL

French Vinegar (Vin Aigre)

Vinegar is one of those stories of an accident turning into a golden opportunity. In the Middle Ages, small boats traveled up the Loire River to Orléans and then on to Paris. Casks of wine were a large part of their cargo, which on the slow journey sometimes turned sour. Savvy dealers bought up this *vin aigre* (sour wine) and began to ferment, bottle, and sell it. By the thirteenth century, France's vinegar trade was bustling. By the eighteenth century, the trade swelled to more than 300 producers. Today there is only one direct descendant still left in Orléans who makes vinegar the traditional way from high-quality wine and cider.

French Roasted Walnut Oil (Huile de Noix)

English walnut trees fill the eastern Loire Valley, where walnut oil production has long been a tradition. Producers grind walnut flesh into paste, roast the paste, then press out the oil. The oil's quality depends on freshness of the nuts, length of roasting time, and the pressing conditions (less oil extracted equals a nuttier flavor. French cooks relish walnut (and hazelnut) oil in vinaigrettes and to season or garnish soup, rice, pasta, French green lentil salad, cooked or raw vegetables (asparagus), fish, poultry, and fruit dishes. It's excellent with lettuce greens and soft rounds of goat cheese (*chevre*) or over roasted peaches and basil. Walnut oil, high in omega 3 fatty acids, is not a cooking oil. It must be kept quite cold because it goes rancid quickly. Look for the traditional French roasted walnut oil with its delicate, nutty flavor and topaz color.

LETTUCE WITH WALNUT OIL (SALADE À L'HUILE DE NOIX)

4 servings

8 to 10 ounce head bibb or butter lettuce
2 ounces walnuts, 1/2 cup broken
2 ounces French bread, 1-1/2 to 2 cups diced into 1/2- to 3/4-inch cubes

Walnut Oil Vinaigrette

2 tablespoons French cider vinegar, more to taste
   or 2 tablespoons red wine vinegar
Optional: 2 teaspoons Dijon mustard
6 tablespoons French roasted walnut oil

1 Remove lettuce leaves, wash and dry. Tear large leaves in half, but leave smaller ones whole to yield 8 to 10 cups loosely packed. Place lettuce in salad bowl and refrigerate.

2 Heat oven to 375 degrees F. Spread walnuts on sheet pan and bread on another. Toast nuts and bread until fragrant and golden. Remove from oven and cool.

3 **Prepare walnut oil vinaigrette:** Whisk together vinegar and mustard if using. Slowly whisk oil into vinegar and mustard. Season with salt. Taste and adjust with more oil, if desired.

4 **To Serve:** In a large mixing bowl, toss lettuce with enough vinaigrette to just lightly coat the leaves. Toss walnuts and bread croutons with lettuce. Season salad with salt and freshly ground black pepper. With tongs, divide leaves onto 4 serving plates and pile high. Scatter the croutons and walnuts lying at the bottom of the bowl over the top of the lettuce. Serve immediately.

REVIEW QUESTIONS

1. Discuss the reasons why France created a world-class cuisine.

2. What are the countries that border France?

3. Name the French chefs who contributed to modern French cuisine.

4. What does AOC stand for and what does it do?

5. Discuss the regions of France and their important dishes and foods.

6. What is an emulsified sauce? Name two emulsifiers.

7. Discuss the rules of sautéing.

CHAPTER SIX

ITALY: GENEROUS AND GENUINE

This chapter will:

- Introduce the history of Italy, its geography, cultural influences, and climate.

- Introduce Italian culinary culture, its regional differences, and dining etiquette.

- Reveal how this peasant cuisine became a great Mother cuisine, and the influences of the Silk Road on it.

- Discuss Italian dry and fresh pastas, Italian produce, and tomatoes.

- Identify the foods, flavor foundations, seasoning devices, and favored cooking techniques.

- Teach the unforgettable, important techniques and dishes of Italy.

FIGURE 6.1 Map of Italy.

An Italian Love Affair

Colman Andrews writing in Saveur Cooks Authentic Italian *waxes poetic on the world's love affair with Italian cuisine, connecting our attraction with the "generosity" of its spirit, its ingredients, its abundance and simple, but naturally striking presentation. Andrews happily notes that "Italy, more than any other country" transformed the North American continent's native foods like tomatoes, peppers, beans, zucchini, and potatoes, and "gave them back to us in a far more savory form."*

Due to Italy's geography—a long, vulnerable coastline, rich soil, good climate, and easy access from the north through the mountains—her history is one of migration and invasion. The people who came through the region left major impacts on the food and culture. The first migrants were *Mycenaeans* (Cretan) around 1400 BCE. Around 800 BCE, the *Phoenicians*, who originated in the eastern Mediterranean, and the Greeks arrived. The Greeks introduced grape and olive cultivation, helped develop the written language, and around the fifth century BCE, named the land *Fitalia*, meaning *land of cattle*.

The Etruscans were probably Italy's most influential culture. Historians think they originated from Asia Minor (Turkey). The Etruscans flourished around Florence and Rome, and by the sixth century BCE they dominated much of Italy. The Arabs ruled Sicily for more than two centuries and left their mark in language, food and cooking, varied agriculture methods, irrigation, and silk manufacture.

Italian history can be outlined by two periods of unity separated by 1,500 years of division. Rome conquered the Italian peninsula from the sixth to third centuries BCE, and spread out to dominate the Mediterranean and Western Europe over the next two centuries. Julius Caesar was dictator from 49 to 44 BCE.

Italy's Roman Empire declined and fell in the fifth century, leaving the previously united region open to invasion. Italy broke into smaller regions, including the Papal States governed by the Pope. Powerful trading city-states, Florence, Venice, and Genoa, emerged, setting the stage for the Renaissance. Their domination continued and was fraught with civil wars between the domestic and foreign Byzantium, and invasions from Arabs, Hungary, and Normans (people of Frankish and Nordic origin in Normandy).

Marco Polo returned from his voyage on the *Silk Road* at the end of the thirteenth century to bring revolutionary new ideas from the East, which benefited the Renaissance. Civil wars continued to plague the Italian peninsula. The fifteenth century saw the High Renaissance with Michelangelo and Leonardo da Vinci. In the sixteenth century Spanish explorers brought tomatoes, chilies, corn, and beans to Europe and the Italian city-states. Trade shifted to the Atlantic in the seventeenth and eighteenth centuries, and Italy came under Spanish, French, and Austrian domination.

Napolean first attempted to conquer the Italian city-states at the end of the eighteenth century; at the dawn of the nineteenth century, he set up a short-lived kingdom. Napolean's efforts served to stoke Italy's unification and independence movement, but it left Italy divided: apart from Sardinia-Piedmont, Tuscany and the north were ruled by the Austro-Hungarian Habsburgs. The French Bourbons ruled the southern *Kingdom of the Two Sicilies*.

Italy's process of *unification* of its diverse city-states began around 1815 with the Congress of Vienna and the end of Napoleon's rule. In 1849, a Roman Republic was declared and Pope Pius IX fled Rome. After the Second War of Independence (1859), Piedmont annexed northern Italy and ceded Nice and Savoy to France. A king of Italy was named in 1861 and parliamentary elections were held. By 1870 the kingdom of Italy acquired Rome by force and Rome and Latium were annexed. In 1871 Italian unification was complete. In 1946 a referendum overwhelmingly voted to abolish the monarchy. Italy has been a democratic republic since the modern constitution in 1948.

LANGUAGE, PHILOSOPHY, AND RELIGION

Italian is the official language of Italy, a Romance language, and direct descendant of Latin. The Tuscan dialect of Florence has been promoted as the standard because of Florence's history of economic power.

Ninety percent of Italy's population is Roman Catholic and 2 percent is Jewish, Muslim, and Orthodox and Eastern Rite Catholic. Supernatural beliefs stretching back to antiquity mix with Catholicism. In Sicily, Arabic and Greek influences have been incorporated into Christian beliefs. Catholic feast days and the church have long influenced the Italian diet and the names of special dishes.

GEOGRAPHY AND CLIMATE

A little larger than Arizona, with a population of almost 58 million, the Italian peninsula is surrounded by the Mediterranean/Tyrennian Sea on its west coast, the Ionian in the south, and the Adriatic Sea on the east. Rolling green hills dotted with vineyards, cypress, fruit, and olive trees dominate Italy's rural landscape. Two major mountain ranges cross Italy, the northern Alps and its backbone, the Apennine range.

Northern Italy, which borders Austria, Switzerland, and France, has hot summers and cold, wet winters with snow in the high mountains. Summer in central Italy can be hot and winters will occasionally get very cold, with rare snowfalls. Southern Italy, with a sunny Mediterranean-influenced climate enjoys long, dry, hot summers and mild, sunny winters.

FARMING AND AGRICULTURE

With just 5 percent of land under cultivation, Italy doesn't grow enough food for self-sufficiency. Italy's main agricultural strength lies in olives, wine, and tomatoes. Small- and large-scale northern farming cooperatives produce wine, prosciutto, pork, poultry, honey, Parmigiano-Reggiano, mozzarella and gorgonzola cheeses, Chianna beef, dry pasta, potatoes, sugar beets, dairy products, apples, rice, corn, and balsamic vinegar. Southern farms produce wheat, wine, tomatoes, oranges, lemons, fresh fruit and vegetables, seafood, Marsala wine, and olive oil.

ITALIAN CUISINE: CUISINE OF HOME AND FAMILY

Modern Italian cuisine arose from both rich and poor tables. Even today, cooks in the poorer south use local olive oil and, without local wheat or much meat, make egg-less pastas dressed with tomato or vegetable sauces, while cooks in the richer north use lard, butter, and olive oil and make egg-rich fresh pastas with meaty or creamy sauces.

The cuisine we know today as Italian is confident, natural, and fully appealing to the senses, but it took many centuries to develop. Influences on Italian food and culture trickled down from the Greeks to the Etruscans to the Romans and finally to Western civilization. The Greeks and Etruscan cuisines were highly developed with baking, sauce-making, preserving in honey and salt, and grilling. They spread cooking techniques and the use of legumes and cereal grains like barley, millet, rye, and farro to the Romans.

The Arabs influenced Italian cuisine, especially southern, with cooking techniques like rice cooking (pilaf and risotto), and foods like durum wheat (for dry pastas), rice, sugar cane, cotton, pistachios, grilled and skewered lamb, spices, macaroni, raisins, and oranges.

For 2,000 years the peasant diet was based on buckwheat, millet, farro, and eventually corn. Seasonal produce, bread, soup, and polenta made up daily meals. Game, fish, meat, eggs, and poultry came to the table on feast days or Sunday, if at all. The monotony of limited food pushed peasant cooks to be creative, but dishes stayed close to home. Indeed, their old names survive today: every village and hamlet had a name for their style of stuffed pasta, which varied with the skill of the cook and seasonal ingredients.

The aristocracy, church, and wealthy merchant class and their desire for culinary pleasure spurred chefs to reach beyond local foods and techniques. Peaking between the fifteenth and seventeenth century, this grand cuisine and gastronomic Renaissance developed new techniques, refined old ones, and incorporated new fruits, vegetables, animals, and spices. The result was a more complex and richer cuisine. Frequent exchanges between the wealthy and poor tables also began to inspire Italian peasant cooks.

At the beginning of the nineteenth century, cookbooks and a rise in the middle class during the Industrial Revolution spread culinary tips, new foods and methods throughout the insular city-states of Italy. A cohesive Italian cuisine began to form around the mid to late nineteenth century after Italy's *unification*, when the peninsula's diverse and often warring city-states finally came together into one country. Pelligrino Artusi, with his post-unification book, *Science in the Kitchen and the Art of Eating Well*, helped to create the new Italian culinary standard. Unlike France, there was no system of schooling to codify cuisine. Artusi identified and clarified hidden familial and regional recipes. In so doing, he helped to knit together diverse peasant family tables and the elite aristocratic cuisine into *la cucina di casa*: the seductive and sincere Italian cuisine of home and family.

ITALIAN REGIONAL CUISINE

1. **Northwest—Liguria, Val d'Aosta, Lombardy, Piedmont—European Influences**
Rich and prosperous, this scenic area is inland and mountainous, except for Liguria, which is a narrow strip between the Alps and Mediterranean. Sunny, warm *Liguria* is famous for seafood, herbs, and small gardens with fabulous produce. Frugal and mostly vegetarian, this region is known for pesto and walnut sauce. French-influenced *Val d'Aosta*, with the highest income in Italy, has a refined and elaborate cuisine with meat and meat-based soups, butter, game, buckwheat, cheese, and dishes like game marinated (*in salmi*) or stewed in red wine. *Lombardy* offers a huge range of quality ingredients from the Alps, lakes, and fertile Po plains like rice, veal, *gorgonzola*, and *mascarpone*. Dishes like *pizzoccheri* (buckwheat tagliatelle with vegetables), *risotto alla Milanese*, and *osso buco* show Lombardy's rich, unobtrusive cuisine. *Piedmont*, known as a region of epicures, grows Italy's asparagus. Piedmontese cooks prepare elaborate *bollito* with four meats, several vegetables, lentils, and four sauces, pasta with egg yolks, and creamy *fonduta* (cheese, butter, eggs, and milk with local truffles).

2. **Northeast—Veneto, Trentino-Alto Adige, Friuli-Venezia Guilia—Cosmopolitan Influences**
This area offers both mountains and sea. *Veneto* is home to cosmopolitan Venice, seat of financial and maritime power. Gifted with fertile plains, and seasonings brought from around the world, Veneto is known for delicate, refined dishes like *risi e bisi* (rice and peas), polenta, and grilled Treviso radicchio. *Trentino-Alto Adige*, a mountainous region with clean air and Bavarian-style food, is known for fine cooking. Game, pork, trout, and *speck* (pickled, smoked ham), sauerkraut, and thick hearty soups are favorites. *Friuli-Venezia Guilia* is a region with two cuisines—peasant and cosmopolitan; both enjoy pork and dairy products like *San Daniele prosciutto*, and *frico*, a thin, crisp grated cheese "pancake." Austro-Hungarian-Slavic influences enrich fish dishes, *jota* (bean soup with cabbage, pork fat, cumin, and bay), *settemplice* (frittata with eggs and herbs), cod with raisins and pine nuts, *goulash*, and horseradish.

3. **Center—Tuscany, Emilia-Romagna, Lazio, Umbria, The Marches—The Heartland**
The central portion of Italy offers fertile agricultural land, harmonious, rolling green landscapes, and an abundance of produce, meat, dairy products, and wine. *Tuscany*, with its Etruscan culinary legacy, excels in the *divina proportione*—harmony and restraint in food and in art. Like its language, Tuscany is Italy's model cuisine with great olive oil, bread, beans, and produce. It's known for ancient, rustic dishes like grilled steak, peas with prosciutto, roast pork loin, *coniglio agro-dolce* (sweet-sour rabbit), and *cacciucco* (fish stew). *Emilia-Romagna*, a prosperous farming region with fertile farmland, is known for rich, creamy dishes, *Parmigiano-Reggiano* cheese, *prosciutto di Parma*, and fresh egg pastas like tortellini, cappelletti, ravioli, and hundreds of others. *Fritto misto* (mixed fry) and *piada* (crisp flatbread) display this region's vitality and love of great food. *Lazio*, the home of the capital Rome, maintains a connection with its past through ancient balanced, commonsense cooking. Grapes (and wine), olives, figs, and wheat play a top role in cuisine along with chicory with anchovies, artichokes *alla Romana* (garlic and mint), *saltimbocca* (sautéed veal, sage, and prosciutto), lamb, gnocchi, fettuccine, and spaghetti *alla carbonara*. *Umbria*, known for pure ingredients, blends an austere and a simple approach to food. Strong olive oil and olives unite a peasant onion soup, spit-roasted lamb, and thick pasta with garlic cooked in oil and an aristocratic pheasant with olives. The full-flavored conservative cuisine of the *Marches* dates back to Roman times with traditional recipes handed down from generation to generation. *Vincisgrassi* (lasagna of chicken liver and meat, lamb brains, prosciutto, mushrooms, and cheese with béchamel), roasted

baby pig, *brodetto* (fish soup), and stuffed and breaded deep-fried olives show off the inventiveness of local cooks.

4. **South—Campania, Abruzzi, Molise, Calabria, Basilicata, Apulia—Dominated by the Sea**
This Mediterranean land specializes in hearty, spicy dishes made with dry pastas, tomatoes, eggplant, seafood, lamb, and pork. Romantic *Campania* (and Naples) is the birthplace of pizza. Its peasant and aristocratic traditions unite in the use of olive oil and dishes like spaghetti with tomato sauce and dry macaroni with meat sauce. More than half of *Abruzzi* and *Molise* is mountainous with a small strip of flat land along the coast. The people of this poor region have perfected their culinary skills with *maccheroni alla chitarra* ("guitar" cut fettuccine), *brodetto di pesce* (fish soup), lamb, *mortadella*, and simple, economical soups made with pantry leftovers. *Calabria* is a picturesque but violent region of river, mountain, and sea. Cabbage soup, *pancotto* (broth, bread, and garlic), fish, figs, olives, and almonds nourish people living on the edge of survival. *Basilicata* has foods and dishes with flavors of the Near East and Greece: pasta with milk and saffron; eggplant with olives, anchovies, and capers, mixed vegetable dishes, and dry pasta with chickpeas or lentils. *Apulia* has developed a complex cuisine with flavors of the Middle East. Vegetables lead the Apulian diet in dishes like *maritata* (layered bitter greens, fennel, and cheese simmered with broth), *calzoni* and *panzerotti* (savory baked pies), and *orecchiette* with vegetables. Dry pastas, oysters, fish, mozzarella, and pecorino cheeses come from here.

5. **Southern Islands—Sicily and Sardinia—Arabic Influences**
The food and culture of these two large southern islands, near the north African coast, display Islamic, Norman, Greek, Spanish, German, Roman, French, and Byzantine influences. With its unique geography and history, *Sicily* seems unrelated to Italy. It is the birthplace of wheat, flour, macaroni, and pastries. Pasta with sardines, couscous, citrus fruits, Spanish *caponata*, *cannoli*, meat pies and garlic, bay leaf, aniseed, mint, cinnamon, and cloves dominate. In *Sardinia*, a region of sea, rivers, mountains, and plains, the food of past and present coexist. The region produces milk-fed grilled piglet, *cassola* (fish broth with twelve species plus chili), *pastu mistu* (baked turkey stuffed with duck, chicken, partridge, and lark), sheep milk pecorino, and cow's milk *fiore* (sheep milk pecorino).

DINE AT HOME IN ITALY

When invited to an Italian home for dinner, it's rude to decline unless there is good reason. Italians have some of the best food and family socializing in the world; they rarely dine at home with anyone other than family. Dress up and bring a gift like quality chocolate or wine. It's okay to be late—15 minutes is normal, but more might put the cook's timing off. Sit down when invited and don't begin eating until the host or hostess does. Take only a small amount of food. Seconds are encouraged. Hold the fork in the left hand and knife in the right. Use fork and knife for everything, including fruit and cheese. Wrists go on the table, but not elbows. When done politely but persistently refuse more food and place the fork and knife onto the plate.

The food will come in courses. First, *antipasti* (before pasta) like melon with prosciutto, fried zucchini blosssoms, *carpaccio*, or maybe crostini with liver. Second comes the *primo* or *minestra* like risotto, soup, *or* lightly dressed pasta (these would never be eaten together). Third is *secondo* with *contorni*: a main course of fish, game, or meat with vegetable dishes and possibly a salad.

FIGURE 6.2 Tuscan countryside.
Source: Anna-Mari West/Fotolia.

Sometimes *formaggio*, a cheese course, then *frutta* or *dolce*, a sweet course of fresh or marinated fruit, will follow. Lastly come caffé (espresso) then *digestivo* like *grappa*, *limoncello*, brandy, or liqueurs and biscotti for dipping in Vin Santo, Moscato, or Marsala. Never leave the table until the host or hostess does. Profuse compliments are always good form.

COMMON ITALIAN COOKING TOOLS

Knife, pots and pans, pasta machine, rolling pins, meat grinder, potato ricer, and much more.

TASTES OF ITALY

Fat: Olive oil, butter, lard

Sweet: Sugar, many types of honey like chestnut, blossom, heather, citrus, and rosemary

Sour/Alcohol: White wine vinegar, red wine vinegar, balsamic vinegar, many varieties of citrus fruit: lemon, orange, blood orange, green lemon, and mandarin orange

Salty: Sea salt, mustard, olive paste, olives, capers, anchovies, and anchovy paste

Spicy-Hot: *Pepperoncini* (fresh red and green chilies), black pepper, cayenne pepper, paprika, dried red chili flakes, horseradish

Spice: Coriander, cinnamon, clove, aniseed

Aromatic Seasoning Vegetables: Onion, carrots, celery, garlic, tomatoes

Herbs, Seasonings, and Condiments: Italian parsley, tarragon, chives, rosemary, bay leaves, thyme, sage, summer savory, marjoram, oregano, fennel, basil, lavender, mint, borage, fennel

Other Important Foods: Olives, wheat, farro, cream, milk, cow and goat milk cheese, white beans, lima beans, fava beans, chickpeas and flour, buckwheat, Arborio style and long-grain rice, corn, nuts, many fruits (figs, citrus, apples, pears, plums, grapes, berries), dried fruits, wild mushrooms, chestnuts, chestnut flour, see *Italian Vegetables*, broccoli, arugula, eggplant, zucchini, beans, lettuces, leafy greens, meat (Chianina beef, cured meats, pork, rabbit, duck, chicken, capon, turkey, boar, wild game), seafood (*bottarga* [dried, salted fish roe cake], squid, scallops, crabs, shrimp, mussels, clams, abalone, cuttlefish, razor clams, many varieties of fish)

Popular Dishes: Risotto, polenta, polenta nera (buckwheat polenta); dry, fresh, and stuffed pasta, fish soup, pizza, *bruschetta* (grilled bread with toppings), *piadina* (lard and flour flatbread), *calzone* (stuffed turnover), *carpaccio* (paper-thin, pounded sliced beef), *polpettone* (meatloaf), lasagna Bolognese, *osso buco* (braised veal), *pollo alla cacciatore* (chicken hunter's style), *scallopine piccata* (veal or chicken with lemon-caper sauce), *braciole di manzo* (braised beef rolls), *pesce spada agrodolce* (sweet-sour swordfish), *vitello tonnato* (veal with tuna sauce), *biscotti* (twice-baked cookies), *arancini* (cheese-filled rice balls), *melanzane involtino* (rolled, stuffed eggplant), *risi e bisi* (rice with peas), *panini* (sandwiches), *zabaglione* (whisked, sweet egg custard), *cannoli* (cream-stuffed tube-shaped pastry), *sformato* (savory or sweet custard), *tiramisu* (layered dessert with mascarpone and ladyfingers), *panna cotta* (cream gelatin), *semi-freddo* (semi-frozen dessert), *gelato* (ice cream), *sorbetto* (fruit sorbet)

Drinks: Coffee, many wines, beer, *cynar* (artichoke liqueur), brandy, *limoncello* (lemon liqueur), *marsala*, *Campari* (bitter liqueur), *grappa* (fiery liqueur produced from grape skins), *Amaretto* (almond flavored liqueur), *sambuca* (anise-flavored liqueur)

FIGURE 6.3 Sheep herder in Abruzzi, Italy.
Source: Ciaobucarest/Fotolia.

ITALIAN CHEESE (FORMAGGIO)

Italians are serious about cheese. There are more than 400 varieties. Almost every village makes one. Sheep, goat, and cow milk cheeses vary from fresh (soft mozzarella, mascarpone, and ricotta) to long-aged like the beautiful Parmigiano-Reggiano, gorgonzola, and Asiago. *Dolce* describes a young, sweet cheese; *medio* describes a stronger, more aged cheese, and *piccante* is a hard, aged pungent, nutty cheese, suitable for grating or eating in thin slices.

Hard Cheeses

Asiago (Veneto, Trentino-Alto, Adige/Südtirol)

A cow milk cheese (cows graze in Alpine meadows) of two types: fresh and ripened. The fresh cheese is sweet and delicate with a hint of acidity, similar to yogurt and aged 20 days. The ripened cheese is aged a year. It is similar to Parmesan: firm and smooth or hard and crumbly depending on how long it has aged. Flavors range from fruity, nutty, and toasty to pungent.

Grana Padano (Emilia-Romagna, Lombardy, Piedmont, Trentino, and Veneto)

A grainy hard, firm cow milk cheese aged 12 to 24 months, which takes on a more complex, nutty flavor and firm texture the longer it's aged. Similar to Parmigiano-Reggiano. *Grana* is the term for hard cheeses first produced in the Po Valley. Parmigiano-Reggiano is the most famous grana.

Parmigiano-Reggiano (Parma, Reggio Emilia, Modena, Bologna, and Mantua)

A firm, granular raw cow milk cheese, with tiny grains of crystallized salt, aged on average 2 years. Its sweet, nutty complex flavor is best enjoyed as a table cheese paired with pears and walnuts, but it is also delicious freshly grated onto pasta, soup, in risotto, or paired with balsamic vinegar. The hard rinds are simmered in stews or soups. Considered Italy's premium cheese.

Pecorino Romano or Sardo (Sardinia, Lazio, and Tuscany) or Siciliano (Sicily)

An aromatic, pleasantly sharp, hard sheep milk cheese aged 8 to 10 months. Pecorino Romano is tart and salty and used for grating; Sardo is not as salty and usually eaten by itself or in sandwiches. Southern Italians used pecorino with olive oil, garlic, and tomato-based dishes.

Medium to Firm Cheeses

Fontina Val d'Aosta (Italian Alps and Other Regions)

Depending on age, a soft to firm cow milk cheese with a natural orange rind and nutty to pungent, earthy flavor. Fontinas can carry hints of mushroom, herb, or fruit and go well with meat and truffles. Traditionally, young Fontina whipped with eggs and cream is known as *fonduta*.

Gorgonzola (Piedmont and Lombardy)

A cow or goat milk green-veined blue cheese, aged 3 months, that ranges from buttery to firm. It is salty, crumbly, and pungent. Used in risotto, polenta, or on short pasta and pizza as one of the four *quattro formaggi*. Dolcelatte is a sweeter gorgonzola made for export.

Montasio (Friuli-Venezia, Giulia, and Veneto)

A mild, nutty cheese made from cow milk that has been skimmed of the cream used for mascarpone. It is semi-aged and creamy (5 to 10 months) to fully aged and firm (more than 10 months) and resembles Asiago in flavor and texture. Used to make *frico* and *fondue*.

Mozzarella (Campania and Other Regions)

Mozzarella is a generic term Italian cheeses made by stretching and cutting the curds. *Mozzarella di bufala* is made from water buffalo milk and *fior de latte* from cow milk. A sweet, mild-tasting white semi-soft cheese, it is usually eaten the day it's made or brined up to one week; vacuum-sealed it lasts longer. Factory produced *low-moisture* or partially dried mozzarella is firmer and more elastic, but not as delicately flavored as fresh mozzarella and it keeps a month.

Provolone (Southern Italy)

A semi-hard cow's milk cheese produced in long pear, sausage, or cone shapes that is made plain or smoked. Taste varies depending on aging (4 month minimum) from very mild to very sharp. Grilled or melted, it is seasoned with oil and spices.

Robiola (Lombardy and Piedmont)

A cow, goat, sheep milk (or blend) soft-ripened cheese (0 to 20 days) with a brownish rind. Generally served as a table cheese with oil, salt and pepper, in fondue or on pizza, it is creamy, fatty, tangy, pungent, and lush.

Taleggio (Lombardy, Piedmont, and Veneto)

A strongly aromatic, mild-tasting soft cheese with a fruity tang and a thin, salt-studded rind. One of the oldest type of soft cheeses, it is aged 6 to 10 weeks, and washed weekly to prevent an orange crust from forming. It may be grated and served with tomato bruschetta, arugula, or radicchio or melted into risotto or polenta.

Soft Cheeses

Mascarpone (Originated near Milan)

A milky-white, creamy, and nutty-sweet triple-cream spreading cheese, mascarpone is neither pressed nor aged: the cream is coagulated with a starter culture for about 12 hours, and drained until thick. A quick version can be made by coagulating cream with fresh lemon juice. It is commonly used in *tiramisu*, with fruit, and stirred into risotto instead of butter or Parmigiano-Reggiano.

Ricotta (Many Regions)

A sheep or cow milk cheese made from whey leftover from Pecorino Romano making. Fresh ricotta is sweet, creamy, and grainy but spreadable. Used in cheesecake, either by itself or beaten smooth and mixed with sugar and seasonings, or to fill stuffed pastas and cannoli, on pizza, pasta, and in lasagne. Some ricottas are made with goat or water buffalo milk. *Ricotta salata* is pressed, salted, and dried for grating and shaving. *Ricotta informata* is baked until charred on the outside or browned all the way through and *ricotta affumicata* is smoked. *Ricotta scanta* is a strong, aromatic ricotta aged 3 to 4 months. See *Special Methods* for a recipe.

ITALIAN CURED MEATS (SALUMI)

Out of a need to conserve meat after the slaughter of a large animal, Italian cooks learned to preserve meat and they have been preserving it for centuries with great success. In the region of Parma in northern Italy, Roman cooks noticed how drying breezes air-cured hams very well while the indigenous bacteria imparted a nutty flavor. The southern region of Basilicata made spicy pork sausages that Romans adored.

Italians now make more than a hundred varieties of cured meats and sausages like mortadella, prosciutto cotto, coppa, guanciale, lardo, salame, soppressata, speck, and many more. Although pork is the clear favorite, Italians also cure beef, veal, goat venison, boar, horse, and sheep. The methods of curing are salting or brining, air-drying, and smoking. Sometimes the methods are combined. Italian cooks offer uncooked, sliced *salumi* as appetizers.

Bresaola

Sweet, musty *bresaola* is salted, air-dried, beef aged 2 or 3 months until firm and almost purple. Lean and tender, it is made from top round of beef. Bresaola originated in Valtellina, in the Alps of the northern Lombardy region. The name comes from the diminutive *bresada*, or braised.

Coppa

The muscular portion of the pig's neck is cured in brine, stuffed with cow intestines, and matured for 6 months for coppa. It is wrapped in wine-soaked cloth for storage. Good sliced thinly for antipasto.

Cotechino

A seasoned, raw pork sausage made throughout northern Italy, but is a specialty of Modena. It must be cooked. The regions of Lombardy, Molise, Trentino, and Veneto have declared cotechino one of their traditional foods.

Culatello

This northern Italian ham is considered the most refined variety of prosciutto. The fatty pork "rump" of the rear legs is trimmed away from the bone, seasoned with spices and salt, and stuffed into a pig bladder. The culatello is tied into a pear shape, then hung and air- and temperature-cured for about 1 year. Culatello di Zibello, recognized by the EEU, has been granted an appellation and is a handmade artisan product only from the 75-square-mile foggy, fertile

FIGURE 6.4   Prosciutto hams.
Source: Comugnero Silvana/Fotolia.

(Continued)

(Continued)

region of Bassa Parmense between Cremona and Ferrara along the Po River. Culatello pairs well with melon or fresh figs.

Lardo

This mountain specialty is made from pork fatback layered with salt and seasonings like rosemary, juniper, sage, oregano, and black pepper, and salt-dried or cured until silky-smooth and delicate tasting. The best-known lardo is from Tuscany, where it is eaten on toast, with tomatoes or olives or melted on polenta.

Mortadella (Bologna)

This large Bolognese cooked sausage is made with ground pork and other types of meat and long strips of fat, which give it a speckled look when cut. Mortadella may be seasoned with white wine, garlic, peppercorns, or pistachios. It should be sliced thinly for best flavor.

Pancetta

Similar to unsmoked bacon, pancetta is salt- and spice-brined pork belly meat shaped two ways and dry-aged: *rotolada* (rolled into a cylinder) or *stesa* (slab). Thinly slice rotolada or dice stesa into small cubes and use similarly to bacon. The seasonings for Italian pancetta vary widely from region to region—there are highly seasoned versions in southern Italy. In North America pancetta is cooked before using.

Prosciutto Cotto (Boiled Ham)

Pork legs for prosciutto cotto are first boned, then brined. Traditionally the hams are cooked in metal pots with spring-loaded tops that compress them into a ham shape as they oven cook. Prosciutto cotto originated in the northern regions of Emilia-Romagna and Lombardy.

Prosciutto Crudo

Prosciutto is made from salted, air-dried, unsmoked, aged pork rear legs (usually organic). Several regions of Italy produce hams that vary in flavor and texture depending on indigenous flora and climate: Parma, Modena, San Daniele, and Tuscany. Prosciutto di Parma is an outstanding ham from pigs that enjoy a diet of chestnut and whey from the making of Parmigiano cheese. All prosciuttos are salt-cured and then hang in a series of temperature and humidity controlled rooms to dry. The cut side of the ham is covered with lard and aged about 12 months. The resulting ham is smooth, nutty, and slightly salty.

Salami

Salami is the general name for a group of cured sausages made with ground meat and fat, usually pork, and sometimes beef, boar, goose, or turkey. Mortadella, coppa, and soppressata are salami. Similar to bologna but with a more complex flavor, *mortadella* is made with finely ground pork mixed with whole peppercorns and cubes of fat. It's shaped into a thick cylinder and cooked. *Coppa* is salted and aged pork shoulder rolled into the shape of a short cylinder. *Soppressata* is peppery, cured, aged salami from Calabria, in southern Italy.

Speck

Salt- and air-cured (as for prosciutto), cold-smoked then aged pork leg. Speck is rare among Italian cured meats because most are not smoked.

ITALIAN FLAVOR FOUNDATIONS

Italian Signature Aromatic Vegetable Combo: Soffritto

Onion and garlic form the most basic soffritto, sometimes with parsley and tomato.

Signature Seasonings

Liquid/Paste

Marsala

This nutty-flavored fortified wine is produced in the region surrounding the city of Marsala in Sicily. It is made similarly to Spanish sherry. Marsala is made from three main white grape varietals. It contains about 15 to 20 percent alcohol by volume. Marsala is classified according to color, length of aging, and sweetness. **Color:** golden or *oro*, amber or *ambra*, and ruby or *rubino*. **Aging:** *Fine* (less than a year), *Superiore* (2 years), *Superiore Riserva* (4 years), and *Vergine e/o Soleras* (5 years). **Sweetness:** dry or *secco*, semi-dry or *semisecco*, and sweet. Marsala is used in cooking and the famed *zabaglione* whisked custard. Traditionally it was served between the first and second courses. It goes well with cheeses, nuts, fruits, and desserts.

Olive Oil

See *Glossary*.

Animal

Anchovies (Alici)

Anchovies are an important part of Italy's flavor building repertoire. The best-flavored Sicilian anchovies are packed in salt, often in a glass jar. Anchovies mute into meat dishes, adding flavor to tomato sauce, vegetables, or toast. Look for the meatiest anchovies; rinse to remove salt. Scrape off skin and remove bones. Pat dry and layer with olive oil in a shallow container. Anchovies keep 1 week refrigerated in oil. Chop anchovies finely and infuse into simmering olive oil or soffritto for an undercurrent of rich flavor. They are an important component of *bagna cauda* (warm vegetable dip of anchovies, garlic, oil, butter, and often, cream). Don't cook anchovies over high heat; they harden and turn bitter. (See chapter *Spain*, section *Signature Seasonings* for more on Spanish anchovies.)

Pancetta

See *Cured Meats*.

FIGURE 6.5 Caper plant.
Source: fotogiunta/Fotolia.

FIGURE 6.6 Caper berries.
Source: Jiri Hera/Fotolia.

Vegetable/Fruit

Capers

A favorite of Sicilian and Mediterranean cooking, capers are part of most Italian kitchens. They are small, unopened buds of the Mediterranean bush, *Capparis spinosa L.*, closely related to the cabbage family, but they look more like a rose bush. Caper bushes grow wild and are also cultivated throughout the Mediterranean. Pickled in vinegar or preserved in salt (which brings out their flavor), European cooks consider the smallest capers (*nonpareilles*) the best. Some make a caper substitute with immature nasturtium seed pods (not flower buds) pickled in vinegar. Capers have a sharp, mustard-like, peppery flavor, which adds tang to pasta sauces, pizza, salad, meat, fish, and anchovies. Their unique flavor comes

(Continued)

(Continued)

from mustard oil or *methyl isothiocyanate.* Use capers whole, crushed, or chopped. Rinse salted capers to remove excess salt, or drain pickled capers—save the salty caper pickling liquid for use in sauces and dressings.

Garlic

Long associated with Italian and Mediterranean cooking, garlic goes into countless dishes. Its deep, rich flavor is the trademark of Italian food. Loosen skin with a light smack or drop in boiling water a few seconds. See *Glossary* for more information on garlic. Chopping increases garlic flavor: enzymes (*allicin*) mix to form classic scent and flavor:

- For gentle aroma and flavor, use whole cloves.
- For more flavor, use smashed cloves.
- For deeper flavor, use sliced garlic.
- For the deepest flavor, use minced garlic.

Herbal/Spice

Calaminta (Nepitella)

Tuscan cooks use this tiny and tender-leafed herb, which tastes like a cross between basil, mint, and oregano, to flavor porcini, artichokes, and zucchini.

FIGURE 6.8 Rosemary.
Source: Ian O'Leary/DK Images.

Rosemary

This woody, strong-scented herb is an evergreen with long, narrow leaves. It is native to the Mediterranean. It is part of the mint family and shares the fragrant, menthol kick along with a pleasant pungency and slight bitterness. Italian cooks use sprigs to flavor roast meats or roasted potatoes, in pasta sauces, and in specialty breads like focaccia. Use this powerful herb with a light hand.

Sage (Salvia)

This strongly aromatic, earthy-flavored herb has been used as food and medicine for centuries. Fresh sage leaves may be chopped or finely sliced for game dishes, risotto, or the classic Tuscan dish of cannellini beans stewed with garlic and tomatoes. Sage sautéed in butter is a classic Roman sauce. Whole leaves may be batter dipped and deep-fried or fried naked for a tasty appetizer.

FIGURE 6.7 Italian parsley.
Source: atoss/Fotolia.

Italian Parsley

This flat-leafed variety of parsley is more flavorful and pungent than the curly variety. Authentic Italian food requires Italian parsley.

FIGURE 6.9 Sage leaves.
Source: Clive Streeter/DK Images.

ITALIAN VEGETABLES

Italian cooks deeply respect vegetables. Tomatoes, cauliflower, broccoli, potatoes, spinach, Swiss chard, wild greens, asparagus, carrots, peas, escarole, endive, and radishes grace Italian tables. See *Glossary* for more information on *Lettuces and Other Salad Greens*. These are a few of Italy's favorites:

Artichokes (Carciofi)

The flower bud of a Mediterranean thistle-like plant in the sunflower family, the artichoke has been eaten for millennia. They range from about 1-½ inches to 4 or 5 inches in diameter. Fresh artichokes have leaves that cling tightly to their body, a fresh, light-colored stem end, and, when pressed, are firm at the base of the leaves. Artichokes darken after cutting; rub cuts with lemon juice to prevent it. The vegetable may be boiled, steamed, or braised. Remove the inner choke after boiling or steaming. It sits directly on top of the prized artichoke heart. Italian cooks stuff artichokes: Snip off the thorny ends of each leaf, pull apart leaves to get to the center, and scrape out the choke. Stuff the cavity and steam vegetable until tender, about 20 minutes. Breadcrumb, cheese, and herb stuffings are popular.

Asparagus

See *Glossary*.

Broccoli Rabe or Rapini (Cime di Rapa)

This green vegetable with leggy stems and small florets is a wild cousin of broccoli, but it differs in use and taste. The whole stalk of rapini is eaten, while many cooks discard broccoli stems. Broccoli is sweet, but rapini can be very bitter; preblanching tames it. Like

FIGURE 6.11 Broccoli rabe or rapini.
Source: chiyacat/Fotolia.

broccoli, overcooked rapini turns into a yellow mush. In southern Italy, rapini is typically paired with orecchiette and sausage or blanched and braised with olive oil, garlic, red chili flakes, and optionally, anchovies.

Cardoons (Cardoni or Cardi or Cynara)

A tall, thistle-like plant in the aster family, cardoons can still be found in the wild. The cultivated plant resembles overgrown celery and tastes like a combination of artichoke, celery, and salsify (oyster plant). The tough outer ribs must be removed before preparing. Cardoons brown when cut and exposed to air; rub with lemon. The vegetable is often preblanched for quicker final cooking.

Dandelion, Italian (Cicoria)

A type of slightly tart chicory, cicoria is a dark green leafy vegetable prepared like kale or spinach.

Fennel (Finoccio) (fee-noh-key-oh)

Originally a wild plant, this onion-like bulb with tall fronds has a delicate taste of anise or licorice and the freshness and crunchy texture of celery. Italian cooks shave it raw into salads, braise, deep-fry, grill or gratinée, or boil the bulb and purée, then use it to make

FIGURE 6.10 Artichokes.
Source: Anna Sedneva/Fotolia.

FIGURE 6.12 Cardoons.
Source: Picture Partners/Fotolia.

(Continued)

(Continued)

FIGURE 6.13   Dandelion greens (cicoria).
Source: Socanski/Fotolia.

FIGURE 6.15   Monk's beard (agretti).
Source: Only Fabrizio/Fotolia.

Monk's Beard (Agretti)

A slightly bitter and salty grass that grows in salt marshes, agretti is served in Roman restaurants and homes in the spring. It looks like a knotted pile of spaghetti or seaweed. When fried in oil and tossed with chili flakes, its texture is chewy and crisp. Some cooks toss the blanched vegetable with lemon and garlic.

Puntarelle (Catalogna Chicory)

The young shoots of this long, serrated and narrow-leaf bitter Roman green

are prized. It may be used in salad or pounded into pesto.

Radicchio (*rah-dee-key-oh*)

Radicchio is a mildly bitter-tasting leafy vegetable in the chicory family. Very popular in Italy, the main varieties are *radicchio di Verona* or *rosa di Chioggia*, which looks like a small head of white and burgundy lettuce, and *radicchio di Treviso*, which resembles a large burgundy and white Belgium endive. Italian cooks dress raw sliced or torn radicchio with olive oil and salt, mix it with other greens and grill it, or sauté it in dishes like risotto with red wine. Radicchio becomes unpalatably bitter if not watered enough as it grows. Soak radicchio in cold water to reduce bitterness. Store radicchio in a cool and dry spot, trim it sparingly, and use a ceramic knife or tear by hand to avoid browning.

Salsify or Oyster Plant (Scorzobianca or Scorzonera)

This long, narrow, white root vegetable has the delicate flavor of oysters and looks like a parsnip. Varieties have grey, pale gold, or black skin (scorzonera). Italian cooks prepare salsify as a vegetable, use in soups or stews, in a gratin, or as a croquette or fritter.

FIGURE 6.14   Fennel bulb.
Source: Philip Dowell/DK Images.

custardy timbales. The long fronds are tough and inedible but provide their delicate flavor to stocks. Purchase bulbs that are blemish-free.

FIGURE 6.16   Puntarelle.
Source: uckyo/Fotolia.

(Continued)

(Continued)

FIGURE 6.17 Radicchio.
Source: Africa Studio/Fotolia.

FIGURE 6.18 Salsify or oyster plant.
Source: Barbro Bergfeldt/Fotolia.

Savoy Cabbage (Cavolo Verza)

This cabbage has bubbly-textured leaves but is similar-looking to plain cabbage. It's great for stuffing because the leaves pull away easily from the head. Purchase heavy heads with bright and glossy leaves. Italians stuff Savoy cabbage with pork sausage, breadcrumbs, and herbs, and serve with the cooking broth. It also graces minestrone or bean

FIGURE 6.19 Savoy cabbage.
Source: Ian O'Leary/DK Images.

FIGURE 6.20 Italian plum tomatoes.
Source: © Annto/Shutterstock.

soup, pasta, or rice or may be braised with chestnuts and/or sausage.

Tomatoes

Although tomatoes are native to South America, Italy finally claimed them by the nineteenth century. Italians have a

tomato for every use from the plum-shaped, firm and sweet San Marzano for sauce, drying, and canning, to the small, sweet cherry tomatoes, the oblong Roma for canning, and the round Napoli and Sardo for sauces, to the salad-only pear-shaped Palla di Fuoco or deep-red, meaty Cuore di Bue. Italians avoid using tomatoes out of season and have devised ways to have them available year round: Tomatoes show up as tomato concentrate (paste), canned (peeled whole or crushed), as strained purée, and sun-fried. Never refrigerate tomatoes; they will lose all flavor. Choose tomatoes for a dish by flavor.

FIGURE 6.22 Male zucchini blossoms.
Source: nito/Fotolia.

FIGURE 6.21 Cavolo nero (tuscan kale).
Source: Picture Partners/Fotolia.

(Continued)

(Continued)

Tuscan Kale or "Black Cabbage" (Cavolo Nero)

A leafy green, which is also called dinosaur or lacinato kale for its very green, bubbly-textured long leaves, cavolo nero responds well to blanching, braising, or steaming. Italian cooks and chefs blanch whole leaves 2 to 3 minutes, drain, and chill. To serve, they'll braise garlic in olive oil then add the cooked, chopped kale. One pound serves 2 to 4 people. Italians also put cavolo nero in soups, mix it into polenta, and serve it braised on grilled bread.

Zucchini Blossoms

Italian cooks gifted the world when they brought zucchini and squash blossoms into the kitchen. There are two types of blossoms: the male with only a stem attached and the female, which is attached to the zucchini. The male is said to be best for eating. Blossoms from other summer squash varieties may be used as well.

ITALIAN SHELL BEANS (FAGIOLI)

Whenever possible, use dried beans instead of canned. Beans prepared from dried have a richer, sweeter flavor without a mealy consistency. Italians, especially Tuscans, love beans and use them for bean salads, in soups, dips, and stews.

Chickpea (Ceci)

The round, buff-colored chickpea goes well in Italian pasta, rice, and farro dishes and are great in cold bean salads, dips, and long-cooking stews. Italians use chickpea flour for large pancakes called farinata. Chickpeas complement figs, nuts, parsley, onions, and lemons.

Corona Judiones (Sweet White Runner Bean)

A large, broad, flat white Mediterranean bean that triples in size when cooked, the corona looks like a large lima bean. It has a meaty, creamy texture.

Cranberry Beans (Borlotti)

Often paired with sage and garlic, these beans have a red and white mottled skin. Slightly nutty, borlottis pair well with bitter greens, tomato sauces, and hearty soup and stew.

Fava Bean, Horse Bean, or Broad Bean (Fave)

Sometime in March the large pods of fava beans arrive at southern Italian tables. The glistening, pale green, young legumes are eaten raw with Pecorino or fruit at the end of a meal. Favas last through May; as they age, favas are braised or added to soups and pasta dishes. They have a buttery texture, slight bitterness, and nutty flavor. The spinach-like, young leaves are also eaten. Fava bean purée with wild chicory is a typical Puglian dish. To prepare favas, first remove the beans from the large, spongy pods and parboil to loosen their tough, exterior shell. Remove the shell before adding favas to other dishes. Fava pods range in size from about 8 to 12 inches; 1 pound whole pods yields about 4 ounces (3/4 cup) raw, unskinned fava beans.

Edible Lupine Beans (Lupini)

These beans look similar to yellow lima beans after processing. Like olives, lupinis are bitter and inedible until cured. Because of a high alkaloid content, lupini beans are soaked in brine and rinsed until the bitterness dissipates. These beans can be found dried or pickled in jars. Italians snack on, marinate, or toss lupinis into salad. Some people react to the bitter alkaloids that are left after soaking, so it's wise to eat small amounts.

Marrow Bean

A large plump, pillowy, round white bean that, when cooked, has a creamy, meaty texture with a flavor reminiscent of smoked bacon. It goes well with braised meats, soups, stews, or served as a side dish.

White Kidney Beans (Cannellini)

These delicate, nutty-flavored all-purpose beans take on the flavor of what they're cooked with. They pair well with strong flavors like rosemary and lemon or basil and shrimp or tuna. Italian cooks use them for antipasti, soups, and with pasta.

ITALIAN MUSHROOMS (FUNGHI)

Italians in northern and central Italy forage many types of mushrooms. In addition to these, they also eat morels, chanterelles, saffron milk caps, and oyster mushrooms. See chapters *France* and *Spain* for more information on mushrooms.

Black Truffle (Tartufi)

See *French Mushrooms*. Italy's black truffles come from Umbria, where there are several varieties.

Imperial Mushroom (Fungho Imperiale)

This is a prized delicious Italian mushroom, but part of the sometimes deadly amanita family. It has short, thick stems and thick cap. The cap underside and stem are yellowish and the top of the cap tan to brownish red. Called "food of the deities," the imperial has a meaty flavor.

Porcini Mushrooms (Funghi Porcini) (*foon-ghee pour-chee-nee*)

These mushrooms are used both dried and fresh. Fresh mushrooms can be thinly sliced and eaten raw in salads or cooked as part of another dish, strengthening the savory flavor of a dish. Italians often slice and fry or grill them brushed with olive oil. Fresh porcini make a particularly good creamy pasta sauce. The dried mushrooms have a concentrated

FIGURE 6.23 Porcini mushroom.
Source: morchella/Fotolia.

umami flavor. Avoid crumbled pieces or mushrooms with pinholes from worms. Soak dried porcini in hot water until soft. Chop before using. Save the soaking water, strain, and use in a dish: it retains much of the dried mushrooms' flavor. Fresh porcini bottled in olive oil are a versatile and tasty product.

White Truffle (Tartufo Blanco or Alba Madonna)

The northern Italian region of Piemonte is known for the most treasured fungus, the white or Alba truffle. It may be found in other regions of north and central Italy. These musky and nutty fall fungus grow symbiotically with oak, hazel, poplar, and beech trees and can be the size of a walnut up to a man's fist (1 pound). The flesh is white or cream-colored and highly aromatic, with tinges of garlic and ripe

FIGURE 6.24 White truffle.
Source: Giuseppe Porzani/Fotolia.

cheese, and flavorful when dug up and harvested after the spores are matured and released. Truffle hunters use specially trained pigs or dogs to locate truffles. Due to its rarity and high cost, the pungent truffle is grated or shaved over top of risotto, soup, eggs, and pastas. Truffles are also inserted under the skin of poultry the day before roasting.

SEASONING AND PASTE MIXTURES

Italian Flavor Methods

Italian cooks favor three key techniques to build flavor from *odori* or aromatic vegetables: *battuto*, a raw chopped odori or vegetable mixture, *soffritto* (sautéed battuto), and the very important method *insaporire* (infusing flavor). Lard was the original choice for sautéing soffritto, but in recent times healthier olive oil and tasty butter have pushed lard off center stage. *Insaporire* happens when the cook infuses main ingredients—meat or vegetables—with a soffritto over heat.

BATTUTO

Onion and parsley were the original components of battuto, with optional garlic, celery, and carrot. A battuto of some sort forms the base of most Italian pasta sauces, risotto, broths, soups, sauces, and meat or vegetable dishes. Pesto and gremolada are also forms of raw or *crudo battuto*.

Signature Technique: Italian Soffritto

1 Choose ingredients and dice evenly. Choose onions, celery, carrots, and garlic or just onions and garlic. Diced pancetta (or prosciutto) is a tasty addition.

2 Heat a skillet over moderate heat with olive oil, lard, or a combo of half unsalted diced butter and olive oil. (Reduce fat if using pancetta.)

3 Heat fat. (Add pancetta, if using, and when fat begins to render/melt from it, add onions.) Add onions and cook them until soft and translucent, about 5 minutes. This step is very important: when onions, which are high in glutamates, are cooked long enough, they break down and release the glutamates for extra big, savory flavor.

4 If using, add celery, carrots, or leeks and cook until soft, 4 to 5 minutes.

5 Stir in garlic and cook until slightly golden. Garlic burns more easily than harder vegetables so it should be added after them, but before wet ingredients. Watch garlic carefully; if it burns, it will become bitter.

6 Stir in remaining ingredients like chopped tomato or chopped parsley and cook until soft.

GREMOLADA

To preserve its fresh flavor, Italian cooks stir gremolada, a chopped and dry or lightly moist raw mixture, into soup or stew at the last minute, sprinkle it over hot vegetables or hot pizza, or stir it into olive oil. Notice the balance of pungent herb, sparkling citrus, garlic, and oil or nuts. Classic gremolada traditionally goes over osso buco (braised veal).

Classic Gremolada

Yields about 1/4 cup

1/2 ounce trimmed Italian parsley, 1/4 cup minced
1/4 ounce garlic, 1 large clove, 1-1/2 teaspoons peeled and minced
Zest of 1 medium lemon, preferably organic, 2 to 3 teaspoons minced zest

Mint and Walnut Gremolada

Yields about 1/2 cup

1/4 ounce mint leaves, 2 tablespoons chopped
1/4 ounce trimmed Italian parsley, 2 tablespoons minced
1/4 ounce garlic, 1 large clove, 1-1/2 teaspoons peeled and minced
1 ounce walnuts, 1/4 cup broken pieces
    or 1 ounce toasted pine nuts, 1/4 cup
Zest of 1 medium lemon, preferably organic, 2 to 3 teaspoons chopped zest

Optional Additions
    2 tablespoons olive oil
        or 2 to 4 tablespoons cream
            or 1 to 2 tablespoons walnut oil
    2 to 3 tablespoons fresh lemon juice

1 Finely chop each ingredient by hand and mix together *or* pulse-grind ingredients in food processor until chunky-smooth.

2 **Optional Additions:** Stir olive oil and lemon juice or cream or nut oil into gremolada before tossing on vegetables. Season with salt and ground pepper.

Vary! Improvise!

☞ *Prepare a sage, fennel, celery leaf, or wild leek gremolada.*

☞ *Toss gremolada with finely shaved fennel, sliced ripe tomatoes, or stir into vinaigrette.*

Saucing Pasta

- Moderation is key to saucing pasta. The sauce should not pool on the bottom of the vessel or serving bowl. A good rule of thumb **per person** is between 1 and 2 tablespoons oil or melted butter sauces, and 3 to 4 tablespoons thicker sauces like *Sugo alla Bolognese* per person.
- Stir the sauce into the pasta in a serving bowl so it is evenly coated. Pasta and sauce complement each other so neither should dominate.
- A grating of good cheese can enhance tomato-based, meat-based, and cream sauces. There's no set rule for vegetable or fish-based sauces, but Italians veer away from adding cheese to seafood dishes. Don't overwhelm a dish with cheese: use 2 to 3 teaspoons freshly grated Parmigiano-Reggiano or high-quality hard Italian cheese per serving.

SAUCE

Italian Sauces

Italians feel that food should be prepared to bring out its best flavor. They don't rely heavily on sauces as the French do. *Sugo* and *salsa* both mean sauce, but salsa is served separately to accompany a dish, and sugos or pasta sauces are considered part of a dish, not a separate sauce. *Besciamella* (béchamel), tomato sauces, and meaty *ragus* of many types, sauces made from walnuts or anchovies and bread or mushrooms, green sauce, and mayonnaise are Italy's most popular.

ITALIAN WHITE SAUCE (BESCIAMELLA)

This Italian version of béchamel sauce is a building block for lasagne.

Yields about 1-1/2 cups

1-3/4 cups whole milk
3 tablespoons unsalted butter
Scant 1 ounce unbleached all-purpose flour, 3 tablespoons
Pinch of freshly grated nutmeg

1 Place milk in a small saucepan and heat over medium-low heat until hot. Melt butter in a 2-quart sauce-pan over medium-low heat. Stir in flour, and cook, stirring constantly until roux bubbles and becomes fragrant but not colored, 2 to 3 minutes. Whisk hot milk into roux, and bring mixture to a simmer.

2 Reduce the heat to low and simmer white sauce, stirring with a spoon or heatproof spatula, taking care to scrape corners and the bottom of the pan, until sauce thickens, 6 to 8 minutes for a single batch, 10 to 12 minutes for a double batch.

3 Remove pan from the heat, and stir in 1/2 teaspoon salt and nutmeg. Sauce should be used within 30 minutes. If sauce cools and thickens too much, whisk in a small amount of hot milk to thin to a usable consistency.

Source: Joyce Goldstein, *Fine Cooking* magazine, December 1, 2006.

ITALIAN GREEN SAUCE (SALSA VERDE)

This sauce has a flexible list of ingredients, but is essentially a thick, fresh herb vinaigrette. Serve salsa verde with grilled lamb, chicken, or pork, steamed green beans, boiled potatoes, or with Italian bollito misto (mixed boil). Parsley, capers, anchovies, vinegar, and olive oil are constants in this delicious green sauce.

Yields about 1-1/3 cups, 6 to 8 servings

2 ounces Italian parsley tough stems removed, 2 cups packed
1/2 ounce mint leaves, 1/2 cup packed
1/2 ounce fresh basil leaves, 1/2 cup packed
1-1/2 ounces drained capers, 1/4 cup rinsed and drained
2 anchovy fillets, rinsed
1 ounce day old country-style bread, 1/2 cup cubed

1/4 ounce garlic, 1 large clove peeled
3 to 4 tablespoons red wine vinegar
1/2 cup extra virgin olive oil

To reduce the saltiness of capers and anchovies: Soak in warm water 10 minutes. Drain and rinse before using.

1 Pulse-chop parsley, mint, basil, capers, anchovies, bread, and garlic with 3 tablespoons red wine vinegar in bowl of food processor until almost smooth. With machine running, drizzle in oil. Add more vinegar to taste.

2 Season sauce with salt and freshly ground pepper. Set sauce aside 1 hour to develop flavor. Before serving, taste sauce and season again with salt or more vinegar.

CLASSIC BASIL PESTO (BATTUTO ALLA GENOVESE)

Pesto alla Genovese (of Genoa) is a green sauce that was born in the northwestern Italian region of Liguria, where the Mediterranean/Ligurian Sea warms the land enough to grow olives. (Further inland, Piemonte cannot grow olives.) Chef Guliano Bugalli says that basil, garlic, olive oil, pine nuts, or walnuts and Pecorino or Parmigiano cheese are the true, traditional ingredients. Toss on freshly cooked pasta, potatoes, or vegetables.

Yields about 1 cup

2 ounces fresh basil leaves, 2 cups packed
1/2 ounce trimmed Italian parsley, 1/2 cup packed
1/2 ounce garlic, about 2 large cloves, 1 tablespoon finely chopped
1 ounce toasted *or* raw pine nuts, 1/4 cup
1/3 cup extra virgin olive oil

For Serving

1 to 2 ounces mixed shredded Parmigiano-Reggiano and/or Pecorino Romano, 1/4 to 1/2 cup

1 **Prepare ingredients:** Pull leaves from herbs stems, discard stems, then rinse leaves and spin or blot dry. To soften garlic flavor, use less, or blanch whole, unpeeled cloves in boiling water 30 seconds to 1 minute and peel. Toast nuts if desired and cool before using—it will bring out their best flavor.

2 **Purée or pound herbs, garlic, and nuts together:** Purée in food processor until smooth; scrape down sides several times. Originally, cooks pounded pestos in a mortar with a pestle, a method that produces a greener—and some say finer—pesto than the more modern food processor. To mimic the mortar and pestle, place herbs into a heavy plastic baggie and pound them with a meat pounder before processing in food processor.

3 **Add oil:** With processor running, pour oil into herb-nut purée in a thin stream and purée until very smooth. Scrape pesto out into bowl, taste, and season with a little salt (cheese will add saltiness) and freshly ground pepper. Pesto may be frozen at this point—a thin film of oil poured over the top will keep the pesto from oxidizing black.

4 **To Use:** Grate cheese, if using, and toss it with pesto. Adding cheese just before serving assures that the cheese will taste its best. Before tossing pesto on pasta or vegetables thin it with cream, or pasta or vegetable cooking water.

Vary! Improvise!

☞ *Lower Fat:* Reduce oil to 1/3 cup and thin sauce with 2 to 3 tablespoons water or stock.

Quick Italian Herb-Butter Sauces

Italian butters sauces are essentially herb-infused melted butter. Stuffed pastas (especially tortellini) are sometimes sauced with melted butter and herbs.

- For 1 pound pasta, stuffed pasta or gnocchi, melt 6 tablespoons diced unsalted butter.
- Toss in 12 to 15 large fresh sage leaves or other herbs, and simmer over low heat 3 to 4 minutes.

Set Aside to Cool

- When pasta is ready, reheat butter over low heat and toss in hot cooked pasta.
- Turn pasta out onto platter. Garnish with 1/4 to 1/2 cup shredded Parmigiano-Reggiano cheese. Or simply dress fresh pasta or ravioli with melted butter and cheese.

Signature Technique: Building an Exceptional Tomato Sauce

1 **Flavor build:** Prepare *Soffritto*. Cook battuto in oil, or oil and butter, to bring out more flavor components, reduce moisture, brown, and intensify flavor. Cut battuto vegetables larger for longer cooking and to keep flavors individual. Cut battuto small for short cooking and to integrate flavors into a whole.

2 **Employ flavor boosters:** Start with *umami* foods—diced pancetta or prosciutto—or slip in a little diced anchovy, dried or fresh mushrooms, or tomato paste.

3 **Start with fresh tomatoes in season, if not use high quality canned:** Taste them. Italian cooking expert Lynne Rosseto Kasper divides fresh tomatoes into 3 categories according to taste; she advises mixing them for best flavor. Correct bland tomatoes with balsamic or red wine vinegar, or with a pinch of sugar if too acidic.

   • **Mellow-rich tomato:** rich and round flavored like Beefsteak or Carbon

   • **Brash tomato:** lots of sugar and acid kick like Red Currant and Early Cascade

   • **Sweet tomato:** lots of sweet and less acid high like Roma, orange and yellow tomatoes

   Cold destroys tomato flavor. Whole canned tomatoes in tomato purée or their own juice are a better choice when tomatoes are not in season since they are picked ripe. Taste test American brands like Muir Glen, Red Pack, Hunt's, and Contadina.

4 **To seed or not to seed.** Seeding fresh tomatoes is unnecessary; sauces cooked with the seeds are actually sweeter because of the sweet gel surrounding the seeds. Many Italian cooks chop tomatoes, cook them, and pass through a food mill to remove seeds and skin. The flavor elements of the tomato cook in the sauce.

5 **The size of a pan influences cooking.** Wider pans cook faster (more individual bright flavor); narrower pots cook more slowly and lose less moisture (less surface area). Slower cooking mellows flavors; short cooking allows individual flavors to remain strong.

6 **Deglaze the soffritto.** Use red wine or meat stock for a hearty sauce or white wine, vegetable or poultry stock for lighter flavor and Marsala or vegetables juices for a sweet sauce. Cook sauce down to remove the raw alcohol harshness.

7 **What happens afterwards counts.**

   • Leave it alone. This type of sauce is a rustic, hearty individual. Take care to chop ingredients carefully.

   • Pass through a food mill. An elegant, refined sauce good on delicate foods and on pizza.

   • Purée. Blenders and food processors add air, but are fast and convenient.

8 **Follow the basics.**

   • Don't burn the garlic.

   • Choose herbs add them in layers: Strong flavored rosemary, sage, bay leaves, oregano, and thyme can cook long, but the delicate mint, basil, marjoram, and chives go in at the end.

   • Investigate flavor builders: olives, pine nuts, orange zest, whole and ground meat, Parmigiano-Reggiano rind, anchovies, capers, or sun-dried tomatoes.

   • End well: Whisk extra virgin olive oil, butter, creamy cheese, or delicate herbs for a pleasing "top" flavor.

   • Preserve summer tomatoes. Wash, core, and toss ripe tomatoes in plastic freezer bags and freeze. Or slice into 1/2-inch rounds and brush liberally with olive oil. Roast at 425 degrees F on a nonaluminum pan until they begin to color. Cool and freeze.

9 **Keep them right.** Use raw sauces immediately. Keep cooked sauces no more than 4 to 5 days. Freeze sauces no more than a month. Thaw in the refrigerator, and heat gently.

Vary! Improvise!

☛ *In winter, use other greens like spinach and arugula.*

☛ *Experiment with other oils like walnut, hazelnut, or avocado.*

☛ ***Anne Bianchi's Sage Pesto:*** *Good with beans, gnocchi, and bean soup. Purée 1/2 ounce sage leaves, about 1/2 cup; 1/2 ounce Italian parsley leaves, about 1/2 cup; 1 large clove garlic, peeled; 1 ounce toasted pine nuts, 1/4 cup; and 1/4 cup olive oil. Garnish with or stir in 1 ounce freshly grated Parmigiano-Reggiano cheese, about 3 to 4 tablespoons.*

Tomatoes Rule Southern Italian Sugos

Sugo alla marinara (an American name) is known as *sugo finto* in southern Italy, or as *pummarola* in Naples. Sugo di pomodoro is a simple southern sauce of tomato, oil, onion, and/or garlic and herbs.

TWO NEAPOLITAN TOMATO SAUCES (SUGOS)

Serve either sauce tossed on pasta with grated cheese on the side.

Yields enough for 1 pound pasta, 4 to 6 servings.

Neapolitan Sugo alla di Pomodoro

Yields 3 to 3-1/2 cups

3 to 4 tablespoons olive oil
1/2 ounce garlic, about 2 large cloves, crushed and peeled
2 pounds plum tomatoes, about 3-1/2 to 4 cups diced
   or 28 ounces canned whole plum tomatoes with sauce, diced
1/2 ounce Italian parsley, 1/4 cup packed
1/4 ounce basil leaves, 6 to 8 large leaves, 1/4 to 1/3 cup torn

Sugo Pummarola

Yields about 3-1/2 cups

3 tablespoons extra virgin olive oil
8 ounces red onion, 2 cups finely diced
1-1/2 ounces celery, 1 stalk, heaping 1/4 cup trimmed and finely diced
3-1/2 ounces carrot, 1 medium, 1/2 cup peeled and finely diced
Optional: 1/2 ounce garlic, 2 cloves, 1 tablespoon peeled and minced
2 pounds plum tomatoes, about 3-1/2 to 4 cups diced
   or 28 ounces canned whole plum tomatoes with sauce, diced
1/2 ounce Italian parsley sprigs, 1/4 cup packed
1/4 ounce basil leaves, 6 to 8 large leaves, 1/4 to 1/3 cup torn

1 Heat olive oil in a 4-quart nonreactive saucepan over medium heat.

Neapolitan Pomodoro
Add garlic and cook until it begins to color; add tomatoes and parsley.

Pummarola
Add onion, celery, and carrot to oil and sauté until lightly colored. Add garlic and cook 1 minute. Stir in tomatoes and parsley.

2 Simmer sauce:

Neapolitan Pomodoro
Partially cover pot and simmer sauce 15 minutes; stir in basil. Remove garlic and parsley sprigs if desired.

Pummarola
Simmer sauce uncovered 20 to 30 minutes, adding water if necessary to keep sauce moist. Stir in basil.

3 Pass the sauce through food mill and back into saucepan. Reduce sauce over medium heat until thick. Season with salt and pepper to taste.

Vary! Improvise!

☞ ***Make it Tuscan Pommarola:*** *Pour in olive oil then layer in onion, celery, carrot, garlic, parsley, basil, and to-matoes. Do not stir; simmer 1-1/2 hours and pass through food mill. Stir 2 tablespoons butter into hot sauce.*

NORTHERN ITALIAN MEAT SAUCE
(SUGO ALLA BOLOGNESE)

Bologna is the heart of Emilia-Romagna. This rich region produces some of the best food in Italy. The Accademia Italiana della Cucina *studied* sugo Bolognese *and set up strict guidelines for authentic Bolognese. This recipe comes close to their decree, but there are many more versions.*

Yields 6 cups, enough for about 3 pounds pasta

2 pounds lean chuck steak, diced into 1-inch cubes
   or 1 pound beef and 1 pound veal or lean pork shoulder, cubed
8 ounces pancetta, 1-1/3 cups diced into 1/4-inch cubes
7 ounces onion, 1-1/3 cups peeled and diced into 1/4-inch cubes
5 ounces celery, 1 cup diced into 1/4-inch cubes
8 ounces carrot, 1-1/3 cups peeled and diced into 1/4-inch cubes
2 cups dry white wine
1/4 cup tomato paste mixed with 1/2 cup water
1/2 cup canned crushed tomatoes in purée *or* tomato purée
3/4 to 1 ounce Italian parsley, 3 large sprigs
3 cups milk

For Serving 4 to 6

1 pound dry pasta, boiled al dente

Garnish: Shredded Parmigiano-Reggiano cheese

1 **Grind the meat:** In two batches, place cubed meat into food processor fitted with a blade. Pulse-chop until meat is finely chopped but not pasty. Scrape out into bowl.

2 **Cook battuto:** Heat a large saucepan over medium heat and add pancetta. When pancetta is golden and most of the fat has rendered, stir in onions, celery, and carrots. Cook vegetables until soft and lightly colored, 10 to 15 minutes.

3 Add meat to cooked vegetables, and cook until it is no longer pink, 6 to 8 minutes. Break it up as it cooks. Add wine and turn up heat to medium-high. Cook until wine is almost evaporated, 15 to 20 minutes. Stir in tomato paste in water, tomato purée, and parsley. Bring to a boil and cook 5 minutes.

4 Reduce heat to low. Stir in milk. Partially cover pan. Simmer sauce until creamy, thick, and reduced by about 2/3 volume to about 6 cups, about 2 hours. Taste sugo and season with salt and fresh pepper. Remove parsley. (If beef is not lean, excess fat may pool on top of the sauce; skim it off.)

5 **To Serve 4 to 6:** Toss 2 cups sauce with hot, cooked pasta (or pour over hot, cooked polenta). Reserve the remainder of the sauce for another dish. Garnish with Parmigiano-Reggiano cheese. Refrigerate sugo up to 5 days or freeze 6 months.

SPECIAL METHODS

Antipasti

The first course of an Italian meal can either be hot or cold antipasti. Antipasti, similar to Spanish tapas, can be many things, some quite simple:

- **Vinegar-pickled vegetables** like baby onions or artichoke hearts
- **Vegetables dressed in oil** like white bean salad, fried eggplant, or zucchini
- **Salt-cured or salty food** like olives or salt-dried tomatoes
- **Meat-based** like sliced cured meat: prosciutto, mortadella, or salami
- **Fish or seafood-based** like seafood salad, raw oysters, or marinated mussels

- **Bread-based** like crostini (toasts with topping), focaccia, or bruschetta (grilled bread with topping)
- **Cheese**, usually served at the end of the meal, is less common, but ricotta salata or buffalo mozzarella dressed in olive oil might be offered

FRESH RICOTTA CHEESE (RICOTTA FRESCA)

Ricotta is Italian for "recooked." Traditionally, liquid whey (leftover from making cheeses like mozzarella) is mixed with an acid coagulant and simmered to produce ricotta. Since whey isn't easily available, this method offers an additive-free alternative with whole milk. The cheese is technically similar to Indian paneer. The cream may be omitted, but it gives a smoother mouth feel to the ricotta. Ultra-pasteurized milk does not work well for cheesemaking; organic milk is often ultra-pasteurized.

Yields about 2 cups cheese, about 1 pound

1/2 gallon regular pasteurized or raw whole milk
1/2 cup heavy cream
1 teaspoon kosher salt
3/4 teaspoon citric acid powder

1 Line nonreactive strainer or colander with several layers of cheesecloth. Set strainer or colander over nonreactive bowl.

2 Combine milk, cream, salt, and citric acid powder in 6-quart nonreactive saucepan. Over medium-low heat, bring mixture to 180 to 190 degrees F, about 15 to 20 minutes. With a clean, heatproof rubber spatula, scrape the bottom periodically to prevent scorching.

3 As the milk simmers it will begin to curdle and separate. When the whey is yellow-green and slightly milky-cloudy, remove pan from the heat. Gently run the spatula around the edge of the curds. Do not stir. Cover pan and rest 10 minutes without disturbing.

4 Gently ladle curds into prepared strainer or colander; too much movement will toughen the curds. (If milk has scorched, leave very bottom curds in pan.)

5 Drain curds: Either leave curds in strainer or tie two opposite corners of cheesecloth together, then the remaining two opposite corners together. Hang curds from wooden dowel or spoon handle over a bowl. Drain curds until the cheese has the desired consistency. Drain until whey stops dripping to yield a moist ricotta; longer for a drier ricotta, about 20 to 30 minutes. Use immediately for best flavor, or place ricotta in an airtight container and refrigerate up to 1 week.

6 To Use: Season ricotta with salt. Spread on bread, toss with hot pasta, serve as antipasti drizzled with fresh herbs and good olive oil, as dessert drizzled honey and sprinkled with grated chocolate, or with figs or fresh berries.

Source: *Artisan Cheese Making at Home* by Mary Karlin.

Ricotta Tips

- Do not use ultra high temperature (UHT) milk; it has been heated to 275 degrees F and is less suitable because it produces a smaller yield and curd. Organic milks are often UHT.
- The acid has the most impact on yield, texture, and flavor.
  - Citric acid gives a high yield and produces a clean flavor.
  - Buttermilk produces ricotta with a tart flavor and sticky, creamy curd.
  - Fresh lemon juice varies in acidity so more might be needed for proper curding; it produces ricotta with a citrus flavor. Citric acid powder can be substituted.
  - White distilled vinegar produces a clean flavor and fine-textured curd.
- Draining time of curds depends on desired texture and ultimate use:

Soft Curds
Cream-cheese-like moist and creamy cheese with small, tender curds is best for immediate use while still warm as antipasti or chilled for dessert.

Dry Curds
Cottage-cheese-like small, tender curds, moist and spreadable but not runny. Best for moist uses like lasagna or ravioli and dips, or noncooked sweet fillings.

Very Dry Curds
Firm, dry, crumbly curds are good for molding into firm shapes. Best for use in pancakes, gnocchi, or tarts and tortas.

Vary! Improvise!

☞ *Goat Milk: Substitute goat milk for cow milk.*

ITALIAN ART

Pasta is the symbol of Italy, and certainly one of its most enduring gifts to world cuisine. Oretta Zanini de Vita, author of *Encyclopedia of Pasta*, scoured public and private archives and interviewed hundreds of elderly Italians over ten years trying to catalog and make sense of Italian pastas for her book. She discovered how Italian women have produced "hundreds of different shapes" with simple dough and an unrivaled creative brilliance. She passionately believes that Italian pasta "is a gift to gastronomic culture on par with what the Florentine Renaissance gave to art."

Italian Pasta

Italians serve pasta mainly as a first course followed by second and third courses of meat, fish, vegetables, or pizza. Pasta does not dominate a meal and portions are small—about 2 ounces dry per person. One pound of dry pasta yields about 8 to 9 cups cooked and will serve 6 to 8. Too much pasta leaves no space for the remaining meal.

Italian cooks made the first pasta with wheat flour and water. Parts of Italy still make fresh pasta without egg. In southern Italy, dried pasta was first made by hand. Workers stomped the tough semolina flour and water dough with their feet, and women with rolling pins shaped it! By the sixteenth century, simple machines began to speed up the process, and pasta came to the poor.

The structure in pasta comes from the gluten in flour, and from eggs. Dough with egg needs less structure from flour, so northern Italian egg-rich handmade pastas use softer wheat *farina tipo 00* flour. Northern style handmade pasta rarely uses the high-gluten durum wheat or semolina flour—it's best for machine-kneaded dry pastas without egg.

- Substitute 1/3 total volume of low or no-gluten flours, like buckwheat or chestnut for wheat flour, to tenderize and flavor fresh pasta dough.
- Chickpea flour adds flavor, strong structure, and extra protein.
- Too much whole egg with higher gluten flour can produce dough tough. Less egg (or just yolks) with more water and oil will produce tender dough.
- Northern Italians sometimes use all yolks and a little olive oil for very rich pasta dough.

ITALIAN FLOURS

By law, in Italy the word *farina* may only refer to the soft wheat flour called *tipo 0* or *00*. It's similar to unbleached or all-purpose white flour mixed with a little cake flour. *Semolina* is hard wheat flour. *Sfarinato* refers to flours made from non-wheat foodstuff like chestnuts or chickpeas. Northern and southern cooks make the chickpea flatbread snacks called *socca* or *panelle*. Northern Italians dry chestnuts over an open fire before grinding them into a delightful, smoky-nutty flour. Chestnut *papardelle* is classically paired with earthy flavors like duck, leeks, sage, mushrooms, or rabbit.

SIGNATURE RECIPE

HANDMADE PASTA DOUGH

Dough with egg will turn black overnight. Anoint it with olive oil, wrap tightly in a plastic bag, and refrigerate up to 1 day. Fresh pasta will yield about 50 percent more weight after boiling: 1 pound fresh pasta will yield around 24 ounces cooked. One pound of fresh pasta yields 5 to 6 cups cooked and serves 6. Prepare firmer dough if using pasta machine or stuffing dough; prepare softer dough if rolling dough by hand.

Food processor method yields about 25 ounces dough

15 to 16 ounces unbleached or all-purpose white flour, 3-1/3 cups
1 teaspoon kosher salt
9 fluid ounces beaten egg, about 5 large
2 teaspoons olive oil

Chestnut Pasta Variation

About 6-1/4 ounces Italian chestnut flour, 1-1/4 cups
About 10 to 11 ounces unbleached or all-purpose white flour, about 2-1/4 cups

1 *Choose a method.*

Food Processor Method (Yields a Firmer Dough)
Slide flour and salt into a food processor. Beat eggs with olive oil in measuring cup with spout. With machine running, pour a thin stream of egg into flour. Stop the machine periodically as egg is added to test dough. Pinch dough and when it holds together, stop adding egg. Don't make dough so soft and sticky that it rolls around in the processor and forms a ball. Dough should be in loose crumbles, and just come together when pressed, about the consistency of playdough.

Bowl or Table Method (Yields a Softer Dough)
Pour flour into a bowl *or* pile it on a worktable. Make a high-sided "well" in the center of flour. Crack eggs into well and add salt and optional olive oil. Beat eggs with a fork and then slowly begin to bring some of the flour in from the sides. Keep beating egg, and bringing in flour, until dough is soft and pliable.

2 **Knead dough:** With a dough scraper, scrape dough and knead it until dough is the consistency of playdough. Well-kneaded dough should feel smooth and resilient—and spring back when poked.

3 **Rest dough:** Cover dough and rest in a cool place (not refrigerator) 30 minutes to 1 hour. Dough (gluten) is sufficiently relaxed when it will not spring back when poked.

4 To cook pasta see *Signature Technique: Cooking Pasta* in *Simmer, Stew, Poach, Boil, and Steam.*

PASTA OF MANY COLORS

Italian chef and author Mario Batali loves to color his pastas, as many modern and traditional cooks do all over Italy. His favorites include purées of blanched chives, lemon thyme, yellow or red beets, and roasted red peppers. Batali recommends finely chopping or puréeing herbs or cooked vegetables. Mix 2 to 3 tablespoons vegetable purée per pound of pasta into eggs before adding flour.

- **Herb Pasta:** fresh Italian parsley, basil, thyme, or rosemary leaves
- **Green Pasta:** cooked, press-drained and puréed spinach or blanched chive purée
- **Red Pasta:** tomato paste or cooked, peeled, and puréed red bell pepper
- **Purple Pasta:** beet purée or red wine

FIGURE 6.25 Pasta rolling procedure.

Source: Richard Embery, Pearson Education.

Signature Technique: Fresh Pasta Rolling Protocol

1 Cut dough into four equal pieces. Cover 3 pieces and set them aside; otherwise dough will form a dry, crackly skin. With a rolling pin, on a lightly floured work surface, roll 1 piece of dough to an even rectangle. This allows it to more easily pass through machine rollers.

2 Set pasta machine at its widest setting. Roll dough through once. Fold it in half or thirds onto itself and roll it though again. Take care to square the dough as evenly as possible each time. Repeat this folding and kneading process up to 10 times to achieve smooth, tender dough.

3 **Without folding dough:** Put dough through rollers. Move machine setting progressively smaller. Roll dough through once on each setting until it reaches the thickness you desire. Usually the thinnest setting allows you to see your hand through the dough. Flour pasta sheet lightly and cut into desired shape:

- Fettuccine: Roll dough sheet slightly thicker than thinnest setting. Cut into 1/2-inchwide strips.
- Tagliatelle: Roll dough sheet slightly thicker than thinnest setting and dry 15 minutes. Roll into a flat roll 3 inches wide. With a sharp knife, cut dough into strips 3/4-inch wide.
- Quadrucci: Cut tagliatelle crosswise into small squares.
- Pappardelle: Roll dough sheet slightly thicker than thinnest setting and cut by hand with knife or pizza cutter 1-1/2 inches wide.
- Orecchiette: Roll pasta dough into long 1/2-inch wide log and slice off 1/4-inch-thick pieces. Press each with a floured thumb to form an "ear."

4 Shake out cut pasta and dust well with flour to keep from sticking.

- Typically pasta machines produce 5-1/2- to 6-inch-wide sheets. Blanch in boiling water before using for lasagna. Or prepare filled pastas or cannelloni.

- Thinner pasta works well for delicate pasta sauces. Medium-thick is good for heartier sauces. The dough will puff up and thicken somewhat as it cooks and absorbs water.
- Fresh Italian parsley or basil leaves make a stunning mosaic pasta. To make pasta with leaves rolled inside, remove all stems from herbs and pat them very dry. Press or crush thick veins in basil. Roll pasta to desired thickness—not too thin or herbs will poke through. Cut or fold pasta exactly in half crosswise. Dough should be slightly sticky. Arrange fresh herbs in one layer, about an inch apart, on half the dough. Place or fold the other half pasta sheet on top to cover herbs, and press to secure. Roll through the same thickness setting.

MATCHING PASTA SHAPE WITH SAUCE

Oretta Zanini de Vita in *Encyclopedia of Pasta*, relegates Italian pastas into 7 categories:

- **Pasta Corta:** fresh or factory dried short pastas like penne, cavatelli, and rigatoni
- **Pasta Lunga:** fresh and factory long forms like spaghetti, fettuccine, and tagliatelle
- **Pasta Ripiena:** stuffed pastas like ravioli, tortellini, and agnolotti
- **Pastina:** tiny pasta shapes cooked in broth
- **Gnocchi and Gnocchetti:** round or long shaped dumplings
- **Strascinati:** hand or factory made pasta disk like orecchiette
- **Unusual Shapes:** lasagna

Zanini de Vita has discovered that the way Italians pair pastas and sauces is guided mainly by tradition, which is dictated by local ingredients, the season, and the church calendar. Cooks created dishes from what was available. Eventually the dishes became tradition and lodged into church law. Zanini de Vita points out that there is nothing wrong with certain combinations (like clam sauce with rigatoni instead of linguine), but because they just aren't done they "still have the power to shock." It seems that tradition has "entered the national DNA" so that "Italians instinctively" put together the correct sauce and pasta.

In general, fine and delicate pastas go best with fine, delicate sauces, and hearty or large pasta shapes go best with heavier meaty sauces. Prepare vegetables and other ingredients to mimic pasta shapes. Slice vegetables into long thin pieces for long thin pasta and into similar sized cubes or short shapes for thick or short pastas. **Most important:** The pasta should support the sauce.

Fresh Home-Made Pasta

Light and silky, fresh pasta tends to absorb sauce more than dried. Slick, strong flavored olive oil sauces tend to obscure its fine texture and deaden its flavor. Match fresh pasta with subtle seafood, meat or vegetable sauces with butter or enriched with cream. *Linguine* and *fettuccine* go well with butter and cheese-based sauces. Wide pasta like *paparadelle* goes well with meaty, chunky sauce. Fresh (or dry) *orecchiette* (little ears or coin-shapes) go well with chunky vegetable and meat sauces.

Dry Factory-Made Pasta

Firm, compact, and grainy, dry pasta holds up to firm and bold sauces based on seafood and a variety of light vegetable sauces based on olive oil. Italians know that different shapes capture and absorb sauce differently. Thin *spaghetti* and *trenette* pair well with olive-oil-based seafood, pesto-based or thinner tomato sauces. Thicker or butter-based tomato sauce goes best with *thick spaghetti*, *bucatini/perciatelli* (long narrow tubes), and smaller odd shapes. Larger ridged hollow tubes like *rigatoni* and *penne*, or *conchiglie* (shells) stand up to meat, beans, and chunky sauces. *Fusilli* handles dense, creamy sauces or fine meat sauces, which cling to its twisted shape.

PAIR A PASTA AND SAUCE

Taking into consideration the information above, pair one of the sauces with a dry pasta.

Classic Dry Pasta Sauces

Aglio e olio: olive oil and garlic

All'amatriciana: tomato and pancetta or guanciale (pork cheek), red chili, and pecorino cheese

Alla napoletana: tomato sauce with meat

Carbonara: pancetta or guanciale, Pecorino or Parmigiano-Reggiano cheese and soft egg

Sugo di pesce: tomato sauce with fish

Pesto: herbs, garlic, and olive oil

Fagiolini e patate al pesto: pesto, green beans, and potatoes

Al ortolano: seasonal vegetables

Al pomodoro e basilico or al pomodoro crudo: raw tomatoes, garlic, and basil

Aglio-olio peperoncino: garlic, oil, and red pepper flakes, anchovies optional

Ragù di fungi misto: mixed mushroom ragu

Alle vongole bianco: clams, white wine, clam juice, and garlic

Con la mollica: anchovies and oil-toasted breadcrumbs

SIMMER, STEW, POACH, BOIL, AND STEAM

Italian Soup

Modern Italians divide soup into:

Zuppa: One-dish meal, dense, rich, bean, tomato, or fish soups eaten over bread

Farinate: Dense vegetable soups thickened with polenta

Minestra: First course, substantial soups, vegetable soups, and "dry" soups (moist pasta dishes) like *pasta e fagioli* (pasta and beans) with rice or pasta as an ingredient

Minestrone: Filling, substantial "big soups" or stews with many ingredients

Brodi: Broths served over fried croutons, or simmered with rice or pastina (which can turn brodo into minestra)

Pancotti, Passate, and Creme: Bread soup, purée soups, and cream soups

Freshly made broth or *brodo* underlies many Italian soups. Most Italian kitchens prepare chicken (*brodo di pollo*), beef (*brodo di manzo*), or meat broth (*brodo di carne*). Chef and cookbook author Lynne Rossetto Kasper recommends preparing brodo from a capon (castrated rooster) or turkey wings and beef shank bones for best flavor. Vegetable broth is also gaining popularity.

Italian soup is flexible. Tomato purée, olive oil, Parmigiano-Reggiano cheese rinds, or ground chestnuts boost soup flavor. Wise and thrifty Italian cooks use seasonal ingredients when they are most abundant and flavorful: spring asparagus, summer tomatoes, and fall kale and mushrooms.

- *Northern Italian* soups tend toward generous, hearty soups based on rich *brodo* (broth) or water with rice, meat, seafood, mushrooms, or cheese.
- *Southern* soups tend to be pasta-rich, based on olive oil, garlic, and tomato.
- *Central Italian* (Rome and Tuscany) soups are bean rich and often poured over toasted bread.
- *Near the Riviera*, soups tend to be lighter, with fish, seafood, herbs, and greens.

MEAT BROTH (BRODO DI CARNE)

The technique for preparing broth is the same as for making French-style stock, except that broth is made with bones and meat. Meaty shank bones add good flavor. Use stock in place of water to yield an extra rich brodo.

Yields about 2-1/2 to 3-1/2 quarts

5 pounds chicken parts, skinned and rinsed
   or 5 pounds turkey wings
      or 3 pounds cracked beef and veal bones **plus** 2 pounds lean beef (top round)

Battuto

About 12 ounces onions, 2 medium, 3 cups medium diced
4 ounces carrots, 1 cup peeled and medium diced
About 4 ounces celery, 4 to 6 stalks, 1 cup medium to large diced
3 ounces garlic cloves, about 12 large cloves peeled and rinsed

1/4 ounce Italian parsley stems
2 whole cloves
1 bay leaf, preferably fresh
Optional: 1-1/2 pounds fresh plum tomatoes, about 4
   or 14-1/2 ounce can plum tomatoes, about 1 cup drained

1 Place meat and bones in 8- to 10-quart stockpot. Cover chicken with 4-1/2 to 5 quarts cold water. Cover turkey wings or beef with 1-1/2 gallons (6 quarts) cold water. Bring water to a boil over medium heat. Lower heat and simmer meat 30 minutes. Skim away as much foam as possible.

2 Immerse **battuto** (onions, carrots, celery, and garlic), parsley stems, cloves, bay leaves, and optional tomatoes into pot. Simmer chicken broth until fragrant, 3 hours. Simmer turkey wing or meat and bone broths 6 hours or longer. If stock boils, the impurities will emulsify into the stock and cloud it. Keep the level of water 2 to 3 inches above solid ingredients.

3 Remove pot from heat and cool stock slightly. Ladle stock through china cap lined with cheesecloth; quickly chill it down. Discard bones and vegetables. Reserve meat for soup garnish or another dish. Refrigerate stock until fat congeals on top, 4 to 8 hours. Skim and discard fat. Ladle stock into storage containers. Refrigerate stock no more than 4 days. Freeze stock for longer storage up to 6 months.

4 **To Serve:** Throughout Italy brodos are served in small cups or garnished with fried croutons or simmered with pastina, tortellini, or dumplings to serve as a first course for holiday meals.

Vary! Improvise!

There are many soups that may be prepared from one brodo:

☛ *Pastina:* Cook tiny pasta in broth and garnish with grated Parmigiano-Reggiano.

☛ Garnish hot brodo with strips of prosciutto and herbs or sprigs of watercress.

☛ *Stracciatella:* Heat 2 quarts beef brodo. Whisk together 3 eggs, 1/4 cup grated Parmigiano-Reggiano, and 1/4 cup semolina flour or cream of wheat. Whisk into simmering broth 2 to 3 minutes.

☛ Simmer sliced escarole or chicory in broth and garnish with grated Pecorino.

☛ Simmer sliced, sautéed mushrooms or soaked and sliced, dried porcini mushrooms in brodo. Garnish with parsley.

☛ *Brodo di Marsala:* Whisk together 4 eggs and 1 cup dry marsala. Bring 6 cups brodo to a boil, remove from heat, and whisk egg mixture into broth. Season with salt and pepper.

Don't Toss That Rind

Italian cooking teacher and author Lynne Rossetto Kasper admonishes against wasting the rind of the excellent Parmigiano-Reggiano cheese. She simmers it into soups, stews, and braised dishes where it enhances, enriches, and deepens flavor with an umami-rich character. The rind is hardened cheese without wax; a 4-inch square is enough to flavor 4 to 5 quarts of soup.

FIGURE 6.26 Parmigiano Reggiano.
Source: heros1973/Fotolia.

Fish Soups and Stews: Place Dictates

Mediterranean cooks are enthusiastic about seafood soups and stews made with glisteningly fresh, local seafood. With many miles of coastline in easy reach, Italian and nearby Mediterranean cooks have numerous variations on seafood-based soups and stews, depending upon the varieties of fish, seafood, seasonings, and vegetables.

Fish soups had humble beginnings, based on the fishermen's leftover small, bony but tasty fish. Home cooks in port towns around Naples, Genoa, Provence, Catalonia, and Valencia developed many stews and soups from the seafood that local markets held. Using more types of fish and shellfish will develop deeper and more complex flavor.

In Italy the two main *zuppa de pesce* are the stew-like Adriatic *brodetto*, the Tuscan *cacciucco* (ka-choo-koh), and the Rivieran/Ligurian *ciuppin* (mother of San Francisco's cioppino). Cacciucco uses a variety of fish and shellfish with a *strained stock* of fish heads and bones or with the meat *ground* through a food mill, and served in broth over toasted bread. Sardinians prepare *fregula*, a kind of chowder with clams. Some cooks serve seafood soup/stew in two courses: broth in bowls with toast, then the fish on a platter. Italian cooks love squid for its deep flavor. Stews and soups are best made with firm fish like halibut and turbot—tender fish like sole and flounder fall apart during cooking.

CANNED PLUM TOMATOES

A 14-1/2-ounce can of plum tomatoes will yield about 1 cup drained whole tomatoes and 1/2 cup juice or purée.

A 28-ounce can of plum tomatoes will yield approximately 2 cups drained whole tomatoes and 1 cup juice or purée.

A 35-ounce can of plum tomatoes will yield 2-1/2 to 3 cups drained whole tomatoes and 1 to 1-1/2 cups juice or purée.

ITALIAN FISH SOUP-STEW (BRODETTO OR ZUPPA DI PESCE)

Most every town along Italy's Adriatic coast prepares fish soups similar to this. Food historian Clifford Wright has said that the most likely precursor to the Provençal bouillabaisse was likely an Italian fish stew. Though Italians call this soup, it is more stew. Tomato, olive oil, and wine are the constants, forming a base with onion, garlic, red chili flakes, and parsley.

Yields 9 cups, 6 to 8 servings

3 pounds assorted whole fish *like* turbot, halibut, cod, shark, mullet, monkfish, grouper, red snapper, or sea bass, filleted, skinned, and diced into 1-inch cubes
 or 2 pounds fish fillets, skinned, boned, and diced into 1-inch cubes

1 pound extra large (26/30) shrimp, 3/4 pound shelled and deveined
1 pound cleaned squid, bodies sliced into 1/2-inch-wide rings and tentacles left whole
1 dozen littleneck clams, 11 to 12 ounces (to yield about 2 ounces meat)
1 dozen mussels, 11 to 12 ounces (to yield about 2 ounces meat)
1/3 cup olive oil
4 to 5 ounces onion, 1 cup peeled and finely diced
1/4 to 1/2 ounce garlic, 1 to 2 large cloves, 1/2 to 1 tablespoon peeled and minced
3/4 ounce trimmed Italian parsley, 3 tablespoons chopped
Two strips or lemon zest from 1/2 lemon
1 cup dry white wine
16 ounce can whole plum tomatoes and juice, 2 cups diced with juice
    or 1 pound ripe tomatoes, 2 cups peeled and diced
Red chili flakes or freshly ground black pepper

Garnish: Chopped Italian parsley

For Serving

Grilled or toasted country bread

1 **Prepare seafood:** Wash fish, shrimp, and squid, and pat dry. Remove heads and set aside. Cut fish into 2- to 3-inch pieces. Scrub clams and mussels; discard any that won't close when tapped.

2 **Cook shellfish:** Place 1/2 cup water, clams, and mussels in 10- to 12-inch-deep (6-quart) Dutch oven. Cover pan and place on high heat. Turn shellfish frequently and transfer from pan to a bowl as they open. Remove meat from shells, place in small bowl, and cover with juices left in bowl and pan, about 1/2 cup. Leave sand or grit behind.

3 **Prepare sauce base:** Pour olive oil and onion into 11-inch (6-quart) Dutch oven. Place on medium heat and cook onion until soft, 5 to 8 minutes. Add garlic and cook until golden. Stir in parsley and lemon zest, cook 2 minutes, and pour in wine. Simmer until reduced by half and stir in tomatoes. Reduce heat to low, cover the pot, and simmer sauce 25 minutes.

4 **Increase flavor; simmer fish heads if available:** Place fish heads in tomato sauce and simmer until tender, but no more than 20 minutes. Remove heads with slotted spoon to a bowl. Remove all meat and chop finely or pass through food mill and stir into tomato sauce. *Or* simmer fish heads separately into a rich broth with fish bones then strain.

5 **Cook squid:** Stir squid rings and tentacles into sauce and simmer until tender when fork-probed, 30 to 45 minutes. Stir in liquid covering shellfish, but not the meat. Taste sauce and season with salt and chili flakes.

6 **Cook firm fish, delicate fish, and shrimp:** Place firmest fish into the simmering sauce and stir occasionally, 3 minutes, then add delicate fish and simmer 2 minutes. Gently fold in shrimp and simmer 2 to 3 minutes. Gently fold in clam and mussel meat. Simmer 1 minute more and remove from heat. Stir in a little water if sauce or stock looks thick, though the texture is more like a stew.

7 **To Serve:** Spoon or pour brodetto into warm serving vessel or ladle into warmed soup plates. Garnish brodetto with parsley and serve with grilled bread.

Vary! Improvise!

☞ *Check Lynne Rossetto Kasper's* Brodetto with Onions Stewed in Vinegar *in* The Splendid Table.

Vary! Improvise!

☛ **Go South:** Season soup with red chili flakes and drizzle with parsley oil.

☛ **Sicilian:** Substitute fresh fava beans (2 pounds fava pods yield 2 cups shelled beans) for white beans, and simmer in chicken stock with onion and fennel bulb until soft. Season with chopped fennel fronds. Serve drizzled with olive oil and toasted croutons.

☛ **Spanish** cooks prepare a chickpea purée with onion, carrot, leek, garlic, smoked paprika, and chicken stock. Garnish the soup with ingredients like sautéed porcini mushrooms, shrimp, or green herb oil and cubes of crisp bacon or jamon.

Long and Delicious Fava Beans

Sometime in March the large pods of fava beans arrive at southern Italian tables. Diners eat the glistening pale green young beans raw with pecorino or fruit at the end of a meal. Favas last through May. As they age they might go onto a sauté of onions and parsley and braise with wine, stock, or water. With more liquid they become a pasta sauce, a lot more liquid and it's soup.

Two pounds fresh fava pods yield 2 cups shelled beans.

FIGURE 6.27 Fresh fava bean in pod.
Source: Vidady/Fotolia.

PURÉED BEAN SOUP (VELLUTATA DI FAGIOLI)

Tuscans are called the "bean-eaters," but all of Italy enjoys beans and bean soups. This soup is typical of Southern cucina povera cooking and of Tuscan bean soups. Northern cooks top bean soup with gremolada. Southern cooks like to season the soup with red chili flakes. The garnish makes this plain-Jane soup come alive.

Yields 9 cups, 6 to 8 servings

1 pound dried cannellini (white kidney) beans, chickpeas, or borlotti beans, 2-1/3 to 2-1/2 cups
   or 6 cups cooked beans with 1-1/2 to 2 cups cooking liquid
1 large sprig fresh sage
1 large sprig fresh rosemary
6 to 8 tablespoons extra-virgin olive oil

Garnish

8 ounces pancetta (or thick-cut bacon), 1-1/2 cups 1/4-inch cubes
2 ounces country bread, about 2 slices, cut into 1/2-inch cubes

Soffritto

8 to 9 ounces onion, 2 cups peeled and finely diced
3/4 ounce garlic, about 3 large cloves, 4-1/2 tablespoons minced
5 ounces carrot, 3/4 cup trimmed and finely diced
3 to 4 ounces celery, 3/4 cup trimmed and finely diced

1 **Soak and cook beans:** Pick through beans and discard stones. Soak beans overnight in 2 quarts cold water and 2 teaspoons kosher salt or quick-soak with salt and covered in boiling water for 1 hour. Drain soaked beans and place in 6-quart pot. Add, sage, rosemary, and 2 quarts cold water, cover, and bring to a boil. Lower heat to a simmer and cook until beans are tender, 45 minutes to 1 hour. Cool beans and cooking liquid to warm. Remove herbs, scrape leaves into soup, and discard stems.

2 Heat 2 tablespoons oil in a 10 to 11-inch skillet over medium heat. Add pancetta, and fry until lightly browned. Remove pancetta with slotted spoon to a bowl, set aside. Heat pan again over medium and add 2 tablespoons oil. Add bread cubes and cook until golden. Remove bread from skillet, and set aside in bowl with pancetta.

3 Reheat pan with 3 tablespoons oil over medium heat and add **soffritto** ingredients. Cook vegetables until tender and slightly golden. Scrape into cooked beans with 1 to 2 cups water, and simmer uncovered until creamy, 15 to 20 minutes. Cool.

4 Transfer beans to blender (in batches) or food processor and purée in machine until smooth. An immersion blender doesn't produce as fine a purée as a blender or processor, but works well for large batches. Scrape purée into saucepan. Rinse out blender or processor with a little water and add to bean purée as necessary to achieve a creamy purée soup consistency. Season to taste with salt and pepper.

5 **To Serve:** Reheat soup over low heat. Ladle hot soup into bowls, sprinkle with croutons and pancetta, and drizzle each bowl with a little olive oil.

Vegetable Soups

The main ingredients of a good Italian soup are water or good stock—*brodo*—plus a combination of tasty vegetables, meat, and anchovy or even a Parmigiano-Reggiano rind to simmer in the broth. Sauté aromatics and meats to bring out their flavor, or just simmer ingredients in stock, garnish, and serve. Taste, taste, and taste soup again before serving. For every serving calculate 1 to 1-1/4 cups broth and 1/4 to 1/3 cup vegetables plus seasonings.

ONION SOUP FROM TUSCANY (CARABACCIA)

Harmon-Jenkins says that this fourteenth century recipe for onion soup is much like what is prepared in Tuscany now and that it's a good example of how the simple, tasty cooking of humble farmhouse cooks has persisted over centuries.

Yields 2 quarts, 6 to 8 servings

2 ounces pancetta, about 1/3 cup finely diced 1/4-inch cubes
2 tablespoons olive oil
5 to 6 ounces trimmed carrots, 2 medium, 1-1/4 cups peeled and finely diced
4 ounces trimmed celery, 2 to 3 medium stalks, 1 cup finely diced
1/2 ounce Italian parsley, 1/4 to 1/3 cup packed, chopped leaves and tender stems
2 pounds red or yellow onions, halved and peeled, 8 cups finely slivered or sliced
1/2 cup dry white wine
6 cups chicken stock
4 ounces 1/4- to 1/2-inch thick sliced country *or* ciabatta bread, 4 slices toasted and halved
1 to 1-1/2 ounces Pecorino or Parmigiano-Reggiano cheese, 1/3 cup freshly grated

Garnish: Chopped Italian parsley

1 Heat pancetta and oil in large saucepan over medium heat. Cook until pancetta begins to brown and melt, 3 to 4 minutes. Stir in carrots, celery, and parsley and cook until soft, 5 minutes. Stir in onions, lower heat, and cover pan. Simmer onions until soft, 30 to 45 minutes. Check onions every 10 to 15 minutes. If the liquid has evaporated and onions start to brown, add 1/4 cup water. The onions should not brown, but reduce to a soft, lightly colored mass.

2 Uncover pot and pour in wine. Turn heat to up to high and cook onions uncovered until wine evaporates, 3 to 5 minutes. Pour in stock and simmer soup partially covered 20 minutes. Taste soup and season with salt and pepper.

3 **To Serve:** Place 1/2 slice toast in each bowl, sprinkle with cheese and parsley, and ladle hot soup over top.

Source: *Flavors of Tuscany* by Nancy Harmon Jenkins.

Vary! Improvise!

☞ *Substitute dry Marsala for white wine for a nutty glow.*

☞ *Use red onions and red wine in place of yellow onions and white wine.*

SOUTHERN ITALIAN SPICY SOUP WITH EGGPLANT (ZUPPA PICCANTE ALLE MELANZANE)

Southern Italian farmers eat this soup hot in winter and at room temperature in summer. Smaller eggplants contain less of the bitter seeds.

Yields about 3 quarts, 6 to 8 servings

2 pounds small eggplants, 5 cups stemmed and diced into 1/4-inch cubes
5 tablespoons olive oil, more as needed
5 to 6 cups chicken or vegetable stock *or* water
8 to 9 ounces red onion, 2 cups peeled and finely diced
3 to 4 ounces carrot, 1 medium, about 1/2 cup finely diced
1/2 ounce garlic, 2 large cloves, 1 tablespoon finely minced
1/4 ounce trimmed Italian parsley, 2 tablespoons chopped
1/4 cup dry white wine
1-3/4 cups cooked chickpeas (from 1 cup dried)
    or 15-ounce can chickpeas, drained
2 tablespoons red wine vinegar
    or freshly squeezed lemon juice, more to taste
16 ounces canned, diced tomatoes with liquid, 2 cups
1/4 ounces basil leaves, 6 to 8 large, 1/4 cup torn
    or 2 to 3 teaspoons chopped fresh rosemary leaves

Garnish

Scant 1/4 ounce mint leaves, 3 tablespoons shredded or torn
3-inch dried red chili, stemmed, seeded and finely diced
4 ounces *ricotta salata* or ricotta cheese, 1 cup crumbled

1 **Degorge eggplant:** Toss eggplant with 1 tablespoon kosher salt. Rest until eggplant exudes water, 20 minutes. Rinse, drain, and blot eggplant very dry.

2 **Brown eggplant:** Heat a heavy 12-inch skillet with 3 tablespoons oil; sauté eggplant in batches until browned and tender, adding oil as needed. Deglaze with a little stock or water if skillet becomes too browned. Scrape eggplant and liquid into bowl; set aside.

3 **Prepare soup:** Heat a 5- to 6-quart soup pot over high heat with 2 to 3 tablespoons oil and sauté onion until golden, 5 to 7 minutes. Reduce heat to medium and add carrot, garlic, and parsley; cook until tender, 4 to 5 minutes. Pour in wine and cook until almost dry. Add chickpeas and 1 tablespoon vinegar or lemon juice and cook 4 to 5 minutes. Stir tomatoes, basil, or rosemary into soup and simmer until it slightly thickens, 3 to 4 minutes. Add eggplant and enough stock, chickpea cooking liquid, or water to make a thick soup, about 3-1/2 to 4 cups. Bring soup to a boil, lower heat, and simmer until rich tasting, 15 minutes.

4 Taste soup, and season with remaining vinegar or lemon juice, salt, and pepper.

5 **To Serve:** Mix mint, chili, and cheese together. Ladle soup into bowls and garnish with mint-cheese mixture.

Source: *The Italian Country Table* by Lynne Rossetto Kasper.

Vary! Improvise!

☛ **Use Another Garnish:** *Goat cheese and oregano or parsley-lemon gremolada.*

☛ **Summer Squash:** *Substitute yellow summer squash for eggplant. No need to degorge.*

☛ **Smoother:** *Purée all or part of the soup.*

Minestrone: Regional Classic

Italian dishes change from region to region, city to city, town to town, and even house to house. Minestrone is no exception. Joe Famularo says in *Italian Soup Cookbook* that cooks on the Italian Riviera use fresh basil and other herbs to flavor minestroni. In northern

Italy, cooks add rice, but in Tuscany and Umbria, beans take the place of rice. Milanese cooks prefer kidney beans, potatoes, zucchini, savoy cabbage, peas, and rice; in Emilia-Romagna they use cannellini beans and fresh green beans without rice. Most minestroni are vegetarian, but Romans use beef, beef stock, kidney beans, and pastina. In Abruzzi, minestroni is prepared with pork, fennel bulb, lima beans, peas, spinach, and mint. Southern Italian cooks include oil, garlic, tomatoes, and pasta into minestroni. All cooks can agree on one thing: The vegetables must be fresh and in season.

MINESTRONE

Minestrone typically includes seasonal vegetables and lots of leafy greens and vegetables. It is a thick soup that is ingredient-flexible. Sometimes cooked rice or pasta is added. The classic northern base is Roman beans (borlotti or cranberry beans) and their broth.

Yields 11 cups, 6 servings

4 tablespoons olive oil, *divided*
6 to 7 ounces red onion, 1 medium, 1-1/2 cups peeled and finely diced
5 ounces carrots, 2 medium, 3/4 cup peeled and medium diced
2-1/2 ounces celery, 1 large stalk, 1/4 to 1/3 cup medium diced
1/4 teaspoon red pepper flakes
1-1/2 teaspoons minced fresh rosemary
14-1/2 ounce can whole peeled tomatoes, 1 to 1-1/2 cups drained and finely diced
8 ounces potato, 1 large, 1 cup peeled and medium diced
8 ounces Savoy cabbage, 3 cups cored and thinly sliced
    or 8 ounces escarole
15-ounce can Roman (borlotti) beans or cannellini beans, 1-1/2 to 1-3/4 cups drained
    or 1-3/4 cups cooked beans
8 ounces green beans, 2 cups trimmed and cut into 1-inch pieces
1/2 ounce garlic, 2 large cloves, 1 tablespoon peeled and minced
1/2 ounce fresh basil leaves, 1/4 cup thinly torn

For Serving

3 to 4 ounces Parmigiano-Reggiano cheese, 3/4 to 1 cup grated

1 In a 6-quart pot, heat 2 tablespoons oil over medium heat. Stir in onion, carrots, celery, red pepper flakes, rosemary, and 1-1/2 teaspoons kosher salt. Cook, stirring occasionally, until onion begins to brown, 5 to 8 minutes. Stir in tomatoes and cook until most of the juice evaporates Stir in potato, cabbage, beans, and 6 cups water (or bean cooking water if available). Bring to a boil and simmer soup 10 minutes.

2 Stir in green beans and garlic. Reduce soup to a simmer, and cook until green beans are tender, about 10 minutes. Season soup to taste with salt and freshly ground pepper.

3 **To Serve:** Just before serving, stir in basil. Ladle hot soup into bowls and garnish each with cheese. Drizzle each bowl with 1 teaspoon of remaining olive oil.

Source: *Everyday Food*, October 2008.

Vary! Improvise!

☛ *Swap zucchini for green beans, Tuscan kale for cabbage, and chickpeas for cannellini beans.*

☛ ***Borlotti Beans:*** *Soak and cook 1 cup (6-1/2 ounces) borlotti beans in place of canned cannellini beans. Use bean cooking water in place of the 6 to 7 cups water.*

☛ ***Enrich:*** *Use 6 to 7 cups chicken or vegetable stock in place of the water.*

Braising and Stewing

Braising and stewing techniques are similar throughout Europe. See chapter *France* for information on braising and stewing.

LAMB AND ARTICHOKE STEW

This traditional Easter peasant dish is popular in northern Italy in the spring when lamb is most tender. Lamb, artichoke hearts, prosciutto, rosemary, and sage make a great combo served over soft polenta, rice, or pasta.

Yields 3 quarts, 6 to 8 servings

Olive oil for sautéing
3 pounds lamb top sirloin or lean lamb leg, diced into 1-inch cubes
Flour as needed
1 cup dry white wine
8 to 12 ounces leek, 1 large
6 to 8 ounces carrots, 1 cup peeled and medium diced
5 ounces celery, 1/2 cup trimmed and finely diced
1/2 ounce garlic, 2 large cloves, 1 tablespoon finely chopped
1/8 ounce fresh rosemary leaves, 1 tablespoon chopped
Scant 1/8 ounce fresh sage leaves, 1 tablespoon finely sliced
1/2 teaspoon dried red chili flakes, more to taste
2 to 3 ounces prosciutto, 4 to 6 tablespoons diced
4 cups chicken stock
3 tablespoons tomato paste
18 ounces frozen plain artichoke hearts, 3 cups thawed
Zest of one lemon
1/2 cup fresh lemon juice, to taste, about 2 lemons

Garnish: 1 ounce trimmed Italian parsley, 1/2 cup coarsely chopped

1 Heat 3 tablespoons oil in a 6-quart Dutch oven over medium-high heat. Season lamb with salt and pepper. When oil shimmers but before it smokes, dip lamb in flour, shake off excess, and add to the oil. Reserve 3 tablespoons flour and set aside. Quickly brown meat, and remove with slotted spoon or tongs to a bowl. Deglaze pot with wine, and boil 1 minute. Scrape deglazed liquid into bowl with lamb.

2 Trim leek root end (but don't cut off). Slice leek down its length and wash under cold water. Drain leek and trim away toughest green leaves. Finely slice leek cross-wise, and discard root end to yield about 3 cups sliced leek.

3 Heat Dutch oven again with 2 tablespoons oil and when oil shimmers, add leeks, carrots, and celery. Cook vegetables, stirring often, until tender, about 10 minutes. Add garlic, rosemary, sage, pepper flakes, and prosciutto, and cook 3 to 4 minutes. Sprinkle vegetables with the reserved 3 tablespoons flour, and cook 1 minute. Add lamb and its deglazing liquid, broth, and tomato paste to the vegetables, and stir well. Simmer over low heat until lamb is tender, 45 minutes to 1 hour.

4 Stir in artichoke hearts, and simmer stew 5 minutes. Stir in zest, lemon juice, and season with salt and freshly ground pepper to taste.

5 **To Serve:** Ladle stew into bowls. Sprinkle parsley over the top of stew. Drizzle with olive oil.

Vary! Improvise!

☞ **Lamb and Fennel Stew:** *Substitute 2 bulbs fennel for artichokes. Slice off tops and a thin slice off the bottom. Place fennel bulb on its bottom and slice it in half so there are 2 thin halves. Lay a half bulb flat side down and dice into 1/2-inch cubes; sauté with leeks, celery, and carrots. Omit tomato paste and sage.*

BRAISED VEAL SHANKS (OSSOBUCO)

Ossobuco is a Milanese specialty of white wine and vegetable-braised veal shanks. The shanks were a less expensive, tough but flavorful cut, perfect for braising. Usually garnished with gremolada, Milanese cooks serve ossobuco garnished with gremolada preceded by risotto alla Milanese or with soft polenta or mashed potatoes. The modern version boasts tomato paste or tomatoes. White ossobuco was seasoned with cinnamon, bay leaves, and classic gremolada.

6 servings

4 pounds trimmed 1-inch thick cross-cut veal shanks
Olive oil for sautéing
Optional: 1/4 cup white or red wine for deglazing
4 to 5 ounces onions, 1 cup peeled and diced 1/2-inch
4 ounces carrot, 1/2 cup peeled and diced into 1/2-inch cubes
About 3 ounces celery, 1/2 cup trimmed and diced into 1/2-inch cubes
4 sprigs rosemary
2 sprigs thyme
1 cup white or red wine
4 cups veal or chicken or beef stock
2 tablespoons tomato paste

Gremolada

1/2 ounce Italian parsley, 3 tablespoons trimmed and chopped
Zest of 1 lemon, 1 tablespoon

For Serving

Soft cooked *Polenta*

1 Preheat oven to 325 degrees F. Blot shanks dry and season with salt. Heat a sturdy 6- to 8-quart ovenproof pot or casserole over medium-high heat with just enough oil to coat its bottom. Sauté shanks until browned, about 2 to 3 minutes per side. Pull them out with tongs as they brown and set in a bowl. If casserole bottom is very browned, pour off excess oil and deglaze with 1/4 cup red wine; scrape browned bits into bowl with shanks.

2 Reheat casserole over medium heat with a little more oil. Add onions, carrots, and celery. Brown the vegetables. Add 1 cup wine and deglaze the pan by scraping the bottom with a wooden spoon. Bring the liquid to a boil, add tomato paste, and reduce wine 1 minute.

3 Remove casserole from the heat. Add rosemary sprigs and place shanks and their liquid on top of the vegetables. Add enough stock to come up halfway the sides of the shanks. Cover casserole, place in oven, and cook until shanks are almost falling-from-the-bone-tender, 2-1/2 to 3 hours. Alternatively, simmer shanks on top of the stove over very low heat.

4 Transfer meat to a warm platter or bowl, and cover loosely with foil. Keep warm.

5 **Prepare the sauce:** Strain the cooking liquid through a fine strainer, and press down on the vegetables to extract juice. Pour juice into a 12-inch sauté pan and over medium heat, reduce the juices by half, skimming off the fat. The juices should coat the back of a spoon. Return juices that have come out of shanks to the sauce. Taste sauce, and season with salt and pepper if necessary. Mix together parsley and lemon zest for gremolada and set aside.

6 **To Serve:** Pile soft polenta on platter or plate and arrange shanks on top. Pour sauce over meat and garnish with gremolada. Serve.

Vary! Improvise!

☛ *Substitute lamb shanks for veal.*

☛ *Add 1 ounce crushed and peeled garlic cloves to vegetables as they sauté.*

BRAISED STUFFED CABBAGE ROLLS
(POLPETTE DI VERZA)

Pestata is a verb that means to crush, grind, or pound. This purée of aromatics becomes a flavor foundation. The technique works particularly well in long-simmering dishes.

Yields 6 cups stuffing, 12 large rolls, 6 servings

4 ounces Italian country style bread, 2-1/2 cups diced into medium cubes
2 cups warm chicken stock

Pestata

2 ounces pancetta, 1/4 cup diced into 1/2-inch cubes
8 to 9 ounces onion, 1 large, 2 cups diced into 1-inch cubes
4 ounces carrot, 1 large, 1/2 cup, diced into 3/4-inch cubes
2 ounces celery, 1 large rib, 1/4 cup diced into 1-inch cubes
3/4 ounce garlic, 3 large cloves, peeled

Stuffing

3 tablespoons extra-virgin olive oil
1 cup dry white wine
2 pounds loose sweet Italian sausage (or removed from casings)
1 large egg, lightly beaten
1/2 ounce trimmed Italian parsley, 1/4 cup chopped
Optional: 3 ounces Parmigiano-Reggiano, 1/2 cup grated

Cabbage and Sauce

2-1/2 pounds Savoy cabbage, 1 large head
3 tablespoons extra-virgin olive oil
2-1/2 teaspoons kosher salt
1 cup dry white wine
3 to 3-1/2 cups hot chicken stock

Garnish: 1/2 ounce trimmed Italian parsley, 1/4 cup chopped

For Serving

Hot, cooked rice, potatoes, or creamy *Polenta*

1 **Prepare the stuffing:** Place bread into a bowl and pour the stock over it. Soak bread until very soft, about 10 minutes depending on bread. Squeeze stock from bread and place into large mixing bowl. Reserve excess stock; there should be at least 1 cup from squeezing. Reserve; this will be used later for braising.

2 **Prepare pestata:** Place pancetta, onion, carrot, celery, and garlic into food processor. Pulse-grind until meat and vegetables are fine-textured, just short of a purée, to yield about 2 cups.

3 Preheat the oven to 375 degrees F. Fill a 6-quart pot with water, and bring to a boil.

4 **Prepare stuffing:** Pour 3 tablespoons olive oil into a 10- to 12-inch heavy sauté pan or 8-quart Dutch oven, and set over medium-high heat. Stir in half the **pestata**, about 1 cup, and cook, stirring frequently, until it dries and sticks to pan. Season with 1 teaspoon kosher salt, and pour in the white wine. Bring to a boil, and cook until the wine has evaporated completely, but pestata is still moist. Remove pan from heat, and scrape pestata into bowl with soaked bread to cool until lukewarm. Fold in sausage and mix with hands to break up the raw meat. Work in egg, chopped parsley, and optional grated cheese into a loose stuffing. Refrigerate stuffing until needed.

5 **Prepare the cabbage:** Pull off and discard bruised or torn outer leaves. Remove core of cabbage, and separate 12 of the largest leaves from the head. Keep them whole. Lay each leaf flat with outer side up. Shave off the raised ridge of the rib at the leaf base with a sharp paring knife. (This may also be done after blanching the leaves.) Finely dice some of the remaining cabbage leaves to fill 4 cups, and set aside. Drop the whole leaves into the boiling water, and blanch until soft and tender, 3 to 4 minutes. Drain leaves, and pat dry.

6 **Prepare the sauce:** Return the sauté pan or Dutch oven to the stove. Pour in 3 tablespoons olive oil and heat over medium-high heat. Stir in remaining **pestata**, and cook until it begins to stick, about 4 minutes. Toss in reserved diced cabbage and 2 teaspoons kosher salt. Stir and cook cabbage until wilted, 5 minutes. Pour in white wine, raise the heat, and bring to a boil. Lower heat and simmer the sauce 10 minutes. Scrape sauce into half hotel pan or leave in Dutch oven.

7 **Construct cabbage rolls:** Lay out each softened leaf with its shaved rib side down. Form 1/2 cup stuffing into a plump log, and lay it in the middle of the bottom of the leaf. Roll the bottom of the leaf over the filling, tuck the sides in, and roll up tightly the rest of the way.

8 Fit rolls snugly into the half hotel pan or Dutch oven, seam side down, on top of the sauce. Measure reserved stock and add enough fresh stock to make 4 cups; pour over rolls. The rolls should be almost submerged. Bring pan or Dutch oven to a boil, and cover with foil or lid. Set pan or Dutch oven into the oven to braise 1 hour.

9 Remove lid, and gently push rolls down into sauce. Bake, uncovered, until sauce and reduced and tops of rolls are lightly browned, 20 to 30 minutes.

10 **To Serve:** Place 1 or 2 rolls in warmed, flat soup bowl. Spoon some sauce over top and garnish rolls with parsley. Serve with rice, potatoes, or polenta.

Source: *Lidia Cooks from the Heart of Italy* by Lidia Bastianich.

INVOLTINI AND BRACIOLE

Involtini and the southern *braciole* are thin slices of meats like beef, veal, or pork that are stuffed and rolled. In the rest of Italy "braciole" simply means "slices of meat." Cooks insert a toothpick through the rolls so they hold together during browning and braising. A classic involtini is thinly sliced and pounded veal or beef rolled with prosciutto and sage.

Other rolled foods include:

- *Cabbage* stuffed with meat and rice simmered in tomato sauce or meat broth
- Roasted *red bell peppers* rolled around puréed tuna, capers, anchovies, and olive oil
- Browned *eggplant* stuffed with ricotta, herbs, and pecorino
- *Swordfish fillets* with breadcrumbs, olive, capers garlic, and parsley

FIGURE 6.28　Involtini di melanzane.
Source: SCPixBit/Fotolia.

Poaching in Italy

Poaching enjoys popularity in Italy and Spain as it does in France. See chapter *France* for *Poaching Technique*. Old Roman recipes reveal that ancient Italians prepared dishes like pheasant dumplings poached in water seasoned with *garum* (a liquid similar to fish sauce).

SARDINIAN POACHED STUFFED CHICKEN (POLLO RIPIENO)

The broth from this dish is sometimes used to poach walnut-sized meatballs, which are served with the chicken and stuffing. The broth may also be used to prepare a meatball and pasta soup, which Sardinians serve as a first course or primo. The use of raisins and spices in this savory dish shows the Arabic-Moroccan influence in Sardinia.

Yields about 3-1/2 quarts broth, 6 servings

Three 1-3/4 to 2 pound Cornish game hens

Stuffing

Yields about 2 cups

4-1/4 ounces raisins, 3/4 cup
1/2 teaspoon saffron threads
3 ounces dry, coarse breadcrumbs, 1 cup
1-1/2 ounces coarsely chopped walnuts, 1/3 cup
3 tablespoons unsalted butter, room temperature
1 teaspoon honey *or* 2 teaspoons sugar
1/2 teaspoon ground cinnamon
Zest of 1 lemon, about 1-1/2 teaspoons, lemon cut into 6 wedges and reserved
1 large egg, about 1/4 cup whisked

2 to 3 ounces celery, 1 medium stalk, 1/3 to 1/2 cup trimmed and diced into 1/4-inch cubes
6 to 7 ounces onion, 1 medium, 1-1/2 cups peeled and diced into 1/4-inch cubes
4 to 5 ounces carrot, 1 medium, 3/4 to 1 cup peeled and diced into 1/4-inch cubes
1-1/2 ounces oil-packed sun-dried tomatoes, 1/4 cup diced into 1/4-inch cubes
1/4 ounce Italian parsley, 2 large sprigs
1/4 ounce whole mint sprigs, 2 large

Garnish

1/4 ounce trimmed Italian parsley, 2 tablespoons chopped
1/2 ounce mint leaves, 4 tablespoons finely sliced, *divided*

1 Rinse hens in cold water, drain, and pat dry with paper towels.

2 **Prepare the stuffing:** Place raisins in a small bowl and cover with 1 cup hot water. In another small bowl, mix saffron with 2 tablespoons hot water. Set both aside 10 minutes. In a large mixing bowl rub together breadcrumbs, walnuts, and butter with fingers. Mix in honey or sugar, cinnamon, and lemon zest. Drain raisins, and reserve water. Fold raisins and the saffron-water into the stuffing. Season with freshly ground pepper and 3/4 teaspoon kosher salt. Whisk egg with 1/4 cup raisin-soaking water and mix into stuffing. Add up to 1/4 cup more raisin-soaking water to yield a moist stuffing that will hold together.

3 **Stuff the bird:** Pack a 1/2-cup dry measure with stuffing and invert onto palm of a hand. Place stuffing into body cavity of one bird. Repeat with two remaining birds. Divide remaining 1/2 cup stuffing, form into balls, and pack into neck cavities. With thread and needle, sew cavities closed. Unfold cheesecloth to a single layer and cut a 32-inch square. Set aside.

4 **Poach the birds:** Scatter celery, onion, carrot, tomatoes, and herbs around the bottom of an 8- to 10-quart Dutch oven or heavy pot with 11- to 12-inch diameter. Drape cheesecloth on top of the vegetables with edges hanging out of pot. Wedge birds in the center of the cheesecloth, bring up two opposite corners of the cheesecloth and tie together loosely; repeat with remaining two corners. Cover birds with 3 quarts cold water; it should fully cover them. Bring to a boil over medium heat. Reduce heat, partially cover pot, and simmer birds at a low bubble until an instant-read thermometer inserted into the stuffing in the cavity reads 165 degrees F, 1 to 1-1/4 hours.

5 Lift birds in cheesecloth from pot, drain, and transfer to a hotel pan. Remove cheesecloth, squeeze lightly, and discard. Cool chickens slightly, and remove thread. Slice chickens in half, cover, and keep warm. Remove parsley and mint sprigs from broth and skim away excess fat. Taste broth and season with salt and pepper.

6 **To Serve:** Ladle hot broth into soup bowls, and **garnish** with parsley and half the mint. Serve soup as the first course with lemon wedges to squeeze into soup. Place chicken halves on warm platter and garnish with remaining mint. Serve as the second course.

Source: *Italian Slow and Savory* by Joyce Goldstein.

Vary! Improvise!

☞ *Roasted Stuffed Hens: Preheat oven to 400 degrees F. Stuff just the body cavities of four hens with 1/2 cup stuffing each. Truss hens and place in baking pan. Roast hens until browned, 20 minutes, and lower heat to 350 degrees F. Roast until internal temperature reaches 165 degrees F, about 1 hour longer.*

FIGURE 6.29 Fresh halibut poached in crazy water (ippoglosso aqua pazza).

FRESH HALIBUT POACHED IN CRAZY WATER (IPPOGLOSSO AQUA PAZZA)

Chef Rina Tonon of Café Cortina in Detroit learned this dish from her family on the Italian island of Ponza. It's 40 miles off the coast between Rome and Naples and the namesake of a small archipelago called the Pontine Islands. Once dubbed the "Pearl of Rome," this small island was a summer retreat for the ruling elite. If serving the fish with the crazy water, precision cut the vegetables.

4 servings

Crazy Water Court-Bouillon

Yields about 5 cups

1 cup white wine
4 ounces onion, 1 small, 1 cup slivered
3 to 4 ounces carrot, 1 medium, about 1/2 cup sliced
3 ounces fennel stalks, 1/2 cup trimmed and sliced
2 ounces celery, 1/4 cup trimmed and finely diced
Zest of 1 organic lemon *and* juice of 1/2 lemon
1 large bay leaf
5 stems Italian parsley
Optional: 1 sprig thyme

Four 5-ounce halibut fillets

Battuto

Yields about 1/2 cup or 4 fluid ounces

1 tablespoon finely chopped Italian parsley
1 teaspoon chopped mint leaves
1 teaspoon chopped tarragon leaves
1/2 teaspoon minced garlic
1 tablespoon drained and chopped pickled pepperocini
1/4 teaspoon hot red chili flakes
1 large lemon, 2 to 3 tablespoons fresh lemon juice
2 tablespoons extra virgin olive oil
4 slices country bread
1/4 ounce garlic, 1 large clove peeled and halved lengthwise

1 Pour 1 quart cold water and **crazy water court-bouillon** ingredients: wine, vegetables, lemon zest and juice, bay leaf, parsley stems, and optional thyme, into covered 4-quart saucepan. Bring to a boil, lower heat, and simmer 20 minutes. Remove pan from heat and steep 10 minutes.

2 Season fish with salt, and rest 15 minutes at room temperature before poaching.

3 Mix together **battuto** ingredients in small bowl. Season with salt. Set aside.

4 Strain court-bouillon and pour into 10- to 11-inch high-sided sauté pan that will fit the fish in one layer. Place fish into court-bouillon; it should cover or almost cover the fish. Bring to a simmer and poach fish until cooked through. It should flake when probed with the tip of a knife, 5 to 8 minutes.

5 Grill or toast bread slices. Rub with garlic clove.

6 **To Serve:** Carefully remove fish fillets with flat spatula. Don't break them. Place fish into serving bowls or flat soup plate. Divide battuto equally and spoon on top of fish. If desired, ladle hot court-bouillon with vegetables around fish. Serve with grilled or toasted bread.

Source: Rina Tonon, *Hour Detroit* magazine, April 2009.

Vary! Improvise!

☞ *The battuto is startlingly good on most fish, even canned—try it on other seafood like salmon.*

☞ *After straining court-bouillon, simmer 1/2 cup slivered fennel bulb and 1 small carrot, finely sliced, until tender.*

Stuffed Pasta (Pasta Ripiena)

Stuffings for pasta can be meat, vegetable, or fish-based, and may include a creamy cheese such as ricotta. *Ravioli* are the classic stuffed pasta made from Emilia-Romagna in the north to Sardinia in the south, but *tortelli, agnolotti, cannelloni,* and *panzarotti* are popular too. The technique doesn't change much around Italy, but the shapes and fillings do. The basic shapes for large and small stuffed pastas fall into less than a dozen types—but with head-spinning variation: *square, triangular, round, half round, half round with ends pinched* together (*cappelletti*), *oblong, oblong with twisted ends,* and *open-ended logs* (*cannelloni*).

MEAT STUFFED AGNOLOTTI

This is a classic meat-based filling from Piemonte (Piedmonte) in northern Italy. Make it with left-over cooked lean meat or sausage.

Yields about 3-1/4 to 3-1/2 cups filling; 28 ounces weight, about
130 to 150 agnolotti

---

16 to 18 ounces trimmed boneless pork shoulder
2 tablespoons extra virgin olive oil or butter
3 ounces onion or leek, 1/2 cup peeled or trimmed and minced onion or leek, white only
4 ounces carrot, 1/2 cup peeled and finely diced
3 ounces celery, 1/2 cup trimmed and finely diced
1 teaspoon chopped fresh thyme leaves
1/2 cup white wine
10 ounces frozen chopped spinach, 3/4 to 1 cup thawed and squeezed dry
1 large egg
1/2 ounce trimmed Italian parsley, 1/4 cup finely chopped
1 recipe *Signature Technique: Handmade Pasta Dough* (made in food processor)

For Serving

Sauce of choice: herb butter, tomato or butter and cheese

1 Preheat oven to 375 degrees F. Place pork on baking pan and oil meat. Place pan in oven and roast pork until it measures 145 degrees F internal temperature. Remove from oven and cool. Remove excess fat and dice meat finely to yield 2-1/2 to 3 cups.

2 **Prepare filling:** Heat olive oil in 10-inch skillet over medium heat. Add onion or leek, carrot, celery, and thyme. Cook vegetables until soft and beginning to brown. Deglaze with white wine and cook until almost dry. Stir in meat and scrape mixture into bowl to cool. Scrape meat and vegetable mixture into a food processor, purée it with spinach, egg, and parsley until smooth. Taste filling and season with salt and pepper. Scrape stuffing into piping bag fitted with 1/2-inch plain tip.

3 See *Fresh Pasta Rolling Protocol*. Divide (firm) pasta into 4 equal pieces. Roll each quarter into two equal sheets on thinnest or next to the thinnest setting, flouring lightly as necessary to keep dough from sticking. Sheets should be about 5-1/2 to 6 inches wide and around 17 inches long. Dough should be slightly moist on up side so the dough sticks together when folded. If not, lightly spray with water.

4 On both sides of the long edge of one 5-1/2- to 6-inch-wide sheet of pasta, 1 inch in from edge and evenly spaced with 3/8 to 1/2 inch (the width of an index or baby finger) between filling blobs: squeeze 1 rounded teaspoon, 1-inch blobs of filling (each weighing about 1/5 ounce). Roll edge over filling toward the center, and seal each by "burping" and pressing in between each blob of filling with floured fingers. Repeat with opposite side.

5 Cut a straight line lengthwise down the center. Cut each agnolotti free by cutting crosswise with pasta cutter. Press edges of agnolotti to secure and place them, not touching, on a lightly floured sheet pan. Cover with a towel until ready to cook. (Agnolotti maybe frozen in one layer on a sheet pan at this point and placed into a freezer container. To cook: Place agnolotti straight from freezer into boiling water.)

6 **To Serve:** Bring 8 quarts water to boil with 2 tablespoons kosher salt. Boil agnolotti until al dente, 2 to 3 minutes. Remove with slotted spoon into bowl and toss with **sauce of choice**. Serve immediately.

Vary! Improvise!

☛ *Prepare filling with 1 pound of any sort of cooked meat, liver, fish, or poultry.*

☛ *Roll extra pasta into thin sheets and cut into fettuccine.*

☛ *Cut out 2-inch circles from dough, place a blob of filling in center, fold in half, and seal edges.*

FIGURE 6.30 Meat stuffed agnolotti procedure.

Signature Technique: Cooking Pasta

An exchange student in Italy in the 1970s watched her new "mother" busily cooking dinner and offered to help. Her "mother" eyed the young American suspiciously, but told her she could cook the pasta. The student boiled water and tossed in dry pasta. When it was done she was about to pour it into a colander; her "mother" came over to test the pasta. Mom took one bite, hauled the large pot over to the window, and tossed its entire contents out onto the street! The student's Italian culinary training had begun.

Dry Pasta

- Use 4 to 6 quarts cold water per pound of dry pasta. Bring it to a strong boil before adding pasta. Cover the pot to bring the water to boil quicker. Salt the water after it boils.

- Don't waste precious olive oil in the water. Oil in water does not keep the pasta from sticking, but it does keep the foam down. Sauce hot pasta immediately or drizzle oil or butter and toss after it drains to keep it from sticking.

- Stir whole pasta into water. Italians prefer long strands of pasta. Bring water to a boil again and stir occasionally to keep pasta from sticking to the pot and to separate strands. Do not cover pot. Maintain a moderate boil.

- Start timing when the water returns to a boil. Most dry pasta cooks in 8 to 12 minutes.

- Italians prefer pasta with an almost crunchy bite, but Americans prefer it slightly more cooked. To experience *al dente*, which means "to the tooth," bite on a strand of pasta: there should be some resistance and pasta should be chewy but not soft, when bitten. To watch al dente form, cut open a strand of spaghetti after boiling 6, 8, and 12 minutes. When a pinprick of uncooked pasta remains, it's done.

- Be quick to drain the pasta. Leave pasta slightly moist. Don't rinse cooked pasta unless it's specified in a recipe—as for pasta salad. For some dishes, cooks toss slightly undercooked pasta into hot sauce to finish cooking. The simmering helps pasta to absorb flavor. Dry pasta about doubles in weight after cooking.

- Toss al dente pasta into a bowl and moisten with sauce, but don't over-sauce. Italians do not drown pasta in sauce. They toss pasta with just enough sauce to coat it without the sauce pooling on the bottom of the serving vessel. Use the pasta cooking water to moisten a sauce that's too dry or to warm a serving bowl.

- A good pasta dish should wait for no one. Serve now.

Fresh Pasta

- For each pound of fresh pasta, bring 6 to 8 quarts salted water to a moderate boil.

- Shake excess flour off pasta and place into boiling water. Stir pasta gently and maintain heat at a moderate boil. Thin pasta takes 1 to 2 minutes; thick pasta takes 2 to 4 minutes.

- If cooking frozen fresh pasta like ravioli, don't thaw. Toss directly into boiling water and cook 30 to 60 seconds longer or more. Test one to be sure.

- Drain pasta. Toss with or into sauce (see above).

Signature Technique: Gnocchi

Although there are many ways to prepare gnocchi, the most common are with potato (and flour or breadcrumbs), flour alone, cooked polenta, ricotta (and flour or dry breadcrumbs), and squash (with ricotta or flour and/or breadcrumbs). Egg is optional. Gnocchi, literally meaning "dumpling," can also be made with other flours like potato, semolina, chestnut flour, or chickpea flour.

Potato Gnocchi

- Use the proper potato. Italians use all-purpose or boiling potatoes. They fall in between new potatoes and baking potatoes: Yukon Gold and Yellow Finn are excellent and russets are fine.

- Do not overcook the potato. Use a cake tester to probe for doneness. Baking or microwaving the potato is a drier method; boiling potatoes whole is the traditional method. Cooking time will vary from 40 to 60 minutes depending on method used. Rice potatoes through food mill; do not purée in food processor, which will make them gummy. Use potatoes immediately while they are still very warm.

- Potatoes should be hot when adding flour—it reduces the amount of flour needed. Add as much flour as necessary for a moist dough that holds together when rolled into a snake. When mixing dough and flour, regularly scrape up dough stuck to the board and incorporate. Dust hands and work surface lightly to keep the dough from sticking.

Polenta Gnocchi

- Prepare firm *Polenta* with no more than 3 cups liquid (milk and/or water) per cup of cornmeal.

- Cool slightly and stir in egg yolks and desired cheese. Season with salt and pepper.

- Pour polenta into oiled sheet pan to 1/4-inch thickness. Cool completely. Cut polenta with a 1-inch-diameter round cutter into disks.

- Oil or butter ovenproof baking vessel. Arrange an overlapping (fish scale) layer of polenta disks, pour a small amount of desired sauce over and a little grated or shredded cheese. Arrange a second layer in the same manner and continue until all the polenta disks are used. Finish with cheese on top. Bake in preheated 375 degree F oven until browned, 20 to 30 minutes.

Ricotta Gnocchi

- Use whole milk ricotta. Drain in strainer, if desired. Mix ricotta with grated or shredded cheese and flour or fine, dry breadcrumbs and flour until a light dough forms. It may be slightly sticky. Improvise by seasoning with fresh or dry herbs, spices, pesto, lemon zest, or porcini dust.

- Handle ricotta gnocchi carefully. They tend to be delicate and break easily once cooked.

Winter Squash Gnocchi

- Winter squash gnocchi, because of their high water content are best made with baked squash and flour and/or breadcrumbs and optional egg yolk and seasonings into a softer and stickier dough than potato.

- Instead of rolling the dough into a shape they are best formed with two teaspoons and dropped into boiling water.

1 **Pay Attention:** Gnocchi can easily end up as leaden dough balls. The main aim is to produce gnocchi that come out as light as possible. Pay attention to the dough and develop a feeling for it.

2 **Dry Ingredients:** Moisture is the enemy of gnocchi. Rid ingredients of as much moisture as possible. If adding cooked spinach, squeeze it until very dry. Less moisture means using less flour, which results in lighter gnocchi.

3 **Don't Overwork Dough:** Knead dough lightly until smooth but still slightly sticky; overworking the dough will make it heavy.

4 **Cut Dough:** Divide the dough into four parts. With the palms of the hands, roll each piece into a snake a little less than 1 inch thick. Cut the rope crosswise into 1/2- to 3/4-inch logs. Sprinkle the logs lightly with flour. Dust hands with flour.

5 **To Cook:** Bring at least four quarts of salted water to a boil.

6 **Form Gnocchi:** Hold a fork or ridged wooden gnocchi roller in one hand. Dust a finger or thumb of the other hand with flour. With one log pressed against the tines of the fork or roller, with the finger or thumb, press the dough gently into the fork or roller, rolling it downward along the tines. Gently flip the ball of dough off the fork away from the tip for gnocchi with ridged surfaces on one side and a deep indentation on the other. Either cook gnocchi or freeze immediately.

7 **Test Cook:** Drop a few gnocchi into gently boiling water. This is the test batch. They should rise to the surface after 2 to 4 minutes. If not, give them a gentle stir to loosen off the bottom of the pan. After they rise, scoop out with a wire skimmer or slotted spoon and drain well. Adjust cooking time for remaining gnocchi accordingly.

8 **To Serve:** Slide cooked gnocchi into a pan with a warm sauce or onto a serving platter and spoon sauce (and cheese) over gnocchi.

POTATO GNOCCHI WITH SAGE BUTTER

Many Italians boil potatoes and add eggs to gnocchi. The additional moisture requires more flour and results in heavier gnocchi. This recipe uses starchy potatoes like russets and bakes them, which rids them of excess moisture and gives a lighter, roasted flavor. The eggs are optional and depend entirely on personal taste. Pair gnocchi with Pesto, Salsa Verde, a herbed tomato sauce, or gratinée with Fontina cheese.

Yields 2 pounds dough, about 100 gnocchi, 6 to 8 servings

Gnocchi

2 pounds (preferably organic) baking *or* russet potatoes, scrubbed and dried
Olive oil
6 to 7 ounces all purpose flour, 1-1/4 to 1-1/2 cups
1 teaspoon kosher salt
Optional: 1 to 2 large egg yolks

Sage Butter

3 ounces unsalted butter, 6 tablespoons diced small
12 to 15 fresh large sage leaves, sliced

FIGURE 6.31 Shaping gnocchi with wooden gnocchi board.
Source: uckyo/Fotolia.

About 2 ounces Parmigiano-Reggiano cheese, 1/2 cup freshly shredded

1 **Prepare dough:** Heat oven to 400 degrees F. Rub potatoes with oil and place in oven on baking dish. Bake potatoes until a metal skewer pierces them easily, about 1 hour. Peel hot potatoes (hold on a fork or skewer) and dice. Place potatoes into a food mill and rice while still warm into large mixing bowl. Sprinkle salt over potatoes. While very warm, knead in optional yolks. Sift 1-1/4 cups flour over potatoes. Dust work surface and hands with remaining flour. Knead dough until smooth. Form dough into a thick log. Use immediately.

2 **Form dough:** Cut dough into 4 even pieces about 1/2 pound each. Keep 3 pieces covered. Roll 1 out into an even 25-inch log 1/2- to 3/4-inch wide. Cut log into 1-inch lengths. Holding a wooden gnocchi paddle or fork in one hand, press each gnocchi against the ridged surface. Roll it off with a thumb or index finger to make an indentation in each dumpling.

3 Place gnocchi on a lightly floured baking sheet and cover with a clean, dry towel. Don't let them touch or sit very long. Repeat with remaining dough. (Freeze dumplings not using immediately. No need to thaw. Toss directly into boiling water.)

4 Bring 4 quarts water with 1 tablespoon salt to a rolling boil in a 6-quart pot. In a 12-inch high-sided skillet, heat butter and sage leaves together over medium-low heat until butter begins to bubble and sage leaves wilt, 3 minutes. Remove from heat and set aside.

5 Lower heat under water to a low boil and add 1/3 of the gnocchi. Cook until they float. Pull them off as soon as they surface with a slotted spoon, drain well, and drop into warm sage butter. Repeat with remaining gnocchi.

6 **To Serve:** Immediately transfer gnocchi to serving dish or plates, and sprinkle with freshly shredded or grated Parmigiano-Reggiano cheese and freshly ground pepper.

Source: *Cook's Illustrated.*

Vary! Improvise!

☞ *Ricotta Gnocchi: Knead together 1 pound ricotta cheese, 4 ounces/1 cup shredded Parmigiano-Reggiano or pecorino cheese, salt and pepper, and about 1 cup flour (or about 1/2 cup dry breadcrumbs and flour) until a light dough forms. Divide dough into 4 pieces. Dust with flour. If gnocchi are soft, refrigerate 20 minutes. Roll each piece into 1/2-inch-wide snake. Cut each "snake" into 1-inch lengths and proceed as for potato gnocchi. Pair with a tomato or mushroom sauce or herb butter sauce.*

FARRO: ANCIENT GRAIN

This ancient Tuscan grain is similar to the wheat berry. It was called *puls* and served as gruel to troops of the Roman Empire. Farro is grown near Lucca and around the mountainous Garafagnana region of Tuscany, and in Abruzzo, where cooks boil it like pasta in lots of water. Modern farro has been "pearled" or polished so it cooks in 20 to 30 minutes to al dente: tender but slightly chewy. Cooks prepare cooked farro into farro salad, simmer the cooked grain in soups or stews, or serve it as a pilaf cooked with flavorings. Ground farro (puls) can be made into polenta. Farro has a nutty taste similar to barley that pairs well with roasted butternut squash, roasted chestnuts and sage, or sautéed shallots and mushrooms and toasted hazelnuts.

FIGURE 6.32 Farro.

Soure: Marek/Fotolia.

Italian Rice for Risotto

Arborio is most readily available Italian rice outside Italy. Italians (except Venetians) favor *Canaroli*, the "king of rices." Italians classify risotto rice into three types:

- **Superfino** rice like *Canaroli* and *Arborio*: very starchy and make the creamiest risotto. Canaroli has a fat kernel, and Arborio a longer grain.
- **Fino** and **Semifino** rice like *Vialone Nano* (most popular with the Venetians) is a little smaller.
- **Comune**, the smallest kernel (and the least expensive) rice, generally used in the area where it is grown.

FIGURE 6.33 Arborio rice.
Source: rafer76/Fotolia.

Italian Risotto

Though rice, brought in by Arabs, was first grown in southern Italy, it is the northerners who are known for risotto. Rice cultivation was established in the northern Po valley by the early sixteenth century. The first risotto recipe appeared in print early in the nineteenth century. Risotto is Italy's riff on rice pilaf. Both pilaf and risotto use flavoring devices like sautéed onions or other aromatic vegetables, stocks and broths, and seasonings like herbs or spices, but the similarities end there. Pilaf uses long-grain rice, never stirred, so the rice ends up fluffy and separate. Risotto uses starchy, short-grain rice that it is vigorously stirred throughout cooking to end up with slightly firm rice bound together in a creamy, flavorful sauce.

- **A good risotto depends on the right rice:** No substitutes. It's possible to improvise risotto-style dishes with finely diced potatoes, barley, and even short-grained brown rice, but they are not risotto: risotto is made with Italian rice. Never wash Italian rice. The starch is important to the dish.
- **Choose the condimenti:** Condimenti give individual risotto its character: meat, seafood, cheese, or aromatic vegetables. In spring prepare risotti with shrimp, asparagus, and lemon or spinach and cheese, in summer with zucchini, tomatoes, corn, and basil, and in winter with dried porcini, red wine, rosemary, and cheese.
- **Cut vegetables near the size of a rice kernel or bite-sized:** Rice is the star.
- **Cook them right:** Precook meat and seafood, save juices, and add to the cooking broth, discard shells, and set aside meat to stir in at the end. Peel and thinly slice artichokes and keep in acidulated water (water with fresh lemon juice) until ready for use. Blanch or precook hard or green vegetables for inclusion at end so they don't over or under cook.

SIGNATURE RECIPE

ITALIAN RISOTTO

For 4 to 6 servings

Yields about 8 cups

3 tablespoons fat (olive oil/butter)
4 ounces onion, 1/2 cup peeled and finely diced
Optional: 1/2 cup wine
10-1/2 ounces Arborio or other risotto, 1-1/2 cups
6 cups hot stock *or* liquid
1-1/3 ounces Italian hard cheese, about 1/3 cup shredded

For 2 to 4 servings

Yields about 4 cups

7 ounces Arborio or other risotto rice, 1 cup
3 cups hot stock *or* liquid

For 6 to 8 servings

Yields about 10 cups

14 ounces Arborio or other risotto, 2 cups
6 to 8 cups hot stock or liquid

1 Cook the aromatic vegetable base: Most risotti begin with diced onion cooked in butter or olive oil or a combination of butter and oil. Carrots, leeks, celery, garlic, or mushrooms may come next. Cook vegetables over moderate heat until tender.

2 Heat chicken, beef, fish, or vegetable stock (and mushroom soaking water) in saucepan until boiling: Add spices like saffron to flavor and bloom in the stock. Lower heat to simmer, add a ladle to the pot, and keep it to the side of the risotto cooking pot. Homemade or unsalted canned chicken stock has the best flavor, but vegetable stock, clam juice, or fish stock, mushroom soaking water, or shrimp shell broth are acceptable, depending on risotto's other ingredients.

3 Sauté the rice first: Stir uncooked rice into sautéed aromatic vegetable base and cook 1 minute to harden outside layer of starch on rice. Stir in wine and cook till dry.

4 Stir no more than 1/2 cup hot liquid into rice at a time: When a spoon runs across the bottom of the pot, a clear wake should remain. Keep risotto at an even low boil. (For 1-1/2 cups rice there should be about 11 broth additions in 15 to 20 minutes or about every 2 minutes.)

5 *Stir risotto evenly and constantly* until the stock is almost completely absorbed before the next 1/2-cup increment of stock: Too much liquid and the rice will swim around and won't get enough friction to form its important creaminess.

6 Scrape around edges and bottom of pot: Ladle in 1/2-cup portions of liquid and watch the heat. If the rice seems to be absorbing the liquid too quickly, turn down the heat. If the rice seems to be absorbing liquid too slowly, nudge the heat up. Add water if stock is used up.

7 Keep track of cooking times: Larger kernel superfino rice like Canaroli and Arborio take 25 to 30 minutes to cook while the smaller fino and semifino rice like Vialone Nano take between 20 and 25 minutes. Warm the serving plates.

8 *Stir in garnish vegetables*, and those that will overcook or turn off-color (like spinach, zucchini, green beans, peas, or asparagus) to cook for the last 5 to 10 minutes. Or precook garnish vegetables by grilling, sautéing, blanching, or steaming. Add them at the very end to retain color and texture.

9 Taste the risotto, and season with salt and pepper. The risotto is finished when a spoonful of it is creamy, well-seasoned and the rice still offers some resistance to the tooth. The rice should not be crunchy or mushy but somewhere in between. Risotto should be little wetter and looser than when it is served; risotto cools as it thickens.

10 Fold in garnishes: cooked seafood, vegetables, butter, cheese, oil, pesto, or fresh herbs.

11 Serve risotto immediately—on preheated plates. Give guests the 5-minute warning and have them at the table when the risotto is ladled. Because of its creamy starch, this dish is best served hot. It will harden into a paste and the rice kernels will lose texture.

Nontraditional but Faster Risotto

It's certainly not traditional, but in *The New Italian Cooking*, authors Franco and Margaret Romagnoli have found that a pressure cooker can be used to prepare an acceptable risotto. Cook the soffritto as usual in the bottom of a pressure cooker, add rice, wine, and all but 1/2 cup broth. Seal pressure cooker with lid, and bring pressure to high. Cook 8 minutes, run cooker under cold water, and remove lid. Over low heat, stir in final garnishes and 1/2 cup hot broth. Stir briskly to create starchiness and finish cooking.

Risotto Ahead

Italian chefs cook risotto 12 to 14 minutes, spread it out to a thin layer in a sheet pan and place in freezer to chill down immediately then refrigerate in serving portions. When an order comes in the risotto portion goes into a little olive oil or butter and is finished with hot broth until done.

Vary! Improvise!

☛ **Mushroom Risotto (Risotto con Funghi):** *1/2 ounce dried porcini, soaked; 2 cups diced onion, 1 tablespoon minced garlic, 8 ounces sliced mushrooms, 1-1/2 to 2 cups Arborio rice, red or white wine.*

☛ *Prepare risotto with solidly good combinations:*

* *lamb, artichoke hearts, and lemon*
* *roasted vegetables*
* *asparagus and shrimp*

Easy Bake Polenta

Los Angeles Times food writer Russ Parsons shares an easy way to prepare polenta: Preheat an oven to 350 degrees F. Pour water (4 cups water per cup of polenta cornmeal) into a wide 4- to 5-quart ovenproof pan and whisk in polenta and butter. Bake polenta uncovered for 1 hour and 20 minutes. Stir the polenta after 40 minutes and place back in oven, stir again after 40 minutes, and continue to bake 10 minutes longer. Before serving, remove pan from oven, cover, and rest the polenta 5 minutes. Stir in grated cheese or more butter as desired. Season with salt and pepper to taste.

FIGURE 6.34 Polenta (Italian cornmeal).
Source: Comugnero Silvana/Fotolia.

CREAMY RICE FROM MILAN (RISOTTO ALLA MILANESE)

Risotto alla Milanese from is the northern city of Milan. Saffron gives this risotto its distinctive golden color. Traditionally it also contained ox bone marrow, which butter has now replaced. Colorful, spiced dishes, designed to impress the rich and powerful, were popular with medieval Europeans; they show an Arab influence.

Yields about 8 cups, 4 to 6 servings

4 tablespoons butter, *divided*
1 tablespoon extra virgin olive oil
4 to 5 ounces onion, 1 cup peeled and finely diced
6 cups chicken stock
1/4 teaspoon crumbled saffron
10-1/2 ounces Arborio, Canaroli, or other short-grain Italian risotto rice, 1-1/2 cups
About 4 ounces Parmigiano-Reggiano cheese, 1 cup freshly shredded

1 Heat 2 tablespoons butter and olive oil in 6-quart pot. Cook onion over medium heat until tender and golden.

2 Heat chicken stock in small covered saucepan over low heat. Place a ladle nearby. Mix saffron in small bowl with 1/2 cup hot broth; set aside.

3 Stir rice into sautéed onion base and cook over medium heat 1 minute to harden outside layer of starch on rice. Stir in wine and cook until dry.

4 Stir no more than 1/2 cup hot liquid into rice at a time. Don't forget the saffron broth. When a spoon is run across the bottom of the pot, a clear wake should remain. Keep risotto at an even low boil over medium to medium-low heat. Keep track of cooking times. Larger kernel superfino rice like Canaroli and Arborio take 25 to 30 minutes to cook while the smaller fino and semifino rice like Vialone Nano take between 20 and 25 minutes.

5 Stir risotto *evenly and constantly* until the broth is almost completely absorbed before the next 1/2-cup increment of broth. Too much liquid and the rice will swim around and won't get enough friction to form its important creaminess. If the rice seems to be absorbing the liquid too quickly, turn down the heat. If the rice seems to be absorbing liquid too slowly, nudge the heat up.

6 Warm the serving plates.

7 Taste the risotto and season with salt and pepper. The risotto is finished when a spoonful of it is creamy, well-seasoned and the rice still offers some resistance to the tooth. The rice should not be crunchy or mushy but somewhere in between. Risotto should be little wetter and looser—as risotto cools it will thicken.

8 **To Serve:** Fold in remaining butter. Serve risotto *immediately* on warm plates topped with cheese or in a serving bowl on the side. Give guests a 5-minute warning and have them at the table when risotto is ladled. Serve immediately while hot.

SIGNATURE RECIPE

ITALIAN POLENTA

For authentic Italian polenta, use Italian cornmeal. American cornmeal is too finely ground and results in a polenta with less texture. In large northern Italian and Roman kitchens, there's no time to stand around stirring polenta. Instead, chefs cook a large pot and leave it to simmer all evening. The polenta forms a protective crust on the bottom (which is later discarded), and the remaining polenta stays soft and creamy. The double boiler or slow-cooker method is a good alternative.

For 4 to 6 servings

Yields about 5 cups

5 to 6 ounces polenta cornmeal, 1 cup
3-1/2 to 4 cups water, stock or milk, *divided*
Optional: 2 tablespoons butter

For 8 to 10 servings

Yields about 10 cups

10 to 12 ounces polenta, 2 cups
8 cups water, stock or milk, *divided*
Optional: 4 tablespoons butter

For 12 to 15 servings

Yields about 15 cups

15 to 18 ounces polenta, 3 cups
3 quarts water, stock or milk, *divided*
Optional: 6 tablespoons butter

1   Fit an 11-inch diameter, 6- to 8-quart pot with a stainless steel bowl and lid to make a double boiler that will hold the volume of polenta and liquid. Alternatively use a 6-inch and a 4-inch hotel pan for large volumes. Pour 2 inches water into bottom of pot or hotel pan. It should not touch the bottom of the polenta bowl or top hotel pan. Bring water to a simmer.

2   Fill another saucepan with water or stock. Bring to a boil.

3   For **1 cup of polenta**, measure 3 cups boiling water or stock, or hot milk into top bowl of double boiler or top hotel pan. Do not add salt; it can keep cornmeal from becoming creamy.

4   Whisk polenta into hot liquid. Cover bowl or hotel pan, and simmer polenta until it absorbs all the liquid, about 15 minutes. Stir polenta with a spoon or heatproof spatula and add more liquid as needed: 3-1/2 to 4 cups boiling liquid **per cup dry polenta** is usual for polenta that will be cooled and sliced. Add up to 5 cups boiling liquid **per cup dry polenta** for soft, mashed potato-like polenta.

5   Simmer polenta covered 1 to 1-1/2 hours, stirring occasionally. Polenta should be creamy and taste full-flavored and sweet. It may be held covered over simmering water 30 minutes or longer.

6   To Serve: Stir soft butter or cheese into cooked polenta, and season with salt to taste. Serve immediately, or keep covered and warm in double boiler.

Vary! Improvise!

☞ *Board It:* Italian tradition is to pour polenta onto a board (or platter), cut with a string, and top with tomato sauce, vegetables, or vegetable sauce or meat sauce.

☞ *Polenta Gnocchi:* Pour hot cooked polenta made with milk into an oiled baking dish 1/2-inch thick, spread with wet spatula, cool until firm then cut into rounds. Layer the cutouts with cheese or tomato sauce and bake.

☞ *Polenta Bolognese:* Serve soft polenta topped with Bolognese Sauce.

☞ *Soft Serve Polenta:* Serve soft-cooked polenta with mushroom ragu or Italian lamb shanks.

☞ *Lasagna Polenta:* Prepare polenta, pour in 1/2-inch layers in pan, and cool. Slice into 3-inch squares and stack them to form lasagna on a plate.

☞ *Chestnut or Chickpea:* Prepare polenta with part chickpea or chestnut flour.

☞ *Herb-Fry:* Stir fresh herbs into polenta before it cools into cakes. Slice and fry in oil or butter.

☞ *Polenta Fries:* Spread cooked polenta into greased pan 1/2-inch thick with wet spatula. Chill. Slice into French fry shapes, brush with clarified butter or oil, and bake on parchment covered pan at 450 degrees F until golden, 20 minutes.

☞ *Polenta Croutons:* Cube polenta and sauté until golden in butter or oil or both.

☞ *Polenta Crostini:* Cut out shapes of cooked polenta, slather with oil, and grill. Top with olive purée.

SAUTÉ, PAN-FRY, AND DEEP-FRY

SIGNATURE RECIPE

VEAL MARSALA

This simple recipe is a classic Roman dish that has withstood the test of time. Marsala, a nutty fortified wine, is made in Sicily, but beloved throughout Italy.

Yields about 4 fluid ounces sauce, 2 servings

About 1 to 1-1/4 ounces all-purpose flour, 1/4 cup
9 to 10 ounces veal cutlets *or* scallopini
5 teaspoons olive oil, divided
1/2 ounce shallot, 1 small, 1 tablespoon minced
Optional: 1 ounce cremini mushrooms, 3 small, 1/3 cup halved and thinly sliced
1 cup dry Marsala
1 ounce cold unsalted butter, 2 tablespoons diced
1/8 ounce trimmed Italian parsley, 1 tablespoon chopped

1 Place flour in a shallow bowl. If veal cutlets are thick, butterfly them open. Pound lightly until they are about 1/4-inch thick. Season with salt on both sides.

2 In a 12-inch skillet, heat 4 teaspoons oil over medium heat. When oil is hot, dredge veal in flour and shake off excess. Lay cutlets in hot pan and sauté until golden brown and slightly pink inside, 1 to 3 minutes per side. Remove cutlets and keep warm.

3 Reheat skillet over medium heat and add 1 teaspoon oil. Stir in shallots and optional mushrooms. Cook until soft. Add Marsala to skillet and cook until reduced by half.

4 Remove pan from heat and cool 30 seconds. Whisk in butter and parsley. Taste sauce and season with salt and freshly ground black pepper.

5 **To Serve:** Plate cutlets and spoon sauce over them. Serve immediately.

Vary! Improvise!

☞ *Replace veal with boneless, skinless chicken breasts or slices of pork tenderloin.*

☞ *Cover each cutlet with a sage leaf and prosciutto before sautéing and it's saltimbocca; roll the sage-prosciutto cutlets up before browning, secure with a toothpick, and they're involtini.*

FRIED ZUCCHINI BLOSSOMS

Though Mexican cooks were the first to eat squash blossoms, Italian cooks were probably the first to batter and deep-fry them.

To prepare blossoms for cooking, snap off inside stamens, if desired, and bristly outer leaves at the base. Cut stem to 1 inch and shake out bugs. Store blossoms on a moist paper towel in an airtight container up to one day.

The simplest way to enjoy blossoms: Dip in tempura-style batter. Shallow-fry blossoms on both sides in hot oil until golden. Season with salt. Blossoms stuffed with cheese or meat may be handled the same way or wedged into an oiled pan, covered, and baked at 350 degrees F until tender.

Fritto Misto

Italian *fritto misto*, or mixed fry, can be made with meat, vegetables, shellfish, or fish tossed in flour or a batter and deep-fried in fresh olive oil. Italians everywhere consider fritto misto a refreshing summer dish. Fried calamari is popular.

FRIED CALAMARI

This dish shows off the simple goodness of Italian cooking: a quick dusting of flour and a short dip into hot oil turn calamari into an addiction.

4 to 6 servings

1 pound cleaned squid (calamari)
Vegetable oil for deep-frying
All-purpose flour for dusting
Lemon wedges
    or *Salsa Verde*

1　Slice squid bodies into 3/8-inch wide rings. Slice tentacles blobs in half. Blot squid dry and set aside.

2　Spread flour in a large bowl, set near stove. Line a half-sheet pan with paper towel and set near stove. Pour oil into wok or 4-quart saucepan until about 3 inches deep or preheat deep-fryer. Set a deep-fry thermometer on pan. Heat oil to 365 degrees F.

3　When oil nears temperature, toss a handful of squid in flour, place in strainer, and shake off excess flour. Slide squid into hot oil and fry about 30 seconds. Don't overcook the calamari or they'll turn to rubber. Immediately transfer fried calamari to sheet pan and sprinkle with salt.

4　**To Serve:** Pile warm calamari on serving plates or platter. Serve with lemon wedges or *Salsa Verde.*

FIGURE 6.36　Fried calamari.
Source: littleny/Fotolia.

Deep-Fried Risotto Croquettes (Arancini)

Though many Italians won't eat leftovers, leftover risotto never goes to waste. It is transformed into the deep-fried, stuffed Italian rice croquette snack known as *riso di arancini.* Cooks mix cold rice with eggs, Parmigiano cheese, parsley, and sautéed garlic. They form balls with the rice mixture and stuff each with a cube of mozzarella and sometimes prosciutto. The balls go into beaten egg and breadcrumbs, are fried in olive oil, and served with marinara sauce.

FIGURE 6.35　Cheese-filled arancini.
Source: msheldrake/Fotolia.

Pan-Toasted Breadcrumbs

Toasted breadcrumbs are the ideal crunchy addition or garnish for pastas and vegetables. Use them in place of cheese. Here's how to prepare 1-1/3 cups:

Heat 4 tablespoons olive oil in a 12-inch skillet over medium heat. Stir in 1-1/2 cups fresh breadcrumbs (made from about 3 ounces country-style bread with crusts). Stir constantly, and cook until the crumbs turn golden and crunchy, 5 to 8 minutes.

GRILL, GRIDDLE, ROAST, BROIL, BAKE, AND BARBECUE

ITALIAN GRILLED OR BROILED FISH

Some of the best seafood comes from the northeastern Italian coast, along the Adriatic, and from Sardinia in the south. Grilling or broiling is a simple, fast, and flavorful way to serve fish that was alive just hours ago. In Sicily and Calabria swordfish is typically cubed, marinated, skewered, grilled, and served with salmoriglio. These two methods come from Marcella Hazan.

Flavor-Marinating Before Cooking

One pound of fish steaks, large fillets, skinned and boned thin fillets, fish steaks, or paillards
2 to 3 teaspoons olive oil
1/2 teaspoon finely chopped rosemary leaves
2 to 3 teaspoons fresh lemon juice
Optional: 1 teaspoon lemon zest

1 Rub raw edges of fish steaks or top of fillet (with skin attached) with olive oil, sprinkle with salt and finely chopped herbs, and drizzle with freshly squeezed lemon juice (and lemon zest). Allow fish to marinate 15 to 20 minutes.

2 Grill or broil fish over moderate heat until tender and opaque, 5 to 8 minutes depending on thickness of fish.

3 **To Serve:** Season with salt, pepper, and more lemon juice, if desired.

Salmoriglio: Marinade-Sauce After Cooking

This sauce is good on lamb as well as fish.

Sauce

1 tablespoon kosher salt
3 to 4 teaspoons freshly squeezed lemon juice
1/2 teaspoon dried, crushed oregano leaves
or 1 tablespoon minced fresh oregano leaves
3 to 4 teaspoons olive oil, more to taste

One pound of fish steaks, large fillets, skinned and boned thin fillets, fish steaks, or paillards

Olive oil for rubbing fish

1 Whisk together **sauce** ingredients.

2 Slice thick salmon fillets into 1/4- to 1/2-inch thick paillards or dice swordfish or tuna into 1-inch cubes, rub with olive oil, sprinkle with a little salt. If grilling, place fish slices in grilling basket or on fine grilling grate and thread cubes onto skewers.

3 Grill or broil fish until done on first side, 2 to 3 minutes and flip to finish cooking remaining side.

4 **To Serve:** Arrange fish on platter and gently poke fillets. Spoon **sauce** over. Serve hot.

Chianina Bistecca Alla Fiorentina

In Tuscany, *bistecca alla Fiorentina* (T-bone or Porterhouse steak) is a popular dish; the steak is brushed with plain olive oil, seasoned with salt and pepper, and grilled. A squeeze of fresh lemon juice is the only garnish. The meat comes from the prized and ancient *Chianina* (*key-ah-nina*) oxen, which are lean, tasty, have extensive, well-defined muscling, and grow quickly. The steaks are aged to develop complex flavor; they are never cooked more than rare or medium-rare (about 125 degrees F). To approximate bistecca alla Fiorentina, start with naturally raised or grass-fed beef without hormones or antibiotics. Look for a richly marbled, dry-aged steak cut 2-1/2- to 3 inches thick. The outside of the thick steak will sear well on the hot grill while the inside stays rare and tender. Rest it 5 to 10 minutes before serving.

FIGURE 6.37 Chianina cow of the Tuscan maremma.

Source: cristal/Shutterstock.

REVIEW: GRILLING

1. Get into the habit of cleaning grill grates and lids religiously with a rag dipped in oil and a wire-bristled brush. Dirty grates stick and leave food tasting like last week's meal.

2. Most grill experts recommend wood-based charcoal. Petroleum-based coal leaves a gasoline aftertaste. When coals are covered with a gray ash, level them and replace the grate and preheat it 5 minutes. A gas grill should preheat with lid down on high 15 minutes. Lightly oil clean grate with paper towel dipped in vegetable oil.
   Direct or Indirect Cooking: Direct heat cooks food directly over the heat source. For indirect heat cooking, move coals to the outer perimeter of grill or to two sides, and place a heatproof pan (aluminum) in the center of coals to catch drippings. Place food over pan and cover grill. Indirect cooking is perfect for slow roast-grilling large pieces like a whole turkey

or chicken into perfect smoked tenderness.
   To check the temperature of your grill, hold your hand 5 inches above cooking grate:

   Hot will take 2 seconds to pain.
   Medium-hot will take 3 to 4 seconds.
   Medium will take 5 to 6 seconds.
   Medium-low will take 7 seconds.

3. Prep ahead and have everything necessary on a nearby table: charcoal, chimney starter, long-handled tongs and spatula, spray bottle with water, clean platters, brushes, large fork, instant-read thermometer, oiled paper toweling, prepped food, seasonings like salt and pepper.

4. Since the surface of food cooks quickly, the food should be tender, thin cuts. Foods for broiling and grilling can be marinated or brined to increase moisture and flavor.

5. Remove food from refrigerator 30 minutes before cooking. Cold

food sticks more readily and cooks unevenly. For rare tuna or beef, freeze fish, steaks, or burgers 15 to 20 minutes so they stay cold and rare in the center while the outside browns.

6. To prevent flare-ups: trim excess fats from meat and scrape excess off marinades back into pan. Blot just-washed food dry. Oil food lightly to keep it moist.

7. Salt meat on both sides just before it goes on the grill. Salt-brine or marinate poultry for flavor, texture, and juiciness.

8. To create grill marks, don't move food until it is seared and releases naturally, about 2 minutes. Rotate food 45 degrees to create crosshatch.

9. Don't press and flip food often. Have patience and pay attention. Rest meat after grilling to allow outer heat to equalize throughout the food, and to finish cooking.

MEAT THICKNESS	INCHES FROM HEAT	DEGREE OF DONENESS
	Rare/Medium	
1/2 to 3/4 inches	1	3 to 4 minutes per side/4 to 5 minutes
1 inch	2	4 to 5 minutes per side/6 to 7 minutes
1-1/2 inches	3	5 to 6 minutes per side/7 to 8 minutes

Home broilers average 500 degrees F. Commercial broilers range from 1,000 F to 1,200 F. To compensate for the difference, leave the door of home broilers ajar when broiling. Determine distance of food from the heat source depending on its thickness. In general, thin cuts of meat, fish, or vegetable should be broiled 1 to 2 inches from the heat source so that they cook quickly and brown. Thicker cuts need to be 3 to 4 inches from the heat source so they may cook through without burning.

Italian Seasonal Grilled Vegetables and Fruits

Seafood is not the only food Italians enjoy grilled. Grilling concentrates the flavor of vegetables and fruits.

- Cut vegetables no more than 1/4- to 1/2-inch thick. Steam or preblanch thicker cuts, or firm vegetables before grilling. Consider carrots, celery, summer squash, bell peppers, eggplant, fennel bulb, corn soaked in husk or on ear, tomatoes, onions, potatoes, cauliflower, mushrooms, and turnips. Coat vegetables with olive or canola oil and salt before grilling over medium heat.
- Consider grilling halved and cored or pitted apples, peaches, plums and pears, whole figs, or slices of pineapple, mango, and bananas. Brush with melted butter. Grill fruit cut side down then flip. Sprinkle with brown sugar and grill until sugar caramelizes and fruit is tender.

RICOTTA AND SPINACH BAKED CANNELLONI

It's possible to prepare this dish without preboiling the pasta. The dough will absorb liquid so the rolls should be covered with a liquid sauce; check periodically and add liquid if needed.

Yields one half hotel pan or 9-inch by 12-inch baking pan, 16 to 20 rolls, 6 to 8 servings

1 recipe *Signature Technique: Handmade Pasta Dough* (some may be leftover)
3-1/2 to 4 cups *Neapolitan Sugo Pummarola* or *Sugo di Pomodoro*

Stuffing

Yields about 4 cups

1 tablespoon butter *or* olive oil
2 to 3 ounces onion, 1/2 cup peeled and finely diced
2 pounds fresh spinach *or* 20 ounces thawed frozen leaf spinach
16 ounces ricotta cheese, 2 cups
2 egg yolks
Grated nutmeg

4 ounces Parmigiano-Reggiano cheese, 1 cup shredded

1 Prepare **pasta dough** and set aside in plastic baggie or plastic wrap. Prepare desired **sugo**. Set aside until needed.

2 Heat butter or oil in small skillet. Stir in onion and cook until soft and transfer to bowl to cool.

3 If using fresh spinach, place spinach into 8-quart pot with 1/4 cup water and bring to a boil. Cover and steam half the spinach, periodically turning it with tongs to cook evenly. Transfer to a strainer

set over a bowl. Repeat with remaining half of spinach. Drain spinach. Place on cutting board and chop finely. Squeeze out excess moisture to yield 2 cups. Cool spinach. If using frozen spinach, thaw overnight in refrigerator or in microwave. Chop and squeeze-drain excess liquid through strainer to yield 2 cups.

4 Mix cooked onion, spinach, ricotta, egg yolks, and nutmeg together. Season filling with salt and pepper to taste. Bring a large pot of water to boil for cooking noodles, and set out a bowl of cold water near the stove.

5 Roll pasta into long, wide, and thin sheets. Lay each on a lightly floured cutting board and cut each sheet into 3-inch by 4-inch squares. Drop pasta rectangles into boiling water and cook 1 minute. Transfer them to cold water 20 seconds, drain, and place on a sheet pan covered with parchment.

6 Preheat oven to 400 degrees F. Oil or butter the bottom of a half hotel pan or 9-inch by 12-inch baking pan. Lay one cooked pasta sheet onto work surface and spread 3 to 4 tablespoons filling along the wider edge and roll up. Repeat with remaining dough. Wedge stuffed cannelloni, seam sides down, into prepared pan.

7 Reheat sauce to near boiling. Pour hot sauce over cannelloni and cover with parchment and aluminum foil (tomato eats through aluminum). Bake until bubbly and very hot, about 20 to 30 minutes. Uncover pan, and sprinkle rolls with cheese. Bake until a golden crust forms, about 15 minutes. Remove pan from oven.

8 **To Serve:** Rest cannelloni 15 minutes before serving. Gently loosen cannelloni and divide into 6 to 8 servings. Serve hot.

Signature Technique: Northern Italian Lasagna

Lasagna is one of Italy's earliest pastas. It makes creative leaps from region to region with fillings from apples, to cinnamon-scented ragú to deep-fried broccoli. Best-known lasagnas might be composed of square to wide, long noodles layered with various fillings then baked. The tastiest lasagnas use homemade fresh, egg-rich dough rolled paper-thin, perhaps layered with Bolognese meat sauce for Lasagna Bolognese or ricotta and meatballs, or a mushroom sauce, then topped with besciamella (béchamel) sauce and baked.

The Essential Elements

Freshly made *Handmade Pasta Dough*
Bolognese Sauce or meat sauce
Besciamella (Béchamel sauce)
Grated cheese

1 Prepare the *Essential Elements*. Roll pasta into wide, long medium-thick sheets.

2 **Cook the fresh noodles:** Set a bowl of ice water next to the stove. Bring a large pot of water to a boil. Stir in salt. Slide a few pasta sheets into the boiling water. Cook until tender, 2 minutes. Transfer noodles to ice water. Drain pasta sheets, and layer on parchment up to 2 hours.

3 **Assemble the lasagna:** Cut all pasta sheets with scissors to fit the pan, measure how many layers they will yield, and set them aside. Lightly butter or oil a cooking vessel. Spread a small amount of sauce on the bottom. The amount of pasta will determine how many layers the lasagna will have. The more layers of pasta, the less sauce and cheese each will use.

4 Cover sauce on bottom of pan with slightly overlapping cooked pasta sheets. If there will be three layers, divide sauce and cheese into three; if four layers, divide sauce and cheese into four. Spread meat or tomato sauce over first layer of pasta. Drizzle with besciamella, and spread evenly with spoon or spatula. Sprinkle with cheese. Top with another layer of pasta. Repeat 2 to 3 times or more ending with sauce, béchamel, and cheese. The assembled lasagna may be prepared up to 1 day before baking or frozen up to 4 months. Bring to room temperature before baking.

5 **To Bake:** Preheat oven to 350 degrees F. Place lasagna on a sheet pan and place in oven. Bake until lasagna browns on top and bubbles at the edges, 45 to 55 minutes. Remove pan from oven and rest lasagna 15 minutes before cutting and serving.

LASAGNA BOLOGNESE

Yields one half hotel pan, 6 to 8 servings

1 recipe (6 cups) *Northern Italian Meat Sauce (Sugo alla Bolognese)*
1/2 to 3/4 recipe (12 to 18 ounces) *Handmade Pasta Dough*
Triple recipe (5 cups) *Italian White Sauce (Besciamella)*
5-1/4 to 6 ounces Parmigiano-Reggiano cheese, 1-1/2 cup freshly grated
1 tablespoon olive oil or unsalted butter

1 Prepare *Northern Italian Meat Sauce (Sugo alla Bolognese),* preferably a day ahead.

2 **On the day of assembling:** Prepare *Handmade Pasta Dough.* Rest dough 20 to 30 minutes. Just before rolling, bring a large pot of water to boil for boiling pasta. Season boiling water with salt.

3 **To roll dough:** Cut dough into two equal pieces. Keep one covered. (The aim will be to roll out dough into wide, long sheets suitable for lasagna.) Flatten one piece of dough into an even rectangle with a rolling pin. Starting on the widest setting, roll dough through once. Fold dough over and roll through widest setting again. Work to shape sheet as evenly rectangular as possible. Repeat the folding and rolling through the widest setting until dough is smooth and squared. Without folding, begin to roll sheets through each successively smaller setting on machine until the second to the last or a medium-thin thickness is reached. Dough should be slightly thicker than the thinnest setting.

4 Place a bowl of cold water and a parchment-covered sheet pan near the stove. Slip pasta sheets into boiling water and boil 1 to 2 minutes. Transfer pasta to cold water, then immediately drain. Lay pasta sheets out on parchment paper. Cut pasta sheets with scissors to fit a 3-inch-deep half hotel pan, and set back onto sheet pan. Measure how many layers the pasta will yield; it should be three or four. If using three layers, each layer will be thicker than if using four pasta layers.

5 Prepare *Besciamella.* Set aside. Grate or shred cheese and set aside.

6 **To assemble lasagna:** Preheat oven to 350 degrees F. Lightly oil or butter bottom and sides of half hotel pan. Spread 1/2 cup sauce on bottom of pan. Proceed with three or four layers of pasta, sauces, and cheese:

Three Thicker Pasta Layers
Cover bottom with first layer of pasta, allowing edges to overlap about 1/2 inch. Spread a scant 2 cups *Meat Sauce* over pasta. Spread 1-1/2 cups *Besciamella* evenly over meat sauce. Sprinkle 1/3 cup cheese evenly over besciamella. Top with second layer of pasta and repeat. Cover with a third layer of pasta and finish with 2 cups besciamella and remaining cheese.

Four Thinner Pasta Layers
Cover bottom with first layer of pasta, allowing edges to overlap about 1/2 inch. Spread 1-1/3 cups *Meat Sauce* over pasta. Spread 1 cup *Besciamella* evenly over meat sauce. Sprinkle 1/3 cup cheese evenly over besciamella. Top with second layer of pasta and repeat. Cover with a third layer of pasta and repeat. *Last Layer:* Cover with a fourth layer of pasta, remaining meat sauce, 2 cups besciamella, and end with 1/2 cup cheese.

7 Place pan in oven and bake until golden and bubbly, 45 to 55 minutes. Remove lasagna from oven and cool 15 minutes to allow it to set before cutting.

Source: *Fine Cooking* and Joyce Goldstein.

Vary! Improvise!

☞ *Sprinkle each layer of meat sauce with red pepper flakes.*

☞ *Substitute another firm or hard cheese like imported Pecorino-Romano or Grana Padano.*

☞ **Vegetarian Lasagna:** *Mix 1-1/2 pounds whole milk ricotta, 20 ounces frozen chopped spinach, thawed and drained (or 2 pounds fresh spinach, cooked and drained), 2 large eggs, and 1/2 cup grated parmesan cheese. Sauté 1/2 cup onion and 1 tablespoon minced garlic until soft. Cool and stir into mixture. Season with 1 teaspoon salt, ground black pepper, and a little nutmeg. Use as a filling along with 4-1/2 to 5 cups Sugo Pummarola or a simple tomato sauce.*

SAVORY BAKED CUSTARDS AND PIES: SFORMATO, TORTA SALATA, AND TORTINO

Savory puddings called *sformati* are popular in Italian kitchens. They begin with besciamella or eggs, milk, and flour to bind puréed vegetables. Sformati are often baked in individual ovenproof cups to a tender custard-like texture, and unmolded. *Torta* are savory pies, and are a specialty of Liguria and Piedmont, but they are also prepared from Rome to Sardinia. Torta may be a one- or two-crusted with a pie or yeast crust and baked tall in a round, springform pan. Like a pie, they are best served at room temperature. When prepared without a crust in a buttered and breadcrumbed baking dish, a torta becomes a *tortino*. Fillings for tortas and tortinos might include cooked Arborio type rice to help thicken. A famous Easter torta includes ricotta cheese, eggs, cheese, and chopped, cooked vegetables.

FIGURE 6.38 Sformato di erbette, an antipasti of the northern region of Trentino Alto Adige.

Source: Comugnero Silvana/Fotolia.

BIG MEATBALLS (POLPETTONE)

All over Italy cooks prepare polpettone—literally "big meatballs." More like a meatloaf, polpettoni are braised (sometimes stuffed) on top of the stove in memorable sauces like tomato or porcini mushroom. Different regions make different types: Bolognese cooks use ground beef, pancetta, cinnamon, and nutmeg, Neapolitan cooks mix ground pork, salame, and mortadella, and stuff polpettone with hard-cooked eggs. Florentines use ground veal and Ligurians make all vegetable polpettoni. See Fred Plotkin's Paradise: Life and Food on the Italian Riviera *for his Ligurian vegetable polpettone.*

Yields 2 medium meat loaves, 8 to 12 servings

3 ounces dried porcini mushrooms, 3 cups
4 ounces stale country style bread crusts removed, 4 thick slices
1 cup whole milk or chicken stock
2 pounds ground lean beef
1 pound lean ground pork
4 ounces prosciutto, 1/2 cup chopped
4 large eggs
Freshly grated nutmeg
1/2 ounce garlic, 2 large cloves, about 1 tablespoon peeled and minced
1 ounce trimmed Italian parsley, 1/2 cup finely chopped
16 ounces onions, 4 cups thinly sliced
1/2 cup olive oil, *divided*
About 3 ounces unbleached all-purpose flour, 2/3 cup
1 cup dry white wine, more as needed
1 cup tomato sauce *or* tomato purée

For Serving

Cooked, soft, warm *Polenta*

1 Soak porcini in 4 cups boiling water until soft 10 to 20 minutes. Drain mushrooms, reserve the liquid, and rinse them lightly to remove any dirt still clinging. Strain liquid through coffee filter, and chop mushrooms coarsely. Place mushrooms back into mushroom liquid. Reserve.

2 Tear bread into small pieces and soak in milk or stock until soft. Place beef, pork, and prosciutto into a large mixing bowl. Mix in eggs, nutmeg, garlic, parsley, 1 tablespoon kosher salt, and freshly ground pepper. Squeeze excess liquid from bread, crumble it, and knead bread into meat well. Divide meat evenly into two large meatballs. Form meat into two compact ovals, like loaves of bread, and set aside.

3 Preheat oven to 350 degree F. Heat an 8-quart heavy pot or Dutch oven over medium heat with 1/4 cup olive oil. Add onions and sweat over medium-low heat until soft, 10 minutes.

4 Heat 12-inch skillet over medium-high heat and add 1/4-cup oil. Spread flour on a sheet pan and roll meatballs in it. Shake off excess. Add meatballs to skillet, and brown on all sides. Move onions aside and transfer both meatballs into 8-quart pot. Cover with onions.

5 Add mushrooms with their soaking liquid to the hot skillet to deglaze. Remove skillet from heat and pour mushrooms and liquid over meatballs and onions. Bring to a boil, lower heat, and cover pot or Dutch oven. Simmer meatballs gently 1 hour, or place in oven to bake 1 to 1-1/2 hours. Add small amounts of water or wine if liquid in pot reduces too far and dries.

6 Uncover pan. Pour tomato sauce over meatballs and simmer until sauce is thickened, 30 to 45 minutes more. Remove pan from oven or stovetop. Cool meatballs to room temperature in sauce.

7 **To Serve:** Remove meatballs and slice as thinly as possible without breaking. Taste sauce and season with salt and pepper. Lay slices artfully on a platter and spoon lukewarm sauce over them. Tuscans eat polpettone at room temperature with soft polenta.

Source: *The Flavors of Tuscany* by Nancy Harmon Jenkins.

STUFFED PORK LOIN WITH ROASTED VEGETABLE AND BALSAMIC SAUCE

Stuffed meat and vegetables are popular in both Italy and Spain. This dish is simple but highly satisfying. Serve it with polenta.

Yields about 5 cups sauce, 6 to 8 servings

14 to 16 ounces carrots, 2 cups trimmed, peeled, and sliced 1/4-inch thick diagonally
4 ounces celery, 2 to 3 medium stalks, 1 cup diced into 1-inch lengths
12 ounces red onions, 3 cups peeled and diced into 1-inch cubes
8 ounce leek, 1 large, 1-1/2 cups white and tender green halved lengthwise; sliced into 3/4-inch lengths
1 tablespoon chopped fresh thyme leaves
4 tablespoons olive oil, more as needed
3 pound pork loin with fat cap
2/3 ounce basil, about 12 large leaves, divided
4 ounces thinly sliced prosciutto
4 to 5 tablespoons balsamic vinegar
3 cups chicken stock, more as needed

1 Preheat oven to 400 degrees F. In mixing bowl, toss carrots, celery, onions, leeks, and thyme with olive oil. Pour vegetables (about 9 cups total) into a hotel pan or stainless steel roasting pan, and place in oven to roast until they begin to soften, 20 to 30 minutes.

2 Meanwhile, butterfly pork tenderloin or loin lengthwise, so it lies on work surface, open flat like a book. Season inside of meat with salt and pepper. Lay 6 basil leaves on open loin and lay prosciutto over top of them. Roll to enclose filling. Tie with butcher's string.

3 Lower heat in oven to 350 degrees F. Rub meat with oil if it has no fat cap. Season meat with salt. Place on top of vegetables in hotel pan with fat cap side up. (Alternatively, brown meat first.) Place pork into oven and roast until internal temperature registers 145 to 150 degrees F. If vegetables begin to over-brown, pour 1/2 cup stock on them and give them a stir. Remove meat from pan, place in warm spot, and cover with foil to finish cooking, rest and keep warm while sauce is made.

4 Test vegetables. They should be very soft. If not, continue to roast until tender. Pour 4 tablespoons balsamic vinegar over vegetables and remove from oven. Scrape vegetables into a food processor with 6 basil leaves. Purée until chunky-smooth. Slowly add about 2-1/2 cups hot chicken stock until sauce is spoonable, but still thick like salsa. Adjust flavors with salt, pepper, and more vinegar if necessary, for a slight tang. Scrape sauce into small saucepan.

5 **To Serve:** Heat sauce over low heat. Add more stock as necessary to maintain the desired consistency. Remove strings from warm meat, slice it thinly, and plate or platter it. Spoon sauce over and serve immediately.

Source: Toscana Saporita Cooking School and Sandra Lotte, Viareggio, Italy.

Vary! Improvise!

☛ *Substitute a large turkey breast or 3 pounds boneless, skinless chicken breasts for the pork loin.*

POTATO, ROSEMARY, AND OLIVE FOCACCIA
(FO-KA-CHEE-AH)

The addition of potato gives his focaccia a moist, deep, and satisfying flavor.

Yields one 13-inch by 18-inch commercial half sheet pan, about 3-1/4 pounds dough, 12 servings

Dough

10 to 11 ounces baking potato, washed and dried
   or 6 ounces warm mashed potatoes, 1 cup
1/2 teaspoon vegetable oil
1/4 ounce active dry yeast, 2-1/2 teaspoons
1/2 cup extra virgin olive oil *plus* 2 tablespoons, *divided*
24 to 25 ounces unbleached all-purpose flour, 5 cups spooned into measure and leveled
1 teaspoon salt

Topping

1/4 to 1/3 ounce fresh rosemary leaves, 2 tablespoons coarsely chopped
2-1/2 ounces pitted Kalamata olives, 1/2 cup halved lengthwise
1/4 cup extra virgin olive oil

1   Preheat oven to 400 degrees F. Rub potato with oil. Place in oven and bake potato until tender, about 1 hour. Peel potato. *Alternatively*, steam the potato: Set up steamer basket in 4-quart saucepan with water, and place on medium heat. Peel potato and dice into 1-inch cubes. Rinse and place potato into steamer. Steam potato until very soft, about 10 minutes. Place cooked potato into food mill fitted with a fine blade and "rice" into bowl. Cool hot potato until just warm. Lightly pack potato into 1 cup measure.

2   In the bowl of an electric mixer fitted with dough hook combine yeast, 1 cup warm potato, 2 cups lukewarm water, and 1/2 cup oil. Add flour and salt and mix at low speed for several minutes, scrape down at least once. The dough will be sticky and rough. Remove bowl from mixer, scrape dough off sides and hook, and cover bowl. Let dough rise in a warm spot until doubled, about 45 minutes to 1 hour.

3   Coat a commercial half-sheet pan with remaining 2 tablespoons olive oil. With oiled hands, scrape dough onto sheet pan and press evenly into pan. If dough feels too elastic, let it rest a few minutes and it will soften. Press rosemary and olives evenly into surface of dough. Allow dough to rest in a warm spot 30 minutes. Preheat oven to 425 degrees F.

4   Press fingers lightly into dough at 2-inch intervals. Mix 1/4-cup olive oil with 2 tablespoons water and drizzle across dough. Shake pan to moisten dough evenly. Place pan into oven and bake focaccia until golden, about 25 minutes.

5   Remove pan from oven. Cool focaccia in pan 10 minutes. Loosen edges and transfer focaccia to cutting board. Slice focaccia in half parallel to the longest edge. Slice each half into 1- to 1-1/2-inch wide focaccia fingers. Arrange on platter and serve.

Source: The Institute for Culinary Education.

SALAD AND VEGETABLE METHODS

Salads/Ensalada/Insalata

Italian cooks, like the French, serve green salads after the main course to cleanse the palate. Wine does not pair well with vinegar, so serving salad after the meal makes sense. Although *vinagretas* are popular in Spain and Italy, greens are often just tossed with freshly squeezed lemon or good red or white wine vinegar and olive oil.

ITALIAN THREE COLOR SALAD
(INSALATA TRI-COLORE)

This simple insalata was designed to honor the colors of the Italian flag: green, red, and white. Store leftover clean greens in plastic baggies or large plastic bin with lid, layered with paper towel. Dry greens well before dressing. Soggy greens make poor salads.

Yields about 8 cups, 4 to 8 servings

8 ounces radicchio, 1 medium head, 8 cups torn leaves washed and dried
5 ounces romaine heart, 4 cups torn leaves washed and dried
3 to 4 ounce Belgian endive, 1 small head, 4 cups washed and dried
3 to 4 tablespoons extra virgin olive oil
2 to 3 tablespoons red wine vinegar *or* freshly squeezed lemon juice

1 Tear radicchio and romaine leaves into large bite-sized pieces. Place dry lettuces in bowl.

2 **When ready to serve salad:** Slice endive in half lengthwise. Remove core with a small V-cut and thinly slice endive lengthwise. Toss radicchio, romaine, and endive with olive oil and salt. Toss with red wine vinegar (or fresh lemon juice) to taste. Toss with freshly ground black pepper. Taste and adjust seasonings.

3 **To Serve:** Pile salad on serving plates and serve immediately.

MEDITERRANEAN COOKS LOVE LEFTOVER BREAD

Italian and Spanish cooks eat crusty bread fresh daily. They love their bread so much that, ever thrifty, they have devised many ways to use the leftovers. Day-old bread serves as soup thickener (gazpacho and garlic soup), as toasted or fried croutons for soup or salad, as fresh or dried breadcrumbs to bread fried foods, cubed for the bread salad *panzanella*, and as Spanish *migas*. In addition to panzanella, Tuscans prepare *ribollita*, vegetable soup re-boiled with bread, and *pappa al pomodoro*, puréed tomato bread soup.

SOUTHERN ITALIAN CAPRESE SALAD (INSALATA CAPRESE)

Insalata Caprese, salad meaning in the style of Capri, a small island off the coast of Campania, is a simple salad of sliced fresh mozzarella, tomatoes, and basil drizzled with olive oil. Italians serve Caprese as a first course antipasto and not, as most salads, at the end of a meal. Caprese is made with local fresh buffalo mozzarella, a Campanian specialty. Buffalo mozzarella, best eaten soon after making, doesn't travel well. Substitute fior di latte, a quality cow milk mozzarella.

6 servings

2 pounds ripe tomatoes, 4 large tomatoes
1 pound fresh mozzarella, preferably buffalo milk mozzarella
8 large, fresh basil leaves
Extra virgin olive oil

For Serving

Country bread

1 Slice tomatoes into 1/4-inch-thick rounds and arrange them overlapping on a platter. Slice mozzarella into 1/4-inch-thick rounds. Slide a slice of mozzarella in between each tomato slice.

2 Tear basil leaves into pieces by hand and scatter on top.

3 **To Serve:** Drizzle salad with extra virgin olive oil and season with salt and pepper. Serve with bread.

FIGURE 6.39 An Italian style panzanella.
Source: Erica/Fotolia.

ITALIAN BREAD SALAD (PANZANELLA)

There was panzanella before tomatoes: a sixteenth-century poet described the leftover bread salad and it contained only bread, cucumber, onion, basil, and arugula. Though panzanella is made from stale bread, it doesn't mean that it takes hand-me-down ingredients. This salad, like most of Italian dishes, reflects the quality of its components. The sweeter the tomatoes and cucumbers and the better the bread, the better the outcome. Don't prepare panzanella if winter tomatoes and commercial soft white bread are all that are available. Country bread is the star and summer tomatoes the support.

Yields 6 to 7 cups, 4 servings

5 ounces day-old artisan country bread, 4 cups cubed 3/4-inch
1 pound tomatoes, 2 large, 2 to 3 cups cubed 3/4-inch
1/2 ounce fresh basil leaves, 1/2 cup packed
8 ounces English cucumber, 1-1/3 cups peeled and cubed 1/2-inch
1 ounce sweet red onion, 3 to 4 tablespoons thinly sliced, more to taste
1/2 ounce trimmed Italian parsley, about 1/4 cup chopped
4 tablespoons extra virgin olive oil
2 to 3 tablespoons red wine vinegar

*Slice bread and let it dry for a day. Don't place bread in plastic where it will stay soft and turn moldy. Italian cooks advise drying the bread enough that it crumbles and resembles couscous.

1 **Toast bread:** Italians use day-old salt-free artisan or country bread for panzanella. They don't usually toast it. If only fresh bread is available, toast it to dry and give the salad extra flavor and crunch. Preheat oven to 400 degrees F. Spread bread cubes on half-sheet pan and place in oven. Bake bread until it begins to color, 10 to 12 minutes. Remove pan from oven and cool bread cubes. Gently crumble bread.

2 **Soften bread with tomatoes:** Toss tomatoes and bread into large mixing bowl. Rest them until the bread absorbs tomato juices and softens, 10 to 15 minutes. Some recipes call for soaking bread in water briefly, but water dilutes the flavor of the salad. Tomato juices enhance it.

3 **Fold in remaining ingredients:** Tear basil leaves by hand. Fold basil, cucumber, onion, and parsley into bread and tomatoes. Drizzle olive oil and fold into salad. Season salad with salt, freshly ground pepper, and vinegar to taste. Toss gently. Refrigerate salad or leave at room temperature until ready to serve, no more than 15 to 20 minutes.

4 **To Serve:** Taste salad again, and adjust the seasonings. Pile salad onto serving plate and serve.

SOUTHERN ITALIAN EGGPLANT RELISH (CAPONATA)

Caponata is the sweet-sour Italian version of Spanish pisto Manchego and French ratatouille. The secret of great caponata is the same as great ratatouille: cook each vegetable separately, combine, and rest overnight before serving so flavors can develop.

Yields 4 to 4-1/2 cups, 6 to 8 servings

8 ounces eggplant, 1 medium, 2-1/2 to 3 cups diced 1/2-inch cubes
5 tablespoons olive oil, *divided*, more as needed
4 to 5 ounces onion, 1 cup peeled and finely diced
4 to 5 ounces celery, 1 cup finely diced
8 ounces tomato, 1 large, about 1 cup skinned and diced into 1/2-inch cubes
Optional: 1 anchovy fillet, minced
2 tablespoons red wine vinegar, more to taste
1/2 to 3/4 ounce drained capers, 2 to 3 tablespoons
2-1/2 ounces large green pitted (pimento-stuffed okay) Italian olives, 1/2 cup diced
2-1/2 ounces pitted Kalamata olives, 1/2 cup diced
1/2 ounce trimmed Italian parsley, 1/4 cup chopped

Optional Ingredients

3 ounces red bell pepper, 1/2 medium, 1/2 cup roasted, peeled, seeded, and diced
About 1 ounce toasted pine nuts, 2 tablespoons
About 1 ounce golden raisins, 2 tablespoons

For Serving

Rustic bread toasts

1 Toss diced eggplant with 1 tablespoon kosher salt, and place in a colander to drain, 20 minutes. Rinse eggplant and blot dry.

2 Heat a deep 11- to 12-inch skillet over medium-high heat, and add 3 tablespoons oil. When oil is hot, add eggplant, and sauté until browned and tender. Transfer eggplant to a bowl. Add 2 tablespoons oil to pan, and heat over medium heat. Add onions and cook until tender, 5 to 8 minutes. Add celery and tomatoes with juice (and optional anchovy). Cook until vegetables are tender and tomatoes soften, about 5 minutes. Stir in vinegar and cook 1 minute. Scrape vegetables into bowl with eggplant.

3 Fold in capers, olives and parsley (and **optional ingredients**). Taste caponata and season with salt, pepper, and more vinegar if necessary. Chill overnight for best flavor or rest 1 hour at room temperature.

4 **To Serve:** Bring caponata to room temperature if refrigerated. Eggplant absorbs flavor like pasta, rice, or beans do. Taste and re-season with vinegar, salt, and pepper if necessary. Mound caponata into bowl and serve with slices of toasted rustic bread.

Vary! Improvise!

☞ *Use other seasonal ingredients, but with restraint—this is a simple salad—don't overload it.*

☞ ***Summer Bread Salad:*** *Plums, onion, Italian parsley, arugula, and bread*

☞ ***Winter Bread Salad:*** *Wilted cabbage, carrots, Italian parsley, red onion, and bread*

☞ *Roast ingredients for winter bread salad: butternut squash, red bell peppers, and zucchini*

Vary! Improvise!

☞ *Dice everything into 1/8-inch cubes. Serve caponata piled on top of two-bite crostini toasts.*

☞ *Add 1/2 teaspoon sugar and 1/2 cup water when adding the vinegar, for more sauce texture and sweet-sour flavor.*

☞ *Add torn basil leaves to the relish.*

☞ ***No Nightshade:*** *Substitute zucchini or yellow squash for eggplant.*

Italian Mixed Boiled Vegetables (Bollito Misto di Verdura)

Though boiled vegetables may not sound as appetizing in English, the Italian version of seasonal vegetables properly cooked in chicken broth and served with the robustly primal green sauce might change some minds. Choose from an array of fresh new potatoes, baby onions, carrots, broccoli rabe, asparagus, summer squash, and zucchini. Boil vegetables until tooth-tender and drain. Arrange on large platter artistically and serve with *Italian Green Sauce* or garlic mayonnaise (aioli). Reserve hot broth for another use, or serve it as first course soup.

Vary! Improvise!

☛ **Potatoes and Green Beans:** *Blanch vegetables then sauté with olive oil and garlic; mash and cook potatoes until browned.*

☛ **Southern Italy:** *Along with garlic, sauté 2 tablespoons golden raisins and 2 tablespoons pine nuts. Remove them when golden. Toss with vegetables before serving.*

BLANCHED, SAUTÉED GREEN VEGETABLES (VERDURAS VERDES)

Blanching then sautéing green vegetables with garlic, is a classic Italian and Spanish technique. It's especially good for taming and sweetening strong-flavored vegetables like kale, rapini, or escarole while setting their green color. Though i contorni is the Italian phrase for side dishes, these vegetables will take center stage.

Yields about 4 cups, 4 to 6 servings

2 pounds kale, rapini, broccolini, chicory, or escarole, washed and trimmed, but left whole
3 tablespoons extra virgin olive oil
1/2 ounce garlic, 2 large cloves, 1 tablespoon peeled and sliced thinly
Optional: Dried red chili pepper flakes

1 Bring water to a hard boil. Blanch leafy green vegetables whole. Immerse completely. Don't fill blanching water more than half full of vegetables; too many vegetables will turn them army green. Turn vegetables periodically with tongs so that they cook evenly. Test vegetables with the tip of a knife, by tasting or by pressing a fingernail on the thickest part of the stem. When crisp-tender, the vegetables are done, 3 to 5 minutes. Don't overcook.

2 Refresh vegetables in cold or ice water, and drain by pressing lightly. Slice or dice vegetables or leave them whole (like rapini).

3 **To Serve:** Heat olive oil over medium low heat in a large sauté pan. Add garlic and simmer gently until garlic softens, but doesn't brown. Raise heat to medium and add vegetables. Toss and cook until tender and heated through, 3 to 4 minutes. Season with salt and pepper or chili flakes.

CAULIFLOWER WITH GOLDEN RAISINS AND PINE NUTS (CAVOLFIORE CON L'UVETTA E I PIGNOLI)

Raisins, pine nuts, garlic, and parsley are a classic Southern Italian combination, which show the region's Arabic influence. Use the combo with cooked broccoli, fennel, leeks, carrots, or kale.

Yields 5 cups, 4 to 6 servings

2-1/2 pounds cauliflower, about 1 medium head
   or 1-3/4 pounds trimmed head, about 7 cups small florets
1/2 cup olive oil
2 ounces golden seedless raisins, 1/3 cup
2 ounces pine nuts, 1/3 cup
1/2 ounce garlic, 2 large cloves, 1 tablespoon peeled and minced
1 tablespoon freshly squeezed lemon juice, more to taste
1/2 ounce trimmed Italian parsley, 1/4 cup chopped

1 Remove cauliflower leaves and cut vegetable into small bite-sized florets. Set up steamer basket in 5- to 6-quart pot with water. Bring to a boil. Or use commercial steamer. Add cauliflower and steam until tender, 4 to 5 minutes. Transfer cauliflower to mixing bowl.

2 Pour olive oil into deep, lidded 12-inch sauté pan or heavy 5- to 6-quart pot, and heat over medium heat. Stir in raisins and cook until they puff and brown. Remove immediately with slotted spoon to cauliflower bowl. Stir pine nuts into hot oil, and cook until golden. Remove immediately to bowl with raisins. Stir in garlic and cook until it begins to color.

3 Immediately stir in cauliflower, raisins and nuts and 1 teaspoon kosher salt. Cover pan and reduce heat to low; stir occasionally. Simmer cauliflower until very tender, about 5 minutes. Remove pan from heat and rest cauliflower 5 minutes to absorb flavors. Uncover pan or pot, stir in lemon juice, and season with salt and pepper to taste.

4 **To Serve:** Reheat cauliflower gently. Toss with parsley and serve.

Source: *Marcella's Italian Kitchen* by Marcella Hazan.

Vary! Improvise!

☛ *Season cauliflower with red wine vinegar at the end instead of lemon juice.*

☛ *Simmer cauliflower with lemon zest.*

☛ *Sauté diced prosciutto in oil after nuts and simmer with cauliflower.*

FENNEL WITH CHEESE AND PROSCIUTTO (FINOCCHI ALLA PARMIGIANA CON PROSCIUTTO)

This is a Roman recipe from Lazio.

Yields one half hotel pan, about 6 servings

3 pounds trimmed fennel, about 4 fat bulbs
3 ounces thinly sliced prosciutto
1/4 cup olive oil or melted butter
3 ounces grated or shredded Parmigiano-Reggiano cheese, 1 cup

1 Fill a 5- to 6-quart pot full of water and bring to a boil. Stir in 1 tablespoon kosher salt.

2 Trim away a thin slice off the bottom of each fennel bulb. Set a bulb on the bottom and slice in half so the bulb becomes two mirror halves. Lay a half on the flat side. Slice each half bulb into three pieces lengthwise so that each piece has the root end keeping it together. Drop fennel into boiling water, and lower heat to a gentle boil. Cook fennel until tender, 10 to 12 minutes. Transfer fennel wedges to colander with slotted spoon or tongs, and drain.

3 Slice prosciutto crosswise into strips, about 1/4-inch wide to yield about 3/4 cup.

4 Set an oven rack in the middle of oven; preheat to 400 degrees F. Coat the bottom of a 10-inch by 12-inch half hotel pan with 2 tablespoons olive oil or melted butter. Arrange drained fennel wedges in one layer. Season fennel with 1 teaspoon kosher salt and freshly ground pepper. Arrange prosciutto strips over and in between fennel. Drizzle remaining olive oil or butter over fennel. Sprinkle cheese evenly over fennel. Place pan into the oven, and bake until the top is crusty and golden and the prosciutto is crisp, 30 to 40 minutes.

5 **To Serve:** Cool fennel slightly so it sets. Serve fennel hot or at room temperature.

Source: *Lidia's Italy* by Lidia Bastianich.

Vary! Improvise!

☛ **Dairy-Free:** *Substitute 1 cup fresh breadcrumbs tossed with 2 tablespoons olive oil in place of cheese. Bake until breadcrumbs are browned and crisp.*

☛ *Substitute other Italian cheeses like Grana Padano for a different taste and texture.*

SOUTHERN ITALIAN FRIED SQUASH WITH MINT (ZUCCA GIALLA CON LA MENTA)

This scapeche *method is an Italian favorite for vegetables. With a little sugar added to the vinegar it becomes* agrodolce *(sour-sweet); both methods are used all over southern Italy. It is similar to the Spanish* escabeche *method of frying fish in olive oil, and marinating in vinegar and seasonings. Italian* zucca *look like enormous butternut squash, but are bland and not sweet.*

Yields 4 to 6 servings

2 to 2-1/2 pounds butternut squash or Italian *zucca*
1 cup olive oil
1/3 cup red wine vinegar
1/2 ounce mint leaves, 1/4 cup torn or finely sliced
1 ounce garlic, about 4 large cloves, 2 to 3 tablespoons peeled and finely sliced

1 Remove stem and bottom end from squash. Peel it with vegetable peeler. Cut squash crossways to separate the neck from the rounded seed-bearing base. Slice the two pieces in half lengthwise; scrape out seeds and discard. Slice each piece of squash crosswise into 3/16-inch half moons to yield 7 to 8 cups.

2 Lightly oil the bottom of a nonreactive 1-1/2-quart loaf pan (5 inches by 9 inches) and place next to the stove. Heat oil in a heavy 11- to 12-inch skillet over medium-high heat. When the oil is rippling hot but not smoking, fry the squash in 3 to 4 batches until bubbly and lightly browned, 1 to 2 minutes per side.

3 Transfer squash to loaf to form the first layer of 5 or 6 layers of fried squash. Season squash with salt and pepper, drizzle with vinegar, mint, and garlic. Continue to fry squash and layer in pan with salt, pepper, mint, and garlic. Reserve leftover oil and reuse for other frying.

4 Fold a half sheet of parchment paper to fit inside loaf pan. Place it on the squash. Cut a piece of heavy cardboard to fit inside the loaf pan and set on top of parchment. Place a 2-pound weight on top of cardboard to weight squash as evenly as possible. Marinate squash at room temperature 4 hours. Or refrigerate squash overnight and bring to room temperature before serving. The weighting is unnecessary, but makes a nice presentation when unmolded.

5 **To Serve:** Unmold squash onto platter. If it comes apart slightly, re-form it. Slice "loaf" into 4 to 6 pieces with a very sharp knife. Serve squash as a side dish with meat, or as an antipasto with prosciutto, cheese, and olives.

Source: *My Calabria* by Rosetta Constantino and Janet Fletcher.

Signature Technique: Stuffed Artichokes (Carciofi Ripieni)

Artichokes are widely cultivated in Sicily. They might be simmered in water and oil, baked, broiled, stewed, or stuffed. A typical Eastern Sicilian stuffing would include breadcrumbs, capers, garlic, parsley, and cheese and sometimes anchovies. In other parts of southern Italy cooks might add black olives, currants, pine nuts, or almonds. In Messina, cooks might use cured meats or fresh sausage meat with breadcrumbs, cheese, garlic, and capers.

1 Choose large (6 to 8 ounces) artichokes for stuffing. They should be tightly closed and look fresh and moist. One or one-half artichoke will serve one person as an appetizer or side vegetable.

2 **Trim:** Strip small, tough leaves off bottom of artichoke. Slice off stem at the base of the artichoke; peel stem and rub cut on artichoke plus stem with lemon to keep it from browning. Slice off top 1/2- to 1-inch of artichoke with a very sharp knife and rub cut sides with lemon. With scissors, snip off needle sharp ends of each leaf. Pull apart leaves like a flower to reveal the inside. Scrape out

Vary! Improvise!

☞ *Substitute zucchini and yellow summer squash for butternut squash. Slice thinly in lengthwise strips on a mandoline. Fry zucchini until browned, and layer into a loaf pan. Heat vinegar, garlic, and mint before pouring over squash for* zucchine a scapece.

☞ ***Less Fat:*** *Instead of frying, substitute olive oil-brushed and grilled or cast-iron grill-pan-grilled slices of eggplant or squash.*

☞ ***Don't Press It:*** *Instead of layering fried squash into a loaf pan, use an 8-inch by 13-inch gratin dish and make three layers. Do not press, just marinate 4 to 8 hours before serving.*

FIGURE 6.40 Trimmed artichokes.
Source: Dorling Kindersley/DK Images.

choke, the fine downy thistle on the inside of the artichoke, but don't dig into the meaty heart. Discard choke, and drizzle artichoke with lemon juice.

3 **Stuff:** Prepare 4 to 5 tablespoons stuffing per artichoke. See *Stuffing Ideas* below. Fill center of artichokes with stuffing and press closed. Press a small amount of the stuffing into the base of each leaf and press artichoke back into shape.

4 **Cook:** Pour about 1-1/2 inches of water in a saucepan or Dutch oven—the artichokes should fit into the pan comfortably standing up, and not too tightly; use two pans if necessary. Add lemon juice (and herbs if desired) the water. Drizzle top of each artichoke with 1/2 teaspoon oil. Cover the pot tightly and steam the artichokes over low heat until they are tender to the core when pierced with a skewer, 30 to 45 minutes. With a slotted spoon, transfer artichokes from pan to a platter. Serve warm or at room temperature. Artichokes may be carefully sliced in half or into quarters to reveal the stuffing. Instruct guests to pull off leaves and scrape fleshy bottom of leaf and stuffing with teeth to eat.

5 **Alternatively:** Prepare 4 to 5 cups tomato sauce in a 6-quart Dutch oven instead of water, and simmer in covered pan until artichokes are tender.

Stuffing Ideas

For 8 artichokes

- Toss together 2-1/4 cups fresh breadcrumbs made from day-old bread, 3/4 cup chopped parsley, 1/2 cup (1 ounce) grated pecorino or grana padano cheese, 1 tablespoon chopped oregano, and 2 ounces mashed anchovies. Moisten with oil if necessary so stuffing holds together. Season stuffing with salt and pepper.
  - Substitute toasted and chopped pine nuts for the anchovies.
  - Add 2 tablespoons currants, soaked 10 minutes and drained.
  - Add 2 teaspoons minced garlic to the stuffing.
  - Substitute black olives, pitted and chopped for anchovies.
- Prepare meat stuffing with loose, raw sweet or hot Italian sausage, herbs, breadcrumbs, cheese, and garlic.

REVIEW QUESTIONS

1. What is a soffritto? What are its components?

2. Name two Italian sauces and describe them.

3. Describe the procedure for preparing and rolling fresh pasta dough.

4. In general terms, discuss how to pair dry pastas with sauce.

5. Name two cured Italian meats.

6. Discuss the main cultural influences on Italian cuisine.

7. In general, how does the food of northern Italy differ from the food of the south?

CHAPTER SEVEN

SPAIN: IBERIAN LAND OF CONTRASTS

This chapter will:

- Introduce the history of Spain, its geography, climate, and major cultural influences from the North African Moors.

- Reveal Spain's influences on Latin American cuisines through conquest of Mexico and Puerto Rico.

- Introduce Spanish culinary culture, its twelve distinct culinary regions, and dining etiquette.

- Identify Spanish foods, flavor foundations, seasoning devices, and favored cooking techniques.

- Discuss the influences that resulted in the rise in popularity of Spanish cuisine.

- Teach the techniques and the beloved, classic dishes of Spain.

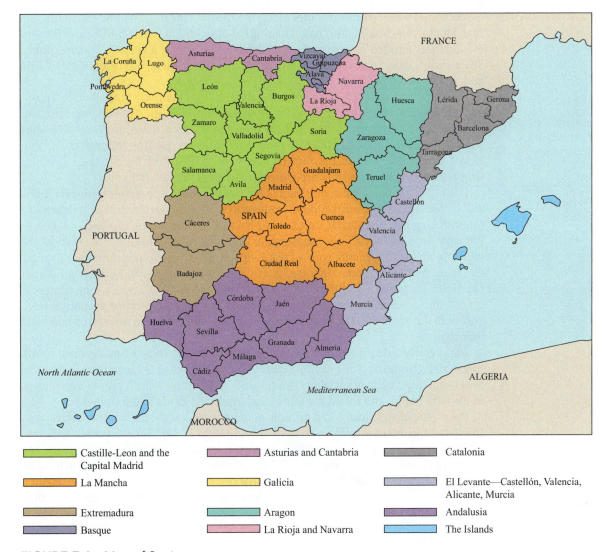

FIGURE 7.1 Map of Spain.

Politics over Poetry

In Moorish Spain, Richard Fletcher relates that Muslims, Jews, and Christians thrived together in Medieval Spain, sharing learning for more than 300 years, contributing poetry, art, architecture, music, cuisine, science, agriculture, medicine, engineering, navigation, and textile expertise. The peak of this enlightened, creative period was during the Mediterranean Middle Ages. Spain's peaceful, multifaith and multicultural civilization was destroyed by a campaign for political power and conquest of land, which led to religious extremism and puritanism (against Muslims and Jews). To comprehend Spain and the Iberian Peninsula, Fletcher writes that this "incredible Islamic legacy" must be considered.

Diversity rooted in history and preserved by geography is a fundamental part of Spanish culture. The second largest country in Western Europe (after France), Spain is a country of spectacular landscapes from the Atlantic Ocean and the Balearic and Mediterranean Sea coastlines, to high sierra and fertile river valleys rich with fruit and almond trees, grapes, vegetables, olives, and oaks. Its Old World village charm mixes with modern architecture like Frank Gehry's Guggenheim Museum in Bilbao. Spain's earthy traditional dishes have been turned on their heads by daring, artistic Spanish chefs like Calalonian Ferran Adrá.

Modern humans first arrived on the Iberian Peninsula about 30,000 BCE. The two main people were the *Iberians* and *Celts*. *Basque* people occupied the western Pyrénées. Around 500 BCE to 300 BCE, seafaring *Phoenicians* (from around ancient Syria) and

Greeks traded with Spanish colonies along her Mediterranean coast. The expanding Roman Empire captured Iberian coastal trading colonies (210 BCE to 205 BCE) and Romans eventually controlled the entire Iberian Peninsula. For half a century Romans united Spain with Roman law, language, Christianity, and roads. Rome brought goods to Spain and, in turn, exported grain, wine, olive oil, wool, and gold.

East-Germanic tribes of *Visigoths* fought and migrated their way through Italy, France, and the Iberian Peninsula. They ruled *Hispania* from 475 to 711, building four new Spanish cities. Muslim/Moorish invasion from North Africa felled the Visigoth Empire (they fled north), and southern Spain came under Muslim rule. The cultured and sophisticated *Moors* (969 to 1031) contributed to every aspect of Spanish life: language, learning, irrigation, cotton manufacture, rice-growing, and great culinary skills.

In 1492, the united Christian armies of the *Catholic Kings of Spain* under *King Ferdinand* and *Queen Isabella* pushed the Moors south and finally conquered the last independent Moorish kingdom. Eventually, unconverted Jews and Muslims were expelled or killed. At the same time, under Catholic sponsorship, Columbus encountered the New World and began Spain's global empire with a great influx of wealth and foods important to modern Spanish cooking from conquered Mexico, Central America, and Caribbean islands like Cuba, Hispaniola, and Puerto Rico. Ferdinand and Isabella began a long process of uniting the independent regions of Spain into one kingdom, continued religious intolerance with the brutal Spanish Inquisition, and united with European powers through royal marriages.

Napoleon invaded Spain in 1808. His defeat resulted in a more liberal Spanish constitution and restoration of the King of Spain. The king refused to abide by the constitution, thus beginning a cycle of social unrest and weak government, which caused a revolution in the New World, and forced the sale of Spanish-held Florida to the United States.

Polarized politics, debt, social turmoil, and desire for less church and monarchist control led to the devastating Spanish Civil War (1936 to 1939). General Franco took over after the war as dictator for nearly four decades. It was a time of fascism, censorship, and social conservatism. Franco died in 1975 and King Juan Carlos I became monarch. Spain established a new democratic constitution that began a process of liberalization. Spain is now a stable, democratic, constitutional monarchy, a committed Roman Catholic nation, and a part of the European Union.

LANGUAGE, PHILOSOPHY, AND RELIGION

Spanish is Spain's official language, but other languages like Basque, Catalan, Galician, and Aranese have recognized status in specific regions. Arabic or Berber is spoken by the Muslim population. About 75 percent of Spaniards are Roman Catholic, 22 percent follow no religion, and 2 percent are Muslim. Only 15 percent of Spanish Catholics regularly attend church. Food and family celebrations still revolve around Catholic feast days with pilgrimages, celebrations of saints, and religious rituals like Easter Holy Week and the festival of San Fermin (with bullfighting) in Pamplona.

GEOGRAPHY AND CLIMATE

About the size of California and Maine, with 52 million people, and located in southwestern Europe, Spain occupies 84 percent of the *Iberian Peninsula* (Portugal makes up the remainder) and all of the Balearic Islands and the Canary Islands. Spain is blessed with one of the sunniest and warmest climates in Europe, which supports diverse and contrasting habitats of wildlife and landscape. The majority of Spain enjoys a Mediterranean climate with long, hot, dry summers, with rainy periods in spring and fall and cold, but not snowy winters. A high arid plateau rimmed by mountains, the Meseta Central, dominates the land along with lowland river valleys and narrow coastal plains. The remainder of Spain consists of subtropical islands, and the *Pyrénées* and *Sistema Penibétuco* mountain ranges. Their highest peaks qualify as alpine climates.

FARMING AND AGRICULTURE

Though Spain is a large country, less than half its land is suitable for growing food. Most of the soil is poor, the terrain tends to be rough and rocky, and rainfall tends to be inadequate with summer droughts. *Latifundios* (large estates), located mostly in the south, hold most of Spain's farms, and north and northwestern *minifundios* (small plots) hold only a small portion. Irrigated farms produce rice, corn, wheat, barley, fruit (citrus, apples and stone fruit trees, berries, and grapes), raisins, nuts, olives, sunflowers for oil, saffron crocus, and numerous vegetables. Legumes, potatoes, sugar beets, tomatoes, eggplant, and chilies, mainly for smoked paprika (*pimentón*), thrive. Europe imports much of Spain's produce. Spanish farmers raise pork, poultry, and beef, and produce sherry, cheese, and great cured hams like *Ibérico* and *Serrano*. Fishing provides a providence of seafood.

SPANISH CUISINE: EARTHY WITH A MOORISH ACCENT

Traditional Spanish food has long been considered plain and earthy. Its fresh, natural flavor relies on excellent ingredients with a minimum of seasoning. Cooks enhance the intrinsic flavors of fresh food without disguising them. Geography, topography, and climate determined what, when, and how people cooked and ate. Those nearer the sea naturally ate more seafood, and those who did not ate salt cod. Those in the north grew cold, hardy fruits like apples, quince and pears, and beans. In the south and along the warm eastern coast of the Mediterranean, people grew rice and oranges. Those in the mountainous and inland regions hunted game and wild mushrooms, and raised and consumed more pork, lamb, and cheese. Much like neighboring France, Spanish cuisine is born of people in close touch with their land: it is a *cocina del terreno*.

Travel was difficult and often nearby villages or *pueblos* were isolated from each other. Regions developed fierce, individualistic pride. Every region refined distinctive ways to prepare similar dishes. Despite this, all Spanish cooks share the use of olive oil, garlic, parsley, tomatoes, peppers, almonds, chocolate, eggs, wine, bread as binder, ground nuts as sauce flavoring, dried beans, peas, and lentils; fish and shellfish; and a *cazuela* (flat earthenware dish) for slow simmering.

Spanish cooking is an ancient blend of many foreign influences. The Phoenicians, Greeks, Carthaginians, Celts, Romans, Jews, and Visigoths left their culinary touches. Phoenician traders brought salt cod, fishing know-how, and fish soups. Greeks introduced olives, olive oil, and chickpeas. Romans introduced grapes and wine. The greatest legacy was that of the *Moors* (North African Muslims) who had contact with Africa, Persia, the Middle East, and India. During eight centuries of rule they brought untold riches into Spain: *spices* like cumin, saffron, coriander, nutmeg, and cinnamon; sugar cane and sugarmaking, *citrus* like oranges and lemons, almonds, *fruits* like apricots, peaches, pomegranates, quince, figs, and melons; rice, wheat, and *vegetables* like artichokes and eggplant. The Moors also brought their culinary knowledge of *pastry-making* with fritters, marzipan, and desserts with almonds, citrus, and cinnamon; grilled kebabs and meatballs, *gazpacho*, hearty stews, pasta-making, rice preparation (*paella*), and the combination of spices and fruit in savory meat and seafood dishes.

After the Moors, the most significant influence came from Columbus's voyage to the West Indies and Spain's eventual conquest of Mexico and many Caribbean islands. Spain's pantry exploded with the addition of Mexican and Central American riches: tomatoes, chocolate, peanuts, chilies, peppers, potatoes, beans, vanilla, squash, zucchini, and corn. Home cooks and chefs embraced these influences and, with an ingenuity born in the cauldron of creativity, incorporated them into their simple, savory, satisfying cuisine.

Spanish cuisine is also a cuisine of the mother—*cocina de la madre*. Generations of female cooks handed down simple, earthy dishes in a straight line from the many Greek,

Roman, Jewish, and Moorish influences. Modern Spanish cooks and chefs treasure and still prepare traditional recipes graced by a mother's or grandmother's special touches.

Spain's history of creatively incorporating new foods has given birth to a renaissance in Spanish cuisine. As Spanish food writer Penelope Casas says, "Traditional does not imply uniformity and lack of variety." The new wave of Spanish home cooks and chefs, with chefs Ferran Adrià, Juan Mari Arzak, Santi Santamaria, and Carme Ruscalleda leading the pack, have proved her right. Their new takes on traditional Spanish food are rocking the culinary world. The *New York Times* speculated on the possibility that Spanish cooking might even sometime soon overtake French cuisine.

THE TWELVE REGIONS OF SPANISH CUISINE

Although it isn't any larger than Texas, Spain is filled with imposing snow-capped mountain ranges, vast plains, forests, wetlands, and desert, which comprise many uniquely distinct culinary regions. In the *The New Spanish Table*, author Anya von Bremzen divides them into twelve.

1. **Castille-Leon and the Capital Madrid: Austere and Elegant Cradle of Modern Culture**
   The largest region, this is a place of plains, mountains, valleys, hilltop castles, and small villages. Charcuterie, beans, chickpeas, lentils, and garlic add to the austere, delicious, and elegant dishes: *cocido* (stew), *albondigas en salsa* (meatballs), and *tortillas* (thick egg and potato omelets).

2. **La Mancha Rural Plains**
   A windswept plain of windmills, vineyards, olive trees, and sheep, this region is fond of *pimentón*, garlic, saffron, and vegetables. Famous dishes include *pisto Manchego* (ratatouille) *sopa de ajo* (garlic and bread soup), and *migas* (fried breadcrumbs with chorizo, garlic, and more).

3. **Extremadura: Wild and Majestic**
   This broad, harsh, but majestic territory shares borders with Portugal. Its rustic, peasant cuisine consists of pork, lamb, and game, bread, dried *ñora* peppers, and local *pimentón de la Vera*, and *jamón Ibérico* (ham from pigs fed acorns) in dishes like potatoes *en escabeche* and lamb stew.

4. **Basque: Independent and Pastoral**
   A region with green hills and wide, sand beaches, Basque country shares borders with, and is influenced by, France. Its cuisine is hearty and uncomplicated with *bacalao* (salt cod), wild mushrooms, vegetable dishes, squid in onion sauce, and *marmitako* (bonito fish and potato stew).

5. **Asturias and Cantabria: Rocky, Scenic Northern Coast**
   This northern area has a scenic, rocky coast with the *Picos de Europa*, Europe's last mountain wilderness area. The mountain cuisine centers on fish, farming, sausage, and cheese with dishes like *fabada* (bean stew), *pescado* or *pollo en la sidra* (fish or chicken in cider), rice pudding, and clams with white beans. Apple and pear orchards thrive here; Asturias is known for *sidra* (hard cider).

6. **Galicia: Green and Rainy**
   This region, with estuaries, lagoons, rocky coves, and deep green countryside jutting into the Atlantic, shows Celtic influences that may have come by contact with maritime traders. Simple seafood dishes, eggs, dairy, beef, potatoes, and turnip greens sustain the inhabitants. Galicia is the home of *empanadas*, *caldo gallego* (pork, turnip green, and bean soup), and boiled octopus with pimentón.

7. **Aragon: Rugged and Remote**
   This region, with the Pyrénées Mountains, contains a strong, rustic cuisine. It's known for lake trout, lamb, pork, olive oil and fruit trees, particularly peaches, and dishes like *chilindrón* (chicken or lamb in red pepper sauce), ham with tomato sauce, and partridge with chocolate sauce.

8. **La Rioja and Navarra: Vines and Vegetables**
   Grape and vegetable growing is this region's largest industry. Artichokes, asparagus, leeks, chard, lettuce, white beans, *piquillo peppers*, and potatoes figure prominently. Stewed and fried vegetable *menestras* (stews) and asparagus in vinaigrette are favored dishes.

9. **Catalonia: Elegant, Modern, and Robust**
   French-influenced, this is a region of Mediterranean coast, walled medieval villages, Roman ruins, and the Pyrénées Mountains. Roman, Arabic, and Italian influences have contributed to its distinct, elegant but robust cuisine. Favored dishes are *samfaina* (ratatouille), toasted pasta casserole, *suquet* (seafood in tomato), fish stews, grilled foods with *allioli* (garlic mayonnaise), and *romesco* (nut and tomato sauce).

10. **El Levante—Castellón, Valencia, Alicante, Murcia: The Garden of Spain**
    This region along the Mediterranean Sea has acres of fertile farmland with groves of oranges, lemons, and almonds, rice paddies, and fishing. Traditional dishes are *paella*, rice dishes, *fideuá* (pasta paella), *turron* (almond honey nougat), marzipan, eel in garlic sauce, and *horchata* (drink made from "chufa nut" tubers, cinnamon, and sugar).

11. **Andalusia: Moorish-Arab Legacy**
    Andalusia has a diverse landscape from the continuous coast on both the Atlantic and Mediterranean to the high peaks of the Sierra Nevada Mountains. About the size of Portugal and at Spain's southern tip, Andalusia is known for beaches, white hilltop villages, sherry, seafood, many types of *gazpacho*, *pescaíto frito* (fried fish), spinach with garbanzos, and its use of Arab foods, spices, and cooking techniques.

12. **The Islands—The Balearics (Mallorca, Menorca, and Ibiza) and the Canaries: Lush, Tropical**
    The Balearics, off Spain's eastern Mediterranean coast, are three lush, romantic islands set in azure waters. The food shows Phoenician, Greek, Roman, and Arabic influences in dishes like *tumbet* (layered vegetable casserole), lobster stew, stuffed vegetables, and *coca* (topped flatbread). *The Canary Islands*, off the coast of southern Morocco and 1,000 miles from Spain, are a series of small, lush, tropical, volcanic islands with Iberian, African, and Spanish-Caribbean influences. Avocado, yam, pineapple, papaya, tomatoes, potatoes, fish, and bananas are staples. Favored dishes are *sancocho* (fish, potato, and yam stew), *mojo* sauces, *tortilla de platanos* (omelet with bananas), and *gofio* (toasted grain porridge).

DINE AT HOME IN SPAIN

As in Italy, meals are important gathering times. *El desayuno* (breakfast) is a light meal of coffee and toast or thick hot chocolate and deep-fried *churros*. Between 10.30 a.m. and noon, many take a coffee break. *La comida* (lunch) starts at 2 and goes until 4 or 5 P.M. It is the main meal of the day with several courses, but always an appetizer and main course, bread, drink (wine or beer), and dessert. *La merienda* (snack) is a meal to hold people until dinner and is often substantial like tapas, sandwich, fruit, or pastry. *La cena* (dinner) is typically around 8 to 10 or 11 P.M. *La cena* is lighter than lunch—often soup, salad, or tapas.

It's probable that if invited to dine with a family, it will be at the midday meal, or for a late supper with friends and family at a restaurant or tapas bar. Don't be more than 15 minutes late. When meeting, shake hands, or if a cheek is offered, touch yours to each of the other person's cheeks. Don't hug anyone you don't know well.

Dress elegantly (and conservatively) with good, clean shoes, no shorts. Bring a gift of nicely wrapped wine, pastry, or chocolate. If there are children present, bring them something too.

Older people are highly respected in Spain so treat them with dignity. Keep wrists on the table (no elbows) and maintain eye contact when conversing. Avoid religion, politics, and the Spanish Civil War—instead talk about food, cooking, and family. The host or hostess will seat you and give the first toast—as honored guest you should toast them later in the meal.

First course will probably be soup. Spanish people love soup and eat it almost daily. Second course might be a rabbit, fish, or seafood dish, lamb, or chicken. Bread is ever-present. Vegetables and salads, courses on their own, come next. The dessert with flan, fresh fruit, or ice cream follows with coffee then brandy and an optional cigar. Wine is the Spanish drink of choice. Wait until the host or hostess rises from the table before you leave. Thank your hosts.

TASTES OF SPAIN

Fat: Olive oil, butter, lard

Sweet: Sugar, honey

Sour/Alcohol: Red, white, and sherry vinegar; lemon; sweet, bitter, and blood oranges; red and white wine, sherry

Salty: Sea salt, olive paste, green and black olives

Spicy-Hot: Black pepper, chilies, *pimentón* (smoked paprika)

Spice: Saffron, coriander, cinnamon, clove, aniseed, cumin

Aromatic Seasoning Vegetables: Onion, garlic, tomato, carrot, shallot, celery

Herbs, Seasonings, and Condiments: Italian parsley, oregano, thyme, rosemary, cilantro, chives, bay leaves, sage, fennel, basil, chorizo, *membrillo* (quince paste), squid ink

Other Important Ingredients: Olives, cream, milk, cow and goat milk cheese, white beans, lima beans, black beans, wheat, couscous, Valencian *calasparra* and *bomba* short- and medium-grain rice, long-grain rice, almonds, hazelnuts, pine nuts, carob, fruit (grapes, peaches, pears, figs, apricots, kiwi, cherries, and apples), potatoes, tomatoes, peppers, eggplant, green beans, artichokes, cabbage, artichokes, Swiss chard, zucchini, squash, peas, asparagus, mushrooms, fennel, spinach, cardoons, meat (lamb, pork and pork products, beef, chicken, turkey, goose, pigeon, sausages, rabbit, wild game, pheasant), seafood (*bacalao* [dried salt cod], octopus, frog's legs, many crustaceans and shellfish like snails, crabs, clams, mussels, squid, and shrimp, and many fish like anchovies, tuna, and swordfish)

Popular Dishes: Paella, empanada, tapas, *fabada* (Asturian bean stew), *pescado en escabeche* (fish marinated in vinegar), *pollo chilindrón* (chicken braised with red peppers), *conjondongo* (bread salad), *xató* (composed salad), *churros* (fried choux pastries), *cocido Madrileño* (chickpea-based stew), *olla podrida* (meat and bean stew), *migas* (fried breadcrumbs and seasonings), *pescado frito* (fried seafood), *croqueta de jamón* (ham croquettes), *turron* (almond nougat), leche frita (fried milk), flan (caramel custard), candied fruit

Drinks: Coffee, tea, red and white wines, beer, sangria, sidra (hard cider), sherry, cava (sparkling wine)

COMMON SPANISH COOKING TOOLS

Cazuela (glazed earthenware dish for stovetop cooking), mortar and pestle, paella pan, *plancha* (iron grill for hearth or wood-fire cooking)

SPANISH CHEESE (QUESO)

Spain is an important cheese-producing country with more than 100 diverse varieties from fresh to extra cured and fermented to blue-veined. Twelve or more carry the D.O.P. (Denominacion de Origen Protegida) status. Each region has a specialty: the northern coast features cow milk cheeses, Inland, sheep milk cheeses dominate, and along the Mediterranean coast goat milk cheeses are most popular. Mixed milk cheeses are also produced.

Cabrales/Valdeón

These two are less pungent blue cheeses and are similar to Gorgonzola: dense, rich, and naturally aged. They can be made with just cow milk or a mixture of sheep and cow milk. The cylindrical Cabrales is softer; Valdeón is firmer. Their flavor is slightly acidic. As they age they can become very strong. Good with red wine, sherry, cured meats, and in sauces or stews.

Garrotxa

This is a creamy, pressed goat milk cheese from Catalonia made from unpasteurized milk and was originally produced only in the Garrotxa area of Catalonia. It has a firm, white interior with a few holes, a natural grey mold rind, and is produced in small 1 kilo wheels. The flavor is milky, delicate, and slightly nutty with a clean, smooth finish. Garrotxa pairs well with sparkling wine, Champagne, whites, and many Iberian varietals like sherry and port.

Idiazábal

This famous cylindrical, cone, or octagonal Basque sheep milk cheese is made from unpasteurized milk. It may be pressed, semi-cured, and or fully cured and can be found smoked. The aged cheese tends to be strong flavored with a dry, chewy, and crumbly texture. Good paired with grilled meat dishes, salads, toasted bread, and full-bodied wines.

Mahón or De Maó

These are a type of rectangular, semi-soft cow milk cheeses produced on the Balearic Island of Minorca. They vary from fresh, semi-cured, to aged. The rind may be rubbed with olive oil and crusted with pimentón. It has a smooth, yellow, and oily rind similar to Gouda and has holes throughout. It tastes slightly salty and acidic and becomes stronger as it ages. Good over pasta, potatoes, vegetables, or as a tapa sprinkled with rosemary and olive oil.

Majorero

This aged, aromatic goat cheese is produced on the Canary Island of Fuerteventura. It's produced in large, cylindrical drums three ways: an oil-rubbed natural rind, pimentón-rubbed, or roasted cornmeal-rubbed ("gofio"). The rind goes from white to brown-beige and the cheese has a slightly crumbly, gummy texture, which melts in the mouth. It is buttery and acidic, making it good as a tapa drizzled with rosemary and olive oil or grated over pasta or vegetable dishes.

Manchego

This famous cheese is traditionally made from the whole milk of sheep from La Mancha. It is available made from pasteurized milk (factory) or from unpasteurized milk (artisan farmhouse). Manchego is a firm, compact cheese with some holes, semi-cured and mild, or well-cured and sharp. Manchego's buttery but piquant flavor goes well with olives, bread, tomatoes, bread, and red wine.

Roncal

This is a sheep milk cheese from the Pyrenees that is similar to Manchego and Pecorino that is made with the rich sheep milk of Lacha and Rasa breeds. It is only made in one of seven villages in the Valle de Roncal. Roncal has nutty and piquant flavors with a firm, chewy texture. Serve as a tapa or dessert cheese paired with red or white wine.

Tetilla (Queso de Perilla or Queso de Teta)

This half pear-shaped cheese from Galicia is made from whole cow milk. Tetilla has a smooth, yellow rind; its interior is soft, thick, and creamy interior with a few holes. The flavor is mild with slight pungency. It's served with crackers, fruit, and quince paste or used for cooking, stuffing, and melting into sandwiches and sauces.

Torta del Casar

This strong-scented, soft, creamy sheep milk cheese is from the Extremadura region made only with the milk of Merino and Entrefina sheep. The milk is curdled with a coagulant from the pistils of the cardoon, a wild thistle, which leaves a slight bitterness. Its flavor is rich, very pungent, and slightly salty. Aged a minimum of 60 days, the ripe cheese is creamy in the center; traditionally the top is sliced off and the inside of the cheese scooped out with bread.

Zamorano

This is a high-quality, robust ewe milk cheese with an oily, engraved rind and a straw-colored interior dotted with crystals. This buttery, intense cheese has an aftertaste of nuts. Good with crackers, olives, and full-bodied wine.

SPANISH CHARCUTERIE (CHARCUTERÍA)

Spain produces numerous pork products with flavorings and ingredients unique to each region. The charcuterie falls into two main types: *cooked products* and *raw products*, which are dried or cured or smoked.

Dry-Cured

Dry-cured hams and charcuterie have been produced throughout southern Europe since Roman times by salting, which extracts moisture, and then air-curing. During curing natural microbial flora work on the meat and enhance flavor, texture, and color. Spain, Portugal, France, and Italy have delicious hams made with various breeds of pigs and curing methods. Overall, Spanish hams have a more uniform texture, more intense flavor, firmer texture, and less moisture than other cured hams. They are best served with piquillo peppers, *membrillo* (quince paste), or a crisp, fruity wine or sangria.

Jamon Serrano (Mountain Ham)

Similar to Italian prosciutto, Serrano is an unsmoked, dry-cured ham. The majority of Serrano hams come from the white Landrace pig. After slaughter, the rear legs are trimmed and cleaned, rubbed with salt, stacked in piles, and covered with more salt. The salt and pressure help to draw off moisture. After two weeks, the salt is washed off and the hams hang to dry. Traditionally, after about six months they were transferred to special drying sheds called *secaderos* at high elevations, where the cool, dry

FIGURE 7.2 Jamon iberico hanging at a butcher shop in Spain.
Source: Danilo Ascione/Shutterstock.

conditions necessary for curing are best. The jamon Serrano cures for another 6 to 18 months, depending on size. Although the modern curing process is temperature and humidity controlled, each ham is still handled individually.

Jamon Ibérico and Jamon Ibérico de Bellota

There are two types of Ibérico ham: Jamón Ibérico, which is made from grain-fed free-range *pata negra* (black-hoof or Ibérico pig), and the prized Jamón Ibérico de Bellota, or acorn-fed *pata negra* (Bellota means acorn). The latter, the king of dry-cured hams, is expensive and rare. The pigs roam through oak forests the autumn before slaughter, and eat a diet of acorns, which helps deliver extraordinary flavor. De Bellota hams have a richly

complex taste, distinct marbling, deep red color, and robust, sweet, nutty flavor with monounsaturated fat. Ibérico hams reach their peak after about two years of curing, protected by a huge amount of fat and enhanced by microbial flora, which further enhance flavor and aroma. The best hams are chosen to cure another 6 to 12 months.

Chorizo

All chorizo sausage is made with ground pork and usually pimentón. It's made throughout Spain and it varies depending upon the meat grind, size, meat density, length of curing, and other seasonings. The simplest chorizo is a very firm, thin sausage with pork, pimentón, and salt, which is hung in temperature and humidity controlled rooms to air-cure. Serve thinly sliced

FIGURE 7.3 Jamon serrano.
Source: Andrew Buckin/Fotolia.

FIGURE 7.4 Chorizo.
Source: Roger Dixon/Dorling Kindersley.

with cheese and fruit, fried in olive oil with bread, or simmered in stews.

Fuet

Fuet means "whip" in Spanish. This thin, long, and intensely flavored, salami-like Catalonian sausage has a texture similar to chorizo, but is seasoned with lots of black pepper instead of pimentón. Spanish cooks traditionally serve fuet whole on a wooden board with a knife, and allow guests to cut slices.

Lomo Embuchado

This dry-cured pork loin, a beloved Spanish delicacy, is dusted with pimentón, wrapped, and cured 2 months or more. Thinly sliced lomo is chewy, meaty, lean, and intensely flavorful. Drizzle lomo with extra good olive oil or pair it with fruit like pears or apples, grilled piquillo peppers, or fatty foods like olives or cheese.

Lomo Embuchado Ibérico de Bellota

This rare and expensive meat product is made similarly to lomo embuchado, but with a large difference: the loin comes from wild-roaming, acorn-fed *patas negras* or black-hoof Ibérico pigs. Color and marbling are richer than lomo embuchado, with dense texture and nutty flavor. Serve it alone.

Tocino de Pancetta

Spanish pancetta (see chapter *Italy*, *Italian Cured Meats* [*Salumi*]).

Lacón

Cured pork hocks/forelegs. Lacón is traditionally cooked with turnip greens (lacón con grelos) or simmered with beans or in stews like *Fabada*.

Cooked

In the warmer Mediterranean regions, most pork products are cooked first and, instead of the beloved pimentón, black pepper is more often the seasoning of choice. Majorcans and Canary Islanders favor pimentón. In the northern, mountainous, rainy region of Spain, cooked and smoked pork products are typical.

Morcilla (Black Sausage)

Morcilla is a delicious blood sausage. Pork blood mixed with rice and flavored

FIGURE 7.5 Morcilla.
Source: Pabkov/Fotolia.

with garlic, onion, pimentón, and salt gives it a meaty texture. Sometimes morcilla is flavored with cinnamon and walnuts. Morcilla is commonly sliced and fried in olive oil until the edges crisp. It is also added to stews.

Butifarra

This Catalonian boiled sausage is made with fine-ground lean pork and garlic. It is reminiscent of American soft salami with lots of garlic. Butifarra pairs well with pickles, sharp cheese, and spicy peppers. Serve it thinly sliced on bread or diced for snacking.

MAGICAL MEMBRILLO

Spanish cookbook author Janet Mendel calls *membrillo* (*mem-BREE-yo*) or quince paste magical. She likes to dissolve homemade or Spanish membrillo in a small amount of hot water and season it with sherry vinegar for a quick sauce, great with duck and pork. She suggests making membrillo into a sorbet with orange zest, adding that the high amount of pectin creates a creamy, smooth texture. If an abundance of quince is available, make it into an incomparable house-made quince paste: Simmer diced quince in water until soft, drain and purée, then

FIGURE 7.6 Membrillo.
Source: Nito/Fotolia.

mix with equal parts sugar by volume, a little lemon juice, and vanilla bean. Simmer in saucepan until garnet-colored and very thick like peanut butter. Transfer paste to oiled pan and place in a 200 degree F oven until hardened and firm. Cool and store in refrigerator up to 1 year.

SPANISH FLAVOR FOUNDATIONS

Spanish Signature Aromatic Vegetable Combo: Sofrito

Sofrito or the Catalan *sofregit* (soo-frah-geet) consists of finely diced onions, garlic, tomatoes and parsley (sometimes bell peppers), and olive oil. The vegetables, starting with onion, cook slowly in olive oil until golden and thick to form an aromatic *flavoring base*, *sauce*, or *cooking medium*. Sofrito is useful either as a stand-alone tomato sauce (toss with cooked pasta or serve with rice or eggs) or as an important ingredient in other dishes like *empanada, paella*, stew, or fish soup.

Important Herbs

Italian parsley, bay leaves, oregano, rosemary, cilantro, and thyme

Signature Seasonings

Liquid/Paste

Vino de Jerez (Sherry)

Sherry is a fortified wine made mainly from the white Palomino grape grown and fermented around the town of Jerez, Spain, also known as the "sherry triangle." This region is known for the unique bacteria, which give Spanish sherry its characteristic nutty flavor. The name "sherry" came from the anglicized version of Jerez. After fermentation, sherry is fortified with brandy. Because the grape sugar is allowed to completely ferment into alcohol, it is initially dry. Sugar is added later. Sherry ranges from dry and pale *fino, manzanilla* and *manzanilla pasada* (aged), to *amontillado* (darker than fino and lightly sweetened) and the darker, more alcoholic and heavier *oloroso*, which is aged longer than fino or amontillado. *Amoroso* is a sweetened oloroso. Cream sherry and *jerez dulce* (sweet sherry) are blended sweet sherries.

Vinagre de Jerez (Sherry Vinegar)

This pungent vinegar is made from sherry wine and must be produced in the "sherry triangle" around Jerez, Spain. *Vinagre de Jerez* must age at least 6 months in wood. *Vinagre de Jerez Reserva* ages 2 years in wood and the newer *Vinagre de Jerez Gran Reserva* ages at least 10 years in wood. The best sherry vinegars are deep and complex. Spanish cooks use sherry vinegar in soup (gazpacho and salmorejo), stew, sauces, and dressings, as well as on salads.

Sidra (Fermented Apple Cider)

Natural "hard" Spanish cider production takes place mainly in the northern regions of Asturias, Galicia, and Basque country, where the cooler climate is good for growing apples. Fermentation is slow and cool and lasts until the cider reaches 4.5 percent alcohol. It is siphoned into new chestnut barrels where residual sugar gives some carbonation and typically aged 6 months. Spanish cider has a dominant wild yeast flavor; some have dry, tannic finish, while others are sweet and bubbly. Sidra is used to poach fish or chicken, in stews, and pairs well with hearty casseroles, steak, cod, sausages, and cheeses. Sidra is served in pubs that specialize in it called *sidrerías* and *chigres*. Asturian cider is usually sweeter with a light sparkle; it tends to complement the chorizos and seafood. Basque sidra is usually drier and somewhat austere, which is softened in bars where they pour it from great height to aerate and enhance.

Animal

Anchoas (Preserved Anchovies)

These tiny fish come oil-packed or salt-packed in cans and bottles. The Iberian Peninsula is known for the best anchovies in the world, especially from L'Escala on the Mediterranean coast of Catalonia, where they are known as *anxovas*, and from Cantabria on the Bay of Biscay west of the Basque region, where they are called *bocartes*. The strong flavor of anchovies is due to the curing process, which involves salting, applying pressure, and storing in barrels at 50 degrees F from 6 to 10 months. A properly cured anchovy should be reddish-tan, firm (but not hard), and immersed in clear oil. The best Spanish anchovy fillets are packed in extra virgin olive oil. Anchovies are pure umami. (See chapters *France* and *Italy* for more information.)

Boquerón (White Anchovies)

These uncured, fresh "white" anchovies are usually sold filleted and marinated in oil and vinegar. They work well as a garnish or on salads and toast as a tapa. Boquerónes are popular in Sicily as well.

FIGURE 7.7 White anchovies.
Source: Lsantilli/Fotolia.

Vegetable/Fruit

Capers

A favorite of Mediterranean cooking, capers are small unopened buds of the Mediterranean bush *Capparis spinosa L.*, closely related to the cabbage family, but they look more like a rose bush. Caper bushes grow wild and are also cultivated throughout the Mediterranean. Pickled in vinegar or preserved in salt (which brings out their flavor), European cooks consider the smallest capers (*nonpareilles*) the best. Capers have a sharp, mustard-like, peppery flavor, which add tang to vinaigrette, sauces, salads, and meat and fish dishes. Cooks in the Mediterranean pair them with anchovies. Use capers whole, crushed, or chopped. Rinse salted capers to remove excess salt, or drain pickled capers—save the salty caper pickling liquid for use in sauces and dressings.

Ñoras

This small, round, sweet red pepper is dried and sometimes ground. Ñoras are used whole or shredded in stews.

Smoky Spanish Paprika (Pimentón)

Earthy-mild to spicy-hot, pimentón is made from small red peppers that are smoke-dried and ground. Spanish cooks use it in chorizo,

FIGURE 7.8 Dried nora peppers.
Source: nito/Fotolia.

in sauces, on chicken or octopus, and on eggs. The most famous pimentón, La Vera, is produced in Extremadura, which has warm, dry summers that are good for growing peppers. There are three types of pimentón:

- Dulce or Sweet
- Agridulce or Medium-Hot
- Picanté or Hot

Piquillo Peppers (Pimentos de Piquillos)

This triangular, 3-inch long, red pepper is mildly spicy and roasted in wood-burning ovens to give it an intense aroma. It is peeled and canned in jars. These versatile peppers may be eaten straight from the jar, with vinaigrette, stuffed, or made into a sauce.

Seville Orange (Bitter/Sour Orange or Bigarade)

This bitter orange with its thick rind is not eaten fresh, but used only for marmalade. A native of Vietnam, the Seville orange was brought to Spain by the Moors and thrives in Seville, with its warm southern climate. The Latin former Spanish colonies use the juice to flavor ceviche.

Herbal/Spice

Italian Parsley
See *Italy Signature Seasonings*.

Saffron (Azafran)
Saffron is the slow-roasted or sun-dried stigma threads of a special crocus. The La Mancha region of Spain leads the European saffron market with this distinctive, honey-earthy-bitter spice. Cooks use saffron in paella and fish soups. Soak threads in warm or hot water 15 to 20 minutes before using. Avoid ground saffron, which is not always pure, and often has less flavor.

FIGURE 7.9 Piquillo peppers.
Source: Ben Fink/Dorling Kindersley.

FIGURE 7.10 Seville or bitter orange.
Source: Reika/Shutterstock.

SPANISH WILD MUSHROOMS

All Spanish cooks love to forage, and Girona is a region in Catalonia that has some of the best mushroom hunting in Spain. Catalan cuisine is based on foraging and mushrooms are prized food. With around 100 edible varieties, taking into account flavor and texture, about 15 are excellent, 35 to 40 are very good and more than 40 are edible. These are the most common and best tasting. For more information on specific mushrooms see *Italian Vegetables* in chapter *Italy* and *French Mushrooms and Fungus (Champignons)* in chapter *France*.

Chanterelles

See *Italian Mushrooms* or *French Mushrooms* in chapter *Italy* or *France*.

Morels

See *Italian Mushrooms* or *French Mushrooms* in chapter *Italy* or *France*.

Niscalos (Saffron Milk Caps and Red Pine)

These mushrooms are prolific in Girona. Milk caps have a short stem, a 5-inch fleshy, thick, vase-shaped cap and color ranging from yellow to orange and are highly delicious.

(Continued)

(Continued)

Rovellos (Cepes or Porcini)

This is the famous creamy bolete known to most in North America as porcini.

Truffles

See *Italian Mushrooms* or *French Mushrooms* in chapters *Italy* or *France*.

FIGURE 7.11 Niscalos (mushrooms).
Source. Hemeroskopion/Fotolla.

SEASONING AND PASTE MIXTURES

SPANISH ADOBO

Adobo is Spanish for "seasoning" or "marinade." It also refers to the marinade or seasoning mix. Food marinated or seasoned with adobo has been "adobada."

Basic Spanish Adobo Marinade

2 to 3 tablespoons white wine vinegar or sherry vinegar
3/4 ounces garlic, 3 large cloves, 4-1/2 teaspoons minced or mashed
1/2 to 3/4 teaspoon ground cumin
1 teaspoon dried *or* 1 tablespoon fresh chopped oregano
Optional: 1 teaspoon sweet or smoked paprika
Optional: 1-1/2 teaspoons minced fresh thyme leaves
Optional: 1/8 teaspoon cayenne

One pound of firm fish, chicken breast, or pork loin, diced into 1-inch cubes

1 Mix together **adobo marinade** and optional ingredients. Toss with cubed fish or meat.

2 Marinate meat 2 hours at room temperature and fish 20 to 30 minutes, or refrigerate 1 to 4 hours. Bring fish or meat to room temperature and blot dry.

3 Adobo Cooking Options:

For deep-fried tapa "en adobo": Toss meat or fish with salt, then in a mixture of flour and cornmeal. Deep-fry in an olive oil/canola oil mix until done, 5 minutes.

For grilled tapa en adobo: Blot meat or fish dry, season with salt, and rub with olive oil. Skewer meat or fish cubes and grill over medium heat until almost cooked through.

SAUCES

Spanish cooks, like cooks in Italy and France, prepare a base of aromatic vegetables like onion, garlic, and tomato, and cook it down into a thick sauce. This sofrito or sofregit is just one of the fundamental sauces of Spanish cuisine. Others are *béchamel, samfaina, picada, romesco, salsa Española, vinaigreta, salsa verde* (green sauce), *mojos, pisto, marinera,* tomato sauce (like southern Italian *sugo pummarola*), and *allioli* (mayonnaise). Many types of stew begin with a version of sofrito/sofregit, which provides a savory base for fish, meat, poultry, and vegetable dishes. Spanish cooks say mayonnaise originated with an eighteenth-century Minorcan cook.

SIGNATURE RECIPE

SPANISH SOFRITO OR CATALAN "SOFREGIT" (*SOO-FRAH-GEET*)

The longer sofrito cooks, the more flavor it develops. Plan on 30 minutes to 1 hour for proper sofrito. Make extra and store for use in other dishes. Some cooks add smoky Spanish paprika, herbs or dried, sweet red peppers called ñora.

Yields 1-1/2 to 2 cups

Basic Sofrito

4 tablespoons olive oil
8 to 9 ounces onions, 2 cups peeled and finely diced
1 pound ripe tomatoes, 2 large
1/4 ounce garlic, 1 large clove, 1-1/2 teaspoons peeled and finely minced
1/8 ounce trimmed Italian parsley, 1 tablespoon minced

Another Sofrito

1/4 to 1/2 cup olive oil
6 to 7 ounces onion, 1 medium, 1 to 1-1/2 cups finely diced
8 ounces ripe tomato, 1 large
1/2 ounce garlic, 2 large cloves, 1 tablespoon peeled and minced
6 ounces red bell pepper, 1 medium, about 1-1/3 cups stemmed, seeded, and finely diced

1 Heat olive oil in an earthenware casserole or 4-quart saucepan. When oil is hot, add onion and turn heat to low. Cook onion until it goes translucent, turns golden, and begins to brown, 15 minutes. Some cooks allow onion to cook longer and to caramelize. Stir often so onions cook evenly.

2 While onions cook, slice tomatoes in half around their equators. Grate cut side of tomatoes on large holes of box grater set over plate or bowl until all pulp is gone and only tomato skin remains. Discard tomato skin. 1 pound tomatoes yield about 1-1/3 cups tomato pulp. One half pound yields about 5 fluid ounces tomato pulp. Set tomato aside.

3 Add garlic (and bell peppers if using) to onions and cook until soft, 3 minutes.

4 Add tomato pulp to onions and garlic, stir, and partially cover pan. Simmer sauce until jam-like, 30 minutes, stirring occasionally. *To caramelize sofrito more fully,* uncover cooking vessel and allow moisture to evaporate. Watch carefully as sofrito thickens and starts to brown and stick. Add small amounts of water as necessary to keep it from burning.

5 (Stir in parsley if using.) Season sofrito with salt and pepper to taste.

Grate Tomatoes

Many Spanish recipes call for peeled, seeded, and chopped tomatoes. Across the Mediterranean cooks slice tomatoes through the "equator," some squeeze out seeds, and then grate the tomato on the large holes of a box grater set on a plate or in a bowl. The tomato flattens and when the peel is shorn of its tasty pulp, it may be discarded. A coarse tomato purée will be in the bowl, perfect for most cooking uses. **1-1/2 pounds tomatoes yields about 2 cups grated pulp.**

FIGURE 7.12 Tenerife, Canary Islands.
Source: Thierry GUIMBERT/Fotolia.

CANARY ISLANDS MOJO SAUCE

The cooking of Spain's Canary Islands arises out of native and imported ingredients (Africa is nearby), and some dishes, like mojo, came from Portuguese immigrants. A popular uncooked sauce, mojo is similar to thick vinaigrette or thin chutney. It accompanies "wrinkled" potatoes, boiled or fried fish, roasted chicken, roasted maize meal, or traditional sancocho (seafood stew). Mojo will strengthen the flavor of mild dishes and cooks sometimes simmer fish in it.

There are two main types of mojo: the red picón and bravo—or the green mojo verde and mojo de cilantro. All mojos employ olive oil, vinegar, or citrus, and sometimes breadcrumbs, raw garlic, ground cumin, or smoked paprika. Fresh or dried red picona peppers and dried chili form the base of red mojos; green mojos have cilantro or Italian parsley and, sometimes, green bell peppers, or avocado.

Each sauce yields 1-1/2 to 2 cups

Green Mojo de Cilantro

1/2 to 1 ounce garlic, 2 to 4 large cloves, peeled and crushed
1/4 to 1/2 teaspoon ground cumin
1 to 1-1/2 ounces cilantro, 2 cups lightly chopped
1/2 cup olive oil, *divided*
Optional: 6 ounces ripe avocado, 1 small, pitted and peeled
2 to 4 tablespoons sherry vinegar

Spicy Red Mojo Picón

1/2 to 3/4 ounce garlic, 2 to 3 large cloves, 3 to 4-1/2 teaspoons peeled and crushed
1 tablespoon ground cumin
1 tablespoon smoked paprika
3-inch dried red chili, stemmed and seeded, chopped
1 tablespoon olive oil
12 ounces red bell peppers, 2 medium, about 2 to 2-2/3 cups, stemmed, seeded, and diced

1/2 to 1 cup olive oil, as needed
Sherry vinegar, to taste

1 Gather ingredients and prep them.

2 For smooth mojo, place garlic, spices, and chili into blender or food processor with kosher salt and 1 tablespoon oil, and process to a paste.

   Green Mojo: Add cilantro and optional avocado to blender with paste and purée.

   Red Mojo: Add a quarter of diced bell pepper to blender with paste, and process until smooth. Add remaining bell pepper in 3 parts and blend each time until sauce is smooth.

3 With machine running, drizzle in remaining olive oil gradually. Season with vinegar, salt, and freshly ground pepper to taste. If not using sauce the same day, store in a glass jar covered with a thin layer of olive oil, seal tightly, and refrigerate.

Vary! Improvise!

☞ *Thicker Sauce: Remove crusts from one slice white bread and tear bread into small pieces. After adding olive oil, alternately add small pieces of the bread and small amounts of water or broth until sauce is thick, but not as thick as a paste.*

ALLIOLI (GARLIC EMULSION)

Spanish cooks make traditional allioli without egg. A modern version uses one egg. Sprouted or prepeeled garlic can be bitter or watery and may adversely affect the emulsification. Be patient, emulsions take time. A little mashed potato or fresh, white breadcrumbs will stabilize the sauce if it won't emulsify easily.

Yields about 1-1/3 cups thick sauce

2 ounces fresh garlic cloves, about 8 large cloves, about 4 tablespoons peeled and minced
2 to 3 tablespoons freshly squeezed lemon juice, 1 large lemon
1 cup extra virgin olive oil

1 **Mortar with pestle:** Pound minced garlic and 1 teaspoon kosher salt in a large mortar with a pestle. When garlic is completely crushed into a wet paste, *slowly* drip oil into it while stirring and pounding. Finished paste will resemble a waxy mayonnaise. Stir in lemon juice. Paste will whiten and lighten. To thin paste, stir in cold water.

2 **Blender:** Place minced garlic and 1 teaspoon kosher salt into blender. Purée and scrape down until garlic becomes a wet paste. With machine running, add 1/2 tablespoon lemon juice and 1/4 cup oil *in a thin stream*. Repeat with remaining lemon juice and oil in 3 more batches. The sauce should be the consistency of thick mayonnaise. Taste and adjust flavors with lemon juice or salt as needed. Thin with cold water.

3 **To Serve:** Serve with fish, broiled meat, vegetables, paella, or rice. Store garlic sauce in refrigerator. It will keep several days refrigerated.

Vary! Improvise!

☛ *Quince Allioli: Melt quince paste with water until it forms a thick purée. Cool and fold into allioli to taste.*
☛ *Saffron Allioli: Steep 1/8 teaspoon crumbled saffron in 1 tablespoon hot water until cool. Fold into allioli.*

PICADA

Picada is one of the four important Catalan "sauces" along with sofrito, samfaina, and allioli. Romesco sauce is a newer addition. All five may be used as a straight sauce, added to a sauce or added to other dishes like soup or stew to garnish or provide flavor. Picada adds a nutty finish, similar to French persillade and Italian gremolada or pesto. A basic picada consists of 1 part chopped toasted almonds, hazelnuts, or pine nuts, or a combination, 1/2 part minced parsley, 1/4 part minced garlic, and sometimes olive oil and/or toasted bread, pounded together in mortar with pestle. Catalan cooks often stir picada into fish soup to thicken and add complexity.

SPANISH ROMESCO SAUCE

Romesco sauce originated in the Spanish Mediterranean coastal city of Tarragona, 60 miles southwest of Barcelona. Its important signature ingredients are mortar-pounded garlic, nuts (almond, pine nuts, hazelnuts), bread, and since the seventeenth century, tomatoes and peppers or chilies, all seasoned with vinegar and olive oil. Everything goes better with romesco sauce.

Yields about 2 cups thick sauce, 6 to 8 servings

3 ounces blanched whole almonds, 3/4 cup
   or 1/4 cup each almonds, pine nuts, and hazelnuts
1-1/2 ounces country bread, about 1-1/2 slices toasted and torn
6 ounces tomato, 1 medium, sliced in half through its equator
1/2 ounce garlic, 2 large cloves, peeled
3/4 teaspoon pimentón (smoked paprika)
1-1/2 inch dried red chili, stemmed and seeded
   or 1/8- to 1/4-teaspoon cayenne pepper
2 tablespoons red wine vinegar, more as necessary
1/3 to 1/2 cup extra virgin olive oil

1 Preheat oven to 375 degrees F. Spread almonds on a sheet pan and bread on another. Place pans in oven and toast each until golden, 6 to 10 minutes. Spread and roast hazelnuts and pine nuts on separate pans, 10 minutes. Rub skin off hazelnuts as much as possible.

2 Rub tomato with olive oil and roast cut side down in baking dish until wrinkled and tender, 15 to 20 minutes, and peel. Cool ingredients.

3 Crush nuts, bread, garlic, chili or cayenne, and 1/2 to 1 teaspoon kosher salt together in mortar or purée in food processor. Add tomato, smoked paprika, and vinegar. Purée-pulse to a smooth paste. Slowly whisk, or drizzle olive oil in with machine running. Taste sauce and season with more salt or vinegar. If mixture is too thick, thin with warm water. Rest romesco 20 to 30 minutes at room temperature and taste again before serving.

4 **To Serve:** This marvelous sauce may function as a stew base for seafood, or as a cold sauce for raw or cooked, hot or cold vegetables, rice, paella, rice or pasta dishes, meat, or eggs. Prepare sauce a day ahead. Refrigerated, it will keep for a week.

PERSISTENT AND PREVAILING FOAM

Foams, considered by many modern critics as a sure-to-fade fad, have been around since the first cook whipped egg whites or cream or prepared *zabaglione* and *sabayon*. Modern gastronomy's foam sauces, first featured by Spanish chef Ferran Adriá, are still a source of delight to many. They start with liquid infused with a strong flavor essence like carrot, beets, asparagus, coconut, foie gras, or fish. Some chefs aerate liquids with an immersion blender and carefully scoop off the evanescent foam, or froth liquid through a nitrous oxide-fitted foamer.

Chefs stabilize foams before aeration with gelling substances dissolved in rich flavored liquid—lecithin, unflavored gelatin, or agar-agar.

Foam sauces are simple affairs: Bring infused milk almost to a boil, remove from heat and drop in diced, cold unsalted butter while puréeing with an immersion blender. Or mix cold water with rice vinegar, wasabi powder, and lecithin granules, and immersion blend until foamy. Allow foam to rise. Spoon it off gently onto a bowl of fish soup or a seared tuna or salmon fillet.

SPECIAL METHODS

FIGURE 7.13 Typical Spanish tapas bar.
Source: © Travel Pictures/Alamy.

Spanish Tapas and the Basque Pintxo

Article I. The word *tapas* is derived from the Spanish verb *tapar*, "to cover." Originally they came from Southern Spain during a time when bars covered glasses of wine or sherry with bread and ham to keep out flies, and indeed they still accompany a beverage. Tapas have exploded into a wide variety of appetizers or snacks, cold (mixed olives, ham, and cheese) or warm (fried baby squid, or simmered shrimp). Tapas can be social drinking appetizers eaten standing up or a quick meal. In the Basque region all tapas are called *pintxos* (thorn or spike) whether arranged with skewers, toothpicks, or not.

Tapas reveal the way in which Spanish cuisine is changing. In *Tapas*, Joyce Goldstein says that modern tapas are precisely cut, decoratively arranged, and often deconstructed: elements of a traditional dish are offered in different combinations, served at different temperatures, or presented differently.

Signature Technique: Ways to Tapa

Most tapas bars include items that appear everywhere in Spain: a selection of local and national cheeses, serrano (sometimes Ibérico) ham, cod purée, patatas bravas (fried potatoes with tomato), albondigas (meatballs), grilled bread with tomato, egg tortilla, a cazuela of sizzling shrimp, and pulpo a la Gallega (Galician octopus). These are top favorites that represent three major tapas categories outlined by Joyce Goldstein in Tapas: cosas de picar (finger food), pinchos (skewered food), and cazuelas (fork food).

- *Cosas de picar include things that can be eaten with the hands in one or two bites: slices of sausage or ham, cubed cheese, fried marcona almonds, tortilla, olives, marinated sardines or anchovies, fritters, croquettes, small empanaditas, tartaletas (savory tartlets), bocadillos (mini sandwiches), and tostas (food spread on bread) like olive paste, allioli, or fresh tomato with anchovy or cheese, piquillo pepper, or serrano ham.*
- *Pinchos include food cooked on skewers or served on skewers or with toothpicks. Pinchos are traditional in northern Spain and popular in Basque country. The beloved Gilda pincho is pickled Basque pepper, guindilla peppers, anchovy fillets, pitted manzanilla olives, and white anchovies on a skewer. Pincho moruno (Moorish) is a highly seasoned grilled pork kebab. Wedges of Manchego cheese with quince preserve or sautéed chorizo chunks become pinchos when piled onto toothpicks.*

TAPAS TRADITION

Cookbook author and chef Joyce Goldstein, writing in *Tapas: Sensational Small Plates from Spain*, has found that tapas "originated in the wine-growing regions of Andalusia" and were probably heavily influenced by the meze tradition of the Moors (Muslims) who lived in the region from the eighth until the fifteenth centuries. Goldstein points out that although chef Ferran Adriá and his culinary explorations have influenced young Spanish chefs, traditional tapas are still very popular because Spaniards refuse to "give up their favorite way to eat."

• *Cazuelas* include foods made in a cazuela (shallow baking dish) or cooked with a sauce, and which need utensils for eating. Smaller versions of main dishes like arroz negro, stuffed peppers, fideuá (noodle paella), and fabada asturianas (bean and meat stew) are often served as tapas.

TAPA 1: COD POTATO PURÉE OR DONKEY CHOKERS (BRANDADA OR ATASCABURRAS)

Yields 5 to 6 cups, 4 to 6 servings

8 ounces salt cod
1-1/4 pounds baking potatoes, about 5 cups peeled and cut into large dice
1/2 ounce garlic, 2 large cloves, 1 tablespoon peeled and minced
1/4 cup *plus* 1 tablespoon extra virgin olive oil, *divided*

Garnish: 1/8 to 1/4 ounce trimmed Italian parsley, 1 tablespoon chopped

For Serving

4 to 6 ounces 1/4 to 1/2-inch-thick slices country bread, 4 to 6 slices toasted and cut in half

1 Soak and rinse cod per instructions for *Shredded Salt Cod with Tomatoes and Olives*. Place cod in small saucepan and cover with cold water. Bring to a simmer and cook until cod flakes easily, about 5 minutes. Drain, reserve 1 cup cooking water, and set aside. Remove and discard skin and bones from cod. Flake meat and set aside.

2 Place potatoes in saucepan and cover with cold water. Bring to boil, lower heat and simmer until potatoes are very tender, 10 to 15 minutes. Put potatoes through ricer.

3 Place garlic into large bowl. Gradually add potatoes and mix to smooth paste. Stir in 1/4-cup oil and 1/2 cup reserved cooking liquid. The purée should be thick. Thin with cooking liquid as necessary. Fold flaked cod into purée.

4 **To Serve:** Plate *brandada*, and drizzle with remaining olive oil. Garnish with parsley. Serve with toast.

Vary! Improvise!

☞ *Sinful Spanish Stuffed Potatoes:* Using the Tapa 1 recipe: Bake 6 small scrubbed potatoes. Cook cod with 1 cup milk or water, garlic and olive oil. Purée. Scoop out baked potatoes, leaving shells, and mash with cod. Stuff potatoes with potato-cod mixture. Top potatoes with allioli (garlic mayonnaise).

☞ Substitute flaked, skinned, and boned smoked whitefish for cod. Do not soak or cook.

TAPA 2: FIERY FRIED POTATOES (PATATAS BRAVAS)

This recipe originally comes from a Madrid bar that is renowned for it. The sauce may be used on octopus or shrimp.

Yields about 4 cups, 4 to 6 servings

1-1/2 pounds waxy, boiling potatoes
Olive oil for frying

Sauce

1 teaspoon hot pimentón (smoked paprika)
1/2 teaspoon hot red pepper flakes
1/2 teaspoon Tabasco sauce (or Chipotle Tabasco sauce)
1 teaspoon red wine vinegar
1/2 cup tomato purée or sauce

1 **Boil potatoes:** Place potatoes in medium saucepan and cover with cold water. Bring to a boil over medium-high heat. Lower heat and slow-boil potatoes uncovered until fork-tender, 15 to 25 minutes. Drain potatoes, and cool. Peel potatoes, and dice into 1-inch cubes to yield about 3 cups.

2 Preheat oven to 300 degrees F. Line a half-sheet pan with parchment paper and set aside.

3 **Deep-fry potatoes:** Pour 1-1/2 inches oil into a heavy, deep 10- to 11-inch pan. Heat pan over high heat until oil becomes very hot: oil should ripple and should register about 365 degrees. Add the potatoes and fry until golden, about 10 to 15 minutes. Do not stir for at least 2 minutes—potatoes will stick and break. Remove potatoes with slotted spoon and drain. Reserve frying oil. Place potatoes on prepared sheet pan and sprinkle with kosher salt. Place pan in oven to stay warm.

4 **Prepare sauce:** Pour 3 tablespoons of the frying oil into a 2-quart saucepan. Heat over low heat. Stir in pimentón, pepper flakes, Tabasco, and vinegar. Blend well with a heatproof rubber spatula, and remove from heat. Pour tomato purée or sauce into a blender and scrape in pimentón mixture. Purée them together on medium speed until sauce is smooth and light colored, about 1 minute.

5 **To Serve:** In a warmed serving bowl, fold together hot potatoes and sauce from blender. Taste potatoes, and season with salt if necessary. Serve potatoes while hot.

Source: *The Cuisines of Spain* by Teresa Berrenechea.

TAPA 3: SPANISH POTATO PIE (TORTILLA)

FIGURE 7.14 Spanish potato pie.
Source: Ildi/Fotolia.

In Spain, a tortilla is a round egg cake often with other ingredients like potatoes, peppers, asparagus, ham, or artichokes. Beloved Spanish tortillas make satisfying, quick picnic, brunch, lunch, dinner, or snack dishes. Tortillas, cut into chunks, are one of Madrid's favorite tapas.

Yields about 4 cups batter; one 10-inch tortilla, 4 lunch servings

1/2 cup olive oil
1-1/2 pounds baking potatoes, about 3 cups peeled and diced into 1/2-inch cubes
6 ounces onion, 1-1/2 cups finely sliced
1-1/2 cups lightly whisked eggs, 6 to 7 large
Optional: 2 ounces serrano ham, 1/2 cup diced
    or 2 ounces dry chorizo, 1/2 cup diced

For Serving

Allioli

1 Heat oil in a deep 10-inch nonstick skillet over medium heat. Add potatoes and turn to coat evenly in oil. Season potatoes with 1-1/2 teaspoons kosher salt. Reduce heat to medium-low, cover skillet, and cook potatoes until tender but not brown, about 15 minutes. Stir potatoes occasionally so they cook evenly.

2 Remove potatoes from skillet with slotted spoon and transfer to a bowl to cool. Heat oil remaining in skillet over medium and add onion. Cook until slightly golden, 10 to 12 minutes. Transfer onions to potatoes in bowl with slotted spoon; set skillet aside with remaining oil.

3 Whisk eggs with 1/2 teaspoon kosher salt and freshly ground pepper. Fold eggs and optional meat into cooled potatoes and onions.

4 Remove 1 tablespoon oil from skillet and set aside. Heat skillet with remaining oil over medium heat, and when hot, pour in egg-potato mixture; press lightly to even out top. Without stirring, cook tortilla until edges of egg are set, 3 to 4 minutes; tilt pan to move runny egg from center to sides. Cover skillet, reduce heat to medium-low, and cook tortilla until egg is almost set in the center, 8 to 12 minutes. Remove lid. Place a large plate over tortilla and invert it onto the plate.

5 Add 1 tablespoon reserved oil to skillet and heat over medium heat. When hot, reduce heat to medium-low, slide tortilla back into skillet and cook until egg is completely set and lightly golden, about 5 minutes.

6 **To Serve:** Slide tortilla onto serving dish and serve hot or room temperature. For lunch, cut tortilla into 4 wedges. For tapas, cut into 1- or 2-inch squares and pierce with toothpicks. Serve with allioli, if desired.

Vary! Improvise!

☞ *In place of part of the potatoes, or along with them, add other types of vegetables like olives, artichokes, mushrooms, asparagus, bell peppers, or seafood like shrimp or tuna.*

TAPA 4: SKEWERED MEATBALLS (PINCHOS DE ALBONDIGAS)

Yields about 4 generous cups raw meat, 40 to 50 meatballs

2 pounds ground pork shoulder butt
1/2 ounce garlic, 2 large cloves, 1 tablespoon peeled and minced
2 to 3 ounces onion, 1/2 cup peeled and minced
1/2 ounce trimmed Italian parsley, 1/4 cup minced

Spice Paste

1 tablespoon kosher salt
1/4 teaspoon ground cayenne pepper
1 teaspoon smoked paprika (*pimentón*)
1 teaspoon sweet paprika
1/2 teaspoon ground cumin
1/2 teaspoon dried thyme
1/2 teaspoon dried oregano
Grating of fresh nutmeg
1 tablespoon red wine vinegar

Flour for dredging meatballs
1/2 cup olive oil for frying
Half of 7 ounce jar piquillo peppers, drained and patted dry
   or 3 ounces roasted red peppers, 1/2 to 2/3 cup

1 Mix pork, garlic, onion, and parsley together in large bowl.

2 *Prepare* **spice paste:** Combine kosher salt, spices, and vinegar in a small bowl and stir to a paste. Knead **spice paste** into meat with gloved hands. Rest meat 1 hour at room temperature or, for best flavor, refrigerated overnight. Fry one small patty of meat to test for salt. Form 1-1/2 to 2 tablespoons meat into balls. Dredge in flour and pat off excess. Place on sheet pan.

3 Preheat oven to 375 degrees F. Over medium heat, add enough oil to cover bottom of a 12-inch skillet. When the oil is hot, fry meatballs in batches until browned, 4 to 5 minutes. Place on parchment-covered sheet pan and place in oven to finish cooking.

4 **To Serve:** Slice peppers into long, 1/4-inch-wide strips. Spear a meatball. Fold pepper into thirds and spear with toothpick. Arrange filled skewers on serving platter. Serve warm or at room temperature.

Vary! Improvise!

☛ *Prepare meatballs with ground fish, turkey, chicken, or shrimp.*

☛ *Skewer other foods with the meatballs, but choose them by color.*

☛ *Make each skewer an art project with layered colors and flavors.*

FIGURE 7.15 Cazuela with shrimp, garlic, chili.
Source: uckyo/Fotolia.

TAPA 5: SIZZLING SHRIMP CAZUELA (GAMBAS AL AJILLO)

Yields about 2 cups, 6 to 12 appetizer servings

8 ounce loaf fresh country bread, 1 small
6 tablespoons olive oil
1/2 ounce garlic, 2 large cloves, peeled and crushed
Two 1-inch dried whole red chilies, crushed, more to taste
   or 3-inch long narrow fresh red chili, stemmed and seeded
1 pound 36/40 shrimp, 12 ounces peeled and deveined, blotted dry
1/4 teaspoon smoked Spanish paprika
1 lemon, cut into 6 wedges

Garnish: Chopped Italian parsley

1 Slice bread into 3/4-inch cubes and set aside in covered bowl or baggie.

2 Heat oil, garlic, and chili in a 2- to 3-quart heatproof casserole over medium-low heat. Brown garlic and discard, but keep chilies or chili. Toss shrimp in hot seasoned oil and cook just until opaque, 2 to 5 minutes. Toss with paprika. Season shrimp with salt and fresh lemon juice, to taste.

3 **To Serve:** Set out hot shrimp in casserole. Garnish with parsley. Place lemons and bread cubes on the side. Or spear shrimp and bread cubes onto bamboo skewers, plate, and drizzle bread with sizzling shrimp oil.

TAPA 6: GALICIAN OCTOPUS (PULPO A LA GALLEGA)

Some Spanish people feel that this could be the world's best tapa. It's the signature dish of Galicia. Cooked on a hot plate with potatoes, it's called pulpo a la plancha. *Some cooks toss the octopus into a boiling copper kettle, which turns the purplish octopus an orange hue.*

Yields about 2 cups, 4 to 6 servings

1 pound frozen octopus (freezing tenderizes it), thawed overnight in refrigerator
1/4 to 1/3 cup olive oil
1 teaspoon *pimentón* (smoked paprika)

1 Cover octopus with water and bring to a boil. Lower heat and simmer it partially covered 1 hour. Drain and cool octopus.

2 **To Serve:** Slice octopus into 1-inch chunks and dress with olive oil. Sprinkle with paprika and 1/2 teaspoon salt. Serve on toothpicks.

TAPA 7: CATALONIAN TOMATO TOASTS (PAN CON TOMATE)

Use firm, crusty country bread for this tapa. There is nothing like the combo of olive oil, seasonal tomato, bread, and salt. Traditional Spanish restaurants bring the bread, tomatoes, and oil to the table and allow diners to make their own pan con tomate. *Top* pan con tomate *with cheese or smoked ham, preserved sardines or sausage, or leave it plain and serve with potato tortilla or grilled meat.*

4 servings

4 ounces country bread, four 1/2-inch-thick oblong slices
1/2 ounce garlic, 2 large cloves, peeled, halved lengthwise, and crushed lightly
16 ounces very ripe, juicy tomatoes, 2 large
Spanish extra virgin olive oil
Optional: Sliced serrano ham and/or Spanish cheese

1 Toast or grill bread. Rub bread with garlic.

2 Slice tomatoes in half around the middle. Rub flesh onto bread generously.

3 **To Serve:** Drizzle bread with olive oil and season with crunchy sea salt. Serve immediately, or top with sliced Spanish ham or cheese and serve.

Vary! Improvise!

☞ *Prepare cazuela with fish cubes, scallops squid rings, or cubes of chicken or turkey breast.*

☞ **Vegetarian Cazuela:** *Dice eggplant into 1-inch cubes. Salt and rest cubes 15 minutes. Rinse and blot dry. Prepare as for shrimp, and cook eggplant until tender.*

FIGURE 7.16 Galician octopus.
Source: KarSol/Shutterstock.

FIGURE 7.17 Catalonian tomato toast.
Source: Kondor83/Fotolia.

Vary! Improvise!

☞ *Similar to bruschetta, tomato bread can be home to a large number of tasty toppings like grilled vegetables or smoked chicken or fish. Change the tomatoes to grilled peaches and top with Serrano ham for an untraditional tapa.*

Signature Technique: Puréed Soup

While puréed soups may strike some as glorified baby food, with correct consistency and skilled seasoning they can be memorable. Purées can be creamy without cream, making them excellent low-fat food. Their refinement positions them as a splendid first course. Spanish tomato gazpacho is the classic cold puréed-chunky soup-salad.

- **A blender makes the finest purées,** the food processor comes in second, and a food mill or an immersion blender third, but for large batches immersion blenders save on cleanup and time. Pounding ingredients with a mortar and pestle was the time-honored and time-consuming tradition of Spanish cooks.

- **Consistency is everything with a puréed soup.** Too thick and they feel gloppy and too thin and they don't satisfy. The proper consistency is like heavy cream.

- Starchy vegetable-based purée soups thicken upon standing so be prepared to thin with more liquid. Bread and nuts commonly bind and thicken Spanish soups.

- **Some like it hot:** The easiest hot purée soups are made by simmering ingredients together until tender, and puréeing them in the same pot. The cook may opt to strain cooked vegetables and purée in a blender or processor with a small amount of liquid, scrape purée into a clean pot, and stir in cooking liquid.

GAZPACHO: NO RESPECT

Gazpacho, originating in Andalusia before Roman times, was belittled as a primitive, provincial dish born in peasant fields (*Gaspa* is Italian for "remains" and *acho* is derogatory.) Things changed when, in the seventeenth century the Spanish finally accepted tomatoes, cucumbers, and peppers (from Columbus). In Madrid gazpacho comes with mayonnaise. Cordobans garnish with hard-cooked egg and ham, and in Extremadura gazpacho comes with ham. Andalusians eat *gazpacho ajo blanco.* Winter gazpacho is hot and thick, and in summer it's a puréed cold salad.

FIGURE 7.18 Andalusia, Spain.
Source: arenaphotouk/Fotolia.

RAW TOMATO AND VEGETABLE SOUP
(GAZPACHO ANDALUZ)

This is a dish best made with seasonal ripe tomatoes. Use a can of V-8 juice to boost flavor if winter tomatoes are all that's available. Gazpacho may be served warm or hot.

Yields 10 cups, 8 to 10 servings

2 ounces white artisan or country-style bread, 1-1/4 cups cubed and toasted
2-1/2 pounds summer-ripe tomatoes
1/4 ounce garlic, 1 large clove, 1-1/2 teaspoons minced
12 ounces English cucumber, about 1-1/2 cups peeled, seeded, and diced
4 to 5 ounces yellow or green bell pepper, about 3/4 cup seeded and diced
2 to 3 tablespoons sherry vinegar or red wine vinegar
1/4 cup extra virgin olive oil, more as needed
Torn basil leaves

Garnishes

2 ounces toasted country bread cubes, about 1-1/4 cups
6 ounces yellow or green bell pepper, about 1 cup finely diced
2 ounces Serrano ham or prosciutto, 1/4 cup finely diced
2 large hard-cooked eggs, finely diced
1/2 large avocado, about 1/2 cup finely diced

1 **Toast bread in oven:** Though it's not traditional, toasting gives the soup richer flavor. Spread bread cubes on sheet pan and place in 375 degree F oven until golden. Soak bread in 2 cups cold water until soft, 5 to 10 minutes. Drain bread, set aside, and reserve water.

2 **Peel and seed tomatoes:** Save seeds and juice and pass through strainer; reserve juice. Two and a half pounds juicy tomatoes will yield about 4 packed cups peeled, seeded, and diced tomato and up to 1 cup juice. Add the juice before adding water to the soup as it is puréed.

3 **Purée ingredients:** Place soaked bread and garlic into food processor, and purée until evenly chopped. Add tomatoes, cucumber, and bell pepper. For chunky soup, pulse-purée vegetables until soupy but with texture. For smooth soup purée ingredients until smooth.

4 **Adjust consistency:** Slowly pour the strained tomato juice, half the vinegar, salt, and part of the bread-soaking-water to achieve flavor and consistency desired: somewhere between a soup and a stew. With machine running, slowly pour in oil, or whisk in oil by hand. Season with 2 teaspoons kosher salt, and black pepper, if desired.

5 **Garnish and chill:** Stir basil and *garnishes* into soup or place **garnishes** and croutons in separate bowls for garnish at the table. Chill soup 1 to 4 hours, or in winter heat it gently, don't boil. Taste and adjust salt, pepper, oil, and vinegar.

6 **To Serve:** Ladle soup into bowls. If **garnishes** are separate, instruct diners to garnish at the table. Drizzle soup with an excellent olive oil, if desired.

Vary! Improvise!

☞ *Salmorejo: Gazpacho Cream from Córdoba, Andalucía:* For classic Salmorejo Cordobés, purée 1/4 pound country bread cubes (soaked 5 minutes in water and squeeze-drained), 2 pounds ripe peeled, seeded tomatoes, garlic, and vinegar until creamy. Slowly process in 1/2 cup oil until emulsified and creamy. Garnish soup with Serrano ham and hard-cooked eggs. Serve as soup, sauce, or dip.

☞ *Contemporary Gazpacho:* Try green tomatoes and green bell pepper for green gazpacho and yellow peppers and yellow tomatoes for yellow gazpacho. Improvise with fresh tart cherries or green or purple plums in place of tomatoes.

☞ *Salad Inspiration:* Use the flavors of a favorite salad as inspiration for an improvised gazpacho: escarole with grilled pears and blue cheese, Caesar salad, Greek salad; avocado, orange, and black olive with Romaine; bacon, tomato, and arugula or apple, walnut, and endive.

GARLIC AND ALMOND SOUP WITH GRAPES (GAZPACHO AJO BLANCO)

The Overnight Stay

The flavor of any soup, chili, or stew improves, softens, marries, and mellows upon standing. Cooks know that a good chili tastes better the next day: the flavors transform overnight from discordant to harmonious. Even an hour or two at room temperature makes a difference. Chilling slows the process.

Vary! Improvise!

☛ **Substitute** *sliced fresh figs and toasted Marcona almonds for grapes as garnish.*

☛ **Substitute** *diced tart apples for grapes.*

☛ **Puréed Salad Two:** *Add and purée watercress, spinach, arugula, radicchio, or lettuce for green gazpacho.*

☛ **Another Nut:** *Prepare gazpacho ajo blanco with macadamia nuts, Brazil nuts, pine nuts, pistachios, hazelnuts, cashews, or pumpkin seeds. Toast for richer flavor.*

Soak almonds overnight for finer purée. Toasting is optional, but it removes the raw bread flavor. Make soup 4 hours ahead for best texture and flavor. This gazpacho predates the tomato variety: prepare it when tomatoes are out of season.

Yields 1 quart, 4 servings

2 ounces sliced white country style bread: pugliese, ciabatta, or artisan
4 ounces whole blanched almonds, toasted, 1 cup
1/2 ounce garlic, 2 large cloves, blanched 1 minute in boiling water and peeled
2 ounces whole green grapes, about 12 or 1/2 cup
4 tablespoons olive oil
3 tablespoons sherry vinegar, more as needed

Garnish: 4 ounces green seedless grapes, 1 cup halved lengthwise

1 *Toast and soak bread:* Heat oven to 400 degrees F. Place bread on baking sheet and place in oven. Toast until golden and remove from oven. Tear bread into small pieces and soak in 2 cups water until soft, 5 minutes. Drain bread and reserve the soaking water.

2 Purée almonds, garlic, 1/2 teaspoon kosher salt, and whole grapes in food processor or blender until smooth. Add drained bread and purée until smooth, adding enough reserved soaking water to yield a heavy-cream soup consistency. With machine running, slowly pour in oil in thin stream then vinegar.

3 Scrape soup into bowl. Rinse out processor or blender bowl and lid with a little reserved water and stir into soup. Taste soup and season with more salt or vinegar as necessary. Add more water to achieve desired consistency. This should yield about 4 cups soup. Rest or refrigerate soup 30 minutes to 1 hour to allow flavor to develop.

4 **To Serve:** Ladle soup into soup plates and **garnish** with sliced grapes.

SIMMER, STEW, POACH, BOIL, AND STEAM

Spanish Soup

In Spain, soup is called *la comida de cuchara* or "spoon food." It is a popular lunch first-course or light dinner. *Sopa* is soup, *caldo* is broth, *crema* is a cream or puréed creamy soup, *cocido* is boiled dinner. *Potaje* is thick soup with legumes. Spanish cooks prepare rustic or refined, cold and hot soups based on bread, water, olive oil, seafood, potatoes, legumes, and ham, relying less on stock than French and Italian cooks.

Modern Spanish chefs like Ferran Adriá have taken Spanish soup a step further, "doing new things with old concepts," by deconstructing it into its parts. For instance, Adria freezes gazpacho into lollipop-shaped popsicles. "I'm not confined by classic techniques," he says. Adriá serves pea soup in a glass flute filled with hot liquid on top and cold on the bottom. Waiters instruct diners to drink it in one long sip.

SPANISH GARLIC SOUP

Everywhere in Spain and Italy cooks prepare a version of this soup. Some country cooks use water, not stock. That requires fresh garlic, great water, superb bread, and the best farm eggs.

Yields 9 to 10 cups, 4 to 6 servings

4 tablespoons olive oil
3 ounces garlic, 12 large cloves, crushed and peeled
4 ounces dense country bread, 4 thick slices, about 3 cups diced into 1/2-inch cubes
4 teaspoons smoked Spanish paprika
2 quarts chicken stock
4 to 6 large eggs

1 Heat oil and garlic over medium heat in 4-quart saucepan. Cook garlic until it browns completely, remove from pan with slotted spoon, and discard. Fry bread cubes in oil until golden, remove with slotted spoon, and set aside. Stir smoked paprika into saucepan, place on medium heat, and cook 2 to 3 seconds. Immediately pour in stock. Bring to a boil, lower heat, and simmer stock 10 minutes.

2 Break 4 (or 6) eggs, one by one, into small mixing bowl, and gently slide into simmering broth. Poach until white is firm, but when pressed, the yellow is still tender and liquid, 2 to 3 minutes.

3 Divide toasted bread cubes among 4 to 6 serving bowls. Remove eggs from saucepan with slotted spoon and place on top of bread. Taste broth and season with salt and pepper, if necessary.

4 **To Serve:** Ladle hot broth over egg and bread. Serve.

Vary! Improvise!

☞ *Crack raw eggs onto bread into ovenproof bowls, ladle hot stock over top, and place in 350 degree F oven until egg is poached.*

☞ ***Spanish Sopa de Picadillo:*** *Brown bread cubes. Heat chicken stock and 4 tablespoons dry sherry and boil 1 minute. Add 4 ounces diced Serrano ham and 2 diced, hard-cooked egg to broth. Garnish with toasted bread cubes and mint leaves.*

FISH SOUP-STEWS OF SPAIN AND THE MEDITERRANEAN: PLACE DICTATES

In Catalonia, *sofrito* or *sofregit* starts many seafood soups, and *picada* finishes them. Andalusian cooks use local hake, grouper, and tuna. Basque cooks make *porrusalda* with leeks and salt cod. Catalonians prepare *suquet*, a *juicy* seafood stew with monkfish, hake, clams, squid, shrimp, mussels, saffron, and almonds, and the classic *marmitako*, a stew of onion, potato, dried and fresh bell peppers, tomato, and tuna. In the Balearics, cooks prepare *burrida*, a seafood soup-stew common all around the Mediterranean, with skate in alioli-enriched stock. Provençal cooks make *bourride* and serve it with *rouille*; Ligurian cooks serve *burrida* with fried bread.

BASQUE TUNA AND POTATO STEW (MARMITAKO)

Prepare the base ahead and cook the fish gently in heat just before serving. This stew is a good use for frozen or strong-flavored tuna; the sauce is assertive. Notice the use of Mexican chilies. When Spain conquered Mexico, many Mexican foods infiltrated Spanish cuisine.

Yields about 8 cups, 4 to 6 servings

1 ounce dried ancho chilies, about 2, stems removed
1 pound skinned and cleaned fresh tuna
2 pounds russet potatoes, peeled
3 ounces green bell pepper, 1/2 medium
1/4 cup olive oil
6 to 7 ounces onion, 1-1/2 cups peeled and finely diced
1/2 ounce garlic, 2 large cloves, 1 tablespoon peeled and finely minced
1 tablespoon paprika
1 tablespoon tomato paste
2 to 3 tablespoons freshly squeezed lemon juice, 1 large lemon

1 Cover chilies with boiling water in small mixing bowl. Set aside until soft, 30 minutes. Drain chilies. Slit them open and rinse away seeds. Discard stems. Scrape out flesh with a paring knife to yield 2 tablespoons purée, and set aside. Discard skins.

2 Dice tuna into 3/4-inch cubes, sprinkle with 1 teaspoon kosher salt, and set aside in refrigerator until ready to use.

3 Dice potatoes into 1-inch cubes and place in a bowl of cold water to yield about 5 cups. Stem, seed, and slice green bell pepper lengthwise into 1/4-inch-wide strips to yield about 2/3 cup.

4 Heat olive oil in heavy 6-quart pot over medium heat. Stir in onion, garlic, bell pepper, and ancho chili flesh. Cook until vegetables soften and blend, 5 to 7 minutes. Stir in potatoes, paprika, and tomato paste. Season with a little salt and cover vegetables with 1 quart cold water. Bring stew to a boil, lower heat, and simmer partially covered until potatoes are tender, 30 to 45 minutes. Mash a few potatoes against the side of the pot to thicken stew.

5 **Just before serving:** Bring stew to a boil. Lower heat and stir in tuna. Simmer until opaque, but still slightly pink, 4 to 5 minutes.

6 **To Serve:** Taste stew and season with lemon juice and salt. Ladle stew into bowls and serve immediately.

Source: *The Cuisines of Spain* by Theresa Barrenechea.

Vary! Improvise!

☞ *Prepare marmitako with salmon instead of tuna.*

☞ *Substitute red bell pepper or strips of carrot for green bell pepper.*

FIGURE 7.19 Besalu, Catalonia, Spain.
Source: knet2d/Fotolia.

SPANISH RABBIT STEW WITH CHOCOLATE (CONEJO CON CHOCOLAT)

FIGURE 7.20 Rabbit cut into pieces.
Source: Gary Ombler/DK Images.

Catalonians first added chocolate (from Mexico) to savory dishes like this one during the flourishing seventeenth-century chocolate trade with the Antilles. Prepare a day ahead for best flavor.

4 to 6 servings

2 cups full-bodied dry red wine
1-1/2 ounces garlic, 6 large cloves, crushed lightly, peeled, and halved
3 pounds skinned rabbit, cut into 8 pieces
   or 4 pounds bone-in chicken breasts and thighs, 3-1/2 pounds skinned

Seasonings

1 sprig fresh thyme
1 sprig fresh rosemary
1 bay leaf
6 black peppercorns
2-inch stick cinnamon

About 1 to 1-1/4 ounce all-purpose flour, 1/4 cup
8 tablespoons olive oil, as needed, *divided*
8 to 9 ounces onion, 2 cups peeled and diced into 1/4-inch cubes
5 to 6 ounces carrot, 3/4 to 1 cup peeled and diced into 1/4-inch cubes
1/2 to 1 cup good, dry sherry *or* brandy
1-1/2 to 2 cups chicken stock
1 to 2 teaspoons grated orange zest
1 ounce bittersweet chocolate, 1/4 cup chopped or grated

For Serving

1 pound wide noodles, boiled and hot, or good bread

1 **Marinate:** Mix 2 teaspoons sea or kosher salt, wine, garlic, and rabbit or chicken in a stainless steel bowl. Tuck in **seasonings**. Cover bowl and refrigerate meat 4 hours. Turn pieces periodically *or* leave at room temperature 1 hour. Remove meat from marinade and pat dry. Set liquid and **seasonings** aside for later use.

2 **Sauté:** Pour flour into a large bowl and set aside. Heat 2 tablespoons oil in a 10- to 11-inch heavy 5- to 6-quart casserole or Dutch oven over medium-high heat. Stir in onion and carrot and cook until soft and lightly browned, 5 to 7 minutes. Scrape into a mixing bowl, and set aside.

3 Reheat casserole or Dutch oven over high heat and add 3 tablespoons oil. Lower heat to medium-high. Working in batches of a single layer of meat, toss meat in flour, shake off excess, and fry until evenly browned. Transfer browned meat to bowl with vegetables. Repeat frying process with more oil and remaining meat and flour. Drain excess fat from casserole and set casserole onto burner.

4 Pour sherry into casserole to deglaze, boil 30 seconds, and scrape up browned bits off bottom. Pour in marinade liquid and **seasonings** and 1-1/2 cups chicken stock. Bring liquids to a simmer and skim off foam and fat. Transfer meat and vegetables to casserole.

5 **Simmer:** Liquid should just cover meat. If it doesn't, pour in more stock. Bring casserole to a boil, and cover with lid slightly ajar. Lower heat and simmer, skimming occasionally, and turning meat so it cooks evenly, until it is noticeably tender, 1 hour. With slotted spoon, transfer meat to a clean bowl and keep warm.

6 **Reduce and season sauce:** Remove **seasonings** (herbs and cinnamon) and discard. Increase heat to high and reduce sauce by half, 7 to 10 minutes. Remove pan from heat, stir in orange zest. Taste sauce and season with salt and pepper. Stir in chocolate until it melts and mixes evenly. Return meat to casserole to heat through. Simmer on low heat several minutes if meat is not still warm, but don't boil.

7 **To Serve:** Transfer meat and sauce to warmed serving vessel. Serve with wide noodles or just bread and a vegetable or salad. Leftover sauce makes a great pasta sauce paired with goat cheese.

Ala Chilindron

When this term pops up on a Spanish menu it means something cooked with fresh and (sometimes dried) bell peppers, tomatoes, and onion. Lamb, chicken, and pork are simmered *ala chilindron*. It is a typical dish from northeastern Spain (Aragon, Navarra, and the Basque region), probably of Moorish origin.

FIGURE 7.21 Asturias coast (Costa Verde), Spain.
Source: david hughes/Fotolia.

ASTURIAN BEAN STEW (FABADA)

Like French cassoulet, an Asturian fabada or stew usually contains a variety of meats, at least one smoked, chorizo, and the famed morcilla or blood sausage. This one has additional chicken. Fabada simmers long and slow to infuse the beans with meaty flavor.

Yields 12 to 13 cups, about 6 servings

1 pound *fabes*, large white dried Asturian beans also called broad beans
   or 1 pound cannellini beans (white kidney beans)
      or 1 pound dried large lima beans
4 ounce slab smoked bacon
   or 4 ounce slab Spanish pancetta
12 ounces onions, 2 medium, *divided*
2-1/2 to 3 ounce head garlic, 2 ounces peeled cloves, about 8 large, *divided*
4 cups chicken stock
3 pounds chicken legs and thighs, 2-1/2 pounds skinned
1/4 cup olive oil
1 teaspoon smoked paprika
Pinch of saffron, crushed
8 ounces chorizo sausage

1 **Prepare beans:** Soak beans by quick soak or overnight method (see *Glossary*). Drain and discard soaking water from beans. After soaking there should be 4 to 5 cups drained beans. Pour beans into a heavy 6-quart pot. Halve and peel one onion and nestle into beans. Remove one clove of garlic, and set aside for later use.

2 **Blanch bacon:** Fill a medium saucepan with water and bring a boil. Immerse bacon in the boiling water 5 minutes, drain off water, and set bacon aside. Pour remaining garlic cloves, blanched bacon, and chicken stock into pot with beans. Bring to a boil, lower heat to low boil, and skim foam, 15 minutes. Nestle chicken into the beans, and lower heat to a bubbly simmer.

3 Finely dice remaining onion to yield about 1-1/2 cups. Peel and mince reserved garlic clove. In a 10-inch sauté pan, heat olive oil over medium heat, cook onion until soft and browned, 10 to 15 minutes. Add

garlic, cook 1 minute and stir in paprika and saffron. Scrape and stir mixture into simmering chicken and beans; rinse pan with 2 cups water and pour over beans. Simmer chicken and beans uncovered on low heat, adding water or stock as necessary to keep beans just covered with liquid, 1-1/2 hours.

4 Place whole chorizo in a small saucepan, cover with cold water, and bring to a simmer. Poach chorizo 5 minutes. Drain. Push chorizos into stew under the liquid; add another cup or more water if necessary. Simmer stew uncovered 30 minutes longer; do not stir stew. Remove pot from heat, cover, and rest 1 hour. Discard onion halves if desired.

5 **To Serve:** Remove bacon and chorizo; slice bacon thinly and chorizo into 1/2-inch chunks. Mix chorizo back into stew. Ladle stew into bowls and garnish with bacon.

SALMON POACHED IN CIDER (SALMÓN EN SIDRA)

Fish dishes in Italy, France, and Spain are often paired with boiled potatoes. The combination of sidra and potatoes is memorable. Notice how cider is reduced and used as a sauce with the fish, a technique also common to French cooking. Hard Spanish cider from Asturias, a region known for apples, is also used for braising chicken, anchovies, fish, or chorizo.

4 servings

24 ounces skinned, boned salmon fillet, cut into four 6-ounce pieces
 or 4 six-ounce salmon steaks
Flour for dredging
4 tablespoons olive oil, *divided*
1-1/2 cups hard dry apple cider
 or 1-1/4 cups sparkling white wine *plus* 4 tablespoons apple juice

For Serving

Boiled redskin or yellow Finn potatoes, halved or quartered

Garnish: 1/4 ounce trimmed Italian parsley, 2 tablespoons finely chopped

1 Preheat oven to 400 degrees F. Sprinkle kosher salt over salmon and rest at room temperature 15 minutes. Blot dry.

2 Heat a heavy, ovenproof 10-inch skillet over high heat with half the oil. Dredge 2 fillets in flour and shake off excess. Place the 2 fillets into hot oil and sear 2 minutes on each side. Transfer to parchment-covered sheet pan or plate. Heat skillet with remaining 2 tablespoons oil. Dredge, shake, and sear remaining two fillets in the same way. Return first two fillets to skillet. Pour cider over them and place skillet in oven to bake until fish are opaque when tested with tip of knife, 10 to 15 minutes.

3 **To Serve:** Remove fish from oven and baste with cider. Transfer fish to plates or a platter with potatoes. Reduce cider over high heat by half; scrape up bits in skillet. Taste sauce and season with salt and pepper. Spoon sauce over fish and garnish with parsley.

Source: *The Cuisines of Spain* by Teresa Barrenechea.

Vary! Improvise!

☛ *Authentic Flavor: Omit the chicken. Increase smoked bacon slab to 8 ounces or add 4 ounces lacón (Spanish cured pork hock). Add 8 ounces morcilla sausage in step 3.*

Signature Technique: Spanish Rice or Pasta (Paella or Fideuá)

Paella may be Spain's best-known culinary achievement. Paella is juxtaposed between Italian risotto and French pilaf like a middle sister. Paella was originally made outdoors by Valencian cooks over a wood fire, and always in the traditional thin-bottomed carbon steel paella pan. Use this same technique and substitute the thin, broken angel hair or vermicelli noodles called fideos for rice to make fideuá, similar to Mexico's sopa seca or "dry soup." The dry noodles are often toasted in hot oil before cooking.

The three best-known types of paella are paella Valenciana *(meat and poultry),* paella de marisco *(seafood), and* paella mixta *(mixed), but many other types exist.*

1 Choose the proper amount of rice (or elbow macaroni) for desired servings and the proper sized pan. The layer of raw rice (or fideos) should never be more than 1/2-inch deep.

Paella Proportions

Use approximately 1/4 to 1/2 cup uncooked rice per person

1/2-pound poultry, meat, or seafood per person/serving

Liquid should be double the volume amount of unwashed, raw rice.

Measure across top of pan from edge to edge; pan expands in diameter not depth:

12- to 13-inch paella pan serves 3 to 4 or 1 to 1-1/2 cups rice

14- to 15-inch paella pan serves 4 to 6 or 2 to 2-1/2 cups rice

16- to 18-inch paella pan serves 8 to 12 or 3 to 4 cups rice

2 **Keep ingredients simple.** Don't overload paella. Flavor-saturated rice is the star.

3 **Prep all ingredients before starting to cook:**

- Pour broth into saucepan with saffron.
- Cut meat and vegetables into bite-sized pieces.
- Soak dried mushrooms in boiling water until tender, 15 minutes.

4 **Choose the right rice.** Look for medium-grain Spanish paella rice like *calasparra* or *bomba*. It's fine to substitute Italian risotto-type rice like *Arborio*, but no other type. Don't wash rice.

5 **Cook the meat, seafood, and vegetables:**

- Brown meats or just cook seafood over medium heat until nearly cooked and push to outside of pan, or set aside in a bowl.
- Cook vegetables in batches: firmer ones first and set aside. Cook tender ones second and push to outside of pan or set aside.
- Artichokes darken paella so add toward end of cooking time.

6 Cook the sofrito in the center of the pan until thick and concentrated. Stir in smoked paprika if using, or other seasonings like dried whole chilies. This is the foundation of paella's flavor.

*At this point it's permissible to stop if necessary.

Forty to 45 minutes before diners will sit down: Preheat oven to 400 degrees F or lidded charcoal or gas grill to medium/medium low and start cooking rice. Rice will take 20 minutes to cook and 20 minutes to rest.

7 Heat rice-cooking broth or water in saucepan and put a ladle into it. Have extra.

8 Return browned meat and cooked vegetables (and cooked legumes) back to sofrito in pan. Add fresh herbs like rosemary or thyme, rice, and proper amount of broth or water. Shake pan to even out rice and ingredients.

9 Bring paella to boil over burner or burners set on medium. Rotate pan every minute or two so rice cooks evenly, until stock is level with rice but still soupy, about 7 to 10 minutes. If liquid evaporates too quickly, add a little more. Don't stir rice at all; this is not risotto.

10 Transfer pan to bottom of oven or kettle grill uncovered, and bake until rice is tender, but al dente. Rice will exhibit a pin-sized bit of white at its core. Traditionally paella was cooked outdoors over a wood fire. Reproduce this by setting it on a wood-charcoal fired grill, which will give heat more even than stovetop burners, dry the rice less than an oven, and grace the paella with an authentic smoky flavor. Paella should bubble merrily on either grill or in oven. The bottom of the pan should be close to the heat source.

*Check for the socarrat: Soccarat comes from the verb socarrar, "to toast lightly." It is the bottom caramelized crust that sticks to a paella pan. Spanish diners love the crust. Pay attention, sniff and poke at bottom. There should be some resistance and a delicate toasted smell.

11 **Remove pan from oven or grill.** To create a socarrat: Set pan onto burners and cook over medium-high heat until it forms. Check after 2 minutes. Drizzle paella with a little of remaining broth or a little water if top rice looks dry or crunchy. Cover pan with foil or parchment and a towel. Rest rice 15 to 20 minutes.

12 **To Serve:** Uncover rice and rest another 5 minutes. Rice texture improves dramatically as it stands. Artfully garnish paella with strips of roasted bell pepper, herbs, artichokes, and serve it in its own pan.

- Serve paella with lemon wedges. Don't store leftover rice in pan. It will blacken. Reheat paella in microwave or steamer.

FIGURE 7.22 Valencia, Spain port.
Source: Alex Tihonov/Fotolia.

CLASSIC PAELLA (PAELLA VALENCIANA)

The sofrito flavoring this paella is made of tomatoes, garlic, saffron, and bell pepper. Valencia lies along the southeast coast of Spain, on the Mediterranean. Moorish influences made this Spain's most famous rice-growing region and the birthplace of paella.

6 to 8 servings

1 recipe *Roasted Romesco Sauce* or *Allioli*
2 pounds chicken thighs, skin and fat removed
1-1/2 pounds skinned rabbit, cut into 8 pieces
   or 2 pounds chicken thighs, skin and fat removed
1-1/2 teaspoons smoked sweet Spanish paprika, *divided*
2 ounces garlic, 8 large garlic cloves, 4 tablespoons peeled and minced, *divided*
8 ounce red bell pepper, 1 large
1 pound ripe tomatoes, 2 large
   or 1-1/2 cups tomato purée
6 to 8 cups chicken stock
1 pinch saffron, crushed
5 to 6 tablespoons olive oil, *divided*
1/4 pound green beans, 1 cup stemmed and diced into
1-1/2-inch lengths
8 ounces frozen baby lima beans, 1 cup thawed
9- or 10-ounce package frozen artichoke hearts
Cayenne pepper
14 ounces short- or medium-grain rice like Arborio, 2 cups
1 sprig rosemary

1 **Prepare Romesco Sauce.** Set aside. In a mixing bowl season chicken and rabbit with salt, pepper, 1/2 teaspoon paprika, and 2 tablespoons minced garlic. Marinate 15 minutes.

2 Roast red bell pepper until blackened. Peel, seed, and stem pepper, and cut long 1/4-inch-wide strips. Halve tomatoes through their equators. Place cut side onto the coarse side of a box grater, and grate until only the skin of the tomato is left, to yield about 1-1/2 cups purée.

3 **Heat stock for rice:** Pour chicken stock and saffron into a medium saucepan, cover, and bring to a simmer.

4 **Begin paella:** Pour 4 tablespoons oil into 14- to 15-inch paella pan and heat over medium until hot. Brown chicken and rabbit until 3/4 done, about 7 minutes. Remove meat to a mixing bowl. Stir green beans, limas, and artichokes into paella pan. Sauté vegetables until browned, about 3 minutes. Transfer to bowl with meat.

5 Add 2 tablespoons oil to pan, and cook remaining garlic until tender, 30 seconds. Reduce heat and add tomato purée. Stir and cook until reduced and thickened, about 5 minutes. Stir in remaining 1 teaspoon paprika and a pinch of cayenne. Add meat and vegetables to tomatoes and mix well.

6 Preheat oven to 425 degrees F (or gas grill). Stir rice and rosemary into pan and stir to coat with tomato mixture. Stir in 4 cups stock and set pan on two burners *or* on gas grill. Shake pan to distribute rice evenly. Cook paella over medium heat until stock is level with rice but rice is soupy, 7 minutes. Rotate pan every minute or two so rice cooks evenly if using stovetop burners. If liquid absorbs too quickly, add more stock. Do not stir rice!

7 Place paella in oven if using stovetop burners. If using gas grill, place pan in grill and cover with lid. Bake paella uncovered (or with piece of parchment weighted on top) until rice is tender but *al dente*, 10 to 15 minutes. Check rice (at the bottom) periodically and spoon on more stock if rice is too crunchy. (To make *soccarat* refer to *Signature Technique: Spanish Rice or Pasta*.)

8 Remove paella from oven. Taste rice, and season with salt if necessary. Sprinkle with 1/4 to 1/2 cup stock, garnish with roasted red pepper strips, and cover with parchment and foil. Rest paella in warm spot 15 to 20 minutes. Uncover paella and rest 5 minutes. Rice texture improves as it stands. Serve.

Source: *The New Spanish Table* by Anya von Bremzen.

Vary! Improvise!

☞ *Prepare a paella with 1-1/2 pounds diced monkfish instead of meat.*

☞ *Prepare a paella with 2 to 4 ounces Serrano ham, 12 to 16 ounces fresh mushrooms, 1 cup Manchego cheese and basil, and 1-1/2 cups rice.*

☞ ***Untraditional:*** *Stir garlic mayonnaise or sour cream into an artichoke, mushroom, and chicken paella at the end.*

FIGURE 7.23 Classic paella (paella valenciana).

VEGETABLE PAELLA (ARROZ DE VERDURAS)

This recipe comes from a Valencian cook and restaurateur who credits the paella's success to garden-fresh vegetables. Reserve mushroom soaking water for the broth and mix with chickpea cooking liquid, vegetable broth, or water.

6 servings

---

1 ounce dried porcini mushrooms, 1 cup, soaked in 1 cup boiling water
3 cups vegetable stock *or* chickpea cooking broth
1/8 teaspoon crumbled thread saffron
1/4 cup olive oil
3 ounces carrot, 1/2 cup peeled and diced into 1/2-inch cubes
1/4 pound green beans, preferably broad flat beans, 1 cup halved and ends trimmed
5 to 6 ounces zucchini, 1 medium, about 1 cup, diced into 1/2-inch cubes

Sofrito

6 to 7 ounces onion, 1 small, 1-1/2 cups peeled and finely diced
3/4 ounce garlic, 3 large cloves, 4-1/2 teaspoons peeled and minced
12 ounces red bell peppers, 2 medium, 2-2/3 cups stemmed, seeded, and diced into 1/2-inch cubes
6 ounces chopped whole canned tomatoes, 3/4 cup

1 teaspoon *pimentón*, Spanish smoked paprika
1 small sprig rosemary
15-ounce can cooked chickpeas, about 1-1/2 cups drained
   or 1-1/2 cups cooked chickpeas
10-1/2 to 14 ounces Valencian short-grain or Arborio rice, 1-1/2 to 2 cups

1 **Soak mushrooms:** Bring 1 cup water to boil, remove from heat, and stir in mushrooms. Soak until soft, 15 minutes, drain and strain mushroom liquid into stock or broth. Chop mushrooms lightly and set aside. Preheat gas oven to 400 degrees F or electric oven to 450 degrees F.

2 When ready to cook, combine stock or broth and saffron in a small saucepan. Cover and keep warm over low heat.

3 **Prepare paella:** Heat half the oil in a 13- or 14-inch paella pan over high heat. Add carrots, mushrooms, green beans, and zucchini, and stir-fry until seared and wilted, 5 to 7 minutes. Transfer to bowl. Add remaining oil to pan and prepare **sofrito**: Cook onion, garlic, and bell peppers until soft, 5 minutes, then add tomatoes. Cook until tomatoes are reduced and pasty. Stir in paprika and return carrots, green beans, and zucchini to pan. Stir in reserved mushrooms and cook over high heat 1 minute.

4 Taste and season vegetables with salt. Pour in broth. Bring to a boil. Stir in rosemary, chickpeas, and rice, and boil over medium heat until rice is no longer soupy but enough liquid remains to continue cooking rice, 8 to 10 minutes. Do not stir rice!

5 **Bake paella:** Transfer paella to oven and cook, uncovered, until rice is almost al dente, 10 to 12 minutes in gas oven, 15 to 20 minutes in electric. Or cook over gas grill as described for *Classic Paella Valenciana.*

6 **To make socarrat crust:** Return paella to stovetop over medium-high heat. Cook without disturbing rice, 2 minutes, until a crust forms on the bottom of pan (don't let it burn). Check by carefully lifting edge of rice with spatula. Sprinkle rice with a little stock. Cover paella with foil and towels. Rest paella in a warm place covered 15 minutes and uncovered 10 minutes. Serve.

SIGNATURE RECIPE

FRIED FISH IN VINEGAR MARINADE (PESCADO EN ESCABECHE)

Originally Spanish and Italian cooks without refrigeration used escabeche or scapeche to preserve food so the amount of vinegar was much higher. Today the method of frying food and marinating 24 to 36 hours is mainly about flavor. The vinegar-spice marinade cuts through oil and imparts a spicy-tang. Use escabeche for boneless, skinless chicken breast or seafood. In the areas of southern Italy that had Spanish rule, cooks prepare vegetables and fish alla scapeche.

Yields about 8 cups, 4 to 6 servings

2 pounds thick fish fillets like halibut or salmon
Olive oil for frying
Flour for dredging
Optional: 12 to 16 ounces baby redskins

Vegetables

8 to 9 ounces onion, 2 packed cups peeled and finely slivered
6 ounces red or yellow bell pepper, about 1 cup finely slivered
6 ounces carrot, 2 medium, about 1-1/2 cups peeled and finely sliced
1/2 ounce garlic, 2 large cloves, 1 tablespoon peeled and finely sliced

Marinade

3/4 cup white wine vinegar
1/2 teaspoon peppercorns
1/2 teaspoon dried thyme
1/2 teaspoon coriander seed
2 teaspoons kosher salt
2 large bay leaves
1/2 teaspoon hot pepper flakes

For Serving

8 to 12 ounces clean, dry lettuce leaves *or* hot, cooked rice

Garnish: 1/4 ounce trimmed Italian parsley, 1/4 cup chopped

1 Wash fish. Remove and discard skin from fish unless skin is very thin. Blot dry fillets dry and sprinkle on both sides with kosher salt. Rest fish at room temperature 30 minutes. Blot dry.

2 **Fry the fish:** Heat 1/4-inch olive oil in heavy 12-inch skillet (nonstick is fine) over high heat. When the oil shimmers but doesn't smoke, lower heat to medium or medium-low for thick fillets. Dredge fillets in flour and shake off excess, and place in hot oil. Brown each side, about 2 minutes per side for thin protein, and 5 minutes for thicker proteins. Fish should be just cooked, and flake when probed with a fork. Remove skillet from heat and transfer cooked food to a half hotel pan or 4-quart shallow serving casserole. Strain oil from skillet and reserve.

3 **Optional baby redskins:** It is traditional to serve fish *en escabeche* with boiled potatoes. If desired, cover redskin potatoes with cold water and bring to a boil. Boil until tender, 8 to 10 minutes. Cool potatoes and slice 1/4-inch thick. Slide potatoes into casserole with fish.

4 Reheat skillet over medium heat and add 3 tablespoons strained oil. Add **vegetables** and cook, without browning, until tender, 5 minutes. Add 2 cups water and **marinade** to vegetables in skillet, and bring to a boil. Lower heat, and simmer mixture 5 minutes. Remove skillet from heat. Spoon vegetables and marinade over fish and optional potatoes. Set aside to cool at room temperature. Cover pan or casserole with plastic wrap and refrigerate for 24 to 36 hours before eating.

5 **To Serve:** Remove pan or casserole from refrigerator 30 minutes before serving. Arrange fish *en escabeche* on salad greens and **garnish** with parsley. Or, if not using potatoes, serve fish with hot, cooked rice and spoon **marinade** over rice. Drizzle with more olive oil, if desired.

Vary! Improvise!

☞ *Try different vinegars like sherry, rice, red wine, or flavored vinegar, or substitute lemon juice and zest.*

☞ *Experiment preparing escabeche with steamed, boiled, or fried starchy vegetables, other meats like pork or poultry, or with other types of steamed or fried seafood like scallops or shrimp.*

THREE SPANISH FRIED FAVORITES

Pescado Frito

Spanish *pescado frito* or fried fish is a favorite of the port towns of Cadíz and Málaga, Andalusia, where cod and baby squid vie for attention with hake and dogfish. The seafood is sometimes battered or often just tossed in fine semolina flour before frying in olive oil, and served plain.

Migas

A traditional dish of peasants and shepherds in the field, migas demonstrate the Spanish flair for turning simple into satisfying. Breadcrumbs form the base of migas; the rest is up to the cook's imagination. Garlic, chorizo, and pancetta brown in olive oil, then day-old breadcrumbs (moistened for a couple hours or overnight) go into the pan and cook until browned. Cumin, caraway, hot pepper flakes, or smoked paprika might season migas along with pomegranate seeds, fresh grapes, or strips of roasted red pepper. Many cooks serve migas as a side with fried eggs, roast meat, or grilled pork chops.

Fried Padrón Peppers (Pimientos de Padrón)

These bite-sized, fragrant, emerald-green, triangular chili-peppers can vary from mild to spicy-hot (as their season progresses they become very hot). Galician cooks like to fry them whole in olive oil until very tender, and serve them sprinkled with coarse sea salt as a tapas or appetizer. These fried peppers are playfully known as Russian roulette peppers because around 1 in 10 will be searingly hot.

FIGURE 7.24   Migas with chorizo.
Source: Algecireño/Shutterstock.

FIGURE 7.25   Padron peppers.
Source: Lorenzo Vecchia/Dorling Kindersley.

FIGURE 7.26   Fried padron peppers.
Source: mipstudio/Fotolia.

GRILL, GRIDDLE, ROAST, BROIL, BAKE, AND BARBECUE

Spanish Calçotada

Spring comes to Catalonia, Spain, in February and March. Whole towns celebrate by holding calçotadas (*kal-so-tadas*). These are gatherings where sweet and young leek-like grilled spring onions or calçots (*kal-sots*) meet *Romesco Sauce*, a thick, savory sauce made with roasted almonds or hazelnuts, garlic, chili, tomato, and smoky Spanish paprika.

Catalonian etiquette requires attendees to pick up a calçot, char-grilled over grapevine cuttings, dip the white bulb into the sauce then into their mouths. (Bibs are useful.) Competitions spring up to see who can eat the most in an allotted time. Grilled meat, dessert, coffee, and convivial conversation follow.

FIGURE 7.27 Grilling çalcots.
Source: Honeyboy Martian/Fotolia.

GRILLED SPRING LEEKS AND ROMESCO SAUCE (CALÇOTS AMB ROMESCO)

4 servings

Romesco Sauce
1-1/2 to 2 pounds large, fat spring grilling green onions, about 1 dozen
Olive oil

1 Prepare *Romesco Sauce*.

2 Preheat a gas or charcoal grill to medium heat. Brush green onions with olive oil. When coals are hot, grill green onions until tender, juicy, and blackened, 5 to 10 minutes, depending on thickness.

3 **To Serve:** Arrange onions on serving platter and *Romesco Sauce* in bowls. Instruct guests to peel the green onions, and dip into sauce before eating.

The Moorish Influence

The effects of the Moorish (Muslim) oc-cupation of Spain, from AD 711 to 1492, were most pronounced in Andalusia. Sugar, spices like saffron, cumin, cinna-mon, nutmeg, coriander, and aniseed, almonds, figs, citrus fruits, melons, rice cultivation, and eggplant are just a few of the many Moorish contributions to the Spanish pantry.

FRUIT AND NUT STUFFED PORK TENDERLOINS (SOLOMILLO DE CERDO MUDÉJAR)

Stuffed meats served with roasted vegetable sauces are popular in both Italy and Spain. The recipe below is simple but highly satisfying, typical of a cuisine with five centuries of creative Moorish and Mediterranean influences. In 1502, when the Spanish Catholic kings won back Granada from the Arabs, they decreed that Muslims must convert (and eat pork) or leave. This dish came from cooks who chose to stay. Mudéjar means Muslim.

4 servings

1-1/2 pounds pork tenderloins, about 2
2 ounces pitted dates 1/4 cup
1 ounce walnut halves, 1/4 to 1/2 cup
5 tablespoons olive oil, *divided*
16 ounces tomatoes, 2 medium-large, about 2-1/2 cups diced
6 to 7 ounces onion, 1-1/2 cups peeled and medium diced
4 ounces carrot, 3/4 to 1 cup peeled and sliced 1/4-inch thick
1-1/2 ounces celery stalk, about 1/2 cup diced into 1-inch cubes
1/2 cup dry sherry or dry white wine
1-1/2 teaspoons fresh thyme leaves
1-1/2 teaspoons fresh rosemary leaves
2 teaspoons sherry vinegar
1/2 cup hot chicken stock

For Serving

Hot, boiled potatoes

1 Preheat oven to 350 degrees F. Butterfly pork tenderloins lengthwise, so they lie on work surface opened in half flat. Season with salt and pepper.

2 Alternate dates and walnuts in a row down the crease on both. Season meat with salt and pepper. Fold up meat to enclose filling. Tie with butcher's string at 1- to 2-inch intervals along the length of the tenderloin.

3 Oil outside of meat with 1 tablespoon oil, and place on half hotel pan or 10-inch by 12-inch by 2-inch roasting pan. In a mixing bowl, toss tomatoes, onion, carrot, and celery with 3 table-spoons oil. Cover tenderloins with vegetables. Place pan in oven. Roast pork until internal temperature registers 150 degrees F, about 45 minutes. Remove meat from pan and scrape vegetables off and back into pan. Cover meat and place meat in warm spot, to finish cooking, rest, and keep warm.

4 Scrape vegetables from roasting pan into a 4-quart saucepan and stir in sherry and herbs. Bring to a boil, lower heat to medium, and simmer until vegetables are very tender and liquid is reduced, 5 to 7 minutes.

5 Purée sauce in blender or food processor with remaining tablespoon oil and part of the sherry vinegar. Pour in enough stock to achieve a salsa-like consistency. Taste sauce and season with salt, pepper, and more sherry vinegar, if desired. Scrape sauce back into saucepan and simmer to reheat.

6 **To Serve:** Remove strings from meat. Slice tenderloins into 1/2-inch-thick medallions on the diagonal. Arrange meat on plates or platter, spoon sauce over, and serve with potatoes.

Source: *The Cuisines of Spain* by Teresa Barrenechea.

Vary! Improvise!

☛ *This method invites different combi-nations of fillings and of vegetables for the roasted, puréed sauce. Devise a cre-ative combination of dried fruits, nuts, and/or herbs to line the meat.*

☛ *Substitute boneless turkey breast for pork.*

Empanada

Empanadas are large, flat, two-crust pies filled with savory foods. The filling usually begins with a base called *zaragallada*: onions and peppers (sometimes tomatoes and saffron) cooked until thick in olive oil. Pork, seafood, shellfish, game, or chorizo then goes into the base. Though empanadas originated in Spain and Portugal, they are also part of regions where Spain had a large influence: South America, Caribbean, and Mexico.

SIGNATURE RECIPE

TENDER, FLAKY EMPANADA DOUGH

Bread dough, short-crust pastry, or puff pastry can be used for empanadas, depending on the occasion and the filling. Empanadas may be shaped round, oblong, or into small turnovers and baked in a casserole, paella pan, or on a sheet pan. Substitute diced butter or freshly rendered lard for half the oil for more flavor and flakiness.

Yields about 26 ounces dough for one 12- to 14-inch empanada, 8 to 12 servings
Will accommodate 8 to 10 cups thick filling.

1 teaspoon active dry yeast
1/2 teaspoon sugar
2/3 cup lukewarm water
4 ounces extra virgin olive oil, plus extra for bowl and pan
1 large egg yolk
2 teaspoons kosher salt
1 pound unbleached white flour
Optional Egg Wash: 1 large egg yolk beaten with 1 tablespoon water

1 **Prepare dough:** Stir together yeast, sugar, and water in large bowl. Rest until foamy, 5 minutes. Whisk in oil, egg, and salt. Stir in flour, in 3 batches, until well incorporated.

2 Turn dough out onto lightly floured counter, or keep in bowl, and knead until smooth and elastic, 5 minutes. Dough should be pliable and oily. Remove dough from bowl and lightly oil bowl. Divide dough into two slightly unequal parts, shape into balls, and place back in bowl, rolling to coat balls with oil. Rest in warm spot 30 minutes to 1 hour. Dough will not rise much.

Signature Technique: Construct an Empanada

1 **Prepare 8 to 10 cups filling.** Cool to lukewarm.

2 **Construct empanada:** Preheat oven to 375 degrees F. Roll out the larger piece of dough to a thin 12- to 14-inch diameter round. Oil a 14-inch round paella pan or pizza pan and fit dough on or in it. Pile filling on dough, but leave a 1- to 1-1/2-inch border clear around the edge.

3 Roll out second piece of dough to a slightly smaller diameter. Set on top of filling. Wet the outermost edges of the bottom dough. Flip the bottom edge up all the way round, and seal dough by rolling and pressing it into a consistent, attractive shape. Make 3 slashes (vents) in top of empanada and, if desired, paint with optional egg wash.

4 **Bake:** Place empanada into oven and bake until filling is oozy and crust is golden brown, 40 minutes to 1 hour. Cool empanada 15 to 20 minutes before slicing into wedges.

Vary! Improvise!

☛ *Prepare Dough Ahead* Rub dough balls with olive oil and place in plastic baggies. Refrigerate overnight. Return to room temperature before using.
☛*Saffron Dough* Crush a large pinch saffron and steep in 3 tablespoons hot water, then mix with oil, egg, and salt.

FIGURE 7.28 Galician tuna empanada.

TUNA AND BELL PEPPER EMPANADA FROM GALICIA (EMPANADA GALLEGA DE ATUN)

Prepare filling and dough a day ahead. Assemble and bake 2 hours before serving.

14-inch empanada, 8 to 12 servings

1 recipe *Tender, Flaky Empanada Dough*, plus flour for dusting.
1/3 to 1/2 cup olive oil
1/2 ounce garlic, 2 large cloves, 1 tablespoon peeled and minced
1 pound onions, 2 large, 4 cups peeled and thinly sliced *or* slivered
18 ounces red bell peppers, 3 medium, 4 cups cored, seeded, and thinly sliced
6 to 7 ounces green bell pepper, 1-1/3 cups cored, seeded, and thinly sliced
8 ounces ripe tomato, 1 large, halved around equator and flesh grated
2 teaspoons sweet Spanish paprika
1 pinch saffron, crushed and steeped in 2 tablespoons hot water
18 ounces olive oil-packed tuna, drained and flaked
1/2 ounce trimmed Italian parsley, 1/4 cup minced
5 ounces pitted manzanilla *or* large pimento-stuffed green olives, 3/4 cup sliced
Egg Wash: 1 large egg yolk whisked with 1-1/2 teaspoons water

1 Prepare **empanada dough**, and set aside to rise. Divide dough into 2 balls, one slightly larger.

2 **Prepare filling:** Heat a 12-inch skillet over medium heat and add oil. Add garlic and cook until soft, 45 seconds to 1 minute. Add onions and cook until soft, 5 minutes. Add bell peppers and cook until soft, 7 to 8 minutes. If skillet begins to dry, add a little water or olive oil. Reduce heat and simmer vegetables until very soft, but not colored, 10 minutes. Stir tomato, paprika, and saffron into skillet, and cover. Simmer vegetables until thick and jam-like, 15 to 20 minutes. Cool mixture. Stir in tuna and parsley. Taste filling and season with salt and black pepper.

3 Preheat oven to 375 degrees F. Dust counter with flour and roll out larger dough ball into 15-inch circle. Transfer dough onto a 14- or 15-inch round paella or pizza pan. Spread filling onto dough and keep it 1 inch from edges. Scatter olives over top of the filling.

4 Roll out second dough ball to a slightly smaller circle, 12- to 13-inch diameter, and fit on top of filling. Fold up edges of bottom crust over top crust and crimp with fork or fingers. Brush top of empanada with egg wash and make decorative slits with knife into dough. Bake empanada until golden and filling oozes through slits, 45 minutes to 1 hour.

5 **To Serve:** Remove empanada from oven and cover with clean cotton towel or foil (to soften crust). Cool to lukewarm. Cut empanada into wedges and serve.

Source: The *New Spanish Table* by Anya von Bremzen.

SALAD AND VEGETABLE METHODS

Salads (Ensaladas)

Spanish serve salads at home, casually as a snack, tapa, or lunch. They don't have a fixed place in a Spanish meal. Catalonians prepare salads of grilled vegetables and the beloved *xató*. Olive oil plus sherry vinegar, lemon or white or red wine vinegars are favored in Spanish salads.

CATALONIAN SHREDDED SALT COD SALAD
(ESQUEIXADA DE BACALAO)

This dish is a classic Spanish ensalada. Look for salt cod or bacalao that is white, not yellow. To test cod's readiness, pinch and taste a piece of fish from the thickest section to gauge its saltiness. Soak cod longer and change water more often to rid it of excess salt.

4 to 6 servings

8 ounces dried salt cod
4 tablespoons extra virgin olive oil, more as necessary, *divided*
2 tablespoons sherry or red wine vinegar
1 ounce green onions, about 2, 1/4 cup thinly sliced, *divided*
1 pound ripe plum tomatoes, about 4 large or 6 medium
6 to 8 ounces red or green bell pepper, about 1 medium, 1-1/2 cups stemmed, seeded, and finely julienned

Garnish

1-1/4 ounces Spanish or Greek pitted black olives, 1/4 cup, sliced
Coarse sea salt

1 **Thirty-six hours before serving:** Place cod in bowl, skin side up, and cover with cold water. Refrigerate. Change water 3 to 4 times in the 36-hour soaking time to de-salt cod.

2 Drain cod. Bring a small saucepan of water to boil. Remove from heat and stir in salt cod; rest 3 minutes. Drain fish, pat dry, and shred cod into small strips. Whisk together 3 tablespoons olive oil and vinegar. Toss with cod and green onions. Season with salt and pepper if necessary. Set fish aside to marinate 1 hour in refrigerator.

3 Slice tomatoes in half around their equators, and grate on box grater set on plate or in bowl until all that remains is the skin. Discard skin and mix remaining 1 tablespoon olive oil with tomato pulp.

4 Pour boiling water over bell pepper strips and rest 10 minutes; drain and blot dry. Toss shredded cod with bell peppers. (**Alternatively**, the traditional way is to toss together cod, bell peppers, tomato, and olives.) Taste mixture, and season with salt and freshly ground pepper.

5 **To Serve:** For each serving or one large platter, drizzle half the tomato pulp on plates or platter. Arrange shredded cod-bell pepper mixture over it. Spoon remaining tomato pulp on top. Garnish with olives and sprinkle with sea salt. (**Alternatively**, chill traditional tossed salad, and arrange 4 to 6 portions on plate.) If desired, drizzle each salad with 1/2 to 1 teaspoon olive oil.

Source: *Made in Spain* by José Andres.

FIGURE 7.29 Salt cod.
Source: Luis Santos/Fotolia.

SPANISH XATÓ: A CELEBRATED AND ROBUST SALAD

Xató is Catalonia's version of the French *Niçoise* salad. It's usually composed of escarole or frisée tossed with garlicky *romesco sauce*. Spanish green or black olives, anchovies, smoked whitefish, salt cod, or tuna are decoratively arranged over or around greens. Xató is so popular that Catalonians have created a festival around it called a *xatonada*. Held during *Carnival*, villages place long tables on their plazas to hold the thousands who come to consume it.

FIGURE 7.30 Two elements of xato.
Source: nito/Fotolia.

EXTREMADURAN BREAD AND TOMATO SALAD (CONJONDONGO)

Chef José Andres says that Spain is the king of cold dishes. This refreshing dish is a prime example.

Yields about 6 cups, 4 servings

4 ounces rustic white bread, about 3-1/2 cups diced into 3/4-inch cubes
1 pound ripe tomatoes, 2 medium large, *divided*
1/8 ounce garlic, 1 medium clove, 1 teaspoon peeled and minced to a paste
1/4 teaspoon Spanish smoked paprika
1/4 to 1/3 ounce trimmed Italian parsley, 2 tablespoons finely minced
5 tablespoons extra virgin olive oil, *divided*
1 tablespoon sherry vinegar
6 ounces green bell pepper, 1 medium, 1-1/4 cups stemmed, seeded, and diced 1/2 inch
1/2 ounce green onion, about 1, 2 tablespoons thinly sliced
5-1/2 ounces large green pimento stuffed olives, 1 cup sliced crossways
   or 5-1/2 ounces pitted green olives, 1 cup quartered

1 Preheat oven to 400 degrees F. Spread bread on sheet pan and toast until golden, about 10 to 12 minutes; cool.

2 Slice half (8 ounces) of the tomatoes in half through the equator. Grate on cut side until pulp is gone and only skin remains. Discard skin. Pour pulp into fine strainer and drain, but reserve tomato liquid, to yield 1/2 cup strained pulp. Dice remaining half pound of tomatoes into 3/8-inch cubes to yield about 1-1/4 cups diced tomatoes.

3 Mix garlic, paprika, parsley, and a pinch of salt in large mixing bowl. Whisk in 4 tablespoons olive oil and vinegar. Toss in diced tomatoes and reserved juice from drained pulp, bell pepper, green onion, and olives. Toss to mix well. Season with salt to taste, and set aside 20 minutes.

4 **Fifteen minutes before serving:** Toss toasted bread into bowl with vegetables and dressing. Rest until bread absorbs the moisture and expands, about 15 minutes.

5 **To Serve:** Spread 2 tablespoons tomato pulp on each of 4 plates, and drizzle each with remaining olive oil. Top each plate of oil-drizzled tomato pulp with 1/4 of the salad. Serve.

Source: *Made in Spain* by Spanish chef José Andres.

Vary! Improvise!

☛ *Toss salad with tomato purée and diced tomatoes.*

Spanish Vegetables (Verduras)

Like their Italian neighbors, Spanish cooks love and respect vegetables. The Spanish rarely serve vegetables with the main course. Instead, vegetable dishes shine alone as a carefully prepared separate course. Spanish cooks braise vegetable medleys called *pistos*; prepare baked casseroles known as *menestras, tumbets,* and gratins; stuff peppers; deep-fry battered eggplant; sauté wild mushrooms, spinach, greens, green beans, or chicory; and grill asparagus and peppers.

ONION, GARLIC, EGGPLANT, TOMATO, BELL PEPPERS, AND ZUCCHINI

This famous vegetable combo is beloved in all of Spain, Italy, and France:

Pisto

Though eggplant is optional to pisto, both pisto and samfaina always include olive oil, onion, garlic, bell peppers, and tomatoes. Both use green bell peppers and some cooks might add diced potato, squash, diced Serrano ham, vinegar, fresh basil, or oregano.

Samfaina

One of four important Catalan sauces (with *allioli, sofregit,* and *picada*) samfaina's collection of onion, garlic, eggplant, tomato, and bell pepper can be cooked until silky and sauce-like or cooked only until vegetables are tender and still retain texture.

FIGURE 7.31 Mallorcan tumbet.
Source: Monkey Business/Fotolia.

Tumbet

A Mallorcan casserole of potatoes, eggplant, zucchini, and red bell peppers. Each vegetable is sautéed in oil separately, layered with tomato sauce then baked.

Pisto Bilbaina

This Basque pisto uses less tomato and has zucchini as the main ingredient. It's drier than most ratatouilles.

French Ratatouille

A little fussier than pisto or samfaina, the vegetables for ratatouille are peeled, seeded, and diced. They are often sautéed separately, then simmered together for a short time. See chapter *France.*

Italian Caponata

More like a complex salad, the vegetables for *caponata* (celery instead of zucchini) are cooked separately, mixed with capers, olives, parsley, wine vinegar, and olive oil. Some versions include anchovy, pine nuts, and raisins.
(See chapter *Italy.*)

Southern Italian Ciambotta

This summer vegetable stew is similar to ratatouille. It consists of eggplant, zucchini, bell peppers, potatoes, garlic, tomatoes, basil, and red pepper flakes. The vegetables are generally browned separately in olive oil, then simmered in garlic and tomatoes for a short time.

Peel a Pepper

For crunchy sautéed or raw peppers without skin, Spanish cooks use a very sharp vegetable peeler. Roasting peppers to remove skin slightly softens them and removes their crunch.

Pisto Manchego: Spanish Mother of Ratatouille

Pisto Manchego (*pee-stow man-chay-go*) was the mother of *ratatouille*. Though the French lay claim to this vegetable braise of onion, garlic, tomato, bell pepper, eggplant, and zucchini, it originated in Don Quixote's *La Mancha* region, south of Madrid in the harsh, hot, and arid central region. Manchegans call it by its Moorish-Arabic name, *alboronia*.

Though La Mancha translates to "the scar," the region is one of Spain's major crops producers: agriculture thrives on the soil and in the climate; pisto came out of its bounty. *Samfaina* is the Catalan version, sometimes with grilled or roasted vegetables. Mallorcans in the Balearic Islands layer and bake this vegetable combo (plus potatoes) into *tumbet*. When *pisto* moved north and east into Italy, it was transformed into *caponata*. Much later *pisto* moved into southern France to become the favorite *ratatouille*.

Pisto, samfaina, and tumbet can serve as an appetizer, side dish, tapa, be eaten hot or cold on its own, or on toast. Pisto and samfaina also serve, much like *sofrito*, as a base for a main dish stewed with salt cod or chicken, with chorizo or hard cooked eggs, or as an egg-poaching medium. Valencians spread it on *coca*, a flatbread pizza, with tuna and pine nuts.

SIGNATURE RECIPE

SPANISH SUMMER VEGETABLES (PISTO OR SAMFAINA)

Simmer pisto or samfaina slowly to allow time for the natural vegetable flavors to merge and mingle. The simmering vegetables form a silky stew, and as they break down they release rich flavor. Prepare this ahead. It tastes better as it sits, reaching peak after a day or two. Proportions are up to the cook. It's traditional to peel the eggplant, but that takes away many nutrients. For less seeds, choose small eggplant.

La Mancha Style *Pisto Manchego*

Yields 3-1/2 cups

---

16 to 18 ounces eggplant, about 6 cups diced into 1-inch cubes
8 ounces zucchini, about 2 cups diced into 1-inch cubes
4 tablespoons olive oil, *divided*
4 to 5 ounces onion, 1 cup peeled and diced into 1/2-inch cubes
8 ounces green bell pepper, 1-1/4 cups, stemmed, seeded, and diced 1/2-inch cubes
1/2 ounce garlic, 2 large cloves, 1 tablespoon peeled and minced
1 pound ripe tomatoes, 2 to 2-1/2 cups, cored, peeled, and diced into 1/2-inch cubes
2 teaspoons red wine vinegar

Catalan Style *Samfaina*

Yields 3 cups

---

7 to 8 ounces Japanese eggplant, 3 cups diced into 1/2-inch cubes
7 ounces zucchini, 1-1/2 cups trimmed and diced into 1/2-inch cubes
4 tablespoons olive oil, *divided*
6 to 7 ounces onion, 1-1/2 cups peeled and diced into 1/2-inch cubes
4 to 5 ounces red bell pepper, 1 cup stemmed, seeded, and diced into 1/2-inch cubes
1/2 ounce garlic, 2 large cloves garlic, 1 tablespoon peeled and minced
8 ounces tomato, about 1 large, 1 to 1-1/2 cups peeled, seeded, and diced 1/2 inch

1 Toss eggplant and zucchini with 1 tablespoon kosher salt. Rest vegetables 20 to 30 minutes. Rinse well, drain, and pat very dry.

2 Heat 2 tablespoon olive oil in a deep 12-inch skillet over medium-high heat. Sauté eggplant and zucchini until tender and lightly colored, 5 to 8 minutes. If skillet browns, deglaze with 1 to 2 tablespoons water and cook until water evaporates. Remove vegetables with slotted spoon and set aside.

3 Heat skillet over medium heat, add 2 tablespoons oil, and stir in onions. Cook until soft, 5 minutes, and add bell pepper. Simmer until the peppers are just tender, 5 minutes. Stir in garlic and tomatoes, cover skillet, and reduce heat to low. Simmer mixture until tomatoes begin to break down, 15 to 20 minutes. Stir frequently.

4 Return zucchini and eggplant to skillet, and:

Pisto: Simmer 40 minutes, stirring occasionally and adding small amounts of water if necessary. The zucchini and eggplant should soften and break down.

Samfaina: Simmer until very tender, about 10 minutes.

5 Season mixture with salt and pepper. Stir vinegar into **Pisto**. Taste.

6 **To Serve:** Serve *Pisto Manchego* or *Samfaina* hot or room temperature, as a light lunch with toasted bread or as an appealing side dish.

Vary! Improvise!

☞ *Thin either mixture with chicken or beef stock to make a thick soup or stew.*

☞ *Spread on a half baguette and top with Spanish egg tortilla.*

☞ *Use as an omelet filling.*

☞ *Use to garnish a soup.*

☞ *Stew chicken or fish in either mixture.*

GREEN BEANS CASTILIAN STYLE
(JUDÍAS VERDES A LA CASTELLANA)

Yields about 6 to 7 cups, 6 servings

18 ounces red bell peppers, 3 medium
1-1/2 pounds green beans, stems trimmed, about 6 cups beans cut into 2-inch lengths
2 tablespoons olive oil
3 ounces Serrano ham *or* prosciutto, 1/2 cup diced
1/2 ounce garlic, 2 large cloves, 1 tablespoon peeled and finely sliced
1/8 to 1/4 teaspoon ground cumin seed
1/8 to 1/4 teaspoon hot red pepper flakes

1   Roast bell peppers on top of gas burner until evenly blackened, but not charred. Cool in bowl. Peel, seed, and slice them into strips the width and length of a green bean. Steam green beans until just tender, 5 minutes. Reserve 1/2 cup steaming water, and set aside.

2   Heat oil in 12-inch skillet over medium heat. Add ham and garlic and fry until golden, about 1 minute. Add cumin, pepper flakes, and beans and heat through, about 2 to 3 minutes. Season beans with salt and pepper. Stir in bell peppers and reserved steaming water. Simmer uncovered until most of liquid evaporates, 10 to 12 minutes. Taste and adjust flavors.

3   **To Serve:** Serve bean and bell pepper dish warm or at room temperature.

Source: *Cooking From the Heart of Spain* by Janet Mendel.

CAULIFLOWER WITH GARLIC AND ALMONDS
(COLIFLOR CON AJO DORADO Y ALMENDRAS)

Yields about 6 cups, 6 to 8 servings

2-1/2 pound head cauliflower, 1-3/4 to 2 pounds trimmed
3 tablespoons olive oil, more to taste
1-1/2 ounces garlic, 6 large cloves, about 3 tablespoons peeled and finely sliced crosswise
About 1 ounce slivered almonds, 3 tablespoons
1 teaspoon sweet Spanish paprika
1 tablespoon red wine vinegar, more to taste
1/2 ounce trimmed Italian parsley, 4 tablespoons coarsely chopped

1   Cut cauliflower into small bite-sized florets to yield 6 to 7 cups. Steam cauliflower until very tender, 5 to 6 minutes. Place cauliflower in mixing bowl, and keep warm. Reserve cooking water.

2   Heat oil in a 9-inch skillet over medium heat. When hot, add sliced almonds. Cook until golden. Transfer almonds to cauliflower bowl with slotted spoon. Add sliced garlic to the skillet, and cook until golden. Transfer garlic with slotted spoon to bowl with cauliflower and almonds.

3   Remove skillet from heat, stir in paprika, vinegar, parsley, and 3 to 4 tablespoons reserved cauliflower cooking water. Taste vinaigrette and season with salt, more vinegar or oil.

4   **To Serve:** Toss vinaigrette on warm cauliflower. Taste and adjust seasonings. Pile cauliflower into serving bowl and serve warm.

Source: *Cooking From the Heart of Spain* by Janet Mendel.

REVIEW QUESTIONS

1. What is a Spanish sofrito? Name its ingredients. Discuss the procedure for preparing it.

2. How did Columbus's voyage to the West Indies and Mexico impact Spanish cuisine?

3. What is pimentón?

4. What were some of the foreign influences on Spanish cuisine? What culture made the greatest impact?

5. What does "en escabeche" mean?

6. What is pisto or samfaina?

7. What country has borders with Spain? What Spanish region does it most affect?

CHAPTER EIGHT

GREECE AND TURKEY

This chapter will:

- Introduce the intertwined and turbulent histories of Greece and Turkey, their geographies, cultural influences, and climate.

- Discuss the importance of the Silk Road, the expulsion of Christian Greeks from Asia Minor, and the Ottoman Empire on both Greek and Turkish cuisines.

- Introduce Greek and Turkish culinary cultures, their diverse regional variations, and dining etiquette.

- Identify foods, dishes, and techniques that cross between countries.

- Identify the foods, flavor foundations, seasoning devices, and favored cooking techniques of both Greece and Turkey.

- Teach the techniques and recipes for the luscious, long-lived dishes of Greece and Turkey.

GREECE: GREAT BEAUTY, GODS, WARS, AND DEMOCRACY

FIGURE 8.1A Map of Greece and Turkey.

Early Celebrity Chefs

Greek cookbook author Rosemary Barron writing in Flavors of Greece doesn't wonder how it was possible that in a rich and complex culture like ancient Greece "food and its preparation would not have been taken seriously." She points out that ancient Greece, known as the cradle of Western civilization, had well-developed social and political systems and a "rich intellectual and cultural life." Ancient Greeks looked upon the culinary arts as both creative and scientific, and "throughout the ancient world" Greek chefs were as highly regarded as are modern-day French chefs. Barron credits the abundant and creative ancient Greek kitchens for first establishing "the principles and practice of fine cooking and gastronomy."

Known for ancient archeology and architecture, Greece is home to the Acropolis, the amphitheater of Epidaurus, the palace at Knossos, and the ancient Greek Orthodox monasteries overlooking the azure Aegean Sea artfully piled atop Mount Athos. Its many spectacular natural sights, from sea coast and mountains, Santorini's caldera and the Samaria Gorge on Crete, to the gray rock pinnacles of Meteora, make this a country of captivating beauty.

Greece lies at the meeting point of three continents, *Europe, Asia* and *Africa*—and in the middle of three seas, the *Mediterranean, Ionian,* and *Aegean*. Greek settlements on the Balkan Peninsula date from prehistoric times, and the contributions and customs first

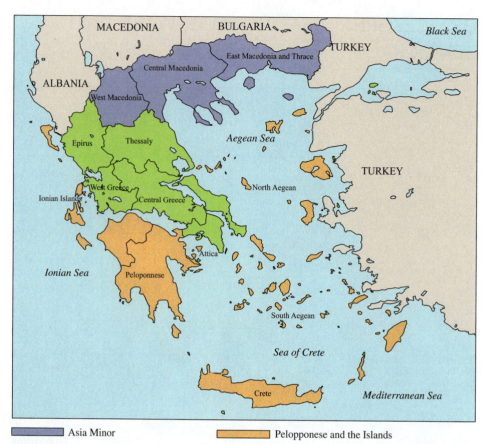

FIGURE 8.1B Map of Greece.

born there are still alive today. Western law, government, math, entertainment, literature, science, architecture, and what and how we eat have their roots in ancient Greek culture.

Three of the earliest advanced European civilizations developed in Greece from 3300 BCE to 1150 BCE: the *Cycladic* on mainland Greece and Crete, *Minoan* on Crete, and the *Myceneaean* on the Greek mainland. The Minoans and Mycenaeans were great shipbuilders and traders known for fine pottery and cloth. The sophisticated Minoan civilization is credited with laying the foundation for the successful economy of classical Greece with their organized trade, arts, and food cultivation. The Mycenaeans conquered the Minoan civilization. They transferred many Minoan cultural influences to mainland Greece and transformed Greek culture.

During the Greek Dark Ages (1200 BCE to 800 BCE) a collapse of Mycenaean civilization, possibly from famine, invasion, or environmental catastrophe, caused the destruction of culture and cities. Literature, art, record-keeping, and trade slowed to almost a halt. By the eighth century BCE more than 1,500 Greek city-states (cities surrounded by villages) arose across the Greek peninsula, to Asia Minor, southern Italy, and the Black Sea. During the *Classical Period* Mediterranean trade renewed and people again began to study. The Greek alphabet was created and the sciences, art, theater, and literature flourished.

Two city-states, *Sparta* and *Athens*, became most powerful. The Spartans were great warriors. The Athenians, with the first democratic government, were great thinkers, artists, poets, writers, and cooks. Athenians *Euclid* and *Pythagoreas* invented geometry, the great philosopher *Socrates* encouraged students to think for themselves, and *Sophocles* and *Euripides* wrote plays still popular today, that were performed in the first theaters (outdoor amphitheaters). The peak *Classical Period* or golden age lasted for most of the fifth and fourth centuries BCE. It was an important time of learning for scholars, scientists, and cooks. The Sicilian-Greek gourmet *Archestratos* wrote the first cookbook around 330 BCE.

In the sixth century BCE, the Persian Empire had begun a long period of war and conquest of Greece. The Greeks defeated them in 479 BCE. The *Peloponnesian War* (431 BCE to 404 BCE) between Sparta and Athens followed. When Phillip II, ruler of Macedonia, died, his son *Alexander the Great* became king. Alexander led the Greek armies to conquer Persia, Egypt, and parts of India. Alexander's death in 323 BCE ended the *Classical Period* and ushered in the *Hellenistic Period*. Though the empire split apart, Alexander had enlarged the world for Greek youth. Many immigrated to new cities in the east, and spread Greek culture and cuisine.

In 146 BCE, the Romans annexed Greece to the Roman Empire. Roman rule was a mixed bag: The Romans respected Greek writing, politics, thought, science, mathematics, language, and culinary skills. They spread them throughout the Western world, where they continue to shape lives. Romans brought an end to warfare, but Roman civil war struggles left Greece weakened.

Invasions by the Byzantine Empire, Normans, Franks, and Turkish-Ottomans followed from second and third centuries through the fifteenth century. For more than a millennium *Byzantium* was a major cultural and military power until the Fall of Constantinople to the Ottoman Turks in 1453. Greeks revolted and finally threw off Turkish rule with the Independence War from 1821 to 1829. In 1831 an independent Greece was established.

In 1923, Turkey and Greece enforced the largest compulsory population exchange of the twentieth century, based on religious beliefs. A million Christian refugees from Muslim Turkey (Asia Minor) settled in the Greek islands and mainland, bringing influences of French, Turkish, and Armenian cuisines with dishes like *moussaka, tzatziki,* and kebabs.

In 1975, the Greek monarchy was abolished with the creation of a democratic constitution. 1n 1981, Greece became the tenth member of the European Union, which raised its standard of living. However Greece has recently experienced some severe economic setbacks.

LANGUAGE, PHILOSOPHY, AND RELIGION

Today, 98 to 99 percent of the population speaks Greek, which is based on classical Greek and very close to the language spoken from the fifth century BCE.

Religion was important to ancient Greeks and remains important to modern day ancestors who are 98 percent Orthodox Christians. Muslims comprise around 1 percent of the population; the remaining fraction is Catholic, Jewish, Old Calendar Orthodox, Jehovah's Witness, Mormon, and Protestant. Most Muslims, Greece's only recognized minority, live in the northern region of Thrace, near Turkey.

Ancient Greeks believed in a pantheon of gods who played a part in all that happened on Earth. Mythology came from Greek literature about the gods, who ruled over special areas of life. The Parthenon in Athens was built to honor Athena, the goddess of war and wisdom. Sports held religious meaning in ancient Greece. They honored important leaders, celebrated gods, and prepared men for battle. The first games were held in the valley of Olympia around 776 BCE.

GEOGRAPHY AND CLIMATE: MEDITERRANEAN, MOUNTAIN, AND ISLAND

The mountainous Greek mainland, located in southeastern Europe on the southern Balkan Peninsula and perched on the rim of the Mediterranean, is about the size of Louisiana. Eighty percent of the peninsula is mountainous. *Mount Olympus* (9,570 feet) is the highest peak. The Greek peninsula juts out into three seas scattered with 1,400 islands (227 inhabited) that form the remainder of Greece: *Crete* in the Mediterranean, the *Dodecanese, Lesbos, Chios,* the *Saronic Island,* and the *Cycladic Islands* in the Aegean Sea, and the *Ionian Islands* in the Ionian Sea.

Greece has three climate zones. The southern, coastal, and island *Mediterranean* climate has mild, wet winters and hot, sunny summers. The mountainous *alpine* climate has cool, wet summers and cold winters with snowfall. The *temperate* climate of northern Macedonia and Thrace has cold, damp winters and hot, dry summers with frequent thunderstorms.

FARMING AND AGRICULTURE

Agriculture in Greece suffers from a lack of natural resources: only 20 to 30 percent of its land is arable, most food is grown on small, family-owned farms, and rainfall is low. Despite these setbacks, abundant wild greens and herbs, dear to every Greek kitchen, supplement a large choice of fruits, nuts, legumes, citrus, and vegetables like tomatoes, cucumbers, eggplant, and artichokes. Farms on the northern plains of Thessaly, Macedonia, and Thrace grow corn, wheat, barley, sugar beets, and cotton. Olives and their oil, grapes, melons, tomatoes, peaches, and oranges are exported. Goats, sheep, pigs, honeybees, cattle, chicken, rabbits, and pigeons are important livestock for the production of meat, honey, milk, and feta cheese. Fishing, not as vital as it once was due to overfishing and pollution, still plays an important role in the Greek diet, along with poultry and lamb.

GREEK CUISINE: MASTERS OF WHEAT, GRAPE, AND OLIVE

Greece's ancient ancestors were hunter-fisher-gatherers. They baked in clay ovens, grilled over wood fires, or roasted in embers. Modern Western and Greek cooking had its genesis with the rise of the *Minoan* civilization. The advanced, organized Minoan civilization developed on Crete and Santorini from about 2700 BCE to 1400 BCE. At their peak, Minoans built the foundations of modern Greek society and its cuisine. Primarily naval traders, the Minoans had frequent contact with mainland *Mycenaean* Greece, Cyprus, Syria, Anatolia, Egypt, North Africa, Mesopotamia, and westward to Spain. The influence of these cultures led Minoans to transform their simple beginnings into a civilization and food culture that became the framework for classical Greece and Europe.

Minoan cooks valued fresh local ingredients. The core of Minoan cuisine was the lush variety of native foods available on Crete like *horta* (greens), grapes, olives, pears, quince, figs, poppies, lettuce, celery, asparagus, wild artichoke, wild leeks, purslane, wild mustard, wheat, barley, chickpeas, fava beans, lentils, bay leaves, oregano, thyme, and carrots. Wild and domesticated animals like honeybees, deer, boar, cattle, sheep, pigs, rabbits, and goats contributed honey, meat, and milk. Fishermen brought in fish, shrimp, octopus, and other seafood. Minoan cooks were sophisticated: they knew how to roast meat and stew it with wild greens, make fruit pastes, the forerunner of Spanish *membrillo*, from quince and other fruit, process olives to be edible and for oil, grind wheat for bread, make the resinated wine *retsina*, and infuse milk with herbs and olive oil with saffron.

Around 1400 BCE, the Minoan civilization gave way to the invading Greek mainland Mycenaeans. The Mycenaeans, strongly influenced by the Minoans, transformed their mainland culinary culture. Later, classical Greeks studied gastronomy seriously. They established the underpinnings of the dining arts and refined many of the sauces and cooking techniques still in use in Greece and the West. When classical Greece declined, the Roman Empire replaced Athens as the heart of the civilized world. Greek chefs were in demand, and from them the Romans developed the foundations of Italian cuisine.

Greece has long been an intersection of East and West, absorbing dark invasions, trade, disaster, conquests, migrations, and settlements. Over centuries, Persian, Byzantine, Frankish, Slavic (Balkan), Roman, Venetian, and Turkish foods and techniques, like paprika, lemons, tomatoes, bell peppers, and potatoes, influenced the continually evolving Greek cuisine. As the Byzantine Empire in Constantinople grew, Greek chefs spread their expertise through the Balkans. During occupation, the Ottoman-Turks changed the names of Greek dishes, which has led to the sometimes mistaken belief that many Greek dishes are Turkish in origin. During the occupation Greek chefs fled to monasteries and instead of the monks' traditional tall black hats, they wore tall white *toques*, now the symbol of all professional chefs.

In addition to the Minoan diet, the mainstays of modern Greek cuisine are vegetables (tomatoes, eggplant, zucchini, bell peppers, onions, garlic, green beans, okra, potatoes, and fennel), fruits (lemons and oranges), herbs (mint, oregano, parsley, dill, sage, basil, and thyme), feta cheese and yogurt, wheat for bread and pasta, rice, barley, bulgar, many types of honey, lamb, nuts (walnuts, pine nuts, and almonds), and a rich variety of legumes.

Greek cuisine is the preeminent Mother cuisine of the Mediterranean basin. Rather than a grand cuisine, Greek cooks have formed an earthy cuisine full of character, soul, and satisfaction. Stovetop and outdoor grill or spit cooking is still the norm in villages, with baking often confined to the after-hours village baker's oven. Stewing, frying, and large casseroles are favored. Despite Greeks' love of meat, they have developed a large variety of meatless vegetable and grain dishes—especially on Greek Orthodox Crete. Meat is expensive and the Greek Orthodox religion requires fasting from meat and dairy about half the year. Inventive vegetarian dishes like *pites* (vegetable pies), *lathera* (oil-braised vegetables or beans), vegetable and rice *dolmades*, and *kefthedes* (grated vegetable fritter balls) resulted.

REGIONAL GREECE

Greece's mountainous and far-flung island geography has hampered communication and travel. Few people in or out of the country have a complete picture of "Greek" cuisine. Bread, olive oil, and wine unite all of Greece, and feta and other cheeses, pork and sausages, breads, and many pastries for festivals and holy days are produced throughout the country. No table is complete without them. Three styles of cooking underlie Greek cuisine: the northern mountainous *pan-Balkan* cooking of itinerant shepherds, cooking of the *Peloponnese and the Islands*, and the cuisine of *Asia Minor*.

1. **Pan-Balkan: Earthy and Dairy-Rich**
   Nomadic shepherd cuisine, influenced by Turkey and Bulgaria, came mainly from what goats or sheep could provide, and what could be foraged: butter, milk, yogurt, cheese, meat, wild greens and herbs, and supplemental grain. Transportable *pites* (pita) or pies, *trahana* (milk-based dry pasta), cheese, and roasts formed daily meals.

2. **Pelopponese and the Islands: Profusion of Olives**
   The Pelopponese is a large peninsula in the southern Greek mainland. Coast and mountains shaped this simple, direct cuisine with its famous Kalamata and Nafplion cracked green olives, olive oil, figs, wine and vinegar, raisins, artichokes, eggplant, citrus groves (with lemons for *avgolemono* sauce), tomatoes (and tomato sauce with cinnamon), one-pot meals with lots of olive oil, and a profusion of vegetables. The Pelopponese produce about a third of Greece's olive oil.

   An important stopping point for East and West trade, the *Ionian Islands* off the west coast of Greece sit on two fault lines and experience earthquakes. They endured Roman, Byzantine, Venetian, Ottoman Turkish, French, Russian, and British occupations until 1864, when they became part of Greece. They developed a cuisine that takes a culinary lead from Venice with tomatoes, peppers, corn, squash, green beans, potatoes, *sofrito* made with fried veal, puddings, tarts, spaghetti in a beef-tomato sauce, and a sort of *zabaglione*.

   Except for *Crete* and *Ionian Islands*, the hundreds of Greek islands tend to be dry with little vegetation. Inhabitants grow small gardens and subsist on vegetables, legumes, fish, and a little meat. Their inventive island cuisine is founded on the trinity of grain, grapes, and olives. Simplicity and economy rule, with much wild foraging and dishes like *horta*, lentil soup, grilled fish, and *pastitsio*. There may not be a great variety of foods, but what they have is very tasty.

   Crete, largest of the Greek islands, is blessed with a wealth of agriculture, but its cuisine is still simple, economical, and very satisfying. Cretan cuisine is the soul of Greek cooking and much of it has not changed since Minoan times. Cretans are blessed with a healthy diet rich in vegetables, fruits, legumes, grains, and herbs with a minimum of meat.

3. **Asia Minor: Lush and Complex**

Four great empires, Persia, Byzantine, Arab, and Ottoman-Turk, influenced the complex cooking of Asia Minor Greeks, many of whom were wealthy and able to travel and to hire French cooks. After the massive population exchange with Turkey in 1923, they came to reside mainly in the northern states of *Macedonia* and *Thrace*. The Greeks of Asia Minor contributed dishes like stuffed vegetables, spicy peppers, eggplant caviar, layered casseroles, baklava, the use of butter and oil, roast beef, ragout, and soufflé. This influence shifted Greece's unadorned peasant cuisine from traditional, spare food into lush *moussakas*, *kebabs*, and rice-stuffed pepper *dolmades*.

DINE AT HOME IN GREECE

Invited to dine in a Greek home, it's okay to be slightly late. Bring a small gift of flowers, pastry, or good wine, and expect to be treated with genuine warmth and hospitality. Even the poorest Greek will invite guests into his or her home and ply them with the best food in the pantry. It is *filoxenia* (*fil-ox-en-ee'-ah*) or "love of strangers" that underlies Greek hospitality. Most Greeks consider it a high honor to have guests. Dinner will likely be a late, noisy affair. It would appear rude not to join in.

Meal patterns vary: Rural dwellers drink an early coffee for breakfast, then lunch on soup, bread, cheese, olives, tomatoes, and cucumbers. Dinner is similar with the addition of meat. Urban dwellers start the day with Turkish coffee or tea, sometimes bread with marmalade, or a bakery *spanakopita*. Lunch at 2 p.m. is considered a main meal, but many urban dwellers grab light soup or sandwich. They snack on *mezethes* (olives, spreads, soup, dolmades) and pastries between lunch and dinner. Greeks dine late, around 9 or 10 p.m. In the country, people love to cook and eat outdoors. The food isn't fancy, but they eat well. The host always serves meat, a vegetable, and salad with wine.

The host or hostess will beckon guests to a seat. The eldest person will be served first. Don't begin eating until the host or hostess lifts a fork. Dinner might begin with a *meze* like *tzatziki*, *kefte* (meatballs or vegetable fritters), *spanokopita* (spinach or cheese pies), *horta* (boiled wild greens), *dolmades* (stuffed grape leaves), feta with oregano and olive oil, or octopus. Or the table will include mezethes with a salad like *horiatiki salata* (tomatoes, cucumbers, onions, olives, and feta), one or more main dishes like *stifado* (stewed dish), *plaki* (braised fish or legumes), or a casserole like *moussaka* or grilled lamb. Vegetable and grain dishes like rice pilaf or *briami* (roasted mixed vegetables) will accompany them. Soup comes with winter meals: *avgolemono* (egg-lemon), fish, lentil, or tripe. Dessert is usually fresh fruit.

It's common for people to share food from their plate or to serve guests. Take small portions: taking large portions insults the hosts and other diners, and tells them the guest is worried there won't be enough food! Expect long reaches, convivial bumping with lots of laughter and talk, not a quiet, insulated dining experience. As in many European countries, Greeks eat with a fork in the left hand and knife in the right, with elbows off, but wrists and hands on, the table. Be sure to finish *everything* on the plate. Taking seconds will please the hostess. Compliment the food and offer to help clear up after the meal.

TASTES OF GREECE

Fat: Olive oil, butter

Sweet: Honey, sugar, *petimézi* (grape must syrup)

Sour/Alcohol: Lemon, orange, Seville orange, red wine vinegar, *verjuice* (unripe grape juice)

Salty: Sea salt, capers, olives, anchovies

Spicy-Hot: Black pepper, red chili, mustard

Spice: Allspice, anise, bay leaf, caraway, cardamom, cinnamon, clove, coriander, cumin, ginger, juniper, *mahlepi* (cherry pits), mustard seed, nutmeg, mace, saffron, vanilla, bay leaf

Aromatic Seasoning Vegetables: Onion, garlic, green onions, shallots, *sélino* (wild "Italian" celery)

Herbs, Seasonings, and Condiments: Oregano, dill, mint, basil, parsley, marjoram, basil, mountain thyme, rosemary, lime blossom, orange blossom water, rose water, *mastic* (resin), rose geranium, bay laurel

Other Important Foods: Wheat, *pligoúri* (cracked wheat), *avarósitos* (cornmeal), rice, barley, sesame, fruit (grapes and grapes leaves, raisins, pomegranates, figs, currants, apples, plums), nuts (almonds, pistachios, poppy seed, walnuts, chestnuts), lettuce, cucumbers, zucchini, eggplant, cabbage, lentils, broad beans, chickpeas, eggs, tomatoes, wild fennel, feta cheese, yogurt, *hórta* (wild and cultivated greens), wild mushrooms, seafood (fish of many varieties, mussels, shrimp, salt cod), meat (lamb, poultry, rabbit)

Popular Dishes: *Dolmades* (stuffed things), savory pies, *spanokopita* (spinach-filo pie), octopus, *avgolemono* (egg-lemon soup), *pastitsio*, shrimp with feta and tomato, plaki-style and grilled fish, stuffed vegetables, *taramasalata* (fish roe spread), spoon fruits (preserves), *souflaki* (grilled and shaved meat in a pita), *saganaki* (Greek fried cheese), *arnáki frikassé* (fricassee of spring lamb), grilled octopus, *moussaka* (layered eggplant casserole)

Drinks: Turkish coffee, tea, herbal tisane, beer, fruitade, red wine, retsina, ouzo, brandy

COMMON GREEK COOKING TOOLS

Outdoor grill, casserole, clay pot, *satz* (flat iron cooking surface), mortar and pestle; long, thin, straight rolling pin (wooden dowel)

GREEK CHEESE

More than a dozen varieties of cheese are commercially available. Many more honest and predictable local cheeses are produced from goat and sheep milk that tastes of the animals' wild grazing.

Feta

The Greek national cheese, feta, which in Italian means *slice*, is a tangy and moist, but crumbly, brined curd sheep or goat cheese ranging in density from soft to hard. Milk mixed with rennet is allowed to curdle and separate. The curds are transferred to a special mold or cloth bag, and left to drain. The cheese is cut into large slices that are salted and packed in brine-filled barrels for several months. When feta is removed from the brine, it dries out rapidly so it is often sold in brine or water. Feta is eaten as a table cheese, in salads, and in sweet and savory pastries like the phyllo-based dishes *spanakopita* (spinach pie) and *tyropita* (cheese pie). Feta goes well with olive oil and vegetables and can be cooked or grilled for garnish or as a sandwich.

Graviéra

This cheese is a Greek version of the firm, creamy, yellow Swiss *Gruyere* cheese made from cow milk. Graviéra is made from sheep milk in the same style; the flavor ranges from nutty to assertive.

Halloumi

This moist, sharp, crumbly, sheep or goat cheese originated in Cyprus during Medieval Byzantine times. It has a high melting point and is often grilled or fried. Cypriots often wrapped it in mint to keep it fresh and add flavor.

Kasseri

This goat milk Cheddar-style cheese is firm, oily and yellow, melts well, and has a mellow tang. Kasseri is used for fried *saganaki*, *pastitsio*, and *moussaka*.

Kefalotiri or Kefalograviéra

This traditional cheese, made with both sheep and goat milk, is very hard and used for grating over pastas and frying. It is salty and sharp similar to Regato and Parmesan. Kefalotiri, ripened minimally for three months, acquires sharp aroma and a rich salty tang.

Manouri and Anthotyri

These fresh, creamy ewe milk cheeses are served with fruit or honey or for cheesecake and sometimes salted and served plain like feta.

Mizithra

A tangy, sharp goat or sheep cheese traditionally made from unpasteurized whey, mizithra may come unsalted and semi-soft or lightly salted and semi-hard for grating.

Telemes

This cheese is made the same way as feta, but with cow milk instead of sheep or goat milk.

GREEK OLIVES (ELIÉS)

FIGURE 8.2 Olive trees on Crete.

Source: Dimitri Maureau/Fotolia.

FIGURE 8.3 Kalamata olives.

Source: Barbara Dudzinska/Fotolia.

Olives have their origins in prehistoric Greece. Some historians believe that they originated on Crete about 3500 BC in the Early Minoan times. Five olive cures are used in Greece: brine, dry, oil, water, and lye, on more than a dozen olive varieties. Olives are selected based on the year of harvest, the type, and the size. Their size varies from very small to giant called as "mammoth." Olives are measured by their number per liter of net content. One liter can hold from 80 to 400 olives.

Ionian

Green brine-cured olives from Peloponnese with smooth, firm and buttery flesh.

Agrinion

This is a large, green Greek olive with very tender flesh.

Kalamata

Large, almond-shaped black or purple water-cured and brined olive, the Kalamata is rich, meaty, and fruity.

Nafplion

Small green, dense, salty brine-cured olives from Peloponnese

Thassos

Sun-dried and salt- and vinegar-cured black olive from Thassos. It looks like a raisin and tastes salty and rich.

FIGURE 8.4 Thassos olives.

Source: Flavia Morlachetti/Shutterstock.

GREEK FLAVOR FOUNDATIONS

Greek Signature Aromatic Vegetable Combo

Olive oil, onion, and/or garlic plus lemon juice and mountain oregano (rigani)

Greek Herbal Quartet: Oregano, dill, thyme, and mint

Lathorigano: Cooking with olive oil and oregano

Signature Seasonings

See *Turkish Signature Seasonings.*

Liquid/Paste

Olive Oil
See *Glossary.*

Verjuice
The juice of unripe grapes used as a sour element, much like vinegar or lemon juice used in Persian and Middle Eastern cuisine on salads, soups, and braised dishes. Verjus has the added benefit that it may be served with wine.

Animal

Cured Meats
Many of Greek cured meats differ only slightly from island to island. These are a few favorites: Cretan *apaki* (vinegar-marinated and smoked pork), *louza* (salt pork stuffed into intestines and air-cured) from the Cycladic Islands, *siglino* (salted, cooked, and smoked pork loin) from the Pelopennese and, *pastourma* (salt-cured beef), which came from Armenian cuisine but is widely enjoyed by Turks, Greeks, and Lebanese. Pastourma arrived in Greece through the migration of Greeks who once resided in Constantinople (Turkey) and Asia Minor.

Vegetable/Fruit

Capers
Small, unopened buds of the Mediterranean bush, *Capparis spinosa L.*, capers are closely related to the cabbage family, but look more like a rose bush. Caper bushes grow wild and are cultivated throughout the Mediterranean. Pickled in vinegar or preserved in salt (which brings out their flavor), cooks consider the smallest capers (*nonpareilles*) the best.

Lemon
The Greek pantry is not complete without fresh lemons. Their fragrant sour juice perfectly complements Greek olive oil. The Arabs probably introduced them to the Mediterranean, having brought them from Persia around the eleventh century. Lemons soon became more popular than vinegar and the juice from tart fruits like unripe grapes (*verjus*) and pomegranates used previously.

Olives
See *Greek Olives.*

Herbal/Spice

Greek Oregano
Greek oregano tends to be spicier with a tongue-numbing intensity not found in other oregano. Its leaves are furry and gray-green.

Mahlepi or Mahlep
An aromatic spice with the flavor of bitter almond and cherry ground from inner seed of cherry pits, *mahlepi* is used to flavor Greek and Mediterranean cookies, egg-rich yeast cakes, and cheese cake.

FIGURE 8.5 Mastic dripping from a tree.
Source: Steliost/Shutterstock.

Mastic
Mastic is a hardened, gummy resin from a Mediterranean shrub with a slight pine or cedar flavor. It's used to season liqueurs, confections, bread, pastries, and Greek spoon sweets. Turkish cooks use it to coat *doner kebab.* It is sometimes called arabic gum, but should not be confused with gum arabic, which is a different substance.

FIGURE 8.6 Bundles of thyme at a Greek market.
Source: Paul Cowan/Shutterstock.

STILL A PARADISE

Greece, with its myriad islands, sun-drenched landscape, startling blue waters, and daunting rocky shores, never fails to captivate. The islands teem with wild things: herbs, edible greens, carob trees, capers, and many forms of animal life. With water, just about any vegetable grows happily there: zucchini, eggplant, tomatoes, garlic, artichokes, bell peppers, and onions plus grapes. Goats and sheep provide milk and meat. Olive, fig, pomegranate, orange, lemon, quince, loquat, and almond trees supply Greek cooks with a luscious, diverse pantry. Though the surrounding seas have been depleted they manage to feed the population with Mediterranean-celebrated seafood of many varieties like sea urchin, octopus, spiny lobster, rockfish, sea bass, bream, grouper, eel, tuna, red mullet, picarel, shark, and hake.

FIGURE 8.7 Rocky Greek Island shore.
Source: Olga Lipatova/Shutterstock.

SAUCE

Greek Salsa

Sauces in both Greek and Turkish cuisine are not elaborate or long cooked. Cooks prepare them just before they are served to preserve fresh flavor. Since food is simple, flavorful, and fresh there is less need for saucing.

SIGNATURE RECIPE

EGG-LEMON SAUCE (GREEK *AVGOLEMONO* OR TURKISH *TERBIYE*)

This sauce, a light and fluffy savory whisked custard-like sabayon or zabglione, is the most loved Greek flavoring. It goes especially well with cruciferous vegetables and strong-flavored meats. Turks and Greeks use it over all kinds of stuffed dolma. Two cups will thicken and embellish 3 to 5 pounds grilled or roasted meat, fish, vegetables, or meatballs, 40 dolmades, 20 stuffed cabbage, and soup or stew for 6 to 8.

Yields 2 cups, 6 to 8 servings

Basic Proportions

1 cup hot meat, fish, or vegetable stock
    or simmering/stewing broth drained from a dish
3 large whole eggs, 5 liquid ounces
    or 5 liquid ounces egg yolks, 6 to 7 large yolks
1/4 cup freshly squeezed lemon juice, about 1 large lemon or 2 smaller

FIGURE 8.8 Lemon trees.
Source: Kostiantyn Ablazov/Shutterstock.

1 Bring stock or broth to a boil and remove from heat 1 minute before using.

2 There are two ways to prepare this sauce:

One: Whisk whole eggs or egg yolks in stainless bowl (that will set over simmering pot of water to create a double boiler) until pale and frothy. Whisk in lemon juice.

Two: Separate whites from yolks. Whisk whites until soft peak. In another bowl (that can set over simmering pot of water to create a double boiler), whisk yolks with lemon juice until pale and frothy. Fold whites into yolks.

3 Slowly whisk in hot stock or broth to temper eggs. Place bowl over (not in) simmering water *or* pour back into saucepan that held broth. Simmer sauce over *low* heat. Whisk sauce until visibly creamy and thickened, 6 to 10 minutes, and remove from heat.

4 **To Serve:** Taste sauce and season with salt, if necessary. Use sauce immediately or keep warm 30 minutes in thermos or warm spot. Chill overnight and bring to room temperature or warm gently in double boiler over simmering heat.

Source: *The Olive and the Caper: Adventures in Greek Cooking* by Susanna Hoffman.

Vary! Improvise!

☞ *Season avgolemono with herbs, Dijon mustard, or chili.*

☞ *What other seasonings would enhance this sauce? Dijon mustard, sage, or rosemary?*

FIGURE 8.9 Old olive oil press at a Greek home.
Source: ShopArtGallery/Shutterstock.

LEMON AND OLIVE OIL SAUCE (GREEK LADOLEMONO OR TURKISH ZEYTINYAGI VE LIMON SALÇASI)

This lemon vinaigrette is a natural partner for grilled, fried, or poached seafood. Olive oil, fresh lemon juice, oregano, and salt are its most basic Greek form. The mustard plant and seed came to Greece around the same time as grapes, before 1000 BCE, to flourish between rows of grapevines and grains. Turks use this sauce without mustard and oregano, but with parsley.

Yields 6 fluid ounces, enough for 2 to 3 pounds seafood

1/4 cup freshly squeezed lemon juice, about 1 large lemon or
2 smaller
Optional: 1 tablespoon Dijon mustard
  or 1/2 to 1 teaspoon ground mustard powder
1 tablespoon crushed, dried oregano
  or 1/2 ounce trimmed Italian parsley, 1/4 cup minced
4 ounces extra-virgin olive oil

1 Whisk together lemon juice, optional mustard, and oregano or parsley in a small bowl.

2 Slowly pour and whisk oil into lemon mixture in a thin stream. Season sauce with salt and pepper. Whisk sauce before serving.

GREEK GRAPE LEAF AND HERB SAUCE

This sauce is flexible and adaptable. Double the capers if no grape leaves are available. Substitute basil for mint. Use 2 teaspoons dried oregano in place of fresh. Add lemon zest.

Yields about 2 cups, about 6 servings

About 1 ounce preserved grape leaves, rinsed well, 1/2 cup stemmed and coarsely chopped
3 ounces trimmed Italian parsley, about 1-1/2 cups lightly chopped and packed
1/2 ounce fresh mint leaves, 1/4 cup packed
1/4 ounce fresh oregano leaves, 2 tablespoons
1/2 ounce garlic, about 2 large cloves, 1 tablespoon peeled and chopped
Juice of 1 large lemon, 3 to 4 tablespoons fresh lemon juice, more as needed
1 to 1-1/2 ounces drained capers, 3 tablespoons
2 ounces trimmed green onions, about 4, 1/2 cup chopped
1/2 to 1 cup extra virgin olive oil

1   Place all ingredients, **except olive oil**, in food processor. Purée until smooth. With machine running, slowly add oil as is necessary to get mixture to a fine purée.

2   Taste sauce and adjust flavors with salt, pepper, and lemon juice. Rest sauce 1 hour before serving.

3   Serve with grilled lamb or pork. Keep refrigerated in a tightly closed jar for up to 1 week.

Source: *The Complete Meat Cookbook* by Bruce Aidells.

SIGNATURE RECIPE

GREEK GARLIC SAUCE (SKORTHALIÁ, SKORDALIA, OR AYIATHA)

Greeks eat skorthaliá, a thick garlicky purée, as a dip or emulsified sauce with fried or poached fish or vegetables: beets, eggplant, and zucchini. At its most basic, skorthaliá combines pounded garlic with thickeners: either day-old dampened breadcrumbs, boiled and mashed potato, ground almonds or walnuts, or even cooked squash with red wine vinegar or lemon juice. Olive oil is beaten in to make a thick garlic mayonnaise. Egg yolks are optional.

4 to 6 servings

Potato-Based

Yields 1-1/2 cups

8 ounces potato, about 1-1/2 cups peeled and diced
1/3 ounce garlic, 2 medium cloves peeled
2 tablespoons red wine vinegar
1/3 to 1/2 cup olive oil

Nut-Based

Yields 1-1/2 to 2 cups

2 ounces blanched, slivered almonds *or* walnuts, 1/2 cup toasted and chopped
1/3 ounce garlic, about 2 medium cloves, peeled
2 to 3 tablespoons red wine vinegar
    or 2 to 3 tablespoons freshly squeezed lemon juice
1/2 to 3/4 cup olive oil

1 *Prepare potato or nut base:*

Potato

Dice potato into 1-inch cubes and place in saucepan. Cover with cold water and bring to a boil. Boil potato until tender, 8 to 10 minutes. Drain and peel. Place potato into ricer and rice potato into a mixing bowl. Mince or mash garlic with 1/2 teaspoon salt to smooth paste and add to potato.

Nut

Grind nuts smooth in blender or food processor. Add garlic and 1/2 cup water and purée until smooth.

2 *Finish skorthaliá:*

Potato

Stir vinegar into potato base. Slowly, slowly, whisk oil into potato base.

Nut

Add vinegar or lemon juice to blender, and purée nut base again until smooth. With machine running, *slowly* pour olive oil into nut base.

3 **To Serve:** Skorthaliá should be the consistency of thick mayonnaise. Adjust consistency with water. Taste sauce and season salt and pepper and more vinegar or lemon juice. Rest skorthaliá 30 minutes or up to overnight for best flavor.

FIVE IMPORTANT GREEK SAUCES

Ladolemono: "vinaigrette" with mustard, fresh lemon juice, and olive oil

Avgolemono: whisked egg and lemon juice "sabayon" or savory "custard"

Skorthaliá: potato-, nut-, or bread-based garlic and olive oil "mayonnaise"

Tzatziki: dip or sauce made with yogurt and grated cucumber

Besamel: béchamel made with flour, butter or oil, and milk

YOGURT-CUCUMBER-GARLIC SAUCE (TZATZIKI)

Serve Greek tzatziki as a sauce or dip with toasted pita, with grilled or fried fish or chicken, or with boiled, sliced beets, fried eggplant, or zucchini. Twelve ounces cucumber yields about 1 cup peeled, squeeze-drained grated cucumber.

Yields 2 cups, 4 to 6 servings

16 ounces plain Greek or whole milk yogurt, 2 cups
12 to 14 ounce English cucumber, 1 cup peeled, seeded, and grated
1/2 ounce peeled garlic, 2 large cloves
2 tablespoons fresh lemon juice, about 1/2 large lemon, more to taste
  or 2 tablespoons red wine vinegar, more to taste
1/3 ounce fresh dill, mint leaves, or trimmed Italian parsley, 2 to 3 tablespoons chopped
  or mixture of chopped dill, mint, and parsley
2 tablespoons olive oil, *divided*

1 **Prepare yogurt:** Line a strainer with dampened cheesecloth and set it over a bowl. Pour yogurt, preferably whole milk, into it. Refrigerate 1 to 2 hours; it should reduce volume by half. Drink or discard watery whey. (Whey is full of beneficial bacteria.)

2 **Prepare cucumber:** Peel, seed, and grate cucumber. Squeeze grated cucumber and drain.

3 Mince garlic until pasty with a little salt to soften its flavor. Combine yogurt, cucumber, and garlic. Stir in lemon juice or vinegar and herbs then whisk in 1-1/2 tablespoons olive oil. Taste tzatziki, and season with salt to taste.

4 **To Serve:** Chill tzatziki 1 hour to blend flavors. Taste again and re-season. Place mixture in serving bowl. To garnish, drizzle with remaining olive oil.

Vary! Improvise!

☛ *Greek Beet Tzatziki: Boil 1/2 pound beets until tender. Cool. Peel and grate or finely dice beets (yields about 1 cup) and mix with 1 cup drained yogurt, 2 cloves minced garlic, 1/2 cup chopped Italian parsley, 1/4 cup chopped dill, 2 tablespoons fresh lemon juice, and salt and pepper.*

☛ *Enrich: Stir 1 to 2 tablespoons tahini into yogurt after it has been drained.*

SPECIAL METHODS

HANDMADE FILLO DOUGH

This dough, made with olive oil, is prevalent in most of Greece. Fillo dough is best made with higher-gluten flours (bread flour or King Arthur all-purpose). They result in a dough stronger than one made with softer all-purpose flour like White Lily. The softer (lower protein or gluten) the flour, the less water needed, so add the water slowly, as needed.

Yields approximately 1-1/2 pounds dough

Enough for 12- to 14-inch round cake pan or half hotel pan and *8 to 10 cups filling.*
About 15 ounces unbleached all-purpose white flour, 3 cups, more for rolling
1/2 teaspoon kosher salt
1 cup plus 2 tablespoons warm water
3 tablespoons olive oil
4-1/2 teaspoons red wine vinegar *or* fresh lemon juice

Yields approximately 2 pounds dough

Enough for two 9-inch round pies, one 18-inch round cake or pizza pan or one 9-inch by 12-inch baking dish and *10 to 12 cups filling.*
About 20 ounces unbleached white flour, 4 cups, more for rolling
1-1/2 teaspoons kosher salt
1-1/2 cups warm water
1/4 cup olive oil
2 tablespoons red wine vinegar *or* fresh lemon juice

1 Mix flour and salt together in large bowl.

2 Mix liquid ingredients (but reserve some water) together and pour into flour. Mix together to a moist dough, using the reserved water as necessary.

3 Knead dough in bowl or on work surface until tender and resilient, 10 minutes. Dust with flour as necessary to keep dough from sticking.

4 Cover dough with damp towel or plastic wrap. Rest 30 minutes to 1 hour in warm place. Refrigerate in airtight zipper baggie up to 3 days; bring to room temperature before using.

Source: *The Glorious Foods of Greece* by Diane Kochilas.

Vary! Improvise!

☞ *Northern Greek Macedonians prepare a flaky version of this dough with 1 tablespoon olive oil and water. The slightly rolled dough then is brushed with melted butter, folded, and chilled, similar to puff pastry. It is brought to room temperature before the final rolling.*

COMMERCIAL FILLO PASTRY

The paper-thin fillo (or phyllo) dough makes Greek and Turkish savory and sweet pastry-baking speedy and easy.

Three to 4 sheets commercial phyllo equals 1 sheet homemade dough.

1 pound commercial fillo yields about 32 sheets (14-inch by 18-inch).

- **Krinos**, about 22 sheets per pound, is light and thin for crisp, delicate layers in desserts like baklava.

- **Athens** (Number 4) fillo is slightly thicker and holds up to custard fillings.
- **Kontos** (Number 5) fillo is heftier, an all-purpose dough for tart shells and mini-fillo cups.
- **Apollo** (Number 7) fillo is sturdy; good for oblong, round, or individual pies like spanakopita.
- **Zagorisio** or **Apollo** (Number 10 or Country-Style) fillo is the thickest, about 10 sheets to the pound, good for hearty, rustic pies like hortopita.

Signature Technique: Handling and Stuffing Commercial Fillo Pastry

1 Thaw commercially made frozen fillo overnight in refrigerator. Speeding up this process results in gummy sheets, which stick together and crack.

2 Rest unopened package at room temperature 1 hour before using.

3 Clarify butter, if using. Removing watery milk solids results in crisper fillo.

4 Set up a station. Unroll sheets and cover with large piece of plastic wrap plus a damp towel over top. Stay away from fans or blowers. Dry fillo is brittle, breakable fillo. If you need to cut fillo, use sharp scissors.

5 Avoid wet fillings. Cook fillings through and thicken so there is no weeping moisture. Sprinkle finely ground bulgar, ground nuts, or dry breadcrumbs on the bottom of the pastry to absorb moisture.

6 Work quickly. Remove a sheet and brush or spray with clarified butter or olive oil, cover lightly and evenly, but don't drench. If a sheet tears, just piece it together.

7 Layer sheets with finely ground nuts or fine dry breadcrumbs for extra crispness.

8 Before baking, score top of finished fillo casserole to serving-size pieces with damp knife. Bake in preheated 400 degree F oven until fillo is deeply golden, 20 to 30 minutes.

9 Wrap remaining rolled up sheets in plastic, seal tightly and refrigerate up to 1 month.

10 Prepare different shapes:

Individual Triangles
Butter, crumb, and stack three 14-inch by 18-inch sheets fillo. Slice longer side into four 4-1/2-inch-wide strips and cover with plastic wrap. Spoon 2 to 3 tablespoons filling on one end of strip 1 inch from end. *Make a Flag Fold:* Fold in corner of that end to form a triangle. Then fold in that triangular edge to form another triangle. Continue folding until you have a triangular pastry. Transfer pastries to baking sheet and brush with butter. Bake.

Logs
Butter and crumb three 14-inch by 18-inch sheets fillo. Along the length of one long side, stopping 2 inches short of each end, lay a 1-1/2-inch log of filling. Roll log over once, tuck side ends in neatly, and finish rolling. Transfer log to parchment-covered sheet pan. Liberally butter logs. Make shallow cuts on a diagonal for 3/4- to 1-inch pieces. Bake logs immediately.

Oblong Casserole Pies
Heavy fillings need eight 14-inch by 18-inch sheets, buttered, crumbed, and layered on the bottom of a casserole. Lighter fillings need six. Spread filling over them and butter, crumb, tuck, and layer six to eight sheets on top. Bake.

Round Pies
Tightly overlap and layer sheets like flower petals on greased round baking pan with sheets hanging off lengthwise from center. Spread filling up to within 1 inch of edges. Top with more layers of fillo and flip up sides, buttering liberally. Brush top liberally with melted butter, and cut a vent for steam to escape. Bake.

GREEK AND TURKISH MEZETHES

These small plates of tasty morsels, served throughout Turkey and Greece in homes and tavernas, entice the appetite before meals and slow alcohol absorption during drinking. In Greek tavernas, every carafe of anise-y ouzo comes with a plate of *mezethes*. Depending on the season and region, a diner might get roasted chickpeas, grilled octopus, marinated olives, cubes of feta cheese, *taramosalata* (fish roe spread), slices of spanakopita or tiropita (cheese pie), or dolmades. In Turkish cafes or homes, dinners begin with an array of dolma, small chopped salads, manti (stuffed pasta), borek, and cacik.

FIGURE 8.10 Mezethes at a Greek taverna.
Source: Studiovd/Shutterstock.

SIMMER, STEW, POACH, BOIL, AND STEAM

Greek and Turks love soup. They eat them as a starter or as a full meal at breakfast, lunch, or dinner. Greek *soupa* are generally simple and hearty with satisfying ingredients like lentils, sesame paste, yogurt, milk, eggplant, bulgar wheat, *tarhana*, cabbage, greens, beans, lamb, seafood, or chicken.

GREEK EGG-LEMON SOUP (SOÚPA AVGOLEMONO)

This classic soup shows off the beloved Greek combination of lemon and eggs.

Yields about 6 cups, 4 servings

1 quart chicken broth
2-1/3 ounces short- or medium-grain white rice, 1/3 cup, rinsed and drained
2 whole eggs
Juice of one large lemon, about 4 tablespoons, more as needed

Garnish: 1/4 ounce trimmed Italian parsley, 2 tablespoons chopped

1 Mix chicken broth and rice in a 2-quart saucepan. Bring to a boil over medium heat. Lower heat, cover pan, and simmer rice until al dente, about 10 minutes.

2 **Just before serving:** Whisk eggs and half the lemon juice together with a pinch of salt in a bowl. Remove saucepan with rice and broth from the heat and let it cool 1 minute. Slowly whisk 1/2 cup hot broth into eggs and lemon juice to temper. Pour and whisk egg-broth-lemon mixture into hot broth and rice. If broth is too hot or eggs too cold, the eggs can curdle.

3 **To Serve:** Reheat soup, but simmer, don't boil. Taste soup and season with salt, freshly ground pepper, and more lemon juice to taste. It should be very lemony, but balanced and refreshing. Ladle into bowls and garnish with parsley.

Vary! Improvise!

☞ *Stir 1/2 cup finely diced cooked chicken breast into soup after rice is cooked.*

GREEK SESAME SOUP (TAHINÓSOUPA)

For a smooth, sophisticated version of tahinósoupa, cut tomatoes in half on their equators, and grate pulp into bowl instead of dicing. Discard skins.

Yields about 2 quarts, 6 to 8 servings

1-1/2 quarts vegetable stock *or* water
1-1/4 ounces garlic, 5 large cloves, 2-1/2 tablespoons peeled and minced
2-1/3 ounces white long-grain rice, 1/3 cup
About 1-1/4 pounds tomatoes, 2 cups peeled, seeded, and diced, juices and seeds reserved
2 lemons, 1 zested and both juiced, about 1/2 cup fresh lemon juice
4 ounces sesame paste (*tahini*), 1/2 cup

Garnish: 1/2 ounce trimmed Italian parsley, 1/4 cup finely chopped

1 In a 4-quart saucepan, bring stock or water, garlic, rice, and tomatoes to a boil over medium heat. Lower heat, partially cover pan, and simmer until rice is tender, 10 to 12 minutes. Stir in lemon zest and remove soup from heat.

2 Whisk tahini with half the lemon juice and 1 cup hot broth until creamy. Pour tahini mixture back into rice-tomato-broth and whisk well to incorporate.

3 **To Serve:** Taste soup and season with salt, freshly ground pepper, and more lemon juice to taste. Ladle hot soup into bowls and garnish with parsley.

GREEK SHRIMP AND BELL PEPPER SOUP WITH GARLIC SAUCE (GARITHÓSOUPA ME SKORTHALIÁ)

Yields about 2 quarts, 4 servings

1-1/2 pounds 21/25 shrimp (with heads if possible), peeled and deveined
2 cups Samos or Muscat wine *or* fruity white wine
1 large bay leaf
1 sprig rosemary
3-inch dried red chili pepper, stemmed and seeded
Zest of 1 lemon
12 ounces red bell peppers, about 2 medium
3 tablespoons olive oil
8 to 9 ounces onions, 2 cups peeled and finely slivered
1/4 ounce garlic, 1 large clove, 1-1/2 teaspoons peeled and minced
4 to 5 ounces celery, about 2 stalks with leaves, 3/4 to 1 cup finely chopped
1 tablespoon torn mint *or* basil leaves
4 slices Greek *paximáthia* bread rusk
   or 4 to 8 ounces sliced and toasted whole wheat bread
Skorthaliá Sauce

1 **Prepare the broth:** In a 5- to 6-quart saucepan, pour 1 quart cold water, shrimp shells and heads, herbs, chili, lemon zest, and 1/2 teaspoon kosher salt. Bring broth to a boil and simmer 20 minutes. Rest 5 minutes off heat. Strain through damp cheesecloth. Discard shells and seasonings and reserve broth.

2 Chop shrimp if desired, or not, and set aside.

3 Roast peppers until blackened. Place in bowl and cool slightly. Peel off skin with hands or paper towels. Remove stems and seeds peppers (seeds will make the soup bitter). Slice half the peppers into thin strips and set them aside. Dice, then purée, remaining peppers in food processor until smooth. Set purée aside.

4 **Prepare the soup:** Heat a 5- to 6-quart heatproof casserole over medium-low heat. Add oil and onions; cook until onions soften, 5 to 8 minutes. Stir in bell pepper strips, garlic, and celery. Simmer vegetables until soft, 8 to 10 minutes. Stir in bell pepper purée and shrimp stock and bring to a boil. Turn off heat, and stir in shrimp. When shrimp have turned opaque, 1 to 2 minutes, sprinkle soup with mint or basil. Taste soup and season with salt if necessary.

5 **To Serve:** Spread 1 slice of bread with *Skorthaliá Sauce* and place in bottom of each bowl. Ladle hot soup over top and serve.

Source: *Recipes From a Greek Island* by Susie Jacobs.

GREEK SQUID STEW WITH FENNEL AND GREEN OLIVES (SOUPIES ME MARATHO KAI ELIES)

Squid needs either very short or very long cooking to avoid rubberiness. To speed up this stew from Crete, add squid at the very end, turn off heat, and cook 1 minute. Greek cooks prepare this stew with 4 cups chopped wild fennel instead of cultivated fennel bulbs.

Yields about 9 to 10 cups, 4 to 6 servings

2 pounds cleaned squid bodies and tentacles
1/2 to 2/3 cup olive oil
8 to 9 ounces onion, 2 cups peeled and finely diced
About 20 ounces trimmed fennel bulbs, 2 large, halved lengthwise, 8 cups finely sliced
1-1/2 teaspoons crushed fennel seed
1 ounce trimmed dill, 1/2 cup chopped
5 to 6 ounces large green olives, 1 cup pitted, quartered, and rinsed
2 teaspoons flour
2 large lemons, about 1/2 cup fresh juice, *divided*

For Serving

Hot, cooked rice or bread

1   Slice squid into 1-1/2–inch-wide rings and lightly chop tentacles.

2   Heat olive oil in 6-quart casserole over medium heat. Stir in onions, fennel, and fennel seed and cook until soft, 8 to 10 minutes. Season with 1/2 teaspoon kosher salt. Stir in squid rings and tentacles and 1 cup water (or liquid from frozen thawed squid). Bring to a simmer, cover casserole, and simmer over low heat until squid is tender, 1 hour.

3   Fold in half the dill and all the olives and simmer stew 10 minutes. Turn heat up and bring stew to a low boil. Whisk in flour and 1/4 cup lemon juice. Cook, stirring with spoon or heatproof spatula until thickened, 3 minutes. Stir in remaining dill.

4   **To Serve:** Remove casserole from heat and taste. Adjust flavors with salt, pepper, and remaining lemon juice. Serve stew warm or at room temperature with rice or bread.

Source: *The Glorious Foods of Greece* by Diane Kochilas.

Braising

Braising on top of the stove is an important technique in both Greece and Turkey. The signature oil-braised *ladera* or *zeytinyağli* make luscious vegetarian dishes. Greek and Turkish cooks also braise seafood, stuffed grape or cabbage leaves and greens in broth, tomato, or *avgolemono* sauce or water.

SIGNATURE RECIPE

OIL-BRAISED VEGETABLES (GREEK LADERA OR TURKISH ZEYTINYAĞLI)

Ladera, lathera, or zeytinyağli, is an olive-oil-stewed or braised dish, usually vegetarian, made with one or more vegetables cooked in an olive-oil-based sauce with onion, tomatoes, and garlic. More olive oil results in a richer dish. This combo of beans and potatoes is popular in the Greek Peloponnese.

4 to 6 servings

1/2 to 1 cup olive oil
8 to 9 ounces onion, 2 cups finely diced or slivered
Optional: 1/4 to 1/2 ounce garlic, 1 to 2 large cloves, 1-1/2 to 3 teaspoons peeled and minced
2 pounds fresh green beans, washed and stemmed
   or 2-1/2 pounds other vegetables like eggplant, zucchini, peas, and carrots
1-1/2 cups tomato sauce
   or grated fresh tomato pulp from about 1-1/4 pounds tomatoes, 2 large
8 ounces red skin potatoes, washed and sliced into 8 wedges

1 Heat olive oil over medium heat in a 6-quart pot or a deep 12-inch skillet. Stir in onion and cook until softened, 5 to 7 minutes. Add garlic, if using, and cook 1 minute.

2 Meanwhile, slice green beans into 2-inch lengths to yield about 7 to 8 cups. (If using eggplant, dice into 1-inch cubes or slice zucchini 1/2-inch thick.)

3 Add green beans to onions and stir well to mix. Cover pan and simmer 2 to 4 minutes. Uncover pan and stir in tomato, potatoes, and salt and pepper plus 1 cup water. Bring vegetables to a boil, reduce heat to medium-low and partially cover pan. Simmer until beans and potatoes can be cut with a fork, 45 minutes to an hour. Stir occasionally, but don't add water, it will thin the sauce. Don't stir vegetables in the latter stages of cooking to avoid breaking up potatoes.

4 **To Serve:** Taste dish and season with salt and pepper if necessary. Serve warm or hot.

Vary! Improvise!

☞ **Other vegetables may be prepared this way:** *leeks, carrots, cabbage, beets, cauliflower, eggplant, or zucchini.*
☞ *Omit potatoes and increase green beans to 2-1/2 pounds total.*

Braised Casserole (Greek Plaki)

Greek *plaki* are meze dishes classically made in a flat pan or casserole with fish or beans seasoned with onions, garlic, and tomato. The sauce can be the juices released from braising or an avgolemono sauce stirred in at the end.

GREEK BRAISED SWORDFISH (PSARI PLAKI)

6 servings

2-1/2 pounds swordfish steaks
   or skinned and boned salmon, sea bass, tilapia, cod, snapper, or halibut fillets
2 tablespoons freshly squeezed lemon juice, about 1/2 lemon, more to taste

1/4 cup olive oil
8 to 9 ounces onions, 2 cups peeled and finely slivered
About 2-1/2 ounces celery rib, 1/2 cup finely sliced
1/4 ounce garlic, 1 large clove, 1-1/2 teaspoons peeled and minced
1 pound tomatoes, about 2 medium, 1-1/2 to 2 cups diced
1/2 ounce trimmed Italian parsley, 4 tablespoons chopped
1/2 cup white wine

Garnish: Italian parsley sprigs

1 Cut fish into serving sized pieces and arrange in baking dish. Marinate fish fillets in lemon juice 15 minutes prior to baking.

2 Preheat oven to 350 degrees F. Season fish with salt.

3 Heat olive oil in 10- to 12-inch skillet over medium heat. Cook onion and celery until tender, 5 to 7 minutes. Stir in garlic and tomatoes and simmer until tomatoes soften, 5 to 7 minutes. Stir in parsley and wine.

4 Oil an 11- to 12- inch skillet and lay fish in it. Top fish with cooked vegetable mixture, chopped Italian parsley (or other herbs of choice). Simmer fish, covered, on top of the stove, 10 to 15 minutes, *or* uncovered in oven until fish flakes, 15 minutes. A whole fish will take twice as long. Taste plaki and season with more salt, freshly ground pepper, and lemon juice.

5 **To Serve:** Transfer fish and vegetables to serving platter and garnish with parsley sprigs.

Vary! Improvise!

☞ *Prepare a plaki with onions, garlic, tomatoes, and 3 pounds shrimp, shelled. Top with crumbled feta at the end.*

☞ **Egg-Lemon Fish:** *Omit the garlic from the vegetable sauté. Transfer cooked fish and vegetables from baking dish to serving dish and prepare avgolemono sauce with braising liquid (or extra fish stock). Pour sauce over fish and vegetables just before serving.*

☞ **Other Vegetables:** *Substitute or add leeks, carrot, potato, celery root, zucchini, summer squash, and eggplant for onions, celery, and tomato.*

GRAPE LEAVES THREE WAYS

Cooks who live near wild or organic cultivated grapes can harvest fresh grape leaves from May or June through August. Look for tender, large leaves nearest the tip of the vine. Experts suggest picking only the top three leaves, but they tend to be small. Pick early in the season for tender leaves. The older tough ones work, but need longer blanching. To use: remove stems, wash leaves, blanch leaves in boiling water 1 to 3 minutes, depending on toughness, and blot dry before using.

Refrigerate blanched, fresh grape leaves up to 7 days. Or layer them flat into freezer zipper baggies, and freeze up to 6 months. Thaw before using.

Jarred or plastic-vacuum-packed brined leaves are an alternative to fresh. Leaves in jars are often so tightly wrapped that it's difficult to remove them. Press a butter knife in around the edges and invert bottle to drain liquid and shake. Be persistent—eventually they will shake loose. Unroll

extra leaves and store flat in batches or in freezer baggies or containers. Blanched, fresh, or preserved leaves stay fresh refrigerated 1 week and frozen up to 6 months.

A 16-ounce jar preserved grape leaves yields 45 to 50 useable leaves. Large leaves (5 inches) take 3 to 4 tablespoons filling, medium leaves (4 inches) take 1 to 2 tablespoons filling, small leaves (3 inches) take 2 teaspoons to 1 tablespoon filling.

FIGURE 8.11 Stuffing grape leaves.

Source: David Murray and Jules Selmes/Dorling Kindersley.

FIGURE 8.12 Pan of stuffed grape leaves.

Source: Dorling Kindersley/Dorling Kindersley.

SIGNATURE RECIPE

GREEK STUFFED AND BRAISED GRAPE LEAVES (DOLMADES)

Fig leaves were probably the first leaves that Greeks stuffed, followed by grape leaves. Now Romaine lettuce, cabbage, chard, and collards provide Greek and Turkish cooks with leaves for stuffing. The techniques for all are similar and the stuffings often are interchangeable with those for fillo. Blanched until tender, grape leaves can be stuffed with goat cheese and eaten without further cooking. The Glorious Foods of Greece offers a recipe from Rhodes for grape leaves stuffed with bulgar, tomatoes, and cumin.

Yields 40 to 50 dolmades, 6 to 8 servings

Meat and Rice Dolmades

Yields about 4-1/2 cups filling

2 to 3 tablespoons olive oil
4 to 5 ounces onion, 1 cup peeled and finely diced
Optional: 1 tablespoon tomato paste
1 pound ground beef
8 ounces lean ground lamb
7 ounces short-grain rice like Arborio, 1 cup
1/2 ounce dill, 4 tablespoons trimmed and chopped
1/2 ounce trimmed Italian parsley, 1/3 to 1/2 cup chopped
Optional: 1 large egg

50 grape leaves, 1 pound jar
16 ounces chicken stock

Squash and Rice Dolmades

Yields 4 cups filling

1/2 cup olive oil
1-1/2 pounds red onions, 5 cups peeled and finely diced
1 pound butternut squash, peeled and seeded, 6 cups coarsely shredded and packed
5-1/4 ounces short- or medium-grain rice, 3/4 cup
2 ounces trimmed Italian parsley, 1 cup chopped
3 ounces mint leaves or trimmed dill, 1/2 cup chopped
    or 3 to 4 tablespoons dried mint 50 grape leaves, 1 pound
2 cups vegetable stock or water, as needed
Juice of 2 large lemons, about 1/2 cup

Sauce

Avgolemono Sauce or *Latholemono Sauce*

1 Prepare Filling.

Meat Rice Filling

Heat olive oil in small skillet and sauté onion over medium heat until soft. Stir in optional tomato paste and cook 1 minute. Cool. In a mixing bowl, mix together beef, lamb, rice, dill, 1 tablespoon kosher salt, and parsley. If using, knead in egg. Scrape cooled onion and tomato paste into meat and rice. Season filling with freshly ground pepper and more salt if necessary. Taste filling before using: Fry a small patty. Season highly with salt and pepper.

Squash Rice Filling

Heat olive oil in large skillet over medium heat and add onions. Cook until soft, 7 minutes. Add squash and cook until tender, 5 to 7 minutes. Stir in rice and remove skillet from heat. Season filling with 2 to 3 teaspoons kosher salt and freshly ground pepper, to taste. Cool filling to lukewarm. Stir in parsley and mint.

2 **Prepare leaves:** Rinse brined grape leaves or fresh grape leaves (or Savoy cabbage or other leaves). Rinse tender leaves or blanch firm or fresh leaves in boiling water until flexible. Tender fresh or brined leaves take 1 minute and tough fresh leaves 3 minutes. Cut away stems. Lay leaves shiny side down. Blot dry. The longer grape leaves are blanched upfront, the less time they need to simmer in the pot.

3 **Fill leaves:** Place **1 to 2 teaspoons filling for small leaves** or **1-1/2 to 2 tablespoons for large leaves** on the base, near the stem. Shape filling into cigar shape. Fold leaf sides over filling neatly, then roll from bottom up. Don't roll too tightly: uncooked rice swells. Arrange dolmades, seam side down, snugly in round casserole, pot, or deep skillet in two layers.

4 **Cook dolmades:** Pour hot water or stock and fresh lemon juice if using, in around the sides of the casserole. The liquid should barely cover dolmades. Cut a circle of parchment to fit casserole and place over dolmades and weight with an inverted plate that is slightly smaller than casserole. Bring liquid to a boil, lower the heat, and simmer **meat dolmades** 45 minutes and **squash dolmades** 20 minutes. Rest dolmades off heat 20 to 30 minutes.

5 **To Serve:** Remove the plate. The options are:

- Serve stuffed grapes leaves plain, warm or at room temperature.
- Drain off as much liquid as possible and use part to make *Avgolemono Sauce*. Pour hot sauce over dolmades in pan and shake to distribute. Serve.
- Cool dolmades to warm, and transfer with slotted spoon to platter. Prepare *Avgolemono* or *Ladolemono* sauce and pour over dolmades on platter.

Sources: *The Olive and the Caper: Adventures in Greek Cooking* by Susanna Hoffman and *The Glorious Foods of Greece* by Diane Kochilas.

WHO INVENTED STUFFED CABBAGE?

Many cultures claim to have invented stuffed cabbage: Persian, Russian, Ukrainian, and Polish. Cultivated cabbage arose from the wild mustard plant, prevalent in and native to Mediterranean. The ancient Greeks (and Romans) knew about cabbage as early as 600 BCE, so it's likely that ancient Greek cooks win the honor.

Signature Technique: Stuffed and Braised Cabbage

Loose-leafed cabbages like Savoy peel off more easily than tightly packed heads: it's possible to pull them off the heads before boiling. Larger heads yield more leaves, but smaller ones are easier to boil. Choose heavier cabbages; they have more moisture and are fresher.

A 4-pound head yields 15 to 20 useable large leaves and more small ones.
A 9-pound cabbage or two 4-1/2 pound heads yield about 40 large useable leaves and more small ones.

1   Pull away blemished leaves and discard. Cut out cabbage core with a long, thin-bladed knife, and discard.

2   Bring a large nonaluminum pot of water to boil and add salt. (Cabbage will discolor aluminum and aluminum will off-flavor cabbage.) Set up an ice bath if desired.

3   Insert a long-handled two-prong fork into the cabbage core and drop the cabbage into the boiling water. To keep the cabbage submerged, place a heavy metal lid (nonaluminum) on top. Later it will stay submerged on its own.

4   Boil cabbage 5 to 7 minutes and, working with tongs, loosen leaves from core. Keep in boiling water until tender, 1 to 3 minutes. Drop leaves into a colander set over a bowl to cool and drain, or immerse briefly in ice water and drain. Drape drained leaves in a pile on a parchment- or paper towel-covered sheet pan before the next batch comes.

5   Continue boiling the cabbage and pulling off the next layer of leaves as they soften and the rib turns flexible. Stop when there is only a small baseball-size core left.

6   *Shave* off the rib on the back of the leaves. Leaves that are larger than a dinner plate may be cut in half with ribs removed.

7   Set a cabbage leaf, stem end nearest the edge of the counter with the inner leaf cupping up. Lay the filling at the bottom and middle of the leaf. Use 2 tablespoons filling for smaller cabbage leaf (the size of a woman's hand) and 1/4 cup for larger ones. Bring the sides in neatly, and roll up cabbage leaf from the bottom. Lay cabbage rolls seam side down, snugly against each other in layers into prepared casserole. Cover rolls with excess leaves before baking. Weight rolls with inverted plate.

8   Pour boiling water, stock, or tomato purée mixed with water in around the edges of the rolls. Cover pan. Simmer on top of the stove 1 hour, or place into 350 degree F oven to bake until tender, 1 hour.

GREEK STUFFED CABBAGE ROLLS (LAHANODOLMADES)

Serve lahanodolmades *with avgolemono sauce with yogurt. Fillings range from rice with pork, beef, or lamb seasoned with pine nuts, currants, mint, allspice, chili flakes, or grated cheese. Turkish cooks make stuffed cabbage called* sarma.

Yields 19 to 20 rolls with 1/4 cup filling

Filling

Yields almost 5 cups

1/4 cup olive oil
1 pound onions, *divided*: 8 ounces finely diced, 8 ounces finely sliced, 2 cups each
1 pound ground beef
8 ounces ground lamb

7 ounces medium-grain rice, 1 cup, rinsed and drained
1 ounce dill, 1/3 cup stemmed and chopped
1 tablespoon kosher *or* sea salt

3-1/2 to 4-pound Savoy or green cabbage
5 cups chicken stock
Avgolemono Sauce

For Serving

Greek Greens (Horta) or Country-Style Greek Salad

1 Heat olive oil in 11- to 12-inch skillet over medium heat. Add **diced onion** and cook until soft. Cool. Mix meat, rice, dill, salt, and pepper with cooled, diced onion. Knead to mix thoroughly.

2 Prepare cabbage and roll dolmades as directed in *Signature Technique: Stuffed Cabbage.*

3 Line the bottom of a lidded casserole with the **sliced onion**. Fit stuffed cabbage rolls on layers snugly on top. Cover dolmades with plate that leaves a margin of 1 inch. Pour water or chicken stock to almost cover, and bring to a boil. Lower heat, cover, and simmer 45 minutes. Remove casserole from heat. Cool to warm.

4 Drain cooking liquid from dolmades. Prepare *Avgolemono Sauce* with cooking liquid.

5 **To Serve:** Remove plate, and pour egg-lemon sauce over cabbage rolls. Shake gently to distribute *or* serve rolls warm on platter with sauce ladled over. Serve with *Greek Greens* or *Country-Style Greek Salad.*

BRAISED LAMB WITH ARTICHOKES (AGINARES ME KREAS)

Quick to prepare, this dish was thickened and finished with avgolemono sauce *made with the stew's cooking liquid. Many Greeks are turning to this recipe's lighter version.*

Yields about 6 cups, 4 servings

1/4 cup olive oil
1-1/2 pounds boneless, trimmed lamb shoulder or leg, diced into 1-inches cubes
8 ounces onion, 2 cups finely diced
1/4 ounce garlic, 1 large clove, 1-1/2 teaspoons peeled and minced
2 cups chicken stock, more as necessary
Two 9-ounce boxes frozen artichoke hearts, about 4 cups thawed
  or 8 medium artichokes, peeled and trimmed down to hearts and rubbed
    with lemon
1/4 cup fresh juice, about 1 lemon, more as needed
2-1/2 to 3 ounces trimmed dill, 2 cups finely chopped, *divided*
To Serve: Bread or hot, cooked rice

1 Heat oil in 5- to 6-quart casserole over medium-high heat. Season meat with salt, brown it in batches, and transfer to bowl. Stir onions into casserole, lower the heat to medium, and cook until soft, 5 to 7 minutes. (If pan gets too browned, deglaze with a little water and allow liquid to evaporate.) Stir in meat, juices, garlic, and chicken stock.

2 Lower heat, cover casserole, and simmer stew until meat is tender, 45 minutes to 1 hour.

3 Stir artichoke hearts into stew with half the dill, 1/4 cup lemon juice, salt, and a little water if liquid doesn't partially cover meat. Partially cover casserole, and simmer until artichokes are tender, 10 to 15 minutes for frozen and 25 to 30 minutes for fresh.

4 **To Serve:** Stir in remaining dill. Taste stew and season with salt, pepper, more lemon juice. Serve with bread or rice.

Vary! Improvise!

☞ *Prepare this and finish it by making* Avgolemono Sauce *with some of the stew's cooking liquid.*

Pitting Olives

Smash an olive lightly with the side of a chef's knife or mallet to loosen its pit. Don't lose any pits, or a customer or guest may lose a tooth.

Pilaf

Pilafs made with rice, bulgar, *freekeh*, wheat berries, or barley show the Ottoman and Persian influences in Greek and Turkish cooking. *Pilavlar* is one of Turkish cuisine's most important dishes and often served as a course by itself, much like Indian *biryanis*. It can be filled with various vegetables, meatballs, dried fruits, beans, or nuts and seasoned elaborately with spices. Grains for pilaf should be sautéed in oil until the outer starch layer hardens before adding liquid. This will keep the grains separate, an important characteristic of a good Turkish or Greek pilaf.

GREEK SPINACH RICE PILAF (SPANAKÓRIZO)

This pilaf is a national Greek favorite. Traditionally long-grain rice is favored for fluffy pilafs, but many Greeks prefer medium-grain rice for a chewier texture.

Yields about 4 to 5 cups, 4 to 6 servings

2 pounds baby spinach leaves, washed and drained
   or 2 cups cooked and chopped, drained spinach
4 tablespoons olive oil
12 to 13 ounces onions, 3 cups peeled and finely diced
7 ounces long- or medium-grain rice, 1 cup
1 lemon, zested and juiced
1 ounce trimmed Italian parsley, 1/2 cup finely chopped
1 ounce trimmed dill, 1/2 cup finely chopped

1 Dice spinach into 1-inch squares. Pour spinach and 1/4 cup water in a 4- to 5-quart saucepan and heat over medium-high heat. Cover and steam spinach, turning occasionally with tongs, until it wilts, 2 to 4 minutes. Drain-press spinach well to yield about 2 cups drained, chopped spinach. Set aside.

2 Bring 2 cups water to a boil in a saucepan and set aside.

3 Heat oil over medium-low heat in 5-quart saucepan and add onions. Sauté until soft, 8 to 10 minutes. Stir rice, 1/2 teaspoon kosher salt, and zest of 1 lemon into onions and cook 1 minute. Add 2 cups boiling water to rice and bring to a boil, cover pot, and lower heat. Simmer rice 15 minutes. Remove pan from heat and rest 10 to 15 minutes. Carefully fold parsley, dill, and spinach into rice with a fork.

4 **To Serve:** Taste rice and season with salt and pepper. Season pilaf with freshly squeezed lemon juice just before serving.

GREEK TRAHANA: THE FIRST PASTA?

Trahana, a sort of handmade sourdough noodle, is one of the oldest foods in the Greek and Turkish repertoire. (Turks call it *tarhana*.) Consisting variously of semolina flour, bulgar, or emmer (*farro*) mixed with soured milk, yogurt, or, in Thrace and Turkey, tomatoes, sesame, herbs, peppers, or onions, the mixture was kneaded into dough and formed into small noodles or pebbles, then sun-dried. An ancient shepherd's food, it was a way of preserving leftovers and of having winter food on hand to put into soup broth, stew, pies, stuffing, or porridge. Some food historians think trahana may have preceded pasta: ancient Greeks were trahana porridge eaters long before they ate bread. Since Greek chefs were Rome's most popular, it's probable that Greek chefs introduced Romans to the first pasta.

SAUTÉ, PAN-FRY, AND DEEP-FRY

Greek Keftéthes

Meat, vegetables, eggs, flour, breadcrumbs, potatoes, and split peas can, alone or together, form the base of *keftéthes*. These savory Greek (or Turkish) fried patties, balls, or fritters are similar to Middle Eastern *kofte*, *kibbeh*, or *falafel*.

GREEK ZUCCHINI FRITTERS (KOLOKYTHÁKIA KEFTÉTHES)

This keftéthe can be found in most Greek tavernas. It is the poor man's meatball. Make it with other kinds of grated cooked or raw vegetables.

Yields about 2 cups batter, enough for sixteen 2-tablespoon balls (about 1-inch diameter) or eight 1/4-cup patties (1-1/2 to 2 inches)

16 ounces zucchini, 3 medium, about 3 cups trimmed and grated or shredded
5 to 6 ounces onion, 3/4 cup peeled and minced
2 ounces hard *myzithra*, *kefalotyri*, Pecorino Romano, or Parmesan cheese, 1/2 to 3/4 cup grated
2 ounces *paximáthia*, 3/4 to 1 cup finely ground, as needed
    or dry, toasted whole grain bread, 3/4 to 1 cup finely ground, as needed
1/2 ounce trimmed Italian parsley, 1/4 cup finely chopped
1/4 ounce mint leaves, 2 tablespoons chopped
    or 1 teaspoon dried oregano
2 large eggs, *divided*
Olive oil and canola oil for frying

For Serving

Tzatziki Sauce

1 Toss zucchini and onion with 2 teaspoons kosher salt and transfer to strainer. Drain vegetables 30 minutes. Squeeze excess moisture from vegetables to yield about 1-1/4 cups.

2 In a mixing bowl, mix zucchini and onion with cheese, 1/2 cup breadcrumbs, herbs, 1 beaten egg, and 1 teaspoon kosher salt. Season with freshly ground black pepper. Mixture should be firm enough to form balls and moist enough to hold together without being overly sticky or dry. Allow batter to rest 5 minutes: breadcrumbs take time to absorb moisture. Adjust batter with more breadcrumbs, part of the second beaten egg or water, if necessary, to achieve desired consistency.

3 With oiled hands, form 2-tablespoon or 1/4-cup sized balls or patties. Set aside on parchment-covered sheet pan. Refrigerate until ready to cook to firm the balls or patties, at least 15 minutes.

4 In a heavy 10- to 12-inch skillet, heat half olive and half canola oil about 1-inch deep over medium-high heat. When oil is hot (360 degrees F) but not smoking, drop balls into oil and fry until very brown, 3 to 5 minutes per side. Work in batches. Drain keftéthes on paper towels and keep warm.

5 **To Serve:** Transfer warm keftéthes to serving platter. Serve with tzatziki sauce on the side.

FIGURE 8.13 Yogurt cucumber sauce. (kolokythákia keftéthes) with zogurt cucumber sauce (tzatziki).

Vary! Improvise!

☛ *Add crushed chickpeas to keftéthe mixture.*

☛ *Roll keftéthe balls in fine, dry breadcrumbs before frying.*

GRILL, GRIDDLE, ROAST, BROIL, BAKE, AND BARBECUE

FIGURE 8.14 Meat kabobs.

Source: Anton Petrus/Shutterstock.

GREEK MEAT KEBABS

Greek kebabs include grilled, roasted, and stewed skewers of large or small cuts, cubes or ground meat of lamb, beef, goat, chicken, pork, or seafood, and falafel. Prepare kebabs with chunks of boneless, gristle- and fat-free lamb from sirloin, leg, or shoulder, pork loin, or boneless, skinless chicken breast. Oregano and garlic give Greek kebabs their signature flavor.

1 pound trimmed meat yields 2 to 4 servings

1 pound trimmed lamb, pork, or chicken

Marinade

1 tablespoon olive oil
Zest and juice of 1/2 lemon, 1-1/2 to 2 tablespoons
1 teaspoon dried oregano
   or 1 tablespoon chopped fresh
Optional: 1 teaspoon dried mint
   or 1 tablespoon chopped fresh
1/2 ounce garlic, 2 large cloves, 1 tablespoon peeled and finely minced
Optional: Fresh bay leaves

For Serving

Rice *or* pita bread
Grape Leaf and Mint Sauce
1 lemon, quartered

1 **Prepare meat:** Remove excess fat and gristle from meat. Dice meat into 1- to 1-1/2 inch cubes.

2 **Whisk together marinade.** Toss with meat and refrigerate chicken or pork to marinate 1 hour. Marinate beef or lamb 2 hours in refrigerator up to 8 hours. Heat grill or broiler to medium-high.

3 **If using bay leaves:** Bring a small saucepan of water to a boil. Remove pot from heat and rest leaves in hot water 5 minutes. Drain.

4 Shake off excess marinade from meat or seafood. Thread an equal number of cubes of meat, with bay leaf in between each if using, per metal skewer. Season meat with salt and pepper.

5 Place skewers on grill or 3 to 4 inches from broiler. Grill meat, turning every 2 minutes, until meat is done and lightly charred, about 10 minutes. Meat should reach medium rare to medium (130 to 135 degrees F for lamb or beef, 155 degrees F for pork, and 165 degrees F for chicken).

6 **To Serve:** Transfer kebabs to serving platter or plate. Serve meat atop rice *or* folded into pita bread. Place grape leaf and mint sauce and lemon wedges on the side.

GRILLED GRAPE OR FIG LEAF WRAPPED FISH

Fresh grape or fig leaves perfume and protect the delicate flesh of fish. Both Greeks and Turks employ this method. Sometimes small fish are skewered backs to bellies and grilled. The yield of small fish differs depending on bone structure; bony snappers have a low yield of meat.

4 servings

Four 12- to 16-ounce whole mackerel, branzini, snapper, striped bass, herring, sardines, or river trout, gutted and scaled; head on or off, as desired
   or four 6-ounce fish steaks like salmon, swordfish, or snapper

FIGURE 8.15 Fig leaf wrapped fish.

1 large lemon, about 4 tablespoons juice
16 to 20 preserved *or* fresh grape leaves
    or 8 to 12 large fig leaves
2 to 4 tablespoons olive oil

For Serving

Lemon and Olive Oil Sauce

1   Season fish inside and out with lemon juice and kosher salt.

2   If using preserved leaves, rinse and pat dry. If using fresh grape or fig leaves, bring a small pot of water to boil and blanch leaves until flexible, 30 seconds to 1 minute. Rinse with cold water, drain leaves, and spread out. Blot dry.

3   Brush each fish or fillet with olive oil. Wrap each with grape or fig leaves to fully cover fish, leaving head and tail exposed on whole fish. Brush leaves with oil. Place fish on platter, cover with plastic wrap, and refrigerate fillets or steaks 15 to 20 minutes and whole fish 30 minutes to 2 hours.

4   **To cook:** Build a medium fire in a charcoal grill or heat a gas grill to medium. Clean and oil grill grates. Remove fish from refrigerator 15 minutes before cooking. Transfer fish to grill and cook first side until leaves are charred and crisp, and fish is flaky. Turn fish once with a metal spatula, and cook second side until it is cooked through and flaky, and leaves are charred and crispy, 8 to 15 minutes total depending on thickness of fish.

5   **To Serve:** Transfer fish to a platter and unwrap blackened leaves and skin. Serve meat from fish drizzled with *Lemon and Olive Oil Sauce*.

GREEK GRILLED OCTOPUS (HTAPOTHI STI SKHARA)

Octopuses have keen eyesight and are highly intelligent, probably more than any other inverte-brates, but their lifespan is only 6 months to 5 years. Greeks love octopus as an appetizer or meze. For a chewier but more flavorful grilled octopus, simply brush tentacles with olive oil and grill until skin is dark and leathery. Serve with sea salt and lemon juice or dip in ouzo. When an octopus is killed, fishermen beat it against rocks or concrete—50 or more times—to break it down, but freez-ing also tenderizes octopus.

4 to 6 servings

4 to 5 pounds octopus, fresh, or frozen and defrosted overnight in refrigerator
2 cups white wine
1/3 to 1/2 cup olive oil
1/2 cup fresh lemon juice, 2 to 3 lemons
2 tablespoons dried oregano

1   **If the octopus comes with its head:** Snip the head sack with scissors just enough to get to the innards. Pull innards out under running water. The beak can be removed after boiling. It can be found under the head and at the center where the tentacles meet. Frozen octopus usually will come cleaned.

2   **Cook octopus:** Rinse octopus well and place in an 8-quart pot with wine. Slowly bring it to a boil, lower heat, and simmer 45 minutes to 1 hour, depending on thickness of legs. Octopus puts out lots of moisture and loses volume during cooking.

3   **Marinate:** Whisk together olive oil, lemon juice, and oregano in small bowl. Drain octopus legs. Pour marinade over and toss to coat evenly. Cool octopus. Refrigerate, tightly covered, overnight, tossing in marinade at least once.

4   **Preheat a grill:** Drain octopus from marinade, season with salt, and arrange on grill. Reserve mari-nade. Grill octopus until browned/blackened and crunchy, 4 to 5 minutes per side.

5   **To Serve:** Taste marinade and adjust flavors with salt, pepper, lemon, or olive oil. Slice octo-pus into bite-sized pieces and arrange on serving platter. Drizzle with marinade, salt and freshly ground pepper, and serve.

FIGURE 8.16   Grilled octopus.
Source: rj lerich/Shutterstock.

FIGURE 8.17   Small octopus.
Source: Madlen/Shutterstock.

Vary! Improvise!

☞ *Instead of using the marinade, pre-pare a vinaigrette with olive oil, red wine vinegar, salt, and pepper, and pour over the cooked octopus.*

Savory Greek Pita or Fillo Pies

Nomadic shepherds in the mountainous northern and mainland regions of Greece first developed a choice array of pites—flat and round, square, triangular or coiled, large or hand-size—designed for easy transport. Now cooks everywhere in Greece make them. Prepare pites on or in a sheet or cake pan or in a skillet, with commercial or handmade dough in large or individual-size pies.

Tiropita: cheese, usually feta or other local cheese, and egg

Hortopita: cooked and seasoned wild greens and herbs, sometimes with cheese, egg, or breadcrumbs, rice or bulgar

Prasopita: leek and cheese

Kreratopita: meat filled, usually pork, lamb, or occasionally, beef.

Kotopita: chicken

Kremmythopita: onion with bacon or nuts

Spanakopita: spinach, herb, and feta and/or egg

Makaronopita: macaroni and cheese

Kolokithopita: zucchini, feta, eggs, and herb

Signature Technique: Filling and Rolling Greek Fillo Pies (Pita or Pitta)

1 Prepare dough according to *Signature Technique: Handmade Fillo Dough* and allow it to rest while preparing the filling.

    For two 9-inch pies, prepare 2 pounds dough.

    For one 14-inch round or 9-inch by 12-inch pie, prepare 1-1/2 pounds dough.

2 Preheat oven to 400 degrees F. Divide dough into 3 slightly larger balls and 3 smaller balls. Cover them so they don't dry and crust over. (One 3-1/2- to 4-ounce ball of dough will roll out to about 15 inches.)

3 With a 20-inch long, 7/8-inch wooden dowel, roll out 1 larger dough ball to a 6- to 8-inch diameter on a well-floured surface. Cover with plastic wrap and rest dough 5 minutes to relax gluten.

4 **Flour dough well.** Wrap nearest edge of dough around pin. Roll with slight pressure until 1/2 inch of far edge is left. Turn pin 90 degrees and unroll, applying slight pressure, onto floured surface. Repeat process of rolling dough onto pin with pressure 1/2 inch up to edge, turning 90 degrees and unrolling with pressure, until dough is 2 inches larger in diameter than the pan you are using. This will take around 10 to 15 turns. Dough will be 1/16-inch thick and wrinkled.

5 Oil or butter pan. Roll finished dough around dowel. Brush off excess flour and transfer to pan.

6 Unroll dough in or onto pan. Brush dough with olive oil. This is the first layer. Repeat rolling and turning process with two larger dough balls. Lay each sheet of dough into pan over first layer of dough and brush with oil.

7 Toss fine cracked wheat or toasted breadcrumbs over bottom to soak up juices. Spread filling evenly over dough up to 1 inch from edge.

8 Roll out remaining 3 smaller dough balls. Cut them to fit into inside diameter of pan to cover filling. Brush each layer with olive oil.

9 Fold up hanging edges of dough or twist edges up decoratively. Brush edges and top of crust with remaining olive oil. Slash a vent into top of pie.

10 Place pie in oven and bake 30 minutes. Reduce heat to 375 degrees F and bake pie until golden, 20 minutes to 30 minutes more. Cool pie slightly before cutting.

FIGURE 8.18 Handmade fillo dough rolled with wooden dowel.

Source: gulaysakalli/Shutterstock.

GREEK PITA: MIXED GREENS (HORTÓPITA) OR SPINACH (SPANOKOPITA)

Greeks, especially Cretans, are obsessed with wild greens, called horta. *Crete has more than 300 varieties edible wild green "weeds." Tough greens wilt by half; delicate greens wilt even more.*

Yields 8 to 10 cups

Handmade Fillo Dough or 1 pound commercial fillo
1-3/4 to 2 pounds tough greens like kale, about 20 packed cups stemmed and chopped
    or 4 pounds tender greens like baby spinach, Swiss chard, or arugula
1/2 cup olive oil
About 20 ounces green onions, about 40 large or 7 bunches, 5 cups trimmed and
finely sliced
    or 2 to 2-1/2 pounds leeks, 4 to 5, 5 cups trimmed to white and tender green,
        finely sliced
2 lemons, zested
3 to 4 ounces trimmed Italian parsley, about 2 cups finely chopped
2 ounces trimmed dill, 1 cup finely chopped
Optional: 8 ounces feta, about 2 cups crumbled
Olive oil for brushing between phyllo layers
For constructing pie: 3 to 4 tablespoons fine cracked wheat or toasted breadcrumbs

1 Prepare *Handmade Fillo Dough* or thaw commercial fillo overnight.

2 Chop greens coarsely. Place greens in 2 batches, into large pot with 2 cups water, cover, and, over high heat, toss and cook until wilted and tender, 4 to 5 minutes for tough greens and 2 to 3 minutes for tender greens. Pour greens into colander set over bowl to drain. Press firmly to remove excess liquid. Save liquid for soup or vitamin-rich drink.

3 Heat large skillet and add olive oil and green onions or leeks. Cook over medium heat until just soft, 5 to 7 minutes. Stir in lemon zest and scrape onion or leek mixture into large mixing bowl.

4 Fluff greens and stir them, along with parsley, dill, optional feta, into onions or leeks. Juice one zested lemon and stir 2 tablespoons lemon juice into onions or leeks. Season filling with salt and pepper. Cool to room temperature, taste, and re-season before using.

5 **To Use:** Stuff or roll fresh made or commercial dough according *to Signature Technique: Filling and Rolling Greek Fillo Pies* or *Tips for Handling and Stuffing Commercial Fillo Pastry.*

FIGURE 8.19 Traditional Greek spinach pita.
Source: kanvag/Shutterstock.

GREEK PITA: ONION, TOMATO, AND NUT (KREMMYDOPITA ME TOMATES)

Yields about 10 cups

Handmade Fillo Dough or 1 pound commercial fillo dough
1/3 cup olive oil
2-1/2 pounds red onions, about 5 large, 10 cups finely slivered or sliced
About 2 pounds tomatoes, 4 medium
    or 4 cups tomato purée or finely diced tomatoes
About 9 ounces toasted walnuts, 1-1/2 cups lightly chopped

For Constructing Pie

Olive oil for brushing layers
4 tablespoons fine cracked wheat *or toasted breadcrumbs*

1 Prepare *Handmade Fillo Dough* or thaw commercial fillo overnight.

2 Heat olive oil in deep 12- to 14-inch skillet. Cook onions over medium heat until soft, 8 to 10 minutes. Season onions with salt.

3 Meanwhile, slice tomatoes around their equators. On a box grater, grate tomatoes on cut side until the skin is all that's left to yield 3-1/2 to 4 cups tomato pulp. Pour tomato pulp into onions. *Alternatively*, stir in tomato purée or diced tomatoes. Simmer over medium-low heat until moist but no longer wet, 10 to 15 minutes Taste mixture and season with salt and pepper. Cool mixture to lukewarm. Stir in nuts.

4 Use filling to stuff or roll fresh made or commercial dough according to *Signature Technique: Filling and Rolling Greek Fillo Pies* or *Tips for Handling and Stuffing Commercial Fillo Pastry*.

Source: *The Glorious Foods of Greece* by Diane Kochilas.

Layered Casseroles

Moussaka and *pastitsio* are two examples of Greek comfort food: rich, layered casseroles that vary according to region, season, and cook, from meat to meatless and with cheese or not, eggplant, peppers, potato, artichokes, squash or zucchini, and béchamel. The Greek *pastitsio* derives from the Italian *pasticcio*, which translates to "hodgepodge." Its four essential components are *pasta, meat filling, béchamel sauce*, and *cheese*. They are layered in an oiled pan and baked until golden, much like moussaka. Bucatini can stand in for Greek Number Two pasta. It is boiled al dente, and tossed with olive oil and cheese. Ground beef, veal, or lamb make up the meat sauce much like the one for moussaka, and the béchamel is mixed with grated Greek *kefalotyri* cheese and egg yolks.

SIGNATURE RECIPE

GREEK MOUSSAKÁ

Although most of the world knows moussaka as Greece's national dish it arrived in Greece in the early twentieth century with the mass exodus of Greeks from Asia Minor and Turkey. Turkish and Greek cooks prepare this beloved newcomer for special celebrations. Potatoes are optional, but decrease the eggplant if they are used.

Yields 3-inch deep half hotel pan *or* 9-inch by 12-inch oblong baking dish, 9 to 12 servings

4 pounds eggplant, about 4 medium, rinsed and stem-tops trimmed away
1/4 cup plus 2 tablespoons olive oil, *divided*, more if eggplant is fried

---

Vary! Improvise!

☞ *Substitute toasted pine nuts or pecans for walnuts.*

2 pounds lean ground lamb *or* veal
16 ounces onion, 4 cups peeled and medium diced
1/2 ounce garlic cloves, 2 large, 1 tablespoon peeled and minced, more to taste
1/2 cup white or light red wine
2 tablespoons tomato paste
28-ounce canned whole plum tomatoes, about 2 cups drained and diced
1 teaspoon dried oregano
1/4 teaspoon ground allspice
1/4 teaspoon cinnamon

Greek Béchamel

3 ounces unsalted butter, about 6 tablespoons
About 2-1/3 ounces flour, 8 tablespoons
4 cups whole milk
3 large egg yolks
1/4 teaspoon ground nutmeg

4 ounces grated Romano or firm Greek cheese, about 1 cup

1 Cut eggplants lengthwise into 1/3-inch-thick slices. Sprinkle salt on eggplant and set aside for 30 to 45 minutes. Rinse and blot dry. There are **three ways** to prepare the eggplant or chosen vegetables: **fry**, **bake**, or **broil**. Frying is traditional, but baking or broiling concentrates vegetable flavor and uses less fat.

Fry Vegetables/Eggplant
Spread two sheet pans with paper towels and set by stove. In a large skillet over medium heat, add 1/4 cup olive oil. When oil shimmers, add eggplant or vegetable in one layer. Fry in batches, adding more oil as necessary. Fry eggplant or vegetable until tender and translucent. Place on sheet pans to drain.

Bake or Broil Vegetables/Eggplant
Preheat oven to 450 degrees F, or preheat broiler with door ajar. Brush eggplant/vegetable slices with 1/4 cup olive oil and lay them on parchment-covered sheet pan/s. Bake or broil vegetables on both sides, in batches if necessary, until tender, 8 to 10 minutes per side.

2 **Prepare meat sauce:** Place meat in a skillet and sauté over medium-high heat. Break up and brown meat, 7 to 10 minutes. Pour off excess fat and discard. Pour meat into a mixing bowl, set aside, and wipe out skillet. Over medium heat, reheat skillet with 2 tablespoons oil and add onion. Sauté onion until soft, 5 to 7 minutes. Stir meat into onions. Add garlic and cook 1 minute. Stir in wine, tomato paste, tomatoes, oregano, allspice, and cinnamon. Bring sauce to a boil, reduce heat, and simmer sauce uncovered until thick and not noticeably wet, 30 to 45 minutes. Too much liquid in the sauce will result in a soupy-wet moussaka. Taste sauce and season with salt and pepper. There should be about 6 cups sauce.

3 Preheat oven to 350 degrees F.

4 **Assemble the casserole:** Grease a half hotel pan with olive oil. Cover bottom with 1/3 the eggplant (vegetable) slices, overlapping as necessary. Spoon 1/3 the meat sauce over them and spread to cover evenly with a spatula. Cover meat sauce overlapping with 1/3 the vegetable slices. Spread remaining meat sauce evenly over eggplant (vegetable) slices. Layer remaining eggplant (vegetable) over meat sauce. Press lightly with spatula to compact the layers.

5 **Prepare Greek béchamel:** Melt butter in a medium-sized saucepan over a medium-low heat. Whisk in flour and simmer roux 2 to 3 minutes. Slowly pour in milk, whisking continuously to remove lumps. Bring sauce to a boil and lower heat. Simmer until sauce is thick, 2 to 5 minutes. Remove saucepan from heat and season béchamel with nutmeg, salt, and freshly ground pepper. Beat eggs and whisk a spoonful of hot béchamel into them. Scrape eggs into hot sauce and whisk well. Pour béchamel over meat layer to completely cover and spread evenly with spatula. Sprinkle top with cheese.

6 **Bake moussaka:** Place moussaka into oven and bake until top is lightly browned, 1 hour. Remove pan from oven and cool moussaka 1 hour before cutting. Or chill and reheat the next day for fuller flavor.

Vary! Improvise!

☛ *Devise a vegetarian moussaka.*

☛ *Substitute part or all of the eggplant for long slices of 1/4-inch-thick cut zucchini or yellow potatoes, roasted bell peppers, or artichoke hearts.*

☛ *Sprinkle 2 tablespoons of the 4 ounces grated cheese on top of each layer of meat sauce.*

☛ *Prepare individual moussakas.*

☛ *Sprinkle breadcrumbs in the bottom of the oiled pan to soak up juices and firm up moussaka.*

PAXIMATHIA

In Greece, leftover slices of country bread (often seasoned with anise and coriander seed) never go to waste. They were turned into paximathia: long, slow, dry-toasted bread slices, which evolved to preserve bread, and to make it easier for farmers and shepherds to carry it with them for lunch. Paximathia store indefinitely. A quick soak in wine or water and olive oil softens paximathia and, with some cheese and olives, they make a satisfying meal, or a simple snack dipped into coffee and tea. Bakeries, instead of home cooks, now produce paximathia. They have many uses in the Greek kitchen, from bread salad and crunchy crumb toppings to thickening soup and for pitta fillings. The best paximathia are made from coarse, dense-textured bread made with barley or chickpea flour. To make them, slice bread into 1/2- to 1-inch-thick slices and bake in a preheated 250 degree F oven until bread is dried but still slightly flexible.

Greek Briami

Briami is an earthy, classic Greek dish of baked vegetables seasoned with oregano and garlic. The name comes from the Persian *biryan*, a rice and vegetable pilaf. (Indian cooks transformed it into *biryani*, a layered, baked casserole of spiced meat or vegetables and rice.) Turks have a similar dish called *turlu*. It's sweet-savory with cinnamon, coriander, fenugreek, mint, and dill. Like most stewed dishes, briami and turlu taste best the day after they're made. To many Turks, turlu is a lamb or chicken and vegetable casserole. Yet in other regions turlu is all-vegetable. Egyptian cooks make a similar meatless dish called *turli*.

SIGNATURE RECIPE

GREEK SUMMER BRIAMI

Fragrant fennel grows wild around Greece. Substitute milder cultivated fennel plus fennel seed. This dish is Greece's answer to ratatouille.

Yields about 10 cups, 8 to 10 servings

About 24 ounces eggplant, 2 medium, 4 cups diced 1-inch cubes
About 1 pound zucchini, 4 medium, 4 cups diced 1-inch cubes
About 18 ounces green bell peppers, 3 medium, 4 cups cored, seeded, and diced 1-inch cubes
1 pound tomatoes, 2 medium, 2 to 3 cups diced 1-inch cubes
16 ounces onions, 2 large, 4 cups diced 1-inch cubes
About 20 ounces trimmed fennel bulbs, 2 medium halved lengthwise, 8 cups 1-inch cubes
3/4 ounce garlic, 3 large cloves, 4-1/2 teaspoons peeled and finely sliced crosswise
1 cup olive oil
1 tablespoon fennel seed, crushed
1/2 teaspoon red chili flakes
1 teaspoon dried oregano
   or 1 tablespoon fresh oregano

Garnish: 1/2 ounce trimmed dill or Italian parsley, 1/2 cup chopped

1 Toss eggplant and 1 tablespoon kosher salt in mixing bowl. Set aside 30 minutes. Rinse eggplant and pat dry. Preheat oven to 400 degrees F.

2 Toss eggplant, zucchini, bell peppers, tomatoes, onions, fennel, garlic, oil, spices, oregano, and 1 tablespoon kosher salt together in large baking dish or stainless hotel pan. Place in oven to bake. After 20 minutes, toss vegetables. Continue to bake briami until vegetables are tender, 40 to 50 minutes total. Season to taste with salt and freshly ground pepper.

3 **To Serve:** Pile vegetables onto platter or serve in baking dish. Garnish with dill or parsley.

Vary! Improvise!

☞ *Slice vegetables. Slice eggplant 1/4-inch thick and salt-wilt as in step 1. Blot dry and brown in oil. Toss remaining vegetables separately with seasonings and oil. Layer vegetables into casserole and bake.*

☞ *Add or substitute green beans, artichokes, or okra.*

SALAD AND VEGETABLE METHODS

COUNTRY STYLE GREEK SALAD (HORIATIKI SALATA)

This classic salad depends on the vegetables in season, but it always features tomatoes and cucumbers and olives. Serve it with rustic main dishes like grilled lamb.

Yields about 8 cups, 4 servings

1 small head leafy lettuce, 4 to 5 ounces, 4 to 5 cups sliced leaves
Optional: 1/4 ounce trimmed parsley, 2 tablespoons chopped
2 ounces sweet or red onion, 1/4 cup thinly sliced
6 ounces tomato, 1 small, cut into 8 wedges
7 ounces cucumber, 1 small, 1 cup peeled, halved lengthwise and sliced crosswise 1/4-inch thick
2-1/2 to 3 ounces green bell pepper, 1/2 small, 1/2 to 2/3 cup cored, seeded, and thinly sliced
2 ounces feta, 1/2 cup crumbled
16 small Kalamata olives, 1/2 cup pitted

Dressing

1/3 cup extra-virgin olive oil
2 tablespoons red wine vinegar
1/4 teaspoon dried Greek oregano, crumbled

For Serving

Greek country bread

1 Combine lettuce and optional parsley. Arrange lettuce and parsley as a bed on a plate, in a bowl, or on a platter. Arrange tomatoes and cucumbers around edges and top with pepper, onion, feta, and olives. Chill until ready to serve. Whisk together oil, vinegar, and oregano. Season with salt and pepper. Rest **dressing** 10 minutes.

2 **To Serve:** Pour **dressing** over salad, and serve salad with bread.

Source: Cretan cook Stathis Stamatakis.

FIGURE 8.20 Greek salad.
Source: Barbara Dudzinska/Fotolia.

Mediterranean Bean Salads

Cooks all around southern Europe and the Mediterranean prepare legume salads. Their flavor improves with time. Season them highly: starchy legumes are notorious for absorbing flavor. Canned legumes have a tired, tinny flavor, so prepare them with soaked and cooked legumes.

GREEK COUNTRY BEAN SALAD

Yields about 2 cups, 2 to 4 servings

6 ounces dried chickpeas, 1 cup
    or 2 to 2-1/2 cups drained, cooked chickpeas
3 ounces trimmed green onions, about 6, 1/2 to 2/3 cup finely slivered
    or 4 ounces red onion, 1/2 cup peeled and finely diced
2 small anchovies, finely chopped
    or 2 tablespoons lightly chopped capers
3 ounces green olives, 8 large, about 1/2 cup smashed, pitted, and quartered lengthwise
1/2 ounce trimmed Italian parsley, 1/4 cup packed lightly chopped
1 to 3 tablespoons red wine vinegar
4 to 6 tablespoons olive oil

Garnish: Chopped Italian parsley

1 *Prepare chickpeas:* Soak dried chickpeas overnight or quick-soak with 2 teaspoons kosher salt. See *Glossary* under Beans. Drain chickpeas, and cover with fresh, cold water. Bring chickpeas to a boil, lower heat, cover, and simmer until tender, 40 minutes to 1 hour. Cool chickpeas until just warm, and drain off liquid (it may be used as a base for vegetarian soups).

2 Prepare and toss together green onions, anchovies, green olives, and parsley. Leave onions raw or cook slightly before adding to legumes. Here are four methods to soften their raw bite:
   * Place onions in a strainer and pour boiling water over.
   * Microwave onions briefly, about 30 seconds to 1 minute.
   * Toss 8 ounces sliced onion with 1 teaspoon kosher salt, rest 15 minutes, squeeze-drain.
   * Sweat or sauté onions in a little olive oil.

3 Toss onion, anchovy or caper, olive, and parsley mixture into warm chickpeas.

4 Dress salad with vinegar and oil, to taste. Season salad well with salt and freshly ground pepper. Taste. Rest salad 1 hour, taste again, and re-season if necessary.

5 **To Serve:** Pile chickpea salad high on serving platter. Garnish with extra parsley, and serve at room temperature.

SIGNATURE RECIPE

GREEK GREENS (HORTA)

Heaping platters of simmered Greek greens are served steaming hot, straight from the cooking pot or pan, or cooled to room temperature like a wilted "salad." Greeks drink the nutrient-rich cooking water.

Yields about 2 to 3 cups, 4 to 6 servings

2 pounds tender chicory greens, dandelion, spinach, kale, chard, or leafy amaranth
1 lemon, 3 to 4 tablespoons fresh lemon juice
1/4 cup olive oil

1 Wash greens thoroughly to remove grit. Remove stems and finely slice them. Leaves stay whole.

2 Bring an 8-quart pot of water to a boil for blanching, or set an 8-quart pot with lid on burner. Tough greens, like dandelion, turnip, collards, and kale, need to boil longer. Cook them separately. Tender greens, like spinach, chard, watercress, beet greens, sorrel, baby endive, and arugula, are better *steam-wilted* with barely any liquid or *sautéed*. Purslane, Asian greens, and the Asian "choys" can go either way.

COOK'S VOICE: STATHIS STAMATAKIS

Jeweler and Homecook, Crete, Greece

"On Crete the greens are so flavorful that after we boil, drain and put them on a platter, we just drizzle them with a little lemon, salt and olive oil."
Source: Courtesy of Stathis Stamatakis.

FIGURE 8.21 Cretan wild greens.
Source: Paul Cowan/Shutterstock.

To Boil

Immerse greens and stems and cook until very tender, 5 to 7 minutes. Press and drain greens well, place on chopping board and coarsely chop. Transfer to serving bowl.

To Steam-Wilt

Chop greens and place in pot with a little water. Cover and heat over high heat. Steam greens until reduced and tender, 2 to 6 minutes. Drain and transfer greens to serving bowl.

3 Whisk together lemon juice, olive oil, and 1/4 teaspoon kosher or sea salt in small bowl. Pour over greens, toss, and serve warm or at room temperature. Taste greens and season with more salt and freshly ground pepper.

Unity and Diversity: A Culinary Foundation

Turkish cookbook author Ayla Algar writes that Turkey's culinary traditions have been stamped throughout history "by unity and diversity." Traditions established by the Ottomans and their palace cuisine provided the unity while local flavor preferences, regional growing climates and outside influences have provided diversity. Istanbul has kept and cultivated the classic palace cuisine best. Family and other connections moved the culinary knowledge and creativity from Istanbul out to the country provinces. Local cooks incorporated this new culinary knowledge into their repertoire where it became "the foundation for a common national cuisine."

Food First

Turkish cookbook writer Ghillie Basan observes in Classical Turkish Cooking *that for inhabitants of Turkey, life "revolves around food." Food surrounds them: it's in the air, on the skin, in the kitchen and in the street. Favorites like fried mussels, stuffed lamb's intestines and doner grill scent the air. Sweet shops display "syrupy baklava" and "meze play havoc with willpower." Basan notes that Turks always make time to eat!*

Vary! Improvise!

☛ *For more flavor, toss hot greens with sliced Kalamata olives and minced fresh garlic.*

☛ ***Another Way: Sauté:*** *Over medium heat, heat 1/4 cup or more olive oil and 4 or more cloves minced garlic in large skillet. Cook until garlic is soft, 1 to 2 minutes, and add 1/4 cup or more pitted olives and chopped tender greens. Cook, turning with tongs, until greens are tender, 2 to 4 minutes. Remove greens from skillet and season with lemon juice, salt, and pepper.*

TURKEY: STRADDLING TWO CONTINENTS

The history of Turkey and the history of its cuisine parallel each other. Movement and survival are at their roots. The diverse tapestry of Turkish tastes is as beautiful, earthy, and pleasurable as its people and landscape. Turkey's active geological past has resulted in a land of many natural wonders, from coastal parks with areas of pristine coastline and beaches and blue waters full of shipwrecks and hidden coves, inland marshes, lakes, waterfalls, volcanic hot springs, mountains, forests, and canyons to hundreds of colored-frescoed cave churches and underground cities to the magical moon-like landscape of *Cappadocia* with undulating white valleys and fairy chimneys. Ruins of Greek temples and Roman spas, Christian mosaics, Ottoman mosques, and the Valen aqueduct fill southwestern Turkey.

Advanced societies inhabited the area of modern-day Turkey (*Anatolia* or *Asia Minor*) starting about 6000 BCE. They formed shifting empires that rose and fell with invasions, power struggles, war, and bloodshed. The *Hittites*, a warrior race from Europe and Central Asia, were the first recorded settlers, eventually ruling Anatolia, Mesopotamia, and Syria from 1500 BCE until 550 BCE. They cultivated wheat, dairy, peas, lentils, beans, grapes, figs, and pomegranates, and cooked meat on skewers. Greek migrations to Anatolia began around 1000 BCE.

In 513 BCE, the Persian Empire conquered Anatolia and Thrace, ruling until 331 BCE. They brought infrastructure, a Royal Road that connected Anatolia's western coast to the Persian capital, and many foods: stews with meat and fruit, apricots, artichokes, eggplant, citrus, rice, yogurt, basil, cilantro, oranges, pistachios, melons, cucumbers, and spices like caraway, sumac, turmeric, and coriander. The Royal Road linked into routes to India and Central Asia, which encouraged contact between India, Mesopotamia, and the Mediterranean.

North: Black Sea
Northwest: Marmara and Istanbul
West: Aegean
South: Mediterranean
Southeast: Southern Anatolia
East: East Anatolia
Central: Central Anatolia

FIGURE 8.22 Map of Turkey.

Alexander the Great marched out of Macedonia and, in a series of decisive battles, conquered Anatolia from the Persians. He created one of the largest empires in history, knitting together Greece in the west, the Mediterranean and the Persian Empire up to the Danube in the north, Egypt to the south, and east into parts of the Indian Punjab. The expansion of Alexander's empire into Central Asia opened the *Silk Road* and trade between East and West.

When Alexander died in 323 BCE, his generals divided the empire amongst themselves. Anarchy and conflict followed until the first century BCE when the Roman Empire absorbed Anatolia, bringing peace and cultural exchange for almost four centuries.

In 330, Roman emperor Constantine the Great moved the Empire's capital from Rome to Byzantium in Thrace, which he renamed *Constantinople* and proclaimed the seat of the Eastern Roman (*Byzantine*) Empire. The central Asian Turko-Persian *Seljuks* ruled Persia, Syria, and Anatolia from 1071 to 1095. They battled the Eastern Romans and ousted them from Anatolia, converting the people from Christianity to Islam and the Greek language to Turkish. European Crusades and Mongol invaders won temporary control during 1095 until 1300, but fell apart with the steady growth of the *Ottoman Turkish Empire*.

Osman I, the leader of the Ottoman Turks, founded the dynasty that established the Ottoman Empire. It spanned three continents and ruled Southeastern Europe, the Balkans,

Western Asia, the Fertile Crescent, and North Africa from 1326 to 1923. Determined and well organized with an advanced army and navy, the Ottomans were at the center of the East and West for six centuries. In 1453, Constantinople became the center of Ottoman culinary culture. Sultan Mehmet II held feasts in his Topkapi Palace. His chefs created sophisticated dishes, which became part of the famous, opulent Ottoman Palace cuisine while Islamic art, architecture, and literature flourished.

The Ottoman Empire peaked during the reign of Suleiman the Magnificent, from 1520 to 1566. Suleiman brought the five major Muslim cities and the Balkan provinces from Croatia to Austria under his control, expanded into Europe and into much of North Africa. As the Empire conquered more territories and adapted and adopted their foods and cooking techniques, the cuisines of the far-flung Empire expanded to include variations of *dolma*, *kofte*, *kebab*, *borek*, *baklava*, yogurt, and Turkish coffee. For more than 400 years, Greece was part of the Turkish Ottoman Empire and many classic Greek dishes still bear Turkish names.

Ethnic uprisings and economic and civil strife weakened the vast Ottoman Empire, which lasted until the end of World War I, when the Allies defeated it. The Turkish national movement under leader Mustafa Kemal Pasha (*Atatürk*) won the War of Independence and abolished the sultanate. The Republic of Turkey succeeded the Ottoman Empire in 1923. Under Atatürk, Turkey went through reforms: secularism was instituted into the constitution, women were given the right to vote, and Constantinople's name was changed to *Istanbul*.

Modern Turkey is a parliamentary representative democracy. Membership in NATO and a desire to be in the European Union tie Turkey to the West, a radical departure from the Ottoman Empire. Like the two bridges spanning the Bosphorus, modern Turkey's land, customs, politics, and culture balance on the cusp of East and West, Asia and Europe.

PHILOSOPHY AND RELIGION

About 98 percent of Turkey is Muslim. The vast majority are Sunni Muslim with a substantial Shi'a Muslim minority. Sufi Muslim or mystical dervish orders, suppressed by law, are still active in certain areas. Since Turkey is a secular country, proselytizing by any religious group is not allowed and religious freedom is a constitutional right. The state maintains mosques and Muslim religious property, and leases it to religious leaders. The state also provides Muslim religious education in schools. Christians, Jews, and Greek Orthodox make up the remaining religious minority.

GEOGRAPHY AND CLIMATE

Turkey, the size of Massachusetts and Texas combined, lies on two continents and an earthquake zone with recurrent tremors: southeast Europe (*Thrace*) and southwest Asia (*Anatolia* or *Asia Minor*). Turkey is bordered to the northwest by Greece and Bulgaria, to the east by Georgia, Armenia, and Azerbaijan and Iran, and to the south by Iraq and Syria. Four seas surround the country: the *Mediterranean* to the south, the *Aegean* to the west, the *Sea of Marmara* between the European and Asian land masses, and the *Black Sea* to the north.

Turkey is comprised of the low, rolling hills of European Thrace, fertile river valleys that connect to the Aegean, warm Mediterranean plains of Antalya and Adana, the narrow Black Sea shore, and rugged mountain ranges surrounding and intersecting the semi-arid Anatolian high plateau. The highest point is *Mount Ararat* (16,949 feet) with more than another 100 peaks at 10,000 feet or higher; the largest lake is Lake Van. Eastern Anatolia is the source of the Tigris and Euphrates Rivers.

Turkey's southern Mediterranean and western Aegean coasts, as far north as Izmir, enjoy a Mediterranean climate with hot summers and mild winters and an annual rainfall as high as 50 inches. The Black Sea coast is temperate with warm summers and mild winters and moist with up to 87 inches annual rainfall. The central Anatolian plateau has hot, dry summers and cold winters and annual rainfall up to 30 inches, usually during fall and winter. With the exception of some warmer valleys, the eastern third of Turkey is snowy with long winters and mild summers and rainfall up to 20 inches.

FARMING AND AGRICULTURE

In years with good rainfall, Turkey's fertile soil and temperate climate can produce enough food to feed its population and still export. Forty percent of Turkish people are engaged in agriculture and animal husbandry. About 38 percent of Turkey is arable, with about 90 percent planted in dry grains. The average farm is between 10 and 12 acres. Wheat, hazelnuts, figs, apricots, yellow sultana raisins; vegetables like eggplant, peppers, chilies, and tomatoes; grapes, quince, tobacco, olives, pistachios, and tea are some of Turkey's largest crops. Barley, maize, sugar beets, sunflower seeds, cotton, and oranges are lesser crops. Anatolia produces cattle, sheep, poultry, eggs, and wool. Coastal fish farms produce and export frog's legs, shrimp, snails, and crayfish. Turkey is one of seven countries authorized to grow opium poppies for refining and export of pharmaceutical opiates.

TURKISH CUISINE: THE MASTERS OF MEAT AND WHEAT

Turkey has been favored throughout history because of its climate and location. Central to Europe, Asia, and Africa, Istanbul was a major hub on the ancient *Silk Road*, one of civilization's oldest active trade routes connecting Europe, the Middle East, Africa, and China. Phoenician, Central Asian Hittite, Roman, Byzantine, Arab, Persian, Chinese, Uighur, Georgian, and Greek traders, and Islamic Turkoman *Seljuk* conquerors, came through with foods, cooking techniques, and tools. These early influences formed the wheat, rice, and vegetable foundation of Turkish cuisine. By 3500 BCE, Cretan Minoans cultivated and introduced olives for eating and oil, and grapes for wine-making. Persians introduced pastries, sugar, and rice as well as many fruits and vegetables.

Turks first brought the Calicut pepper from India to the Eastern Mediterranean. They use it to prepare a spicy chili and pepper paste called *biber salçasi*. Although ancient Near East cultures made yogurt, Turks pride themselves for having named it and introduced it to the rest of the world.

Modern Turkish cooking is a combination of two cuisines: the early traditional, nomadic *Anatolian* and the later, more elaborate cuisine of the *Ottoman Empire*. Pastoral, nomadic Anatolians enhanced native vegetables, fruits, nuts, olive oil, herbs, and the many varieties of fish that came from the three seas surrounding the Anatolian Peninsula. They developed dishes like roasted meat, grilled kebabs, yogurt and cheese, *manti* (dumplings), *bugra* (ancestor of fillo-stuffed *börek*), stuffed vegetable *dolmades*, leavened and unleavened wheat breads either baked in clay ovens (*tandir*), fried on a griddle (*sac*), or buried in embers (*gömmeç*). These cooks sought to enhance, not cover their remarkable fresh food, and favored simple seasonings: cumin, garlic, mint, garlic, oregano, dill, and sage. Eventually, spices like allspice, cinnamon, black pepper, and chilies were incorporated.

Culinary pursuits took on greater importance during Ottoman times, and triggered a refinement and enlargement of Turkish cuisine. The cuisine of the rich and elite Ottoman kitchens, unlike humble Turkish food, required hundreds of cooks to prepare its elaborate dishes like lamb, rabbit, duck, or pigeon kebabs skewered on eggplant stalks, *cerkez tavugu* (chicken with walnut sauce), *pilav* (rice or grain, often with eggplant and meatballs), *piyazlar* (chopped salads), salads with rose petals and the expensive olive oil-simmered dishes (*zeytinyaglilar*) like the eggplant dish *imam bayaldi*. Chefs were brought in from regions that specialized in certain dishes. They often spent whole careers refining one or several techniques for kebabs, pilafs, milk pudding, pastries, breads, candy, drinks, or soups.

Though officially just Muslim, Ottoman Topkapi Palace culture included many religions and ethnicities. The result was a synthesis of foods and dishes from three continents. Ottomans fused the flood of new ingredients with Middle Eastern, Balkan, and traditional Turkic elements from Central Asia, to create a cuisine that persists today.

Desserts, many directly from Ottoman times, fall into three categories: *fruit and vegetable-based* like *compote*, such as pumpkin cooked in syrup or *asure* (wheat pudding or fresh fruit with topped with clotted cream); *milk-based* like rice pudding or *keskul* (milk pudding with coconut); and *pastry-based* like baklava, *kadayif* (shredded fillo pastry), *revani* (soft, sweet semolina cake), *helva* (halva), and Turkish delight.

Although the late nineteenth century saw the emergence of restaurant dining in Turkey, the most varied and interesting food is still made at home by women. Dining together reinforces the ties of family and friendship on which Turks place great importance. Despite that, modern Turkey has a modern and diverse food culture. Travel writer Jenny White comments that Istanbul's restaurants reveal the "tug-of-war between religion and secularism that permeates Turkish society." She has seen that what foods Turkish people choose to eat and where they choose to dine are serious matters.

From habits formed during the Ottoman Empire, a desire for authentic food and because of Muslim taboo foods, each type of food has its own restaurant: fast food, meat (*kebabs*), *meyhane* (wine bars), the home-style and alcohol-free *lokanta*, the *muhallebiciler* specializing in milk-based puddings, the *pastahaneler* for European pastry, and shops that sell only *baklava*.

REGIONAL TURKEY

Turkey consists of seven geographic and culinary regions.

1. **North: Black Sea**
   This temperate zone of high rainfall, lush greenery, rocky Caucasus Mountains and cool, coastal Black Sea is home to tea, hazelnut, tobacco, and corn farming. *Hamsi* (sardine-like fish), corn, and hazelnuts make up a substantial part of the diet along with numerous vegetables like collards and fruits like cherries. It's known for crisp *fillo* filled with custard and *guli corbasi* (soup with beans, lamb, and greens). Legend has it that Amazon female warriors once lived in this region.

2. **Northwest: Marmara and Istanbul**
   The Bosphorus, the Sea of Marmara and the Dardenelle Straits separate this ancient Roman region from the rest of Turkey. The lush, rolling fields feature fruit orchards, vegetable gardens, Ottoman architecture, broad beaches, wine festivals, thermal springs, vineyards grown for Sultana raisins and wine, and sunflowers for seed and oil. The culinary center of Turkey, Marmara supplies the best chefs in the country. It features pasture-fed lamb and lamb kabobs, use of chestnuts in stews, rice or bulgar pilafs, *tarhana corbasi* (ancient pasta soup), *dolma* with rice and sour cherries, *ayva dolmasi* (melon stuffed with minced lamb, rice, almonds, and pistachios), *basti* and *kalye* (buttery vegetable stews with meat), *turşu* (pickled vegetables), and many desserts. It is rich in vegetables, herbs, and fish. Istanbul is known for the meze *midye* (pilaf-stuffed mussels).

3. **West: Aegean**

Full of seaside resorts, thermal springs, and the famous cities of Troy and Ephesus, the Aegean region is a treasure trove of Ionian culture with ancient temples of Artemis and Apollo. The western region consumes more seafood than lamb or chicken and has a mild climate good for growing figs, peaches, vegetables, herbs, and olives and producing olive oil. Greens like purslane are popular. Dishes like *zeytinyaglilar* (olive oil-braised vegetables), a light Aegean-style *moussaka*, yogurt with cucumbers and dill, dried bean casserole, *gozleme* (stuffed and baked thin pastries), and milk-based sweets are favored.

4. **South: Mediterranean**

This sunny region of ocean, beach, and Roman ruins has a cuisine rich in vegetables, seafood, herbs, olive oil, smoky eggplant purée with pomegranate syrup, *piyaz* (Turkish bean salad with walnuts and sumac), *sis köfte* (grilled meatballs), *doner kebab* (spit grilled lamb), and *teretorlu balik* (fish with tarator sauce) made with local grouper or red mullet. Fruit like bananas, oranges, pomegranates, cherries, strawberries, and apricots are abundant and many are made into the beloved Antalyan jam. This region's specialties include an orchid drink (*salep*), goat and cow milk ice-cream, *hibeş* (chickpeas with cumin and tahini), *tirmis* (boiled lupine seeds), and many types of *cive* (vegetable stews) like tomato stews with wheat.

5. **Southeast: South Anatolia**

This hot and desert-like region is the oldest cultural settlement in Anatolia, where the prophet Abraham is believed to have lived. It is best known for spicy kebabs, mezes, and dough-based desserts such as baklava and *kadayif* and *künefe* (shredded fillo desserts). Turkish southeastern food reflects hotter and spicier Middle Eastern-Arabic influences with fresh and dried chilies, peppers, cumin, nigella, sumac, za'atar, and sesame. It's known for special varieties of kebab, *lahmacun* (lamb-topped flatbread) and pistachio baklava, melons, eggplant and lentil stews, *freekeh* (unripe wheat), pomegranates and their syrup, lamb tail fat, butter, olive oil, *kaytaz boregi* (savory patties topped with ground meat, onions, and pepper paste), ispanakli borek (pastries stuffed with spinach a white cheese called *cokelek*), *oruk* (baked oval shaped bulgur patties filled with ground meat, walnuts, and onions), and onion and *sumac* salads. *Tandir* oven-baked breads and *kisir* (fine bulgur salad), as well as stuffed and raw *köfte* (meatballs), Aleppo pepper flakes (*pul biber*), a semi-moist, hot, flaked red pepper, and *biber salçasi* (chili and pepper paste) are favorites.

6. **East: East Anatolia**

This is an area of remote and unspoiled beauty: rugged snowcapped mountain ranges, remote plateaus, colorful lakes and riverbeds, and historic Turkish architecture. Noah's Ark is believed to have come to rest on this region's highest peak, Mt. Ararat. Livestock farming employs most people and produces butter, yogurt, cheese, honey, and meat. Winters are long and cold. To survive, residents dry fruit, wild herbs, and grain, and consume *yayla corbasi* (hot yogurt soup), herbed meatballs, and hot tea. Clay-oven (*tandir*) cooked kebabs, fried *böreks*, meat and vegetable dishes, and *helva* (halva) date back to the Ottoman feasts.

7. **Central: Central Anatolia**

Turkey's rural heartland, this high plateau is known for pasta, and specialties like *keşkek* (ground mutton or chicken stewed with boiled, mashed wheat, and chickpeas), *manti* (dumplings), *gözleme* (stuffed flatbreads), *etliekmek* (a long meat or cheese topped pizza), *tirit* (cubed flatbread layered with yogurt, onions, lamb, butter, and sumac), *firin* (mutton kebab), many soups like okra, vermicelli, milk or lentil soup with mint, stuffed vegetables, and stuffed grape or cabbage leaves. The city of Konya was home to the mystic whirling dervishes.

DINE AT HOME IN TURKEY

Invitations to dine in a Turkish home are rare. It is customary to dress modestly, be on time, and to bring a gift. Since Turkey is mainly Muslim, give flowers, pastries, or chocolate, not alcohol. Shake hands if a hand is extended and maintain eye contact while speaking. Guests remove shoes at the door in a Muslim home, even if the hosts say it's not necessary. They will provide a choice of slippers by the door.

Guests are likely to be seated at a table, but in the country they may be seated on the floor around a communal array of food on a low table. The head of the family or the honored guest is usually served first, but it shows good manners for guests to insist that the most senior diner is served before them. Turkish meals are animated and social. Guests take only what food they will finish, and to ask for seconds is a high compliment to the host and hostess. Food is commonly eaten with the *right hand* only. Spoons, knives, and forks are also used, with the fork in the left hand and knife in the right. Guests never speak with food in their mouth, point, pick their teeth, or show the soles of their feet. All are considered rude.

The meal might begin with an array of *meze*, starting with cold and moving to hot: roasted eggplant purée with yogurt, *dolma*, *barbunya pilaki* (stewed kidney beans), stewed mussel *pilaki*, or cheese *borek*—or these might be served as side dishes. A hot or cold soup will follow: lentil, rice, and bulgar, yogurt soup, or lamb and vegetable soup. Pilaf, generally made of rice, bulgar, or vermicelli, is popular as a course or as a side with meat and chicken. Cooked or raw *kofte* (ground meat or vegetable balls grilled, simmered, or baked) and *sis kebabs* grilled chunks of lamb, fish, or chicken, a casserole like *kuzu güveç* (braised lamb) and vegetable dishes like stuffed peppers or eggplant, and spinach, leeks, green beans, or artichokes braised in olive oil are popular.

Bread accompanies every meal, usually *ekmek* (crisp sourdough baguette) or flatbread. Guests eat heartily, clean their plate, and when finished, place their knife and fork side by side on the plate. Desserts and *cay* (tea) or Turkish coffee are served at the end of a meal. Turks have a sweet tooth, so be prepared.

TASTES OF TURKEY

Fat: Olive oil, butter, sunflower oil, corn and canola oil, sesame, peanut, hazelnut, and walnut oils

Sweet: Honey, sugar, grape syrup

Sour/Alcohol: Red and white wine vinegar, lemon and citrus, sour plums, pomegranate, yogurt molasses/syrup, unripe grape syrup, yogurt, sumac, tomato paste

Salty: Sea salt, olives

Spicy-Hot: Red and green chilies, black pepper, chili paste

Spice: Allspice, cinnamon, paprika, cumin seed, nigella, clove, coriander, fenugreek, saffron, sumac, black and white poppyseed, jasmine flowers, *mahleb*, *mastic* (acacia resin)

Aromatic Seasoning Vegetables: Onions, garlic, leeks, carrots, tomato

Herbs, Seasonings and Condiments: Parsley, oregano, mint, thyme, dill, bay leaf, rose petals, rose water

Other Important Foods: Hulled wheat, rice, bulgar, millet, barley, *yufka* (thick phyllo dough), *kadayif* (shredded phyllo dough), *kaymak* (very thick, cuttable cream), tahini, sesame, almonds, chestnuts, hazelnuts, pine nuts, pistachios, walnuts, eggplant, zucchini, tomato, potato, green and red bell peppers, cucumbers,

COMMON TURKISH COOKING TOOLS

Mortar and pestle, *tandir* (tandoori-type underground oven), grill, *sac* (griddle)

FIGURE 8.23 Greek satz or Turkish sac or iron griddle.
Source: uwimages/Fotolia.

spinach, artichokes, cauliflower, cabbage, green beans, fruit (melons, plums, apricots, dates, figs, apples, grapes, raisins, currants, quince), legumes (chickpeas, fava beans, white beans, and red lentils), fish and seafood, meat (lamb, veal, chicken, sheep, goat, beef), *sujuk* (spicy raw beef sausage), *pastirma* or *basturma* (cured beef)

Popular Dishes: *Borek* (stuffed fillo roll), dolmas, pilaf, *manti* (dumplings), braised lamb, *bildircin izgara* (quail grilled on fig leaves), pilaf, *köfte* (meat or vegetable balls), döner kabob, *sis kebab* (shish kebab), *kokoreç* (grilled lamb intestines), baklava, *karni-yarik* (lamb-stuffed, braised eggplant), *patlican salatasi* (roasted eggplant salad), *midye tavasi* (mussel brochettes with tarator), *kalamar tava* (fried squid), *imam bayildi* (oil-braised, vegetable-stuffed eggplant)

Drinks: Black tea, Turkish coffee, wine, beer, *raki* (anise flavored alcohol), lemonade, *aryan* (salty yogurt drink), kefir, *salgam* (fermented turnip juice), *boza* (fermented bulgar), millet wine, herbal teas (orchid root, nogay, and mirra), rose "sherbet"

TURKISH CHEESE (PEYNIR)

Turkish cuisine has many varieties of cheese, most of which fall into six types divided by method, location, and climate. Generally, wintery climates produce harder, saltier cheeses and warmer coastal regions produce lighter cheeses.

Beyaz Peynir or White Cheese

Produced in the Marmara regions and most of Turkey, the popular *beyaz peynir* is made in various ways from sheep or cow milk. These cheeses resemble soft feta, but are curdled with a vegetarian coagulant and mature 3 to 6 months in salt water. Beyaz peynir is essential for breakfast and börek.

Tulum

Produced in northeastern Anatolia and the Aegean regions, tulums are made from sheep and goat milk. The Anatolian is a strong, yellowish cheese, smooth, creamy, and without holes. Tulums mature in 3 months, usually in animal skins or stomachs. Aegean tulums age in salt water and are higher fat, harder, saltier than white cheese, with small holes.

Kasar

Produced in the Middle Anatolian and Thrace regions, the two types of *kasar*—old and *fresh*—are similar to cheddar or Greek *kasseri*. Made with sheep milk, the dark yellow, moderately fatty kasar cheese is immersed in hot water, kneaded, and cooked.

It ages in cylindrical molds 1 month or more. Old kasar is a rich, aged yellow cheese, cold-aged in sacks 6 months

Mihalic

Mostly produced around Bursa and Balikesir, *mihalic* cheeses are made from high-fat cow or sheep milk. It is similar to kasar cheese, but is harder, white and riddled with small holes, and is similar to Parmesan. It is grated, melted, or eaten by itself.

Lor and Çökelek

Created from boiling the whey generated during kasar and mihalic production, this inexpensive cheese is unsalted and used fresh or preserved by sun-drying or in goatskin bags or in jars. It is often mixed with walnuts or tomato paste and used as a spread, in desserts, or in börek filling.

Otlu Peynir or Herbed Cheese

Produced mainly in Eastern Anatolia, this white sheep or goat milk cheese is flavored with local herbs like mint, wild garlic, bay leaves, dill, or lavender and matures 2 to 3 months.

Special Cheese: Kars Gravyer

Produced in Eastern Anatolia, the special *kars gravyer* is made from cow milk. It's similar to Gruyere and Emmental, creamy, pale yellow, and full of large holes. It matures in 10 months.

TURKISH FLAVOR FOUNDATIONS

Turkish Signature Aromatic Vegetable Combo

Olive oil or butter, onion, carrots, garlic

Turkish Herbal Quartet: Mint, parsley, bay leaf, and dill

Signature Seasonings

See *Greek Signature Seasonings*.

Liquid/Paste

Olive Oil

Turks favor fruity, green oil from the first pressing. They use it for salads, and a less expensive oil for their braised olive oil dishes called *zeytinyaglilar*. See *Glossary*.

Pomegranate Molasses

The juice of pomegranates, simmered to a thick, tart syrup. Look for types with no sugar added. Used to give sweet, fruity, tart flavor to anything from soups, stews, and vegetables to marinades.

FIGURE 8.24 Pastirma or basturma.

Source: Roger Dixon/DK Images.

Animal

Pastirma or Basturma

Spice-rubbed, dry-cured beef much like Italian dry-cured meats (prosciutto and bresaola), thinly sliced and used in sandwiches, as a meze or as flavoring in beans or scrambled eggs.

Vegetable/Fruit

Turkish Chilies

Turkish cooks cultivate and use a wide variety of capsicums. They use them fresh, dried, and coarsely ground. None are searingly hot.

FIGURE 8.25 Aleppo chili flakes.

Source: elena moiseeva/Shutterstock.

- **Long green pepper:** This tender chilipepper is 6 to 7 inches long and slightly curvy. Its flavor is mild to hot; Hungarian peppers may be substituted.
- **Aleppo pepper:** This dried, coarsely ground chili slightly oily chili is bright red, medium-hot. It has a fruity, sweet, rounded flavor with a chili kick, and tastes slightly of cumin, chocolate, and salt.
- **Kirmizi pepper:** This is the long, red cayenne pepper. It is used fresh and dried. It is ground until grainy, not powdery.
- **Maras pepper:** This is a bright red chili with an acidic fruity flavor and medium heat.
- **Urfa pepper:** This dark, sultry red-brown chili has hints of earth, clay, and smoke.

Sumac

Aromatic sour berry soaked in water and pressed for juice, or dried and ground and used in salads and dressings, meat dishes, or marinades to impart a sour flavor like lemon or vinegar. Dried ground sumac serves as a topping as part of the Middle Eastern za'atar spice mix (with sesame and dried ground thyme) or as a topping for flatbreads and grilled or fried meat dishes.

FIGURE 8.26 Sumac plant.

Source: Melinda Fawver/Shutterstock.

Herbal/Spice

Turkish Bay Leaf

The dark green, broad Turkish bay leaves are far milder and more complex than the long and narrow California bay leaves, which are not a true bay genus. California bay leaves have a very strong, eucalyptus-like flavor and are not good for cooking. Turkish bay leaves grow wild on the mountains of western Turkey near Izmir. They add a subtle, sweet herbaceous perfume to dishes. Use fresh bay leaves whenever possible.

FIGURE 8.27 Dried Turkish bay leaves.

Source: Nicholas Piccillo/Fotolia.

FIGURE 8.28 Istanbul grand bazaar, one of the largest and oldest covered markets in the world.
Source: MasterLu/Fotolia.

SEASONING AND PASTE MIXTURES

Turkish Infused Fat: Yüzüne

Much like an *Indian tempering*, a *yüzüne* is melted butter infused most commonly with mint and black pepper. Turkish cooks pour it over a dish as a garnish. Cook in parts of the Eastern Mediterranean heat paprika in butter or oil and pour the reddened fat over a dish to finish.

Butter-yüzünes are used on dishes served warm, and oil-yüzünes on dishes served cold.

TURKISH SPICE BLEND (BAHARAT)

Baharat is used throughout the Mediterranean, Middle East, and North Africa as an all-purpose flavor enhancer for seafood, meat, and vegetables. Turkish cooks add savory and mint to their version. Rub it on meat prior to grilling, sprinkle into an eggplant dish, kofte, or pilaf or infuse into butter (yüzüne) or oil (baharatli zeytinyagi) and drizzle over a dish as a final flourish.

Yields about 1/3 cup

---

3 tablespoons dried, crumbled summer or winter savory
    or 3 tablespoons dried thyme
2 tablespoons dried, crumbled mint leaves
1 to 2 tablespoons black peppercorns
1 tablespoon cumin seed
1 tablespoon coriander seed
1 teaspoon whole allspice
1/2 to 3/4 whole nutmeg, chopped, or 1 teaspoon ground nutmeg
1/4 teaspoon ground cinnamon

1 Grind ingredients to powder. Keep in tightly covered jar 4 to 6 months stored in cool, dark spot.

SIGNATURE RECIPE

TURKISH RED CHILI AND PEPPER PASTE (BIBER SALÇASI)

Turks invaded India and first brought the Calicut pepper to the Eastern Mediterranean. They spread it to the rest of the Ottoman Empire; now Tunisians, Syrians, Georgians, Macedonians, and Greeks love them. In late summer, Turkish cooks harvest and prepare this paste.

Yields 1 cup

1-1/2 pounds sweet red bell peppers
1-1/2 pounds mildly-hot red chilies
  or 3 pounds any combination chilies and peppers depending on your desire for heat
2 tablespoons olive oil

1 Preheat grill or broiler. Wash and dry chilies and peppers. Grill or broil them until the skin blackens. Peel away blackened skin and rinse chilies and peppers; drain. Halve peppers and chilies lengthwise and remove stems, seeds, and membranes.

2 Chop chilies and peppers coarsely. Place in food processor with 1-1/2 tablespoons kosher salt. Grind, in pulses, until coarsely but evenly ground to yield about 4 cups.

3 Pour 2 cups chili-pepper purée into each of two heavy 10- or 11-inch sauté pans. Simmer over low heat, folding purée with heatproof spatula until purée is the consistency of tomato paste, 30 to 45 minutes.

4 Scrape paste into 8-ounce canning jar and cover with oil to keep out mold. Seal tightly with lid and refrigerate up to 3 months. Wait 1 week before using. *Alternatively*, freeze paste in 1-tablespoon drops on parchment-covered sheet pan and freeze in zipper baggies up to 6 months.

5 **To Use:** Spread on bread or thin with water or oil and use as a dip. Or use in stews and soups in the same way as tomato paste.

Vary! Improvise!

☞ *Mild Walnut-Pepper Spread (Cevizli Biber):* Grind 8 ounces (2 cups) walnuts with 3 to 4 tablespoons Red Chili and Pepper Paste. Purée with 2 to 3 tablespoons olive oil and thin with water. To soften it further, purée 1 slice of bread in with walnuts.

☞ *Add other seasonings to the paste.*

☞ *Spread paste on a plastic sheet in a dehydrator and dehydrate instead of simmering paste.*

FIFTEEN LAYERS OF TURKISH CUISINE

- **Mezeler:** appetizers
- **Dolmalar:** vegetables and green leaves stuffed with vegetables, fruit, rice, bulgar, or meat
- **Çorbalar:** soups
- **Salatalar or piyazlar:** salads
- **Baklagiller:** bean, lentil, and pea dishes
- **Zeytinyağli Sebzeler:** vegetables simmered in olive oil and often served cold
- **Pilavlar:** pilafs, usually with rice or bulgar
- **Etli Sebzeler:** vegetables cooked with (usually small amounts) meat
- **Börekler:** fillo stuffed with meat, cheese, or vegetables
- **Pideler:** flat breads, often with cheese, meat, or vegetables
- **Kebaplar:** any sort of kebabs from meat chunks to meatballs that are skewered to pot-simmered
- **Kofteler:** vegetable fritters and meatballs
- **Balik ve Deniz Ürünleri:** fish and seafood dishes
- **Tatlilar:** desserts
- **İçecekler:** all drinks alcoholic and nonalcoholic like Turkish coffee, Turkish tea, raki, and ayran

SAUCE

Turkish *Soslar*

Sauces in both Greek and Turkish cuisine are not elaborate or long cooked. Cooks prepare them just before they are served to preserve fresh flavor. The simplest of Turkish sauces (*sosu*) is yogurt with minced garlic and salt. It's served over grilled meat, vegetables, pilaf, and savory stuffed fillo. Tomato sauce is another Turkish favorite. Since food is simple, flavorful, and fresh, there is less need for saucing.

Turkish Egg-Lemon Sauce (Terbiye)

See *Greece: Sauce*

Turks and Greeks use this fluffy sauce over all kinds of stuffed *dolma*.

Turkish Lemon and Olive Oil Sauce (Zeytinyagi Ve Limon Salçasi)

See *Greece: Sauce*

This lemon vinaigrette is a natural partner for grilled, fried, or poached seafood. Turks use this sauce without mustard and oregano, but with parsley.

SIGNATURE RECIPE

TURKISH NUT SAUCES (TARATOR)

These two sauces, similar to Greek skorthaliá, are made in many parts of the Eastern Mediterranean.

Hazelnut Tarator

Yields 1-1/2 thick cups to 1-3/4 thin cups

1 to 2 ounces crustless fresh bread, about 1 cup coarsely chopped breadcrumbs
1/2 ounce garlic, about 2 large cloves, 1 tablespoon peeled and chopped
About 4 ounces hazelnuts, 1 cup
    or 4 ounces pine nuts *or* chopped walnuts, about 3/4 cup
1/4 cup fresh lemon juice, about 1 large lemon
1/2 cup olive oil

Walnut-Spice Tarator

Yields 2 cups

1/2 ounce peeled garlic, 2 large cloves, 1 tablespoon peeled and chopped
8 ounces chopped walnuts, about 2 cups
1 teaspoon paprika
2 teaspoons ground coriander
2 tablespoons pomegranate molasses
2 tablespoons red wine vinegar
1/2 ounce trimmed Italian parsley, 4 tablespoons finely chopped

1 Prep food:

Hazelnut

Soak bread in water to soften, 5 minutes. Drain and gently squeeze out excess water.

2 Grind ingredients in food processor:

Hazelnut

Place bread, garlic, nuts, and lemon juice in food processor. Process until finely purée. Add 1/2 cup cold water and 1/2 teaspoon kosher salt and purée until smooth.

Walnut-Spice

Pour garlic, walnuts, paprika, and coriander into blender or food processor and process until finely puréed. With machine running, add pomegranate molasses, vinegar, 1 teaspoon kosher salt, and 1 cup warm water. Purée until smooth. Add up to 1/2 cup more warm water to achieve a thick, pourable sauce.

3 Finish sauce:

Hazelnut

With machine running, pour oil in a thin stream into mixture.

Walnut-Spice

Scrape sauce into bowl and fold in parsley.

4 **To Serve:** Taste sauce and re-season. Transfer sauce to bowl and refrigerate 30 minutes to 1 hour before serving. Taste again, re-season sauce if necessary, and serve.

TURKISH YOGURT-CUCUMBER-GARLIC SAUCE (CACIK)

Turkish cacik is Greek tzatziki's diluted cousin. Serve cacik as a salad or soup with meat and vegetable dishes. Omit garlic for a mild version.

Yields 3 to 3-1/2 cups, 6 to 8 servings

16 ounces whole milk *or* goat milk yogurt, 2 cups
About 6 ounces English cucumber
1/2 ounce garlic, 2 large cloves, peeled
1/2 ounce mint leaves, about 1/2 cup finely chopped

Garnish: Extra virgin olive oil

1 **Prepare yogurt:** Beat yogurt in medium mixing bowl; do not strain.

2 **Prepare cucumber:** Lightly peel, halve lengthwise, seed and finely slice cucumber to yield 1 cup. Toss with 1/2 teaspoon kosher salt, and set cucumber aside 5 minutes. Gently squeeze and drain off liquid.

3 Mince garlic until pasty with a little salt to soften its flavor. Combine yogurt, cucumber, and garlic. Stir in lemon juice or vinegar and herbs. Taste cacik and season with salt to taste.

4 **To Serve:** Chill cacik 1 hour to blend flavors. Taste again and re-season. Place mixture in serving bowl. Garnish with a drizzle of olive oil if desired.

Vary! Improvise!

☛ *Turkish Cold Yogurt Soup: Dilute cacik with 1/2 cup water and a few ice cubes for summer soup. Taste and re-season before serving.*

SPECIAL METHODS

RED LENTIL AND BULGAR BALLS (MERCIMEK KÖFTESI)

Vegetarian kofte are made with cooked ground vegetables or lentils and bulgar, breadcrumbs, or rice. They can be molded in various shapes and stuffed or not and deep-fried or not. This fresh favorite is served rolled into lettuce leaves. It's the perfect canvas for a host of flavors. The constants are lentils and bulgar. The kofte will firm and flavors meld as they cool, after 1 hour.

Yields 5 cups, about 30 (2 tablespoons plus 2 teaspoons each) *kofte*

7 ounces split red or pink lentils, 1 cup
2 tablespoons olive oil, plus more for rolling
8 to 9 ounces onion, 2 cups peeled and finely diced
1/2 ounce garlic, 2 large cloves, 1 tablespoon peeled and minced
1 tablespoon *Turkish Red Chili and Pepper Paste*
    or 1 tablespoon tomato paste
    or 1 tablespoon chopped sun-dried tomato
About 5 ounces fine-grain bulgar, 1 cup
Optional: 1 ounce trimmed green onions, about 2 large, 4 tablespoons finely minced
1 ounce trimmed Italian parsley, 1/2 cup finely chopped
1 lemon, juiced, 2 to 4 tablespoons
Olive oil for shaping

To Serve

1 pound head Bibb or Boston lettuce, about 30 whole, small lettuce leaves
Choice of fresh herb leaves and sprigs: Italian parsley, mint, cilantro leaves, or tarragon
Onion-Sumac Salad

1 Pour lentils in 4-quart saucepan with 3 cups water. Bring to a boil, reduce heat, and partially cover pan. Simmer lentils until mushy, 30 minutes. Stir occasionally to keep lentils from sticking to bottom of pot and burning.

2 Heat oil in 10-inch skillet over medium heat and cook onion until soft, 5 to 7 minutes. Add garlic and cook 1 minute longer.

3 **Prepare kofte mixture:** Stir onion-garlic mixture and red pepper paste into lentils. Slightly over-salt lentils; the lentils and bulgar absorb salt. Remove saucepan from heat and fold in bulgar and green onions. Set aside 30 minutes to allow bulgar to absorb moisture. Stir in parsley. Season mixture with fresh lemon juice, salt and pepper, to taste.

4 **Shape kofte:** With oiled hands, place 2 heaping tablespoons of the mixture in the middle of the palm of one hand. Squeeze lightly into an elongated oval and smooth the outer surface. Finish shaping kofte.

5 **To Serve:** Place each kofte on top of a lettuce leaf. Arrange in a sun-ray pattern on a large serving platter. Garnish each kofte with herb leaves. Serve with onion-sumac salad. Eat kofte rolled up in lettuce leaf with herbs.

Source: The Cooking of the Eastern Mediterranean by Paula Wolfert.

Vary! Improvise!

☛ *Season kofte differently with toasted, ground cumin, or coriander seed, toasted nigella seed or curry powder.*
☛ *Cook 2 to 3 tablespoons grated carrot with onions and garlic.*
☛ *Fold 1 tablespoon tahini or 2 tablespoons finely chopped walnuts into lentil-bulgar mixture.*
☛ *Roll kofte in finely ground nuts.*

SIMMER, STEW, POACH, BOIL, AND STEAM

Greek and Turks love soup, and eat them as a starter or as a full meal at breakfast, lunch, or dinner. Turkish *corbasi* are generally simple and hearty with satisfying ingredients like lentils, sesame paste, yogurt, milk, eggplant, bulgar wheat, *tarhana*, cabbage, greens, beans, lamb, seafood, or chicken.

HOT YOGURT SOUP (YAYLA OR YOGURT CORBASI)

If this soup boils, it will curdle. Reheat it gently.

Yields about 7 cups, 4 to 6 servings

2 tablespoons clarified butter, *divided*
4 to 5 ounces onion, 1 cup peeled and finely diced
About 2/3 ounce all-purpose flour, 2 tablespoons
1 quart chicken *or* beef stock
About 4 ounces drained, canned chickpeas, 1/2 cup
    or 1-3/4 ounces dry chickpeas, 4 tablespoons, 1/2 cup cooked
About 1-3/4 ounces long-grain rice, 4 tablespoons, washed and drained

Yüzüne Garnish

1 teaspoon crumbled saffron threads
    or 2 teaspoons crumbled dried mint leaves *or* 2 tablespoons fresh mint leaves

1-1/2 cups thick whole milk yogurt

1   Heat 1 tablespoon butter over medium heat in saucepan. Add onion and cook until soft, 5 to 7 minutes. Stir in flour and cook 1 minute. Whisk in stock and bring liquid to a boil. Stir in cooked chickpeas and rice. Lower heat, cover pan, and simmer soup 20 minutes, stirring occasionally.

2   **Prepare *yüzüne garnish*:** Heat 1 tablespoon clarified butter in small sauté pan until foamy. Add either saffron or mint. Cook 10 seconds. Remove pan from heat but keep warm.

3   Whisk yogurt smooth in small mixing bowl. Slowly whisk 1/2 cup hot stock into bowl. Remove pan from heat and whisk yogurt into hot soup. Taste soup and season with salt and freshly ground pepper.

4   **To Serve:** Ladle soup into bowls and drizzle each with a little **yüzüne garnish**.

RED LENTIL AND MINT SOUP (EZOGELIN CORBASI)

Yields about 6 cups, 4 to 6 servings

2 tablespoons olive oil
2 tablespoons diced unsalted butter
8 to 9 ounces onion, 2 cups finely diced
1/2 ounce peeled garlic, 2 large cloves, about 1 tablespoon peeled and minced
About 4 ounces tomato, 2/3 cup peeled and finely diced
2 tablespoons tomato paste
2 tablespoons sweet paprika
1/2 teaspoon cayenne pepper
About 10-1/2 ounces split red lentils, 1-1/2 cups
About 3-1/2 ounces long-grain white rice *or* 2-1/2 to 3-ounces fine-grained bulgar, 1/2 cup
2 cups chicken stock *or* water, more as needed
1 tablespoon dried mint, crumbled

Yüzüne Garnish

2 tablespoons diced unsalted or clarified butter
1/2 teaspoon sweet paprika
1 tablespoon dried mint

1 large lemon, cut into 6 wedges and seeded

1 Heat oil and butter in 4-quart saucepan over medium heat. Stir in onion and cook until soft, 5 to 7 minutes. Stir in garlic and cook 1 minute more. Stir in tomato and paste, paprika, pepper, lentils, rice (if using), and stock or water. Bring soup to a boil, lower the heat, cover saucepan partially, and simmer soup 30 to 35 minutes, stirring occasionally to scrape lentils off bottom of pot.

2 Add bulgar (if using) and mint. Simmer soup 10 minutes. Adjust consistency with more water or stock as desired. Taste soup and season with salt. Prepare **yüzüne**. Melt butter in small sauté pan over medium heat until foamy. Stir in paprika and mint and sizzle 20 to 30 seconds

3 **To Serve:** Ladle hot soup into bowls and drizzle warm *yüzüne* over top. Serve with lemon wedges.

Source: *The Sultan's Kitchen: A Turkish Cookbook* by Özcan Ozan.

Vary! Improvise!

☛ *Stir cream or thick yogurt into soup just before serving.*

Braising

Braising on top of the stove is an important technique in both Greece and Turkey. The signature oil-braised Turkish *zeytinyağli* make luscious vegetarian dishes. Turkish cooks also braise seafood, stuffed grape or cabbage leaves and greens in broth, tomato or egg-lemon sauce, or water.

Turkish Oil-Braised Vegetables (Zeytinyağli)

See *Greece: Simmer, Stew, Poach, Boil, and Steam*
Zeytinyağli is an olive-oil-stewed or braised dish, usually vegetarian, made with one or more vegetables cooked in an olive oil-based sauce with onion, tomatoes, and garlic. More olive oil results in a richer dish.

Signature Technique: Stuffed and Simmered Bell Peppers or Tomatoes

Use seasoned bread, rice, or bulgar with chickpeas or leftover pilaf to stuff tomatoes.

1 **Prepare the vegetables:** Slice 1/4- to 1/2-inch tops from even-shaped medium bell peppers or large, round tomatoes. Reserve.

   Bell Peppers
   Scrape out cores and seeds from peppers and rinse. Turn peppers over to drain.

   Tomatoes
   Scoop out innards, leaving 1/4-inch thick tomato shell intact. Press tomato innards over strainer set in bowl and reserve liquid. Salt tomato insides and turn them over on a plate to catch the juices.

2 **Prepare a filling:** Choose from grape leaf fillings or pilafs. (Use reserved tomato liquid in filling if desired. If not, save for later or another use, like soup.)

3 **Stuff:** Fill each tomato or pepper with *1/2 to 3/4-cup filling*. Place their caps on top of each.

4 **Cook:** Arrange stuffed vegetables into large, wide pot in one layer, tightly packed. Pour strained tomato juice, broth, or water around the edges of tomatoes but not on them. Bring water or broth to a boil, lower heat, and cover pot. Simmer vegetables until they are soft but not falling apart: 25 minutes for peppers and 15 to 20 minutes for tomatoes.

   Alternatively, arrange stuffed vegetables in one layer into oiled baking dish. Preheat oven to 375 degrees F and bake peppers or tomatoes until golden and tender, 30 to 35 minutes.

FIGURE 8.29 Eggplant.

Source: Simon Bracken/DK Images.

FIGURE 8.30 Turkish stuffed, braised eggplant (Imam Bayildi).

Vary! Improvise!

☛ *Large Eggplant:* Cut large eggplants completely in half lengthwise. Make shallow crosshatch in flesh side, salt as in step 2, rinse, and blot dry. Fry halves on both sides as directed for whole eggplants. Stuff slits and cover cut top of eggplant with filling before simmering or baking.

☛ *Lamb or Beef Karniyarik:* After cooking and removing onions, add 1/2 pound ground lamb or beef to skillet. Cook until done and stir into onion-tomato stuffing.

TURKISH STUFFED, BRAISED EGGPLANT (IMAM BAYILDI)

A favorite dish across the Ottoman Empire, imam bayildi *means "the imam fainted," probably from the cost of the olive oil in this dish. It's one of the best-known Turkish* zeytinyaglilar *or olive oil-simmered dishes. A heartier variation, called* karniyarik, *contains minced lamb or beef.*

6 servings

2-1/2 pounds Italian eggplant, preferably 6 six-inch-long eggplants
1 cup olive oil, *divided*
8 to 12 ounces long green Italian peppers, 3 small, about 2 cups stemmed, seeded, and halved lengthwise
12 to 14 ounces onions, 3 cups slivered *or* thinly sliced
1-1/2 ounces garlic, 6 large cloves, 3 tablespoons peeled and finely sliced, more to taste
1 to 1-1/2 pounds ripe tomatoes, 2 to 3 cups peeled and diced
1 ounce trimmed Italian parsley, 1/2 cup finely chopped
1/2 ounce trimmed dill, 1/4 cup chopped
2 tablespoons fresh lemon juice, about 1/2 large lemon

Garnish: 1/4 ounce trimmed Italian parsley, 2 tablespoons chopped

For Serving

1 lemon, sliced into 6 wedges
Crusty bread

1 Imam bayildi may be cooked on stovetop or in oven. If using oven, preheat to 375 degrees F.

2 Peel eggplant skin lengthwise at 1-inch intervals to make stripes. Leave stem on. *Make a pocket:* Cut a deep lengthwise slit along the side of each eggplant, but don't cut all the way to the ends or puncture all the way through the skin. Sprinkle eggplants inside and out with kosher salt and set aside in bowl to soften, 20 minutes. Rinse eggplant, squeeze gently, and blot with paper towels.

3 **Brown eggplant and peppers:** Heat 1/2 cup oil in a 12-inch ovenproof skillet, over medium-high heat. Fry eggplant on all sides until golden brown, 4 to 6 minutes. Remove eggplants from skillet to drain on paper towels. Fry peppers until crisp-tender, 2 minutes, and set aside. Wipe out skillet.

4 In the same skillet, add remaining 1/2 cup oil and over medium-high heat. Stir in onion and garlic, and cook until soft, 5 minutes. Transfer onions to a mixing bowl and toss well with tomatoes, parsley, and dill. Season mixture with salt and freshly ground pepper to taste.

5 Arrange eggplant back into skillet (or casserole) side by side with slit side up. Gently open the slit. Stuff each eggplant equally with onion-tomato-herb filling. Pour excess filling over top and sprinkle with lemon juice. Lay 1/2 green pepper on top of each eggplant or crisscross peppers if there are extra.

6 Bring mixture to a simmer and cover skillet or casserole. Cook over low heat, or place in preheated oven and bake, until eggplant is soft, 40 to 50 minutes. Add 2 to 4 tablespoons water or juice to skillet as necessary if tomatoes are not juicy. There should be no more than 3 to 4 tablespoons oil and liquid remaining at the end of cooking.

7 **To Serve:** Transfer eggplants to platter. If there is excess liquid, boil to reduce to 3 to 4 tablespoons. Spoon juices over eggplants, cool, and garnish with parsley. Serve eggplant at room temperature with lemon wedges and crusty bread.

Turkish Braised Casserole (Pilaki)

See *Greece: Simmer, Stew, Poach, Boil, and Steam*

Turkish cooks, using a base of olive oil onion, garlic, carrot, potato, tomato or tomato paste, and sugar, make fasulye pilaki with white beans or barbunya pilaki with pink borlotti beans. Fish or mussel pilaki is a classic Turkish meze eaten with bread. Serve pilaki cold or at room temperature garnished with parsley and lemon.

TURKISH BRAISED MUSSELS (MIDYE PILAKISI)

Celery root may be a surprise, but Turks boil it or grate it raw and dress into salads or add to stews. Some versions of mussel pilaki add golden raisins. Frozen prepared mussels in the shell are ideal for this dish.

Yields about 7 cups (4 cups sauce and 3 cups mussel meat), about 4 servings

4 pounds mussels, scrubbed and bearded just before cooking
6 to 7 ounces onion, 1-1/2 cups peeled and finely diced
3/4 ounce garlic, about 3 large cloves, smashed and peeled
1/2 cup olive oil
About 3 ounces carrots, 1/2 cup peeled and finely diced
About 8 ounces potatoes, 1 cup peeled and finely diced
About 2 ounces celery root, 3/4 cup peeled and finely diced
12 ounces tomato, 2 medium, about 1-1/2 cups peeled and diced
2 teaspoons flour
1 ounce trimmed Italian parsley, 1/2 cup finely chopped
2 tablespoons fresh lemon juice, about 1/2 lemon

For Serving

Lemon wedges, seeded
Country bread

1 If using fresh mussels, pour 1 cup water in wide 6- to 8-quart pot. If using frozen mussels, reduce water to 1/2 cup. Bring to a boil over high heat. Add mussels and cover pot. Steam 1 minute and give them a stir. Cover and steam until they open, 1 to 2 minutes. Remove them as they open to a mixing bowl. Reserve all juice and cooking liquid. Reserve pot.

2 Remove mussels from shells and set aside. Strain reserved mussel juice and cooking liquid, and set aside 1 cup. Reserve or freeze any remaining cooking liquid for other seafood dishes.

3 In 6- to 8-quart pot, heat olive oil over medium heat. Add onion and garlic and cook until tender but not browned, 5 minutes. Stir in carrots, potatoes, and celery root and cook until tender, 5 minutes. Pour in 1 cup reserved mussel cooking liquid, bring to a simmer, lower heat, cover pot, and simmer until vegetables are tender, 10 minutes.

4 Uncover pot and whisk in tomato and flour. Season with salt. Simmer pilaki sauce over medium heat, uncovered, until moist, slightly thickened, and reduced, 4 to 5 minutes. (If sauce gets too thick, stir in a little mussel cooking liquid or water.)

5 **To Serve:** Stir in mussels, remove pot from heat and stir in parsley. Taste mussels and season with lemon juice, more salt if necessary, and freshly ground pepper. Serve with lemon wedges and bread.

Source: *Classical Turkish Cooking* by Ayla Algar.

FIGURE 8.31 Wrapping plain rice sarma.

Source: Taratorki/Fotolia.

TURKISH RICE, CURRANT, AND NUT-FILLED GRAPE LEAVES (SARMA)

Romaine lettuce, cabbage, chard, and collards provide Greek and Turkish cooks with leaves for stuffing. The techniques for all are similar and the stuffings often are interchangeable with those for fillo.

Yields about 4-1/2 cups filling, about 40 to 50 dolmades, 6 to 8 servings

Filling

4 tablespoons olive oil
10 to 12 ounces onions, 2-1/2 cups peeled and finely diced
7 ounces short-grain rice, 1 cup
1-3/4 cups vegetable stock or water
About 1-1/2 ounces currants, 1/4 cup
Optional: Zest of 1 lemon
1-1/2 ounces toasted pine nuts, 1/4 cup
1/2 ounce trimmed Italian parsley or dill, 4 tablespoons chopped

50 grape leaves, 1 pound jar
Juice of 1 large lemon, about 1/4 cup
Avgolemono Sauce or Latholemono Sauce

1 *Prepare* filling: Heat olive oil in 4-quart saucepan over medium heat. Stir in onions and cook until soft, 5 to 7 minutes. Stir in rice and cook 1 minute. Stir in stock or water and 1 teaspoon kosher salt and bring to a boil. Lower heat, cover pot, and simmer rice 5 minutes. Remove rice from heat and rest 10 minutes. Toss rice into bowl with currants and optional lemon zest. Cool. Fold in nuts and herbs. Taste rice and season with salt and pepper.

2 **Prepare grape leaves:** Rinse brined grape leaves or fresh grape leaves (or Savoy cabbage or other leaves if desired). Rinse tender leaves or blanch firm or fresh leaves in boiling water until flexible. Tender fresh or brined leaves take 1 minute and tough fresh leaves 3 minutes. Cut away stems. Lay leaves shiny side down. Blot dry. The longer grape leaves are blanched upfront, the less time they need to simmer in the pot.

3 **Fill leaves:** Place *1 to 2 teaspoons filling for small leaves* or *1-1/2 to 2 tablespoons for large leaves* on the base, near the stem. Shape *filling* into cigar shape. Fold leaf sides over filling neatly, then roll from bottom up. Don't roll too tightly: uncooked rice swells. Arrange dolmades, seam side down, snugly in round casserole, pot, or deep skillet in two layers.

4 **Cook sarma:** Pour hot water or stock and fresh lemon juice if using, in around the sides of the casserole. The liquid should barely cover sarma. Cut a circle of parchment to fit casserole and place over sarma and weight with an inverted plate that is slightly smaller than casserole. Bring liquid to a boil, lower heat, and simmer sarma 20 to 30 minutes. Rest sarma off heat 20 to 30 minutes. Remove plate.

5 **To Serve:** The options are:

- Serve stuffed grapes leaves plain, warm or at room temperature.
- Drain off as much liquid as possible and use part to make *Avgolemono Sauce*. Pour hot sauce over sarma in pan and shake to distribute. Serve.
- Cool sarma to warm, and transfer with slotted spoon to platter. Prepare *Avgolemono* or *Ladolemono* sauce and pour over sarma on platter.

CIRCASSIAN POACHED CHICKEN IN WALNUT SAUCE (ÇERKEZ TAVUGU)

The Circassians are one of the oldest indigenous peoples of the Caucasus. Russia deported and killed many Attéghéi or Adighe (Circassians). Most now live in Turkey and the Middle East. Circassian cooks are the only ones in Turkey who use cilantro. Make this ahead for best flavor.

8 to 12 servings

5 pounds chicken breast, leg, or thigh parts
8 to 9 ounces onion, peeled and quartered with root end intact to hold onion quarters together
6 ounces carrots, 1 cup peeled and coarsely chopped
8 peppercorns
2 bay leaves
3 ounces whole cilantro or Italian parsley sprigs, about 6 large sprigs

Garnish

1 tablespoon olive or walnut oil
2 teaspoons paprika

Walnut Sauce

Yields about 3-1/2 cups

1-1/2 ounces crustless white bread, 1 cup torn and packed
8 ounces shelled and broken walnuts, 2 cups
1/2 ounce garlic, 2 large cloves, peeled
1 tablespoon paprika
1/4 teaspoon Aleppo pepper
   or pinch of cayenne pepper
4 tablespoons juice, 2 medium lemons, more to taste

Garnish: Cilantro or Italian parsley leaves

1 **Cook chicken:** Remove skin and fat from chicken pieces, and discard. Rinse chicken and place in 6-quart pot. Pour 5 cups cold water into pot with chicken. Add 1 teaspoon kosher salt, onion, carrots, peppercorns, bay leaves, and cilantro or parsley sprigs. Bring to a boil, lower heat, partially cover pot, and simmer until chicken is cooked through and tender, 30 to 45 minutes.

2 Transfer chicken from pot to a bowl and cool. Remove bones and gristle from cooled chicken and discard. Shred meat or dice into bite-size pieces and set aside in mixing bowl to yield about 8 cups. Remove onion from broth and reserve for sauce, but remove and discard its root. Boil broth until reduced by about half to about 2 cups. Cool slightly and strain. Reserve broth.

3 **Prepare garnish:** Meanwhile, heat 1 tablespoon oil over low heat in small skillet, and stir in 2 teaspoons paprika. Set aside.

4 **Prepare walnut sauce:** Grind reserved cooked onion, bread, walnuts, garlic, and paprika plus Aleppo or cayenne pepper in a food processor until smooth. With machine running, add lemon juice and 1-1/2 cups reserved stock to make a finely puréed, thick sauce of pouring consistency. Taste sauce and season with salt and more lemon juice to taste. Adjust consistency with remaining stock, as needed.

5 **To Serve:** Mix half of the sauce with the reserved chicken. Arrange chicken mixture on a serving platter and pour remaining sauce into bowl for passing at the table. Drizzle chicken with hot paprika oil and garnish with lots of cilantro or parsley leaves. Serve cold or at room temperature. (Use leftover sauce on rice or freeze and use for another dish.)

Vary! Improvise!

☞ **Season:** *Season walnut sauce with ground coriander, allspice, or fresh thyme.*

☞ **Other Meat:** *Prepare this dish with turkey parts or thick white fish fillets and fish cooking broth.*

Pilaf

Pilafs made with rice, bulgar, *freekeh*, wheat berries, or barley show the Ottoman and Persian influences in Greek and Turkish cooking. *Pilavlar* is one of Turkish cuisine's most important dishes and often served as a course by itself, much like Indian *biryanis*. It can be filled with various vegetables, meatballs, dried fruits, beans, or nuts and seasoned elaborately with spices. Grains for pilaf should be sautéed in oil until the outer starch layer hardens before adding liquid. This will keep the grains separate, an important characteristic of a good Turkish or Greek pilaf.

ANCIENT FOOD: FREEKEH

Known in Turkey and the Arabic countries to North Africa, *farik* or *freekeh* is immature, green durum wheat, harvested, dried, and set on fire to roast the grains. Once they are threshed and sun-dried, the grain looks like green bulgar. With an earthy, smoky flavor, it is high in protein and fiber. Turks rarely cook freekeh on its own. Instead they mix it with bulgar or grain, chickpeas, lamb, or chicken to soften its strong, assertive taste.

BULGAR WHEAT PILAF WITH WALNUTS (PILAV)

Bulgar is made from steamed and baked-dry wheat kernels that are ground into fine, medium, and coarse textures. Because it's precooked, bulgar needs little or no cooking, only moisture. It absorbs flavor beautifully. Greeks and Turks love bulgar and use it in many dishes.

Yields about 4 cups, 4 to 6 servings

1 tablespoon olive oil
1 tablespoon unsalted butter, diced
8 to 10 ounces onion, 2 cups peeled and finely diced
5 ounces medium coarse bulgar, about 1 cup
1 bay leaf
5 to 6 ounces toasted walnuts, 1 cup finely chopped
2 ounces trimmed Italian parsley, 1 cup chopped, *divided*

1 Heat a 4-quart saucepan over medium and add oil and butter. When butter melts, add onion and cook until soft, 7 minutes.

2 Bring 1-1/2 cups water to a boil in small saucepan or kettle. Add bulgar to onions and stir and cook 1 minute. Pour in 1-1/2 cups boiling water, bay leaf, and 1/2 teaspoon kosher salt. Bring pilaf to a boil, lower heat, cover, and simmer 5 minutes. Remove pot from heat and rest pilaf 10 minutes. Fold in walnuts and all but 1 tablespoon parsley with fork. Fluff bulgar, don't stir.

3 **To Serve:** Taste bulgar and season with freshly ground pepper and more salt as necessary. Pile pilaf into serving bowl and garnish with reserved parsley.

Vary! Improvise!

☞ *Add other combinations of nuts, dried fruits, and herbs.*
☞ *Sauté other vegetables with onions like finely chopped chard, finely diced carrots, or tomatoes.*
☞ *Toss 1 cup cooked, drained chickpeas into cooked onions with the bulgar.*
☞ *Substitute dill for parsley.*

COOK'S VOICE: MELTEM K. CERVANTES

Turkish Foodie and Writer
New York City

"When I lived in Turkey, as I prepared *mercimek köftes* (lentil and bulgur patties) with my mom, enjoyed *içli köfte* (stuffed bulgur shells) at a restaurant, or a fresh serving of *kisir* (bulgur salad) with my family at tea-time, I took this ingredient, a native of the Eastern Mediterranean for granted . . . It is so ingrained in the culture and the Turkish cuisine that you cannot effectively cover (Turkish food) without dedicating some time to bulgur."

Source: Reprinted with permission of Meltem K. Cervantes.

TURKISH PALACE RICE PILAF

The Ottoman Empire once stretched from Baghdad to Budapest. Their cuisine, heavily influenced by Persia, peaked in the fifteenth and sixteenth centuries. The Topkapi Palace in Istanbul, home to sultans for over 400 years, is synonymous with the excesses of the last days of the Empire, and rich pilafs were a favorite. The sweet and savory combination of rice, currants, nuts, and spices is ubiquitous all around the Mediterranean basin where the Ottoman Empire flourished.

Yields about 7 cups, 4 to 6 servings

14 ounces long-grain white rice like jasmine or basmati, 2 cups
3 to 4 tablespoons clarified butter, *divided*
About 1 ounce blanched whole almonds, 1/4 cup
About 3/4 ounce pine nuts, about 3 tablespoons
About 3-3/4 ounces dried currants, 3/4 cup
1/2 teaspoon ground cinnamon
3 cups chicken stock or water
8 ounces trimmed green onions, about 16 large, 1 to 1-1/2 cups finely sliced
7 black peppercorns
3 whole cloves
1/4 teaspoon saffron
1/2 ounce trimmed Italian parsley, 4 tablespoons minced

1 Soak rice in cold water 15 minutes. Drain.

2 Heat 1/2 tablespoon clarified butter in 4 quart saucepan over medium-high heat and add almonds. Fry until golden, 2 to 3 minutes. Remove almonds with slotted spoon into small bowl. Add 1/2 tablespoon butter and pine nuts. Fry pine nuts until colored, 1 minute. Remove with slotted spoon and place in bowl with almonds. Remove pan from heat and add currants; stir 1 minute and scrape into bowl with nuts. Toss cinnamon into nut-currant mixture. Reserve saucepan.

3 Bring 3 cups stock or water to boil in 2-quart saucepan, cover, and set aside.

4 Heat 1 tablespoon clarified butter in reserved 4-quart saucepan over medium heat and add green onions. Cook until green onions are tender and wilted but bright green, about 1 minute. Scrape into bowl with nuts and currants.

5 Heat remaining tablespoon butter in saucepan over medium high heat and stir in drained rice, 1-1/2 teaspoons kosher salt, peppercorns, cloves, and saffron. Cook until rice begins to stick to pan and whiten slightly, 1 to 2 minutes. Stir in boiling stock or water, bring rice back up to boil, lower heat, and cover pan. Cook rice 12 minutes, turn off the heat and rest rice 10 minutes.

6 **To Serve:** Fluff rice and gently fold in green onion-nut-currant mixture and parsley. Taste rice and season with more salt as necessary. Serve immediately.

Source: *The Ottoman Kitchen* by Sarah Woodward.

TURKISH DUMPLINGS: MANTI

Manti are a type of dumpling made with flour and water dough, usually filled with spiced lamb, beef, chicken, or even quail, boiled or steamed and topped with yogurt and mint-infused butter or sumac. Manti probably originated in Central Asia and came to Anatolia by Turkic and Mongol horsemen who carried frozen or dried manti as sustenance. There are many different types and sizes of Turkish, Central Asian, and Caucasian manti.

FIGURE 8.32 Manti.

Source: Steshkin Yevgeniy/Shutterstock

SAUTÉ, PAN-FRY, AND DEEP-FRY

Turkish Borek

These savory pastries are a large and beloved part of Turkish cuisine. The best *borek* use homemade dough rolled and stretched very thin, but commercial fillo dough can take its place. Fillings vary from feta, eggs, and herbs to ground veal with chilies, tomatoes, dill, and parsley and beyond to lamb and pistachio, spinach and onions, or the ubiquitous chicken with cumin seed, pine nuts, chilies, and currants. Borek can be baked, or fried as the "cigar" rolls below. All are luscious and make a perfect light lunch or meze.

TURKISH CIGAR ROLLS (SIGARA BOREGI)

The yogurt-garlic sauce is popular served with grilled and stuffed vegetables, pilafs, cooked greens, and boreks. It is mild flavored. Spark it up with a little sumac or fresh lemon juice and Lebanese dried red pepper: aleppo, kirmizi, maras or urfa.

Makes about 31 with 1-1/2 tablespoons filling each to about 40 with 1 rounded tablespoon

Yogurt-Garlic Sauce (Sarmisaki Yogurt Sos)

1 cup thick whole milk yogurt
1/2 ounce garlic, 2 large cloves, 1 tablespoon peeled and minced

Filling

Yields about 3 cups

12 ounces feta cheese, 3 cups well crumbled
1 ounce trimmed Italian parsley, about 4 tablespoons finely minced
1 ounce trimmed green onions, 2 large, 4 tablespoons finely minced
1 large egg yolk

About 8 ounces commercial fillo: eight 14-inch by 18-inch sheets (each sheet yields 4 rolls)
Olive oil for frying

1 **Make the sauce:** Mix together yogurt, garlic, salt and freshly ground pepper, to taste. Rest sauce at room temperature or in refrigerator.

2 **Prepare the filling:** In a bowl, mix crumbled feta, parsley, green onions, egg yolk, and freshly ground black pepper.

3 **Prepare fillo:** For 32 rolls: Stack 8 sheets of fillo. On the long (18-inch) side, cut four 4-1/2-inch wide strips (they will be 14 inches long). Keep fillo covered. Wrap unused sheets and refreeze or refrigerate up to 1 week. For sturdier rolls with double the fillo see *Vary! Improvise!*

4 **Fill rolls:** Near short end of one strip, place 1-1/2 tablespoons feta mixture. Fold up sides so they almost meet in the center over filling. Roll up fillo to form a cigar shape. Moisten edge and seal cigar. Place on sheet pan, seam side down. Cover tightly with plastic wrap. Repeat with remaining strips and remaining filling.

5 Over medium-high heat, heat 1/4-inch oil in 10-inch skillet. When oil is wavy but not smoking, place rolls in. They should sizzle. Fry rolls until evenly golden and crisp, about 1-1/2 to 2 minutes per side. Drain on paper towels. Reheat rolls in 350 degree F oven 5 to 10 minutes.

6 **To Serve:** Transfer rolls to serving platter. Serve hot as an appetizer or meze with *Yogurt-Garlic Sauce* on the side.

Turkish Mücver

Meat, vegetables, eggs, flour, breadcrumbs, potatoes, and split peas can, alone or together, form the base of *mücver*. These savory Turkish (or Greek) fried patties, balls, or fritters are similar to Middle Eastern *kofte*, *kibbeh*, or *falafel*.

TURKISH FRITTERS (MÜCVER)

Yields about 2-1/2 cups batter, enough for twenty 2-tablespoon-sized balls (about 1-inch diameter) or ten 1/4-cup-sized patties (1-1/2 to 2 inches)

16 ounces zucchini, 3 medium, 3 cups trimmed and grated or shredded
4 ounces green onion, about, 8, about 1 cup finely diced
2 ounces feta, about 1/3 cup crumbled
About 4-1/2 ounces all-purpose flour, 1 cup, more as needed
1/2 ounce trimmed Italian parsley, 1/4 cup finely chopped
1/4 ounce mint leaves, 2 tablespoons chopped
  or 1 tablespoon dried mint
1 large egg, beaten
Olive oil and canola oil for frying

For Serving

Cacik or *Yogurt-Garlic Sauce (Sarmisaki Yogurt Sos)*

1 Toss zucchini and onion with 2 teaspoons kosher salt and transfer to strainer. Drain vegetables 20 to 30 minutes. Strongly squeeze out excess moisture to yield about 1 cup zucchini.

2 In a mixing bowl, toss zucchini and green onion with cheese, 1 cup flour, herbs, egg, and 1 teaspoon kosher salt. Season with freshly ground black pepper. Mixture should be just firm enough to form balls. Adjust with more flour if necessary.

3 With oiled hands, form zucchini mixture into 1-, 2-, or 4-tablespoon-sized balls (or patties) and roll into flour. Set balls or patties aside on parchment-covered sheet pan and refrigerate until ready to cook, at least 15 minutes.

4 In a heavy 10- to 12-inch skillet, heat half olive and half canola oil 1-inch deep over medium-high heat. When oil is hot (360 degrees F), but not smoking, drop fritters into oil and fry until brown, 3 to 5 minutes per side. Work in batches. Drain mücver on paper towels and keep warm.

5 **To Serve:** Transfer warm mücver to serving platter. Serve with *Cacik* or *Yogurt-Garlic Sauce (Sarmisaki Yogurt Sos)* on the side.

Vary! Improvise!

☞ *Sturdier Rolls: Instead of making rolls with one strip of fillo, layer 2 strips together, fill, and roll. This will require another 8 sheets fillo, about 1 pound total.*

☞ *Freeze rolls cooked or uncooked for later use.*

☞ *Change the herb or cheese.*

☞ *Instead of rolling, fold the borek flag-like into triangles and fry.*

GRILL, GRIDDLE, ROAST, BROIL, BAKE, AND BARBECUE

Turkish Kebobs (Sis Kebab)

The word *kebab* is from Persian; it originally meant fried meat. This technique probably originated with cooks who were in short supply of cooking fuel. For Turkish *sis kebab*, cooks skewer chunks of meat, seafood, vegetable, or seasoned meatballs (*köfte*) onto different styles of metal skewers, and grill them. Like their Greek counterparts, Turkish cooks marinate cubed lamb in olive oil, lemon, and herbs *or* Persian-style yogurt, tomato paste, cayenne, and paprika.

Köfte or meatballs threaded onto a flat skewer (shish) and grilled are known as *shish köfte*. Turkish köftesi are balls or patties, usually meat but sometimes made of cooked lentils, bulgar, and seasonings, related to Middle Eastern *kibbeh kabobs*, Georgian *kotelettis*, and Indian *kofta*. Chef Paula Wolfert recommends removing *köfte* made with low-fat meat from skewers when half-done. To maintain juiciness, she simmers them in a sauce until finished, much like Indian cooks do with *kofta curry*.

TURKISH FISH KEBABS

1-1/2 pounds trimmed protein yields about 4 servings

1-1/2 pounds firm white fish like swordfish, 1- to 1-1/2-inch-thick slab

Marinade

4 tablespoons fresh lemon juice, 1 to 2 large lemons
4 tablespoons extra virgin olive oil
1 teaspoon paprika
For Skewering: 16 fresh bay leaves

For Serving

Rice *or* pita bread
Walnut Tarator
1 lemon, quartered

1 **Prepare fish:** Remove excess fat and gristle from meat. Dice fish into 1- to 1-1/2-inch cubes.

2 **Whisk together marinade:** Toss with fish and marinate 10 to 15 minutes. Heat grill or broiler to medium-high.

3 **Bay leaves:** Bring a small saucepan of water to a boil. Remove pot from heat and rest leaves in hot water 5 minutes. Drain.

4 Shake off excess marinade from meat or seafood. Thread an equal number of cubes of meat or seafood, with bay leaf in between each if using, per metal skewer. Season meat or seafood with salt and pepper. Place skewers on grill or 3 to 4-inches from broiler. Grill fish and turn and baste with marinade, until just done, 6 to 8 minutes for swordfish cubes.

5 **To Serve:** Transfer kebabs to serving platter or plate. Serve atop rice *or* folded into pita bread with *Walnut Tarator* and lemon wedges on the side.

NORTHERN TURKISH GROUND MEATBALL KABOBS (KOFTE)

It's also traditional to serve köfte with a choice of hummus, sliced onions, salad greens, bulgar pilaf, pickles, or Warm Eggplant Salad.

Yields about 3 cups, enough for eight 2-1/2-inch patties *or* twenty-four 1-inch patties

1-1/2 pounds lean ground lamb or beef
1/3 ounce Italian parsley, 1/3 cup minced
1/2 ounce garlic, 2 large cloves, 1 tablespoon peeled and minced
1 teaspoon *Turkish Spice Blend* (*Baharat*)
2-1/2 teaspoons kosher salt
1/4 teaspoon Aleppo chili pepper
   or 1 teaspoon *Turkish Red Chili and Pepper Paste*, more to taste
1 tablespoon all-purpose flour
4 tablespoons soda water

For Shaping

Olive oil
4 or 8 flat-sided long metal skewers

For Serving

2 lemons, quartered into wedges, seeded
Turkish Flatbread
Parsley or mint leaves
Turkish Chopped Salads

FIGURE 8.33 Northern Turkish ground meatball kabobs (kofte) and Southern Turkish adana kabob top of photo: Lebanese flatbread (khobz arabi) right of photo: Turkish chopped salad: green olive and walnut salad (yetyin piyazi).

1 **Mix ground meat with seasonings:** Mix meat, parsley, garlic, baharat, salt, pepper, or chili and pepper paste, flour, and soda water until well blended. Soda water or plain water lightens the meat texture. Chill meat 1 hour.

2 Heat a grill or broiler. Place a small bowl of olive oil, meat, sheet pan, and metal skewers on work surface.

3 **Shape meat:** Oil hands lightly. Divide meat into 8 equal-sized balls (about a heaping 1/3 cup each). Mold 2 balls onto each of 4 metal flat skewers. Or shape each into fat oval or round patties.

4 Grill or broil meatballs over medium-low heat until firm and crusty on one side, 4 to 6 minutes. Turn once and finish remaining side until meat is cooked through to desired doneness.

5 **To Serve:** Remove meatballs from skewer and serve with chopped salad or yogurt, Turkish flatbread and *ayran* (yogurt drink whisked with water and salt).

Source: *The Cooking of the Eastern Mediterranean* by Paula Wolfert.

Chef at Hasan Kolcuoğlu Restaurant Adana, Turkey

"The Adana kebab is made with male mutton and hand-minced. Tomato paste and various spices should never be added to the meat, only salt and red pepper. Otherwise, (the) good traditional flavor is spoiled. It is served with green vegetables and onion salad. Also, spicy turnip juice, which is as famous as Adana kebab, should not be forgotten."

Source: Courtesy of Sabhattin Kolcuoğlu.

Vary! Improvise!

☞ Prepare kabob with ground chicken. Add 2 tablespoons olive oil if using breast meat.

SOUTHERN TURKISH ADANA KABOB

This long, spicy, ground meat kabob comes from Adana, on the Mediterranean in south-central Turkey. Some cooks add finely ground fresh breadcrumbs, flour, or egg white to strengthen the meat mixture. Kirmizi biber or oiled, roasted red chili is the traditional seasoning.

Yields about 5 cups, 8 servings

3 ounces trimmed Italian parsley, 1 cup minced and loosely packed
2 to 4 three-inch dried red chilies, about 1 tablespoon stemmed, seeded, and minced
   or 1 to 2 tablespoons *kirmizi biber*
      or 2 to 4 teaspoons red chili or Aleppo chili flakes
3/4 ounce garlic, 3 large cloves, 4-1/2 teaspoons peeled and minced
2 teaspoons kosher salt
1 teaspoon freshly ground black pepper
2-1/2 pounds ground lamb

For Shaping

Olive oil
4 or 8 flat, wide and long metal sword-skewers

For Serving

2 lemons, quartered into wedges, seeded
Turkish Flatbread
Parsley or mint leaves
Turkish Chopped Salads

1 **Mix ground lamb (or meat) with seasonings:** Place parsley, chilies, and garlic in food processor and process until evenly minced. Add meat and process parsley mixture, salt, pepper with lamb until evenly distributed. Slap and knead meat until dough-like, 5 minutes. Refrigerate meat 1 hour to overnight.

2 Heat a grill or broiler. Place a small bowl of olive oil, meat, sheet pan, and metal skewers on work surface.

3 **Shape meat:** Oil hands very lightly. Make 8 balls about 1/2 heaping cup, the size of a large egg, and set on sheet pan. Mold each meat "egg" onto a skewer and pat into a long, narrow sausage about 3/4-inch wide. Set skewer on sheet pan and finish preparing remaining kabobs.

4 Grill or broil Adana kabobs until done, 2 to 3 minutes per side.

5 **To Serve:** Remove Adana kabobs from skewers and slice into serving-sized pieces. Serve meat with lemons, flat bread, parsley or mint, and chopped salads.

DONER KEBAB, THE ROTATING ROAST

Originating in Turkey or the Middle East, this giant "kabob" made of ground lamb or various meats packed onto a vertical spit, reaches around the world. Also known as Arabic *shwarma* or Greek *gyro*, in Turkey it's known as *doner kebab*. Each country serves it slightly differently. The meat is roast/grilled and sliced off when cooked. Turks and Greeks serve it as a sandwich in a pita with lettuce, tomato, onion, and *cacik* or *tzatziki*. *Arab shwarma* is served in pita, with tahini sauce, garlic mayonnaise, or hot sauce.

FIGURE 8.34 Doner kebab with sliced meat.

Source: Faraways/Fotolia.

TURKISH BAKED STEW: GUVECH

This quintessential Turkish stew consists of lamb (or other meat or seafood) layered with green beans, zucchini or eggplant, potatoes, tomatoes, bell peppers, and pearl onions in a lidded clay pot. It is seasoned with garlic and thyme or spices. Guvech was originally baked in the coals of a *tandir* oven (much like an Indian *tandoori* oven): the secret to a sensational guvech is slow cooking. Guvec may also be meatless.

Turkish Filled Boats (Pide) or Topped "Pizza" (Lahmacun)

Pide is an ancient, traditional Anatolian dish. A thin-crusted flatbread dough shaped to resemble a boat is filled with a variety of richly flavored, aromatic items like ground lamb or braised meat, fish, or vegetables, feta cheese, spicy red peppers, *pastirma* (spicy Turkish pastrami), *sucuk* (spicy Turkish pepperoni), potatoes, and onions with cheese or even shrimp. Pide are baked in a wood fire oven until the crust is crunchy and browned.

Lahmacun, originally from Armenia, resemble pide, but their shapes differ. Lahmacun are thin and round and the typical ground meat topping is pasty. Lahmacun is often served rolled up with fresh Italian parsley or mint while pide are sliced.

TURKISH FLATBREAD DOUGH

Lower-gluten all-purpose flour produces a tender, soft dough that works well for flatbreads, pide, or lahmacun.

Yields two 10-inch flatbreads *or* eight 6-inch by 12-inch oval pides *or* eight 8-inch round lahmacun

Yields about 2 pounds dough

Sponge

4 teaspoons active dry yeast
1/2 teaspoon sugar
1/2 cup lukewarm water
About 2-1/2 ounces unbleached all-purpose flour, 1/2 cup

Dough

1 teaspoon kosher salt
3 tablespoons olive oil
1 cup lukewarm water
14 to 17 ounces unbleached flour, 3 to 3-1/2 cups
Olive oil for oiling dough

1 **Prepare the sponge:** Mix yeast, sugar, and water together in a large mixing bowl and rest until foamy, 10 minutes. Stir in 1/2 cup flour and cover bowl. Set in warm spot 30 minutes to rise.

2 **Prepare the dough:** Make a well in the center of the sponge and pour in salt, olive oil, and water. Stir to mix and immediately stir in 3 cups flour. Gather up dough (it will be rough) into a ball and knead until dough is tender, moist, and springy, 3 to 5 minutes. The oil in the dough should keep it from sticking, but if the flour is low in gluten, the extra 1/2 cup flour will be needed. Dough should be moist and soft but not sticky. Oil dough, place in bowl, cover with plastic wrap, and set aside to rise in warm spot until doubled, about 1 hour.

3 **Press and divide dough:** Press dough to deflate. For **plain flatbreads**, divide dough into 2 balls (about 16 ounces each). For **pide** or **lahmacun**, divide it into 8 equal balls (about 4 ounces each). Cover dough and rest it 5 to 10 minutes.

   *Dough may be refrigerated 1 day in zipper baggie. After 1 hour in refrigerator, press and deflate dough. Bring dough back to room temperature 30 minutes before using.

4 **Choose a bread and shape according to instructions.** Prepare *Glaze for Plain Flatbreads, Cheese Filling for Pide,* or *Meat Topping for Lahmacun* for chosen bread. For filling or topping recipes see *Turkish Flatbread Glaze, Filling and Topping.*

Source: *Classical Turkish Cooking* by Ayla Algar.

FIGURE 8.35   Glazed flatbread (pide).
Source: OZMedia/Shutterstock.

Glazed, Filled, and Topped Flatbreads: Pide and Lahmacun

The glaze, filling, and topping are just a few of the many that Turkish cooks have created ranging from spicy sausage and tomato to onions and leeks or potatoes, onions, chilies, and cumin to bananas with sour cream and honey! Fillings for *borek* and *pide* are often interchangeable.

PLAIN GLAZED TURKISH FLATBREAD (PIDE)

1 recipe *Turkish Flatbread Dough*
2 large eggs, about 1/2 cup beaten
2 tablespoons nigella *or* sesame seeds

1 Thirty-minutes before baking, place overturned sheet pan or quarry tiles into oven and preheat to 475 to 500 degrees F.

2 On lightly floured work surface, roll flatbreads out into a 10-inch round. Transfer to a half sheet of parchment paper. Dip fingers in egg and press and drag them across the flatbread. Sprinkle with nigella or sesame seeds. Holding two ends of dough disk, stretch it into 9-inch by 15-inch oval. Slide parchment and dough onto pan or hot tiles and bake until golden, 5 to 8 minutes.

3 Remove flatbread from oven, and wrap in clean dry towel or cotton napkin. Repeat process with second dough ball. Eat flatbread immediately while warm.

Source: *Classical Turkish Cooking* by Ayla Algar.

CHEESE-FILLED FLATBREAD (PEYNIRLI PIDE)

Filling

Yields about 4 cups

About 12 ounces feta, cottage, or goat cheese, 3 cups well crumbled
1 ounce trimmed dill, 1/2 cup chopped
1 to 2 ounces trimmed green onions, 2 to 4 large, 1/4 to 1/2 cup finely minced
2 large eggs, about 1/2 cup lightly beaten

1 recipe *Turkish Flatbread Dough*

1 Thirty-minutes before baking, place overturned sheet pan or quarry tiles into oven and preheat to 475 to 500 degrees F.

2 Mix **filling** ingredients together.

3 On lightly floured work surface, roll, shape, and stretch 1 dough ball into a 6-inch by 12-inch oval. Transfer to half sheet of parchment. Spread 1/8 of cheese filling (about 1/2 cup) on oval, leaving a 1/2-inch border along the edges. Fold up edges and pinch both ends to form an open canoe shape. Slide parchment and dough onto hot pans or tiles, and bake until golden and crusty, 6 to 8 minutes.

4 Remove pide from oven and brush with oil or butter. Keep warm in covered serving dish or hotel pan covered with foil. Repeat process with remaining 7 dough balls. Serve pide in slices while hot, or reheat wrapped in foil.

Source: *Classical Turkish Cooking* by Ayla Algar.

FIGURE 8.36 Cheese-filled pide.
Source: oocoskun/Fotolia.

Vary! Improvise!

☞ *Filled Pide-Kapelli Roll dough as for pide, fill, and fold longest edges up to cover filling. Pinch edges to seal "boat" shut.*

FIGURE 8.37 Preparing a traditional Turksh lahmacun with meat.

Source: Brian Chase/Shutterstock.

Vary! Improvise!

☞ *Prepare zucchini or eggplant filling for pide. Dice zucchini or eggplant (salt, rest, and drain eggplant). Sauté onion and garlic in olive oil and add zucchini or eggplant. Cook until tender and stir in tomato paste, parsley or mint, and red pepper flakes. Cool and season with salt and pepper.*

SPICY MEAT-TOPPED "PIZZA" (LAHMACUN)

Topping

Yields 7 to 8 cups

16 ounces ground lamb
6 to 9 ounces red onion, 1-1/2 to 2 cups finely diced or minced
1/2 ounce garlic, 2 large cloves, 1 tablespoon peeled and minced
28-ounce can peeled tomatoes, about 2 cups squeeze-drained and finely diced, juice reserved
2 to 3 ounces peppers *or* chilies, 1/2 cup stemmed, seeded, and finely diced
1 teaspoon Aleppo chili
    or red pepper flakes
1/2 ounce trimmed Italian parsley, 1/2 cup chopped
1/4 ounce mint leaves, 1/4 cup chopped

1 recipe *Turkish Flatbread Dough*
Olive oil for brushing top of dough

Garnish

Italian parsley leaves
Fresh lemon juice

1 Thirty-minutes before baking, place overturned sheet pan or quarry tiles into oven and preheat to 475 to 500 degrees F.

2 **Prepare topping:** Knead meat, onion, garlic, tomatoes, peppers or chilies and flakes, parsley, and mint together. Season with 1 teaspoon kosher salt and freshly ground pepper. (In Armenia cooks grind the ingredients together until filling has the consistency of hummus before spreading and baking.) Topping should be loose enough to spread easily, but not watery. Stir in a little reserved tomato juice, if necessary.

3 On lightly floured work surface, roll 1 ball into an 8-inch round 1/4- to 1/8-inch thick. (For thicker, chewier dough make them smaller and thicker.) Transfer rounds to half sheet of parchment. It's possible to make *lahcumun* into small, thick, bite-sized rounds for party food (they are called *findik lahmacun*, meaning the size of a walnut).

4 Brush top of dough with olive oil and spread 1/8 of meat topping (about 1 cup) into a thin layer to the edges. Slide parchment and dough onto hot pans or tiles. Bake until golden and meat is done, 5 to 7 minutes. Lahmacun should be crisp at the edges and softer under the topping.

5 Stack lahmacun in a hotel pan in warm spot to keep warm. Repeat process with remaining 7 dough balls.

6 **To Serve:** Serve lahmacun hot, rolled up with fresh parsley and a squeeze of lemon juice. Reheat extras wrapped in foil.

Source: *Classical Turkish Cooking* by Ayla Algar.

FIGURE 8.38   Lahmacun.

Source: khz/Shutterstock.

BELOVED TURKISH BREAD: SIMIT

FIGURE 8.39   Simit, traditional Turkish bread.

Source: bernanamoglu/Fotolia.

Simit, a crisp, chewy, twisted clay-oven baked ring studded with sesame seeds, is highly popular with Turkish people. Simit is sold throughout Turkey by vendors who carry them by tray loads or in special carts. For a recipe go to *Classical Turkish Cooking* by Ayla Algar.

SALAD AND VEGETABLE METHODS

SIGNATURE RECIPE

TURKISH CHOPPED SALADS (PIYAZLAR)

Onion and Sumac (Sogan Piyazi)

Yields 1-3/4 cups

8 to 10 ounces red onions, 2 cups peeled and finely slivered or sliced
3/4 teaspoon kosher or sea salt
1 teaspoon sumac powder
1/4 teaspoon ground red or Aleppo pepper
2 ounces trimmed Italian parsley, 1 cup coarsely chopped

Eggplant Salad

Yields about 3 cups

2 to 3 ounces onion, 1/2 cup peeled and slivered
1/2 teaspoon kosher or sea salt
1-1/2 pounds eggplant
3 tablespoons fresh lemon juice, 1 large lemon, more to taste, *divided*
About 1 pound tomatoes, 2 medium-large, 1-1/2 cups grilled, peeled, seeded
Optional: 2 teaspoons slivered medium-hot green chili
1 ounce green bell pepper or Italian green pepper, 1/4 cup seeded and slivered
1/3 to 1/2 ounce trimmed Italian parsley, 3 tablespoons chopped
2 tablespoons olive oil

Green Olive and Walnut (Zetyin Piyazi)

Yield 2-1/2 cups

About 15 ounces pitted or pimento-stuffed big green olives, 2 cups quartered
lengthwise and sliced crosswise
4 tablespoons olive oil
About 6 ounces walnuts, 1-1/2 cups finely chopped
2 ounces trimmed green onions, 4 large, 1/2 cup finely chopped
2 ounces stemmed Italian parsley, 1 cup chopped
1 to 2 teaspoons *Turkish Red Chili and Pepper Paste*
    or 1/2 teaspoon Aleppo pepper, to taste
4 teaspoons pomegranate molasses
2 tablespoons fresh lemon juice, 1/2 large lemon

1 Choose a salad. Gather and chop the ingredients. Ingredients must be diced, slivered, or chopped finely enough so they can be scooped with pita or bread.

2 Marinate and cook ingredients:

Onion and Sumac Salad *or* **Eggplant Salad**
Toss raw onion with salt and leave to wilt 15 minutes. Lightly squeeze and drain.

Eggplant Salad
Grill or broil eggplant over low heat until skin blackens and interior is soft, 20 to 30 minutes. Remove skin and stem, dice flesh into 1-inch cubes, and toss with 1 tablespoon lemon juice. Scrape eggplant into strainer set over a bowl. Drain well. Grill or broil tomatoes until skin shrivels, then peel, seed, and dice them. Drain.

3 **Finish salads:** Toss or fold together remaining salad ingredients (remaining lemon juice for eggplant) for chosen salad. Taste and adjust flavors. They should be bright and assertive.

4 **To Serve:**

Set *Green Olive* or *Onion Sumac* salads aside 1 hour to overnight in refrigerator before serving.

Set *Eggplant Salad* aside 15 minutes. Taste and re-season. Reheat *Eggplant Salad* if necessary and serve warm drizzled with olive oil.

Source: *The Cooking of the Eastern Mediterranean* by Paula Wolfert.

Mediterranean Bean Salads

Classic *piyaz* or Turkish bean salads with white beans and salt-wilted onion dressed with oil, vinegar, and pepper flakes may have additions like tomatoes, parsley, hard-boiled eggs, green onions, or sumac. In southern Turkey, along the Mediterranean, tahini and garlic find their way into bean salads.

TURKISH WHITE BEAN SALAD (FASÜLYE PIYAZI)

Yields about 8 cups, 6 to 8 servings

About 21 ounces white beans like Great Northern, 3 cups
 or 7 cups drained, cooked white beans
8 to 9 ounces red onion, 2 cups finely slivered, tossed with salt 15 minutes, and drained
2 to 3 ounce Italian or Cubanelle pepper, 3/4 cup stemmed, seeded, and thinly sliced
About 2-1/2 ounces pitted black Kalamata olives, 1/2 cup diced
1/4 ounce mint leaves, 1/4 cup chopped
1 ounce trimmed Italian parsley, 1/2 cup chopped
1/2 cup red wine vinegar, more as needed
1/2 to 3/4 cup olive oil

Garnish: Chopped Italian parsley

1 **Prepare legumes:** Quick-soak beans by covering with boiling water and 1 tablespoon kosher salt for 1 hour. Drain, and rinse beans. Place beans into 4-quart saucepan, cover with cold water, and bring to a boil. Reduce the heat, cover pot, and simmer beans until tender, 40 to 60 minutes. Cool beans, and drain off liquid (it can be used as a base for vegetarian soups).

2 **Prepare salad ingredients:** Onion, pepper, olives, and herbs.

3 Leave onions raw or cook them slightly before adding to legumes. Here are 4 methods to soften their raw bite:

- Place onions in a strainer and pour boiling water over.
- Microwave onions briefly, about 30 seconds to 1 minute.
- Toss 8 ounces sliced onion with 1 teaspoon kosher salt, rest 15 minutes, squeeze-drain.
- Sweat or sauté onions in a little olive oil.

4 Toss onion, pepper, olives, and herbs into warm, cooked beans. Dress salad with vinegar and oil. Season salad well with salt and freshly ground pepper. Taste. Rest salad 1 hour, taste again and re-season if necessary.

5 **To Serve:** Pile bean salad high on serving platter. Garnish with extra parsley, and serve at room temperature.

WARM TURKISH TAHINI AND POMEGRANATE BEANS

Serve this bean salad with rice, on salad greens, or as a side dish. Make it a day or two ahead and re-warm before serving. Cilantro imparts a subtle meatiness.

Yields 7 cups, 6 to 8 servings

About 21 ounces dry cannellini (white kidney) beans, 3 cups
   or 7 cups drained, cooked cannellini beans
2 teaspoons cumin seed
1 teaspoon paprika
2 to 3 teaspoons olive oil
About 1 ounce walnuts, 1/4 cup
1/2 ounce garlic, 2 large cloves, 1 tablespoon peeled and minced
4 tablespoons fresh lemon juice, 1 to 2 lemons
2 tablespoons red wine vinegar
2 tablespoons pomegranate syrup
3 tablespoons Arabic (loose) tahini
1 tablespoon bean cooking water *or* water
1 ounce cilantro, 1/2 cup finely sliced
   or 1 ounce trimmed Italian parsley, 1/2 cup coarsely chopped

1 Quick-soak beans by covering with boiling water and 1 tablespoon kosher salt for 1 hour. Drain, and rinse beans. Place beans into 4-quart saucepan, cover with cold water, and bring to a boil. Reduce the heat, cover pot, and simmer beans until tender, 40 to 60 minutes. If using precooked or canned beans, drain. Preheat oven to 375 degrees F.

2 Heat a small sauté pan over medium heat and add cumin seed. Toast seeds dry, shaking pan, until fragrant, 1 minute. Pour onto small plate and set aside. Reheat pan and add paprika and oil. Remove pan from heat and set aside.

3 Spread walnuts on sheet pan and place in oven. Toast walnuts until fragrant and roasted, 12 to 15 minutes. Remove pan from oven. Pour nuts into small bowl and cool. Chop lightly, and set aside.

4 Drain cooked warm beans or pour cold beans into a heavy pot over low heat, heat gently until warmed through, and remove from heat. Fold in garlic, lemon juice, vinegar, pomegranate syrup, tahini, water, 2 teaspoons kosher or sea salt, and toasted cumin seed. Taste beans, adjust flavor. Fold in cilantro or parsley.

5 **To Serve:** Pile warm beans into a serving bowl, garnish with walnuts and paprika oil. Serve.

Vary! Improvise!

☞ *Substitute sumac powder for paprika.*

REVIEW QUESTIONS

Greece

1. What are the three core foods that Greek cuisine has relied upon for centuries?
2. What is a meze? Name one.
3. What were early cultural influences on Greek cuisine?
4. How is olive oil produced?
5. What are dolmades?
6. What are two types of fillo dough? Discuss how they are made.
7. Name one island that is part of Greece. Discuss its cuisine.

Turkey

1. Discuss the main influences on the formation of Turkish cuisine. What are the two cuisines that make up modern Turkish cooking?
2. Discuss foods that Turks and Greek share.
3. What are four herbs used most often in Turkish cooking?
4. What is sumac? How is it used?
5. What is a kofte? How is it made?

UNIT III

EASTERN MEDITERRANEAN (CAUCASUS) AND MIDDLE EAST

CHAPTER NINE

LEBANON: THE HEART OF THE MIDDLE EAST

CHAPTER TEN

THE MIDDLE EAST AND CAUCASUS: PERSIA-IRAN AND REPUBLIC OF GEORGIA

LEBANON: THE HEART OF THE MIDDLE EAST

This chapter will:

- Introduce the long history of Lebanon, its geography, religious and cultural influences, and climate.

- Discuss Lebanon's important location at the edge of the Fertile Crescent, bordering the Eastern Mediterranean.

- Introduce Lebanon's culinary culture, its influence on other Middle East and Eastern Mediterranean countries, its two main culinary regions and dining etiquette.

- Identify Lebanese and Middle Eastern foods, flavor foundations, seasoning devices, and favored cooking techniques.

- Teach the techniques and succulent dishes of the Lebanon and the Middle East.

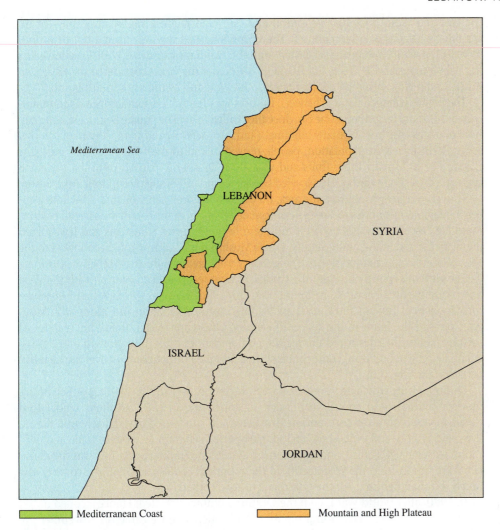

| Mediterranean Coast | Mountain and High Plateau |

FIGURE 9.1 Map of Lebanon.

Small Country, Big Influence

Author Claudia Roden describes Lebanon in Arabesque: A Taste of Morocco, Turkey and Lebanon *as "less than half the size of Wales." She muses how the cooking can differ so much in a country so small. Lebanon may be small, but it is a country of vast contrasts from a Muslim and Christian population with differing culinary needs, a long, narrow Mediterranean shore to tall mountains with deep, valleys. The regions produce food and dishes from three climate zones: warm Mediterranean, cold and snowy mountains and isolated valleys, where cooks still follow ages-old culinary traditions with local food. Famed village dishes from the mountains and valleys have spread to other parts of Lebanon and to the rest of the world. Roden observes that these simple dishes have formed the menu of Lebanese restaurants everywhere.*

This lush, rugged, and fertile land is tiny: only 30 miles wide and 135 miles long. Since ancient times, out of proportion to its size, Lebanon has played an important part in history. Centrally located in the Middle East, Lebanon lies along the eastern Mediterranean coast on the edge of the Fertile Crescent, where historians believe Western civilization began, and in the center of the *Silk Road*, an ancient East-West crossroads. Famous for its temperate climate, varied geography, abundant produce, and cedar, pine, and olive trees, *Lebanon* comes from the root word *lubnan* or "white," and refers to Lebanon's snowy peaks.

The first settlers to the modern-day Lebanon were Semitic Canaanites, later called *Phoenicians*. The Phoenicians developed the first Western alphabet. They established city-states along the Mediterranean coastline from which they navigated, and traded spices, grains, preserved foods and wine, and acted as commercial and cultural middlemen between the East and West. Phoenicia's location and rich land made it highly appealing for invasions by a series of other cultures. The Egyptians ruled the area from 1484 BCE until 1150 BCE. A short independence lasted until the Assyrians came in 857 BCE, followed by the Babylonians and Persians. In 333 BCE, Alexander the Great conquered the Egyptian-influenced region, bringing the first taste of the West and a culinary sophistication.

The Romans merged the area between the northern Taurus and southern Sinai Mountains (often called the *Levant*) into one province they called *Syria*. They made Beirut a leading cultural center by constructing many buildings (and a law school) and giving it Roman colonial status. With increased population, people moved inland to the fertile foothills and grew grapes, figs, and many other fruits and vegetables. Prosperity reigned until the mid-sixth century, when severe earthquakes leveled coastal towns and brought economic devastation.

Though Muslims conquered the area, they mostly ignored Lebanon and it became a haven to religious minorities seeking safety from persecution. At the end of the seventh century, Maronite Eastern Catholics settled in northern Lebanon. Later, Christians and Jews joined them. By the end of the ninth century, Druze Muslim missionaries brought followers to the southwestern Anti-Lebanon slopes. Their dietary rules greatly influenced Lebanese cuisine.

The eleventh century brought the *Crusaders*, who reconnected Lebanon with the West and made it part of Jerusalem. By the mid-thirteenth century, the Egyptian *Mameluks*, former slaves of Turkish and Circassian descent, captured Lebanon and, along with Mongols, ravaged the land. In the sixteenth century, Ottomans ousted them, but a series of earthquakes further destroyed the region, and epidemics caused by drought and famine decimated the population. Trade routes shifted and the Portuguese took over the lucrative Lebanese trading routes.

Ottoman rule, which arose in the sixteenth century, began the shaping of Lebanon's modern borders, and contributed much to enrich the cuisine. Southern feudal lord *Fakhr el-Deen II* annexed surrounding provinces and conquered city-states Beirut, Sidon, Tyre, and Tripoli, and unified the region. He opened Lebanon to Western trade and education with French, British, and Italian missionaries and trading posts. Silk was the major Lebanese export from the seventeenth to the twentieth century. In 1860 the country saw much sectarian fighting, but the Ottomans restored order.

In 1920, after World War I, with the Ottoman Empire defeated, France stepped in, set borders, and declared Lebanon a republic. Full independence came on November 26, 1941, but the French stayed until 1946. Lebanon began to rebuild trade and regain prosperity. From 1975 to 1990, a major civil war set Lebanon back. The country is slowly trying to rebuild. Sectarian violence and conflict continue to plague the region.

LANGUAGE, PHILOSOPHY, AND RELIGION: ISLAM AND CHRISTIANITY SIDE BY SIDE

Lebanon's official language is Arabic, but many people speak English, French, or Greek. The country is divided into Christianity and Islam. The *CIA World Factbook* reveals that almost 60 percent of Lebanese are Muslims (Sunni, Shi'a, Druze, Sufi, and Alawites). The population balance tipped in the favor of Sunni Muslims when Sunni Kurds migrated from Syria and Turkey. (Shi'a Muslims now constitute the Muslim majority.) Sunni Bedouins were granted citizenship and the Civil War caused many Christians to flee. The remaining Christians, mostly Maronites, Greek Orthodox, Armenian Apostolic, Melkite Greek Catholics, Assyrian Church of the East, Syrian Orthodox, and Chaldean Catholics, number almost 40 percent.

GEOGRAPHY AND CLIMATE: SMALL BUT VARIED

Stretched along the western coast of the Mediterranean Sea, with Syria along its north and eastern backside and Israel to the south, Lebanon is smaller than Connecticut. Lebanon's main cities—the capital Beirut, Tripoli, and Sidon—lie along the narrow Mediterranean coastal plain. Two parallel mountain ranges, the Lebanon and Anti-Lebanon, run the length of Lebanon with the fertile *Bekáa Valley* and the *Litani River* in between.

Lebanon's climate is as varied as its food. Between the temperate Mediterranean coast and snowy mountain ranges, Mediterranean swimming and mountainous snow skiing are less than an hour drive away from each other. In general, summers are long, hot, and dry, and winters are cooler and rainy. Summers along the coast are hotter and more humid with heavy dew, but with little rainfall. Winters are cooler with good rainfall. Inland dwellers see a greater variation in temperature. Summers are hot, but cool down at night, and winters are more severe with frost and snow. In the mountains, snow covers the highest peaks year-round.

FARMING AND AGRICULTURE: FERTILE CRESCENT

Although Lebanon is the smallest country in the Middle East and cropland is limited due to rugged terrain, it is able to produce most of its own food. The land alternates between two lowlands and two highlands running parallel to the sea from north to south: the *Mediterranean coastal strip* or maritime plain, *western Lebanon range*, the *central plateau* or Bekáa Valley, and the *eastern Anti-Lebanon range*.

Good rainfall, good soil, sun, and warm temperatures along the coastal plain and foothills result in crops like bananas, citrus, dates, grapes, almonds, hazelnuts, abundant vegetables like zucchini, tomatoes, eggplant, and peppers. Fish and seafood come from the Mediterranean Sea. Ninety percent of the population lives in cities in the maritime plain. The central plateau and mountains contain only 10 percent of the population and over half the arable land. They receive less rain and colder winters, but produce wheat, wine grapes, some vegetables like greens, and fruits and nuts like apples, apricots, peaches, plums, and walnuts. Terraced farming in the mountains produces figs, olives, sheep, and goats.

LEBANESE CUISINE: MASTERS OF A CULINARY CROSSROADS

Lebanon resides in the heart of the Eastern Mediterranean-Middle East. Its pre-Biblical cuisine, representative of the region's best cooking, is the epitome of the Mediterranean diet and has had a profound influence on all who taste it. The genius of this cuisine is simplicity, its bond with the earth and the sea, and the exotic, robust flavors of the Middle and Far East paired with the sophistication and subtlety of Western and European cuisine.

For most of its history the region of Lebanon has been ruled by a succession of foreigners who influenced its cuisine: Greeks, Persians, Romans, Egyptians, and Turks. Greek Alexander the Great and Ottoman Turks introduced flatbread, olive oil, phyllo and baklava, stuffed vegetables, grilled meats, coffee, and nuts. Rice, dates, and many spices came from travelers criss-crossing the region on the Silk Road from China to Rome and back. In the twentieth century the French introduced flan, croissants, and refined the cuisine's strong flavors.

Arab-Muslim-Ottomans provided exotic flavors like rose flower water and spices, lemon and olive oil for dressings and marinades, yogurt, lamb instead of pork, nuts in sweet and savory dishes, and the *mezze* tradition. Lebanese cooks are known throughout the Arab world for their elaborate *mezze*, small dishes served before the main meal or as the meal. French, Jews, Romans, and the Maronite Catholics brought butter, cream, wine, vinegar, new vegetables like chard and truffles, dried fruit with meat, beef and meat stews, pomegranates, and pasta.

The food of the entire Eastern Mediterranean-Middle Eastern region is a celebration of life: fresh, flavorful, and diverse. In the country, produce comes from home gardens and in the city, from the *souk* (street market shop). Large feasts on nonreligious holidays and religious holy days also shape Lebanese cuisine. Muslims fast from sunrise to sunset during Ramadan; in the evening people stay up late to dine on soup, tabbouleh, fattoush, hummus, and *fatteh* (soaked bread layered with chickpeas and topped with tahini and yogurt). Some sweets and drinks are made only during Ramadan. (Christians sometimes dine at night in restaurants with Muslim friends during this time.) End of Ramadan feasts feature meat and include chicken with almond rice, grilled lamb, platters of dates, and *tamar hindi*, a tamarind drink.

Eastern Catholics observe Lent with lean, meatless dishes like *m'jaddara* (rice, lentils, and browned onions). They celebrate Easter, their most important holiday, with *moghrabiyeh* (Lebanese couscous with lamb shanks and chicken), lamb in yogurt sauce over rice and toasted vermicelli, *kibbeh bil-saneeya* (meat and bulgur pie), *shoraba zingood* (vinegar-sour soup), *selak* (rice-stuffed chard), eggplant stuffed with minced meat, onion, and spices and *ma'amoul*) (date or walnut-stuffed semolina cookies).

Though there are many similar dishes between cuisines of Arab region, the preparations and ingredients can vary markedly. For instance, Iraqis uses sesame oil instead of olive, and Syrians simmer *kibbeh* in pomegranate syrup instead of Lebanon's tahini-onion sauce. The ubiquitous Lebanese chickpea dip, *hummus*, seasoned with *tahini* (sesame paste), lemon and sometimes garlic, is made in other parts of the Arab and Mediterranean world with olive oil instead of tahini, and seasoned with cumin. Bedouin (desert tribes), Indian, and Pakistani cuisines strongly influenced the food of the Gulf States.

With their focus on fresh vegetables, fruits, herbs, sheep and goat milk, wheat, and seafood, the Lebanese consume less meat, butter, and cream. The meat they do consume is lamb, poultry, rabbit, and wild game. Beef isn't common because cattle need grazing land, which is unavailable. Most Lebanese avoid pork and Muslims eat only *halal* meat and fish (see *Glossary*). *Khobz arabi* (flat bread), *labneh* (yogurt), and the national dish, *kibbeh* (lamb pounded with bulgar wheat), fresh or cooked vegetables and legumes, and large amounts of garlic and olive oil form the basis of Lebanese cuisine. This cuisine doesn't contain a large repertoire of sauces. Instead it focuses on cooking techniques like grilling, baking, marinating, and sautéing, and a variety of seasonal produce, herbs, and spices. The flavor and the freshness of raw ingredients produce a surprisingly varied and satisfying cuisine.

Kibbeh, the national dish, takes many forms: *kibbeh nayeh* (raw kibbeh or lamb tartar), *kibbeh bil-saneeya* (pan-layered and baked kibbeh), and *kibbeh ras* (fried kibbeh "footballs" or balls). The last two often contain a filling of cooked lamb and pine nuts. *Za'atar* is a popular seasoning mixture of wild thyme, sesame seeds, and sumac. Mixed with olive oil, it is painted onto flatbreads and baked to become *man'oushe bi-za'tar* (za'atar-topped flatbread). This is a common breakfast food and is often topped with other ingredients like yogurt or mint. Bread has a sacred status in Middle Eastern cuisine; za'atar flatbread is considered "brain food" and given to school children on exam days.

Wine and an anise-flavored liqueur, *arrack*, the national drink of Lebanon, are produced in the Bekáa valley fruit-growing region. Drinks are always served with *mezze* like pickled vegetables, hummus, *baba ganouj* (roasted eggplant dip), pita bread, tabbouleh, grilled marinated seafood, skewered meats, cheese, a variety of cooked and raw salads, and fruit.

Breakfast is usually flatbread, yogurt, cheese, tomatoes, olives and olive oil, fruit, and honey. Country folk eat lunch between 1 p.m. and 3 p.m. It is the largest meal, often with a small assortment of mezze and main entrée. Hummus, olives, and nuts are common with kibbeh, kebabs, *kefta* (meatballs) and pickles, salads or vegetable dishes, and fruit. Dinner is between 8 p.m. and 11 p.m., when city dwellers eat their main meal.

REGIONAL LEBANON

Lebanon's small size keeps its food and cooking techniques mostly homogeneous, but two distinct regions do exist: the flat, temperate, and sunny Mediterranean *coast* with abundant seafood, citrus, and fresh produce the year round, and the *mountain* and *high plateau* regions that experience cold winters. Mountain and plateau cooks prepare sheep and goat meat and yogurt, and preserve many foods. They pickle cauliflower, cucumbers, and grape leaves; dry apricots, figs and apples, and dehydrate tomatoes into paste. Many cooks simmer pomegranate juice into syrup; and make cheeses and *kishik*, the fermented and dried bulgar and yogurt powder used for sauces, salads, porridge, and soup.

DINE AT HOME IN LEBANON

The Lebanese have a tradition of hospitality to guests so guests may be invited to dine in a private home. Meals are social occasions. Since honor, dignity, and reputation are all-important to Lebanese, try not to offend. Dress well. Greet the host and hostess with a smile, their name and title, direct eye contact, a handshake (when offered), and the greeting *"marhaba."* Bring flowers, candy, or pastry, or to non-Muslims, wine or liqueur. In a Muslim home, guests give the gift to the host with the right hand, not the left.

Greet elders first and maintain only short eye contact with them, but do look people in the eye—it's a sign of honesty. Avoid discussing politics, religion, and civil war unless the host or hostess brings it up. Wait to be told where to sit for dinner. Table manners are formal; hold the fork in the left hand and the knife in the right. Arabic bread is essential to every meal and it's permissible to use the bread as a scoop with the *right* hand.

The dinner table will be crowded with delicious and filling food on the table all at once. Try a little of everything, but don't overeat on the first helping. It's expected that guests will take second and third helpings to compliment the host and hostess.

The most popular meals are *mezze* buffets offering as many as forty small dishes from olives and cheese to kebabs, *yaprak dolma* (stuffed grape leaves), marinated chicken or lamb kebabs, *kibbeh*, *fatayer* (stuffed savory pastries), *tabbouleh*, salad, roast chicken with garlic sauce, fried cauliflower with tahini, *m'jadderah* (rice or bulgar and lentils), and *falafel* (deep-fried chickpea balls). A traditional dinner might start with soup, like chard with lentil, and flatbread. Mezze-type dishes follow. Next come platters of fish with tahini sauce or cardamom chicken or lamb with rice and dishes like spinach with caramelized onions, *shish barak* (stuffed, baked pastry pies with yogurt sauce), cabbage rolls, green beans or okra simmered in olive oil, and tomato or fava beans with lemon and garlic.

Adults will drink beer, wine, or *arak* (if not Muslim), and children will drink *limonada* (lemonade), fresh fruit juice, or *jellab* (date- or raisin-based soft drink with pine nuts). Fresh fruit—melon, oranges, apples, grapes, persimmons, or figs—ends most Lebanese meals. For special occasions, pastries like *baklava* with pistachios and rosewater or *atayef bil jawz* (pancakes stuffed with walnuts) and *ahweh* (strong, thick coffee with sugar and cardamom) provide a celebratory ending.

FIGURE 9.2 Mount Lebanon.
Source: siphotoart/Fotolia.

TASTES OF LEBANON

Fat: Olive oil, butter, clarified butter, vegetable oil, sheep tail fat, *dehen* (seasoned sheep tail fat)

Sweet: Sugar, honey, pomegranate molasses, grape molasses, carob molasses

Sour/Alcohol: Lemon, orange, bitter orange, red or white wine vinegar, pomegranate syrup, sumac powder, yogurt, *kishk* (fermented and powdered yogurt and bulgur)

Salty: Salt, olives

Spicy-Hot: Red chili pepper flakes, white and black pepper

Spice: Aniseed, cumin, allspice, cinnamon, saffron, cardamom, bay leaves, nutmeg, cloves, *mastic*, *mahlab* (ground cherry kernels), *za'atar* (spice blend of thyme, sesame, and sumac), mastic, seven-spice blend

Aromatic Seasoning Vegetables: Onion, garlic, carrot, celery, green onions

Herbs, Seasonings, and Condiments: Italian parsley, mint, cilantro, oregano, orange blossom and rose flower waters, rose petal jam

Other Important Foods: Sesame seed, *tahini* (sesame paste), nuts (pine nuts, pistachios, almonds, walnuts), *burghul* (bulgar wheat), short-grain rice, *freekeh* (roasted green wheat), fillo pastry, chickpeas, lentils, fruit (apricots, cherries, quince, dates, figs), olives, grape leaves, cabbage, eggplant, zucchini, tomatoes, cucumbers, romaine, artichokes, okra, green beans, fish, meat (lamb, chicken, goat), *pastirma* or *basturma* (spice-rubbed, dry-cured beef)

Popular Dishes: *Khobz arabi* (flatbread) and *khobz marquq* (paper-thin flatbread), baklava, *hummus* (chickpea and tahini dip), *baba ghanouji* (eggplant dip), *kibbeh* (dish with lamb and bulgar), *fattoush* (salad with dried or toasted flatbread), *labneh* (strained yogurt), *m'jaddarah* (lentils, rice, and crisp-fried onion), *tabbouleh* (bulgar wheat salad), *falafel* (deep-fried chickpea balls), *mezze* (any dish served in small portions as appetizer), *shawarma* (shaved grilled meat)

Drinks: *Ayran* (yogurt drink), tea, Arabic and Turkish coffee, *arak* (anise-flavored liqueur), lemonade, beer, wine, *jallab* (drink made with ice, grape molasses, and nuts)

COMMON LEBANESE COOKING TOOLS

Mortar and pestle, *saj* (overturned wok-like pan)

LEBANESE AND ARABIC CHEESE

Many of the cheeses eaten in Lebanon are eaten throughout the Middle East.

Akkawi

This white, smooth-textured brined cheese can be mildly salty or not, depending on the producer. It is usually made using cow milk, but can be made with goat or sheep milk. Akkawi originated in Palestine, but is produced on a large scale in Lebanon, Syria, and Cyprus. It is a favorite cheese for the table; it pairs well with fruit.

Gibneh Bulgharieh (Bulgarian Cheese or Feta)

See chapter *Greece and Turkey*, section *Greek Cheese*.

Halloum or Halloumi

This cheese, similar to mozzarella, is produced with a mixture of goat and sheep milk. It has a high melting point and is often grilled or fried. Halloumi pairs well with fresh foods like salads and fruits like watermelon.

Jibneh Arabieh (Arab Cheese)

This simple cheese has an open texture and a mild taste. Bedouins first made it using goat or sheep milk, but now it's made from cow milk. Jibneh Arabieh can be found on the table or used for cooking.

Shanklish, Surke, or Sorke

This cow or sheep milk cheese is sometimes prepared with spices in the cheese. The cheese is formed into balls and covered in za'atar or Aleppo chili powder and aged and dried. Shanklish varies greatly in its texture and flavor depending on aging. Fresh cheeses are softer and milder tasting. Aging progressively hardens the cheese, and the older a cheese gets the more pungent it becomes. Shanklish is often eaten as a mezze with tomato, olive oil, and sometimes onion.

LEBANESE FLAVOR FOUNDATIONS

Lebanese Signature Aromatic Vegetable Combo

Onions and garlic

Signature Seasonings

Liquid/Paste

Tahini (Middle Eastern Unroasted Sesame Paste)

Tahini is an oily, ground, hulled sesame seed paste. Stir the oil back into sesame seed mass before using. Tahini should be loose, not peanut-butter-thick like Asian sesame pastes.

Animal

Labneh

Labneh is a strained, thick, whole milk yogurt cheese, like smooth cream cheese, made with goat, sheep, or cow milk. See recipe *Yogurt Cheese (Labneh)*.

Qawarma (Lamb Confit or Rillettes)

Quwarma is minced lamb simmered in and preserved in fat from the tail of the fat-tailed sheep. It is prepared in the fall and stored in earthen jars, where it is allowed to cool. The covered jars are stored in a cool spot throughout winter. It is cooked with dried *kashk* (bulgur fermented with milk and labneh) for breakfast, fried with eggs, or eaten on bread like French rillettes.

Pastirma or Basturma

See chapter *Greece and Turkey*, section *Turkish Flavor Foundations*, *Signature Seasonings*. This is spice-rubbed, dry-cured beef, often used for mezze or breakfast dishes.

Vegetable/Fruit

Sumac

The sour red berry of a wild Mediterranean bush that is used in Arabic cooking to add a fruity, sour taste. Dried berries are crushed to a powder and sprinkled into dishes during or after cooking. Dried, whole berries can be macerated in hot water to release flavor. See chapter *Greece and Turkey*, section *Greek or Turkish Flavor Foundations*, *Signature Seasonings* for more information.

Herbal/Spice

Za'atar Herb and Za'atar Blend

There are several varieties of aromatic herbs called za'atar (and other names in other parts of the Mediterranean and Middle East) that taste like a cross of oregano, savory, and thyme. There is also a blend, popular in Lebanon, that consists of 2 parts dried thyme, 1 part sumac, 1/2 part toasted sesame seeds and salt. Some cooks substitute dried oregano, savory, or marjoram for part of the thyme to give a more complex flavor. Lebanese and Middle Eastern groceries sell the prepared za'atar blend.

FIGURE 9.3   Fresh za'atar herb.
Source: Ekaterina Lin/Fotolia.

FIGURE 9.4   Za'atar blend.
Source: Roger Dixon/DK Images.

SEASONINGS AND PASTE MIXTURES

Lebanese Brown-Fried Onions

Brown-fried onions are so important in the Lebanese kitchen that they have names for the cuts of brown-fried onions. Cooks cut onions two ways and soft-brown or crisp-brown them. The onions are used as flavoring or garnish: crisp-fried slivered onions are called *basal mhammar*, and soft fried diced onions are known as *te'leyeh*. Use basal mhammar with greens and lemon or to garnish rice and lentils. Te'leyeh can be used as a base to many dishes like lentil soup or stews. Fried onions need about 1/2 cup oil per 1-1/2 pounds or 6 cups diced or sliced onion. Heat oil over medium-high heat and fry onions until soft and browned or crisp and browned, 10 to 20 minutes or more. Remove onions with slotted spoon. To re-crisp *crisp-browned* onions, heat in skillet or microwave.

LEBANESE 7-SPICE BLEND

This spice mixture gives a dish the taste of the Eastern Mediterranean. Try it as a rub on pork, chicken, lamb, and fish. Rub onto meats 2 hours before cooking, 15 to 20 minutes for seafood.

Yields about 2 tablespoons

1 teaspoon ground or whole allspice
1 teaspoon ground or whole black pepper
1 teaspoon ground cinnamon
1 teaspoon ground or whole cloves
1 teaspoon ground or whole fenugreek
1 teaspoon ground ginger
1 teaspoon chopped or ground nutmeg

1 Though whole spices are more flavorful, using ground spices is quicker. Mix together ground spices *or* grind whole spices in spice grinder, and mix together.

2 *For more flavor:* Lightly dry toast each whole spice in a small sauté pan over medium heat until fragrant. Do not brown or burn the spices. Pour into a small bowl to cool. Grind spices. Mix together and store in airtight jar in cool, dark spot or refrigerate.

SAUCE

LEBANESE GARLIC SAUCE (TOUM)

Lebanese cooks prepare this fluffy, emulsified garlic sauce ahead to have on hand for pairing with roast chicken, chicken shawarma, and shish tawook (chicken skewers). It also goes beautifully with lamb, beef, and goat or fish. Use toum to garnish dishes that need a dose of garlic after they are cooked.

Yields about 1-1/3 cups thick sauce

2 ounces fresh garlic cloves, about 8 large cloves, peeled, 4 tablespoons minced
2 to 3 tablespoons freshly squeezed lemon juice, 1 large lemon
1 cup sunflower *or* canola oil *or* half olive/half sunflower

1 **Mortar with pestle:** Pound minced garlic and 1 teaspoon kosher salt in a large mortar with a pestle. When garlic is completely crushed into a wet paste, slowly drip oil into it while stirring and pounding. Finished paste will resemble a waxy mayonnaise. Stir in lemon juice. Paste will whiten and lighten. To thin paste, stir in cold water.

2 **Blender or food processor:** Place minced garlic and 1 teaspoon kosher salt into blender. Purée and scrape down until garlic becomes a wet paste. With machine running, add 1/2 tablespoon lemon juice and 1/4 cup oil *in a thin stream*. Repeat with remaining lemon juice and oil in 3 more batches. The sauce should be the consistency of thick mayonnaise. Taste and adjust flavors with lemon juice or salt as needed. Thin with cold water.

3 Store garlic sauce in refrigerator. It will keep several days refrigerated.

*Neutral oils taste lighter than olive oil. Do not use sprouted or prepeeled garlic; it can be bitter and watery. Use the freshest garlic available. There are two ways to prepare this sauce. Be patient: successful emulsions take time.

Vary! Improvise!

☞ *Some Lebanese cooks add mashed potato to stabilize garlic sauce.*
☞ *Substitute red wine vinegar for lemon juice.*
☞ *If a fluffy sauce can't be achieved easily in the blender, add an egg white to garlic before adding oil and lemon juice.*

SIGNATURE RECIPE

TAHINI SAUCE (TARATOUR)

Use more lemon juice for an added kick.

Yields 1/2 cup, 3 to 4 servings

1/4 cup Middle Eastern-style tahini
1/4 cup freshly squeezed lemon juice, about 1 large lemon

Optional Seasonings

1/8 ounce garlic, 1 small clove, 3/4 teaspoon peeled and minced
1/2 teaspoon ground cumin
1/2 ounce trimmed Italian parsley, 1/4 cup chopped

1 Whisk tahini with 1/4 cup warm water. It will seize then soften. Whisk in lemon juice to taste. Season with salt.

2 If **optional seasonings** are used, rest sauce 20 to 30 minutes.

Vary! Improvise!

☞ *Use other herbs or powdered sumac in this dressing.*
☞ *Stir in roasted tomato or red bell pepper purée or a dash of hot sauce.*

COOK'S VOICE: FOUAD KASSAB

TheFoodBlog.com Writer

"Tahini is the Lebanese culinary cure-all. If disaster befalls the Lebanese, we reach for tahini. Let me see: we've got chickpeas with tahini, eggplants with tahini, snails with tahini, fish with tahini, falafel with tahini, shawarma with tahini, molasses with tahini, kibbeh with tahini, eggs with tahini, cake with tahini. And of course, silver beet stalks (Swiss chard) with tahini."

SPECIAL METHODS

Lebanese Mezze

In humble homes and major restaurants, *mezze* are a feast of texture, color, and flavor that represent the best of Lebanese cuisine. Although these little appetizer-size plates of foods and dips served with drinks appear throughout the Mediterranean basin and Arab world, Lebanon is known for its huge variety and number. Almost anything (except soup) can be turned into mezze.

Smooth Hummus

For very smooth hummus, Lebanese cooks spread cooked chickpeas on a cloth and lightly run a rolling pin over to split them open. Split chickpeas go into a large bowl filled with water and the skins that rise to the surface are scooped off with a strainer. The chickpeas are drained.

FIGURE 9.5 Hummus.
Source: karam miri/Fotolia.

Vary! Improvise!

☞ *Fold diced roasted red bell pepper or chopped Italian parsley into finished hummus.*

☞ *Flavored bean dips are crazy-popular. How would you work this basic method to include other combos of beans, fat, seasonings, and acid?*

☞ *Fry a little ground lamb or pine nuts in olive oil and strew on top of hummus in place of sumac and oil.*

MEZZE 1: HUMMUS CHICKPEA AND TAHINI DIP (HUMMUS BI TEHINE)

Hummus is the quintessential Lebanese mezza. Mediterranean tahini tends to be very loose and watery while American or Asian sesame paste tends to be thicker, more like peanut butter. Adjust the flavor of hummus with more or less garlic, tahini, or lemon juice to suit tastes.

Yields about 6 cups

14 ounces dry chickpeas, 2 cups
　　or 5 cups cooked, drained chickpeas, cooking water reserved
3/4 to 1 cup fresh lemon juice, 4 to 6 lemons
1 cup "loose" Mediterranean tahini
　　or 3/4 cup sesame paste
Optional: 1/4 ounce garlic, 1 large clove, 1-1/2 teaspoons peeled and finely minced

Garnish

Ground sumac or ground cumin
Extra virgin olive oil

1　Soak dry chickpeas overnight or quick-soak (soak in boiled water 1 hour) with 2 teaspoons kosher salt. Drain, rinse, and cook in fresh water until tender, 45 minutes to 1 hour. Drain cooked chickpeas, and reserve cooking water.

2　Pour warm chickpeas into food processor. Grind into a purée, 4 to 5 minutes. Add 1/2 cup lemon juice (garlic if using) and tahini. Continue to grind chickpeas. If necessary, add enough cooking water to help facilitate puréeing, about 1/2 cup. Purée 4 to 5 minutes.

3　Season hummus with 2 to 3 teaspoons kosher salt, and continue to purée until hummus is smooth, 5 to 10 minutes. Taste hummus. If desired, season with salt and more lemon juice. Garlic flavor will take time to come through. Purée should be a soft, creamy paste; it will firm somewhat as it sits. The longer hummus is puréed, the fluffier and creamier it will be.

4　Scrape hummus into a mixing bowl and cover. Rest hummus at room temperature or refrigerate 1 hour to allow flavors to mingle. Taste again and re-season if necessary.

5　**To Serve:** Pour hummus in serving dish. Make a swirling indentation in the center with the back of a spoon. Garnish with a dusting of sumac or cumin and a healthy drizzle of olive oil. Serve.

MEZZE 2: EGGPLANT AND TAHINI DIP (BABA GHANOUJI)

Yields 2 cups

1 to 1-1/4 pounds eggplant
1/4 cup Middle Eastern-style (thinner) tahini
1/4 cup fresh lemon juice, about 1 large lemon, more to taste
Optional: 1/4 ounce garlic, about 1 large clove, 1 to 1-1/2 teaspoons peeled and finely minced

For Serving

Arabic Flatbread (Khobz Arabi)

1　Slice stem off eggplant. Roast whole on a grill or on top of low gas flame, turning frequently, until the skin is evenly black and crisp and the inside is very soft. Alternatively, broil the eggplant. Set eggplant into a bowl and cover. Set aside to cool.

2 Pick off blackened skin and discard. If there are excess bits of skin, rinse eggplant lightly and drain. Dice eggplant finely and evenly to yield about 1-1/2 cups.

3 Stir together tahini, lemon juice, 1/2 teaspoon kosher salt, and optional garlic. Fold in diced eggplant. Taste and adjust seasonings. Rest baba ghanouji 30 minutes and taste again.

4 **To Serve:** Pile baba ghanouji in serving dish and serve with flatbread.

Vary! Improvise!

☞ *Add 2 tablespoons chopped Italian parsley.*

☞ *Reduce tahini to 3 tablespoons and add 1/2-cup whole milk yogurt, 2 cloves minced garlic, plus lemon juice to taste.*

☞ *Chop roasted eggplant and toss with salt, minced garlic, and lemon juice. Arrange on plate and drizzle with olive oil.*

FOUL MEDAMAS

Eggplant and chickpeas are not the only foods made into tasty dips. Lebanese cook transform dried fava beans (foul) into another soul satisfying dip with garlic, lemon juice, cumin, and olive oil called *foul medamas*.

FIGURE 9.6 Dried fava beans.
Source: NinaM/Shutterstock.

The World of Kibbeh

Kibbeh is the national dish of Lebanon and Syria, but many countries in the Mediterranean region prepare it. There are four basic types: **raw**, **patties**, **stuffed balls**, or **layered in a pan** and baked. Kibbeh can also be sautéed, deep-fried, or simmered in a sauce and made with meat or meatless. All kibbeh contains bulgar and onion. Except for the vegetarian versions of potato, pumpkin, and fish, kibbeh is usually made with lamb.

Traditionally, women use a stone mortar and a heavy pestle called *jorn* and *modaqqa* to rhythmically pound meat and bulgar until smooth and pasty—music to the ears of waiting diners. Today, a food processor quickly does the job. *Kibbeh nayeh* (raw kibbeh) is made with fresh, lean lamb leg, trimmed of fat and gristle, and pounded very smooth. Households serve it mounded on a platter, drizzled with olive oil, and garnished with mint and slivered onion. Arabic flat bread/pita serves as a scoop.

PAYING ATTENTION TO KIBBEH

Lebanese chef and author Kamal Al-Faquih says in *Classic Lebanese Cuisine* that when making kibbi "the moisture-to-bulgar ratio" is all-important. He suggests paying attention to the feeling of the kibbi dough: when it feels damp, add a little bulgar, and if it feels dry drizzle in a bit of water. Al-Faquih advises against using a food processor to grind kibbi. He prefers the texture of bulgar that a meat grinder produces to that of a food processor.

SPICED RAW GROUND LAMB AND BULGAR (KIBBEH NAYEH)

Bulgar dampens the flavor of the meat. For a meatier flavor, adjust the proportions to a little less bulgar and a little more meat.

Yields 2 to 2-1/2 cups kibbeh, 12 (3 tablespoon) balls *or* 8 to 10 (1/4-cup) patties
4 servings

10 ounces lean lamb *or* beef, diced into 1-inch cubes
2-1/2 ounces fine bulgar, 1/2 cup
3 ounces onion, 3/4 cup grated or finely diced
1-1/2 teaspoons ground cumin
1-1/4 teaspoons ground cinnamon
1-1/4 teaspoons ground allspice
Optional: 2 to 4 tablespoons freshly squeezed lemon juice, 1 large lemon

For Serving

Chopped Italian parsley
Chopped green onion or slivered red onion
Arabic Flatbread (Khobz Arabi)

1 Set up a meat grinder with a fine blade. Grind meat through grinder twice to yield about 1 cup plus 2-1/2 tablespoons ground meat. Place into mixing bowl.

2 Pour bulgar into fine strainer and rinse with cold water. Rub with hands to soften bulgar, then squeeze to drain bulgar well.

3 Mix bulgar and onion with meat in mixing bowl. Grind mixture through fine blade of meat grinder until smooth. Place ground mixture into bowl and knead in spices, optional lemon juice, 1 teaspoon kosher salt, and freshly ground pepper. Mixture should be very smooth, pasty, and doughy; if not, grind it again. Taste kibbeh and adjust flavors.

4 **To Serve:** Mound kibbeh into shallow dish or plate. Make a slight indentation on the top. Draw grooves in a design on the raw kibbeh mound with the tines of a fork. Decorate with chopped parsley, green onion, or slivers of red onion. Alternatively, form kibbeh into 12 (3-tablespoon-size) balls and place on platter. Serve kibbeh with flatbread and eat with bits of parsley and green onion or onion.

Source: *Lebanese Mountain Cookery* by Mary Laird Hamady.

Vary! Improvise!

☞ *Kibbeh Kras or Baked Patties: Form the raw kibbeh into 1/4-cup patties 1-1/2 to 2 inches diameter and 1/2 inch thick. Preheat oven to 350 degrees F. Place patties on oiled sheet pan and brush with oil. Bake kibbeh until golden, 15 to 20 minutes. Broil to brown further. Serve with yogurt and Arabic bread.*

COOK'S VOICE: FOUAD KASSAB

TheFoodBlog.com

"When it comes to Middle-Eastern food, yoghurt is the reigning champion. When it comes to cooked yoghurt dishes, *kibbeh b' laban* (yoghurt kibbeh) is an absolute favorite, but when eaten fresh, there's nothing that beats *labna*. Strained through muslin, yoghurt lets go of its whey to become incredibly creamy, and the longer you strain it, the thicker and richer it gets. This is labna: wheyless yoghurt that is salted and eaten in every single Lebanese home, every single day at every single breakfast."

YOGURT CHEESE (LABNEH)

Use labneh in cooking, in savory and sweet dishes. To keep labneh longer, roll it into 1-inch balls, place in cheesecloth in the refrigerator, and change cheesecloth daily until no moisture exudes from them, then immerse balls in olive oil.

Yields 1 to 2 cups

1 quart whole milk live-cultured yogurt (without additives)

1 Line a strainer with several layers of cheesecloth. Set strainer over a bowl (to catch the liquid whey).

2 Whisk yogurt with 1 teaspoon kosher salt and pour into strainer. Refrigerate. Check consistency of yogurt after 8, 12, and 24 hours. Twenty-four hours is most common, but some cooks strain labneh 2 days. The yogurt will become increasingly thick (and yield less) the longer it drains. Refrigerate cheese, and use within a week.

3 **To Use:** Combine labneh with herbs, za'atar, olive oil, or nigella or toasted sesame seeds and serve as a spread. Or, with oiled hands, roll labneh into bite-sized balls and roll in spices or seeds for a mezze. Drizzle labneh with olive oil and mint and serve as a mezze. Spread labneh and black olives on Arabic bread and roll up for a sandwich.

FIGURE 9.7 Plain labneh.
Source: Lilyana Vynogradova/Shutterstock.

SIMMER, STEW, POACH, BOIL, AND STEAM

LEBANESE LENTIL AND SWISS CHARD SOUP (ADAS BI HAMOOD)

Yields 6-1/2 to 7 cups, 4 to 6 servings

About 3-1/2 ounces brown lentils, 1/2 cup, picked through for stones and rinsed in strainer
10 to 12 ounce bunch Swiss chard
3 tablespoons olive oil
8 ounces onion, 2 cups diced into 1/4-inch cubes
1 teaspoon ground coriander
1-1/2 teaspoons flour
1/2 ounce garlic, 2 large cloves, 1 tablespoon peeled and finely minced into paste
1/2 ounce cilantro leaves and tender stems, about 1/4 cup finely sliced
2-1/2 to 3 tablespoons freshly squeezed lemon juice, 1 medium lemon

1 In a small saucepan, combine lentils, 1/2 teaspoon kosher or sea salt, and 4 cups water. Bring to a boil over high heat, reduce heat to low, cover, and simmer lentils 20 minutes.

2 Cut away stalks from chard. Slice each leaf in half lengthwise, then slice leaves crosswise into 1-inch slices to yield about 8 cups sliced, lightly packed leaves. If not, make up the remainder with finely sliced stems. Set aside.

3 Heat olive oil in 4- to 5-quart soup pot over medium-high heat. Add onions, coriander, and 1/2 teaspoon kosher or sea salt. Sauté until onions are soft and brown, 7 to 10 minutes. Stir in flour and cook 1 minute. Stir garlic and Swiss chard into onions. Cook and stir until Swiss chard has wilted, 5 minutes. Stir in 2 cups water, cilantro, and cooked lentils with their cooking water.

4 Bring soup to a boil, reduce heat to low, and simmer partially covered 10 minutes. Remove soup from the heat and set aside to cool 5 minutes. Stir in lemon juice to taste. Adjust with salt and pepper.

5 **To Serve:** Reheat soup and ladle into bowls. Serve. This soup tastes best if prepared a day in advance to allow the flavors mellow. Freeze soup up to 1 month.

Source: *Classic Lebanese Cuisine* by Kamal Al-Faqih.

LEBANESE CHICKEN SOUP (SHOURABAT DJAJ)

Home cooks prepare their soup with a whole chicken, but that requires cooling the stock and skimming the fat.

Yields 8 to 9 cups, 4 to 6 servings

2 quarts chicken stock
3-inch cinnamon stick
2 large, preferably fresh, bay leaves
1/2 teaspoon whole allspice
6 ounces onion, 1 medium, 1-1/2 cups peeled and finely diced
12 to 14 ounces boneless, skinless chicken breast, 2 medium
2 ounces broken vermicelli, 1/2 cup
1 ounce trimmed Italian parsley, 1/2 cup finely sliced and packed
Optional: 8 ounces tomato, 1 medium, 1 to 1-1/2 cups seeded and diced

For Serving

Ground cinnamon
2 lemons, cut into 8 to 12 wedges

1 Pour stock into 4-quart saucepan. Bring to a boil. Stir in cinnamon stick, bay leaves, allspice, and onion. Lower heat and simmer soup uncovered 20 minutes.

2 Meanwhile, slice chicken breast into 1-inch "worms," and set aside. Prepare remaining ingredients.

3 **Five minutes before serving:** Bring stock to a boil. Lower heat and stir in chicken, vermicelli, parsley, and optional tomato. Simmer 2 minutes and remove pan from heat.

4 **To Serve:** Ladle soup into bowls. Serve with a small bowl of ground cinnamon and lemon wedges with which each diner may garnish the soup.

Lebanese Stewing and Braising

Lebanese cooks prepare many stuffed and braised foods like grape leaves and cabbage. The basic stuffing of rice and lamb or rice and herbs so popular in Greek and Turkish cooking are favorites. Some cooks fashion stuffed grape or cabbage leaves into enticing long, narrow rolls measuring 3 to 4 inches long by 1/2 inch wide.

FIGURE 9.8 Kibbeh balls.
Source: pseudopixels/Shutterstock.

STUFFED LAMB AND BULGAR BALLS SIMMERED IN TAHINI SAUCE (KIBBEH ARNABIEH)

Kibbeh-making skills show in how thin their walls are before stuffing. Instead of simmering in the sauce, deep-fry these stuffed balls and serve with tarator (tahini) sauce.

4 to 6 servings, 8 to 12 kibbeh

1 recipe *Raw Lamb and Bulgar (Kibbeh Nayeh)*

Stuffing

Yields almost 1 cup

2 tablespoons butter *or* olive oil
2 ounces pine nuts, 1/3 cup
3 ounces onions, 3/4 cup peeled and finely diced or slivered
1/2 teaspoon cinnamon

Tahini-Onion Sauce

Yields 6 to 6-1/2 cups

1/4 cup olive oil
8 ounces onions, 2 cups peeled and finely diced
1 cup tahini, 8 ounces
1 cup freshly squeezed lemon juice, 4 large lemons
3 tablespoons cornstarch *or* arrowroot

For Serving

Cooked rice

Garnish: Chopped parsley

1. Prepare *Raw Lamb and Bulgar (Kibbeh Nayeh)* as directed.

2. *Prepare* stuffing: Heat butter or oil in medium skillet over medium heat. Add pine nuts and cook until golden; remove to bowl with slotted spoon. Stir onions into skillet and cook until lightly golden and soft, 10 to 12 minutes. Pour pine nuts into onions along with cinnamon, 1/2 teaspoon kosher salt, and ground black pepper. Simmer 2 to 3 minutes. Taste and adjust flavors. Cool.

3. *Stuff* kibbeh nayeh: Set a bowl of cold, salted water out. Divide raw kibbeh into 10 (1/4 cup) or 12 (3 plus tablespoons) balls. With damp fingers, poke a finger into one ball and shape into an open "pierogi." Stuff 1 tablespoon filling into hole and pinch meat closed along the open side, using a little water to help. Shape into "football" and set aside. Repeat with remaining kibbeh and filling.

4. *Prepare* tahini-onion sauce: Heat oil in a 3-quart saucepan over medium-high heat. Stir in onions and sauté until browned, 10 to 15 minutes. Stir in 4 cups cold water, bring to a boil, and lower heat to a simmer. Whisk together tahini and lemon juice. Whisk tahini mixture into onion and water. Simmer until onions soften further, 5 to 7 minutes. Dissolve cornstarch into 3 to 4 tablespoons cold water and whisk into simmering sauce. Cook until sauce thickens, 3 to 5 minutes. Season sauce with salt to taste.

5. **To Serve:** Place kibbeh into simmering sauce; they should be completely covered. Partially cover saucepan and simmer kibbeh until done, 30 to 40 minutes. Serve with cooked rice. Garnish with parsley.

Source: *Lebanese Mountain Cookery* by Mary Laird Hamady.

Vary! Improvise!

☞ *Stuff kibbeh with cooked ground meat instead of onions and pine nuts.*
☞ *Substitute chopped walnuts for pine nuts in stuffing.*

RICE OR BULGAR WITH LENTILS AND CRISP ONIONS (M'JADDARAH)

This dish is popular in the Arab world. Lebanese mountain cooks prepare it with bulgar, but else-where it's prepared with rice if a family can afford it. The proportions of rice to lentils vary from place to place—some with more rice and less lentils. Some recipes purée the lentils and in others they are left whole. The browned onions give this dish its distinct flavor. Don't reduce the oil.

Yields about 10 cups, 8 to 10 servings

8 to 9 ounces brown or green lentils, 1-1/4 cups
1/2 cup olive oil
1-1/2 pounds onions, 6 cups finely slivered
8 to 9 ounces long-grain rice, 1-1/4 cups rinsed and drained
   or 8 ounces medium bulgar, about 1-1/4 to 1-2/3 cups

1 **Cook the lentils:** Pick out stones, rinse lentils, and drain. Pour into 4-quart saucepan with 4 cups cold water and bring to a boil. Lower heat and simmer lentils until just tender, 20 minutes.

2 Bring 2 cups water to a boil for adding to rice and lentils later.

3 **Fry the onions:** Heat oil in a heavy 12-inch skillet, over high to medium-high heat. Stir in on-ions and sauté until they begin to brown. Lower heat to medium-high and cook onions, stir-ring or folding them periodically, until deeply and evenly browned and crisp, 20 to 30 minutes. Watch carefully. The onions can quickly go from very browned to black. Transfer onions with slotted spoon to bowl to cool. Pour 2 tablespoons water into hot skillet to deglaze and reserve liquid.

4 **If using rice:** Stir rice, deglazing water from skillet, 1 teaspoon kosher salt, and 1-1/2 cups boil-ing water into lentils. Lower heat and cover saucepan. Simmer rice and lentils 15 minutes exactly. Remove pan from heat. Let rice and lentils rest 10 minutes without disturbing.

   If using bulgar: Place bulgar into a mixing bowl and stir in 1-1/4 cups boiling water plus deglazing water. Cover bowl and allow bulgar to rest and absorb water, 15 to 20 minutes. Fold in lentils.

5 Pour half the fried onions and all their oil on top of the rice or bulgar, but don't mix them in. Cover pot or bowl. Rest in warm spot 10 minutes and up to 20 minutes.

6 **To Serve:** Remove lid from saucepan or bowl and fluff-fold onions and the rice-lentil or bulgar-lentil mixture together with a large fork. Pile *m'jaddarah* into bowl or onto platter and top with remaining half of onions. If the reserved onions have lost their crispness, reheat in skillet, or micro-wave them on paper towels 30 seconds before using.

Source: *The New Book of Middle Eastern Food* by Claudia Roden.

Vary! Improvise!

☞ *Add ground cumin, allspice, or chili powder to lentils as they cook.*

LEBANESE RICE AND VERMICELLI PILAF (PILAU)

Yields about 8 cups, 4 to 6 servings

3 tablespoons clarified butter
  or 2 tablespoons unsalted butter, diced, *plus* 1 tablespoons olive oil
1-1/2 to 2 ounces pine nuts, 1/3 cup
3 ounces vermicelli or thin spaghetti, 1 cup broken into 1/2-inch pieces
13 to 14 ounces long-grain rice, 2 cups

Garnish: Ground cinnamon

1 Bring 4 cups water to boil in a small saucepan.

2 Heat butter or oil over medium heat in heavy 4-quart saucepan. Add pine nuts and cook until golden. Transfer nuts with slotted spoon to small bowl and set aside. Add spaghetti or vermicelli to hot butter or oil and cook until lightly browned, 5 minutes. Stir constantly to avoid burning.

3 Stir rice into pan, and cook briefly to coat in oil and harden outside of rice kernel. Season rice and noodles with 1-1/2 teaspoons kosher salt. Stir in 4 cups boiling water. Return rice to a boil. Cover pot, reduce heat to low, and simmer 15 minutes. Remove pot from burner and rest pilaf undisturbed 10 minutes.

4 **To Serve:** Uncover and fluff rice gently with a fork. Pile pilaf into a serving dish. Garnish with toasted pine nuts and a generous dusting of ground cinnamon.

MOGHRABIEH: LEBANESE COUSCOUS

Lebanese rolled semolina couscous looks like giant pearls. It is larger than Moroccan (or Israeli) couscous, about the size of a pea, and needs soaking and longer steaming or cooking. Lebanese cooks prepare *moghrabieh* into a stew-like dish of the same name with chicken and/or lamb, chickpeas, and spices. While the stew simmers the soaked couscous steams over it, catching the vapors and plumping and tenderizing them with chewy flavor.

FIGURE 9.9 Stuffed zucchini simmered in tomato sauce (koossa meche banadoora).

STUFFED ZUCCHINI SIMMERED IN TOMATO SAUCE (KOOSSA MEHCHE BANADOORA)

The first time making this dish, it's easiest to use large zucchini. Narrower zucchini with a 1-1/4- to 1-1/2-inch diameter are more tender, and they don't need to be cut as the larger ones do. If the fresh tomatoes are not ripe, stir in 2 tablespoons tomato paste.

Yields about 1-1/4 cups meat-rice filling and 3 cups sauce, 6 servings

3-1/2 ounces medium-grain rice like Arborio, 1/2 cup
About 4 pounds large zucchini, six 8-inch long with 1-3/4- to 2-inch diameter
8 ounces raw ground lamb *or* beef
1/2 teaspoon ground cinnamon
1/4 teaspoon ground allspice
Optional: 1/2 teaspoon pomegranate molasses

Sauce

3 to 4 tablespoons olive oil
8 ounces onion, 1 large, 2 cups peeled and finely sliced
28-ounces canned whole plum tomatoes, 2 cups drained and chopped
　　or 2 pounds ripe tomatoes, peeled, seeded, and diced, 2 cups
1-1/2 ounces garlic, about 6 large cloves, peeled and halved or quartered lengthwise
3 cups chicken or meat stock or water
1 tablespoon dried, crushed mint
　　or 1/4 ounce fresh mint leaves, 2 tablespoons finely sliced

For Serving

Lebanese Rice and Vermicelli Pilaf (Pilau)
Lebanese Flatbread (Khobz Arabi)

1　**Prepare the filling:** Rinse rice and place in small bowl. Cover with cold water and soak rice 15 minutes. Drain rice well and pour into medium mixing bowl. Knead in meat, 1/2 teaspoon kosher salt, freshly ground pepper, cinnamon, allspice, and optional pomegranate molasses until spices are evenly distributed. Cover bowl and place into refrigerator until ready to use or overnight. Before using, mix filling with 1 to 2 tablespoons water to loosen it up.

2　**Core the zucchini:** Fill a mixing bowl with cold water and 1 tablespoon kosher salt. Lightly trim ends of zucchini. Measure each zucchini and cut exactly in half: about 4 inches long. Drop zucchini into salted water. With an apple corer (inner diameter 3/4 inch) or long vegetable corer, core out the middle seed-pulp, but take care not to go all the way through the end of the zucchini. The walls of the zucchini will be about 1/4-inch thick. If using an apple corer, split the cored column in half with a butter knife and give it a twist to dislodge the core. Place zucchini back into salted water until all the zucchini are cored.

3 **Stuff the zucchini:** Shake each zucchini dry as it is used. It's easiest to stuff zucchini with a teaspoon of filling at a time and gently tamp the filling into the cavity; each zucchini will take about 3 to 5 teaspoons filling. Leave 1/4-inch headspace. The rice will expand as it cooks. (If there is filling left over, roll into balls and simmer with zucchini.)

4 **Simmer the zucchini:** Heat oil in the bottom of a heavy 6- to 8-quart pot over medium heat. Stir in the onion and cook until soft and golden, 7 to 10 minutes. Stir in tomatoes and simmer mixture 5 minutes. Wedge zucchini (and the leftover meatball) in one layer on top of tomatoes; set any remaining zucchini on top. Wedge garlic in between zucchini. Pour in stock or water. It should almost cover zucchini. Bring to a boil, lower heat, cover pot partially with lid, and simmer zucchini until tender, about 45 minutes. Turn zucchini periodically so they cook evenly. Test zucchini for tenderness by poking with a cake tester or small bamboo skewer.

5 **Reduce sauce:** Carefully transfer zucchini to platter with slotted spoon. Bring sauce in pot to a boil over medium heat, and reduce until somewhat thickened to about 3 cups, 15 to 20 minutes. Stir in mint. Taste sauce and season with salt and pepper, to taste.

6 **To Serve:** Spoon sauce over platter of zucchini. Or plate two stuffed zucchini per person and pour about 1/2 cup sauce over and around each plate. Serve zucchini hot, warm, or room temperature. Serve with pilaf or flatbread.

Vary! Improvise!

☛ *Slice cooked, stuffed zucchini into 1/2-inch thick slices just before serving.*

☛ ***Different Garlic:*** *In place of sliced garlic cloves, it's also traditional to stir 1 tablespoon mashed garlic or Lebanese Garlic Sauce (Toum) into tomato sauce along with mint, and simmer 1 to 2 minutes before serving.*

☛ ***Vegetarian:*** *Stuff zucchini with leftover Rice or Bulgar with Lentils and Crisp Onions (M'jaddarah).*

LEAN AND EXTRA-LEAN MEAT

The U.S. Department of Agriculture says that extra-lean ground meat should have no more than 5 percent of the total weight as fat. Lean ground meat is less than 10 percent fat of total weight. This does not apply to ground beef: "lean" ground beef can go as high as 22 percent fat, and "extra lean" as high as 17 percent fat. Since most ground beef is labeled in supermarkets after it crosses state lines, the fat content of beef varies a lot, and often contains more than labeled. In many states, ground beef does not have to be labeled with fat percentages.

LEBANESE CABBAGE ROLLS (MEHSHI MALFOUF)

Notice how cold water is kneaded into the filling; this keeps the meat from forming into hard logs. The converted rice holds its shape during the long cooking. See Glossary for more information on converted rice. These rolls are left open on the ends. If using dried mint, use the freshest available. For more information on stuffed cabbage, see Signature Technique: Stuffed and Braised Cabbage in chapter Greece.

Yields 3 to 3-1/4 cups filling; enough for 32 to 35 medium rolls (1-1/2 tablespoons filling), 6 to 8 servings

6-1/2 ounces uncooked converted (parboiled) rice, 1 cup
1/2 teaspoon ground cinnamon
1/2 teaspoon ground allspice
1/2 teaspoon dried mint
8 ounces ground lamb
8 ounces ground beef (85/15 or 80/20)
1/4 cup olive oil or melted butter
1 tablespoon freshly squeezed lemon juice
Two 3-1/2 pound heads green cabbage
1-1/2 ounces garlic, 6 large cloves, 3 tablespoons peeled and minced
2 to 3 teaspoons dried mint
    or 2 to 3 tablespoons finely sliced mint leaves
1/4 cup freshly squeezed lemon juice, 1 large lemon
Optional: 2 to 3 cups tomato sauce, hot

1 **Prepare the filling:** Mix rice with dry spices: 1 tablespoon kosher salt, 1/2 teaspoon ground pepper, cinnamon, allspice, and mint. In a large mixing bowl, knead together meat and rice with olive oil or melted butter, lemon juice, and 1/4 cup cold water until evenly mixed. Cover bowl and refrigerate 30 minutes. Mix in 1/4 cup cold water. If filling is too firm, add up to 2 tablespoons more cold water. *If preparing filling ahead:* Mix spices with meat and olive oil; add rice, lemon juice, and water as directed just before using.

2 **Boil the cabbage:** Fill a large stockpot with enough cold water to easily cover the cabbage. Bring to a boil. Core the cabbages. Immerse one into the boiling water. After several minutes the leaves will begin to flower out. Detach leaves with tongs and a small knife. Boil leaves until almost tender, 1 to 3 minutes. Repeat with second cabbage. Continue detaching and boiling leaves until there are 30 or more. Set them into a colander to drain. Transfer each batch to a bowl to cool. Reserve cabbage cooking water. Use leftover cabbage hearts for another dish.

3 **Trim the leaves:** Lay each leaf down onto a cutting board rib side up. Shave off the thick outside rib. Reserve trimmings and place on the bottom of a 6- to 8-quart pot. Place 4- to 6-inch leaves into a bowl, and set aside. Cut very large (7-inch or more) leaves in half along the rib. (If rib is very tough it may be lightly trimmed off.)

4 **Stuff and roll:** Place a whole cabbage leaf on work surface with stem end facing nearest the counter edge with inside of leaf facing up. Form a long, narrow log (3 to 4 inches) with 1-1/2 tablespoons stuffing. Set it at an angle off to the right of the stem/rib. Roll up the cabbage leaf; leave ends open. The filling will expand slightly so don't place stuffing too near the ends of the cabbage "cigar." For the halved leaves, lay the leaf on the work surface with the rib parallel and nearest to the edge of the counter. Lay the log of stuffing parallel to and at the bottom near the cabbage rib. Roll up without folding in edges. As they are made, place a snug layer of cabbage rolls on top of rib trimmings in pot, seam side down. Sprinkle with 1 teaspoon kosher salt, half the garlic, half the mint, and half the lemon juice. Arrange a second layer of rolls crosswise to the first. Sprinkle with 1 teaspoon kosher salt and remaining garlic, mint, and lemon juice.

5 **Simmer rolls:** Ladle 3 cups cabbage cooking water or boiling water over cabbage rolls. It should almost cover them. Cover rolls with excess leaves and place a plate on them. Bring to a boil over medium heat, immediately reduce heat to a simmer. Cover pot. Simmer until cabbage is very tender, 1 hour. Remove pot from heat. Rest rolls in pot 30 minutes. If not using immediately, carefully transfer rolls to hotel pan and arrange in one layer to cool. Refrigerate.

6 **To Serve:** Carefully transfer hot stuffed cabbage to a platter or individual plates. Optionally, ladle about 1/4 cup tomato sauce over each serving. Serve cabbage hot.

Vary! Improvise!

☞ **Oven-Bake:** *Preheat oven to 350 degrees F. Arrange rolls in a half hotel pan as directed in recipe. Ladle enough boiling cabbage water over rolls to almost cover. Cover pan with parchment and foil. Bake in oven until rolls are tender, about 1 hour.*

☞ **Lamb:** *Eliminate the beef and use all lamb.*

SAUTÉ, PAN-FRY, AND DEEP-FRY

LEBANESE PAN-FRIED FISH WITH TAHINI SAUCE (SAMAK BI TEHINE)

This dish, popular along the Mediterranean Lebanese coast, is usually made with floured and crisp-fried red mullet. For a lighter dish, bake or steam fish fillets instead.

4 servings

3 ounces tahini, 1/3 cup
3 to 4 tablespoons fresh lemon juice, 1 large lemon
1/4 ounce garlic, 1 large clove, 1-1/2 teaspoons peeled and finely minced
24 ounces fish fillets like red mullet, snapper, trout, or white fish, skin on
4 tablespoons olive oil, more as needed
Flour for dredging

Garnish

Chopped Italian parsley
1 lemon, wedged into 4 to 6 pieces

1 **Prepare tahini sauce:** Whisk tahini, 1/3 cup lemon juice, 1/3 cup warm water, and garlic together. Season with salt and pepper. Taste sauce after 15 minutes and adjust flavors with more lemon or salt. Consistency should be like pancake batter.

2 Wash and blot fish dry. Season with salt and pepper.

3 Heat oil over medium-high in heavy 12-inch skillet. When oil is hot, dredge fillets in flour and shake off excess. Lay fillets skin side down into oil in one layer and sauté until golden, 2 to 3 minutes. Turn fillets and finish cooking remaining side, 1 minute. If all the fillets will not fit into the pan without crowding, fry them in batches with extra oil. Drain fish on paper towel. (Keep warm in preheated 200 degree F oven if necessary.)

4 **To Serve:** Plate fish and serve with tahini sauce. Garnish with parsley and lemon wedges.

Vary! Improvise!

☛ *Prepare this dish with nontraditional salmon.*

☛ **Pomegranate-Olive Sauce:** *Prepare a sauce with 6 tablespoons olive oil, 3 tablespoons pomegranate syrup, and minced garlic instead of tahini-lemon. Good with fried eggplant too.*

LEBANESE FALAFEL DISPUTE

Falafel, a deep-fried fava and chick-pea patty popular in Lebanon, is the object of a cultural quarrel between Israel and Lebanon, as hummus and tabbouleh were the previous year. Israel is accused of claiming the dish as its own. Lebanon set the tabbouleh record. On Sunday May 9, 2010, in Fanar, east of Beirut, Lebanon, over 300 Lebanese chefs prepared a huge plate of falafel to register a confirmed world record, and settle the dispute once and for all. *www.yalibnan.com*

Signature Technique: Fava and Chickpea Balls (Falafel)

- Traditionally, falafel balls or patties are made from dried fava beans and chickpeas that have been soaked 12 hours and ground.

- When making deep-fried falafel balls or patties the texture and consistency of the falafel mixture is most important. The ideal mixture holds together when formed into a patty or ball. If it doesn't, add water to correct a too-dry mixture or flour for a too-wet mixture.

- Canned legumes produce less flavorful, runny "dough."

- A blender or food processor yields wetter dough than a meat grinder.

- Dried fava beans are available with or without skins. Favas with skins must be skinned after soaking. Prepare falafel with all chickpeas if dried fava beans are unavailable.

- Freeze uncooked or cooked patties individually and transfer to freezer baggies up to 3 months.

- Serve falafel tucked into *Arabic Bread* (pocket or pita bread) with *Tahini Sauce (Taratour)*, sliced tomato, mint, parsley, and onions mixed with salt and sumac powder.

FIGURE 9.10 Frying falafel.
Source: DemarK/Shutterstock.

FIGURE 9.11 Pita stuffed with falafel.
Source: Nir Darom/Shutterstock.

FAVA BEAN AND CHICKPEA BALLS (FALAFEL)

Yields 3 cups falafel "paste" (twenty-four 1-ounce/2 tablespoon balls or twelve 2-ounce/1/4-cup patties), 4 to 6 servings

6-1/2 ounces dry, split, and skinned fava beans, 1 cup
7 ounces dry chickpeas, 1 cup
1 ounce onion, 1/4 cup peeled and diced
1 ounce garlic, 4 large cloves, 2 tablespoons peeled and minced
1 ounce trimmed parsley, 1/2 cup chopped
1 ounce cilantro, 1/2 cup finely sliced
1 tablespoon ground coriander
2 teaspoons ground cumin
1/2 teaspoon paprika
1/4 teaspoon red chili powder
Unbleached white flour, as necessary
1/2 teaspoon baking soda
Oil for frying, about 4 cups

Garnish

Arabic Bread (Khobz Arabi)
Tahini Sauce (Taratour)
Mint leaves, parsley leaves, sliced tomatoes, slivered green onions

1 Rinse fava beans and cover with cold water and 1 tablespoon kosher or sea salt. Repeat in separate bowl with chickpeas. Soak beans 12 hours.

2 If the fava beans have skins, slit with a small paring knife and peel them. Rinse favas and chickpeas, drain, and pat dry well; if beans are too wet, the dough will be runny.

3 Combine raw soaked beans, onion, garlic, parsley, and cilantro in a mixing bowl. Grind mixture though meat grinder or grinder attachment on a standing mixer fit with a fine blade. Grind mixture a second time. To clean out grinder, push a piece of parsley through grinder.

4 Knead spices (not baking soda), 2 teaspoons kosher salt, and a little black pepper into bean "dough" until well mixed, 2 minutes. The dough will be somewhat coarse but should hold together, like cooked polenta. Adjust with a little water for dry falafel and a little flour for wet falafel. Cover dough and rest 2 hours at room temperature or refrigerate until 1/2 hour before frying.

5 **Half an hour before frying:** Knead in baking soda. Heat oil in wok or deep-fryer to 365 degrees F over medium-low heat. Set up two half-sheet pans: one lined with parchment for uncooked falafel and one lined with paper towel for fried falafel.

6 **Shape falafel:** With wet hands, form balls the size of a walnut, about 2 tablespoons. For patties, flatten balls gently. Place on prepared sheet pan.

7 **Fry falafel:** Slide falafel into hot oil in batches and fry until richly browned, 5 minutes. Remove with slotted spoon and drain on paper towel-lined sheet pan. (Keep falafel warm in a 200 degree F oven.)

8 **To Serve:** Tuck warm falafel into opened half pieces of warm *Arabic Bread* with *Tahini Sauce*, mint, parsley, tomatoes, and green onions.

Source: *Alice's Kitchen* by Linda Dalal Sawaya.

Vary! Improvise!

☞ *Bake or Broil:* Brush the balls or patties with olive oil and bake in preheated 400 degree F oven 20 minutes, then broil to brown them.

☞ *Sesame Flavor:* Roll balls into unhulled sesame seeds before frying.

GRILL, GRIDDLE, ROAST, BROIL, BAKE, AND BARBECUE

LEBANESE GRILLED MEATS

Shish Tawook
Marinated chicken cubes skewered and grilled.

Shish Kebab
Marinated lamb or beef cubes skewered and grilled.

Shawarma
Chicken, lamb, or beef stacked onto large, upright turning spit, grilled, and sliced off. Usually made into sandwiches with pita or flatbread.

Kefta/Kafta
Ground chicken, lamb, or beef made into meatballs and skewered *or* molded onto skewer and grilled.

FIGURE 9.12 Lamb kefta.
Source: mipstudio/Fotolia.

LEBANESE MEATBALLS (KEFTA)

This is the popular meatball of the Middle East.

Yields 3 cups raw meat mixture, enough for twelve 1/4-cup balls, six 1/2-cup balls, or four 3/4-cup patties, 4 servings

1-1/4 pounds ground lamb
   or 1-1/4 pounds ground goat or ground sirloin
6 ounces onion, 1 cup finely minced or grated
1 ounce trimmed Italian parsley, 1/2 cup finely chopped, packed
1/2 teaspoon cinnamon
1/2 teaspoon allspice
2 teaspoons kosher salt

For Serving

Arabic Bread (Khobz Arabi), Tabbouleh and *Tahini Sauce (Taratour)*

1   Mix lamb, onion, parsley, cinnamon, allspice, and salt together in mixing bowl. Season meat mixture with freshly ground pepper. If possible, refrigerate meat 1 to 4 hours for flavors to mingle.

2   Form seasoned meat into patties, balls, or football shapes. The cooking methods are similar to kibbeh: they may be molded onto wide, flat skewers and grilled or broiled. The patties or balls may be fried, baked, stuffed, or baked or simmered in sauce.

3   **To Serve:** Place hot kefta on platter, and serve with *Arabic Bread, Tabbouleh,* and *Taratour.*

LEBANESE LAMB OR CHICKEN KEBABS (SHISH KEBAB OR SHISH TAWOOK)

Greeks, Turks, and Moroccans as well as many other Middle Eastern cuisines have kebabs in their repertoire.

4 servings

1-3/4 to 2 pounds trimmed lamb meat from leg
   or 1-3/4 to 2 pounds boneless, skinless chicken breasts or thighs

Seasonings

1 ounce garlic, 4 large cloves, 2 tablespoons peeled and minced
2 tablespoons olive oil
4 tablespoons fresh lemon juice, 1 large lemon
1/8 teaspoon ground cinnamon
1/2 teaspoon ground allspice

For Serving

Arabic Bread (Khobz Arabi) or Lebanese Rice Pilaf
Lebanese Salad with Sumac Dressing
Lebanese Garlic Sauce

1 Dice meat into generous 1-inch cubes.

2 Mix meat with **seasonings** and marinate overnight refrigerated or 1 to 2 hours at room temperature. (Longer is better.) Turn meat periodically in marinade.

3 Bring meat to room temperature. Preheat grill. Thread meat onto metal skewers and season with salt and pepper. Grill meat until done as desired.

4 **To Serve:** Remove meat from skewers. Serve on or with *Arabic Bread* or *Lebanese Rice Pilaf*, *Lebanese Salad with Sumac Dressing* and *Lebanese Garlic Sauce*.

FIGURE 9.13 Lebanese savory pies (Fatayer).

LEBANESE SAVORY PIES (FATAYER)

Fatayer are small savory "pies" usually found stuffed with meat, spinach, or cheese. A beloved part of Middle Eastern cuisine, they can be found in Turkey, Syria, Lebanon, and Jordan. The classical dough is a yeast dough (aajeen), but for speed, some cooks make short crust dough sometimes with baking powder. These savory pies can be hors d'oeuvres, part of a larger meal, or serve as snack food anytime.

Yields about 20 "pies"

Dough

Yields about 20 ounces

1 teaspoon active dry yeast
1/2 teaspoon sugar
About 12 ounces all-purpose flour, 2-1/2 to 2-3/4 cups, extra for kneading and rolling
1 teaspoon kosher salt
3 tablespoons olive oil, *divided*

Spinach Filling (Fatayer bi Sabanekh)

Yields 2-1/4 cups

1 pound baby *or* trimmed fresh spinach, washed and drained
   or 10-ounces frozen chopped spinach, about 1 cup thawed and drained
2 to 3 tablespoons olive oil
4 ounces onions, 1 cup peeled and finely diced
2 tablespoons freshly squeezed lemon juice, 1/2 large lemon
Optional: 1-1/2 ounces toasted pine nuts, 1/4 cup

Feta Cheese Filling

Yields about 2-1/4 cups

2 to 3 tablespoons olive oil
3 to 4-1/2 ounces trimmed green onions, 6 to 9 large, 3/4 to 1-1/4 cups finely chopped
12 ounces feta, 2-1/4 cups finely diced
1-1/2 teaspoons sumac powder, more to taste
2 to 3 tablespoons fresh lemon juice, 1 large lemon, more to taste

Olive oil for brushing finished fatayer

1 **Prepare dough:** In a small bowl, mix yeast, sugar, and 1/2 cup lukewarm water and let it rest 5 minutes. Combine flour, salt, and 2 tablespoons oil evenly in large mixing bowl. Stir yeast mixture and an additional 1/2 cup lukewarm water into flour. Knead dough with a little more flour 1 to 2 minutes. Form into a ball. Pour remaining tablespoon oil in clean bowl and roll dough in it. Cover bowl loosely with plastic wrap. Set dough aside in a warm spot to rise until doubled, 1 to 1-1/2 hours.

2 **Prepare a filling:**

Spinach

If using fresh spinach, chop spinach and place in an 8-quart pot. Bring to a boil over medium heat. Cover and steam 1 minute. Uncover and turn spinach with tongs. Cook just until it wilts evenly. Place cooked spinach in fine strainer, cool it, then squeeze dry to yield about 1 cup. Chop fresh spinach and place in small bowl. Heat oil in 10-inch skillet over medium heat. Sauté onion until golden, 5 to 7 minutes. Remove pan from heat and stir in fresh or thawed spinach. Season spinach with salt, pepper, and lemon juice, to taste. Stir in optional nuts and place mixture back into bowl to cool.

Feta Cheese

Heat oil in 9- to 10-inch skillet over medium heat and stir in green onions. Cook until wilted down, about 2 minutes. Remove skillet from heat. Transfer onions to mixing bowl; cool slightly. Stir in feta, sumac, and lemon juice. Season with salt and pepper. Taste and adjust flavors.

3 **Press dough down:** Lightly knead olive oil in bowl into dough. Form dough into a 20-inch log. Scale out 1-ounce balls *or* cut log into 20 (1-ounce) pieces. Set pieces on lightly floured workspace and cover with plastic wrap.

4 Preheat oven to 375 degrees F.

5 *Form the fatayer:* Fatayer dough works best when kept moist, so avoid the use of too much flour. Lightly dip cut sides of dough into flour and shake off excess. Roll dough into *4-inch circles*. Lightly dampen the edges of the circle of dough.

6 **Fill the Fatayer:** Place dough circle on work surface. Place 2 tablespoons filling in the center—it will be quite full. Form the triangle by stretching up two edges of the dough and pinching together with right thumb and forefinger. Pull up dough edge from opposite side and pinch dough together from top down to corner to form two more seams for a total of three seams. Finish with remaining dough and filling.

7 **Bake fatayer:** Place finished fatayer on parchment-covered sheet pan. Brush lightly with olive oil. Bake until lightly browned, 20 to 25 minutes. Brush fatayer with a little water as soon as they arrive from the oven.

8 **To Serve:** Serve fatayer warm or at room temperature as a snack, mezze or with other luncheon dishes.

Vary! Improvise!

☞ *For Lenten* fatayer, *cooks fill the dough with seasoned mashed chickpeas.*
☞ *For 2 bite hors d'oeuvres: Prepare each fatayer with 1/2 ounce dough (instead of 1 ounce) and half the filling.*

LAMB AND BULGAR CASSEROLE (KIBBEH BI-SANIYEH)

Kibbeh bil-Saniyeh *is made traditionally in a round pan and is best made with boned and skinned leg of lamb. Use preground meat or grind meat through meat grinder or in a food processor.*

Yields 9-inch by 11-1/2-inch by 2-inch half-hotel pan, 6 to 8 servings

24 ounces boned and trimmed lamb leg meat (silver-skin and fat removed)
   or 24 ounces lean beef

Stuffing: For 7 ounces of the ground lamb

Yields 3 cups

1-2/3 ounces pine nuts, 1/3 cup
1/4 cup unsalted butter
   or 1/4 cup olive oil
1 pound onions, 4 cups peeled and finely chopped
2 teaspoons ground cinnamon
2 teaspoons ground allspice

Kibbeh Shell: For 17 ounces of the ground lamb

Yields 4 cups

6 ounces onion, peeled, halved, and each half quartered
1 tablespoon ground cinnamon
1 tablespoon ground allspice
Optional: 4 to 5 tablespoons fresh lemon juice, 1 to 2 medium lemons
7 ounces fine bulgur, about 1-1/2 cups

2 to 3 tablespoons melted butter or olive oil

1 Grind the meat. Skip this step if using preground meat.

   Meat Grinder Method: Cut lamb into chunks to fit into the tube of a meat grinder. Pass all the meat through once, then again. Push a piece of onion through to clean the grinder.

   Food Processor Method: To grind the meat in a food processor, dice it evenly, and pulse-chop until evenly ground but with some texture. Too-pasty meat makes the shell difficult to shape. Remove meat from processor.

2 Divide meat into two separate batches each weighing: 7 ounces and 17 ounces.

3 Prepare the stuffing: Spread pine nuts on baking sheet and roast until golden, 5 minutes. Leave onion on. Melt butter or heat oil a deep 12-inch skillet over medium heat. When hot, stir in onion and cook until soft, 5 to 7 minutes. Add **7 ounces ground meat** and constantly stir it to break it up until it is completely cooked, 2 to 3 minutes. Stir in spices and cook 1 minute. Remove pan from heat and season with salt and pepper to taste. Stir in pine nuts.

4 **Prepare kibbeh shell:** Pulse-chop onion pieces in food processor until very fine. Add 17 ounces **ground meat**, cinnamon, allspice, lemon juice, finely ground pepper, and 2 teaspoons kosher salt. Lightly pulse-chop together until smooth. Taste and adjust seasonings.

5 Fill a mixing bowl with salted cold water, and set aside. Place bulgar in bowl, cover in cold water, and wash in two changes of cold water; drain well. Knead bulgar and (shell) meat together with clean hands. Dip hands occasionally into the cold salted water to moisten the hands and the **kibbeh**. Add a little water to the kibbeh to soften it and knead until mixture is smooth, 2 to 4 minutes. Taste and adjust the seasoning if necessary.

6 Preheat oven to 400 degrees F.

7 **Assemble kibbeh:** Rub a half-hotel pan (9-inch by 11-1/2-inch by 2-inch) with oil or butter. Divide kibbeh shell mixture into two equal pieces. Set one aside. Moisten both hands in cold salted water. Divide one of the half pieces of kibbeh and flatten pieces onto the bottom of the oiled pan to an even 1/2-inch thick. Smooth entire layer with wet fingers. Spread the stuffing evenly over the bottom layer.

8 **Make the top layer of kibbeh shell:** Cover and overlap the back of an inverted half-sheet pan with plastic wrap. With damp hands, divide remaining ball of kibbeh shell into four pieces. Pat the pieces into an oblong matching the dimensions of the half-hotel pan, about 1/2-inch thick. Use a little cold water to "glue" the pieces together, if necessary, and to smooth the entire layer.

9 Carefully line up the sheet pan and kibbeh oblong with the half-hotel pan and flip it onto the top of the filling. With wet fingers, smooth and piece together any cracks.

10 **Finish the dish:** Cut the pie into serving size pieces all the way through with a damp knife. Draw shallow geometric patterns on top of each piece if desired. Run a knife around the edge to loosen meat from the edges. Drizzle top of kibbeh with melted butter or oil. Place pan into oven and bake until golden, 30 to 45 minutes.

11 **To Serve:** Remove kibbeh from oven, and let it rest 15 minutes to firm up before cutting and serving.

Source: *Lebanese Cuisine* by Anissa Helou.

Vary! Improvise!

☛ ***Lebanese Kibbeh "Pizza":*** *Prepare the bottom with 2/3 cup bulgar, 1 pound ground lamb, and 6 ounce onion, puréed. Season with cinnamon, salt, and pepper. Press into an oiled 11-inch tart part and brush with 2 tablespoons olive oil. Slice into wedges and bake at 375 degrees F until browned. Prepare onion-pine nut stuffing for Stuffed Lamb and Bulgar Balls Simmered in Tahini Sauce (Kibbeh Arna-bieh). Season with 1 tablespoon pomegranate molasses. Pile onto baked meat shell, cut and serve.*

FIGURE 9.14   Arabic bread.
Source: Simon Smith/DK Images.

ARABIC BREAD (KHOBZ ARABI)

This bread is also known as pocket or pita bread.

Yields about 24 ounces dough, eight 6-1/2- to 7-inch pitas

2-1/4 teaspoons active dry baking yeast
1 teaspoon sugar
14 to 15 ounces all-purpose flour, about 3 cups plus extra for kneading and rolling
    or 4-1/2 to 5 ounces whole wheat flour, 1 cup *and* 9 to 10 ounces unbleached white
       flour, 2 cups
1-1/2 teaspoons kosher salt
2 tablespoons olive oil, *divided*

1   Dissolve yeast in 1/2 cup warm water. Add sugar and stir until dissolved. Let sit until yeast is frothy, 5 minutes.

2   Combine flour and salt in large bowl. Make a depression in the middle of flour and pour in yeast water and 1 tablespoon oil. Slowly stir in 2/3 cup warm water. Mix with wooden spoon or hands until dough comes together into a ball.

3   Place dough on well-floured surface (with up to 1/4 cup flour) *or* in mixer fitted with dough paddle (on low speed) and knead until dough is smooth, earlobe soft and elastic, 10 to 15 minutes. Dough should spring back when pressed.

4   Coat large bowl with remaining 1 tablespoon oil. Place dough in bowl and turn dough to coat evenly. Cover bowl loosely with plastic wrap and set in a warm place to rise until doubled, 1 to 1-1/2 hours.

    To get the pita to puff, three things are important:
- Knead long enough to develop the gluten structure of the dough.
- Roll the dough evenly.
- Bake on a very hot surface (oven and baking surface preheated 30 minutes).

5   **Thirty minutes before baking:** Preheat oven to 450 degrees F. Place one full-sheet pan or two half-sheet pans on bottom rack of oven upside down. Press down dough and roll into an even 8-inch log. Slice into 8 equal pieces *or* scale out 8 scant 3-ounce pieces. Cover with plastic wrap and rest dough 5 minutes.

6   Generously flour work surface. Lay cut sides of 1 dough slice into flour. Roll out into an even round 6-1/2- to 7-inches diameter. Repeat rolling with 3 more dough balls. Place dough rounds on half sheets of parchment and let them rise 5 to 7 minutes.

7   Open oven and slide dough rounds on the hot sheet pan/s or onto pizza stone. Bake until bread puffs and browns slightly, 5 minutes. Do not open oven door. Flip pitas with tongs and bake second side, 3 to 5 minutes. Remove each pita with a spatula, and repeat process with remaining 4 dough balls.

8   **To Serve:** Serve flatbread warm, or cool fully and store. To soften, wrap bread in a towel while warm. Flatbread can be refrigerated 1 week and frozen 1 month in freezer bags.

Vary! Improvise!

☛ *Add herbs or ground spices to dough.*
☛ *Roll flatbreads in sesame seeds before baking.*

FIGURE 9.15   Thick za'atar bread.
Source: Terry Davis/Shutterstock.

FLATBREAD TOPPED WITH ZA'ATAR (MANAQISH OR MAN'OUSHE BI-ZA'ATAR)

This is popular street and breakfast food. In Lebanon, za'atar flatbreads are either baked in an oven or cooked on a saj—an inverted wok placed over charcoal, wood fire, or gas burner.

1 recipe *Lebanese Flatbread (Khobz Arabi)* dough
6 tablespoons *Signature Seasonings: Za'atar*
    or 6 tablespoons commercial za'atar mixture
6 tablespoons olive oil

For Serving

Labneh (strained whole milk yogurt)
Olives

1 Prepare pita dough as directed in *Lebanese Flatbread (Khobz Arabi)*. Mix together *za'atar* and olive oil. After rolling dough into 1/4-inch-thick rounds, press with fingers to dimple dough. Paint or spoon and spread za'atar mixture over dough to the edges. Sprinkle with kosher salt.

2 Cook in one of two ways:

- In preheated 400 degree F oven until browned.
- On preheated cast-iron skillet or griddle over medium to medium-low heat. Place pita, topping side up in hot skillet *or* on griddle. Cover with lid. Cook until dough is cooked through and the bottom is crisp and golden, 3 to 5 minutes.

3 **To Serve:** Cut flatbread, and serve with bowl of labneh and a bowl of olives.

Vary! Improvise!

☛ *Roll the dough super thin, paint with za'atar mixture, and bake until browned and crisp.*

PAPER-THIN BREAD (KHOBZ MARQUQ)

Marquoq is a paper-thin bread made with a yeast dough. The dough "bakes" on a hot *saj*, a convex metal disk, which looks like an overturned wok. The bread is the same as Persian-Iranian *lavash* bread. For a recipe, consult chapter *Persia-Iran and Republic of Georgia*.

FIGURE 9.16 Paper-thin bread (khobz marquq).
Source: YuG/Shutterstock.

SALAD AND VEGETABLE METHODS

THREE LEBANESE SALADS (SALATA)

These dressings make cooked or raw vegetables addictive.

Yields enough for 5 to 6 cups vegetables *or* raw greens

Lebanese Yogurt Dressing

Yields 1 cup

1/4 ounce garlic, 1 large clove, peeled
8 ounces whole milk yogurt, 1 cup
Optional: 1 teaspoon or more tahini

Garnish: 2 tablespoons olive oil

Lebanese Sumac Dressing

Yields 1/2 cup

1/4 cup extra virgin olive oil, more as needed
1/4 cup freshly squeezed lemon juice, 1 large lemon
    or 1/4 cup cider vinegar
1 tablespoon ground sumac

Lebanese Tahini Dressing

See *Lebanese Tahini Sauce (Tarator)*

Salad Ingredients

Arugula, purslane, tomatoes, carrots, zucchini, lettuce, diced potatoes, chickpeas, steamed green beans, finely sliced cabbage, dandelion greens, roasted eggplant cubes, or sliced cucumbers.

1 *Prepare Yogurt Dressing:* Finely mince or mash garlic with salt. Whisk together yogurt and optional tahini. Taste and adjust flavors. Season highly with salt. Consistency of dressing should be like pancake batter.

2 **Prepare Sumac Dressing:** Whisk together olive oil, lemon juice or vinegar, and sumac. Season with salt and pepper to taste.

3 **Prepare Tahini Dressing:** See *Lebanese Tahini Sauce (Tarator)* and thin with water to achieve dressing consistency, like cream.

4 Rest dressings 20 minutes and taste again. Adjust flavor and texture if necessary. Choose **salad ingredients** and prepare 5 to 6 cups for each dressing.

5 **To Serve:** Toss dressing on chosen salad ingredients. For tougher vegetables like cabbage, refrigerate 30 minutes to give vegetables time to soften. Garnish salad tossed with **Yogurt Dressing** with olive oil.

LEBANESE SIMPLE SALAD

Like the French, Lebanese love salad. Their "simple salad" is made from sliced or torn romaine hearts, lightly peeled and thinly sliced small cucumbers, and wedged ripe tomatoes. Sumac or tahini dressings dress the vegetables.

ARABIC BREAD AND VEGETABLE SALAD
(FATTOUSH)

The name fattoush *is derived from an Arabic word meaning small crumbs. Some Lebanese cooks leave herb leaves whole and some chop them.*

Yields about 8 cups, 4 to 6 generous servings

Lebanese Sumac or Lebanese Yogurt Dressing
Two 7-inch Arabic flatbread or pita breads, about 3 cups toasted, cooled, and broken apart
1-1/2 ounces green onions, about 3 large, 3/4 cup finely chopped
or 4 ounces red onions, 1 cup peeled and thinly sliced
1/2 ounce mint leaves, 1 cup lightly packed
5 ounce romaine heart, washed and dried, 4 cups sliced into 1/2-inch ribbons
1/2 ounce trimmed curly parsley, 1 cup loosely packed lightly chopped
6 ounces cucumber, 1 cup peeled, seeded and diced or sliced into half moons
4 to 5 ounces red bell pepper, 1 cup stemmed, seeded and diced into 1/2-inch squares
16 ounces tomatoes, 2 medium-large, 2 to 3 cups diced into 1/2-inch cubes

Garnish: Sumac powder

1 Whisk **Dressing** together and set aside to rest.

2 Toast flatbread and cool. Break into 1/2- to 1-inch pieces and set aside.

3 To soften raw red onions, toss and knead lightly with salt, rest 20 minutes, and drain before using. Toss green onions or red onions, mint, romaine, parsley, cucumbers, bell pepper, and tomatoes in bowl.

4 **To Serve:** Toss salad with toasted flatbread and **Dressing**. Pass a small bowl of sumac powder for each diner to sprinkle on the salad.

PARSLEY AND BULGAR SALAD (TABBOULEH)

Many American versions of this famous salad feature more bulgar than parsley or mint. Traditionally, tabbouleh is green with more parsley and mint than bulgar. Many Lebanese use curly parsley. The flavor is not as dominant as Italian parsley. Wash herbs the day before and wrap in paper toweling or clean cotton towel, or they'll turn to mush when chopped.

FIGURE 9.17 Tabbouleh.
Source: Matthew Cole/Fotolia.

Yields 4 cups, about 4 servings

1-1/4 to 1-1/2 ounces fine bulgar, 1/4 cup
8 ounces tomato, 1 medium-large, 1 to 1-1/2 cups diced 1/4-inch cubes
4 tablespoons lemon juice, *divided*, about 1 large lemon
2 ounces trimmed curly parsley *or* Italian parsley
1/4 to 1/2 ounce mint leaves, 1/2 cup finely sliced
   or 2 tablespoons dried mint
1 ounce trimmed green onions, 2 large, 1/4 cup finely chopped, more to taste
4 tablespoons olive oil
4 to 5 ounces romaine lettuce heart, whole leaves washed and dried

1 Place bulgar in strainer, rinse under warm water, and drain. Place bulgar into mixing bowl and stir in tomato and half the lemon juice. Soak bulgar 20 minutes in tomatoes and lemon juice.

2 Roll parsley into a ball on cutting board and chop finely and evenly to yield about 3 cups. (Pulse large amounts in food processor.)

3 Fold parsley, mint, green onions, and olive oil into bulgar and tomatoes. Season salad with salt and freshly ground black pepper. Rest tabbouleh salad 20 minutes. Season tabbouleh with salt, pepper, olive oil, and remaining lemon juice, to taste.

4 **To Serve:** Pile tabbouleh high on a large platter and arrange romaine leaves around it. Scoop salad with romaine leaves.

Vary! Improvise!

☞ **Wheat Allergic:** *Substitute cooked or soaked quinoa or cooked basmati rice for bulgar.*

☞ *Add a small dice of vegetables like peeled and seeded cucumbers or pitted olives.*

☞ *Add cooked chickpeas to tabbouleh.*

FIGURE 9.18 Okra.
Source: Roger Phillips/DK Images.

OKRA WITH TOMATOES AND ONIONS (BAMIEH BI ZEIT)

Serve dish warm as a side dish with rice and chicken or at room temperature as a mezze salad.

Yields about 6 cups, 4 to 6 servings

1 pound medium-sized okra
8 ounces small boiling onions *or* shallots, tops trimmed off
5 tablespoons olive oil, *divided*
3/4 ounce garlic, about 3 large cloves, peeled and quartered lengthwise
1 pound tomatoes, about 2 cups peeled, cored, and diced medium
1 ounce cilantro or trimmed parsley, 1/4 cup finely sliced
1 tablespoon pomegranate molasses

For Serving

Hot cooked rice
Lebanese Lamb or Chicken Kebabs (Shish Kebab or Shish Tawook)

1 Bring small saucepan of water to boil. Meanwhile, pare top stems off okra, but don't cut lower into pod. Wash okra, drain, and set aside. Drop onions or shallots into boiling water until skins loosen, 3 to 5 minutes. Rinse with cold water, drain, and peel. Set aside.

2 Heat 3 tablespoons oil in a deep 11- to 12-inch skillet, over medium-high heat. Stir in onions or shallots and garlic. Cook vegetables, shaking skillet periodically, until they begin to brown evenly, 5 minutes.

3 Stir in okra, lower heat to medium, and sauté until it begins to soften, 5 minutes. Stir in tomatoes and season with salt and pepper. Reduce heat to low, cover pan, and simmer 5 minutes. Remove lid and simmer until okra is tender and sauce is thickened and reduced, 5 to 10 minutes. Stir in herbs, remaining olive oil and pomegranate molasses. Taste and adjust seasonings.

4 **To Serve:** Serve okra warm or at room temperature as a side dish with rice, lamb, or chicken or as a mezze salad.

Source: *Arabesque: A Taste of Morocco, Turkey & Lebanon* by Claudia Roden.

REVIEW QUESTIONS

1. Name two cultures that influenced Lebanese cuisine.

2. Discuss kibbeh and its various forms.

3. Discuss the fats that are used in Lebanese cuisine.

4. What is za'atar?

5. What is bulgar? How is it prepared?

CHAPTER TEN

THE MIDDLE EAST AND CAUCASUS: PERSIA-IRAN AND REPUBLIC OF GEORGIA

This chapter will:

- Introduce the rich and varied histories of Iran and Georgia, their diverse geographies, cultural influences, and climates.
- Introduce the culinary culture, regions, and dining etiquette in Iran and Georgia.

- Discuss the importance of religion and the Silk Road on both cuisines.

- Discuss the importance of the *supra* and *tamada* on dining etiquette in Georgia.

- Identify the foods, flavor foundations, seasoning devices, and favored cooking techniques.

- Teach the techniques and the marvelous, creative dishes of ancient Persia, Iran, and the Republic of Georgia.

IRAN AND PERSIA: EXOTIC AND INFLUENTIAL EMPIRE

Once the Center

In the introduction to The Legendary Cuisine of Persia *by Margaret Shaida, Gregory Lima, who started an English-language newspaper in Tehran in 1958 and lived there many years, observes that although "Persia is no longer at the center of the world," it once was. He muses that perhaps when caravans with Chinese silk, Indian saffron, Arabic frankincense and Roman gold crossed Iran, people have might asked, "Where is the center of the world?" Lima's answer is that surely was Iran with her fine wine, profound poets and delightfully delicious food.*

Modern Iran is extremely rich in natural resources. They have the second largest oil and gas reserves in the world and large quantities of low-grade uranium. But Iran has given the world more than just oil: ancient Persians created highway systems, engineered subterranean mountain-to-desert aqueducts called *qanats* and windmills, contributed great poets like Rumi and Omar Khayyam, mathematicians, astronomers, miniature painters,

FIGURE 10.1A Map of Iran and the Republic of Georgia.

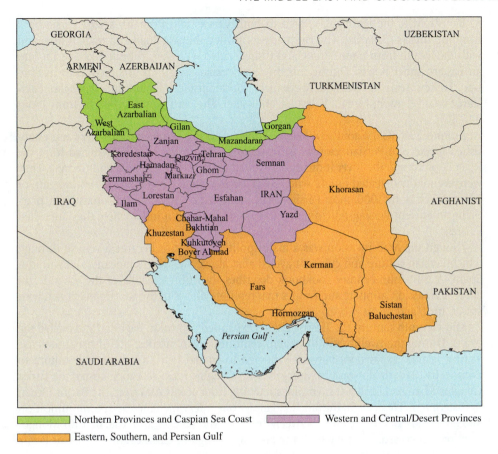

FIGURE 10.1B Map of Iran.

amazingly skilled carpet weavers, and disseminated a cuisine that influenced all who came in contact with it.

Around 3000 BCE, the first known well-developed culture to inhabit the southern area of modern-day Iran was the *Elamite*. Around 1500 BCE, the *Aryans*, descended from semi-nomadic Central Asian tribes, settled nearby in the area called Fars or Pars and were called *Persians*. The Persians established dynasty rule. From 580 BCE to 529 BCE, Cyrus the Great of the Achaemenid Dynasty began the Persian Empire's period of greatest glory. Cyrus conquered the northern Persian region of Media, Lydia in Turkey, and Babylon in Mesopotamia; his son Cambyses continued with the acquisition of Egypt.

Darius I took over in 521 BCE and expanded the Persian Empire to the world's largest at the time. It ranged from India, to central Asia, the Caucasus, and Egypt. Persians influenced religion and philosophy and introduced their cuisine into captured countries. Darius built Persepolis, Persia's fifth capital city, a road system, created a postal system, coins, and a consistent system of weight and measure. In 486 BCE Darius died, and his son Xerxes ruled Persia. Xerxes conquered Greek land, but eventually the Greeks destroyed his fleet, and the Empire went into a slow decline.

In 330 BCE, Alexander the Great came from Greece and Macedonia to conquer the wealthy but weak Persia. Persia remained under Greek rule (*Seleucid*) for almost 160 years. During that time Greek and Persian cultures mingled, exchanging ideas, architecture, food, and culture. The sophisticated, diverse, and exotic cuisine of the Persians fascinated the Greeks, whose food was notably plain.

By 171 BCE, the *Parthians*, related to both Greeks and Persians, seized Persia back from the Greeks (*Selucids*). The Parthians controlled the Silk Road and trade routes, and with the wealth from trade (Rome and China traded with Persia) built Persia again into an Eastern super power. During this time the Persian kingdom occupied areas in Iran, Iraq, Turkey, Armenia, Georgia, Azerbaijan, Turkmenistan, Afghanistan, Tajikistan, Pakistan, Syria, Lebanon, Jordan, Palestine, and Israel. The Parthians ruled Persia from about 247 BCE.

Around 224 BCE, a southern Persian tribe called the *Sassanians* took over and established the second Persian Empire. At its peak the Sassanian Empire stretched from the River Euphrates to the River Indus and included modern-day Armenia and Georgia. They were eventually defeated in 642 when Arab forces invaded, bringing the new religion of Islam to Persia. By 1000, most Persians had converted to Islam. Many Zoroastrians, practicing an ancient Persian religion, fled to Gujarat in western India where they are called *Parsees*.

Though the Arab invasion was a major political defeat, it became a vehicle through which Persian culture and cuisine traveled afar, along the Mediterranean coast and into Spain. A thirteenth-century cookbook describes the culinary skills of the magnificent court of Abassid Caliphate and recipes that replicate dishes of the Sassanian era rich with spices, fruit, and meats.

Mid-eleventh century, the Turkish *Seljuks* expanded control to Baghdad and ousted the Arabs. During the twelfth and thirteenth centuries, the Crusades, the Christian defense against Islamic expansion, perversely helped to spread Persian cuisine and culture to Europe. In 1220, the far-eastern Mongols, with Genghis Khan as leader, ousted the Turks. Genghis Khan had built a vast empire stretching from across Asia from the Pacific Ocean to eastern Iran. He brought the Silk Road under one rule, which increased communication and trade and expanded culture between the West, Middle East, and Asia. By 1501 Mongol domination ceased, but they took the language, religion, cuisine, and culture of Persia with them into India and become Moghuls.

The third Persian Empire started with Ismail Safavi in 1501. He gradually unified a dislocated country under one rule. The Safavids remained in power until 1736. At their height they controlled an empire that extended from Afghanistan and Pakistan in the East to parts of modern-day Turkey and Iran. This was a golden era for Persian art and architecture: Persian extravagance and luxury fascinated Europeans. Seventeenth-century travel writer Jean Chardin observed, "Saffron was the best in the world. . . . Melons were regarded as excellent fruit, and there were more than 50 different sorts. . . . After melons the finest fruits were grapes and dates, and the best dates were grown in Jahrom."

From 1587 to 1629, Safavi's descendant Shah Abbas the Great built schools, encouraged crafts and Persian carpet making, and finished the beautiful capital Isfahan. From 1779 to 1857, the Persians were involved in a civil war and eight wars with the Russians, Turks, and Afghans. After the Persian Revolution (1906 to 1911), the Qajar Dynasty was defeated. The Pahlavi Dynasty (1925 to 1979) followed with much political unrest centered around oil, and the countries who wanted it: Russia, Britain, and the United States. In 1979 an Islamic Revolution put the cleric Ayatollah Khomeini in control. He declared Iran an Islamic Republic and killed the ruling shah's associates. Iran became a conservative Islamic country. In 1980, Iraqi ruler Saddam Hussein, seeing Iran's turmoil, invaded. The war destroyed much of Iran and killed more than a million people.

After Khomeini died in 1989, moderate clerics won the next two presidential elections. They relaxed Khomeini's hostility to the West and hoped to improve women's status, but powerful conservatives blocked them. In 2005, Mahmoud Ahmadinejad, a confrontational, conservative Muslim, was elected president of Iran's more than 70 million people. Iran's relations with the West continue to be tense.

LANGUAGE, PHILOSOPHY, AND RELIGION: ISLAM RULES

Persian ethnicity dominates with 51 percent of the population; Azeris, Gilakis, Mazandaranis, Kurds, Arabs, and Armenians comprise the remainder. The main language is Persian (*Farsi*) and Persian dialects along with a smaller portion of Turkic and Turkic dialects, Kurdish, Luri, Baluchi, and Arabic.

Iran is 99 percent Muslim (mostly Shi'a and a few Sunni), with the remaining 1 percent Baha'i, Christian, Jewish, and Zoroastrian. Baha'i and the ancient Zoroastrian faith originated in Iran and have had a profound influence on them. Other faiths have the right to practice, but all women must cover arms, legs, and head, as is required for Muslim women. Islam is a monotheistic (one God) religion with followers of the prophet Muhammad who practice the "five pillars of Islam," which includes the belief in one God, and Muhammad as messenger, praying daily, giving to the poor, fasting during Ramadan, and making a pilgrimage to Mecca, Muhammad's birthplace (in 570).

GEOGRAPHY AND CLIMATE: THE BRIDGE THAT LINKS ASIA AND EUROPE

Twice the size of California, Oregon, and Washington combined, 90 percent of Iran falls within an earthquake zone. Iran's landscape varies; much is arid with rugged, barren mountains and harsh deserts, which have shaped Iran's circumstances. The Caspian Sea coast has fertile lowlands where rainfall is high. The populous Northern and Western regions are most mountainous, with the Caucasus, Zagros, and Alborz ranges. Iran's highest peak, *Mount Damavand* (18,406 feet), is the highest mountain on the Eurasian landmass west of India. Eastern and central Iran has salt lakes and desert basins; the largest is Dasht-e Kavir.

Iran has a diverse climate with four seasons. It is mostly arid or semiarid, ranging from subtropical in the south to subpolar at higher elevations. The northwest is the coldest region, where winters see heavy snow and below freezing temperatures. On the northern Caspian Sea coast temperatures rarely go below freezing and rarely exceed 80 to 85 degrees F; it is often foggy and humid with dense rain forests. Winter brings chill winds from Siberia to the interior basin or Iranian Plateau. The southern and Gulf coast region has warm winters and scorching summers with high humidity.

FARMING AND AGRICULTURE

Though Iran's climate is mostly semi-arid with much desert, it has good soil. With underground *qanats* bringing snowmelt and rainwater from the mountains, many desert cities and foothill regions are lush with produce. Central Iran grows dates and pistachios; northern Iran grows rice and olives and fresh fruit. Vegetables and herbs grow all over. Because of the dry air, many foods like limes, herbs, raisins, apricots, tomatoes, and legumes are preserved by drying. Less than half of Iran's crops are irrigated and only about one-fourth of Iran has enough rain for agricultural production. The remaining three-fourths receives less than 10 inches of rainfall per year.

IRANIAN CUISINE: MASTERS OF THE EXOTIC

Iranian cuisine is often referred to as "Persian," but modern Iranian food is a mixture of ancient Persian and other cultures. Iranian-Persian cuisine, one of the oldest and richest with strong influences of the Ottomans, Turkey, and Greece, is not the same as most Middle Eastern cuisines. Throughout centuries, the Persian Empire freely mingled its rich culture through war, and trade along the Silk Road with China, India, Rome, and Eastern Europe. The result is a vibrantly delicious, exotic cuisine unlike any other. The early sophistication of Persian cuisine is due in part to the frequent contact that ancient Persians had with other cultures. It likely helped to inspire and perfect their culinary artistry.

Grapes, lemons, pomegranates, melons, cucumbers, spinach, and roses originated in Persia, and Persian growers refined many other types of trees, fruits, vegetables, and culinary flowers. The Greeks took lemons, pomegranates, pistachios, and many Persian desserts to the Mediterranean. The Christian Crusades returned to Europe with rose petal jam, pomegranate, quince, barberries, and mulberries, and the Arabs adopted and spread the use of rice, eggplants, spinach, oranges, lemons, and tarragon. The unique flavors of lamb, sour cherries, pomegranates and syrup, plums, dates, and figs mingled in Persian cuisine with dried limes, tarragon, cilantro, basil, dill, tamarind, barberry, saffron, rosewater, and fenugreek leaves.

Early Greeks wrote about Persia's abundance of wheat, barley, rye, livestock, onions, garlic, beets, capers, apple juice, honey, almond oil, raisins, nuts, and aromatic spices and herbs. An eleventh-century historian noted that Persians marinated dishes with wild birds and other game, fish, lamb, and veal in vinegar, mustard, stock, garlic, dill, and green and black cumin, or in yogurt. They were flavored with spices, and stewed, broiled, or roasted. Meat was marinated in pomegranate juice and barbecued chicken sweetened with sugar, tinted with saffron, then skewered and grilled. Stuffed grape leaves; puddings made of rice, milk, honey, butter, eggs, and rosewater; and sweets scented with rose and orange flower water were also popular. These foods and dishes still define Iranian cooking.

Religion has helped to shape Persian and Iranian cuisine. Pork, fish without scales, and alcohol are absent. Cooks rely on poultry, game, sheep, and lamb, which inspired many meat dishes like kebabs and stews as well as yogurt and fruit drinks.

Persians who followed Zoroaster around 600 BCE (Zoroastrians) believed that the balance of life between good and evil influenced every part of life. This constant struggle could manifest in disease caused by body imbalances. Food became instrumental in maintaining health. Many modern Iranians still follow this way of cooking by classifying foods like animal fats, chicken, wheat, sugar, and dried fruits and vegetables as "heating," and beef, fish rice, dairy, fresh vegetables, and fruits as "cooling." To achieve balance, chicken (heating) might be served with a garnish of pomegranate seeds (cooling). Mothers, knowing their children's constitutions, might, for example, feed a child with a hot constitution, cooling foods to achieve balance.

Whether they cook at home or in the palaces of Persian kings, women have dominated Iranian cuisine throughout its history. Iranian men rarely cook, and they expect expert cooking from women. The best food is served in homes. Restaurant food is limited to mainly kabobs and rice or foreign foods like pizza and hamburgers, so Iranian cuisine isn't well known in much of the world.

Cooking is naturally linked to the seasons and it would seem odd to most Iranians to eat a food out of season. Although each household always has its distinctive touches, a visitor arriving during cherry season would find every household serving dishes made with seasonal produce like *albalo polow* (rice with sour cherries and chicken) or cold soup with yogurt, mint, and cucumber. Conserving food is an important part of the Iranian kitchen and of winter meals. Dried legumes, dried herbs, jams, *torshii* (pickles), and methods for preserving fruit, vegetables, meat, fish, dairy, and tomato paste have been developed and passed on by women from generation to generation.

Iranian cuisine is characterized by the use of spices, in particular cinnamon and saffron, the liberal use of oil (a mark of generosity), vibrant color, and by long simmering times. Rice dishes are Iranian cooks' trademark. Plain boiled rice (*kateh*) is cooked so that it acquires a distinctive golden crust. Iranian rice *polows*, studded with bits of meat, nuts, fruit, flavored with saffron and with a golden crust, are delicate and refined.

Iranian cuisine reveals its dualistic character (light and dark, sweet and sour, hot and cold) in the trademark *khoresh*, a savory stew with meat and split peas often combined with fruit, grain, or nuts, and in thick soups called *ash*. Long, slow cooking is very important because it melds the flavors of khoresh and ash into subtle, satisfying food, which is rarely hot-spicy, and always fragrant. *Biryani* (baked dishes), *nan* (flatbread), and *kofteh* (meatballs) are also important. Tea is a national favorite with sweets. Biscuits, baklava, and *falooda* (ice cream and crushed ice desserts) feature poppyseeds, pistachios, chickpea flour, rosewater, orange blossom water, pistachios, and honey.

Records from the Safavid period describing Persian cooking reveal that little has changed since that time except the addition of *kebabs* (meat on skewers). The methods for kebab making were imported to Persia from the Caucasus. As more Persians, mainly the aristocracy, began to travel out of the country, table manners and entertainment were affected. By the twentieth century, more Iranians traveled abroad. Consequently, Persian restaurants and food products became available in cities outside Iran. Persian people with families and work living a high-paced lifestyle away from Iran began to take shortcuts to the traditional Persian long cooking; that lifestyle and cuisine has filtered into modern Iran.

REGIONAL IRAN

The people, land, and the cuisines of Iran are quite diverse. High mountain ranges between plateaus meant little contact between communities. Until the twentieth century, roads and railways were undeveloped so travel was difficult. Consequently, Iranian food has remained largely regional and seasonal. From the Caspian Sea, and fresh fish daily, to rice fields, luscious citrus groves, and tea plantations, Iran may be divided into three main culinary regions:

1. **The northern provinces of Gilan and Mazandran and Caspian Sea Coast**
   This very green, foggy, and wet region is known for fish and seafood, small salted fish similar to anchovies, smoked or salted fish roes and the famed Iranian caviar, olives and olive oil, rice paddies, pomegranate syrup, lamb, and tea. Pickled garlic and walnut dip are a favorite. Brown-crusted rice and butter *kateh* is common and often eaten for breakfast with jam and milk or cheese and garlic. Fish roe is often served with eggs or in egg-cake *koo-koos*. Long-grain nutty rice from Gilan is considered the best in the country. *Morghe toursh* (sweet-sour chicken), *zeitun parvarden* (olives in walnut paste), garlic *mast* (yogurt), *mirza ghasemi* (mashed eggplant, squash, garlic, tomato and egg), and *fesenjan* (chicken with walnuts and pomegranate) are favorite dishes.

2. **The western and central desert provinces; the cities Esfahan and Yazd**
   This region is home to Esfahan the jewel of Iranian art and architecture and Yazd, considered the pearl of the central desert region. This region is known for *fesenjan*, *ash-e reshte* (noodle soup with beans and vegetables), *gaz* (nougat mixed with chopped pistachios or other nuts), *faludeh* (sorbet made of rice flour, grated fruit, and rosewater), and a honey toffee called *shohan-e asali* flavored with cardamom and saffron and coated with nuts. *Yogurt khoresh* is served as a sweet or side dish here, unlike other Iranian khoreshs, which are meaty stews. Central Iranians enjoy bread, yogurt, and soft cream for breakfast. In Yazd (central Iran), Kerman, and Azerbaijan, *bghm* features chunks of goat or mutton fried with onions seasoned with turmeric and cinnamon then sprinkled with tarragon and mint or saffron, and topped by thick yogurt or kashk. *Ghormeh sabzi* (herb stew), *khoresh khalol* (lamb stewed with almonds), and *gheimeh* (split-pea stew) are traditional in the western provinces.

3. **The eastern, southern, and Persian Gulf provinces of Khorsan, Baluchistan, Fars, and Khouzestan; the cities of Shiraz and Persepolis**
   This region, with its relaxed pace of life and Indian, Arabic, and African culinary influences, is a world apart from the rest of Iran. British, Armenians, Jews, and Germans

have also left their mark. Southern Iran and its Gulf area are renowned for seafood, dates, and *halvah*. *Ghaliyeh mahi* is a popular spicy whitefish soup with cilantro, garlic, and tamarind along with *khoresh bamieh khuzestani* (okra stew with tamarind), *maygoo polow khuzestani* (spicy shrimp and rice pilaf), and *dal adas* (red lentil soup with tamarind sauce). Southern Iranians eat bread, cheese, and dates for breakfast.

DINE AT A HOME IN IRAN

Iranians are a highly hospitable people with family at the core of their social structure, but if invited, guests should check to see if the invitation is for the man or, if married, both spouses. Muslim men and women often socialize separately. Show respect by arriving on time and greeting the hosts with *salaam*, meaning "hello." Bring elegantly wrapped flowers or pastry, and apologize for the gift's inadequacy. Dress conservatively: no short skirts or pants or revealing tops.

When entering an Iranian home, guests should ask if they should remove shoes. Greet elders first and shake everyone's hand. It is inappropriate to ask about the host's wife or female relatives. Do accept offers of food or drink, but first decline. This is *taarof* (a system of polite manners): first declining what is offered until your hosts' insistence becomes greater than yours.

In a traditional home, guests are shown to a room spread with carpets covered with a covering call a *sofreh*. This is covered with a white cloth and bordered with cushions and dinner plates. Guests wash hands and remove shoes before entering this room. Some households use table and chairs. The guest is accorded a place of honor, so wait to be seated.

There will be an abundance of food served family style, all at once, with main dishes concentrated in the center, surrounded by smaller dishes containing appetizers, condiments, side dishes, as well as bread, nearest to the diners. Say *nush-e jan* or "food of life," which roughly translates to *bon appétit*. Try a little of each dish that comes around; second and third helpings will be offered. Iranians typically eat with a spoon or other cutlery.

For lunch or dinner, rice will be central: either brown-crusted buttery basmati *chelow* or a *polow* (parboiled rice layered with seasoned vegetables, meat, legumes, or seafood and steamed). A rich, stew-like *khoresh* of vegetables and herbs long cooked with chicken, duck lamb, beef, or fish or a thick soup called *ash* and eggy *koo-koo* might be included. Cooked vegetables like stuffed peppers, cabbage, quince, tomato, or eggplant with a sweet-and-sour sauce, and yogurt-vegetable salads may accompany the rice and stew or soup. Pickles, flatbreads like *lavash* or *sangak* (bread), yogurt, and mineral water will be ever present. When finished, leave some food on the plate to signal fullness.

Coffee and tea (often from a samovar) but no alcohol will follow the meal. Fresh fruit and exotic and delicious sweets like milky rosewater-cardamom custard garnished with pistachios, baklava, saffron halva, saffron ice cream, or saffron rice pudding and many types of candy and cookies will accompany the coffee or tea. Iranians drink clear tea, their national drink, with a sugar cube on the tongue that dissolves with each sip. In summer, *sharbats*, fruit or flower syrups on ice, are popular. Thank your hosts profusely and compliment them on the fine cuisine and company.

FIGURE 10.2 Iranian village at the edge of the desert and mountains.
Source: gaelj/Fotolia.

TASTES OF IRAN AND PERSIA

Fat: Olive oil, clarified butter, fat-tailed sheep-tail fat, vegetable oil

Sweet: Sugar, honey, crystallized sugar

Sour/Alcohol: *Ghureh* (unripe grapes), *torshi-e ghureh* (pickled unripe grapes), *gard-e ghureh* (dried unripe grapes), *ab-e ghureh* (juice of unripened grapes), shirch-e angur (grape syrup or paste), *limu omani* (dried limes), lime, lemon, *somagh* (ground sumac berries), whey, *kashk* (dried buttermilk), barberries, tamarind, *rob-e anar* (pomegranate molasses or paste), *alu bukhara* (dried golden Persian plums), rob-e narenji (Seville orange syrup or paste)

Salty: Salt

Spicy-Hot: Black pepper, chilies

Spice: Bay leaves, saffron, turmeric, cardamom, cinnamon, coriander, cloves, ginger, nutmeg, paprika, caraway, anise, celery seed, cumin, *siah daneh* (nigella seed), white or black poppy seed, sesame seed, angelica powder and seed, *salep* (dried orchid root), *kari* (curry powder), sumac, vanilla

Aromatic Seasoning Vegetables: Onion, garlic, green onions, leeks, tomatoes, shallots

Herbs, Seasonings, and Condiments: Persian purple basil, cilantro, dill, fenugreek, cilantro, angelica leaves, marjoram, oregano, parsley, pennyroyal, savory, spearmint, tarragon, fresh and dried mint, tangerine peel, *gole-e sorkh* (dried rose petals) and rosewater, leek or garlic chive, chives, bay leaf, summer savory, bahar narenj (orange blossoms), gol-e beh (quince blossom)

Other Important Foods: Chickpea flour, wheat, *barghul* (cracked wheat), rice, barley, *reshteh* (linguine-like noodles), fish, caviar, meat (lamb, venison, veal, chicken, partridge, duck), eggs, rice flour, cheese, yogurt; legumes (lentils, yellow split peas, kidney beans, fava beans, broad beans, chickpeas), fresh and dried fruit (apples, cherries, quince, apricots, plums/prunes, peaches, pomegranate, watermelon, melons, figs, raisins, jujubes, dates, tamarind, barberries), eggplant, rhubarb, cauliflower, nuts (walnuts, pistachios, hazelnuts, almonds), squash, sesame seeds, radishes, watercress, wild olives

Popular Dishes: *Tah chin* (parboiled rice mixed with saffron, yogurt, and egg yolks and layered in a baking dish with chicken or lamb, baked, and a golden, crisp crust), *khoresh* (thick stew), *polow* (layered rice pilaf), *ash* (thick soup), *koo-koo* (egg cake), *borani* (yogurt appetizer), *seer* (pickles), *shashlik* (skewered, grilled meat)

Drinks: *Chay* (tea), *sharbet* (fruit or flower juice, sugar water and ice), *dugh* (yogurt drink)

COMMON IRANIAN AND PERSIAN COOKING TOOLS

Deeg (saucepan), tandoor oven, mortar and pestle, rice cooker cooking.

IRANIAN PANIR AND TABRIZ CHEESE (FETA CHEESE)

Cheese is an important part of the traditional Iranian diet, particularly white, brined cheeses like panir (feta) or Tabriz. Cheese is eaten as a side dish or for breakfast and along with yogurt and milk never used for cooking. The traditional Iranian breakfast is flatbread and cheese with tea. The white, semi-soft Tabriz (Lighvan) is the most popular. Prepared from sheep milk, Tabriz is tart and full of holes. The name comes from Lighvan, a village in Tabriz, where it is made. The milk is curded with rennet. The curds are packed into triangular cloth bags and drained. The triangular block of cheese is stored in an earthenware vessel, covered with salt, and cured for two days. Tabriz is eaten while still fresh.

IRANIAN-PERSIAN FLAVOR FOUNDATIONS

Iranian Signature Aromatic Combo

Onions, parsley, and mint

Herbal Combination

Herbs or *sabzi* are very important to Persian cooking. The combo of Italian parsley, leek chives, and cilantro is often used in ash and some khoresh.

Signature Seasonings

Liquid/Paste

Ab Ghureh (Verjus or Unripe Grape Juice)

This is the juice of unripe grapes, which Iranian cooks press, and preserve by adding a little salt and bringing the juice to a boil. This sour, fruity juice is used in place of vinegar or citrus for a refreshing sparkle.

Rob-e Anar (Pomegranate Molasses/Syrup)

Pomegranate molasses is made by boiling down the juice of a variety of tart pomegranates to form a thick, dark reddish syrup that Turkish, Persian, and Arabic cooks use to give their dishes a tart, fruity, and pungent tang. It goes well with walnuts, beans, poultry, and seafood. Mix it in salad dressings or used as a meat marinade. It keeps indefinitely; look for sugarless varieties. Fresh pomegranate juice and seeds are used.

Animal

Persian Fat-Tailed Sheep Fat (Donbeh or Liyeh)

Sheep were one of the first domesticated animals in Persia. The Baluchi, Awassi, or fat-tailed sheep were developed there for milk, meat, and wool. Their tail was bred, primarily to obtain a soft fat for meat cooking, to a wide, beavertail-like flap or a long kangaroo's tail with fat deposits along its length. Though the use of the tail fat is in decline, and is rarely used, there are hundreds of fat-tail breeds. The tail fat has a more delicate flavor than the body fat, and it leaves a pleasing fragrance and richness in Persian meat dishes that is impossible to duplicate.

Kashk

There are two main kinds of kashk: drained yogurt and ground grain combined with curdled milk or yogurt. In modern Iran, kashk is drained yogurt similar in texture to a tahini-like sour cream. It's available liquid or dried. Dried kashk must to be soaked and softened before using in cooking. Kashk was traditionally prepared from the whey left over from cheese production.

Vegetable/Fruit

Barberries or Oregon Grapes (Zereshk)

Persians have long used the tiny, tart and tasty barberry in cooking. The fruit is high in pectin, malic and citric acid, bright red-colored when fresh, good for regulating blood pressure and has anti-fungal and anti-inflammatory properties. Persian groceries sell barberries dried. Before using, soak them in cold water 15 minutes and rinse to remove sand and impurities. Strew into a dish of rice, couscous, or pot-roasted chicken for a burst of gorgeous color and fruity-tart flavor.

Whole Dried Limes (Limu Omani)

These whole limes are boiled in brine and dried. Added to stews or soups they impart musk and citrus notes. They may also be purchased in a powdered form (gard-e-limu-omani).

Tomato Paste (Rob-e Gojeh Farangi)

When tomatoes are in season, many Iranian cooks still prepare their own tomato paste. Iranian cooks use the paste to add color and bright flavor to dishes all winter long.

Herbal/Spice

Angelica (Golpar)

Generally the ground seeds of this plant are used to season bean dishes. They add a fragrant sweetness.

Chives (Tareh)

Chives used in Iran are similar to the flat garlic chives used in Asia.

Dried Rose Petals or Buds (Gole-e Sorkh)

These fragrant petals or tiny buds add their aromatic perfume to beverages, yogurt salads, desserts, sweets, and spice mixtures.

FIGURE 10.3 Fresh barberries.
Source: mch67/Fotolia.

FIGURE 10.4 Dried barberries.
Source: Vidady/Fotolia.

Fenugreek Leaves (Shambabileh)

Also used in Georgian cuisine, fresh and dried fenugreek leaves are the green herbs that grow from fenugreek seeds. They are mildly bitter.

Sumac

See *Signature Seasonings: Lebanon*

FIGURE 10.6 Angelica herb leaf and stems.
Source: Marilyn barbone/Fotolia.

FIGURE 10.5 Dried limes.
Source: Dave King/DK Images.

FIGURE 10.8 Dried rose buds.
Source: matka_Wariatka/Fotolia.

FIGURE 10.7 Chives (tareh).
Source: JIANG HONGYAN/Shutterstock.

FIGURE 10.9 Fenugreek leaves.
Source: Neil Fletcher/DK Images.

SEASONING AND PASTE MIXTURES

IRANIAN SPICE INFUSION (NA'NA DAGH)

This method, similar to Indian tempering, can be used as a final flourish on soups, ash (thick soup), kashké bademjan (eggplant spread), and borani (yogurt appetizer). Na'na daghs are often included in, not separate from, recipes. They are a way to create complex flavor and used as a final garnish.

Vary! Improvise!

☞ *Alternatively, crisp-fry slivered shallots or onions and use as na'na dagh topping*

☞ *Another popular Persian na'na dagh combo is dried mint, cinnamon, and black pepper.*

2 tablespoons clarified butter, ghee or oil
Optional: 1 teaspoon turmeric
2 tablespoons crushed dried mint leaves
    or 6 tablespoons finely sliced fresh mint leaves

1 Heat butter, ghee, or oil in small skillet over medium heat. When hot, stir in optional turmeric and cook 15 to 20 seconds.

2 Remove skillet from heat and stir in mint. Do not burn the mint. Immediately pour over dish to garnish.

PERSIAN SPICE MIXES (ADVIEH)

Similar to Indian garam masala, advieh is a blend of herbs and spices individual to each cook or household. It literally means "medicines." Chilies, peppers, garlic, or ginger never appear. Each region uses differing ingredients: cooks of the Persian plateau and Northwest use rose petals. Azerbaijani cooks include rose petals, cinnamon, cardamom, black pepper, marjoram, nutmeg, and for dishes other than rice, caraway seed.

Central Persia (Delicate)

Makes 4-1/2 teaspoons

1 teaspoon ground cinnamon
1 teaspoon ground nutmeg
1 teaspoon ground cardamom
1 teaspoon dried, ground rose petals
1/2 teaspoon ground cumin

Persian Gulf (Hearty)

Makes 2-1/2 to 3 tablespoons

2-1/2 teaspoons coriander seed
2 teaspoons ground cinnamon
1 teaspoon cumin seed
1/2 teaspoon caraway seed
1/4 teaspoon cardamom seed
1/4 teaspoon black peppercorns
1/4 teaspoon whole cloves
1-1/2 teaspoons ground turmeric

1 Grind or mix spices together. Keep in an airtight container and store in a cool place.

Source: *The Legendary Cuisine of Persia* by Margaret Shaida.

FIGURE 10.10 Dried rose petals.
Source: © Ivary Inc./Alamy.

IMPORTANT CHARACTERISTICS OF PERSIAN COOKING

- Persian cooking takes into account the senses.
  Color: Yellow/orange from turmeric and saffron and red from barberries and tart cherries contrast with white rice.
  Flavor: Spices are much used, but are never hot or overpowering. Sweet and sour is a favorite flavor contrast.
  Texture: Dried fruits and nuts contrast with delicate rice.
  Scent: Onions fried in oil and fresh or dried herbs are a typical Iranian culinary scent.
- Most Persian dishes begin with onions. They are fried until soft and golden.

- Many Persian dishes require long cooking or marinating. Abgusht, ash, halim, and khoresh simmer until they "fall into place" (*ja oftadan*). Chicken kebabs marinated overnight take on deep, rich flavor. Rice left to slow cook acquires a tasty crust while the grain elongates and separates.
- Persian dishes are endless variations on simple themes. Once the basic methods of Persian dishes are learned, they are varied depending on local ingredients and the season.

SAUCE

Persian Sauce

Persians don't have the typical repertoire of sauces like Western-influenced cooks. They rely mainly on thick, long-cooked stews called *khoresh* to provide flavor and act as a sauce for *chelow* (seasoned rice). Sweet-sour combinations of lemon juice or vinegar or tamarind, and sugar like the ones below garnish stuffed vegetables.

PERSIAN SWEET-SOUR SAUCES FOR STUFFED VEGETABLES

Sweet and sour is an important signature flavor combination of Iranian cuisine.

Northern Lemon Sauce

Yields about 12 fluid ounces

3/4 cup freshly squeezed lemon juice, 2 large lemons
1/4 teaspoon saffron softened in 2 teaspoons warm water
3/4 cup chicken *or* vegetable stock
1/4 cup sugar, to taste

Central Vinegar Sauce

Yields about 12 fluid ounces

3/4 cup red wine vinegar
3/4 cup chicken *or* vegetable stock
1/4 cup sugar, to taste

Southern Tamarind Sauce

Yields about 16 fluid ounces

4 ounces tamarind paste, 1/2 cup packed
1-1/3 cups hot chicken or beef stock, more as needed
   or 1-1/3 cups hot water
1/2 cup sugar, to taste
To Thin Sauce: 1/2 to 3/4 cup chicken or vegetable stock

Garnish: 2 to 4 tablespoons cold unsalted butter, diced

1 *Prepare sauce of choice:*

Northern
Mix together lemon juice, saffron-water, stock, and sugar.

Central
Mix vinegar, stock, and sugar together.

Southern
Soak tamarind in hot stock or water until soft, 15 minutes. Knead paste into liquid. Scrape purée through strainer and discard pits and fiber. Yields about 1 cup. In a small saucepan, mix tamarind purée with sugar to taste and simmer until sugar melts. Thin the sauce with chicken or vegetable stock to the consistency of thick cream.

2 Pour *Northern, Central,* or *Southern* sauce around stuffed vegetables. Cover and bake vegetables as directed in *Signature Recipe: Persian Stuffed Vegetables.*

3 Transfer stuffed vegetables to platter. Drain hot liquid into a saucepan, bring to a boil, and remove from heat. Whisk in **butter garnish**; do not boil sauce. Taste sauce, and season with sugar and salt and pepper, to taste. Spoon sauce over stuffed vegetables, and serve.

Source: *The Legendary Cuisine of Persia* by Margaret Shaida.

Vary! Improvise!

☞ *Add pomegranate concentrate, to taste, to the Central Vinegar Sauce.*

COOK'S VOICE: MARIAM HABIBI

Paris, France

"Sweet and sour is very important to Iranian cuisine. Different households add different amounts of sugar to taste, but dishes with sour flavors from green grapes, lime, lemon, or vinegar are always cut by sugar. The amount of time a dish needs to simmer is also an important feature of Iranian food. A good khoresh needs a low simmer for at least two hours: the oil will come up and may be removed. We have an old saying that for good taste food must have time for the flavors to set or come together."

SIMMER, STEW, POACH, BOIL, AND STEAM

Persian Soup, Pottage, and Porridge (Abgusht, Ash, and Halim)

Soup in Persia means thick, rich ingredient-laden dishes that bear little resemblance to the liquids that Westerners think of as soup. *Abgusht*, *ash* and *halim* play an important part in feeding large groups, and many are designated for special occasions. Persian soups should be prepared a day in advance for best flavor, garnished, and served with flatbread.

ABGUSHT

Abgusht is a meat-based soup with liquid that is the mainstay of rich and poor. The meat-less version is called *eshkeneh*. After ingredients (like meat, chickpeas, nuts, vegetables, or fruit) in an abgusht simmer, they are usually removed and either placed on a platter or mashed for easy scooping with flat bread. The cooked ingredients are eaten and the strained broth sipped from a small bowl.

ASH

Ash is a beloved, thick, stew-like "pottage." It is favorite winter fare and often serves as a complete meal. Ash usually includes rice or wheat, yellow split peas, meat, and sometimes fruit or nuts simmered until soft and thick.

HALIM

Halim is a really thick *ash* with its slow-cooked ingredients—wheat, lentils, vegetables, seasonings, and meat—puréed into a creamy, blended paste. The halim variation (called *khichra* in India) is popular as street food during Ramadan all the way from Persia to Pakistan and into north India. Some eat it for breakfast.

PERSIAN LAMB SOUP (ABGUSHT)

Abgusht, means the water of the meat, and is one of the most popular dishes in Iran because it is infinitely variable. The secret of a good abgusht is the seasoning and long, slow cooking. Some cooks prefer a less watery soup and simmer the finished soup uncovered until thick.

Yields about 7 cups (3 cups broth and 4 cups paste), 4 servings

1-3/4 ounces dry chickpeas, 1/2 cup
1-1/2 ounces dry red kidney beans, 1/2 cup
   or 1/2 cup each cooked chickpeas and red kidney beans
1 pound lamb shoulder blade steak or leg steak *with bones*
8 ounces onion, 1 large, peeled and quartered
1/2 teaspoon ground turmeric
12 ounces potatoes, 4 medium-small, peeled
3-3/4 ounces drained, peeled, whole canned plum tomatoes, 1/2 cup sliced
1 tablespoon tomato paste
1 teaspoon ground cinnamon
2 whole dried light-colored Persian limes (*limu-omani*), pierced
   or 2 tablespoons fresh lime juice
1/4 teaspoon saffron threads
1/2 teaspoon *Advieh (For Hearty Dishes)*

For Serving

Persian pickles (*Torshi*)
Green onions
Radishes
Fresh tarragon
Fresh basil
Fresh mint
Lavash or Arabic bread

1 Soak chickpeas and beans overnight in cold water with 1 teaspoon kosher salt, or quick-soak: Place in small saucepan, cover with water, and stir in 1 teaspoon salt. Bring to a boil, remove pan from heat, and cover. Set aside 1 hour. If using cooked peas and beans, skip this step.

2 Place meat, onion, and 1 quart water into a 4-quart saucepan. Bring to the boil over medium heat, skimming the froth as it forms. Drain the soaked, dried chickpeas and kidney beans. Stir peas, beans, turmeric, and 1 teaspoon kosher salt into soup. Cover and simmer soup 1-1/2 hours over low heat.

3 (If using cooked peas and beans, add now.) Add the potatoes, tomatoes, tomato paste, cinnamon, pierced Persian limes or lime juice, saffron, and advieh. Bring soup to a boil. Reduce heat and simmer 45 minutes over low heat. Test meat and vegetables with a fork or a knife tip for tenderness. Taste soup and adjust with salt and pepper.

4 **Strain out meat, beans, and vegetables and leave broth in pot.** Discard gristle and bone. Mash meat, beans, and vegetables to a not-fully-smooth "paste" and season with salt and pepper.

5 **To Serve:** Heap paste on serving platter. Garnish with Persian pickles (*torshi*), green onions, radishes, fresh tarragon, basil, and mint. Taste broth, and season with salt and pepper. Ladle hot broth into small bowls. Serve with meat "paste," garnishes, and lavash or Arabic bread. Scoop up paste with flatbread, and sip soup and eat garnishes in between.

Vary! Improvise!

☞ *Add 12 ounces peeled eggplant, diced into 1-inch cubes along with the potatoes.*

POMEGRANATES: FRESH JUICE AND SYRUP

Probably native to Persia, this apple-sized red fruit has a leathery skin that, peeled back, reveals clusters of sweet, ruby red juice-encapsulated seeds embedded in white spongy compartments. Available fresh from September to January, pomegranates keep up to 2 months refrigerated in a plastic bag. Score the skin and immerse the fruit in a bowl of cold water (the juice stains). Break it gently into sections and free the jewel-like seeds. Peel and pick away pith (which will float) and skin and discard. Drain. Seeds will keep several days refrigerated.

To juice: Slice pomegranate in half and juice like citrus; freeze extra juice. High in potassium and vitamin C, the juice has the antioxidant power of green tea and red wine. Fresh pomegranate juice and the sweet-tart, syrupy pomegranate "molasses" concentrate (read the labels for pure juice) are available the year round.

FIGURE 10.11 Pomegranates.
Source: Gary Segraves/Dorling Kindersley.

PERSIAN POMEGRANATE SOUP (ASH-E ANAR)

Ash-e Anar has a taste of the exotic. This thick stew-like soup is better the second day when made with the typical water. Enrich the flavor with stock for deep flavor immediately. It's not strictly necessary to sauté the meatballs, but their flavor jumps up when browned.

Yields 12 cups, 6 servings

7 ounces basmati or medium-grain rice, 1 cup
3-1/2 ounces yellow split peas, 1/2 cup
2 tablespoons ghee or oil
1 pound small yellow onions, peeled and *divided*
1/2 teaspoon turmeric
1/2 teaspoon cinnamon
2 quarts beef *or* chicken stock
2 ounces green onions, about 4, 1 cup finely chopped
2 ounces trimmed Italian parsley, 1 cup chopped
2 ounces cilantro, 1 cup finely sliced
1/2 ounce mint leaves, 1/4 cup chopped
8 ounces ground lamb
   or 8 ounces ground beef
2 to 3 tablespoons oil

Garnish

2 tablespoons ghee *or* oil
4 ounces onion, 1 cup peeled and finely slivered

6 tablespoons pomegranate molasses/syrup, more to taste
2 tablespoons fresh lemon juice, 1/2 lemon, more to taste

1 Wash rice and split peas. Soak separately in warm water 30 minutes. Drain.

2 Finely sliver 12 to 13 ounces onions to yield about 3 cups. Heat ghee or oil in heavy 6-quart pot over medium heat. Add onions and fry until golden, 15 to 20 minutes. Stir in turmeric and cinnamon and cook 1 minute. Stir in stock, drained split peas, bring to a boil, and lower heat. Simmer soup until peas are tender, 20 minutes. Stir green onions, fresh herbs, and salt into soup, and simmer 20 minutes.

3 **Meatballs:** Grate remaining 3 ounces onion and mix well with ground meat. Season with 1 teaspoon kosher salt and pepper, to taste. Scoop 1 tablespoon of meat to make meatballs the size of small chestnuts, about 16. Heat oil in skillet over medium heat. Add the meatballs and brown evenly, 8 to 10 minutes.

4 Stir drained rice into soup and gently drop in meatballs; simmer until rice is very tender, 20 to 30 minutes.

5 **Prepare garnish:** Heat ghee or oil for **garnish** in 9-inch skillet. Fry onion over medium-high heat until browned and crispy, about 10 minutes.

6 Stir pomegranate syrup, lemon juice, and salt and pepper into soup. If soup is too thick, thin with water. Taste. Soup should be pleasantly sweet-sour. Adjust as necessary with pomegranate syrup, lemon, and sugar, if desired.

7 **To Serve:** Ladle hot soup into bowls and garnish with fried onion.

Vary! Improvise!

☞ **Na'na Dagh:** *Some cooks sauté dried mint in ghee and swirl it into each bowl to garnish.*

CULINARY MARRIAGE

In *The New Book of Middle Eastern Food*, Claudia Roden observes that the Arabs (Islam), through war and empire-building conquest, brokered the culinary marriage of Persia, the ancient Mediterranean and the Near East. Arab warriors (Bedouins) had simple cooking styles and austere culinary habits. The aristocratic and opulent brilliance of Persia captivated them. Eventually the Arabs, "infiltrated and diluted" by Byzantine, Persian, Greek, Asian and Egyptian conquered peoples, adopted and spread this marvelous, melded cuisine.

Signature Technique: Persian Meat and Vegetable Stew (Khoresh)

By Western criterion khoresh-ha are long-cooked stews, and Iranians always eat them over rice; they act as sauce for the rice. Indian curries are related to khoresh-ha; both are eaten with rice or flatbread. With their rich combinations of meat, vegetables, fruit and seasonings, these stew-sauces are a distillation of centuries of Persian kitchen culture and experience.

- Butter and lamb fat are traditionally used for khoresh-ha, but for health reasons, oil is often substituted.
- All khoresh start with onions cooked until soft and golden, and meat.
- Spices and garlic cook for a minute or two in the fat to bloom their flavor.
- Water and wet ingredients like tomato or grapes are added and simmered until meat is very tender.
- Some khoresh preserve the texture and flavor of starring ingredients by cooking them separately and slipping them into the stew-sauce at the last minute.
- The basic steps of a khoresh lead to an endless number of variations. This pattern, the same for hundreds of variations, renders a certain simplicity to Persian cuisine.

PERSIAN HERB STEW (KHORESH GHORMEH SABZI)

This is a Persian favorite. Instead of the usual bright top flavor, these long-cooked herbs and meat form a deep, rich, unified flavor. In the north, near the Caspian Sea, cooks prepare it with fish, not meat, which is sautéed separately and slipped into the khoresh at the very end. Substitute fresh-squeezed lime juice if dried Persian limes are unavailable.

Yields about 8 cups, 4 servings

6 tablespoons butter, ghee, or oil, *divided*
8 ounces small yellow onions, 2 cups peeled and finely sliced
1 pound boneless lamb, veal, beef, or boneless, skinless chicken thighs, diced into 1/2-inch cubes
  or sliced into thin strips

Seasonings

1/2 ounce garlic, 2 large cloves, 1 tablespoon peeled and minced
1 teaspoon ground turmeric
1/2 teaspoon saffron soaked in 1 tablespoon hot water
4 whole dried Persian limes, poked all over with tip of knife

Herbs

8 ounce leek, 1 large, trimmed to 4 ounces white and pale green, 1 cup finely diced
2 ounces green onions, 4 large, 3/4 to 1 cup chopped
6 ounces trimmed Italian parsley, 3 cups finely chopped
2 ounces cilantro, 1 cup finely sliced
2 ounces trimmed fresh fenugreek leaves and tender stems, 1 cup finely chopped
  or 3 tablespoons dried fenugreek leaves

15-ounce can red kidney beans, drained
  or 1-1/2 cups cooked kidney beans
4 tablespoons fresh lime juice, 1 large lime, more to taste

For Serving

Chelow, cooked long-grained rice or flatbread

1 Heat 3 tablespoons butter, ghee, or oil in 6-quart saucepan over medium heat. Stir in onion and sauté until golden, 7 to 10 minutes. Stir in meat and cook until browned. Season onions and meat with a little salt. Add **seasonings** and sauté mixture 2 minutes. Cover meat and vegetables with 4 cups water and bring to a boil. Lower heat, cover pot partially, and simmer 30 minutes.

2 Heat remaining 3 tablespoons fat over medium heat in 10- to 12-inch skillet. Fry **herbs** until they darken and become fragrant, 20 minutes. This is very important. If they start to stick or brown too quickly, deglaze with 2 to 3 tablespoons water. Sprinkle herbs with salt. Scrape herbs into khoresh. Rinse skillet with 1/2 cup water, and scrape water into khoresh along with kidney beans. Cover pot, reduce heat, and simmer khoresh until meat is very tender, 1-1/2 to 2 hours.

3 **To Serve:** Stir in lime juice, to taste. Adjust seasonings to taste with salt and pepper. Ladle khoresh into bowls and serve with *Chelow*, rice, or flatbread.

Source: *A Taste of Persia* by Najmieh Batmanglij.

POULTRY AND POMEGRANATE STEW (KHORESH FESENJAN)

To bind the stew properly the nuts must be ground finely but not quite to a paste. The finished stew will be a deep, rich brown and look somewhat like a Mexican mole. For a sweeter fesenjan, add more sugar. For more piquant-sour, add more pomegranate juice. The flavor should be balanced somewhere between sweet and sour.

Yields 8 to 9 thick cups, 6 to 8 servings

1/2 cup olive oil *or* ghee, *divided*
14 ounces onions, 3 cups medium diced
1-1/2 teaspoons ground cardamom
1 teaspoon ground coriander
1/2 teaspoon turmeric
1/2 pound walnuts, 2 cups finely ground
2 cups pure pomegranate juice
2 tablespoons sugar
All-purpose flour, as needed
1-3/4 to 2 pounds boneless, skinless chicken thighs and breast, cut into 1-1/2 to 2-inch cubes
 or 1-3/4 to 2 pounds boneless, skinless duck thighs and breast, cubed 1-1/2 to
  2-inches
2 cups chicken stock
4 ounces dried prunes, 3/4 cup halved, about 12 to 15

For Serving

Chelow or cooked long-grain rice

1 In a heavy 6-quart pot over medium heat, heat 1/4 cup oil or ghee. Stir in onions and cook until soft, 5 to 7 minutes. Add cardamom, coriander, and turmeric, cook 1 minute; stir in walnuts. Cook nuts until fragrant, 5 minutes. Season with 1 teaspoon kosher salt. Stir pomegranate juice and sugar into the pot.

2 Heat 2 tablespoons oil or ghee in a 12-inch skillet. When oil is hot, season half the chicken with salt, toss with flour. Shake off excess flour. Lay chicken in skillet and sauté until browned. Place browned chicken into pot with onion and spices. Repeat browning with remaining 2 tablespoons fat and remaining chicken. Deglaze skillet with stock, bring to a boil, and scrape up bits from pan. Pour into pot with the chicken.

3 Bring stew to a boil, lower heat, and simmer until stew thickens, 1 hour. Skim away foam. Add prunes and simmer stew until thick and chocolatey, 30 minutes to 1 hour. Taste stew and season with salt and freshly ground black pepper to taste.

4 **To Serve:** Ladle stew into bowls and serve with *Chelow* or cooked long-grain rice.

Vary! Improvise!

☞ *Koofteh Fesenjan:* Use 1 pound ground lamb or beef in place of poultry and prepare walnut-sized meatballs. Brown them and simmer as with chicken or duck.

Rice and Wheat

Rice and wheat are central to Persian cooking. Persians have taken rice cooking and pilafs to a high art. Starting from the sixteenth-century royal courts, Persian cooks have been turning out elaborate rice dishes that stun the imagination and satisfy the senses (some were dyed indigo or laced with jewels). Wheat is made into Persian flatbreads.

Persian Rice: Kateh, Chelow (Chelo), and Polow (Polo)

Persian rice, the major staple in Persian cuisine, isn't available in the United States, but long-grained, nutty Indian basmati is similar. No other rice will give you the proper taste and texture: high-quality rice holds its shape, fluffs better, and produces a superior crust. Always pick through rice for stones, and wash rice in at least 3 to 4 changes of cold water. Drain rice and allow it to absorb the surface water 10 to 15 minutes, before parboiling or cooking.

Three Persian Rice Cooking Methods

With these rice methods, Persians demonstrate their ancient cuisine's creativity and knowledge. Their classic rice dishes have influenced the rice cooking of Indian, French, Spanish, Eastern European, and Middle Eastern cultures.

- **Kateh:** Rice is boiled with water and salt uncovered until water is fully absorbed. Butter or oil is drizzled in, the pot covered and allowed to steam until a sticky, compact cake with a golden bottom crust forms. Kateh is often eaten for breakfast with milk and jam.
- **Chelow/Chelo:** The golden-crusted chelow is usually made with **parboiled, drained, and rinsed** rice. A small portion of the rice is mixed with butter or oil, yogurt and/or egg, and saffron and spread over the bottom of the pot to make the prized, golden *tah dig* crust. Some cooks substitute lavash bread *or* sliced potato and layer them in before the rice. The remaining rice is mounded on top and the chelow is steamed over low heat. Chelows typically accompany kebabs or khoresh.
- **Polow/Polo and Tachin:** Polow is a *layered* chelow: Parboiled rice is layered with meat, fruits, and/or vegetables and seasonings and steamed/cooked through. A golden crust forms, usually made with just butter or oil. Polow is typically the central part of a meal served with just an appetizer and dessert. A polow with *tah dig* (egg and yogurt crust) is a *tahchin*. Tachins can be made on top of the stove or baked in the oven in a hotel pan for more of the tasty *tah dig* crust.

Persian chef Najmieh K. Batmanglij recommends a heavy nonstick pot with tight-fitting lid or rice cooker for making Persian rice dishes. If neither is available, she suggests lining the inside of a heavy pot with aluminum foil. Wider pots produce more crust.

SIGNATURE RECIPE

SMOTHERED PLAIN RICE (KATEH)

If using plain long-grain white rice, reduce water to 4-1/2 cups.

6 to 8 servings

21 ounces basmati rice, 3 cups, washed and drained
1/4 cup melted ghee, unsalted butter, or oil
Garnish: finely sliced parsley, mint, or chives

1   Wash rice well in cold water. Pour rice in strainer and drain until needed.

2   In a 5- to 6-quart nonstick pot with 10- to 11-inch diameter, combine rice, 5-1/4 cups water, and 1 tablespoon kosher salt. Over high heat, bring water to a boil. Reduce heat to low and simmer covered until rice has absorbed all the water, 20 minutes. Gently loosen rice sticking to bottom twice during this time with a heatproof rubber spatula.

3   Fold ghee, butter, or oil into rice and lightly smooth it until even on top.

4   Lay a clean cotton towel, cheesecloth, or two layers of paper toweling on top of pot and cover with lid. Towel should not hang too far over or it can be a fire hazard. Cook rice 40 minutes. Remove pot from heat to cool 5 to 10 minutes.

5   **Unmold rice:** Remove lid and towel. Place platter over pot and, holding both tightly together, invert. The rice should come out as a golden-crusted compact cake.

6   **To Serve:** Garnish kateh with herbs. Serve in wedges.

Source: *A Taste of Persia* by Najmieh K. Batmanglij.

STEAMED RICE WITH CRUST (CHELOW TAH DIG)

Tah dig *means "bottom of the pot." Some Iranian cooks lay lettuce leaves instead of potatoes or lavash on the bottom of the pot for a tah dig crust. They look dramatically beautiful when the chelow is unmolded.*

6 to 8 servings

21 ounces basmati rice, 3 cups, washed and drained as for *Smothered Plain Rice*
3/4 cup melted ghee, unsalted butter, or oil, *divided*

Rice-Yogurt Crust

1 ounce plain whole-milk yogurt, 2 tablespoons
1/2 teaspoon ground saffron soaked in 4 tablespoons hot water

Other Optional Tah Dig Crusts

5 to 8 ounces potatoes, peeled and sliced into 1/8-inch-thin rounds
1 lavash bread *or* 10-inch flour tortilla

1 Set a large, fine strainer into a bowl set in the sink. In a heavy 4-quart pot with lid, bring 2 quarts water and 2 tablespoons kosher salt to a big boil. Stir in rice and boil 5 minutes. Loosen rice from bottom of pot with heatproof rubber spatula twice.

2 Pour rice into strainer and drain. Discard cooking water. Rinse rice with 3 cups warm water, and drain again.

3 Form the tah dig or bottom crust. The size of the pot will determine the amount of crust and how much rice, potato, or lavash needed for the first layer.

   • **For Rice-Yogurt Crust:** Whisk together 1/2 cup melted ghee or butter or oil, yogurt, 1/2-cup warm water and 1 tablespoon saffron water. Fold in:

      *For a 5-quart nonstick pot with 9- to 10-inch diameter fold in 2 cups parboiled rice.

      *For a 6-quart nonstick pot with an 11-inch diameter, fold in 2-1/2 to 3 cups parboiled rice.

   Spread seasoned rice mixture on bottom of chosen pot. Proceed with step 4.

   • **For Potato or Lavash Crust:** Whisk together 1/2 cup melted ghee, butter, or oil, 1/2-cup warm water, salt, and 1 tablespoon saffron water. Pour onto bottom of nonstick pot (see sizes above). Whisk mixture to combine before laying in sliced potato *or* lavash slices. Overlap potato or bread in concentric circles to fully cover bottom of pot. Season potato with salt. Proceed with step 4.

4 One large spoonful at a time, and staying away from the sides of the pot, mound remaining parboiled rice into a pyramid on top of *tah dig*. Cover pot with lid and place on medium heat. Cook 10 minutes.

5 Mix 1/2 cup cold water with remaining melted ghee, butter, or oil and pour over rice. Drizzle remaining saffron water over rice. Drape clean cotton towel or 2 layers of paper toweling over pot and cover with lid.

6 *Reduce heat to low* and simmer rice 50 to 60 minutes. Check for *tah dig* by carefully lifting edge of rice and peeking underneath. Cook longer if it hasn't formed. Remove pot from heat and cool 10 minutes before unmolding.

7 **To Serve:** Two options:

   • Unmold *chelow tah dig* onto platter. Place platter over top of pot and, with a hand on both, quickly and smoothly flip the pot onto the platter. The rice and its crust will come out in one piece—if done correctly! If not, follow the next option.

   • *Spoon* rice onto platter and place pieces of the crust around cooked rice.

Source: *A Taste of Persia* by Najmieh K. Batmanglij.

Vary! Improvise!

☞ *Use thinly sliced sweet potato or onion as a crust for chelow.*

☞ **Use a Rice Cooker:** *Reduce water to 4 cups. Combine 1 tablespoon salt, 3 cups rinsed and drained basmati rice, 4 tablespoons oil, and 4 tablespoons ghee or butter. Start rice cooker; after 75 minutes, pour 1/4 teaspoon saffron soaked in 1 tablespoon water over rice, and unplug cooker. With lid on, cool rice in cooker 10 minutes. Remove lid and unmold as for kateh.*

☞ *Prepare flat chelow cakes in small sauté pans.*

☞ **Brown Basmati:** *Increase water to 6-3/4 cups, parboil brown basmati rice 15 minutes.*

Signature Technique: Persian Steamed Rice Pilaf (Polow)

The Indian biryani is very similar to the Persian polow. The method of boiling the rice al dente, layering with seasoned foods, and steaming makes an eye-catching entrée that can be assembled ahead. It's wide open to interpretation.

1 **Prepare a filling:** About 8 to 10 cups filling for 3 cups dry rice.

2 **Parboil rice:** Set a fine strainer into bowl in sink. In a heavy nonstick 6-quart pot with lid, for every **3 cups rice, bring 2 tablespoons salt and 2 quarts water to a big boil.** Stir in rice and boil 5 minutes. Loosen rice from bottom of pot with heatproof rubber spatula twice. Drain rice in fine strainer in sink. Rinse with *3 cups warm water* and drain again. **Three cups dry rice will yield about 7 cups cooked.**

3 **Form the tah dig:** Whisk together 1-1/2 to 2 cups parboiled rice, oil, melted ghee, or butter, 2 tablespoons water or broth, and 1 tablespoon saffron water. Spread seasoned rice mixture on bottom of a 5- to 6-quart *nonstick* pot. Alternatively, follow directions in *Signature Technique: Steamed Rice with Crust (Chelow Tah Dig)* for making crust with lavash, sliced potatoes, or yogurt.

4 **Form a pyramid and first cooking:** Spoon 1/3 of the parboiled rice (almost 2 cups) over tah dig and gently smooth. Continue layering and smoothing 1/2 of filling, 1/3 of parboiled rice (almost 2 cups), the remaining filling and remaining 1/3 of rice (almost 2 cups) into a slightly pyramidal shape. Cover pot and place on medium heat and cook 10 minutes.

5 **Drizzle liquid over rice:** Mix liquid (water or broth) with oil or melted butter (and saffron water) and drizzle over rice.

6 **Second cooking and crust:** Lay clean cotton towel or doubled paper towel over pot and cover with lid. Reduce heat to low and simmer rice 50 to 60 minutes. Check for crust by carefully lifting edge of rice; cook longer if necessary.

7 **Unmold and serve:** Remove pot from heat and cool 5 to 10 minutes. Place serving platter over top of pot and, with a hand on both, quickly and smoothly flip the pot onto the platter. The rice and its crust will come out in one piece if you've done it all correctly. If not, *spoon* rice onto platter and place pieces of the crust around cooked rice.

PERSIAN TOMATO RICE (ESLAMBOLI POLOW)

Yields about 15 cups, 8 to 10 servings

2 pounds tomatoes, peeled and seeded, seeds strained and juice reserved
    or 28-ounce can whole tomatoes, drained and juice reserved
5 tablespoons oil, *divided*
8 ounces onion, 2 cups peeled and finely diced
2 pounds trimmed lamb, beef, or veal stew meat, diced into 1/2-inch cubes
    or 2 pounds boneless, skinless chicken thighs, diced into 1/2-inch cubes
1 ounce garlic, 4 large cloves, 2 tablespoons peeled and minced
1 teaspoon turmeric
1 teaspoon cinnamon
1 ounce tomato paste, 2 tablespoons
19 to 21 ounces basmati rice, 3 cups, washed and drained
Optional: 1/4 cup melted butter

1 Purée tomatoes in food processor or blender. Pour purée into 1-quart liquid measure. There should be 3 cups; if not, add enough reserved juice to make 3 cups and set aside.

2 Heat *1-1/2 tablespoons oil* in a deep 10-inch skillet over high heat. Working in two batches: Add half the meat, season with salt, and sauté until browned. Transfer to mixing bowl. Repeat with *1-1/2 tablespoons oil* and remaining meat. Scrape meat into bowl with first batch.

3 Reheat skillet over medium heat, and add 2 tablespoons oil. Stir in onion and cook until browned, 10 minutes. Stir in garlic, turmeric, cinnamon, and tomato paste; cook 30 seconds. Stir in puréed tomatoes. Season with salt and pepper, lower heat, cover pan, and simmer sauce 30 to 40 minutes. You should have 5 to 5-1/2 cups meat sauce.

4 Parboil rice as directed in *Signature Technique: Persian Steamed Rice Pilaf* to yield about 7 cups drained, parboiled rice.

5 **Prepare optional tah dig:** Follow directions in *Steamed Rice with Crust (Chelow Tah Dig).*

6 **Construct pilaf-polow:** Follow *Signature Technique: Persian Steamed Rice Pilaf* directions for layering rice and tomato-meat sauce. Drizzle with optional butter. Cook as directed in *Signature Technique: Persian Steamed Rice Pilaf.*

7 **To Serve:** Unmold rice onto platter: Place platter over top of pot and, with a hand on both, quickly and smoothly flip the pot onto the platter. The rice and its crust will come out in one piece. If not, spoon rice onto platter and place pieces of the crust around cooked rice.

PERSIAN RICE WITH SOUR CHERRIES AND CHICKEN (ALBALOU POLOW)

Yields about 15 cups, 8 to 10 servings

1/2 to 2 pounds fresh or frozen and thawed pitted sour cherries, 4 generous cups
2 tablespoons sugar, more to taste
2 tablespoons lime juice, 1/2 large lime
1/2 teaspoon ground cinnamon
1/2 teaspoon crushed saffron
1/4 cup olive oil
16 ounces onion, 4 cups peeled and finely sliced
2 pounds boneless, skinless chicken breasts, diced into 1/2-inch cubes
19 to 21 ounces basmati rice, 3 cups, rinsed and drained
4 ounces melted butter, 1/2 cup, *divided*
Optional: 1 lavash bread *or* flour tortillas *or* thinly sliced potato

FIGURE 10.12 Persian rice with sour cherries and chicken (albalou polow).

1 Pour cherries and sugar into a medium-sized saucepan and bring to a boil. Reduce heat and simmer 1 minute if previously frozen and 2 to 3 minutes if fresh. Remove from heat and stir in lime juice. Cool. Drain cherries, and reserve juice (about 1 cup). Stir cinnamon into cherries.

2 Dissolve saffron in 1 tablespoon cherry liquid and set aside.

3 Heat olive oil in 12-inch skillet over medium-high heat. Add onion and cook until golden, 7 to 10 minutes. Remove onion to a bowl with slotted spoon. Reheat skillet and sauté chicken lightly. Add 1/4 cup water and return onions to skillet. Bring to a boil, cover, lower heat, and simmer until chicken is tender, 15 minutes. Cool. Drain cooking juices from chicken and onions; reserve juices.

4 Parboil rice as directed in *Signature Technique: Persian Steamed Rice Pilaf* to yield about 7 cups drained, parboiled rice.

5 Prepare optional tah dig: Follow directions in *Steamed Rice with Crust (Chelow Tah Dig)*.

Rice Crust
Mix 2 cups rice with 1/2 cup melted butter. Spread on bottom of pot.

Lavash or Tortilla Crust
Pour 1/4 cup melted butter and 1/4 cup reserved chicken juices into 5- to 6-quart nonstick pot and whisk together. Cut lavash or tortilla to fit into bottom of pot and lay in neatly.

Potato Crust
See *Signature Technique: Steamed Rice with Crust (Chelow Tah Dig)*

6 Construct pilaf-polow: Follow *Signature Technique: Persian Steamed Rice Pilaf* directions for layering rice, chicken, and cherries, then rice, chicken, and cherries, and finish with rice. Cook as directed in *Signature Technique: Persian Steamed Rice Pilaf* over medium heat 10 minutes.

7 Mix saffron liquid, reserved chicken cooking liquid, and cherry juice together. Drizzle 1/2 cup over rice. Cook polow 40 minutes over low heat, lift lid, and drizzle remaining chicken-cherry liquid over rice (and remaining 1/4 melted butter if using lavash or potato). Cook on low heat 10 minutes more. Rest polow 10 minutes before inverting.

8 **To Serve:** Unmold rice onto platter: Place platter over top of pot and with a hand on both, quickly and smoothly flip the pot onto the platter. The rice and its crust will come out in one piece. If not, spoon rice onto platter and place pieces of the crust around cooked rice.

Vary! Improvise!

☞ Substitute lamb for chicken and apricots for cherries.
☞ **Vegetarians:** Omit chicken. Substitute chickpeas.
☞ **Substitute Meatballs:** Prepare tiny meatballs from 2 pounds seasoned, ground meat. Brown meatballs and substitute for chicken.
☞ **Festive Dish:** Garnish with toasted slivered almonds and shelled pistachios.

SAUTÉ, PAN-FRY, AND DEEP-FRY

FRIED EGGPLANT SPREAD (KASHK E BADMJAN)

Kashk is a fermented yogurt that looks like tahini, and is very pungent.

Yields about 4 cups eggplant and 2/3 cup yogurt sauce, 6 to 8 servings

2 pounds Japanese eggplant, 4 to 5 medium-small
16 ounces onions, 2 large, 4 cups slivered
3/4 ounce garlic, 3 large cloves, 1-1/2 tablespoons peeled and minced
1/2 cup plus 3 tablespoons olive or vegetable oil, *divided*
1/2 teaspoon turmeric
1/4 teaspoon crumbled saffron

Garnish

1/2 ounce fresh mint leaves, 1/2 cup finely sliced
  or 2 tablespoons dried mint
1/2 cup *kashk*
  or 1/2 cup plain whole milk yogurt

For Serving

Arabic bread

1 Peel eggplant. Rub whole eggplant with 1 tablespoon kosher salt; set aside in bowl 20 to 30 minutes while prepping remaining ingredients. Blot eggplant dry.

2 Heat 4 tablespoons oil in a 5- to 6-quart pan over medium heat. Add eggplant and fry on all sides until browned, 7 to 10 minutes. Transfer eggplant to clean bowl. Reserve remaining oil in pan.

3 Add 1/4 cup plus 2 tablespoons oil to pan, and heat over medium heat. Stir in onions and fry until browned, 12 to 15 minutes. Stir occasionally so onions cook evenly; reduce the heat as they begin to brown. At this point the onions burn easily, so pay attention. Burnt onions are bitter. Transfer 1/3 of browned onions to a small bowl, and set aside for garnish. Stir garlic into remaining onions, and cook 30 seconds. Remove pan from heat.

4 Lay eggplant on top of onion mixture. Add turmeric, saffron, 1 teaspoon kosher salt and 1/2 cup water. Bring to a boil, reduce heat to low, and cover pan. Simmer eggplant until very tender, turning once after 15 minutes for a total of 30 minutes. Remove pan from heat. Lightly mash eggplant and onions. Season to taste with salt and pepper.

FIGURE 10.13 Saffron thread.
Source: Dream79/Shutterstock.

Vary! Improvise!

☞ *Before serving, garnish eggplant with roasted walnuts and chopped dates.*

5 **Prepare garnish:** Heat 1 tablespoon oil in a 6-inch sauté pan over medium-low heat. When hot, stir in mint and immediately remove pan from heat. Scrape mint and oil into a small bowl. Mix kashk or yogurt with 2 tablespoons water to thin in another bowl. Set both aside.

6 **To Serve:** Pile eggplant onto round platter. Drizzle artistically with kashk or yogurt mixture, mint, then reserved onions. Serve with Arabic bread.

GRILL, GRIDDLE, ROAST, BROIL, BAKE, AND BARBECUE

Persian Breads (Persian Nan-e)

Every neighborhood in Iran has bakeries that specialize in the many Persian flatbreads. Like the French, Iranians buy staple flatbreads fresh daily. The best-known flatbread is wafer-thin *lavash*. A thicker, round lavash is called *taftoon* and an even thicker flatbread is called *barbari*. Add whole wheat flour and bake the flatbread on pebbles, and it is called *sangak*. Sweetened, topped with sesame, cumin, nigella, fennel, or poppy seeds or pan-baked breads are part of the multitude of ways Persians prepare flatbreads. Commercial Middle Eastern lavash comes as a large, thin flatbread either cracker-hard or tortilla-soft. Soften hard lavash by misting both sides with water and placing in a plastic bag for 30 minutes.

FIGURE 10.14 Commercially produced lavash.
Source: Lucertolone/Shutterstock.

FIGURE 10.15 Persian flatbread (lavash).

PERSIAN FLATBREAD (LAVASH)

Though this bread is associated with Armenia, it is made in many parts of the Eastern Mediterranean, Georgia, and Middle East. In Iran and Armenia, it is rolled slightly thicker than this recipe, and generally baked in tandoori-style clay ovens.

Yields about 1 pound 10 ounces dough, eight 14-inch breads

2 teaspoons active dry yeast
1 teaspoon honey *or* sugar
1-1/2 cups warm water
16 ounces all-purpose unbleached white flour, about 3 to 3-1/4 cups
1 teaspoon kosher salt
1 tablespoon olive or vegetable oil

1 Dissolve yeast and sugar in water until foamy, 5 minutes.

2 **Mix Dough:** Place yeast and honey or sugar mixture into bowl or mixer bowl.

   By Hand
   Stir in 2 cups flour. Stir constantly in one direction until smooth, 1 minute. Gradually stir in flour and salt until dough is too stiff to mix easily, about 1/2 cup.

   In Mixer
   Fit mixer with paddle. Add 2 cups flour to yeast-water. Mix 60 seconds on low speed and 10 seconds on high. Add 1-cup flour and mix 30 seconds on low and 30 seconds on high speed.

3 Spread 1/2-cup flour (by hand) or 1/4 cup flour (by mixer) on work surface. Gather up dough, turn out onto flour, and with dough scraper, scrape, fold, and then knead in flour 3 to 5 minutes (hand) or 1 to 2 minutes (mixer) for a soft but elastic dough.

4 Pour oil in mixing bowl and roll dough in it to cover evenly. Cover bowl and let dough rise in warm spot until doubled, about 2 hours.

5 **Form balls:** Press down dough, rest it 10 minutes, and divide into 8 equal-sized balls, about 3-1/4 ounces each. Cover with plastic or towel. Keep dough covered at all times when not rolling or it will develop a tough skin.

6 **Roll lavash:** Remove two dough balls from their cover. Roll each to 5 to 6 inches diameter. If dough is hard to roll, set it aside so gluten relaxes; the dough will be easier to roll. Alternating between the two pieces of dough to allow relaxation time, roll the dough rounds until they reach a 14-inch diameter. Repeat with remaining 3 pairs of dough balls.

7 **Cook lavash:**

   Wok Method
   Scrub the outside of a wok (with metal handle/s). Place inverted wok on gas burner over low heat, and dry. Oil wok lightly with paper towel and rub off excess oil. Raise heat under wok to high on gas stove. Carefully roll 14-inch-diameter bread onto rolling pin halfway. Unroll onto wok. Cook bread 15 seconds and carefully turn the fragile bread with fingers or tongs. Cook second side 30 to 40 seconds, turn over, and cook the first side 30 seconds more. Instead of turning the bread to cook on the wok, it may be finished in an oven with the **Oven Method**.

   Oven, Convection Oven, or Deck Oven Method
   Place quarry tiles *or* overturned whole sheet pan on the bottom rack of a regular oven or convection oven. Preheat regular oven to 450 degrees F for 15 to 20 minutes and convection to 400 degrees F for about 10 minutes. A deck oven may also be used; preheat to 400 degrees F. Place lavash onto tiles or overturned sheet pan, and bake until lightly browned, 2 to 4 minutes per side.

8 **To Serve:** Lay cooked lavash immediately onto clean cotton towel. Fold towel and lavash over and keep warm. Serve lavash warm; they dry out when cooled. Freeze cooled lavash in plastic zipper baggies. Dried lavash is good as crackers. Moisten dried lavash by spraying with water and resting in clean cotton towel until lavash is pliable.

Source: *Flatbreads and Flavors* by Jeffrey Alford and Naomi Duguid.

Vary! Improvise!

☞ *Spice It Up: Before baking lavash, paint rolled dough lightly with olive oil, and press on toppings like poppy seeds and orange zest, lemon zest, and rosemary or dried herbs.*

IRANIAN NATIONAL DISH: CHELOW KEBAB

Chelow kebab is simple: a buttery-saffron-scented crusty *chelow* arranged on a platter with grilled lamb or beef kebab. For kebab recipes see chapters *Greece and Turkey* or *Lebanon*. Grilled tomatoes, lavash bread, and powdered sumac (for sprinkling on rice) accompany this tasty fare. Originally from northern Persia, chelow kebab is a favorite bazaar food, where the waiter holds several skewers in his left hand and a piece of flatbread in his right. He places a skewer on rice and, while holding the kabab down on the rice with the bread, quickly pulls out the skewer. *Doogh* or *dugh* is the traditional beverage to accompany chelow kabab. It's a mixture of sour yogurt, salt, mint, and carbonated mineral water.

VOLUME OF PANS

An 8-inch by 2-inch *round* cake pan holds 6 to 7 cups.

A 9-inch by 2-inch *round* cake pan holds about 7 cups.

A 10-inch by 2-inch *round* cake pan holds about 8 cups.

A 12-inch by 2-inch *round* cake pan holds about 15 cups.

A standard *square* half hotel pan holds about 12 cups.

A standard *oblong* full hotel pan holds about 24 cups.

An *oblong* 13-inch by 9-inch by 2-inch pan holds about 15 cups.

An *oblong* 18-inch by 12-inch by 2-inch pan holds about 29 cups.

PERSIAN FRITTATAS (KOO-KOO)

A kookoo, also spelled koo-koo-ye, kuku, or kou-kou, is a Persian egg cake similar to an Italian frittata. Iranians make many variations with a variety of flavorings and cooked ingredients ranging from savory or sweet-sour chicken, lamb, or turkey, zucchini, cauliflower, lima bean, potato, and pistachio, sometimes with the addition of the fruity-sour dried barberry. The deep green koo-koo sabzi, flavored with herbs, is the most popular.

Eggplant Frittata (Koo-Koo Bademjan)

Yields a 10-inch cake, 6 cups batter

3/4 cup olive oil, *divided*
1 pound onions, 4 cups peeled and thinly sliced
2 pounds eggplant, tops trimmed off
1/2 ounce garlic, 2 large cloves, 1 tablespoon peeled and minced
1 cup beaten eggs, 5 large
1/2 ounce trimmed Italian parsley, 1/2 cup chopped
1/4 cup fresh lime juice, 1 to 2 large limes
1 teaspoon baking powder
1 tablespoon all-purpose flour
1 teaspoon kosher salt

1 Preheat oven to 350 degrees F.

2 **Prep:** Peel eggplant with vegetable peeler. Slice eggplant on mandoline or by hand lengthwise into 1/8-inch-thick slices. Cut slices into strips 1 inch wide. If strips are very long, slice in half to yield about 10 cups sliced eggplant.

3 **Sauté:** Heat a 12-inch sauté pan or skillet over medium heat. Add 3 tablespoons oil and onion, and cook until soft and golden, 7 to 10 minutes. Add garlic and cook 1 minute.

4 Scrape onions into 2-quart mixing bowl. Reheat skillet over medium-high heat, add 3 tablespoons oil and half the eggplant. Season eggplant with salt. Cover and cook, stirring occasionally, until eggplant is tender, 4 to 5 minutes. Uncover pan. If bottom of pan browns excessively (it should), deglaze with 1 to 2 tablespoons water and let it cook off. Scrape eggplant into bowl with onions. Repeat with 3 tablespoons oil and remaining eggplant. Scrape eggplant into bowl to yield about 6 cups eggplant-onion mixture.

5 **In mixing bowl:** Whisk eggs with parsley, saffron, lime juice, baking powder, flour, salt, and freshly ground pepper. Whisk well and fold in eggplant mixture.

6 **Bake koo-koo:** Pour 2 tablespoons oil into 10-inch cake pan. Coat bottom and sides evenly. Line bottom of cake pan with parchment and oil both sides. Pour egg-vegetable mixture into cake pan and place pan in oven. Bake until eggs are fully set and top golden, 45 to 50 minutes. To finish koo-koo, see *To Finish Koo-Koos* (after herb koo-koo recipe).

Herb Frittata (Koo-Koo Sabzi)

Yields an 8-inch cake, 3 cups batter

1/4 cup olive oil, melted butter, or ghee, *divided*
5 to 6 ounces trimmed whole green onions, 10 to 12 large, about 2 cups finely chopped
2 ounces trimmed Italian parsley, 1 cup chopped
2 ounces trimmed dill, 1 cup chopped
2 ounces cilantro, 1 cup finely sliced
1-1/2 cups beaten eggs, about 7 large

1 teaspoon turmeric *or Advieh Spice Mix*
1 teaspoon baking powder
1 teaspoon kosher salt

1 Preheat oven to 350 degrees F. Heat a 12-inch sauté pan or skillet over medium heat.

2 **Prep:** Clean and chop green onions and herbs.

3 **Sauté:** Heat 3 tablespoons oil or butter. Add green onions, parsley, dill, and cilantro, and sauté until herbs cook down, 2 to 3 minutes. Scrape herbs (about 2 cups cooked) in mixing bowl, and set aside to cool.

4 **In a mixing bowl:** Whisk eggs with turmeric or *advieh*, baking powder, salt, and pepper until smooth. Stir in cooled herbs.

5 **Bake koo-koo:** Pour 2 tablespoons oil into 8-inch cake pan. Coat bottom and sides evenly. Line cake pan with parchment and oil both sides. Pour egg-vegetable mixture into cake pan and place pan in oven. Bake until eggs are fully set and top golden, 45 to 50 minutes.

Source: *A Taste of Persia* by Najmieh Batmanglij.

To Finish Koo-Koos

To Serve: Cool koo-koo until warm. Run a knife around the edges of the koo-koo and invert onto a plate. Remove parchment. Invert again onto a serving platter so browned side is up. Cut koo-koo into wedges and serve warm or at room temperature.

Vary! Improvise!

☞ *Alternatively, cook koo-koo in an appropriately sized sauté pan on the stovetop. Cook over medium-low heat until bottom is browned and set. Invert koo-koo onto a plate and carefully slide into pan to cook second side until koo-koo is browned and cooked through.*

☞ *Lettuce or Spinach: Substitute chopped lettuce leaves or spinach for part of the herbs.*

☞ *Herb and Berry: Add 1/4 cup chopped walnuts and 1/4 cup currants or dried barberries to the beaten eggs.*

PERSIA'S DELICATE TOUCH

Iranian chef and author Najmieh Batmanglij remarks in *The New Food of Life, Ancient Persian and Modern Iranian Cooking* that a "feeling for the delicate touch" called *letafat* has influenced all of the arts from textiles, copperware, pottery, miniatures, poetry, calligraphy and classical literature, and not the least, Persian cuisine.

FIGURE 10.16 Ancient ornamental teapot.
Source: dunga/Fotolia.

SALAD AND VEGETABLE METHODS

Iranians tend to always have a salad on the table as a side dish. Some people eat it before the main meal, some with the meal and some after. Other salads include a simple lettuce, cucumber, and tomato salad and *shirazi*, a salad of finely diced cucumbers, tomatoes, onions, and dried mint dressed with fresh lemon juice and olive oil.

PERSIAN YOGURT SALAD-APPETIZERS (BORANI)

Cooling borani salads, similar to Greek tzatziki and Turkish cacik, act as Persian appetizer, salad, sauce, and side dish. Yogurt, thickened by draining, is the base for borani. The three most popular Persian boranis are made with cooked eggplant, spinach, or beets.

6 to 8 servings

1 quart whole milk yogurt
or about 2 cups drained

Eggplant (Borani Bademjan)

Yields 4 to 5 cups

1-1/2 pounds eggplant
1/2 cup vegetable oil, *divided*, more as needed
1/4 to 1/2 ounce garlic, 1 to 2 large cloves, 1-1/2 to 3 teaspoons peeled and minced

Garnish: Chopped walnuts

Spinach (Borani Esfanaj)

Yields about 4 cups

1 tablespoon diced unsalted butter *or* olive oil
6 ounces onion, 1-1/2 cups peeled and finely diced
1/4 to 1/2 ounce garlic, 1 to 2 large cloves, 1-1/2 to 3 teaspoons peeled and minced
1-1/2 pounds washed baby spinach, about 12 cups chopped
Na'na Dagh

Beet (Borani Chogondar)

Yields 4-1/2 to 5 cups

1 pound trimmed beets
4 tablespoons fresh lemon juice, 1 large lemon, more to taste
About 1/4 ounce mint leaves, 4 tablespoons finely sliced

Garnish: Mint leaves

1 **Strain yogurt:** Line strainer set over bowl with an overhanging double layer of cheesecloth. Pour in yogurt and place in refrigerator to drain 2 to 3 hours to yield 2 cups drained yogurt.

2 Prep salad ingredients:

Eggplant
Trim eggplant and dice into 1/2-inch cubes to yield about 3 cups. Toss in mixing bowl with kosher salt, and rest eggplant 30 minutes. Rinse eggplant and pat dry. In a 12-inch skillet, heat 1/4 cup oil over medium heat. Fry half the eggplant until browned on all sides. Repeat with remaining oil and eggplant. Drain and cool eggplant on paper towels. *Alternatively:* Poke eggplant and bake or broil until tender; cool, peel, and dice. Blend drained yogurt and garlic together. Season with salt and pepper. Layer 1/2 of the eggplant in serving dish, spread half the yogurt over it, the remaining eggplant, and top with remaining yogurt. *Alternatively:* Fold eggplant and yogurt together.

Spinach

Heat butter or oil in deep 12-inch skillet over medium heat. Sauté onion until soft, 5 to 7 minutes, add garlic, and cook 1 minute then add spinach. Toss spinach and cook until wilted and moisture evaporates. Season spinach with salt and pepper and cool. Toss spinach, onion, and garlic with strained yogurt. Place in serving dish.

Beet

Peel beets and dice into 1/4- to 1/2-inch cubes. Steam beets until crisp-tender, 5 to 7 minutes. Cool. Toss beets with strained yogurt, lemon juice, and mint. Season with salt and pepper.

3   Cover and chill borani 1 hour before serving. Taste borani and adjust seasonings.

4   *Garnish before serving:*

Eggplant

Garnish with walnuts.

Spinach

Prepare *Na'na Dagh* with 1 tablespoon butter or oil and dried or fresh mint. Just before serving, pour over borani.

Beet

Garnish with sliced, fresh mint leaves.

Source: *The Complete Middle East Cookbook* by Tess Mallos.

PERSIAN RAW VEGETABLE AND HERB PLATTER (SABZI KHORDAN)

A platter of fresh herbs and raw vegetables served with flatbread and panir or feta cheese accompany most Persian meals; diners help themselves before, during, and after the meal. A bite-size piece of bread is wrapped around herbs, vegetables, and cheese, and eaten as a refreshing breakfast or snack. For a paneer (panir) cheese recipe see chapter India. Substitute goat milk for cow milk.

4 servings

2 to 3 ounces trimmed red radishes, 1/2 bunch, about 8 radishes
4 ounces green onions, about 8 large
Mint, basil, tarragon, Italian parsley, and cilantro, as desired
6 ounces watercress, 1 bunch, 6 to 8 cups large stems removed
2 ounces shelled walnuts, about 1/2 cup

For Serving

Arabic flatbread or Lavash
Persian goat milk *panir* cheese *or* feta cheese, cubed

1   Wash vegetables and herbs and blot dry. Quarter radishes and trim green onions. If green onions are very large, halve them lengthwise. Remove mint, basil, and tarragon leaves from stems. Trim large stems from parsley and watercress. Soak walnuts in warm water 15 to 20 minutes, and drain.

2   **To Serve:** Arrange ingredients with flatbread and cheese on a large platter. Serve as a first course appetizer or for palate refreshing between course nibbling.

Persian Vegetables

Iranians rarely eat vegetables alone as side dishes. Instead, cooks turn them into khoresh, stuffed vegetables or a salad, combining them with legumes, rice, meat, or cheese, to accompany a meal.

FIGURE 10.17 Quince.
Source: Steve Lee/DK Images.

Signature Technique: Stuffed Vegetables and Fruit

The fillings and shells work in concert to enhance each other's flavor. Cook them until they are very tender. Short- or medium-grain rice works best because it's starchier.

Tomato

An 8-ounce tomato will take 1/2 cup filling.

Slice off tops of tomatoes 1 to 1/2-inch from stems. Scoop out pulp with melon-baller or teaspoon, taking care not to damage tomato shell. Save pulp. Salt insides lightly and drain tomatoes upside down.

Eggplant

A 7- to 8-ounce eggplant will take 1/2 cup filling.

Choose small, round eggplant if possible. Slice off stem ends of eggplant with 1/2-inch eggplant meat still attached. Reserve tops. Scoop out insides of eggplant with melon-baller leaving 1/2-inch-thick walls. Sprinkle with salt inside and drain 20 minutes. Rinse and pat dry.

Potato

A 4-ounce potato will take 1/4 cup filling. An 8-ounce potato will take 1/2 cup filling.

Scrub potatoes or peel. Scoop out insides with melon-baller, leaving a 1/2-inch shell. Slice a small bit off bottom so potatoes sit upright. Use immediately or store in cold water.

Bell Peppers

A 6- to 7-ounce (medium) bell pepper will take 3/4 to 1 cup stuffing.

Bring a small pot of water to boil. Slice off tops of peppers 1-inch from stems; set tops aside. Scrape out ribs and seeds and rinse out seeds. Blanch peppers and tops 2 minutes, remove, and rinse with cold water; drain.

Quince or Apples

A 7-ounce apple or quince will take 1/4 to 1/2 cup filling.

Slice top off quince or firm apples 1/2- to 1-inch from stem; save tops. Scoop out insides with melon-baller leaving 1/2-inch shell. Blanch 30 seconds to 1 minute in boiling water.

Onions

A 6-ounce onion will take about 1/4 cup filling. A 12-ounce onion will take about 1/2 cup filling.

Bring small pot of water to a boil. Slice stem end off onions and discard; leave root end on but trim slightly. Blanch onions until tender, but not falling apart, 2 to 4 minutes; drain. Scoop out insides of onion with teaspoon leaving at least 1/2-inch shell.

SIGNATURE RECIPE

PERSIAN STUFFED VEGETABLES

Stuffing leaves, fruits, and vegetables probably originated with ancient Persians or Greeks and spread via the Silk Road and the Ottoman Empire to the rest of the Mediterranean Basin and beyond. Persian recipes from 500 years ago show that third-century Persian court kitchens stuffed zucchini, eggplant, cucumber, and grape leaves. Persian sweet and sour sauces set their stuffed vegetables apart from the rest of the Middle East. Some cooks prepare half a batch of grape leaves with a savory sauce and the other half with a sweet-sour sauce.

Split Pea and Meat Stuffing

Yields about 6 cups

2-1/2 ounces yellow split peas, 1/3 cup
1/2 cup oil, *divided*
8 ounces onions: 4 ounces finely slivered *and* 4 ounces finely diced, about 1 cup each
1/2 teaspoon turmeric
1 pound ground lamb, beef, or veal (2 to 2-1/2 cups cooked)
About 5-1/4 ounces medium- or short-grain rice, 3/4 cup
2 to 4 ounces green onions, 4 to 8 large, 3/4 to 1 cup chopped
2 ounces trimmed Italian parsley, 1 cup chopped
1/4 ounce tarragon leaves, 1 to 2 tablespoons chopped
1/2 ounce trimmed dill, 4 tablespoons chopped

Vegetarian Stuffing

Yields about 5-1/2 cups

Remove meat from Split Pea and Meat Stuffing *and add:*
1/2 ounce garlic, 2 large cloves, 1 tablespoon peeled and minced
3 ounces pine nuts, 1/2 cup
5-1/2 ounces raisins, about 1/2 cup
1 teaspoon ground cinnamon

Optional: 1 tablespoon dried, crushed savory
Vegetables for stuffing; see *Stuffed Vegetables and Fruit*
Choice of *Persian Sweet-Sour Sauce for Stuffed Vegetables*

For Serving

Bread and yogurt

1 Soak split peas in warm water 1 hour. Drain. Bring split peas and 1 cup water to boil in small saucepan over high heat. Lower heat and cook until tender, 25 to 30 minutes. Drain well; pour into mixing bowl.

2 Heat a 10-inch skillet with 1/4 cup oil over medium-high heat. Sauté **finely slivered onion** until golden and crispy, 15 to 20 minutes. Remove crisp slivered onion with slotted spoon to small bowl; set aside for garnish.

3 Reheat skillet over medium heat; there should be oil remaining. Sauté **diced onions** until soft. Stir in turmeric (and garlic for *Vegetarian Stuffing*) and 1 teaspoon kosher salt. Cook 1 minute. Scrape into mixing bowl with split peas, and set aside.

4 *For meat or vegetarian stuffing:* Heat skillet over medium heat with 2 tablespoons oil and add meat OR for **vegetarian** filling, add pine nuts and raisins. Stir and cook meat until fully cooked OR cook nuts and raisins until they begin to color and the raisins puff. Drain excess fat from meat and discard. Scrape drained meat and optional dried savory OR **vegetarian** nuts and raisins and cinnamon and savory into bowl with cooked diced onions and split peas.

5 Bring 2 cups water to boil. Season with 2 teaspoons kosher salt. Stir in 3/4 cup rice, and boil 5 minutes. Drain well and fold into onion-meat OR **vegetarian** onion-nut-raisin mixture. Mix green onions and herbs with stuffing mixture. Season *Vegetarian Stuffing* with optional lime juice and both stuffings with salt and pepper to taste.

6 Preheat oven to 350 degrees F.

7 **Stuff and cook vegetables:** Prepare a **simmering sauce**. Fill prepared vegetables with stuffing and wedge into ovenproof dish with a lid. Pour **simmering sauce** over and around vegetables. Cover cooking vessel, and bake vegetables until very tender, 1-1/2 hours for onions, 50 minutes to 1 hour for eggplant, peppers, quince, or apples, and potatoes; 30 to 45 minutes for tomatoes.

8 **Prepare sauce:** After vegetables are cooked, cover and rest 30 minutes. Drain hot liquid from vegetables into a small saucepan. Bring to a boil, remove pot from heat, and whisk in butter. Taste sauce and adjust with acid, sugar, salt, or pepper.

9 **To Serve:** Transfer stuffed vegetables to platter or serve in baking dish. Spoon sauce over, into, and around stuffed vegetables. Garnish with reserved crisp-fried onions. Serve with yogurt and bread for a full meal.

Source: *The Legendary Cuisine of Persia* by Margaret Shaida.

Vary! Improvise!

☞ *Add 1 cup cooked, slightly mashed chickpeas to vegetarian filling.*

☞ *Stuff with the Season: Stuff squash blossoms, artichokes, small pumpkins, or blanched Swiss chard or collard greens.*

☞ *Eastern Mediterranean Combos: Devise a stuffing from rice, cabbage, mint, and garlic or ground cooked meat with pomegranate seeds and pine nuts.*

PICKLE AND PRESERVE

There are two types of pickles in Iran: salt water pickles called *shoori* and pickles in vinegar called *torshi*. Torshi is usually made with vegetables like diced eggplant, cauliflower, beets, turnips, and carrots, and pickled several months.

FIGURE 10.18 Persian cucumber.
Source: Le Do/Fotolia.

PERSIAN PICKLED CUCUMBERS (KHLAR SHOOR)

Persians and Arabs eat pickles as refreshing condiments. This pickle is quick and easy—and it tastes better than store bought. The tannins from the leaves give the pickles an extra crunch. Some cultures use fresh black currant or sour cherry leaves.

Yields 2 quarts

2 pounds small unwaxed pickling cucumbers or Persian cucumbers, preferably organic, scrubbed
2 ounces garlic, 4 large cloves, peeled and blanched 20 seconds
2 large sprigs dill with flower heads
    or 4 sprigs dill without flower heads
5 black peppercorns, crushed
6 whole coriander seeds, crushed
Optional: 2 to 3 fresh unsprayed grape, horseradish, or oak leaves, washed

Brine

1 quart nonchlorinated water
1/2 cup white wine vinegar
3 tablespoons kosher salt

1 Rinse scrubbed cucumbers, and drain. Layer blanched garlic, dill, peppercorns, coriander, and leaves into 2-quart glass canning jar or two 1-quart glass canning jars with cucumbers.

2 **Prepare brine:** Bring 1 quart water to a boil in small saucepan. Stir in vinegar and salt. Remove pan from heat and when salt dissolves, immediately pour brine over cucumbers.

3 Seal jars tightly with lid and place jar at room temperature (70 degrees F) 7 to 10 days. Taste cucumbers to determine if they are pickled (sour) enough. Refrigerate pickles when pickled sufficiently. Store up to 6 weeks.

Source: *The New Book of Middle Eastern Food* by Claudia Roden.

PERSIAN PICKLED GARLIC (SEER TORSHI)

Pickled garlic is a handy way to have garlic for seasoning. Many Iranians consider it a medicinal cure for coughs, colds, or high blood pressure—and a delicacy. The longer garlic matures, the better it tastes, becoming sweet and jammy. Some Iranians have garlic pickled more than twenty years! The garlic turns black and utterly sweet.

Yields 1 quart

1-1/2 pounds broken, unpeeled garlic cloves, about 12 large heads, 4 cups cloves

1-3/4 cups white or white wine vinegar
3 tablespoons kosher salt
2 tablespoons honey

1 Peel garlic:
- **Hard Stem Garlic** has fewer but larger cloves with thicker skin. The cloves may be peeled, or soaked in warm water or quickly blanched to loosen the peel before peeling.
- **Soft Stem Garlic** has many smaller cloves with finer skin. The cloves may be used without peeling, or blanched quickly and peeled. Fill a large saucepan with water and bring to a boil. Place garlic in strainer and immerse in boiling water 10 to 20 seconds. Rinse under cold water. Peel garlic and discard peels. Rinse garlic again in strainer under cold running water. Hang strainer and rest garlic cloves in it to drain.

2 **Pack the jar:** Pack garlic cloves in 1-quart glass canning jar.

3 **Prepare the brine:** Mix vinegar with salt and honey in a small saucepan. Simmer over low heat until salt and honey are dissolved. Pour mixture over garlic. Garlic cloves should be completely immersed; if not, add more vinegar and honey.

4 Cover jar with plastic wrap and close tightly with a lid. Place in a cool and dark place 1 month before using, but the garlic may be kept indefinitely. Its flavor will deepen over time.

5 **To Serve:** Serve *seer torshi* with lamb shanks and lima beans, rice polows, or eggplant dishes. Place garlic cloves in small bowls and serve as a condiment with appetizers, meat or cheese, or sliced on salads.

THE REPUBLIC OF GEORGIA: GARDEN OF EDEN

Independent Identity

Florian Muehlfried in Sharing the Same Blood, Culture and Cuisine in the Republic of Georgia, from the Anthropology of Food [Online] recognizes that the Republic of Georgia, a country overrun with Arab, Mongol, Ottoman, Persian, and Russian invaders throughout its history, modified and incorporated foreign culinary knowledge into strong traditions all its own. Thus, food and drink became ritual ways of "preserving nationhood." This "framework of shared meals and drinks" provided Georgians with a way to form a social identity strongly apart from their invaders.

Though the Republic of Georgia is a small, remote county, its twenty-five centuries of history are like its food: rich, abundant, and colorful, overlaid with diverse cultural influences. Forbidding mountains, lush valleys, and fertile lowlands have given Georgia its romantic reputation. Filled with wildfowl, seafood, wild greens and mushrooms, and a profusion of vegetables and fruit trees, Georgia is like a "garden of Eden" to those who have passed through this ancient commercial crossroads of silk and spices.

Slightly smaller than South Carolina, the area of modern-day Georgia has been inhabited since the fifteenth century BCE. Georgians can trace their culture from the various people who invaded or migrated there starting from sixth century BCE.

Attracted by the Georgian agricultural expertise, the Greeks founded colonies along the Black Sea. In the fourth century BCE, Georgia's first native ruler, King Farnvazi (Pharnavaz), imposed order, knit the region together, and introduced literacy and prosperity. Around the third century BCE, the *Kartli* or Iberian kingdom, strongly influenced by both the Greco-Roman and Persian Empires, was established in southeastern Georgia.

In 65 BCE, the Romans under Pompey, desiring more access to Georgia's important trade routes, invaded and ousted the Greeks; Georgia remained under Roman control nearly 400 years. Early Georgia was a battlefield between nomadic horsemen from the northern steppes and the rivals Muslim Persia and Christian Roman-Byzantium. Caught

Western Georgia
Southern Georgia
Central and Eastern Georgia

FIGURE 10.19 Map of Republic of Georgia.

in between, Georgia learned how to blend the culture and cuisine of east and west, yet retain its own strong character.

Georgia adopted Christianity mid-300. This had a large impact on culture and society and tied Georgia to Rome-Byzantium. The continuing power struggles between Byzantium and Persia for the Caucasus, and Georgia's unsuccessful insurrection in 523, resulted in Persian rule over Georgia. In 591, Byzantium and Persia divided Georgia between them. At the beginning of the seventh century their truce collapsed and the eventual result was Byzantine predominance in western and eastern Georgia until Arabs invaded in 645. Arab rule weakened at the beginning of the ninth century and non-foreign Georgian dynasties followed. This established the Georgian Empire and led to her Golden Age (1099 to 1220).

During the Golden Age reign of Queen Tamara (1184 to 1213), Georgia reached the peak of her civilization with architecture, literature, philosophy, sciences, medicine, and the arts and an enlarged territory that included Transcaucasia. Invaders Genghis Khan and the Mongols ended the renaissance. In 1386, the Turco-Mongol Tamerlane invaded and decimated Georgia's population and economy. From the sixteenth century on, a weakened Georgia was trapped between Persia and Ottoman Turkey, who struggled over her territory. In 1783, Georgia, in exchange for protection, became a Russian vassal, and in 1801 Russia annexed Georgia.

Georgia declared independence in 1918. In 1921, the Red Army overthrew Georgia's democracy and forcibly made her part of the new USSR. Under Soviet rule, the country was transformed from an agrarian society to a largely industrial, urban society. In 1989, Soviet troops killed twenty civilians involved in a nationalist protest outside the parliament in T'bilisi. By 1991, Georgian parliament declared Georgia independent of the Soviet Union. In 1992 until 2003, Eduard Shevardnadze, the Soviet Union's foreign minister under Gorbachev, became president of this representative democracy. Reformists opposed Shevardnadze, and after much strife, on January 4, 2004, Mikhail Saakashvili won the presidential election in an overwhelming majority. Georgia is one of the more democratic countries in the region due to reforms by Saakashvili. In 2010, NATO countries reaffirmed support for Georgia's sovereignty, territorial integrity, and its aspirations for NATO membership.

PHILOSOPHY AND RELIGION

The wide variety of people inhabiting Georgia has resulted in a rich array of active traditional religions, of which Georgians are highly tolerant. In T'bilisi, Christians, Muslims, and Jews live in close proximity. Christianity came to Georgia in 330 and roughly 84 percent of Georgians are Orthodox Christians. This has provided a strong national identity despite repeated periods of foreign occupation and attempted assimilation. The remaining population is 10 percent Muslim, 4 percent Armenian Apostolic, and less than 1 percent Roman Catholic, Bahá'í, Lutheran, Seventh Day Adventist, and Baptist. Under Soviet rule, the number of active churches and priests declined, but has rebounded since independence in 1991.

GEOGRAPHY AND CLIMATE

Georgia has a diverse terrain from the humid, subtropical Black Sea shore with abundant vegetation to snow-capped mountain peaks, deep gorges with fast-moving rivers, lush forest valleys, and green alpine meadows turning into the dry steppes. One-third of Georgia is forested with pine, oak, chestnut, beech, alder, fir, ash, linden, apple, pear, nut, and eucalyptus trees and bilberry and holly shrubs.

The Caucasus Mountain regions have cold winters with heavy snow while the southern and coastal areas have milder winters. The east has hot summers while the western Black Sea coast region has warm, Mediterranean-like conditions.

FARMING AND AGRICULTURE

Agricultural land in Georgia is scarce, often mountainous and difficult to work, but highly valued. In 1929, Soviet introduction of collective farms (*kolkhozy*) and state farms (*sovkhozy*) altered the traditional structure of landowning and working by supplying modern equipment, fertilizer, and herbicides. However, private garden plots still produce much of Georgia's food.

Georgians believe that their country's name came from the Greek word *georgios*, meaning "farmer" or "cultivator of land." Most of Georgia's cultivated land is devoted to growing wheat, corn, tobacco, and sugar beets. The rest of Georgian agriculture comprises orchards with citrus and other fruits, vineyards, tea plantations, and private garden plots of vegetables and melons. Wine is an important agricultural product and has been in production since 300 BCE. Eastern Georgia is the center of Georgia's wine industry. Cattle, sheep, goats, poultry, and pigs provide meat, eggs, and dairy products; bees and silkworms provide honey and silk. Black Sea fisheries provide fish like flounder and whitefish.

GEORGIAN CUISINE: THE MASTERS OF NATURAL FLAVOR

Cuisine is central to the life and history of all Georgians. Sandwiched between Russia, Armenia, Turkey, Dagestan, and Azerbaijan, Georgia was in the center of the ancient East-West silk and spice trade routes, and her primary link to the known world. Though many invaders (Persians, Ottomans, and Mongol) and traders (Indian) have left their influences on Georgian cuisine, its true excellence arises from the fertile Georgian soil, natural riches, and abundant culinary ingredients. Citrus, pomegranates, plums, apricots, walnuts, figs, corn, wheat, beans, herbs, spices, eggplant, tomatoes, grapes, and more thrive there.

Georgian culinary techniques are uncomplicated; they originated from rural countryside farm cooking. The cuisine, rich with the natural flavors of fresh food, needs little embellishment. *Matsoni* (buffalo milk yogurt), cow, goat, and sheep cheeses, fresh and pungent herb salads, grilled meat kebabs like marinated *basturma* and *shasklik*, sturgeon in walnut sauce, flattened pan-grilled chicken *tabaka* with cilantro-garlic sauce, and stuffed vegetable *tolmas* (dolmas) are favorites. Fresh sauces made with tart wild plums, walnuts, apricots, or tomatoes or flavored with pomegranate juice; honey, herbs or chilies, bean salads with walnuts or plums, clay oven breads, corn polenta, and fresh, succulent *pkhalis* (walnut-vegetable "patés") are characteristic of a cuisine bursting with tradition, enticing colors, and natural flavors.

Unlike Persians with rice and Armenians with bulgur, Georgians prefer to eat wheat and corn. Instead of the typical Mediterranean lentils, chickpeas, and favas, Georgians prefer New World kidney beans. Walnuts and walnut oil dominate the Georgian kitchen over pine nuts and almonds.

The Georgian landscape alternates between mountain, lowland, and seacoast, creating differing culinary regions: high mountains and alpine pastures, fertile valley lowlands, and sunny, subtropical coasts. Each region offers something special. The mountainous regions feature goat and sheep milk cheeses, wild meat dishes and *akjika* (hot pepper paste), *khinkali* (meat dumplings), *fidjin* (meat pies), and *khachapuri* (cheese-stuffed bread). The valley farmlands produce many vegetables, meat, dairy, poultry, and dry beans. River fish and wine are popular throughout, but the Black Sea coastal region offers more varieties of seafood.

Khachapuri is easily Georgia's most popular dish. Nearly every home, restaurant, or street stall offers this stuffed bread in many variations from *imeruli khachapuri* (flat, round pie with cheese inside), or *megruli khachapuri* (cheese inside *and* melted on top) to *ajaruli* (bread boat holding melted cheese, butter, and egg cracked on top), or stuffed with seasoned beans or meat. They can be made with yogurt dough, puff pastry, or yeast dough, made large or small, and baked in a clay oven, clay pan, or regular oven.

REGIONAL GEORGIA

Some culinary differences exist between western and eastern Georgia. The west emphasizes less meat and more vegetables and the use of walnuts for *satsivis* (walnut sauce). The southwest coast is known for spa-hot springs, tea plantations, bay leaves, and citrus fruits. Western food with fenugreek leaves, tarragon, basil, cilantro, pepper, and chilies is generally hotter and more highly seasoned than the east. Cow milk cheese and *mchadi* (corn bread) or *ghomi* (polenta) and khachapuri are common.

Eastern Georgia favors wheat breads, sheep milk cheese, and heavier meats like lamb and pork. T'bilisi, located in the east, is the capital and largest city, and is considered the culinary capital of Georgia. Seasoning is generally milder than in the west. The eastern Inner-Kartli Plain is the most important agricultural region, specializing in fruit like apples and wine grapes. Tomatoes, potatoes, radishes, squashes, eggplant, beans, cucumber, pomegranates, melons, and cabbage are popular cultivated crops along with berries and wild plums, for the famous *tkemali* sauce.

DINE AT HOME IN GEORGIA

Georgians are passionate about dining and drinking toasts. Their almost obsessive dedication to cooking and hospitality makes the Georgian meal a festive, tasty social event. Guests are highly honored. Indeed, some say that guests are a "gift from God," so expect an invitation to dine and be prepared for a long event. Bring a gift of flowers, sweets, or good chocolate. Entering a Georgian home, guests greet hosts with a handshake and *gamarjoba* or "hello." Address the host and hostess with *batono* (sir) or *kalbatono* (madam) and surname or their first name followed by *batono* or *kalbatono*.

Table manners are relaxed; the host will see to guests' comfort, happiness, and hunger. Elders and guests receive the most honor and are served first. Try a little of every dish, but don't take much; to please the host and hostess, take two to three helpings and eat it all. Table manners are European: fork in the left hand and knife in the right to eat. Keep hands visible and elbows off the table.

A Georgian meal's success depends on variety and abundance. Expect the table to be stuffed with small dishes ranging from appetizers, soup, and vegetables, to meat, fish, and poultry served in many courses: *khachapuri* (stuffed bread), *khinkali* (dumplings), pickles or aromatic herb salads, eggplant with walnut and garlic sauce, fried fish, sautéed mushrooms, cucumber and tomato salad, baked trout, roast sucking pig, green spinach balls, meat casserole, pork kebab, and fried chicken with walnut-garlic sauce served with several sauces, including sour plum *tkemali*, Georgia's national sauce, like a plummy ketchup.

Wine, beer, and mineral water will accompany the meal. Dessert will probably be nuts and fresh fruit. Lively conversation will accompany dinner and even music. Many people play instruments and most sing, so expect to join in the singing after the meal.

The Supra and Tamada

Georgians have great reverence for grapes and wine. As Georgian scholar Darra Goldstein says, "If food is the heart of the Georgian feast, then its spirit resides in wine. For a Georgian, wine evokes both culture and community." Guests often encounter the *supra* or large dinner party with its prescribed wine-toasting ritual presided over by the *tamada* or toastmaster. Though the supra is fraught with important rituals, guests watch others and ask if they don't know what is appropriate. The tamada will make toasts, then select people to make toasts; a *khantsi* (ram or goat horn) full of wine comes to each (male) guest. The guest must drink it all down. The toasts come in a special order: peace, the reason for the gathering, the hostess, parents and ancestors, motherland Georgia, friends, the dead, life, children, the women, each guest, the tamada, a safe journey home, and to future meetings. Beer is never used for toasting. Never propose a toast without permission. If a toast bears on a guest personally, he must wait to drink until everyone has had a drink. Respond with thanks.

FIGURE 10.20 Georgian wine and grapes.
Source: artjazz/Shutterstock.

TASTES OF GEORGIA

Fat: Butter, fat-tailed sheep-tail fat, olive oil, corn or sunflower oil, walnut oil

Sweet: Sugar, honey, grape juice syrup

Sour/Alcohol: Red or white wine vinegar, *matsoni* (yogurt), *machari* (immature wine), *masharabi* (sour, spiced pomegrante syrup), *tkemali* (sour plum), lemon, *tklapi* (dried fruit leather), barberries, *kvatsarakhi* (barberry syrup)

Salty: Salt, olives

Spicy-Hot: Black pepper, fresh and dried chilies

Spices: Bay leaf, caraway, cinnamon, clove, coriander, fenugreek, fennel seed

Aromatic Seasoning Vegetables: Onions, garlic, leek, scallions

Herbs, Seasonings, and Condiments: Basil (purple and green), celery and lovage leaves, cilantro, marigold/calendula petals, dill, fennel leaves, mint, Italian parsley, summer and winter savory, tarragon, wild sage, fenugreek leaves

Other Important Foods: Wheat, wheat berries, corn, cornmeal, millet, kidney beans, cheese, fruit (cherries, apricots, plums, pears, gooseberries, currants, citrus fruits, grapes, feijoada, figs, pomegranates, blackberries, barberries), meat (beef, veal, chicken, lamb, pork, turkey), fish (sturgeon, trout), beets, cabbage, eggplant, cauliflower, spinach, potatoes, mushrooms, purslane, sarsaparilla, nettles, mallow, ramps, tomatoes, pumpkin, almonds, walnuts, hazelnuts, green beans, asparagus, radishes, cucumbers, lentils, beans

Popular Dishes: *Basturma* (marinated, grilled meat**)**, *borani*, (cooked vegetable and yogurt salad), *kharcho* (lamb or beef soup), *churchkhela* (grape juice-dipped and dried nuts) *pkhali* (vegetable puree), *khachapuri* (cheese bread), *khinkali* (dumplings), *chakhokhbili* (chicken stew), *satsivi* (poultry in walnut sauce), *tabaka* (pressed and fried chicken), *kupati* (kidneys stuffed with spiced meat), *mtsvadi* (grilled lamb), *mtsvane lobio niguzit* (bean salad with walnut dressing)

Drinks: Tea, wine, beer, kvass (fermented rye), *chacha* (grain alcohol), vodka, *kefir* (buttermilk or yogurt-type drink), Turkish coffee

COMMON GEORGIAN COOKING TOOLS

Mortar and pestle, *toné* (clay oven), grill, *ketsi* (clay pots), skewers

GEORGIAN CHEESE (KVELI)

Because of unreliable electricity, many Georgian cheeses are preserved in salty brines; the commercial varieties are known as *brindza*. Many Georgians make cheese at home.

Gudiskveli

This salty sheeps milk is made in bags (*guda*) of sheepskin (with the wool inside).

Imeruli

This fresh, mild, white, curded cheese from the Imereti region is made from curded cow milk like *suluguni*, but it is not cheddared or plasticized.

Nadughi, Nodun, or Naduri

This soft, fresh cheese, made from whey, is similar to mild, soft cream cheese-like ricotta. Nadughi is often mixed with mint or tarragon and served as an appetizer.

Suluguni (Pickle Cheese)

This white to pale yellow sheep, cow, buffalo, or goat milk cheese can be made from one or a mixture of milks. It is similar to mozzarella, but strong smelling, moderately salty and sour. Its texture is elastic and dimpled due to two processes called *cheddaring*, in which chunks of cheese are constantly flipped and pressed so cheese becomes dense, fibrous, acidic, and stringy and *plasticizing*, in which the cheddared chunks are mixed with whey or brine. The cheese is cooled, dried, hand-shaped into flat disks and refrigerated in brine to cure for 6 to 48 hours. Georgians use this cheese in khachapuri breads and deep-fry it. *Suluguni shebolili* is smoked.

GEORGIAN FLAVOR FOUNDATIONS

Georgian Signature Aromatic Vegetable Combo

Onions, garlic, peppers, or chilies

Georgian Signature Herbal Combo

Cilantro, Italian parsley, dill, and basil

Signature Seasonings

Liquid/Paste

Immature Wine (Machari)

As grape juice for wine ferments to achieve the proper sourness, the new, sour wine is drawn off. This is used to offset the richness of walnuts and as a souring agent.

Animal

Yogurt (Matsoni)

This pleasantly tart, creamy yogurt is made from whole cow milk or the richer water buffalo milk. Matsoni is used in salads, soups, sauces, and stews to impart a subtle tartness.

Vegetable/Fruit

Sour Plum (Tkemali)

Tkemali grow throughout Georgia. They are made into the famous tkemali sauce with both red and green varieties. The sauce is a balance of sweet and pungently tart. To lower the tartness level, occasionally sweeter types of plums

FIGURE 10.22 Georgian tklapi.
Source: Chubykin Arkady/Shutterstock.

can be used. Traditionally garlic, pennyroyal, cilantro, dill, cayenne pepper, and salt are used in tkemali sauce.

Fruit Leather (Tklapi)

The dried fruit "leather" made from dried tkemali sour plums is used to add refreshing tartness to soups and stews. Sweeter fruit leathers

FIGURE 10.23 Fresh fenugreek.
Source: Hugh Johnson/DK Images.

FIGURE 10.21 Tkemali (sour plums and sauce).
Source: MariyaPhoto/Fotolia.

FIGURE 10.24 Marigold petals.
Source: Elenathewise/Fotolia.

(Continued)

(Continued)

made from apricots or peaches are used for snacking.

Herbal/Spice

Fenugreek Leaves (Utskho Suneli)

The seed and fresh or dried leaves of delicately fragrant fenugreek are used in Georgian cooking. Grow the leaves from seed and dry them, or purchase fenugreek dried or fresh as kasoor methi at Indian markets.

Marigold Petals (Imeretian Saffron)

Young marigold petals are an important flavor device in Georgian cuisine. They impart a sunny golden color and a musky, delicate flowery, slightly bitter flavor. They keep sauces with walnuts and vinegar, which normally turn purple when mixed, yellow-beige. They are part of the Georgian khmeli-suneli spice mix. Grow them or mail-order them.

FERTILE LAND BEGETS FERTILE CUISINE

In *Please to the Table, The Russian Cookbook,* Anya von Bremzen and John Welchman comment that the quality of a cuisine depends on the quality of its food. The Republic of Georgia is no exception. The food of subtropical Georgia is similar to the most fertile areas of the Mediterranean and produces an enticing, exotic cuisine. Georgians grow a rich plethora of citrus, pomegranates, grapes, plums, blackberries, walnuts, figs, corn, shell and green beans, and various herbs. Their ancient expertise with cattle provides excellent local cheese, meat, and dairy.

FIGURE 10.25 Georgian produce.
Source: Oleg Golovnev/Shutterstock.

FIGURE 10.26 Upper Svaneti, Georgia.
Source: vyskoczilova/Fotolia.

SEASONING AND PASTE MIXTURES

GEORGIAN SPICE MIX (KHMELI-SUMELI)

Similar to Indian garam masala and Persian advieh, Georgian cooks might use this seasoning mixture as Indians and Persians do: infused in fat or lightly toasted. Every cook has a mixture of fenugreek leaves, marigold petals, and other herbs and spices for use in stews, braised lamb, vegetable purées, soups, and sour-fruity-spicy sauces, dry rubs, and marinades. Dishes often include individual khmeli-sumeli seasonings tailored to the recipe (as in an Indian curry) rather than a specific mixture like this one.

Yields 3-1/2 tablespoons

1 tablespoon ground coriander
1 tablespoon crumbled dried fenugreek leaves (available in Indian markets as *kasoor methi*)
1/2 teaspoon ground fenugreek seed
1 teaspoon dried marigold petals *or* 1/4 teaspoon saffron
1 teaspoon dried mint
1 teaspoon dried savory or oregano
1 teaspoon dried tarragon

1 Grind ingredients together in spice grinder. Pass through fine strainer to remove large pieces.

2 Seal in glass jar with tight lid. Keep in cool, dark spot up to 3 months.

Vary! Improvise!

☞ *Other common khmeli-sumeli seasonings include dried dill, dried parsley, bay leaf, and small amounts of paprika, ground black pepper, ground cloves, and/or cinnamon.*

GEORGIAN HOT PEPPER-HERB PASTES OR RELISHES (ADZHIKA)

Georgians prepare adzhika as a thicker paste or as a thinner salsa-like relish, and use it as a condiment with grilled meats or with bread and cheese. Try thick adzhika as a rub for roast pork or lamb, as marinade, or as thin adzika a last-minute sauce to spice up roasted meat or a vegetable or grain dish.

Tomato, Herb, and Pepper Adzhika
The tomato makes this version of adzhika more like salsa.

Yields about 3 cups

1 ounce garlic cloves, 4 large, 2 tablespoons peeled and minced
2 ounces jalapeños, 2 large, 1/3 cup stemmed, seeded, and diced
12 ounces red or green bell peppers, 2 medium, 2 cups cored, ribbed, seeded, and diced
12 ounces plum tomatoes, fresh or canned and drained, 2 cups diced
1 ounce trimmed Italian parsley, 1/2 cup chopped
1-1/2 ounces cilantro, 3/4 cups finely sliced
1/4 ounce trimmed dill, 2 tablespoons chopped
3 tablespoons red wine vinegar

Green Herb and Pepper Adzhika
Celery leaves give this a different and refreshing flavor.

Yields 12 fluid ounces

1/2 ounce cilantro, 1/4 cup finely sliced
1/2 ounce trimmed Italian parsley, 1/4 cup lightly chopped
1/4 cup packed celery or lovage leaves, 1/4 cup lightly chopped
About 1/4 ounce basil leaves, 2 tablespoons torn or finely sliced
About 1/4 ounce mint leaves, 2 tablespoons lightly chopped
1 ounce mild, long thin green chilies, 1/4 cup stemmed, seeded, and diced
6 ounces green or yellow bell pepper, 1 medium, 1 cup stemmed, seeded, and diced
1 ounce garlic cloves, 4 large, 2 tablespoons peeled and minced
2 to 3 tablespoons red or white wine vinegar

1 Pour ingredients into food processor with 1 teaspoon kosher salt:

Tomato, Herb, and Pepper
Pulse-grind 10 seconds. Scrape down and repeat pulse-grind and scraping down 5 more times.

Green Herb and Pepper
Grind 10 seconds. Scrape down and repeat grinding and scraping down 5 more times.

2 Taste adzhika; add more salt and vinegar to taste. Cover and refrigerate adzhika overnight or 24 hours before using. Taste again and adjust flavors with more salt and vinegar, as necessary. Keeps fresh 7 to 8 days refrigerated.

Sources: *Flatbreads and Flavors* by Jeffrey Alford and Naomi Duguid and *The Cooking of the Eastern Mediterranean* by Paula Wolfert

Vary! Improvise!

☞ *No basil? Double the mint. No mint? Double the basil.*
☞ *Thicker Adhizka: Drain puréed ingredients from step 1 in cheesecloth-lined strainer before adding vinegar.*

SAUCE

Georgian Sauces

Georgians make use of what their local climate provides to create their many distinctive sauces: most notably *tkemali* with green plums and others including walnuts, herbs, garlic, spices, pomegranates, blackberries, tomatoes, cherries, and barberries. Thickened by boiling fruit juices or with ground walnuts, fruit, or vegetables, all Georgian sauces are tart and some are slightly spicy. Cooks freely alternate sauces between meat, fish, and vegetable dishes; some are eaten smeared on bread.

GEORGIAN PLUM SAUCE (TKEMALI)

Tkemali is the universal Georgian condiment used as much as Americans do ketchup. Georgian plums are similar to the tiny green Mirabelle plum, and very tart. This sauce is a good use for hard, American supermarket purple plums or fresh "prune" plums in season: the color is stunning. The addition of lime or lemon adds an appropriate tart-fruitiness. Prepare in small portions for immediate use or larger batches for freezing or canning.

Yields 2 cups

FIGURE 10.27 Georgian plum sauce (tkemali).
Source: MariyaPhoto/Fotolia.

1 pound firm or unripe purple plums, halved, pitted, and diced
1/2 teaspoon ground coriander
1/2 teaspoon ground fenugreek
1/3 to 1/2 ounce garlic, 1-1/2 to 2 large cloves, 2 to 3 teaspoons peeled and minced
1/2 to 1 teaspoon chili flakes
   or 1/4 teaspoon cayenne pepper
2 to 3 tablespoons fresh lime or lemon juice, 1 large lime or lemon
1/4 ounce cilantro, 2 tablespoons finely sliced
Optional: 1 tablespoon minced mint leaves

1 Pour 3 tablespoons water, plums, coriander, fenugreek, and garlic into small saucepan. Bring to a boil, lower heat, cover pot, and simmer plums until tender, 15 to 20 minutes. Cool plums to just warm.

2 Purée plum mixture in food processor or blender until smooth. To thicken sauce, place back in saucepan and simmer until slightly thickened. Scrape sauce into bowl and stir in salt, chili or cayenne, lime juice, and herbs. Rest sauce 1 hour. Taste again and adjust flavors. Cool sauce to room temperature and refrigerate up to 1 week.

Vary! Improvise!

☞ *More Flavor: Toast whole spices and grind before adding to plums.*
☞ *Substitute tart greengage plums.*

GEORGIAN BLACKBERRY SAUCE (MAKVALI)

This tart, refreshing summer sauce is great with roasted or grilled pork or chicken, but it would do beautifully on a piece of grilled fish.

Yields 1-1/3 cups

12 ounces ripe or frozen (thawed) blackberries, about 2-1/4 cups
    or 1-1/4 cups seedless, unsweetened blackberry purée
1/8 ounce garlic, 1 small clove, 1 teaspoon peeled and minced
1-inch hot red or green chili, minced
    or 1/8 to 1/4 teaspoon dried red chili flakes
1/4 ounce trimmed dill, 2 tablespoons chopped
1/4 to 1/2 ounce cilantro, 2-1/2 tablespoons finely sliced
3 to 4 teaspoons fresh lemon juice, 1 large lemon

1. Purée blackberries. Scrape purée through a fine strainer into a bowl, and discard seeds to yield about 1-1/4 cups purée.

2. Mix blackberry purée with garlic, chili, and herbs. Season to taste with lemon juice and salt. Rest sauce 1 hour at room temperature before serving.

GEORGIAN APRICOT, WALNUT, AND CILANTRO SAUCE (KINDZIS SATSEBELA)

This sweet-pungent sauce is the best-known Georgian sauce, and a mainstay of its cuisine. Serve it with grilled meat or chicken, cooked beans, grains, or vegetables or slather it on bread. Use intense-tasting dried apricots, or the sauce won't be flavorful.

Yields about 2 cups

2 ounces dried apricots, about 1/3 cup diced
    or 2 ounces sugar-free apricot fruit leather
        or 4 ounces fresh ripe apricots, about 3 medium, halved and pitted
4 ounces chopped walnuts, 1/2 cup
1/2 ounce garlic, 2 large cloves, 1 tablespoon peeled and finely chopped
3 ounces cilantro, 1-1/2 cups finely sliced
3 ounces mixed: trimmed Italian parsley and dill, basil leaves and tarragon leaves, total 1-1/2 cups finely chopped
1 to 2 ounces trimmed green onions, 2 to 4 large, 1/4 to 1/2 cup finely chopped
4 tablespoons freshly squeezed lemon juice, 1 large lemon
1/8 teaspoon cayenne pepper
    or 1/2 teaspoon chili flakes
3/4 to 1 cup walnut *or* olive oil

1. Soak dried apricots or fruit leather in 1 cup boiling water until soft, about 1 hour, or overnight. Drain and reserve soaking water. Chop fresh apricots if using instead.

2. Pour walnuts and garlic into food processor and pulse-grind until coarsely mixed, about 30 pulses. Add apricots and 1/4 to 1/2 cup soaking water, herbs, green onions, lemon juice, and 1 teaspoon kosher salt. Purée sauce until almost smooth. With machine running, pour oil into purée in a slow, thin stream to make a thick sauce. Season with cayenne, chili flakes, or freshly ground black pepper if desired.

3. Rest sauce 1 hour before serving. Taste and adjust flavoring with lemon or salt, and consistency with leftover soaking water or water. Sauce will keep refrigerated up to 3 days.

Source: *The Georgian Feast* by Darra Goldstein.

GEORGIAN GARLIC SAUCE (NIORTSKALI)

Traditionally served with Chicken Tabaka or grilled fish, this is more jus than sauce. Serve it at room temperature or hot.

Yields about 1 cup, 2 to 4 servings

1 cup chicken broth
1 to 1-1/2 ounces garlic, 4 to 6 large cloves, 2 to 3 tablespoons peeled and finely minced
1/4 teaspoon sweet paprika
Pinch of cayenne pepper or chili flakes

Garnish: 1/2 ounce cilantro, 1/4 cup finely sliced

1 In a 1-quart saucepan over low heat, bring chicken broth to a simmer. Whisk in garlic, paprika, and cayenne or chili flakes. Simmer 1 minute, and remove from heat.

2 **To Serve:** Reheat mixture, if desired. Just before serving, stir in cilantro, and season sauce with salt to taste.

SATSIVI: GEORGIAN WALNUT SAUCE

Satsivi, a favorite Georgian nut sauce, is a paste of walnuts, sautéed onions, coriander, and garlic, puréed with broth, perfumed with cinnamon and paprika, and served cold with cooked chicken, turkey, fish, or vegetables. The dish originated in Circassia, directly north of Georgian Abkhazia. The Cherkess/Circassians were displaced by war and slavery. Most escaped to Turkey, where they are a persecuted ethnic minority, bringing with them this sauce. Unlike the Georgian sauce, the Turkish version uses bread to bind. (See the *Circassian Chicken in Walnut Sauce* recipe in chapter *Greece and Turkey*.)

SIMMER, STEW, POACH, BOIL, AND STEAM

Georgian Soups

Georgians love soup and divide them into three categories: meat, meatless-vegetable, and dairy based. Many soups are thickened with flour and/or eggs. *Matsoni* (rich, sour clabbered milk-yogurt), vinegar, or tart fruit juice provides Georgian soups with their characteristic tart flavor. The most popular soups in a Georgian cuisine are *khashi*, *kharcho*, and *chikhirtma*, but there are many more. Vegetarian bean, hot yogurt, or asparagus and cold fruit soups are also popular.

KHASHI

Khashi is a rich, fiery beef soup made from tripe and calf foot and seasoned with garlic and milk, khashi is eaten by many Georgians for breakfast—and as a cure for a hangover.

KHARCHO

Kharcho is a beef-based soup with rice, ground walnuts, and *tklapi* (dried sour plum fruit leather) garnished with garlic, cilantro, and basil. A vegetarian version is made with tomatoes and walnuts.

CHIKHIRTMA

Chikhirtma is a clear garlicky broth made with poultry (chicken or turkey) or lamb, thickened with flour and eggs whisked with lemon juice, and seasoned with saffron, mint, cilantro, parsley, fennel, or basil. Similar to Greek *avgolemono*, this soup has no rice, and lots of spice.

SATATSURI

Satatsuri is a meatless, spring asparagus soup thickened with eggs and seasoned with parsley, cilantro, and dill.

LOBIANI

Lobiani is a meatless vegetable-bean soup seasoned with garlic, *adzhika*, herbs, and *tkemali*.

SHECHMANDI

Shechmandi is a vegetarian yogurt-based soup similar to Turkish *corbasi*; it is made with *matsoni* and herbs, and thickened with flour and eggs.

GEORGIAN BEEF AND HERB SOUP (KHARCHO)

Kharcho is the premier soup of Georgia. Prepare it with beef, lamb, or chicken. Khmeli-suneli, fresh herbs, and something pungent like apricot fruit leather, lemon juice, tkemali sauce, or vinegar is a feature of all kharchos. Goldstein says that kharcho tastes best served the day it is made. If preparing it ahead, add fresh herbs just before serving for a fresher taste.

Yields about 10 cups, 6 to 8 servings

---

2 pounds lean stewing beef, cut into 1/2-inch cubes
1 pound cracked veal or beef bones, rinsed well
   or 3 pounds chicken parts, skinned
      or 2 pounds lamb stew meat, diced into 1/2-inch cubes *and* 1 pound cracked lamb
      bones, rinsed well
2 bay leaves
1/2 ounce Italian parsley, about 2 to 3 large sprigs
1/4 teaspoon whole black peppercorns
2-1/2 ounces apricot leather
   or 2-1/2 ounces dried apricots, about 1/3 cup diced
      or 2-1/2 ounces fruit juice-sweetened apricot jam, about 1/4 cup plus 1 tablespoon
1 tablespoon fresh lemon juice, 1/2 lemon, more to taste
1-3/4 ounces raw rice, about 1/4 cup
1-1/2 pounds onions, 3 large, 6 cups peeled and finely diced
2 tablespoons unsalted butter
   or butter and oil mixed
1 ounce garlic, 4 large cloves, 2 tablespoons peeled and finely minced
1/4 teaspoon red chili flakes, more to taste
1/4 teaspoon paprika
2 to 3 teaspoons *Khmeli-Suneli*

Garnish: 1/8 to 1/4 ounce each fresh herbs, about 2 tablespoons sliced or chopped: cilantro, trimmed parsley, and dill *or* mint leaves

---

1 **Prepare broth:** Cover beef and bones (*or* chicken *or* lamb and bones) with 2 quarts cold water and bring to a boil. Skim away foam and simmer 10 to 15 minutes. Stir in bay leaves, parsley, and peppercorns; simmer 1-1/2 hours. Strain stock into 6-quart soup pot. Discard bones, skin, and gristle. If using chicken, dice meat into bite-sized pieces. Reserve meat and set aside. Skim off fat that rises to the surface and discard. (At this point, broth may be cooled, and chilled overnight. Remove fat on top and proceed.)

2 **Prepare apricot purée:** In a small mixing bowl, cover apricot leather, if using, or jam with 1 cup boiling water. Rest 30 minutes, and stir until creamy. If using dried apricots, soak in 1 cup boiling

water 1 hour (or overnight) and purée until very smooth. Stir lemon juice into apricot purée and set aside.

3 **Finish soup:** Bring strained broth to a boil, stir in rice, and simmer 10 minutes. Meanwhile, heat butter in 12-inch skillet and stir in onions. Sauté onions over medium heat until soft, but not browned, 5 to 7 minutes. Add garlic and 2 teaspoons kosher salt. Cook 1 minute. Scrape onion-garlic mixture into soup, and simmer 10 minutes. Place reserved meat into the soup. Stir in chili flakes, paprika, khmeli-suneli, apricot purée, and freshly ground pepper. Simmer soup 10 minutes. Taste soup and adjust seasonings.

4 **To Serve:** Stir **garnish** herbs into soup. Ladle hot soup into serving bowls.

Source: *The Georgian Feast* by Darra Goldstein.

GEORGIAN LEMON-EGG CHICKEN SOUP (CHIKHIRTMA)

This delicious soup is similar to Greek avgolemono and probably originated in Greece.
The yellower the egg yolks, the brighter the soup.

Yields 7 cups, 4 to 6 servings

1-1/2 quarts chicken stock
1 pound raw boneless, skinless chicken breasts
2 tablespoons unsalted butter *or* oil
4 to 5 ounces onion, 1 cup peeled and finely diced
1 ounce garlic, about 4 cloves, 2 tablespoons peeled and finely sliced
1-1/2 tablespoons all-purpose flour
1/2 teaspoon ground coriander seed
1/8 teaspoon ground fenugreek seed
1/4 teaspoon red pepper flakes
1/8 teaspoon saffron, crushed and softened
1/3 cup large egg yolks, about 3 large
1/4 cup fresh lemon juice, 1 large lemon, more to taste
1/4 to 1/2 ounce cilantro, 3 tablespoons finely sliced, more as desired
1/4 to 1/2 ounce mint leaves, 3 tablespoons finely sliced, more as desired
1/4 to 1/2 ounce basil leaves, 3 tablespoons finely sliced, more as desired

1 In a small saucepan, heat chicken stock to a simmer. If using, add raw chicken breasts, partially cover pot, and simmer until chicken is tender and just cooked through. Remove breasts, cool, and dice, or slice into 1-inch slivers to yield about 1-1/2 cups. Reserve stock.

2 Melt butter or oil in a 4- to 6-quart soup pot over medium heat. Stir in onion and cook until tender, 5 to 7 minutes. Add garlic and cook until soft, 2 minutes. Sprinkle in flour, coriander, and fenugreek, and cook 1 minute. Whisk in reserved stock, and raise heat to high. Stirring constantly, bring soup to a boil, reduce the heat, and add red pepper flakes and saffron. Season soup with salt. Simmer 5 minutes.

3 Whisk egg yolks and lemon juice together in small mixing bowl. Gradually whisk 1 cup hot soup into them. Remove boiling soup from heat. Slowly whisk egg mixture back into soup.

4 **To Serve:** Stir herbs and reserved chicken breasts into hot soup. Taste soup, and season with salt, pepper, and fresh lemon juice. Ladle soup into bowls and serve hot.

Source: *Please to the Table* by Anya von Bremzen and John Welchman.

Vary! Improvise!

☛ Add finely chopped lemon zest from 1 lemon (preferably organic) with red pepper flakes and saffron.

GEORGIAN VEGETARIAN TOMATO AND WALNUT SOUP (BOSTNEULIS KHARCHO)

Georgians consider this soup a vegetarian version of the popular kharcho. If the tomatoes are not ripe, add a tablespoon of tomato paste.

Yields 10 plus cups, 6 to 8 servings

4 tablespoons unsalted butter, diced
12 ounces onions, 3 cups peeled and finely diced
4 ounces broken walnuts, 1 cup
3/4 ounce garlic, 3 large cloves, 1 tablespoon peeled and minced
1 teaspoon coriander seed
1 teaspoon red pepper flakes, less to taste
   or Adzhika
1-1/2 pounds ripe tomatoes, 3 cups diced
   or 3 cups drained and diced canned whole tomatoes
3 ounces vermicelli pasta, 1 cup broken into 1-inch pieces
2 tablespoons lemon juice or red wine vinegar
1/2 ounce trimmed Italian parsley, 1/4 cup chopped
1/2 ounce cilantro, 1/4 cup finely sliced

1 In a 6-quart soup pot over medium heat, melt butter. Stir in onions and sauté until golden, 7 to 10 minutes.

2 Pour walnuts, garlic, 3/4 teaspoon kosher salt, coriander seed, and red pepper (or *Adzhika*) into food processor and pulse-grind until fine. Scrape walnut paste into onions. Rinse out food processor with 2 cups warm water, and reserve. Simmer walnut paste 2 minutes. Stir tomatoes into onion-walnut mixture, reduce heat to medium-low to low, and simmer until tomatoes break down, 5 to 7 minutes.

3 Pour 4 cups cold water plus reserved 2 cups water from food processor into onion-walnut-tomato mixture, and bring to a boil. Stir vermicelli into soup, reduce the heat, and simmer soup 10 minutes. If soup is too thick, stir in water as needed.

4 **To Serve:** Stir in lemon or vinegar and herbs and remove pot from heat. Taste and adjust flavors with salt and pepper. Ladle soup into bowls and serve hot.

Source: *The Georgian Feast* by Darra Goldstein.

Vary! Improvise!

☛ *Substitute 1/2-cup long-grain rice for the vermicelli.*
☛ *Add 2 to 3 teaspoons khmeli-suneli spice blend with other spices for more flavor.*
☛ *Add 1/4 cup chopped dill with other herbs.*

GEORGIAN CHICKEN STEW WITH HERBS (CHAKHOKHBILI)

It's traditional to fry the chicken with skin on, but this way is just as tasty with lower fat.

Yields about 10 cups, 6 servings

4-pound chicken
   or 3 pounds skinned chicken parts, about 8 pieces
3 tablespoons unsalted butter, *divided*
4 tablespoons olive oil, *divided*
Flour for dusting chicken
16 ounces onions, 4 cups peeled and finely diced
1/2 ounce garlic, 2 large cloves, 1 tablespoon peeled and minced
Optional: 1-1/2 teaspoons ground marigold leaves
2 teaspoons ground coriander
2 pounds ripe plum tomatoes, about 4 cups peeled seeded and diced
   or two 28-ounce cans whole plum tomatoes, about 4 cups drained and diced

Herbs

1/2 ounce trimmed Italian parsley, 4 tablespoons chopped, *divided*
1/2 ounce cilantro, 4 tablespoons finely sliced, *divided*
1/2 ounce tarragon leaves, 4 tablespoons chopped, *divided*
1/4 ounce mint leaves, 2 tablespoons finely sliced, *divided*
1/4 ounce basil or dill leaves, 2 tablespoons sliced or chopped, *divided*

1/2 teaspoon dried chili flakes, more to taste

For Serving

Cooked rice

1   Wash and pat chicken dry. Cut whole chicken into 8 pieces. (Two thighs and two legs plus each breast cut in half.) Remove skin and fat from chicken parts and discard. Season meat with salt.

2   Heat a 12-inch skillet over medium-high heat with 1 tablespoon butter and 1 tablespoon oil. When hot, dredge half the chicken pieces in flour, shake off excess, and place in hot pan. Brown chicken on both sides. Set chicken aside in mixing bowl. Repeat with remaining chicken parts and 1 tablespoon each butter and oil.

3   In a 5-quart casserole, heat 1 tablespoon butter and 2 tablespoons oil over medium heat. Stir in onions and cook until golden, 7 to 10 minutes. Stir in garlic, marigold, and coriander, and cook 1 minute. Place chicken into casserole on top of onions and pour in tomatoes. Bring mixture to a boil, lower heat, and simmer partially covered until chicken is done, 40 to 50 minutes.

4   **To Serve:** Stir in half the **herbs** and the chili flakes, and simmer 5 minutes. Season stew with salt and pepper to taste. Stir in remaining **herbs**. Serve chakhokhbili with hot rice.

Vary! Improvise!

☛ Simmer peeled and cubed potatoes with chicken.

GEORGIAN FISH IN CILANTRO SAUCE (TEVZI KINDZMARSHI)

This simple, plain-Jane dish is surprisingly tasty and refreshing. It tastes best in the heat of a Georgian summer. Very low fat, this dish could be considered spa cuisine.

Yields 4-1/2 cups, 4 to 6 servings

1-1/2 pounds boned and skinned whitefish, flounder, catfish, or halibut fillets
1 bay leaf
1 teaspoon sugar
2 ounces peeled onion, 1/2 cup finely diced

Sauce

1/2 cup white wine vinegar
1 ounce cilantro, 1/2 cup finely sliced
1/2 small red chili, sliced

1   **Prepare fish:** Slice fish into 1-1/2 inch strips. Cut an 11-inch circle from parchment paper. Place 1-1/2 cups cold water, 1 teaspoon kosher salt, bay leaf, sugar, and onion into a deep 10-inch skillet. Set fish into pan and press parchment circle on top. Bring to a simmer over medium heat. Reduce heat to low, and poach until fish turns opaque and begins to flake, 6 to 8 minutes. With slotted metal spatula, transfer fish and onion to a 2-quart serving dish. Reserve poaching broth.

2   **Sauce:** In a bowl mix vinegar, cilantro, and chili with 1-1/2 cups reserved (warm) fish poaching broth. Season mixture with salt and pepper to taste. Pour over the fish and cool to room temperature. Cover and refrigerate fish and sauce overnight or at least 2 hours. This dish tastes best the next day when flavors mingle.

3   **To Serve:** Spoon cold or room temperature fish and sauce into soup plates or bowls.

Source: *The Classic Cuisine of Soviet Georgia* by Julianne Margvelashvili.

Vary! Improvise!

☛ **More Color:** Simmer a brunoise of onion, leek, celery, red bell pepper, and carrot in Step 1.
☛ Substitute fresh lemon juice for vinegar.
☛ **Boost Flavor:** Substitute fish stock for water in step 1.
☛ **More Herbs:** Reduce cilantro to 1/4 cup and add 2 tablespoons each chopped fresh dill and tarragon leaves.

Georgian Rice and Dumplings

Wheat is central to Georgian cuisine. Georgians eat rice and corn, but whole-wheat berries and wheat flour are most esteemed. They make the flour into numerous breads, noodles, and dumplings.

LAMB, RICE, AND POTATO PILAF (SHILAPLAVI)

Georgian pilaf, borrowed from the Persians, mixes rice with legumes, vegetables, fruit, and/ or meat. This is a Georgian favorite and a combination all their own. Goldstein says that this is categorized as a "white pilaf."

Yields 7 to 8 cups, 6 to 8 servings

1 pound trimmed lamb leg or shoulder
1 tablespoon olive oil
1 teaspoon caraway seed
1 pound onions, 3-1/2 to 4 cups peeled and finely diced
7 ounces long-grain rice, 1 cup
4 tablespoons unsalted butter, diced
12 ounces potatoes, 1-1/2 to 2 cups peeled and diced into 1-inch cubes
1/2 ounce trimmed Italian parsley, 1/4 cup chopped

1 Dice lamb into 1-inch cubes. Place into 10-inch skillet and season with 1/2 teaspoon salt. Cover skillet and cook meat over low heat until juicy, 10 to 12 minutes. Uncover skillet and add oil. Raise heat to high, stir in caraway and onions. Cook meat mixture until liquid evaporates and onions begin to color, 10 to 15 minutes.

2 Wash rice in cold water and drain. Pour into small saucepan with 1 cup cold water and 1/2 teaspoon kosher salt. Bring to a boil over high heat. Lower heat, cover rice, and simmer until water is absorbed, 5 minutes. Remove pan from heat, rest rice undisturbed 5 to 10 minutes. Uncover pan and fluff rice.

3 In a 5-quart nonstick pot, melt butter over medium heat. Remove pot from heat and arrange potatoes in a single layer and season with 1/2 teaspoon kosher salt and a few grinds of pepper. Top potatoes with 1/2 to 2/3 of cooked rice. Layer the meat mixture, parsley, salt, and pepper over the rice. Smooth remaining rice over the meat. Drizzle 1 cup water over rice and meat.

4 Place pot back onto medium heat. Arrange a cotton towel over top of the pot and cover with a lid. Reduce heat to low, and simmer rice until tender, 40 minutes to 50 minutes.

5 **To Serve:** Do as the Persians, and invert the pilaf onto a platter to show off the browned potatoes and rice.

Source: *The Georgian Feast* by Darra Goldstein.

GEORGIAN MEAT DUMPLINGS (KHINKALI)

Georgian dumplings, relative to Ukrainian pierogi, *Turkish* mandu, *and Chinese soup dumplings, are large, pleated, and stuffed with several kinds of filling. Ground lamb is favored in the mountainous regions; elsewhere a mixture of ground beef and pork is used. Less common are cheese, greens, or mushroom fillings. Meat fillings are beaten and emulsified with broth, and when* khinkali *are cooked, the juices are trapped inside.*

Yields about 23 ounces dough for 15 large (1-1/2 ounces dough per 6-inch) dumplings

Yields about 3 cups filling

15-3/4 ounces unbleached all-purpose flour, 3-1/2 cups, plus extra for rolling

Filling

1/2 pound ground beef
1/2 pound ground pork
2 to 3 ounces onion, 3 tablespoons grated
1-1/2 teaspoons caraway seed
1/4 teaspoon freshly ground black pepper
1/8 teaspoon hot paprika
1 cup cold beef or chicken stock *or* water

FIGURE 10.28 Georgian khinkali dumplings.
Source: Gayvoronskaya_Yana/Shutterstock.

1 **Prepare the dough:** Combine flour and 1 teaspoon kosher salt in food processor. With machine running, slowly pour in 1 cup warm water. (Warm water makes tender dough.) Process until dough comes together in a mass, 45 seconds. Scrape dough out onto work surface and knead lightly by hand to form a soft, pliable dough. Place dough in bowl and cover tightly with plastic wrap; rest 30 to 40 minutes.

2 *Prepare the* **filling:** In a large mixing bowl, combine ground meats, onion, caraway, pepper, paprika, and 1 teaspoon kosher salt. With one hand, beat in cold broth or water 2 tablespoons at a time, until well incorporated. The filling should be loose, but not sitting in liquid.

3 **Roll dough:** Roll dough into 15-inch log and cut into 15 equal pieces; cover. Dip both cut sides of a piece of dough into flour and shake off excess. Roll into 6-inch (large) circle. Repeat with remaining dough. Lay lightly floured dough circles on a sheet pan; cover with plastic wrap.

4 **To stuff:** Place about 2 heaping tablespoons filling in the center of a round. Make accordion pleats: Moving clockwise around the edge of the wrapper, overlap/fold dough, and bring up toward the center. Overlapping the previous fold, continue all the way around the filling (20 or more pleats shows expert pleating) until filling is completely enclosed. Holding dumpling firmly in one hand, twist the pleats together at the center, and press to seal. Cut off excess topknot dough with scissors. Place dumplings 1/2- to 1-inch apart on lightly floured, parchment-covered sheet pan.

5 **Cook the dumplings:** Over high heat, bring a 6-quart pot of water to a boil. Stir in 2 to 3 tablespoons kosher salt. Carefully add dumplings and stir gently 30 seconds to 1 minute so they don't stick to the bottom of the pot. Lower heat to a low-boil/high-simmer and cook dumplings until tender, about 8 minutes.

6 **To Serve:** Remove dumplings with slotted spoon to warmed serving vessel and sprinkle with freshly ground black pepper. Serve immediately while hot. To eat, bite the bottom off a dumpling, suck the juices, then eat the dumpling. Discard the tough dough "handle" at the top, where the pleats meet. To reheat dumplings, sauté them in butter until the bottoms are browned.

Source: *The Cooking of the Eastern Mediterranean* by Paula Wolfert.

FIGURE 10.29 Georgian flattened chicken.
Source: Guy Shapira/Shutterstock.

Vary! Improvise!

☞ *Season hen under the skin or salt-brine it overnight: Dissolve 1/2 cup kosher salt in 9 cups water for a brine.*

☞ *Remove the rib cage or glove-bone hen before cooking.*

Kupati: Georgian Pork and Pomegranate Sausages

Pairing meat and fruit is one of the hallmarks of Georgian cooking. *Kupati* are pork and pomegranate sausages seasoned with dill, cilantro, and cinnamon, and are popular for breakfast in the fall when fresh pomegranates are in season. The meat mixture is traditionally stuffed into sausage casings, but it may be cooked as patties or molded onto flat skewers and grilled for *kofta*. Georgians serve the sausage as hors d'oeuvres or on bread for a sandwich.

SAUTÉ, PAN-FRY, AND DEEP-FRY

SIGNATURE RECIPE

GEORGIAN FLATTENED CHICKEN (TABAKA)

This is a classic Georgian dish, simple but flavorful.

1 to 2 servings

Georgian Garlic Sauce or Georgian Plum Sauce
1-1/2 pound Cornish game hen
1/4 ounce garlic, 1 large clove, peeled and crushed
1 to 2 tablespoons oil

For Serving

Cooked warm rice and steamed green beans

1 Prepare *Georgian Garlic Sauce or Georgian Plum Sauce.*

2 Place the hen breast side up on cutting board. Pat dry. Slice or cut through breastbone to separate rib cage. Turn hen over and lightly pound with a small skillet to flatten. Sprinkle hen liberally with salt on both sides, then rub with garlic clove.

3 Over medium-high heat, heat a 10- to 12-inch well-seasoned cast-iron skillet. (For large batches, cook several at a time on a flat-top gas griddle.) Add oil to skillet. When it shimmers, place hen into skillet and coat both sides. Cook hen skin side up 5 minutes, then flip to skin side down. Place a heavy weight or brick covered in foil to weight down hen. Lower heat to medium-low, and cook hen until brown and crusty, 20 minutes. Turn hen and replace weight. Cook on remaining side until hen is cooked through, juicy and golden, 10 to 15 minutes.

4 **To Serve:** Transfer hen to plate and ladle sauce over. Serve with rice and green beans.

GRILL, GRIDDLE, ROAST, BROIL, BAKE, AND BARBECUE

GEORGIAN MARINATED MEAT GRILLED ON SKEWERS (BASTURMA)

Mtsavadi, grilled skewers or plain lamb, beef, or pork, is the most common grill in Georgia. Basturma is made with less tender cuts marinated overnight before grilling. This marinade works equally well with pork. In Turkey and Lebanon basturma is a spice-rubbed, dry-cured beef eaten in thin slices, much like prosciutto or bresaola (Italian dry-cured beef).

Yields 1-1/4 cups marinade; serves 4 to 6

1 cup pomegranate juice
1/4 cup olive oil
1 bay leaf, preferably fresh, bruised
1/2 ounce garlic, 2 large cloves, 1 tablespoon peeled and minced
2 pounds trimmed boneless lamb shoulder or leg, cut into 2-inch cubes
    or 2 pounds boneless beef sirloin, cut into 2-inch cubes
1 pound eggplant, 4 to 5 cups diced into 2-inch cubes

For Serving

Georgian Plum Sauce, Georgian Garlic Sauce or Georgian Apricot, Walnut and Cilantro Sauce
Bread and Lavash Bread

1 **Marinate:** In large mixing bowl mix juice, oil, bay leaf, and garlic. Fold in meat and cover with plastic wrap. Refrigerate 12 to 24 hours.

2 **Eggplant:** Toss eggplant with 1 tablespoon kosher salt and rest 30 minutes. Drain and pat eggplant dry. Steam eggplant until slightly tender, 2 minutes. Set aside.

3 **Preheat rill:** Drain meat from marinade and place on skewers alternating with eggplant cubes. Season meat and eggplant with salt and freshly ground pepper. Grill until eggplant is cooked through and meat is cooked to desired doneness: medium to medium-rare takes 8 to 10 minutes.

4 **To Serve:** Arrange meat on platter with Georgian sauce or sauces on the side. Serve with lavash bread.

Source: *The* Georgian Feast **by Darra Goldstein.**

Vary! Improvise!

☛ *Bigger Flavor: Beef for basturma is often marinated overnight in grated onion, minced garlic, finely sliced cilantro and basil, olive oil, and fresh lemon juice. To strengthen the flavor of this marinade, add 1/2 cup or more minced onion, 2 to 3 tablespoons cilantro, 1 to 2 tablespoons fresh basil, more olive oil, and 1/4 cup or more fresh lemon juice.*

FIGURE 10.30 Another Georgian speciality: shashlik.
Source: Svitlana-ua/Shutterstock.

Georgian Breads

The best-known Georgian bread is the cheese-filled *khachapuri* made with either yeast dough or a yogurt-baking powder dough. Khachapuri are filled with cheese or mashed beans or potatoes and onions *or* greens and herbs, and traditionally baked in a clay griddle over an open fire. The baking powder and yeasted versions are pleated over the filling or made into "boats" and filled with cheese and egg. Georgians are also fond of a rustic, simple, clay-griddle-cooked corn bread called *mchadi*.

Georgian Filled Breads (Khachapuri)

The most popular khachapuri filling is made with cheese from the Georgian region of Emereti, hence the name "Emeruli." The technique is similar to Indian *stuffed paratha*, which are cooked on a cast-iron or steel griddle.

FIGURE 10.31 Khachapuri.
Source: SK/Fotolia.

TWO DOUGHS FOR GEORGIAN FILLED BREADS (KHACHAPURI)

Yogurt Dough

Yields 36 to 38 ounces dough, 8 breads about 4 to 4-1/2 ounces each

18 ounces unbleached all-purpose flour, 4 cups, plus more for rolling, *divided*
1-1/2 teaspoons baking powder
1/2 teaspoon kosher salt
2 cups plain whole milk plain yogurt

Yeast Dough

Yields about 24 ounces dough, 6 breads about 4 ounces each

4-1/2 teaspoons active dry yeast
1/2 teaspoon sugar
1 cup lukewarm milk
15 to 16 ounces flour, 3-1/3 to 3-1/2 cups, plus more for rolling
1 tablespoon sugar
2 teaspoons kosher salt
2 ounces unsalted butter, 4 tablespoons, softened, more for bowl

1 **Prepare a filling:** See *Three Fillings for Georgian Filled Breads.*

2 **Prepare a dough:**

Yogurt Dough
In a large mixing bowl, blend 1 cup flour, baking powder, and salt. Stir in yogurt until evenly mixed. Continue to stir in 2-1/2 cups flour, bit by bit, until dough is not too sticky. Pour remaining 1/2-cup flour onto work surface and scrape dough onto it. With a bench scraper to help, knead flour into dough until soft and elastic, 3 minutes. Scrape dough into bowl and cover.

Yeast Dough
In a small mixing bowl, blend yeast, sugar, and milk. Rest until yeast softens and bubbles, 5 minutes. In a large mixing bowl, stir together 3 cups flour, sugar, salt, butter, and yeast-milk mixture until smooth. Gather dough into a ball. Sprinkle 1/2-cup flour on work surface and with bench scraper, knead dough on it until smooth and elastic, 5 to 10 minutes. Butter or oil a bowl and roll dough ball in it. Cover bowl with plastic wrap and place in warm place to proof until doubled, 1-1/2 to 2 hours. Press dough down and re-cover.

3 **Preheat oven to 400 degrees F:** Line one (for yeast dough) or two (for yogurt dough) half-sheet pans with parchment paper. Lightly oil them.

4 **Roll dough:** Roll dough into an even 12-inch log. Cut in half. Divide **yogurt dough** into 8 equal balls. Divide **yeast dough** into 6 balls. Keep dough balls covered. Flatten 1 dough ball on a lightly floured surface with a hand. With a floured rolling pin, roll dough into 6- to 7-inch diameter.

5 **Fill, pleat, and press breads:** Place 2 level tablespoons filling in center of dough circle. (Overfilled breads tend to leak.) Draw the sides of dough up over filling: make small pleated folds and pinch together. Continue all the way round the dough circle so the filling is completely enclosed. Seal top by pinching and twisting, then lightly press with a hand to flatten khachapuri. Flip bread and gently hand-flatten or roll the other side into: **yogurt bread:** 6-inch diameter or **yeast bread:** 5-inch diameter.

Vary! Improvise!

☛ **No Bake:** *Paint yogurt breads with sunflower or olive oil and cook in a cast-iron pan over medium-low heat until both sides are golden.*
☛ **Shiny Crust:** *Brush yeast bread with egg yolk mixed with a few drops of water before baking.*
☛ **Whole Wheat:** *Substitute half of the white flour for whole wheat bread flour.*

6 **Bake breads:** Place breads as they are made on prepared sheet pans. Place **yogurt bread** pleated side down. Place **yeast bread** pleated side up. Poke **yogurt breads** a few times to keep them from puffing up. Bake stuffed bread until brown speckled or lightly golden, 15 to 25 minutes. Remove breads from pan and keep warm until ready to serve.

7 **To Serve:** Cut breads in half and serve warm or at room temperature. Cool uncut breads completely before freezing in zipper baggies. Thaw and reheat in 400 degree F oven until warm.

Source: *Flatbreads and Flavors* by Jeffrey Alford and Naomi Duguid.

SIGNATURE RECIPE

THREE FILLINGS FOR GEORGIAN FILLED BREADS

Cheese (Emeruli)

Yields 1 cup

4 ounces mild Cheddar cheese, 1 cup grated and chopped
2 ounces feta cheese, 1/3 cup crumbled
1 ounce plain whole milk yogurt, 2 tablespoons
1 large egg

Red Bean (Lobiani)

Yields 1 cup

1 tablespoon olive oil
1/4 ounce garlic, 1 large clove, 1-1/2 teaspoons peeled and minced
8 ounces drained, cooked small red or kidney beans, 1-1/4 cups
1/4 to 1/2 ounce cilantro, 3 tablespoons finely sliced

Potato and Herb (Ossetinski)

Yields about 1-1/2 cups

8 ounces small- to medium-sized waxy potatoes
1 tablespoon olive oil
4 to 5 ounces onion, 1/2 cup peeled and finely diced
1/2 ounce trimmed Italian parsley, 1/4 cup finely chopped
1 ounce cilantro, 1/2 cup finely sliced
1 ounce mint leaves, 1/2 cup sliced leaves
Optional: 1 ounce feta, 3 tablespoons crumbled

1 Prepare a filling:

Cheese
Blend together **cheese** filling ingredients and set aside.

Red Bean
Heat olive oil over medium heat in 10-inch skillet or small saucepan. Add garlic and beans and cook 5 minutes. Cool. Stir in cilantro. Season with salt and pepper.

Potato and Herb
Boil potatoes until fork-tender, about 10 to 15 minutes. Cool. Peel and dice potatoes into 1/2-inch cubes to yield about 2 cups. Heat oil in small skillet over medium heat and cook onion until golden, 7 to 10 minutes. Break up potatoes with fork, but don't mash. Stir onion into potatoes, and cool. Stir in herbs and optional cheese. Season potatoes with salt and pepper to taste.

Source: *Flatbreads and Flavors* by Jeffrey Alford and Naomi Duguid.

Vary! Improvise!

☞ *Devise a filling of beet or other greens and dill with sautéed onion.*

FIGURE 10.32 Clay oven in the Republic of Georgia.
Source: © jane schreibman/Alamy.

SALAD AND VEGETABLE METHODS

Georgian Vegetables

Georgians love vegetables in many forms cooked or uncooked. Because of the many fasting days in the Orthodox Church calendar, Georgians, like Greeks, have learned to make delicious dishes without meat, eggs, or dairy. Simple techniques result in a variety of dishes like cooked vegetable *boranis*, vegetable "paté" purées called *pkhalis*, and vegetable or bean salads dressed with oil and vinegar.

TWO GEORGIAN RED BEAN SALADS (LOBIO)

The "salads" may be mashed and used to stuff khachapuri breads.

14 ounces dry small red or kidney beans, 2 cups rinsed and drained

---

Red Beans in Sour Plum Sauce (Lobio Tkemali)

Yields 4 to 5 cups

Georgian Plum Sauce (Tkemali), divided
1/2 ounce cilantro or trimmed Italian parsley, 1/4 cup finely sliced
2 tablespoons walnut, sunflower, or good olive oil, *divided*

Optional Garnish

6 to 9 ounces red onion, 1-1/2 to 2 cups peeled and thinly sliced or slivered
4 to 6 ounces pickled mild banana peppers, about 6 slices
8 ounces feta, about 2 cups cubed
5 ounces Kalamata olives, 1 cup pitted

Red Beans with Walnuts (Lobio Nigozit)

Yields 7 cups

4 tablespoons sunflower or olive oil
8 to 9 ounces onion, 2 cups peeled and finely diced
4 ounces walnuts, 3/4 to 1 cup finely ground
1 tablespoon ground coriander
3 tablespoons dried summer savory
1 ounce garlic, 2 large cloves, 1 tablespoon peeled and minced
1 teaspoon *Khmeli Suneli*
1 ounce trimmed celery or lovage leaves, about 1/2 cup chopped
1/4 cup red wine vinegar
Optional: 1 ounce cilantro, 1 cup finely sliced
Garnish: Cilantro or Italian parsley leaves

FIGURE 10.33 Lovage.
Source: Dave King/DK Images.

1 Pour dry beans into large pot and cover with water. Stir in 2 tablespoons kosher salt. Soak beans overnight or quick soak: Bring beans and water to a boil, remove pot from heat. Cover and rest beans 1 hour. Drain. Cover beans with 4 cups fresh ----water and bring to a boil. Lower heat, cover pot, and simmer beans until tender, 40 minutes to 1 hour.

2 Season beans:

Sour Plum Sauce

Drain beans. While warm toss beans with 1/2 cup or more plum sauce or mash beans lightly with 1/2 cup or more *Georgian Plum Sauce (Tkemali)*. Toss or mix beans with cilantro or parsley, and season with salt and pepper. Stir in 1 tablespoon oil.

Walnuts

Do not drain beans. Heat 10- to 12-inch skillet on medium heat. Add oil and sauté onion until golden, 5 to 8 minutes. Add ground walnuts and cook until toasted, 3 minutes. Add coriander, savory, garlic, and khmeli suneli. Cook 1 minute. Deglaze with up to 1/2 cup bean water, if necessary. Toss mixture into beans and simmer 5 minutes. Season with salt to taste. Cook beans uncovered until about a fourth of the beans break down and the liquid has absorbed or thickened. Stir in celery or lovage leaves and vinegar. Stir in optional cilantro. Taste and adjust flavors.

3 **To Serve:** Mound beans in serving vessel and:

Sour Plum Sauce

Drizzle beans with remaining 1 tablespoon oil. Serve with remaining plum sauce and garnishes on the side. Each diner mixes them into the salad as they desire.

Walnuts

Garnish with cilantro or parsley leaves, and serve.

FIGURE 10.34 Summery savory.
Source: David Murray/DK Images.

FIGURE 10.35 Winter savory.
Source: Dave King/DK Images.

GEORGIAN VEGETABLE PATÉ/PURÉE (PKHALI/ MKHALI)

Pkhalis are made with many types of vegetables and seasonings; each lends its own distinctive flavor. Herbs, walnuts, garlic, and pomegranate juice and/or vinegar flavor this quintessential Georgian vegetable "paté." Spinach and beets are the favorites, but cauliflower, leeks, peppers, green beans, radish greens, cabbage, nettles, and onion can become pkhalis. Traditionally served molded into an oval, pkhalis are cross-hatched and garnished with pomegranate seeds, slivered red onions, sour cream, or walnut oil. Cut them like a pie and eat with a fork or spread on crackers or toast. They should taste tart and refreshing.

Beet Paté (Mtsvane Charkhils Pkhali)

Yields 2 cups

1 pound trimmed beets
2 ounces walnuts, 1/2 cup broken
3/4 ounce garlic, 3 large cloves, peeled
1 ounce trimmed dill, 1/2 cup chopped
1/2 ounce trimmed Italian parsley, 1/4 cup chopped
1/2 teaspoon ground coriander
1/2 teaspoon hot paprika
2 tablespoons red wine vinegar, more to taste

Green Bean Paté (Mtsvane Lobios Pkhali)

Yields 2-1/2 cups

1 pound trimmed green beans
2 ounces walnuts, 1/2 cup broken or lightly chopped
3/4 ounce garlic, 3 large cloves, peeled
1 ounce cilantro, 1/2 cup finely sliced
1 ounce trimmed Italian parsley, 1/2 cup chopped
1 teaspoon crushed, dried summer savory
    or 1 tablespoon chopped fresh summer savory
1 tablespoon red wine vinegar

Spinach Paté (Mtsvane Ispanakhi Pkhali)

Yields 2 cups

1 pound baby spinach, washed and drained
2 ounces walnuts, 1/2 cup broken
1/2 ounce garlic, 2 large cloves, 1 tablespoon peeled and minced
1 ounce cilantro, 1/2 cup finely sliced
1 ounce trimmed Italian parsley, 1/2 cup chopped
1 ounce trimmed green onions, 2 large, 1/4 cup chopped
1/2 teaspoon ground coriander
1 tablespoon red wine vinegar

Garnish

Walnut or good olive oil or sour cream
Toasted and chopped walnuts
Pomegranate seeds *or* pomegranate syrup

For Serving

Fresh country bread *or* toasted slices of baguette or other rustic bread

1 Cook vegetables until very tender. To hold together into a "paté," the vegetables must be drained and excess liquid squeezed out:

Beets
Preheat oven to 400 degrees F. Trim beets and scrub. Rub with oil, wrap with foil, and bake whole until fork-tender, 1 to 1-1/2 hours. Peel and grate beets to yield 1-1/2 cups.

Green Beans
Trim away stem ends. Steam beans until tender, 5 to 7 minutes. Cool under cold water and drain. Chop into 1-inch lengths to yield 3-1/2 cups.

Spinach
Steam spinach until fully cooked, 2 minutes. Drain and squeeze out excess liquid; reserve liquid. Chop spinach finely and evenly to yield about 1 cup.

2 *Grind* **walnut-garlic base:** In a food processor, grind walnuts and garlic until coarse. Add herbs (cilantro, Italian parsley, dill, and/or green onions) and dry spices as called for in each recipe. Grind to a fine paste and transfer paste to mixing bowl. No need to clean processor. Then:

Beets
Add grated beets to food processor and pulse-grind just until they hold together, but still have texture. Combine with **walnut-garlic base**.

Green Beans
Add beans to food processor and grind until "paté" holds together, but with texture. Combine with **walnut-garlic base**.

Spinach
Combine **walnut-garlic base** with spinach. Stir in 1 tablespoon reserved cooking water, if necessary, until pkhali achieves a paté texture.

3 Scrape pkhali into mixing bowl. Season with salt, pepper, and more vinegar, to taste. Rest pkhali 1 hour and taste again; adjust seasonings. Oil a 3- to 4-cup ramekin and pack pkhali into it *or* form paté into a high-mounded smooth oval on serving plate. Cover, and refrigerate 1 hour or overnight.

4 **To Serve:** Bring pkhali to room temperature and invert ramekin on serving platter. Drizzle pkhali with walnut oil *or* sour cream *and* garnish with fresh pomegranate seeds (or drizzle with pomegranate syrup if fresh are unavailable) and toasted walnuts. Serve with fresh bread or toast.

Vary! Improvise!

☞ *For richer taste, double the walnuts and toast them.*

☞ *Toast the coriander.*

☞ *Season each vegetable patés differently. Devise other seasonings that would harmonize like lemon, lime, or pomegranate syrup to add acid zest.*

GEORGIAN WALNUT-HERB STUFFED GREEN TOMATOES

4 to 8 servings

Four (large) 8-ounce firm green *or* red tomatoes

Sauce

Yields about 1/2 cup

1/2 ounce trimmed Italian parsley, 1/4 cup finely chopped
1/2 ounce trimmed dill, 1/4 cup finely chopped
1/4 ounce basil leaves, 2 tablespoons finely sliced, more to taste
2 teaspoons balsamic vinegar, more to taste

Filling

Yields about 2 cups

8 ounces walnuts, 2 cups lightly chopped
1/4 ounce garlic, 1 large clove, 1-1/2 teaspoons peeled and minced
1/2 ounce cilantro, about 1 cup lightly packed sprigs
1 teaspoon powdered marigold leaves
1/2 ounce basil leaves, about 1/4 cup torn
2 teaspoons balsamic vinegar
Pinch of ground hot paprika or cayenne pepper

Cilantro leaves for garnish

1 Grill or broil tomatoes over medium-low gas flame, charcoal, or under broiler until skin is blistered and meat is tender, 3 to 5 minutes for red tomatoes and 10 to 15 for green. Place green tomatoes in large mixing bowl, cover with plate and cool. Cool red tomatoes on parchment-covered sheet pan, stainless half hotel pan, or a plate. Peel tomatoes, and discard skin.

2 **Core tomatoes:** Slice off tomato tops, reserve, and carefully run a paring knife around the inside edge of the tomato to release its insides. Holding the tomato firmly to keep it from splitting, scoop out tomato insides with a melon baller, leaving thick tomato walls. Press pulp through fine strainer and reserve tomato liquid. Sprinkle inside of tomato with salt.

3 **Sauce:** In a small saucepan, combine parsley, dill, and basil with balsamic vinegar and enough reserved tomato liquid to make a thick sauce, about 5 tablespoons. Season sauce with salt and pepper. Heat sauce to lukewarm, and set aside.

4 **Filling:** In a food processor, combine **filling** ingredients and 3 to 4 tablespoons reserved tomato liquid. Pulse-grind until combined; filling should be chunky, not pasty, but it should hold together. Arrange tomatoes on serving platter and stuff each with 1/4 of filling. Cover with reserved tops. Cover platter and set aside for 1 hour.

5 **To Serve:** Before serving, drizzle tomatoes with reserved sauce (about 2 tablespoons per tomato), garnish with cilantro, and serve.

Source: *The Cooking of the Eastern Mediterranean* by Paula Wolfert.

Vary! Improvise!

☞ *Toast the walnuts.*

☞ ***Not Grandmother's Cabbage Rolls:*** *Using the filling ingredients, grind walnuts and garlic to a paste with a little tomato liquid, stir in herbs, and season with vinegar, salt, and pepper. Boil 10 to 12 large Savoy cabbage leaves until tender, drain, and trim off outside of large rib. Overlap leaves 1 inch on top of half sheet of parchment on work surface to form a long cabbage sheet. Spread with walnut paste, leaving 1/2-inch margins free on sides and 1 inch on bottom and top. Roll up as for strudel, tucking in ends. Rest roll at room temperature 30 minutes. Chill. Slice roll into 3/4- to 1-inch-wide "sushi"-sized rolls. Serve at room temperature. Garnish with mayonnaise and/or pomegranate seeds.*

PICKLE AND PRESERVE

GEORGIAN PICKLED GARLIC (MZHAVE NIORI)

Pickled garlic is a handy way to have garlic for seasoning. Many Georgians consider it a medicinal cure for coughs, colds, or high blood pressure.

Yields 1 quart

1-1/2 pounds broken, unpeeled garlic cloves, about 12 large heads, 4 cups cloves
12 black peppercorns
2 small (1-inch) dried red chilies, stemmed and seeded
1/2 teaspoon dry-toasted coriander seed
4 tablespoons kosher salt
1/2 cup unsweetened pomegranate juice
1-1/4 cups red wine vinegar

1 *Peel garlic.*

- **Hard stem garlic** has fewer but larger cloves with thick skins. The cloves may be peeled, or soaked in warm water or quickly blanched in boiling water to loosen the peel before peeling.

- **Soft stem garlic** has many smaller cloves with finer skin. The cloves may be used without peeling, or blanched quickly and peeled. Fill a large saucepan with water and bring to a boil. Place garlic in strainer and immerse in boiling water 10 to 20 seconds. Rinse under cold water. Peel garlic and discard peels. Rinse garlic again in strainer under cold running water. Hang strainer and rest garlic cloves in it to drain.

2 **Pack the jar:** Place peppercorns, chilies, and coriander in clean 1-quart glass canning jar. Pack in garlic tightly.

3 **Prepare the brine:** In a small saucepan, bring salt, pomegranate juice, and vinegar to a boil. Pour over garlic. Press garlic to completely immerse in liquid. Tightly screw on lid.

4 Store jar at room temperature (68 to 70 degrees F) 3 to 4 weeks before using.

5 **To Serve:** Place garlic cloves in small bowls and serve as a condiment with appetizers, meat, or cheese, or sliced on salads.

REVIEW QUESTIONS

Iran/Persia

1. What is the reason for the early sophistication of Persian cuisine?

2. What other cultural influences shaped Persian-Iranian cuisine?

3. What was the Silk Road?

4. Name two important Persian dishes.

5. What are the three main Persian rice dishes? Describe one.

Republic of Georgia

1. What cultures left their influences on Georgian cuisine?

2. Discuss the foods and herbs important to Georgian cuisine.

3. Name one Georgian sauce and describe it.

4. What is the premier soup of Georgia? What are its main ingredients?

5. What are the supra and the tamada?

UNIT IV

AFRICA AND LATIN AMERICA

CHAPTER ELEVEN

AFRICA

This chapter will:

- Introduce the changing, turbulent histories of Morocco, Ethiopia, and Senegal, their geographies, cultural influences, and climate.

- Discuss the importance of tagine, couscous, w'et, injera, thiebou jen, maafe, and fufu.

- Introduce North, East, and West African culinary cultures, their diverse influences, and regional variations and dining etiquette.

- Identify foods, dishes, and techniques that cross between countries.

- Identify the foods, flavor foundations, seasoning devices, and favored cooking techniques of Morocco, Ethiopia, and Senegal.

- Teach techniques and recipes for beloved, long-lived African dishes.

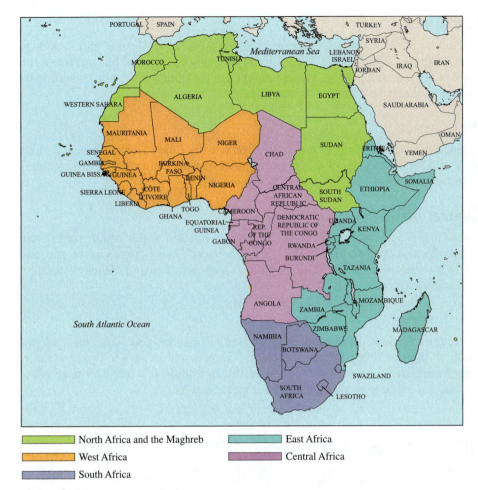

FIGURE 11.1A Map of Africa.

Africa, with fifty-four sovereign states, is, after Asia, the second largest and second most populated continent in the world. The Mediterranean Sea surrounds Africa to the north, the Suez Canal and the Red Sea along the Sinai Peninsula to the northeast, the Indian Ocean along the southeast, and the Atlantic Ocean to the west. The hottest of continents, Africa sits on the equator and is the single continent that bridges both northern and southern temperate zones. Many scientists consider eastern Africa as the birthplace of humans; the earliest Homo sapiens discovered dates back 200 thousand years.

Most African states are republics operating under some form of presidential rule. Few have been able to maintain democracy permanently; they struggle with constant military coups and the resulting dictatorships. African states or countries can be divided up into five *regions*:

North Africa and the Maghreb

Hugging the Mediterranean basin, this region includes seven countries: Algeria, Libya, Morocco, Tunisia, Egypt, and—often included—Sudan and Western Sahara. The first four are called the *Maghreb*. Egypt, straddling two continents with its Sinai Peninsula in Asia, is a *transcontinental* country. The people of the Maghreb belong to both Berber and Arab ethnolinguistic groups.

East Africa

Nineteen countries make up this region from Tanzania, Kenya, Uganda, and Rwanda to Eritrea, Ethiopia, and Somalia. East Africa is strikingly scenic with the continent's two tallest peaks, Mount Kilimanjaro and Mount Kenya, the world's second largest freshwater lake, Lake Victoria, and the world's second deepest lake, Lake Tanganyika.

West Africa

Despite the wide variety of cultures from Nigeria, Ivory Coast, Liberia, Mali, and Sierra Leone to Senegal, this region of sixteen countries displays similarities in dress, cuisine, music, and culture not seen in groups outside the region.

Central Africa

Comprising eleven countries in central and southwest Africa, this region ranges from Malawi, Zambia, and Zimbabwe to Angola, Cameroon, and Congo. One of the most biodiverse regions in the world, this region is in danger of environmental devastation due to deforestation.

South Africa

Five countries, Botswana, Lesotho, Nambia, South Africa, and Swaziland, make up this region of diverse ecoregions from grasslands, bushveld, and savanna to riparian (water) zones, which are home to great numbers of African wildlife. It is home to many native peoples, and has been heavily settled by Europeans and Asians.

NORTH, EAST, AND WEST AFRICA: MOROCCO, ETHIOPIA, AND SENEGAL

This chapter includes Morocco, Ethiopia, and Senegal because they have three of the most engaging, inspiring, and representative cuisines of the vast multicultural continent of Africa.

NORTH AFRICA

MOROCCO: THE JEWEL OF NORTH AFRICA

A Long Love Affair

In Couscous and Other Good Food From Morocco, *chef Paula Wolfert speaks with deep love of Morocco with its music, the great and exotic cities of Marrakesh, Fez, and Tangier, the pre-Saharan oases, the country souks (open air markets), the variable landscape, and the simple hospitable Moroccan people and their food. She considers Moroccan food "one of the world's great cuisines." To Wolfert, Morocco is a place that touches her with "a deep longing to return."*

From whitewashed fishing ports on the Mediterranean and Atlantic, the Sahara desert, High Atlas Mountains, and deep, craggy valleys, to Roman ruins and great imperial cities with winding streets and ancient medinas and souks, Morocco's colorful, exotic culture is

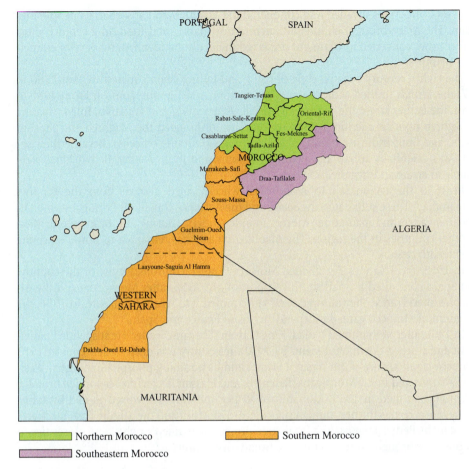

Northern Morocco

Southern Morocco

Southeastern Morocco

FIGURE 11.1B Map of Morocco.

filled with enticing sights, scents, and flavors. Arabs know Morocco as *al-Maghreb al-Aqsa*, meaning "the farthest west." Ruled for many centuries by *Berber* kings who could trace their ancestry to Paleolithic times, Morocco once was the center of Moorish kingdoms that included much of Spain and North Africa.

The region of Morocco on the north coast of Africa was probably first inhabited by people similar to Neanderthals. Nomadic Homo sapiens from the Mediterranean basin moved in after the last Ice Age. Around the sixth century BCE, mariner-trader Phoenicians established settlements on the shores of the *Maghreb*. The greatest was Carthage, where the Phoenicians paid the indigenous ruling peoples, the *Imazighen*, also called Berbers, to bring in raw materials. Carthaginians grew wheat, likely introduced grapes, and developed a fish salting and preserving industry and an anchovy liquid called *garum*, which they exported to Italy and Europe.

In the mid-third century BCE during the Punic Wars, the Roman navy, fighting the Carthaginians over Sicily, eventually destroyed Carthage. Romans introduced economic development, roads, and agricultural skills. They placed Juba II and then his son Ptolemy on the throne. In AD 40, Caligula had Ptolemy assassinated and annexed the Maghreb region to the Roman Empire. Berber rule overshadowed Carthage and Rome, and after the fall of Carthage, the Berbers refused to integrate into the Roman Empire, causing constant friction with Rome.

From the second to fourth centuries, many slaves and Berbers converted to Christianity. During the fifth century, Vandals, Visigoths, and Byzantine Greeks conquered the region of Morocco, but the Berbers remained in the mountains, unconquered.

In 647, the Arabs invaded and conquered the Maghreb and absorbed its people into Islam. The Arabs brought culture: art, architecture, dance, and food. In a century, most Berber tribes converted to Islam but preserved their cultural identity and developed their own Islamic sect.

The eighth century began a cycle of rising and falling Islamic dynasties. From 780 to 917, the *Idrisids* unified Morocco and broke from Arab Empire control. From 1061 to 1554, the Berber kings, the *Almoravids, Almohads, Merenids,* and *Wattasids,* ruled, creating a Maghreb political identity for the region. They dominated the Maghreb and Muslim Spain, and built exquisite mosques and *madrassas* (Quranic schools). Because their society was essentially tribal, and prized autonomy and individuality, Berber kings were unable to create an integrated society.

In 1559 the region fell to Arab tribes who claimed descent from the Prophet Muhammad. These sultanates, the *Saadis* and the *Alaouites,* fought off Portuguese and Ottoman invaders and maintained Moroccan independence during European colonization of other countries in the region. The Alaouite dynasty has remained in power since the seventeenth century.

In 1912, the Treaty of Fez divided Morocco: France controlled most of the country, and Spain controlled a small southwest portion. In 1955, after Moroccans and the Allies pressured France, they allowed King Mohammed V to return from exile. In 1956, the Kingdom of Morocco gained independence from France and Spain.

In 1961, after Mohammed V died, King Hassan II became leader. He suspended parliament and cracked down on dissent. By 1970 the country was deep in debt, but in 1973 Morocco claimed part of the Western Sahara and its booming phosphate industry. Western Saharans and many Moroccans dissented, and Hassan II's regime responded brutally. When Hassan died in 1999, Mohammed VI became king. He vowed to end brutality. Today Morocco has the best human rights record in Africa and the Middle East. Elections, state-taught Berber languages, a legal code protecting women's rights, and closer ties to Europe have brought Morocco into the twenty-first century.

LANGUAGE, PHILOSOPHY, AND RELIGION

The official language of the more than 32 million Moroccans is an Arabic dialect peculiar only to Morocco. Fewer than a quarter of the people (mostly in remote mountains) still speak one of the Berber languages, *Rifi, Tamazight,* and *Tashilhit.* French is the language of diplomacy; some Spanish is also spoken.

Morocco's official religion is Islam. Most Moroccans are Sunni Muslims with a few Sufis. Moroccan law assures freedom of religion, but Christianity (mostly Roman Catholic) and Judaisim are a very small minority. Moroccans deeply respect the royal family and believe that their lineage comes directly from the Prophet Muhammad.

Religion affects law and order. Morocco is declared a Muslim nation in the constitution, and the king is called *Amir El Mouminin* (leader of the faithful). The Islamic faith binds the country together. Its people consider the Koran their holy book and the mosques as social and religious centers. It is illegal to attempt to convert a Muslim, and Muslims who do convert are punishable by law.

GEOGRAPHY AND CLIMATE

Morocco is essentially a central spine of mountains flanked by deserts and plains. Slightly larger than California, Morocco lies across the Strait of Gibraltar on the Mediterranean and looks out onto the Atlantic from Africa's northwest shoulder. Algeria borders it to the east and Mauritania to the south. The Atlantic coast is a fertile plain and the Mediterranean coast is mountainous. The Atlas Mountains, running northeastward from the south to the Algerian frontier, average 11,000 feet elevation and are often snow-capped year round with below-zero temperatures in winter.

Morocco's climate is mostly mild and subtropical. Prevailing west winds shape weather in the Maghreb: the winds drop most of their moisture on the northern slopes and coastal plain, with little left for the desert scrub of the southern slopes that fade south into the true desert of the Sahara. Sea and ocean breezes cool the coastal areas in summer and warm them in winter. Inland temperatures get quite hot in summer and cold in winter. Northern Morocco is very wet in winter and the inland south can get bitterly cold and dry.

FARMING AND AGRICULTURE

Aside from drought years, Morocco mostly produces what it consumes. Severe variations in rainfall have motivated governmental dam and irrigation projects that provide almost half of Morocco's water resources. Only a quarter of Morocco's land is arable with the bulk of farming as subsistence on plots less than twelve acres. Moroccans grow wheat and grain, olives, almonds, peanuts, citrus, grapes, dates, legumes, many vegetables, and industrial sugar beets, sugar cane, cotton, and oil seeds.

MOROCCAN CUISINE: THE MASTERS OF SAVORY AND SWEET

The Moroccan diet is rooted in the simple cuisine of ancient Berber tribes. It is based primarily on maize, barley, sheep and goat milk, cheese and butter, honey, lamb, couscous, and wild game. Morocco's Islamic-Arabic legacy enriched the tribal cuisine: Through Islam, Moroccan food absorbed the tastes and techniques of Persia, the Ottomans-Turks, and Spain. Muslims abstain from pork and alcohol, so cooks turned to *halal* lamb and chicken (see *Glossary*), and mint tea.

Morocco is best known for its fascinating mix of exotic spices and for successfully mixing savory and sweet. Sugar or honey season many meat and vegetable dishes and, as in Persian cuisine, fruit is often paired with meat. Highly aromatic seasonings and harmonious, subtle food combinations appear in the dynamic but delicate *tagines* (braised dishes slow-cooked in clay vessels with pointy, conical lids), *b'stilla* (spiced pigeon, egg, and almond fillo "pie"), *harira* (spicy bean and meat soup), *méchoui* (tender, spiced, slow-grilled meat), and dishes made with the national food *couscous* (fluffy, durum wheat "pasta"). Bread, a mainstay, bakes in outdoor conical ovens called *tannours*. *Harissa*, although Tunisian in origin, is made with dried red chilies, garlic, salt, coriander seed, cumin, and oil, and is a popular condiment.

Slow-cooked tagines, with their richly complex, reduced sauces, reveal a graceful marriage of flavors and a balance of sweet with salty, savory, and spicy so important to Moroccan cooks. Tagines come in a multitude of meat, seafood, vegetable, and seasonings combinations. The most famous contains *chicken, green olives*, and *preserved lemon*. Seasonal produce, fat, spices, and cooking methods distinguish tagines: *m'quali* contains oil in a yellow sauce seasoned with saffron and ginger; *m'hammer* is made with oil or butter in a red sauce seasoned with cumin and paprika. Ingredients are occasionally browned before simmering, or just simmered together.

Situated on the Mediterranean basin, Moroccan cuisine is more Mediterranean than African, though it was connected to Africa and the Far East through the West and Central African spice trade. Constant cultural exchange with Spain, and Morocco's prime trading location, drew culinary riches from other lands. Olives, citrus fruits, and grapes came via Phoenicians, Greeks, Romans, and Carthaginians. Garlic, cinnamon, coriander, cardamom, saffron, cumin, turmeric, sesame, and *ouarka/warqa* (fillo-like thin pastry) came via Egypt and Central Asia. The Ottomans contributed stuffed *dolma* and honey and almond pastries. The British introduced black tea in the nineteenth century. Moroccans mixed it with mint for an essential drink.

In the seventeenth century, Sudanese black female slaves called *Dadas*, became domestics in rich homes. They developed into respected (but underpaid) culinary professionals, putting their stamp on Moroccan cuisine and presiding over kitchens in great homes as well as important events. Women continue to rule Morocco's cuisine: great Moroccan food is made at home, not in restaurants. Food is abundant and served with generous, genuine hospitality.

Moroccan cuisine is arguably the most refined and exciting in North Africa. The combination of creative, sophisticated dynastic court kitchens, diverse cultural influences, geographical and agricultural riches that echo those of France, and refined cooking techniques, contributed to the development of a full-flavored, vital culinary style.

REGIONAL MOROCCO

Though many dishes are common throughout Morocco, seasonings, styles, and specific ingredients vary by geography, climate, and history. Cuisine differs in the rural countryside from the Berber mountain highlands and to large cities and the Mediterranean and Atlantic seacoasts. The three cities of Fez, Tetouán, and Marrakesh are considered Morocco's culinary capitals with Tangier, Safi, and Rabat as secondary capitals. All show strong Euro-Mediterranean influences. In the largely Berber northern Rif Mountains and Middle Atlas region and the southwestern Souss and the pre-Saharan plains, the food is more elemental-Berber.

Northern Morocco (with Tangier and Tetouán), just across the Straits of Gibraltar from Spanish Andalusia, has Berber, Andalusian, Mediterranean, and Ottoman influences that show up in buttery pastries like *baklava* and *b'stilla*. *Byesar* (dried fava bean purée), fish tagines, *tagra* (fish, tomatoes and paprika oil), and *maraks* (vegetable tagines). Meknes is known for mint, olives, and quince, and Fez for citrus. The Middle Atlas region is known for Berber couscous made with barley, for liver brochettes and *mechoui* (Berber-style roasted lamb).

Southern Morocco (with Marrakesh, Safi, and Essaouira) shows the distinct culinary stamp of pre-Saharan-Africa, Atlantic-West Africa, and Senegal with Portuguese, French, and British influences. Signature southern dishes include fish couscous, *tegree* (dried and spiced mussels), fish kebabs, dishes with dates, spicy Senegalese tagines, *amalou* (almonds, honey, and argan oil purée), camel and gazelle meat dishes, *tangia* (lamb stew with garlic and cumin), bluefish dishes, and *asidah* (corn porridge). Agadir is known for oranges and lemons; Marrakesh for pomegranates, Souss for almonds, lamb and za'atar; and eastern Erfoud for its dates.

DINE AT HOME IN MOROCCO

Dress well when invited to dine at a home in Morocco; it shows respect towards the hosts. Bring a small gift of pastry, nuts, figs, dates, or flowers for the hostess and a small gift for each child. Don't bring alcohol to Muslim homes. More conservative Moroccans may not entertain mixed-sex groups. If in doubt, ask. When entering a Moroccan home, guests remove shoes. Guests might be led into a rose-scented inner courtyard with a glistening cobalt blue mosaic-lined tinkling fountain. Shake each of the men's hands, moving right to left. Wait for women to extend a hand; if not, a nod of the head is fine. Take time to converse about friends or general topics.

At urban homes guests may be seated at a table. In a traditional setting they'll likely sit on cushions spread around large, ornate brass, copper, or silver trays placed on knee-high wooden stools. The guest of honor will probably sit next to the host. Before dining, a washbasin will come around to each diner. Guests hold their hands over the basin so that the scented water can be poured over them, then dry their hands on the towel offered.

Wait until the host blesses the food and begins to eat. Hospitality is an important North African tradition. Guests will be offered a lavish display of food from a communal bowl or plate. Guests eat only from the section of food directly in front of them. Don't reach across to grab something from another side. The best pieces will come to guests. The ever-hospitable hosts will urge guests to eat as much as they can. Use a piece of bread or the thumb and first two fingers of the right hand only. Don't wipe hands on the napkin, only the mouth. Water may be served from a communal glass, but guests may ask for their own glass or for a soft drink. Coffee or mint tea made with black tea, local mint, and lots of sugar will be offered.

The washbasin will come around again signaling the end of the meal. Compliment the meal and the host and hostess's hospitality. Remember to say good-bye to each person when leaving, especially the respected and revered elderly.

TASTES OF MOROCCO

Fat: *Smen* (fermented, clarified butter), olive oil, argan oil, vegetable oil

Sweet: Sugar, confectioner's sugar, honey

Sour/Alcohol: Lemon, lime, vinegar

Salty: Capers, black and green olives, preserved lemons

Spicy-Hot: Ginger, fresh and dried red chilies, green chilies, black and white pepper, paprika, cayenne pepper

Spice: *Ras el hanout* (spice mix), cinnamon, nutmeg, clove, cumin, saffron, coriander, turmeric, allspice, aniseed, sesame seed, caraway, cardamom, black cumin, *melegueta* (grains of paradise), mace, lavender, cubeb pepper, za'atar, gum arabic, fenugreek, licorice, honey dates (sweet fruit)

Aromatic Seasoning Vegetables: Onion, garlic, ginger, chilies

Herbs, Seasonings, and Condiments: Feta, *mska* (gum Arabic), sesame paste, cilantro, mint, Italian parsley, marjoram, fresh and dried rosebuds and petals, rosewater, orange flower water

Other Important Foods: *Warqa* (thin dough), semolina and couscous, wheat, barley, rice, corn, sugar beets, fennel, potatoes, tomatoes, okra, fish, seafood, eggs, meat (lamb, goat, chicken, pigeon, duck, beef), eggplant, zucchini, bell peppers, *melokhia* (spinach-like green), Swiss chard, cardoons, turnips, lentils, chickpeas, fava and white kidney beans, fruit (citrus fruits, dates, prunes, raisins, apricots, apples, quince, peaches, melons), purslane, nuts (almonds, walnuts, pistachios)

Popular Dishes: *Tagine* (fish, chicken, beef, lamb), *b'stilla*, *couscous*, *harira*, vegetable salads

Drinks: Mint tea, tea, fresh orange juice, almond milk drink, apple milk drink, beer, wine, *qahwa kahla* (Turkish-style black coffee), *qahwa meherris* (coffee with a little milk), *helib meherris* (milk with a little coffee), *ahwa nus-nus* (half coffee, half milk) and *qahwa helib* (café au lait), grey verbena or basil tea

FIGURE 11.2 Traditional Moroccan market.
Source: Mariusz Prusaczyk/Fotolia.

COMMON MOROCCAN COOKING TOOLS

Mortar and pestle, earthenware pots and dishes, *cous-cousière*, tagine (earthenware casserole with conical lid)

FIGURE 11.3 Couscous steamer.
Source: Pierrette Guertin/Fotolia.

MOROCCAN FLAVOR FOUNDATIONS

Moroccan Signature Aromatic Vegetable Combo

Spanish onions and garlic

Signature Seasonings

Liquid/Paste

Argan Oil

Beloved by Moroccans, this rare, dark and nutty oil is made from the roasted kernels of the fruit of the ancient Moroccan argan tree. This strong tree grows wild in semi-desert and is highly adapted to arid conditions. Moroccans use the oil cosmetically, medicinally, and for cooking, salads and dipping.

Olive Oil

See *Glossary*.

Orange Flower Water and Rose Flower Water

Moroccan cooks use these fragrant waters in sweet and savory dishes: tagines, salads, and cakes or confections. It takes seven pounds of Bergamot orange blossoms or rosebuds to make one gallon of the water. They are traditionally distilled in an alambic.

Animal

Moroccan Preserved Meat (Khelea)

Because of the climate, before refrigeration, North Africans could rely on preservation methods like salt or sun dehydration and storage in fat (much like the French confit). Moroccans make a preserved meat, usually beef, similar to Greek or Turkish *basturma* called *khelea, chele, kleehe,* or *khlii*. Strips of meat marinate in cumin, coriander, garlic, and salt, and sun-dry several days. The meat is cooked in animal fat, oil, and water. Packed in cooking fat, khelea will keep up to two years at room temperature. Rural families still store large quantities of meat this way. They rely on khelea to season eggs or lentils, to form the flavor base of soups and stews or for traveling.

Fermented Fresh Butter (Zebda)

This fresh butter is quite pungent, but not as strong as the fermented *smen* or rancid *boudra*. Milk is allowed to sour and churned. The leben (buttermilk) is drained away and zebda or butter solids remain. It is used for cooking.

Vegetable/Fruit

Preserved Lemons

See *Preserved Lemon* recipe. These silky, salt- and lemon-juice-pickled lemon rinds add a flavor that is characteristic of Moroccan cuisine.

FIGURE 11.4 Argan oil and nuts.
Source: luisapuccini/Fotolia.

FIGURE 11.5 Orange flowers.
Source: ANCH/Shutterstock.

Rinse lemons before using; both rinds and pulp may be used, but the rind is the prize. It may be sliced into salads, or simmered in tagines, soups, and stews.

Herbal/Spice

Black Pepper (Elbezar)

Black pepper is used liberally and extensively in Moroccan cuisine. Always freshly ground, it goes in at the beginning of cooking.

Cilantro (Qsbour)

See *Glossary*.

Cinnamon

Two types of cinnamon are popular in Morocco, the light, delicate Ceylon cinnamon and the stronger, tougher cassia cinnamon. They are used in desserts and savory dishes.

Cubeb Pepper or Java Pepper

Cubeb is a pungently aromatic spice similar in appearance to peppercorns, but with the stem attached. Its flavor can be acrid, slightly bitter, and persistent. Some describe its flavor as a cross between warm, woody allspice and black pepper. It can be confused with the Ashanti or "false cubeb," which grows in Central Africa; its flavor is fresher and not as bitter and its shape is elongated. Arab trade via India brought the cubeb to Europe and Africa. Moroccan cooks use it in savory dishes, ras el hanout, and in *markouts* (semolina diamonds with honey

FIGURE 11.6 Cubeb peppercorns.
Source: Dave King/DK Images.

FIGURE 11.7 Moroccan mint.
Source: Dave King/DK Images.

and dates). For best flavor, crush the spice just before using.

Cumin Seed (Kamoon)

An important spice, cumin seed is used extensively, but delicately, with fish and chicken dishes and with *mechoui*; it is also mixed into *kefta* (meatballs).

Fenugreek Seed (Hellbah)

This mild and tiny legume-seed smells delicately of maple. It grows in Morocco. Berber cooks heat it before grinding to bring out its burnt sugar and celery flavor.

Moroccan or Nana Mint (Liqama)

Moroccans favor the milder spearmint (versus the assertive peppermint) variety of mint with its mild, clear flavor. To prepare Moroccan tea, the mint is mixed with Gunpowder green tea. See Mint in *Glossary*.

Moroccan Parsley (Maadnous)

Moroccans use a flat leaf variety of parsley, but it is milder than Italian flat leaf parsley. Substitute half or all of the parsley with curly leaf parsley for a more authentic flavor.

Gum Arabic (Mska)

Strong scented, but usually mild-flavored gummy sap-resin from the acacia tree, gum Arabic is a natural emulsifier and used to bind and thicken soft drinks, candies, marshmallows, and gelato-type desserts.

Saffron (Safran)

The most expensive spice in the world, saffron is the stamen of the saffron crocus. It takes a

FIGURE 11.8 Turmeric root.
Source: sommai/Fotolia.

football field of flowers to produce a pound. Saffron has a bitter, beguiling taste, grassy hay-like fragrance, and transmits an intense yellow hue to foods with which it's cooked. It thrives in the Mediterranean and possibly originated in Persia.

Spanish Green Aniseed

This spice has a warm and strongly licorice flavor that Moroccans pair with bread, cookies, and fish.

Spanish Paprika

Mild to spicy red paprika made from ground, dried *Capsicum annuum* red bell or chili peppers go into Moroccan tagines, tomato dishes, and charmoula marinade.

Turmeric (Quekoum)

This powder is ground from the dried root of a tropical rhizome. It imparts a bitter, astringent taste (which long cooking softens) and an intense yellow hue.

SEASONING AND PASTE MIXTURES

FIGURE 11.9 Moroccan spice shop.
Source: Radar_Mark/Shutterstock.

MOROCCAN SPICE MIXTURE (RAS AL HANOUT)

Ras al Hanout literally means "top of the shop." This spice mixture can contain anywhere from nine to nineteen or more seasonings. It's not necessary to toast the spices for this seasoning, but the flavors will be more intense and satisfying with toasting.

Yields about 1/3 cup

1 teaspoon allspice berries
1 whole nutmeg, chopped
2 teaspoons black peppercorns
1-1/2 teaspoons whole mace
   or 1-1/4 teaspoons ground mace
1 three-inch stick cinnamon
2 teaspoons cardamom seeds (not pods)
   or 1-1/2 teaspoons ground cardamom
2 teaspoons ground ginger
2 teaspoons kosher salt
1 teaspoon ground turmeric
1/2 teaspoon saffron threads
Optional: 5 small, dried rosebuds (available in Arabic markets)

1 Roast each whole spice (not ground spices or rosebuds) individually in small skillet (without oil) over medium heat until fragrant and lightly toasted, 3 to 4 minutes.

2 Spread spices on sheet pan or plate to cool. In small batches, grind to a powder in spice/coffee grinder. Mix ground mixture together well and store in tightly sealed jar in freezer or refrigerator.

Source: *Cooking at the Kasbah* by Kitty Morse.

Smen

Similar to Indian ghee and Ethiopian spiced butter, the earthy seasoned, aged Moroccan butter, *smen* tastes and looks somewhat like Roquefort cheese. It's an acquired taste, but a teaspoon or two gives couscous or a tagine a truly traditional, authentic Moroccan flavor. Substitute equal parts olive oil and butter.

To Make Herbed Smen: Simmer 1 pound diced, unsalted butter with 2 teaspoons dried oregano over low heat in a heavy pot. Butter will melt, separate and clear. Skim away foamy white milk solids and strain butter through cheesecloth-lined strainer several times until perfectly clear—smen will turn rancid if all the milk solids are not removed. Scrape smen into pint glass canning jar and stir in 1 tablespoon sea salt. Rest butter at room temperature until pungent, up to 2 weeks. Refrigerate up to 6 months.

MOROCCAN TAGINE SPICE MIXTURE (LA KAMA)

Use a teaspoon or two of this spice mixture from Tangier to season meat tagines, eggs, roasted potatoes, soups like harira, vegetable dishes and salads, and as a rub on chicken or lamb.

Yields about 4 teaspoons

1 teaspoon ground ginger
1 teaspoon ground turmeric
1 teaspoon freshly ground white pepper
1/2 teaspoon ground cinnamon
1/2 teaspoon ground cubeb pepper
1/4 teaspoon freshly grated nutmeg

1 Mix together spices. Store in a small, tightly closed jar in a cool, dark place—the freezer or refrigerator—up to 6 months. Some cooks dry roast whole pepper, cinnamon, and cubeb before grinding for more flavor.

Source: *Mediterranean Clay Pot Cooking* by Paula Wolfert.

SAUCE

PAULA WOLFERT ON MOROCCAN SAUCES

There are eight major cooking sauces in Moroccan cuisine: m'qalli, m'hammer, m'ghdour, marka, dalaa, emchermel or (m'charmel), massal, and k'dra. The spice structure and cooking methods differentiate them. Five are garnished with preserved lemon and olives, but they may also be made with artichokes, fava beans, okra, or quince instead.

M'qalli, the most common tagine sauce, is made with pepper, turmeric, saffron, salt, and ginger. Spices and meat are heated in warmed oil and infuse flavor into the meat. Onion (to thicken) and tomato are sometimes added. Traditionally m'qalli is garnished with lemon and olives, but most can be garnished with sweet fruit like prunes or figs instead. Cinnamon is added to sweet m'qallis.

K'dra is a lighter yellow sauce with onions, butter, saffron, and pepper.

M'hammer means reddish and is made with chicken, lamb, or beef, predominately colored with paprika.

Emcharmel (or emshmel or m'charmel) is a red sauce with paprika, garlic, cumin, and cilantro.

FIGURE 11.10 Harissa.
Source: FOOD-pictures/Fotolia.

HARISSA

Harissa originated in Tunisia, where it is used liberally as seasoning, a spread on bread, or as a dipping sauce with olive oil. In Morocco, it's a side sauce, and added to taste.

Yields about 1-2/3 cups

3 ounces dried ancho chilies, about 6
1 ounce dried guajillo chilies, about 6
1 ounce garlic, about 4 large cloves crushed and peeled
2 teaspoons ground cumin
2 teaspoons ground coriander
2 teaspoons ground caraway
1/2 cup olive oil

1 With gloves on, slit open each chili with small knife or with scissors. Remove stems and all seeds. Rinse away seeds and veins. Place chilies into a medium bowl and cover with warm water. Weight with a small plate. Soak chilies until soft, 20 to 30 minutes. Drain well.

2 Pour chilies, 1 teaspoon kosher salt, garlic, and spices into food processor. Purée until chilies break up. Pour in 1/4 cup water and continue to purée until very smooth, 3 to 5 minutes. With machine running, pour oil into chili purée in a thin stream (like chili mayo). Taste and add more salt if necessary.

3 Transfer harissa into 1-pint glass jar. Pour a little oil over top to seal and close tightly with lid. The flavor of harissa improves as it sits. It may be used after 1 to 2 hours, but longer is better. Refrigerate and use within 6 months. Cover with more oil after each use.

MOROCCAN CHARMOULA OR CHERMOULA SAUCE

Throughout the country Moroccan cooks use charmoula or chermoula sauce as a marinade for fish. It traditionally contains cilantro, Italian parsley, garlic, cumin, paprika, chili, and lemon juice, and in some regions cooks add ground ginger or caraway.

Yields 3/4 cup, 4 to 6 servings

1-1/2 ounces cilantro, 1 cup packed
1 ounce garlic, about 4 large cloves crushed and peeled
1-1/2 teaspoons ground cumin
1/2 teaspoon ground caraway
1-1/2 teaspoons paprika
1/2 teaspoon ground chili powder
    or 1- to 1-1/2-inch dried red chili, broken
4 tablespoons freshly squeezed lemon juice, 1 large lemon
3 to 4 tablespoons olive oil

1 Blend ingredients together in food processor or blender with 1 teaspoon kosher salt and 2 tablespoons to 1/4 cup water until smooth.

Vary! Improvise!

☞ Substitute half the cilantro for trimmed Italian parsley.
☞ Use charmoula as a dressing on wilted cabbage or salad greens.
☞ Marinate chicken or shrimp in charmoula before braising, baking, or grilling.

SPECIAL METHODS

FAVA BEAN PURÉE (BYESAR)

This Berber dish is a kissing cousin to Middle Eastern chickpea hummus.

Yields 4 cups, 8 or more servings

8 ounces dried fava beans with shells, 1-1/2 cups
3/4 ounce garlic, 3 large cloves, peeled
1 teaspoon cumin seeds
2 tablespoons freshly squeezed lemon juice, about 1/2 large lemon
2 to 3 tablespoons extra virgin olive oil
1/2 teaspoon za'atar, dried thyme *or* dried marjoram *or* dried oregano

For Serving

Dry-toasted and ground cumin seed mixed with salt
Green olives
Arabic Bread (see *Lebanon*)

1   Soak fava beans and 1 tablespoon kosher salt overnight, covered in cold water or quick-soak with boiling water and salt for 1 hour. Discard beans that float. Drain beans.

2   Slit each bean with a paring knife, and push bean out of skin. Discard skins. Pour beans, garlic, and cumin into 4-quart saucepan. Pour in enough cold water to cover beans. Bring beans to a boil over high heat. Reduce heat and simmer beans, uncovered, until tender, 30 to 45 minutes, depending on age of beans.

3   Drain beans, and reserve cooking water. Pour beans, garlic, and lemon juice into food processor. Purée beans until they are smooth, slightly soupy, and the consistency of whipped cream. Add a little reserved cooking water as necessary. Season purée with about 2 teaspoons kosher salt, to taste.

4   **To Serve:** Warm byesar (bean purée), and swirl onto serving plate. Mix olive oil and za'atar or thyme or marjoram or oregano together in a small saucepan. Warm them gently and drizzle over byesar. Serve byesar with cumin for dipping, green olives, and Arab bread for scooping.

Source: *Couscous and Other Good Food From Morocco* by Paula Wolfert.

FIGURE 11.11   Dried fava beans with shell.
Source: Luis Bras/Fotolia.

Vary! Improvise!

☞ *Substitute about 1 cup (6-1/2 ounces) dry, shelled fava beans for dry favas with shells.*

☞ *Roasted Fava Beans:* *Soak 8 ounces shell-on dried fava beans overnight with 1 to 2 teaspoons kosher salt. Drain. Preheat oven to 350 degrees F. Make a slit in the top of the skin of each bean. Spread favas out on a half sheet. Salt them liberally and roast like chestnuts until skins pop open when squeezed and the insides are soft and tender, 45 minutes to 1 hour. Eat favas as a snack, or shell and use for byesar.*

AMALOU

Amalou is a smooth, thick blend of roasted, whole almonds, which are crushed by machine (or ground in a food processor). Moroccan argan oil (olive oil may be substituted) is slowly added to form a thick liquid consistency. Amalou is seasoned with honey to taste. It is used as a spread on *khboz* (bread) or fried breads, and stirred into hot, cooked breakfast cereal. To make a facsimile, use 1/2 pound almonds, about 1/2 cup oil, 2 to 3 tablespoons honey, and 1/2 teaspoon kosher salt.

FIGURE 11.12 Goats eating argan nuts.
Source: Heiko Löffler/Fotolia.

SIMMER, STEW, POACH, BOIL, AND STEAM

Soup

Moroccans like their soups spicy and rich, and often consume them for dinner. Variations of the hearty *harira* are eaten year round like *chorba bil hamus* (chickpeas, lamb shank, and spices) and a thickened caraway flavored milk soup called *harira karouiya*. Medicinal soups dosed with various spices and herbs to help with childbirth or to stave off colds are popular.

MOROCCAN LEGUME SOUP WITH MEAT (HARIRA)

Harira soups are chockful of legumes (chickpeas, lentils, and beans), herbs, and spices, with meat and vegetables adding flavor. Ingredients and seasonings vary, but the addition of a tadawira, the flour and water or sourdough batter, gives the soup a velvety texture. Eaten as a one-dish meal for dinner or breakfast, during Ramadan cooks accompany harira with honey cakes. In the winter, maquoudas (pancakes) accompany harira.

Yields about 24 cups, 12 to 18 servings

7 ounces chickpeas, 1 cup
Optional: 2 marrowbones, blanched in boiling water 1 minute
1 pound trimmed lamb or beef shoulder or neck, 2 cups diced into 1/2-inch cubes
16 ounces onions, 4 cups peeled and diced into 1/2-inch cubes
About 5 ounces brown lentils, 3/4 cup rinsed
16 ounces tomatoes, about 2-1/2 cups peeled and diced
   or 28-ounce can crushed tomatoes
4 ounces celery, about large 4 stalks, 1-1/4 cups diced into 1/2-inch cubes
1 tablespoon tomato paste
1 teaspoon ground black pepper
1 teaspoon ground ginger
Two 3-inch cinnamon sticks
1/2 teaspoon saffron
   or 1 teaspoon turmeric
Flour Paste: 1-1/2 ounces all-purpose flour, 5 tablespoons
5 ounces orzo pasta *or* broken vermicelli, 3/4 cup
4 tablespoons lemon juice, 1 large lemon
1-1/2 ounces cilantro, 3/4 cup finely sliced
1/2 ounce trimmed Italian parsley, 1/2 cup chopped

For Serving

3 lemons, quartered
24 to 36 dates

1 **Prepare chickpeas:** Rinse, drain, and cover with cold water and 2 teaspoons kosher salt. Bring water to a boil, remove from heat, cover, and rest 1 hour to quick soak *or* soak chickpeas overnight in cold water. Drain and rinse. Place blanched bones, meat, onions, and soaked chickpeas into a heavy 8-quart pot. Cover with 13 cups cold water and bring to a boil over medium-high heat. Remove scum that rises. Cover pot partially and lower heat. Simmer 1 hour.

2 **Simmer soup:** Remove bones and discard. (Inner bone marrow may be spooned back into soup for deeper flavor.) Stir lentils, tomatoes, celery, tomato paste, pepper, ginger, cinnamon sticks, and saffron or turmeric into soup. Bring to a boil and lower heat. Simmer soup until lentils soften, 15 minutes. Season soup with salt.

3 **Prepare tadawira:** Pour flour into small saucepan and whisk in 2 cups cold water; beat until smooth. Place on medium heat and stir constantly until mixture thickens. Lower heat and simmer flour-water mixture 10 minutes.

4 Slowly stir flour mixture into simmering soup. Simmer soup while stirring energetically to achieve a slightly thickened, light and creamy texture, 2 to 3 minutes. At this point, harira can be cooled and refrigerated up to two days.

5 **Ten minutes before serving:** Stir pasta into soup and simmer until tender, 5 to 7 minutes. Stir in lemon juice, cilantro, and parsley.

6 **To Serve:** Ladle soup into bowls and serve with lemon wedges and dates.

Source: *Arabesque: A Taste of Morocco, Turkey & Lebanon* by Claudia Roden.

Vary! Improvise!

☞ *Vegetarian Harira: Omit meat and bones. Use vegetable broth or water and decrease liquid from 13 cups to 10 cups.*

☞ *Chicken Harira: Substitute 1 pound boneless, skinless chicken thighs for meat and 2 quarts chicken stock and 6 cups water for the 13 cups water.*

Cooking Teacher and Cookbook Author
California

"I am very partial to unglazed earthenware tagines and glazed flameware tagines. The meat and vegetables benefit from the steamy environment with moisture recycling from the cool cone tip back into the stew and will cook to a similar level of tenderness as they reabsorb the moisture floating under the cone. At this point the hot clay dries out and the top and bottom turns into a portable oven. The contents continue to bake and develop a deep rich sauce at the bottom, and the meat and vegetables develop a toasty shield. This is the old Berber method; many variations exist. If you'd like to simulate the patina of an antique tagine, you can burnish the (unglazed) pot by rubbing the clay inside and out with a mixture of 1/2 cup olive oil and 3/4 cup wood ash from the fireplace. Place in a cold oven, set the temperature to 250°F, and bake for two to three hours. Turn off the heat and let the pot cool in the oven. Repeat for deeper browning."

FIGURE 11.13 Traditional Moroccan tagine.
Source: picturepartners/Shutterstock.

Moroccan Tagine

Tagines are slow-cooked, assertively flavored braises, traditionally cooked in a vessel of the same name. The traditional tagine vessel is unglazed terracotta with a flat, round base with low sides and sits over hot coals in a brazier. A tall, conical lid rests inside the base and is designed to return moisture to the dish. *Cook's Illustrated* tested terracotta tagines against Dutch ovens and concluded that "more important than the shape of the pot were the lid's weight and fit."

Tagine braises come in differing styles and flavor combinations in different regions of Morocco, but all share the rich, complex, fruity-savory flavor of a reduced sauce that is a signature of these slow-cooked dishes. Most tagines don't require meat to be browned (probably because a terracotta vessel can crack over high heat), but like most braises and stews, meat is cooked until falling-off-the-bone tender.

The combination of ingredients is crucial to a great tagine and there are dozens. Paula Wolfert divides tagines into *fragrant* (preserved lemon and olives), *robust* (browned meat and toasted, strong seasonings like cumin and paprika), or *meat and fruit* combos. Morocco is blessed with a year-round growing climate that produces a plentiful pantry for tagine-making: olives, lemons, quince, apples, pears, prunes, dates, and apricots, plus honey, nuts, and seeds and a multitude of spices and herbs. Cinnamon, saffron, coriander, and ginger are used for *aromatic warmth*. Turmeric and paprika are used for *color* and cumin and the spice mixture *ras el hanout* for robust, *deep flavor*.

FIGURE 11.14 Tagine slow cooking over charcoal at an outdoor restaurant.
Source: rj lerich/Shutterstock.

Signature Technique: Prepare a Tagine

- Choose a wide, sturdy cooking vessel with a heavy, tight-fitting lid.

- Choose a strategic blend of ingredients like lamb with caramelized onions and pears (or quince or apricots), chicken thighs with dates (or prunes) and almonds or with preserved lemon and artichoke hearts, or fish with tomatoes, preserved lemons, and olives.

- Choose more flavorful, long cooking cuts of meat like shank, thighs, neck or shoulder, and meat that braises well like chicken, turkey, meatballs, fish, beef, root vegetables, or legumes.

- Choose bone-in and dark meat for richer flavor, but first remove the skin for less fat.

- Toast spices in fat for deep, robust flavor.

- Cook the tagine on low heat.

- Add olives or preserved lemon for the last 10 minutes of braising time. It preserves their individual aromatic flavors and keeps the olives from becoming bitter.

- Season salty tagines with honey or confectioner's sugar for balance. Season sweet tagines with salt and black pepper for balance.

CHICKEN, PRESERVED LEMON, AND OLIVE TAGINE (TAGINE DJAJ BI ZAYTOUN WAL HAMID)

This tagine is light, flavorful, and refreshing: a good starter tagine for diners unfamiliar with Moroccan flavors. There are seven classic versions of this famous combination of chicken, lemon, and olives. Paula Wolfert considers djej emsharmel (chicken with lemon, green olives, onion, paprika, cumin, saffron, ginger, chicken liver, cilantro, and parsley) the most important of the seven classic versions of chicken with lemon and olives.

Yields about 8 cups, 4 servings

3 tablespoons olive oil
12 to 13 ounces onions, 2 medium, 3 cups peeled and finely diced
3/4 ounce garlic, about 3 large cloves, 1-1/2 tablespoons peeled and minced
1/2 teaspoon saffron
1/2 teaspoon ground ginger
4 pounds bone-in chicken breasts and thighs, 3-1/2 pounds skinned
2 tablespoons fresh lemon juice, 1/2 large lemon
5 ounces green olives, about 12 large, 1 cup
1 *Preserved Lemon*, about 1/3 cup slivered
1/2 ounce cilantro, 1/4 cup finely sliced
1/2 ounce trimmed Italian parsley, 1/4 cup chopped

1   In an 11- to 12-inch-wide, heavy 6-quart pot or tagine dish, heat oil over medium heat. Stir in onions and reduce heat to low or medium-low. Cook onions until soft, 10 to 15 minutes. Stir in garlic, saffron, and ginger.

2   Season chicken with salt and pepper and place on top of the onions. Pour in 1 cup water and bring tagine to a boil. Lower heat to a simmer and cover pot or tagine dish with heavy lid. Turn chicken periodically so it cooks evenly.

3   After 30 minutes, remove chicken breasts, transfer to a bowl, and set aside. Simmer remaining chicken thighs and leg until very tender, 20 to 30 minutes. Return chicken breasts to pot. Stir in lemon juice, olives, and preserved lemon. Simmer tagine uncovered until the sauce thickens, about 10 minutes. Taste sauce and season with salt, pepper, or lemon juice if desired. If sauce is still watery after 10 minutes, don't continue to cook tagine: it will overcook the chicken and the olives will turn bitter. Instead, transfer solid ingredients to a serving dish or bowl and reduce sauce on its own until thick. Reunite all ingredients and heat through before serving.

4   **To Serve:** Stir in cilantro and parsley. Transfer chicken and sauce to a serving dish or serve in tagine dish. Arrange preserved lemon and olives on top for presentation.

Source: *Arabesque: A Taste of Morocco, Turkey & Lebanon* by Claudia Roden.

CHICKEN, SPICE, AND PRESERVED LEMON TAGINE

This dish is dark and appealing, but strong flavored—very North African. It reveals how different two tagines with similar ingredients can be.

Yields about 8 cups, 4 servings

1 teaspoon saffron threads
3/4 ounce garlic, about 3 large cloves, 1-1/2 tablespoons minced
3 tablespoons olive oil, *divided*
16 to 18 ounces red onions, 2 large, 4 cups peeled, halved, and slivered
3-1/2 pounds chicken breasts, thighs and legs, 3 pounds skinned
2 teaspoons ground ginger
1 teaspoon ground cinnamon
1/2 teaspoon ground turmeric
1 tablespoon lime or lemon juice, 1/2 lime or lemon
1/2 teaspoon fresh ground black pepper
3 ounces Moroccan purple or Greek Kalamata olives, 1/2 cup
1 *Preserved Lemon*, about 1/3 cup pulp discarded and peel slivered
1/2 ounce cilantro, 1/4 cup finely sliced

1 Place saffron in a small heavy skillet over low heat and dry-toast it until fragrant, about 1 minute. Cool saffron in a small bowl and crumble. Mix garlic with saffron and 1 teaspoon kosher salt. Set aside.

2 Pour 2 tablespoons oil into a 12-inch tagine dish, 6-quart heavy, covered casserole or 12-inch heavy, deep skillet. Scatter onions over oil.

3 In a large mixing bowl, toss chicken with remaining tablespoon oil, the garlic and saffron, ginger, cinnamon, turmeric, lime or lemon juice, and pepper. Arrange chicken pieces over onions in tagine, and scrape marinade onto chicken.

4 Pour 3/4 cup water into tagine and bring to a simmer. Lower the heat and simmer dish covered until chicken is cooked through and tender, about 30 to 45 minutes. Check tagine occasionally so that it maintains liquid. Add olives, and simmer covered no more than 10 minutes.

5 **To Serve:** Season dish with salt to taste. Sprinkle with preserved lemon and cilantro and serve.

Source: *Peggy Markel's Culinary Adventures, Gourmet,* November 2009.

Vary! Improvise!

☞ *Prepare tagine with large green olives.*

FIGURE 11.15 Casablanca.
Source: aadur/Fotolia.

FISH TAGINE WITH CHARMOULA (HUT TUNGERA)

Moroccan cooks mostly prepare fish with charmoula sauce. For fish tagines, they criss-cross carrot, celery, or bell pepper strips on the bottom of the tagine or cooking vessel to form a bed that keeps the fish from sticking. This dish is memorable made with tender, juicy halibut. Often hut tungera contains sliced potatoes, which are dipped into charmoula and set on top of the fish.

6 servings

FIGURE 11.16 Fish tagine with charmoula (hut tungera).

Charmoula Sauce
2-1/2 pounds trimmed firm, white-fleshed fish like halibut or monkfish, skinned and boned
12 ounces green or red bell peppers, 2 medium
1 pound ripe tomatoes, 2 medium-large

Sauce Ingredients

6 tablespoons olive oil
2 tablespoons reserved *Charmoula Sauce*
1 teaspoon ground ginger
1/4 teaspoon saffron mixed in 1/3 cup hot water

5 ounces large green pitted olives, 1 cup
1/2 *Preserved Lemon*, 1/2 cup slivered and inner skin discarded

1 Prepare *Charmoula Sauce*. Remove 2 tablespoons for tagine sauce and set aside in small mixing bowl.

2 Cut fish into 6 portions and rub liberally with the remaining **charmoula sauce**, 4 to 6 tablespoons. Refrigerate fish 15 to 20 minutes to marinate.

3 Grill peppers over gas flame or char-grill until skin is blackened. Place in bowl, cover, and cool. Peel and core peppers, remove all the bitter seeds. Slice peppers into long 3/8-inch-wide strips. Grill tomatoes over flame or char-grill until skins blacken slightly and shrivel evenly, 30 to 60 seconds. Peel tomatoes, core, and dice into 1/2-inch cubes to yield 2-1/2 to 3 cups. Discard peels and set tomatoes aside.

4 Criss-cross pepper strips in one layer on the bottom of a heavy, 12-inch wide deep pan or tagine dish. Place fish on top of peppers.

5 Mix together **sauce ingredients**. Pour over fish and arrange tomatoes on top. Bring dish to a simmer over medium heat. Reduce the heat, cover, and simmer tagine until fish is cooked through and flakes, 20 to 25 minutes.

6 **To Serve:** Transfer fish to warm serving vessel. Bring sauce to a boil in pan or a small saucepan and cook over medium heat until thickened and slightly reduced. Stir olives and preserved lemon into sauce and simmer 5 minutes; pour sauce and vegetables over fish in serving vessel. *Alternatively to serve in tagine:* Drain liquid from tagine dish and pour into small saucepan, bring to a boil, and cook on medium heat until thickened and slightly reduced. Stir olives and preserved lemon into sauce and simmer 5 minutes; pour back over fish and serve in tagine dish.

Source: *The Momo Cookbook* by Mourab Mozouz.

FIGURE 11.17 Todra valley and Atlas mountains, Morocco.
Source: Moreno Novello/Fotolia.

LAMB, DATE, ALMOND, AND PISTACHIO TAGINE

Moroccans serve this tagine with couscous rubbed with harissa. The couscous is formed into a high pyramid, the peak flattened and formed into a well into which the lamb tagine is ladled. This lamb should be moist and tender, the tagine, sweet and fragrant, and the harissa, mildly spicy. Pair the lamb and couscous with a salad of cubed honeydew melon and mint.

Yields about 4 cups, 4 to 6 servings

2 tablespoons clarified butter *or* olive oil *or* a mixture
8 to 9 ounces onion, 2 cups peeled and finely diced
1 teaspoon ground turmeric
1/2 teaspoon ground ginger
1 teaspoon ground cinnamon
1-1/2 pounds trimmed lean lamb, from shoulder, neck, or leg, diced into 3/4-inch cubes
4 ounces Medjool dates, 1/3 cup pitted
1/2 tablespoon dark honey

Garnish

1 tablespoon olive oil *or* clarified butter or a mixture
1 ounce blanched almonds, 2 tablespoons
1 ounce shelled pistachios, 2 tablespoons
1/2 ounce trimmed Italian parsley, 1/4 cup finely chopped

For Serving

Harissa
Buttered, steamed *Couscous*

Vary! Improvise!

☞ *Substitute goat meat, beef, or boneless, skinless chicken thighs for lamb.*

☞ *Figs and Walnuts: Substitute 1/2 to 3/4 cup quartered, dried white figs for the dates and garnish with 1/4 cup walnuts (instead of almonds and pistachios) plus diced fresh tomato and cilantro instead of parsley.*

1 Melt clarified butter or heat oil in a heavy 11-inch 6-quart casserole dish or tagine dish over medium heat. Add onions and sauté until golden. Stir in turmeric, ginger, and cinnamon and cook 30 seconds. Fold meat into onions and spices to coat. Pour in 1-1/2 cups water and bring to a boil. Reduce heat, partially cover vessel, and simmer gently until meat is tender, 45 minutes to 1 hour.

2 Stir in dates and honey. Cover pot partially with lid and simmer 30 minutes. Taste tagine and season with salt and lots of black pepper.

3 **Prepare garnish:** Heat olive oil or butter over medium heat in a 7-inch skillet. Stir in almonds and pistachios and cook until the almonds roast to golden.

4 **To Serve:** Arrange nuts over lamb and dates, and garnish dish with parsley. Serve with buttered couscous, and harissa on the side for each diner to add.

Source: *Tagines and Couscous* by Ghillie Başan.

VEGETABLE, TOMATO, AND CARAMELIZED ONION TAGINE (TAGINE MAKFOUL)

This classic Moroccan dish, usually made with beef, lamb, or goat stewed with savory spices, is topped with a makfoul: caramelized onions, tomato, and honey. This recipe omits the traditional meat in favor of summer-fresh vegetables. Vegetable tagines are scarce in the bigger cities, but Berber communities serve them often.

Yields about 8 cups, 6 to 8 servings

Makfoul

Yields about 1-3/4 cups

2 tablespoons butter
1 to 2 tablespoons olive oil
1 pound onions, 4 cups peeled, halved and finely sliced or slivered
3 tablespoons honey
1 teaspoon cinnamon
1 pound fresh plum tomatoes, cored, 3 cups thinly sliced
Optional: Freshly squeezed lemon juice

Tagine

2-1/2 pounds vegetables:
1 pound red-skin potatoes
1 pound green beans (*or older, starchy sugar snap peas*)
8 ounces carrots

1/4 cup olive oil
1 pound onions, about 2 large, 4 cups peeled and finely diced
1/2 ounce garlic, 2 large cloves, 1 tablespoon peeled and minced
1-1/2 teaspoons ground ginger
1 teaspoon turmeric
2 teaspoons Ras el Hanout
1/2 teaspoon coarsely ground black pepper
1/4 teaspoon saffron threads
3-inch cinnamon stick
1/4 ounce trimmed Italian parsley, 2 tablespoons chopped, more to taste
1/4 ounce cilantro, 2 tablespoons finely sliced

1 **Prepare makfoul:** Heat butter and oil in deep 11- to 12-inch pan or skillet over medium heat. Stir in onions and cook mixture, stirring occasionally, until onions soften and brown, about 20 minutes. Stir in honey, cinnamon, and top onions with tomatoes. Cover pan, and continue to cook and occasionally stir makfoul until tomatoes disintegrate. Uncover and cook until juices evaporate and mixture thickens, 30 to 40 minutes total. Season with salt, pepper, and optional lemon juice, and set aside.

2 **Prepare vegetables:** Scrub potatoes, and dice into 1/2- to 3/4-inch cubes. Remove stem from beans or peas. Slice green beans, if using, in half. Slice carrots in half lengthwise and slice crosswise into 1/2-inch chunks. Set vegetables aside in mixing bowl.

3 **Prepare tagine:** Heat olive oil in 6-quart pot or tagine over medium heat. Stir in onions and cook until onions soften and begin to brown, 10 to 15 minutes. Stir in garlic, ginger, turmeric, ras el hanout, pepper, saffron, cinnamon, and 1-1/2 teaspoons kosher salt. Cook 1 minute.

4 Stir in vegetables and about 1 cup water. Bring to a simmer, lower heat, partially cover pot and simmer vegetables, stirring occasionally, until tender, about 10 minutes. Add more water (1/4 to 1/2 cup) as necessary. Resulting dish should be moist with a thick sauce. Stir in parsley and cilantro and simmer 1 to 2 minutes. Taste dish and season with salt and pepper as necessary.

5 **To Serve:** Platter vegetables and top with **makfoul** or leave vegetables in tagine cooking vessel and top with **makfoul**.

Vary! Improvise!

☛ *Stir 1 cup cooked chickpeas into vegetables or substitute for potatoes or beans.*

☛ *Change the vegetables to suit personal tastes. Substitute butternut squash for carrots and/or potatoes.*

FIGURE 11.18 Steamed couscous.

Couscous

The *grain* called couscous is made from semolina flour. The Moroccan national *dish* called couscous is a stew of meat and/or vegetables over which hard wheat semolina couscous, barley, millet, sorghum, breadcrumbs, crushed acorns, or maize (corn) are steamed. The stew is then served over the fluffy (never gummy or gritty) cooked grain.

Beloved throughout the Maghreb, this dish of Berber origin exists in many variations, from spicy or spicy-sweet to sweet or simple, with vegetables, fruit, lamb, fish and fennel, or chicken. Food writer Paula Wolfert notes that couscous is often served as lunch, but rarely served as an evening meal or as a main course. Instead, it has traditionally been served at the end of many courses so the guest will achieve total satisfaction.

The traditional Arabic clay or aluminum vessel used to make couscous dishes is called a *kiskis* or *couscousière*. It consists of two parts: a tall, bottom pot-bellied vessel for the broth, meat, and vegetables and a perforated top vessel, which fits snugly over the bottom. The holes allow steam to rise, cook, and flavor the couscous. Create a couscousière by seating a colander snugly into a tall pot so that the bottom of the colander is several inches away from simmering liquid.

SIGNATURE RECIPE

COUSCOUS

Never purchase couscous labeled instant.

Yields 6 cups steamed couscous

12 ounces couscous, 2 cups
1 teaspoon kosher salt
Oil for hands

1 **Wash and dry:** Pour couscous into a large mixing bowl with 6 cups cold water (3 times the amount of couscous). Stir with hand and immediately drain through fine strainer. Dump couscous into a 2-inch-deep stainless steel hotel pan, smooth out, and leave to absorb water, swell and dry, 10 to 15 minutes.

2 **Lift, rub, and rake:** Lift couscous with cupped hands, rub gently, and let it fall back into the pan to break up lumps. Lifting and raking couscous with fingers helps it to swell evenly.

3 **Prepare cheesecloth for sealing steamer:** Measure the circumference of your stewing pot and cut a 3-inch-wide strip of cheesecloth or aluminum foil to fit it all the way around the edge. Fold it in half so it is a long 1-1/2-inch strip. Arrange foil on edge with half overlapping into the pot, OR dampen cheesecloth and dredge it through flour. Gently twist it and place cheesecloth along the entire top edge of stew pot. Set steamer snugly on top of foil or cheesecloth to seal steam in.

4 **First steaming:** Couscous should be steamed at least twice. Layer cheesecloth into the top steamer and pour in the couscous. Over moderately boiling liquid, *without covering*, steam couscous 20 minutes. Periodically rake and toss couscous so it steams evenly.

5 **Rest and cooling off period:** Transfer couscous in cheesecloth to hotel pan. Still in cheesecloth, spread it out. For 2 cups couscous, sprinkle with 1 teaspoon kosher salt and 1/2 cup cold water. Oil your hands, and briefly repeat the lifting, rubbing, and raking to distribute the water and break up lumps. Smooth couscous out and allow it to rest, cool, and dry 10 to 15 minutes.

*At this point, if necessary, couscous may be covered with a damp towel allowed to wait several hours before the final steaming.

*If at any point stew is fully cooked but couscous is not, steam couscous over boiling water.

6 **Second and final steaming:** Transfer couscous back into the steamer. Steam uncovered over gently boiling liquid 20 minutes and toss periodically to ensure even cooking. The couscous should be tender—not al dente, but not mush-soft. Grains should be moist, fluffy, and separate. If necessary, at this point couscous can rest in a 200 degree F oven, back in the hotel pan, covered, up to 15 minutes.

THE MAKING OF COUSCOUS

Traditionally, for centuries, groups of women have hand-prepared couscous. It is labor intensive: they sprinkle water over freshly ground semolina flour made from two inner parts of husked and crushed hard wheat. They roll the resulting mixture into small pellets or balls and sprinkle them with more flour to keep the balls separate. The balls are strained and whatever falls through is dampened, rolled, floured, and strained again. The couscous is spread out and sun-dried. Most modern couscous production is mechanized, but in some rural areas women still make it by hand.

Couscous: Stew with Pebble Pasta Steamed over Top

In Morocco, the *dish* called couscous is a combination of the stew with a flavorful broth in the bottom of the couscousiére served over or mixed with the *couscous pasta* or grain that has been steamed on top. The couscous grain (or another starch like barley grits, corn couscous, or crushed acorns) takes on flavor from the stew's steam. There are many types of this remarkable, simple signature dish. Harmonious spicy-sweet combinations of lamb, chickpeas, vegetables, or dried fruit with spices and herbs transform it to something soul-satisfying.

SEVEN VEGETABLE COUSCOUS (KSEKSÜ BIDAWI)

This vegetable mixture for couscous is stew-like, while a tagine is braised and liquids reduced.

Yields about 14 cups (about 8 cups vegetables and 6 cups broth), 6 to 8 servings

3-1/2 ounces chickpeas, 1/2 cup
    or 1 cup drained, (canned) cooked chickpeas
1/4 teaspoon crushed saffron
18 ounces onions, 3 medium, peeled and wedged into fourths or eighths
1-1/2 pounds tomatoes, 3 medium, 3-1/2 to 4 cups peeled and diced
2 teaspoons freshly ground pepper
3 tablespoons olive oil
6 tablespoons unsalted butter, diced, *divided*
18 ounces couscous, 3 cups
10 ounces cabbage, half a small head, quartered and cored
7 ounces carrots, 1 cup halved or quartered lengthwise and cut into 1-inch lengths
6 ounces zucchini, about 1 cup quartered lengthwise and cut into 1-inch lengths
5 ounces small to medium turnips, wedge-cut into fourths or eighths
5 ounces shelled and skinned fava beans, about 1 cup fresh or frozen
    or 5 ounces shelled lima beans, about 1 cup fresh or frozen
Scant 2 ounces golden raisins, 1/3 cup
1/2 ounce trimmed Italian parsley, 2 tablespoons minced
1/2 ounce cilantro, 2 tablespoon finely sliced
1/4 teaspoon red chili flakes

1 **Chickpeas:** Wash chickpeas. Soak overnight in cold water and 1 tablespoon kosher salt, or quick soak in boiling water and 1 teaspoon kosher salt for 1 hour. Drain and rinse chickpeas. Cover with cold water and bring to a boil. Cover saucepan and simmer chickpeas until tender, 40 to 60 minutes. Drain chickpeas and reserve cooking broth. Pour into the bottom of a couscoussiére or steamer.

2 **Cook stew:** Layer in saffron, onions, tomatoes, pepper, and 6 cups total mixture of chickpea cooking broth and cold water. Bring to a boil, lower heat, and stir in olive oil and 4 tablespoons butter. Cover pot and simmer mixture over medium-low heat 30 minutes.

3 **Couscous:** Prepare and steam couscous following instructions in *Signature Recipe: Couscous*.

4 **Steam couscous:** Add cabbage to chickpea stew. Line top steamer with damp cheesecloth and transfer couscous into it for the first steaming. Simmer cabbage until tender, 15 to 20 minutes. Remove pot from heat. Transfer couscous in cheesecloth to pan (keep it in cheesecloth) and toss with 1 teaspoon salt and 1/2 cup cold water (follow instructions). Add carrots, zucchini, turnips, favas or limas, and raisins to stew, and season with salt to taste.

5 **Twenty minutes before serving:** Return couscous in cheesecloth to steamer and place steamer over stew pot. Bring to a boil, lower the heat, and simmer vegetables and steam couscous (turning it occasionally) until tender, 15 to 20 minutes. Transfer couscous to a mixing bowl and rub with remaining 2 tablespoons butter. Pile couscous onto a deep platter. Stir herbs into stew and taste the broth; adjust seasonings if necessary.

6 **To Serve:** With a slotted spoon, transfer vegetables to top of couscous. Drizzle a little broth over them. Pour remaining hot broth into a spouted serving vessel, and stir in red chili flakes. Serve immediately while everything is hot. Each diner should pour a little broth over couscous to moisten it to taste.

Source: *Café Morocco* by Anissa Helou.

COOK'S VOICE: FOREST REBECCA OLSON

Empire, Michigan

"Along the coast of Morocco the seafood was outstanding. I loved all the tea stands serving mint tea with the leaves left in the bottom of the glass. The waiter would shave sugar from a large dark cone to your preference. My most memorable meal was with a poorer family who served a large platter of couscous with squash and something that resembled sheep intestines. I can not recommend the recipe . . . No utensils needed . . . Only one hand was used to eat with . . . or face being publicly shamed."

LAMB AND SQUASH COUSCOUS

This is simple, hearty, and straightforward food for a crowd.

Yields 4 quarts, 8 to 12 hearty servings

3-1/2 ounces dried chickpeas, 1/2 cup
   or 1-1/2 cups drained cooked chickpeas
1-1/2 pounds couscous, 4 cups
2 pounds lamb shoulder chop, fat trimmed away
   or 1-1/2 pounds boneless lean lamb neck or leg, diced into 3/4-inch cubes
2 pounds Spanish onions, 8 cups slivered
1-1/2 teaspoons freshly and coarsely ground black pepper
1 teaspoon ground ginger
1/8 teaspoon saffron
1/2 teaspoon ground turmeric
8 ounces softened unsalted butter, 1 cup, *divided*
1 pound carrots, peeled, halved *or* quartered lengthwise and cut into 2-1/2-inch lengths
2 ounces sugar, 1/4 cup
7-1/2 ounces large black raisins, 1-1/2 cups
1-1/2 pounds butternut squash, 5 cups seeded, peeled, and diced into 1-inch cubes.
Garnish: 1 teaspoon cinnamon

1 **Chickpeas:** Wash chickpeas. Soak overnight in cold water and 1 tablespoon kosher salt, or quick-soak in boiling water and 1 teaspoon kosher salt for 1 hour. Drain and rinse chickpeas. Cover with cold water. Bring to a boil, lower heat, cover pot, and simmer chickpeas until slightly firm, 30 minutes. Drain, and reserve cooking water and chickpeas separately.

2 **Couscous:** Begin the preparations for steaming couscous following instructions in *Signature Recipe: Couscous.*

3 **Stew:** Place lamb in bottom of a couscousiére or a tall stockpot. Pour in 1 teaspoon kosher salt, onions, black pepper, ginger, saffron, turmeric, 4 ounces butter, 6 cups water (or chickpea cooking water), and drained chickpeas. (Add canned or fully cooked chickpeas toward the end of cooking.) Bring stew to a boil, cover the pot, lower the heat, and simmer 1 hour. (Set a colander into stockpot for steaming couscous.)

4 **Steam couscous:** Layer colander with cheesecloth. Pour couscous into couscousiére or colander and set over top of stew for first steaming. Remove and rest couscous. Stir carrots, sugar, and raisins into broth and simmer 30 minutes. (Dish can be prepared to this point and cooled then refrigerated until next day.)

5 **Thirty minutes before serving:** Stir squash into hot stew (and canned or fully cooked chickpeas). Continue to cook stew over medium heat while steaming couscous a second time for 20 minutes.

6 **Scrape** hot couscous into large mixing bowl and rub with remaining 4 ounces butter while breaking up lumps. Pile couscous onto large, deep platter. Make an indentation in the center. Taste stew and season with salt, pepper, and cinnamon.

7 **To Serve:** With a slotted spoon, transfer meat and vegetables to center indentation in the couscous. Dust with a little more cinnamon, if desired. Strain broth into serving bowl and drizzle some over couscous. Serve couscous, meat, and vegetables with broth on the side for diners to add as they wish.

Source: *Couscous and Other Good Food From Morocco* by Paula Wolfert.

SAUTÉ, PAN-FRY, AND DEEP-FRY

FRIED FISH IN CHARMOULA (HOUT MAQLI BIL CHARMOULA)

4 servings

Four 7-ounce fillets of firm, white-fleshed fish like bream (fresh water bluegill or sunfish)
   or salt water snapper, haddock, cod, or turbot
1 teaspoon ground cumin
Charmoula Sauce
Olive oil for frying
Flour

1 Rub fish with cumin and sprinkle with kosher salt.

2 Mix together **charmoula sauce**, and season with salt to taste. Set aside.

3 In a deep 10-inch skillet, heat 1/2 inch oil to 360 degrees F. Dredge fish in flour, shake off excess, and slide into the hot oil. (Do not dredge in flour ahead of frying.) Fry fish until golden, turn, and fry on remaining side until golden and fish flakes when probed. Drain on paper towels.

4 **To Serve:** Transfer fish to serving dish and pour charmoula sauce over. Serve fish hot, or refrigerate fish in sauce to chill and marinate 1 hour to overnight. Turn fish several times to marinate evenly.

Source: *Arabesque: A Taste of Morocco, Turkey & Lebanon* by Claudia Roden.

GRILL, GRIDDLE, ROAST, BROIL, BAKE, AND BARBECUE

MECHOUI: MOROCCAN LAMB ON A SPIT

Mechoui is a specialty of the Berbers. Simple and succulent, cooks make a paste of garlic, ground coriander, cumin and paprika, and butter. They rub it into slits made in a whole lamb and all over the meat. The lamb roasts on a spit. The perfect mechoui is browned and crisp on the outside and falling-apart-tender inside. Mechoui should be eaten with the hands.

AMFOUER WITH ARGAN

In *The Momo Cookbook: A Gastronomic Journey Through North Africa*, chef Mourad Mazouz shares the Moroccan way of rescuing and transforming leftover bread in a "couscous-like way." Moroccans bake bread at home daily, and purposely retain the leftovers for amfouer, an easy and satisfying way to prepare a meal on busy days. The stale bread, moistened, seasoned, and steamed, much like couscous, is served hot, crowned with cold tomato and grilled pepper salad, and drizzled with local argan oil. The exotic-flavored argan oil is never heated and rarely mixed with lemon juice or vinegar.

Foolproof Bread Baking

The simplest way to tell when a loaf of bread is done is to check its internal temperature with an instant-read thermometer. Soft, pillowy breads with fat should be baked to around 180 to 190 degrees F. Drier, crusty breads can go up to 200 to 210 degrees. Poke the thermometer into the bottom center of the loaf for an accurate measure of its internal temperature.

Moroccan Bread

Moroccans love baking. They bake savory "pies" loaded with juicy meat, fruit, and vegetables surrounded by a crisp, buttery crust, a kind of "pizza" stuffed with fat, herbs, and spices and bread. Moroccans consider bread sacred and make several different types. Paula Wolfert says that Moroccan breads are hearty and flavorful with whole grains, chewy, and soft-crusted to act as a "fork" to eat with and to absorb juices from a tagine.

BREAD OF MOROCCO (KSRA OR KHBOZ)

Moroccans use bread as a utensil: to sop up juices and bits of food, so this bread is dense and delicately flavorful.

Yields about 31 ounces dough, two 6- to 6-1/2-inch round loaves, each about 14 ounces

2-1/4 teaspoons active dry yeast
1 teaspoon sugar
16 to 17 ounces unbleached flour, 3-1/2 cups
4 to 5 ounces whole wheat flour, 1 cup
2 teaspoons kosher salt
2 teaspoon sesame seeds
2 teaspoons aniseed
1/2 cup lukewarm milk
1 tablespoon olive oil *or* melted, unsalted butter
Optional: Cornmeal for sheet pan

1 Mix yeast with 1/4 cup lukewarm water and sugar. Let yeast rise until doubled and bubbly, about 10 minutes.

2 Mix flours, salt, and seeds in large mixing bowl or bowl of a mixer fitted with dough hook.

3 Stir yeast mixture, milk, and about 3/4 cup water to achieve a firm, nonsticky dough. Knead dough in mixer on slow speed 7 to 8 minutes or by hand 5 to 10 minutes. Form dough into 2 equal balls, about 16 ounces each, and rest 5 minutes covered with damp cotton towel.

4 Sprinkle a parchment-covered half-sheet pan with optional cornmeal. Grasp one ball of dough and transfer to a deep bowl. Holding the bowl with one hand, rotate dough against the side of the bowl with the other hand and form dough into a cone shape. Rub cone all over with half the oil or butter.

5 Place dough cone onto one side of sheet pan. Flatten the tip of the cone to form a 5-inch-diameter round disk with a raised center. Repeat process with second ball of dough.

6 Cover dough balls with damp cotton towel, and rest in warm place to rise until doubled, about 2 hours. When dough does not spring back when poked, it is ready for baking.

7 **Thirty minutes before dough is ready to be baked:** Preheat oven to 400 degrees F. Prick dough with fork all around the edges. Place pan in the middle of the oven and bake bread 15 minutes. Lower the heat to 300 degrees F and bake bread until it sounds hollow when knocked on the bottom or the internal temperature reaches 190 to 200 degrees F, about 35 to 40 minutes.

8 **To Serve:** Remove bread from oven and cool on racks. Cut in wedges to serve.

Source: Couscous and Other Good Food From Morocco by Paula Wolfert.

Vary! Improvise!

☞ *Khboz Mikla: Flatten circles of the dough and cook on a griddle (the Moroccan earthenware griddle is called a mikla) until browned on both sides. Serve with butter and honey.*

☞ *Campfire Snakes: Take this bread on the next camping trip or outdoor catering job. Roll 8 snakes of dough and wind each onto the end of a thick, long stick; grill over coals until baked through and browned, 8 to 12 minutes.*

MOROCCAN PIZZA: KHBOZ BISHEMAR

Chef and cookbook writer Paula Wolfert relates how cooks in Marrakech flatten (approximately 1/8 of ksra) dough balls to 8-inch by 14-inch rectangles, lay a filling of diced beef or lamb suet, chopped parsley, onion, cumin, chili, and paprika onto the dough. The dough is folded over the filling and flattened and stretched back to the original size. It's folded one more time, right side over and left side under, and allowed to rise 45 minutes. The bread package is pricked on both sides, placed on a hot griddle to fry in the fat that releases from the filling. The packets become golden, crisp, and infused with the seasonings and fat.

BRIK, BRAEWAT, AND TRID

Brik, *braewat*, and *trid* are poplar Tunisian and Moroccan savory pastries made with the thin Moroccan pastry leaves called *warka*, similar to thin crepes or thick fillo leaves. *Brik* is a deep-fried pastry turnover filled with soft egg, meat, tuna and capers, or mashed potatoes. *Braewat* is a small, stuffed pastry triangle filled with ground fish or spiced meats or sweet fillings like rice pudding or ground almonds and cinnamon. *Trid*, similar to b'stilla, is made with layers of warka filled with saffron-spiced chicken, sugar, and cinnamon, but no almonds or eggs.

B'stilla (*Bis-stee-ya*)

B'stilla is an extravagant Moroccan meat pie from Fez that consists of layers of thin, crisp *warka* dough, which is thicker than phyllo dough—closer to crisp spring roll wrappers. See Glossary for more information on warka, warqa, or ouarka. B'stilla is a savory-sweet dish made with chicken simmered in spice-broth, bones removed, and meat shredded. Lemony eggs cook in the broth. Eggs and meat are layered with crunchy toasted almonds, cinnamon, and sugar. Traditionally made with squab (baby pigeon), this dish is nothing short of a culinary revelation. Other regions prepare b'stilla with finely chopped lamb or beef, and there is even a sweet version made with custard.

FIGURE 11.19 Moroccan chicken pie (b'stilla).

SIGNATURE RECIPE

MOROCCAN CHICKEN PIE (B'STILLA)

Thaw frozen fillo overnight in refrigerator for best results. It's common in Morocco to drain the eggs, but here they are slightly thickened with cornstarch or flour to keep the chicken moist. For more information on handling fillo dough see chapter Greece and Turkey.

Yields 2-inch high, 13-inch round pie, about 12 servings

Chicken Filling

Yields about 7 cups boned shredded meat (about 2 pounds) and about 3-3/4 cups broth

2 tablespoons olive oil
8 ounces onion, 2 cups finely diced
5 pounds bone-in chicken thighs and breasts, 4 pounds skinned
1/2 ounce trimmed Italian parsley, 1/4 cup chopped
1/2 ounce cilantro, 1/4 cup finely sliced
1/4 teaspoon ground turmeric
1 teaspoon freshly ground black pepper
1/4 teaspoon saffron, toasted crushed
1 teaspoon ground ginger
6 inches cinnamon sticks, about 2

Almond Mixture

Yields 3 cups

15 to 16 ounces toasted blanched almonds, 3 cups
2 ounces confectioner's sugar, 1/2 cup
2 teaspoons ground cinnamon

1/2 pound unsalted butter, scant 1 cup clarified
1/4 cup freshly squeezed lemon juice, about 1 large lemon
10 large eggs, 2 to 2-1/4 cups lightly beaten
1 tablespoon cornstarch or flour
1 pound frozen fillo sheets, *thawed overnight*

Garnish: Ground cinnamon and powdered sugar

1 Preheat oven to 400 degrees F.

2 **Prepare filling:** Heat oil over medium heat in 6-quart pot. Stir in onion and cook until golden, 6 to 8 minutes. Stir in chicken, 3 cups cold water, parsley, cilantro, turmeric, black pepper, saffron, ginger, and cinnamon sticks. Bring to a boil, reduce heat, and cover the pot. Simmer chicken until very tender, 45 minutes to 1 hour.

3 Spread almonds on sheet pan and roast in oven until golden, 10 to 15 minutes; cool. Pour almonds into food processor and pulse-grind until coarse. Pour into mixing bowl and stir in sugar, cinnamon, and a pinch of kosher salt; set aside.

4 Dice butter into small cubes and clarify. Skim away white foam; set aside.

5 With a slotted spoon, transfer chicken and bones to mixing bowl to cool. There should be about 3-1/2 to 4 cups broth left in pot. Discard cinnamon stick. Remove chicken bones from meat, and discard. Shred chicken finely. Taste and season with salt and pepper, and set aside.

6 Bring broth to a boil and reduce by about half to 1-3/4 to 2 cups. Stir in lemon juice. Whisk eggs with cornstarch or flour and 1 teaspoon salt. Slowly pour eggs into simmering broth. When eggs are lightly scrambled, remove pan from heat and season with freshly ground pepper.

*Dish may be prepped to this point 1 day in advance and refrigerated.

7 Raise oven heat to 425 degrees F. Fold 4 whole fillo leaves in half, place on two sheet pans, and place in oven to crisp, 1 to 2 minutes. (If using commercial fillo with half sheets, use 8 half sheets.) Remove and set aside.

8 **Construct b'stilla:** Unroll fillo and place on work surface. Cover with plastic wrap and damp towel. Place 13- to 14-inch paella or cake pan on counter and butter inside bottom and sides liberally. Lay 1 sheet fillo on bottom and lay 6 more sheets radiating like flower petals from center, overlapping and hanging out over edge of pan. Brush leaves inside pan (not the parts outside pan) with clarified butter.

9 Evenly spread chicken into pan. Cover with eggs. Top with the 4 crisp, folded sheets and butter them. Cover crisp sheets with almond-cinnamon-sugar mixture. Radiating from center and overlapping, cover nuts with 4 sheets fillo and butter them.

10 Fold up sheets that are hanging outside the pan and brush with butter. Layer 2 or 3 more sheets on top of pie and neatly tuck them under like tucking sheets in while making a bed. Brush well with butter. Seal any leftover fillo and freeze.

11 Place b'stilla into oven and bake until golden, about 20 minutes. Remove from oven. Shake pan to loosen. Place 12-inch by 17-inch sheet pan over b'stilla and, with two hands, invert pie onto sheet pan. Brush the top of the b'stilla with melted excess butter; place pan into oven. Bake until golden, 10 to 15 minutes. Remove b'stilla from oven and cool slightly. Place large serving platter over b'stilla and, with two hands, carefully invert pie onto platter.

12 **To Serve:** For decoration, place powdered sugar in fine strainer and tap evenly over top. Lay a stencil on top of b'stilla and repeat with ground cinnamon. Serve b'stilla warm. Freeze unbaked b'stilla pies in freezer bags up to 2 months. Don't thaw before baking; just bake 10 minutes longer.

Source: *Couscous and Other Good Food From Morocco* by Paula Wolfert.

EXOTIC MARRAKECH MARKETS

Blogger Alice Hou (An American in London) shares her experiences watching "the Snake Guys, storytellers, musicians and henna artists" in the open-air markets of Marrakech. By evening every day, they moved out and hundreds of tables appeared by stalls with open-air kitchens. As the dinner rush ensued, the smell of grilled kebabs, simmering harira soup, snails, merguez sausages, and sheep's head filled the air.

FIGURE 11.20 Merguez sausage.
Source: shellyagami-photoar/Shutterstock.

FIGURE 11.21 Warm chickpea salad.
Source: Elzbieta Sekowska/Shutterstock.

SALAD AND VEGETABLE METHODS

Signature Technique: Moroccan Salad

Moroccans are genius with (mostly cooked) vegetable salads similar to French crudités salads (see France). The Moroccan combinations are exotic and delicious:

- Sweet potatoes with olives and preserved lemons
- Carrots with cumin or *harissa* or oranges
- Young fava beans with lemon and olive oil
- Fennel with red onion and citrus
- Cooked beets with cumin, cinnamon, lemon, and rosewater
- Eggplant simmered with tomatoes and garlic
- Roasted green and red bell peppers
- Zucchini with onions, garlic, mint, and lemon
- Cooked pumpkin cubes with cinnamon, garlic, and lemon.
- Diced tomato, cucumber, and onion

MOROCCAN SWEET POTATO SALAD
(SLADA BATAT HALWA)

Yields 5 cups, 4 to 6 servings

4 tablespoons olive oil
12 ounces onion, 3 cups peeled and diced
1 teaspoon ground ginger
1 teaspoon ground cumin
1 teaspoon paprika
2 pounds orange sweet potatoes, 6 cups peeled and diced into 1-inch cubes
3 ounces green olives, 7 large olives, 1/2 cup halved lengthwise
1/2 preserved lemon, 3 tablespoons slivered peel
3 to 4 tablespoons lemon juice, 1 large lemon
1 ounce trimmed Italian parsley, 1/2 cup chopped

1 Heat oil over medium heat in deep 12-inch skillet or 6-quart Dutch oven. Stir in onions and cook until golden, about 20 minutes. Stir in ginger, cumin, and paprika, and season with salt. Cook 1 to 2 minutes. Stir in sweet potatoes and 1 cup water.

2 Bring mixture to a boil, lower heat, and simmer potatoes, turning once after 5 to 7 minutes. Cook potatoes until tender and liquid is reduced to a thick sauce, 5 to 7 minutes more. Do not stir potatoes too much or they'll fall apart. Add 1/2 cup water if potatoes begin to dry.

3 **To Serve:** Transfer potatoes to mixing bowl with slotted spoon—leave the liquid in pan. Reduce liquid over medium-high heat until syrupy and thick. Stir in olives, preserved lemon, lemon juice, and season with salt to taste. Fold mixture with parsley into potatoes. Pile potato salad into serving vessel.

Source: *Arabesque: A Taste of Morocco, Turkey & Lebanon* by Claudia Roden.

MOROCCAN BLACK OLIVE, ORANGE, AND RED ONION SALAD (SLATA BORTOKAL BIL ZAYTOUN)

In Morocco, bitter Seville oranges are used for this salad. The sweet Navels are more to North American tastes. An 11-ounce orange yields about 7-1/2 ounces peeled fruit, about 1 cup sliced.

Yields about 5 cups, 4 to 6 servings

3-1/2 ounces black oil-cured olives, about 3/4 cup pitted
1 teaspoon orange zest, about 1/2 to 2/3 of an orange
1/8 teaspoon crushed red chili flakes
3 tablespoons fresh lemon juice, about 1 lemon
3 tablespoons extra virgin olive oil
   or 3 tablespoons argan oil
6 ounces 1 medium red onion, 1-1/2 cups peeled, halved, and very thinly sliced
4 large navel oranges, preferably organic

Garnish: 1/4 ounce trimmed Italian parsley, 2 tablespoons chopped, more to taste

1. **Prepare dressing:** Smack olives with side of a chef's knife to loosen pits. Remove and discard pits; tear olives in half. In a small bowl, toss olives with zest, chili, lemon juice, and oil. Marinate at room temperature 30 minutes to 1 hour.

2. **Salt-wilt onion:** Toss onion with 1 teaspoon kosher salt and mix well; set aside 20 minutes. Knead onion occasionally to encourage wilting. Rinse onion and squeeze out excess liquid; set aside.

3. Peel oranges, removing outside membrane. Slice oranges into 1/4-inch-thick rounds. Arrange oranges overlapping on a serving dish and chill.

4. **To Serve:** Sprinkle sliced onions over oranges. Evenly arrange olives and marinade over onions and oranges. Garnish with parsley.

Vary! Improvise!

☞ *Sprinkle salad with feta cheese.*
☞ *Whisk 1/2 teaspoon ground cumin into olive oil.*
☞ *Dust salad with paprika.*
☞ *Substitute blood oranges for navel oranges.*

PICKLE AND PRESERVE

MOROCCAN PRESERVED LEMONS (HAMAD M'RAKAD)

Traditionally made, Moroccan preserved lemons are quartered through their skin to within 1/2-inch of bottom and top so they hold together. Stuffed with salt, they are packed into a glass jar and sealed. Within a few days lemon juice will fill the jar. The method below, with cut and squeezed lemons, is a way to get a higher yield of skin and to ensure that the lemons will be completely covered with lemon juice from the start. The salty juice and the saturated, tasty skin of the lemon are both delightful. Slice or dice the skin and toss in hot rice, salads, dressings, stuffings, or as soup or stew garnish.

Yields 1 quart

2 ounces kosher salt, 6 tablespoons, *divided*
About 30 ounces lemons, preferably organic, 7 medium

1 Pour 1 tablespoon salt on the bottom of a wide-mouth glass 1-quart canning jar.

2 Slice lemons in half through their equators and squeeze lemons to juice them, but not fully: leave some pulp. Set juice aside in a measuring container with a spout. It should yield about 1-1/4 to 1-1/2 cups.

3 Divide 3 tablespoons salt among the lemon halves, and rub them inside with it. Pack lemon shells tightly into jar. Sprinkle remaining 2 tablespoons salt over lemons and pour fresh lemon juice over the salt until the lemons are covered, leaving 1/2 to 1-inch headspace. Seal jar tightly with plastic lid, or a piece of plastic wrap and metal lid.

4 Set jar on nonreactive pan to catch overflow juices. Leave lemons in a warm spot 7 days or longer to mature. Shake jar daily to distribute salt. Check lemons for tenderness, and refrigerate when lemon skins are softened and slightly broken down. The lemons are usable, but taste best after 3 weeks of refrigeration. The lemons will improve in flavor up to 6 months. Preserved lemons keep refrigerated for 1 year. Rinse the lemons to reduce saltiness.

5 **To Use:** Before using lemons, rinse off salt and scoop out and discard inside pulp. If lemons develop a white yeasty-looking mold, rinse it off. It is not harmful.

FIGURE 11.22 Preserved lemons.
Source: Steve Lee/DK Images.

EAST AFRICA

ETHIOPIA: THE LAND OF BREAD AND HONEY

A Genuine Revelation

Phillip Briggs writing in Ethiopia *(Bradt Travel Guide) recounts his surprise and revelation at seeing Ethiopia, calling it a country that "confounds every expectation." Instead of a "vast, featureless desert," he found awesome landscapes and a varied climate. Instead of a land devastated by decades of civil war, he found a country that showed few signs of war. Instead of "human degradation and abject poverty," he found a culture that loved itself and its history with an "infectious" pride and self-esteem.*

Ethiopia is a land of ancient civilization, impressive architecture, and fascinating legends. Most of modern Ethiopia is poor, but its long history left it with many treasures: pre-Christian tombs, medieval stone churches, monasteries with religious artifacts, and

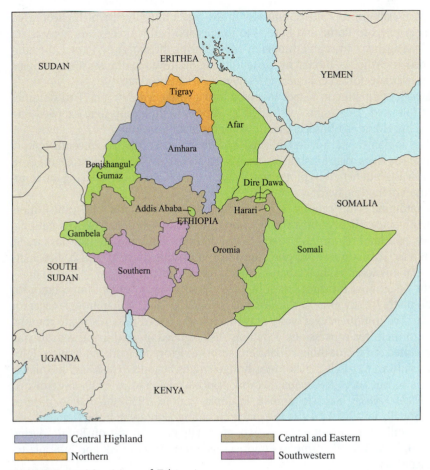

Central Highland

Northern

Central and Eastern

Southwestern

FIGURE 11.23 Map of Ethiopia.

seventeenth-century castles. The captivating landscape features canyons, chasms, gorges, and high plateaus. Natural riches include the Simien Mountains and Lake Tana, source of the Blue Nile, and the Danakil Depression, one of the lowest, hottest, and most inhospitable places on the planet.

Most paleo-anthropologists agree that human life probably began around Ethiopia. The oldest hominid was discovered there in 1974. Ethiopia's first known civilization was the *Punt*, who traded gold, myrrh, ivory, and slaves with Egyptian trading ships attracted to the coastal region. By 2000 BCE, the Punt had strong trade with Southern Arabia. This first historical instance of Southern Arabia mixing with East Africa had an enormous impact on East Africa's language and culture.

About 400 BCE, the *Aksumite* civilization, along with Persia, Rome, and China, was one of that era's *four most powerful ancient kingdoms*. Well-organized, the cosmopolitan Aksumites were agriculturally, technically, and artistically advanced. They built obelisk monuments and introduced Christianity. For nearly a millennium under the Aksumites (and the legendary Queen of Sheba), Ethiopia became an important *Silk Road* commercial crossroads and trading port with sea routes around the horn of Africa and the Indian subcontinent. At the peak, from third to sixth century AD, Egypt, Arabia, India, Syria, Byzantium, and Rome traded silk, olive oil, spices, and wine for Aksumite grain, gold, emeralds, and ivory. The Islamic Empire took control of sea trade and eventually the Aksumite economy slumped into isolation and a dark age.

The *Zagwe* ruled from around 1137 to 1270. All that's left of this mysterious dynasty are rock-hewn churches. During the Ethiopian Middle Ages, Yekuno Amlak killed the Zagwe king and established the *Solomonic* dynasty, which lasted 500 years. During this time, contact with Byzantium increased, which strained relations with Ethiopia's Muslim neighbors.

The French established the first embassy in the fifteenth century, which encouraged Ethiopians to travel to Rome and Europe to join established churches. An angry Islam declared jihad against Christian Ethiopia in 1490. During the sixteenth century, the Ethiopian Christian-Orthodox monarchy, close to being destroyed by the Muslims during a costly tragic war, was forced to appeal to Portuguese Jesuits for help.

The *Oromos*, originating in Kenya, migrated into a weakened Ethiopia. Two centuries of conflict followed. The Jesuits, who tried to impose Catholicism, were expelled and Ethiopia all but closed her borders to Europe for more than a century.

A new Ethiopian capital was established and by the end of the seventeenth century thriving markets drew rich Muslim merchants. Palaces hosted extravagant events with sumptuous feasts, but nefarious plots created chaos. Civil war ensued, reducing the country to a cluster of feuding fiefdoms.

By the mid-nineteenth century, the Robinhood-like *Tewodros* defeated rival princes to become Emperor. He became a strong, innovative leader who established a national army, roads, and land reform and attempted to unify the land and abolish slave trade. Angry at the lack of European support, Tewodros imprisoned several British diplomats and European missionaries; in retaliation, the British defeated him.

With the opening of the Suez Canal in 1869, Ethiopia again gained importance for its position on this passageway to the East and beyond. By 1885, Italian troops, eager for conquest, arrived in Eritrea. Eventually King *Menelik* was forced to sign a treaty granting the region to them for concessions. Relations disintegrated and Ethiopia went to war. Menelik defeated the encroaching Italians in a surprise victory. Menelik modernized Ethiopia with a railway, electricity, telephones, bridges, roads, schools, banks, and hospitals.

Menelik's cousin's son, *Ras Tafani*, became prince regent, and in 1930 was crowned Emperor *Haile Selassie*. Selassie unified Ethiopia, but in 1935 the Italian dictator Mussolini brutally invaded Ethiopia to expand his empire. Ethiopian troops fought back, but were woefully under-equipped. In 1940, after Italy declared war on Britain during World War II, Britain finally came to Ethiopia's aid. Selassie returned, and Ethiopia regained independence.

Dissatisfaction with Selassie's rule led to his imprisonment in 1974. Derg military leader colonel *Mengistu* assumed power. Under his rule, Ethiopia suffered financial ruin, drought, and appalling famine. By 1991, violent opposition forced Mengistu to flee and today's Democratic Republic of Ethiopia was formed under former rebel leader Zenawi. In 1999, long simmering military conflict between Ethiopia and Eritrea lead to thousands of deaths. Tensions still remain. Today, Ethiopia's wobbly economy, exploding population, joblessness, and overwhelming poverty have put a massive strain on the depleted soil and food production.

LANGUAGE, PHILOSOPHY, AND RELIGION

Amharic once was the language of primary school instruction. In 1991 the constitution of the Democratic Republic of Ethiopia gave citizens the right to develop local, ethnic languages and teach them in primary school. Ethiopia has more than 75 indigenous languages, most of them Afro-Asiatic and Nilo-Saharan. English is the most widely spoken foreign language; it is used in secondary school and university.

Ethiopia has been predominately Orthodox Christian since the fourth century and the religion now comprises about half the population. Islam is second with about a third of the population. Protestants, and traditional beliefs like animism, make up the remainder. Ethiopia is the spiritual homeland of the Rastafari movement with its pan-African Reggae music. The constitution provides freedom of religion, but this freedom is not always respected. It is considered a crime to turn one religion against another or to form religion-based political parties.

Ethiopia follows its own calendar based on the Eastern Coptic calendar and has a seven- to eight-year gap behind the Gregorian calendar. Ethiopian New Year begins at the end of August. Unlike conventional time with the start of the day at midnight, the Ethiopian day begins at dawn, so 7 a.m. East African Time is 1 a.m. Ethiopian time.

GEOGRAPHY AND CLIMATE

Ethiopia sits on two plateaus, the northern Amhara and the arid, rocky, and sparsely populated eastern Somali; the Chercher, Aranna, and Chelalo mountains and the Great Rift Valley bisect both. Most of the rural population originally lived south of Addis Ababa in the rugged lowland coffee-growing provinces of Sidamo and Goma Gofa. Today the population is visible in all directions.

Ethiopia's climate varies from cool to quite cold in the highlands to extremely hot in the lowlands. Although Ethiopia sits near the equator, its climate isn't typically tropical because most of its elevation is around 5,000 feet. The climate can be divided into three zones: the *cool zone* with over 8,000-foot elevations, freezing temperatures and afro-alpine vegetation in parts of the northwestern plateau; the *temperate zone* with 5,000- to 8,000-foot elevations, moderate temperatures, and most of the population in the low areas of the plateau; and the *hot zone* with elevations below 5,000 feet and temperatures that can reach over 100 degree F. Seacoast and river valleys have high humidity. Annual rainfall is heaviest in the southwest, light in the Great Rift Valley and the Ogaden, and almost zero in the extreme heat of the Denakil Depression.

FARMING AND AGRICULTURE

Agriculture is Ethiopia's most important source of income, engaging around 85 percent of the population despite having only about 12 percent arable land. Ethiopia exports coffee, leather hides and skins, legumes, oilseeds, beeswax, honey, and tea. Meat, produce, grains, and dairy are produced domestically. Coffee is the most important export, employing one-fourth of the population; Ethiopia has Africa's largest number of livestock, and exports of beeswax and honey. Environmental issues (drought, soil degradation, and deforestation) and poor infrastructure hinder self-sufficiency.

ETHIOPIAN CUISINE: THE MASTERS OF RURAL AND RUSTIC

Silk Road traders coming by way of the Indian Ocean and the Red Sea first influenced Ethiopian and Eritrean cuisine with nonindigenous ingredients: Ginger, turmeric, pepper, fragrant spices, and culinary techniques came from Asia and India. The Arabs introduced Persian foods, cooking techniques, and a refined use of spices. Portuguese traders brought chilies, peppers, potatoes, and tomatoes in the fifteenth century. Ethiopia's mountainous terrain made transportation and invasion difficult, so the neighboring countries of Sudan, Uganda, Kenya, and Somalia had much less influence.

Religion has played an important part in shaping the cuisine. Christians live mainly in northern Ethiopia and Muslims in the south. Both Christians and Muslims favor vegetarian (and vegan) dishes and abstain from pork. Orthodox Christians abstain from meat and dairy 200 days a year: twice a week as well as during Lent. Consequently, Ethiopia, much like India, developed a complex and satisfying vegetarian cuisine based on grains, dried peas, lentils, and beans. In modern Ethiopia, the more affluent eat more meat—chicken, beef, lamb, and goat.

At its heart, Ethiopian cuisine is rural, rustic, and deeply comforting. It is the hottest-spicy food in Africa with the signature *berbere* (*bear-bear-ray*)—ground chili and spice powder *or* ground chili and spice paste. Mildly spiced berbere mixed with wine or water becomes a table condiment called *awaze.*

Two stews form the backbone of Ethiopian meals: *w'et*, seasoned with spicy berbere and *niter kibbe* (spiced ghee), or the mild *alich'a* seasoned with turmeric, garlic, and ginger. These long-simmered, thick stews similar to Indian curries are made with various meats, seafood, legumes, or vegetables. As with Indian curries, a blending of seasonings and the berbere or seasoning mixtures provides a classic "Ethiopian" taste.

Ethiopia is often called the land of bread and honey, and Ethiopians eat what their land provides. Honey is collected by ancient beekeeping techniques. Ethiopians grow *t'eff*, sorghum, millet, wheat, and maize for porridge and breads. The signature spongy, sourdough *injera* flat bread, a staple at most meals, is made from flour ground from t'eff in a process similar to South Indian *dosa*. T'eff is high in iron, calcium, potassium, and minerals. Like grapes, t'eff contains symbiotic yeasts that encourage a flavorful fermentation. Local wild herbs, spices, flowers, leaves, legumes, and aromatic roots provide flavor contrasts and combinations for a variety of relishes, sides, and main dishes.

REGIONAL ETHIOPIA

Although there are distinct regional variations in Ethiopian cuisine, they were absorbed into a national cuisine popular in central Ethiopia and its capital, Addis Ababa. Skilled palace cooks in the early twentieth century declined to share their knowledge with the common people, but when the monarchy collapsed in 1974, many of the aristocracy were bankrupted. They were forced to open restaurants and food-related businesses, thus new dishes spread out to the general public.

Despite the fact that Ethiopia is a blend of the central highland Amhara, eastern Oromos, northern Tigrays, southwestern Gurages, and dozens of other indigenous people, most Ethiopian restaurants abroad feature dishes from the Amhara north-central highlands (and Eritrea). Consequently, throughout the country, people eat pretty much the same food. From Amhara came *doro w'et* (chicken stew with hard-boiled eggs); from Oromo, buttered barley porridge; from Tigrayan, baked bread; and from Gurage, *kitfo* (raw ground beef seasoned with spiced butter).

With a large population of Orthodox Christians (Copts) and Muslims, who both observe many fasting days, cooks have developed many vegetarian and vegan dishes. Muslims and Copts developed dishes without pork.

DINE AT HOME IN ETHIOPIA

If invited to dine in an Ethiopian home, consider it an honor—the sharing of food from a common plate conveys loyalty, family, and friendship. Punctuality isn't stressed, but extreme lateness is an insult. Remove shoes at the door. Greet the host warmly with the greeting *tena yistiligne* and a light handshake; wait for the hostess to extend her hand. Inquire about family and health. Greet elders first with a bow. Use the honorific *ato* for men, *woizerit* for married women, and *woizrity* for single women. Bring a modest gift like flowers or fruit and give it with the right hand. Don't bring alcohol to Muslim homes.

Guests are seated on a low divan or stools around a *mesob*, a handmade wicker hourglass-shaped table with a domed cover. A woman, possibly dressed in a traditional *shama* (white cotton robe-like dress), will bring a water pitcher, a basin, and a towel before and after the meal. She'll pour warm water over guests' right hand after which they wipe hands on the towel.

A platter covered with spongy-soft, sour *injera* flatbreads will arrive at the table. An assortment of *w'ets* (stews) and vegetables will be spooned onto the injera: *alicha-sega w'et*—beef cubes in butter; *doro w'et*—chicken and egg cooked in a spicy red-brown sauce; *misir w'et*—spicy pink split lentils; *tikil-gomen*—spiced cabbage, carrots, and potatoes; and *fosoli*—sautéed and spiced green beans, carrots, onions, and garlic. Wait for the eldest guest to begin eating. Using the right hand only, tear off a piece of injera and use it to either dip into or fold up some of the stews.

The host or hostess might place a tasty morsel or two into a guest's mouth; it's called *gursha* and is a sign of respect. (Smile widely.) If offered *kitfo* (seasoned raw meat) at the end of the meal, it's an even higher honor. (Try it!) If the hosts are Christians, during the meal guests might be treated to *t'ella* (homemade beer), whiskey, or *tej* (an amber honey mead-like brew). The hand washing will be repeated after dining.

SACRED COFFEE RITUAL

After dinner guests may be invited for a formal coffee ritual, which can take an hour or more. In most parts of Ethiopia, the coffee ceremony takes place in the morning, at noon, and in the evening. It is the main social event within the village and a time to discuss the community, politics and life, and to gossip.

The sacred Ethiopian coffee ritual starts with guests seated on pillows with incense burning. Someone will wash and roast the green coffee beans over charcoal, then grind and mix them with boiling water in a clay coffee pot, which imparts a delightful flavor. In the first round, *abol* or *awol*, small handle-less cups will be filled with a little sugar and coffee and handed to the eldest person first. Inhale the aroma before tasting and sip slowly. The coffee pot will be refilled with boiling water and the weaker second round of coffee, or *tona*, is served. Boiling water added a third time to the grounds produces an even weaker third round, or *baraka*. It is impolite for a guest to retire until he or she has consumed at least three cups; the third round is thought to bestow a blessing that will transform the spirit.

TASTES OF ETHIOPIA

Fat: Butter, spiced clarified butter, spiced oil, roasted flax oil; olive, cottonseed, safflower, corn, soybean, and sesame oils

Sweet: Honey, sugar

Sour/Alcohol: Lemon, orange, vinegar, *t'ej* (honey wine), *berz* (un-fermented t'ej)

Salty: Salt

Spicy-Hot: *Berbere* (spiced red chili powder or paste), black pepper, Anaheim chilies, jalapeño chilies, Serrano chilies, cayenne chilies, bird's eye chilies, ginger, mustard seeds, *awaze* (red chili paste)

Spice: *Bishop's weed* (ajwain), anise, false cardamom, cardamom, coriander, cumin, nutmeg, turmeric, rue seed, cloves, cinnamon, *black cumin* (nigella), fenugreek seed, fennel seed

Aromatic Seasoning Vegetables: Red shallots, Italian purple onion, white onions, garlic, gingerroot

Herbs, Seasonings, and Condiments: Fenugreek leaves, hibiscus leaves, flaxseed, sacred basil, oregano, mint, cilantro, savory, dill leaves, rue seed and leaf

FIGURE 11.24 Ethiopian pitcher for coffee boiling.
Source: nik7ch/Shutterstock.

COMMON ETHIOPIAN COOKING TOOLS

Large wooden mortar and pestle, grinding stones, *mitad* (flat clay pan for injera cooking), clay cooking vessels

FIGURE 11.25 Ethiopian artisanal pottery.
Source: Erwan Guillard/Fotolia.

Other Important Foods: Meat (lamb, beef, *qwant'a* [dried beef], kidneys, tripe and liver, chicken), fish, eggs, grain (barley, wheat, oats, *t'eff* [millet-like grain], emmerwheat, millet, sorghum, rice), legumes (chickpeas, chickpea flour, *shiro mi'tin* [spiced chickpea flour mixed with other bean or pea flours], lentils, broad beans, kidney beans, split peas), collard greens, kale, tomatoes, bell peppers, Italian frying pepper, pumpkin, nettles, beets, *ayib* (soft cheese), *irgo* (yogurt), false banana stem, sweet potatoes, potatoes, cabbage, cottonseeds, carrots, okra, fruit (guava, prickly pear, bananas, dates), coconut, sunflower seeds

Popular Dishes: *Injera* bread, *kitfo* (spiced raw beef or raw fish), *alich'a* (mild stew), *w'et* (spicy stew), *fitfit* (stew made with torn leftover injera bread), *t'ibs* (meat or fish cooked in spices)

Drinks: Coffee, *t'ej* (honey mead made with special hops called *gesho*), wine, *t'ella* (Ethiopian beer), tea, barley tea, coffee leaf tea, *suff* (sunflower seed drink), *telba* (flaxseed drink), *berz* (unfermented t'ej), fenugreek and honey tea

FIGURE 11.26 Grinding stones.
Source: Jaggat/Shutterstock.

ETHIOPIAN CHILIES

Hot chilies and paprika are important traditional crops in Ethiopia because they provide color and pungent, spicy flavor. To Ethiopians, food without chilies has little flavor. Ethiopians grow diverse Capsicum species; below are several of the most important. Fresh green chilies are eaten as a vegetable or with other foods. Dried, ground chili flavors and colors stews (w'ets) and vegetable dishes. Ethiopian cooks in North America substitute jalapeño, serrano, and Cubanelle or Anaheim chilies for fresh chilies, and dried and ground cayenne, paprika, or Mexican chili replace the African varieties.

Bako Local

This spicy cayenne-type chili is tapered and smooth. It grows to about 5 inches long and about 1 inch wide.

Berbere

This chili matures from green to a 6-inch-long by 3/4-inch-wide red chili. Its pods swell slightly in the middle. When dried and ground the berbere chili has a rich, smokey flavor and aroma that make it an important Ethiopian variety. It is part of the spice paste called berbere.

Mareko Fana

This milder pepper is a variety of the berbere chili; it grows 6- to 7-inches long. It is used as part of the spice paste called berbere.

Mitmita

This narrow, hot red chili is about 3 inches long. It is often dried and blended with other spices before milling into powder.

FIGURE 11.27 Ethiopian valley.
Source: Arapov Sergey/Shutterstock.

FIGURE 11.28 Market in southern Ethiopia.
Source: © Sabena Jane Blackbird/Alamy.

ETHIOPIAN FLAVOR FOUNDATIONS

Ethiopian Signature Aromatic Vegetable Combo

Red shallot or onion, garlic, ginger, and chili

Traditional dishes were almost exclusively prepared with shallots, but due to cost and convenience, the modern cuisine has adopted the less intense yellow and red onions. Shallots and onions are the most important vegetable in the Ethiopian diet. Wealthy and poor Ethiopian households eat them daily. The amount depends on preference. Red shallots are prized.

Ethiopian Signature Seasonings

Liquid/Paste

T'ej (Mead or Honey Wine)

This fermented honey wine is used to flavor the famous berbere and w'ets. Usually, homemade t'ej is available throughout Ethiopia. T'ej has a high alcohol content, but is quite sweet depending on length of fermentation. It is flavored with the powdered leaves and twigs of *gesho*, a hops-like bittering agent that is a species of buckthorn. Gesho balances the sweetness with bitter-dryness that complements the complex flavors of Ethiopian food. *Berz* is the sweeter, less-alcoholic version, and is aged for less time. Sweet white wine may be substituted.

Vegetable/Fruit

Chilies

See *Ethiopian Chilies*.

Shallots

Ethiopians prize the purple, oval shallots. Cheaper and less flavorful red or white onions have replaced shallots in restaurants.

Herbal/Spice

These are only a few of the seasonings that Ethiopian cooks use.

FIGURE 11.29
Cayenne chilies.
Source: Dave King/DK Images.

Berbere Powder

Ground red berbere chili powder spiced with ground cardamom, fenugreek, ginger, coriander, cinnamon, clove, allspice, black pepper, and nutmeg plus garlic. It can be made as a dry mix or combined with oil and red wine or water to make a paste. To soften its bite, cooks substitute paprika for some of the chili.

Cardamom Seed (Elettaria Cardamomum or True Cardamom)

This ancient and pricey spice originated in south India. About 18 seeds reside in each green or brown pod. The crushed or ground seeds are hauntingly pungent, aromatic and warm with sweet lemony, camphor undertones that work well in sweet or savory dishes. See chapter *India, Indian Flavor Foundations*.

Cayenne Pepper

A highly pungent, hot powder ground from the large red, dried cayenne chili.

Ethiopian False Cardamom (Korerima)

This cardamom is native to Ethiopia and is grown in the southwest region. It is a large brown pod with sharper and harsher tasting seeds than true cardamom. It pairs well with spicy Ethiopian cuisine.

Bishop's Weed (Ajwain or Carom Seed)

This assertive spice, a member of the dill, caraway, and cumin family, is also used in Indian cuisine. The seeds resemble caraway and cumin seeds, but are slightly smaller, with a strong and spicy thyme, celery, and cumin

(Continued)

(Continued)

FIGURE 11.30 Ethiopian false cardamom pods.
Source: Dave King/DK Images.

flavor and fragrance. See chapter *India, Indian Flavor Foundations.*

Rue Seed and Leaf

The bitter seeds and blue-cheese flavored leaves are used in Ethiopian, Greek, and Mediterranean cooking and pair well with citrus. Ethiopian cooks season porridge with the seeds and use small amounts of the leaves in egg, meat, cheese, and fish dishes.

FIGURE 11.31 Rue plant.
Source: Birute Vijeikiene/Fotolia.

Ethiopian Black Cumin (Nigella)

Nigella seed is a small, black pungent-flavored seed used in India where it is called *kalonji*. It has a nutty, pleasant and enticing aroma, but somewhat bitter taste. See chapter *India, Indian Flavor Foundations.*

Fenugreek Seeds

These small legumes are square and a pale bronze color. Their warm, penetrating scent is maple-like and, indeed, the seeds are used commercially for making fake maple syrup. Their ground flavor is bittersweet, much like burned sugar, with an aftertaste of celery or lovage.

Sacred or Holy Basil (Hot Basil)

Closely related to sweet basil, the many types of holy basil have been used as a valued culinary and medicinal herb in India, Southeast Asia, and Africa. The variety used in Ethiopia is reddish-purple under leaves and on stems. The leaves are smaller and slightly hairy and have a peppery taste of camphor, anise, and mint that becomes more pronounced upon cooking. Ethiopians use dried holy basil shoots.

FIGURE 11.32 Sacred or holy basil.
Source: Dave King/DK Images.

SPICE AND PASTE

MITMITA

Another of the pantheon of spicy-hot Ethiopian seasonings, mitmita is similar to the Indian garam masala mixture, which makes use of (sometimes roasted) sweet spices like clove, cardamom, cinnamon, and black peppercorns. The orange-red mitmita powder, at its most basic, contains the small, dried, ground mitmita chili and roasted ground cardamom, roasted ground cloves, and salt. Occasionally dried holy basil, roasted, ground cumin, or ground ginger is added. Mitmita can be used as a condiment for dipping or sprinkling, for cooking or as a seasoning for kitfo (raw beef), or cooked fava beans.

Yields about 5-1/2 tablespoons

8 ounces fresh mitmita chili *or* bird's eye chilies
   or 1 ounce dried red chilies, 3/4 cup (3/4 ounce) broken, stemmed, and seeded
      or 3 tablespoons ground Korean red chili
         or 1 tablespoon cayenne powder and 2 tablespoons sweet paprika
1 tablespoon cardamom seed
Optional: 1 teaspoon cumin seed
1/2 teaspoon whole cloves
1 tablespoon kosher *or* sea salt

1 If using fresh chilies, dehydrate in dehydrator overnight or on racks in dry spot. Remove stems and seeds.

2 In a small skillet, dry roast cardamom, optional cumin, and cloves separately, and cool.

3 In batches, grind broken chilies, *if using*, and spices to a fine powder in a spice grinder. Mix with salt and ground chili *if using*, and store in airtight container.

FIGURE 11.33 Ethiopian chilies.
Source: © imagebroker/Alamy.

SIGNATURE RECIPE

SPICY-HOT RED CHILI AND SPICE PASTE (BERBERE)

Berbere is a basic ingredient in Ethiopian cuisine and is important to many dishes. The amount of berbere in a dish determines its spiciness. Western berbere lacks certain seasonings like rue and sacred basil.

Yields about 2-3/4 cups

Spices I

2 teaspoons cumin seed
1-1/2 teaspoons coriander seed
1 teaspoon cardamom pods, crushed lightly
   or 1/2 teaspoon cardamom seed
1 teaspoon fenugreek seed
1/2 teaspoon black peppercorns
1/2 teaspoon nigella seed
1/2 teaspoon chopped nutmeg, about 1/4 whole nutmeg
1/4 teaspoon whole cloves
Optional: 1/4 teaspoon crushed cinnamon stick
Optional: 1/4 teaspoon whole allspice

Spices II

5-1/4 to 5-1/2 ounces sweet Hungarian paprika, 1-1/2 cups
1-3/4 ounces, hot red chili powder like cayenne or Korean red chili, about 1/2 cup

4 ounces red onion, 1/2 cup peeled and finely diced
  or 3 ounces shallots, 3 medium, 1/2 cup peeled and diced
1 ounce garlic, 4 large cloves, crushed and peeled
About 1 ounce gingerroot, 2 tablespoons peeled and finely chopped
1/4 cup t'ej or dry red wine
Vegetable or olive oil for storing

1 Dry-pan roast **Spices I** in heavy 2- to 3-quart saucepan. Heat pan over medium-low and toast cumin, coriander, cardamom pods (if using cardamom seeds, toast with nigella mixture), fenugreek, and peppercorns. Stir constantly and toast until *fragrant* and one shade darker, 1 to 2 minutes. Pour spices into small mixing bowl to cool. Remove outer shell from cardamom and discard. Place seeds in with other spices.

2 Heat pan again and toast nigella, nutmeg, cloves, and optional cinnamon and allspice until fragrant. Scrape spices into bowl with other toasted spices. Cool. Grind spices to a powder in spice/coffee grinder.

3 **Combine Spices II:** paprika, red chili powder plus 1 tablespoon kosher salt in 2- to 3-quart saucepan. Toast over medium-low heat until fragrant, stirring constantly, 1 to 2 minutes. Remove pan from heat.

4 **Into a blender:** Pour all of **Spices I** and 4 tablespoons of the **Spices II** mixture, onion or shallots, garlic, ginger, wine, and 1/2-cup warm water. Blend to a smooth paste. Scrape paste into saucepan with remaining **Spices II**. Rinse out blender with 1 cup warm water and whisk water into spice mixture in saucepan. Heat saucepan over low heat. Simmer paste, folding and stirring occasionally, until fragrant and thick, 20 minutes.

5 Pack berberé into a wide-mouth 12-ounce glass jar. Cool paste to room temperature and cover with oil. Seal jar with lid, and refrigerate. Replenish oil each time the paste is used. Refrigerated and covered with oil, it will keep 5 to 6 months.

Source: *Foods of the World, African Cooking* by Time-Life Books.

Vary! Improvise!

☞ **Milder:** *Play with the proportion of paprika to chili powder. For a very mild version, increase paprika to 2 cups and decrease cayenne or ground chili to 2 tablespoons. For a true Ethiopian taste, go half and half.*

☞ **More Authentic:** *Dehydrate the 4 to 8 ounces diced red onion or shallot. Toast and grind with Spices I.*

☞ **Spread or Dip:** *Simmer 1/2 cup berbere with 1/4 cup t'ej or Riesling wine and 2 tablespoons oil for 15 minutes. Stir in lemon juice to taste and thin with water to a spreadable paste.*

SIGNATURE RECIPE

ETHIOPIAN SPICED BUTTER (NIT'IR QIBE OR NITER KIBBE)

Similar to Indian ghee, nit'ir qibe, seasons a range of Ethiopian dishes. Ethiopian cooks also prepare spiced oil called yetenet'tere zeyt.

Yields about 1-1/2 cups

Spices

1 teaspoon fenugreek seeds
3 green cardamom pods, crushed
1-1/2-inch long cinnamon stick, lightly crushed
1/2 teaspoon chopped whole nutmeg
3 whole cloves
2 teaspoons ground turmeric

1 pound unsalted butter, finely diced
4 to 5 ounces red onion, 1/2 cup minced
   or 3 ounces shallots, about 3 medium, 1/2 cup peeled and finely diced
3/4 ounce garlic, 3 large cloves, crushed and peeled
1 ounce gingerroot, 1 tablespoon peeled and minced

1. **Dry-pan roast spices:** Place fenugreek, cardamom, cinnamon, nutmeg, and cloves together in a heavy 2-quart saucepan. Cook over low heat. Stir constantly until fragrant, 1 to 2 minutes. Stir in turmeric and remove pan from heat. Turmeric should turn a shade darker, but don't burn it.

2. Immediately place butter into saucepan with spices and place back over low heat. Stir in onion or shallots, garlic, and gingerroot. Simmer butter over *very* low heat, *without stirring*, until milk solids clump, turn golden, and butter oil is clear, 30 to 45 minutes.

3. Line a fine strainer with several layers of folded cheesecloth and set over heatproof bowl. Strain hot nit'ir qibe through cheesecloth. Pick up edges of cheesecloth and gently squeeze out hot butter. There should be no solids in the butter. If there are, strain through clean cheesecloth a second time.

4. Transfer butter to clean 1-pint glass canning jar, seal, and refrigerate. Spiced butter will keep 2 to 3 months refrigerated.

COOK'S VOICE: MENKIR TAMRAT

Ethiopian-Born Passionate Cook East Bay, California

"I've seen what Ethiopian cuisine is capable of being, but I can't get it here. Vietnamese, Korean, Chinese, and other Asian cuisines, I've been told, are almost as good in the United States as they are there, because all the ingredients are now grown right here. You can't say the same for our cuisine . . . I had tried to make berbere using off-the-shelf chilies, but it just wouldn't come out right. I didn't realize that (using authentic peppers) made that much difference—in color, in heat, and in taste."

Source: From *Edible East Bay* by Patricia Hayse Haller.

Vary! Improvise!

☞ ***More Flavor:*** *Ethiopian chef and Chicago restaurateur Zenash Beyene sautés the onion until golden in some of the butter, adds garlic and ginger, and cooks until soft, adds spices, and cooks for a few minutes then simmers with the remaining butter.*

FIGURE 11.34 Flaxseed and oil.
Source: Elena Schweitzer/Fotolia.

ROASTED FLAXSEED PASTE (YETELBA LIQUT')

Affluent Ethiopians use plain roasted and ground flaxseed powder to thicken and flavor w'ets or stews. They spread the savory or sweet paste on bread as a snack or breakfast.

Yields 1-1/3 to 1-1/2 cups paste

5 ounces flaxseed, 1 cup

Savory Seasonings

2 tablespoons olive oil
1/2 teaspoon *Mitmita*, more to taste
1/2 teaspoon garlic powder
1 teaspoon honey
Optional: 3 to 4 tablespoons freshly squeezed lemon or lime juice

Sweet Seasonings

1/2 teaspoon cinnamon
Honey, to taste

1 Place flaxseed in a 10-inch skillet and heat over medium-low heat. Dry-roast seeds until they crackle and pop; don't over-roast. Seeds can be dry roasted or until they become popcorn fragrant, 5 to 12 minutes, depending on tastes. A seed should easily crush under a fingernail. Remove skillet from the heat and spread seeds onto a plate to cool.

2 Grind flaxseed in small batches in a spice grinder until finely powdered. (If using plain powder, pour powder into a jar. Seal tightly and refrigerate or freeze. Use to enrichen and thicken w'ets.

3 **To Use:** Pour toasted, ground seeds into a bowl and stir in either **savory seasonings** or **sweet seasonings**. Slowly stir in enough water to make a spreadable paste similar in consistency to peanut butter, about 1 cup. Season paste with salt (and if desired, freshly ground pepper) to taste. Rest paste in refrigerator 30 minutes to 1 hour. Taste again and re-season if necessary.

Source: *Exotic Ethiopian Cooking* by Daniel J. Mesfin.

FIGURE 11.35 T'eff plant.
Source: cdkeyser/Fotolia.

SPECIAL METHODS

Injera: Spongy Ethiopian Flatbread

Injera is to Ethiopians what flatbreads and roti are to Middle Eastern and Indian diners. Injera works as platter, starch, *and* utensil. A 16-inch injera set on a tray serves as a platter lining for small mounds of w'ets, salads, and numerous other dishes. Diners gather round and tear off pieces of injera and use it to enfold and convey bits of vegetable or stew to their mouths.

Injera is made with a millet-type cereal grain called *t'ef* or *t'eff—genus Eragrostis* or lovegrass, and it is more a poured sourdough pancake than hand-rolled or baked bread. T'eff is an Ethiopian staple high in iron, calcium, and minerals. It has symbiotic yeast, as on the surface of grapes and cabbage, which after several days of fermentation gives a sourdough flavor to the batter without the addition of yeast. (See *Glossary* under *T'eff* for more information.) Traditionally made on a flat clay griddle with a cover called a *mitad*, injera can also be successfully made in a heavy nonstick skillet with a lid.

SIGNATURE RECIPE

TWO TO THREE-DAY FERMENTED INJERA

In the United States, Ethiopian cooks and restaurant chefs use the Bethany Housewares 16-inch nonstick electric griddle with a lid for cooking their injera. They set it at its maximum 500 degrees and pour a cup or so of batter, roll it around, place the lid on, and cook the injera about 2 minutes on one side only. The cook scoops the injera onto a thin, flat, woven wicker round, and transfers it to a cotton tablecloth to cool. When fully cooled, the injera are stacked and wrapped in plastic wrap. As with pancakes, the pan needs to heat evenly before it will produce a top-notch injera, so the first one might not be the best.

Yields about 3-1/2 cups batter, four to six 12- to 13-inch-diameter injera

Starter

7 to 7-1/2 ounces unbleached flour, 1-1/2 cups
2-1/2 to 2-3/4 ounces t'eff flour, 1/2 cup
2-2/3 cups nonchlorinated or bottled spring water
1/4 teaspoon active dry yeast

Daily Feed/Injera Batter

About 3 ounces unbleached white flour, 10 tablespoons, *divided*
5/8 ounce t'eff flour, 2 tablespoons

1 **Prepare the starter:** Pour flours into 2-quart bowl, and vigorously whisk in water and yeast. Cover bowl with a cotton towel or cheesecloth. Set starter aside in a warm spot (70 to 80 degrees F) 24 hours.

2 **After one day of fermentation:** Whisk 2 tablespoons white flour into starter and cover; ferment 24 hours.

3 **After two days of fermentation:** Sniff batter. It should be bubbly and smell delicately sour. For a typical, strongly sour injera, whisk in 2 tablespoons white flour and ferment the starter another 24 hours.

4 **After two or three days of fermentation:** Whisk remaining white flour and the 2 tablespoons t'eff flour into *starter* to make *batter*. The batter should run off a spoon but coat it well—about the consistency of heavy cream. The batter should spread, with tilting, when poured into the pan like a slightly thick crepe batter.

5 **Cooking injera:** Heat a 12- to 13-inch nonstick pan over medium to medium-high heat. Sprinkle surface of pan with a pinch of kosher salt. Do this for each injera.

6 Pour 2/3 to 3/4 cup batter from a spouted measuring cup in the center. Rotate the pan so the batter covers the entire surface of pan evenly.

7 *Immediately cover pan with lid* and lower the heat to medium. Covering the pan will retain moisture and keep injera from cracking. Cook injera one side only without browning, 1 to 2 minutes. If injera cooks too long, it will become overly gummy and disintegrate. The characteristic *ain* bubbles should appear.

8 When the top is set and the edges begin to curl, lift edge of injera and slide flat silicone spatula under. Gently pick it up with hands and transfer injera to clean cotton towel or parchment-covered sheet pan to cool slightly. The injera will feel tender and slightly gummy, but as it cools, it will firm up and become stretchy-spongy.

9 Finish cooking remaining injera. Allow them to cool before stacking. Wrap tightly in plastic wrap and leave at room temperature up to 6 days. Do not refrigerate.

Storing Injera

Make only as much injera as needed for 5 to 6 days. Cool freshly cooked injera completely and stack in large zipper bags at room temperature. Injera bread stored in the refrigerator becomes brittle and dry.

FIGURE 11.36 Rolled injera bread.
Source: Otokimus/Shutterstock.

Vary! Improvise!

☞ *Search out ivory t'eff flour and use in place of dark t'eff flour.*
☞ *Use equal parts t'eff, barley flour, and unbleached white flour instead of t'eff and white.*

FIGURE 11.37 Cooking injera traditionally on a mitad (or mogogo).
Source: PhotoStock-Israel/Alamy.

FIGURE 11.38 Lefse pan used for making injera bread.
Source: Bethany Housewares, Inc.

FIGURE 11.39 Lefse pan lid.
Source: Bethany Housewares, Inc.

INJERA FROM SOURDOUGH STARTER

Yields 10 to 11 cups batter, ten to eleven 12-inch-diameter injera

Sourdough Starter

Yields 3 cups

9 to 10 ounces unbleached white flour, 2 cups
2-1/2 to 2-3/4 ounces t'eff flour, 1/2 cup
2 cups lukewarm non-chlorinated *or* bottled spring water
2 ounces unwashed organic grapes with chalky bloom, about 12

Daily Feed

2-1/4 ounces unbleached white flour, 1/2 cup

Injera Batter

2 cups *Sourdough Starter*
14 to 15 ounces unbleached white flour, 3 to 3-1/3 cups
5-1/2 to 5-2/3 ounces t'eff flour, 1 cup
5 cups lukewarm nonchlorinated *or* spring water

1 **One week before using prepare Sourdough Starter:** Vigorously whisk (about 100 times) together white flour, 1/2 cup t'eff flour, and water in a 2-quart mixing bowl. Drop grapes into batter, drape bowl with cheesecloth or clean cotton towel, and place in warm spot (70 to 80 degrees F) with good air circulation.

2 **Daily:** Vigorously stir the **Sourdough Starter** batter. Agitation stimulates yeast activity. After 2 to 3 days (and before stirring), there should be tiny bubbles that release on the surface of the batter. (If after 3 days there is no visible yeast activity, stir in 1/4 teaspoon active dry yeast.)

3 **Daily feed the sourdough starter:** When yeast activity is noticeable, pick out fruit and discard. Vigorously stir in 2 tablespoons white flour every day for the next 4 days. The batter will thicken and rise. The batter is ready when thick, bubbly, and sour smelling.

4 **One day before cooking prepare** *Injera Batter:* Whisk together 2 cups sourdough starter, white and t'eff flour, and 5 cups water in a mixing bowl. Batter should coat a spoon well, but run off. If batter is too thin, whisk in more white flour. Cover bowl with cheesecloth or towel and set aside to ferment at 70 to 80 degrees F for 24 hours.

5 Batter should be slightly thicker than the consistency of crepe batter. Stir in water or add a little flour as necessary. Cook injera as for *Two to Three-Day Fermented Injera* starting at step 5.

Source: *Wild Fermentation* by Sandor Ellix Katz.

Maintaining the Sourdough Starter

Whisk 2 cups lukewarm water and 1 cup unbleached white flour into remaining 1 cup of starter, cover and leave to ferment 12 to 24 hours. Refrigerate starter. Feed every 4 to 5 days by whisking in 2 tablespoons white flour.

ETHIOPIAN BEAN AND SEED PURÉE (ELIBET)

In Ethiopia, broad beans (fava) are cooked in many ways; they come in green, beige, or brown. Beige beans deliver a creamy colored elibet.

Yields 4 cups, 6 to 8 servings

8 ounces dried broad beans, dried shell-on fava beans, *or* large dried lima beans, 1-1/2 cups
2-1/2 ounces sunflower seeds, 1/2 cup
3 to 4 tablespoons lemon juice, 1 large lemon
1/2 ounce garlic, 2 large cloves, 1 tablespoon peeled and minced
2 tablespoons sunflower oil
   or 2 tablespoons olive oil

For Serving

Injera bread or Arabic flatbread

1 Cover beans with cold water and 2 teaspoons kosher salt and soak overnight or quick-soak in boiling water and 2 teaspoons kosher salt for 1 hour. Drain, rinse, and drain beans. Peel tough outer skins from favas, and discard. Place peeled favas or lima beans into 4-quart pot, and set aside.

2 Rinse sunflower seeds with cold water. Pour into blender with 1-1/2 cups cold water, and purée until smooth. Pour sunflower seed purée into pot with beans. Rinse out blender with 1 cup cold water and pour into beans. Bring mixture to a boil, lower heat, and cover pot. Simmer bean and seed purée until beans are very tender, about 45 minutes. Cool mixture to lukewarm.

3 Pour bean-seed mixture into food processor. Add lemon juice, garlic, 1 teaspoon kosher salt, and oil. Purée mixture until smooth, about 5 minutes. Taste purée and adjust seasonings.

4 **To Serve:** Pile *elibet* into serving vessel and serve with injera or pita. Refrigerate up to 4 days or freeze.

Source: *Haile-Mariam Yewoineshet, http://www.yewoinfamilyrecipes.com/.*

ETHIOPIAN BUTTERMILK CHEESE (AYIB OR IAB)

Made from buttermilk, this lightly tangy soft white curd cheese (similar to Indian paneer) is often flavored with herbs and spices and served as a last course in lieu of dessert. High-fat buttermilk with no additives from a local dairy makes the best cheese.

Yields 3 cups, 1-1/2 pounds

3 quarts buttermilk

Optional Spices

2 ounces *Nitir Kibbe*, 1/4 cup
1/4 ounce garlic, 1 large clove, peeled and halved
1/4 teaspoon ground black pepper
1/8 teaspoon ground cardamom

1 Heat buttermilk in 6-quart pan over *very* low heat and stir occasionally until an instant-read thermometer measures 120 to 145 degrees F (but no higher, or the cheese will take on a cooked flavor). The whey will separate and large mass of curds will form float on top, 25 to 30 minutes.

2 **If making spiced cheese:** In a small pan on low heat, simmer nitir kibbe with garlic 1 to 2 minutes. Remove pan from heat and cool butter. Remove garlic and discard.

3 Set up a strainer lined with cheesecloth over bowl or saucepan. Pour buttermilk curds through and drain 1 hour without pressing. Discard whey or use to cook greens. The cheese is ready for use.

4 **For optional spiced cheese:** Crumble cheese and mix with seasoned nitir kibbe, 1 teaspoon kosher salt, pepper, and cardamom. Set aside at room temperature until ready to use, or refrigerate up to 1 week.

FIGURE 11.40 Ethiopian mesob (wicker table with lid).
Source: © Jeff Greenberg/Alamy.

Vary! Improvise!

☞ *Serve with Berbere paste (or stir a little Berbere into elibet) for a spicy variation.*

☞ *Substitute about 1 to 1-1/4 cups shelled dry favas (6-1/2 to 8 ounces) for shell-on.*

Vary! Improvise!

☞ *Stir 4 tablespoons lemon juice into buttermilk before simmering for a tarter flavor.*

☞ *Herbed Ayib: Fold in a mixture of fresh and/or dried herbs like parsley and basil. Season with salt and pepper.*

ETHIOPIAN SPICED BEEF (KITFO OR KITFO LEBLEB)

This dish is usually served raw. In this recipe it is mostly uncooked, so the beef should be high quality, freshly ground just before serving, using scrupulously clean equipment.

Yields 2 cups, 4 to 6 servings

1 pound trimmed boneless sirloin *or* top round steak
4 tablespoons *Nitir Kibbe*
1/4 to 1/3 ounce garlic, 2 medium cloves, 2 to 3 teaspoons peeled and minced
Optional: 2 to 3 teaspoons *Mitmita*

For Serving

Injera or Arabic flatbread

1 Chill meat grinder attachment or food processor bowl and blade. Dice meat into 1/2- to 1-inch cubes. Put through meat grinder with coarse blade *or* into food processor and pulse-grind until meat is coarsely chopped. Alternatively, chop meat into an even 1/8- to 1/4-inch dice.

2 Heat *nitir kibbe* over low heat and add garlic and optional *mitmita*. Simmer 1 to 2 minutes.

3 Kitfo may be prepared three ways: raw, warm, or cooked to medium-rare.
   - Raw: Fold warm nitir kibbe mixture into raw meat. Season with 1 to 1-1/2 teaspoons kosher salt.
   - Warm: Remove pan from heat, and stir in meat until just warm. Season with salt.
   - Cooked: Simmer meat, stirring to cook it evenly, until medium-rare. Season with salt.

4 **To Serve:** Immediately mound kitfo into bowl or onto platter on top of injera.

SIMMER, STEW, POACH, BOIL, AND STEAM

ETHIOPIAN SOUP

Ethiopian kitchens seem to always have a pot simmering over an open fire or charcoal brazier, but soup isn't a large part of the cuisine. Harry Kloman, author of *Mesob Across America: Ethiopian Food in the U.S.A.*, says, "Soup is sort of a Western-influenced adaptation. *Misir shorba*, literally, lentil soup, is sometimes served at restaurants.

The Recipe of Love, an Ethiopian cookbook by Aster Ketsela Belayneh, who owns a restaurant in Toronto, has recipes for such soups as beef barley, ox tongue, kidney bean, lamb and lentil, lentil and potato, and even chicken soup with wine. But again, these are adaptations, not 'native' cuisine per se."

FIGURE 11.41   An Ethiopian home.
Source: Pascal RATEAU/Fotolia.

W'et and Alich'a: Ethiopian Stew

The most common meal for Ethiopians is injera and a stew of meat, legumes, or vegetables. Thick and creamy stews or *w'ets* and *alich'as* lie somewhere between the Western idea of sauce and stew. Seasoned with browned shallots or red onions, garlic, ginger, various spices, berbere, or niter kibbe, w'ets are hearty, spicy, and highly flavorful while alich'as are flavorful, but with less spicy-heat, and usually seasoned with turmeric. Good for eating with injera and hands, these dishes are made with lamb, poultry, or beef, but never pork. They form the main course of a meal. Muslim and Christian cooks prepare vegetarian-vegan w'ets and alich'as on fasting days.

Signature Technique: Ethiopian Stew (W'et or Alich'a)

An Ethiopian stew may be either a spicy we't seasoned with berbere or a mild alich'a seasoned with turmeric.

1 Classical Ethiopian cooks dry-sauté shallots or red onions over medium to medium-low heat in a heavy earthenware pan **without fat** until soft, 7 to 15 minutes. If using metal, when the bottom of pan browns, deglaze with a small amount of water. Keep cooking onions until the bottom of pan browns again and deglaze with water. Repeat this process once or twice more until shallots or onions are browned, moist, and very soft.

2 Stir in oil or clarified/spiced butter (*nitir kibbe*). Ethiopian cooks minimally use 1 to 2 tablespoons oil or butter per serving. Not only are oils and butter an Ethiopian's main source of dietary fat, they also enrich vegetarian dishes, carry flavor, and keep food from sticking.

3 Simmer onions in oil or spiced butter 2 minutes over medium heat.

4 Berbere should always be cooked in fat before adding wet ingredients. Ethiopian cooks refer to the flavor of uncooked berbere as *kulait*. Stir in berbere spices or paste (or turmeric for an alich'a) and dry spices, and cook over medium to medium-low heat until moist-roasted or very dry-roasted, anywhere from 20 minutes to 1 hour. Stir in puréed fresh garlic and ginger.

5 One by one, stir in other ingredients like vegetables, legumes, and meat and simmer in fat for a few minutes to infuse flavor.

6 Add liquid as necessary to form a thick sauce, and simmer until ingredients are fully cooked. Many stews are cooked so that a thick purée-sauce forms, which makes them easier to eat with injera.

7 Taste the stew and season with salt and pepper. For more flavor, drizzle stew with *nitir kibbe*.

COOK'S VOICE: PROFESSOR JAMES C. MCCANN

Head of African Studies Center, Boston University Boston, Massachusetts

"Dry frying (shallots) is an important step. Using oil (to brown shallots) is cheating. Clay cooking pots are treated with 'gomen zer' (mustard oil from Ethiopian kale seed) to reduce sticking and season the pot. In a dish like *doro w'et*, the butter is added for flavor at the end, not for sautéing. Use of oil is a modern, urban affectation. *Nug* or niger seed oil is commonly used, but has historically been relatively scarce, and recently, hard to get in Ethiopia."

Source: James McCann, STIRRING THE POT, Ohio University Press © 2009. Used with permission of James McCann.

FIGURE 11.42 A: Injera bread topped with Ethiopian chicken stew (doro w'et), chickpea flour "fish" in spicy sauce (yeshimbra asa), and simple spiced collard greens (ye gomen kitfo). B: Onions and shallots browned without fat for Ethiopian chicken stew.

ETHIOPIAN CHICKEN STEW
(DORO W'ET)

Ethiopian cooks say that the chicken must be a freshly killed hen and divided into 12 parts. Some cooks soak the skinned chicken in cold water-salt brine for 30 minutes prior to cooking.

Yields about 2-1/2 quarts, 8 servings

5 pounds chicken legs, thighs, and breasts, about 4-1/2 pounds fat and skin removed
2 tablespoons fresh lemon or lime juice, 1/2 large lemon or lime
1-1/2 pounds shallots or red onions or a mixture, 6 cups finely diced
3 to 4 tablespoons vegetable oil
1 cup *Berbere*
1/4 cup tomato paste
1-1/2 cups *tej* or dry red wine
 or 1 cup red wine plus 1/2 cup sherry
1-1/2 ounces garlic, 6 large cloves, 3 tablespoons peeled and minced
1/2 to 3/4 ounce peeled gingerroot, 4 teaspoons minced
1/2 teaspoon crushed ajwain seed (also called bishop's weed)
Optional: 1/4 teaspoon crushed nigella seed (also called Ethiopian black cumin)
3/4 to 1 cup *Nitir Kibbe*
1 teaspoon ground cardamom or 1-1/2 teaspoons crushed seeds
1/2 teaspoon freshly ground black pepper
8 large eggs

For Serving

Injera bread *or* cooked long-grain rice

1   Rinse skinned chicken parts and pat dry. Make two 1-inch slits on each piece of chicken and place into large mixing bowl. Sprinkle with 2 teaspoons kosher salt and drizzle lime or lemon juice over chicken. Mix well and set aside.

2   Heat 6- to 8-quart heavy pot over medium heat. Stir in onion and cook, stirring occasionally. After 5 to 10 minutes, onion will begin to brown and stick to pan; stir in 2 tablespoons water and scrape onion from pan. Continue this process of browning and sticking and deglazing with water until onions are completely soft and browned, 20 to 30 minutes.

3   Stir oil, bebere, tomato paste, and red wine into onion. Cook over medium-low heat until mixture is very browned and dryish, about 30 minutes. Cooking the berbere long enough is an important step. Stir in garlic, ginger, ajwain, and optional nigella. Lower the heat and simmer mixture 5 minutes. Stir in **niter kibbe**. Simmer on low 15 minutes. (This should yield about 3-1/2 cups thick base sauce. It may be refrigerated at this point, and used within four days.)

4   Stir chicken into thick base. Simmer mixture 10 to 15 minutes to infuse flavor into chicken.

5   Stir in enough water, about 1-1/2 cups, to form a thick, pourable sauce. Partially cover pot and simmer chicken 15 minutes. Remove lid. Stir in cardamom and black pepper, and simmer chicken, stirring occasionally, until very tender and sauce is thickened, about 30 minutes. Remove pot from heat.

6   **While chicken simmers:** Place eggs into small saucepan and cover with cold water by 1-inch. Bring to a boil. Remove pan from heat, cover pan, and time eggs exactly 10 minutes. Drain hot water and run cold water over eggs. Crack ends of eggs and rest in cold water 10 to 15 minutes. Drain and peel eggs, leaving them whole. Refrigerate if not using immediately.

7   **To Serve:** Gently fold hard-cooked eggs into chicken stew. Simmer 5 minutes, and remove pot from heat. Serve doro we't hot with injera or cooked long-grain rice.

Vary! Improvise!

Ethiopian Meat Stew (Sega We't)

☞ *Substitute 2 to 2-1/2 pounds boneless, trimmed lamb leg or beef instead of chicken. Reduce onions by half. Dice meat in l-inch cubes and brown on all sides before simmering. Omit water.*

☞ ***Less heat:*** *Substitute sweet Hungarian paprika for part of berbere.*

☞ ***More heat:*** *Mix ground cayenne with berbere.*

SPICY LENTIL STEW (MESIR WE'T)

Drizzle lentils with nitir kibbe *to boost their flavor.*

Yields 6 to 7 cups, 6 servings

14 ounces red lentils, 2 cups, rinsed and drained
8 to 9 ounces red onions, 2 cups peeled and finely diced
4 tablespoons sunflower or olive oil
2 tablespoons *Berbere*
8 ounces tomato, 1 medium-large, about 1 cup cored and diced into 1/2-inch cubes
1/2 ounce gingerroot, 1 tablespoon peeled and minced
1/2 ounce garlic, 2 large cloves, 1 tablespoon peeled and minced

For Serving

Injera bread

1 Pour lentils and 4 cups cold water into 4-quart saucepan. Bring to a boil, lower heat, cover pot, and simmer lentils 15 minutes; stir occasionally to keep bottom from sticking.

2 Heat oil in a 4-quart saucepan over medium heat. Stir in onions and cook until soft. Stir in berberé and tomatoes. Simmer berberé until fragrant and thick, adding water as needed to keep berberé from burning and sticking, 30 to 40 minutes. Stir in ginger and garlic; simmer 2 minutes. Scrape cooked lentils into mixture.

3 Stir a little water into lentils if they are too thick. Bring spiced lentils to a simmer, cover partially, and simmer over low heat 20 minutes, stirring occasionally to prevent sticking. Lentils should not be too runny. Season lentils with salt and black pepper to taste.

4 **To Serve:** Pile lentils onto platter covered with injera bread and serve.

FIGURE 11.43 Brown lentils.
Source: lapas77/Fotolia.

FAUX MIT'IN SHIRO POWDER

Although the traditional way to make mit'in shiro is with spices toasted whole and ground, this shortcut of mixing ground spices is probably the way many Ethiopian restaurants prepare it. Alter the seasonings to your taste. For every 4 ounces (1 cup) plain chickpea flour, stir in 4 tablespoons mit'in shiro powder.

Yields 1/2 cup, enough for 8 ounces (2 cups) chickpea flour.

2 tablespoons mild ground red chili (Korean chili powder), more if more heat is desired

  or 2 tablespoons ground cayenne pepper (spicier)

2 tablespoons paprika

2 teaspoons ground ginger

2 teaspoons garlic powder

2 teaspoons ground fenugreek

1 teaspoon ground coriander

1/2 teaspoon ground cardamom

1/4 teaspoon ground allspice

1/4 teaspoon ground nutmeg

1/8 teaspoon ground clove

1/8 teaspoon ground cinnamon

ETHIOPIAN SPICY CHICKPEA FLOUR STEW (YESHIMBRA SHIRO W'ET)

Ethiopian cooks use two types of chickpea flour, mit'in shiro and shiro powder. Shiro powder is plain chickpea flour. Mit'in shiro is an orange mixture of chickpea flour (and sometimes other legumes like fava and split peas) blended with important Ethiopian spices and herbs like ground cardamom, bishop's weed, black cumin, dried holy basil, garlic powder, and ground ginger. This popular, tasty dish is quick and easy to prepare, economical, and highly nutritious.

Yields about 3 cups thick or 3-1/2 cups thinner, 6 servings

5 ounces shallots or red onions or a mixture, 1 cup peeled and finely minced
4 tablespoons sunflower oil
2 tablespoons *Berbere* paste
1/4 ounce garlic, 1 large clove, 1-1/2 teaspoons peeled and minced
1/4 teaspoon Ethiopian *black cumin seed* (nigella)
2 ounces plain chickpea flour, 1/2 cup
2 tablespoons *Faux Mit'in Shiro Powder*
1/4 teaspoon cardamom powder
Optional: 1 tablespoon freshly squeezed lemon juice

For Serving

Injera bread or cooked rice

1 Heat a 2-quart saucepan over medium to medium-low heat. Stir in onion and cook until tender without oil. When bottom of pan becomes very brown, drizzle in 2 tablespoons water, and continue to cook onions. Repeat this process with 2 tablespoons water twice more. Onions should be soft and brown, 15 to 20 minutes. (To speed browning, "cheat" and use half the oil to brown the onions.)

2 Stir in oil, berbere, garlic, and black cumin seed. Simmer on low heat 7 minutes. Stir in 1 cup water, and bring to a boil.

3 Sift chickpea flour into a small bowl and slowly whisk 1 cup cold water into it until no lumps remain. Slowly whisk mixture into simmering spice mixture. Bring mixture to a boil, lower the heat, partially cover pan, and simmer stew 30 minutes. Stir stew occasionally and add water (1 to 1-1/2 cups) as necessary to keep stew the consistency of slightly thinned sour cream. Stir in cardamom, and season stew with salt and pepper. Simmer 10 minutes more.

4 **To Serve:** Taste w'et and adjust flavors with salt, pepper, and optional lemon juice. The stew should be smooth and thick, but if it thickens too much, thin with boiling water. Serve shiro w'et warm with injera or rice.

Vary! Improvise!

☞ Substitute 2 tablespoons Nitir Kibbe *for 2 tablespoons of the oil.*

☞ *The "bone structure" of shiro w'et makes a great start for vegetarian dishes. How might it be varied?*

FIGURE 11.44 Deep-fried chickpea "fish" fritters.

CHICKPEA FLOUR "FISH" IN SPICY SAUCE (YESHIMBRA ASA)

These fish are traditional Lenten food, so oil is used instead of spiced butter. They are often served with spicy lentil salad and injera.

Yields 4 to 5 cups, 4 to 6 servings

Chickpea "Fish" Fritters

Yields about 12 ounces dough, about sixty 1-inch by 1-1/2-inch "fish" or about thirty 1-inch by 3-inch "fish"

About 11 ounces plain chickpea flour *or* plain Indian besan, 3 cups
1 teaspoon coarsely ground white or black pepper
2 ounces shallot or onion, 4 tablespoons peeled and finely minced
1/4 ounce garlic, 1 large clove, 1-1/2 teaspoons peeled and minced

Chickpea flour for rolling
3 to 4 cups vegetable oil for deep-frying

Sauce

8 ounces red onions, 2 cups peeled and finely diced
   or 4 ounces shallots and 4 ounces red onions, 2 cups peeled and finely diced
1/4 cup sunflower oil
1/2 cup *Berbere*
1/2 ounce garlic, 2 large cloves, 1 tablespoon peeled and minced
1/2 teaspoon ground cardamom
Optional: 1/4 teaspoon nigella seed (Ethiopian black cumin)
1/4 ounce gingerroot, 1 teaspoon peeled and grated

For Serving

Injera bread or hot, cooked rice

1 **Fish dough:** Sift chickpea flour and pour into mixing bowl. Make a well in the center and pour in 2 teaspoons kosher salt, pepper, onion, and garlic. Stir ingredients together and *gradually* add cold water in 2 tablespoon increments until dough just comes together, about 1/2 to 3/4 cup water. With oiled hands, knead until dough forms a smooth, compact ball the consistency of playdough. Wrap dough in plastic and set aside to rest 15 minutes.

2 **Roll fish:** Cut a large square of plastic wrap and set on work surface; sprinkle with chickpea flour. Roll out half the dough on flour to an even 1/4-inch thickness. With a 1-inch by 1-1/2-inch to 1-inch by 3-inch fish-shaped cutter, or by hand, cut out fish shapes. Repeat with second half of dough. Re-roll scraps and use. Set fish onto parchment-covered sheet pan, and cover loosely with clean cotton towel.

3 **Fish fry:** Heat fresh oil in deep-fryer or 4-quart saucepan (to 2- to 3-inch depth). When oil reaches 360 degrees F, fry 4 to 5 fish at a time until puffed and golden, 3 to 4 minutes. Maintain heat around 350 degrees F. Turn fish frequently so they fry evenly. Transfer to paper towels to drain. Chickpea fish may be fried 1 day ahead, and refrigerated until needed.

   • **Baked fish:** The chickpea flour fish may be baked instead of deep-fried, but they won't have the light texture of deep-fried "fish." Stir in 6 tablespoons oil into flour before adding water. Preheat oven to 375 degrees F. Cut out chickpea fish shapes, place on baking sheet and into oven to bake until golden, about 25 minutes.

4 **Dry-fry onions for sauce:** Heat a heavy, deep 11- to 12-inch skillet or 6-quart pot over medium heat. Stir in onions *without fat* and cook, stirring constantly, until soft and browned, 20 to 30 minutes. If onions brown too quickly, lower the heat or sprinkle with water to deglaze.

5 **Sauce:** Stir oil into skillet with onions and cook 1 minute. Stir in berbere, garlic, cardamom, nigella, and ginger and reduce heat to low. Cook paste 10 to 15 minutes, stirring constantly, until fragrant. Pour in 2 cups water. Continue to stir and cook mixture until it thickens slightly. Season with salt. Leave sauce slightly chunky, or purée until smooth with an immersion blender.

6 **Add fish:** Immerse the "fish" into the sauce, reduce heat, partially cover pan, and simmer mixture 30 minutes. Check sauce for consistency. Fish will absorb liquid and thicken sauce. Stir in water as necessary to maintain a sauce that will coat a spoon and run off.

7 **To Serve:** Transfer chickpea fish to heated platter, and spoon sauce over them. Serve with injera or rice.

Source: *Foods of the World, African Cooking* by Time-Life Books.

ANOTHER ETHIOPIAN BREAD: DEFO DABO

Defo Dabo is a giant Ethiopian yeast bread made for every important occasion. Baked in a traditional clay pan, this bread symbolizes sharing and festivities. Its extra large size serves a multitude of friends, family, neighbors, and relatives—and so helps to strengthen ties between people.

SALAD AND VEGETABLE METHODS

ETHIOPIAN LENTIL SALAD (AZIFA)

Spice this up with a little Mitmita, *or by substituting sliced and browned shallots for the green onions.*

Yields 5-1/2 to 6 cups, 4 to 6 servings

14 ounces brown lentils, 2 cups

Dressing

4 tablespoons sunflower *or* olive oil
4 tablespoons fresh lemon *or* lime juice, 1 large lemon or lime
2 teaspoons Dijon mustard
1/2 teaspoon garlic powder
1/2 ounce trimmed parsley, 1/4 cup chopped
1/4 ounce basil leaves, 2 tablespoons finely sliced

8 ounce ripe tomato, 1 medium-large, 1 to 1-1/4 cups finely diced
1 ounce trimmed green onions, about 2 large, 1/4 cup chopped
1 ounce jalapeño chili, 1 medium, 2 tablespoons stemmed, seeded, and finely diced, more to taste

For Serving

Injera Bread
Simple Spiced Collards and/or *Ethiopian Ginger Spiced Vegetables*

1 **Cook lentils:** Rinse lentils and place in 4-quart saucepan. Cover with 6 cups water. Bring to a boil over high heat, reduce heat, and simmer lentils until just tender, 20 minutes. Pour lentils through strainer, discard cooking water, and pour lentils into mixing bowl to cool.

2 **Prepare dressing:** In a medium bowl, whisk together oil, lemon or lime juice, mustard, garlic, parsley, and basil. Fold in tomato, green onion, and chili. Mix dressing and vegetables with lentils and lightly mash the lentils. Taste salad, and season with salt and freshly ground pepper. Rest lentils at room temperature 1 hour to develop flavor.

3 **To Serve:** Pile room temperature lentils onto platter spread with injera. Serve with other dishes like *Simple Spiced Collards* and/or *Ethiopian Ginger Spiced Vegetables* and rolled up injera bread.

Source: Haile-Mariam Yewoineshet, http://www.yewoinfamilyrecipes.com/.

ETHIOPIAN GINGER-SPICED VEGETABLES (YATAKLETE KILKIL)

Yataklete kilkil, also known as yatakilt alich'a, is a popular mild-flavored Lenten vegetarian dish.

Yields 6 cups, 4 to 6 servings

1 pound new potatoes, about 6 small, 3 cups (peeled if desired) diced into 3/4-inch cubes
8 ounces carrots, about 4 medium, 2 cups peeled and cut into 1/4-inch rounds
12 ounces green beans, about 3 cups trimmed and halved
4 tablespoons sunflower or olive oil
12 to 14 ounces onions, 3 cups peeled and diced
1/2 to 3/4 ounce garlic, 2 to 3 large cloves, 1 to 1-1/2 tablespoons peeled and minced
1-1/2 ounces gingerroot, 1-1/2 tablespoons peeled and minced
1 teaspoon turmeric
1/2 teaspoon ground coriander
1/2 teaspoon ground cumin

Garnish

1/4 teaspoon ground cardamom
1/4 teaspoon ground nutmeg

1 Set up 6-quart pot with steamer and water. Steam potatoes until tender, about 10 minutes. Steam carrots, then green beans, until crisp-tender, 4 to 5 minutes. Reserve steaming water. Cool vegetables, and set aside in bowl.

2 Heat oil in 6-quart pot over medium heat. Add onion and cook until soft, 5 to 7 minutes. Stir in garlic, ginger, turmeric, coriander, and cumin and cook until garlic and ginger are soft, 3 to 4 minutes.

3 Stir in cooked vegetables, cardamom, nutmeg, and 1 cup reserved steaming water. Simmer over medium-low heat, partially covered, 15 to 20 minutes. Season with salt and freshly ground black pepper. Serve hot or at room temperature.

Vary! Improvise!

☞ *Different Vegetables: Use whatever is seasonally available like cauliflower, cabbage, zucchini, green beans, or bell peppers.*
☞ *Classic Vegetable Combos: Onion, potato, green beans, and carrot, or onion, potato, cabbage, and carrots with turmeric.*
☞ *More Heat: Stem, seed, and finely dice 1 jalapeño chili. Cook with garlic and ginger.*

FIGURE 11.45 Women vegetable sellers.
Source: derejeb/Fotolia.

GOMEN (ETHIOPIAN GREENS)

Vegetables are an important part of the Ethiopian diet. Ethiopia is known for a diversity of native wild and cultivated food plants and vegetables, which have been grown traditionally in home gardens. Two brassicas native to Ethiopia, *Brassica carinata* and *Brassica nigra*, are similar to collards or kale, two leafy brassicas. (Brassicas are members of the mustard family along with cabbage.) Brassica carinata, also called *loshuu*, grows throughout eastern and southern Africa in both lowland and highland conditions. Seeds of high-potential crops like Brassica and Amarantus have been collected and preserved in an Ethiopian national genebank.

SIMPLE SPICED COLLARD GREENS (YE GOMEN KITFO)

Simple, but exotic and spicy, the layers of flavor in this dish can be complex or simple depending upon what is available.

Yields 4 cups, about 4 servings

1 pound trimmed, stemmed collard greens
3 tablespoons *Niter Kibbe* or clarified butter
   or vegetable oil
1/2 teaspoon cardamom powder (double if not using *mitmita*)
1/8 teaspoon nigella seed
1 teaspoon garlic powder
   or 1/2 ounce garlic, 2 large cloves, 1 tablespoon peeled and minced
2 teaspoons *Mitmita*
   or 1 teaspoon chili flakes, 1/4 teaspoon ground cumin, and 1/8 teaspoon ground clove

1   Wash and drain collards. Stack leaves and make a lengthwise cut. Slice collards into 1/2-inch ribbons and then crosswise into squares. You should have about 10 cups.

2   Bring 2 quarts cold water to a boil in a 6-quart pot. Stir in collard greens and stir occasionally. Boil collards until very, very tender, about 20 to 30 minutes. Drain collards into colander and rinse with cold water. Drain well. Rinse out pot and wipe dry.

3   Set pot back on burner over medium heat. Stir in butter or oil, cardamom, nigella, garlic, freshly ground black pepper, and cook spices 30 to 60 seconds. Stir in **mitmita** and collards and toss until warmed through. Season with salt and black pepper to taste. Serve with injera bread.

Vary! Improvise!

☞ **Collards with Ethiopian Cheese (Yegomen Kitfo):** Add 1/2 to 1 ounce ginger, 1 tablespoon peeled and minced, to butter or oil, and cook briefly. Fold 6 to 8 ounces unsalted, un-spiced homemade Ethiopian buttermilk cheese (ayib), 3/4 to 1 cup crumbled, or 8 ounces unsalted farmers cheese into collards with spiced butter and mitmita.

FIGURE 11.46 Southern Ethiopia.
Source: Jan Martin Will/Shutterstock.

WEST AFRICA

THE REPUBLIC OF SENEGAL: GEM OF WEST AFRICA

Cultural Mélange

Condé Nast Traveler travel and music writer Amy Wilentz, in L'Afrique, Mon Amour, wrote that Senegalese food exhibits a "grand historico-cultural mélange." This mélange translates into cuisine touched with a French influence of cream, mustard, onion, and garlic; Muslim attributes with halal meat and marinated, grilled fish and chicken and an absence of pork, joined with the African bedrock of spicy-heat, peanuts, and root vegetables. Wilentz points out that despite all this culinary melding, Africa still dominates in all things Senegalese, cascading over all recent culinary arrivals and "making them its own."

Senegal is a sunny semi-tropical country on the North Atlantic Ocean known for its striking landscape, beaches, wildlife, urban cultural scene, and five World Heritage sites. Elegant women with intensely hued fabric wound around their heads wear bold and brilliant clothing in colors that echo the region's many tropical fruits and vegetables. Roasted peanuts scent the air of Senegal's vibrant markets. Baobab trees, the sacred symbol of Senegal, dot the ancient landscape.

Paleolithic and Neolithic axes and arrows, stone circles, and ceramic, copper, and iron artifacts found in the West African region that is modern Senegal reveal that it has been inhabited since ancient times. Several waves of migrating people moved there from the north and east, possibly from the region of Egypt. Gold, salt, and cloth gave the earliest empire, the *Soninke*, power and wealth while the camel expanded the trade on the Trans-Saharan route.

During the Middle Ages the *Wolof, Serer*, and *Toucouleur* tribes migrated in from the north. During the eleventh century, North Africans traded foods, cinnamon, cloves, mint, wool, pearls, and copper for slaves and gold, and converted the Toucouleur to the Islamic faith.

Over centuries, the land that is modern Senegal shifted among several kingdoms. During the fifteenth century, Portuguese traders explored the region, probably introducing New World chilies, tomatoes, and potatoes. Coconuts, maize, cassava, pineapple, guavas, and peanuts arrived in Africa with various explorers and traders during the sixteenth through eighteenth centuries.

A group of states called the Wolof established the *Jolof Empire*, which disintegrated by the seventeenth century. During the seventeenth century, French and Dutch traders established settlements at the mouth of the Senegal River and on Gorée Island near Dakar. They traded wheat and pepper for ivory and slaves. From the Seven Years' War in the eighteenth century until the nineteenth century Napoleonic Wars, France and Great Britain struggled for control of the rich region of Senegal and Gambia (Senegambia). In 1815, the Congress of Vienna awarded possession of Senegal to the French. By the middle of the nineteenth century, France had moved inland, exporting slaves, ivory, and gum Arabic. By the end of the century, Senegal became the seat of government for French West Africa and an official French colony complete with its current borders. The French governor built railroads and increased peanut production.

In 1946, Senegal and French West Africa became citizens of the French Union. In 1958, under De Gaulle, Senegal become autonomous, but in 1959 joined the Sudanese Republic to form the Federation of Mali. Senegal withdrew a year later to become an independent republic and elected African nationalist and Roman Catholic Lésopold S. Senghor president and Mamadou Dia prime minister. Senegal maintained close economic, political, and cultural ties to France.

Drought, famine, a declining economy, and political unrest aimed at Senghor plagued Senegal in the 1970s. Senghor helped establish the West African Economic Community, linking six former French colonies. A separatist movement from the southern province of Casamance arose early in the 1980s. It grew into an insurgency with guerilla fighting. Senghor finally yielded power to president Abdou Diouf in 1981. In 2000, Abdoulaye Wade of the Senegalese Democratic Party defeated Diouf's Socialist rule.

Senegal adopted a new constitution in 2001 limiting presidential terms to five years and establishing a unicameral parliament. The southern Djola rebel separatists agreed to sign a peace treaty with the government in 2004, ending West Africa's longest civil war. However, conflict continues from splinter groups. Despite this, modern Senegal is among the most stable democracies in Africa with a population of over 12 million residents, refugees, and asylum seekers. Senegal serves as a diplomatic and cultural bridge between the Islamic and black African worlds.

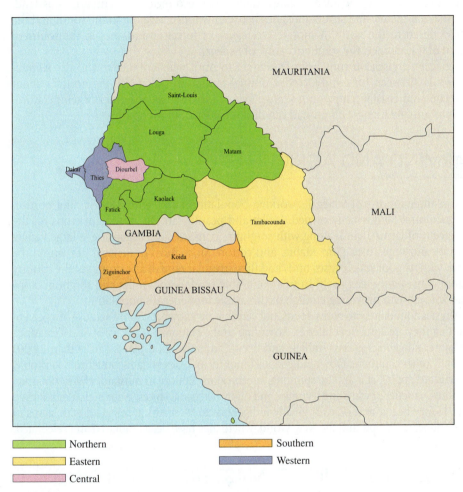

Northern   Southern
Eastern   Western
Central

FIGURE 11.47 Map of Senegal.

LANGUAGE, PHILOSOPHY, AND RELIGION

French is the official, administrative language of Senegal, but understood by only a fraction of the population. A multilingual country, the twelve ethnic groups of Senegal speak around 36 languages, but *Wolof* is the most widely recognized and understood. In the north, *Balanta-Ganja, Hassaniyya, Mandjak, Mankanya, Serer-Noon, Pulaar,* and *Seereer-Siinin*—and in the south, *Jola-Fonyi, Mandinka,* and *Soninke*—are also recognized as national languages.

Most Senegalese are religious and Senegal is a tolerant secular state. The constitution guarantees freedom of religion and interfaith marriage is common. The majority of the population is Sufi Muslim; the rest are Roman Catholic or Protestant or follow traditional animistic beliefs. Although the Toucouleurs were the first to convert to Islam, in the nineteenth century, many Senegalese converted as a way of resisting the traditional French colonial aristocracy. Most people follow key traditional values: *kersa* (respect for others), *tegin* (good manners), and *terranga* (hospitality).

GEOGRAPHY AND CLIMATE

Senegal sits on the westernmost point of West Africa on the Atlantic Ocean. Northern Senegal is a land of low, rolling plains that rise to foothills in the southeast. Its northern border is the Senegal River and the Gambia and Casamance are also important rivers. Dakar, the capital, lies on the Cap-Vert peninsula, the westernmost point of continental Africa. Senegal's vegetation zones range widely with mangroves and tropical rainforest. In northern Senegal, the *Sahel*, a large, transitional eco-region of semi-arid grassland, savanna, flat plains, and shrublands, lies between wooded savanna to the south and the Sahara desert to the north. A mosaic eco-region of forest-savanna lies in the southern region of Casamance, the southern "arm" of Senegal.

Senegal's dry season runs from December to April with hot, dusty, and dry *harmattan* winds. Between June and October, annual rainfall in Dakar and the north is about 24 inches and coastal temperatures range from 75 to 86 degrees F. Interior temperatures are substantially higher and rainfall can double or triple in the south.

FARMING AND AGRICULTURE

Almost three-fourths of Senegal's working population farms with a substantial portion of agricultural land tribally owned. Millet and peanuts are the dominant crops on the 11 percent of farmed land, along with sorghum, corn, cassava, sugarcane, a large variety of fruits and vegetables, gum Arabic, and cotton. Since most of Senegal lies within the Sahel, with its poor soil, locusts, birds and flies, irregular rainfall and droughts, the country cannot consistently feed itself. In years of ample rainfall, the millet and sorghum crops just come close to providing enough of this staple for Senegal's population.

Africa is abundant with native foods, but very few are known, possibly because of a perception that they are somehow inferior. According to the National Academy of Sciences, Africa has more indigenous grains—millets and rice—and native food plants (more than 2,000) than any other continent. Other indigenous foods include desert dates, butterfruit, kei apple, figs, custard apples, star apples, spirulina, mushrooms, Ethiopian mustard, Hausa potatoes, tiger nuts, varieties of yams and legumes, and many herbs and spices. Watermelon, black-eyed peas, kidney beans, and okra, originally indigenous to West Africa, migrated with slaves to the Caribbean, Europe, and the New World, where they have been embraced and celebrated.

SENEGALESE CUISINE: MASTERS OF MELDING FOREIGN WITH NATIVE AND NEW WITH OLD

Early European settlers drew colonial borders in West Africa without regard to tribal culture. Consequently, West Africa is home to dozens of distinct regional cuisines that cut through countries; Senegalese cuisine may be the culinary gem of them all.

Ancient, tribal food preparation methods underlie West African cuisine. From antiquity, cooking over wood fires or fire pits with stones, and grinding with stones has been part of rural Senegalese cooking custom. Frying, simmering, roasting, and steaming foods wrapped in banana, plantain, corn, or cocoyam leaves are commonly favored methods.

The first peoples hunted and gathered, which gave way to food cultivation and sheep, goat, and cattle herding. Bustling, colorful open-air markets, mostly in the hands of independent women traders, offer palm oil, palm wine, ducks, chickens, fresh beef, mutton, and many herbs, spices, fruits, and vegetables.

Simple, rustic cooking methods like grilling, frying, and the one-pot stew still rule the typical Senegalese meal. Most of West Africa and Senegal eat slow-cooked stews with many vegetables and a little meat or fish over rice, sorghum couscous, or with pounded cooked yam or plantain. Peanuts, onions, garlic, chilies, and tomatoes season the stews. Palm oil, with its reddish hue, is the favorite cooking medium, and cooks use it liberally.

The ubiquitous West African groundnut stew called *maafe* is made with beef, mutton, goat, or chicken and vegetables like sweet potatoes, cassava, carrots, or turnips, and served with the nationally beloved white long-grain rice, or bread.

Though Portugal, Britain, the Middle East, the Americas, Vietnam, and especially North Africa and France have influenced the cuisine, in its heart Senegalese food retains African roots. The French influence shows up in the use of mustard, garlic, green onions, salads eaten after the main course, dishes like fondue; cooking methods like marinating; and in extravagant desserts that combine French technique with native ingredients. Islamic traders from the Middle East and North Africa brought couscous and seasonings like cinnamon, nutmeg, and orange flower water. From the Americas came chilies, tomatoes, peanuts, corn, and cassava (yuca/manioc). In turn, West African slaves carried black-eyed peas and okra, as well as their cooking techniques and dishes, to the New World via the Caribbean islands and Mexico.

The people of Senegal and West Africa rely mainly upon peanuts, palm oil, rice, cassava, yams, millet, black-eyed peas, tropical fruit, and seafood. Chicken, lamb, and beef are popular, but because of a mainly Muslim population, pork is absent. Breakfast might be dinner leftovers, sweetened sour milk, bean cakes, or fried or roasted plantains, and coffee or tea. Lunch might be soup with greens, okra, and smoked or dried shrimp and crayfish. For dinner, *yassa* dishes are popular: marinated and grilled, or simmered chicken or fish in lemon, onions, and sometimes mustard. *Fu-fu* is a popular dish of boiled and pounded white yams or plantains. Senegalese dip starchy balls of fu-fu into stew, and swallow them whole. Side dishes of various greens, plantain, and cassava chips and millet cakes are popular. Rich, sweet desserts like banana and yam fritters, *cinq centimes* (peanut butter cookies), *dege* (couscous pudding), banana glace, and coconut candy combine African ingredients with French technique.

Senegal is crossed by many rivers and sits on the Atlantic Ocean so fish and seafood are abundantly available. Fresh fish is fried, grilled, or simmered. Because of the West African heat, much of Senegal's catch is salted, dried, pickled, or smoked. Preserved fish, shrimp, and crayfish keep months and are used as seasonings. Salted fish is de-salted and cooked, similar to salt cod in Italy and France. Dried and smoked snails, flounder, catfish, mussels, shrimp, and crayfish are tossed directly into stews and sauces for deeper flavor.

The country's national dish is called *thiebou jen* (*cheb-oo jen*). It features fish stuffed, marinated, and simmered in a spicy vegetable, tamarind, and tomato sauce—with revered rice cooked in the resulting broth. This vegetable-fish stew reveals the harmonious combination of European influences and uniquely African ingredients that is the surprise and delight of Senegalese food.

FIGURE 11.48 Baobab tree.
Source: GoLo/Fotolia.

REGIONAL SENEGAL

Northern Senegal has a well-developed cuisine due to the strong European and North African influences. The beloved *thiebou jen* and *dem à la St Louis* (stuffed mullet) originated in the northwestern coastal city of Saint-Louis. The central coastal city of Dakar has been heavily influenced by foreign cuisines with dishes like French baguettes, fondue, and *thiou* (bouillabaisse with African vegetables), Moroccan couscous, and mint tea as well as other international tastes. The western coastal region prepares many dishes with fish, seafood, chilies, ginger, and cayenne.

The southern provinces like Casamance are touched by Guinean influences (and their love of milk, curds, and whey) and prepare dishes like *soupou kandia* (soup with okra) and *chicken yassa*. Eastern Senegal shows influences from its closest neighbor, Mali, with dishes like millet couscous and *maafe* (groundnut stew).

FIGURE 11.49 Dakar, Senegal.
Source: bertauxn/Fotolia.

In rural regions, people rarely eat away from their homes. On special occasions they may go from house to house partaking of neighbors' food offerings. Whey, curd and milk, vegetables, cereals, and sweet potatoes are common parts of the village diet. Bananas, coconuts, melons, and watermelons are beloved everywhere.

DINE AT A HOME IN SENEGAL

Greet the host and hostess with a prolonged handshake and inquire about their and their family's welfare—keep communication positive and the gaze soft and lowered. Cross-gender touch is not strict as in other Muslim countries, but some very religious females may refrain from touching men. Address the host and hostess by their professional or honorific title in French along with their first or surname. Since gifts are not common, if you bring one, keep it small: fruit or chocolate. Remove shoes and wash hands before entering the dining area. Since water has strong ritual importance in dry regions of West Africa, it is often the first thing a host offers guests.

Wait to be seated—seating has a formal hierarchy. Guests are seated on a mat on the floor or at a low table; if on a mat, sit cross-legged with feet off the mat. Women or men might eat in separate rooms or at separate tables. Wait to eat until the eldest male begins. Dishes with rice such as *thiou au poulet* (chicken stew), *maafe* (meat and peanut stew), or the fish stew, *thiebou jen*, might be offered in communal bowls. Jollof rice, boiled rice, couscous, roasted meat, beans, and rice garnished with fried plantains, cabbage, or okra might appear.

All the food will be served at the same time. Dip into it with the first three fingers of the right hand only. Guest eat only from the section directly in front of them. Taste a little of everything and take second helpings to compliment the hostess. Leave just a bit of food on the plate to signal satiety—a small burp is not out of place. Do praise the cook (and Allah).

A dessert of fruit will be followed by tea or coffee. At most meals it is improper etiquette to eat and drink at the same time, so eat first and drink afterward. Guests never pour their own drinks: they wait to be served. Tea is served in three rounds. The first tea is unsweetened. A little sugar is added to the second cup, and the third cup is very sweet, mirroring the development of friendship. Always accept the three cups, and sit and converse until guests disperse.

FIGURE 11.50 Senegalese tea pot.
Source: CptHaddock/Fotolia.

FIGURE 11.51 Fresh sorrel rosella (roselle).
Source: Venus Angel/Shutterstock.

TASTES OF WEST AFRICA AND SENEGAL

Fat: *Palm oil* (reddish saturated oil from palm kernal rich in vitamin A), peanut, coconut, plain sesame, corn, shea, and vegetable oils

Sweet: Sugar, honey

Sour/Alcohol: Lemon, lime, orange, vinegar, tamarind, *bouye* (sour fruit of baobab tree a.k.a. monkey fruit), *sorrel* or *rosella* (See *Glossary*.)

Salty: Sea salt

Spicy-Hot: Red chilies, black pepper, Scotch Bonnet (habañero) chilies, paprika

Spice: Grains of paradise, cloves, allspice, Moroccan ras el hanout mixture

Aromatic Seasoning Vegetables: Onions, carrots, garlic, green onions

Herbs, Seasonings, and Condiments: Parsley, cilantro, thyme, orange flower water, preserved lemons

Other Important Foods: Peanuts, couscous, cabbage, millet-couscous, rice, millet, *fonio* (tiny grain), yam, plantain, *cassava* (yuca), black-eyed peas (40 varieties), hubbard squash, chickpeas, coconut milk, eggplant, mango, okra, spinach-like leaves of rosella plant, tomato, tomato paste, *athieke* (yuca flour), *diaxatou* (African bitter eggplant), peanut flour, *guedj* (dried fermented fish), *kong* (smoked catfish), *yet* (dried fermented conch), okra, nutty Djola red rice, green almonds, avocado, mango, fish (tilapia, red snapper, and many others), seafood (crab, shrimp, prawns), meat (lamb, chicken, goat)

Popular Dishes: *Thiéboudienne* or *ceebu jën* (fish and rice stew), *fu-fu*, groundnut stews, *akara* (black-eyed pea fritters), *jollof* rice (rice pilaf with meat, vegetables, and tomato), *salatu niebe* (black-eyed pea salad), *kaldou* (stew), *dibi* (simmered, grilled lamb), *bassi-salté* (meat cooked with tomato sauce, vegetables served with couscous), chicken *yassa*, *tempra* (grilled ceviche), *sombi* (rice pudding), banana glace (sweet soup), *fundaye* or *fondé* (sweet yogurt and millet), banana fritters, cheese or chocolate fondue

Drinks: *Toufam* (yogurt thinned with sugared water), mint tea, palm wine, fresh or fermented, home-roasted coffee with pimento, sorghum or millet beers, *kola nuts* (Muslims abstain from alcohol, so many chew this mild stimulant originally used to flavor Coca-Cola.)

COMMON SENEGALESE COOKING TOOLS

Tourniere (hibachi-like grill), large wooden mortar and pestle, clay and metal cooking vessels

FIGURE 11.52 Stacks of West African pottery.
Source: trevor kittelty/Shutterstock.

FIGURE 11.53 Senegalese handmade baskets.
Source: GoLo/Fotolia.

SENEGALESE FLAVOR FOUNDATIONS

Senegalese Signature Aromatic Vegetable Combo

Onion, garlic, green onions

Signature Seasonings

Liquid/Paste

Dende Oil (Red Palm Oil)

Used in Brazilian and West African cooking dende oil is made from the kernel of the palm fruit. The oil is thick and red-orange in color with a nutty flavor and high in saturated fat. West African cooks use it for frying, and to flavor stews, rice, and sauces.

Animal

Bouillon Cubes

Commercially made bouillon cubes are essential ingredients in much of Senegalese cooking. Although they contain MSG, they add a lot of flavor quickly and for a low cost. Different bouillons impart different flavors. Popular brands include Maggi, Adja, and Jumbo. Adja comes tomato-based or plain.

Dried and Smoked Fish

Dried, salted fish are used in West Africa as seasoning, much like anchovies or fish sauce might be used in Western and Asian cuisine. They may be substituted.

Guedge: A musty, deeply funky, fermented, dried-fish

Yete: A dried giant snail, with a leathery texture and a slightly smoky smell

Kong: Smoked-dried catfish

Vegetable/Fruit

Tamarind (Dvakhar)

Tamarind adds sweet-sour balance. As in other cultures, it is softened in warm water or broth, strained, and sweetened to soften the sour bite. Lime is sometime substituted for tamarind.

FIGURE 11.54 Palm oil fruit.
Source: nui7711/Fotolia.

FIGURE 11.55 Senegalese salted fish.
Source: beatrice prève/Fotolia.

Scotch Bonnet Chili

One of the hottest chilies in the world, this little chili has about 40 times the heat of a jalapeño chili. Mainly used in West Africa and the Caribbean, it is cousin to Mexico's habañero and tastes slightly different. The colors range from unripe green, to ripe orange and red.

Herbal/Spice

Melegueta Pepper (Grains of Paradise)

Native to West Africa, and about the size of cardamom seeds (with a bit of their flavor), these pungently spicy, warm, and slightly bitter seeds are crushed or added whole to many dishes in place of the more irritating black peppercorns.

(*Continued*)

FIGURE 11.56 Senegalese smoked fish.
Source: beatrice prève/Fotolia.

FIGURE 11.57 Tamarind.
Source: Popova Olga/Fotolia.

FIGURE 11.58 Scotch bonnet chilies.
Source: Ian O'Leary/DK Images.

FIGURE 11.59 Melgueta pepper or grains of paradise.
Source: Dave King/DK Images.

SEASONING AND PASTE MIXTURES

SENEGALESE SEASONING BLEND (NOKOS)

Used in Wolof households mainly for the preparation of thiebou jen and thiebou niebe (rice and black-eyed peas), this pounded or ground paste also flavors other dishes like grilled chicken. Some versions add green bell pepper, green onion, or rosella leaf powder. The commercially made Maggi Nokos imitates the flavors of handmade nokos.

Yields about 1/4 cup

1/4 ounce Scotch Bonnet chili, 1/2 medium chili, 1-1/2 teaspoons stemmed, seeded, and minced
1/4 ounce garlic, 1 large clove, 1-1/2 teaspoons peeled and minced
2 to 3 ounces onion, about 1/4 cup peeled and finely minced
4 Maggi chicken *or* vegetable bouillon cubes
1/2 teaspoon freshly ground black pepper

1 Pound chili, garlic, onion, and bouillon cubes in a mortar with a pestle until pasty and smooth *or* purée in small food processor. Mix with black pepper.

Source: *Yolele! Recipes From the Heart of Senegal* by Pierre Thiam.

ROFF (*RAWF*)

This popular Senegalese condiment is widely used as a fish stuffing. To use it as a mild condiment, use half a chili.

Yields about 3/4 cup

1 fragrant bay leaf
3 ounces cilantro *or* trimmed Italian parsley, about 2-1/2 cups finely sliced *or* a mixture
of both
1/2 ounce Scotch Bonnet chili, 1 whole, halved, stemmed, and seeded
1/2 ounce garlic, 2 large cloves, 1 tablespoon peeled and minced
2 to 3 ounces trimmed green onions, 4 to 6 large, 1/2 to 3/4 cup chopped
1 Maggi chicken bouillon cube, crumbled
1 tablespoon oil

1 Toast bay leaf over flame and cool. Set aside.

2 Pulse-purée cilantro and/or parsley, chili, garlic, and green onions in small food processor until finely chopped. Crumble bouillon cube and bay leaf into sauce in food processor, and purée until sauce is chunky-smooth. With machine running, pour in oil and purée a few seconds to mix. Taste sauce and season with salt and freshly ground black pepper, if desired.

3 **To Serve:** Pour roff into a bowl and use to stuff (marinate) fish or pass as a condiment with rice, beans, and fish.

SIMMER, STEW, POACH, BOIL, AND STEAM

Senegalese Soups

Senegalese soups and stews are spicy, nutritious, rich, and full-bodied with vegetables, meat, fish, or peanuts. Cooks prepare simple, rustic soups by boiling ingredients in a clay pot over an open fire or a charcoal brazier. They often season soup with curry powder, yogurt, lemon, paprika, coriander, and herbs, and thicken with vegetables, legumes, and/or peanuts. The West African *soupi kandja*, the ancestor of Louisiana gumbo, is made with meat and shrimp, okra, and chilies. *Plassas*, the ancestor of the Caribbean *callaloo*, is made with beef, sometimes seafood, ground peanuts, yuca, or sweet potato greens, okra, and chilies.

SENEGALESE SPICY SOUP (PEPPE')

This simple soup is usually eaten spicy-hot and used as a cure for hangovers. West Africans think of it as Westerners do chicken soup—as a cure for colds, flu, and just plain comfort. Nigerians add dried, ground crayfish, equivalent of Thai fish sauce. West African grocers sell ready-made pepper soup seasoning.

Yields about 6 cups, 4 to 6 servings

5 to 6 ounces yuca, about 1-1/2 to 2 cups peeled and cubed
8 ounces onions, 2 cups peeled and diced
1/4 ounce garlic, 1 large clove, peeled and crushed

FIGURE 11.60 Cassava (yuca) root.
Source: Will Heap/DK Images.

1/2 Scotch Bonnet chili, seeded and stemmed
1 bay leaf, preferably fresh
2 pounds scaled and gutted whole fish like tilapia, snapper, grouper, catfish, or sea bass
    or 1 pound fish fillets
4 tablespoons lime fresh juice, about 1 large lime, more to taste

1 Pour yuca, onions, garlic, chili, bay leaf, and 1 quart cold water into 4-quart saucepan and over medium heat, bring to a boil. Lower heat and simmer 20 minutes.

2 If using whole fish, remove fish heads for use in stock or another dish. Cut fish into several large pieces and place into saucepan with water and vegetables. Simmer on very low heat until fish is just opaque. Remove fish with slotted spoon into mixing bowl. Discard bay leaf, fish skin, and bones. Reserve fish meat in another bowl. Pour broth through a strainer into large heatproof bowl. Remove chili, finely dice it, and stir into strained broth. Transfer vegetables in strainer into food processor and purée until smooth.

3 **To Serve:** Pour broth and vegetable purée back into saucepan, and bring to a simmer. Stir in reserved fish and remove pan from heat. Stir in lime juice to taste, and adjust seasonings with salt and freshly ground pepper. Serve soup hot.

Vary! Improvise!

☞ *Garnish soup with cilantro leaves or chopped Italian parsley.*

☞ ***Make It Meat:*** *Substitute 1 pound boneless, skinless meat and dice into bite-sized pieces. Senegalese cooks mix beef with oxtail, tripe, intestines, and hooves.*

DELICIOUS HANDS

In Senegal, the Wolof people believe that good flavor comes more from the hand than a spoon. A high compliment to a Senegalese cook is "Your hand is delicious."

Senegalese Fish Stew

Fish stews are popular with Senegalese. *Caldou* is a fish stew from the southern region of Casamance, where the indigenous nutty Djola rice is cultivated. Made with tomatoes and onion and served with rice, it reveals the Portuguese influence on the region. Served with *baguedi* (okra purée), it is pure Senegal. *Thiou* is a sort of West African bouilliabaise, similar to *thiebou jen,* but without rice.

FIGURE 11.61   Senegalese women waiting for returning fishermen.
Source: guy barbacetto/Fotolia.

FIGURE 11.62   Senegalese crab.
Source: jespel/Fotolia.

Stuffed Fish and Rice (Thiebou Jen, Thiéboudienne, Tiébou Dienn)

Pronounced *cheb-oo-jen*, this national dish of Senegal is eaten throughout the country—always in a large group of family or friends. This dish is perfect for a crowd—it's somewhat labor intensive, but feeds many. Cooks choose ingredients by the season, availability, cost, personal preference, and the occasion.

Stripped to its essentials, thiebou jen is fish and long-grain or the local West African Djola rice, but the dish typically includes oil, fresh and dried seafood like herring and mussels, parsley or cilantro, *Roff*, garlic, and vegetables like pumpkin or squash, turnip, cassava, tomato, carrot, okra, eggplant, onion, chilies, and bell peppers.

There are two types of thiebou jen: red-tomato-based (*thiebou jen xonkh*) or simple-white (*thiebou jen weex*). A variety of sauces may accompany this dish. The fish in thiebou jen can be simmered in the broth or fried in oil and simmered on top of the vegetables. Many Senegalese discard the vegetables, which they use only as flavoring for the broth.

MODERN CHANGES TO THIEBOU JEN

Roff

Purée of Italian parsley or cilantro, dried, ground red chili or Scotch Bonnet chilies, ground black pepper, garlic, and green onion. It is stuffed into slits into fish flesh and left to marinate before fish is cooked.

Nokos

A spicy mixture added to the broth after fish and vegetables are strained out, but before the rice is cooked in the broth.

Beugeudie

A sauce made of boiled hibiscus water or *rosella* (a type of hibiscus also called sorrel) ground with cooked okra and whipped into a smooth, thick sauce. It is served with thiebou jen and spooned on to taste.

Ceebu Goor-Jigeen

The combination of cooked white rice paired with tomato sauce.

Diaga

A tomato-based sauce with small fish, beef, or sheep and carrot and onion meatballs.

SIGNATURE RECIPE

FISH STEW WITH RICE (THIEBOU JEN)

This dish was probably the precursor to Louisiana jambalaya. Traditional recipes call for yete (dried large snail) or guedge (dried, smoked fish) to enrich the flavor of this stew. Fish sauce is a Western substitution.

Yields 4-1/2 to 5 quarts, about 12 servings

Roff

4 pounds whole red snapper, cleaned and cut crosswise into 1-inch steaks
   or 2 pounds fish fillets
   or 3-1/2 pounds skinned chicken parts (see Senegalese Rice with Chicken- Thiebou Yap below)

1/2 ounce tamarind paste, 1 tablespoon packed
1/2 cup palm or peanut oil

1 pound onions, 4 cups peeled and medium diced

1/2 ounce garlic, 2 large cloves, 1 tablespoon peeled and minced

6 ounce green or red bell pepper, 1 medium, 1 cup cored, seeded, and medium diced

4 tablespoons tomato paste

28-ounce can diced tomatoes, about 3 cups

8 ounces carrots, trimmed and scrubbed

8 ounces sweet potato *or* butternut squash, peeled

8 ounces yuca, peeled

4 cups fish stock, chicken stock *or* water

1 tablespoon fish sauce

1/2 ounce Scotch Bonnet chili, 1 medium, stem removed but left whole

8 ounces green cabbage, diced into 2-inch squares

7 to 8 ounces okra, stem ends trimmed

1/4 cup fresh lime juice, about 1 large lime

21 ounces long-grain, basmati or African broken rice, 3 cups, rinsed and drained

Optional Garnish: 1/4 to 1/2 ounce cilantro or trimmed Italian parsley, 2 to 4 tablespoons finely sliced

1   **Marinate fish:** Prepare **roff**. Cut 1-inch-long, shallow pockets in fish and stuff with **roff**. Smear some paste over exposed flesh (but not skin). Place fish in a bowl, cover, and refrigerate 45 minutes. (If using chicken, marinate at room temperature 45 minutes or overnight.)

2   Pour 1/4 cup hot water over tamarind paste and knead. Set aside 15 minutes and scrape pulp through strainer. Discard seeds and fiber. Set pulp purée aside.

3   Pour oil into an 8-quart Dutch oven or stockpot over medium heat. Stir in onions, minced garlic, bell pepper, and 1 teaspoon kosher salt. Cook over medium heat until vegetables are soft, 5 to 7 minutes. In a medium bowl, whisk tomato paste with 1/2 cup water. When onions begin to brown, stir in diluted tomato paste and tomatoes. Cook uncovered, stirring occasionally to keep vegetables from burning, until vegetables have thickened and reduced, 20 to 30 minutes.

4   **Meanwhile, cut vegetables:** Depending on their size, halve or quarter carrots lengthwise and cut cross-wise into 1-1/2 to 2 inch sticks to yield 2-1/2 to 3 cups. Dice sweet potato or squash into 1-inch cubes to yield 2-1/2 to 3 cups. Dice yuca into 1-inch cubes to yield 1-1/2 cups.

5   Stir stock or water and fish sauce into stew. Bring stew to a boil, lower the heat, and fold in Scotch Bonnet chili, carrots, sweet potato or squash, and yuca (if using chicken, stir it in now). Simmer stew until vegetables are tender (and, if using, chicken is cooked through), about 30 minutes.

6   Fold in cabbage and okra. Cover and simmer until vegetables are tender, 10 to 15 minutes. (Chicken should be very tender if using.) Using tongs or slotted spoon, carefully transfer vegetables (and chicken) from stew to a platter or serving bowl. Keep warm. Stir in lime juice and remaining roff paste.

7   **If using fish:** Lower fish into broth and simmer until just done, 5 to 7 minutes. Remove fish and discard bones and skin. Place fish meat on platter with vegetables and keep warm.

8   Measure remaining liquid: there should be 5 cups; if not, add water to make up the difference or pour off excess into a small bowl. Pour broth into a heavy 4-quart saucepan and bring to a boil over high heat. Stir in rice, cover pan, reduce heat to low, and simmer until tender and broth has been absorbed, 12 to 15 minutes. Rest rice 5 minutes.

9   **To Serve:** Place a portion of rice onto each plate. Arrange 1 or 2 pods of okra, some fish (or chicken if using), carrot, sweet potato or squash, yuca, and cabbage on top of or around rice. Discard chili. Spoon any reserved stew liquid over each plate. Garnish with optional parsley or cilantro, and serve.

Vary! Improvise!

☞ *Senegalese Rice with Chicken (Thiebou Yap):* Substitute 4 pounds chicken parts, about 3-1/2 pounds skinned but bone-in, for the whole fish, or substitute 2 pounds boneless, skinless chicken for fish fillets. Simmer chicken with carrots, sweet potato, and yuca about 30 minutes.

☞ *Other Vegetables* Substitute eggplant diced into 1-inch cubes, or 2-1/2 pounds of other seasonal, local vegetables.

WEST AFRICAN RICE AND BEANS

Rice and beans are celebrated staples around the world. Africa was the progenitor of many rice and bean dishes that made their way to the southern United States and Caribbean. Northern Senegalese *thiebou niebe* (black-eyed peas with rice) morphed into southern American Hoppin' John.

FIGURE 11.63 Black-eyed peas.
Source: fkruger/Fotolia.

RICE AND BLACK-EYED PEA STEW (THIEBOU NIEBE)

This classic stew is from Gorée Island near Dakar. Sengalese cooks serve it with barbecued prawns and a very spicy carrot and chili relish called goût de piments et de carotte. *This is a simplified version of thiebou niebe. Other versions add cabbage, winter squash, okra, and eggplant.*

Yields about 7 cups, 6 servings

14 ounces basmati rice, 2 cups
7 ounces black-eyed peas, 1 cup
2 tablespoons peanut, sunflower, palm oil, *or* vegetable oil
4 to 5 ounces onion, 1 cup peeled and finely diced
2 tablespoons tomato paste
6 ounces plum tomatoes, 2 medium, about 1 cup medium dice
1 tablespoon *Nokos*
8 ounces yuca, 1-1/2 cups peeled and medium dice
8 ounces carrots, 1-1/2 cups scrubbed or peeled and medium dice
8 ounces sweet potatoes, 1-1/2 to 2 cups peeled and medium dice
Optional: 1/2 ounce Scotch Bonnet chili, 1 medium, stemmed
2 tablespoons fish sauce

1 Rinse rice and soak in bowl with cold water to cover and set aside 1 hour. Rinse black-eyed peas and soak in another bowl with cold water to cover and set aside 1 hour. Drain each and keep separate.

2 **Prepare the stew:** Heat oil over medium heat in 8-quart pot. Stir in onion, tomato paste, diced tomatoes, and *nokos*. Season with salt, bring to a boil, lower heat, cover pot, and simmer 15 minutes. Pour in 4 cups water and bring to a boil. Stir in black-eyed peas, yuca, carrots, sweet potato, and optional whole chili. Bring to a boil, lower heat, partially cover pot, and simmer vegetables until tender, about 30 minutes. Fold in fish sauce and taste stew for seasoning with salt.

3 **Cook the rice:** Drain rice and pour into 4-quart saucepan with 3 cups cold water and 1/2 teaspoon kosher salt. Bring to a boil, lower the heat, cover pan, and simmer rice 15 minutes. Remove pan from heat and leave rice 10 minutes undisturbed.

4 **To Serve:** Mound rice on platter and artfully spoon vegetables and stew broth over top.

SIGNATURE RECIPE

WEST AFRICAN CHICKEN AND GROUNDNUT STEW (MAAFE)

This stew probably originated among the Bambara people of Mali, but it's beloved in Senegal.

4 to 4-1/2 quarts, 8 to 12 servings

8 ounces unsalted roasted peanuts, 1-1/2 cups
5 pounds chicken parts: legs, thighs, and breasts, 4-1/2 pounds with skin and fat removed
Flour for dredging
Palm or vegetable oil for frying
12 ounces onion, 2-1/2 to 3 cups peeled and diced into 1/2-inch cubes
6 to 7 ounce red bell pepper, 1 medium, 1-1/4 cups 1/2-inch dice
3/4 ounce garlic, about 3 large cloves, 1 to 1-1/2 tablespoons peeled and minced
16 ounce can diced tomatoes, 2 cups with liquid
    or 3/4 to 1 pound ripe tomatoes, 2 cups diced, *plus* 2 tablespoons tomato paste
1 to 1-1/2 teaspoons ground cayenne

1-1/2 pounds sweet potatoes, 5 cups peeled and diced into 3/4-inch cubes

1-1/2 pounds turnips, 4 medium turnips, 4 cups peeled and wedged or diced into 3/4-inch cubes

1 pound baby spinach, about 12 to 16 cups lightly chopped
   or 1 pound Swiss chard leaves, stems removed and 1-inch dice
      or 8 ounces green cabbage, about 3 cups diced into 1-inch squares

For Serving

Cooked white rice

1 **Prepare peanut mixture:** (Preheat oven to 325°F if using oven.) Pour peanuts into food processor and grind until fine, 2 to 3 minutes. Pour in 1/2 cup water and grind 1 minute more. Scrape peanut mixture into bowl and rinse out bowl with 1 cup water; stir rinsing water into peanut mixture and set aside.

2 **Brown the chicken:** Season chicken with salt. Pour flour into bowl. Heat 3 tablespoons oil in 12-inch skillet over medium-high heat until hot. Dredge chicken in flour and shake off excess. Place chicken in hot oil without crowding. Brown both sides. Repeat in one or two batches more. Use more oil as is necessary. Transfer browned chicken to a bowl. Deglaze skillet with 1-1/2 cups water and scrape bits off bottom of pan; pour deglazing liquid into bowl with chicken.

3 **Prepare stew:** Heat 2 to 3 tablespoons oil in 6- to 8-quart heavy ovenproof pot over medium heat. Stir in onion and bell pepper and sauté, stirring occasionally, until onion begins to brown, 7 to 10 minutes. Stir in garlic; cook 1 minute. Stir in peanut mixture, tomatoes, cayenne, 2 teaspoons kosher salt, and chicken with juices. Bring stew to a simmer. Partially cover pot with lid and braise chicken on low heat until tender, 45 minutes to 1 hour. *Alternatively*, place pot in oven and bake/braise until tender, 45 minutes to 1 hour. Remove pot from oven or burner. With tongs, transfer chicken to a 4-quart serving dish. Cover and keep warm.

   *Maafe may be made 1 day ahead to this point. Cool it, uncovered, in a shallow pan, then cover and refrigerate. To finish maafe, reheat chicken in sauce, then transfer chicken to serving dish before cooking vegetables in sauce.

4 Stir sweet potatoes and turnips into sauce and simmer on top of stove over medium-low heat, uncovered, until vegetables are tender, 15 to 20 minutes. Transfer cooked vegetables with a slotted spoon to serving dish with chicken.

5 Bring sauce to a boil over medium heat, and cook uncovered until thickened and reduced to about 4 cups; stir frequently. If using spinach, remove pot from heat, stir in spinach and wait until it wilts, 2 to 3 minutes. If using chard or cabbage, simmer in sauce until very tender, 5 to 7 minutes. Remove from heat. Taste sauce and season with salt.

6 **To Serve:** Spoon sauce over chicken on serving dish, and serve stew with cooked rice.

Vary! Improvise!

☛ **Vegetarian:** Omit chicken and use more vegetables.

☛ **Lamb It Up:** Prepare maafe with 2 to 2-1/2 pounds lamb diced into 1-1/4-inch cubes, instead of chicken.

SIGNATURE RECIPE

WEST AFRICAN FUFU

In West Africa, fufu balls act as utensils: diners who eat with their hands form balls from the starchy mass and dip them into stews. Fufu should be unseasoned—and delicately fruity to balance spicy dishes.

Yields about 3 cups

1 pound soft and very ripe plantains, 3 large, 2-2/3 cups peeled and sliced

2 tablespoons red palm oil
   or peanut oil

1 Fill a 4-quart saucepan with cold water and bring to a boil. Stir in plantains and lower heat to medium; boil plantains until tender, 5 to 7 minutes. Remove with slotted spoon and drain. Transfer plantains to food processor and purée with oil and 1 teaspoon salt until smooth. The purée will firm as it cools.

2 **To Serve:** Serve fufu warm or reheat slightly before serving.

FIGURE 11.64 Ripe plantains.
Source: Barnabas Kindersley/DK Images..

Vary! Improvise!

☛ Prepare fufu from African yams, yuca, cooked short-grain rice or fermented cassava flour.

☛ Experiment with other starchy vegetables like green bananas or grains.

MASHED PLANTAINS WITH COCONUT (NOIX DE COCO BANANE PLANTAIN)

This dish is done in many ways throughout sub-Saharan Africa, but the lime juice instead of lemon marks it as coming from Dakar, the capital of Senegal.

Yields about 4 cups, 8 servings

1-1/2 pounds unripe, green plantains, 3 medium-large
    or 1-1/2 pounds unripe, green bananas 1 ounce trimmed green onions, 2 large, about 1/4 cup finely sliced
1/2 ounce Scotch Bonnet chili, 1 medium, 1-1/2 to 2 teaspoons stemmed, seeded, and finely diced
    or 1 ounce jalapeño chili, 1 medium, 2 tablespoons stemmed, seeded, and finely diced
4 to 5 ounces grated fresh coconut, 1 cup
    or 3 ounces unsweetened, dry, shredded coconut, 1 cup*
4 tablespoons thick coconut milk
4 tablespoons fresh lime juice, about 1 large lime

*If using dried, unsweetened coconut, soak in warm water 15 minutes, and drain before using.

1 Cut the ends off plantains or bananas and slit skin down the length of the fruit. Peel skin off and discard. Slice fruit into 1/2-inch-thick coins to yield about 3 cups.

2 Bring a 3-quart pot of water to boil. Salt the water and stir in plantains or bananas. Lower the heat and slow-boil fruit until very tender, 30 minutes or more. Drain fruit and pour into large mixing bowl. Coarsely mash hot fruit and fold in onions and chilies. Stir in grated coconut and coconut milk. Combine thoroughly.

3 **To Serve:** Season dish with salt and lime juice to taste. Serve warm.

Source: www.celtnet.org.uk/

SAUTÉ, PAN-FRY, AND DEEP-FRY

SIGNATURE RECIPE

WEST AFRICAN BLACK-EYED PEA FRITTERS (ACCARA OR AKARA)

These deceptively simple fritters pack big flavor. They should be tender with a crunchy outside crust.

Yields about 8 cups batter, eighty-five to ninety 1-1/2-inch fritters

1 pound black-eyed peas, about 2-1/2 cups
2 to 3 ounces onion, 1/2 cup peeled and diced
1-1/2 to 2 ounces gingerroot, 2 tablespoons peeled and minced
1/2 to 1 teaspoon ground cayenne
Oil for deep-frying

For Serving

Hot pepper sauce or *Roff*

1 Rinse beans with cold water, drain, pour into large bowl, and cover with cold water. Soak beans overnight. (Do not quick-soak.) Rub beans back and forth vigorously with hands to remove some skins, which will rise to the surface. Pour them off and drain beans.

2 Pour 1 tablespoon kosher salt, drained beans, onion, ginger, and cayenne into a food processor. Grind to a coarse purée. Pour in 1 cup water, and purée until beans form a smooth, fluffy batter. Thicker batters tend to produce firm, cakey fritters; looser batters produce light, fluffy fritters.

3 Heat oil to 365 degrees F. For each akara, drop a rounded tablespoon of batter into hot oil. Fry until brown, turn, and brown second side. Transfer akara to paper-towel-lined sheet pan to drain. Keep them warm.

4 **To Serve:** Transfer akara immediately to serving vessel. Serve with hot pepper sauce or *Roff*. Fritters may be made ahead and reheated in 375 degree F oven until hot, 10 to 15 minutes.

Vary! Improvise!

☛ *Toss 1 cup chopped cilantro or 1 chopped carrot in processor with beans and onion.*

☛ *Fold finely diced bell pepper or finely sliced green onions into batter.*

GRILL, GRIDDLE, ROAST, BROIL, BAKE, AND BARBECUE

A KEY TO AFRICAN FOOD

Fear of African food has led many people to avoid it. Cookbook author and culinary historian Jessica B. Harris thinks that the old Senegalese dish called chicken yassa is an important key that "opens the door for some people" to African food. Chicken yassa, with simple ingredients, is non-threatening. Its brilliant flavor comes from first being marinated, then grilled, and finally, stewed. Harris notes that all three techniques contribute to this "strange and wondrous" dish.

FIGURE 11.65 Chicken yassa in Senegal.
Source: © dbimages/Alamy.

SENEGALESE CHICKEN (YASSA GINAAR)

This is a deeply flavorful recipe. Some recipes call for olives, carrots, and Dijon mustard to be simmered with the chicken.

Yields about 10 cups, 6 to 8 servings

6 pounds bone-in chicken breasts, legs, and thighs
1-1/4 to 1-1/3 cups fresh lime juice, 5 large to 7 medium limes
5 tablespoons peanut *or* olive oil, *divided*
2 chicken bouillon cubes (preferably Maggi), mashed
36 ounces onions, about 4 medium-large, 8 to 9 cups halved and sliced 1/4-inch thick
1/2 ounce Scotch Bonnet chili, about 1, halved, stemmed, and seeded

For Serving

Cooked rice

1 Remove skin and excess fat from chicken parts and discard to yield 5-1/4 to 5-1/2 pounds chicken.

2 Zest 3 limes. Pour lime juice and zest into large mixing bowl. Stir in 2 tablespoons oil and bouillon cubes until dissolved. Transfer onions and chicken to bowl and rub mixture into chicken parts. Cover bowl and marinate 1 hour at room temperature or 2 hours refrigerated. Turn chicken halfway during the marinating time. Remove chicken and drain excess marinade back into bowl.

3 Place chicken onto parchment-covered sheet pan or in mixing bowl and season with salt. Set a strainer over another bowl and pour marinade through. (Allow onions to drain while chicken cooks.) Reserve both onions and marinade separately.

4 Preheat broiler or grill over high heat. Working in batches, grill or broil chicken pieces, turning once, until browned but not cooked through. Set chicken aside in a bowl.

5 Heat remaining 3 tablespoons oil in a heavy 8-quart pot over medium heat. Add reserved drained onions, cover, and cook until soft and browned, 25 to 30 minutes. Sugars from the lime juice will caramelize on the bottom of the pan; stir onions and scrape bottom of pan occasionally. Pour marinade and the chili into onions. Transfer grilled chicken and any collected juices to pot, and tuck chicken into onions. Bring to a boil, lower heat, and simmer, partially covered, until chicken is cooked through, 30 to 45 minutes. Turn chicken once or twice so it cooks evenly.

6 **To Serve:** With tongs, transfer chicken to a platter. Taste sauce and season with salt if necessary. Pour or spoon onion sauce over top of chicken. Serve with rice.

Source: *Yolele! Recipes From the Heart of Senegal* by Pierre Thiam.

SALAD AND VEGETABLE METHODS

SENEGALESE SALAD OF BLACK-EYED PEAS (SALATU NIEBE)

Black-eyed peas don't need long soaking and cooking so they're ideal for meals in the heat of Africa or summer.

Yields 8 cups, 6 to 8 servings

14 ounces black-eyed peas, 2 cups
8 ounce fresh tomato, 1 medium-large, 1 to 1-1/3 cups peeled and cubed 1/4-inch
8 ounces cucumber, about 1-1/4 cups peeled, seeded, and cubed 1/4-inch
6 ounce red or green bell pepper, 1 medium, 1 cup cored, seeded, and cubed 1/4-inch
3 ounces trimmed green onions, about 6, 2/3 to 1 cup finely sliced
1-1/2 to 2 ounces trimmed Italian parsley, about 1 cup coarsely chopped

1/2 ounce Scotch Bonnet chili, 1 medium, 1 tablespoon stemmed, seeded, diced, more to taste
  or 1 ounce serrano chili, about 2, 2 tablespoons stemmed, seeded, and finely diced
1/2 cup peanut, vegetable, *or* olive oil
1/3 cup fresh lime juice, 1-1/2 large limes

1 Rinse black-eyed peas, and soak in cold water 1 hour. Drain. Pour peas into 4-quart saucepan with 1 quart cold water. Bring to a boil over high heat. Lower heat to a simmer and cover. Simmer until peas are tender but not splitting, about 30 minutes. Strain peas, season with salt, and set aside.

2 In a large mixing bowl, toss together tomato, cucumber, bell pepper, green onions, parsley, and chili. Fold oil, lime juice, salt, and freshly ground black pepper. Fold in cooked black-eyed peas. Cover salad and allow flavors to develop 1 hour. Taste and season with more lime juice, salt, or pepper.

3 **To Serve:** Pile salad into serving vessel and serve chilled or at room temperature.

Source: *Yolele! Recipes From the Heart of Senegal* by Pierre Thiam.

SENEGALESE SHRIMP AND AVOCADO SALAD (SALADE AVOCAT AUX CREVETTES SENEGALAISE)

This salad brings to mind a French Salade Niçoise, *the classic composed salad. Senegalese cooks often stuff prawn or shrimp salads into avocado halves and serve as appetizers.*

4 servings

7 ounces black-eyed peas, 1 cup
2 ounces onion, 1/4 cup peeled and finely diced
3 tablespoons oil, *divided*
6 tablespoons fresh lime juice, 1-1/2 to large limes, *divided*
2 large eggs
6 ounces red bell pepper, 1 medium
  or 2 ounces canned sliced red pimento
12 ounces 26/30 shrimp, 20 peeled and deveined
  or 12 ounces 21/25 shrimp, 12 peeled and deveined
8 to 10 ounce avocado, 1 large, halved, pitted, and peeled
4 ounces cleaned and dried torn lettuce or baby greens, about 4 cups
4 to 5 ounces plum tomatoes, sliced into twelve 1/8-inch-thick rounds

Garnish: Italian parsley leaves

1 Soak black-eyed peas 1 hour in cold water. Drain peas, pour into 2-quart saucepan, and cover with water. Bring to a boil, lower heat, and simmer peas until tender, about 30 minutes. Cool peas and drain to yield about 2-1/2 cups cooked peas. Measure 2 cups drained peas and set the extra 1/2 cup aside for another use. Toss 2 cups drained peas with onion, 2 tablespoons oil, and 2 tablespoons fresh lime juice. Season with salt and pepper; set dressed peas aside.

2 Place eggs into 2-quart saucepan and cover with cold water. Bring to a boil, cover pan, and remove pan from heat. Time eggs 12 minutes. Remove eggs from hot water, crack the ends, and place in bowl of cold water 10 minutes. Peel eggs and quarter lengthwise into 8 wedges. Set aside.

3 Roast bell pepper over flame or under broiler until evenly blackened. Set aside in bowl, covered, until cooled. Peel pepper and discard stem, skin, membranes, and all seeds. Slice into thin julienne to yield about 1/2 cup, and set aside.

4 Steam shrimp or prawns until just cooked through and opaque, 3 to 5 minutes. Remove from steamer and cool. Refrigerate until needed.

5 Dice peeled avocado halves into 3/8- to 1/2-inch cubes and toss with 4 tablespoons lime juice and 1 tablespoon oil. Season with salt and pepper.

6 Line up 4 large salad plates or shallow bowls. Lay a fourth of the lettuce on each plate. *On each plate:* Pile 1/2-cup black-eyed peas in the center. Spoon a fourth of avocado mixture over peas and greens. Arrange 3 slices of tomato, 2 quarters hard-cooked egg, and 5 to 6 shrimp or 3 to 4 prawns around the sides. Arrange sliced bell peppers (there will be some left over) or pimento slices across the top of the salad.

7 **To Serve:** Garnish salad with parsley leaves. Serve with salt and pepper grinder on table. Advise diners to toss salad before eating.

SENEGALESE CHILI AND CARROT RELISH
(GOÛT DE PIMENTS ET DE CAROTTE)

This is a much less hot, but still quite spicy, version of an Indo-Chinese-Senegalese relish. Like all West African chili-based condiments, it's served with every meal. Halve the amount of chilies to decrease the heat even further.

Yields about 2 packed cups

3 tablespoons vegetable oil
1 ounce Scotch Bonnet chilies, about 4, about 1/4 cup stemmed, seeded, and finely diced
2 ounces shallot, 1/2 cup peeled, halved, and finely sliced
16 ounces carrots, about 4 large, 4 cups peeled and shredded
1 tablespoon brown sugar
Optional: Fresh lime juice

1   Heat oil in a 3-quart saucepan over medium-low heat. Stir in chilies and shallot. Cook until soft, 3 to 5 minutes. Meanwhile, chop shredded carrots lightly. Stir carrots and brown sugar into saucepan, and cook until carrots are soft, about 3 minutes.

2   Stir in 1/3 cup water and bring mixture to a simmer. Cook, uncovered, until the water has evaporated and the mixture is moist but not browned, 5 minutes. Season relish with salt and optional lime juice, to taste.

3   **To Serve:** Remove pan from heat and transfer relish to bowl to cool. Store relish in refrigerator up to 1 week. Consume in small amounts with Senegalese meals.

REVIEW QUESTIONS

Morocco

1. In what cuisine is the Moroccan diet rooted? Name two other cultural influences on Moroccan cuisine.

2. What are three important Moroccan cooking fats?

3. Discuss the Moroccan procedure for preserving lemons.

4. Name three important Moroccan dishes.

5. What is the famous Moroccan spice mixture? Name two spice ingredients in it.

6. What is a tagine?

7. What is couscous? Discuss how it's made and prepared in Morocco.

Ethiopia

1. From where did the first the nonindigenous ingredients in Ethiopian cuisine come?

2. Name one Silk Road culture and an ingredient it brought to Ethiopia.

3. What are the two stews that form the backbone of Ethiopian cuisine? How do they differ?

4. What is injera? From what grain is it made?

5. What is berbere?

6. How is Ethiopian spiced butter made?

7. What is dry-frying? How is it used in Ethiopian cuisine?

Senegal

1. Why and how were Senegal and West Africa an important influence on Caribbean, Mexican, and American Southern cuisine?

2. What is Senegal's national dish? How is it prepared?

3. Name two important cooking fats in Senegalese cuisine.

4. What chili is most popular in Senegal? What spice?

5. What is fufu and how is it eaten?

6. What legume is the most common in Senegal? Name one dish made with the legume.

CHAPTER TWELVE

THE WEST INDIES OR CARIBBEAN ISLANDS

This chapter will:

- Introduce the changing, turbulent histories of the Caribbean island countries, their geographies, cultural influences, and climate.

- Discuss the importance of Africa and Spain to the cooking of the Caribbean.

- Introduce Caribbean culinary culture, its diverse regional variations, and dining etiquette.

- Identify foods, dishes, and techniques that cross between countries.

- Identify the foods, flavor foundations, seasoning devices, and favored cooking techniques of the Caribbean.

- Teach favorite classic dishes of many of the Caribbean islands.

A Unique and Vital Crossroads

In A Concise History of the Caribbean, *B. W. Higman observes that history of the Caribbean Islands "look(s) both ways," toward the Americas and toward Africa and Europe. The islands' varied and inventive cultures became "vital sites in the creation of the modern western world." Columbus arrived in the islands first during his 1492 voyage, and the Spanish established their first colonies there. The small islands with long coastlines and easy passage between them made the Caribbean Islands "the ideal sites for economic exploitation."*

Situated in the tropical blue Caribbean Sea, southeast of the Gulf of Mexico and North America, east of Central America, and north of South America, the sweeping crescent arc of the Caribbean chain comprises more than 7,000 islands. Also known as the West Indies, the islands range from flat and dry, mountainous and rainforest-lush, to vacation paradise blessed with year-round fishing and sun-drenched sugar-sand beaches of unequaled beauty.

The Caribbean island countries, a geopolitical subregion of North America, are divided into three main groups: *The Lucayan Archipelago* includes the independent Commonwealth of the Bahamas with Andros and Grand Bahama plus British Bermuda and the Turks and Caicos. *The Greater Antilles*, with 90 percent of the Caribbean landmass, includes Cuba, the largest island, and Havana the largest city, Hispaniola (half Haiti and half Dominican Republic), Jamaica, and Puerto Rico. *The Lesser Antilles* forms an arc from Puerto Rico to South America; it is further divided into Windward and Leeward Islands. The Leewards include Guadeloupe, St. Kitts, and Nevis, Virgin Gorda and the British

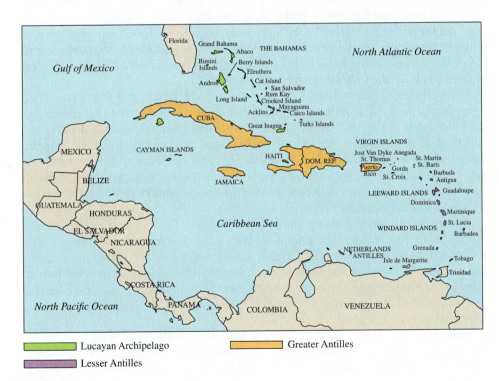

FIGURE 12.1 Map of Caribbean Islands.

and U.S. Virgins. The Windwards include Martinique, St. Lucia, Grenada, Barbados, and Trinidad-Tobago.

Archeological evidence suggests that humans, called the *Casirimoid*, first occupied Cuba and Hispaniola in the Caribbean around 4500 BCE. Various other peoples migrated over from Central and South America. In 1492, when explorer Christopher Columbus (under the auspices of Spain) arrived in the Caribbean, two main *Amerindian* native peoples lived on the islands: the gentle farmer-hunter-fisher *Taíno-Arawaks* and the war-like *Caribs*. Both migrated from South America north along the Lesser Antilles to the Greater Antilles during the thirteenth century.

Columbus and crew came seeking gold and spices, but in 1493, on the second of four trips, he returned with farmers and missionaries. They enslaved the native people, stole crops and women, demanded taxes, and nearly wiped out the population with unstinting labor and European diseases. The native people who survived the onslaught proudly kept their culture alive. Starting in 1493, Spain claimed the entire Caribbean, but settled Hispaniola, Puerto Rico, Jamaica, Cuba, and Trinidad. Soon Portuguese and Spanish ships claimed territories of Central and South America, founding colonies based on gold and gem discoveries.

Britain, the Netherlands, and France, desiring to establish colonies, fought the Spanish for Caribbean territory from the early seventeenth century for centuries onwards. The years between 1640 and 1680 were also a ripe time for English, French, and Dutch pirates, better known as *buccaneers*, who were often licensed by their governments to attack Spanish ships for spoils.

Early in the seventeenth century, European colonials instituted a plantation system to grow sugar cane. The Spanish began to import African slaves to augment the dwindling Amerindian slave workforce (and Europeans) killed off by diseases. Africans began to outnumber Europeans and the native population because they were more resistant to malaria. Slave rebellions were common. By mid-eighteenth century, sugar was Britain's largest, most profitable import. By the nineteenth century, slavery, increasingly expensive and difficult to maintain, was abolished and workers were paid wages. Plantation dependence left workers with only agricultural skills and limited opportunities for education and growth. It left the Caribbean nations impoverished.

During the eighteenth century, Spain, the Netherlands, Britain, and France continued to battle over these rich islands and many of them changed hands, traded for other mainland territories. In the 1823 *Monroe Doctrine*, an angry president Monroe declared the Americas off limits to European countries. He wanted the newly independent colonies free of European intervention, and to ensure U.S. national security. The Doctrine persisted for almost two centuries and gave the United States great influence over Caribbean nations. At the end of nineteenth century, after the Spanish-American War, Cuba became independent and Puerto Rico became a U.S. colony.

During the twentieth century, the failed *West Indies Federation* attempted to knit British-controlled islands into a unified state. Jamaica, Trinidad and Tobago, Barbados, Bahamas, and many other islands gained independence. As European colonial powers de-colonized the Caribbean region, the United States expanded into it. Though the United States invaded and occupied Hispaniola for almost two decades and was accused of interfering in elections, it became the Caribbean's main, reliable consumer of exported goods.

Strategic interest in Caribbean trade routes has kept America's interest into the twenty-first century. Desiring economic security, in 2000 the Caribbean nations signed the *Caribbean Basin Trade Partnership* and welcomed U.S. trade and subsequent involvement in the global free market. Caribbean economies are still strongly linked to the United States and Europe through trade, foreign remittance (Caribbean people working elsewhere transferring money home), and foreign investments.

LANGUAGE, PHILOSOPHY, AND RELIGION

The Caribbean countries are home to many languages. English is spoken in the northern, central, and eastern islands; Spanish in the western and central Caribbean, Dutch in southeastern Caribbean, French in the central and eastern islands, and *Papiamento*, a Portuguese-Creole language, mainly in the southern islands. There are several native languages, but many have become extinct. English, Spanish, Dutch, and French are considered national languages.

The Caribbean islands are predominately Christian, but newer religions like Haitian voodoo, Jamaican Rastafarianism, Cuban Santeria, and the Spiritual Baptists in Trinidad are flourishing. Europeans, Africans, and Asians have affected the religious and philosophical beliefs, and Caribbean people have adopted and modified them to fit their lives. Rastafarianism is based on the belief that the once-emperor of Ethiopia is the "Lion of Judah" and would lead African people back to the "Promised Land" in Africa. Santerians combine African and European beliefs, one of which is animal sacrifice and the blood poured on sacred stones through which they feed the gods. Spiritual Baptists practice an elaborate mourning ceremony in which they deprive themselves by fasting and lying on dirt floors to discover their true rank in the church.

Afro-Caribbean religions have both a belief in a Supreme Being and a pantheon of deities who serve as intermediaries between God and mankind. Music, magic spells, dance, and chanting are important activities. Most believe that dead ancestors influence events from the Beyond, that objects can be invested with supernatural forces, and that animals, plants, and trees have a will and soul and can be summoned for help.

GEOGRAPHY AND CLIMATE

The geography of the Caribbean chain ranges from flat, dry, and unmemorable to volcanoes, huge bays of stunning aquamarine water, rocky shores, mountains, and rain forest.

The Caribbean Islands, which lie close to the equator, have a climate that ranges from tropical to subtropical, moderated by the prevailing northeast tradewinds. The region is plagued with the possibility of hurricanes from June to November. Elevation determines the climate on each island. Those at sea level maintain a constant temperature of 75 to 90 degrees F. Higher elevations tend to get lower temperatures. The rainy season goes from May through October and the dry season from November through March. Windward islands have higher rainfall; leeward sides are drier.

FARMING AND AGRICULTURE

From foundations built on a plantation economy scarred by centuries of slavery, the Caribbean economy has relied on strong exports of agricultural goods. Small-scale farmers are hobbled by inequality and a marginal role in agriculture exacerbated by rising food imports. Agriculture mainly provides food domestically and is the main land-use activity in the islands. Sugarcane is still an important crop on some islands along with bananas, citrus, coffee, yams, sweet potatoes, cassava, *callaloo* (greens), sweet and hot peppers, tomatoes, cucumbers, corn, pumpkin, plantains, avocados, mangoes, pineapples, soursop fruit, breadfruit, akee, melons, legumes, tobacco, coconuts, cocoa, ginger, and peanuts. Though they do not have an abundance of natural resources, fishing, timber, and mineral mining are a strong part of the region's economy.

WEST INDIAN-CARIBBEAN CUISINE: THE MASTERS OF FUSION

Situated on a main trade route, the Caribbean Islands have been subjected to a complex, multicultural fusion process that shows up in their food. The islands served as a central stopping place for ships trading spices, foods, and goods from Spain, France, Britain, the Netherlands, Africa, Indonesia, and China, as well as Mexico and Central and South America. In *Beyond Gumbo*, Jessica B. Harris says, "Créole food is undeniably the true food of the Western Hemisphere, a food created from an international larder of ingredients and a world of techniques that make something rewarding from difficult circumstances."

The first influence on Caribbean cuisine came from the primitive Amerindians who cultivated corn, cassava (for bread), sweet potatoes, beans, peanuts, bell peppers, and chilies that came from Mexico. Taking advantage of the lush island bounty, many people hunted, fished, and gathered guava, pineapples, and cashew fruit. The Amerindian legacy was the creation of Caribbean *barbacoa* (barbecue) and one-pot stews.

The second influence came from Europe and her empire. The first settlers were Spanish. They brought very different kinds of food: flour, cows, chicken and pigs, oil, vinegar, rice, and wine. They also brought plants and seeds to grow crops like breadfruit, limes, oranges, lemons, bananas, coconuts, tamarind, sugarcane, onions, garlic, ginger, chickpeas, cilantro, eggplant, coffee, and sugarcane for sugar and rum, which were native to other countries with whom they traded or had conquered. Avocado, chayote, and chocolate eventually migrated from Mexico via the Spanish. The Spanish left a particularly strong influence on Cuba, Puerto Rico, and the Dominican Republic. Spanish cooks brought the technique for paella, which became *asapao*, their marinated fish dish called *escabeche*, which translated into the Jamaican *escovitch*, rice and broth dishes, and the flavoring sauce *sofrito*, which Caribbean cooks prepare with onion, bell pepper, garlic, tomatoes, annatto, and cilantro.

The British brought high tea and "black cake" and "rum cake" along with many of their favorite foods to the islands like bacon and eggs, roast beef, pancakes, sponge cake, rice pudding, kidney pie, Irish stew, Yorkshire pudding, hot cross buns; Scottish haggis, which became Barbadian *jug-jug*; Cornish pasties, which became Jamaican "patties"; and smoked fish. The French brought culinary methods for fish soups and stews (*blaff* and *court-bouillon*), *fricassee*, and seasonings to many French-influenced islands like St. Martin, Guadeloupe, and Martinique. The Dutch brought Edam cheese, which developed into *keshy yana* (shrimp-stuffed Edam cheese). Originally from India and Southeast Asia, bananas and plantains came to the Caribbean Islands with a Portuguese monk in 1516.

The third influence came in the early seventeenth century during the slave trade. African slaves, mainly from West Africa, brought native foods like okra, pigeon peas, kidney beans, black-eyed peas, and watermelon. Their cooking techniques and style are the basis of modern Caribbean-Creole cuisine that can be seen in popular dishes like Jamaican *jerk*, which came directly from a West African preslavery hunting-tribe called the Cormantee, *callaloo*, a soup of meat and stewed greens, fish cakes, *foo-foo* (mashed booked cassava, yam, or plantain), *cou-cou* (cornmeal with okra), *bammi* (cassava bread), and saltfish and ackee (a fruit that tastes like scrambled eggs and is combined with salt-cod).

The fourth influence came after the slave trade was abolished in 1838. Indentured workers came from India and China to work in the fields and plantations. They brought with them dishes like *colombo* (curry dish), mango chutney, *dhalpour* (roti bread), rice dishes like *pelau* (meat, vegetables, and rice in one dish), stir-fried dishes like sweet and sour, Chinese spare ribs, and noodles. These immigrants wove their native foods like mangoes, eggplant, ginger, wheat flour, rice, soy sauce, and curry powder deeply into the local Caribbean diet.

No matter the island, home-cooked Caribbean meals always begin with staple local ingredients: fresh fish and seafood, vegetables, beans, tropical fruits like coconut, papaya, lime, and mango, and chicken—and end with spiced-up flavor. The fruity Scotch Bonnet chili, reputed to be the hottest, is prized. Caribbean cooks are flexible: they take what they know, and combine it with what they have and what they have learned from other cultures. They use spices in unique ways: allspice in jerk marinades and sauces for meat and poultry, chilies in chocolate cake and fruit sauces, cinnamon and raisins with pork *picadillo*, or oregano and garlic with orange juice marinades.

Jessica B. Harris says that the "creolized cuisine" or melting pot cuisine of the West Indies and Latin America, formed by the mixing of native-American, Spanish, French and African peoples, can be characterized by twelve elements: **rice and broth dishes**; **hot sauces**; **dumplings and fritters**; **high seasoning and brightly colored foods** (the use of turmeric and annatto); **seasoning foundations** like sofrito; **okra**; **pork and all its parts**; flavoring with **dried, smoked, and pickled things** (as in West Africa), **sweets made with nuts**; **fruit pastes**; **and the use of cane sugar**; and **women chefs and cooks**. Caribbean cuisine started at home with women, and women continue to rule professional and home kitchens. They have united the many disparate cuisines of these beautiful islands into a mosaic of big, bright Caribbean flavor.

REGIONAL CARIBBEAN

The Lucayan Archipelago includes the independent Commonwealth of the Bahamas with Andros and Grand Bahama plus British Bermuda and the Turks and Caicos. Conch dishes reign in the Bahamas: conch fritters, salad, and chowder. Fish and grits, baked bonefish, peas and rice, and *jonnycake* (corn cake) are also popular throughout this region. These islands don't grow much produce, so freshly caught seafood and imported foods are important.

The Greater Antilles, with 90 percent of the Caribbean landmass, includes Cuba, the largest island, and Havana the largest city, Hispaniola (half Haiti and half Dominican Republic), Jamaica, and Puerto Rico. Cuban cuisine fuses Spanish and Caribbean with its black bean soup, *moros y cristianos* (black beans and rice); slow-cooked dishes seasoned with garlic, cumin, oregano, and bay leaves, fried plantains, *ropa vieja* (shredded beef), pork with onions, and tropical fruits. Haitians depend upon *du riz a pois or diri ak pwa* (rice and beans), *griot* (fried pork), sweet potatoes, manioc, yams, corn, sugarcane, manos, peanuts, and sesame.

Cooks in the Dominican Republic prepare *arroz con pollo* topped with stewed red kidney beans, pan-fried or braised beef, green salad, shrimp, empanadas, *tostones* (twice-fried sliced plantains), or the popular Dominican *mangú* (mashed boiled plantains). Jamaica is known for its spicy jerked meats and fish, ackee and saltfish, *fish tea* (brothy soup), *callaloo* stew, roasted breadfruit, stewed or roasted beef, boiled yam or plantains, rice and peas, or *escovitched* fried fish. Puerto Rican cooks prepare many Spanish-influenced dishes: roasted whole pork, grilled chickens, *arroz con pollo* (rice and chicken), *mofongo* (boiled, mashed plantain seasoned with pork cracklings), *surullitos* (deep-fried corn sticks), *tostones*, paella, *gandules* (pigeon peas), and *pasteles* (a yuca or plantain tamale filled with picadillo).

The Lesser Antilles is divided into *Windward* and *Leeward Islands*. The Leewards include Guadeloupe, St. Kitts, and Nevis, Virgin Gorda, and the British and U.S. Virgins. The Windwards include Martinique, St. Lucia, Grenada, Barbados, and Trinidad-Tobago. Barbadians love flying fish and *cou cou* (cornmeal and okra loaf). French Caribbean islands of St. Barts, Martinique, and French St. Martin combine French technique and Creole cooking with Caribbean chilies and seasonings in *blaff* (poached fish), *court-bouillon* (fish poached in spicy tomato sauce), *boudin* (spicy pig's blood sausage), *callaloo* stew, and rum punches. Trinidad, Grenada, Martinique, and Guadeloupe are home to *colombo* (meat or vegetable curry), *roti* (flatbreads), *oildown* (fish-coconut stew), and *pelau* (pilaf) while Saint Kitts and Nevis and Saint Lucia specialize in coconut dumplings and salt cod. *Crapaud* or "mountain chicken," a type of frog, is the national dish of Dominica. Cassava bread, land crabs, river crayfish, and locally raised livestock like goat, pig, and cow, as well as many imported foods and homemade sweets and coconut desserts, round out the *Lesser Antilles* diet.

FIGURE 12.2   Caribbean Island view.
Source: pavel Chernobrivets/Fotolia.

DINE AT HOME IN THE CARIBBEAN ISLANDS

The people who populated the islands and their ancestry largely helped to determine the dining customs in each region of the Caribbean Islands, but most of the islands follow continental etiquette. (On many islands, lunch is the main meal and dinner is lighter, as in Spain.) If invited to dine at someone's home, dress up (no beach attire allowed) and plan to arrive slightly late, unless it is a business meeting. In much of the Caribbean, meals are informal, but it depends: the more formal a gathering, the stricter the manners.

Greet the host and hostess with a gentle handshake and use a title with their surname, not their first name. Bring a gift of pastries, good chocolate, or flowers (avoid black or purple, which is associated with death). West Indians show a reserved face; they save smiles and laughter for family and friends. Guests should not be disturbed if they don't elicit smiles right away. When introduced by good friends or relatives, guests are often given the same treatment as the friend or relative: a kiss and a hug.

Men should hold doors open and allow women and the elderly to enter a room first, and rise when a woman enters the room. Usually the honored guest will be invited to sit to the right or left of the host and hostess. Eat when the host or hostess says *Buen provecho!* Keep hands visible, but no elbows on the table. Hold the fork in the left hand and knife in the right to eat. Pass dishes to the left. Politely try a bite of everything, but take only what can be eaten—it's impolite to leave food on the plate. Fish or seafood will likely feature in any meal: it will be cooked in different ways depending on the island. The meal may begin with *asopao* (rice and chicken soup) or *ceviche* (raw, marinated fish). The main dish might be fried fish patties, Jamaican jerked chicken, or a goat curry. Rice and possibly a vegetable like *callaloo* (greens) will accompany the main dish.

Guests don't leave the table before the entire meal is finished; it may insult the hosts. When finished, lay the knife and fork parallel to each other across the plate, or lay them on either side of the plate. Well-mannered guests toast the hosts with *salud*, which means "to your health." Thank the host and hostess and compliment the meal before exiting the table.

TASTES OF THE CARIBBEAN

Fat: Vegetable and peanut oil, palm oil, coconut oil, lard, fatback

Sweet: Sugar, sugar cane, cane syrup, molasses

Sour/Alcohol: Lime, tamarind, cane vinegar, vinegar, *amchar* (green mango powder), Seville orange (sour)

Salty: Salt, soy sauce

Spicy-Hot: Fresh chilies—Scotch Bonnet, jalapeño, *melegueta* peppercorns, cayenne and chili powders, red pepper flakes, black and white pepper

Spice: Annatto, mustard powder, allspice, clove, cinnamon, coriander, garlic powder, turmeric, ground ginger, cumin, nutmeg, mace, paprika, curry powder, celery salt, star anise

Aromatic Seasoning Vegetables: Onions, garlic, tomato, *escallions* (green onions), carrots, shallots, celery, bell peppers

Herbs, Seasonings, and Condiments: Thyme, marjoram, bay leaf, oregano, chives, parsley, cilantro, *shadon or chandon beni* (culantro), *cassareep* (cooked cassava juice, brown sugar and spices) *pick-a-peppa sauce* (Jamaican mango-tamarind-pepper), hot pepper sauces, salsas, jerk seasonings, Angostura bitters, vanilla

Other Important Foods: (See *Vegetables and Fruits of the Caribbean*), rice, coconut, avocado, fruit (papaya, mango, melon, pineapple, plantains, bananas), seafood (saltwater fish, conch, flying fish, grouper, marlin, pompano, king mackerel, oysters, red snapper, shark, tilapia, *bacalao* [salt cod], salted mackerel, herring or haddock, sea urchin, land crabs), meat (chicken, goat, seafood, sausage, oxtail, salted beef, pork), legumes (pigeon peas, kidney beans, black beans, pink beans, broad beans, butter beans, black-eyed peas, peanuts), arrowroot (starchy thickener), *turrón* (Spanish almond nougat)

Popular Dishes: *Asopao* (soupy meat or seafood stew), *arroz con pollo* (rice and chicken), *arroz con gandules* (rice with pigeon peas), *lechón* (roasted pig), *alcapurria* (meat stuffed banana or yautía fritter), *ceviche* (raw marinated seafood), chutney, *colombo curry* (spicy gravy-based dish), *escovitch* (fried or poached fish marinated), *Jamaican jerk* (spice rubbed chicken, pork, or other protein), *paella, roti, stamp and go* (codfish patties fried in heavy batter seasoned with onions, annatto, and chilies), *callaloo* (soup or stew with greens), *mondongo* (tripe stew), goat curry or stew, *buñuelos* (sweet fritters), *flan* (custard caramel)

Drinks: Coffee, tea, *mawby* (bark boiled with spices), rum, *Mojito Cuban cocktail* (rum, lime, and soda)

COMMON CARIBBEAN COOKING TOOLS

Pilón (mortar and pestle), dippers, spoons, bowl and serving pieces made from dried *calabash gourd, anafre* (portable burner)

CARIBBEAN CHEESE

Non-Melting White Cheese

The most popular cheeses in the Caribbean Islands are fresh, mild, creamy white types. When heated, the fresh white cheeses of the Caribbean (and Mexico) soften without melting. This characteristic is essential in many Hispanic dishes for stuffing, frying, and tossing the cubed cheese into hot dishes. Most cheese becomes gooey during cooking, but even after long cooking, these white cheeses do not. Traditionally, nonmelting cheeses were produced by local artisans and brought to market wrapped in banana leaves.

Queso Blanco or Queso de País

Queso blanco is a traditional fresh, white cow milk cheese like a cross between salty cottage cheese and Italian mozzarella. The curd is traditionally coagulated with lemon juice, which imparts a creamy, crisp citrus flavor.

Queso Para Freir

This Caribbean cheese is similar to queso blanco, white and crumbly, but saltier. It is often used for frying because it resists melting even better than queso blanco.

Melting Cheese

Caribbean melting cheeses are generally smooth-textured, mild-flavored with slight acidity. These cheeses do not separate into solids and oils when heated.

Queso Media Luna or Queso de Papa

A popular melting cheese in Puerto Rico, this common Caribbean cheese is a Colby-type cheese with an orange hue and firm, moist texture. The smooth mild to tangy flavor makes it good for snacking or baking.

Aged, Grating Cheese

Hard-grating cheeses are made by salting fresh cheese and aging in the heat up to a year.

Duroblando

A strong-flavored, firm Caribbean cheese with a mildly smoked flavor. It is used for grating similar to Mexican cotija.

Cultured Cream

Like Mexican cuisines, Caribbean cuisines use thick, fresh cultured creams to add richness, to garnish savory dishes such as quesadillas and enchiladas, as toppings on desserts, and as thickeners in sauces and gravies.

Crema Agria or Crema Centro Americana

Similar to crema Mexicana, this is a thick, rich cream with a tangy flavor, which makes it an ideal garnish for savory dishes.

VEGETABLES AND FRUITS OF THE CARIBBEAN

Though many of these fruits and vegetables are not native to the Caribbean, they thrive in the tropical climate and are prized throughout the islands.

Vegetables

Ackee
A large Jamaican pink fruit that looks like a mango or guava. Toxic when unripe, the ackee's ripe yellow flesh resembles scrambled eggs. Jamaicans pair it with saltfish for a national breakfast dish. Ackee is available canned.

Boniato or Batata
This tropical tuber is a type of sweet potato with sweet, white or orange flesh, and pink to purple skin.

Calabaza or West Indian Pumpkin
A very large, round, yellow-skinned squash similar to Hubbard, acorn, and butternut squashes.

Callaloo
The large green leaves of dasheen or taro plant or the leaves of Chinese spinach. Substitute fresh large spinach leaves for callaloo.

Cassava, Yuca, Tapioca, or Manioc
A large, long brown root vegetable with hard starchy white flesh that when boiled is similar to potato. Two varieties exist: bitter and sweet. The sweet version is dried and ground into cassava flour, which is used to make tapioca and a Caribbean bread called *bammie* or *pain de kassav*.

Christophene or Chayote
A pale, green pear-shaped tropical fruit with edible skin and pit that has the flavor of zucchini when cooked.

Cocoyam, Dasheen, Taro, Malanga, Yautia, or Tannia
Tropical brown-skinned *corms* (swollen underground stems) with edible leaves, the cocoyam or taro and related species are toxic when raw, but sweet and nutty when boiled or roasted with white flesh.

Hearts of Palm
Literally the tender heart of a palm tree that is boiled until tender. It is served on salads or as a vegetable. Its texture

FIGURE 12.3 Ackee fruit.
Source: Blacqbook/Shutterstock.

FIGURE 12.4 Boniato.
Source: Will Heap/DK Images.

FIGURE 12.5 Calabaza.
Source: Argonautis/Fotolia.

(Continued)

FIGURE 12.6 Cassava/yuca.
Source: Dorling Kindersley/DK Images.

FIGURE 12.7 Chayote squash.
Source: Lorenzo Vecchia/DK Images.

FIGURE 12.8 Taro root.
Source: Will Heap/Dorling Kindersley.

and taste are similar to a delicate asparagus. Hearts of palm come canned.

Jicama

See *Glossary* or chapter *Mexico*.

June Plum or Golden Apple

This Caribbean plum is related to stone fruits like peach and apricot. It is large, oval, and lime green when harvested with the complex flavors and

FIGURE 12.9 Hearts of palm.
Source: ChantalS/Fotolia.

aromas of pineapple, mango, apple, and melon. Its flesh is cream-colored, slightly acidic, and firm; it may be eaten raw or cooked. The skin ripens

to red and orange. It complements pork products. The June plum thrives in tropical and subtropical regions and is mainly grown in South America and the Caribbean, specifically Jamaica.

Okra

The most prized vegetable of the Caribbean, okra came to the Caribbean with West African slaves. Its long, narrow green pods are slightly fuzzy and pointed. When sliced and cooked, they produce a mucilaginous liquid that is prized for its thickening ability.

Yam or Ñame

A tropical tuber similar to sweet potato, but much less sweet and much, much larger.

See *Glossary*.

FIGURE 12.10 Yam or ñame.
Source: Turbojet/Shutterstock.

Fruit

Breadfruit

A large, round, cannonball-sized, green-skinned starchy fruit that is used unripe or ripe as a starch in Caribbean dishes, breadfruit must be cooked before eating and is roasted whole or fried as chips. Use potatoes as a substitute.

Carambola or Star Fruit

A slightly tart, translucent star-shaped fruit, which Caribbean cooks use for the tart juice. Two varieties exist—pale yellow and pale green; the yellow is sweeter.

(Continued)

(Continued)

FIGURE 12.11 Breadfruit.
Source: singphoto/Fotolia.

FIGURE 12.13 Cashew fruit.
Source: denchat/Fotolia.

FIGURE 12.12 Star fruit.
Source: Roger Phillips/Dorling Kindersley.

Cashew Fruit
Literally the red pear-shaped fruit that produces the cashew nut, the fruit is juicy and sweet with hints of mango, green bell pepper, and citrus.

Cherimoya or Custard Apple
The size of a grapefruit with green skin that gives slightly to pressure when ripe, cherimoya flesh is white, soft, and sweet with a sherbet-like texture and flavor of banana, pineapple, papaya, peach, and strawberry.

Guava or Guayaba
An apple-sized, oval fruit with taste of strawberry, banana and pineapple,

FIGURE 12.14 Cherimoya, custard apple.
Source: joefotofl/Fotolia.

unripe green guava is tart-flavored and ripe guava is yellow, red, purple, or almost black and sweet when ripe. The creamy flesh of this Mexican native ranges from white, yellow, and salmon to intensely pink.

Jackfruit
A huge fruit that tastes of pineapple and custard with a custardy texture. Unripe, it is often cooked. Jackfruit is related to the stinky but prized Southeast Asian durian fruit.

Papaya
There are two varieties of papaya: the small and pear-shaped Hawaiian, and the very large and long Mexican variety. Both have green skin when unripe

FIGURE 12.15 Guava.
Source: Vinicius Tupinamba/Shutterstock.com

FIGURE 12.16   Jackfruit.
Source: Vinicius Tupinamba/Shutterstock.com

FIGURE 12.19   Caribbean pineapple.
Source: 强子/Fotolia.

FIGURE 12.17   Papaya.
Source: Malyshchyts Viktar/Fotolia.

and yellow skin that gives upon pressing, when ripe. Their flesh is sweet and creamy, similar to a cantaloupe, pale salmon-pink, and filled with round, black, peppery seeds. The smaller fruit is slightly more intense. The large variety is eaten raw and green or sometimes cooked.

Passion Fruit or Parcha
A small, round fruit, the size of a tennis ball, that is bright yellow with soft to firm juicy flesh filled with many seeds. Its juice is used in drinks and the flesh in desserts.

Pineapple
A tropical fruit with brown skin topped with long, spiky, green leaves that give it the look of a pinecone. It has very sweet, pale yellow flesh that

sometimes has hints of coconut. Raw pineapple contains bromelain, a powerful enzyme that breaks down protein.

Plantain
A large starchy banana, plantains must be cooked before eating. Cooks use them unripe or ripe for various dishes. The unripe fruit is starchy and delicate flavored when cooked; the ripe fruit, called *amarillo*, is slightly sweet with a lovely fruity note.

FIGURE 12.18   Passion fruit.
Source: Tim UR/Shutterstock.com

FIGURE 12.20   Ripe plaintains.
Source: Barnabas Kindersley/ Dorling Kindersley.

(Continued)

(Continued)

FIGURE 12.21 Mamey sapote.
Source: kmiragaya/Fotolia.

FIGURE 12.24 Soursop.
Source: Shariff Che'Lah/Fotolia.

FIGURE 12.25 Tamarind.
Source: Popova Olga/Fotolia.

Mamey Sapote

A beloved native Mexican fruit with brown, sandpapery skin, its creamy flesh tastes of peach, cinnamon, maraschino cherry, and pumpkin.

Mango

Many varieties of mango exist and their sweet yellow flesh, with hints of carrot, peach, coconut, and melon, is used in different ways: ripe in desserts or in drinks and unripe in hot sauces and chutneys.

Sapodilla or Naseberry

A kiwi-sized native South and Central American fruit with golden-brown skin and pink-brown, slightly grainy pulp, which tastes of pear, apple, and cinnamon. Chewing gum was made from the tree's sap, known as *chicle*.

Soursop or Guanábana or Brazilian Pawpaw

A native Caribbean fruit with pale yellow or green skin covered with small spines. Its creamy white flesh tastes of strawberry, pineapple, and sour citrus overlying coconut or banana.

Tamarind

A long brown pod filled with large seeds surrounded by a sticky, tart-sweet flesh, tamarind pulp flavors chutney, juices, and stews.

FIGURE 12.22 Mango showing flat pit.
Source: Lorenzo Vecchia/Dorling Kinderlsey.

FIGURE 12.23 Sapodilla.
Source: sayhmog/Fotolia.

CARIBBEAN FLAVOR FOUNDATIONS

Caribbean Signature Aromatic Vegetable Combo

Sofrito

Onion, garlic, green bell pepper, tomato, and cilantro

Sofrito ingredients are finely diced or puréed before cooking with lard and/or pork. Sofritos are cooked ahead and refrigerated for easy addition to many dishes. Dominican and Cuban cooks generally prepare sofrito with tomato or tomato paste and sometimes season it with vinegar.

Alcaparrado

A mixture of green olives, capers, and pimientos used to season many dishes.

Recaito (Green Sofrito)

Ajies dulces, green bell pepper, garlic, *culantro (recao)*, and cilantro. This Puerto Rican flavoring base, similar to sofrito, doesn't usually contain tomatoes. Cooks grind the ingredients into a purée *before* cooking. Puerto Ricans fry recaito with salt pork or oil infused with annatto as a base seasoning like sofrito or stir recaito in at the end of cooking.

Caribbean Herbal Combo/ Bouquet Garni

Thyme, bay leaf, and marjoram.

Caribbean Signature Seasonings

Liquid/Paste

Achiote Oil

Oil into which achiote or annatto seed has been infused, imparting a orange glow and pleasant and mildly saffron-bitter flavor.

Angostura Bitters

Made in Trinidad, this bitter alcohol-based liquid is a mixture of herbs and seasonings like gentian. Known for its digestive qualities and often used in cocktails, Caribbean cooks season savory and sweet dishes with Angostura Bitters.

Jerk Seasoning

Although dry jerk mixes are available, they aren't used much in Jamaica. Instead cooks employ jerk pastes and marinades with ground allspice and Scotch Bonnet chilies as main ingredients.

Palm Oil

Used in Brazilian, Caribbean, and West African cooking, palm oil is made from the kernel of the palm fruit. The oil is thick and red-orange in color with a nutty flavor and high in saturated

FIGURE 12.26   Dende oil palm.
Source: sarot/Fotolia.

FIGURE 12.27   Palm oil fruit.
Source: nui7711/Fotolia.

fat. cooks use it for frying, and to flavor stews, rice, and sauces.

Animal

Lard

See chapter *Mexico Signature Seasonings*.

Vegetable/Fruit

Ajies Dulces (Sweet Chilies)

This rich-flavored chili is similar in shape and size to a Scotch Bonnet, but mostly lacks the hot intensity. The small, light-green aji dulce chili ripens to red or yellow, and is used green or ripe. Caribbean cooks freeze rather than dry this chili to preserve its flavor. It is an important part of the Puerto Rican *recaito*.

FIGURE 12.28   Ajies dulces.
Source: Margaret M Stewart/Shutterstock.

(Continued)

(Continued)

FIGURE 12.29 Scotch bonnet chilies.
Source: Ian O'Leary/Dorling Kindersley.

FIGURE 12.30 Jamaican allspice berries.
Source: Barbara Dudzinska/Fotolia.

Scotch Bonnet Chili

This very hot, small chili is found mainly in the Caribbean, West Africa, Grenada, Trinidad, Jamaica, Barbados, Guyana, Surinam, Haiti, and the Caymans. It ripens from green to yellow and red and is mainly used ripe. Scotch Bonnets are about 40 times hotter than a jalapeño and sweeter than their Mexican relative, the *habañero*. Caribbean cooks place whole Scotch Bonnets to simmer in soups and stews for flavor with less heat, or seed and mince them for more heat in sauces and condiments.

See *Vegetables and Fruits of the Caribbean.*

Herbal/Spice

All-Purpose Caribbean Seasoning

Used throughout the islands, this ubiquitous seasoning contains salt, chili powder, onion powder, ground coriander, dried thyme, ground allspice, and ground black pepper. Commercial varieties contain MSG. Caribbean cooks use it to season one-pot dishes, fish, meat, or vegetables.

Allspice

Predominately grown in its native Jamaica, these aromatic dried brown berries are an important part of jerk seasoning.

FIGURE 12.31 Annatto seed.
Source: David Murray/Dorling Kindersley.

Annatto/Achiote

Red seed used to color and flavor cooking oil, some think to resemble the orange West African *dende* oil (red palm oil). Seeds that turn brown are old and flavorless.

Bajan Seasoning

Barbadian mixture used to season chicken and fish dishes that can consist of all or part dried thyme, marjoram, green onions, chives, garlic, parsley, basil, Scotch Bonnet chili, clove, black pepper, paprika, and salt.

Basil

European sweet basil is preferred.

FIGURE 12.32 Culantro/saw leaf herb.
Source: Dave King/Dorling Kindersley.

Chandon Beni (Culantro)

See *Glossary.*

Cinnamon or Cassia

Pale inner bark of cinnamon tree mostly grown on Grenada. Cassia is a coarse cousin. In Barbados, cinnamon is known simply as "spice." See chapter *Mexico, Mexican Flavor Foundations.*

Clove

Aromatic, unopened bud of tropical evergreen indigenous to the Spice Islands mostly grown on Grenada.

Cumin

Aromatic brown seed from the parsley family often used in Caribbean curry powders.

Ginger

Used fresh and dried, this Asian native happily grows in Jamaica, where cooks add it to curry, and use it fresh to make ginger candy and ginger beer.

Jamaican Peppermint (Menta de Palo)

Although traditional mint is used in the Caribbean, cooks also use another class of mints from the summer and winter savory family that taste similar to peppermint. Jamaican peppermint is one of the best known. It is actually a woody shrub that grows wild in Jamaica, Puerto Rico, Costa Rica, Trinidad, and other Caribbean islands. Jamaicans grind the leaves to season meat or use it in place of traditional mint in desserts, drinks, and tea.

FIGURE 12.33 Melegueta pepper or grains of paradise.
Source: Dave King/Dorling Kinderlsey.

Melegueta Peppercorns or Grains of Paradise

See *Glossary.*

Mustard Seed

Jamaican cooks use yellow mustard seed whole or ground to add a sparky, pungent flavor to stews and curries.

Nutmeg and Mace

Nutmeg, a nutty, sweet aromatic spice, is a seed and mace its aromatic red webbed covering. Grown on Grenada, nutmeg comes from a tall tropical evergreen.

Sazón

A commercial seasoning (used mainly in Puerto Rico) made with ground coriander, cumin, pepper, annatto seed, garlic powder, salt, and often, MSG.

- To prepare Puerto Rican sazón: Dry-toast and grind 1 tablespoon each coriander, cumin, and black peppercorns, and mix with 1 tablespoon each ground annatto and garlic powder plus 2 teaspoons kosher salt.
- **Dominicans** prepare a wet sazón with onions, bell pepper, garlic, oregano, scallion, parsley, and cilantro.

Thyme

Frequently used in Caribbean herb mixtures fresh or dried, this aromatic, meaty herb is a relative of mint.

Turmeric

Sometimes called *saffron* in the Caribbean, turmeric is an acrid, orange-yellow root that looks like ginger. It may be used fresh grated or dried and powdered. It adds a deep orange hue to food.

SEASONING AND PASTE MIXTURES

Caribbean cooks are wild about rubs, sauces, and seasonings, which they call *sazón*. They are almost always spicy with heat, herbs, and locally grown chilies. Sauces are either bottled or puréed and used fresh or cooked before serving. Marinade liquids, pastes, and rubs are applied to fish, meat, or fowl. Liquid marinades are usually thinner than sauces and are sometimes thickened into a sauce with arrowroot or cornstarch.

ACHIOTE-ANNATTO OIL (ACEITE DE ACHIOTE)

Infusing annatto (achiote) seeds into hot olive oil turns the oil a brilliant orange with mild, nutty, aroma that adds color and a little flavor to rice, beans, soups, stews, and braises. Brush it on fish or chicken before baking or grilling, or begin a sauté with it.

Yields 1 cup

1 cup olive oil *or* vegetable oil
2 tablespoons achiote (annatto) seeds

1 Heat oil and annatto seeds in a 1-quart saucepan over low heat until seeds sizzle. If seeds are overheated, they will blacken and the oil will turn green. Dump it and start again.

2 Remove pan from heat and cool. Strain oil and store at room temperature 1 day and in refrigerator up to 1 week.

There are other versions of this commercial seasoning available with ground ginger, clove, oregano, and ground mustard seed.

Yields 3-1/2 tablespoons

1 tablespoon kosher salt
1-1/2 teaspoons garlic powder
1-1/2 teaspoons onion powder
1-1/4 teaspoons dried, crushed thyme
1 teaspoon ground red chili powder
3/4 teaspoon ground black pepper
1/2 teaspoon ground allspice
1/4 teaspoon ground coriander

1   Mix salt and ground spices together. Seal in glass jar.

Jamaican Jerk Marinade, Sauce, and Rub

The key ingredients of this well-known Jamaican seasoning are allspice (Jamaican *pimento*) and Scotch Bonnet chilies. *Jerk Rub* is a moist, intense flavoring best rubbed on pork, meat, or game 1 hour before cooking. *Jerk Marinade*, with spices, garlic, chilies, vinegar, soy sauce, and oil, is best used on chicken, fish, and ribs. Prepare *Jerk Sauce* and serve as a sauce or table condiment over cooked beef, pork, fowl, or fish.

SIGNATURE RECIPE

JAMAICAN JERK MARINADE AND JERK SAUCE

Yields 3/4 to 1 cup, depending on chilies; use 1 to 2 tablespoons per pound meat, fish, or fowl

1 teaspoon freshly ground allspice
1/2 teaspoon freshly ground nutmeg
1/2 teaspoon ground cinnamon
2 ounces trimmed green onions, about 4 large, 1/2 cup chopped
    Spicy-hot: 2 ounces Scotch Bonnet chilies, about 4, halved and stemmed
    or *Mildly spicy-hot:* 1 to 2 ounces serrano chilies, 2 to 4 medium, halved and coarsely chopped
1/2 cup distilled white vinegar
1/4 cup soy sauce
2 tablespoons vegetable oil
1 tablespoon kosher salt
1/4 teaspoon garlic powder
For Jerk Sauce: 2 tablespoons to 1/2 cup distilled white vinegar, to taste

1   *To prepare* **Jerk Marinade:** Pour ingredients into blender and purée until smooth and liquid, about 2 minutes.

2   *To use* **Jerk Marinade:** Spread marinade evenly over fish, fowl, or meat. Marinate fish in refrigerator 15 minutes and chicken or meat 1 to 8 hours. Pour unused marinade into a glass jar and tightly cover. Refrigerate up to 6 months.

3   *To prepare* **Jerk Sauce:** Pour **jerk marinade** into a small saucepan. Add distilled white vinegar to taste. Bring sauce to a boil, cover pan, and reduce heat. Simmer sauce 15 minutes. Cool sauce, transfer to glass canning jar with tight lid, and refrigerate. Refrigerated, the sauce will keep several months or more. Use on beef, pork, fish, and fowl.

Source: *Island Barbecue* by Dunstan Harris.

SIGNATURE RECIPE

JAMAICAN JERK RUB

Yields 1/3 to 1/2 cup depending on chilies

3 ounces lightly trimmed green onions, about 6, 2/3 to 1 cup coarsely chopped
1 tablespoon kosher salt
1 teaspoon freshly ground allspice
1/2 teaspoon freshly ground nutmeg
1/4 teaspoon ground cinnamon
Spicy-hot: 2 ounces Scotch Bonnet chilies, about 4, halved and stemmed
    or Mildly spicy-hot: 1 to 2 ounces serrano chilies, 2 to 4 medium, stemmed
    and coarsely chopped
1 teaspoon freshly ground black pepper
Optional: 1 tablespoon distilled white vinegar

1 Place ingredients into wet grinder or blender. Process ingredients to a paste. If using a blender, add 1 tablespoon white vinegar or water to aid in blending.

2 Scrape rub into jar and cover tightly. Refrigerate up to 2 months.

Source: *Island Barbecue* by Dunstan A. Harris.

SAUCE

CARIBBEAN-STYLE SOFRITO

Sofrito varies wildly from island to island, but in Cuba its basic foundation includes onions, bell peppers, garlic, and often tomato with accents of optional cilantro, oregano, ground cumin, and bay leaves. Some recipes add pork products like ham, and olives or capers for extra flavor.

Yields about 2 cups

3 to 4 tablespoons oil
6 to 7 ounces onion, 1 medium, 1-1/2 cups peeled and finely diced
1 ounce garlic, 4 large cloves, 2 tablespoons peeled and minced
6 to 7 ounce green bell pepper, 1 cup cored, seeded, and finely diced
Optional: 1/4 teaspoon ground cumin
Optional: 1 teaspoon crushed dried oregano
7 ounces tomatoes, 1 cup finely diced
2 bay leaves
Optional: 1/4 ounce cilantro, 2 tablespoons finely sliced

1 Heat oil in a 10- to 11-inch skillet over medium heat. Add onion, garlic, and bell pepper and cook until vegetables are tender, 5 minutes. Sprinkle with optional cumin or oregano.

2 Stir in tomatoes and bay leaves. Simmer until tomatoes break down and the liquid reduces, 5 minutes. Remove bay leaves and season sofrito with salt and freshly ground black pepper to taste. Stir in optional cilantro.

Vary! Improvise!

☞ *Blend It: Place coarsely chopped raw ingredients, except oil and bay leaf, into blender, and process to a coarse purée. Place in storage container and top with oil. Refrigerate. Scoop out sofrito and cook (with bay leaf) as needed. Refrigerate up to 4 days for best flavor.*

FIGURE 12.34 Cubanelle pepper.
Source: Bert Folsom/Fotolia.

PUERTO RICAN GREEN RECAITO

Culantro is called recao in Puerto Rico, and recaito means "little culantro." Culantro is the defining flavor of this type of sofrito. Use recaito for soups, stews, Cuban black beans, rice pilafs, or Puerto Rican pot roast or when less liquid than sofrito or a green color is preferred.

Yields 1-1/4 to 1-1/2 cups

6 ounces Spanish onion, about 1 medium, 1-1/2 cups peeled and diced
1-1/2 ounces garlic, 6 to 8 large cloves, peeled
3 ounces *ajies dulces* sweet pepper-chilies, about 6 small
    or 3 ounces Cubanelle or green bell pepper, 1 medium, 3/4 cup cored, seeded, and diced
1 ounce cilantro, 1 cup packed with stems, coarsely chopped
4 leaves culantro
    or increase cilantro by half (1/2 ounce or 1/2 cup packed with stems)

1 Place onion and garlic into food processor or blender. With the machine running, add the remaining ingredients and purée until mixture is velvety. If using blender, add 1/4 cup water to aid puréeing.

2 Refrigerate recaito in storage container or freeze the remainder in small portions. Will keep up to 1 week refrigerated or 2 months frozen.

3 **To Use:** Sauté recaito in lard- or annatto-infused oil at the beginning of a dish as a seasoning base or stir in toward the end of cooking time to provide a fresh top flavor.

Source: Latin chef Daisy Martinez.

FIGURE 12.35 Caribbean version of creole sauce.
Source: Unclesam/Fotolia.

FRESH CARIBBEAN TOMATO SAUCE (SAUCE CRÉOLE)

This fresh sauce comes from Martinique where the cuisine reflects the southeastern Caribbean-Creole mélange of French, Spanish, African, Indian and European influences.

Yields about 2-1/2 cups, 4 to 6 servings

12 ounces tomatoes, 2 medium, 1-1/2 cups finely diced
    or 1-1/2 cups tomato purée
4 to 5 ounces onion, 1 cup peeled and finely diced
1 ounce trimmed celery, 1/4 cup finely diced
1/4 to 1/2 ounce serrano or jalapeño chili, 1-1/2 teaspoons stemmed, seeded and finely diced
1 ounce trimmed green onions, 2 large, 4 tablespoons finely chopped
4 tablespoons fresh lime juice, about 1 large lime
1-1/2 ounces small pimento-stuffed olives, about 1/4 cup finely sliced

For Serving

1-1/2 to 2 pounds baked, broiled or grilled fish

1 Combine tomatoes, onion, celery, chili, green onions, lime juice and olives in a mixing bowl. Season to taste with salt and freshly ground black pepper. Rest sauce 15 to 20 minutes at room temperature, or chill. Taste and adjust flavors.

2 *To Serve*: Transfer sauce to bowl with serving spoon. Serve sauce spooned over baked, broiled, or grilled fish or seafood.

Source: *The Complete Book of Caribbean Cooking* by Elisabeth Lambert Ortiz.

CUBAN MOJO SAUCE

Mojo refers to the Moors who brought oranges to Spain and Latin America. Use this "Cuban National Sauce" as a marinade, warm or room temperature on boiled yuca or potatoes, meat, fish, or sandwiches.

Yields about 1 cup

1/2 cup olive oil, *divided*
1 to 2 ounces onion, 1/4 cup peeled and finely diced
1 ounce garlic, about 2 large cloves, 1 tablespoon peeled and finely sliced
1 teaspoon ground cumin
1/4 cup plus 2 tablespoons (3 fluid ounces) fresh orange juice, about 1 medium orange
1/4 cup fresh lime juice, about 1 large or 2 medium limes, more to taste
1/4 ounce cilantro, 2 tablespoons finely sliced

1 Heat 2 tablespoons oil over medium-low heat in small saucepan. Stir in onion and garlic and cook until golden, 5 to 7 minutes. Stir in cumin and cook 30 to 45 seconds. Stir in orange juice and lime juice. Bring to a boil, remove pan from heat, and pour sauce into bowl to cool.

2 Whisk cilantro and remaining olive oil into warm sauce. Season sauce to taste with salt and pepper and more citrus, if desired.

Vary! Improvise!

☞ *Simplify: Simmer garlic until soft in a little oil, add sour orange juice or orange mixed half and half with lime and cumin, and bring to a boil. Remove mojo from heat and season with salt and pepper.*

DOG SAUCE (SAUCE CHIEN)

From Martinique, this table sauce is classic French Caribbean where it's poured over cooked seafood and poultry. Similar sauces are the Cuban mojo, *the Haitian* ti-malice, *and the Dutch Caribbean* pika. *Use half the chili for less heat.*

Yields 1 cup

3 ounces trimmed green onions, 6 large, 2/3 to 1 cup coarsely chopped
1/2 ounce trimmed Italian parsley, 3/4 cup coarsely chopped
3/4 ounce garlic, 3 large cloves, 1-1/2 tablespoons peeled and minced
1/4 ounce Scotch bonnet chili, 1 small, 1 teaspoon stemmed, seeded, and minced
1/2 cup boiling water
2 tablespoons lime juice, 1/2 large lime
1 tablespoon white wine vinegar
2 tablespoons olive oil

1 Place onions, parsley, garlic, and chili in bowl of food processor. Pulse-chop until vegetables are finely chopped. (Alternatively, finely chop ingredients by hand.)

2 Scrape mixture into mixing bowl and pour boiling water over. Cool slightly. Stir in lime juice, vinegar, and olive oil. Season with salt and pepper to taste.

3 **To Serve:** Serve sauce on the side or poured over fish, meat, or poultry. Refrigerate sauce up to 1 week. Bring to room temperature before serving.

Source: *The Spice Necklace* by Ann Vanderhoof.

Vary! Improvise!

☞ *Stir in 2 to 4 tablespoons finely diced, seeded tomato.*

CARIBBEAN MANGO RELISH

Caribbean mango relish had its beginnings in India. Immigrants from India made it from ripe or unripe mangos, onion or garlic, chili, oil, and salt. Cooks in the southeastern Caribbean islands of Martinique, Guadeloupe, and Trinidad serve mango relish with hot or cold boiled, roasted, or grilled fish or meat. Cooked sweet-and-sour mango chutney, made with ripe or unripe mangos, is popular in Jamaica.

CARIBBEAN MANGO CHUTNEY

Yields 6 cups

2 ounces dried tamarind pulp, 1/4 cup packed
3 pounds unripe mango, 3 large
2 cups malt vinegar
8 ounces granulated sugar, 1 cup
2-1/2 ounces raisins, 1/2 cup
About 3 ounces gingerroot, 1/2 cup peeled and finely diced
1/4 ounce garlic, 1 large clove, 1-1/2 teaspoons peeled and minced
1/4 to 1/2 ounce Scotch Bonnet chili, 1 small to medium, 1 to 2 teaspoons stemmed, seeded, and diced
1/2 teaspoon ground allspice

1 Bring 3/4 cup water to boil in a small saucepan. Remove pan from heat and place tamarind into it. Mash and stir until tamarind softens in water into a purée, 20 minutes. Rub purée through fine strainer, reserve purée, and discard seeds and fibers to yield 2/3 to 3/4 cup tamarind purée.

2 Peel mangos with vegetable peeler. Make a small slice on the bottom or top of one and set mango on one flat end. Remove mango cheeks by keeping knife parallel to and flat against the flat, broad pit. Cut down to remove cheeks. Cut remaining flesh away. Dice mango flesh into 1/2-inch pieces. Repeat with remaining mangos to yield about 7 cups diced mango.

3 Pour mangos and vinegar into a heavy 4- to 5-quart nonreactive saucepan and bring to a boil over high heat. Partially cover pan. Cook mangos 10 minutes, stirring occasionally. Add sugar, raisins, ginger, garlic, chili, allspice, and 2 teaspoons kosher salt. Bring mixture to a boil. Reduce heat to low, and simmer chutney uncovered until thickened and reduced, about 45 minutes. Stir periodically to keep chutney from burning.

4 Remove pan from heat. Cool chutney, place in jars, and refrigerate up to 6 months. Alternatively, check canning information.

Source: Time-Life's Foods of the World *The Cooking of the Caribbean Islands*.

SIMMER, STEW, POACH, BOIL, AND STEAM

Soup

Soups and stews form the backbone of Caribbean cuisine. They serve as a repository for end-of-week leftovers, as comforting tonics to revive, as hearty main meals, and as food for any celebration—birthdays, christenings, graduations, weddings, and wakes. In hot climates it would seem that soups and stews would tend to be lighter, but that's not the case. Caribbean soups and stews are chock full of meat, fish, fowl, seafood, vegetables, beans or noodles and seasonings and run the gamut from brothy to thick, satisfying gumbos. Visitors are offered strained soup as an appetizer. The meat and vegetables are served later for family dinner.

Fish tea, callaloo (in Jamaica called *pepperpot*), and Cuban black bean soup demonstrate the versatility of Caribbean soup. Hot, edible liquids are called *tea*, and the classic Caribbean "fish tea" is a rich fish broth prepared like a fish stock, but simmered with whole Scotch Bonnet chilies, sliced green bananas, tomato, and yam garnished with fresh cilantro or chives. Callaloo is a thick, satisfying soup of meat and greens with coconut milk while Cuban black bean soup employs a flavorful sofrito and ham to produce a rich, creamy soup.

SIGNATURE RECIPE

FISH TEA

If whole fish isn't available, use fish stock instead of water and 1-1/4 pounds fish fillets. If the chilies are broken, cut, or pierced they will make the soup too hot-spicy—keep them whole! Hot, edible liquids are called tea *in the Caribbean, hence the name of this fish broth.*

Yields 10 cups, 6 to 8 servings

2-1/4 pounds cleaned whole fresh red snapper or grouper
   or 1-1/4 pounds snapper, grouper, halibut, or other firm white fish fillets, skinned
1 cup dry white wine
4 to 5 ounces onion, 1 cup peeled and finely diced
3 to 4 ounces carrot, 1 cup scraped and finely diced
1 teaspoon black peppercorns
2 bay leaves
3 sprigs fresh thyme
1 whole Scotch Bonnet chili
5 cups water
   or 5 cups fish stock
12 ounces green, unripe bananas, 2 medium, 1-1/2 cups peeled and sliced 1/2-inch thick
1 pound tomatoes, 2 medium-large, about 2 cups peeled, seeded, and diced
1-1/2 pounds Caribbean yam or taro, about 3-1/4 cups peeled and medium dice
   or 1-1/2 pounds red-skin potatoes, about 4 cups medium dice

For Garnish: Finely sliced cilantro or chives

1 **Broth or tea:** Place fish, white wine, onion, carrot, peppercorns, bay leaves, thyme, whole chili, and water (*or fish stock if using fish fillets*) into 4-quart saucepan. Bring to a boil and lower heat so that broth simmers. Partially cover pan and simmer stock 30 minutes.

   If using fillets: Simmer fillets in fish stock until tender and cooked through, about 15 to 20 minutes. Remove fish, flake into smaller pieces, and set aside. Finish simmering vegetables.

2 **Strain:** Remove lid from pan and remove pan from heat. Cool soup 10 minutes. Strain through fine strainer lined with 2 layers of dampened cheesecloth into a clean 4-quart saucepan. Reserve strained ingredients and allow them to cool. Pick through strained ingredients, pull out fish meat, and set aside. Discard bones, skin, and vegetables. Squeeze gently to extract remaining juice.

3 Stir bananas, tomatoes, and yam or taro or potatoes into strained broth. Bring soup to a boil, reduce heat, and simmer vegetables until tender, 10 to 15 minutes. Season soup with salt and pepper to taste.

4 **To Serve:** Reheat soup. Divide reserved fish between serving bowls, ladle hot soup over fish, and garnish with cilantro or chives.

Source: *Eat Caribbean* by Virginia Burke.

Signature Technique: Caribbean Soup with Greens (Callaloo or Pepperpot)

There are many versions of this beloved and famous Caribbean créole soup-stew—alternately called calaloo, callilu, or callaloo. Caribbean cooks prepare it with young leaves from taro or yautía plants, but spinach (not baby) and chard are good substitutes. Also known as pepperpot in parts of the Caribbean, the distinctions between this soup and the eastern Caribbean callaloo-coconut-crab dish, also called callaloo, have been blurred.

On French Martinique and Guadaloupe, it's thickened with cooked green plantains or green bananas and served with créole rice (boiled white rice) and salt cod salad. Southeastern Caribbeans thicken callaloo with casareep, sweetened cooked cassava juice. In Jamaica this soup is called pepperpot and it's prepared with beef and many root vegetables and served with flat round flour dumplings called spinners.

- Wash, stem, and dice sturdy greens. Place in 6- to 8-quart pot.
- Stir in onion, garlic, thyme sprigs, blanched ham hocks or salt pork, cubed stew beef, and an optional whole Scotch Bonnet chili.
- Cover with chicken or beef stock or water or a combination.
- Bring to a boil, lower to a simmer, and cook until meat is tender, 45 minutes to 1 hour.
- Stir in tender vegetables like spinach greens if using, okra, green onions, crab, if using, and coconut milk.
- Simmer until vegetables are tender, 5 to 10 minutes.
- Season soup with salt and pepper. Remove thyme sprigs and chili.
- Ladle into bowls and serve *or* remove meat and purée vegetables with broth.
- Serve soup as the first course and the meat as the second course with hot sauce on the side.
- Serve with *Foo-Foo* or *spinners* (boiled flour dough dumplings).

FIGURE 12.36 Callaloo from tobago, West Indies.
Source: Robert Harding Picture Library Ltd/Alamy.

CARIBBEAN SOUP WITH GREENS (CALLALOO)

This is more stew than soup. It's traditionally made with water, but boost the flavor with all or part beef stock.

Yields about 6 quarts, 12 to 16 servings

8 ounces smoked ham hock
1 pound stewing beef, 2 cups diced into 1-inch cubes
4-1/2 to 5 quarts water *or* beef stock, or a mixture, *divided*
1-1/4 pounds fresh *callaloo* leaves, about 8 cups stems removed and finely diced
    or 1-1/4 pounds Swiss chard, about 8 cups stems removed and finely diced
        or 1-1/4 pounds baby collards, about 8 cups stems removed and finely diced
            or 1 pound large leafed spinach, chopped
8 to 12 ounces okra, 3-1/2 to 5 cups trimmed whole pods
    or 10-ounces frozen whole or sliced okra
1 pound russet-type potatoes, 3 medium, about 4 cups peeled and diced into 1/2-inch cubes
1/2 ounce whole Scotch Bonnet chili, 1 medium
6 to 7 ounce onion, 1-1/4 to 1-1/2 cups peeled and diced medium
1/2 ounce garlic, 2 large cloves, 1 tablespoon peeled and minced
2 large sprigs fresh thyme
1-1/2 cups canned or fresh coconut milk
4 tablespoons fresh lime juice, 1 large lime, more to taste
1 ounce trimmed green onions, 2 large, 4 tablespoons minced

1 If using, place ham hock into 2-quart saucepan and cover with cold water. Bring to a boil, remove from heat, and allow meat to soak in water 15 to 20 minutes. Drain and rinse ham hock. Place ham hock and stewing beef into heavy 8-quart pot. Cover meat with 2 quarts cold water. Bring to a boil over medium heat, lower the heat, partially cover the pot, and simmer the meat until tender, 1 hour.

2 Remove lid and stir in 2-1/2 quarts water, chosen greens (but not spinach), okra, potatoes, whole chili, onion, garlic, and thyme. Bring soup to a boil, lower heat to a bubbling simmer uncovered, and cook until vegetables soften and soup thickens, 1 to 1-1/2 hours, depending on greens.

3 If using spinach, stir in with coconut milk. Cook with a bubbling simmer until spinach is wilted, 5 to 10 minutes. Remove chili and thyme sprig. Season soup with salt, pepper, and lime juice to taste. Callaloo is traditionally puréed, but may be served without puréeing. To purée: Remove ham hock and beef and purée soup with immersion blender or in batches in a food processor. Adjust soup consistency with water or stock. Shred meat from ham hock, mix with beef, and stir into soup.

4 **To Serve:** Ladle hot soup into bowls, garnish with green onions, and serve.

Source: Island Cooking by Dunstan A. Harris.

CUBAN BLACK BEAN SOUP (SOPA DE FRIJOL NEGRO)

This classic soup is a favorite in Cuba, where the sweet-sour flavor from vinegar and sugar mark it as authentically Cuban.

Yields 9 cups, 6 to 8 servings

1 pound dry black beans, about 2-1/2 cups
2 bay leaves
2 tablespoons Achiote-Annatto Oil
6 ounces onion, 1-1/4 cup peeled and finely diced
1/2 ounce garlic, about 2 large cloves, 1 tablespoon peeled and minced
6 ounces lean ham, 1 cup diced into 1/4-inch cubes
2 teaspoons ground cumin
8 ounce tomato, 1 medium-large, about 1 cup peeled and finely diced
   or 1 cup drained, diced canned tomatoes
2 tablespoons malt or cider vinegar, more to taste
2 cups chicken stock, divided
Optional: 1 tablespoon sugar

Garnish: Finely sliced cilantro or diced hard-cooked eggs

For Serving

Cuban Mojo Sauce

1 Rinse black beans several times in cold water and drain. Pour beans and bay leaves into 4-quart saucepan and cover with 2 quarts cold water. Stir in 1 tablespoon kosher salt and bring beans to a boil. Lower the heat, cover beans, and simmer until very tender, 2 hours or more.

2 Heat a heavy 6-quart pot with annatto oil over medium heat. When oil ripples, stir in onion and garlic. Cook vegetables, stirring constantly, until soft but not browned, 3 to 5 minutes. Stir in ham and cumin and cook until fragrant, 3 to 4 minutes. Stir in tomatoes and vinegar and bring to a boil. Stirring constantly, cook sofrito until it thickens, 5 minutes. Remove from heat.

3 Place 1/3 cooked beans and broth and 1/2 cup chicken stock into blender, and purée until smooth, then pour into sofrito. Repeat with remaining beans and broth in two more batches. Rinse blender with remaining chicken stock and add to pot with sofrito and beans.

   Alternatively, mix beans and their broth and chicken stock into sofrito, and purée with immersion blender until smooth.

4 Bring soup to a simmer and cook until flavorful and heated through, 15 to 20 minutes. Taste soup and season with salt and freshly ground black pepper. If necessary, thin soup with water or more stock.

5 **To Serve:** Ladle soup onto soup plates or into bowls. Garnish with cilantro or hard-cooked eggs and serve with Cuban Mojo Sauce or another hot sauce as desired.

Source: Time-Life Foods of the World The Cooking of the Caribbean Islands.

Vary! Improvise!

☞ Substitute 2-1/2 quarts chicken stock for 2-1/2 quarts water in step 2.

☞ Substitute any dark, leafy greens for the callaloo.

☞ Use other root vegetables in place of potatoes.

FIGURE 12.37 Cuban favorite: roast pork, black beans, and fried ripe plantains.
Source: rgbspace/Fotolia.

Vary! Improvise!

☞ Core, seed, and finely dice 1 small bell pepper (6 ounces) and cook with onions and garlic.

☞ **Vegetarian:** Substitute vegetable stock for chicken, up the garlic and tomato, and omit the ham. Garnish with cheese if desired.

☞ Substitute kidney beans for black beans.

☞ Substitute fresh lime juice for vinegar.

FISH AND COCONUT STEW
(RUNDOWN, RONDÓN, OR OILDOWN)

Rundown varies from island to island and day to day depending on the ingredients the cook "runs down" from the local market or fisherman. This is a simple version. Coconut and lime juice are cornerstones of rundown from Jamaica to Grenada and Barbados; it is often accompanied by roast breadfruit.

Yields about 8 cups, 4 to 6 servings

3 cups thick coconut milk
8 to 9 ounces onion, 2 cups peeled and finely diced
1/4 ounce Scotch Bonnet chili, 1 small, halved and seeded
1/2 to 3/4 ounce garlic, 2 to 3 large cloves, 3 to 4 teaspoons peeled and minced
1-1/2 pounds tomatoes, about 3 cups peeled, seeded, and finely diced
1 tablespoon white wine vinegar
2 large sprigs fresh thyme
1/4 cup fresh lime juice, 1 to 1-1/2 large limes
2 pounds skinned firm or oily fish fillets like mackerel, halibut, bluefish, or Chilean sea bass

For Serving

Plain, cooked rice or *Boiled Green Bananas*

1 Pour coconut milk into deep 10- to 12-inch skillet and bring to a boil over medium heat. After 5 to 8 minutes, the coconut milk should reduce by about half. Fresh coconut milk may begin to separate and look oily—that's fine. Stir in onion, chili, and garlic and cook until soft, 10 minutes. Stir in tomatoes, vinegar, thyme, and season with salt. Bring to a boil. Lower heat and simmer stew 10 minutes. Taste stew and remove chili if no more heat is desired.

2 **Twenty minutes before serving:** Pour lime juice into mixing bowl. Dice fish into 1-inch cubes, and fold into lime juice in bowl. Marinate fish 15 minutes. Drain.

3 Add the fish to the stew, partially cover the pan, and lower the heat. Simmer fish gently until it flakes when probed with the tip of a knife, 5 to 8 minutes, depending on its thickness. Remove pan from heat. Taste sauce and season with salt and pepper.

4 **To Serve:** Spoon rice (if using) into soup plates. Transfer portions of fish onto rice and spoon sauce over. Or serve with boiled green bananas.

Source: *Beyond Gumbo* by Jessica B. Harris.

LE COLOMBO

In the mid-nineteenth century, French sugar plantation owners brought Sri Lankans to the southeastern Caribbean to work. The workers brought with them their beloved dark mustard seeds, coriander, turmeric, saffron, and black pepper and the know-how to make curry dishes, which they called *colombo* after the largest city in Sri Lanka. Though the original *colombo* was likely vegetarian, (most Hindus do not eat flesh), Martinique and Guadeloupe islanders love their colombo with pork, chicken, and fish as well as pumpkin, zucchini, potatoes, or green mangos.

SIGNATURE RECIPE

PORK CURRY (COLOMBO DE PORC)

Colombo is the national dish of Martinique. It's made with chicken, pork, beef, fish, or vegetables. Local restaurants allow diners to choose wine or coconut milk as a base. This rather spicy dish is traditionally served with fried plantains. Because poudre de Colombo *is not easily available in the United States, use a commercial curry powder. Substitute a Scotch Bonnet chili for the jalapeño for more authentic flavor.*

Yields about 12 cups, 6 to 8 servings

1/2 ounce tamarind paste, 1 tablespoon packed
2-1/2 pounds pork from shoulder, like shoulder blade boneless country ribs
   or 2 pounds trimmed pork diced into 1-inch cubes
3 tablespoons fragrant coconut oil *or* vegetable oil
12 ounces onions, 2 medium, 3 cups peeled and finely diced
1/2 ounce garlic, 2 large cloves, 1 tablespoon peeled and minced
1 ounce gingerroot, about 1 tablespoon peeled and minced
2 tablespoons curry powder
1-1/2 cups chicken stock
12 to 16 ounces hard, unripe mango, 1 medium, about 2 cups peeled and diced
into 1/2-inch cubes
8 ounces hubbard *or* butternut squash, about 1-1/2 cups peeled and diced into
1/2-inch cubes
8 to 10 ounces chayote, 1 medium, 1-1/2 to 2 cups peeled, pitted, and diced into
1/2-inch cubes
12 ounces taro, about 2 cups peeled and diced into 1/2-inch cubes
   or 12 ounces red-skin potatoes, about 2 cups scrubbed and diced into 1/2-inch cubes
1 cup coconut milk
   or 1 cup white wine
1 ounce jalapeño chili, 1 medium, 3 tablespoons stemmed, seeded, and finely diced
2 tablespoons freshly squeezed lime juice, 1/2 large lime, more to taste
Optional: 2 tablespoon Madeira or rum
Optional: 1 to 2 teaspoons brown sugar

To Serve: Hot rice or roti (for Indian flatbreads, see chapter *India*)

1   Place tamarind paste into small bowl and mash into 2 tablespoons hot water. Knead occasionally until paste softens. Push through fine strainer. Discard pits and fiber. Set aside the purée, about 2 tablespoons.

2   Remove excess fat from pork and discard. Dice pork into 1-inch cubes to yield 2 pounds meat.

3   Heat 3 tablespoons oil in 6- to 8-quart pot over medium heat. Blot pork dry, season with salt, and toss half into oil. Brown meat, turning to brown 2 sides, and transfer to bowl with slotted spoon. Repeat with remaining meat and transfer to bowl. Drain off fat into small stainless bowl and reserve. The pot bottom should have a golden crust; this will deglaze as the onions cook.

4   Reheat pot with 1 to 2 tablespoons reserved oil (more if using wine, less if using coconut milk). Stir onions into pot and cook, stirring periodically, until golden, 5 to 7 minutes. Stir in garlic, ginger, and curry powder and cook, stirring constantly until vegetables are soft and curry powder is toasted, 2 to 3 minutes.

5   Return pork to pot and cook in spice paste 1 minute. Stir in tamarind purée, chicken stock, mango, squash, chayote, taro or potatoes, coconut milk or wine, and chili. Bring to a boil. Lower heat to a simmer, partially cover pot and simmer colombo until meat is falling apart and vegetables are very tender, 1-1/2 to 2 hours. *Alternatively*, to keep vegetables more intact, simmer pork until tender, 1 to 1-1/2 hours. Stir in vegetables and simmer 1/2 hour more.

6   **To Serve:** Season dish with salt and pep*per, lime juice,* and optional *Madeira or rum, to taste. If colombo tastes too sour, correct w*ith brown sugar. Serve ladled into bowls with rice or roti.

Source: *The Complete Book of Caribbean Cooking* by Elisabeth Lambert Ortiz.

Vary! Improvise!

☞ *Vegetarian:* Omit pork, increase the vegetables and substitute vegetable stock for chicken stock.

☞ *Pumpkin Curry from St. Lucia:* Devise a pumpkin curry with grated coconut, onion, green bell pepper, garlic, gingerroot, curry powder, green chilies, West Indian pumpkin, or hubbard squash and tomatoes.

☞ *Colombo de Poulet:* Substitute 4 pounds chicken parts (skinned and fat removed) for pork.

NO GOAT LEFT BEHIND

Although not wildly popular in the United States, goat is by far the most popular meat in the world, comprising

FIGURE 12.38 Diagram of butchered goat.
Source: Stelios Filippou/Fotolia.

60 to 70 percent of the world's animal protein. Only pregnant goats produce the prized goat milk. Because they gobble milk and produce none, male goats are considered a financial drain. Most males are killed at birth.

Heritage Foods USA has launched *No Goat Left Behind*, a meat distribution initiative dedicated to introducing goat as a delicious meat product in the United States. Billy (male) goats are slaughtered under one year old. Young milk-fed, very lean and tender goat meat from animals four to eight weeks old is called *cabrito*. Stronger flavored meat from animals six to nine months old is called *chevron*. Goats bred for their meat are typically from Spanish and Mexican goat breeds.

Although goat meat is most beloved in the Caribbean, inhabitants of Africa, Asia, Mexico, China, India, France, and Saudi Arabia also relish it. Goat meat is lean and flavorful, milder than lamb, and easier to digest, due to a different molecular structure than other meats. According to the U.S. Department of

Agriculture, goat meat is more than 50 percent lower in fat than similarly prepared beef, but with a similar protein content. The saturated fat content of cooked goat meat is 40 percent less than skinless chicken.

Meat cuts determine cooking methods. Tender cuts can be successfully roasted, broiled, grilled, or sautéed. Less tender cuts respond best to braising and stewing. Because of its low fat, cabrito can toughen when exposed to high, dry cooking temperatures. For best results, cook chevron or cabrito slowly at a low temperature with moisture. Fresh meat should be frozen after three days. Incorporate these cuts into stews, curries, soup, burger, ribs, jerky, and gumbo. Or grill or roast the cuts whole.

- Whole goat
- Shoulder
- Ground, cubed, or finely chopped
- Ribs
- Leg
- Neck
- Tenderloin or backstrap

JAMAICAN GOAT CURRY

This dish reflects a typical Caribbean technique: steam-frying.

Yields about 9 cups, 4 servings

2-1/2 to 3 pounds trimmed, boneless goat shoulder or leg
   or 2-1/2 to 3 pounds trimmed, boneless lamb shoulder or leg
2 tablespoons fresh lime juice, 1/2 large lime
2 tablespoons mild commercial curry powder
2 tablespoons *Caribbean Seasoning*
6 tablespoons sunflower *or* vegetable oil
1-1/2 cups chicken stock, *divided*
8 ounces onion, 2 cups peeled and diced medium
1-1/2 to 2 ounces gingerroot, about 2 tablespoons peeled and minced
1/2 ounce Scotch Bonnet chili, 1 large, 3 to 4 teaspoons halved, stemmed, and seeded
1/2 ounce garlic, 2 large cloves, 1 tablespoon peeled and minced
15 allspice berries
3 ounces red bell pepper, 1/2 medium pepper, about 2/3 cup cored, seeded, and diced
3 ounces green bell pepper, 1/2 medium pepper, about 2/3 cup cored, seeded, and diced

1 ounce trimmed green onions, about 2 large, 2 tablespoons green part only chopped
1/4 ounce trimmed Italian parsley, 2 tablespoons chopped
16 ounces waxy potatoes, about 3 cups diced into 3/4-inch cubes
1/4 ounce cilantro, 2 tablespoons finely sliced, more to taste

For Serving

Cooked, long-grain white rice

1 Rinse meat with cold water and pat dry. Dice into 1-inch cubes. Toss in large bowl with lime juice, curry powder, and Caribbean seasoning. Mix well and cover bowl. Refrigerate and marinate meat 4 hours. *Express Marinade:* Leave meat to marinate at room temperature 1 to 2 hours.

2 Heat a 6-quart heavy pot over high heat. Add oil and lower heat. When oil is very hot and ripples, toss in meat, and turn to coat in oil. Cover pot, lower the heat, and simmer meat 45 minutes. Stir meat occasionally to ensure even cooking and no burning.

3 Stir in 1/2 cup stock, bring to a boil, lower the heat, cover, and simmer meat 30 to 45 minutes. Repeat with 1/2 cup stock and simmer meat 30 to 45 minutes more. Stir in remaining 1/2 cup stock, onion, ginger, chili, garlic, allspice, and bell peppers. Bring to a boil, lower the heat, cover the pot, and simmer meat 1 hour and 45 minutes. Stir occasionally.

4 Stir in green onions, parsley, and potatoes. (Add more stock or water if liquid has evaporated.) Continue to simmer curry until potatoes are tender, 15 to 20 minutes. Taste curry and season with salt and pepper. Stir in cilantro.

5 **To Serve:** Pour curry into serving vessel and serve with rice.

Source: *Caribbean Food Made Easy with Levi Roots* by Levi Roots.

WEST INDIES SHRIMP AND POTATO CURRY

Yields 7 cups, 4 to 6 servings

1-3/4 pounds waxy red-skinned or Yukon Gold potatoes
2 tablespoons sunflower *or* vegetable oil
8 ounces onion, 2 cups peeled and finely diced
1/4 ounce garlic, 1 large clove, 1-1/2 teaspoons peeled and minced
1-1/2 to 2 ounces gingerroot, about 2 tablespoons peeled and minced
2 teaspoons all-purpose *Caribbean Seasoning*
1/4 ounce red Scotch Bonnet chili, 1 teaspoon stemmed, seeded, and finely chopped
4 to 6 ounces green bell pepper, 1 cup seeded and sliced into thin strips
14-1/2 ounce can diced tomatoes, about 1-3/4 cups
1 pound 36/40 shrimp, peeled and deveined
1/2 ounce cilantro, 1/4 cup finely sliced, plus more for garnish
To Serve: Hot, cooked rice

1 Pour potatoes and 1 teaspoon kosher salt into 4-quart saucepan, and cover with cold water. Bring to a boil, lower heat, and boil potatoes until almost cooked through, 8 to 10 minutes. Drain and cool slightly. Peel potatoes and dice into 3/4-inch cubes to yield 6 to 7 cups. Set potatoes aside.

2 Heat oil in 6-quart saucepan over medium heat and stir in onion. Cook until soft, 5 minutes. Lower heat, stir in garlic, ginger, and Caribbean seasoning. Cook until ginger and garlic are soft, 1 to 2 minutes. Stir in chili and bell pepper and cook until soft over medium-low heat. Stir in tomatoes, potatoes, and 1-1/2 cups water. Simmer until sauce thickens and potatoes are very tender, 20 to 30 minutes. Add water as necessary to maintain a medium-thick sauce.

3 **To Serve:** Bring curry to a simmer. Stir in shrimp and simmer until opaque, 2 to 5 minutes. Immediately remove curry from heat, stir in cilantro, and season with salt to taste. Serve with rice, and garnish each serving with more cilantro.

Source: *Caribbean Food Made Easy with Levi Roots* by Levi Roots.

FISH BRAISED IN SPICY TOMATO SAUCE (COURT-BOUILLON DE POISSON)

This dish is pure French Caribbean from Guadeloupe, an island known for its seafood. This dish, with its simple, spicy tomato sauce, is a signature dish of the island.

Yields 2 to 2-1/2 cups sauce, 4 servings

2 one-pound whole sea bream or red snapper
    or 4 six-ounce red snapper or firm white-fleshed fish fillets
2 teaspoons chopped fresh thyme
1/4 to 1/2 ounce Scotch Bonnet chili, 1 small or large, 2 to 4 teaspoons stemmed, seeded, and minced
1/2 ounce garlic, 2 large cloves, 1 tablespoon peeled and minced, *divided*
6 tablespoons fresh lime juice, about 3 medium limes, *divided*
3 tablespoons *Achiote-Annatto Oil*
4 to 5 ounces onion, 1 cup peeled and finely diced
1-1/2 pounds tomatoes, 3 large, about 3 cups diced
    or 3 cups canned diced tomatoes

Garnish: 1/4 ounce fresh chives, 2 tablespoons trimmed and finely sliced, more to taste

For Serving

Hot, cooked rice *or Vinegar-Marinated Green Bananas*

1 Wash fish and pat dry. Mix thyme, chili, half the garlic, and half the lime juice in a medium bowl. Place fish in bowl and rub with mixture. Season fish with salt and pepper. Place in refrigerator to marinate: whole fish 1 hour, fillets 15 to 20 minutes. Drain fish, but retain as much thyme as possible.

2 Over medium heat, heat achiote-annatto oil: For **whole fish**, use a deep 12-inch skillet and for **fillets**, use a deep 10-inch skillet. Add onion and sauté until it begins to soften, 3 to 4 minutes. Stir in garlic, cook 30 seconds and stir in tomatoes. Lower heat and simmer tomatoes until they start to break down, 3 to 5 minutes.

3 Bring a small saucepan with 2 cups water to a boil and remove from heat; reserve. Place fish into sauce and turn to coat all sides. Pour in 1 to 1-1/2 cups of reserved hot water, enough to barely cover fish. Season with salt. Bring sauce to a simmer. Lower the heat, partially cover the pan, and simmer fish until cooked through and flakes when probed with the tip of a knife, 10 to 15 minutes for whole fish and 6 to 8 minutes for fillets.

4 Remove fish from pan and keep warm. Remove skin and bones from whole fish and discard. Push sauce through strainer and pour back into pan to yield about 2 to 2-1/2 cups sauce.

5 **To Serve:** Bring sauce to a simmer. Stir remaining lime juice into sauce, taste, and adjust seasonings. Add fish and heat through *or* transfer fish to 4 soup plates, and pour 1/4 of the sauce over each serving. Garnish with chives. Serve with rice *or Vinegar-Marinated Green Bananas.*

SIGNATURE RECIPE

CREOLE POACHED FISH (POISSON EN BLAFF)

Blaff *and the national dish,* court-bouillon, *are popular in Martinique with its blend of French and Caribbean-Creole cooking. Melegueta peppercorns, also known as "grains of paradise," add zing to this dish; they are native of West Africa and part of the ginger family.*

Yields about 6 cups, 4 servings

1-1/2 to 2 pounds red snapper or other white fish fillets
  or 4 one-pound small whole red snappers, gutted and scaled

> **Marinade**
> 1/2 cup fresh lime juice, about 2 large limes
> 1/4 ounce garlic, 1 large clove, 1-1/2 teaspoons peeled and minced
> 3-inch fresh red chili, 1 to 2 teaspoons stemmed, seeded, and finely chopped

1 cup dry white wine
6 to 7 ounces onion, 1-1/2 cups peeled and finely slivered
1 ounce trimmed green onions, 2 large, 1/4 to 1/3 cup finely sliced
1/4 ounce garlic, 1 large clove, smashed and peeled
1 large sprig fresh thyme
1 bay leaf
1 large sprig Italian parsley
1/2 ounce whole Scotch Bonnet chili, 1 large
1/4 teaspoon *melegueta* peppercorns *or* 3 to 4 whole allspice berries

Garnish: 1/4 ounce trimmed Italian parsley, 2 tablespoons chopped

To Serve: Hot rice *or* sautéed or boiled ripe plantains *or* green bananas *or* Tostones

1 Wash and dry fish fillets or whole fish. Pour marinade ingredients into nonreactive bowl or shallow pan. Place fish fillets in bowl and toss with marinade. Or place whole fish in pan, and rub marinade over and inside cavities. Refrigerate fish. Marinate fillets 15 minutes and whole fish 30 minutes. Cut fillets into serving size pieces to yield about 2 cups. Discard marinade.

2 While fish marinates: Pour wine and 2 cups water into deep 10- to 11-inch skillet or saucepan. Add onion, green onions, garlic, thyme, bay leaf, parsley, chili, and peppercorns or allspice. Cover pan and bring to a boil. Reduce heat and simmer mixture 5 minutes. Remove from heat.

3 Cook fish: Uncover pan, bring liquid to a simmer, and immerse fish in broth. Simmer fish over low heat, partially covered, until the meat flakes when probed with the tip of a knife, 8 to 10 minutes. Remove chili, parsley, thyme, and bay leaf, and discard. Season broth with salt and pepper.

4 To Serve: Transfer whole fish or fillets to four soup plates. Ladle cooking broth over fish and garnish each plate with parsley. Serve with rice or cooked plantains or bananas *or* tostones.

Vary! Improvise!

☞ *Substitute 1-1/2 to 2 pounds boneless, skinless chicken breasts for fish fillets. Dice into serving size pieces before marinating.*

Signature Technique: Caribbean Classic Rice and Broth Dishes

Probably every island in the Caribbean chain prepares some sort of composed rice dish. Derived directly from West African thiébou jen and thiébou niébe and Spanish paella and pilaf, these Creole-Caribbean dishes are very popular.

Caribbean rice dishes include Jamaica's and Barbados's peas and rice, Cuba's black beans and rice, yellow rice and pink beans, Puerto Rico's arroz con gandules (pigeon peas and rice), asopao (chicken and rice "stew") and arroz con pollo, Trinidad's chicken pelau, Guadeloupe's riz aux gombos (rice with okra) and matété crabes (crabs with rice), and Haitian red beans and rice. Arroz amarillo y maíz (yellow rice with corn and olives) is also popular.

Rice and Beans

Though Caribbean cooks put cooked, seasoned red beans or pigeon peas and rice together to cook, this method of tossing them together after the rice is properly cooked allows for more control.

- Cook long-grain white rice using chicken stock or water.
- Season and simmer cooked black beans with oregano, cumin, bay leaf, salt, and pepper.

  or simmer cooked pink beans with annatto oil and sofrito.

  or simmer cooked pigeon peas with annatto oil, ham, and sofrito.
- Serve black beans and rice side-by-side.

  or pink beans and rice or pigeon peas and rice tossed together.

Rice and Meat Casseroles

- Brown meat and/or onions in annatto or plain oil. Transfer meat to a bowl.
- Add *sofrito* or *recaito* to onions or fat, and cook until liquid evaporates.
- Stir in rice and cook until outside whitens and hardens, 5 minutes on medium heat.
- Season with salt and pour in stock.
- Return meat to rice and bring to a boil.
- Boil until craters form and stock is absorbed.
- Cover pot and simmer dish until chicken cooks through, 20 minutes.
- Rest dish 10 minutes, fluff rice, and serve.

Soupy Rice

Follow steps above, but use more broth and less rice.

RICE WITH CHICKEN (ARROZ CON POLLO)

This soul-satisfying dish comes from Puerto Rico, Cuba, and the Dominican Republic and shows their strong Spanish heritage. Latin chef Daisy Martinez uses a paella pan to cook this dish.

Yields 16 to 20 cups, 8 to 10 servings

4 pounds chicken thighs
1/4 cup *Achiote-Annatto Oil*
1 cup *Recaito or Sofrito*
3 ounces pimento-stuffed olives, 1/2 cup sliced
1 teaspoon ground cumin
1/4 teaspoon ground cloves
About 21 ounces long-grain rice, 3 cups
5 cups chicken stock, *divided*

Garnish: 18 ounces red bell peppers, 3 medium, about 1-1/2 cups roasted, peeled, seeded, and sliced into 1/4-inch by 1-1/2-inch strips
   or 1-1/2 cups bottled roasted red peppers, cut into 1/4-inch strips

1   Remove and discard skin and excess fat from chicken, if desired. This is optional and not traditional. Chicken doesn't brown easily without skin: blotting it very dry helps.

2   In a heavy 6-quart pot with a tight-fitting lid or a deep 12-inch braising pan with lid, heat achiote oil over medium-high heat until the oil is very hot but not smoking. Season chicken with salt and pepper. Sauté chicken in two batches. Turn as necessary, until browned on all sides and almost cooked through, about 5 to 7 minutes per side. Remove chicken as it is done and set aside in mixing bowl. Regulate the heat so the chicken browns without burning the oil.

3   Add recaito or sofrito and olives to pot. Raise heat to high and boil *recaito* or *sofrito* until liquid evaporates and it thickens, about 5 minutes, and stir in cumin and cloves. Stir in rice, season with 1-1/2 teaspoons kosher salt, and coat well in *recaito* or *sofrito*. Sauté rice, stirring constantly, until it begins to dry and stick, 5 minutes. Return chicken to pot, pour in 4-1/2 cups stock, and bring to a boil. Cook over high heat until the level of liquid reaches the rice and craters form.

4   Reduce heat to low, cover pot, and cook until liquid is absorbed, the chicken is cooked through, and rice is tender, about 20 minutes. Remove pot from heat and pour in remaining 1/2 cup stock. Rest rice and chicken 10 minutes.

5   **To Serve:** Fluff rice with a fork. Bring *arroz con pollo* to the table in the pan or pile rice and chicken onto a large serving platter. Garnish with red bell pepper strips before serving.

Source: Latin chef Daisy Martinez.

PUERTO RICAN SOUPY RICE AND CHICKEN (ASOPAO)

This dish has been popular for lunch in Puerto Rico for almost a century.

Yields about 12 cups, 8 servings

3-1/2 to 3-3/4 pound chicken
 or 2-3/4 to 3 pounds chicken thighs and breasts
1/4 ounce garlic, 1 large clove, 1-1/2 teaspoons peeled and finely minced
1 teaspoon crumbled dried oregano
4 tablespoons *Achiote-Annatto Oil*
 or 4 tablespoons oil
4 to 5 ounces onion, 1 cup peeled and finely diced
5 to 6 ounce green bell pepper, 1 medium, about 1 cup cored, seeded, and finely diced
3 ounces lean ham, 1/2 cup diced into 1/4-inch cubes, packed
12 to 16 ounces ripe tomatoes, 2 medium, 1-1/2 cups peeled, seeded, and finely diced
 or 1-1/2 cups finely diced drained canned tomatoes
10 ounces frozen peas, 2 cups
2 ounces small pimento-stuffed green olives, 1/3 cup
1/2 to 1 ounce drained capers, 1 to 2 tablespoons
4 to 6-1/2 cups chicken stock
14 ounces raw long-grain rice, 2 cups rinsed and drained
6 ounce red bell pepper, 1/2 cup roasted, peeled, seeded, and sliced into 1/2-inch by 1-inch strips
 or 4 ounces sliced canned pimento, more to taste

For Serving

Tostones

1 Cut whole chicken into legs, thighs, wings, and breasts. Skin chicken if desired. (Skinned chicken won't brown as well; patting it dry helps.) Cut each breast into 2 pieces. Reserve back and wing tips. Pat chicken dry, and place in large mixing bowl. Mix garlic, oregano, and 1 teaspoon kosher salt together in a small bowl, and rub chicken parts with mixture.

2 Place chicken back and wing tips into small saucepan. Cover with 5 cups cold water. Bring to a boil, lower heat, and simmer the mini-stock until it reduces to 2-1/2 cups, about 45 minutes to 1 hour. (If using chicken parts, skip this and use 6-1/2 cups stock.)

3 Heat a heavy 11-inch, 6-quart pot with oil over medium heat. Brown chicken, 3 to 5 minutes per side, and transfer to a clean bowl. Stir onions and green pepper into oil and season with salt. Scrape up any brown bits from bottom of pan and cook, stirring frequently until vegetables soften, 4 to 5 minutes. Stir in ham and cook 1 minute. Stir in tomatoes and cook until mixture thickens and moisture evaporates, 6 to 7 minutes.

4 Return chicken and any juices to pot, and coat in tomato mixture. Reduce heat to low, cover pot tightly, and simmer chicken until tender, 30 to 35 minutes, turning once halfway through cooking time. Transfer chicken pieces to a clean bowl. When chicken cools, remove meat and discard skin and bones. Shred or dice meat into 1-inch cubes. Place peas, olives, and capers in bowl with chicken and set aside.

 *The elements of asopao can be made to this point, refrigerated, and finished the next day.

5 Stir 2-1/2 cups reserved mini-stock and 4 cups stock *or* 6-1/2 cups stock into tomato mixture. Bring to a boil over high heat, stir in rice, lower heat, cover tightly, and simmer rice until tender, 12 to 15 minutes. Remove pan from heat and rest rice 5 to 10 minutes. Mixture should be slightly soupy, but will absorb liquid as rice stands. Fold in reserved chicken, peas, olives, and capers. (If soupier rice is desired, add more stock or water.)

6 **To Serve:** Taste rice and season with salt and pepper. Arrange bell pepper or pimento strips on top as garnish and serve asopao directly from the pot with tostones.

Source: Time Life Foods of the World *The Cooking of the Caribbean.*

TRINIDADIAN CHICKEN PELAU

This pilaf is an important tradition in Trinidad. It's very flavorful and festive.

Yields about 15 cups, 6 to 8 servings

3-1/2 to 3-3/4 pound whole chicken
1 tablespoon malt vinegar
12 to 14 ounces onions, 3 cups peeled and finely diced
1 tablespoon chopped thyme leaves
3/4 ounce garlic, about 3 large cloves, 1-1/2 tablespoons peeled and minced
3 tablespoons vegetable oil
1 ounce brown sugar, 2 tablespoons
6 ounce red bell pepper, 1 cup cored, seeded, and finely diced
8 to 9 ounces pumpkin or butternut squash, 1-1/2 cups peeled and diced
into 1/2-inch cubes
14 ounces long-grain white rice, 2 cups rinsed and drained
1/2 cup thick canned coconut milk
2-1/2 cups chicken stock *or* water
1 whole Scotch Bonnet chili

1 Cut up chicken into legs, thighs, wings and breasts. Slice each breast into 2 to 3 pieces. Remove skin and excess fat from chicken, and discard. Reserve chicken backbone and wing tips for mini-stock. (There should be about 2-1/4 pounds skinless bone-in chicken parts.)

2 Pat chicken dry and place into large mixing bowl. Toss with vinegar, onions, thyme, and garlic. Season with 1 teaspoon kosher salt and pepper. Cover bowl and refrigerate 8 hours or leave at room temperature 1 hour.

3 **Prepare Mini-Stock:** Place the wing tips and chicken backbone into small saucepan and cover with 5 cups cold water. Bring to a boil, lower the heat, and simmer the chicken parts until water reduces by half, 45 minutes to 1 hour. Strain and reserve broth, about 2-1/2 cups.

4 Heat oil in a 6-quart casserole over medium heat. Stir in brown sugar. Cook until it melts, bubbles, froths, and turns a shade darker, 30 seconds to 1 minute. Don't let sugar blacken. Shake marinade ingredients off chicken parts and place into sugar. Cook both sides to infuse into sugar, about 3 minutes per side.

5 Stir in marinade seasonings from chicken, the bell pepper, and pumpkin or squash. Simmer until vegetables begin to soften, 5 to 6 minutes, stirring occasionally. Stir in rice, and season with 1 teaspoon kosher salt.

6 Stir in coconut milk and 2-1/2 cups reserved chicken mini-broth or water. Bring to a boil and reduce heat to a simmer. Tuck in chili and cover casserole. Simmer *pelau* until rice and chicken are tender, 20 to 25 minutes. Remove casserole from heat and rest undisturbed 10 minutes. Uncover casserole and fluff rice before serving. Remove chili and discard.

7 **To Serve:** Pile *pelau* onto platter and serve hot.

Source: *Eat Caribbean* by Virginia Burke.

> ## VERSATILE CARIBBEAN CORNMEAL
>
> In *Eat Caribbean*, Virginia Burke declares that throughout the Caribbean Islands cornmeal has long been a versatile staple that is "cheap, filling and tasty." Cornmeal can be made into many dishes like "porridge, dumplings, pone, fritters, pudding, pastilles and coo-coo." Coo-coo, a Caribbean original, is cornmeal cooked with seasonings, sometimes coconut milk, or mixed with okra, onions, or meat then poured into a mold and cooled. The coo-coo can be sliced and fried or served with other dishes.

SIGNATURE RECIPE

CORNMEAL LOAF (COO-COO/COU-COU OR FUNGI)

The coo-coo with okra is from Barbados, but cooks in Grenada and Trinidad make it too. Many recipes advise 15 to 20 minutes cooking time for cornmeal, but it takes minimally 40 minutes of cooking and stirring to bring out cornmeal's full flavor. For no-stir cornmeal, cook it in a double boiler.

Yields about 3 cups, 6 servings

Basic Plain Coo-Coo

4 cups liquid (water, stock, coconut milk)
7-1/2 ounces cornmeal, 1-1/2 cups
Optional: Unsalted butter

Barbadian Coo-Coo with Okra

4 cups liquid (water, stock, coconut milk)
6 ounces okra, about 12 medium, about 1 cup tops trimmed off and sliced into 1/4-inch-thick rounds
7-1/2 ounces cornmeal, 1-1/2 cups
1 to 2 tablespoons sugar
2 tablespoons unsalted butter, diced

For Serving

Cooked, sliced sweet potatoes, sliced tomatoes, and sliced bell peppers

Grenadian Coo-Coo with Corn and Coconut Milk

2 cups water
2 cups coconut milk
7-1/2 ounces cornmeal, 1-1/2 cups
1/2 cup canned creamed corn
Butter for greasing bowl

1 Prepare one of the three *Coo-Coos*.

Basic Plain

Set up double boiler with large bowl on top and water below. Pour 4 cups boiling water or stock into top of double boiler and set double boiler on medium-low heat. Slowly sift 1-1/2 cups cornmeal into the double boiler. Whisk out lumps.

Cover pan and simmer cornmeal 1 to 1-1/2 hours over double boiler (with simmering water), stirring occasionally. Butter a 1-quart bowl, and set aside. Taste mixture and season with salt. Add optional butter. Turn cooked cornmeal mixture into a buttered bowl and form it into a rounded shape. Cool in bowl.

With Okra

Heat 4 cups boiling water in 4-quart saucepan. Stir okra and 2 teaspoons kosher salt into boiling water, lower heat, and simmer until almost tender, 4 to 5 minutes. Remove okra and set aside. Reserve water.

Set up double boiler with large bowl on top and water below. Pour 4 cups boiling okra water into top of double boiler and set double boiler on medium-low heat. Slowly sift 1-1/2 cups cornmeal into the double boiler. Whisk out lumps.

Cover pan and simmer cornmeal 1 to 1-1/2 hours over double boiler with simmering water, stirring occasionally. Stir in okra after 1 hour. Butter a 1-quart bowl, and set aside. Stir sugar and butter into cornmeal. Taste mixture and season with salt. Turn cooked cornmeal-okra mixture into buttered bowl and form it into a rounded shape. Cool in bowl.

With Corn and Coconut Milk

Pour 2 cups water, 2 cups canned coconut milk, and 2 teaspoons kosher salt into 4-quart saucepan. Bring to a slow boil over medium heat and slowly whisk in cornmeal.

Set up double boiler with large bowl on top. Bring water under double boiler to a boil. Scrape cornmeal and coconut mixture into the double boiler bowl. Cover bowl and simmer cornmeal 1 to 1-1/2 hours over double boiler, stirring occasionally.

Stir in canned corn and continue to simmer and stir mixture 10 minutes more. Taste mixture and season with salt. Butter a 1-quart bowl, and set aside. Turn cooked cornmeal mixture into a buttered bowl and form it into a rounded shape. Cool in bowl.

2 **To Serve:** Invert bowl onto cutting board. Slice loaf, and serve alongside stews as a vegetable dish or on its own for breakfast. Serve Barbadian coo-coo with sweet potatoes, tomatoes, and bell peppers.

Source: *The Complete Book of Caribbean Cooking* by Elisabeth Lambert Ortiz.

CARIBBEAN GREEN PLANTAIN BALLS (FOO-FOO)

As in West Africa, foo-foo balls act as utensils: diners who eat with their hands form balls from the starchy mass and dip them into créole soups and stews. Foo-foo may also be made with boiled and pounded or puréed cassava or yuca (tapioca) root. For a recipe, see chapter *Africa: Senegal*.

Signature Technique: Boiled Green Bananas or Plantains

Boiled green bananas and plantains are a popular side dish in the Caribbean and often replace rice or potatoes. Unripe green bananas are starchier and less sweet than ripe ones, and make a good side for fish or chicken. One medium banana equals about one serving.

1 Wash bananas or plantains and drop into a pot of boiling water. Slow-boil until fruit is tender, 20 to 30 minutes.

2 Slice off ends and peel. Serve whole or mashed into chunks, seasoned or not.

3 *Alternatively*, slice off ends of bananas or plantains, cut into 1-inch chunks, and make a slit through the peel to remove. If peel is very sticky and stubborn, pour boiling water over sliced unpeeled fruit, and rest 15 minutes to loosen skins.

4 Boil sliced, peeled fruit slowly, until tender, 30 to 40 minutes.

SAUTÉ, PAN-FRY, AND DEEP-FRY

Of any cuisine, Caribbean-Creole can probably boast the largest choice of fritters, both sweet and savory, from codfish, bean, meat, and rice fritters to okra, grated sweet potato or yam, pineapple, or pumpkin. Some fritters, like fruit and okra, are battered and fried while others mix cooked and mashed or chopped ingredients with eggs and flour plus seasonings. *Stamp and Go* is a classic savory fritter eaten throughout the Caribbean (and known by different names). Serve fritters with or without a dipping sauce, but serve them immediately or risk them getting soggy.

FIGURE 12.39 Cod fritter.
Source: nito/Fotolia.

CODFISH FRITTERS (STAMP AND GO)

Salt cod was slave food and these fritters could be made in a hurry. This is a Jamaican version.

Yields about 3 cups batter, 24 to 32 fritters, 8 to 10 servings

8 ounces salt cod
1 ounce trimmed green onions, about 2 large, 4 tablespoons minced
1-1/2 to 2 ounces red bell pepper, 1/3 cup finely diced
1/4 ounce Scotch Bonnet chili, 1/2 to 1 teaspoon seeded and minced
6-3/4 ounces flour, 1-1/2 cups
2 teaspoons baking powder
Oil for frying

For Serving

Sauce Chien, bottled Pickapeppa Sauce, or another hot sauce

1   Cover salt cod with cold water and refrigerate 24 to 48 hours. Change the soaking water several times.

2   Drain fish and place in 2-quart saucepan; cover with cold water. Bring to a boil over medium-low heat. Remove pan from heat and drain off water. Pick through fish for skin and bones and discard. Flake the fish and place in mixing bowl to yield about 2-1/2 cups.

3   Heat frying oil to 375 degrees F.

4   Mix fish with green onions, bell pepper, chili, flour, baking powder, and salt and pepper. Stir in enough water to make a slightly sticky batter, about 1 cup. Thinner batter makes lighter fritters; thicker batter makes dense fritters. Drop 1 rounded tablespoon batter per fritter into hot oil. Fry until golden. Drain on paper towel.

5   **To Serve:** Pile hot fritters onto platter and serve immediately with Sauce Chien, bottled Picka-peppa Sauce, or another hot sauce.

Source: *Beyond Gumbo* by Jessica B. Harris.

Vary! Improvise!

☞ ***With Egg:*** *An egg makes rich, cakey fritters. In place of just water, whisk and add 1 large egg and 3/4 to 1 cup water.*

☞ ***Conch or Other Seafood Fritters:*** *Substitute 2-1/2 cups chopped, cooked conch, or other cooked, shredded fish or seafood.*

FIGURE 12.40   A: Squashing tostones after first frying, B: Twice-fried plantains.

Vary! Improvise!

☞ *Plantain Chips:* Peel plantains as for tostones. Thinly slice plantains lengthwise or crosswise on mandoline. Deep-fry until golden and crisp in oil heated to 355 to 360 degrees F. Drain on paper towel and season with salt while still warm.

TWICE-FRIED PLANTAINS (TOSTONES)

Popular in Puerto Rico, tostones have become a Caribbean-Latin American favorite. Some varieties of plantains work better than others: look for short, fat ones with distinct edges. The second dip into saltwater steams and crisps the tostones.

Yields about 16 tostones, 4 to 8 servings

2 pounds large unripe, green plantains
Oil for frying

Mayo-Ketchup

1/2 cup mayonnaise
1/2 cup ketchup

Garlic Oil

1/4 cup oil, preferably olive
1/4 ounce garlic, 1 large clove, 1-1/2 teaspoons peeled and chopped

1 Cut the ends off plantains and slice shallowly through the skin lengthwise in two places to loosen peel. (If peels won't budge, immerse plantains in hot tap water 5 to 10 minutes and drain.)

2 Mix 1 quart cool water with 3 tablespoons kosher salt and stir until salt dissolves. Slice peeled plantains into 1-inch-thick rounds. Immerse plantain slices in salt water and rest 10 minutes. Remove plantains and blot dry. Reserve salt water.

3 Heat 1/2 inch oil in 10- to 12-inch skillet over medium heat until oil sizzles when a plantain hits it. Fry plantain slices in batches until tender and a golden crust forms, but not until overly brown, 2 to 3 minutes per side. If oil gets too hot, turn down the heat or remove pan briefly from burner. Transfer once-fried plantains to paper towel-covered sheet pan to drain. Set skillet with oil aside and reserve.

4 Place a warm plantain on a clean cutting board and put a glass or pie plate on top. Squash plantain an even 1/4-inch thick. (With a glass it's possible to see the plantain as it flattens.) Transfer squashed plantain to sheet pan, and cover with damp towel or plastic wrap. Smashed plantains will keep up to 2 hours tightly wrapped.

5 Reheat oil over medium heat until hot, but not smoking. Dip each plantain into reserved salt water, drain lightly, and place immediately into the hot oil. Fry plantains in batches until golden and crunchy, about 2 minutes per side.

6 **Prepare Mayo-Ketchup and/or Garlic Oil:** Mix mayonnaise with ketchup. Mix oil with garlic and season with salt.

7 **To Serve:** Transfer tostones to paper towel-lined serving dish, season with a little salt, and serve immediately. Serve tostones with mayonnaise and ketchup and/or garlic oil.

Source: Richard Messina and Annie Landfield.

GRILL, GRIDDLE, ROAST, BROIL, BAKE, AND BARBECUE

Signature Technique: Jerk-Cooking

Jerk-cooking is a Jamaican method of wet-marinating or dry-rubbing and smoke-cooking meat slowly over a barbecue; the result is tender meat with a spicy-sweet-smoky flavor. The origin of the name "jerk" has several theories: that it evolved from the Spanish word "charqui" or dried meat to "jerky," or from the process of jerking or poking the meat with holes before marinating. Jerk-cooking's slow-smoke method is an age-old Caribbean practice used to cure meat. It involved marinating or rubbing meats, seafood, or vegetables with a jerk mixture. The traditional method of cooking was in open-ground wood-fired pits. Modern jerk is slow-cooked on grills made from steel drums fired with charcoal.

- Use a coffee grinder to grind whole allspice berries for marinade—they'll taste fresher.

- Rub jerk paste onto food with gloved fingers to get best coverage. Marinate meats in a shallow, nonreactive pan or heavy zipper baggies.

- Don't marinate meat too long: it changes the texture to mushy. Fish can be dipped into marinade and grilled or baked immediately.

- Adjust and dilute marinate with soy sauce, distilled white vinegar, rum, or beer.

- For milder seasoning, remove seeds and membranes from Scotch Bonnet chilies, or use a milder chili like jalapeño or serrano, though the dish will lack the authenticity and intensity of true jerk.

- Keep jerk paste, marinade, or sauce in a tightly sealed glass jar and store paste up to 6 months, and marinade and sauce up to a year.

- When using a gas grill, keep the temperature low. If using coals, when they're ready, push them to the outside edges of the grill. Nestle an aluminum pan in the center of the coals to catch the drippings. Place fish, fowl or meat on grill over pan, cover grill, and roast meat or fish until tender, turning and brushing with marinade periodically.

- For authentic smoked flavor, toss soaked allspice berries, oak, or mesquite wood on the coals (if pimento [allspice] wood isn't available). Don't charcoal or gas alone.

- Soak allspice berries in water 15 to 20 minutes or soak wood chips in water 2 hours before grilling to keep them from burning and to create good smoke.

IT'S IN THE SEASONING

In *Island Cooking,* Dunstan A. Harris asserts that jerk seasoning is what allows "cooks, housewives and entrepreneurs" to recreate the taste of good Jamaican jerk. Traditional pit cooking is no longer necessary; instead Harris notes that excellent jerk "can be made on a grill or in the oven."

FIGURE 12.41 Jerk chicken with rice and red beans.
Source: Rohit Seth/Fotolia.

JAMAICAN JERK CHICKEN

It's traditional to serve Red Stripe beer and hard dough bread (a sort of French bread made with a little dry milk and lard) with jerk chicken. Grilling is the superior method.

6 servings

6 pounds bone-in chicken thighs and breasts
6 tablespoons fresh lime juice, 1-1/2 large limes or 2 medium
1/2 cup *Jerk Marinade plus* 1/2 cup extra for grilling or basting
For Grilling: 2 tablespoons whole dried allspice, soaked 15 to 20 minutes in water
For Baking: 1 tablespoon liquid smoke seasoning

For Serving

Sliced French bread

1. Preheat oven to 350 degrees F. Remove fat and skin from chicken, if desired. Cut breasts in half. Place in large bowl with lime juice. Turn chicken frequently and marinate 10 to 15 minutes. Drain chicken, and discard juice.

2. Pour 1/2 cup **jerk marinade** into bowl with chicken, and toss well. Cover bowl with plastic wrap and marinate chicken at room temperature 1 hour, or refrigerate chicken 3 to 8 hours.

3. Grill or bake marinated jerk chicken:

   Grill: Heat grill to medium-low heat. If using gas grill, place an aluminum pie pan in center of grill. If using charcoal, push hot coals aside so center is free of coals. Place chicken either oven the aluminum pie pan or over the center, coal-free spot. Drain whole allspice and toss on coals. Grill chicken until tender and browned, about 30 to 45 minutes. An instant-read thermometer should register at least 170 degrees F. As chicken is done, transfer to pan, cover, and keep warm.

   Bake: Remove chicken from refrigerator 30 minutes prior to cooking and toss with 1 tablespoon liquid smoke seasoning. Preheat oven to 425 degrees F. Spread chicken onto nonreactive hotel or baking pans. Place pans in oven, cover with parchment and foil, and bake 20 minutes. Lower heat to 275 degrees F and bake chicken until tender, about 1 hour. Periodically baste chicken throughout baking with pan juices. Remove parchment and foil. Broil skin-on chicken until browned, 3 to 5 minutes. Remove pan from oven to cool 5 minutes.

4. **To Serve:** Transfer chicken (and juices) to platter and serve with French bread. Alternatively, transfer chicken to cutting board. Chop meat into bite-sized pieces, discard bones, and transfer meat to platter. Pour pan juices over the meat. Serve.

Source: *Island Barbecue* by Dunstan A. Harris.

JAMAICAN JERK PORK

8 to 10 servings

5 pound boneless pork leg or shoulder
1/4 cup fresh lime juice, about 1 large lime
1 teaspoon garlic powder
1 teaspoon chopped fresh thyme leaves
1 teaspoon coarsely ground allspice
1/4 cup *Jerk Rub*
1/4 cup soy sauce
1/2 ounce Scotch Bonnet chili, 2 teaspoons stemmed (seeded) and finely chopped

For Serving

Rice, salad, or *Festive Coleslaw* and French bread

1 Rub pork with lime juice. Drain meat and pat dry. Place meat in large bowl. Make 1/2-inch deep incisions into meat all over.

2 Mix together garlic powder, thyme, allspice, and 2 tablespoons **jerk rub** in a mixing bowl. Stuff the incisions in the meat with the mixture. Mix remaining stuffing with remaining **jerk rub** and soy sauce. Slather it over the outside of the meat. Cover meat with plastic wrap and refrigerate 3 to 8 hours. Turn meat occasionally in marinade.

3 Remove meat from refrigerator 1 hour before cooking. Preheat oven to 350 degrees F. Transfer pork to hotel pan or nonreactive pan and stuff incisions with the chili. Pour marinade left in bowl over meat. Cover meat tightly with parchment and aluminum foil (parchment under the foil will keep it from reacting). Place meat in oven, and bake until very, very tender, about 4 hours. Uncover pan and bake meat 30 minutes more. Baste meat with pan juices frequently.

4 **To Serve:** Transfer pork to cutting board. Reserve pan juices. Slice meat with a sharp cleaver or chef's knife and arrange on serving platter. Pour pan juices over meat. Serve with salad or *Festive Coleslaw*, rice, and bread.

Source: *Island Barbecue* by Dunstan A. Harris.

Vary! Improvise!

☞ **Baa, Baa:** Substitute boned and butter-flied lamb for pork. Use fresh garlic instead of garlic powder and omit soy sauce and chili.

☞ Roast the pork in a covered grill.

FIGURE 12.42 Another Caribbean pork favorite: whole grill-roasted pig.
Source: Pablo Fernández/Fotolia.

JAMAICAN JERK FISH

6 servings

Six 6- to 8-ounce firm, fish steaks, like kingfish or salmon
1/4 cup lime juice, 1 large lime
4 to 6 tablespoons *Jerk Marinade*

For Serving

French bread

1 Heat grill to hot or oven to 375 degrees F. Swish fish steaks in lime juice, rinse, and pat dry. Place fish in hotel pan or shallow pan that will fit steaks in one layer. Pour **marinade** over fish and turn to coat well. Immediately remove fish from marinade and place into clean pan.

2 Place fish on preheated grill or into oven. Bake or grill fish until it flakes easily, 20 to 25 minutes in the oven and 5 minutes per side on the grill. Baste with marinade during cooking.

3 **To Serve:** Transfer steaks to platter or serving plates and serve with bread.

Source: *Island Barbecue* by Dunstan A. Harris.

CARIBBEAN BEEF "PATTIES"

This beloved street food is more like a Cornish pasty or an empanada. Jamaicans prepare them with shrimp, fish, chicken, ground lamb, or vegetables. Improvise with ground turkey or ground goat.

Yields 11 filled pastries

FIGURE 12.43 Caribbean beef "patties."

Patty Pastry

Yields 32 to 34 ounces pastry

20 ounces all-purpose flour, 4 to 4-1/2 cups
4 teaspoons ground turmeric
1 teaspoon kosher salt
About 10 ounces beef lard or vegetable shortening, 1-1/2 cups
About 5 fluid ounces ice water, less or more as needed

Filling

Yields about 5 cups filling

2 pounds lean ground beef, about 4 cups
1 teaspoon ground allspice
1/2 teaspoon freshly ground black pepper
2 tablespoons vegetable or olive oil
4 to 5 ounces onion, 1 cup peeled and finely diced
1/4 ounce garlic, 1 large clove, 1-1/2 teaspoons peeled and minced

2 teaspoons dried thyme

2 teaspoons to 1 tablespoon tomato paste

1 ounce Scotch Bonnet chili, 2 medium, 2 teaspoons stemmed, seeded, and minced, more to taste

1 ounce fresh breadcrumbs, 1/2 cup, more as necessary

3 ounces trimmed green onions, about 6, about 2/3 cup finely chopped

For glazing: 2 large egg yolks beaten with 1 tablespoon cold water

For Serving

Caribbean Mango Chutney

1 **Prepare** Patty Pastry: Place flour, turmeric, salt, and lard or shortening into food processor. Pulse until evenly mixed. Pour mixture into mixing bowl. Slowly toss with ice water, stopping periodically to press pastry together. Slowly toss with water until pastry just holds together when pressed. Wrap dough in plastic and refrigerate 30 minutes. Remove dough from refrigerator 20 to 30 minutes before rolling.

2 **Prepare** filling: In a medium mixing bowl, mix together beef, allspice, pepper, and season with salt. Set aside. Heat oil over medium heat in a deep 10- to 12-inch skillet. Stir in onion and cook until it begins to color, 5 to 7 minutes. Lower heat and stir in garlic and thyme. Cook 1 minute.

3 Stir in beef mixture. Break up meat and simmer until meat is fully cooked and juices reduce, 5 to 10 minutes. Stir in tomato paste and chili, and cook 1 minute. A little fat and juices will remain. Stir in breadcrumbs to soak them up. Use a little more if necessary, but don't overdo it. Stir in green onions. Taste filling, and season with salt and pepper to taste. Cool.

4 **Divide and roll** patty pastry: Divide pastry into eleven balls roughly 3 ounces each. Roll out into 7-inch rounds about 1/4-inch thick. For easier rolling, place lightly floured ball between two sheets cut from a freezer baggie. Press ball flat in tortilla press. Remove dough still encased in plastic and roll to 7-inch diameter. Peel off only top layer of plastic.

5 **Fill** patties: Scoop a scant 1/2 cup of cooled **filling** into the center of dough round. Leave a 1- to 1-1/2-inch border all the way round. Brush bottom edge with water. Fold pastry in half. If using heavy plastic, use it to help fold the dough over filling. Crimp edges nicely—with a fork if desired. (Peel filled patty off plastic if using.) Line up pastries on parchment-covered sheet pan. Repeat with remaining dough and filling.

6 Bake patties: Preheat oven to 400 degrees F. Refrigerate patties 15 to 20 minutes. Brush top of patties evenly with egg wash and prick with fork on top. Place patties in oven and bake until golden, about 30 minutes. Serve warm or at room temperature with mango chutney.

Vary! Improvise!

☞ **Go Vegan:** *Devise a vegan "patty." Use a quality vegetable shortening or firm coconut oil and whole wheat pastry flour for the crust, and a Caribbean vegetable-coconut mélange for the filling.*

☞ **Go Fishing:** *Shrimp or fish require a sauce to bind them. Create a roux and prepare a thick white sauce with milk or stock.*

☞ **Small:** *Divide dough into 2-ounce balls and press/roll into 5-inch rounds. Fill with about 3 tablespoons filling.*

☞ **Smaller:** *Roll dough out 1/8- to 1/4-inch thick, and cut out small rounds. Fill with 1 to 2 tablespoons filling.*

COOK'S VOICE: FRANCISCO RODRIGUEZ

San Germàn, Puerto Rico

"Piñón was always a big treat in our Puerto Rican family and I always asked my mother to double the olives. When we kids were gone my mother used to prepare piononos: individual rings of fried plantain stuffed with all the ingredients in piñón. They were easier to prepare for just her and my dad. Another memory is waiting for my grandmother to make fresh ground meat empanadas. It began my culinary education for the balance of different flavors. The picadillo (filling) had olives, capers and raisins, which was exotic yet familiar. While living in Spain I discovered that the Moorish influence showed in the use of raisins and other dried fruits and preserves in savory dishes."

Source: Courtesy of Francisco Rodriguez.

FIGURE 12.44 Puerto Rican piononos.
Source: Otokimus/Fotolia.

CARIBBEAN LASAGNA
(PIÑÓN DE PLÁTANO MADURO)

This recipe is a Cuban, Dominican, and Puerto Rican classic. Another fried plantain favorite is a Puerto Rican sandwich of fried plantains pinned together with toothpicks and used as "bread," which is stuffed with roast pork, mayo, lettuce, and tomato.

Yields 2-inch deep, 9-inch by 11-1/2-inch rectangular half hotel pan *or* 9-inch by 12-inch casserole, 9 to 12 servings

10 to 12 ounces green beans
or 2 cups frozen sliced green beans, thawed

Meat Filling (Picadillo)

Yields about 6 cups

3 tablespoons vegetable or canola oil, *divided*
4 ounces ham, about 1 cup diced into 1/4-inch cubes
2 to 3 ounce Cubanelle pepper, 1/3 to 1/2 cup stemmed, seeded, and finely diced
2 to 3 ounces onion, 1/2 cup peeled and finely diced
4 ounces ripe tomato, 1/2 cup diced
    or 1/2 cup drained, diced, canned whole tomatoes
2 pounds lean ground chuck or round
    or 2 pounds lean ground pork
3 ounces small stuffed green olives, 1/2 cup
2 tablespoons capers

About 6 pounds ripe (yellow with black spots) plantains, 8 large
Oil for frying
6 large eggs, about 1-1/2 cups beaten, more as needed

1 Preheat oven to 350 degrees F.

2 Blanch whole green beans until tender, 5 minutes. Drain and rinse under cold water. Drain again. Slice into 1-inch lengths. Alternatively, slice green beans into 1-inch lengths. Steam until tender, 5 minutes. Set beans aside.

3 Heat a deep 12-inch skillet with 2 tablespoons oil over medium heat. Add ham, pepper, and onion and cook until soft, 5 to 6 minutes. Stir in tomatoes and cook until moisture evaporates, 3 to 4 minutes. Stir in meat and reduce heat to medium-low. Simmer meat until cooked through and moisture evaporates, 15 minutes. Drain off fat if desired: pour meat filling into strainer set over bowl and drain. Transfer meat to bowl, taste, and season with salt and pepper. Set aside.

4 Cut ends off the plantains. With shallow, lengthwise cuts, score the skin. This will help to peel the fruit easily. Lay each plantain onto cutting board, and slice lengthwise into 4 long, even slices. Repeat with remaining plantains to yield 32 slices total.

5 Heat oil in 12-inch skillet 1/2- to 3/4-inch deep over medium heat, until very hot but not smoking. Fry plantains in batches of 6 strips until golden, about 4 minutes on the first side and 2 minutes on the second. Transfer strips on paper towel to drain. Repeat with remaining plantains.

6 Beat eggs with salt and pepper, and set aside. Grease a rectangular baking dish with 1 table-spoon oil.

7 Arrange 1/3 of fried plantain strips (about 10) into the pan. Choose half narrow strips and half wide strips. Fit them closely together as when making lasagna. (There will be some space around the edges, don't fret.) Cover plantains with half the meat (3 cups) followed by half the green beans (1 cup) and drizzle 3/4 cup beaten eggs, over the meat. Construct another layer of plantains fit closely together, remaining half of the meat and remaining green beans. Drizzle 1/2 cup beaten egg over. Cover meat and beans with remaining plantains and drizzle remaining 1/4 cup beaten egg over top of casserole.

8 Cover piñon loosely with foil. Place in oven, and bake until heated through, 45 minutes to 1 hour. Remove pan from oven and rest piñon 20 minutes before cutting and serving.

TROUT ESCOVITCH

This is another version of the famed Spanish pescado en escabeche. Cooking the cucumber in vinegar gives it a refreshing pickled flavor. This is made in Jamaica and is a popular street breakfast; it is the perfect balance for baked or fried, mild, whole fish.

4 servings

Escovitch Dressing

10 to 15 allspice berries, about 1/2 teaspoon well-crushed
1 cup cider vinegar
1/2 cup olive or sunflower oil

2-1/2 to 2-3/4 pounds whole trout, four 10-ounce trout, gutted, scaled, rinsed
and patted dry
2 ounces green onions, about 4 large
4 ounces unwaxed pickling cucumbers, 2 small, scrubbed and quartered lengthwise
6 ounce red bell pepper, 1 medium, 1-1/2 cups cored, seeded, and thinly sliced
6 ounce green bell pepper, 1 medium, 1-1/2 cups cored, seeded, and thinly sliced
1/2 ounce garlic, 2 large cloves, 1 tablespoon peeled and finely sliced or minced
1/2 ounce red Scotch bonnet chili, stemmed, seeded, and thinly sliced (use less for less heat)

1 *Prepare* dressing: Mix together allspice, vinegar, and oil. Set aside.

2 Preheat oven to 375 degrees F. Season trout with salt and pepper inside and out. Slice green onions into 1-inch lengths. Separate white from the green tops. Stuff each fish with equal part of white part of green onions. Lay the fish into a hotel pan and scatter green part of green onions, cucumber, peppers, garlic, and chili over and around fish.

3 Pour **dressing** over trout. Cover pan tightly with aluminum foil. Place in oven to bake until fish is cooked through and flaky, 25 to 30 minutes. Place each fish into soup plate and spoon vegetables and liquids over. Escovitch trout may be served hot, at room temperature, or chilled. If chilling baked trout, turn in marinade several times.

Source: *Caribbean Food Made Easy with Levi Roots* by Levi Roots.

Vary! Improvise!

☛ *Fold diced green beans directly into meat filling.*

☛ ***Individual Piononos:*** *Lay a strip of fried plantain on one thin side while still warm, and overlap the ends so that the strip forms a ring. Secure ring with a toothpick. Repeat with remaining plantain strips. Place plantain rings in frying pan with 1/2-inch oil. Pack rings with about 1/4 cup picadillo. Heat oil over medium heat and when hot, pour 1 to 2 tablespoons beaten egg over the meat inside the plantain rings. Cook piononos until egg has solidified, 2 to 4 minutes. Carefully flip each pionono, and cook remaining side. When the toothpick is loose, the piononos are done. Transfer to serving platter. Serve with fresh steamed green beans.*

TRINIDADIAN COCONUT BREAD

This bread is from Trinidad in the southeastern part of the Caribbean chain. Classically it's paired with breakfast buljol (salt cod salad), but it goes equally well with other fish or savory dishes and as morning breakfast with tea and fruit or mango chutney.

Yields 20 ounces dough, one 7-inch round disk

1-1/2 ounces unsweetened, dried, shredded coconut, 1/2 cup
   or about 4 ounces grated fresh coconut, 3/4 cup
9 ounces unbleached white flour, 2 cups
2 teaspoons baking powder
1/2 teaspoon kosher salt
1 ounce sugar, 2 tablespoons
2 ounces cold unsalted butter, 4 tablespoons diced into 1/4-inch cubes
2/3 cup canned coconut milk

1 In small bowl, mix dried coconut, if using, with 1/4 cup hot water; set aside. Preheat oven to 400 degrees F.

2 Pour flour, baking powder, salt, and sugar into food processor. Pulse to mix well. Add butter and pulse until butter and flour mixture looks like cornmeal, 10 seconds. Don't over process.

3 Pour flour-butter mixture into mixing bowl. Stir in coconut and coconut milk. Lightly knead dough until it comes together into a ball. Cover dough with plastic wrap and rest 30 minutes.

4 Flatten dough ball into a 7-inch disk and place on parchment-covered sheet pan. Bake until bread is lightly golden around the edges and skewer comes out clean, about 25 minutes. Remove bread from oven. Cool 20 to 30 minutes. Bread will firm as it cools and cut more easily.

SALAD AND VEGETABLE METHODS

You'd think that a hot climate would revel in salads, but until recently the Caribbean salad referred to sliced tomatoes. Demand has grown in recent years with seafood salads, green salads, cucumber and cilantro salad, coleslaws, and thrilling New Wave salads like jerked chicken salad or watercress with chayote or melon.

FESTIVE COLESLAW

Coleslaw is a Caribbean standard salad. A 5-1/4-pound pineapple yields 6 cups medium-diced or 8 cups large-diced pineapple. A 3-pound cabbage yields about 8 cups grated or shredded.

Yields about 8 cups, 8 to 12 servings

4 to 5 ounces onion, 1 cup peeled and slivered
12 ounces trimmed and cored red cabbage, 2 cups grated or shredded, packed
12 ounces trimmed and cored green or Savoy cabbage, 2 cups grated or shredded, packed
4-1/2 ounces carrots, 1 cup trimmed, peeled, and grated or shredded
2-1/2 ounces dried, unsweetened coconut flakes, 1 cup packed
9 ounces trimmed and cored fresh pineapple, about 1/4 of 5-pound pineapple
1-1/2 cups diced

3 ounces golden raisins, 1/2 cup packed
1/4 ounce Scotch Bonnet chili, 1/2 large chili, 2 teaspoons stemmed, seeded, and finely diced

Dressing

1 tablespoon brown sugar
3 tablespoons white distilled vinegar
1 cup mayonnaise, less to taste

1 Pour 1 quart cold water into a small saucepan and bring to a boil over high heat. Place onion into a strainer and pour the boiling water it while tossing. Drain onion well, and place in mixing bowl.

2 Toss cabbages, carrots, coconut, pineapple, raisins, and chili with onion. Season coleslaw with salt and pepper to taste.

3 Whisk together **dressing** ingredients in small bowl, and pour on coleslaw. Taste and adjust seasonings. Chill salad 1 hour or up to 1 day before serving.

Source: *Eat Caribbean* by Virginia Burke.

Vary! Improvise!

☛ *Toast the coconut in the oven before folding into coleslaw.*

CUCUMBER SALAD FROM MARTINIQUE (CONCOMBRES EN SALADE MARTINIQUE)

Serve this refreshing salad with jerk dishes or grilled or fried food.

Yields 4 to 4-1/2 cups, 8 servings

About 1-1/2 pounds English cucumbers, 2 medium-sized
1/2 ounce Scotch bonnet chili, 1 large, 2 to 3 teaspoons stemmed, seeded, and finely diced
4 tablespoons fresh lime juice, 1 large lime
1/4 ounce garlic, 1 large clove, 1-1/2 teaspoons peeled and minced
1/4 ounce cilantro, 2 tablespoons finely sliced
1/4 ounce trimmed Italian parsley, 2 tablespoons finely sliced

1 Peel cucumbers, but leave thin stripes of green peel on. Slice cucumber in half lengthwise and with a teaspoon, scrape out seeds. Slice cucumbers crosswise into 1/4-inch-thick slices. Toss sliced cucumbers with 2 teaspoons kosher salt, and rest 30 minutes in refrigerator. Drain cucumbers and pat dry.

2 Toss cucumber with chili, lime juice, garlic, cilantro, and parsley. Refrigerate salad and marinate 1 hour. Marinate overnight for best flavor. Taste salad and season with lime, salt, and freshly ground pepper as necessary. Serve chilled.

FIGURE 12.45 Queen conch shells.
Source: Subbotina Anna/Fotolia.

CARIBBEAN CONCH SALAD (LAMBI)

The Bahamas and Turks and Caicos Islands all claim this salad as their national dish. Unfortunately, due to over-fishing, the Caribbean conch is in decline, but squid or abalone make a good substitute.

Yields 3 cups, 4 to 6 servings

8 ounces fresh *or* frozen conch, 2 cups diced into 1/4-inch cubes
   or 8 ounces squid bodies, 2 cups diced into 1/2-inch cubes
2 to 3 ounces onion, 1/2 cup peeled and diced into 1/4-inch cubes
2 to 3 ounces celery, 1/2 cup diced into 1/4-inch cubes
4 ounces green bell pepper, 1/2 cup diced into 1/4-inch cubes
8 ounces ripe tomatoes, 1 cup seeded and diced into 1/4-inch cubes
6 tablespoons freshly squeezed lime juice, about 1-1/2 large limes
4 tablespoons freshly squeezed lemon juice, about 1 lemon
1 ounce jalapeño chili, 1 large, 2 tablespoons stemmed, seeded, and finely diced

For Serving

Bed of lettuce
   or 2 to 3 avocados, halved lengthwise and pitted (1 avocado half per serving)
     or 8 ounce tomato, 1 medium-large, halved and scooped out (per person)

1   Bring 6 cups water to boil. Place conch or squid in colander and pour 4 to 5 cups boiling water over to scald. Drain seafood well, and place in medium, nonreactive bowl. Place onion in colander and pour 1 cup boiling water over and rest 20 to 30 seconds. Drain well. Place in bowl with seafood.

2   Immediately stir in celery, bell pepper, tomato, lime and lemon juices, and chili. Cover bowl and marinate in refrigerator 30 minutes to 1 hour. Season salad with salt and pepper, and adjust flavor with more lime or lemon juice to taste.

3   **To Serve:** Spoon salad onto a bed of lettuce with half an avocado, or into a hollowed out tomato, and serve as a first course or as luncheon main meal.

Caribbean Vegetables

Served in numerous ways, yuca, breadfruit, plantain, green bananas, yams, and taro form the main starchy vegetable offerings of the Caribbean. Okra, callaloo greens, pumpkin, and tomatoes probably top the list of favored vegetables with chayote, onions, bell peppers, and sweet potatoes close on their heels. Cooks often prepare these vegetables simply, by boiling, stewing, or frying.

PAN-STEWED OKRA (QUNGOMBÓS GUISADOS)

Yields about 4 cups, 6 to 8 servings

1-1/2 pounds whole okra
2 tablespoons oil *or* olive oil
6 to 7 ounces onion, 1 medium, 1-1/2 cups peeled and finely diced
1 pound tomatoes, 2 cups cored and finely diced
1 ounce jalapeño chili, 1 medium, 2 tablespoons stemmed (seeded for less heat)
and finely diced
1/2 ounce garlic, 2 large cloves, 1 tablespoon peeled and minced

1   Wash okra and lightly trim off top stem above where it meets the body of the okra. Set aside in bowl.

Vary! Improvise!

☛ *Cook conch or squid very briefly or for a long time. In-between cooking toughens conch and squid. To remedy tough conch or squid, cook it longer and it will soften.*

☛ *Fresh, raw conch can be treated like ceviche: marinate in the lime and lemon juice 30 minutes and stir in remaining ingredients.*

2 Heat oil in 10- to 12-inch skillet over medium heat. Stir in onion and cook until soft but not browned, 5 minutes. Stir in tomatoes, chili, and garlic. Cover pan, lower heat, and simmer sofrito mixture 5 minutes.

3 Uncover pan, stir in okra, and season with salt. Partially cover pan and stirring occasionally, simmer okra until tender, 15 to 20 minutes. Uncover pan and continue to simmer until most of the tomato juice condenses, 5 minutes. Season to taste with salt and pepper.

4 **To Serve:** Pile okra into serving dish and serve warm or at room temperature.

Source: Time-Life Foods of the World *The Cooking of the Caribbean Islands.*

THE WIDE WORLD OF PLANTAINS AND BANANAS

Plantains, the big starchy brother of the diminutive sweet banana, are cooked and eaten while green and very starchy *or* when almost black and very sweet. Green and ripe bananas are treated in much the same way and often serve as stand-ins when plantains are unavailable. Some of the ways that Caribbean cooks have concocted to show off plantains and bananas include:

- **Tostones:** Sliced green plantains, fried, smashed, and fried again

- **Banana or plantain chips:** Thinly sliced green or ripe fruit deep-fried into chips
- **Arañitas:** Shredded green plantain fritters
- **Piononos:** Dough made with cooked, ripe plantains mashed with egg and flour, rolled into balls, stuffed with meat picadillo (spiced meat), and fried. Or fried ripe plantain strips wrapped around picadillo and heat in skillet.
- **Jibarito:** Puerto Rican long slices of fried plantain used as the "bread" for roast pork sandwiches
- **Piñon or pastelon de amarillos:** A sort of baked lasagna of layered meat and fried ripe plantains

- **Pasteles:** Plantain and/or taro paste "tamales" stuffed with meat and annatto-spiced filling steamed in banana or plantain leaves
- **Foo-Foo:** Boiled and mashed ripe or green plantains
- **Mofongo:** Puerto Rican boiled and mashed plantains seasoned with fried pork cracklings; sometimes mofongo is "stuffed" by pressing it into the bottom and sides of a bowl and pouring in stews or sautés.
- **Mangú:** Dominican boiled and mashed green plantains served for breakfast
- **Conquintay:** Dried and ground green plantain flour; used for dumplings or to thicken

FIGURE 12.46 Mofongo.
Source: Montanez/Fotolia.

FIGURE 12.47 Fried sweet plantains.
Source: Lisa F. Young/Fotolia.

VINEGAR-MARINATED GREEN BANANAS
(BANANA ESCABECHE)

Escabeche or escovitch is a traditional method of preparing fish that came directly from Spain and North Africa. Though Cubans and Jamaicans prepare escovitch with fish, this dish substitutes boiled green bananas.

Yields 5 cups, 4 to 6 servings

2 pounds and 10 ounces green unripe bananas, about 6 medium (8-inch long), washed
1/4 cup plus 2 tablespoons olive oil
4 ounces red bell pepper, 1/2 large pepper, 3/4 to 1 cup seeded and finely slivered
4 ounces green bell pepper, 1/2 large pepper, 3/4 to 1 cup seeded and finely slivered
4 to 5 ounces onion, 1 cup peeled and finely slivered
4 tablespoons white wine vinegar
3 tablespoons drained capers
1-1/2 teaspoons fresh thyme leaves

1 Slit green bananas (shallowly) lengthwise and slice off both ends. Place in 4-quart saucepan, cover with cold water, and stir in 1-1/2 tablespoons kosher salt. Bring bananas to a boil and lower heat to a high simmer. Weight bananas with small lid to keep them immersed. Cook until tender, 30 to 40 minutes. Don't be alarmed if a purple scum appears: it may come off the ends of the green banana if they are not trimmed completely away. Rinse bananas under cold water, drain, and set aside to cool.

2 In the meantime, heat oil in 10-inch skillet over medium heat and add peppers and onion. Cook until soft, stirring occasionally, about 10 minutes. Stir in vinegar, capers, and thyme, and season with salt to taste. Remove pan from heat.

3 Peel bananas, discard peels, and slice bananas into 1/2-inch thick rounds. Place bananas into pan with the warm onions and peppers and toss well. Taste and adjust seasonings. Marinate 1 hour or longer at room temperature.

4 **To Serve:** Mound banana escabeche into serving bowl or onto serving platter; spoon some of the vegetables and marinade over top. Serve at room temperature or chilled.

Source: *Beyond Gumbo* by Jessica B. Harris

REVIEW QUESTIONS

1. Into what three main groups are the Caribbean islands divided?

2. What were the four main influences on Caribbean cuisine?

3. Name one Caribbean fruit or vegetable and describe it.

4. What is achiote or annatto? How is it used in Caribbean cuisine?

5. Discuss the process known as "jerk." What are two of the four key ingredients in all jerk marinades?

6. Discuss the twelve elements of Créole cuisine.

CHAPTER THIRTEEN

MEXICO

This chapter will:

- Introduce the changing, turbulent histories of Mexico and the Caribbean countries, their geographies, cultural influences, and climate.
- Discuss the importance of Africa and Spain to the cooking of Mexico and the Caribbean.
- Introduce you to Mexican and Caribbean culinary cultures, their diverse regional variations, and dining etiquette.
- Identify foods, dishes, and techniques that cross between countries.
- Identify the foods, flavor foundations, seasoning devices, and favored cooking techniques of Mexico and the Caribbean.
- Teach some of the influential techniques and beloved dishes of the complex cuisine of Mexico.

The Northern Frontier   The Pacific Coast

The Southern Isthmus of Tehuantepec   The Central Crossroads

The Colonial Plains and Highlands   The Yucatán Peninsula

FIGURE 13.1   Map of Mexico.

MEXICO: LAND OF FASCINATION

Food Culture Developed Early

In Jim Peyton's New Cooking from Old Mexico, *Jim Peyton recounts pre-conquest Mexico City through the eyes of a soldier in Cortes's contingent. The Spanish were surprised at the natives' respect for food and their "rich legacy of recipes." The soldier describes a "great market-place" full of people buying and selling, their voices "heard for more than a league." Many of the soldiers had experienced Constantinople, Italy, and Rome, but had never encountered there such a huge, vibrant market as "well ordered" as in Mexico City.*

Mexico is land of contrasts. Modern industries and the largest city in the world are neighbors to simple farmers in small, remote villages. Mysterious, dramatic ancient ruins compete with serene churches; turbulent political upheavals and bloody wars have been transformed into skilled dance, music, art, and literature. The Mexican landscape ranges from fertile plains, rainforest, desert, and mountains to ancient cities, colonial palaces, and elaborate museums. Prime beaches border the azure Pacific Ocean, the Caribbean Sea, and Gulfs of Mexico and California. Perhaps best of all, this richly fascinating, colorful culture has developed a complex, delicious, and unforgettable cuisine.

Archeological evidence suggests that humans first inhabited Mesoamerica around 10,000 BCE; they likely came from Siberia over the now-submerged Bering Strait. In ancient times, Mexico was warmer and covered with dense forest, but the ancient diet was surprisingly varied with indigenous corn, squash, beans, tomatoes, chilies, peppers, avocadoes, peanuts, papayas, turkey, cacao, tobacco, nopal cactus, and sapodilla fruit. Though agriculture began much earlier, intensive farming began around 1800 BCE.

Ancient Mexico produced five major pre-Hispanic "mother" civilizations: the *Olmec*, *Maya*, the multi-ethnic *Teotihuacan*, *Toltec*, and *Aztec*. They ranged over three main periods: the *Preclassic* (before AD 250), the *Classic* (250 to 900), and the *Postclassic* (900 to 1521). These powerful cultural empires, kingdoms, and city-states influenced trade, art, politics, technology, and religion across and beyond Mexico. Experts consider Classic Maya the most brilliant period because it produced unsurpassed art, architecture, mathematics, and astronomy. Mexicans today owe their heritage, spirituality, and arts to these cultures.

In April 1519, Spanish conquistador Hernán Cortés landed at modern-day Veracruz intent on conquest and religious conversion. By 1521 he had conquered the Aztec Empire in Mexico, due in no small part to smallpox and measles, which killed one-third of the native population—and eventually many, many more. The Spanish conquest of the Yucatán Peninsula and the Mayan civilization in Mexico and Central America began in 1551 and ended around 1697.

From 1521 until 1810, Mexico was known as New Spain. It was part of the *Viceroyalty of New Spain*, which included Cuba, Puerto Rico, the American Southwest, Central America south to Costa Rica, and the Philippines. For 200 years, Aztec rebellions and wars plagued the Spanish colonizers. Colonial law mainly benefited Spain; however, human sacrifice, cannibalism, slavery, and genocide were abolished in Mexico, thus preserving many of its native languages and customs. During three centuries of Spanish rule, Spanish male settlers intermarried with native women to produce *mestizo* or mixed race descendants—the majority population of present-day Mexico.

In 1810, Catholic priest Father Miguel de Hidalgo y Costilla took action against repressive Spanish rule with an armed rebellion. He was executed, but the *Mexican War of Independence* had begun. The rebels finally achieved independence when conservative Spanish-led forces rebelled against a temporarily liberal regime in Spain. After an initial clash, the royalist leader Iturbide switched allegiances and invited the rebel leaders to discuss a renewed independence struggle. By 1821, the result of this alliance, the short-lived Treaty of Cordoba, ended the conflict and gave independence to the Mexican Empire.

The nineteenth century was a period of unstable government caused by the disparity of wealth, land, and power between the Spanish elite (*criollo* or Mexican-born Spaniards) and *mestizo* majority. The struggle over Mexico's territories bordering the United States was another issue. Due to Comanche raids, those territories became isolated from Mexico. The *Mexican-American War* (1846 to 1848) started after the United States annexed Mexican-claimed Texas, and Mexico attacked Ft. Texas. American troops invaded the northern territories and Mexico City, which ultimately forced Mexico to sell half of its territories, New Mexico, and (Alta) California, to the United States.

By the mid-nineteenth century, bloody political battles and the subsequent liberal reforms changed Mexico into a cohesive nation. France invaded Mexico, and Napoleon installed his brother, Archduke Maximilian and Maximilian's consort, Carlota, as emperor and empress. President Benito Juarez had Maximilian executed and became president. After Juarez's death, Porfirio Díaz assumed power, and although this was a time of relative peace and prosperity, social inequalities increased. Blatant election fraud by Díaz caused Mexican civilians to plot his overthrow and triggered the Mexican Revolution (1910 to 1929), a period of bloodshed, shifting allegiances, and legends like Pancho Villa and Emiliano Zapata.

In 1929, the *Partido Revolucionario Institucional* (PRI) was formed and most of the revolutionary generals transferred their armies to the Mexican Army. In 1934, President Lázaro Cárdenas united and reformed Mexico; despite growing accusations of fraud, his successor, Manuel Ávila Camacho, presided until 2000 and the end of PRI rule. Presidents Vicente Fox Quesada (2000 to 2006) and Felipe Calderón Hinojosa (2006 to 2012) followed. Mexico is a federation of thirty-one states and a Federal District, the capital (and largest city) Mexico City. Today Mexico is a member of NAFTA. The country continues to struggle with poverty and the eradication of drugs and vicious drug cartels, which run rampant throughout the country.

LANGUAGE, PHILOSOPHY, AND RELIGION

Mexico's official language is Spanish. Although Mexicans speak over 60 native languages, the most spoken are the Aztec *Nahuatl*, the Mayan *Guarani*, and the Incan *Quechua*. English is spoken near the border towns while other parts of Mexico are home to enclaves that speak Italian, French, German, and Mandarin.

The ancient native religion was *Nahua*, in which multiple deities were worshipped. Despite ritual human sacrifice and cannibalism for the gods, Nahua was theologically advanced. There was a great emphasis on astronomy and mathematics, which native priests used to form calendars for growing crops and predict natural events. The Spaniards brought Roman Catholicism, which temporarily led natives to drop most deities in favor of one "True God." Modern-day religion is varied with a surreal mix of pagan and traditional, incorporating ancient deities like San La Muerte (the skeletal Saint Death) worshipped on Dia de los Muertos (Day of the Dead) with the brown-skinned Virgin of Guadalupe. The Virgin has long symbolized for Mexicans the fusion of their conflicting worlds, knitting family, politics, religion, Indian, Spanish, and Mexican, the colonial past, and independent modern society.

Today, though the majority of Mexicans are still Roman Catholic, a growing percentage have converted to Protestant and Evangelical churches like Lutheran, Methodist, Presbyterian, Assemblies of God, Seventh Day Adventist, Church of Jesus Christ of Latter Day Saints (Mormon), and Jehovah's Witnesses.

GEOGRAPHY AND CLIMATE: MAGICAL

Three times the size of Texas with almost one-third the population of the United States, Mexico contains thirty-one states and a federal district. Flanked by the Pacific Ocean to the west and south, by the Sea of Cortes between Baja California and the mainland, on the east by the Gulf of Mexico, and on the southeastern tip by the Caribbean Sea, Mexico also has borders with the United States, Guatemala, and Belize. Mexico lies within the Pacific Rim's volcano and earthquake-prone *Ring of Fire*.

Desolate, beautiful, and forbidding, northern Mexico contains two large deserts, the *Chihuahuan* and the *Sonoran*, between the *Sierra Madres*, Mexico's two mountain ranges extending south from the U.S. border along the Pacific and Gulf of Mexico. Between them lies the vast *Altiplano Central*, a large plateau, divided into north and central, which sees summer temperatures soaring to 100 degrees F. Home to salt flats, snowy mountains, and dramatic coastlines, the north contains Mexico's largest states and Baja California with its Pacific beaches and famous resorts. The north is generally drier, hot in summer, and colder in winter with near freezing temperatures.

Central Mexico has a milder climate and terrain than the North. Fertile, rolling green hills and blossoming trees signal that, despite low rainfall, this most heavily populated region is the agricultural center of Mexico. It is home to Mexico City and the fertile central Mexican lowlands (*bajío*). The coastal plains are hot and humid year round.

Southern Mexico is a region of rugged terrain, rocky cliffs, valleys, and abundant rainfall with tropical rainforests and savanna. Chiapas has Mexico's highest rainfall with more than 98 inches yearly. In general, Mexico's climate ranges from temperate to tropical depending on altitude, winds, and ocean currents. June through September is hottest and wettest for the entire country. Southern low-lying areas are hotter and humid, while higher areas are cooler and drier. The east and west coasts see hurricanes summer through fall.

FARMING AND AGRICULTURE

Although agriculture (and livestock) employs almost a quarter of the population, it is only a small fraction of the economy. Mexico produces most, but not all, of the meat, fish, milk, eggs, wheat, beans, corn, and sorghum for domestic consumption, and produces sugar, coffee, fruit, cocoa, and vegetables for export.

Mexico has abundant land for crop farming, and government irrigation programs have allowed more of it to be farmed successfully. Land ownership changes instituted in 1992 allow peasants to combine to form larger, more efficient farms. Up until 2008, government cash payments directly to farmers encouraged them to diversify to grow more wheat, sorghum, fruits, and vegetables, instead of the profitable and traditional corn and beans.

MEXICAN CUISINE: THE MASTERS OF CORN, CHILIES, BEANS, AND SQUASH

Known for its colorful variety and big flavors, Mexican cuisine isn't just tortillas, tacos, cheesy refried beans, salsa, guacamole, and chips. Travel to the Mexican interior reveals a vast, complex mother cuisine that rivals the cuisines of Italy, Rome, and China. Though Mexico has contributed substantially to world cuisine with indigenous shell beans, winter and summer squashes, tomatoes, vanilla, chilies, peppers, avocadoes, chocolate, chayote, and jicama, this is a cuisine strongly rooted in the celebrated native *maíz* (corn).

For 10,000 years the entire Mexican culture has had its grounding in corn's cycle of planting, growth, harvest, and preparation. Radically different, ancient maize originally grew wild. Farmers domesticated it into more than sixty native varieties suitable for the widely varied landscapes of Mexico—dry, temperate highlands to moist, tropical lowlands. The Olmec and Mayan cultures developed *nixtamalization*. This process of soaking and cooking corn kernels in wood ash or lime (calcium hydroxide or *cal*) increases bio-availability of protein and amino acids and softens kernels for grinding into *masa* (dough) for the national staple, corn tortillas.

The ancient, delicious, nourishing peasant diet of this agriculture-based society mixed corn and beans with squashes, tomatoes, chilies and peppers, wild greens, and tropical fruits like papaya, pineapple, *pitaya, mamey, zapote,* and *guanábana.* Many supplemented their diet with domesticated turkey, duck, dog and wild deer, peccary, iguana, armadillo, seafood, insects like *chapulines* (grasshoppers), and insect larvae.

Without ovens, the pre-Hispanic native women cooked over open fire, using clay pots. Without fat, they mostly steamed meat by wrapping it in cactus or banana leaves and suspending it over boiling water in a deep pit. The method, still in use today, is called *barbacoa.* Mexican food's unique flavor came from dry-roasting tomatoes, tomatillos, chilies, and spices on clay *comals* or directly over coals. Cooks used the *metate y mano* (volcanic grinding stone) for grinding corn into masa for tortillas and tamales, and the *molcajete* (volcanic mortar and pestle) to grind chilies, spices, and vegetables for *salsas* and *moles* (sauces).

Along with salsas and corn dishes, moles are Mexico's gift to the world, the quintessential Mexican-Spanish invention. Modern moles, with the addition of Spanish spices, raisins, garlic, lard, and sugar, employ a remarkable number of ingredients and culinary know-how. Chilies and their seeds play the most important role with spices, nuts, seeds, lard, bread or tortillas, tomatoes, and dried and fresh fruit as the supporting cast. Chocolate makes a cameo appearance in a very few moles. Every town and every region guards traditional mole recipes that range in texture from soupy-thin to thick and rich, with colors ranging from yellow to red, brown and black. Moles are a cross between a sauce and a stew: cooks simmer cooked meat and poultry and uncooked seafood and vegetables in finished moles.

Modern Mexican cuisine began in 1519, when Spain burst on the scene with rice, beef, pork, chicken, wheat, citrus, onion, garlic, sugar, and many Far Eastern spices like cinnamon, clove, nutmeg, and saffron. Women ruled Mexican kitchens in all but northern Mexico, where ranchers and hunters created many dishes. Working in haciendas and convents with educated and creative Spanish women (and nuns), and in the homes of Spanish soldiers, native women cooks began to meld together ingredients of both Old and New Worlds. The *mestizo* (mixed) and *criollo* (Mexican-born Spanish) children of the kitchens and convents learned to cook, and helped to spread the cuisine.

When traders and slaves came to Mexico from the Caribbean, South America, West Africa, and Portugal, Mexican cooks further assimilated these cuisines. The aristocracy considered the French as masters of good taste and imported French chefs, but their classic techniques became Mexicanized. These techniques set the stage for the new Mexican cuisine and dishes like crepes stuffed with *huitlacoche* (corn fungus), *chipotle* remoulade, cream of avocado and tequila soup, tenderloin with *ancho*-port sauce and snapper with *tomatillo* cream sauce.

"*Nueva cocina mexicana,*" Mexican cookbook author Jim Peyton says, "differs from other styles of nouvelle and fusion cooking in that its ingredients and techniques come, for the most part, from various aspects of Mexican cooking rather than from a combination of other cuisines. [Pre-Hispanic] Mexican cuisine developed on two levels simultaneously, with 'peasant' and 'court' cooking evolving separately. In *nueva cocina mexicana*, these two paths merge, with dishes combining these aspects in various ways."

Mexican cuisine has knit together the early influences of Spain and her conquered lands and many European influences with its native cooking skills and the foods of her rich and poor, urban and village cooks to become one of the world's most diverse and vital cuisines. In 2010, UNESCO named Mexican cuisine an "intangible world cultural heritage."

REGIONAL MEXICO

A large, complex country with major differences in terrain and climate, Mexico has a cuisine that is largely regional and hugely diverse. Mountains separate close neighbors often resulting in delicious but little known regional techniques and dishes. Mexico's post-Hispanic, modern cuisine also varies depending where immigrating people settled. Each of the thirty-one states and Federal District of Mexico City can boast of a rich menu of regional foods and signature dishes. In *Culinary Mexico*, chef Daniel Hoyer divides Mexico into six main culinary regions:

1. **La Frontera (The Northern Frontier)**
   A very rich region, northern Mexico, of which originally Texas and New Mexico were part, is like a movie set with *vaqueros* on horses, sparsely inhabited small towns, and large, modern cities. The mineral-rich soaring Sierra Madres give way to sweeping flat, arid desert good for growing wheat, cattle, goat, and ostrich. Northern Mexico comprises the states that border the United States: Baja California, Chihuahua, Coahuila, Nuevo León, Sonora, Durango, and Tamaulipas. They are known for ranching, manufacturing, high-tech, and music; Coahuila is a grape-growing region. Simple, hearty dishes originated by men who hunted, like *fajitas*, flour tortillas, nachos, *chimichangas*, *charro* (cowboy) beans, *menudo norteño* (tripe soup), *cabrito* (young goat), *burritos*, and *asado de chili colorado* (pork simmered in a chili-based sauce), are well suited to northern Mexico's challenging landscape and climate.

2. **Las Costa Oro (The Pacific Coast)**
   The Pacific coast from Sinaloa, Nayarit, coastal Jalisco, Colima, and coastal Michoacán to Guerrero and the Sierra Madre foothills is a region of rugged, tropical beauty with miles of untouched beaches and a backdrop of volcanoes. Tall evergreens, mountainous jungle, and huge, shiny resorts rub shoulders with small villages, coffee, coconut and agave plantations, seaports, and fishing. Seafood, game, pork, tropical fruits, insects, larvae, worms, parrot soup, and iguana tamales are locally beloved foods. Tequila, *tacos al pastor* (pork with pineapple and chilies), shrimp tamales, char-grilled

chicken on a stick, *ceviche*, pineapple vinegar, *guacamole*, *pozole* (corn and meat stew), bread soup, char-grilled whole fish, squash blossom and corn soup, and *birria* (spicy meat and tomato stew thickened with cornmeal) are specialties of this region.

3. **El Istmo (The Southern Isthmus of Tehuantepec)**
In this region, the Sierra Madre levels out to broad plateau-like ridge with a 735-foot elevation fanned with cool Pacific trade winds known as the *Tehuano*. The northern isthmus is swamp and jungle; the east-central portion is the largest remaining piece of Mexico's tropical rainforest. This is a region of tropical beauty made up of Oaxaca, Veracruz, and western Tabasco. Coastal Veracruz is a place of seafood, big cities, Caribbean music and food influences, and vast spaces with cattle, tobacco, coffee, seafood, and lush greenery. Tabasco is sprinkled with rivers, lakes, and swamps. A place of dense jungle, and banana and cacao plantations, Tabasco is the home of Mexico's mother culture, the *Olmec*, and the cradle of the Mesoamerican civilizations, many of which (like the Maya) still influence the food of this region. The most culturally and culinarily diverse state in the country, Oaxaca, the *Land of Seven Moles*, is a favorite among foodies. Despite the poverty-stricken population, *la cocina oaxaqueña* (the cooking of Oaxaca) is complex and richly flavorful. This region's renowned dishes include iguana, chicken, beef or armadillo tamales, spicy vegetable, chili, and chicken dishes, many Oaxacan moles like *manchamanteles*, Oaxacan mescal, *pollo en escabeche*, snapper Veracruz, potato fritters, peanut and chipotle salsa, *arroz verde* (green rice), and aniseed tamales. Coffee and vanilla are abundant.

4. **La Encrucijada (The Central Crossroads)**
This region encompasses the Valley of Mexico, which was the home of the Aztec empire and is the soul of Mexico. Mexico City (with the sixth largest world population) is a sensual feast. The city and its surrounding states of Hildago, Morelos, Puebla, Tlaxcala, and the Estado de México vibrate with the scents of mole, hot corn tortillas, and chilies and the beat of music. Varied architecture, cathedrals, and Aztec temples mingle with cactus and palm trees. The birthplace of mole, Puebla's specialties include various pre-Hispanic dishes, *chiles en nogada*, and *chalupas*. Tlaxcala, a region of complex climate and rugged terrain dominated by ridges and valleys, is the birthplace of corn tortillas. It shares with mountainous, rugged Hidalgo and Morelos specialties like *barbacoa*, *mixiote*, *tamales*, *tacos*, *quesadillas*, *chilies rellenos*, *xolostle* (chicken in red chili sauce), varieties of edible insects like *escamoles* (ant eggs) and *maguey* larvae, wild mushrooms, squash flowers, *xoconostle* (cactus fruit), *nopal*, and *epazote*. Mountainous Morelos is fruit heaven and many dishes include fruit: chicken in peach sauce, plum *atole* (a corn-based drink), and chicken with apples.

5. **El Centro Colonial (The Colonial Plains and Highlands)**
This is a region of lush, green central plains and mountainous highlands encompassing Guadalajara, Eastern Jalisco, Zacatecas, Guanajuato, Michoacán, Aguascalientes, and San Luis Potosí. The highland region is dominated by mining and agriculture, which gave the people the means to build churches and soaring cathedrals. The culture, food, religion, architecture, and politics of this Mexican heartland were strongly influenced by the Spanish colonial period (mid-1500 to early 1800). Spanish settlers, commercial agriculture, and cattle ranching influenced the cuisine strongly, emphasizing meat, corn, wild herbs, game, fish, insects, fruit, and cactus in dishes like sweet or blue corn tamales, *churipo* (meat stew), *pozole* (hominy and pork stew), *elotes asados* (grilled corn on the cob), and *carnitas* (braised, fried, and shredded pork).

6. **La Tierra Maya (The Yucatán Peninsula)**
This land of the mysterious Mayan and other rich cultures includes Chiapas, eastern Tabasco, Campeche, Quintana Roo, and the Yucatán. Chiapas has high mountains, plains, and low wetlands, but the other states are flatter and fertile with lush, tropical forests and beaches on the Gulf of Mexico and Caribbean Sea. The Yucatan is a place where the traditional Mayan culture melds with the colonial and plantation cultures. The food is Mayan with accents of the Caribbean, Africa, and the Middle East,

and famously seasoned with *tres recados* (three seasoning pastes). Dishes like *papazules* (enchiladas), *panuchos* (puffed, stuffed, and fried tortillas), *sopa de lima* (lime soup), Mayan grilled fish, *carne asada Yucateca* (grilled meat), *brazo de la reina* (queen's arm tamale), *cochinita pibil* (pit-roasted pork), pickled red onions, black beans, and tamales with greens are some of this region's delights.

FIGURE 13.2 Mazatlan Mexico.
Source: Vivid Pixels/Fotolia.

DINE AT HOME IN MEXICO

If invited to dine at someone's home, leave the shorts and flip-flops at the hotel and dress up. It's good etiquette to arrive thirty minutes late, with a gift for the host, hostess, and any children. Flowers (preferably white, as other colors have funereal connotations), sweets, or something from a guest's country are most appreciated. Greet the host and hostess with a handshake. A kiss on the hostess' cheek is acceptable if a guest knows her well. Most of Mexican social life centers on large family gatherings that celebrate christenings, weddings, birthdays, saint days, funerals, or fiestas. Music plays an important role. At large gatherings, guests introduce themselves. At small gatherings, the host will do the honors. Use the restroom before being seated—it's rude to leave the table during dinner.

Wait to be seated. Rest wrists on the edge of the table and keep hands visible at all times. Wait for the hostess to begin eating. Only men give toasts—and only with an alcoholic beverage. Wish everyone *buen provecho* or good dining. During dinner avoid political, racial, and economic topics. Do not eat the last food on a platter without offering it to others first. Some foods are eaten with hands—follow the lead of others.

Mexican meals vary greatly from region to region, but expect a meal with corn, beans, chilies, and meat and in coastal regions, fish and seafood. Mexicans have, for centuries, followed the Spanish way of eating: coffee or hot chocolate and roll for breakfast, a large *comida* (midday meal) around 2 p.m., a snack mid-afternoon, and a light meal of soup for *cena* (dinner). That is slowly changing as more working Mexican families move their largest meal to dinnertime.

Formal midday *comida* traditionally comprised five elements: *sopa* (soup), *sopa seca* (rice or noodles), *main dish* of meat or seafood with tortillas and vegetables, a course of *frijoles* (beans), and a *light dessert* like pudding or fruit to finish. Soups are usually chicken-stock-based with garnishes, and sopa secas might be red or green rice or *fideos* (pasta) cooked in tomato. The main dish might be *pescado a la Veracruzana* (fish Veracruz-style), pork *adobo*, shrimp in pumpkin seed sauce, rabbit, duck, stuffed poblano chilies, or a tomato-based chicken stew. Food to mark a celebration might be *barbacoa* (meat braised in barbecue sauce or pit-cooked), *tamales*, or chicken or turkey *mole* (thick sauce of chilies, nuts, seeds, and spices).

When finished eating, leave a little food on the plate to signal satiety. Place the knife and fork, handles to the right and prongs facing down, across the plate. Praise the meal highly.

TASTES OF MEXICO

Fat: Pork lard, butter, beef tallow; olive, canola, safflower, sunflower, and corn oils

Sweet: *Piloncillo* (raw sugar cone), sugar, honey, agave nectar (cooked syrup from agave plant)

Sour/Alcohol: Lemon, *limon* (lime), Mexican and Key limes, bitter lime, *lima agria* (acidic, fragrant lime), *naranja agria* (bitter orange), *lima dulce* (sweet lime), fruit vinegars, tamarind

Salty: Sea salt

Spicy-Hot: Many types of fresh and dried or smoked chilies, black pepper, paprika, cayenne pepper

Spice: Allspice, *canela* (flaky cinnamon), clove, cumin, coriander, *achiote* (annatto), ginger, aniseed, nutmeg, saffron, *azáfran* (Mexican saffron), turmeric (fresh or dried), *azafrán de bolita* (spice used for yellow color)

Aromatic Seasoning Vegetables: White onion, *cebolla de rabo* (large white onion with green attached), red onions, chilies, garlic, tomatoes, tomatillos

Herbs, Seasonings, and Condiments: *Cilantrillo* (cilantro), *cilantro* (culantro), Italian parsley, marjoram, basil, many types of Mexican "oregano," *epazote*, bay leaf, *hoja santa* (anise-flavored large leaves), Mexican avocado leaf, lemongrass, mint, sage, thyme

Other Important Foods: Wheat, corn, *pozole* (hominy or large kernel corn), amaranth, potatoes, fish, seafood, chicken, duck, turkey, pork, goat, beef, dried shrimp, crab, rabbit, duck, sour cream, cheese, rice, wild and cultivated greens, cabbage, eggplant, zucchini, jicama, pumpkin and squash flowers, *huitlacoche* (corn fungus), *nopales* (cactus paddles), plantains, chayote, *calabaza* (pumpkin), squash, sweet potatoes, bell peppers; legumes (fava beans, chickpeas, lentils, pinto and black beans and many more varieties); nuts and seeds (pecans, walnut, peanuts, almonds, pumpkin seeds, sesame); fruit (apples, peaches, melons, pineapples, guava, plantains, bananas), wraps (fresh and dry corn husks, fresh banana leaves, *mixiote*, the papery leaf shaved from maguey)

Popular Dishes: Tortillas, tacos, quesadillas, tamales, *ceviche*, salsa, *barbacoa* (barbecue), *pozole* (corn and pork soup), *caldo tlalpeño* (chicken-vegetable soup), enchiladas, guacamole, mole sauces, *calabacitas*, chilies rellenos (stuffed poblano chilies), *chilies en nogada* (stuffed poblanos in walnut sauce), *carne adobo* (meat in adobo sauce), *carne asada* (grilled steak), *sopa seca* (dry soup), *frijoles refritos* (well-fried beans), red snapper Veracruz-style, *enfrijoladas* (quesadillas covered with soupy beans), *cochinita pibil* (Yucatanean pit-roasted pork), *cemitas* (Pueblan avocado, bean or meat and cheese sandwiches), *res con rajas de chili poblano* (beef with chili strips), flan

Drinks: *Atole* (corn drink), *horchata* (rice drink), *tejate* (corn flour, mamey pits, cacao and sometimes piquin chili steeped in water, sweetened and whipped to a froth), chocolate, coffee, beer, wine, *pulque* (fermented agave), apple cider, *charanda* (sugar cane spirit), *rompope* (egg nog), tequila, mescal, *aguas frescas* (seasonal fruit waters), fruit punch, herbal teas (lemongrass, chamomile, orange blossom, and hibiscus)

COMMON MEXICAN COOKING TOOLS

Molcajete (volcanic stone mortar with pestle), *metate* (volcanic stone slab and roller for grinding), tortilla press, *cazuela* (earthenware baking dish), *comal* (steel plate for heating tortillas), *molinillo* (wooden chocolate frother)

FIGURE 13.3 Nopales cactus on comal griddle.
Source: © Benedicte Desrus/Alamy.

FIGURE 13.4 Molcajete.
Source: greenfire/Fotolia.

FIGURE 13.5 Tortilla press.
Source: raptorcaptor/Fotolia.

FIGURE 13.6 Metate for grinding corn, sauces, and pastes.
Source: lrafael/Shutterstock.

MEXICAN CHILIES

There are more than sixty varieties of chili eaten fresh, dried, smoked, or pickled in Mexico. Many of the most wonderful, complex-flavored chilies are grown in Oaxaca. About a dozen varieties are most important. As a rule, the smaller the chili, the hotter.

Fresh Chilies

To tell the heat of a fresh chili, slice a bit off the tip and sniff (but not too close!). If the chili gives off a strong, pungent scent, it packs some heat. A mild fragrance signals less heat.

FIGURE 13.7 Jalapeno chili.
Source: Glenn Price/Shutterstock.

Jalapeño

Probably best-known of all chilies, this green chili is grassy-flavored and mildly hot. Smoked and dried jalapeños become the very tasty chipotle. Pickled jalapeños become the habit-forming jalapeños en escabeche; sliced they are called nacho chilies. Look for La Costeña brand.

FIGURE 13.8 Serrano chilies.
Source: Roger Dixon/DK Images.

Serrano

Though it is a smaller cousin to the jalapeño, this chili delivers more heat and is preferred by Mexican cooks. It appears green and sometimes ripened to yellow or red.

FIGURE 13.9 Poblano chili.
Source: Roger Dixon/DK Images.

Poblano

This chili is large, triangular, and deep green. Mildly spicy, Mexican cooks roast, peel, and stuff poblanos for chilies rellenos or slice it (rajas) and cook with cream or vegetables. When dried, poblano chili becomes the fruity and delicious ancho.

FIGURE 13.10 Anaheim chili.
Source: Ronald James/Fotolia.

Anaheim

These large, mild-flavored chilies have tough skins. Many Mexican cooks stuff them. Ripened red Anaheims are called chili colorado. Dried, they are called California chilies. Anaheims are used fresh in sauces.

Habañero

A cousin to the Scotch Bonnet, this small, thin-walled, bonnet-shaped chili has citrusy, fruity undertones, but beware—it packs a hot wollop. It comes in three colors: unripe green,

FIGURE 13.11 Habañero chili.
Source: Roger Dixon/DK Images.

middling ripe yellow, and fully ripe orange or red. Habañeros are about 40 times hotter than jalapeño chilies.

Dried Chilies

The flavor of dried chilies is richer and more concentrated. Most dried chilies benefit from toasting and soaking in hot water to plump them. Dried chilies should be soft, flexible, and smell fruity and sweet, like prunes. Hard, brittle chilies are old and less flavorful.

FIGURE 13.12 Ancho chili.
Source: Dave King/DK Images.

Ancho

This large, purple, flexible, wrinkled, and very flavorful, acid-fruity chili is mildly hot to hot. Sometimes erroneously called pasilla and mistaken for mulato, this chili has a reddish-purple cast held up to the light, and broad shoulders that narrow to a tip.

Cascabel

This is a small, deep red, smooth-surfaced, round chili usually found in the north and central parts of Mexico.

FIGURE 13.13 Cascabel chilies.
Source: Crepesoles/Shutterstock.

It looks a bit like a baby rattle and is pleasantly hot. Seeds can be toasted and ground to give a nutty flavor to sauces.

FIGURE 13.14 Chili de arbol.
Source: Roger Dixon/DK Images.

Chili de Árbol

This long, narrow red chili is thin-fleshed, smooth-skinned, and very hot. It's good with black beans or ground and sprinkled with salt on jicama, cucumbers, or fruit.

Chili Seco del Norte or Largo Colorado

This is a burnished copper-colored north Mexican dried Anaheim, New Mexican, or California chili that is mild to hot. Used in chilaquiles, enchiladas, and carne con chile, many northern cooks brown flour to thicken sauces with it.

FIGURE 13.15 Chipotle chili.
Source: Dave King/DK Images.

Chipotle (Chilpocle)

Chipotles are the very spicy, ripened-red, smoke-dried jalapeño. Larger chipotles are meco and smaller are mora. They are available dried, canned, or canned en adobo.

FIGURE 13.16 Guajillio chili.
Source: Dave King/DK Images.

Guajillo

A large, low-priced long, red chili with skin is tough so it should be strained from sauces. The guajillo has a smooth skin with a crisp, sharp flavor.

FIGURE 13.17 Mulato chili.
Source: Ian O'Leary/DK Images.

Mulato

Easily mistaken for anchos, this chili is flexible, triangular, and large. Its shiny brown skin isn't as wrinkled as the ancho. Its flavor is mild to hot with a sweet undertone. Good for mole poblano.

Pasilla (Negro or Chilaca)

This large, rich-flavored chili has shiny, black skin and puckered surface. It ranges from medium to very hot and may be stuffed, made into sauces, moles, whole, or in strips. The veins and seeds are especially flavorful and are used as flavorings and condiments.

FIGURE 13.18 Pasilla chili.
Source: Philip Dowell/DK Images.

FIGURE 13.19 Fresh pequin chili.
Source: Christine M. Douglas/DK Images.

Piquín

This red chili, which looks like a tiny version of chili de árbol, is the smallest of all chilies. Used fresh or dried, it is found in northern Mexico. It is very hot, but has a complex smoke and citrus flavor.

MEXICAN CHEESE (QUESO)

Soft Cheeses

Fresco
Crumbly soft, white garnishing cheese similar to Muenster or feta that doesn't melt well and is consequently an excellent choice for dishes that need a cheese that softens when heated, but does not become gooey. Good for frying, stuffing, or tossing with hot ingredients.

Panela
Fresh, mild, and milky-flavored soft, porous, spongy cheese similar to ricotta or mild feta.

Requesón
This loose, ricotta-like cheese is used to fill enchiladas and to make cheese spreads. Most requesón is sold wrapped in fresh corn husks; ricotta may be substituted.

Semi-Firm Cheeses

Queso Blanco
This creamy, white cheese made from skimmed cow milk is a cross between cottage cheese and mozzarella. Traditionally it was coagulated with lemon juice, but commercially it is made with rennet. Good for stuffing enchiladas, queso blanco softens when heated but doesn't melt.

Quesillo or Queso Oaxaca
Mild-flavored stretched and rolled string cheese similar to whole milk mozzarella and string cheese made with cow milk. Good for melting and in quesadillas.

Asadero
A northern Mexican tart, soured milk cheese similar to queso Oaxaca.

Chihuahua or Menonita
Of Menonnite origins, this white, mild cheese has a texture similar to cheddar or gouda and is a favorite for melting in dishes like nachos and quesadillas.

Firm Cheeses

Añejo or Cotijo
An aged queso fresco with strong, salty flavor similar to Parmesan, made from goat or cow milk, and used as zesty, grated topping for salads, tacos, and beans.

Enchilado
The reddish *queso enchilado* is añejo or cotijo rubbed with a thin layer of ancho chili on the outside.

Queso Criollo
Very similar to Muenster cheese.

MAÍZ

Maize, from the native Taino word *maíz*, spread over most of the Americas between 1700 BCE and 1250 BCE through native trade networks. Spanish conquerors took it back to Spain in the late fifteenth and early sixteenth centuries. From there, corn spread to the rest of Europe and other parts of the world. Able to grow in diverse climates, corn became, and remains, a hugely popular crop; it is the largest crop grown in the United States. See *Glossary* for types of corn.

Fresh Corn

A favorite of Mexican street food, vendor carts offer giant ears of roasted fresh corn dipped into rich crema Mexicana and sprinkled with chili powder and lime juice.

From Whole Corn

Pozole (Hominy): Lime-treated cooked kernels, skinned and cooked until bursting. Fresh masa dough for tamales is ground from pozole. Masa harina (flour) is ground from dried pozole.

On the cob: Fresh sweet corn roasted and swabbed with butter or cream and drizzled with lime and chili powder.

From Corn Masa Dough

Atole: Flavored drink made with masa.

Tamales: Masa dough with sweet or savory filling wrapped in corn husks or banana leaves and steamed.

Tamal de Cazuela (Tamale Casserole): Masa creamed with butter and egg yolks and lightened with beaten egg white. Layered into a casserole to enfold a filling, and baked.

Gordita: Corn cake or patty, sometimes stuffed with cheese or meat.

Panucho: Deep-fried puffed tortilla, split, stuffed, and deep-fried again.

Sopes: Thick soft, masa turnover or oblongs pinched to create a cup and deep-fried to hold filling.

Chalupa: Crunchy, deep-fried thin, shallow masa cups garnished with meats, beans, cheese, and nopales.

Empanada: Baked stuffed turnover.

Molotes: Masa "samosas" filled with potato and chorizo, fried and garnished.

Memela: Griddle-warmed Oaxacan "pizza" topped with black beans and queso fresco.

Huaraches: Similar to sopes, but with a flat oblong masa base, fried and topped with various meats, cheese, salsas, and cilantro.

Tlacoyas: Fat, torpedo-shaped fried or griddle toasted blue or yellow masa cakes served with salsa. They are often stuffed with beans or cheese, sometimes served with soup or stew.

Polkanes: Stuffed Mayan corn fritters.

Corn Tortillas: Flat-pressed thin, round unleavened "bread" cooked briefly on hot griddle.

With Corn Tortillas

Tostada: Fried flat and topped

Soft Taco: Filled and folded in half or rolled and eaten

Tacos Doraditos: Filled, rolled, and crisp-fried

Enchilada: Stuffed, rolled, and sauced *or* sauced, stuffed, rolled, and sauced

Quesadilla: Cheese stuffed, folded in half and heated

Flauta: stuffed, Rolled (like a flute) and deep-fried

Chilaquiles: Fried tortilla strips baked or simmered with chili sauce and cheese

Totopos: Fried tortilla chips

Chef Advice on Masa

Chef, Chicago restaurateur, and cookbook author Rick Bayless has a long history with corn and the masa dough and flours made from it. Masa is made from corn that has been soaked with calcium hydroxide (slaked lime) and water. Fresh masa dough is ground directly from the soaked corn into a smooth texture for making tortillas and a slightly coarser texture for tamale preparation. Bayless prefers purchasing the whitest masa (this indicates the bitter calcium hydroxide has been washed out) from a tortilla factory. He advises wrapping the dough tightly and refrigerating. It should be used within one day or the dough loses "the plasticity crucial to making light tortillas." Masa dough may be frozen up to a month. If using dried masa harina (flour), Bayless cautions cooks to be aware of the difference between *masa para tamales* and *masa preparada para tamales*. The first is a smooth, plain corn flour. The second is more coarse-textured and often mixed with lard and flavorings.

MASA HARINA AND MASA

Masa harina is corn flour ground from dried, whole corn kernels (hominy or pozole) that have been *nixtamalized* or cooked with lime (calcium hydroxide) or wood ash to soften their outer layer, which is discarded. Masa is the corn dough made from ground, freshly cooked nixtamalized corn or from masa harina. Nixtamalization also makes the amino acids and protein in corn more bio-available—without this process corn can cause *pellagra* from a deficiency of B-vitamins. The cooked corn is dried and ground. Lime or wood ash gives masa flour its characteristic earthy, sweet aroma and flavor. Cooking the corn contributes to the flour's viscosity through starch gelatinization.

FIGURE 13.20 Dried pozole (hominy).
Source: Yai/Shutterstock.

FROM SENSUAL TO PROFOUND

Many recipes may seem simple, but Mexican cookbook author Jim Peyton knows from experience that until "you learn how much work, passion, creativity and trial and error" and how long it took for a recipe to be born there cannot be a true appreciation of a dish. This appreciation transforms simple "sensual pleasure" into a deeper "cultural experience." Mexico's long, interwoven and lush history and its influence on her complex, deeply creative food demonstrates this better than many other cultures.

MEXICAN FLAVOR FOUNDATIONS

Mexican Signature Aromatic Vegetable Combo

White onions (sometimes red), chilies, garlic, and tomatoes

Hierbas de Olor

Thyme, marjoram or Mexican oregano, and bay leaf

The herbal bouquet used to scent and flavor many dishes.

Mexican Signature Seasonings

Liquid/Paste

Adobo

Thick, spicy adobo pastes are used to marinate and coat a meat or seafood for grilling, roasting, and frying. They are often thinned with stock for slow cooking and braising.

Annatto Oil

Oil into which achiote or annatto seed has been infused, imparting a orange glow and pleasant and mildly saffron-bitter flavor.

Animal

Chicharrón (Fried Pork Rind)

Sun-dried and fried pork skin, which is brown, light and crisp. It is simmered in sauces, used as garnish on soup, guacamole, and salad or as a filling.

Chorizo

Spiced pork sausage that is dried; it is usually seasoned with chilies, garlic, thyme, Mexican oregano, marjoram, pepper, cloves, allspice, and, in the Yucatan, annatto, herbs, and bitter orange juice. **Longaniza** refers to sausage made with inferior cuts of meat and sometimes beef.

Lard

Freshly rendered pork fat is the lard of choice in Mexico, but beef tallow (rendered fat) is sometimes used. Leaf pork lard is the highest grade and is rendered from the flavorless fat deposits surrounding the kidneys and inside the loin. It is ideal for flaky pie crusts. Fatback produces the next best grade; it is rendered from hard subcutaneous fat between the back skin and muscle. Soft caul fat produces the lowest grade; it comes from fat surrounding digestive organs. See *Glossary* for more information on how to prepare lard.

Vegetable/Fruit

Avocados

There are three main strains of avocados: Mexican (Criollo), Guatemalan (Fuerte), and

FIGURE 13.21 Chicharrones.
Source: Rafael Ramirez/Fotolia.

FIGURE 13.22 Mexican chorizo.
Source: marekuliasz/Shutterstock.

FIGURE 13.23 Mexican avocado leaf.
Source: Dave King/DK Images.

Caribbean (Florida). The small, native, non-hybridized Mexican is rich and creamy with almond and anise accents. The Guatemalan is less rich and flavorful than the Mexican variety. (Haas is a Mexican-Guatemalan hybrid.) The Caribbean strain is largest with a light, fruity flavor and less fat.

Herbal/Spice

Achiote (Annatto)

The seed of the achiote fruit produces annatto, which comes from the pulp surrounding the seed. Latin American cooks use achiote seeds for coloring foods yellow to orange and to impart its mildly peppery, nutty scent and flavor. Originally from South America, the Spanish adopted annatto from the Aztecs as a stand-in for saffron. See chapter *The West Indes or Caribbean Islands, Caribbean Flavor Foundations.*

Mexican Avocado Leaf (Hojas de Aguacate)

The Mexican avocado leaf is the only one of the avocado strains with aromatic, anise-flavored leaves. (Guatemalan leaves can be toxic in large doses; see **Avocado** above.) Mexican cooks usually toast the leaves and add to dishes (black beans) like a bay leaf, or line a pit or steamer with untoasted leaves when making barbacoa.

Azafrán (Mexican Saffron or False Saffron)

Azafran is the dried flower petals of the safflower plant. It has a slightly bitter flavor and is used to impart color (no flavor) to a dish. True saffron comes from the stamen of a special crocus. **Azafrán de bolita** is a completely different seasoning: a dull, dark brown seed that resembles allspice and is also used to color and slightly flavor food.

Canela (Mexican Cinnamon)

Canela is the Spanish word for cinnamon. Mexico is the world's largest importer of Ceylon (Sri Lankan) cinnamon, also known as

(Continued)

(Continued)

FIGURE 13.24 Mexican flaky canela.
Source: Brigida Soriano/Shutterstock.

true cinnamon. This delicate, sweet, flaky cinnamon is milder than its tough barked, assertive counterpart (*cassia*) and easily ground in a molcajete or spice grinder.

Cilantro

This pungent, aromatic herb looks similar to Italian parsley, but is very tender, lighter green, and fragrant. Leaves and tender stems have a mild flavor while larger stems impart a strong cilantro flavor. It's best sliced finely. Over-chopped cilantro turns to mush.

FIGURE 13.25 Culantro.
Source: Dave King/DK Images.

Culantro

This spiky, long-leafed herb grows in the southern tropical region of Mexico. Too tough

FIGURE 13.26 Epazote.
Source: Dustin Dennis/Shutterstock.

to be used raw, Mexican cooks add it to stock, broth, stew, or rice. Like cilantro, when cooked too long it loses its meaty, complex flavor. Latin and Asian cooks also use culantro.

Epazote (Wormseed or Mexican Tea)

A strong, aromatic native Mexican herb with a wild, tarry flavor, epazote is often paired with beans or added to soup. It is not used raw—always cooked. Dried epazote has little flavor.

Hoja Santa (Yerba Santa, Hierba Santa, or Momo)

This "holy leaf," native to Mexico, has heart-shaped leaves with strong anise flavor. It seasons and wraps tamales, meat, fish,

FIGURE 13.27 Hoja santa leaf.
Source: Dave King/DK Images.

mushrooms, and rice and can be an ingredient in moles; some cooks toast the leaves before using.

Mexican Oregano

Mexican oregano is stronger and less sweet than true Mediterranean oregano and suited to spicy, hot, cumin-flavored dishes and excellent in salsa. Author Diana Kennedy says that there are at least 18 varieties of wild Mexican oregano. They range in flavor from light and minty, marjoram-like to intense-flavored. Look for them in Mexican markets.

Recado Roja (Yucatecan Spice Mixture)

This seasoning paste is used in the Yucatán to season meats, stews, and tamales. Yucatecan cooks use various amounts of mild peppercorns, cloves, allspice, canela, cumin seed, and oregano, then, depending upon the recipe, season it with minced garlic, salt, bitter orange juice or fruit vinegar, and achiote.

A LIGHT HAND WITH GARLIC

Mexican chef and cookbook author Diana Kennedy has noticed that garlic in the southern Mexican states of Oaxaca and Guerrero is smaller and more flavorful. She points out that garlic is used with a very light hand in Mexican food so that the flavor "is not discernible in the finished sauce." Dishes of Spanish origin use garlic with a heavier hand.

SEASONINGS AND PASTE MIXTURES

ACHIOTE PASTE (RECADO COLORADO OR CONDIMENTO DE ACHIOTE)

This paste is usually made with the sour juice of Seville oranges. If available, use 1/2 cup in place of the lime and orange juice.

Yields about 1/2 cup

1/4 cup annatto seeds
1 tablespoon coriander seeds
1 tablespoon dried Mexican oregano
1 teaspoon cumin seed
1 teaspoon black peppercorns
1 teaspoon kosher salt
1/4 teaspoon allspice berries
1/2 ounce garlic, 2 large cloves, 1 tablespoon peeled and finely minced
5 tablespoons fresh lime juice, about 1-1/2 limes
3 tablespoons fresh orange juice, about half of a 5-ounce orange
 or 1/3 to 1/2 cup white vinegar

1 In a spice grinder in batches, grind annatto, coriander, oregano, cumin, peppercorns, salt, and allspice into a fine powder.

2 Blend ground spices with garlic and the juices or vinegar until smooth and pasty. Store in airtight container in refrigerator up to 2 weeks. Freeze until 6 months.

3 **To Use:** Rub achiote paste onto chicken or pork steak and marinate several hours in refrigerator. Rub on seafood or fish and marinate 1 hour in refrigerator. Grill, roast, or fry protein. Or use paste to season rice, soup, stew, or vegetable dishes.

YUCATAN SEASONING PASTE (RECADO YUCATECO)

Prepared at home or purchased in the market, cooks in the Yucatan use different pastes to season many dishes. This paste, also known as recado de bistec, is used to marinate steak.

Yields about 1/2 cup, enough for 5 to 8 pounds meat

1-1/2 tablespoons black peppercorns
1 tablespoon whole allspice
1 tablespoon Mexican oregano
2 teaspoons coriander seed
1 teaspoon whole cloves
3-inches Mexican canela *or* cinnamon stick, broken up
1 tablespoon kosher salt
1-1/2 ounces garlic, 6 large cloves, about 3 tablespoons peeled and minced to a paste
5 tablespoons cider vinegar

1 Grind spices in spice grinder until very fine. Place spices and salt in bowl. Stir in garlic and vinegar plus 1 tablespoon warm water to a thick paste. **If paste will be stored,** blanch peeled garlic in boiling water 30 seconds before mincing to disable bacteria.

2 **To Use:** Rest paste 1 hour before using. Rub on beef, pork, or turkey legs before grilling or roasting. Refrigerate paste up to 2 weeks or freeze up to 1 month.

COOK'S VOICE: ROBERT SANTIBAÑEZ

Chef-Owner Fonda and The Taco Truck and Cookbook Author Brooklyn, New York

"Every cuisine has its special techniques. European techniques don't always work for Mexican cuisine. French cooks rub tomatoes with oil and roast them in the oven, but Mexican cooks roast tomatoes, chilies and tomatillos on a comal (without fat) or directly over the flame as they have for centuries."

Source: Courtesy of Roberto Santibañez, chef-owner of Fonda restaurants in NYC and cookbook author.

BUILDING BLOCKS OF MEXICAN COOKING

These six building blocks consist of simple sauces and two meat mixtures that are the foundation to several classic Mexican dishes. They can give cooks a non-threatening place to begin to learn Mexican cooking and may inspire new uses.

- **Spiced ground meat (*picadillo dulce*)** Use as stuffing for poblano chilies, tacos, burritos, or empanadas.
- **Braised pork shoulder (*carnitas*)** Use this meat shredded as taco, tamale, or enchilada filling.
- **Light tomato sauce (*caldillo de tomate*)** Roasted tomatoes give the sauce a smoky undertone; chilies, herbs, and spices pop the flavor. Use it with stuffed poblanos, sopa seca, soup or stew or to braise fish, meat or meatballs, and poultry.
- **Chipotle paste (*pasta de chipotle*)** Purée a 7-ounce can of *chipotles en adobo* with 2 tablespoons oil, 1-1/2 tablespoons minced garlic, 2 teaspoons coriander, and 1 teaspoon each dried thyme and ground black pepper for a spicy paste that will work as a rub on meat for roasting or grilling, in sauce or soup.
- **Tomatillo sauce (*salsa verde de tomatillo*)** Use this fresh, tart sauce for salsa, tortillas, grilled meat and poultry or in stews, to make chilaquiles and enchiladas, on fish or chicken, or in soup.
- **Red chili adobo (*adobo de chile colorado*)** This sauce, made with the intense flavor of dried chilies creates a stewing sauce for meat stews, a brushing sauce for grilled meats, or a base for Tex-Mex chili con carne.
- **Fresh salsa (*salsa fresca*)** Mexican cooks prepare and use tomato salsa both raw and cooked. Use it as a sauce on fish, in ceviche or guacamole, as a poaching medium, or in soup or vegetable dishes.

Source: *Food and Wine*, December 1994, *Zarela's Kitchen; How to Infuse Your Everyday Cooking with a Mexican Accent.*

FLAVOR TECHNIQUES FOR AROMATIC VEGETABLES

The sharp-flavored white onion is most favored in Mexico. These are ways cooks bring out flavor in aromatic vegetables.

Picada

Onion finely chopped and used as garnish.

Rebanada Delgada

Onion thinly sliced into half-moons, seasoned with lime juice, and used as topping.

Acitronada

Onions fried slowly in oil until soft.

Frita

Oaxacan method of frying onions in oil until very golden.

Enterrada

Onions, chilies, garlic, and tomatoes cooked on hot stones of pit barbecue until charred on the outside and steaming soft on the inside; the vegetables are added to soups, broth, and escabeche dishes.

Asada

Cooking onions, garlic, chilies, tomatoes, or tomatillos on a comal until charred and soft; the vegetables are added to moles and sauces.

SAUCE (SALSA)

Salsas are always on the Mexican table. Walk into a typical taqueria or taco stand and there will be several bowls of condiments like cilantro, chopped onion, chopped tomato, lime wedges and, at the least, fresh or cooked tomato salsa and a green salsa. With these simple additions, Mexicans enhance their meals and season food to personal taste.

Though some characterize Mexican cuisine, with over 60 varieties of chilies, as spicy-hot, salsas, moles, and pastes employ chilies for varying degrees of heat and aromatic flavor. Mexicans make salsas with uncooked ingredients (*salsa cruda*) or with cooked (*salsa cocida*) ingredients—broiled, roasted, grilled, simmered, or boiled. Cucumbers, pineapple, yellow tomatoes, mango, peaches, and papaya make a great base for raw salsas. Roasted pineapple, tomatoes, or peaches make attention-getting cooked salsas.

FIGURE 13.28 An array of Mexican salsas.
Source: *JEREMY*HERMAN*/Fotolia.

To Seed or Not to Seed

Mexicans don't seed fresh green chilies. Many Mexican cooks feel that chilies are the "soul" of Mexican cuisine; when they are seeded, the dish is robbed dish of the chilies' full flavor. However, dry chilies used in moles are seeded. Sometimes a measured amount of those seeds are roasted, ground, and added to the mole.

Tomatoes used for salsa are often seeded to remove extra liquid and yield a less soupy salsa. Strain the seeds and use the juice elsewhere: the gel surrounding the seeds provides intense tomato flavor not to be missed.

Vary! Improvise!

☞ Add 1/4 ounce garlic, 1 large clove, 1-1/2 teaspoons peeled and minced.

☞ **Roasted Tomato Salsa:** Broil tomatoes, onion, 1 large clove unpeeled garlic and stemmed and halved chilies until blistered and soft all the way through. Peel tomatoes and garlic. Coarsely purée vegetables in food processor.

☞ Substitute 1 to 2 canned chipotle chilies for jalapeños. Omit cilantro and lime juice. Purée salsa in blender until smooth.

FIGURE 13.29 Tomatillo.
Source: Lorenzo Vecchia/DK Images.

Signature Technique: Great Salsas

- Prepare salsas 20 to 30 minutes in advance to allow flavors to mingle. Taste and adjust seasonings before serving.

- Dice vegetables neatly and evenly for maximum eye appeal.

- Seed tomatoes to prepare less watery salsas.

- Add enough salt and lime juice or other acid ingredients. These two flavor enhancers bring a so-so salsa to life.

- Don't seed fresh chilies if you want true Mexican (spicy) flavor.

- Serve salsa warm or at room temperature. Cold dulls flavor.

- Follow time-honored principles:

  - *Raw salsas* provide textural and flavor contrast good for fatty or buttery meat, cheese, and fish dishes.

  - *Cooked salsas* are usually smooth and soupy, but because they're cooked they usually taste less of their individual components and more of a unified whole. Cooked salsas aren't so much for contrast; they work more to enhance what they're paired with like roast pork, lamb, or goat.

FRESH SALSA (SALSA FRESCA, SALSA MEXICANA, OR PICO DE GALLO)

Pico de gallo literally means "beak of the rooster" or bitingly sharp, but to Mexicans this sauce is known as salsa Mexicana or salsa fresca. It is found throughout Mexico. Fresh ingredients are essential.

Yields about 2-2/3 cups

1 pound ripe tomatoes*, about 2-1/2 cups seeded and diced into 1/4-inch cubes
2 ounces white onion, 1/3 cup peeled and finely diced
   or 2 ounces trimmed green onions, about 4, about 1/3 cup finely chopped
1/2 ounce cilantro, 1/4 cup finely sliced
2 tablespoons freshly squeezed lime juice, 1/2 large lime, more to taste
1 ounce jalapeño, 1 large, or 1 ounce Serrano chilies, about 2 small, 2 tablespoons stemmed and finely diced, more to taste

*Optionally, roast tomatoes until blistered over gas flame, on grill, or under broiler. Peel, core, and dice tomatoes.

1 Combine tomatoes and juices, onions, cilantro, lime juice, and chili. Season with salt, to taste. Rest salsa 15 minutes to allow flavors to develop.

GREEN TOMATILLO SALSA (SALSA VERDE DE TOMATILLO)

Simple yet versatile, this classic salsa is a tangy and spicy building block of Mexican cuisine. It pairs well with rich food like pork, egg dishes (huevos rancheros) or, when made with cream, in tortilla dishes like chilaquiles or enchiladas. Cooked tomatillos become gelatinous and will thicken sauces. Cooking the prepared salsa will extend its life.

Yields 4 to 4-1/2 cups

2 pounds tomatillos, husked and rinsed

2 ounces jalapeño chilies, 2 large, stemmed
1 teaspoon ground cumin
1/2 ounce garlic, 2 large cloves, peeled
1 ounce cilantro, about 1 cup packed
Optional: 2 ounces onion, 1/2 cup peeled and diced

Thickened Salsa Verde

1 tablespoon olive oil

Salsa de Tomatillo con Crema

1 cup heavy cream

1. Pour tomatillos into 4-quart nonreactive saucepan and cover with cold water. Bring to a boil over high heat. Lower heat and simmer tomatillos and chilies (turn or weight them to cook evenly) until they are tender, but not falling apart and turn a dull olive color, 10 to 15 minutes.

2. Cool tomatillos slightly, and pour half into blender, half the chilies, 1/2 teaspoon cumin, 1/2 teaspoon kosher salt, and half the cilantro. Cover top of blender with towel and purée in short pulses until sauce is smooth with seeds still visible. Don't over-purée. Repeat with remaining vegetables, cilantro, and optional onion if desired. Mix batches together. Season with salt to taste.

3. **Thickened Salsa Verde** (good for tacos and casseroles): Heat olive oil in 4-quart saucepan until hot. Pour in salsa and bring to a high-simmer. Cook until thickened, 5 minutes. This should yield 4 cups. Taste and adjust seasonings. Refrigerate up to 3 days or freeze up to 1 month. Serve salsa warm or room temperature. Salsa may sit at room temperature up to 1 hour.

4. **Salsa de Tomatillo con Crema** (good for tacos, enchiladas, and casseroles): Heat cream in 4-quart saucepan over medium heat. Boil to reduce cream by half; it will coat the back of a spoon. Pour in 4 cups tomatillo salsa and bring to a low boil, stirring occasionally, until thickened and slightly reduced to yield 4-1/2 cups. Sauce will look somewhat curdled, whisk until smooth. Remove pan from heat. Cool sauce to lukewarm. Taste and adjust seasonings. Refrigerate up to 2 days.

FRIED GREEN CHILI SALSA
(SALSA DE CHILI VERDE FRITO)

This unusual salsa is from Oaxaca, but frying the chilies and emulsifying them into a thick sauce shows a Spanish influence.

Yields 1 cup

1/4 cup olive oil
2-1/2 ounces serrano chilies, about 5, stemmed
2 ounces white onion, 1/2 cup peeled and medium dice
1/4 ounce garlic, 1 large clove, peeled

1. Heat oil in 1- to 2-quart saucepan over medium heat. Fry chilies until blistered all over, about 2 minutes per side. Transfer chilies to blender with slotted spoon.

2. Add onion to hot oil and cook until soft and slightly golden, 3 minutes. Transfer with slotted spoon to blender with chilies. Add garlic to hot oil and cook 30 seconds. Transfer to blender. Remove oil from heat and cool until just warm, 10 to 15 minutes.

3. Add 1/4 cup water to blender. Purée vegetables until smooth. Season with 1/2 teaspoon kosher salt. With machine running, *slowly* pour reserved cooking oil in a thin stream into blender until smooth and emulsified. Taste salsa and season with salt as necessary.

4. **To Serve:** Pour salsa into a bowl and serve with grilled chicken, tacos, tamales, or tostadas. Or use salsa as a garnish on soups and stews.

Source: *Truly Mexican* by Roberto Santibañez.

RED CHILI ADOBO (ADOBO DE CHILE COLORADO)

Yields 1-1/4 cups

2 ounces dried whole red chilies: about 2 anchos and 3 guajillos
1/2 ounce garlic, 2 large cloves crushed and peeled, *divided*
2 tablespoons lard *or* oil
1/2 to 2/3 ounce all-purpose flour, 2 tablespoons

1 Wearing gloves, wipe chilies with damp towel. Cut open chilies with scissors and discard stems and all seeds. Heat a cast-iron griddle, pan, or comal over medium heat. When hot, roast chilies until fragrant and slightly puffed, 30 seconds to 1 minute per side. Chilies should not burn or blacken, which will give the sauce an unpleasant, burned flavor.

2 Bring 1-1/2 cups water to boil in 2-quart saucepan. Remove pan from heat and add the chilies. Cover and weight with heatproof plate or bowl to immerse them fully. Soak chilies 10 minutes. Drain, but reserve 1 cup soaking water.

3 Place chilies, 1 clove garlic, and 1 cup soaking water (or water) into blender. Purée until smooth. Pour purée into fine strainer set over a bowl, and scrape as much pulp through as possible. Rinse blender with 2 tablespoons water and pour through strainer. Discard skins in strainer and reserve purée.

4 In a 2-quart saucepan, heat lard or oil over medium-high heat until very hot but not smoking. Add remaining garlic clove and cook until fragrant and slightly colored, about 30 seconds. Discard garlic.

5 Reduce heat to medium. Stir in flour. Cook, stirring constantly, until golden, 1 to 2 minutes. Whisk in chili purée. Reduce the heat, and simmer sauce until thickened 4 to 5 minutes, stirring occasionally. Season with 1/2 to 1 teaspoon kosher salt, to taste.

6 **To Use:** Use this sauce to braise meats like goat, pork, chicken, or turkey. Serve with tortillas. Refrigerate adobo in glass jar up to a month or freeze up to 3 months.

Source: Mexican chef Zarela Martínez.

MEXICAN CREAMY TOMATO SAUCE (CALDILLO DE TOMATE)

Yields about 3 cups

2 pounds ripe tomatoes, about 4 medium-large
3 tablespoons lard *or* olive oil
4 ounces onion, 1 cup peeled and finely diced
3/4 ounce garlic, 3 large cloves, 4-1/2 teaspoons peeled and minced

1 Blister and blacken tomatoes on cast-iron griddle or over gas flame. Cool. Core tomatoes and coarsely chop with skins.

2 Heat lard or oil in heavy 2-quart saucepan over medium heat. Stir in onions and garlic and cook until soft. Add tomatoes and simmer 5 to 10 minutes. Remove pan from heat and cool.

3 Pour tomato mixture into blender and purée sauce until smooth. Scrape sauce through medium-fine strainer set into a bowl. Discard seeds and skins. Season with salt to taste. Refrigerate sauce up to 3 days or freeze up to a month.

Source: Mexican chef Zarela Martinez.

GREEN PUMPKIN SEED SAUCE (PIPIÁN VERDE)

This is not Mole Verde, one of Oaxaca's great moles, which is made with tomatillos, thickened with corn masa and white beans, and seasoned with epazote and hierba santa leaves. It is a Puebla-style sauce (Puebla is north of Oaxaca) made instead with pumpkin seeds.

4 to 6 servings

FIGURE 13.30 Pumpkinseeds.
Source: womue/Fotolia.

Pipián Sauce

Yields about 4 cups

5 ounces hulled, raw green pumpkin seeds, 1 cup
1-1/2 ounces white onion, 1/3 cup finely diced
1-1/2 ounces serrano chilies, 3 medium, 1/3 cup stemmed and sliced
   or 2 to 3 ounces jalapeño chilies, about 3 medium, 1/2 cup stemmed and sliced
1/4 ounce garlic, 1 large clove, peeled
1/2 teaspoon dried Mexican oregano
1/4 teaspoon ground cumin
3 to 4 cups chicken stock, *divided*
2 tablespoons olive oil *or* vegetable oil
1 to 1-1/2 ounces cilantro with stems, 1/2 cup lightly chopped
2 tablespoons fresh lime juice, 1/2 large lime

Pipián Stew

Yields 7 to 8 cups

1-1/2 pounds raw shrimp, peeled and deveined
   or 1-1/2 pounds fish fillets like sea bass, halibut, or snapper, diced into 1-1/2-inch cubes
     or 1-1/2 to 2 pounds boneless, skinless chicken breasts, diced into 1-inch cubes

To Serve

Warm tortillas
Lime wedges

1 **Prepare the sauce:** Preheat oven to 350 degrees F. Spread pumpkin seeds on sheet pan and place in oven to roast until seeds pop, puff, and turn golden. Alternatively, heat a cast-iron skillet over medium heat and when hot, stir in pumpkin seeds. Roast them, stirring and tossing constantly, until puffed and slightly browned, 5 to 8 minutes.

2 Cool seeds and place into spice grinder. Grind into a powder. Pour ground pumpkin seeds into blender jar with onion, chilies, garlic, oregano, cumin, 1 cup stock, and 1 teaspoon kosher salt. Blend mixture until smooth, 3 to 4 minutes.

3 Heat oil in a heavy 5- to 6-quart pot over medium heat, and pour in blended mixture. It will sputter. Rinse out blender with 1/2 cup stock and pour into pot. Simmer sauce, stirring occasionally, until thickened, about 5 minutes. Sauce should be velvety and thickly coat a spoon. Partially cover pot and simmer sauce 20 minutes. Add more stock as necessary to maintain the smooth consistency.

4 Place cilantro and 1/2 cup stock into blender and blend until smooth. Pour cilantro and broth into sauce and simmer over low heat, uncovered, 1 minute. Taste and season sauce with salt and lime juice, to taste.

5 *Prepare* pipián stew: Immerse shrimp, fish, or chicken into simmering sauce. Cook until just done: shrimp 3 to 5 minutes and fish and chicken 7 to 10 minutes. Season with more salt to taste.

6 **To Serve:** Ladle stew into bowls and serve with fresh, warm tortillas and lime wedges, beans, or other vegetable sides. It may also be used as an enchilada filling/topping. This sauce tastes best the day it's made.

Source: *Truly Mexican* by Robert Santibañez.

Vary! Improvise!

☞ *Serve pipián verde over grilled pork tenderloin, chicken breasts, or fish fillets.*

Mexican Mole

Mole comes from the Nahuatl word *molli*, meaning sauce or mixture. A mole is generally thought of as a sauce, but foods are mostly simmered in it so could also be considered a stewing medium. One of Mexican cuisine's best-known dishes, a mole can be complex or simple, but all moles contain chilies. *Pipianes* are moles made predominately with nuts or seeds. The texture of moles ranges from soupy-thin, thick enough to coat a spoon and run off, to just short of gummy—thickly coating a spoon. The colors of a mole may be yellow, red, black/brown, or green. Raw or precooked meat or poultry, vegetables, or seafood are simmered in the finished mole before serving.

Mexican archeologists have found fossilized remains of what they think is mole from the fifth century BCE. Many believe that the origin of modern mole (with raisins and nuts not available until the Spanish arrived) was in a convent in Puebla, near Mexico City. The nuns, working with local female Indian cooks, created this fusion of Spanish and Mexico techniques and flavors to impress a visiting clergyman. It worked, and a star was born.

Mole Poblano, from Puebla, made with fruity dried chilies, nuts, seeds, spices, and a touch of chocolate in which, classically, turkey is simmered, is considered Mexico's national dish. *Mole Negro*, the king of moles, is similar, but darker, more time-consuming, and complex; it contains the herb *hoja santa*. *Mole Amarillo* is the most versatile: it can be the base for chicken, beef, pork, or made vegetarian with just vegetables. The fruity *manchamanteles* contains pineapple, plantain, and apple. *Mole verde* or green mole with tomatillos is the freshest and easiest to make of the many varieties and variations of mole.

Signature Technique: Making Mole

- Gather ingredients and measure them out into small containers set on a sheet pan.

- Organize the kitchen: gather and set out tools and utensils.

- Make a cheat sheet with the steps clearly outlined, and hang it where you can easily see it.

- Prep all ingredients before beginning to construct mole: Prepare stock, poach or roast meat, slice and dice vegetables and herbs, and toast nuts, seeds, spices, or dry herbs.

- Try to reuse pots and pans and blender—it's not always necessary to wash in between.

- Methodically follow each step for constructing mole.

- Taste, taste, taste.

- *Pay attention to texture:* moles should be *thin* or be *sauce consistency* (coat a spoon) or *thickly coat* a spoon. Oaxacan cooks often start with a thicker sauce and thin it more or less, depending on the dish.

OAXACAN GREEN MOLE (MOLE VERDE)

Mole verde is the lightest and freshest-tasting of Oaxaca's "seven moles." Fresh herbs rather than spices distinguish it from other moles. Seeded chilies deliver flavor with less heat.

Yields about 12 cups mole sauce or 15 to 16 cups mole with chicken and beans, 8 to 12 servings

---

3 pounds chicken breast and thighs, about 2-1/2 pounds with skin and fat removed
1-1/2 quarts chicken stock
About 5 ounces small dry white beans, 3/4 cup
    or 1-1/2 cups drained, canned white or navy beans
1 pound tomatillos, husked and washed
1 pound green tomatoes, 2 medium large, cored and chopped

6 ounces white onion, 1-1/2 cups peeled and diced
1-1/2 to 2 ounces garlic, 6 to 8 large cloves, peeled

- **Mildly spicy:** 4 ounces jalapeño chilies, about 4 large, stemmed, halved, and seeded
- **Moderately spicy:** 6 ounces jalapeño chilies, 6 large, stemmed, halved, and seeded
- **Spicy:** 8 to 9 ounces jalapeño chilies, 8 to 9 large, stemmed, halved, and seeded

1/2 teaspoon ground cumin
1/4 teaspoon ground cloves *or* allspice
1 tablespoon sunflower *or* vegetable oil
3-1/2 ounces masa harina for tortillas, 3/4 cup
1-1/2 ounces trimmed Italian parsley, 3/4 cup coarsely chopped
1 ounce epazote leaves, 1/2 cup
  or 2 teaspoons fresh thyme leaves *and* 1/2 ounce cilantro sprigs, 2 large sprigs
1 to 1-1/2 ounces *hierba/hoja santa leaves*, 4 leaves with ribs removed, 1/2 cup coarsely chopped
  or 5 dried leaves

For Serving

Warm corn tortillas

1 **Chicken:** Combine skinned chicken parts and chicken stock in 6-quart pan. Bring to a simmer and cook until chicken is tender, 1 hour. Transfer meat from stock to bowl, and reserve stock. Skim off excess fat. Remove meat from bones and dice into 1-inch cubes to yield about 3 cups. Discard bones, gristle, and veins.

2 **Beans:** Rinse and drain dry beans. Place into 2-quart saucepan with 1 quart water and 1 teaspoon kosher salt. Bring beans to a boil, lower the heat, partially cover the pot, and simmer until beans are tender, 1-1/2 to 2 hours. Drain and reserve beans.

3 **Green purée:** Place tomatillos into 2-quart saucepan and cover with cold water. Bring to a boil, lower the heat, and simmer tomatillos until they turn a shade darker and tender, 10 to 15 minutes. Transfer tomatillos with slotted spoon to large mixing bowl. Add green tomatoes, onion, garlic, jalapeños, cumin, and cloves or allspice to bowl, and mix. *In two batches*, purée vegetables and seasonings in blender, adding 1/2 cup reserved chicken stock to each batch. Purée mixture until smooth to yield about 7 cups. Reserve blender for later use.

4 Heat oil in a heavy 6-quart pot over high heat. When oil shimmers, stir in green puréed mixture from blender—be careful, it will sputter! Lower heat to medium, cover pot partially, and cook purée, stirring constantly until it thickens and reduces, 10 minutes.

5 **Masa:** Meanwhile, place masa harina into small bowl. Whisk in 3/4 cup cold water until smooth. Stir in 2 cups warm stock. Stir masa mixture into green purée. Cook and stir over medium heat until thickened, 15 minutes.

6 **Second purée:** Place parsley, epazote, *or* fresh thyme, cilantro, and hoja santa leaves into blender with 3/4 to 1 cup stock, and purée until smooth. Pour into pot with green purée and reduce heat to low. Simmer mole 15 minutes. Season with salt and pepper, to taste.

7 **To Serve:** Stir meat and cooked beans into mole. Thin with remaining stock or water so sauce just coats a spoon. Heat through, taste, and adjust seasonings. Ladle mole into bowls and serve with corn tortillas.

Source: *Seasons of My Heart* by Susana Trilling.

Vary! Improvise!

☞ **Pork:** *Substitute 1 pound boneless pork shoulder (cubed 1-inch) and 1 pound baby back pork ribs for chicken. Prepare pork stock with ribs.*
☞ **Fish:** *Substitute 2-1/2 to 3 pounds fish fillets and fish stock for chicken and chicken stock. Don't over-cook the fish.*

Dealing with Dry Chilies

1. Gloves on, and with scissors, cut dry chilies open. Remove stems and discard. For some moles, cooks save the seeds to roast, grind, and use as part of seasoning.

2. On a griddle, cast-iron pan, or comal preheated over medium heat, *briefly* toast chilies. They should *not* be blackened, just a slight crackle as you press them down onto the griddle, about 5 to 7 seconds per side. Some recipes call for frying the chilies in hot oil or lard until they puff, less than a minute.

3. Transfer toasted chilies to bowl of warm water and immerse. Place a plate or weight on them to keep immersed. Soak until soft, 20 to 30 minutes.

4. Drain off water. Some recipes call for using the soaking water, but it can be bitter so use small amounts; you decide. Place chilies into blender with a little water, and purée.

5. **Improve Texture:** Pour chili purée into fine strainer and scrape through. Rinse out blender with 2 tablespoons water and pour through strainer and scrape and mash chilies again. Discard skins and seeds in strainer.

6. **Soften Flavor:** Pour purée into saucepan and simmer until thickened slightly.

PUEBLAN MOLE WITH TURKEY (MOLE POBLANA CON PAVO)

Mole is rich and intense. Instruct guests to go easy the first time they try it. It's traditional to use Mexican chocolate, which is spiced and sweetened. For more chocolate punch, substitute good-quality bittersweet chocolate. It's possible to make a shorter version with commercially available dried, ground Mexican chili powders.

Yields 9 to 10 cups mole sauce, 12+ servings as stew or 36 to 40 servings as sauce

Turkey

8 pounds turkey breasts, thighs, and legs
If roasting turkey: 8 cups chicken or turkey stock

Chilies

About 1 cup lard *or* olive oil, *divided*
4 ounces dried *mulato* chilies, about 8
2 ounces dried *ancho* chilies, about 4
1-1/2 to 2 ounces dried *pasilla* chilies, about 6
1/2 ounce dried *chipotle* meco chili, about 2
    or 2 small canned *chipotle* chilies in adobo

Aromatic Vegetables

3 ounce tomato, 1 small, cored
3 ounces tomatillo, 2 medium, husked and rinsed
6 ounces onion, 1 medium, about 1-1/4 cups peeled and sliced 1/2-inch thick
1-1/4 ounces garlic, 5 large cloves, peeled

Seeds and Spices

1-1/2 ounces unhulled sesame seeds, 1/4 cup
1/4 teaspoon coriander seed
1/4 teaspoon whole aniseed
1/4 teaspoon black peppercorns
1/4 teaspoon whole allspice
6 whole cloves
1-inch stick Mexican canela, broken into pieces

Nuts, Raisins and Seeds

3 ounces blanched almonds, 1/2 cup
1 ounce hulled pumpkin seeds, 3 tablespoons
2 ounces raisins, 1/3 cup

Thickeners

1-ounce baguette, 1-inch thick slice
1 stale 6-inch corn tortilla

To Finish

6 ounces Mexican chocolate, 2 disks, about 1 cup finely chopped
    or 6 ounces good quality bittersweet chocolate, 1 cup finely chopped
1 tablespoon sugar, more to taste

Garnish: 1-1/2 ounces unhulled toasted sesame seeds, 1/4 cup

To Serve: Warm corn tortillas, rice and beans

1 Roast or poach turkey parts:

- *To roast*, preheat oven to 350 degrees F. Place turkey into hotel pan and roast until meat is tender and internal temperature reaches 170 degrees F, about 2 hours.

- *To poach*, place turkey into heavy 8-quart pot, cover with 3 quarts cold water (it will also require mirepoix-cut onion, carrot and celery, and bay leaf), and bring to a boil over high heat. Reduce heat to low and simmer turkey until tender, about 1 to 1-1/2 hours. Cool turkey in stock 20 minutes, strain, and discard vegetables. Remove skin and bones, and discard. Cool meat and 8 cups stock (separately), and refrigerate if not using immediately. Skim fat from stock and reserve 2 quarts for this mole. Freeze remaining stock.

2 *Prepare* chilies: Bring 2 quarts water to boil and set aside. With gloves on, wipe chilies clean. With scissors, cut chilies open, remove stems and discard. Reserve 3 tablespoons chili seeds in small bowl. Cut chilies into 2 flat pieces.

3 *Fry and soak* chilies: Heat 1/2 cup lard or oil in a heavy 6- to 8-quart pot or 9- to 10-inch cast-iron fry pan over medium heat until it ripples. Working in small batches, add chilies and cook, turning, until they puff and change color, 30 to 45 seconds for *mulatos* and *anchos*, 45 seconds to 1 minute for *pasillas*, and 1 to 1-1/2 minutes if using *dried chipotles*. With a slotted spoon, transfer chilies to paper towels to drain. Transfer chilies to a large bowl. Discard lard or oil in pot or pan, wipe out, and set aside. Cover chilies with boiling water, weight them with a plate, and steep 20 minutes. Strain chilies and discard all but 2 cups soaking liquid.

4 *Roast* aromatic vegetables: Preheat broiler and position a rack 8 inches from heat. Set tomato cored side up, and tomatillos on a broiler pan. Roast until both are tender all the way through. Turn tomatillos halfway through cooking, 10 minutes, but not tomato. Both should be blackened and tender, about 20 minutes total cooking. Discard tomato skin and place vegetables in bowl.

5 Heat a 9- to 10-inch cast-iron skillet over medium-low heat. Wipe lightly with paper towel dipped in a little lard or oil. Place onion and garlic on skillet. Roast garlic until tender and golden with a few black spots, 8 to 10 minutes. Roast onion until softened and charred on both sides, 10 to 15 minutes.

6 *Roast and grind* seeds and spices: Lightly wipe cast-iron skillet or griddle clean with fat-dipped paper towel. Heat over medium heat and when hot, toast 3 tablespoons of reserved chili seeds until fragrant and 1 shade darker, 2 minutes (don't inhale). Transfer to a small bowl. Place sesame seeds, coriander, aniseed, peppercorns, allspice, cloves, and canela in skillet and toast, stirring occasionally, until fragrant and 1 shade darker, 1 to 2 minutes. Transfer to bowl with chili seeds and cool. Grind seeds and spices in spice grinder in batches and return to small bowl.

7 *Fry* nuts, raisins, and seeds: Set a metal strainer over a medium metal mixing bowl. Heat remaining 1/4 cup lard or oil in cast-iron pan over medium heat until it ripples. One by one, fry nuts, seeds, raisins, and bread, then transfer with slotted spoon to strainer to drain: Fry almonds until golden, 2 minutes. Fry pumpkin seeds until puffed and slightly browned, 1 minute. Fry raisins until puffed, 1 minute. Fry bread on both sides until golden, 3 minutes total. Scrape remaining fat, about 1 to 2 tablespoons, into 6- to 8-quart pot and set aside.

8 Toast the tortilla: Place tortilla directly on gas flame and, with tongs, toast (and turn) until golden with burned spots. Break into 2 or 3 pieces and set bowl. Pour reserved chili soaking water over tortilla and soak 5 minutes. Drain, and discard soaking water.

9 *Purée* chilies: Pour half the soaked and drained chilies into blender and purée with 1 to 1-1/2 cups stock, pour into small bowl, and repeat with remaining chilies and 1 to 1-1/2 cups stock. Scrape purée through strainer. Place skins into blender with 1 cup stock and purée and strain again. Rinse out blender with 1/2 cup stock and pour through strainer. Discard chili skins. Wash blender.

10 Cook chili purée: Heat reserved oil plus more oil, to make about 3 tablespoons total, in pot over medium heat until it ripples. Stir in chili purée and cook, stirring occasionally until slightly thickened, 10 minutes. Cover with spatter screen, it will spit.

11 *Purée* tortilla, fried nuts, raisins, and seeds *and* aromatic vegetables: Working in two batches, in blender combine drained tortilla and fried and toasted nuts, raisins, and seeds with roasted

Vary! Improvise!

☛ **Enchiladas Mole:** *Shred cooked turkey or chicken and toss with a little mole. Fill enchiladas and sauce over them with mole sauce. Drizzle with Crema Mexicana (see Glossary) or thinned sour cream, toasted sesame seeds, and cilantro.*

☛ **Smooth and Sophisticated:** *Stir in a little chopped or grated dark bitter-sweet chocolate before serving.*

tomato, tomatillo, onion, and garlic plus 1 cup stock per batch. Purée until smooth. When chili purée has cooked 10 minutes, pour nut-vegetable mixture into pot. After second batch, swish 1/2 cup stock into empty blender to clean, and pour into pot.

12 **To finish: stir in ground seeds and spices**, and bring to a boil, lower heat to a simmer, and partially cover pot. Simmer mole 45 minutes, adding stock to keep a texture that thickly coats a spoon. Stir in chocolate and sugar, and simmer 10 minutes more. Taste mole and season with salt to taste. Rest mole overnight or 20 minutes for flavors to develop.

13 Stir turkey into mole and simmer until heated through, 15 to 20 minutes. Alternatively, serve mole as a sauce over the meat. Meanwhile, heat small skillet over medium heat and toast sesame seeds until fragrant, 1 to 2 minutes. Set aside.

14 **To Serve:** Spoon mole into bowls and garnish with toasted sesame seeds. Serve with warm corn tortillas, rice, and beans. The mole improves the next day and will keep refrigerated 5 days without meat and 3 to 4 days with. Freeze sauce up to 1 month.

Source: *Truly Mexican* by Roberto Santibañez.

OAXACAN YELLOW MOLE WITH CHICKEN (MOLE AMARILLO DE POLLO)

Nicknamed amarillo (though it is red), this mole is a specialty of Oaxaca's Central Valley and one of the famous Seven Moles of Oaxaca. Thicken this mole with more masa harina and use to season shredded chicken, pork, or beef for empanadas. Amarillo is commonly served with masa dumplings.

Yields about 4 cups sauce and about 12 cups mole with chicken, 6 servings

Chicken and Stock

4 pounds chicken legs, thighs, and/or breasts, 3-1/2 pounds skinned chicken parts
5 cups chicken stock

Vegetables

8 ounces small red skin potatoes, about 6 small, scrubbed
8 ounces green beans, stemmed
10 ounces chayote squash, 1 medium
    or 8 ounces zucchini, about 2 medium

Sauce

1/2 ounce *chilcostle* chiles or *chihuacles amarillos* chilies, about 6
    or 1 ounce *guajillo* chilies, about 6 seeded and deveined
1 ounce *ancho* chiles, about 2 seeded and deveined
1/2 to 3/4 ounce *costeños amarillos* or *chiles de onza amarillo*
    or 3/4 ounce more *guajillo* chilies, about 4 to 6
1/8 teaspoon whole cloves
1/8 teaspoon whole allspice
1/8 teaspoon whole peppercorns
1/8 teaspoon cumin seeds
1 teaspoon Mexican oregano
1 pound tomatoes, about 2 medium
6 ounces tomatillos, about 5 large, husks removed
6 to 7 ounces white onion, about 1-1/2 cups coarsely chopped
1 to 1-1/2 ounces garlic, about 6 cloves, peeled
2 tablespoons lard or oil

Thickener

3 ounces *masa harina for tortillas*, 1/2 cup

Garnish: 3 small, fresh or dried *hoja santa** leaves

For Serving

Warm corn tortillas

*If hoja santa (piper auritum) is not available, substitute lightly toasted and finely ground Mexican avocado leaves or just omit.

1 *Cook the* **chicken:** Place skinned chicken parts into 4- to 5-quart saucepan and cover with stock. Bring to a boil, lower heat, and simmer until chicken is tender, 45 minutes to 1 hour. Cool meat in stock 15 minutes. Transfer meat to mixing bowl to cool.

2 *Prep the* **vegetables:** Halve or quarter potatoes. Slice green beans diagonally into 2-inch lengths to yield 2 cups. Peel chayote. Quarter it lengthwise, and remove pit. Slice each quarter crosswise 1/2-inch thick to yield 2 to 2-1/2 cups. If using zucchini, slice into 1/2-inch-thick rounds to yield about 2 cups.

3 *Cook the* **vegetables:** Bring stock back to a low boil and add potatoes. Cook until potatoes are tender, 8 to 10 minutes. Remove and place in a second mixing bowl. Repeat cooking green beans and chayote until tender, 4 to 5 minutes. Place vegetables into bowl with potatoes, and set aside.

4 **Toast and soak chilies:** Bring 2 cups water to a boil, remove from heat, and set aside. Heat a griddle, 10-inch cast-iron skillet, or comal over medium-low heat. With gloves on, cut dry chilies with scissors and remove stems and seeds. Cut each into 2 pieces. Toast chilies until fragrant and slightly blistered, but don't burn, about 10 to 30 seconds per side. Transfer chilies to a bowl and cover with reserved hot water. Weight with a plate and soak until soft, 15 to 20 minutes. Drain chilies, but reserve 3/4 cup soaking water.

5 **Prepare chili purée:** Transfer chilies, 3/4 cup soaking water, and 3/4 cup fresh water to a blender, and purée until smooth. Scrape purée through fine strainer, discard pulp, and set purée aside. Reserve blender without washing.

6 **Toast spices:** Reheat skillet or comal over medium heat, and toast cloves, allspice, peppercorns, cumin, and oregano just until fragrant but not browned. Cool and grind spices finely in spice grinder. Set aside.

7 **Prepare tomato-tomatillo purée:** Bring a 2-quart pot of water to boil. Blanch tomatoes until skin and meat softens, 3 minutes. Remove tomatoes to a bowl, peel, and discard skin. Stir tomatillos into boiling water, weight with small lid, and simmer until they turn army green and soften, 10 minutes. Transfer tomatoes, tomatillos, onion, garlic, and 1/2 cup reserved stock to a blender and purée until smooth. Scrape through medium-fine strainer, discard skins, and set purée (about 4 cups) aside.

8 **Cook purées:** In a heavy 6-quart pot, heat lard over medium heat until it ripples. Lower heat to medium-low, stir in chili purée, and stirring constantly, fry 10 to 15 minutes. Stir in tomato-tomatillo mixture and ground spices, and continue simmering and stirring 15 minutes more.

9 **Thicken and thin mole:** Whisk masa harina and 1 cup stock together until smooth. Stir masa into mole. Cook, stirring constantly as masa thickens, 15 minutes. Season mole with salt to taste. Stir in enough remaining broth, about 1 cup, to thin mole so that it coats the back of a spoon, the consistency of heavy cream. Stir in hoja santa leaves, remove mole from heat, and keep warm.

*At this point, mole may be used with any meat or vegetables. Or freeze it up to 1 month.

10 **To Serve:** Place meat and vegetables into mole and heat through. Taste and adjust seasonings. Place a piece of chicken and some vegetables into each bowl. Ladle mole sauce over. Accompany with warm tortillas.

Source: *Seasons of My Heart* by Susanna Trilling.

Vary! Improvise!

☞ *Masa Dumplings:* Mix 1 cup masa harina for tortillas with 1/2 teaspoon kosher salt, 5 fluid ounces warm water, and 2 teaspoons lard or oil. Prepare walnut-sized balls and make an indentation in each. Before adding vegetables and chicken to mole, simmer dumplings until cooked through, 5 minutes.

☞ *Refine:* Remove bones from chicken, and discard. Shred meat and stir into mole, or plate with vegetables, and ladle sauce over.

☞ *Beef It Up:* Substitute 2-1/2 to 3 pounds beef and beef stock for the chicken and chicken stock.

☞ *Vegetarian:* Substitute vegetable stock for chicken stock, oil for lard, omit chicken, and double the vegetables.

OAXACA'S SEVEN FAMOUS MOLES

Though mole dishes are made in other parts of Mexico, Oaxaca is known as the "Land of Seven Moles." Chef and cookbook author Susanna Trilling says in her Oaxacan cookbook *Seasons of My Heart* that she knew of six: the king of moles, *Mole Negro*; the brick-red *Mole Coloradito*; the fresh, green *Mole Verde*; the yellow, masa-thickened *Mole Amarillo*; the spicy enchilada sauce *Mole Rojo/ Colorado*; and the fruity *manchamanteles* or tablecloth-stainer.

After years of searching for the missing seventh mole she encountered a rare, spicy mole called *Chichilo Oaxaqeño*, which takes flavor from chili seeds burned on top of a tortilla, soaked, then ground. Trilling realized it must be the missing seventh mole. Some Oaxacan cooks disagree (as might be expected). They consider *Estofado de Pollo (Oaxacan Chicken Stew)* the missing seventh mole. . . .

SPECIAL METHODS

Antojitos

Antojito means *craving* in Spanish. Antojito is the name given to simple, tasty street food, sometimes quite filling and usually made with corn, that falls between a snack, a tapa, and an appetizer. Tacos, tostadas, quesadillas, enchiladas, ceviche, and guacamole all qualify.

SEASONED MASHED AVOCADO (GUACAMOLE)

In Mexico, guacamole is made in a traditional molcajete or volcanic stone mortar with pestle. Purchase rock-hard avocados 4 to 5 days before needed. When they darken and give slightly to pressure, use or refrigerate up to 4 days.

Yields 3 cups

1 pound avocadoes, 2 large
1/2 ounce peeled white onion, 2 tablespoons finely diced
1/2 ounce serrano chili, 1 medium, stemmed and finely diced
6 ounce ripe tomato, 2/3 cup finely diced
1/2 ounce cilantro, 1/4 cup finely sliced, more to taste
2 tablespoons fresh lime juice, 1/2 large lime, more to taste

For Serving

Warm corn tortillas or corn chips

1 Slice avocados in half, remove pits, and evenly cross-hatch flesh of each half. Scoop out cubed avocado with spoon into a bowl or molcajete to yield about 2-1/2 cups.

2 Lightly mash avocados until chunky, but adhering together. Fold in onion, chili, tomato, and cilantro. Season with lime juice and salt to taste. Serve immediately with tortillas or chips.

AVOCADOES

Avocado fruits ripen in a warm spot after they are picked and the little stem is broken away. Plan ahead and buy hard, green avocados up to a week before needed. Ripen them to firm-ripe, and refrigerate. But don't refrigerate before ripe or the flesh will darken and become bitter. Ripe avocados should have a smooth, firm surface that gives just a little, the skin should be tight to the flesh, and the pit should not rattle inside.

Halve the avocado lengthwise and remove the pit. Citrus juice will keep avocados from browning for a short time. To store a cut avocado half overnight, press a wet paper towel to the exposed flesh (or dampen towel with lime or lemon juice) and place into a plastic baggie. It will last one, maybe two days refrigerated.

A large avocado weighs between 8 and 10 ounces. The 8-ounce yields about 1-1/4-cups diced flesh and the 10-ounce yields about 1-1/2 cups.

Signature Technique: Safe and Skillful Mexican Ceviche

Ceviche is a mixture of diced or ground raw fish or shellfish marinated with acidic citrus enhanced with chilies, onions, salt, and fresh herbs like cilantro. Found primarily on the seacoast, this uncomplicated, elegant dish inspires countless interpretations. As with any simple dish, high-quality ingredients and skillful preparation deliver extraordinary results.

Ceviche Safety

- Ceviche's biggest virtue is freshness. Form a relationship with a fishmonger to get the freshest seafood possible.

- Always use fish or seafood from the sea. Freshwater fish tend to have more parasites. James Peterson, author of *Fish and Shellfish*, recommends that unless the fish or seafood has been frozen (most sashimi-grade fish has been frozen) or is certifiably free of parasites, freeze it at least 24 hours. Thaw slowly overnight in the refrigerator.

- Buy the freshest fish available: clear, rounded eyes, red gills, no strong fishy smell, and firm, bouncy flesh.

- Keep everything that will touch the ceviche scrupulously clean, especially hands and cutting board.

- Prepare the seafood the day it is received.

- Avoid feeding ceviche to the very young or elderly, immune deficient, or to pregnant women.

- It's fine to quickly blanch seafood in slowly boiling water several seconds to kill bacteria on the outside surface of seafood.

- Keep seafood refrigerated and very cold at all times.

Ceviche Skills

- **Fundamentals:** Fresh seafood, acidic citrus, and salt.

- **Important Flavorings:** Alliums (onion family), fresh herbs, and an optional garnishing fruits or vegetables like mango, papaya, coconut, tomato, squash, corn, avocado, or bell pepper.

- **Keep it simple:** Since seafood is the star, don't overdo ceviche with too many ingredients. Keep it to the fundamentals and important flavorings plus no more than one more extra ingredient.

- Cut seafood into precise, even cubes about 1/3- to 1/2-inch thick. Mexicans sometimes coarsely grind the fish. Small cuts assure even marinating within 30 minutes. If seafood is cut too large it will take too long to marinate, the outside can become mushy and strongly acidic tasting. For smaller cuts use shorter marinating times. Taste if in doubt.

- Use very acidic citrus to assure proper denaturing of seafood protein. The acid doesn't cook the seafood: it breaks down the protein strands. Seafood flesh should go from soft and transparent to firm and opaque (white).

- Use contrasting colors, textures, and flavors when creating ceviche: tuna, coconut, lime, cilantro, and roasted red bell pepper or shrimp in roasted tomato purée with jicama, lime, and basil.

- Use saltwater fish like red snapper, sole, pompano, scallops, shellfish, squid, sea bass, Chilean sea bass, Gulf shrimp, sashimi-grade tuna or yellowtail, salmon, halibut, flounder, or tilapia.

MARINATED RAW SEAFOOD (CEVICHE)

Leave seeds in the chilies for spicy ceviche.

Yields about 2-1/2 cups, 4 servings

8 ounces skinned sea bass fillets, tuna *or* diver scallops
1/2 to 2/3 cup freshly squeezed lime juice, about 3 large limes
1/2 ounce serrano chilies, 1 medium, about 2 tablespoons stemmed, seeded, and finely diced
1 ounce trimmed green onions, 2 large, 4 tablespoons chopped
1/3 ounce cilantro, about 1/4 cup finely sliced
8 to 9 ounce avocado, 1 medium, 3/4 to 1 cup peeled and finely diced

For Serving

Tortilla chips or warm corn tortillas

1 Dice fish into 1/3- to 1/2-inch cubes to yield about 1 cup. Toss fish in nonreactive bowl with lime juice, chili, green onions, and 1/2 teaspoon kosher salt. Cover bowl, and refrigerate fish 30 to 35 minutes.

2 Drain off most of the lime juice, and discard. Fold cilantro and avocado into fish. Season to taste with salt.

3 **To Serve:** Divide ceviche, and pile into 4 small bowls or martini glasses. Serve with tortilla chips or warm tortillas.

Tacos

In Mexico, tacos are not made with the hard crunchy shells from the grocery store. Instead, cooks prepare them best with soft corn tortillas pressed from fresh masa and hot off the griddle. Head to an outdoor Mexican market and numerous vendors will be selling these delicious *antijitos* filled with goat, cactus, pork, chicken, mushrooms, zucchini, potatoes and chorizo, grilled steak, or pork and onions or many other creative variations. Done correctly, just about anything can become material for a taco. It's customary to douse them lightly with salsa.

Vary! Improvise!

☛ *Stir in 1/4 cup finely diced and drained tomato with the cilantro and avocado.*

☛ *At Frontera Grill, chef Rick Bayless serves ceviche dosed with tequila and topped with a garnish of micro-greens.*

☛ *Make the Chips: Slice corn tortillas into 6 to 8 wedges and deep-fry until golden.*

Signature Technique: Construct a Taco

Constructing a good taco is all about flavor combos and textures. Keep an eye out for favorite combos, or try these:

- Mashed potatoes or chickpeas seasoned with fried onions and crumbled queso fresco.
- *Calabacitas*, cooked to a thick, but not gloppy consistency.
- Blanched and sautéed greens like kale with onion, garlic, and cheese.
- Roasted poblano chili strips, tomatoes, and egg.
- Shredded beef cooked in salsa ranchera and topped with crema Mexicana and queso fresco.
- Shredded, cooked pork cooked with tomatoes, garlic, onion, and chili.
- Shredded grilled chicken with fresh salsa or *Green Tomatillo Salsa*.
- Grilled adobo-marinated flank steak, boneless/skinless chicken breasts, *or* peeled, deveined shrimp with *Fresh Salsa*, *Fried Serrano Chili Salsa*, or *Green Tomatillo Salsa*, diced white onion, cilantro, and lime wedges.
- Lime-brushed skirt steak well-seared with grilled poblanos or serranos and grilled onion.
- Leftover chicken or turkey in mole, shredded lettuce and chopped tomato, cilantro, and lime.

1 Prepare a main filling meat, bean, or vegetable mixture and season highly. Grill, broil, or simmer until thick.

2 Prepare salsas of choice.

3 Choose and prepare condiments like chopped cilantro, finely sliced green or Savoy cabbage, shredded romaine lettuce, chopped tomato, vinegar-pickled red onion slices, chopped white onion, lime wedges, sliced avocados, or sour cream.

4 Prepare 6-inch tortillas from masa dough and cook on a comal or cast-iron skillet or heat premade tortillas.
   - **To steam:** Chef Rick Bayless suggests wrapping stacks of 12 tortillas in clean kitchen towels, set in a steamer, cover, bring to a strong boil 1 minute, then remove from the fire and let stand, covered, 15 minutes.
   - **To microwave:** Line a 9-inch glass pie plate with a lightly dampened cotton towel, stack in 12 tortillas, and wrap. Microwave on half power 4 minutes and rest in microwave 3 minutes.

5 **Filling Tacos:** Place no more than 3 to 4 tablespoons filling into warm 6-inch tortilla. Too much filling obscures the corn flavor of the tortilla, plus it's messy. Top with salsa and/or condiments of choice.

6 **How To Eat a Taco:** Roll up taco and wedge it between index and middle finger on top and thumb, ring and baby fingers on the bottom. Fold up back edge slightly before biting taco.

SHEPHERD STYLE PORK TACOS (TACOS AL PASTOR)

These tacos are the most beloved taco in and out of Mexico. Large hunks of marinated meat are speared onto an upright rotisserie, pressed together, and grilled. The succulent meat is shaved off and put into freshly made corn tortillas.

Yields about 7 cups filling, enough for 28 tacos, 6 to 8 servings

Marinade

3 to 4 tablespoons *Achiote Paste*
   or 2 ounces package commercial achiote paste
2 tablespoons canned *chipotle chiles en adobo*, about 1-1/2, *plus* 2 tablespoons sauce
2 tablespoons vegetable *or* olive oil

1-1/2 pounds boneless pork shoulder, sliced 1/4-inch thick (Mexican butcher cut for tacos al pastor)
   or 1-1/2 pounds trimmed, boneless goat shoulder or leg sliced 1/4-inch thick
8 ounce red onion, 1 medium, 2 cups halved and sliced 1/2-inch thick
Olive or vegetable oil for brushing
Half 4 to 5 pound pineapple, peeled, cored, and sliced crossways 1/2-inch-thick

For Serving

30 six-inch corn tortillas, warmed
2 to 2-1/2 cups *Green Tomatillo Salsa* or salsa of choice

1 **Marinate the pork:** In a blender, combine achiote paste, chilies and their sauce, oil, and 3 tablespoons water. Blend until smooth. Pour marinade onto meat and smear over both sides. Cover and refrigerate meat 1 hour.

2 **Prepare grill:** Light charcoal or preheat gas grill. When coals are gray and very hot, push 3/4 of the coals to one side and set grill grate in place. Or heat one side of a gas grill to high and the other side to medium-low.

3 **Grill onions and pineapple:** Brush onions with oil and season with salt. Lay onions without overlapping on the hotter side of the grill. When the first side of the onions is browned, flip and brown the other side, 2 to 4 minutes total. Transfer onions to cooler side of grill. Brush pineapple slices with oil, lay on hot side in one layer, and grill on both sides until browned and tender. Dice onion and pineapple into 1/2-inch cubes to yield about 1 cup onion and 2 cups pineapple. Place in bowl.

4 **Grill the pork:** Do this in batches, about 1 minute per side. Transfer cooked meat to a cutting board and slice it into 1/4- and 1/2-inch-wide strips to yield 3-1/2 to 4 cups. Scoop into a skillet and set on a low burner to keep warm. Add onions and pineapple to the skillet and toss with meat. Heat through. Taste and season with salt.

5 **To Serve:** Fill warm tortillas with 3 to 4 tablespoons meat-onion-fruit filling each. Top with 1 to 1-1/2 tablespoons salsa.

Source: http://www.rickbayless.com/.

Vary! Improvise!

☞ *Quicker: Choose a flavorful cut of meat—minute steak, skirt, flank, round, or shoulder—and thinly slice. Brush with lime juice, cumin, salt, and oil. Griddle-fry or grill over fast heat until browned and crusty. Finely slice or dice meat, onion, and pineapple.*

☞ *Vegetarian Al Pastor: Substitute portobello mushrooms for the meat. Scrape away the underside dark gills, marinate mushrooms, and grill until tender and juicy.*

FISH TACOS FROM VERACRUZ (TACOS DE SALPICÓN DE PESCADO)

Popular in Veracruz, along Mexico's eastern coast, and in Baja California, these tacos have migrated to California and beyond.

Yields 4 to 4-1/2 cups filling, about 16 tacos

1-1/2 pounds skinned fillets of snapper, mahi-mahi, halibut, or firm, white fish

About 2-1/2 ounces unbleached white flour, 1/2 cup
1/4 cup vegetable oil
2 cups *Fresh Tomato Salsa* or *Green Tomatillo Salsa*

For Serving

16 corn tortillas, warmed
6 to 8 ounces green or Savoy cabbage, 2 cups finely sliced or grated
2 limes, quartered

1 Season fish fillets with salt and pepper. Pour flour into a large bowl, and set near stove. Cover a half sheet pan with paper toweling, and set by stove.

2 Heat oil in 10-inch skillet over medium heat until it ripples. Dredge fish fillets in flour and shake off excess. Place into hot oil and fry both sides until golden, and fish flakes when probed with tip of knife, 1 to 2 minutes per side, or more, depending on thickness of fillets. With tongs or slotted spoon, transfer fish to paper towel-covered pan to drain. Shred fillets and place in warm bowl if using immediately. (This can be done a day ahead and chilled.) Fold in salsa.

3 **Assemble** tacos **and serve:** Place 3 to 4 tablespoons fish mixture into each tortilla. Garnish with cabbage. Serve with lime wedges on the side.

Source: from *Savoring Mexico* by Marilyn Tausend.

FIGURE 13.31   Fish tacos.
Source: JJAVA/Fotolia.

MUSHROOM TACOS (TACOS DE HONGOS)

Chef Diana Kennedy's recipe calls for 2 sprigs fresh epazote, chopped, instead of parsley. After filling and rolling, she secures the tacos with toothpicks and fries them in oil until crisp but still tender.

Yields 2-1/2 to 3 cups filling, 10 to 12 tacos, 3 to 4 servings

2 tablespoons olive or vegetable oil
4 ounces white onion, 1 cup peeled and finely diced
1/2 ounce garlic, about 2 cloves, 1 tablespoon peeled and minced
1 pound mushrooms, cleaned, about 6 cups quartered and thinly sliced crosswise
12 ounces tomatoes, 1-1/2 cups cored and finely diced
1 ounce serrano chilies, 2 medium, 3 to 4 tablespoons stemmed, seeded, and finely sliced
1/4 ounce trimmed Italian parsley, 2 tablespoons finely chopped

For Serving

1/2 to 3/4 cup *crema Mexicana* (see *Glossary*)
12 corn warm tortillas

1 Heat oil in 12-inch skillet over medium heat. Stir in onion and garlic and cook until soft but not browned. Add mushrooms and cook until wilted down, about 5 minutes.

2 Stir in tomatoes and chilies. Season with salt to taste. Bring mixture to a simmer over medium heat. Cook until mushrooms are soft and juices evaporate, about 15 minutes. Stir in parsley and remove pan from heat. Set mixture aside to cool slightly before filling tacos. Taste and adjust seasonings if necessary. Optionally, stir in 1/2 cup crema Mexicana.

3 **To Serve:** Fill each taco with 3 tablespoons filling (and top with 2 to 3 teaspoons *crema Mexicana* if not added to filling).

Source: *The Essential Cuisines of Mexico* by Diana Kennedy.

Vary! Improvise!

☞ *California Variation: Lay a smear of mayonnaise onto the tortilla before the fish goes on.*

☞ *Color: Substitute for or mix purple cabbage with green. Pour boiling water with a little vinegar over finely sliced cabbage to wilt slightly. Drain and blot dry.*

☞ *Rub fish with Achiote Paste and grill instead of flouring and frying.*

Enchiladas

Enchilada comes from the Spanish *enchilar*, which means to immerse in chili. Enchiladas are tortillas softened and warmed in a chili sauce before filling. The word enchilada might bring to mind a casserole of baked enchilada rolls smothered in spicy tomato sauce and cheese, but that's only one version, and generally made for large groups. There's a second, quicker version that may be placed directly on the dining plate:

Immerse the tortilla into the sauce then briefly into hot lard *or* first into hot lard to soften then briefly into the chili-spiked sauce. The tortilla may be filled (or not) with any number of combinations, but shredded chicken with tomatillo-chili-cream sauce, or pork with red chili sauce, or cooked spinach and mushrooms with roasted tomato salsa are good choices. Guacamole, pork adobo, or grilled, leftover lamb are also delicious.

FIGURE 13.32 Enchiladas with green sauce.
Source: kafka/Fotolia.

Signature Technique: Enlightened Enchiladas

- Fresh, day-old, or store-bought fresh, 6-inch corn tortillas are fine enchilada material.

- **Choose a tasty sauce:** Tomato-chili, tomatillo-chili, cooked tomato salsa, *salsa ranchera*, or mole.

- Have fun with the filling. Refer to *Construct a Taco* for filling ideas. Prepare combos with what you have leftover in the kitchen, but keep it simple: let the tortilla and sauce shine. They are equally or more important than the filling; don't overwhelm with too much filling or a too fussily complex filling.

- **Inside-out enchiladas:** It's not always necessary to fill enchiladas—the filling can go on top. Heat them in sauce until flexible and slightly al dente, fold into fourths, and garnish with crumbled cheese, finely diced, raw red onion, and cilantro.

- **For casserole enchiladas:** Brush tortillas lightly melted lard or oil, and over medium heat, cook in 8-inch nonstick skillet briefly *or* place into 350 degree F preheated oven on parchment-covered sheet pan and bake until flexible, about 3 minutes. Stack tortillas and wrap to keep warm.

- *For* **fry** *and dip tortillas:* Fry tortillas as for casserole enchiladas, and dip in warm sauce to soften until flexible, slightly al dente, and warmed through. This is a good method for unfilled enchiladas.

- *For* **dip** *and fry tortillas:* Dip tortilla in sauce. Over medium heat, cook tortilla in 1 teaspoon lard per side in nonstick pan about 20 seconds per side. Place on parchment-covered sheet pan in preheated 350 degree F oven to warm through.

- Fill 6-inch tortilla with 3 to 4 tablespoons warm filling. Plate while warm *or* place in low oven up to 15 minutes, *or* place enchiladas in casserole and drizzle with sauce. Heat through in oven. Remove enchiladas from oven and lightly sprinkle with queso fresco or cotija cheese and raw onion.

CHICKEN ENCHILADAS WITH GREEN TOMATILLO SALSA AND CREAM (ENCHILADAS DE POLLO CON SALSA DE TOMATILLO CON CREMA)

These are the casserole-style tortillas with which most Americans are familiar. One pound of boneless, skinless meat, cooked and shredded equals 2 to 2-1/2 cups.

Yields 12 tortillas, 4 to 6 servings

1-3/4 to 2 pounds split chicken breast with bone and skin,
   or 2-1/2 cups grilled, roasted, or poached and shredded chicken
4-1/2 cups *Salsa de Tomatillo con Crema*
12 six-inch corn tortillas
3 to 4 ounces Chihuahua, Monterey Jack, *or* mild cheddar cheese, 3/4 to 1 cup shredded

For Garnish: Finely sliced cilantro

1. **Roast chicken:** Preheat oven to 400 degrees F. Place chicken breasts into baking pan and place in oven. Bake chicken until instant-read thermometer reads 170 degrees F, 40 to 50 minutes. Remove chicken from oven and cool. Discard skin and bones. Shred chicken into mixing bowl to yield about 2-1/2 cups.

2. Prepare tomatillo salsa with crema. Toss shredded chicken with 3/4 cup warm salsa.

3. Preheat oven to 350 degrees F. Spread 3/4 cup sauce on the bottom of a half-hotel pan, or a 9-inch by 13-inch baking dish, in two rows.

4. Refer to *Signature Technique: Enlightened Enchiladas:* Prepare tortillas for *Casserole Enchiladas.* Stack and wrap tortillas to keep warm.

5. **Assemble:** Working quickly, roll 3 tablespoons chicken filling inside each tortilla and wedge, seam side down, into prepared pan. There should be two rows of a single layer. Ladle remaining 3 cups sauce over top of enchiladas. Sprinkle cheese over top of sauce.

6. **To Serve:** Place enchiladas into oven and bake until hot, and cheese is lightly browned, 15 minutes. Remove pan from oven. Plate enchiladas while very hot, and garnish with cilantro. The enchiladas must be served immediately; they will disintegrate after 15 minutes.

Vary! Improvise!

☞ **No Tomatillos:** Substitute 5 to 6 cups *Mexican Light Tomato Sauce or* thinned *Green Pumpkin Seed Sauce.*

☞ **Vegetarian:** Fill enchiladas with grilled vegetables or sautéed greens and mushrooms instead of meat.

SIMMER, STEW, POACH, BOIL, AND STEAM

Mexican Soup (Sopa)

Mexicans love soup and they eat it at least once a day. Soup often precedes a meal. It can be a bracing street snack, a full meal, or served as midnight fortifier after an evening of drinking. Soup begins with rich, homemade broth made from poultry, pork, or beef often seasoned with onion, garlic, and tomatoes. Mexican cooks have created a vast array of deeply satisfying soups from native beans, fresh and dry chilies, cactus, leftover tortillas, corn, crab, shrimp, hominy, avocados, wild mushrooms, tomatillos, cilantro, squash blossoms, and zucchini, and the Spanish contributions of beef marrow, cheese, melon, almonds, and *crema* (naturally soured cream).

Some favorite combinations:

- Classic clear chicken *consomé* garnished with tomato, toasted chili, fried strips of tortilla, avocado, and herbs (*sopa de tortilla*)
- Intensely flavored shrimp broth
- Richly flavorful *caldos* like the hominy and tripe *menudo*
- Chili-spiked crab soup

- Brothy black bean soup
- Purées of poblano and cream *or* corn chowder

Mexicans also prepare *sopa seca* or dry soup. It begins "soupy," but ends up as a plate of flavorful, simmered, seasoned pasta or rice. In formal meals, much as in Italy with pasta, sopa seca follows sopa. Nowadays one or the other might be served.

MEXICAN COMFORT FOOD: MENUDO AND POZOLE

FIGURE 13.33 White pozole soup.
Source: uckyo/Fotolia.

Originally a food for celebration, menudo has become a meal that knits families: they visit while it long-simmers and prepare side dishes. This traditional and hugely popular Mexican soup-stew is made with chewy tripe (beef stomach) in a clear broth or as *menudo colorado* in a red chili broth.

Menudo is accompanied by tortillas or *bolillos* (buns) and condiments: lime wedges, diced white onion, chopped cilantro, crushed oregano, and crushed chilies. Northern Mexican cooks add *hominy* (nixtamalized whole corn), northwest cooks prepare it without chilies, central Mexican cooks substitute sheep tripe, and in Chihuahua, near the Texas border, menudo is prepared in red chili broth.

Similar to menudo, *pozole* is a soup usually made with pork or chicken instead of tripe, that simmers for several hours. Cooks in Guadalajara prepare the white or clear pozole, red pozole is popular in Michoacán and Jalisco, and *pozole verde* (made with *Pipían Verde*) is popular in Guerrero. A steaming bowl of the lime-infused broth with chewy hominy will clear the sinuses. Crunchy radishes, shredded lettuce or cabbage, diced onion, oregano, chili, and plenty of limes traditionally accompany pozole.

One cup (5 ounces) dried pozole corn (hominy), soaked and cooked, yields about 1 pound or 2-1/2 cups.

SIGNATURE RECIPE

WHITE CHICKEN POZOLE (POZOLE BLANCO DE POLLO)

In the northern Pacific Mexican state of Guerrero, pozole is practically the state dish.

Yields about 11 cups broth with hominy, about 6 servings

5-1/2 ounces dried prepared pozole (hominy), 1 cup
   or 16 ounces cooked fresh or frozen *nixtamal* corn, about 2-1/2 cups
      or 29-ounce can hominy, 3 cups drained
1 ounce garlic, 4 large cloves, smashed and peeled, *divided*
3-1/2 pounds whole chicken, cut up and skin removed
   or 8 to 9 cups chicken stock
1 pound white onion, 4 cups peeled and finely slivered, *divided*
1 tablespoon dried Mexican oregano

Garnish

3 to 4 ounces green, Savoy or napa cabbage, about 3 cups cored and finely sliced
4 ounces trimmed red radishes, 1 to 1-1/2 cups thinly sliced or finely slivered
2 teaspoons dried Mexican oregano

For Serving

1 to 2 tablespoons coarsely ground dried red chilies de árbol
3 limes, each cut into 4 to 6 wedges
Warm corn tortillas

1 Soak **dried pozole** 12 to 24 hours, drain, and rinse. *Or* rinse **fresh or frozen nixtamal corn** and drain. Combine **pozole** or **nixtamal** with 8 cups water, 2 cloves garlic, and 1-1/2 teaspoons kosher salt. Bring to a boil and lower heat to a simmer. Cover pot, and simmer **dried pozole** until tender, 4 to 5 hours to yield about 2-1/2 cups cooked hominy. If using **cooked nixtamal**, bring to a boil, reduce heat, and simmer until tender, about 3 hours. If using **canned hominy**, skip this step and simply open the can and drain off liquid.

2 Bring chicken, 2 cloves garlic (4 cloves if not used with hominy cooking in step one), half the onion, 1 tablespoon oregano, and 10 cups cold water to boil in a 6-quart pot over medium heat. Cover pan partially, and simmer over low heat until chicken is cooked through and tender, 2-1/2 to 3 hours.

3 Transfer chicken to mixing bowl, strain broth, and reserve to yield about 8 cups. Add water or cooking liquid from hominy if it's less than 8 cups to make up the difference. Chill broth and re-move or skim off fat. Cool chicken, and remove meat from bones. Discard skin and bones. Shred or dice chicken and set aside to yield about 3 cups.

4 Combine drained, cooked **pozole** and 1 to 2 teaspoons kosher salt with reserved broth. Bring to boil. Reduce heat and simmer 15 minutes. (*Soup may be prepared 1 day ahead. Cover and chill. Bring to simmer before serving.) Stir onion into hot broth and simmer 5 minutes. Taste soup and season with salt and pepper.

5 **To Serve:** Divide reserved meat, shredded cabbage, sliced radishes, and oregano equally among soup bowls. Ladle hot pozole and broth over the garnishes. Serve soup with ground chili, lime wedges, and warm tortillas.

SQUASH BLOSSOM SOUP
(SOPA DE FLOR DE CALABAZA)

This is a simple version of a classic soup. Many cooks add finely diced zucchini, tomatoes, or mushrooms; or to thicken, masa dough or potatoes; and to garnish, cream, grated cheese, or cilantro. Gardeners pick the male zucchini blossoms (no fruit attached, only a stem), but leave 1 male per 25 female blossoms for fertilization.

Yields about 3 quarts, 8 to 12 servings

3 to 4 tablespoons unsalted butter, diced
12 to 13 ounces onion, 3 cups peeled and finely diced
9 ounce ear of fresh corn, about 8-inches long, 1 cup kernels
   or 1 cup frozen corn kernels
1 ounce garlic, about 4 large cloves, 2 tablespoons peeled and minced
2 teaspoons ground cumin
2 ounces jalapeno, 2 medium, about 4 tablespoons stemmed, seeded, and finely diced
14 ounces fresh squash blossoms
8 cups unsalted chicken stock
3 to 4 tablespoons fresh lime juice, 1 large lime

For Garnish: 1/2 to 3/4 cup *crema Mexicana* (see *Glossary*)

1 Heat a 6-quart saucepan over medium heat and melt butter. Stir in onion, corn, and 1 teaspoon salt (less if stock is salted). Sauté vegetables until soft. Stir in garlic, cumin, and chilies. Continue to cook vegetables, stirring frequently, until tender.

2 Meanwhile, prepare blossoms. There are 4 or 5 small green leaves called *sepals* at the base of the blossom. Pull them off and slice the blossom where the sepals attach, called *receptacle*, the narrowed, slightly rounded bottom part of blossom that attaches to the stalk. As the receptacle is pulled away, the inside *pistil* will come away with it. Discard both *pistil* and stalk (though they may be eaten). Rinse blossoms and drain. Slice blossoms into 3/8- to 1/2-inch crossways slices to yield about 8 cups.

3 Stir blossoms into vegetables, and cook just until wilted, about 1 minute. Stir in stock. Bring to a simmer, and cook soup 5 minutes.

4 **To Serve:** Taste soup and adjust seasonings with salt and lime juice. Ladle hot soup into bowls and top each with 1 tablespoon crema. Serve immediately.

FIGURE 13.34 Male zucchini blossom.
Source: nito/Fotolia.

FIGURE 13.35 Female zucchini blossom.
Source: marco mayer/Shutterstock.

LIME SOUP FROM THE YUCATÁN
(SOPA DE LIMÓN VERDE DE YUCATÁN)

Yields about 10 cups, 4 to 6 servings

Broth

1-3/4 to 2 pounds chicken breasts with bone and skin
1 ounce garlic, 4 to 5 large cloves
4 to 5 ounces onion, 1 cup peeled and medium diced
1/4 teaspoon dried oregano
1/4 ounce cilantro sprigs, 1/4 cup packed
1 ounce serrano chilies, 2 medium, stemmed, halved lengthwise, and seeded

Soup

1 tablespoon vegetable or olive oil
4 to 5 ounces white onion, 1 cup finely diced
1 ounce green onions, 2 large, white and green *divided,* and finely sliced
5 to 6 ounces green bell pepper, 1 small, 3/4 to 1 cup cored and finely diced
8 ounces tomato, 1 medium, 1 cup peeled, seeded, and finely diced
2 key limes, 1/4 to 1/3 cup sliced into very thin rounds
    or 1/2 medium lime, 1/3 cup sliced into very thin half-rounds

To Serve

Oil for deep-frying
2 to 3 six-inch corn tortillas
1/2 ounce trimmed cilantro, 1/4 cup finely sliced
Lime wedges

1 **Prepare Broth:** Remove skin and all fat from chicken. Place chicken in 4-quart saucepan with 7 cups cold water and bring to a simmer. Wipe a 9- to 10-inch cast-iron skillet with oil, and heat over medium heat. Place garlic cloves (in skin) and onion into skillet and cook until soft and browned, 10 to 15 minutes. Transfer vegetables to saucepan with chicken, and stir in oregano, cilantro, and chilies. Bring to a boil and lower heat. Simmer broth until chicken is tender and just cooked through, 20 minutes.

2 Transfer chicken from broth to mixing bowl and cool. Dice or shred meat to yield about 3 cups, and set aside. Discard bones and gristle.

3 Heat clean 4-quart saucepan over medium heat. Pour in oil, onion, white part of green onion, and the bell pepper. Cook until vegetables are soft, about 5 minutes. Stir in tomato and cook 3 to 4 minutes. Set strainer over saucepan and pour in broth. Discard broth vegetables (the garlic is tasty). Stir in the lime slices and bring soup to a simmer for 5 minutes. Remove half the lime slices if desired.

4 Heat frying oil to 365 degrees F. Slice tortillas into 1/4-inch-wide by 1-1/2-inch-long strips and deep-fry until golden. Drain on paper towels.

5 **To Serve:** Bring soup to a near boil. Remove pan from heat and stir in chicken and remaining green onions. Ladle hot soup into bowls and garnish with tortilla strips and cilantro. Serve with lime wedges.

Source: *New Cooking From* Old Mexico by Jim Peyton.

SOUP OF TLALPAN (CALDO TLALPEÑO)

This soup is a classic in central and southern Mexico. It originated as a dish sold at animal-powered tram stops in the early twentieth-century in the village of Tlalpan. Tlalpan is the largest borough of Mexico City and is located on the south side of Mexico City.

Yields 3 quarts, 6 to 8 servings

2 quarts high-quality chicken stock
3/4 pound boneless, skinless chicken breasts
1 pound tomatoes, cored
1 tablespoon olive oil
4 to 5 ounces onion, 1 cup peeled and finely diced
1/2 ounce garlic, 2 large cloves, 1 tablespoon peeled and minced
3 to 4 ounces carrots, 3/4 cup peeled and diced into 1/4-inch cubes
15-ounce can cooked chickpeas, drained
   or 1-1/2 cups cooked chickpeas
4 ounces zucchini, 1 cup diced into 1/4-inch cubes
Optional: 4 epazote leaves
3 ounces fresh or frozen green peas, 1/2 cup
1 tablespoon fresh lime juice, more to taste, 1/2 large lime
1 tablespoon chopped canned chipotle chili, to taste

Garnish: 12 ounces avocadoes, about 2 medium, 1-1/2 to 2 cups peeled, seeded, medium dice

For Serving

2 limes sliced into 6 to 8 wedges

1 Pour stock and chicken breasts into a 2-quart saucepan and bring to a simmer. Cook meat until just done, 15 to 20 minutes. Transfer breasts to a mixing bowl to cool. Reserve stock. Dice chicken into 1/2-inch cubes to yield about 1-1/2 cups, and set aside.

2 Meanwhile, roast tomatoes over gas flame, or broil, until soft and skin blackens. Coarsely chop tomatoes and skin, and place into food mill fitted with fine blade and set over a bowl. Grind tomatoes to yield 1-1/2 to 1-3/4 cups purée, and set aside. *Alternatively,* peel tomatoes, discard peel, and dice flesh into 3/8-inch cubes and set aside.

3 In 4-quart saucepan, heat oil over medium heat. Stir in onions and cook until soft and just starting to brown, 6 to 8 minutes. Stir in garlic and cook 20 seconds. Pour in stock, tomatoes, carrots, chickpeas, zucchini, and epazote. Simmer 15 minutes.

4 **To Serve:** Stir chicken and green peas into soup, and heat through. Season soup to taste with lime juice, chipotle, and salt. Ladle soup into bowls and garnish with avocado. Serve with lime wedges.

Source: *New Cooking From Old Mexico* by Jim Peyton

AVOCADO CREAM SOUP WITH TEQUILA (SOPA DE CREMA DE AGUACATE)

This is a nueva cocina mexicana *recipe. Most recipes for this classic soup call for cream, but this recipe is lighter and easier to prepare. Chill all ingredients except spices for a refreshing hot weather soup.*

Yields 5 cups, 4 servings

1 pound avocados, 2 medium-large
1 cup freshly squeezed orange juice, about two 6- to 7-ounce oranges

2 tablespoons tequila
1/2 ounce serrano chili, 1 medium, 1 tablespoon stemmed and diced
1/2 teaspoon ground cumin
1/4 ounce cilantro, 4 tablespoons finely sliced
3 cups de-fatted chicken stock
3 to 4 tablespoons fresh lime juice, 1 large lime

Garnish

Cilantro leaves
Red chili powder

1 Peel, seed, and dice avocados. Place into food processor with orange juice, tequila, chili, cumin, and cilantro. Purée until smooth.

2 Transfer soup to tureen. Stir in chicken stock and lime juice. Season to taste with salt and more lime juice as necessary. Cover tureen. Refrigerate soup 30 minutes to 2 hours to chill, or serve at room temperature.

3 **To Serve:** Ladle soup into bowls. Garnish with cilantro leaves and a dusting of chili powder. Serve.

Source: *New Cooking From Old Mexico* by Jim Peyton.

Vary! Improvise!

☞ *Vegetarian: Substitute a flavorful vegetable broth for chicken stock.*
☞ *Garnish soup with a dollop of crema Mexicana or a swirl of cream.*

Signature Technique: Mexican Dry Soups (Sopas Secas)

Sopa secas or Mexican dry soups are not soup nor are they completely dry: they begin soupy with stock and tomato sauce, which absorbs into brown-fried broken vermicelli or noodle "nests," tortilla strips, or rice. The starch absorbs the flavor of the cooking medium and becomes a thing apart—a sort of intensified, concentrated "soup." This dish has its roots in Spanish paella—usually made with rice, but also made with noodles called fideos. Mexicans eat sopas secas as a first course or as lunch.

A cross between pasta and pilaf, this homey dish is a great place to improvise. It may be simple or more complex depending on the occasion. Sopa seca's essential building blocks are lard or oil, thin noodles (fideos) or long-grain rice or tortilla strips, tomato-based sauce, and chilies. Prepare the elements of this dish and put them together just before serving.

Noodle Sopa Secas

- For 1 pound short, thin dried vermicelli or Mexican nested *fideo* vermicelli, prepare 3-1/2 to 4 cups tomato-based purée/sauce.

- Brown chorizo or meat, if using, in oil. Remove and drain.

- If noodles are long and not in nests, break into smaller pieces. Wrap in towel to keep noodle bits from flying around.

- Heat 1/2-cup oil in a deep 12-inch pan. Fry noodles over medium heat, tossing or turning occasionally, until golden or a deeper reddish brown. If using nests, fry on one side and turn to fry on second side. Toss broken long noodles with tongs to cook evenly. Or deep-fry the noodles until browned.

- Drain fried noodles on paper towels.

- To finish the dish, heat some of the remaining oil and add sauce. Reduce until thickened enough to coat a spoon if it isn't already thick. Add any garnishes like the fried chorizo, diced fresh tomato or vegetables, and seasonings like fresh herbs or spices.

- Pour in 4 cups stock for 16 ounces noodles. Consistency of sauce should now be like a loose and juicy tomato sauce.

- Stir in fried noodles and coat in sauce. After a few minutes, the nests, if using, will soften: gently pull apart. Stir in any precooked, diced vegetable garnish like zucchini or carrot, meat, or chorizo. The sauce should be bubbling vigorously. Cover pan and cook 5 minutes. Uncover pan and, still bubbling vigorously, cook until noodles are al dente and liquid has been fully absorbed, about 5 minutes more. Remove pan from heat, and rest undisturbed 5 to 10 minutes.

- Serve sopa seca garnished with crumbled Mexican cheese, herbs, crema Mexicana or thinned sour cream, avocados, salsa, or chilies.

- Some people prefer sopa seca made with fideos the next day; keep it no longer than 3 days. Drizzle noodles with a little stock before reheating.

FIGURE 13.36   Mexican-style noodles (fideos secos).

MEXICAN "DRY SOUP" NOODLES (FIDEOS SECOS)

This show-stopping "dry soup" shows off la cucina nueva mexicana at its best.

Yields 10 to 12 cups, 4 to 6 servings

Chili-Tomato Sauce

Yields 3-1/2 cups

8 ounces tomatoes, 2 small or 1 medium-large, cored
4 ounces tomatillos, 4 medium, husked and rinsed well
3/4 ounce guajillo chilies, 4, stemmed, seeded, and deveined
1 to 1-1/2 ounces dried ancho chilies, 2, stemmed, seeded, and deveined
1 ounce canned chipotle chilies in adobo, about 2 tablespoons chopped, more to taste
2 to 3 ounces white onion, 1/2 cup peeled and finely diced
1 to 1-1/4 ounces garlic, 5 large cloves, peeled
2-inch piece Mexican canela (cinnamon), broken
  or 1-inch cinnamon stick
1-1/2 teaspoons cumin seed
  or 2 teaspoons ground cumin
1 teaspoon dried Mexican oregano
1 tablespoon kosher salt
1/2 teaspoon sugar

6 cups chicken stock, *divided*

Noodles

1/2 cup olive or vegetable oil
1 pound thin spaghetti or vermicelli, broken into 2-inch lengths
  or 1 pound Mexican nested *fideos* (vermicelli)

Seasoning

1/2 to 3/4 ounces cilantro, 10 large sprigs

Garnish

12 to 16 ounces avocados, 2 medium to large, pitted, peeled, and finely sliced
4 ounces queso fresco, 1 cup crumbled
   or 1 cup *crema Mexicana* (see *Glossary*)
Green Tomatillo Salsa
1 ounce cilantro, 1/2 cup finely sliced

1 **Prepare the sauce:** Preheat broiler to high and position a rack 8 inches from heat source. Line a sheet pan with foil. Place tomato or tomatoes and tomatillos on pan cored side up. Roast tomatoes and tomatillos until blackened and very soft, turning once after 10 to 15 minutes, and continue to broil on remaining side. Remove to a bowl.

2 **Chilies:** Heat a cast-iron skillet over medium heat. Toast guajillo and ancho chilies until puffed and a shade darker but not blackened, 30 seconds to 1 minute per side. Place in bowl and cover with warm water. Soak until softened, 15 to 20 minutes, and drain. Discard water.

3 **Purée the sauce:** Drop tomato, tomatillos, drained chilies, chipotle chili, onion, garlic, canela, cumin seed, oregano, kosher salt, and sugar into blender with 1 cup stock. Purée mixture until smooth, 3 minutes. Scrape purée through medium-fine strainer into a bowl. Rinse out blender with 1/2 cup stock and pour through strainer. Discard solids, and reserve strained sauce.

4 **Fry the noodles:** Heat oil in 12-inch skillet over medium-high heat. When hot, fry noodles in two batches, tossing or turning with tongs, until they turn reddish-brown, about 2 minutes per side. Transfer fried noodles to paper towel-lined bowl or sheet pan.

5 **Cook the sauce:** Lower heat to medium-low and pour strained sauce into skillet (it will sputter). Fry sauce, stirring frequently, until it thickens enough to coat a spoon, about 5 minutes.

6 **Cook the noodles:** Stir 4 cups stock, cilantro sprigs, and the fried noodles into skillet. Toss to coat noodles in sauce, and immerse them. Bring to a boil, lower heat, and cover skillet. Noodles should bubble vigorously 5 minutes. Uncover pan and simmer vigorously until sauce absorbs and they are tender, 5 minutes more. Toss noodles once or twice during cooking so they cook evenly. Cover skillet, and remove from heat. Rest dish undisturbed 5 to 10 minutes.

7 **To Serve:** Fluff noodles in pan *or* transfer to platter or bowl and pile high. Garnish with avocado and queso fresco or drizzle with *crema Mexicana* and *Green Tomatillo Salsa* and sprinkle with cilantro. Or place the garnishes in bowls and allow diners to garnish each portion. Cooked noodles keep up to 3 days refrigerated. *To reheat:* drizzle noodles with chicken stock, cover, and place in preheated 350 degree F oven until heated through, about 30 minutes.

Source: *Truly Mexican* by Roberto Santibañez.

Vary! Improvise!

☞ *Carnivore:* Add 8 ounces sliced, fried chorizo sausage (see *Signature Technique: Mexican Dry Soups*).
☞ *Vegetarian: Use vegetable stock in place of chicken stock.*
☞ *Toss cooked or grilled diced chicken into simmering noodles.*

OAXACAN SPANISH CHICKEN STEW (ESTOFADO DE POLLO)

This dish may look daunting, but its technique is similar to a European stew. Chef Susana Trilling grinds the sesame seeds very finely on a metate or in a spice grinder; grinding them in a blender gives more texture. This dish could be considered a mole, though Trilling does not.

Yields about 3 quarts with chicken, 8 servings

5-1/2 to 6 pounds chicken legs, thighs, and breasts
3 pounds ripe tomatoes, 6 medium-large
    or 2-1/4 pounds tomatoes and 3/4 pound tomatillos, husked
1-1/2 to 2 ounces ancho chilies, about 3
2-1/2 ounces sesame seeds, 1/2 cup
5 tablespoons sunflower oil, olive oil *or* lard, *divided*
2-1/2 ounces blanched almonds, 1/2 cup
2-1/2 ounces raisins, 1/2 cup
3/4 to 1 ounce garlic, 3 to 4 large cloves, peeled
4 to 5 ounces white onion, 1 cup peeled and diced
2 whole cloves
1-1/2-inch piece Mexican canela (cinnamon) stick *or* cinnamon stick
1/2 teaspoon coarsely ground black pepper
1 teaspoon crumbled, dried Mexican oregano *or* dried oregano
1 large sprig fresh thyme
2 cups chicken stock, *more as needed*
2 tablespoons capers plus 1 tablespoon caper liquid
4 ounces green olives, 1/2 cup pitted

Garnish

Pickled sliced jalapeño or serrano chilies
Chopped Italian parsley

For Serving

Warm corn tortillas

1 Remove skin and fat from chicken; it's not strictly necessary, but it does make the dining experience neater and the mole less fatty. Wash and pat chicken dry.

2 Fill a 4-quart saucepan with cold water and bring to a boil. Core, and blanch tomatoes until skin comes away easily, 1 to 2 minutes. Transfer tomatoes to bowl with slotted spoon. (If using tomatillos, add to simmering water, and cook until dull green and soft, 7 to 10 minutes). Reserve cooking water. Peel tomatoes when cool, seed, but reserve seeds, and dice tomato coarsely to yield about 5 cups.

3 With scissors, cut open dried ancho chilies and remove stems, seeds, and veins. Heat an 8- to 9-inch cast-iron skillet over medium heat. Toast chilies until blistered and aromatic, but not blackened, 30 seconds to 1 minute per side. Transfer chilies to reserved tomato-blanching water to soak 15 to 20 minutes. Drain chilies and reserve.

4 Reheat cast-iron skillet over low heat. Stir in sesame seeds and roast until fragrant and darkened, 4 to 7 minutes. Scrape seeds into small bowl to cool.

5 Reheat cast-iron skillet over medium heat and add 2 tablespoons oil or lard. Stir in almonds, raisins, garlic, onion, cloves, cinnamon, pepper, oregano, and thyme. Cook until onion is soft and remaining ingredients are browned and fragrant, 5 to 7 minutes. Strip leaves off thyme sprig and discard woody stem. Scrape mixture into a second bowl to cool.

6 Working in 2 batches, pour half the tomatoes and half the chilies into blender with 1/4 cup chicken stock. Purée until smooth, 2 to 3 minutes. Repeat with remaining tomatoes, chilies, and 1/4 cup stock. Pour into large bowl and set aside. (At this point the mixture may be strained through a fine-mesh strainer if desired.)

7 Pour sesame seeds and almond-raisin-herb mixture into blender with 1 cup chicken stock and purée until smooth. Pour into bowl with tomato-chili mixture, and rinse out blender with 1/2 cup chicken stock; pour stock into bowl with tomato-chili mixture.

8 Blot chicken parts very dry and season with salt. Heat remaining 3 tablespoons lard or oil in a heavy 6-quart pot over medium heat. Fry chicken parts in two batches until colored, but not cooked through. To better brown skinned parts, dust with flour (or potato flour for gluten-free), shake off excess, and add to hot fat; fry until browned. Transfer chicken to bowl, and set aside.

9 Reheat pot over medium heat, and stir in tomato-chili-almond-raisin-herb mixture. Cook 10 minutes, stirring occasionally. Transfer chicken to sauce and lower heat. Simmer chicken until very tender, 45 minutes to 1 hour.

10 Sauce should just coat the back of a spoon, if it's too thick adjust with more stock or water. Stir in capers, caper liquid and olives. Simmer stew partially covered 10 to 15 minutes longer. Season stew to taste with salt and pepper. Olives can turn bitter if simmered too long.

11 **To Serve:** Ladle stew into bowls and top with pickled chilies and parsley. Serve with tortillas.

Source: *Seasons of My Heart* by Susanna Trilling.

PORK WITH RED CHILI SAUCE (CARNE EN ADOBO)

Yields about 5 cups, 4 to 6 servings

2 tablespoons fresh pork lard *or* vegetable oil
2 pounds lightly trimmed, boneless pork shoulder, diced into 1-inch cubes
1/4 ounce garlic, 1 large clove, 1-1/2 teaspoons peeled and minced
2 cups chicken stock *or* canned low-salt chicken stock
1-1/4 cups *Red Chili Adobo*

For Serving

Warm tortillas
Shredded romaine
Finely sliced radishes

1 Heat lard or oil over high heat in deep 10-inch skillet or heavy 6-quart pot. When the fat ripples, add the pork. Cook until golden, 5 to 6 minutes. Lower heat, stir in garlic, and cook 30 seconds.

2 Stir in stock and **red chili adobo**. Bring to a boil, cover pot, lower heat, and simmer 30 minutes. Remove lid and continue to cook, stirring occasionally, until meat is very tender and sauce has thickened, 35 to 45 minutes.

3 **To Serve:** Season meat with salt, to taste. Serve pork with tortillas, shredded romaine, and radishes.

Source: Mexican chef Zarela Martinez.

BRAISED, FRIED, AND SHREDDED PORK (CARNITAS)

Beloved throughout Mexico, but a specialty of Michoacán, this simple technique begins with meat, fat, seasonings, and something sweet. Some cooks use cola in place of whole milk or sweetened condensed milk. The sugars in them help to brown and caramelize the meat. This is savory, big-flavored food.

Yields about 8 cups, enough for 32 or more tacos

4 pounds fatty pork shoulder (butt), diced into 1-1/2 inch cubes
12 to 13 ounces white onion, 3 cups peeled and finely sliced
Half of a 6 ounce juice orange, halved through its "equator"
1/4 cup fresh pork lard *or* sunflower *or* olive oil
2 ounces garlic, about 8 large cloves, peeled
3 large bay leaves
1 tablespoon sweetened condensed milk
  or 1 cup cola
2 teaspoons dried Mexican oregano, crumbled

For Serving

Warm tortillas
Salsa of choice
Cooked beans of choice
Cooked rice of choice

1 Place 3 cups cold water, 4 teaspoons kosher salt, pork, onion, 1/2 orange, lard or oil, garlic, bay leaves, condensed milk or cola, and oregano into a heavy 6-quart pot. Bring to a boil. Skim foam off and discard.

2 Partially cover pot, lower the heat, and high simmer pork until very tender, 45 minutes. Stir occasionally so pork cooks evenly. Uncover pot, raise heat so pork maintains a high simmer, and cook until water has evaporated, about 2 hours. When the liquid evaporates, only fat will be visible on the bottom of the pot. Discard orange half and bay leaves.

3 Continue frying meat until it browns evenly. If bottom of pan becomes too encrusted and browned, deglaze with a little water and continue to cook. *Alternatively*, preheat oven to 450 degrees F. Transfer meat and fat to hotel pan and roast (stirring occasionally) until meat is evenly browned, 20 to 30 minutes.

4 **To Serve:** Break meat apart or shred. Serve carnitas as a main dish with tortillas, salsa, beans, and rice or as a filling for tacos.

Source: *Truly Mexican* by Roberto Santibañez.

Vary! Improvise!

☞ *Season It Up:* Add 2 sprigs fresh thyme and 6 whole allspice.
☞ *Goat or Lamb:* Substitute goat or lamb shoulder for pork.

Tamales: The Best of Mexico

Versatile tamales are food that signals celebration. Cooks gather friends and family for a *tamalada* (tamale-making party) to prepare hundreds of these packets ideal for fiestas. In northern and central Mexico, cooks wrap the spongy corn batter and spicy fillings in fresh or dried, soaked cornhusks. In southern Mexico, fresh banana leaves act as wrappers for tamales. Both types of tamales are steamed.

Tamales vary in size. The typical tamale might measure 2- or 3-inches wide and 4-inches long. Variations can go from 2-inches wide and 6- or 7-inches long to one so large it holds a whole loin of pork.

Throughout Mexico, cooks prepare a dazzling array of tamales with batters from fresh corn, field corn, plain masa harina, or masa flavored with shredded or puréed squash, strawberry, or pineapple. Tamale fillings can range from sweet and mild to spicy. Two of the most favored fillings are chicken with tomatillo-salsa and pork with red-chili sauce. Tamales may be filled with highly seasoned or sauced beans or shredded beef, cheese and roasted chilies, seafood, raisins, cooked vegetables, peanuts or pine nuts, or *picadillo dulce*. Some tamales are served with more salsa or sauce on the side.

Tamales require three important elements: *masa* or corn "batter," a substantial vegetable, bean, or meat *filling*, and a *sauce* or seasoning. Like good sushi rolls and their balance of rice and filling, tamales must also strike a balance of masa with enough filling and sauce to flavor-saturate the masa, but not overwhelm it.

Signature Technique: Tamale Masa Batter, Filling, and Sauce

Element One

The Masa Batter

Masa Dough or Masa Harina Flour and Liquid, Fat, and Baking Powder

Tamale batters can be made from ground, freshly cooked "nixtamalized" corn (masa), or from dried, ground "nixtamalized" corn flour (masa harina). Fresh masa makes the best tamales, but most cooks in Mexico make tamales from masa harina. Doughs from both fresh and dried masa are treated in the same way for tamale-making, but fresh dough needs less liquid. Liquids used for moistening dough include chicken, beef, seafood, or vegetable stock, fruit juice, coconut milk, milk, cream, fruit purée, or water.

Whipped fat gives tamales a light, rich texture and taste. The ideal fat is freshly rendered pork lard. A good shortening or half shortening and half butter is popular with health conscious Mexican-Americans. Leftover bacon fat mixed with commercial lard boosts flavor. Spectrum Foods makes two organic, nonhydrogenated vegetable shortenings (plain and butter-flavored) excellent for vegans and vegetarians. For lighter tamales, some cooks add a little baking powder to the batter.

Masa Batter Proportions

- Three cups masa harina (15 ounces) plus 3 cups liquid to about 1-1/4 cup lard (7-1/2 ounces)
    or 1-1/4 cups vegetable shortening (7-1/2 ounces)
    or a combination of 3-1/2 ounces shortening and 4 ounces unsalted butter

- Use chicken stock, water, or fruit juice for part or all of the liquid.

- Other additions like puréed canned or fresh squash, shredded vegetables, puréed canned hominy, or fruit help masa to hold moisture so less fat may be used.

- If using canned hominy, use equal parts hominy to masa harina by volume. Grind hominy in food processor before mixing with masa harina. The masa dough will need a little less water.

- For an extra light batter, add about **1 teaspoon baking powder per 3 cups masa harina**.

Basic Masa Batter Method

1 **Prepare masa dough:** In a mixer with paddle attachment *or* in a bowl by hand, beat masa harina and warm or hot liquid together until it forms a soft mass that doesn't crack when rolled into a ball and pressed. Transfer masa dough (from mixer) to bowl and cover. Rest 20 to 30 minutes and allow to cool.

2 **Whip the fat:** Add fat to clean mixer bowl. Set a timer. With paddle attachment, beat fat until fluffy, about 2 minutes.

3 **Beat in masa dough:** Slowly, in 1 to 2 cup increments, add masa dough to beaten fat. *Beat 2 minutes for each addition of masa dough.* Don't skimp on beating: *time it.*

4 **Optional leavening:** Beat in baking powder for a lighter, less dense masa batter.

5 **Adjust consistency of batter:** Thin dough to desired consistency with lukewarm liquid (or fruit purée). Basic masa batter should be at least the consistency of cake batter: thick, but light and frosting-spreadable. Batter can range from thick and creamy to slightly thinner and creamy depending on how much liquid is added. Batters with more liquid tend to be less dense.

6 **Test batter:** Drop 1/2 teaspoon batter into a bowl of cold water. It should float. If not, the fat and masa batter hasn't beaten well enough. Beat longer, but if after 2 minutes the masa batter doesn't float, the batter is still useable, just somewhat heavier. Live and learn.

7 **Optional:** Beat or fold in shredded vegetables. Think color.

*In southern Mexico and Central America the corn masa is cooked with liquid and cooled before beating into the beaten fat.

Element Two

The Filling

- Fillings for tamales should be *fully cooked and highly seasoned.*

- Season fillings with salt, pepper, herbs, spice, and/or chilies OR a sauce or salsa.

- Shredded cooked chicken or pork are the top favorites, but seafood, game, toasted seeds or nuts, legumes, fruit, vegetables, roasted fresh chilies, and cheese, or leftovers make tasty tamales.

- Cooks prefer dark meat poultry or pork for moistness.

Element Three

The Sauce

- Sauce for tamale fillings should have big flavor.

- Fillings (meat, poultry, seafood) may be mixed with sauce/salsa, spooned on top fillings, or served alongside the hot tamales. Choose a flavorful sauce: chili sauce, tomatillo salsa, mole, tomato sauce.

- Fillings are either tossed with salsa, mole, or sauce, or seasoned and topped with a sauce as tamales are constructed.

- For every 4 cups shredded or finely diced meat, season with about 2 cups salsa or sauce.

Devise filling combos with cooked, shredded meat, seafood, or legumes:

Mole Sauce
Green Tomatillo Salsa plain or *con Crema*
Green Pumpkin Seed Sauce
Red Chili Adobo
Red Chili Sauce
Picadillo

PLAIN MASA BATTER

Yields about 6 cups batter, enough for 32 to 48 tamales

15 ounces *masa harina para tamales* or masa harina, 3 cups
3 cups warm chicken or vegetable stock
7-1/2 ounces fresh pork lard, 1 cup
   or 7-1/2 ounces vegetable shortening, 1-1/4 cups
1 teaspoon baking powder

1   Place masa harina into bowl, or bowl of mixer fitted with a paddle attachment. On low speed, or by hand, mix stock and 2 teaspoons kosher salt. Dough should be pliable and tender. Roll a piece into a ball and press. Dough should not crack around the edges.

2   Transfer dough in mixer to bowl. Cover dough and rest it 30 minutes.

3   Add lard or shortening to clean mixer bowl of mixer fitted with clean paddle attachment. Set a timer: Beat fat on high speed 2 minutes. Scrape fat down.

4   On medium speed, add 1/3 of the masa dough to fat in mixer. Beat each addition 2 minutes. Repeat twice more with remaining masa dough, beating 2 minutes each time. Add baking powder and 1/2 to 3/4 cup cold water (or stock) to achieve a thick, creamy cake batter consistency.

5   Test batter consistency, drop 1/2 teaspoon into a cup of cold water. If it floats it's ready. If not, beat 2 minutes more; in a warm kitchen, refrigerate the masa batter 30 minutes to 1 hour before beating 2 to 4 minutes. Use batter immediately or within several hours.

MASA BATTER WITH HOMINY

Yields about 7 cups batter, enough for 37 to 56 tamales

2 cups drained, canned, cooked hominy, about 2/3 of 29-ounce can
10 ounces *masa harina para tamales* or masa harina, 2 cups
2 cups warm chicken or vegetable stock
7-1/2 ounces lard, 1 cup
   or 7-1/2 ounces vegetable shortening, 1-1/4 cups
1 teaspoon baking powder

1   Place hominy in food processor. Process until finely ground. Scrape into bowl, or bowl of mixer fitted with paddle. Fold in masa harina and 2 teaspoons kosher salt. Mix by hand, or in mixer on low speed. Slowly add stock until dough is moist and pliable. Transfer dough to bowl and cover; rest 30 minutes. Wash and dry mixer bowl if using.

2   Add lard or shortening to clean mixer bowl of mixer fitted with a paddle. Set a timer: Beat fat on high speed 2 minutes. Scrape fat down.

3   On medium speed, add 1/3 of masa dough to fat in mixer. Beat each addition 2 minutes. Repeat twice more with remaining masa dough, beating 2 minutes each time. Add baking powder and 1/2 to 3/4 cup cold water (or more stock) to achieve a thick, creamy cake batter consistency.

4   To test batter consistency, drop 1/2 teaspoon into a cup of cold water. If it floats, it's ready. If not, beat 2 minutes more; in a warm kitchen, refrigerate the masa batter 30 minutes to 1 hour before beating 2 to 4 minutes. Use batter immediately or use within several hours.

Vary! Improvise!

☞ **Masa with Shredded Squash:** Increase the fat to 10 ounces for either *Plain Masa Batter* or *Masa Batter with Hominy*. Fold in 4 cups shredded butternut squash (1-1/4 pounds, peeled and seeded) at the end.

TAMALE WRAPPERS

Dried Corn Husks

Loosen husks and soak in warm water until pliable, 1 to 2 hours. Shake husks dry, stack, and rest covered until ready to use.

Fresh Green Corn Husks

These add delicate flavor to fresh corn tamales. Cut leaves near the base of the cob to achieve a slightly cupped end. Peel apart carefully so leaves remain whole. Green husks don't generally require soaking.

Banana Leaves Harvested Fresh

Choose the most tender, flexible leaves and cut off plant with some stem attached. Beware of the staining sap. Carefully cut the leaf off on both sides of the center rib with a very sharp knife. Cut each leaf into the necessary size. The stem can be sliced lengthwise to produce ties. Hold each leaf piece over a flame or hot griddle until it turns bright green (browned is too far) and soft and flexible. Cool before using. Place masa batter on smooth underside of leaf.

Banana Leaves Purchased Fresh

Found in Latin markets, these leaves are already stripped off the center rib. Follow directions for **Harvested Fresh.**

Frozen Banana Leaves

Thaw leaves fully, unwrap and wipe clean with cloth. Follow directions for **Harvested Fresh.** These thicker, tougher leaves will take longer to soften.

FIGURE 13.37 Banana leaves.
Source: vieraugen/Fotolia.

Signature Technique: Assembling and Steaming Tamales

Yields between 40 and 50 tamales

8 cups *Masa Batter*
6 ounces dried corn husks, about 60
5 to 6 cups seasoned or sauced filling (half recipe *Red Chili Pork or Chicken Tamales*)
Optional: Sauce or salsa for serving

1 Soak corn husks in cold water 1 hour in warm water. Drain husks and keep covered with damp towel until needed.

2 Flatten a 6-inch by 9-inch husk (or assemble and overlap several small pieces) with narrower, pointed end up and broader end on the bottom. No need to blot husks; just shake off excess moisture. Some moisture will keep masa batter from sticking to wrapper.

3 Spread 2 to 3 tablespoons batter in a 3- to 4-inch by 4-inch square in the middle of the husk. There should be a 1-inch space on each side and 2-inches on top and bottom.

4 Place 1-1/2 to 2 tablespoons filling in the center of each square of masa batter.

5 Fold in one side of husk over filling and fold second side of husk over the first. Fold down the narrow top end and fold up the broader bottom end. To hold tamale together, tie with string or strips of husk around middle. Some cooks fold up only the bottom end and leave the top end open.

6 Pack tamales (open end up) standing upright and close together into steamer, but not too tightly. Or arrange in 6-inch-deep perforated hotel pan. Finish assembling remaining tamales. (Tamales should be steamed immediately.)

7 If not using commercial steamer, set a collapsible vegetable steamer into heavy stockpot with a tight-fitting lid. (Thin metal pots may scorch tamales sitting around the edges—protect them

with a layer of husks.) The steamer should sit 2 inches above the boiling water. The water should never touch the tamales. If using a commercial steamer, pack tamales upright into 6-inch deep perforated hotel pan.

8 Cover tamales with leftover cornhusks and thin cotton kitchen towel. Cover pot.

9 Place a penny on the bottom of the steaming pot and fill pot with water to come up to 2-inches beneath steamer. A rattling penny will serve as a signal that the steaming water needs to be replenished. (Have kettle of boiling water handy for refills.) Bring water under tamales to a boil, lower heat to a high simmer, and steam tamales until tender, 1 to 1-1/2 hours, depending on the batter.

10 Check tamales after 1 hour. Corn masa should come away from corn husk cleanly when opened. Masa may be soft, but it will firm as it cools. If masa doesn't come away cleanly from husk, steam tamales 30 minutes more, and check again.

11 Rest tamales in pot 10 minutes after steaming to firm up before serving. Steamed tamales keep well 5 days refrigerated or 3 to 4 months frozen. Cool tamales thoroughly before refrigerating or freezing. Steam refrigerated tamales 10 to 12 minutes to reheat. Steam frozen tamales 25 to 30 minutes; do not thaw first.

FIGURE 13.38 Red chili chicken tamales.

FIGURE 13.39 Red chili chicken tamales.

RED CHILI CHICKEN OR PORK TAMALES (TAMALES DE CARNE EN CHILE COLORADO)

Use with cooked shredded pork, chicken, or vegetables.

Yields 4 cups sauce, enough for 8 to 9 cups shredded meat, for about 60 to 70 tamales

4 pounds boneless, skinless thighs
  or 5 to 6 pound pork shoulder

Sauce

2 ounces dried ancho chilies, about 5 large or 8 small
1/2 ounce dried guajillo chilies, about 2 large
6 to 7 ounces onion, peeled and quartered
1 ounce garlic, 4 large cloves, peeled
2 cups vegetable or chicken stock, *divided*
3 tablespoons olive or vegetable oil or lard
2 teaspoons ground cumin
14-ounce can diced fire-roasted tomatoes
  or 1-3/4 cups tomato purée or crushed tomatoes in purée

1 **Prepare meat:** Roast or poach chicken until tender or roast pork shoulder until very tender. Cool meat. Finely shred meat to yield 9 to 10 cups or finely dice meat to yield 8 to 9 cups. Set aside.

2 Bring 6 cups cold water to a boil. Heat a cast-iron griddle over medium heat. Toast chilies until slightly fragrant and slightly softened, about 30 to 60 seconds per side. Transfer chilies to bowl and cool slightly. Cut chilies open with scissors. Remove stem, seeds, and veins, and discard. Pour boiling water over seeded chilies. Soak chilies until soft, 15 to 20 minutes. With tongs, transfer soaked chilies to blender. Discard soaking water.

3 Meanwhile, bring 1 quart cold water to boil over high heat. Lower heat and add onion and garlic. Simmer vegetables until just tender, 15 minutes. Remove vegetables with slotted spoon to a blender (with chilies) with 1/2 cup stock or vegetable cooking water. Reserve remaining cooking water if using instead of stock. Purée mixture until smooth.

4 Heat oil or lard in deep 10- to 11-inch skillet or Dutch oven over medium heat. Add cumin and cook until fragrant, about 1 minute. Slowly pour in purée. (Do not rinse blender.) Cook purée 1 to 2 minutes.

5 Add diced tomatoes to blender and purée until smooth. Pour into sauce in skillet or Dutch oven. Rinse out blender with 1 cup more stock or vegetable cooking water and pour into skillet or Dutch oven. Reduce heat, cover cooking vessel, and simmer sauce 10 to 15 minutes. It should be the consistency of heavy cream. Season sauce with salt and pepper to taste. Cool sauce. It may be refrigerated up to 5 days or frozen up to 2 months.

6 **To use for tamale filling:** Toss sauce with reserved prepared meat. Prepare tamales according to directions in *Signature Technique: Assembling and Steaming Tamales.*

Source: *Tamales 101* by Alice Guadalupe Tapp.

BEAN TAMALES FROM NORTHERN MEXICO (TAMALES DE FRIJOL NORTEÑOS)

Yields about 4 cups bean filling, enough for 32 to 40 tamales

11 ounces pinto or "flor de mayo" beans, picked over for stones, rinsed and drained, 1-1/2 cups

Sauce

Yields about 1-1/2 cups

1/2 ounce garlic, 2 large cloves, peeled
1-1/2 ounces ancho chilies, 2 large
1 teaspoon cumin seeds
5 peppercorns
2 cups vegetable or chicken stock, *divided*
3 tablespoons pork lard or olive oil

5 cups *Masa Batter*
5 ounces dried corn husks, 40 to 50, soaked 1 hour and drained

1 Pour beans into 4-quart saucepan and cover with 6 cups cold water and 1-1/2 teaspoons kosher salt. Bring to a boil, lower heat, and cover pan. Simmer beans until tender, about 2 hours, to yield 4 cups drained, cooked beans.

2 Pour 1 quart cold water into 2-quart saucepan and bring to a boil. Lower heat, add garlic, and simmer 3 to 4 minutes; transfer to a medium bowl. Cover saucepan and keep water at a low simmer.

3 Heat cast-iron pan, griddle, or comal over medium heat. Toast chilies until lightly blistered on both sides, 20 to 30 seconds per side. Cool chilies and cut them open with scissors; discard stem, seeds, and veins. Uncover saucepan with simmering water, and remove from heat. Immerse chilies in hot water. Cover saucepan and soak chilies 10 minutes. Drain chilies and place in bowl with garlic cloves.

4 Toast cumin and peppercorns until fragrant in hot pan, griddle, or comal. Pour into mortar and crush with pestle. Pour cumin and peppercorns, chilies, garlic, and 1/2 cup stock into blender. Purée until smooth.

5 Heat lard or oil in deep 10-inch skillet over medium heat. When hot, stir in chili-spice purée. Rinse blender with 1/2 cup stock and pour into skillet. Lower heat and cook sauce 1 minute. Stir in beans and mash until rough-textured. Cook beans, stirring occasionally, until they thickly fall off a spoon, about 15 minutes. Add remaining stock as needed to maintain a thick but not stiff consistency to yield 4 to 4-1/2 cups. Set beans aside to cool. Season with salt to taste.

6 **Assemble tamales:** See *Signature Technique: Assembling Tamales.* Spread 2 tablespoons of masa dough thinly from upper part of wrapper down about 4 inches. Place about 1-1/2 tablespoons filling down the center of the masa. Wrap as indicated into long, narrow tamales.

7 **To Cook:** See *Signature Technique: Steaming Tamales.* Steam over high heat until dough separates cleanly from husk, 45 minutes to 1 hour.

Source: *The Essential Cuisines of Mexico* by Diana Kennedy.

Beans (Frijoles)

Dried beans are an essential part of Mexican cuisine—beloved by rich and poor—and served at every meal. Black and pinto beans are most associated with Mexican cooking, but in Mexico dried beans come in a delightful variety of flavors, shapes, and colors: black or purple-mottled, deep or pale yellow, pink, mottled-pink, brown, and white. Pinto beans are predominant in north, pale yellow *peruanos* and pale purple *flor de mayo* in central Mexico, while black beans are the favorite south of Mexico City. Prized fresh shell beans (*frijoles nuevos*) arrive at the market still in their pods.

Mexican cooks rarely soak dried beans. Soaking speeds up cooking time and improves texture, but doesn't make much difference in digestibility. (Eat beans daily as Mexicans do and they will be easy to digest.) Since beans absorb water through the small black spot on their sides, they can burst if cooked too quickly. Traditional Mexican cooks simmered beans slowly and long in a clay pot (*de olla*) with onion, lard, and salt, but modern homes use a pressure cooker to save time. Black beans additionally simmer with *epazote*. Contrary to what some cooks believe, salt does not toughen beans, rather the opposite: it tenderizes them, especially in hard water. However, dry beans cooked with tomatoes will toughen beyond redemption.

SIGNATURE RECIPE

BEANS POT-COOKED THE MEXICAN WAY (FRIJOLES DE OLLA)

For every pound of beans (about 2-1/3 cups):

1 Pick through beans thoroughly for moldy beans and stones or dirt and discard. Rinse beans very well and rub to remove as much of the dust or dirt clinging to them as possible. Drain.

2 Pour beans into a heavy 4- to 6-quart saucepan and cover with 2 to 2-1/2 quarts cold water and, for more flavor and tenderness, 1 tablespoon kosher salt. Bring to a boil. (Soaking prevents beans from bursting, but does rob them of flavor—and, in the case of black beans, color.) Immediately lower heat to a simmer. Beans break if cooked on high heat, but if they'll be mashed that may not be important.

3 Optionally, stir in 2 ounces diced onion, about 1/2 cup.

4 Cover or partially cover the pot and simmer beans until tender, 2 to 3 hours depending on the age of the beans—older beans need longer cooking. Test beans by tasting one—it should feel creamy and taste full-flavored.

5 Season beans with salt if necessary, and simmer until completely soft, 15 minutes. Add 2 large sprigs epazote to black beans, and simmer 5 to 10 minutes. Remove and discard epazote. Beans will keep refrigerated up to 5 to 7 days. Reserve broth.

   In the Yucatan, cooks prepare beans (*frijol colado*) with three traditional textures according to use: *aguado* (watery), *espeso* (thick), and *seco* (dry). The cooking time and the amount of cooking liquid, water, or chicken stock added to beans when they are puréed and strained determines their texture.

   • *Aguado* is served in a small bowl as an accompaniment to a meal, and eaten either as soup or drizzled onto meats or tacos.

   • *Espeso* is used for fillings and toppings for tostadas or *panuchos* (puffed, stuffed tortillas).

   • *Seco* is used for the Yucatecan version of refried beans, as an accompaniment to a meal.

SAUTÉ, PAN-FRY, AND DEEP-FRY

MEXICAN SPICED MEAT (PICADILLO DULCE)

Use this as a filling for roasted poblano chilies, tacos, tamales, or enchiladas. Picadillo can be made simply with ground meat, almonds, raisins, and Mexican cinnamon. A variation of this Spanish favorite can also be found in the Caribbean.

Yields 4 to 4-1/2 cups

1/2 cup sherry
3 ounces golden raisins, 1/2 cup packed
3 ounces long green chilies like Anaheim or Poblano
　or 4-ounce can peeled whole green chilies, drained and finely diced
2 teaspoons cumin seed or 2 teaspoons ground cumin
1-1/2 pounds coarsely ground pork shoulder (chili-grind)
　or 1-1/2 pounds coarsely ground beef from round or shoulder
Optional: 2 to 3 tablespoons olive oil
4 to 6 ounces onion, 1 to 1-1/4 cups peeled and finely diced
3 ounces small pimento-stuffed olives, 1/2 cup thinly sliced
3/4 ounce garlic, 3 large cloves, 1-1/2 tablespoons peeled and minced
1-1/2 teaspoons ground Mexican canela
　or 1 teaspoon ground cinnamon
1/4 teaspoon ground clove
1/4 teaspoon ground allspice

1　In a 2-quart nonreactive saucepan, bring sherry and raisins to a boil. Remove from heat and rest 20 minutes.

2　Roast fresh chilies (if using) on gas burner or under broiler until evenly charred. Place in stainless steel bowl and cover. Rest 10 minutes. Remove peels, stems, ribs, and *all* seeds from chilies and discard. Dice chilies finely and set aside.

3　Toast whole cumin seeds or ground cumin in small skillet until fragrant. Ground cumin burns quickly so pay attention. Transfer to small bowl, and set aside.

4　Heat a deep, heavy 12-inch skillet or a heavy 6-quart Dutch oven over medium heat. Stir in meat (and oil if meat is very lean) and 1 teaspoon kosher salt. Cook meat until browned, 7 to 10 minutes. If necessary, pour off all but about 1 tablespoon fat.

5　Stir in raisins and sherry, chilies, cumin seed, onion, olives, garlic, canela or cinnamon, clove, and allspice. Lower the heat, cover cooking vessel partially, and simmer mixture, stirring occasionally, until onions are very tender, 15 to 20 minutes. Taste and adjust seasonings with salt and ground black pepper.

Source: Mexican chef Zarela Martinez.

Vary! Improvise!

☞ *Prepare picadillo with ground dark turkey or chicken instead of pork or beef.*

☞ **Vegetarian:** *Substitute 4 cups cooked, lightly mashed chickpeas for the meat. Sauté the onions, garlic, and spices together in oil until soft, and add the remaining ingredients. Simmer.*

☞ *Omit olives and substitute 1/2 cup slivered, toasted almonds.*

☞ *Omit chilies and double the olives.*

STACKED: TOSTADA

The tostada is a crisp-fried tortilla "plate" topped with a feast of fun flavors and textures. The tortilla should be tender enough to bite into without it disintegrating. One topping shouldn't dominate and the flavors and textures should balance: beans, avocado, and cheese or sour cream for creaminess; meat or fish for savoriness; pickled raw onion, diced tomato, finely sliced romaine or cabbage, sliced or diced radish, and cilantro for crunch; and salsa and pickled jalapeños for heat.

FIGURE 13.40 Carnitas tostada.
Source: JJAVA/Fotolia.

BATTER-FRIED STUFFED POBLANO CHILIES (CHILIES RELLENOS)

Take care not to tear chilies. Prepare and stuff chilies one day in advance and refrigerate, or freeze tightly wrapped up to 1 week. Coating batter has the proportions per two 3-ounce chilies, stuffed: 1 large egg, pinch of salt, and 1 teaspoon all-purpose flour.

6 servings

Mexican Light Tomato Sauce
Six 4- to 5-inch long whole poblano chilies with stems, about 3 ounces each

Stuffing

12 ounces quesillo de Oaxaca, mozzarella *or* Monterey Jack cheese, 2 cups shredded *or* half recipe (2 cups) *Spiced Ground Meat (Picadillo Dulce)*
Optional: 1/2 to 1 cup chicken stock or water for thinning tomato sauce

Coating Batter

3 large chilled eggs, separated
About 2-1/2 ounces unbleached white flour, 1/2 cup
Oil for frying

1 Prepare *Mexican Light Tomato Sauce*. Set aside in saucepan.

2 Wash and dry whole poblanos. Roast chilies over gas flame or under broiler, turning 3 or 4 times, so skin blisters and blackens evenly—but not so much to create white ash. Chilies should be tender. Alternatively, shallow-fry whole chilies in very hot but not smoking lard or oil until dull green and blistered, 1 to 2 minutes per side. Reserve lard or oil for frying stuffed chilies later.

3 Place chilies in a bowl and cover to steam and cool. Remove and discard skin. Make a slit down the length of each chili, but leave the top "shoulders" of the chilies intact. Taking care not to tear chilies, snip veins and remove seeds and veins; discard. Rinse chilies, drain, and pat dry.

4 **Stuff chilies:** Press together 2 ounces (1/3 cup) grated cheese into six "footballs." Insert one into each chili and set aside. *Or* fill each chili with about 1/3 cup picadillo meat stuffing. Slightly overlap sides of chili and pin together with 2 toothpicks. Lightly flatten chilies. (Place meat chilies into freezer 1/2 to 1 hour to firm or even freeze them. Fully frozen chilies will need to be baked slightly longer.)

5 **Just before frying chilies prepare coating batter:** Beat egg whites and 1/4 teaspoon kosher salt to stiff peak in mixer or by hand. Beat yolks into whites then beat in 1 tablespoon flour. Place remaining flour onto plate or into half hotel pan.

6 **Shallow-fry chilies:** Over medium to medium-high heat in a deep 12-inch skillet, bring 3 to 4 inches of oil to 350 degrees F. Preheat oven to 400 degrees F. *When oil is ready:* Roll each stuffed chili in flour, pat lightly to remove excess, and dip into egg mixture to coat evenly. Immediately fry each chili on first side until golden, about 1 minute. Turn and fry remaining side until golden. Chili batter should puff. Transfer chilies to paper towel-covered sheet pan to drain. Remove toothpicks. Chilies may rest up to 20 minutes.

7 **Fifteen minutes before serving:** Place chilies on parchment-covered sheet pan and into oven to heat through and crisp, 15 minutes. (Slightly longer for fully frozen chilies.) Bring tomato sauce to a simmer. Thin with stock or water if necessary to maintain a purée that will coat a spoon.

8 **To Serve:** Ladle or spoon 1/2 cup hot tomato sauce onto each of 6 flat soup plates. Arrange 1 chili on top of each and serve.

Rice (Arroz)

Mexicans consider rice as *sopa seca* or dry soup, so most Mexican cooks think of them together. Sopa secas are generally served after sopas (soups). Rice made its way to Mexico with the Spanish, who got it from the Arabs who ruled northern Spain for a time. In Mexico rice might be cooked with chicken broth, spiked with lime juice, flavored with sautéed aromatic vegetables, tomato, roasted chili or achiote paste, corn, and cheese or a purée of greens and herbs.

Signature Technique: Mexican Fried Rice

1 Wash rice and drain 15 minutes. This allows it to absorb some water before cooking and aids in proper plumping. If rice has added vitamins, refrain from rinsing.

2 Purée aromatic seasoning vegetables and greens like onion, tomato, cilantro, garlic, green onion, or spinach.

3 **Brown the rice:** Mexicans learned from the Spanish to fry medium- and long-grained rice before adding liquid. Frying rice until its outer layer hardens and turns opaque, pale gold, or brown serves to keep rice from clumping and sticking. Browning rice in fat additionally adds flavor crucial to certain rice pilafs.

4 Pour in liquid ingredients plus stock or water. As with most rice, 1 cup dry rice will need 2 cups liquid, and 2 cups or more dry rice will need 1-1/2 cups liquid per cup rice to cook properly. Bring rice to a boil. Lower heat, cover pan, and simmer rice until done: white rice 12 to 15 minutes; brown rice 30 to 45 minutes. Rest rice 10 minutes before serving.

MEXICAN RED RICE (ARROZ A LA MEXICANA)

This version of Mexican rice is from Central Mexico. Garnish it with cilantro, peas, or parsley. For a redder version, substitute 1-3/4 cups tomato purée for fresh tomatoes.

Yields about 6 cups, 4 to 6 servings

14 ounces long-grain white rice, 2 cups
8 to 9 ounces white onion, 2 cups peeled and diced
1/2 to 3/4 ounce garlic, 2 to 3 large cloves, crushed and peeled
2 cups chicken stock *or* water, *divided*
12 ounces summer-ripe tomatoes, about 1-3/4 cups cored and chopped
1 tablespoon tomato paste
4 tablespoons vegetable *or* olive oil

1 Pour rice into strainer and rinse with cold water. Shake dry and rest rice in strainer 15 minutes.

2 Pour onions and garlic into blender and purée until smooth. Add 1 cup stock or water to aid blending. Pour purée into a small bowl, and set aside.

3 Drop tomatoes into blender with tomato paste and purée until smooth to yield about 1-3/4 cup tomato purée.

4 Heat oil over medium heat in 4-quart saucepan. Add rice and cook, stirring occasionally, until golden and popcorn-fragrant, 8 to 10 minutes. Remove pan from heat and stir in onion mixture—it will spit, so be careful. Cook until liquid is absorbed, about 3 to 5 minutes. Pour in tomato, remaining stock or water, and 2 teaspoons kosher salt. Bring to a boil. Lower heat and cover pan. Simmer until rice is tender and liquid is absorbed, 15 minutes. Rest rice without disturbing 10 minutes.

5 **To Serve:** Remove lid, fluff rice, and season with salt and pepper, to taste. Transfer rice to serving bowl, and pile it high.

MEXICAN GREEN RICE (ARROZ VERDE)

Cooks from various regions of Mexico use other green ingredients such as spinach, fresh basil, chives, green onions, celery, green bell peppers, green peas, or jalapeño chilies.

Yields about 6 cups, 4 to 6 servings

14 ounces long-grain white rice, 2 cups
1 ounce trimmed Italian parsley, about 1 cup
1 ounce cilantro, about 1 cup packed
3 ounces romaine lettuce, about 3 large leaves, torn
3 ounces fresh poblano chili, about 1 large, 1/2 cup stemmed, seeded, and diced
   or 4 ounces canned diced green chili, about 1/2 cup
2 to 3 ounces white onion, 1/2 cup peeled and medium diced
1/4 ounce garlic, 1 large clove, 1-1/2 teaspoons peeled and chopped
3 cups chicken stock, *divided*
3 tablespoons vegetable *or* olive oil

1 Pour rice into strainer and rinse with cold water. Shake dry and rest rice in strainer 15 minutes.

2 Pour parsley, cilantro, romaine, chili, onion, and garlic into food processor or blender and purée until smooth. Add 1/4 cup chicken stock or water to aid puréeing.

3 Heat oil over high heat in heavy 4-quart saucepan and stir in rice. Cook, stirring occasionally until rice turns pale gold and smells like popcorn, 5 to 7 minutes.

4 Fold puréed ingredients into rice and fry, stirring bottom of pan constantly, until mixture is almost dry. Fold in remaining stock and 1 teaspoon kosher salt. Reduce heat to medium. Cook rice until stock is absorbed and craters form in rice, 7 to 8 minutes. Cover pan and simmer rice 7 to 8 minutes. Remove pan from heat and set aside 10 minutes undisturbed, with lid slightly ajar.

5 **To Serve:** Fluff rice and taste. Season with salt and pepper as necessary. Serve hot.

Vary! Improvise!

☞ *Devise green rice with local or available ingredients.*

☞ *Intensify: Double the amounts of parsley, cilantro, lettuce, and chili.*

☞ *Emerald Green: Substitute 4 ounces baby spinach for romaine and delete the chili. Cook rice separately from greens, onion, and garlic. To preserve the vivid color, fold puréed vegetables into hot rice just before serving.*

WELL-FRIED PINTO BEANS (FRIJOLES REFRITOS)

Yields about 7 to 8 cups, 6 to 8 servings

1 pound dried pinto beans, about 2-1/2 cups
4 tablespoons fresh pork lard *or* olive oil *or* a mixture
8 to 9 ounces white onion, 2 cups peeled and finely diced
Optional: 1/2 ounce garlic, 2 large cloves, 1 tablespoon peeled and minced

For Serving

Cooked, hot rice and warm tortillas

1 Cook beans as directed in *Signature Recipe: Beans Pot-Cooked the Mexican Way*. Drain beans and reserve cooking broth.

2 In a heavy 12-inch skillet or 6-quart Dutch oven over medium heat, add lard or oil. When hot, stir in onion and cook until soft or soft and golden, 5 to 7 minutes. Stir in optional garlic and cook 1 minute. Stir half the beans into onions, and mash them with 2 cups bean cooking broth. Add remaining beans and mash to a coarse purée the consistency of chunky mashed potatoes. Season beans with salt. When beans sizzle around the edges and begin to dry, remove from heat. Thin beans with additional broth, as necessary.

3 **To Serve:** Pile beans into serving dish and serve hot with rice and tortillas.

Source: *The Essential Cuisines of Mexico* by Diana Kennedy.

"DIRTY" BLACK BEANS FROM THE YUCATAN (FRIJOLES A LA HUACHA)

It's traditional to add a few sliced mint leaves to these beans before serving. In the southern state of Veracruz, well-fried black beans are seasoned with toasted, crumbled Mexican avocado leaves.

Yields 7 to 8 cups, 6 to 8 servings

1 pound black turtle beans, about 2-1/2 cups
1/4 cup pork lard or oil
4 to 5 ounces white onion, 1 cup peeled and finely diced
1 ounce jalapeño chili, about 1 large, 2 tablespoons stemmed, seeded, and finely diced

For Serving

Cooked, hot rice and warm tortillas

1 Cook beans as directed in *Signature Recipe: Beans Pot-Cooked the Mexican Way*. Drain beans, and reserve cooking broth. Mash beans by hand in bowl or purée in batches in blender until smooth, adding a total of 1-1/2 to 2 cups cooking broth as necessary. Pour bean purée into bowl and set aside.

2 In a deep, heavy 12-inch skillet over medium heat, add lard or oil. When hot, stir in onion and chili, and cook until soft, 5 to 7 minutes. Pour in mashed beans or bean purée, and lower heat. Simmer beans until thickened, 5 to 10 minutes. Season beans with salt, to taste. Adjust consistency from thick to very loose, as desired, by either cooking longer or adding more bean broth.

3 **To Serve:** Ladle beans onto plates. Serve with rice and tortillas.

Source: *The Essential Cuisines of Mexico* by Diana Kennedy.

WELL-FRIED (NOT RE-FRIED)

Chef, author and restaurateur Rick Bayless emphasizes that *frijoles refritos* does not translate from Spanish to beans fried *again*. Rather, it translates as coarse or smooth beans "well-fried or intensely-fried."

Vary! Improvise!

☞ *Leave half the beans whole.*

☞ ***Smooth Yucatan Beans:*** *After puréeing beans, push through a strainer to remove skin.*

☞ *Season beans at the end with 1/2 ounce finely sliced cilantro, about 1/4 cup.*

GRILL, GRIDDLE, ROAST, BROIL, BAKE, AND BARBECUE

Mexicans are intensely fond of grilling meat over mesquite and hardwood coals. The signature *carne asada*, meat marinated and slow-grilled over a bed of coals, spit-roasted, or plunged on spits into mesquite and oak charcoal fire pits, can be found throughout the country. Roadside vendors grill *cebollitas* (green onions with large, knobby bulbs) and marinated chicken. Whole restaurants are devoted to grilled steaks or spit-roasted lamb, quail, chicken, chorizo, and ribs. Thin slices of pork leg are smeared with red chili adobo and grilled and served in tortillas with shredded cabbage, salsa, and grilled or pickled red onions. Sides of cactus salad, guacamole, *frijoles de la olla*, and fresh radishes accompany them. Along the southern coasts, spice-rubbed fish are wrapped in fresh banana leaves and grilled.

For a rich Mexican flavor, marinate fish, beef, chicken, poultry, goat, or lamb in lime juice or a *recado* (spicy dry rubs or pastes). Grill whole or sliced ripe plantains and marinated protein, and serve with tortillas and salsas.

GRILLED STEAK AND POBLANO CHILI TACOS (CARNE ASADA CON RAJAS)

6 to 8 servings

2 pounds flank steak, trimmed of silverskin
2 pounds white onions, about 4 large, sliced into 1/2-inch thick rounds, kept intact
1 ounce garlic, about 4 large cloves, crushed and peeled
6 tablespoons fresh lime juice, about 1-1/2 large limes
1/2 teaspoon ground cumin
18 ounces poblano chilies, 6 medium
Oil as needed

For Serving

24 or more corn tortillas, warmed
2 limes, wedged

1 **Marinate meat:** Make shallow cross cuts into flank steak and place in stainless hotel pan. Transfer approximately 6 ounces onions, the garlic, lime juice, cumin, and 1 teaspoon kosher salt to a food processor or blender. Process until smooth. Smear marinade over both sides of meat. Marinate at room temperature 1 hour or in refrigerator up to 8 hours.

2 **Heat a charcoal or gas grill:** When the coals are covered with ash and glowing, place a cooking grate on grill, cover and preheat it 5 minutes. Lay chilies onto grate and grill, turning, until evenly blackened and blistered, 5 minutes. (Don't over-char chilies to a white ash.) Transfer chilies to a metal bowl and cover. With a paper towel, wipe off blackened skin from chilies. Remove stem, seeds, and membranes. Slice chilies into 1/4-inch-wide strips to yield about 1-1/2 cups grilled, peeled, seeded, and sliced chilies. (Alternatively, blacken chilies over gas flame ahead of time.)

3 Brush onion slices with oil and place on grill. When the first side browns and softens, flip with a spatula and grill second side until onion is very tender and browned, 15 to 20 minutes total. Transfer onions to bowl with chilies, season with salt, and keep warm.

4 Lightly scrape away excess marinade and place meat on grill. Cook meat, flipping to brown both sides, to medium or medium rare, 2 to 5 minutes per side, depending on thickness. Rest meat in warm spot, covered, 10 to 15 minutes. Slice steak in half with the grain, then very thinly across the grain for 3 to 4-inch long slices. Mix meat with chilies and onions, or place in separate bowls.

5 **To Serve:** Set warm tortillas, meat, and vegetables and limes out in serving vessels. Instruct guests to construct tacos by filling tortillas with meat, onions, and chili rajas. Squeeze lime over top.

Source: *Mexico One Plate at a Time* by Rick Bayless.

Vary! Improvise!

☞ *Substitute orange juice for lime and spike the marinade with a little ground chili.*

☞ *Use another cut of beef.*

BARBACOA: THE ROOTS OF TEXAS BARBECUE

Although some refer to *barbacoa* as Mexican barbecue, traditionally it is a form of pit steaming and smoking. The pit master places a cauldron of hot water into a 3-foot-deep pit on top of hot coals. A grill with the meat on it goes on top of the cauldron. Vegetables, beans, and spices are sometimes added to the pot for a soup. The pit is sealed and covered with damp earth and the meat slow cooks—sometimes for days depending on its size. Traditionally a cow's head or whole goat, lamb, or pig is wrapped in maguey cactus leaves, cooked barbacoa-style, and served at village festivals and weddings. It's accompanied by various sauces, guacamole, and lime wedges. Nowadays *barbacoa* also refers to meltingly tender, slow-cooked, highly seasoned meat.

ACHIOTE-MARINATED GRILLED FISH (PESCADO DE ACHIOTE)

This makes a good filling for fish tacos.

4 servings

3 tablespoons *Achiote Paste*
1/2 ounce garlic, 2 large cloves, 1 tablespoon peeled and minced
1-1/2 pounds fish fillet like yellow tail, sea bass, or halibut

1 In a large nonreactive bowl, combine achiote paste, garlic, and 1/2 teaspoon kosher salt. Rub fish fillets with paste. Place in stainless hotel pan, cover, and refrigerate fish 30 minutes to 1 hour.

2 Preheat a grill or cast-iron griddle, or heat a 12-inch skillet with olive oil over medium-high heat. Scrape excess achiote paste from fish. Place fish on grill or sauté until fish is cooked through, 4 to 7 minutes per side. Serve fish hot or rest fish before slicing for tacos.

Signature Technique: Mexican Grilled Cheese (Quesadilla)

The quesadilla is probably the most elemental way to get the taste of Mexico. At its simplest, a quesadilla is a tortilla folded in half over shredded cheese and cooked on a griddle until the cheese melts and the tortilla crisps. Like a grilled cheese sandwich, its texture is hypnotic. Mexico has a world of quesadillas: in Oaxaca they are made from fresh masa and look like a calzone.

- Cheese is a constant in precooked tortillas but not necessary in ones formed with fresh, raw masa.

- Sautéed mushrooms, chilies, epazote, squash blossoms, shredded meat or chorizo, and fried potatoes may grace quesadillas.

- Northern Mexican cooks prepare quesadillas with flour tortillas and leftover pork from *tacos al pastor*. In the south, corn tortillas or fresh masa turnovers prevail.

- For 16 six-inch quesadillas, prepare about 12 ounces or 3 cups shredded cheese.

FIGURE 13.41 Quesadilla.
Source: Lilyana Vynogradova/Fotolia.

FRESH MASA TURNOVERS WITH CHICKPEAS (QUESADILLAS DE MAÍZ CON GARBANZOS)

Fresh quesadillas are also filled with a mixture of cooked chilies, green onions, and squash blossoms and served with crema Mexicana.

Yields about 10 large quesadillas

Garbanzo Filling

Yields about 2-1/2 cups

7 ounces dry chickpeas, 1 cup
   or 2-1/2 cups canned cooked chickpeas
1 tablespoon olive or vegetable oil
1/4 ounce garlic, 1 large clove, 1-1/2 teaspoons peeled and minced
1 ounce jalapeño chili, 1 medium, 2 tablespoons stemmed, seeded, and finely diced
1 ounce trimmed green onion, 2 large, 1/4 cup chopped
1/4 ounce cilantro, 1/2 cup loosely packed
1 to 2 tablespoons fresh lime juice, 1/2 lime, to taste

2-1/2 to 5 ounces Monterey Jack cheese, 10 to 20 tablespoons shredded

Dough

Yields 20 to 21 ounces, about 2-1/4 cups

2 cups dry masa harina
1 ounce lard *or* shortening, 2 tablespoons

For Serving

Salsa of choice

1 **Cook the chickpeas:** Wash and drain dry chickpeas. Cover with 2 quarts cold water and 2 teaspoons kosher salt. Bring chickpeas to a boil, reduce heat, and simmer until tender, 2 hours. Cool chickpeas, and drain off cooking liquid to yield about 2-3/4 cups cooked, slightly more than needed.

2 **Prepare the filling:** Place 2-1/2 cups drained chickpeas, oil, garlic, chili, onion, cilantro, and lime juice into food processor. Pulse-purée mixture until chunky smooth. Season with salt and pepper. Add more lime juice, to taste.

3 **Prepare the dough:** Pour masa harina and 1/2 teaspoon kosher salt into mixing bowl. Cut the lard or shortening into flour with fingers, fork, or pastry cutter. For large batches, place flour, salt, and lard or shortening into food processor and pulse until well mixed. Transfer mixture from food processor into bowl.

4 Slowly pour 1-1/2 cups water into dough. It should come together into a soft ball. When a small ball of the dough is pressed it should not crack around the edges. Sprinkle in up to 1/4 cup more warm water if necessary. Knead dough until smooth, 1 minute. Wrap dough in plastic, and set aside 20 minutes. Line a half sheet pan with parchment paper.

5 **Press:** Divide dough into ten 2-ounce balls. Split a plastic freezer baggie into two. Place one plastic sheet onto tortilla press. Place one ball of dough on it and cover with plastic second sheet. Press dough ball to 6-inch diameter, about 1/8-inch thick. Carefully peel off top plastic sheet.

6 **Fill:** While holding the plastic sheet with the flattened dough in one hand, crumble and lightly spread 3 tablespoons filling in the center of the round. *Optionally*, top filling with 1 to 2 tablespoons cheese. With the plastic to aid and support, fold dough in half to create a half moon pastry and press to seal the edge. Carefully peel quesadilla off the plastic and set onto parchment-covered sheet pan. Seal the edges again, neatly, with fork or fingers. To keep quesadilla from drying, cover with plastic wrap. Finish making remaining quesadillas.

Vary! Improvise!

☛ *Substitute 1/2 cup (or more) finely sliced leeks for green onions.*

7 **Cook:** Heat a cast-iron griddle or comal over medium-low heat. Rub hot griddle or comal with oil. Place 2 quesadillas onto it and cover with domed lid. Cook until brown-speckled on one side, 4 to 5 minutes. Turn and cook on second side until brown-speckled, 4 to 5 minutes.

8 **To Serve:** Slice quesadillas in half and place on serving platter with salsa of choice.

Source: *Text © 2005 Daniel Hoyer. Reprint permission* by Gibbs Smith.

TORTILLA CASSEROLE COMFORT FOOD: CHILAQUILES

Chilaquiles likely arose from women who had only some chilies, tomatoes or tomatillos, and some day-old tortillas with which to make dinner. *Chilaquiles*, which means chilies and greens in Nahuatl, is hearty, rib-sticking food like southern Italy's dry pasta with tomatoes. This is the food a mother would make. Start with sautéed onion and garlic simmered in red tomato-purée-and-chili-infused chicken broth or a tomatillo-infused broth. (Add some greens like Swiss chard, and simmer until tender.) Fry cut-up leftover corn tortillas until crisp. Toss them into the broth for a very short simmer. The chips should be softened, but slightly al dente. Spoon sizzling chilaquiles into soup plates and garnish with cilantro, onion, and cheese or Mexican *crema*.

FIGURE 13.42   Chilaquiles.
Source: Irafael/Shutterstock.

Tortillas

In central and southern Mexico the best (not necessarily the biggest) restaurants and taquerias daily prepare tender, aromatic corn tortillas from fresh masa dough. Mexican cooks find hundreds of uses for fresh and day-old tortillas from *quesadillas*, *enchiladas*, and *memelas* to *chilaquiles* and for thickening sauces. In northern Mexico, where wheat flourishes and corn does not, cooks prepare flour tortillas.

Signature Technique: Tortilla-Making

- Heat two griddles, one over medium-low and the second over medium-high heat.

- Roll a piece of masa or flour dough slightly larger than a walnut but smaller than a golf ball, about 1-1/2 ounces, into a smooth ball. Corn tortillas are usually 5 to 6 inches in diameter; flour tortillas are larger.

- Cut a quart size freezer zipper baggie into two large squares. Place one square onto tortilla press, place masa ball slightly higher than center (toward hinge), and cover with the second square of plastic.

- Close the tortilla press and gently press—don't use excessive force. Open the press, turn the tortilla 180 degrees (half the way round), and close the press gently again.

- Remove top piece of plastic and place tortilla face down in one hand with half draping over the baby finger edge of the hand. Peel away remaining sheet of plastic.

- Gently lower bottom half of tortilla and drape onto cooler preheated comal or cast-iron skillet and roll the hand away from under the tortilla.

- Cook tortilla until it releases and is a bit dry around the edges, about 20 seconds, depending on thickness of tortilla. Flip tortilla and cook on second side onto hotter griddle; tortilla should puff slightly and become slightly brown speckled, 30 to 45 seconds. Turn once and cook on remaining side until brown speckled. Like an Indian chapatti-phulka, if a tortilla doesn't puff, it was either cooked too long on the first side or not baked hot enough during the second cooking.

- Remove tortillas as they cook, stack on top of each other, cover with cloth, and keep warm. They will steam and soften, so don't skip this step. (Place tortillas, still wrapped in cotton towel, in an empty ice chest or Styrofoam container to stay warm.)

FIGURE 13.43   Shaping tortillas from fresh masa dough.
Source: Alvaro German Vilela/Fotolia.

FIGURE 13.44 Traditional way to cook tortillas.
Source: karamysh/Shutterstock.

FRESH CORN TORTILLAS (TORTILLAS DE MAÍZ)

Masa harina (treated corn flour) is not the same as fine-ground corn meal. Maseca brand masa harina is a favorite. Store masa flour in a cool, dry place in airtight container and it will last 6 to 9 months.

Yields 32 ounces, about twenty-one 6-inch tortillas

15 ounces masa harina flour for tortillas, 3 cups
2-3/4 to 3 cups baby-bath warm water

1 Pour flour into a bowl. Stir in water, a little at a time, until dough is moist and pliable, like cookie dough. Softer dough yields tender tortillas, but the dough should not be too sticky. Knead dough until smooth and soft. When pressed, a dough ball should not crack around the edges. If it does, knead in a little more warm water.

2 Place dough in a bowl, cover with plastic wrap and rest 5 minutes. Divide dough into 1-1/2-ounce balls for 6-inch tortillas. Roll balls smooth and keep covered. Press masa balls in tortilla press and cook as directed in *Tips for Signature Technique: Tortilla-Making.*

FLOUR TORTILLAS

Yields 14 ounces dough, 9 six-inch tortillas

9 ounces all-purpose flour, 2 cups
Optional: 1 teaspoon baking powder
1 teaspoon kosher or sea salt
2 ounces fresh lard or shortening, 1/4 cup
1/2 cup hot tap water

1 Stir together flour, optional baking powder, and salt in a bowl or food processor. Pulse or cut in lard or oil with a pastry cutter, a fork, or fingers until mixture is evenly mixed and crumbly.

2 If using food processor, transfer mixture into mixing bowl. Slowly pour in hot water. Stir after each addition and pay attention to the texture of the dough as it forms; it should be moist but not wet. Lightly knead dough 30 to 45 seconds, until smooth and elastic. Cover dough with plastic wrap, and set aside to 45 minutes.

3 Roll dough into 1-1/2-ounce balls. Cover with a towel. While dough balls rest, heat a comal or cast-iron skillet over medium-high heat. Follow *Tips for Signature Technique: Tortilla-Making.* In a plastic-freezer-bag-lined tortilla press, press each ball of dough as thin as possible. While still between the two plastic sheets, remove tortilla from press and roll out to a 7-inch diameter. Peel tortilla off plastic sheet. Stretch tortilla lightly.

4 Place tortilla onto hot griddle and cook on each side until is dotted with brown spots, puffy, but still soft, about 40 seconds per side. Tortilla will shrink to 6-inches after cooking. (Tortillas made with 2 ounces dough will roll out to 8-inches and shrink to 7-inches after cooking.)

5 Wrap tortillas in a dampened towel and keep warm in low oven until ready to serve.

Vary! Improvise!

☛ Substitute 1/2 to 1 cup fine whole wheat flour for 1/2- to 1 cup all-purpose.
☛ Substitute 1/4-cup duck fat or 1/4 cup olive oil for lard.

RED SNAPPER VERACRUZ-STYLE (HUACHINANGO A LA VERACRUZANA)

This dish is one of Mexico's most beloved fish dishes. All Mexican cooks have a variation—some simply garnish it with a warmed raw salsa with olives and capers. Veracruz, a major Mexican port city, is in the southeast and lies on the Gulf of Mexico.

Yields 4 cups sauce, 4 servings

3 pounds red snapper with head and tail, cleaned and gutted
   or 1-1/2 pounds red snapper fillets, 4 six-ounce fillets
2 tablespoons freshly squeezed lime juice, about 1/2 large lime
2 pounds firm, ripe tomatoes, about 4 medium-large
5 tablespoons olive oil, *divided*
4 to 5 ounces onion, 1 cup peeled, halved, and thinly sliced or slivered
1/2 ounce garlic, 2 large cloves, 1 tablespoon peeled and minced
2 Mexican bay leaves *or* fragrant bay leaves
1 teaspoon dried Mexican oregano *or* dried oregano
4 ounces pitted big green olives, 1 cup halved lengthwise
2 tablespoons drained large capers
2 ounces pickled sliced jalapeños, 4 tablespoons
1/2 ounce trimmed Italian parsley, 4 tablespoons chopped

To Serve: Cooked long-grain white rice

Garnish: Italian parsley leaves

1 Rinse fish, pat dry, and place into a lightly oiled ovenproof vessel without much excess room around the fish. With a fork, pierce fish flesh all over. Rub fish with lime juice and 1 teaspoon kosher salt inside and out. If using fillets, marinate fish only 5 to 10 minutes before cooking. Refrigerate whole fish 30 minutes to 1 hour while preparing remaining ingredients.

2 Over a gas flame, on a grill, or under a broiler, roast tomatoes just until blistered. Remove skin and halve tomatoes. Press seeds and juices from tomato through strainer, and reserve. Dice flesh into 3/8-inch cubes to yield about 4 cups.

3 Heat 4 tablespoons oil in 12-inch skillet over medium to medium-low heat. Stir in onions, garlic, and 1 teaspoon kosher salt, and cook until soft but not brown, 5 minutes. Stir in bay leaves, oregano, tomatoes and strained juices, olives, capers, and jalapeños. Raise heat to medium-high and cook sauce until slightly reduced, about 10 minutes.

4 **To finish dish:** Remove fish from refrigerator. Preheat oven to 350 degrees F. Pour sauce over fish. Drizzle with remaining 1 tablespoon olive oil. Cover fish with a piece of parchment. Place fish in oven and bake whole fish 20 minutes, then turn and baste with sauce. Bake whole fish until it flakes when probed with tip of a knife, about 20 minutes longer. Bake fillets until fish flakes when probed with a fork at its thickest part, 12 to 15 minutes, longer depending on thickness. Taste sauce and season with salt as necessary. Stir in chopped parsley.

5 **To Serve:** Platter whole fish and spoon sauce over top. For fillets: Mound cooked rice onto 4 plates. Place 1 portion of fish on top. Spoon sauce over fish. Garnish fish with parsley leaves if desired. Serve warm.

Source: *The Essential Cuisines of Mexico* by Diana Kennedy.

Vary! Improvise!

☛ **Restaurant Service:** *Prepare sauce ahead. Brush lime-marinated fish fillet with olive oil and sprinkle with salt. Roast, sauté, or grill fish and plate. Spoon warmed sauce over fish.*

SALAD AND VEGETABLE METHODS

Salads are a modern addition to the Mexican kitchen. Northern tourists, hotels, and resorts have brought them into mainstream Mexico along with olive oil and vinegars, but most people take their lettuce as topping on tostadas, tacos, and other dishes. Cooked vegetables, raw vegetables, or fruit are simply dressed with lime or vinegar, oil, salt, chili, and cilantro. Street vendors sell cubes of lime, chili and salt-dusted mango, jicama, cucumber, and other seasonal fruits and vegetables. Vegetables as a side dish are not a large part of public cuisine, but Mexican homecooks often prepare whole meals with vegetable dishes seasoned with small bits of meat.

FIGURE 13.45 Jicama.
Source: Bert Folsom/Fotolia.

Vary! Improvise!

☞ **No Jicama:** Substitute peeled and cubed turnips or lightly steamed daikon radish.

☞ **Salsa-Salad:** Peel and finely dice jicama, tomatoes, cucumbers, cantaloupe, watermelon, or papaya and toss with diced chilies or red chili powder, salt, lime juice, and cilantro.

SPICY JÍCAMA SALAD (ENSALADA DE JÍCAMA)

Jicama looks like a round, smooth raw potato and is good raw. Its flavor is part apple, potato, and raw water chestnut. Like many root vegetables, jicama is harvested in the fall. This simple salad is at once refreshing and quintessentially Mexican. It can be a vibrant part of any meal, mixing as it does the dynamic hit of lime, chili, and salt to awaken the comforting sweetness of fruit and vegetable.

Yields about 3 cups, about 4 to 6 servings

1 pound jicama, 1 small, about 3 cups peeled and diced into 1/2-inch cubes
4 tablespoons fresh lime juice, about 1 large lime
12 ounces navel orange *or* tangerines, 1 large orange *or* 3 tangerines
1/2 ounce cilantro, 1/4 cup finely sliced
1/2 to 1 teaspoon powdered red chili

For Garnish: Romaine leaves

1 In large non-reactive bowl, toss jicama with lime juice and 1/2 teaspoon kosher salt. Cover and marinate 30 minutes to 1 hour at room temperature. (Jicama may be chilled.)

2 Peel orange or tangerines. Slice orange cross-wise 1/2-inch thick and break sections. Slice tangerines into 3 or 4 pieces and pit. Either fruit should yield about 1 cup.

3 *Fifteen minutes before serving:* Toss orange or tangerines, cilantro and chili with jicama. Taste and season with more lime juice or salt.

4 **To Serve:** *Line platter or bowl with romaine leaves and pile salad on top. Serve immediately.*

Source: *Authentic Mexican* by Rick Bayless.

EDIBLE MEXICAN CACTUS (NOPAL)

Various members of the nopal cactus family produce fleshy tender leaves or paddles that are delightfully crisp and acidic-tasting. Mexicans boil or steam/braise nopales for salads or as a side dish, slice like fingers, and grill on a comal or over charcoal and sandwich them with cheese between for a sort of nopal quesadilla or batter and deep-fry. The downside of this tasty treat is the gooey juice it exudes upon cutting and the hair-thin, or larger, thorns that dot its surface. Freshly picked nopales are firm, rigid, and around 1/4-inch thick. Older nopales, though floppy, are still edible.

FIGURE 13.46 Nopales cactus.
Source: ilumus photography/Fotolia.

MEXICAN CACTUS SALAD (ENSALADA DE NOPALES)

Nopal cactus salad, more a salsa than a salad, is often sold as street food in Mexico. It pairs well with meat, chicken, fish, and seafood dishes and serves well as a taco filling or tostada garnish. Some believe the cactus leaves help fight high cholesterol and diabetes. One pound cleaned nopales yields almost 4 cups cleaned and cut.

Yields 4 cups, 4 to 6 servings

1-1/2 pounds fresh Mexican cactus leaves
3 tablespoons vegetable oil, *divided*
1/2 ounce garlic, about 2 large cloves, 1 tablespoon peeled and minced
1 ounce white onion, 1/4 to 1/3 cup peeled and finely diced
8 ounces tomato, 1 medium large, 1-1/4 cups cored and finely diced
1/4 to 1/2 ounce cilantro, 2 to 4 tablespoons finely sliced
1 ounce jalapeño chili, about 1 large, 2 to 3 tablespoons stemmed, seeded, and finely diced
3 tablespoons fresh lime juice, 1 large lime, more to taste

Garnish

Romaine leaves

Optional: 2 ounces queso fresco, about 1/2 cup crumbled
Optional: Pickled sliced jalapeño chilies

1 **Clean the cactus:** Taking care to avoid the spines, grip a leaf by its base. Hold a very sharp knife or Y-peeler flat against the paddle and shave off the spines and bumps, but not the green skin. Carefully trim the base and shave a thin strip off the outer leaf edges with spines; discard. Rinse nopales and slice into strips 1/4-inch by 1-inch *or* dice into 1/2-inch cubes to yield 5-1/2 to 6 cups.

2 Most Mexican cooks boil nopales to rid them of the gooey juice, but boiling robs the cactus of flavor. This method comes from Diana Kennedy, who learned it from a bus driver in Mexico: Heat 2 tablespoons oil in a deep 11- to 12-inch skillet over medium heat. Stir in garlic and cook until soft, about 30 seconds. Stir in diced nopales and season with a little salt. Cover the skillet, reduce heat to low, and simmer, stirring occasionally, until nopales are almost tender, 5 minutes.

3 Remove lid from skillet and raise heat to medium or medium-low. Cook nopales until the gooey liquid has evaporated, about 5 minutes. (Cook nopales longer for use as a vegetable, then scrape into a bowl, cool, and refrigerate.) Remove pan from heat and cool slightly. Stir onion, tomato, cilantro, and chili into pan. Season with salt, lime juice, and remaining 1 tablespoon oil, to taste. Rest salad 20 to 30 minutes to develop flavors (chill if desired).

4 **To Serve:** Line platter with lettuce leaves. Pile salad onto platter and garnish with optional cheese and chilies.

BRAISED ZUCCHINI (CALABACITAS GUISADOS)

Cooks from the northern state of Sonora to the southwestern state of Michoacán prepare this beloved dish.

Yields 5 to 6 cups, 4 to 6 servings

12 ounces tomatoes, about 2 medium
3 ounces poblano chili, 1 large
   or 1 ounce serrano chilies, about 2
   or 1 ounce jalapeño chili, about 1 large
1/2 ounce garlic, 2 large cloves, 1 tablespoon peeled and minced
   or 2 ounces trimmed green onions, 4 large, about 1/2 cup sliced
1/4 cup vegetable, sunflower or olive oil
2 pounds small zucchini, about 7 cups trimmed and diced into 3/4-inch cubes
6 to 7 ounces white onion, 1-1/2 cups peeled and finely diced
10 ounces fresh or frozen corn kernels, 2 cups
Optional: 1/4 ounce cilantro, 2 tablespoons finely sliced, more to taste

1 Preheat a broiler. Core tomatoes and place core side down on broiler pan. Broil tomatoes until skin is browned and tomato is tender, turning once. Remove from oven, cool tomatoes, and chop with skin; set aside in small bowl.

2 Blacken skin of chili or chilies over gas flame or under broiler. Set aside to cool then peel away skin and discard. Remove stem and seeds. Slice poblano chili into long narrow strips to yield about 1/2 cup. Cut serranos or jalapeños into small dice to yield 3 to 4 tablespoons serrano or jalapeños. Set aside chili in bowl with tomatoes. Stir in garlic or green onions.

3 Heat oil in a deep 11- to 12-inch skillet over medium heat. Stir in zucchini, onion, and corn, and season with salt. Cook vegetables until fully tender, 7 to 10 minutes.

4 Stir in tomato, chili, and garlic (or green onion) mixture, and lower heat to a medium simmer. Cook until tomatoes reduce, about 15 minutes. Season with salt and cilantro, to taste. Serve at room temperature.

Vary! Im¡vise!

☞ *Substitute one or two fresh, green Anaheim chilies for the poblano.*

☞ *Add 1/3 cup chopped epazote leaves to the zucchini as they cook.*

☞ *Creamy: Stir in 1/2 cup crema Mexicana when the dish is finished and off the heat.*

☞ *Omit tomatoes.*

☞ *Chayote: Substitute 2 pounds chayote squash (3 to 4) for zucchini. Peel, pit (save the pit for munching), and slice.*

☞ *Substitute mint for cilantro.*

CHAYOTE SQUASH

A pear-shaped, pale green, smooth-skinned relative of squash, the chayote is known as *mirliton* in Louisiana. It is native to Mexico and many types grow wild, from a pale yellow type to a large and dark green variety with thorns. The vine and root are edible. Refrigerated, chayote will keep a month or longer. Use like any squash: bake whole, braise, fry, or stuff, in soup, stew, or sweetened for desserts. As with most squash, the seeds are edible.

FIGURE 13.47 Chayote squash.
Source: Lorenzo Vecchia/DK Images.

CORN WITH LIME JUICE AND CHILI POWDER (ESQUITES)

This dish comes from Mexico City.

Yields 7 cups, 6 servings

6 large (9 ounce) or 9 medium (7 ounce) ears corn
   or 6 cups corn kernels
3 tablespoons unsalted butter, diced
1/2 ounce serrano chili, 1 tablespoon stemmed, seeded, and finely diced
1 stalk fresh *epazote*
   or 1 teaspoon dried Mexican oregano
5 to 6 ounces queso fresco or queso blanco, 1 cup diced into 1/4-inch cubes
2 tablespoons fresh lime juice, 1/2 large lime, more to taste
1/2 teaspoon ground *piquin* chilies
   or 1/4 to 1/2 teaspoon ground cayenne pepper

1 Strip outer leaves and corn silk from corn. Rinse and drain corn. Slice kernels from ears of corn to yield 6 cups. Set aside in bowl.

2 Heat a deep 10-inch skillet or 5-quart saucepan over medium heat. Melt the butter and stir in corn, serrano, torn leaves from epazote, or dried oregano and 1 cup water. Bring to a simmer, reduce heat to medium-low, and cook, partially covered until corn is tender, about 10 minutes. Remove pan from burner and cool slightly.

3 **To Serve:** Stir cheese, lime juice, and powdered chili into corn. Taste dish and season with salt and lime juice as necessary. Serve warm.

Stuffed Chilies (Chiles Rellenos)

Relleno means stuffed. Mexican cooks are masters of stuffing, but never more so than when they stuff chilies with cheese, meat, or vegetables. The most popular stuffing chili is the mild *poblano*, which originated in Puebla, Mexico. Cooks in Veracruz favor the jalapeño and in Oaxaca, the small, hotter *chile de agua* or reconstituted *chile pasilla oaxaqueño*. The poblano's mild-flavored, dark green pod has thick walls and ranges from 4 to 6 inches long and 2 to 3 inches wide, making it ideal for stuffing. Chilies may be stuffed and closed with a toothpick, then dipped in a fluffy egg batter and fried, covered with a walnut sauce; or stuffed and dipped in flour, fried, and served with a smooth tomato sauce.

Signature Technique: Stuffing Chilies

• Choose chilies that are even and smooth without a curls and bumps. One 3-ounce, 2-1/2-inch by 6-inch poblano chili will take about 1/3 cup stuffing and yield one serving. Anaheims or other large, long chilies will also work.

• Loosen chili skin and peel by either roasting over a flame, under a broiler, or by frying in hot oil until blistered, about 2 minutes per side. It's crucial to cook the chili through until tender but not falling apart. Frying in oil achieves this perfectly—more efficiently than roasting.

• Leave stem intact and carefully make a slit in chili. Carefully remove seeds and membranes by cutting seeds and veins away from base of stem with scissors. Slide fingertips inside to remove veins and seeds. Rinse and drain chilies.

• Place stuffing into chili cavity with a spoon. Filling should be well-seasoned and moist, but not wet. Form 2 ounces, about 1/3 cup, moist grated cheese into a football shape and insert into chili.

• Overlap cut edges of chili and close with 2 toothpicks. Lightly flatten stuffed chili and place in freezer to firm slightly, about 45 minutes or refrigerate overnight. Chilies may be made in advance and frozen up to 1 week before finishing in oven *or* battering and frying. Battered chilies go best with the light tomato sauce, and plain chilies with a richer walnut sauce.

CHILIES IN WALNUT SAUCE (CHILES EN NOGADA)

Soak walnuts overnight for the best textured sauce.

6 servings

4 ounces walnuts, 1 cup broken nuts
Half recipe *Spiced Meat: Picadillo Dulce*
Six 5- to 6-inch-long whole poblano chilies with stems, about 3 ounces each

Garnish

5 to 6 ounce pomegranate, 1 medium, about 3/4 cup seeds
3 to 4 sprigs Italian parsley

Walnut Sauce

Yields about 3 cups

1/2 ounce white bread with crusts removed, about 1/4 cup packed coarse crumbs
1 cup heavy cream
1/4 cup chicken *or* vegetable stock
2 to 3 teaspoons sugar
1/4 teaspoon ground cinnamon
1 cup *crema Mexicana* (see *Glossary*)

1 Place walnuts in bowl and cover with hot tap water. Soak nuts 2 to 8 hours. Drain nuts and rub/peel away as much brown skin from walnuts as possible: less skin means a whiter sauce.

2 Prepare *Picadillo Dulce*.

3 Wash and dry whole poblanos. Roast chilies over gas flame or under broiler, turning 3 or 4 times, so skin blisters and blackens evenly—but not so much to create white ash. Chilies should be tender and cooked through. *Alternatively*, shallow-fry whole chilies in very hot but not smoking oil until dull green and blistered, 1 to 2 minutes per side.

4 Place roasted chilies in a bowl and cover to steam and cool. Or place fried chilies on paper towel-covered sheet pan to cool. Remove and discard skin. Make a 1-1/2- to 2-inch slit down the length of each chili, but leave the top "shoulders" of the chilies intact. Taking care not to tear chilies, snip and remove seeds and veins with fingers; discard. Rinse chilies, drain, and pat dry.

5 Stuff each chili with about 1/3 cup filling. Fold over edges of chili, and pin together with two toothpicks set parallel to the cut. Set aside on parchment-covered sheet pan.

6 **Clean the pomegranate:** Fill a large bowl with cold water. With a chef's knife, make 4 shallow lengthwise cuts from top to bottom of pomegranate, all the way through the skin. Immerse fruit into bowl of water and, using fingers, pry the fruit open. Carefully peel away red seeds from peel and membranes. The seeds will sink and white membranes will float. Discard skin and membranes. Drain seeds, pat dry, and reserve. Use immediately or store in an airtight container up to 3 days. Pick leaves from parsley and set aside.

7 **Purée walnut sauce:** Pour walnuts and bread into blender (for the finest grind) and grind until very fine. Pour in cream and purée until very smooth. Scrape mixture into 1-quart saucepan. Rinse blender with stock. Pour into saucepan along with sugar, cinnamon, and 1/4 teaspoon kosher salt.

8 Preheat oven to 375 degrees F. Place stuffed chilies into oven, cover, and heat through, 7 to 10 minutes. Chili flesh should be tender enough to cut with a fork. Bring sauce to a simmer, stir in crema. Taste and season sauce with salt. Sauce should coat a spoon; it will thicken as it cools.

9 **To Serve:** Line up 6 plates and place a stuffed chili on each. Ladle 1/3- to 1/2-cup sauce over each chili. Sprinkle with pomegranate seeds and parsley. Serve immediately.

WATERY REFRESHERS (AGUA FRESCA OR AGUAS DE FRUTA)

Mexicans are passionate about fresh fruit drinks. Called *aguas frescas*, they refresh the palate. Melon, guava, mango, papaya, passion fruit, pineapple, strawberry, cucumber, prickly pear (*tuna*), tamarind, hibiscus flower, and chia seeds are a few favorites. Fruit, water, and sweetener are essential; lime or other citrus optional. Cucumbers make an especially refreshing agua fresca on a hot day: purée cucumbers with a little water, pour it into pitcher, and add ice cubes. Season with lime juice and a little sugar, to taste.

FIGURE 13.48 Agua fresca made with cantaloupe and carbonated water.
Source: msheldrake/Shutterstock.

PICKLING

MEXICAN PICKLED ONIONS (ESCABECHE DE CEBOLLA)

Onions may be made several days ahead of time and refrigerated until ready to use. They turn a gorgeous shade of pink. Use them on sandwiches, tacos, and any Mexican meat dish.

Yields 5 cups

1-1/3 cups freshly squeezed lime juice, about 5 large limes
2/3 cup freshly squeezed orange juice, about 2 medium juice oranges
1-1/2 pounds red onions, 3 large, 6 cups peeled and sliced 1/8-inch thick

1 Combine lime and orange juice in a medium mixing bowl, and set aside.

2 Bring a small pot of water to boil. Place onions into a nonreactive bowl, pour boiling water over them, wait 10 seconds, and pour the onions through a strainer.

3 Transfer drained onions to the bowl with citrus juices and stir in 2 teaspoons kosher salt. Cover onions, and set aside 1 or more hours. Alternatively, pack onions into clean glass canning jars and refrigerate overnight.

4 **Just before serving:** Drain onions and set out in serving bowl. Pickled onions will last a month or more; the flavor will improve after 3 to 7 days.

Source: *Authentic Mexican* by Rick Bayless.

Vary! Improvise!

☛ *Spice It Up:* Add 1 teaspoon black peppercorns and cumin seed and 2 teaspoons dried Mexican oregano to onions and citrus juices. Blanch 8 cloves garlic and add to onion and juices.

☛ *No Citrus:* Substitute an equal amount of cider vinegar for the lime juice.

YUCATÁNEAN QUICK-PICKLED ROASTED ONIONS (CEBOLLAS ASADAS)

Pickled onions are an indispensable condiment used on many foods in the Yucatán. Cooks there traditionally use naranja agria (sour orange juice) to pickle them.

Yields 1 quart

2 pounds small, unpeeled red-purple onions
   or 2 pounds unpeeled red-purple Italian cipollini onions

Pickling Mixture

1 teaspoon orégano Yucateco
   or 1 teaspoon Mexican oregano
3/4 cup *naranja agria* juice (also known as Seville orange)
   or 6 tablespoons fresh orange juice *and* 6 tablespoons fresh lime juice
1 teaspoon black peppercorns
6 whole allspice
4 whole cloves

Garnish: 1/4 to 1/2 ounce cilantro, 3 to 4 tablespoons finely sliced

1 **Grill onions:** Preheat gas or charcoal grill. Place onions in a grilling basket or on a mesh grill grate, and place over hot coals or gas grill. Roast, turning or shaking occasionally, until onions blacken and insides soften, 10 to 20 minutes depending on size of onions and heat. Place onions into bowl, cover with plate or lid, and cool to room temperature.

2 **Prepare pickling mixture:** Meanwhile, heat a small skillet over medium heat. Add the oregano. Dry-toast oregano until fragrant and transfer to nonreactive mixing bowl. Stir orange or orange and lime juice with oregano. Place peppercorns, allspice, and cloves into mortar and crush finely with pestle. Transfer to bowl with orange juice. Stir in 1 teaspoon kosher salt.

3 Slice off onion root and stem ends. Remove burnt skin and discard. Cut small onions in half and medium onions into 4 to 6 wedges. Fold into bowl with pickling mixture.

4 **If using onions immediately:** Allow onions to marinate at room temperature 30 minutes. If using later, pack into clean 1-quart jar or container and refrigerate up to 1 week. The onions will absorb the citrus juice.

5 **To Serve:** Remove onions from refrigerator 30 minutes before serving. Toss with cilantro and more orange-lime juice, to taste. Serve at room temperature.

Source: Chef David Sterling at Los Dos cooking school; www.los-dos.com/.

REVIEW QUESTIONS

1. Discuss Mexico's contributions to world cuisine.

2. What is nixtamalization? What is its effect?

3. What is a mole?

4. What was one of the two great outside influences on Mexican cuisine?

5. Discuss dried and fresh chilies.

6. What is masa and how can it be used?

7. Describe the process for cooking dried beans the Mexican way.

ASIAN AND INDIAN KNIVES AND CUTS

ASIAN KNIVES AND CUTS

Asian knives are centrally balanced, rather than heavy at the top edge as a French knife. When using an Asian knife, consider it as an extension of the hand. The arm should be a single unit moving from the shoulder, not the wrist. Many Asian knives are carbon steel, which rusts easily, so clean the knife immediately, and store it in a knife case. For safety's sake, never put a knife into a sink with soapy water or onto a table where it could be covered with other items.

Chinese Cleavers

The Chinese cleaver, like the wok, is a desert-island versatile tool. This inexpensive knife with its broad blade is the heart of a Chinese kitchen: it cuts, dices, slices, flattens, cracks, and scoops. A **heavy weight** cleaver will bone out a chicken and crack bones or smash garlic, lemongrass, and ginger with a whack of its back, handle, or side. The **medium weight** cleaver is the best all-round kitchen knife—it will mince, dice, slice, and bone out chicken. The blade can be carbon steel or, more recently, high-carbon stainless steel. Some cleavers are made like Japanese knives with a core of hard steel and layered on the outside with softer steel. Ideally, cleavers should be sharpened after each use.

FIGURE A.1 Meat cleaver.
Source: David Murray/DK Images.

HEAVYWEIGHT BUTCHERING CLEAVER

With a broad, thick blade, grooved handle for better grip when holding handle near its end and a thick blade, this knife typically weighs 1-3/4 pounds. Its top edge is about 1/4-inch wide. Use for heavy bones.

FIGURE A.2 Poultry cleaver.
Source: Gary Ombler/DK Images.

HEAVYWEIGHT POULTRY CLEAVER

Often with a blade curved at the tip, this compact knife can be used in a rocking motion, and turned more easily in tight places. It typically weighs 1-1/2 pounds with a top edge between 1/8- and 1/4-inch. Use for light bones like poultry and fish.

LIGHTWEIGHT VEGETABLE CLEAVER

This is an everyday tool for use in about 90% of kitchen chopping. It can come with narrow or the usual wide blade, which typically weighs about 3/4 pound. The top edge is about 1/8-inch thick. This narrower blade is very light and a bit flimsy in the hand. Use for vegetables and meats or seafood with no bones.

Chinese Cleaver Holds

THE GRAND SLAM

Hold the knife at the handle firmly. Use for whacking bones and smashing garlic.

THE CHOKE HOLD

"Choke up" on the handle and onto the blade. Use for close cutting, slicing, dicing, and rocker mincing.

CHINESE FOOD PROCESSOR

Chinese chef, author, and restaurateur Martin Yan calls the Chinese cleaver "the original Chinese food processor." He advises students to use it to smash, slice, mince, chop, grind, crush, tenderize, and transfer food from board to bowl. The handle may be used to reduce spices to a coarse grind. Yan suggests adding a paring knife to the cleaver, and students will be "ready for just about anything."

ASIAN AND INDIAN CUTS

In addition to basic French cutting techniques like dicing, shredding, and mincing, Asian cooks use vegetable cuts that serve to maximize the surface area for fuller flavor and quicker cooking.

ROUND AND FLOWER CUT

Evenly slice cylindrical vegetables into rounds. For flowers, run a channel tool along the length of a carrot, zucchini, or cucumber about 5 times, evenly spaced around it. Thinly slice into flowers.

FIGURE A.3 Matchstick cut cucumbers.
Source: Paul Williams/DK Images.

HALF MOON CUT

Cut cucumbers, carrots, or daikon radish in half lengthwise, and then slice crosswise.

DIAGONAL CUT

Using a cleaver, slice vegetables like carrots or zucchini on a sharp bias.

MATCHSTICK OR NEEDLE CUT

Make thin diagonal cuts of carrots, gingerroot, burdock, or other vegetable. Stack thin slices on flat side and thinly slice lengthwise into fine needles. Slice thicker slices into larger matchstick.

ROLL OR ROLL WEDGE CUT

Slice a vegetable like carrot or zucchini diagonally, rotate it 1/4 around, or 90 degrees, and slice again; repeat.

SHAVING CUT

Shave peeled carrot or other cylindrical vegetables while slightly rotating vegetable; same as sharpening a pencil.

SLIVER CUT

This cut is used in India on small brown onions. The stem and root end are removed and the onion is cut in half through the root end (not through its equator). After peeling, the onion is laid on a flat side and thinly sliced from stem to root end.

Japanese Knives

There is a great range of price for Japanese knives; they differ in the type of steel and the way the knife is constructed. The most expensive knives are true-forged (hon-yaki) hard carbon steel. Kitchen blades (kasumi-yaki) are usually a thin layer of hard steel covered with thicker layers of (cheaper) soft steel. Therefore only the cutting edge on the less expensive knives is hard steel.

Typically Japanese knives have only one cutting edge on the right. Left-handed knives are available and more expensive. This single blade is said to cut faster and cleaner, with less tearing. Japanese knives are hone-sharpened before each use on a whetstone wet with water only. The stone should be a medium or fine (not coarse) Japanese stone, not a Western stone, free of grooves. The cutting side of a Japanese knife should be sharpened with the angle that is already present from the manufacturer.

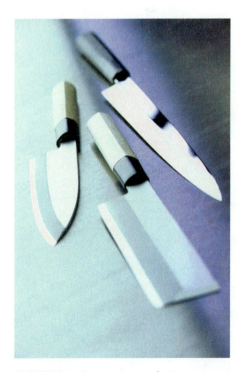

FIGURE A.4 Japanese knives.
Source: Ian O'Leary/DK Images.

VEGETABLE KNIFE (USUBA OR NAKIRI-BOCHO)

This is considered by Japanese cooks to be the most useful kitchen knife of all. It is quite light and is used for paring vegetables, slicing, chopping, mincing, julienne or matchstick, and delicate work. It has rounded ends and a cutting edge on one side.

KITCHEN CLEAVER (DEBA-BOCHO)

This knife is for use on light bones, fish, meat, and poultry and can be from 7-inch to 10-inch lengths with a pointed tip, a cutting edge on one side, and thicker blade than the vegetable knife. It is a versatile knife, performing delicate work as well as the heavier work of bone chopping.

SASHIMI KNIFE (TAKO-BIKI HOCHO OR YANAGI-BA HOCHO)

This knife has a very long, thin blade that is either pointed or blunted at the end. The long blade allows fish to be sliced in one long motion; it is used only for slicing boned fish destined for sushi and sashimi. This knife can be very expensive.

Japanese Knife Holds

CHOKE HOLD

Choking up onto the blade from the handle.

EXTENDED FINGER HOLD

Index finger is stretched out on top of blade

Japanese Cutting Strokes

DRAWING CUT

Place the heel of the knife on food and lightly press (or simply let the weight of the knife do the work) while drawing the blade toward you. This cut is used mostly for cutting sashimi and sushi fish.

PUSHING CUT

Push the center of the blade straight down into the food. This is a good cut for producing a clean edge.

THRUSTING CUT

Used with the usuba knife. Slice or cut with a forward thrusting motion. Try this on cucumber julienne.

Japanese Cuts

PAPER TOWEL CUT (KATSURAMUKI)

This cut is used mainly on daikon radish and cucumbers with a long sashimi or vegetable knife. Cut a daikon or cucumber into 5- or 6-inch lengths. Peel away the skin by stabilizing the knife firmly on the right hand and guiding the daikon under the thumb of the left hand. Discard the skin and repeat, but slicing a thinner sheet, similar to a roll of paper toweling. Keep the sheet as thin as possible (the knife should show clearly beneath the sheet of daikon) without breaking the sheet. Work slowly, smoothly, and steadily. The resulting sheet should be thin enough to see through. The sheets can be cut into strips. Daikon is cut into hair-like strands (ken) and served in a pile with sashimi.

JULIENNE

Peel the vegetable and cut into 3-inch lengths. Cut a thin wafer lengthwise from one side and lay vegetable on the flat side on the cutting board. Slice into 1/16- to 1/8-inch wafers, stack the wafers, and cut into thin or fine julienne.

MATCHSTICKS

Use the same technique as for julienne, but cut into 1/4-inch by 1/4-inch, for soft and delicate vegetables such as mountain yam. For cucumbers used in sushi-maki, cut into 3/8-inch by 3/8-inch by 3- or 4-inch lengths.

SLIVERS

To sliver green onions or negi, slice at a very sharp 45-degree angle, or, if the onion is very wide, slice in half lengthwise, into desired lengths crosswise, and each piece into slivers lengthwise. Place slivers in ice water to curl at both ends, and use to garnish salads, soups, and appetizers.

BEVELED EDGED ROUNDS

Slice vegetables like carrot or daikon into rounds or coins. With a vegetable peeler, round off the two edges of the "coins" by running the peeler around the diameter of both sides of the round at a 45-degree angle.

SASHIMI CUT

With a super-sharp, long chef's knife or sashimi knife, Japanese cooks start at the heel of the knife, and pull it forward toward the cook. A short or less-than-sharp knife will require cutting in several passes, and can produce a misshapen slice of sashimi.

BEEF OR CHICKEN CUTS

Most Japanese and Asian cooks cut meat into bite-sized pieces (1- to 1-1/2-inch cubes) that can be eaten with chopsticks. The meat is easily flavored and cooks quickly. Shabu shabu and sukiyaki require thin slices of beef; partially freeze the meat before slicing.

GLOSSARY

A

Aburage/Age-Dofu (Japanese Deep-Fried Tofu Pockets) This tofu product is deep-fried brown until no soft white tofu remains. In the process, a pocket opens in the center, which is often stuffed. Aburage is simmered in a sweet-soy marinade before making the stuffed inari-zushi. Aburage may be frozen. Before using, blanch it in boiling water and blot dry to remove some of the oil.

Achiote (Annatto) The seed of the achiote fruit produces annatto, which comes from the pulp surrounding the seed. Latin American cooks use achiote seeds for coloring foods yellow to orange and to impart its mildly peppery, nutty scent and flavor. Originally from South America, the Spanish adopted annatto from the Aztecs as a stand-in for saffron.

Ackee See *Caribbean Vegetables and Fruit* in chapter *The West Indies or Caribbean Islands*.

Adobo This Spanish term can mean two different savory seasonings in Latin America. In Mexico it is a thick, spicy paste used to marinate meats before grilling, roasting, or frying. In the Caribbean, adobo is a dry spice seasoning made with garlic powder, onion powder, salt, black pepper, dried oregano, and lemon zest, and used as a condiment or rub. Some Caribbean cooks make a wet adobo rub with raw garlic, black pepper, dried oregano, salt, oil, and vinegar. The word *adobo* comes from the Spanish word *adobar*, which means "to marinate," and *adobado* means "marinated and cooked in adobo sauce." Many Caribbean cooks consider adobo to be the most important seasoning in their kitchens; they use it in red beans and rice, grilled steak, chicken, roast pork, and hamburgers.

Adzuki Beans Small, creamy, red bean used in Japanese and Korean cuisines mainly for sweet fillings and desserts. The Japanese confection *yokan* is made with agar (the jelling agent), sugar, and adzuki bean paste and sometimes flavored with persimmons or chestnuts.

Agar-Agar (Japanese Kanten) Agar is used to thicken and set gelatin-like desserts. It comes in pale sticks, flaked or powdered. It is a tasteless product made from a type of seaweed called *tengusa* that looks like a dry sponge. Like gelatin, agar must be dissolved in cold liquid before bringing to a boil. Traditionally, 1 tablespoon agar flakes is used per cup of liquid, but measurements can vary.

Agave (Mexico) Sweetener produced from the large, spiky, blue agave plant. The sap is expressed from the leaves and cooked to concentrate it to slightly thinner than honey. It is 1-1/2 times sweeter than sugar and higher in fructose. Agave is sold in light, amber, dark, and raw types. Light and raw agave are mild flavored, amber agave tastes slightly caramel, while dark agave tastes deeply caramel.

Alich'a Nonspicy Ethiopian meat or bean stew made with browned onion seasoned with garlic, ginger, and turmeric.

Amaebi Japanese name for cooked "sweet" shrimp destined for use as nigiri sushi. Amaebi have been traditionally the small Alaskan pink shrimp with a clear, sweet aftertaste, but the larger West Coast botan shrimp can be substituted.

Amaretti Small, round, crunchy, sweet almond-flavored Italian cookies.

Amaretto Italian almond liqueur.

Angelica A tall, pleasantly aromatic plant that grows wild in woods and near streams, young angelica shoots taste like a sweet, nutty celery and are prized for salads or stewed; in France the stems are candied. The powdered root has a long history as a medicinal herb. In Persian cuisine the powdered seeds from angelica pods are ground and used as seasoning over legumes and legume dishes to aid in digestion.

Antojito Spicy Mexican street food, usually made with corn, like tacos, quesadillas, enchiladas, ceviche, or guacamole with corn chips.

Argan Oil (Morocco) This rare, dark and nutty oil is made from the roasted kernels of the fruit of the ancient Moroccan argan tree. This strong tree grows wild in semi-desert and is highly adapted to arid conditions. Moroccans use the oil cosmetically, medicinally, and for cooking, on salads and for dipping.

Arrowroot This white, flavorless, starchy powder is obtained from the arrowroot plant (Maranta arundinacea). It is used as a thickener, similar to cornstarch and in the same proportions, in Caribbean soups, stews, sauces, and for glazing. The thickening properties reduce with long cooking so it's usually added toward the end. The maximum thickening occurs just before a dish boils.

Artichoke A relative of the thistle family, this round green vegetable is prized for its tender, sweet heart, but it is protected by layers of thorny leaves. When cut, the artichoke oxidizes and browns; immerse in water with lemon. See *Italian Vegetables* in chapter *Italy*.

Arugula (French Roquette) Spicy, nutty green leafy vegetable that can be used raw or cooked. Greeks harvest it wild.

Asian Sesame Oil Before pressing this seasoning oil, the sesame seeds are roasted, which yields a fragrant, dark oil suitable for salads and seasoning. It is not a cooking oil.

Asparagus, Green and White A perennial flower shoot that is harvested in the spring, asparagus is eaten as a vegetable. Over 300 wild varieties of asparagus exist, but only a few are edible. The three main cultivated culinary types are green, white, and purple. Green asparagus is 6 to 8 inches tall and varies from pencil-thin to a meaty 1/2-inch thickness. Thinner asparagus tend to have more flavor. White asparagus, grown in dark cellars to inhibit development of green chlorophyll, are thick, tender, and more delicate-flavored than the green. Purple asparagus are somewhat smaller than green and slightly fruity-tasting; the color disappears during cooking. Look for very fresh asparagus with tightly closed heads; check the bottom stem for woodiness or dryness. Fresh asparagus are flexible and plump. Choose similar sized asparagus; they cook more evenly. Some chefs peel the bottoms to equalize cooking time. Refrigerate fresh asparagus no more than 2 days like flowers, standing in a bit of cold water.

Aspic French term for clear jelly made from clarified gelatinous stock and used to coat food and keep it moist for buffet: ham, turkey, fish, and small hors d'oeuvres canapes.

Atta or Chapatti Flour (India) Atta is finely stone-ground, nutty flour from soft to medium-hard whole wheat with low to medium gluten content. Western whole wheat flour is not a substitute.

Avocado and Avocado Leaf See *Signature Seasonings* in chapter *Mexico* for the different varieties of avocado and use of avocado leaf.

Azafrán and Azafrán de Bolita See *Signature Seasonings* in chapter *Mexico*.

B

Baccalá (Italy), Morue (France), or Bacalao (Spain) This dry-salted and dried fresh cod came about because sixteenth-century European fishermen, fishing off the coast of Newfoundland, needed to preserve cod long enough to get it home. They found they liked its flavor and texture more than fresh. High quality salt-cod is rarely found in stores: Portuguese, Spanish, Italian, and Greek vendors often carry it. Salt cod must be soaked from 24 to 48 hours in cold water, depending on its thickness. Properly soaked salt-cod is thicker, flexible, and slightly salty. The water should be changed every 6 to 8 hours.

Balsamic Vinegar The traditional method of making balsamic vinegar begins with a reduction of white Trebbiano and Lambrusco grape must (juice). The reduction is aged for a minimum of 12 years and as long as 25 or more in 7 successively smaller wood barrels made from acacia, chestnut, cherry, oak, mulberry, ash, and juniper. They impart a complex flavor and glossy brown color. Commercial balsamic may be produced traditionally, but it's not aged as long. There are three types: *Aceto balsamico tradizionale* (authentic, traditional artisan-produced), *commercial* (produced industrially), and *condimento* (mixture of aceto balsamico tradizionale and commercial).

Balsamic Vinegar, White White balsamic vinegar is a blend of white grape must and white wine vinegar. It is reduced at a low temperature to avoid darkening. Some manufacturers age the vinegar in oak barrels, while other use stainless steel. It tends to be sweet, amber-colored, and is used as a base for many trendy infused vinegars.

Bamboo Shoots This crisp, pale yellow vegetable is the large—up to 5 pounds—young shoot of certain species of bamboo. After cooking and trimming, they look like pale cones. Some species contain cyanide and must be boiled before eating.

Barberry (Persian Zereshk or Oregon Grape) Persians have long used the tiny, tart, and tasty barberry in cooking. The fruit is high in pectin, malic, and citric acid, bright red-colored when fresh, good for regulating blood pressure, and has anti-fungal and anti-inflammatory properties. Persian groceries sell barberries dried. Before using, soak them in cold water 15 minutes and rinse to remove sand and impurities. Strew into a dish of rice, couscous, or pot-roasted chicken for a burst of gorgeous color and fruity-tart flavor. A slightly astringent syrup can be made by combining 2 cups dried barberries with 1 quart water or for a sweet syrup, equal weights of fresh barberries and sugar. Boil 15 to 20 minutes over high heat, and strain through cheesecloth. The syrup may be used to make drinks or as a tart seasoning. It is used medicinally for sore throat.

Basil, Sacred or Holy (Hot Basil) Closely related to sweet basil, the many types of holy basil have been used as a valued culinary and medicinal herb in India, Southeast Asia, and Africa. The variety used in Ethiopia is reddish-purple under leaves and on stems. The leaves are smaller and slightly hairy and have a peppery taste of camphor, anise, and mint that becomes more pronounced upon cooking. Ethiopians use dried holy basil shoots.

Bay Leaves The dark green, broad Turkish bay leaves are far milder and more complex than the long and narrow California bay leaves, which are not a true bay genus. California bay leaves have a very strong, eucalyptus-like flavor and are not good for cooking. Turkish bay leaves add a subtle, sweet herbaceous perfume to dishes. Use fresh bay leaves whenever possible.

Beans, Dry Over 7,000 years ago Mesoamerican and Andean peoples domesticated the common bean or *Phaseolus vulgaris*. Centuries ago, Portuguese traders and Spanish conquerors took them to sub-Saharan Africa and beyond. Now there are thousands of varieties. Excluding broad or fava beans (North Africa and Asia), chickpeas (Middle-East), lentils (Greece), and black-eyed peas or cowpeas (West Africa), Mexico is the origin of the most shell beans in the world. See *Italian Shell Beans* in chapter *Italy* for more information on legumes popular in Europe and the Mediterranean. **To quick-soak beans:** Cover with cold water (and about 1 tablespoon kosher salt per pound of dry beans). Bring to a boil. Remove pan from heat, cover, and rest beans 1 hour. Drain and rinse. Proceed to cook beans with fresh cold water.

Mexicans eat a multitude of legume varieties that stay mostly regional. They vary in color from white (**blanco**), black (**negro**), and beige (**bayo**) to red, yellow, purple, lilac, russet, and coffee. Some varieties are the small, white round *alberjón*, red *sangre de toro*, brown speckled pinto beans, creamy *mantequilla* (butter or lima bean), large, purple-black *ayocote negros*, speckled black and white *vaquitas*, red-speckled *vaquitas rojas*, yellow-tan *amarillos*, pale-yellow, creamy *peruanos*, rust-colored small *ayocote café*, and gray *moros*. Mexican cooks use beans in soup, fritters, as stuffing and toasted, ground to a powder, strained and reconstituted for soup. Caribbean cooks favor pigeon peas (*gandules*), black-eyed peas, and pink and black beans.

Bean Curd See *Tofu*.

Bean Curd Skin (Japanese Yuba) and Bean Curd Sticks, Dried Yuba are thin sheets made by boiling soymilk, removing the skin that forms, and drying it. Yuba is popular fresh or dried in Japanese temple and vegetarian cuisine; restaurants called *yubani* create whole meals with yuba in various forms. Yuba comes in three forms: fresh, half-dried, and fully dried. Like yuba, Chinese bean curd skin is made from boiled soymilk. The dried sheets or skins can be used as wraps, pressed to form logs for vegetarian "meat," or sliced and added to dishes. When the fresh sheets are bunched together and dried they are called bean curd sticks. Chinese cooks use bean curd sticks as a meat product substitute. Bean curd skins and sticks are rehydrated in flavored broth or water before using.

Bean Sauce and Paste, Asian There at least five types of Chinese bean sauce either made with soybeans or black beans: Bean or Brown Bean Sauce is made from the soybean pulp leftover after brewing. Sweet Bean Sauce is the Peking sweetened version. Hot Bean Sauce typically has Szechwan chilies and Asian sesame oil added. The black bean sauces are made from puréed or crushed black beans. Black Bean Garlic has garlic added and Black Bean Chili is spicier with chilies. In addition, Yellow Bean Paste, a sweet, soupy paste is used in Southeast Asian cooking.

Bean Sprouts (Mung Bean Sprouts) These long white sprouts are grown from the pale green mung bean. Blanched 30 seconds and refreshed in ice water they will keep up to 5 days refrigerated. Use in salads and soups or stir-fried.

Belgian Endive (Witloof or Chicory) These pale white, bullet-shaped leafy heads are crisp, refreshing, and slightly bitter. Choose heads with yellow tips; when the tips turn green, the leaves tend toward deeper bitterness. The leaves are great in salads or used as dippers.

Beni Shoga (Japanese Red Pickled Ginger) A red, sweet, thicker-cut pickled ginger used in Japanese cuisine for garnish.

Bento Box (Japan) An elegant boxed lunch made in Japan and Korea, and traditionally packed into black lacquer boxes.

Berbere An Ethiopian spicy powdered blend or paste prepared with dried ground chilies, herbs such as sacred basil, ginger, garlic, shallots, fenugreek, and cardamom. It is an important ingredient in Ethiopian cooking.

Berz Ethiopian unfermented honey wine (t'ej).

Besan (India) See *Chickpea Flour*.

Beurre Manie (France) This thickener is made from equal parts by weight of flour and unsalted butter kneaded together. To use it, cooks whisk bits of beurre manie into a soup, stew or sauce, and simmer in until thickened. Simmer the dish 5 minutes to remove floury taste. For a butter-free thickener, substitute olive oil for butter and stir to a paste. Approximately 1 tablespoon flour and 2 teaspoons butter will thicken 1 cup liquid to sauce consistency.

Bird's Eye Chilies (Thai Chilies) Tiny (about 1/2- to 1-inch long) hot, red, or green chilies used in Southeast Asia.

Black Limes, Dried (Limu Omani) (Persia-Iran) These whole limes are boiled in brine and dried. Added to stews or soups they impart musk and citrus notes.

Bonito A fish from the skipjack family. It is widely used in Japan for preparing dashi or broth. The fish fillets are dried, aged to heighten umami, and shaved before using. Also see *Katsuobushi*.

Bottarga This salted, dried and lightly smoked fish (mullet or tuna) roe is made into a loaf and often coated in beewax. It is favored in Italy and Greece. The briny roe cake is traditionally sliced thinly or ground and sprinkled on seafood pasta dishes.

Breadfruit See *Caribbean Vegetables and Fruit* in chapter *The West Indies or Caribbean Islands*.

Bresaola See *Italian Cured Meats* in chapter *Italy*.

Bresse Chicken (France) The French consider this chicken the queen of chicken. They have blue feet, white feathers, red crests, tender flesh, and rich flavor. These colorful chickens are appellation-controlled, which means they must be a particular breed, fed a particular diet, and raised a particular way in the specific area of Burgundy, France called Bresse.

Broccoli Raab or Rapini See *Italian Vegetables* in chapter *Italy*.

Buckwheat and Buckwheat Flour Buckwheat is a cereal grass seed that is popular in Asia, Eastern Europe, and Brittany. The "groats" are roasted for richer flavor and used in pilafs or noodle dishes or ground into flour. Flour ground from roasted buckwheat imparts a hearty, nutty, and pleasing flavor to dishes. It is popular for Japanese and Korean noodles and in Indian cuisine. Japanese and Koreans use the whole roasted grain to make a smoky, refreshing tea. French cooks in Brittany prepare crêpes from buckwheat flour.

Bulgar Wheat Bulgar is made from wheat berries that are steamed, dried, and crushed or ground. Different grades from very fine to very coarse are available. Fine bulgur is used in recipes with little or no cooking like salads or tabbouleh. It is usually soaked in cool, warm, or boiling water or stock, sometimes with the addition of tomato and lemon juice for 10 to 20 minutes, and fluffed. The proportions are about one cup bulgar to one cup liquid. Medium and coarse bulgur is used in Lebanese kibbeh and baked or cooked meat dishes. Coarse bulgur is ideal for baked casseroles where it holds up with longer cooking times.

Butter (French Beurre) Butter is churned from cream skimmed from cow's milk. It's easily made by over-whisking or over-blending whipped cream: the rapid beating bursts the fat globules, butterfat releases and forms butter. The butter is rinsed, the buttermilk is drained off, and the butter is kneaded into a smooth mass. In French cuisine *beurre clarifié* (clarified butter) has its milk solids removed and is used for sautéing. *Beurre noisette* (brown butter) is whole butter that has been slowly cooked until the milk solids turn nut brown; it is used as a sauce or flavoring as in sauce Meuniére with lemon and parsley. *Beurre noir* (black butter) is butter heated until the milk solids turn very dark. It is used as a flavoring or sauce.

C

Cabbage, Savoy   See *Italian Vegetables* in chapter *Italy*.

Callaloo   This leafy green, used in the Caribbean for its leaves and stems, is from two cultivars: the amaranth family or taro (dasheen) family. It probably had its origins with slaves from West Africa. Callaloo is similar to spinach, but can withstand the heat of the Caribbean, is sweet, and does not turn slimy when cooked. (Callaloo is also the name of a Caribbean stew.)

Carmargue Red Rice (Riz Rouge)   Le riz rouge looks like long-grain brown rice dyed mahogany. Riz rouge is unpolished (its bran is red) with a chewy, somewhat starchy and sticky texture like medium-grain rice, and delicious, mild, nutty flavor. It is grown exclusively in the drained salt marshes of Camargue, a southeastern region of France. French cooks boil red rice like pasta, in a large pot boiling water, until al dente then drain it in a colander.

Candlenuts (Indonesia)   Round, fatty nut used to thicken Indonesian curries and add texture and flavor to many dishes. Substitute macadamia nuts or raw cashews. Candlenuts are toxic when raw and must be cooked before eating.

Capers   A favorite of Sicilian and Mediterranean cooking, capers are part of most Italian kitchens. They are small unopened buds of the Mediterranean bush, *Capparis spinosa L.*, closely related to the cabbage family, but they look more like a rose bush. Caper bushes grow wild and are also cultivated throughout the Mediterranean. Pickled in vinegar or preserved in salt (which brings out their flavor), European cooks consider the smallest capers (nonpareilles) the best. Some make a caper substitute with immature nasturtium seed pods (not flower buds) pickled in vinegar. Capers have a sharp, mustard-like, peppery flavor, which add tang to pasta sauces, pizza, salad, meat, fish, and anchovies. Their unique flavor comes from mustard oil or methyl isothiocyanate. Use capers whole, crushed, or chopped. Rinse salted capers to remove excess salt, or drain pickled capers—save the salty caper pickling liquid for use in sauces and dressings.

Capon   A castrated rooster that is fatty, rich, tender, and meaty.

Carambola   A relative of starfruit, this pale-green to yellow fruit is acidic; its juice gives a tart tang to Indonesian soups, curry, fish, and sambal.

Cardoon   See *Italian Vegetables* in chapter *Italy*.

Cassava   A root plant used in Asia, Africa, the Caribbean, and Mexico also known as yuca, tapioca, cassava, or manioc.

Caviar, Black   Caviar is the salted roe (eggs) of the sturgeon. It comes in various grades depending upon size, color, and flavor. The best is Beluga, Osetra, and Sevruga. Its flavor is rich, earthy, buttery, nutty, and smooth. It is expensive; Beluga is on the endangered list and unavailable. Caviar is prized in France, Italy, and Spain.

Cavolo Nero (Tuscan Kale or Black Cabbage)   See *Italian Vegetables* in chapter *Italy*.

Celeriac (Celery Root)   A knobby, round, and rough-skinned root vegetable that may be eaten raw or cooked. It has a delicate flavor of celery. Celeriac browns when cut and exposed to air; store in acidulated water. French cooks toss raw, shredded celery root with a remoulade sauce for a refreshing crudités. Toss cubes of it into stews or soups in place of parsnips or potatoes. It is eaten in Europe and Turkey.

Cellophane Noodles (Bean Thread, Mung Bean Noodle, Mung Bean Thread)   A clear, thin, wiry noodle made from mung bean starch. Mung noodles have little taste; they are about texture. Deep-fry dry noodles quickly for a crispy garnish or boil water and pour over them to soak until noodles are clear and tender, 10 minutes. Chinese make cold summer salads with cellophane noodles or use them as base to soups and stir-fries. They absorb the flavor of a dish in which they are cooked.

Charmoula or Chermoula   Sauce of Moroccan origin usually used with fish; it contains cilantro, parsley, paprika, chili, lemon juice, and spices.

Chayote or Christophene   A pale, green pear-shaped tropical fruit with edible skin and pit. It has the delicate flavor of zucchini and may be eaten raw or cooked. Mexicans call it *chayote* and in the Caribbean it's called *christophene*.

Chervil   This delicate, anise-flavored herb is related to parsley, but milder. It is popular in France, in egg dishes, omelettes, salad, and soup.

Chestnuts   These shiny brown, starchy edible nuts are used in much of Europe (not all chestnuts are edible). There are three main types: European sweet chestnut, Chinese or Asian chestnut, and the American chestnut. The tasty American breed suffered a destructive blight and is now experiencing a renaissance. Chestnuts are best eaten cooked. The shell should be slit before roasting, baking, or boiling. The shell and skin should be removed when the nut is warm and moist. Chestnuts have many culinary uses from flour to preserves and confections. Chestnuts are used in northern China fresh, as pungent, smoky-dried, or as paste. Soak dried chestnuts in boiling water 3 to 8 hours before cooking.

Chestnut Flour   Chestnut flour is milled from dried chestnuts. Pale gray-tan Italian (and some Corsican) flour is produced from smoke-dried chestnuts. Smoke-drying imparts a delightful sweet, nutty flavor to pasta, cakes, polenta, crepes, and cookies. The cream-colored commercial chestnut flour is ground from chestnuts dried by fans and it lacks the wonderful smokiness of the darker flour.

Chickpea Flour (Ethiopian Shiro or Indian Besan)   Flour ground from dried chickpeas. Chickpea flour can be found in Mediterranean cuisines like southern France and Italy, where it is made into polenta, pasta, and flatbread. Indian cooks use it for fritter batter. Chickpea flour has a rich, nutty flavor and imparts a density to baked goods. Ethiopian cooks prepare a quick cooking high-protein, spiced stew with it called yeshimbra shiro w'et.

Chinese Cabbage   See *Napa Cabbage*.

Chilies   Chilies are used in Asia fresh or dried. Dried red chilies are used in Japanese, Korean, and Chinese Hunan and Szechwan cooking. Fresh chilies are used in Japanese, Korean,

Southeast Asian, and Indian cuisine. See *Signature Seasonings* of each chapter.

Chilies, Mexican Dried and Fresh   See *Mexican Chilies* in chapter *Mexico*.

Chinese Garlic Chive (Gow Choy)   This long, narrow, and wide-leafed pungent garlic-flavored herb is used to season dumpling fillings, stir-fries, and soups.

Chipotles en Adobo (Mexico)   Although most cooks know only the Mexican canned, smoke-dried jalapeños in tomato sauce, the true chipotles en adobo are made from the smoke-dried *mora* chilies (small, ripe jalapeños) simmered in a true adobo made with ancho chilies, garlic, herbs, vinegar, and sugar.

Chorizo   See *Spanish Charcuterie (Charcutería)* in chapter *Spain*.

Cilantro or Mexican Cilantrillo   This pungent, aromatic herb looks like Italian parsley, but is very tender and fragrant. Leaves and tender stems have a mild flavor while larger stems impart a strong cilantro flavor. It's best sliced finely. Over-chopped cilantro turns to mush.

Cloud (Wood or Tree) Ear Mushroom (Asia)   See *Tree Ear Mushroom*.

Cockerel (French Coq)   This is a deeply tasty, meaty rooster. When not available, is often substituted with a hen.

Coconut   This large round seed or drupe comes from the coconut palm. When young, its husk is green and flesh is soft and creamy with nutritious "water" inside. As the coconut matures the husk turns brown and flesh becomes firm and hard. The firm flesh may be dried (copra) and pressed for oil or grated fresh and mixed with hot water to make coconut milk. Purchase heavy coconuts with three "eyes" that are firm and not moldy. One cup grated fresh coconut weighs 4 ounces lightly packed and 5 ounces packed. One and one fourth cups grated fresh coconut equals 1 cup unsweetened, dry, shredded coconut. One cup grated fresh coconut equals 3/4 cup unsweetened, dry, shredded coconut.

Coconut Milk and Coconut Oil   Coconut can be found in many forms: fresh coconut, frozen coconut meat, dried, unsweetened shredded coconut; sweetened coconut meat, coconut "water," canned coconut milk, and instant coconut milk powder. Coconut oil is used in South Indian cuisine. Vegetable-based, it contains no cholesterol, but it hardens at room temperature because of high saturated fat content. Cheaper, chemical-refined coconut oils have no scent or flavor. Purchase virgin, unrefined brands that carry the delicate fragrance and flavor of coconut. Coconut milk comes in several forms. The best flavor is freshly made from fresh, grated coconut, fresh, frozen coconut or unsweetened dried coconut. Second in flavor is unsweetened, aseptic packaged coconut milk in 1 liter boxes. Third is dried, instant coconut milk powder and last in flavor is canned, unsweetened coconut milk in 14-ounce cans. If speed is important, choose aseptic packaged instant or canned. Canned coconut milk lacks aroma and flavor while aseptic is surprisingly delicate and fresh. Instant powdered coconut milk is also good solution, it is aromatic and faster than fresh, and not as thick and fatty as canned or aseptic: buzz it

in a blender with water or whisk into a dish. To prepare coconut milk buzz 2 to 3 cups dried, unsweetened or fresh grated coconut in a blender with 2 to 4 cups boiling water. Rest 10 minutes and strain.

Congee   A thin rice gruel served in all over Asia and Southeast Asia for breakfast. It is loaded with condiments like soy sauce, fresh or preserved vegetables, chili sauce, and herbs.

Converted Rice   See *Rice, Converted or Parboiled*.

Coppa   See *Italian Cured Meats* in chapter *Italy*.

Coulis   This is the French term for a purée of vegetables or fruit used as a sauce, base of a dish, or a garnish. Raspberry or strawberry coulis is made from puréed, strained, and sweetened fresh or thawed frozen raspberries. Bell pepper coulis is made from roasted, peeled, and simmered bell peppers or simmered seeded bell peppers, which are puréed and strained.

Couscous   A tiny pasta rolled from high protein semolina wheat and dried. It is usually soaked and steamed. See *Couscous* in chapter *Africa*.

Crema Mexicana   This is a cultured dairy product, made similarly to crème fraîche, with the consistency of heavy cream and a nutty, tart flavor. Mexicans use crema as a cooling, creamy condiment. For a quick version, mix sour cream with cream or whole milk to thin. To make 1 cup crema Mexicana: Bring 1 cup cream (not ultra-pasteurized) to 86 degrees F. Pour into nonreactive vessel and stir in 1 tablespoon live-cultured buttermilk. Cover and set in warm (70 to 75 degrees F) spot until slightly thickened and pleasantly tart, about 8 to 12 hours. Refrigerate crema and it will thicken to the consistency of sour cream; thin with cream or milk to pourable consistency.

Crème Fraîche   A nutty-tasting thick, cultured cream used in France for cooking and cold dishes. See chapter *France* for a recipe.

Cubeb Pepper or Java Pepper   Cubeb is a pungently aromatic spice similar in appearance to peppercorns, but with the stem attached. Its flavor can be acrid, slightly bitter, and persistent. Some describe its flavor as a cross between warm, woody allspice and black pepper. It can be confused with the Ashanti or "false cubeb," which grows in Central Africa; its flavor is fresher and not as bitter and its shape is elongated. Arab trade via India brought the cubeb to Europe and Africa. Moroccan cooks use it in savory dishes, ras el hanout, and in *markouts* (semolina diamonds with honey and dates). For best flavor crush the spice just before using.

Cucumber, Japanese (Kyuri)   The Japanese cucumber (also used in Korea) is small, about 1 inch diameter and 4 to 5 inches long. It is sweeter and firmer textured than larger cucumbers. Substitute Persian cucumbers.

Culantro or Mexican Cilantro Extranjero   This spiky long leafed herb grows in the southern tropical region of Mexico. Too tough to be used raw, Mexican cooks add it to stock, broth, stew, or rice. Like cilantro, when cooked too long it loses its meaty, complex flavor. Latin and Asian cooks also use culantro.

Currant, White, Black and Red (Europe and Mediterranean) Currants are the small, clustered white, black, or red fruit that grow on low, thorny bushes and are related to the European gooseberry. The jewel-looking fruit is tart and juicy, similar to a sweet cranberry, high in pectin and filled with tiny seeds. *Currant* may also refer to the dried "Zante currant" made from the tiny, juicy, and thick-skinned Black Corinth grape.

Curry Leaves (India) These aromatic and enticing narrow green leaves look like a long, narrow bay leaf. They are indispensable for true South Indian flavor, but can be difficult to find unless an Indian market is nearby.

D

Daikon or White Radish This very long snow-white radish (which comes in spherical and cylindrical shapes) is eaten throughout Asia and India (mooli). It can grow to 6 to 14 inches long and 2 to 4 inches diameter. Japanese cooks grate it and serve with sashimi. It is crunchy and sweet to spicy when raw, but milder when cooked. Chinese cooks preserve the giant radish in salt; Japanese cooks "pickle" it in rice bran for sushi or snacking.

Daikon Sprouts (Japan) Very long, leggy sprouts from daikon (white) radish seeds, which have a slightly spicy flavor.

Dal Indian term for dried beans, peas, and lentils. See chapter *India* for more information.

Dandelion These long, slender, tender green leaves are slightly bitter when young, which increases as they age. Harvest wild unsprayed dandelion leaves or purchase the larger commercially grown leaves.

Dashi Japanese all-purpose broth made by steeping kelp (seaweed) and shaved, dried bonito fish flakes (katsuobushi). For a recipe, see chapter *Japan and Korea*.

Djola Red Rice See *Rice*.

Doenjang/Toenjang Korean fermented soybean paste. See Korean *Signature Seasonings* in chapter *Japan and Korea* for more information.

Dried Seafood (Senegal) Guedj (dried fermented fish), kong (smoked catfish), and yet (dried fermented conch) are used as seasoning in Senegalese cooking. They impart a rich, savory flavor to a dish, much as fish sauce does. Use dried anchovy or fish sauce as a substitute.

E

Edamame (*eh-dah-mam-me*) Young, green soybeans in the pod. Frozen edamame may be simply tossed in boiling water for a few minutes, drained, and tossed with a little Asian sesame oil and salt. The pod is not eaten. Japanese restaurants offer edamame as a predinner snack. Cooks sometimes remove the beans from the pod and toss into cooked rice dishes.

Eggplant (French Aubergine; Italian Melanzana; Spanish Berenjena; Greek Melitzána; Turkish Patlican) Though classified as a vegetable, this important Mediterranean nightshade is a fruit native to India and China. Eggplant comes in various colors, shapes, and sizes: white, green, lilac, orange, red, magenta-striped, and purple; and pinball-sized, round, long and narrow, to small and large pear shapes. In general, choose firm, young eggplant. Japanese long lilac eggplant tend to have fewer seeds, the small purple and white striped eggplant tend to be tender and sweeter than the large purple varieties. Traditionally, sliced eggplant is salted to draw out moisture and soften the cell structure; this helps reduce the amount of oil absorbed while frying. Eggplants may also be stewed, stuffed, grilled, steamed, battered and fried, baked, or roasted and charred like a bell pepper. The skin is edible and nutrient-rich.

Emulsion French vinaigrette and mayonnaise are classic culinary oil-in-liquid (vinegar) emulsions. All emulsions have two phases: a dispersed phase and a continuous phase. In vinaigrette, whisking the *dispersed phase* oil breaks it into tiny droplets, which become suspended in the *continuous phase* vinegar. Emulsions made without emulsifiers are unstable and will separate quickly. Hollandaise, aioli, milk, cream, and pan sauces are other examples of emulsions.

Emulsifiers These are substances that act as a stabilizing intermediary between oil and a watery liquid, allowing the oil to be held in suspension in the liquid indefinitely. Dry and wet mustard, egg, nuts, bread, and starchy vegetable purées like potatoes and garlic (and other pure starch thickeners) can act as emulsifiers. Modernist cuisine employs pure lecithin and agar powder as emulsifiers.

Espelette Chili-Pepper (Piment d'Espelette) This Appellation Controlled special, red French pepper is grown in Espelette near the Spanish-Basque territory where it is central to the cuisine. It has very little heat, but has a robust, lightly smoky flavor. The pepper may be purchased dried, ground, as a purée, or roasted and canned in jars.

Escarole (Italian Scarole) Escarole is a leafy green that has large, sturdy, wavy leaves. They form a loose head with pale yellow leaves inside and darker green leaves outside. Escarole has a slightly bitter flavor. Young escarole leaves can be used in salads; older escarole is prepared as a side dish or cooked in soup.

F

Farro (Emmer Wheat) An ancient Italian grain relative to wheat, einhorn, and spelt, farro is mostly grown in Tuscany and Abruzzo. It is low in gluten and has a robust, nutty flavor and chewy texture. Italian cooks serve the whole grain in salads, soups, and as a side dish. Boil 1 cup pearled farro in 4 cups water until chewy but tender, about 15 minutes and drain. Farro will hold its texture even when overcooked. Farro that is not pearled or hulled must be soaked overnight and simmered for 1 hour or more.

Fat-Tailed Sheep Fat (Donbeh or Liyeh) Sheep were one of the first domesticated animals in Persia. The Baluchi, Awassi, or fat-tailed sheep were developed there for milk, meat, and wool. Their tail was bred, primarily to obtain a soft fat for meat cooking, to a huge, wide, beavertail-like flap or a long kangaroo's tail with fat deposits along its length. Though the use of the tail fat is in decline, there are hundreds of fat-tail breeds. The tail fat has a more delicate flavor than the body fat, and it leaves a pleasing fragrance and richness in Persian and Middle-Eastern meat dishes that is impossible to duplicate.

Feijoa or Pineapple Guava (Mexico and Caribbean)   A thick-skinned, exotic fruit native to South America, the feijoa looks like a large, elongated lime. Peeled, it reveals pale yellow flesh; a cut feijoa reveals 4 seed chambers filled with gelatinous pulp. This fruit has a subtle flavor of pineapple, banana, and strawberry with a hint of mint. Its texture is slightly gritty and scent quite potent. It may be eaten raw or used in preserves and jellies.

Fennel   Both a licorice-tasting pale green seed and a pale green vegetable bulb that tastes mildly of anise. See *Italian Vegetables* in chapter *Italy*.

Fenugreek Leaves (Indian Methi)   These slightly bitter greens, which look similar to wild clover, are grown from whole fenugreek seed. The leaves are used fresh or dried and have a mild flavor similar to fennel and celery. Fenugreek leaves are used in Indian, Persian-Iranian, and Middle-Eastern cuisines.

Feta Cheese   There are three types of feta cheese: Greek, Bulgarian, and French. Greek feta has the most consistent flavor and texture, and is prized by feta lovers. French feta is the mildest tasting and the least salty. Bulgarian feta tends to be tangy to almost fermented tasting, strong and bold. See *Greek Cheese* in chapter *Greece and Turkey* for more information.

Fideos (Spain and Mexico)   Thin Mexican vermicelli noodle that is of Spanish origin. It comes broken into 1-inch lengths or wound into dry "nests." Fideos are used to prepare sopa secas or dry soups.

Fillo or Phyllo   A paper-thin dough used for sweet and savory pastries in Greece, Turkey, and the Middle East. See chapter *Greece and Turkey* for more information.

Fitfit   An Ethiopian dish made with pieces of injera mixed with any type of sauce.

Fish Sauce (Vietnamese Nuoc Mam and Thai Nam Pla)   The best fish sauce is made by fermenting 3 parts anchovies to 1 part salt for one week then recycling the liquid back through the wooden vats daily for a year. High quality fish sauce is intensely meaty and full of umami complexity. The first extraction is used for sauce and dips, the remainder for cooking. Quality Vietnamese nuoc mam is transparent, salty at first taste with a sweet aftertaste.

Five Elements (Wu Xing)   Chinese use this system or theory for describing relationships between five interdependent forces of wood, fire, earth, metal and water, phenomena in the world or body and how to maintain balance and harmony between them. Traditional Chinese medicine uses the five elements diagnostically as part of a way to explain relationships between the body and its environment. Chinese grandmothers use it to treat small maladies. Special restaurants in China, with a pharmacy attached, offer a diagnosis and dishes tailored to balance a malady. For instance, for spleen or stomach-related problems like fatigue, dizziness, and pale complexion, part of the remedy might be to eat earth element foods like millet, cabbage, carrots, chickpeas, lotus seed, pumpkin seeds, spinach and squash.

Wood—Liver and Gall Bladder—Sour

Fire—Heart and Small Intestine—Bitter

Earth—Spleen and Stomach—Sweet

Metal—Lungs and Large Intestine—Spicy

Water—Kidneys and Bladder—Salty

Flours, Asia and India   Although wheat flour is used throughout Asia, cooks also employ starches made from wheat, sago, arrowroot, cornstarch, tapioca, potato, mung bean, and kuzu. Other flours are made from buckwheat, barley, rice, roasted soybeans, dried chickpeas, water chestnuts, and Japanese wild yams. They are used for thickening, coating, and frying, and for dumpling doughs. Most recipes that use starch as a thickener call for mixing them with cold water; some dumpling recipes require hot or boiling water to create the proper texture dough.

Foie Gras (France)   The delicious enlarged liver of force-fed ducks or geese. See chapter *France* for more details.

Fonio (West Africa and Senegal)   This very small, flavorful grain in the millet family is almost exclusively grown in West Africa and part of an ancient, diverse, wild and cultivated species harvested there. Fonio grows quickly in poor soil and offers good nutrition. Two cultivars are black and white. Fonio has a nutrient composition similar to wheat, but contains no gluten. West Africans use fonio prepared like couscous (soaked and steamed), as pilaf, porridge, and in bread and beer.

Fowl (France, Italy and Spain)   Fowl is the name given to edible birds; chicken (French poulet) is the best known. In France, Spain, and Italy many types are eaten like capon, cockerel, duck, goose, guinea fowl, pigeon or squab, poularde, quail, and turkey.

Freekeh (Middle East)   Freekeh is young, green (unripe) wheat berries or cracked wheat that has a nutty, smoky flavor. It is harvested while tender and sun-dried in piles. The piles are lit with fire. The moisture in the green wheat keeps it from burning along with the dry straw and chaff, and the heat roasts it. The wheat is threshed or rubbed, dried and cracked. Modern machinery performs the processing today. Cracked freekeh looks like bulgar. It is popular in the Middle East, where it is often served with lamb, cinnamon, cumin, coriander, and lamb tail fat.

Frisée or Curly Endive   This loose-headed chicory green is crisp and bitter but refreshing. The larger head is similar to escarole but with frizzier leaf edges. The smaller frisée is smaller and frizzier with a yellow heart and darker green outer leaves.

Fruit, Caribbean Tropical   See *Vegetables and Fruits of the Caribbean* in chapter *The West Indies or Caribbean Islands*.

G

Galangal   Resiny, hot, peppery rhizome used as seasoning in Southeast Asia. Looks like ginger root.

Gari (Japanese Sushi Pickled Ginger)   This pale-colored pickled ginger is used as a condiment with sushi. The chapter *Japan and Korea* includes a recipe to prepare it, which is far superior to bottled pickled ginger.

Garlic   There are two main types of garlic: soft stem and hard stem. Soft-stem garlic is planted the last two weeks of December and harvested in June or July. Hard-stem garlic is planted in autumn and harvested in June or July. Soft-stem garlic tends to have more and smaller cloves, which store well and don't readily sprout. Hard-stem is more complex and flavorful with one row of large bulbs, but it tends to sprout quickly. The French pink *ail rose de Lautrec* is a prized soft-stem variety. Hard-stem garlic includes violet Rocambole and Porcelain varieties. Garlic scapes are the curly, fleshy green sprouts that are cut off the hard-stem varieties to allow the plant to retain more nutrients. The scapes are mildly garlicky and can be used like asparagus.

Gingelly Oil (India)   Plain sesame oil from unroasted seeds. May be used for cooking.

Gingko Nuts   Small yellow or white nuts (that turn green after blanching) from the mature gingko tree, these nuts may be found fresh in Japanese markets or canned in Chinese markets. Drain, blanch, and rub away skin of fresh nuts before roasting or using in *Chawan Mushi* (Japanese savory custard), stews, desserts, or grain dishes.

Gingerroot (Asia)   This pungent, hot-sweet rhizome or stem of the ginger plant arrives in markets in early spring and autumn with a thin, brown skin and very little fiber. The skin toughens and thickens and fibrousness increases as it matures (and dries). Very young ginger with pale pink shoots and pale gold, translucent skin is used to make Japanese pickled sushi bar ginger. Refrigerate in open bag; moist ginger rots.

Gomen   Ethiopian word for greens. Collards, mustard greens, and kale are the most similar to some of the varieties indigenous to Ethiopia.

Gooseberry, European   This small, round green or red fruit, the size of a grape, is native to Europe and Asia. The fruit grows on thorny low-growing bushes. It has a thin, fuzzy skin that surrounds a juicy, gel-like interior with seeds. When ripe, the fruit is tender and its flavor is sweet-tart and refreshing. It is rich in pectin, making it an excellent jam ingredient.

Grape Leaves   The leaves of wild or cultivated unsprayed grape leaves are used to prepare stuffed grape leaves in Greece, Turkey, and Lebanon. See *Grape Leaves Three Ways* in chapter *Greece and Turkey* for more information.

Grape Must and Grape Syrup   The fresh juice of crushed wine grapes strained through cheesecloth. It takes about 9 pounds of fresh grapes to produce 1 quart juice. The juice is cooked down until thick and honey-like, for Greek *petimézi*, Turkish *pekmez*, or Italian *vino cotto* (grape syrup), and used as a sweetener.

Green Onion, Scallion, or Spring Onion   These are the pungent young shoots of an onion. An average green onion weighs 1/2 ounce. Both the green and white may be used; the white is stronger and often cooked in a dish. The green is added as a garnish or warmed through.

Guinea Fowl   This black and white spotted bird originated in Africa. It is gamey and flavorful with slightly dry meat. Cooks lard birds with bacon fat or wrap in bacon to give the bird moisture and tenderness.

Gunpowder Green Tea   This green tea is produced in southeastern China, Taiwan, and Sri Lanka. Each leaf is rolled into a pellet that was said to resemble gunpowder grains. Purchase the smallest, tightly rolled, shiny pellets. The tea's flavor is strong and smoky. It is exported to Morocco, where it is prepared with mint and honey and part of social gatherings there.

H

Halal (Islam)   The term used to designate food permissible according to Islamic law. For meat or fish it means slaughtering with a swift, deep incision cutting the carotid artery, windpipe, and jugular veins without cutting through the spine, with a very sharp knife. The animal is hung upside down and its blood is drained; the head must be aligned with Mecca and the slaughter done in the name of God. Foods not considered halal are pork and all its products, improperly slaughtered animals, alcoholic drinks and intoxicants, carnivorous animals, birds of prey, and food contaminated with these products.

Halloumi   See *Greek* or *Lebanese Cheese* in chapters *Greece and Turkey* or *Lebanon*.

Hamachi (Japanese)   Young yellowtail or amberjack fish popular as sashimi or sushi.

Harissa   This spicy sauce originated in Tunisia, but is much loved in Morocco. See *Morocco* in chapter *Africa* for a recipe.

Hazelnut (Filbert)   This nut, popular in Europe and the Mediterranean, is round with a thin, dark brown skin. Hazelnuts are widely cultivated in Spain, Europe, Turkey, Iran, and the Caucasus, where they are used for oil and dessert confections.

Hijiki (Japanese)   This dark seaweed is a tasty, mild-flavored spaghetti-sized tangled mass. Hijiki is soaked in water and will expand to many times its size. After soaking, hijiki is drained and may be simmered in soy and dashi simmering broth or sautéed with tofu, carrot slivers, ginger, and/or burdock root, then seasoned with soy sauce and Asian sesame oil.

Hoisin Sauce (China)   This spicy-sweet, thick, reddish-brown sauce is prepared from soybeans, sugar, flour, vinegar, salt, garlic, chili, and sesame. It's used as a barbecue sauce, marinade, and dipping sauce with Peking duck or moo shu pork and Mandarin pancakes.

Hoja Santa (Yerba Santa, Hierba Santa, or Momo) This "holy leaf," native to Mexico, has heart-shaped leaves with strong anise flavor. It is used to season and wrap tamales, meat, fish, mushrooms, and rice and can be an ingredient in moles; some cooks toast the leaves over a flame before using.

Hominy (Mexico) See *Pozole*.

Honey Honeybees produce honey from flower nectar and pollen they gather. In their stomach it mixes with natural enzymes. The bees deposit the mixture into beeswax honeycomb to mature in the hive (as food for the bees). There are two types of honey: **monofloral**, or those made primarily from one flower, and **multifloral**, those made from a mixture of flowers. Many varieties of honey can be found in the Mediterranean and Europe: citrus, eucalyptus, thyme, chestnut, pine, lavender, acacia, rhododendron, heather, sunflower, and linden tree. It was the sweetener of choice until the seventeenth century, when sugar arrived. Honey was abandoned for a time, but has experienced a resurgence of popularity in recent years. Wild honey can be found in India and Asia.

Huitlacoche (Hongo de Maíz or Corn Mushroom) (Mexico) This gnarly, silver-grey fungus-mushroom grows on unsprayed corn ears and is black on the inside when ripe. It eventually consumes the kernels, synthesizes significant nutrients that don't exist in corn (like lysine), and pushes out the top of the ear. Huitlacoche is smooth and dry with a spongy texture, which turns into an exotic, delicious black purée when cooked, although it may be eaten raw in salads. The fresh-cut mushroom has a nutty, earthy, smoky flavor; as it ages, the flavor gets stronger and less appealing. Purchase it attached to the cob if possible; freeze extras up to 6 months. Huitlacoche goes best with corn, green chilies, epazote, poblanos, and eggs. A simple way of preparing the mushroom is *huitlacoche de Mexicana*, with onions, jalapeño chilies, and tomatoes. Huitlacoche may be eaten as a side dish or stuffed into corn masa dough for *tlacollos* or tamales and fried or steamed, or into tortillas for tacos and quesadillas.

J

Jaggery (Indian Gur) An unrefined, dark, soft, and richly complex cane sugar that tastes of caramel. South Indian cooks melt it and skim off impurities before using in uncooked dishes. Sometimes palm sugar is confused with jaggery.

Jambon Serrano, Jamon Ibérico See *Spanish Charcuterie (Charcutería)* in chapter *Spain*.

Java Pepper or Cubeb Pepper Java pepper is a pungently aromatic spice similar in appearance to peppercorns, but with the stem attached. Its flavor can be acrid, slightly bitter, and persistent. Some describe its flavor as a cross between warm, woody allspice and black pepper. Arab trade via India brought the spice to Europe and Africa. Indonesian cooks use it to flavor many dishes, especially curries.

Jicama (Mexico) A brown-skinned, firm white-fleshed tuber, usually eaten raw. It is slightly sweet and crunchy with the delicate flavor of potato and apple.

Jujube or Chinese Date Ancient Chinese fruit that is a glossy, blood-red, jujubes are sold dried and wrinkled. Purchase soft, pitted red jujubes instead of hard, dried, unpitted ones. They may be eaten dried or cooked into rice or sweet dishes.

K

Kabocha Squash (Japanese Pumpkin) A large round, deep to medium, thin and green-skinned squash with sweet creamy flesh.

Kale, Tuscan (Cavolo Nero) See *Italian Vegetables* in chapter *Italy*.

Kamaboko Kamaboko is the name for a wide variety of Japanese fish products that are made by steaming, puréeing, and molding seafood and binders into cakes. They have the texture of bologna; kamaboko is sliced and sometimes grilled.

Kampyo (Dried Gourd Shavings) This Japanese ingredient is made from dried strips of bottle bush gourd and used as an edible tie or as in ingredient in sushi. The dried strips must be rubbed with salt, washed, and simmered until soft before using. For *futomaki*, the strips are simmered in a dashi and soy-flavored sauce.

Kashk (Persia-Iran) There are two main kinds of kashk: a fermented, drained yogurt and a ground grain combined with fermented milk or yogurt. In modern Iran, kashk is drained, soured yogurt similar in texture to sour cream with a darker color, like tahini. It's available liquid or dried. Dried kashk must to be soaked and softened before using in cooking. Kashk was traditionally prepared from the whey leftover from cheese production.

Katsuobushi, Dried Bonito, or Skipjack (Japan) Katsuobushi is dried, fermented, and smoked skipjack tuna fillets high in umami. Most commonly used as the base for dashi broth along with kelp, kasuobushi is also used to boost the flavor of sauces and to garnish salads. Traditionally, cooks kept large chunks of katsuobushi and shaved them as needed on a tool similar to a wood plane. Now, most katsuobushi is sold as pink shavings in bags.

Kelp Sun-dried seaweed with broad, long leaves used in Japanese and Korean cuisine as a flavoring in dashi broth, soups, and stews. High in glutamic acid (and umami), kelp is a flavor-booster. Glutamic acid was first isolated from kelp, which led to the production of monosodium glutamate. Kelp comes in several grades; purchase the best. It takes 2/3 to 1 ounce to prepare 4 to 5 cups dashi. The white bloom on its surface is salt and minerals; do not rinse them away. Kelp may be lightly scored to release more flavor. Paper-thin shaved kombu strips (mottled white and green) are used for sushi in place of nori or as an edible wrapper.

Ketcap Asin Indonesian salty soy sauce.

Ketcap Manis Indonesian sweetened soy sauce.

Khelea (Moroccan Preserved Meat) Moroccans make preserved meat, usually beef, similar to Greek or Turkish basturma, called khelea, chele, kleehe, or khlii. Strips of meat marinate in cumin, coriander, garlic, and salt, and sun-dry several days and are cooked in animal fat, oil, and water. Packed in cooking fat, khelea will keep up to two years at room temperature.

Kibbeh or Kibbe (Lebanon) Arab dish traditionally made of bulgar and seasonings mixed with minced lamb or beef. It can be shaped various ways, stuffed, or layered and served raw or cooked.

Kikil Ethiopian meat or vegetable boiled with just water or seasoned with onion, garlic, and ginger.

Kinako This roasted soybean flour is often sweetened and used on Japanese tea sweets called *wagashi*.

Kirmizi Biber (Turkey) Oiled, roasted red chili used in Turkey. It may also refer to whole red chilies. The flakes range from mild and sweet to fiercely hot. The chilies are rubbed with olive oil and gently roasted until dark red, which imparts an unmistakable unique flavor and scent.

Kitfo Ethiopian dish of finely chopped raw meat seasoned with mitmita chili or mitmita spice blend and clarified butter. It may be cooked slightly and it becomes kitfo lebleb, rare or lightly cooked.

Knives and Knife Terms (Asia) See appendix, *Asian and Indian Knives and Cuts*.

Kombu (Kelp) (Japan) See *Kelp*.

Konnyaku (Japan) This pearly to gray-toned gelatinous cake comes in 10- to 12-ounce blocks immersed in a bag of water. The noodle form of konnyaku is called *shirataki*; it is some-times made with part tofu. Japanese cooks blanch konnyaku and use in stir-fries, salads, sukiyaki, soups, and stews (it takes on more flavor the longer it simmers). It is made from a tuber-ous root vegetable called "konnyaku potato" and calcium hy-droxide or oxide calcium extracted from eggshells. Konnyaku is 97 percent water and 3 percent glucomannan, or dietary fiber, which has very few calories. It is also rich in minerals and very low in calories. The konnyaku plant is native to In-donesia and is a kind of herbaceous perennial cultivated for food only in Japan. Wild konnyaku grows in Southeast Asia and China. To prepare konnyaku: Bring a small pot of water to a boil. Drain and rinse konnyaku. It is normal to have an unpleasant smell. Slice or dice konnyaku and place in boiling water. Boil 2 to 3 minutes, drain konnyaku, and rest until it is cooled and dried. This is a good way to prep konnyaku for stir-frying.

Kuzu or Kudzu This starch is made from the dried processed kuzu root; it is used for thickening desserts and sauces and is said to have a beneficial effect on digestion.

Kuzu Noodle, Japan Made from kuzu starch, which is consid-ered good for digestion. Boil these pricey noodles until tender and clear. Japanese use them in cold summer dishes because they remind them of ice.

Kvas or Kvass A tart, slightly alcoholic drink fermented from rye bread that is of Russian origin. It is popular in cultures that had Russian influences, like the Republic of Georgia.

L

Labneh Yogurt cheese. See *Signature Seasonings* in chapter *Lebanon*.

Lard Lard is the liquid fat rendered from pork fat, and is widely used in Mexican cooking. Flavorless commercial lard is made from high- and low-quality fat, usually hydrogenated, bleached, and deodorized. Freshly rendered lard has superior flavor. See *Mexican Signature Seasonings* in chapter *Mexico* for more information. To render lard: Finely dice unsalted fat-back into small cubes; discard tough skin. Place cubes in a food processor and process until it resembles ground meat, a few seconds. Place ground fat into a heavy pot over low heat. Scoop off fat as it melts and pour through cheesecloth-lined fine strainer. Stir fat frequently, and cook until cracklings are crisp and golden but not brown. Strain off remaining melted fat through cheesecloth. Store lard in small containers in freezer up to 1 year. The crisp cracklings (chicharróns) can be added to other dishes. One and half pounds of fatback will yield about 1-1/2 cups lard.

Lardo See *Cured Meats* in chapter *Italy*.

Lemongrass This herb has long, narrow, pale green woody stalks with a tender, bulb-like base. It has a refreshing and delicate, grassy, citrus flavor and scent and is used in South-east Asian cuisines.

Lemon Verbena (Lemon Beebrush) A bushy, flowering plant grown in Europe and the Mediterranean with long, narrow leaves highly aromatic with lemon and ginger, lemon verbena is great infused into poultry dishes, sauces, tea, sweets, pud-ding, ice cream, and sorbet.

Lettuces and Other Salad Greens (Europe and the Mediterra-nean) Lettuce is a leafy, edible green, and is part of the large *Compositae* or daisy family. The hundreds of varieties of let-tuces fall into four categories plus a cross: Crisphead or Head-ing, Butterhead, Loose-leaf and Cos (Romaine), and the cross, Buttercrunch. Other greens, not classified as lettuce, are often combined with them to produce salad. See *Mesclun*.

Liaison (France) A liaison is a mixture of egg yolks and heavy cream that is used to thicken and add satiny richness to a sauce, stew, or soup. For medium sauce thickness use 2 egg yolks to 2 or 3 ounces cream to thicken 1-1/2 cups liquid.

Lily Buds, Dried (Tiger Lily Buds or Golden Needles) These are the dried, unopened buds of the yellow or orange tiger lily. Dried, they have a strong scent, but when soaked are mildly floral. Lily buds are used for texture in Chinese moo shu or hot and sour soup. Soak in hot water until tender, 20 minutes, drain, rinse, and shred or use whole.

Lime Leaves (Kaffir or Thai Lime Leaves, Makrut) The South-east Asian lime tree (also known as Kaffir) has small, bumpy, green citrus and distinctive, shiny, firm double leaves. The pungent skin of the limes is used to flavor Thai curry pastes. The leaves are heavenly-fragrant and used to perfume soups, curries, and sauce. The lime juice tends to bitterness and is not often used. The tree is native to Malaysia, India, Laos,

Indonesia, Thailand, and adjacent countries. Lime leaves freeze well.

Longbeans, Chinese These stringless, foot-long deep green beans come in large hanks bound at one end. When fresh (thin, smooth, and deep green), they are sweet and tender with crunch and body. Chinese cooks cut them into 2- to 3-inch lengths and stir-fry.

Lotus Root This large, pinkish rhizome comes from the water lotus plant. When peeled and sliced crosswise it reveals a beautiful cut-out pattern. It is crunchy when raw; Japanese cooks prepare vinegared salads with it. The raw, peeled vegetable must be stored in vinegared water to keep from browning. Steam, boil, or deep-fry (tempura) thin slices for soup, stew, or as garnish.

Lovage This tall, herbaceous plant has leaves that look similar to Italian parsley, but tastes intensely of celery. It is native to much of Europe, southwestern Asia, and the eastern Mediterranean, where the leaves are used in salads and soup, and the roots are cooked as a vegetable or grated into salads.

Lychee (Asia) A rough-textured and thick-skinned red fruit with a large brown pit. Lychee nut usually refers to dried lychee fruit. The fresh fruit peels to reveal a soft, delicately sweet white flesh with a delicate floral flavor, which is lost with canning. Lychees are related to the prickly rambutan.

M

Mâche (Corn Salad, Lamb's Tongue) This wild or cultivated green has tender leaves and very mild, slightly nutty flavor.

Mahlab, Mahlepi, or Mahlep An aromatic spice with the flavor of bitter almond and cherry ground from inner seed of cherry pits, mahlepi is used to flavor Greek and Mediterranean cookies, egg-rich yeast cakes, and cheese cake.

Maize (Corn) Corn originated in Mexico, and *maíz* is the Mexican native Taino word for corn. Five varieties of corn are easily recognized: very hard-grained *popcorn*, hard-starchy *flint corn*, soft starch *flour corn*, *dent* or field corn (used for masa harina) with soft starch covering hard starch and a dented top, and sugary, tender *sweet corn*. Blue or red corn can be flint or dent corn. Like Italian cooks with pasta, Mexican cooks prepare an encyclopedia of dishes with fresh or dried corn. See chapter *Mexico* for more information.

Malt Powder (Korea) Powder made from barley grains that have been soaked, germinated, dried, and ground. This process of malting modifies starches into sugars, which are more easily digested by yeast. In Korea it is used in drinks; the syrup is added to sauces and stews.

Marigold or Calendula Petals The dried bright orange or yellow leaves of the marigold plant are somewhat bitter. The calendula and Tagetes-type marigold are used powdered in Georgian cooking as part of the khmeli-suneli seasoning mixes and to color dishes. Some cooks use dried marigold petals in place of saffron. The petals are anti-inflammatory and are used for skin disorders and to improve digestion.

Masa Mexican term for corn flour or dough made with dried, whole corn kernels that have been nixtamalized or cooked with lime (calcium hydroxide) or wood ash to soften their outer layer.

Mastic Mastic is a hardened, gummy resin from a Mediterranean shrub with a slight pine or cedar flavor. It's used to season liqueurs, confections, bread, pastries, and Greek spoon sweets. Turkish cooks use it to coat doner kebab. It is sometimes called arabic gum but should not be confused with gum arabic, which is a different substance.

Mechoui Moroccan spiced whole lamb cooked until tender on a spit. It is a specialty of the Berber mountain people.

Melegueta or Grains of Paradise Native to West Africa, and about the size of cardamom seeds (with a bit of their flavor), these pungently spicy, warm, and slightly bitter seeds are crushed or added whole to many dishes in place of the more irritating black peppercorns.

Membrillo This Spanish quince paste comes sweetened and reddish-colored in a rectangular block. It can be sliced and served simply with cheese, added to sauces, or used in desserts and is often found in the Caribbean (Puerto Rico and Cuba) and Mexico.

Merek Ethiopian term for broth.

Mesclun In France, mesclun was traditionally baby lettuce leaves mixed with young dandelion and arugula leaves. Today the standard mixture can contain baby oakleaf and romaine lettuce leaves plus arugula, dandelion, watercress, chervil, purslane, Italian parsley, mache, frisée (curly endive), escarole, chicory, and radicchio.

Meze or Mezze (Snacks or Tastes) An offering of small dishes (much like tapas) served as a light lunch or before a main meal in Mediterranean and Middle Eastern cultures of the former Ottoman Empire.

Millet A small, gluten-free, starchy grain (a.k.a. birdseed) from a grass. Millet grown for culinary use in the West is a small, round, pale-yellow-colored grain known as "Proso" millet, but hundreds of varieties exist. Millet is used in India, Asia, in the West, and in Africa, where it most likely originated.

Mint There are hundreds of varieties of mint, but for culinary purposes mints can be divided into **peppermint, spearmint, mild mints**, and other **un-minty** cultivars. Peppermints are very assertive and are often used dried in Middle-Eastern cooking, as oil for desserts, or used sparingly when fresh. Spearmints contain little peppermint, but are double minty without the pungency of peppermint. They are most used in cooking and sold in bunches in the produce section. Mild mints like curly mint and the wooly apple or pineapple mints are slightly minty and tend to have other flavors that shine through, like caraway or pineapple. Un-minty cultivars have little or no mint flavor or scent, like lemon or bergamot mint, which has a citrus scent.

Mirin (Japanese Rice Wine Seasoning) This fortified sweet alcoholic seasoning, when made traditionally, is brewed from rice, koji bacteria, and water and fortified with 80 proof alcohol. Eden brand is traditionally brewed. Low-cost mirins (aji-mirin or mirin-fu) are mixtures of chemicals, molasses, and glucose. Traditional mirin is called hon-mirin or "real mirin." This mirin should be refrigerated and used within several months after opening. Mirin should be brought to a boil before using to remove raw alcohol flavor.

Miso (Japanese Fermented Bean and Grain Paste) Live, lactobacillus-rich paste traditionally made from cooked soybeans and rice (or other grains and legumes) fermented with koji. Japanese cooks use miso to flavor soup broths, as part of sauces, and to marinate foods. See chapter *Japan* for more information.

Mixiote (Mexico) A shaved leaf fiber from the maguey leaf, mixiote is used like parchment paper to wrap and cook pre-Hispanic tamales, meats, fish, and poultry. It lends its flavor to dishes and becomes crisp when cooked.

Monosodium Glutamate (MSG) Also known as sodium glutamate or MSG or L-glutamate, this white crystalline salt is the sodium salt of glutamic acid, a naturally occurring nonessential amino acid. Commercially it was made from wheat gluten by three methods: hydrolysis of vegetable proteins with hydrochloric acid, direct chemical synthesis, and bacterial fermentation. Currently it is synthesized by bacterial fermentation from sugar beets, sugar cane, tapioca, or molasses. MSG is used in Asian cooking to enhance the flavor of food, much like salt.

Mortadella See *Cured Meats* in chapter *Italy*.

Mska (Gum Arabic) Strong scented, but usually mild-flavored gummy sap-resin from the acacia tree, gum Arabic is a natural emulsifier, thickener, and stabilizer. It is used to bind and thicken soft drinks, prepare candies and baked goods, and flavor foods.

Mung Bean Sprouts See *Bean Sprouts*.

Mushrooms (Asia) See *Japanese Mushrooms* in chapter *Japan and Korea*.

Mushrooms, Wild and Cultivated (Europe) See *Italian Vegetables* in chapter Italy, *French Mushrooms and Fungus (Champignons)* in chapter *France*, and *Spanish Wild Mushrooms* in chapter *Spain*.

Mustard Oil (India) This spicy, strong-smelling oil, similar to horseradish, is pressed from black mustard (Brassica nigra), brown mustard (Brassica juncea), and white mustard seed (Brassica hirta). East Indian cooks use mustard oil as a main cooking oil, while north Indian, Nepalese, and Bangladeshi cooks use it for specific dishes. Indian cooks heat mustard oil to the smoking point and cool before using to mellow and release the pungent smell. Mixing mustard oil with canola eliminates the need for this process. Mustard oil adulteration (the addition of argemone oil, a poison) has occasionally been reported in India.

Mustard Powder (Hot, Yellow) Dried, ground seed from the yellow mustard plant. To bring out its pungent, spicy flavor, the powder must be mixed in equal parts with water and allowed to rest 10 minutes. For a thinner version use 1 part mustard powder to 1-1/2 parts water. Temperature of the liquid is the key: hot liquid will produce mild mustard, and cold liquid produces hot mustard. Chinese mustard is made with water and mustard powder. Cover mustard after preparing; it will lose pungency as it sits.

N

Napa Cabbage (Chinese Cabbage) This wide, oblong, torpedo-shaped head can reach 12 inches long and weigh 5 or more pounds each. It is white to pale green with broad leaves that have a wide rib surrounded by a thin crinkly skirt. They are tightly packed. Koreans favor this cabbage for kim chi.

Natto (Japan) Cooked soybeans, which are left whole and injected with Aspergillis mold. They ferment and produce gooey, sticky, soft soybeans reminiscent of blue cheese or tempeh. Natto is served in sushi bars.

Nigella (N. Sativa) This pale blue flower has sharp-tasting, aromatic, nutty seeds that look like tough black sesame seed. They are erroneously called black caraway, black onion seed, and fennel flower; in India nigella is known as *kalonji*. It is used in Europe and the Middle East as a seasoning for bread, Armenian string cheese, and on pastries.

Nitir Kibbe Ethiopian clarified butter simmered with herbs and spices. It isn't usually used at the start of a w'et, but rather added midway and simmered. However, kitfo, when cooked, is simmered lightly in nitir kibbe.

Nokos (Senegal) Pounded or ground Senegalese seasoning paste made with bouillon cubes, garlic, onion, and Scotch Bonnet chilies and used mainly to season thiebou jen (rice and fish stew) and thiebou niebe (rice and black-eyed pea stew).

Noodles (Asia) Noodles are beloved food all over Asia. They fall into three categories: wheat (somen, egg noodles, wontons, udon, soba, and ramen), rice, or "other" starches like tapioca, mung bean starch, kuzu, yam, potato starch, or Asian sweet potato starch (rice, tapioca, cellophane, kuzu, harusame, and Korean sweet potato starch). In each category noodles can be fresh or dried, thin vermicelli or up to wide, flat ribbons. Heavier sauces with large pieces of meat do well with heavier noodles and, conversely, thinner noodles are best with more delicate sauces and smaller shreds of meat or vegetables. Fresh noodles keep 3 to 4 days refrigerated and 1 month frozen. Keep dried noodles in a cool, dry, dark place up to 1 year.

Nori (Laver or Korean Kim) Originally this algae was harvested in Tokyo Bay, washed and, like handmade paper, laid on bamboo or wood frames to dry. The modern process has been mechanized to produce the toasted, dark green (or unroasted purple), paper-like sheets. A sheet of nori measures about 7-1/2 by 8 inches. Expensive brands are heavier shiny.

Each sheet has a shiny side and a rough side with lines that run the shorter length of the sheet. Keep nori packed in a dark, cool, dry spot in an airtight container up to 6 months. Pass limp nori over a gas flame to toast, crisp, and bring out flavor. Ao-nori is flaked nori used as a condiment.

O

Olives   There are two main types of edible olives: green and black. Olives are too bitter to eat when first picked from November to January. Green (unripe) olives may be crushed and soaked in changes of water for several days then preserved in brine. Black (ripe) olives are cured several months in brine or layered with coarse salt until shriveled and tender. Greek and Turkish oil-cured black olives are layered with coarse salt and cured until soft and fruity. They are then rinsed, dried, and packed in oil.

Olive Oil   This highly prized cooking oil is produced in many Mediterranean, Middle Eastern, and Arab countries. Pressing olive oil is an age-old process. It begins with picking green or ripe olives. The olives are ground into a paste or *pomace* with big millstones or modern steel drums. Workers spread the paste onto cocoa fiber mats, which they stack on top of each other in a column and put into a press. The press separates oil/water from paste: water causes oil to deteriorate quickly. Since oil is less dense than water, traditional producers allowed gravity to separate oil from water. The faster process of centrifugation has replaced gravity. Spain tops olive oil production, Italy is second, and Greece ranks third; together they produce about 75 percent of the world's olive oil. Turkey, Spain, Tunisia, France, Portugal, Syria, Morocco, and the United States also produce olive oil. The first cold pressing is known as *extra virgin* and the second cold pressing is called *virgin*. The remaining pressings produce oils that are called *pure* or olive oil. They are pressed with chemical solvents and heat and have little use in the kitchen. Store olive oil tightly capped in a cool, dark spot. Use within a year of purchase.

Orange Flower Water (France, Spain, Morocco)   Orange flower water is a clear water that is distilled from fresh bitter (Seville) orange blossoms. It is used to flavor cookies, cakes, cocktails, and baklava. Moroccan cooks use orange and rose waters in sweet and savory dishes: tagines, salads, and cakes or confections. It takes seven pounds of Bergamot orange blossoms or rosebuds to make one gallon of the water. They are traditionally distilled in an alambic.

Oshinko   The term for Japanese vegetables pickled in rice bran (nuka) or pickled in salt and vinegar. Napa cabbage, daikon radish, eggplant, cucumber, carrot, or burdock root are commonly pickled. They may be part of a sushi roll.

Ouarka (Morocco)   See *Warqa*.

Ouzo   A popular licorice-flavored Greek and Turkish liquor, ouzo turns white when mixed with water. It is served in Greek tavernas with small plates of food.

Oyster Sauce (China)   This rich and concentrated thick, brown sauce is made from soy sauce and oyster extract. Its smoky flavor and high umami make it popular in dipping sauces or on stir-fries. Look for the best.

P

Palm Hearts (Hearts of Palm)   Hearts of palm are the fresh, edible inner stems or shoots harvested from several varieties of palm trees. The heart is harvested from a year-old tree when it is about 5 feet tall with a 4-inch diameter. The hearts may be eaten raw and are available canned. They have a mild flavor and tender flesh similar to artichokes or white asparagus.

Palm (Red) Oil or Dende Oil   Used in Brazilian and West African cooking, dende oil is made from the kernel of the palm fruit. The oil is thick and red-orange in color with a nutty flavor and high in saturated fat. West African cooks use it for frying, and to flavor stews, rice, and sauces.

Palm Sugar (Southeast Asia)   Palm sugar is the sap of the coconut palm tree, which is cooked down to crystalline form and used as a sweetener in soups, sauces, and desserts.

Pandanus Leaf or Screwpine   Though not easily available in the West, the fragrant pandan leaf is worth searching out in Asian markets (or growing indoors). Its flavor, subtle and nutty, adds an exotic hint to the dishes of Malaysia, Indonesia, Thailand, Singapore, and Sri Lanka. Known as "screwpine," this plant forms rosettes of long, arching spiny yellow leaves, 18 to 30 inches long, maturing from all green, to green with pale yellow stripes. Simmer 1 leaf per cup coconut milk.

Panko (Japan)   Crunchy, flaky, dried white breadcrumbs used in Japanese cooking, often for breading and deep-frying.

Pasta (Italy)   Dry pastas, mostly made with semolina flour and water, can be divided into four basic categories, each with many entrants: long shapes or *pasta lunga*, short shapes or *pasta corta*, tiny shapes or *pastina*, and stuffed, filled, or baked shapes like ravioli and lasagna. See chapter *Italy* for more information.

Paximáthia (Greece)   Slices of bread, oven-dried into rusks so they last indefinitely. Paximáthia are used to thicken soups or other dishes, as crumbs for salad or toppings, and as travel or snack food; they last indefinitely. Substitute dry, toasted whole wheat bread. See chapter *Greece and Turkey* for more information.

Piloncillo (Mexico)   The dark brown hard sweetener is made from raw sugar cane juice, which is cooked and poured into conical molds. Oaxacans pour it into round molds that look like panela cheese so it is called *panela* in Oaxaca.

Pimentón   Spanish smoked paprika. See *Signature Seasonings* in chapter *Spain*.

Piquillo Peppers   See *Signature Seasonings* in chapter *Spain*.

Plantain   See *Vegetables and Fruits of the Caribbean* and *The Wide World of Plantains and Bananas* in chapter *The West Indies or Caribbean Islands*.

Plum Sauce or Duck Sauce (China)   This thick, jammy sauce is made from a type of fruit species related to both plums and apricots, but more closely to the apricot and the Japanese umeboshi plum. The apricot-like plums, sugar, vinegar, salt, ginger, chili, and garlic yield a clear yellow sauce with light, sweet, and tart flavor. It is especially good with poultry, spring rolls, and egg rolls.

Polenta   Polenta is a coarsely-ground yellow corn meal used in northern Italy for a cornmeal mush of the same name.

Pomegranate   An ancient fruit arrives to markets from September to February. When broken open, its leathery red skin reveals a network of fleshy white veins filled with juicy, garnet nuggets that each house a small seed. Lightly score the skin and break the fruit apart. Place it into a bowl of cold water and separate the seeds from the skin and papery veins, which will float. The seeds or arils can range in flavor from sweet to slightly sour. Pomegranates may be juiced or the seeds used as garnish.

Pomegranate Molasses or Syrup   The juice of pomegranates simmered to a thick, tart syrup. Look for types with no sugar or preservatives added. It is used to give sweet, fruity, tart flavor to anything from soups, stews, and vegetables to marinades.

Porcini   A prized mushroom eaten throughout Europe. See *Italian Vegetables* in chapter *Italy*.

Poularde   A French term for a young, fatted chicken with tender, delicate meat.

Poulet   A French term for chicken. The best are from Bresse, France. See *Bresse Chicken*.

Potato and Yam (Asia)   Though Asians use white potatoes, yams and sweet potatoes are also popular. Japanese and Korean cooks use several types of the gluey, stringy *mountain yam*, a red-skinned white-fleshed sweet potato and a thin-skinned field yam or tuber. Indian, Indonesian, and Chinese cooks use white and sweet potatoes, and in India, Vietnam, and Indonesia, purple yams are popular.

Pozole or Hominy Corn   Corn kernels that have been nixtamalized or cooked with lime (calcium hydroxide) or wood ash to soften their outer layer then dried. To use dried pozole, it must first be soaked 12 to 24 hours, drained, rinsed, and cooked until tender, 4 to 5 hours. Canned hominy doesn't have the sweetness of the fresh kernels or dried and cooked. Pozole is also the name of a Mexican soup with hominy as a main ingredient. One cup dried pozole (hominy) corn soaked and cooked yields about 1 pound or 2-1/2 cups. See chapter *Mexico*.

Prosciutto   See *Italian Cured Meats* in chapter *Italy*.

Purslane   The wild or cultivated succulent plant has red stems with small green, oval, fleshy leaves. It can range in flavor from very mild to nutty; it is crunchy when raw. Purslane is rich in alpha-linolenic acid, an essential fatty acid.

 Q

Quanta or Qwanta   Ethiopian beef or fish jerky.

Queso   The Mexican term for cheese. See *Mexican Cheese* in chapter *Mexico*.

Quince   This fruit looks similar to a squat, yellow-green apple or pear, to which it is related. Quinces are high in pectin, very tart, hard, fragrant, and inedible unless cooked. Moroccan cooks use the fruit to deepen flavor in meat tagines and stews. Arabic and Middle Eastern cooks stuff quince and bake them, simmer quince in meat dishes, and cook them with sugar into quince jam.

 R

Radicchio   This burgundy-red and white-veined, round-headed or long, narrow-headed leafy chicory has a refreshing bitterness. Versatile, it can be torn into salads for contrast, grilled, braised, sautéed, or as part of risotto. See *Italian Vegetables* in chapter *Italy* for more information.

Radish, White   See *Daikon*.

Ramen   Dried, wavy noodles compressed into square cakes and packaged in cellophane with a seasoning packet. They are popular for a quick, inexpensive meal.

Ras el Hanout   Literally "top of the shop." Moroccan spice mix that can contain up to 40 spices and herbs.

Rice, Asia (Chinese Mee, Korean Bap, and Japanese Kome)   Rice, the seed of a type of grass that was probably first cultivated in Southeast Asia and China 8,500 years ago, is a staple for two-thirds of the world and most of India. Asian countries produce many varieties of rice. But most rice isn't exported; it stays local. Rice is cultivated in 2 to 4 inches of water; consequently it requires very level fields or paddies. The shallow water heats up quickly and retains heat, protecting the young plants. Rice is sown mid-April, the fields are flooded for about 1 month while the rice geminates. The water is drained to allow plants to root deeper, and flooded again. The rice will flower and set seed if conditions are right. After harvest the rice is hulled, polished, and dried.

The rice starches *amylose* and *amylopectin* compose 90 percent of rice. **Amylose** does not gelatinize during cooking, so rice containing higher levels result in fluffy, separate grains after cooking, which tend to harden after rice is cooled. Long-grain white rice has the most amylose and the least amylopectin, so it is the least sticky with the lowest glycemic index. **Amylopectin** is the waxy, stickier starch that is higher in medium, short-grain, and sticky, glutinous rice. Short and sticky rice has almost no amylose. High amylopectin rice has a characteristic opaque white grain, while higher amylose grains are clearer. Occasional varieties of Thai sticky rice may look like long grain, but the grain will exhibit the opaque white color that identifies it as containing high amylopectin. There are three most basic rice types (commonly called long-, medium-, and short-grain) categorized by amylose (starch) content, but many more hybrids exist: *Indica*, with long slender grains high in amylose that cook into separate fluffy grains, *Javanica*, with a middling amylose content and stickiness, and *Japonica*, with shorter, plump, medium-low amylose, high amylopectin grains that cook into sticky clumps. Japanese and Koreans use mainly medium-grain rice. Southeast Asians and Chinese like short-, medium-, and long-grain rice. Indians prefer long-grain parboiled or long-grain aged basmati.

Use the correct rice: long grain for fluffy dishes and short grain for stickier dishes. Wash rice and drain well. Choose a heavy pot with lid and never add more than 2 inches of rice. Use the proper amount of water; older rice needs slightly more. Don't excessively peek at or stir the rice. Allow cooked rice to rest 10 to 15 minutes before fluffing. This allows the rice to harden a bit.

Rice, Europe and Mediterranean The Italian and Spanish medium-grain rice, because it is a cultivar of *japonica* short-grain rice, is slightly stickier, good for paella and risotto. The plumper short-grain and glutinous rice are very sticky. Italian risotto type rices are also used for arancini, omelets, stuffings and desserts. They fall into four categories: *Riso superfino* is a premium group of rice has high starch content and large grains; this rice takes the longest to cook. It makes creamy risotto and may be used for salad, timbales, or side dishes. Arborio and Canaroli are two types. *Riso fino* is a standard rice similar to superfine but with smaller grains. It is used for risotto, soup, salads, and side dishes. Vialone is a prized Venetian variety. *Riso semifino* has smaller, thicker grains than fino and is very starchy. It cooks faster than the others and stays intact so is used in soups and side dishes. Maratelli, Vialone nano, and Padano are examples. *Riso commune* is the fourth type with small, round kernels. It cooks quickly and is the least expensive type, generally used in the region where it is grown. Spanish rice tends to be smaller grained and acts like Italian rice. Three types are prized for paella and pilaf: *bomba*, *calasparra*, and *granza*. Bomba is an ancient, small-kernel rice prized for paella. It expands in width like an accordion rather than longitudinally and can absorb three times more liquid than similar rice. Calasparra is a small-kernel grain rice that will absorb twice more liquid than similar rice, and granza is a prized, rare rice used for paella.

Rice, Converted or Parboiled This is long-grain brown rice that has been soaked and pressure steam-cooked, which forces nutrients from the bran into the starchy grain. The rice is then dried and polished like white rice. Converted rice has a beige, glassy look and takes slightly longer to cook than white rice, but it keeps its shape during long cooking and is more shelf stable.

Rice (Latin America and West Africa) Mexican and Caribbean cooks favor long- and medium-grain white rice. **Djola Red Rice** is a long-grain rice grown in Senegal; the reddish-colored bran coating gives it its name.

Rice Flour Fine white rice flour comes from two types of rice: long grain and glutinous or sticky. Fresh and dried noodles, batters, and desserts are made from long-grain rice flour. Dumplings, buns, pudding, and pastries like the Japanese tea ceremony sweets called *wagashi* are made with the sweeter glutinous rice flour. Japanese rice flours are *joshinko*, *mochiko*, and *shiratamako*. Joshinko is ground from plain short-grain rice and used for sweets. Mochiko is a pre-steamed glutinous rice ground into flour. Mochiko is used for mochi and thickening.

Shiratamako is made from uncooked glutinous rice flour and used for sweets. Mix mochiko or shiratamako with cool water before using.

Rice Noodles Rice noodles, used throughout Asia, can be found fresh or dried. Thai cooks use dried thin or medium rice sticks for pad Thai, and Vietnamese use various rice noodles for "bun" salads, noodle soups like tom yum and pho, stir-fries, and salads. Chinese toss them with dressing, shredded cooked chicken, and cooked greens. Wide noodles do well in stir-fries and soup. Made from long-grain white rice flour and water, these noodles turn opaque white after cooking. They cook very quickly—a blessing in countries with scarce fuel. Soak dry noodles in warm water until flexible, 15 to 20 minutes. They may be stir-fried (with liquid) or dipped in boiling water for a few seconds then put into soup or stir-fried. Though typically made with rice flour and water, some producers add other starches to rice noodles, like wheat gluten or tapioca flour. Read labels. Rice noodles are made by extruding rice paste and steaming or by steaming rice slurry into sheets and slicing. Prepare fresh rice wrappers or noodles by mixing rice flour with water and salt to a thin, crepe-like batter. Steam thin layers of it ladled in oiled baking tins until firm.

Vermicelli: Fine and wiry, like angel hair

Thin Rice Sticks: Like opaque, narrow fettuccine, they also come in Medium and Wide

Rice Sticks: Wide, flat, thin noodles

Rice Chip Slices (Korea): Thick slices of large snakes of noodle dough sliced on the diagonal and dried. Soak till tender and simmer in stew or stir-fry.

Sliver Pin Rice Noodles: Hand-rolled 2-inch long, these are coated with oil and resemble bean sprouts. Used to make Cantonese stir-fry with chicken, scallions, soy sauce, and black pepper.

River Rice Noodles: Wide, flat noodles made from rice flour, wheat starch, and water

Fresh Rice Noodle Sheets: Chinese dim sum specialty; thin layer of steamed rice flour batter

Rice-Sesame Seed Wafers (Vietnam) Vietnamese rice and sesame seed wafers are called *banh trang me*. They are deep-fried or microwaved until puffed and cracker-like. They are served topped with fresh salads.

Rice Vinegar (Japan) Mild, light-colored, and subtly sweet vinegar made from white or brown rice. Strong, astringent, Western vinegar is not a good substitute. Japanese produce several strengths of high-quality rice vinegar. See *Signature Seasonings* in chapters *Japan and Korea* or *China* for more information.

Rice Wine (Chinese Shaoxing Wine) This nutty, amber, rice wine is brewed from glutinous rice, millet, and yeast and aged 10 to 100 years. Similar in alcohol content and full-bodied flavor to sherry, Shaoxing wine is used for drinking, marinating, and cooking. Dry sherry may substitute. Avoid salted varieties.

Roff Senegalese condiment used as a seasoning-stuffing for fish.

Rosewater   Rosewater is a watery by-product from the distillation of rose oil for perfume. It is used to flavor desserts and rice dishes in Greece, Turkey, Iran, Lebanon, and France.

Roux   Classically this thickener is made from equal parts flour and unsalted butter by weight and cooked together before use; some recipes use 3 to 4 ounces flour to 2 ounces whole, unsalted butter. The amount of flour determines thickening ability. Butter coats protein or gluten strands to keep flour from lumping, and adds flavor. An old chef's rule says 1 pound roux to 1 gallon milk/stock for medium thickness. A *white roux* is cooked briefly with no color. A *blonde roux* is light colored and nutty. A *brown roux* is dark and very nutty. The darker the roux, the less it thickens.

S

Sago   This starch is extracted from the sago palm or sago cycad mainly in Indonesia. Sago pearls are used for desserts and may be used interchangeably with tapioca. Noodles and white bread are made from sago starch.

Saké (*sah-kay*) (Japan)   The big four flavors of Japanese cuisine are **dashi**, **shoyu** and **miso**, and **saké**. Saké is a brewed alcoholic drink made from sushi rice, water, and koji (fungus Aspergillus oryzae). It is called rice wine, but more accurately is a rice beer. Japanese saké makers take pride in the water quality. Cheaper saké is served hot; the more expensive brands are served chilled. Brewing methods and ingredient quality, the rice used and how much it is polished, strained, or aged, determine saké type and quality. Flavor of saké is measured according to residual sugar and alcohol content. Ratings are from plus 10 to minus 10: Plus 10 or **karakuchi** is the driest. Minus 10 or **amaguchi** is the sweetest.

Salam Leaf   Many Indonesian and Malaysian recipes call for the subtly flavored salam leaf, from the cassia (cinnamon) family, and suggest that deprived cool-climate cooks substitute bay leaves. Bay leaves are nothing like this aromatic and slightly sour/astringent salam leaf. Available fresh only in Indonesia and Malaysia (the tree grows wild there), salam leaves are available dry in some Southeast Asian groceries catering to Indonesians. Cooks fry the leaves in oil to bring out their delicate flavor. Some cooks substitute the more flavorful Indian curry leaves.

Salsify or Oyster Plant   See *Italian Vegetables* in chapter *Italy*.

Salumi   The Italian term for cured meats.

Sambal   A fragrant Indonesian wet spice paste that melts easily into stir-fries, marinades, soups, and sauces.

Sashimi   Japanese sliced raw fish eaten raw with condiments.

Sazón (Caribbean)   A commercial seasoning (used mainly in Puerto Rico) made with ground coriander, cumin, pepper, annatto seed, garlic powder, salt, and often, MSG.

Seaweed or Sea Vegetables   Chinese, Japanese, and Korean cooks use various types of sea vegetables, from the most popular agar (kanten), kelp, nori, and wakame to hijiki, arame, and iwanori.

Sélino (Greek Wild Celery)   This wild "Italian" celery, as Greeks call it, looks like large-stemmed Italian parsley with a strong, pungent flavor. It is not used raw as a vegetable but rather as an herb, cooked into Greek dishes. It is now found cultivated. Lovage is a similar plant and may be a substitute.

Semolina   A somewhat coarse, pale yellow flour made from the high-gluten, high-protein durum wheat endosperm. It is used in southern Italy mainly to prepare dry pastas. In other countries it's used to prepare couscous or porridge; in Greece it is cooked with grape juice to produce a sweet confection.

Sesame Oil, Plain   Oil pressed from unroasted white sesame seeds, this oil makes a fine cooking oil. It is called gingelly oil in India. It should not be confused with Asian sesame oil, which is pressed from roasted seeds.

Sesame Seed Paste, White and Black   Chinese and Japanese cooks use black or white sesame seed paste made from roasted sesame seeds. Mediterranean sesame paste (tahini) made from unroasted seeds is not a good substitute.

Shallot (Asia, French Eschalot, Italian Scalogno, and Spanish El Chalote)   The shallot is closely related to garlic and onions, and looks like a small, brown onion. Historians believe that shallots originated in Central or Southeast Asia and traveled from there to India and the Mediterranean. Asian and Indian shallots are small and reddish-purple. The large, often elongated European-style shallot has coppery skin with multi bulbs. The prized French grey shallot is pear-shaped with tough, thick, gray-blue, wrinkled skin and creamy purple flesh with a sweet (never bitter), rich flavor. It is considered the "true shallot." In India small yellow onions and shallots are interchangeable; shallots are prized for their strong flavor and quick browning. Southeast Asian groceries sell dry, fried shallots for use as garnish.

Sheep Tail Fat   See *Fat-Tailed Sheep Fat*.

Shark's Fin (China)   Shark's fin is valued for its gelatinous properties. Sold in packets of transparent threads, dried shark's fin is simmered in soup or cooked with eggs. It should be soaked in boiling water 30 minutes to soften it before using.

Shichimi (Japanese Seven Spice Mixture) (Japan)   This spicy condiment is a mixture of ground red chili (togarashi), sansho pepper, dried orange peel, black hemp or white poppy seed, nori flakes, and sesame seeds. It comes in various spicy strengths and is most often used on rice, in soup, and on noodles.

Shiitake (Dried) or Dried Black Mushrooms   These popular, meaty, umami-rich brown mushrooms become concentrated and strong-flavored when dried. They come in many different sizes and grades. Soak them in warm water until soft, 20 to 30 minutes, discard stems or use for stock, and slice the caps for soup and stir-fry. Incorporate the very flavorful soaking liquid into the dish.

Shirataki (Japan)   See *Konnyaku*.

Shiro   Ethiopian term for chickpea flour. See *Chickpea Flour*.

Shishi-Togarashi (Lion Pepper) (Japan) Small (3-inch long), green, sweet, and mild-flavored Japanese pepper that is deep-fried or grilled; often served as a side dish. Green bell peppers may be substituted.

Shiso (Perilla) With its cinnamon-like, minty, apple, and basil flavor, the fragrant green shiso or perilla leaf keeps food bright-tasting and fresh. Asians believe it has antiseptic properties. Japanese use shiso with raw fish, in dressings, on salads, added to red miso and saké, to mayonnaise, or with rice or noodles. Koreans call perilla "wild sesame" and use it to wrap bulgogi or season it and to wrap rice. Both green or purple/red varieties are easy to grown in a small pot on a windowsill.

Shrimp, Dried Tiny to small dried shrimp are used in many Asian cuisines. Southeast Asian cooks use them in soup, vegetable dishes, and fried rice. Fresh shrimp are salted and dried to intensify their flavor. Chinese use dried shrimp to enhance vegetable dishes. The best are bright pink and about 1 inch from head to tail. Avoid older, gray-colored shrimp. To soften their flavor, soak in sherry or Shaoxing wine. They keep indefinitely.

Shrimp Paste Pungent seasoning paste made from ground, salted, and fermented shrimp. Though it smells like long-neglected gym socks, when cooked this flavoring device delivers an exotic salty, smoky flavor. The best fermented salted shrimp pastes come from Thailand. They are known as *kapi* in Thailand, as *mam tom* or *mam ruoc* in Vietnam, and as *trasi*, *terasi*, or *belacan* in Malaysia and Indonesia. It is available in firm cakes, which should be roasted before using, and also a softer version in tubs.

Smen A very strong, cheesy, fermented clarified butter, sometimes seasoned with herbs, eaten in Morocco.

Snow Peas and Pea Shoots This bright green, crisp and sweet, green flat, almost crescent-shaped pod may be eaten raw or slightly cooked. Sugar snap peas are a good substitute. Snow pea shoots and tendrils are a popular edible green available in Asian markets.

Sorrel A large green-leafed vegetable-herb with a pleasant, tart, lemony taste, sorrel is one of the first spring arrivals. Sorrel was developed in Italy and France in the Middle Ages. It is frequently used in salads, puréed in soups and sauces (France and Italy), or mixed with potatoes (Belgium), eggs (Spain), or other vegetables like spinach and chard (Greece).

Sorrel (Flor de Jamaica or Rosella) Caribbean sorrel is not the same as the European green, leafy, tart herb. It is a small, fleshy red plant in the hibiscus family, which is used to make jam, jelly, chutney, sauce, and syrup. In Senegal the leaves are used as a spicy version of spinach and to flavor the national stew called thiéboudienne.

Soy Sauce, Shoyu, and Tamari (Japan, Korea, and China) Japanese soy sauce is richly colored and full-bodied to light and thin but salty. Japanese shoyu (soybeans and wheat) and tamari (soybeans) are the most refined soy sauces. To make Japanese tamari, soybeans are soaked, then pressure cooked until soft. Wheat is roasted and cracked. The soybeans and wheat are combined and ground, then passed through an extruder and scraped into nuggets. The nuggets are coated with Aspergillus mold (koji) and placed into an incubator for 2 days where they change from white to yellow and become covered with the koji mold. This koji mash is mixed with a salty brine and allowed to ferment about 6 months (some longer and in cedar casks for more complex flavor). The brined mash (moromi) is now a thick paste (miso was originally made this way, and tamari was simply a by-product of production). The moromi is pressed three times: first with a gravity press, second with a light press, and third with a heavy press. The soy sauce or tamari is poured into a settling tank, where it stays for a week to allow the fine particulate to settle. The soy or tamari is pulled from the top and blended to achieve a consistent flavor. It is then pasteurized to kill mold and bacteria, and bottled. The soy/wheat solids are distributed as cattle feed, and the soybean oil that occurs is piped off and sent to oil processors. Chinese soy sauces are densely flavored, very salty and range from thick and dark to thin and light. Low-sodium soy sauce is brewed soy sauce that has the sodium content reduced through dialysis by 35 to 40 percent. The cheapest soy sauces are not brewed. They are made from hydrolyzed vegetable protein, hydrochloric acid, caramel, and corn syrup plus preservatives. They are generally thick and dark and can taste yeasty and metallic.

Soba (Japan and Korea) Japanese soba noodles are sometimes made with wheat and buckwheat or with just buckwheat (a non-gluten grain). Korean buckwheat (naengmyon) is made with buckwheat flour and Korean sweet potato starch, which makes them chewier than Japanese soba. Japanese cooks make the nutty flavored soba tea from coarsely ground roasted buckwheat grains.

Somen, Japanese (Chinese Sun Mian) Japanese somen are very thin, straight dried pasta made from wheat flour. The Chinese versions are thin, round, dried noodle nests.

Squash Flowers (Flor de Calabacita) These bright yellow flowers from the summer squash are used raw or cooked in Mexican cuisine. The unsprayed male flowers (without a squash attached) are picked, and the green sepals around the bulb are removed, but a little stalk may be left. Bugs are shaken out. The flowers may be lightly rinsed and patted dry, but this will soften them. The flowers may be stuffed and fried, chopped, and sautéed as a side dish or filling for quesadillas or tacos, or simmered in soup.

Star Anise The seeds of this 8-pointed star-shaped, brown spice have a mildly licorice-fennel flavor and are used in red-cooked dishes.

Straw Mushrooms (Asia) A pale brown mushroom grown in China in beds of rice straw, this mushroom is mostly found canned in the West. It has a pleasant, slippery texture and mild taste.

Sugar Cane A tall, stout, perennial grass native to Southeast Asia, the fibrous stalks of sugarcane are rich in sugar. About 90 percent of the world's sugar is processed from sugarcane. The cane may be used as a skewer for grilled foods, chewed, or pressed to extract the sweet juice, crystallized into rock sugar, or evaporated into thick cakes called jaggery or gur in India.

Sumac (Lebanon, Middle East)   Sumac is the sour red berry of a wild Mediterranean bush that is used in Arabic cooking to add a fruity, tart taste. Dried berries are crushed to a powder and sprinkled into dishes during or after cooking. Dried, whole berries can be macerated in hot water to release flavor.

Summer Savory   This is a green, leafy herb with a robust, pungent, peppery, savory flavor reminiscent of dill and thyme that goes well with beans, tomatoes, fish, and cooked vegetables. It may be used fresh or dried. Summer savory is used Roman, French, Iranian, Georgian, Greek, and Turkish cuisines. **Winter savory** is related: both are in the rosemary-thyme family. Winter savory is a semi-evergreen and more pungent than summer savory; it goes well with beans and meat. Winter savory loses its potency when long-cooked.

Surimi (Imitation Crab)   Imitation crabmeat used in Japanese cuisine. It may be constructed of pollock, egg white, potato starch, and sugar. Use within 3 days of opening.

Sweet Potato, Asian   See *Potato and Yam (Asia)*.

Sweet Potato/Yam Noodles, Korea   Similar to cellophane noodles, these are made with Korean sweet potato starch and mung bean starch; soften in warm water 10 minutes before using. The similar Japanese harusame noodles are made from potato starch, sometimes cornstarch, and water. Cover with boiling water and let stand 10 minutes. Drain and use.

Szechwan Pepper, Sansho, Prickly Ash, or Fagara   The Szechwan peppercorn is a small reddish spice with an outer husk and an inner dark seed. Japanese use a close relative called sansho. The husk is used for seasoning and the bitter seeds discarded. Whole Szechwan pepper and sansho are often lightly dry-toasted before use. Szechwan pepper isn't hot, it is citrusy and mouth-numbing. Duck, chicken, and pork dishes go well with Szechwan peppercorns, which are made into a roasted Szechwan salt good for dipping.

Different varieties of this spice are used in China, Japan, Korea, Tibet, Indonesia, Bhutan, Goa, and Nepal. Sansho's lemony-fragrant leaves, kinome, are used in Japanese cooking, dried or fresh, with bamboo shoots or as soup garnish.

T

Tahini (Middle Eastern Unroasted Sesame Paste)   Tahini is an oily sesame paste made from raw or lightly toasted unhulled sesame seeds. Stir the oil back into sesame seed mass before using. Chinese sesame paste is made from roasted sesame seed.

Tamarind   This long, brown pod is harvested from tamarind trees, which grow in temperate climates. Fresh, the interior of the pod is filled with a fruity-tart pulp and seeds. Dried tamarind pulp, with the consistency and scent of dates, retains the fruity, sour flavor. Tamarind gives an acidic flavor to many dishes across Southeast Asia and India, and is used as the basis of sauces, as thickener, and as flavor enhancer. It comes in various forms: dried block, concentrate, liquid concentrate and powder. The dried block is soaked in water and strained

to remove seeds and stringy pod, Four ounces *block* tamarind (1/2 cup packed) simmered with 1-1/4 to 1-1/2 cups hot water equals about 1 cup strained tamarind. Tamarind *concentrate* is commercially cooked, strained, and reduced to a sticky tar. The best Indian brand is Tamicon. Tamarind concentrate is less fruity, darker, and tarter tasting, but easy to use. Use about 2 tablespoons per cup water. Thai *liquid tamarind concentrate* is usually found in Thai markets and used as seasoning. It doesn't have the flavor or thick consistency for Indian dishes. Tamarind *powder* is dried and powdered tamarind. Sprinkle into dishes to add tart flavor.

Tangerine Peel, Dried (China)   Chinese cooks prize this dried, gnarly brown peel for the bright, floral citrus flavor it gives to soup, stew, chicken dishes, and red-cooked dishes. Soak in water and scrape off the bitter, white pith before using.

Tapioca Flour or Starch   Ground from the tuber of the cassava (also called yuca or manioc) plant, tapioca is as popular in Asia as cornstarch for use as a thickener. This starch becomes stringy when boiled but freezes very well. Mix into slurry as with cornstarch or arrowroot and cook only until liquid boils and clears. It is also made into wrappers similar to Vietnamese and Thai rice paper wrappers. When steamed tapioca starch becomes chewy and translucent.

Tapioca Noodles, Cambodia and Vietnam   Made from tapioca flour and water, these noodles are similar to rice sticks but chewier. Soak and cook like rice noodles.

Tapioca Pearls and Seeds   In Southeast Asia, tapioca starch is made into many colorful shapes, from oblong to square and round. The most common are small, white "seeds" or larger balls or "pearls" used in soups, drinks, or desserts. Large tapioca pearls retain a delightful chewy tenderness when cooked, and are part of tapioca pearl drinks like fruit or bubble tea. Vietnamese boba (bubble tea) is a thick, sweet drink made of coffee, tea, or fruit-ice slushies, sometimes with cream, coconut milk, or evaporated milk, and chewy tapioca pearls Tapioca pearls can be found black, white, and colored. Pearls and tapioca "seeds" may be used in savory dishes, added to soup at the last minute, used as a pilaf, or stirred into vegetable dishes. Chefs have used them as faux caviar or to thicken consommé. Use about 1 tablespoon tapioca seeds per cup of stock and simmer until translucent, 15 minutes. In India, tapioca seeds are called *sago* or *sabudaana*. Among other uses, sago is made into *sabudaana khichadi*, a sort of sago pilaf with chilies, cumin seeds, potatoes, ground peanuts, and cilantro. To prepare tapioca pearls: In a 6-quart saucepan, bring 8 cups water to a strong boil. (Pearls will disintegrate in anything less than boiling water.) Stir 1 cup (6 ounces) dry tapioca pearls. Cover the pan tightly, and reduce heat so the water continues to boil heartily. Boil pearls 50 minutes, turn off heat, and rest the pearls until translucent and chewy, 30 to 45 minutes. Immediately drain pearls and rinse with cold water. Not all pearls cook the same. Some may take less time, so keep an eye on them as they boil. There may be a few pearls with white spots depending on the quality of the tapioca. In a separate container, prepare the marinade: Mix 1-1/2 cups cold water with 1/3 to 1/2 cup sugar, to taste, or use other sweeteners like brown sugar, jaggery, honey, or maple syrup. Instead of water, experiment with other liquids like wine, coffee, tea, or juice and an optional flavoring like vanilla or almond extract. Pour pearls through strainer to drain. Gently stir them into the marinade. The pearls will absorb more marinade the longer they sit. Taste test for texture and flavor. Refrigerate cooked pearls and use within two days. Yields 2-1/2 to 3 cups tapioca pearls.

Tarama (Carp Roe) This fish roe is blended with bread, lemon juice, and olive oil to form taramosalata, a fluffy purée and beloved Greek meze.

Taro This small to very large, round shaggy brown tuber houses a mild, sweet white flesh that can be baked, braised, boiled (and mashed), stewed, or fried. Peel taro before cooking. It can become slimy and irritate the skin; keep in water after peeling. For less gluey texture, boil and drain taro.

Tea (Camellia Sinensis) (Asia and India) There are numerous types of tea from the same plant. Grades and quality depend on weather, size of leaf, where it grows on the plant, when it is picked, and fermentation-oxidation time. The highest quality tea is picked at the end of September, the dry season. Although in many places it is still done by hand, a machine called CTC (crushing, tearing, curling) is also used to turn fresh green tea leaves into the crumbly black stuff of tea bags. In approximately 20 hours, 4 kilos of fresh leaves end up weighing 1 kilo. The machines crush the leaves to release the cell moisture. As the leaves are crushed, fermentation-oxidation begins. This is a natural process aided by enzymes present in the tea that activate on contact with air. Fans and heat aid in the withering and drying. This is when the aroma develops and caffeine increases, while the tannins break down. The tea is sifted and at this point graded into **Leaf**, **Broken**, **Fannings**, and **Dust**. Fannings and Dust are used for tea bags.

Tea, Green (Chinese or Japanese Cha) For green tea, (Camellia sinensis) leaves are steamed or heated after plucking to make them soft and stop natural fermentation-oxidation. They are rolled and dried until crisp. They remain green and the tea has a grassy, fresh, clean taste. Gunpowder and Dragonwell are two types of Chinese green tea. Green tea is the main tea that Japanese drink. Its quality depends on what part of the plant the leaf grows and in what season it was picked. *Gyokuru* tea is from the best young leaves that are picked from the very top of the plant. Use hot water to brew, about 170°F to 180°F. *Matcha* is powdered green tea used for Japanese tea ceremony; it is whisked into hot water with a special bamboo whisk. *Sencha* is from medium-quality green tea leaves. Use very hot but not boiling water, about 180°F to 200°F. *Genmaicha* is generally sencha tea mixed with puffed, roasted rice. Brewed like sencha, it has a light, nutty flavor. *Bancha* and *hoji-cha* are made from the cheaper tea stems and coarse leaves. They have an earthy, strong flavor. Hoji-cha is roasted bancha tea, which gives it a slightly bitter, smoky flavor. Boiling water is used to brew them both.

T'eff (Ethiopia) This tiny, gluten-free grain is a staple in Ethiopia, where it originated. It is cooked similarly as millet and quinoa, but is much smaller, and cooks in less time. T'eff is ground into a khaki-colored flour, and used for the important Ethiopian injera bread. There are three main varieties of t'eff,

each with characteristics best suited to specific conditions: red-brown, mixed (red, brown, white), and white. Red-brown t'eff is the least expensive, least preferred, and has the highest iron content. The mixed variety has less iron and consequently a milder flavor. White t'eff is the mildest, most expensive, and most prized. Injera made with it stays fresh longer.

Tempeh Traditional in Indonesia, tempeh is prepared by mixing cooked, whole soybeans with beneficial bacteria and forming it into cakes, which are allowed to ferment. The result is a whole soybean cake bound by a beneficial white mold. The fermentation process and use of whole beans makes tempeh easier to digest and gives it higher levels of protein, fiber, and nutrients than any other soy product. Its firm texture and earthy flavor increase as the tempeh ages. It may be fried, baked, or sautéed.

Thickeners and Binders European cooking draws on a huge vocabulary of thickeners for sauces and soups. The most successful imbue soup with flavor while adding body. They may be starch, starch with fat (roux or beurre manie), or egg and cream (liaison).

Tibs Ethiopian dish of beef, lamb, chicken, or fish sautéed and/or pan-fried with or without onion, fresh chilies, and other seasonings and prepared juicy or dry according to individual preference. Lega tibs is tender beef or lamb sautéed medium-rare.

Tofu or Dou-Fo (Japanese or Chinese Soybean or Bean Curd) Soymilk, prepared from soaked, boiled, puréed, and strained soybeans, is curded, traditionally with nigari (primarily magnesium chloride from seawater) or with calcium chloride or calcium sulfate, scooped into molds and pressed. The curding agent and pressing determine the texture. Tofu usually comes in white blocks that range from silken-soft to very firm. After pressing, tofu is immersed in water and chilled. Water leaches out its sweetness: before immersion in water, fresh-made tofu is custard-sweet and tender. Tofu may be frozen to increase texture; thaw by immersing in boiling water. Weight or press tofu in toweling 20 to 30 minutes to expel water. Tofu comes in forms besides fresh: freeze-dried, fermented (stinky), flavored and pressed, and deep-fried pockets (aburage).

Tomato This sweet, complex vegetable-fruit, which genetic evidence shows originated in South America, and spread to Mesoamerican civilizations in Mexico, now comes in many shapes, colors, and sizes. To substitute canned tomatoes for fresh (or vice versa):

> One 28-ounce can of whole tomatoes equals about 3 cups undrained tomatoes and about 2 to 2-1/2 cups drained tomatoes OR 2 pounds fresh tomatoes.

> One 14-1/2- to 16-ounce can of whole tomatoes equals 1-1/2 to 2 cups undrained tomatoes and about 1 to 1-1/4 cups drained tomatoes OR 1 pound fresh tomatoes.

Tomatillo (Tomate Verde or Husk Tomato) A small, pale green or purple-fleshed vegetable-fruit covered with a pale green husk, like tomatoes, tomatillos are in the nightshade family. They may be used raw in salad or salsa, but tomatillos are very tart and are usually cooked when used in Mexican cuisine. The purple variety tends to be sweeter than the green. The cooked fruit may be chopped or puréed and made into a salsa or added to a dish for a bright, fresh taste. To cook tomatillos: Remove husk and rinse off sticky residue. Immerse tomatillos into simmering water and cook until tender, but not split, about 10 minutes, and drain. Or tomatillos may be griddle-roasted over medium heat until charred and soft.

Tree Ear Mushrooms (Wood or Cloud)   A fungus that when soaked becomes rubbery and crunchy. They are relatively tasteless; Chinese cooks value them for their texture and color. Soak 30 minutes, swish and wash until clean, and drain. Store in cold water up to 8 hours before using.

Truffles   See *Signature Seasonings* in chapter *France* or *Italy*.

Tulsi   The seeds of Southeast Asian holy basil that become gelatinous when soaked and are used to prepare a beverage.

Tuna (Maguro), Toro, Chutoro and Akami, Japanese   Maguro is the Japanese name for tuna. Akami is the red tuna that comes from the upper region of the fish. Two types of fatty tuna from the Bluefin tuna are prized for Japanese sushi and sashimi: the most fatty, toro, and chu-toro, a medium-fatty tuna. Toro is cut from the underside or fatty belly of the tuna; it is peach-colored and luscious. Chu-toro comes from the fatty region close to the dorsal fin in the middle and back of the fish, between akami and toro. It is less marbled than toro.

U

Udon, Japanese   Medium-thick noodle that is now usually made commercially. When Japanese homecooks prepare udon, the dough is so stiff that common practice is to knead and stomp them with their feet.

Umami   Umami is the Japanese term for deep, rich, savory flavor. Umami has been hailed as a "new" discovery: the fifth taste after sweet, sour, salty, and bitter. (Spicy-hot, pungent, and astringent are sensations.)

Umeboshi (Japanese Pickled "Plums")   Although the fruit of this Japanese "pickle" is called a plum, it is really a species of apricot. Unripe apricots are soaked in brine and packed in red shiso leaves, which add flavor and color, then aged. The flavor of umeboshi is fruity-salty-tart and oddly refreshing. Japanese use them as tonic, for breakfast food, in dipping sauces, as marinade, and paired with rice dishes like sushi and onigiri. To make umeboshi paste, finely chop or purée pitted "plums." The best umeboshi cost the most, and are found refrigerated in Japanese markets.

V

Vegetables, Caribbean   See *Vegetables and Fruits of the Caribbean* in chapter *The West Indies or Caribbean*.

Verjuice (Europe and Mediterranean)   The pressed juice of unripe grapes, verjuice is used to add tartness in place of citrus or vinegar.

Vinegar (Europe and Mediterranean)   Traditional French and European vinegar production begins with good wine, which is pumped into casks with a small amount of old vinegar and a compressed, gelatinous mass of vinegar bacteria known as the *mother*. The casks age in dark cellars at around 80 degrees F, until the bacteria transform the alcohol into acetic acid, about 3 weeks. Young vinegar is very sharp so it is stored in wooden casks to mature, soften, and pick up deeper aroma. Large commercial operations accelerate this process. Red wine, white wine, champagne and sherry are popular vinegars. See also *Balsamic Vinegar*. The fruity cider vinegar is produced from pressed apple juice with the same process as traditional wine vinegars. It tends to be more acidic than other vinegars. The fruity and tangy French cider vinegar is made from juice pressed from apples in the Brittany, Normandy, and Limousin regions.

W

Wakame   Subtly sweet, thin, bright green, slippery-textured, this sea vegetable is often used in Japanese salads and soups.

Warqa, Warka, or Ouarka (Morocco)   These paper-thin, crisp Moroccan pastry dough leaves are similar to fillo dough and are traditionally used to make b'stilla. Warqa are made by first kneading bread flour and water to form a soft dough. A special, heavy flat pan (like an upside-down flat skillet) is set onto a charcoal brazier and rubbed with a scant bit of butter. The ball of dough is tapped around the hot surface leaving a film of dough that covers the entire surface. The dough is cooked a few seconds until the edges come away from the pan then peeled off. This is more difficult than it sounds. For detailed instructions refer to *Couscous and Other Good Food From Morocco* by Paula Wolfert.

Wasabi (Sabi)   This sushi bar condiment is a type of pale green, perennial rhizome originally grown only in northern Japan. True wasabi is only distantly related to horseradish, mustard, kale, watercress, and cabbage. Most sushi bar wasabi is a powdered and reconstituted mixture of dried, ground horseradish, food coloring, and mustard. Real wasabi is more complex and mellow than the faux product: it has a mildly spicy first taste but a smoother finish. Considered a delicacy, Japanese chefs use a special sharkskin grater to grate real wasabi, and diners must request it.

Water Chestnuts and Water Chestnut Starch/Flour   Asian groceries often sell fresh water chestnuts, which are far superior to canned. They are sweet and nutty, a combination of jicama and chestnut. Rinse these small brown knobs well to rid them of mud. Just before using, peel away the thin, outer brown skin with a paring knife and rinse. Blot dry and slice or dice as necessary. Eat water chestnuts raw, lightly steamed, or quickly stir-fried. Water chestnut starch is used as a deep-fry coating.

Watercress   This peppery green has thick bottom stems and leafy tops with emerald green thumbnail-sized leaves. Harvested wild in running streams, wild watercress can harbor snails with liver flukes; cultivated watercress is a fine alternative.

W'et An Ethiopian stew with thick sauce that is made with a base of browned shallots or onions, ginger, garlic, tomato, and berbere spice paste. It can have meat or beans added. It is reminiscent of an Indian curry crossed with a Mexican mole.

Wheat, Cracked Whole wheat berries that have been crushed for quicker cooking to three textures: fine, medium, and coarse. Cracked wheat requires cooking. It is not a substitute for *bulgar* (steamed, dried, and cracked wheat). Also see *Bulgar*.

Wheat Starch This fine, white powder is wheat flour with most of the gluten removed. Asian cooks use it to prepare batters and dumplings. When steamed it turns soft, shiny, and opaque white.

Wild Greens In many parts of the Mediterranean, people gather wild food. Purslane, nettles, mallow, and ramps (wild leeks) are particularly beloved. These spring foods are considered nourishing and cleansing. The island of Crete is known for its enormous number of wild greens, more than anywhere else in the world.

Wing Beans (Goa or Asparagus Bean) (Asia) This long, green bean with four frilly edged "fins" running along its length grows well in tropical climates. The bean pods are about 6 to 9 inches long, and when young, a waxy translucent green with the sweet, grassy flavor of asparagus. The entire plant is edible from roots and leaves to flowers and seeds. The leaves may be used like spinach and the immature beans pickled or stir-fried.

Winter Melon (White Gourd, Ash Gourd, Fuzzy Melon) This very large, bland, watery-sweet melon has pale green skin and snow-white flesh. Chinese cooks prize winter melon for its texture and translucence in soup, stir-fry, braised, or steamed dishes, filling for mooncakes or as a vegetable, sometimes paired with pork products. In Southeast Asia, winter melon is made into candy or fruit drinks and in India it is used in curries. The large melon seeds are a favorite of Chinese.

Wonton Wrappers (China) This square wrapper is made with wheat flour and water. Wontons, either steamed, boiled, or fried, are made by filling and folding a wrapper in half into a triangle or by bringing up four corners together and sealing.

Y

Yam (True Yam) This edible starchy tuber, native to Africa and Asia, differs from the sweet potato and is not related. It has thick skin that can be rough or smooth and vary in color from pale to brown to purple. There are many varieties: they range in size, but are often very large—up to 5 feet long. The flesh color may range from white, yellow, and pink to purple. Yams contain less sugar and moisture than sweet potatoes. See *Potato*.

Yam, Japanese Mountain This long, tan colored, rare and prized tuber has flesh that when grated raw is starchy and gluey. Raw, it can be used as a binding agent or as a digestive. The flavor is slightly nutty, but bland. Dried slices are cooked in soups. Dried grated yam is used as flour for noodles.

Yellow Bean Sauce (Vietnam) See *Bean Sauce*.

Yogurt A staple of the Turkish and Greek diet, yogurt is milk cultured by beneficial bacteria. The bacteria break down the milk and make it more digestible while imparting a tart tanginess.

Yuca, Tapioca, Cassava or Manioc A large, long brown root vegetable with hard starchy white flesh that when boiled is similar to potato. Two varieties exist: bitter and sweet. The sweet version is dried and ground into cassava flour, which is used to make tapioca pearls and the Caribbean bread called bammie or pain de kassav. Senegalese and West African cooks use the vegetable to make fufu, a boiled and pounded starchy dish similar to sticky, creamy mashed potatoes.

Yukari (Japan) Salted preserved red shiso leaf.

Yuzu (Japanese Citrus) A fragrant but sour gnarly-skinned Japanese citrus the size of a tangerine. Its aromatic rind is slivered and used as garnish; the juice is used to season dishes. Yuzu is also available as a bottled juice or dry powder.

Z

Za'atar Herb and Za'atar Blend There are several varieties of aromatic herbs called za'atar (and other names in other parts of the Mediterranean and Middle East) that taste like a cross of oregano, savory, and thyme. There is also a blend, popular in Lebanon, that consists of 2 parts dried thyme, 1 part sumac, 1/2 part toasted sesame seeds, and salt. Some cooks substitute dried oregano, savory, or marjoram for part of the thyme to give a more complex flavor. Lebanese and Middle Eastern groceries sell the prepared za'atar blend.

Zebda (Moroccan Fermented Fresh Butter) Zebda is not as strong as the fermented smen or the even more rancid boudra. For zebda, milk is allowed to sour and is then churned. The leben (buttermilk) is drained away and zebda or butter solids remain. It is used for cooking.

Zucchini (Italian: Zucchino; French: Courgette) Although this plant originated in Central and South America, it was the Italians who hybridized it into the modern plant. This tender, green (and sometimes bright yellow) summer squash can grow very large, but when it is harvested over an inch diameter it is woody and flavorless. Look for small, firm, taut, plump, shiny-skinned zucchini with tender (not hard) skin with no blemishes. Hard skin signals an old zucchini that will be bitter, stringy, and seedy. Check zucchini ends for mushiness. Don't peel zucchini, but do trim away ends.

Zucchini Blossoms See *Italian Vegetables* in chapter *Italy*.

REFERENCES/BIBLIOGRAPHY

GENERAL REFERENCES

Bon Appetit
Cook's Illustrated
Everyday Food
Fine Cooking
Gourmet
http://about.com
http://en.wikipedia.org
http://www.cooksillustrated.com
http://www.everyculture.com/
http://www.finecooking.com
http://www.foodandwine.com
http://www.foodbycountry.com/
http://www.gourmet.com
http://www.infoplease.com/
http://www.marthastewart.com/
http://www.saveur.com
On Food and Cooking by Harold Mc Gee
Paula Wolfert's World of Food by Paula Wolfert
The CIA World Factbook: https://www.cia.gov/library/
    publications/the-world-factbook/
The Complete Meat Cookbook by Bruce Aidells and Denis Kelly
The New Food Lover's Companion by Sharon Tyler Herbst
The New Making of a Cook by Madeleine Kamman
The New York Times food section
The Oxford Companion to Food by Alan Davidson

ASIA AND INDIA

A Taste of Thailand by Vacharin Bhumichitr
Andrea Nguyen: www.vietworldkitchen.com/
Asian Dumplings by Andrea Nguyen
At Home with Japanese Cooking by Elizabeth Andoh
Authentic Vietnamese Cooking by Corinne Trang
Beyond the Great Wall: Recipes and Travels in the Other China by
    Jeffrey Alford and Naomi Duguid
China, Japan, Korea, Culture and Customs by John and Ju Brown
Chinese Noodles, Dumplings and Breads by Florence Lin
Classic Chinese Cuisine by Nina Simonds
Classic Food of China by Yan Kit So
Classic Indian Cooking by Julie Sahni
Cooking Along the Ganges by Malvi Doshi
Cooking teacher Jyoti Agarwal, Gourmet Desire,
    New Delhi, India
Cooking teacher Nimmy Paul, Cochin, Kerala, India
Cooking teacher Shakila Amberkar, Mumbai, India
Cooking teacher Sreedevi Olappamanna, Kerala, India
Cracking the Coconut by Su-Mei Yu
Culture Cheese Magazine

Dakshin: Vegetarian Cuisine from South India by Chandra
    Padmanabhan
Elizabeth Andoh: www.tasteofculture.com/ and http://
    washokufood.blogspot.com/
Flavours of Korea by Marc and Kim Millon
*Florence Lin's Complete Book of Chinese Noodles, Dumplings and
    Breads* by Florence Lin
Food of Japan by Shirley Booth
Foods of Asia by Kong Foong Ling, Ming Tsai, and Chiong Liew
Grains, Greens, and Grated Coconuts by Ammini Ramachandran
Growing Up in a Korean Kitchen by Hi Soo Shin Hepinstall
Hot Sour Salty Sweet: A Culinary Journey Through Southeast Asia by
    Naomi Duguid and Jeffrey Alford
In Clay's Kitchen: http://www.panix.com/~clay/cookbook/
Indonesia Dining and Cooking: http://indonesiaeats.com/
Into the Vietnamese Kitchen: Treasured Foodways, Modern Flavors by
    Andrea Nguyen and Andrea Quynhgiao Nguyen
Japanese Cooking: A Simple Art Shizuo Tsuji
Korean Home Cooking: http://www.koreanhomecooking.com
Land of Plenty: A Treasury of Authentic Sichuan Cooking by Fuchsia
    Dunlop
Madhur Jaffrey's Flavors of India: Classics and New Discoveries by
    Madhur Jaffrey
New Salads, Quick, Healthy Recipes from Japan by Shinko Shimizu
Nobu: The Cookbook by Nobuyuki Matsuhisa
Practical Japanese Cooking by Shizuo Tsuji
Quick and Easy Korean Cooking by Cecilia Hae-Jin Lee
Real Thai by Nanci McDermott
Revolutionary Chinese Cookbook, Recipe from Hunan Province by
    Fuschia Dunlop
Sushi at Home by Kay Shimizu
Takashi's Noodles by Takashi Yagihashi and Harris Salat
Thai Food and Travel: http://www.thaifoodandtravel.com/
The Art of Chinese Cuisine by Hsiang Ju Lin and Tsuifeng Lin
The Art of Indian Vegetarian Cooking by Yamuna Devi
*The Asian Grocery Store Demystified, A Food Lover's Guide to All the
    Best Ingredients* by Linda Bladholm
The Classic Cuisine of Vietnam by Bach Ngo and Gloria
    Zimmerman
The Complete Asian Cookbook by Charmaine Solomon
The Food of China by E. N. Anderson
The Great Curries of India by Camellia Panjabi
*The Indian Grocery Store Demystified, A Guide to All the Best
    Ingredients in the Traditional Foods of India, Pakistan, and
    Bangladesh* by Linda Bladholm
The Japanese Kitchen by Hiroko Shimbo Beitchman
The Key to Chinese Cooking by Irene Kuo
The Korean Table by Taekyung Chung and Debra Samuels
The Modern Art of Chinese Cooking by Barbara Tropp
The Wisdom of the Chinese Kitchen by Grace Young
Time-Life Foods of the World *Chinese Cooking*
Time-Life Foods of the World *Pacific and Southeast Asian Cooking*

Time-Life Foods of the World *The Cooking of India*
Time-Life Foods of the World *The Cooking of Japan*
Washoku: Recipes from the Japanese Home Kitchen
    by Elizabeth Andoh

EUROPE, MEDITERRANEAN, MIDDLE EAST, CAUCASUS

France

A Flavor of Normandy: Exploring the Tastes, Techniques, and Traditions of the Finest Regional Cooking in the World by Carole Clements
A Mediterranean Feast by Clifford A. Wright
A Taste of France by Robert Freson
All About Braising: The Art of Uncomplicated Cooking by Molly Stevens
Around My French Table by Dorie Greenspan
Cookwise by Shirley Corriher
Culinaria France edited by Andre Domine
French Regional Cooking by Anne Willan
Julia's Menus for Special Occasions by Julia Child
La Varenne Pratique by Anne Willan
Le Guide Culinaire by Georges Auguste Escoffier
Mastering the Art of French Cooking (Volumes 1 and 2), Knopf, 1971, Julia Child
Mastering the Art of French Cooking by Julia Child
On Cooking: A Textbook of Culinary Fundamentals by Sarah R. Labensky and Alan M. Hause
Recipes from a French Country Kitchen: The Very Best of Real French Regional Cooking by Carole Clements and Elizabeth Wolf-Cohen
Sauce by James Peterson
Techniques of Fine Cooking from the Institute for Culinary Education, New York, New York
The Balthazar Cookbook by Keith McNally
The Country Cooking of France by Anne Willan
The Essentials of Wine by John P. Laloganes
The HerbFarm Cookbook by Jerry Traunfeld
The New Making of a Cook by Madeleine Kamman
The Paris Cookbook by Patricia Wells
The Soups of France by Lois Anne Rothert
The Wonderful Food of Provence by Jean-Noel Escudier and Peta J. Fuller
Time-Life Foods of the World *The Cooking of Provincial France*
Vegetables by James Peterson

Italy

A Taste of Tuscany by Sandra Lotti, publisher Maria Pacini Fazzi, Lucca, Italy
Cucina del Sole by Nancy Harmon Jenkins
Cucina Siciliana by Clarissa Hyman
Culinaria Italy edited by Claudia Piras and Eugenio Medagliani
Encyclopedia of Pasta by Oretta de Vita

Flavors of Tuscany by Nancy Harmon Jenkins
From the Tables of Tuscan Women by Anne Bianchi
Glorious Soups and Stews of Italy by Domenica Marchetti
Good & Garlicky, Thick & Hearty, Soul-Satisfying More-Than-Minestrone Italian Soup Cookbook by Joe Famularo
Italian Slow and Savory by Joyce Esersky Goldstein
Italian Soup Cookbook by Joe Famularo
Lidia Bastianich: www.lidiasitaly.com/
Lidia Cooks from the Heart of Italy by Lidia Bastianich
Lidia's Italy by Lidia Bastianich
Lynne Rossetto Kasper: www.splendidtable.org/
Marcella's Italian Kitchen by Marcella Hazan
Prosciutto, Pancetta, Salame by Pamela Sheldon Johns, Joyce Oudkerk Pool
Rustic Family Cooking from Italy's Undiscovered South: My Calabria by Rosetta Constantino and Janet Fletcher
Saveur Cooks Authentic Italian with Colman Andrews
Solo Verdura, The Complete Guide to Cooking Tuscan Vegetables by Anne Bianchi
The Essentials of Classical Italian Cooking by Marcella Hazan
The Fine Art of Italian Cooking by Giuliano Bugialli
The Food of Italy by Waverly Root
The Italian Baker by Carol Field
The Italian Country Table by Lynne Rossetto Kasper
The Splendid Table: Recipes from Emilia-Romagna, the Heartland of Northern Italian Food by Lynne Rossetto Kasper
Time-Life Foods of the World *The Cooking of Italy*
Toscana Saporita Cooking School and Sandra Lotti, Viareggio, Italy
Zuppa: Soups from The Italian Countryside by Anne Bianchi

Spain

Cooking from the Heart of Spain by Janet Mendel
Culinaria Spain edited by Marion Trutter
Culinary Institute of America *Worlds of Flavor Spain*: http://www.worldsofflavorspain.com/
Delicioso! The Regional Cooking of Spain by Penelope Casas
José Andres: www.josemadeinspain.com/
La Cocina de Mama: The Great Home Cooking of Spain by Penelope Casas
Made in Spain by José Andres
Moorish Spain by Richard Fletcher
My Kitchen in Spain by Janet Mendel
Tapas: Sensational Small Plates from Spain by Joyce Esersky Goldstein
The Cuisines of Spain by Teresa Berrenechea
The Food of Spain and Portugal: A Regional Celebration by Elizabeth Luard
The New Spanish Table by Anya von Bremzen
Time-Life Foods of the World *The Cooking of Spain and Portugal*

Greece and Turkey

A Mediterranean Feast by Clifford Wright
Classic Turkish Cooking by Ghillie Basan and Jonathan Basan
Classical Turkish Cooking: Traditional Turkish Food for the American Kitchen by Ayla Esen Algar

Flavors of Greece by Rosemary Barron
Greek Cooking for the Gods by Eva Zane
How to Roast a Lamb: New Greek Classic Cooking by Michael Psilakis
Recipes from a Greek Island by Susie Jacobs
The Arab Table: Recipes and Culinary Traditions by May Bsisu
The Complete Meat Cookbook by Bruce Aidells
The Cooking of the Eastern Mediterranean by Paula Wolfert
The Food and Wine of Greece: More Than 300 Classic and Modern Dishes from the Mainland and Islands by Diane Kochilas
The Foods of the Greek Islands: Cooking and Culture at the Crossroads of the Mediterranean by Aglaia Kremezi
The Glorious Foods of Greece by Diane Kochilas
The Olive and the Caper: Adventures in Greek Cooking by Susanna Hoffman and Victoria Wise
The Ottoman Kitchen: Modern Recipes from Turkey, Greece, the Balkans, Lebanon, and Syria by Sarah Woodward
The Sultan's Kitchen: A Turkish Cookbook by Özcan Ozan
Time-Life Foods of the World *Middle Eastern Cooking* by Harry G. Nickles

Lebanon

Alice's Kitchen: Traditional Lebanese Cooking by Linda Dalal Sawaya
Anissa Halou: http://anissas.com/ and http://www.anissas.com/blog1/
Arabesque: A Taste of Morocco, Turkey, and Lebanon by Claudia Roden
Classic Lebanese Cuisine by Kamal Al-Faqih
Fouad Kassab: www.thefoodblog.com.au/
http://jennifermclagan.blogspot.com/2012/03/fat-tailed-lamb.html
Lebanese Cuisine by Anissa Helou
Lebanese Cuisine by Madelain Farah
Lebanese Mountain Cookery by Mary Laird Hamady
Mediterranean Street Food: Stories, Soups, Snacks, Sandwiches, Barbecues, Sweets, and More from Europe, North Africa, and the Middle East by Anissa Helou
Odd Bits: How to Cook the Rest of the Animal by Jennifer McLagan
Sheep with Two Tails, in The Cooking Medium, Oxford Symposium on Food History 1986 by Jill Tilsley-Benham
The New Book of Middle Eastern Food by Claudia Roden

Iran-Persia and Georgia

A Taste of Persia by Najmieh Batmanglij
Amazon link to *Medieval Arab Cookery*: http://www.amazon.co.uk/Medieval-Arab-Cookery-Maxime-Rodinson/dp/0907325912
Flatbreads and Flavors by Jeffrey Alford and Naomi Duguid
Florian Muehlfried, from *Sharing the Same Blood, Culture and Cuisine in the Republic of Georgia*, in the *Anthropology of Food* [Online]
Irakli Metreveli, *Agence France-Presse*, April 28, 2011, *Georgia Rediscovers Ancient Culinary Traditions*: http://linkgeorgia.com/2011/04/georgia-rediscovers-ancient-culinary.html

My Persian Kitchen: http://mypersiankitchen.com/
Persian Cuisine from Javane's Kitchen: http://javanehskitchen.wordpress.com
Persian Cuisine by M. R. Ghanoonparvar
Please to the Table by Anya von Bremzen and John Welchman
The Classic Cuisine of Soviet Georgia by Julianne Margvelashvili
The Complete Middle East Cookbook by Tess Mallos
The Cooking of the Eastern Mediterranean by Paula Wolfert
The Georgian Feast by Darra Goldstein
The Legendary Cuisine of Persia by Margaret Shaida
The New Book of Middle Eastern Food by Claudia Roden
The New Food for Life by Najmieh Batmanglij

AFRICA AND LATIN AMERICA

A Taste of Africa: Traditional & Modern African Cooking by Dorinda Hafner
Arabesque: A Taste of Morocco, Turkey, and Lebanon by Claudia Roden
Beyond Gumbo: Creole Fusion Food from the Atlantic Rim by Jessica B. Harris

Morocco

Cafe Morocco by Anissa Helou
Christine Benlafquih: http://moroccanfood.about.com/bio
Cooking at the Kasbah by Kitty Morse
Couscous and Other Good Food from Morocco by Paula Wolfert
http://www.gourmet.com/recipes/adventureswithruth/2009/10/chicken-tagine-with-lemons-olives-and-coriander
Peggy Markel's Culinary Adventures: www.peggymarkel.com/morocco.html
Tagines and Couscous by Ghillie Başan
The Momo Cookbook by Mourab Mozouz
The North African Kitchen by Fiona Dunlop

Ethiopia

Conservation and Use of Traditional Vegetables in Ethiopia, Zemede Asfaw Faculty of Science, Addis Abeba University, Addis Abeba, Ethiopia
Ethnomed: More About Ethiopian Food: http://ethnomed.org/clinical/nutrition/more-about-ethiopian-food-teff
Exotic Ethiopian Cooking by Daniel J. Mesfin
Haile-Mariam Yewoineshet: www.yewoinfamilycooking.com
Menkir Tamrat
Mesob Across America: Ethiopian Food in the U.S.A. by Harry Kloman
Professor James C. McCann, Head of African Studies Center, Boston University
Time-Life Books Foods of the World *African Cooking*
Wild Fermentation by Sandor Ellix Katz
Zenash Beyene, Ethiopian chef and owner of Chicago restaurant Ras Dashen

Senegal

Celtnet Senegalese Recipes and Cookery: www.celtnet.org.uk/recipes/senegal.php

Duffy, Megan, *Ceeb ak Jën: Deconstructing Senegal's National Plate in Search of Cultural Values* (2009), Kenyon College, Senegal Arts and Culture, ISP Collection, Paper 669

http://digitalcollections.sit.edu/isp_collection/669

http://www.worldtravelguide.net/senegal/food-and-drink

Sky Juice and Flying Fish: Traditional Caribbean Cooking by Jessica B. Harris

The Africa Cookbook by Jessica B. Harris

Travel and Music Writer Amy Wilentz, *L'Afrique, Mon Amour*, November, 2007, Condé Nast Traveler: http://www.cntraveler.com/features/2007/11/L-Afrique-Mon-Amour

Yolele! Recipes from the Heart of Senegal by Pierre Thiam

The Caribbean Islands

A Concise History of the Caribbean by B. W. Higman

Caribbean Cooking by John DeMers

Caribbean Food Made Easy with Levi Roots by Levi Roots

Creole Cooking: The Taste of Tropical Islands by Sue Mullin

Daisy Martinez, Latin Chef and Cooking Teacher: www.daisymartinez.com/

Eat Caribbean by Virginia Burke

Heritage Foods USA and the No Goat Left Behind project: http://heritagefoodsusa.com/ventures/goat.html

Island Barbecue by Dunstan A. Harris

Island Cooking by Dunstan A. Harris

New World Kitchen: Latin American and Caribbean Cuisine by Norman Van Aken

Puerto Rican Cookery by Carmen Aboy Valldejuli

The Art of Caribbean Cookery by Carmen Aboy Valldejuli

The Complete Book of Caribbean Cooking by Elisabeth Lambert Ortiz

The Complete Caribbean Cookbook by Pamela Lalbachan

The Spice Necklace: My Adventures in Caribbean Cooking, Eating, and Island Life by Ann Vanderhoof

Time Life Foods of the World *The Cooking of the Caribbean Islands* by Linda Wolfe

Mexico

Authentic Mexican by Rick Bayless and Deann Groen Bayless

Culinary Mexico by Daniel Hoyer

David Sterling, Cooking Teacher Yucatan: http://www.los-dos.com/

Food and Wine, December 1994, *Zarela's Kitchen; How to Infuse Your Everyday Cooking with a Mexican Accent*, by Zarela Marinez

Food from My Heart, Macmillan, 1992, by Zarela Martinez

From My Mexican Kitchen: Techniques and Ingredients by Diana Kennedy

Jim Peyton: www.jimpeyton.com

Mexconnect, search on Karen Hursh Graber: http://www.mexconnect.com/

Mexican Everyday by Rick Bayless and Deann Groen Bayless

Mexican Family Cooking by Aida Gabilondo

Mexico One Plate at a Time by Rick Bayless

My Mexico: A Culinary Odyssey with More Than 300 Recipes by Diana Kennedy

New Cooking from Old Mexico by Jim Peyton

Rosa's Mexican Table by Roberto Santibañez

Savoring Mexico: Recipes and Reflections on Mexican Cooking (Williams Sonoma) by Marilyn Tausend

Seasons of My Heart by Susana Trilling

Tamales 101 by Alice Guadalupe Tapp

The Art of Mexican Cooking by Diana Kennedy

The Essential Cuisines of Mexico by Diana Kennedy

The Mija Chronicles: A Quick Guide to Mexican Beans: http://www.themijachronicles.com/2010/06/a-quick-guide-to-mexican-beans/

Time-Life Foods of the World *Latin American Cooking*

Truly Mexican by Roberto Santibañez

Well-Filled Tortilla Book by Victoria Wise and Susanna Hoffman

Williams-Sonoma Collection: Mexican by Marilyn Tausend

Zarela Martinez: www.zarela.com

INDEX